W9-BDQ-941

African American National Biography

African American National Biography

SECOND EDITION

HENRY LOUIS GATES JR.
EVELYN BROOKS HIGGINBOTHAM

Editors in Chief

VOLUME 1: AARON – BLAKE, "BLIND" ARTHUR

OXFORD
UNIVERSITY PRESS

OXFORD
UNIVERSITY PRESS

Oxford University Press is a department of the University of Oxford.
It furthers the University's objective of excellence in research, scholarship,
and education by publishing worldwide.

Oxford   New York
Auckland   Cape Town   Dar es Salaam   Hong Kong   Karachi
Kuala Lumpur   Madrid   Melbourne   Mexico City   Nairobi
New Delhi   Shanghai   Taipei   Toronto

With offices in
Argentina   Austria   Brazil   Chile   Czech Republic   France   Greece
Guatemala   Hungary   Italy   Japan   Poland   Portugal   Singapore
South Korea   Switzerland   Thailand   Turkey   Ukraine   Vietnam

Oxford is a registered trademark of Oxford University Press in the UK and certain other countries

Published in the United States of America by
Oxford University Press
198 Madison Avenue, New York, NY 10016

Library of Congress Cataloging-in-Publication Data
African American national biography / editors in chief Henry Louis Gates Jr., Evelyn Brooks Higginbotham. – 2nd ed.
p. cm.
Includes bibliographical references and index.
ISBN 978-0-19-999036-8 (volume 1; hdbk.); ISBN 978-0-19-999037-5 (volume 2; hdbk.); ISBN 978-0-19-999038-2 (volume 3; hdbk.);
ISBN 978-0-19-999039-9 (volume 4; hdbk.); ISBN 978-0-19-999040-5 (volume 5; hdbk.); ISBN 978-0-19-999041-2 (volume 6; hdbk.);
ISBN 978-0-19-999042-9 (volume 7; hdbk.); ISBN 978-0-19-999043-6 (volume 8; hdbk.); ISBN 978-0-19-999044-3 (volume 9; hdbk.);
ISBN 978-0-19-999045-0 (volume 10; hdbk.); ISBN 978-0-19-999046-7 (volume 11; hdbk.); ISBN 978-0-19-999047-4 (volume 12;
hdbk.); ISBN 978-0-19-992077-8 (12-volume set; hdbk.)
1. African Americans – Biography – Encyclopedias.   2. African Americans – History – Encyclopedias.
I. Gates, Henry Louis.   II. Higginbotham, Evelyn Brooks, 1945-
E185.96.A4466 2012
920'.009296073 – dc23
[B]
2011043281

1 3 5 7 9 8 6 4 2
Printed in the United States of America
on acid-free paper

Editorial and Production Staff

Contents

African American National Biography

List of Entries

Bond, Scott
Bonds, Barry Lamar
Bonds, Margaret Jeannette Allison
Bonner, Marita Odette
Bontemps, Arna Wendell
Booker, Cory A.
Booker, James Carroll III
Booker, Joseph Albert
Booker, Kinney Ibis
Boone, Clinton Caldwell, Sr.
Boone, Eva Roberta (or Mae) Coles
Boone, Sarah
Boothe, Charles Octavius
Borde, Percival
Bostic, Earl
Boston, Absalom
Bottoms, Lawrence Wendell
Bouchet, Edward Alexander
Bouey, Harrison N.
Bousfield, Midian Othello
Boutelle, Frazier Augustus
Bowden, Artemisia
Bowe, Riddick
Bowen, John Wesley Edward
Bowen, Ruth Jean
Bowen, Uvelia Atkins
Bowens, Beverly ElizabethDodge
Bowers, Thomas J.
Bowie, Lester
Bowles, Charles
Bowles, Eva Del Vakia
Bowling, Frank
Bowman, Euday Louis
Bowman, James E., Jr.
Bowman, Laura
Bowman, Thea
Bowser, David Bustill
Bowser, Mary Elizabeth
Bowser, Rosa
Boyce, Mildred L.
Boyd, Gerald M.
Boyd, Henry Allen
Boyd, Richard Henry
Boyer, Frances
Boykin, Keith
Boyne, Thomas
Boynton Robinson, Amelia
Bozeman, Sylvia Trimble
Brace, Jeffrey
Bradford, Alex
Bradford, Mark
Bradford, Perry
Bradley, Aaron Alpeora
Bradley, Buddy

Bradley, David
Bradley, Edward
Bradley, Thomas
Bradley, Wallace "Gator"
Bradshaw, Tiny
Brady, St. Elmo
Brady, Xernona Clayton
Bragg, George Freeman, Jr.
Bragg, Janet
Braithwaite, William Stanley Beaumont
Branch, Frederick Clinton
Branch, Mary Elizabeth
Branch, Wallace
Branche, George Clayton
Brandon, Barbara
Brandon, Brumsic, Jr.
Branson, Herman Russell
Branton, Wiley Austin
Brashear, Carl Maxie
Brashear, Donald
Braud, Wellman
Brawley, Benjamin
Brawley, Edward McKnight
Brawley, James P.
Braxton, Anthony (Delano)
Brazier, Arthur
Brewer, John Mason
Brewster, William Herbert
Brice, Carol Lovette
Bricktop
Bridgewater, Cecil
Bridgewater, Dee Dee
Briggs, Bunny
Briggs, Cyril Valentine
Briggs, Martha Bailey
Brimmer, Andrew Felton
Briscoe, Marlin
Briscoe, Neliska Ann "Baby"
Bristol, Johnny
Bristow, Lonnie Robert
Broadnax, Wesley Jerome
Brock, Lou
Brock, Ralph Elwood
Brodhead, John Henry
Bronson, James H.
Brooke, Edward
Brooks, Avery
Brooks, Carolyn Branch
Brooks, Elizabeth Carter
Brooks, Gwendolyn
Brooks, Hallie Beachem
Brooks, Lucy Goode
Brooks, Owen

Brooks, Shelton
Brooks, Tyrone
Brooks, Walter Henderson
Broonzy, Big Bill
Broteer (Venture Smith)
Broughton, Virginia E. Walker
Brown, Ada
Brown, Addie
Brown, Anne
Brown, Arthur McKimmon
Brown, Benjamin
Brown, Buster
Brown, Cecil
Brown, Charles
Brown, Charlotte Eugenia Hawkins
Brown, Chuck
Brown, Clara (Aunt Clara)
Brown, Clarence "Gatemouth"
Brown, Claude
Brown, Cleo
Brown, Clifford
Brown, Cora
Brown, Corrine
Brown, Dorothy Lavinia
Brown, Earl
Brown, E. C. (Edward Cooper)
Brown, Elaine
Brown, Emma V.
Brown, Ernest "Brownie"
Brown, Everett
Brown, Frank London
Brown, Fredi Sears
Brown, George S.
Brown, Grafton Tyler
Brown, H. Rap
Brown, Hallie Quinn
Brown, Henry "Box"
Brown, Homer S.
Brown, James
Brown, James
Brown, Jeannette Elizabeth
Brown, Jesse
Brown, Jesse Leroy
Brown, Jill
Brown, Jim
Brown, Joan Myers
Brown, Joe
Brown, John
Brown, John Mifflin
Brown, Josephine
Brown, Kate
Brown, Larry
Brown, Lawrence
Brown, Lawrence, Jr.

McFerrin, Robert, Sr.
McGee, Charles Edward
McGee, Henry Wadsworth
McGhee, Brownie
McGhee, Frederick Lamar
McGhee, Howard B. "Maggie"
McGinty, Doris Evans
McGirt, James Ephraim
McGruder, Aaron
McGuire, George Alexander
McGuire-Duvall, Edith
McJunkin, George
McKaine, Osceola
McKane, Alice Woodby
McKay, Claude
McKay, Nellie Y.
McKegney, Tony
McKenzie, Vashti Murphy
McKinlay, Whitefield
McKinney, Cynthia
McKinney, Ernest Rice
McKinney, Nina Mae
McKinney, Roscoe Lewis
McKinney, William (Bill)
McKissack, Pat
McKissick, Floyd Bixler
McKoy, Millie and Christine McKoy
McLaurin, George W.
McLean, Jackie
McLendon, Johnny
McLin, Lena
McMillan, Terry
McNair, Barbara
McNair, Denise
McNair, Ronald Erwin
McNair, Steve
McNairy, Francine
McNatt, Rosemary Bray
McNeely, Cecil James (Big Jay)
McNeil, Claudia
McNeill, Robert H.
McPhatter, Clyde
McPhatter, Thomas Hayswood
McPherson, Christopher
McPherson, James Alan
McQueen, Butterfly
McRae, Carmen
McShann, Jay
McTell, Blind Willie
McWhorter, John
Meachum, John Berry
Meadows, Lucile Smallwood
Mease, Quentin Ronald "Quent"

Mebane, George Allen
Mebane, Mary Elizabeth
Meek, Carrie Mae Pittman
Meek, Kendrick B.
Meeks, Gregory
Melvin, Chasity
Melvin, Harold
Memphis Minnie
Memphis Slim
Menard, John Willis
Mendez, José
Menéndez, Francisco
Mercer, Mabel
Meredith, James Howard
Meriwether, Louise
Merrick, John
Merriweather, "Big Maceo"
Metcalfe, Ralph Harold
Metoyer, Augustin
Metoyer, Louis
Mfume, Kweisi
Michaux, Lewis H.
Michaux, Lightfoot Solomon
Micheaux, Oscar
Mickens, Ronald Elbert
Middleton Hairston, Jeanne
Mifflin, James
Milai, A. Sam
Milburn, Amos
Milburn, Rodney "Hot Rod"
Miles, John "Mule"
Miles, Lizzie
Miley, Bubber
Miller, Bebe
Miller, Cheryl
Miller, Dorie
Miller, Gertrude C. Hood
Miller, Kelly
Miller, Loren
Miller, May
Miller, Robert
Miller, Thomas Ezekiel
Millinder, Lucky
Mills, David
Mills, Florence
Mills, Harry and Herbert Mills
Mills, Stephanie
Milton, Little
Milton, Roy
Ming, William Robert "Bob," Jr.
Mingus, Charles, Jr.
Minkins, Shadrach
Minor, Jane

Mitchell, Abbie
Mitchell, Arthur
Mitchell, Arthur Wergs
Mitchell, Bert Norman
Mitchell, Blue
Mitchell, Bobby
Mitchell, Charles Lewis
Mitchell, Clarence Maurice, Jr.
Mitchell, Elvis
Mitchell, George
Mitchell, John, Jr.
Mitchell, Joseph E.
Mitchell, Juanita Jackson
Mitchell, Littleton Purnell
Mitchell, Matt
Mitchell, Parren
Mitchell, Walter M.
Mitchell-Bateman, Mildred
Mix, Sarah Ann Freeman
Mobley, Hank
Mollison, Irvin C.
Mollison, Willis E.
Molyneaux, Tom
Mongoula, Nicolas
Monk, Thelonious
Monroe, Vernon Earl "The Pearl"
Montana, Allison Marcel "Tootie"
Montgomery, Benjamin Thornton
Montgomery, Isaiah Thornton
Montgomery, Little Brother
Montgomery, Ralph
Montgomery, Wes
Montgomery, William Thornton
Montjoy, Zilpah
Moody, Anne E.
Moody, Charles David
Moon, Harold Warren
Moon, Henry Lee
Mooney, Paul
Moore, Aaron McDuffie
Moore, Acel
Moore, Amzie
Moore, Archie
Moore, Cecil Bassett
Moore, Charles
Moore, Dorothy Rudd
Moore, Frederick Randolph
Moore, Gwen
Moore, Harry Tyson
Moore, John Jamison
Moore, Johnny Dizzy
Moore, Kevin (Keb' Mo')
Moore, Lenny

Preface to the Second Edition

In early January 2008, as the first print editions of the eight-volume, 4,080-entry *African American National Biography* (*AANB*) were dispatched to book stores and libraries across the globe, Illinois's junior U.S. senator, BARACK OBAMA JR., emerged as the front runner in the Democratic Party's presidential primary. The *AANB*'s editorial team had completed all entries in late Fall 2007. For Senator Obama, as for several hundred living people represented in our pages, we knew that any final assessment would necessarily be tentative and subject to future update. In Obama's case, author Randall Kennedy of Harvard Law School speculated that, as of late 2007, "whether Obama would become the first black to win the presidency was unclear," but also noted that his candidacy was "a serious effort, as opposed to merely a symbolic one." That assessment was borne out a year later, in January 2009, as President Obama took the oath of office. That same month, Oxford University Press completed the digitization of the full *AANB* to its online website, the African American Studies Center (AASC) http://www.oxfordaasc.com. Four months later, we added the first fifty new entries to the AASC, including an entry on the first African American First Lady, MICHELLE OBAMA, authored by Professor Darlene Clark Hine of Northwestern University. Since that date we added a further 700 new entries online, and will continue to add a minimum of 300 new entries annually to the AASC. In this essay all existing *AANB* entries are marked in SMALL CAPS; all new *AANB* entries are marked in **BOLD SMALL CAPS**.

The 751 new *AANB* entries continue our effort to capture the African American experience in all its complexity: from the world of politics we have essays on mayors **CORY BOOKER** of Newark, New Jersey, **MICHAEL NUTTER** of Philadelphia, and **SHIRLEY FRANKLIN** of Atlanta. In art, we have several cartoonists from the golden age of the black press in the mid-twentieth century: **JACKIE ORMES**, **CHESTER COMMODORE SR.**, and **AHMED SAMUEL MILAI**. New entries in sports include baseball's **DON NEWCOMBE** and **DARRYL STRAWBERRY**, basketball coach **C. VIVIAN STRINGER**, track star **EVELYN ASHFORD**, and NASCAR's **WILLY T. RIBBS**. Also included are football legends **RONNIE LOTT** of the National Football League (NFL) and **MICHAEL "PINBALL" CLEMMONS**, deemed too small for the NFL, but whose speed and agility made him one of the greats of the Canadian Football League. As in our earlier edition, the field of education enjoys a nearly equal split between women and men. These include the early classical scholars, **WILEY LANE** and **DANIEL BARCLAY WILLIAMS**, **ALBERTA VIRGINIA SCOTT**, the first African American graduate of Radcliffe College, and **VIRGINIA RANDOLPH**, a pioneer of industrial and vocational education in the progressive Era South. Among the more unusual additions is **BARNEY HILL**, a post office worker who gained notoriety by claiming to have been abducted by extraterrestrial aliens. Another postal worker, **HOMER SMITH**, is one of several entries on African Americans who sought a better life in the Soviet Union in the 1930s. Smith would help modernize the Soviet postal system.

This second edition of the *AANB* also includes substantial updates to entries on many important figures, including both Obamas, former Secretaries of State CONDOLEEZZA RICE and COLIN POWELL, and poet ELIZABETH ALEXANDER, who recited her "Praise Song for the Day" at President Obama's inaugural. The new edition also records the deaths of many prominent African Americans since 2007, among them: JOHN HOPE FRANKLIN, the Reverend PETER GOMES, DOROTHY HEIGHT, FRED SHUTTLESWORTH, DERRICK BELL, BENJAMIN HOOKS, PERCY SUTTON, **STEPHANIE TUBBS JONES**, **ROY DeCARAVA**, LENA HORNE, EARTHA KITT, ABBEY LINCOLN, KOKO TAYLOR, GIL SCOTT-HERON, ALBERTINA WALKER, TEDDY PENDERGRASS, SOLOMON BURKE, **LEVI STUBBS**, and MICHAEL JACKSON.

Perhaps less well known among the *AANB* subjects who have recently died is VERNON J. BAKER, one of eighty-seven African American winners of the nation's highest military award, the Medal of Honor. During World War II Baker was awarded the Purple Heart, the Bronze Star, and the Distinguished Service Cross for his heroics behind the vaunted Gothic Line in 1945, when, under intense German bombardment, he led the 360th and 361st Regimental Combat Teams through mine fields near Viareggio, Italy, to capture both of the original objectives of the mission. It was not until 1997, however, after a lengthy campaign for recognition, that Baker and six other African Americans received the Medal of Honor for their heroics in World War II. Baker received his in person from President Bill Clinton; Private **GEORGE WATSON**, Sergeant **EDWARD A. CARTER JR.**, Private WILLY F. JAMES JR., Sergeant **RUBEN RIVERS**, First Lieutenant **CHARLES L. THOMAS**, and First Lieutenant JOHN FOX received their awards posthumously. All of these servicemen—and indeed all eighty-seven winners of the Medal of Honor, including **ROBERT SWEENEY**, one of only nineteen American servicemen to win the award twice—are now included in this new edition of *AANB*.

Our new edition also includes many African American military figures who may not have won the Medal of Honor, but whose achievements are significant. Among these are **OLIVER CROMWELL**, who participated in Washington's crossing of the Delaware and fought for the Patriot cause at Trenton, Brandywine, Monmouth, and Yorktown. Cromwell is one of forty-seven military entries in this edition authored by Glenn Allen Knoblock, whose work ensures the sacrifices of black military personnel will always be remembered. Also of note is Sara Bruya's fascinating essay on **MINGO SANDERS**, of the Twenty-fifth Infantry's bicycle corps, which in 1896 completed a round-trip bicycle expedition from Fort Missoula, Montana, to St. Louis, Missouri, to test the military applications of that new vehicle. That Sanders was partially blind because of an explosion makes his achievement even more surprising. It was, however, in the Spanish American War that Sanders most distinguished himself. Although one-quarter of the American troops in Cuba were African American, it was Colonel Teddy Roosevelt who claimed most credit for the American victory at San Juan Hill. During the battle, Roosevelt summoned Sanders and requested that his troops surrender some of their rations to help feed the weary "Rough Riders." Sanders obeyed his superior officer, a devotion to duty not reciprocated by Roosevelt, when as U.S. president in 1906 he included Sanders among 167 black soldiers dishonorably discharged (without trial) following an incident at Brownsville, Texas, when a white bartender was shot and killed. There was no evidence that any of the soldiers was involved in the shooting. Despite a spirited campaign to reverse Roosevelt's decision—which in part prompted W.E.B. DU BOIS to support Woodrow Wilson, and other blacks to support William Henry Taft in 1912—Sanders and other members of the Twenty-fifth would not receive an honorable discharge until 1972.

This second edition also includes Zoe Trodd's fine entry on **LEWIS SHERIDAN LEARY** to ensure that the *AANB* includes all of the African American allies of John Brown at Harper's Ferry, including JOHN ANTHONY COPELAND, DANGERFIELD NEWBY, SHIELDS GREEN, and the only black survivor, OSBORNE PERRY ANDERSON. Anderson would later recall that Leary was "generous-hearted and companionable," "brave to desperation," and ready to die for "the most holy principles." Copeland was Leary's nephew, and Leary's widow, Mary Patterson Leary, later married the noted Ohio abolitionist CHARLES HENRY LANGSTON, who was in turn the older brother of JOHN MERCER LANGSTON, the first black U.S. Congressman from Virginia. Mary and Charles Langston would have an even more famous grandson, the writer LANGSTON HUGHES. Indeed, as the *AANB* continues to grow, readers will be able to trace the many family, kin, and other networks of association among people of color. The African American Studies Center has begun to highlight these links through a series of family trees. In addition to FREDERICK DOUGLASS, for example, the *AANB* has entries on his first wife, ANNA MURRAY DOUGLASS; his daughter, ROSETTA DOUGLASS SPRAGUE; sons FREDERICK DOUGLASS JR. and **LEWIS HENRY DOUGLASS** (in a new essay by Donald Yacovone); granddaughter FREDERICKA DOUGLASS SPRAGUE PERRY; and grandson JOSEPH HENRY DOUGLASS, an accomplished concert violinist.

Other notable families who provide several entries to the *AANB* are the Tanners, Mossells, and Bustills. Among the new entries for this edition is **SARAH E. TANNER** (1840–1914), a teacher at Avery Institute, who married Bishop HENRY TUCKER TANNER, and was the matriarch of a family that included a son, the renowned painter HENRY OSSAWA TANNER, and a daughter, HALLE TANNER JOHNSON, the first woman licensed to practice medicine in Alabama. Another daughter, Mary Louisa Tanner, would marry **AARON ALBERT MOSSELL II**, the first African American graduate of the University of Pennsylvania Law School. One of their daughters, SADIE TANNER MOSSELL ALEXANDER, would go onto be the first African American women to earn a Ph.D. and to graduate from Penn Law School. She would barely know her father, however, since he left the family and the country when Sadie was one year old. After working briefly in Africa, Aaron Mossell became a leading trade union leader in Cardiff, Wales, and was also a delegate to the 1945 Pan African Conference in Manchester. While in Wales, Aaron Mossell entertained the actor-singer PAUL ROBESON, who was greatly revered in that nation for his support for Welsh coal miners. It helped that Robeson was a relative. Robeson's mother, Maria Louisa Bustill Robeson, was the sister of GERTRUDE ELIZABETH BUSTILL MOSSELL, wife of Aaron's elder brother, **NATHAN FRANCIS MOSSELL**, who was the first black graduate of Penn Medical School. The Bustills were themselves descended from the abolitionists

Grace Bustill Douglass, Robert Douglass, and Sarah Mapps Douglass. Other new *AANB* entries include **Charles Wesley Mossell,** a missionary to Haiti, a brother of Nathan and Aaron, and Mary (Mazie) Campbell Mossell, daughter of Gertrude and Nathan, and a noted Philadelphia clubwoman.

Finally, the new edition of the *AANB* allows us to showcase the first entries inspired by teacher Terry Vara-Dannen and her students at the Hartford University High School of Science & Engineering. After attending an *AANB* workshop sponsored by the Gilder Lehrman Foundation, Ms. Vara Dannen encouraged her students to craft their own *AANB* essays on local figures from Connecticut. The success of these entries prompted us, in conjunction with Oxford University Press and the Gilder Lehrman Foundation, to launch a broader outreach program to more than forty high schools. Gilder Lehrman has plans to continue the outreach to even more high schools in the years ahead. The process has been enriching for all: the students have had access to the full *AANB* through Oxford's site, and have had a chance to turn insights from primary resources and background reading into well-crafted essays. The very best of them will leave high school having already been published in a major reference work. Among these are four essays focused on Hartford's Primus family, all written by students in Ms. Vara Dannen's class. Chaitali Korgaonkar and Robert Smieja wrote on the family patriarch, **Holdridge Primus,** who sought his fortune in the Gold Rush, and who became the most prominent business, civic, and religious leader of late-nineteenth-century Hartford. Jennifer Ky gave us a fine piece on Holdridge's son, **Nelson Primus,** who struggled to make a career as an artist, while Joshua Sibblies wrote on Nelson's sister, **Rebecca Primus,** who served as a teacher during Reconstruction. We also include an entry by Jasmine Ali on Rebecca's friend, correspondent, and probable lover **Addie Brown**, a free-born northern working-class woman. As Ms Ali noted:

> Addie Brown's correspondence with Rebecca Primus is of historical significance on several counts: it is a loving exchange between two African American women, a New England domestic and an early Reconstruction educator, a rarely documented nineteenth-century same-sex relationship. In addition, Brown's letters illustrate the vibrant social fabric of Hartford's African American community and churches, while Primus's letters document the struggles of a young teacher starting a school all alone in the South in the years immediately following the Civil War.

This second edition of the *AANB* reflects once again the excellent partnership between Harvard's Du Bois Institute and Oxford University Press. At Harvard, Steven Niven has continued as *AANB* Executive Editor, with primary responsibility for identifying and editing our new entries. We would like to thank him for his unwavering commitment to this project since 2002. We also would like to express our appreciation to Vera Grant, Donald Yacovone, Abby Wolf, Tom Wolejko, and Amy Gosdanian of the Du Bois Institute for their assistance and support. Verity Harding and Rhae Lynn Barnes, graduate students at Harvard, provided excellent research assistance. At Oxford University Press, Senior Editor Tanya Laplante, Editor Robert Repino, and Associate Editor Adam Rosen have overseen the expansion of AANB online, a process which includes recruiting new scholars and shepherding manuscripts through the publication process. Along with Steven Niven and Robert Repino, Eric Stannard managed the production process for the second edition, while Tony Aiello, Lynley Wheaton, and Ryan Abrecht all contributed to the first edition's timely and successful completion. Finally, additional thanks go to James Basker and Richard Gilder at the Gilder Lehrman Foundation and to Harriet Zuckerman at the Mellon Foundation for their continued support of the *AANB*.

HENRY LOUIS GATES JR.
CAMBRIDGE, MASSACHUSETTS, NOVEMBER 2012

Preface to the First Edition

When I was an assistant professor of Afro-American Studies and English at Yale in the late 1970s and early 1980s, I met the great historian John Wesley Blassingame Sr. every morning for breakfast at the Naples Pizza Shop. Situated near the geographical center of the Yale campus, Naples had become the actual center of African American intellectual life at Yale by the time I returned there in 1975, after graduate school at the University of Cambridge—all because John Blassingame, for reasons that he took to his grave, preferred Naples to every other restaurant in New Haven.

Every morning John and I would meet, sometimes alone, sometimes with other colleagues such as the economists Donald Brown and Gerald Jaynes, the philosopher KWAME ANTHONY APPIAH, the historian Peter Ripley, the sociologist Hardy Frye, and the anthropologist John Brown Childs—all regulars during their time at Yale. (Throughout the *African American National Biography*, subjects profiled elsewhere are highlighted in SMALL CAPS.) We talked about everything from last night's basketball game to contemporary politics to historical events. We argued as though our lives depended on it: over questions such as whether BOOKER T. WASHINGTON and W. E. B. DU BOIS could have forged a strategic alliance or whether "Booker T." was an "Uncle Tom." While I was in the process of ascertaining the race of HARRIET E. WILSON, African American literature's first woman novelist, it was to Blassingame, at Naples, that I would bring the results of my research and seek his counsel about new leads to pursue. It was there that we celebrated with a slice of pepperoni pizza and a glass of beer when Blassingame became satisfied that Wilson was, as I had expected and as she claimed to be, a black woman and a novelist.

Blassingame was the first African American scholar to write a full-length study of the history of slavery from the viewpoint of the slaves themselves. Using slave narratives, which at painstaking length he attempted to authenticate, "Blass" (as we called him, with enormous affection and respect) re-created the morals and manners and the life and times of what he termed, brilliantly, "the slave community." And it was at Naples that he and I would plot—fantasize about, actually—the future of the fledgling field of Afro-American Studies in the decades ahead.

Upon one thing we agreed early on: We had to find a way to map the field with reference works, sophisticated reference works such as biographical dictionaries; encyclopedias of history and culture; scholarly editions of texts; collected works of authors who had published essays primarily in periodicals; collected papers projects for major canonical figures like Washington, Du Bois, MARCUS GARVEY, and FREDERICK DOUGLASS; bibliographies; and concordances—in short, all of the foundational reference works that, taken together, bring a field of study into the realm of the scholarly. It is upon reference works such as these that any discipline of study is constructed and through which a field is defined, and "Afro-Am" (as we called it then) was no exception. Indeed, we were determined that we would be part of the generation that eliminated forever the curse of scholars of African American Studies: that each successive generation was forced to reinvent the proverbial wheel, repeating the research undertaken by earlier scholars, of which we remained unaware. It was nothing less than a textual legacy of memory that we hoped to leave to our colleagues and contemporaries, and to our intellectual heirs. So we embarked upon projects, major and minor, with alacrity and a sense of excitement difficult for our students—who now take reference works and research collections such as these for granted—even to begin to understand.

The *African American National Biography* was born out of Oxford University Press's partnership with the American Council of Learned Societies, which resulted in the *American National Biography* (*ANB*) and was originally conceived as a supplement to the *ANB*. In 2001 Casper Grathwohl at Oxford University Press asked me to select a figure included in the ANB about whom Americans should know more, and then to write an essay about her or his accomplishments for the book *Invisible Giants* (2002). When I looked for my first and second choices through whom to fulfill this assignment—JAMES MCCUNE SMITH and WILLIAM SANDERS SCARBOROUGH—I was surprised to find they were not among the many thousands of biographies in the ANB. As I searched more widely for other African American historical figures, I realized that a second biographical dictionary would be necessary to cover all of the African American figures essential to narrating the complex story of African American history. When I suggested the idea to Grathwohl and to my coeditor, Evelyn Brooks Higginbotham, they quickly agreed to embark upon this project. The result is the *African American National Biography*.

HENRY LOUIS GATES JR.
CAMBRIDGE, MASSACHUSETTS, OCTOBER 2007

Introduction

The impulse to collect and codify the lives and achievements of African Americans has a long and curious history. Faced with allegations that blacks were innately intellectually inferior to Europeans and therefore fit by nature only to be slaves, opponents of slavery during the Enlightenment seized upon a novel idea. They decided that a most efficacious way to refute these spurious and quite dangerous charges was to marshal dramatic biographical evidence about the lives and times of blacks who had distinguished themselves in some way, but especially in the arts and sciences. Since 1808, when the antislavery activist Abbe Henri-Christophe Gregoire published *De la litterature des negres*, well over 300 black biographical dictionaries have been published—their rather colorful titles ranging from *God's Image in Ebony* (1854) and *The Colored Aristocracy of St. Louis* (1858), to *Progress of a Race* (1897), *Negro Stars in All Ages of the World* (1890), and *The African Abroad* (1913).

Given that its origins were deeply and directly political, the genre of the black biographical dictionary lent itself readily to hyperbole and wishful thinking, sometimes for patently ideological reasons, and sometimes because imagination had to do the work of research and historical fact. JOEL AUGUSTUS ROGERS's *World's Great Men of Color* (1947) is one of the best examples, its overly zealous researcher applying a touch of the tar brush to such well-known historical figures as Alessandro de Medici, John VI of Portugal, and Robert Browning. Still, a surprising number of African Americans have only survived as part of the historical record because some enterprising and well-intentioned foe of slavery or advocate of the Negro's equal rights made a concerted effort to record what they did and how they did it as one of the stories in one of these curious biographical dictionaries, thereby countering claims about what was possible for a Negro to achieve "by nature." In the story of the collective life of the race, as narrated through the achievements contained in these individual lives, was proof that the person of African descent was fit to be something more than a slave. We might think of this as antislavery (and later, civil rights) agitation by biography.

If Rogers's work represents an extreme form of the genre in which almost everybody who did anything historically significant in the West turns out to have been recently descended from one African or another, at the other extreme stand biographical dictionaries created by white scholars, in which blacks have traditionally been dramatically underrepresented. Until its most recent edition, the *Dictionary of American Biography* included only 120 African Americans, while *Notable American Women* (NAW) included only 41 black women (the most recent edition of NAW, however, has made significant progress in correcting this problem). Clearly, a "comprehensive biographical dictionary based on scholarly research," as RAYFORD WHITTINGHAM LOGAN and Michael R. Winston put it in their seminal *Dictionary of American Negro Biography* (*DANB*, 1982), was urgently needed to fill this hole in the official historical record, and the supremely scholarly dictionary—consisting of 626 entries—that Logan and Winston produced began to do just that.

The study of history itself has changed considerably since the 1980s, when Logan and Winston edited the *DANB*. When that dictionary was published, African American Studies had just begun to emerge as a vibrant field of study in the academy, despite the fact that black historians had been publishing pioneering research at least since W. E. B. DU BOIS earned his Ph.D. in History at Harvard in 1895 (his thesis was published a year later). In the last three decades, historical methodology has increasingly explored and accepted new types of evidence, such as slave narratives and oral testimony, and these have given rise to new interpretive frameworks that focus on the significance of broad social movements, rather than merely the "great man" or "great woman" theory of historical agency. More recently, attention to popular culture has provided a wealth of insight into the lived experience of persons who, like most slaves and women, did not necessarily leave many written records. But most important of all, without a doubt, the Internet and digitization projects such as those being undertaken by Ancestry.com and Google.com, which are scanning millions and millions of pages of original historical documents, manuscripts, and books, have resurrected a multiplicity of names of individuals known only to their peers, now long gone. These digitization projects have rescued the historically obscure from a certain purgatory; they were lost, and now are found. Or, more accurately, students and scholars can now "find" these people and begin to piece together the stories of their lives because their names and what they did have been preserved in some historical document: a will, a tax record, a birth or death certificate, a deed—documents that we can retrieve in seconds and then study through the magic of the world wide web. So many broad conclusions about what actual human beings did or felt in any given historical period—and we are thinking here of the whole of American history, not just African American history—will have to be reconsidered, inductively, based upon the emergence of this Alexandrian library of historical data.

*   *   *

With the idea of expanding the *American National Biography* (*ANB*) and at the same time updating Logan and Winston's volume, and relying on the revolution in research in African American Studies since 1982, we launched with Oxford University Press the largest black biographical encyclopedia project to date—the *African American National Biography* (*AANB*)—and published in 2004 the book *African American Lives* to introduce readers to a sample of the 4,100 biographies that fill the pages of these eight printed volumes.

If choosing the 600 biographies that filled *African American Lives* proved a daunting task, selecting more than 4,000 entries for the full-length *African American National Biography* was much more so. This aspect of the project was a constant negotiation between the editors and our contributors, the authors of all of these entries—a debate that lasted until the very last entry was sent to the printer and no time remained to debate the historical importance of this individual or that, and whether that individual would be included in this incarnation of the project, and who might be the best author to write his or her biography in the time allowed. From the beginning, though, we realized that even an eight-volume reference work would, necessarily, omit important historical actors, especially since the digital revolution is enabling the rediscovery of people who have been suspended for decades, even centuries, in the amber of dusty, obscure archives. To confront the issue, we planned with the reference publisher at Oxford, Casper Grathwohl, to build on online component of *AANB*. Eventually, this "online edition" became the centerpiece of Oxford University Press's reference program in African and African American history and culture, the online African American Studies Center. Working with a database that currently includes more than 12,500 names of African Americans, the online *AANB* will continue to grow beyond the 4,100 biographies published in this edition. We next plan to publish an additional 2,000 biographies, and this work has already begun.

Our efforts have been made easier by the decision to include entries on living subjects. Though doing so required more editorial work to ensure our entries are up to date, it also allowed the *AANB* to capture the unprecedented contributions of African Americans to the life of the nation since World War II, and especially since the civil rights revolution of the 1960s opened up new avenues of opportunity for people of color. Thus the *AANB* includes not only MARY MCLEOD BETHUNE, LOUIS ARMSTRONG, PAUL ROBESON, and FLORENCE GRIFFITH JOYNER, but also COLIN POWELL, TONI MORRISON, HANK AARON, QUINCY JONES, OPRAH WINFREY, and HARRY BELAFONTE. Living subjects also include several presidential cabinet secretaries, federal judges, congressional leaders, and candidates for the presidency of the United States; Nobel and Pulitzer Prize winners; musicians, artists, and entertainers in every genre; Olympic and world-champion athletes, as well as prominent writers, activists, religious leaders, scientists, inventors, and educators.

The sheer scope of *AANB*, however, also enabled us to unearth the stories of unheralded black Americans, many of whom had never before appeared in a biographical dictionary. *AANB* is thus a work of recovery, meant to place individuals of specific historical significance (or notoriety) side by side on the page with those outstanding figures about whom most of us know something, so that readers can discover the lives of not just MARTIN LUTHER KING JR. or MALCOLM X, but also the first black woman poet, the slave LUCY TERRY; the frontierswoman Stagecoach Mary (MARY FIELDS); MAJOR TAYLOR, a world-champion cyclist and the first black international athletic superstar; and the Alabama midwife, MARGARET CHARLES SMITH, who delivered more than 3,500 babies between 1948 and 1976.

AANB is a work that tells the story, for the first time, of the broadest swath of the black people who lived and breathed and made our collective history—the history of African America—people whose contributions marked their place and time, and people whose contributions have transcended their place and time. In a significant sense, the simplicity and serendipity of arranging subjects in alphabetical order serves as a powerful educational tool. Readers curious about the writer JAMES BALDWIN may find equally fascinating the adjacent entries on MARY LOUISE BALDWIN, the principal of the famed, all-white Agassiz School in Cambridge, Massachusetts, and VERNON JOSEPH BAKER, winner of the Medal of Honor for his heroism as a soldier in World War II. Those interested in the history of music and hip-hop will undoubtedly be drawn to the entry on SNOOP DOGGY DOGG, but we hope that they will find equally fascinating the nearby entry on VALAIDA SNOW, a jazz musician and singer who is one of two *AANB* subjects to have been interned in a Nazi concentration camp (the other is LIONEL ROMNEY).

*   *   *

The literary critic and biographer ARNOLD RAMPERSAD demonstrated in an important essay published in the *Yale Review* several years ago that the biographical impulse among African Americans—as measured by the publication of life histories of black individuals by black authors—has been surprisingly minimal. Few blacks, Rampersad found, had written full-length biographies of black subjects. On the other hand, African Americans excelled at writing autobiographies, starting with autobiographical slave narratives. Extraordinarily, many black authors have published autobiographies as their first books; usually, one writes an autobiography after one is established as a public figure, someone about whose life general readers might naturally be curious. But in the black literary tradition, writers have often used autobiographies to establish themselves as public figures. One need think only of MAYA ANGELOU's canonical *I Know Why the Caged Bird Sings* to illustrate the point. Moreover, many black authors have embraced the form so thoroughly that they have published multiple autobiographies, texts that at times contradict important facts asserted in a previous autobiography. FREDERICK DOUGLASS and W. E. B. DU BOIS are probably the two best examples of this practice.

Though there have been many attempts over the last 200 years to put in place a biographical record of African American lives, as evidenced by the more than 300 collective biographies of black people that have come and almost entirely gone, now, thanks to Oxford University Press, we can at long last publish the definitive biographical dictionary, recording the contributions of an unprecedented number of historically significant African Americans, individual subjects whose contributions to American history have long deserved to be recorded. As we have seen, black biographical dictionaries have often operated as important and iconographic acts of hero-production and hagiography, as testaments to the intellectual capacities of "the Negro." Nurses and churchmen, clubwomen and fraternal orders, free citizens and slaves, sleeping-car porters and freemasons—each provided their piece of the collective biographical history of their contemporaries and peers. But the *AANB* stands upon the foundation that the pioneering editors of these biographical dictionaries constructed. The *AANB* stands heir to the tradition that they, collectively, so nobly and fearlessly created.

The *AANB* would also not have been possible without the efforts of the more than 1,700 contributors whose expertise and desire to tell these great stories appears on every page. The incredible diversity of subjects covered in the *AANB* is a testament to the broad range of our contributors, which includes professors and graduate students at major research institutions, as well as independent scholars and freelance writers. Authors came from all regions of the United States, and the participation of writers from Canada, the Caribbean, Europe, and Africa reflects the deep interest in African American history throughout our world.

The *AANB* is the largest act of historical recovery in the history of African American Studies, full of colorful characters like Colonel ALLEN ALLENSWORTH, who founded an all-black town in California in 1808; MARY ELLEN PLEASANT, a legendary woman of influence and political power in Gold-Rush and Gilded-Age San Francisco; ALICE OF DUNK'S FERRY, who died in Philadelphia at the age of one hundred sixteen, a female slave and an Episcopalian; and RICHARD POTTER, "a celebrated Ventriloquist and Professor of Legerdemain," who owned a two-hundred-acre estate in Andover, Massachusetts, before his death in 1835. Even Joel A. Rogers—most appropriately—is in our collection of distinguished black lives, along, of course, with the great historical figures of our people. All the individuals whose lives are recollected and analyzed in these pages played crucial roles in the collective history of black people. And, indeed, the strength of *AANB* is that, taken together, the lives recorded tell a richer and fuller story of black life in America than was ever possible, such as one of my favorites, the Honorable THEOPHILUS B. MORTON, "a great race man and leader among the people," as his contemporary biographer put it, and a messenger to a district judge in San Francisco. Morton was a person of vital importance to his community, but someone whose contributions to American history had long been forgotten or minimized—until now. T. B. Morton will now be remembered forever for all he did for his people, no matter how modest those contributions might seem in the twenty-first century, when black people have achieved so very much. The list of subjects in *AANB*, the depth of coverage of the marvelously colorful and sometimes quirky people whose lives actually make up the "Black Experience in America," is astonishing, even to its editors. Their stories, long buried in those dusty archives that contain the raw material of history, will never be lost again. And that is what scholarship in the field of African American Studies should be all about.

Finally, we wish to thank the many and incredibly generous individuals and foundations that supported the research, writing, and publication of *AANB*, and without whom this massive undertaking would have been impossible. The American Council of Learned Societies wholeheartedly supported this "expansion" of the *AMERICAN NATIONAL BIOGRAPHY* and assisted us in innumerable ways, especially during the phase that culminated with the publication of *AFRICAN AMERICAN LIVES*. Additional thanks to Harriet Zuckerman and the Mellon Foundation; Richard Gilder and Dr. James Basker at the Gilder-Lehrman Foundation; Donald and Susan Newhouse, members of the National Advisory Board of the Du Bois Institute; Dr. Irma McClaurin and Monica Hilliard at the Ford Foundation; and the Educational Netcasting Corporation.

HENRY LOUIS GATES JR.
EVELYN BROOKS HIGGINBOTHAM
EDITORS IN CHIEF

Editorial Note

Work on the *African American National Biography* (*AANB*) began early in 2002 in the Barker Center at Harvard University with the compilation of a database containing the names of 12,500 African Americans. These ranged from ESTEBAN, who in 1528 was the first African to set foot in North America, to the tennis star SERENA WILLIAMS, born in 1982. By September 2002, HENRY LOUIS GATES JR. and EVELYN BROOKS HIGGINBOTHAM had assembled a ten-member editorial board of eminent scholars and selected Dr. John K. Bollard as the *AANB*'s first managing editor. John Bollard created a collegial and intellectually stimulating work environment at the *AANB* offices established at 69 Dunster Street in Cambridge, and instituted the highest standards for all who would work for the project. He was assisted by Lisa Rivo and two other associate editors and senior writers: Sholomo Ben Levy and Steven Niven. Over eighteen months, this team completed the first stage of *AANB*, the *African American Lives* project. In addition to writing eighty entries for *African American Lives* and more than 200 biographies for the full *AANB*, Levy, Niven, and Rivo solicited and edited contributions from a wide range of scholars and writers.

In the summer of 2005 the *AANB* underwent a major reorganization, with Kate Tuttle serving as executive editor until August 2006. Together, Tuttle and Niven in the Harvard offices of the *AANB* and Anthony Aiello at Oxford University Press in New York reorganized the project staff, created a board of seventeen subject-area experts to assist the editors in chief and senior editorial staff in the review and approval of entries, added renowned scholars to the advisory board to ensure that we were keeping an eye on both the forest and the trees, and somehow assigned, collected, reviewed, revised, approved, and edited more than 3000 new biographies in the last three years of the project. The final year of the project proved the most challenging. In August 2006 Steven Niven followed Kate Tuttle as the Harvard-based *AANB* executive editor.

The editorial staff of the *AANB* has made a special effort to ensure that a number of topics received due coverage in these pages, notably the role of African Americans before the nineteenth century and in the exploration of the frontier and westward expansion; the sustained and memorable, but often neglected, role of blacks in science, medicine, and technology; and the contributions in every sphere and historical period by African American women. While 28 percent of our entries are biographies of women, we expect that this figure will be higher in the growing online edition of the *AANB*. In some categories, the numbers of women are even higher: 38 percent of our activists and 44 percent of our writers are women. Slightly more than half of all of the educators featured in the *AANB* are women.

The full diversity of all 4,100 subjects can be gleaned from the list indexes arranged by a variety of topics, including subject category, occupation, and realms of renown; place of birth; and medal and award winners. All entries also contain a Further Reading section, which lists relevant biographical sources and, where available, obituaries and manuscript collections. Any autobiographies by the subject of the entry are listed first in the Further Reading section.

The *AANB* reflects the perseverance, creativity, and achievements of black Americans over five centuries. Legal and extralegal impediments—such as slavery, segregation, and racial violence—limited, but could not fully prevent, African Americans' participation in our national life. Thus, while there would be no African American Chairman of the Joint Chiefs of Staff until COLIN POWELL in the 1990s, Powell built on the efforts of black military figures from the Revolutionary War (including CRISPUS ATTUCKS, PRINCE ESTABROOK, CATO CARLISLE, SCIPIO AFRICANUS, and PRIMUS HALL); the Civil War (among them ROBERTS SMALLS, ANDRE CAILLOUX, PRINCE RIVERS, BRUCE ANDERSON, JOHN LAWSON, and WILLIAM CARNEY); as well as HENRY O. FLIPPER, the first black graduate of West Point; the Buffalo Soldiers CATHY WILLIAMS, CHARLES VEALE, JOHN DENNY, and SAMUEL GARLAND; and the twentieth-century military leaders CHARLES YOUNG, BENJAMIN O. DAVIS SR., BENJAMIN O. DAVIS JR., CHARITY ADAMS EARLEY, HAZEL JOHNSON-BROWN, and HARRIET M. WEST WADDY. The famed pediatric neurosurgeon BEN CARSON and the U.S. Surgeon General DAVID SATCHER likewise built on the legacy of the slave physicians CESAR and ONESIMUS and the nineteenth-century medical pioneers DANIEL HALE WILLIAMS and WILLIAM WARRICK CARDOZO.

And when ROSA PARKS refused to give up her seat on a Montgomery, Alabama, bus in December 1955, she followed a precedent set by, among others in these volumes, BAYARD RUSTIN, JACKIE ROBINSON, BENJAMIN DAVIS JR., HOMER PLESSY, IDA WELLS-BARNETT, Congressman ROBERT BROWN ELLIOT, SOJOURNER TRUTH, JAMES W. C. PENNINGTON, and DAVID RUGGLES. Ruggles refused to give up his seat in a New Bedford, Massachusetts, railcar in 1841, a year after the railway was established in that town. Even the seemingly twenty-first-century cause of reparations for slavery, as advocated by DEADRIA FARMER-PAELLMANN, has its precedent in the remarkable work of CALLIE HOUSE, born a slave in 1861, a leading light in the Slave Mutual Relief, Bounty and Pension Association, which boasted 300,000 members in 1915. A similar pattern emerges in the categories of sports and entertainment. TIGER WOODS stands on the shoulders of fellow golfers TED RHODES and CHARLIE SHIPPEN; the NFL coaches TONY DUNGEE and LOVIE SMITH owe a debt to pioneering college coaches such as EDDIE ROBINSON of Grambling State; CHRIS ROCK follows in a long line of comedians that includes BILL COSBY, RED FOXX, and MOMS MABLEY.

The *AANB* also acknowledges those African Americans who paid the greatest price, losing their lives solely because of their color. Among these are two slave women named CELIA, one from Florida and one from Missouri, both executed for killing their masters in self-defense; the Reconstruction politicians CHARLES CALDWELL and NOAH PARKER, both assassinated in Mississippi in 1875; and ANTHONY P. CRAWFORD and SAM HOSE, lynching victims during the "nadir," as the historian RAYFORD W. LOGAN has described it, of American race relations between 1880 and 1915. You will also find entries on the victims of racist resistance to the post–World War II Second Reconstruction: EMMETT TILL, MEDGAR EVERS, VERNON DAHMER; JIMMY LEE JACKSON, MALCOLM X, and MARTIN LUTHER KING JR. The youngest subjects in the *AANB* and also the most tragic are ADDIE MAE COLLINS, DENISE MCNAIR, CAROLE ROBERTSON, and CYNTHIA WESLEY, victims of the 1963 church bombing in Birmingham, Alabama. For the first time in any biographical dictionary, each of these young women, memorialized in SPIKE LEE's documentary *4 Little Girls* (1997), has a separate entry.

Tom Wolejko at Harvard and Jody Benjamin and Ryan Abrecht at Oxford University Press worked wonders during the final months of production, locating contributors to remind them of their due dates, making sure the most crucial entries were submitted, and ensuring the most efficient and timely flow of entries among contributors, subject editors, executive editors, copyeditors, and proofreaders. In the final seven months of production, Dr. Donald Yacovone, research manager at the Du Bois Institute, and Julie Wolf of QWERTY Editorial Inc. joined the editorial staff to ensure that we met our goal of at least 4,000 high-quality entries by June 2007.

Anthony Aiello, *AANB*'s co-executive editor at Oxford University Press, joined the project in 2004 and was involved with all aspects of development and production: coordinating the efforts of the various teams and offices involved in completing *AANB*, maintaining the project schedule and budget, reviewing manuscripts, managing the art research and image acquisition, and otherwise acting as the point of contact for everyone working on *AANB*. Responsibility for the copyediting, proofing, and printing of *AANB*'s nearly 4,100 entries lay primarily with Martin Coleman and Nancy Tan. Coleman's unflappability and expertise with managing encyclopedia production was most welcome throughout the always difficult editing and composition of a project of such scope, and Tan's completion of the final production stages was a superhuman effort. Coleman and Tan's constant vigilance and attention to detail ensured that entries met our editorial demands for accuracy and excellence while also making sure that production goals and publication deadlines were being met.

*   *   *

Working with Professors Gates and Higginbotham has been a privilege and an honor. The passion they bring to this vitally important work and the excellence they have demanded of the project staff and the scholars and experts who have contributed to *AANB* have made each day its own learning experience, as we have tackled large issues such as whom to include and whom to exclude and why, of race, of naming, and smaller issues like the length of entries, the handling of bibliographies, or whether to hyphenate "African American." Through it all, the *AANB* has been a communal effort that we hope will open doors to previously unexplored spaces in American history.

STEVEN J. NIVEN
ANTHONY AIELLO
EXECUTIVE EDITORS

African American National Biography

Aaron (1811?–?), a former Virginia slave who became an antislavery lecturer, used no last name. Almost nothing is known about him outside of the record contained in his episodic, forty-eight page memoir. He did not provide any information about his parents other than that "hard work and hard usage … killed them" (*Light and Truth*, 6). He recorded that he had lived in Maryland and Kentucky, but that for most of his time as a slave he lived in Virginia, owned by a master with seven other slaves, three of whom were female. Aaron's owner proved especially cruel, preferring to personally punish his slaves rather than send them out for a whipping. During the summer he forced his three female slaves to work all day and then spend the entire night cooling him and his family with fans while they slept. Aaron was forbidden to go to church, although he often did so despite his master's commands and received beatings for his disobedience or would be locked up in a cellar for days without food or water. Aaron did not indicate when or what particular incident prompted him to run away when he was twenty-nine or thirty years of age, but he did reveal that he left a wife behind when he fled from Virginia to Lancaster, Ohio, a small town southeast of Columbus.

Aaron remained in Lancaster for about four years before his former owner learned of his whereabouts and sent slavecatchers to retrieve him. To outfox his pursuers, Aaron said that he walked backward through a swamp, leaving footprints that would lead his pursuers in the wrong direction. He was imprecise about his travels while escaping further north—perhaps to protect the few who aided him—but said that by the time he published his memoir he had traveled in twelve Northern states and one hundred miles through Canada. His experience in the North, probably during the early 1840s, affirmed the message of the black abolitionist movement that most Northerners hated slavery and the slave. "I have traveled through about all of the free States," he said. "I have been mobbed in a great many places" (*Light and Truth*, 41). Sometime after his departure from Ohio, he was shunned from Elizabethtown, New Jersey, and probably would have died from exposure if not for one family that allowed him to sleep in a barn. In most towns, he found that even abolitionist families treated him coldly, preferring that he freeze to death rather than sleep in their homes.

After leaving New Jersey, he conducted an extensive antislavery tour of New England. Probably traveling mostly by foot, Aaron wandered from Massachusetts to Maine, from Connecticut to Rhode Island, seeking a place to speak, meals, donations, and a warm spot by a fireplace to sleep. His travels appeared to begin well in Foxboro, Massachusetts. He encountered sympathetic Universalists, possibly led by Reverend Charles W. Mellen, who "treated me like a brother, minister and all" (*Light and Truth*, 4) and even helped pay for the publication of his memoir in 1845. Eventually, he succeeded in speaking in thirty-two churches and in numerous halls, schools, and private homes, many undoubtedly arranged by friends he had made in the antislavery community. George Benson, William Lloyd Garrison's brother-in-law, for instance, accompanied Aaron to Providence, Rhode Island. In Portland, Maine, he addressed an audience of seven to eight hundred people, very likely the largest he attracted.

But most of his New England tour only revealed the depth of the region's racial prejudice. At one point, Aaron's lecturing had brought him somewhere between forty-eight and seventy-five dollars, which, when he arrived in Providence, he placed in the hands of a white tavern owner for safekeeping. When Aaron retrieved his cash the next morning, only twenty-five dollars remained. Aaron heard of a wealthy white man from the city who traveled south every winter, each time taking a different black boy with him as a servant. Although every year the man claimed his servant had died during his visit, he in fact had sold all of them into slavery. In Hallowell, Maine, Aaron learned that the city could boast of at least fifty-two solid antislavery families, but none would give him a place to sleep or a scrap of food. In Braintree, Massachusetts, the birthplace of John Quincy Adams, Aaron discovered a minister who had recanted his abolitionism after marrying a woman from the South who owned 160 slaves: "slavery is not so bad as he formerly thought it was" (*Light and Truth*, 35).

Aaron had gained great familiarity with the Bible (although he could not read), the antislavery movement, and antislavery politics. While he condemned most of the North as steeped in racial animosity and hypocrisy—"wolves clothed in sheep's clothing"—he spoke knowledgeably and approvingly about the Liberty Party, a small antislavery political party with strongholds in southeastern Massachusetts, parts of northern New England, and western New York, Michigan, and Ohio. It was, to Aaron, a trusted enemy of slavery: "it makes the abolition of slavery the paramount vital interest of this nation …" (*Light and Truth*, 11–12). His tour brought him to countless hamlets, where he would seek assistance and an opportunity to talk about his experience in slavery. Unable to write, he used his travels to find people willing to write portions of his memoir for him, usually a widow or a wife whose husband was away at work. More often than not, when the husband returned from work, he would chase Aaron from his house. Aaron's reliance upon others to write his text accounts for its meandering quality and constant shifts between the first and third person narrator. But it also allowed him to support his stances with quotations from newspapers, books, poems, the Bible, political leaders, white abolitionist leaders, and other slaves, including an account of Toussaint L'Ouverture and a portion of the slave narrative of MOSES GRANDY's, which concludes his brief work.

The first page of the memoir reveals an image of Aaron, a woodcut of a slight, dark-skinned man in what appears to be a turban. How true a representation it is cannot be known, but the depiction clearly sought to present the author as a respectable, perhaps foreign-born—if not slightly exotic—individual worthy of sympathy and support. Perhaps sold at some of Aaron's later appearances, the pamphlet was aimed at white audiences and drew upon the authority of the printed word to serve as irrefutable evidence of the evils of slavery and racial prejudice.

FURTHER READING

Aaron. *Light and Truth of Slavery. Aaron's History* (1845).

LAURA MURPHY

Aaron, Hank (5 Feb. 1934–), baseball player and executive, was born Henry Aaron in the Down the Bay section of Mobile, Alabama, the third of eight children of Herbert Aaron and Estella (maiden name unknown). His parents had left the Selma, Alabama, area during the Depression for greater opportunity in Mobile's shipbuilding industries. In 1942, as the family grew and Down the Bay became more crowded with wartime job seekers, the Aarons moved to a rural suburb of Toulminville. Working as a boilermaker's apprentice, Herbert Aaron suffered through the frequent layoffs that plagued black shipyard workers before wartime demand dictated full employment. Ever resourceful, Herbert Aaron bought two lots in Toulminville, hired carpenters to frame out the roof and walls of a house, and set about with his family to find materials to finish the property. The Aarons continued to live in the house even as Henry achieved superstardom.

Making balls from such scavenged materials as tape and tin cans and using them by himself or in frequent games with his playmates, young Henry loved baseball. His younger brother Tommie became a professional player, later joining Hank on the Milwaukee Braves in 1962. While the big leagues were still a dream, Henry was developing the skills and techniques of success by tossing bottle caps into the air and hitting them with a broomstick. This regimen encouraged him to hit with his weight shifted to his front foot, a stance that resulted in the consistently good contact between ball and bat that set him apart from other hitters. From his earliest playing days, players and coaches wondered at the size and strength of Aaron's wrists. Henry's notable qualities were not limited to his batting

Hank Aaron, Atlanta Braves' outfielder, bats during spring training in March 1974. (AP Images.)

stance, however. Herbert Aaron had instilled in his son qualities of pride, determination, and respect exercised without attracting attention. Henry later recounted that, when he left home to play baseball, his father told him that "nobody would want to hear what I had to say until I proved myself" (Aaron and Wheeler, 17). After JACKIE ROBINSON broke the color barrier in the major leagues in 1947, the thirteen-year-old Henry skipped school to listen to Brooklyn Dodgers broadcasts on a pool-hall radio. Five years later he left Alabama for Indiana to play for the Indianapolis Clowns in the Negro American League. Aaron's world expanded even further when the Major League Boston Braves purchased his contract from the Clowns in 1952. Having just missed out on signing Willie Mays, the Braves front office acted quickly with Aaron and sent him to their Class C Northern League farm team in Eau Claire, Wisconsin. Despite bouts of homesickness and the difficulties of playing shortstop in the minor leagues, he fared well in Eau Claire. He hit .336 to finish second in the league, earning a trip to spring training in 1953 with the parent Braves club, now moved to Milwaukee. Reassigned to second base,

Aaron was sent to the Class A Sally League team in Jacksonville after manager Ben Geraghty learned that he was willing to become the first black player in the league. Along with outfielder Horace Garner and shortstop Felix Mantilla, Aaron integrated the Deep South league. Geraghty respected and supported Aaron, who hit a league-leading .362 and won the Most Valuable Player award. That winter, Aaron began playing the outfield.

During the summer of 1953, Aaron met Barbara Lucas and enjoyed spending time with her family. The couple married on 6 October, and a daughter was born a year later. Four other children followed.

When the Braves left fielder Bobby Thomson broke his leg during spring training for the 1954 season, Aaron was given the opportunity to start in his place. He responded by hitting .280 and winning the job permanently. Clearly, the Braves had a bona fide major leaguer. During that first season, the Braves traveling secretary Donald Davidson began calling Henry "Hank," and the name stuck. At the end of the season, Aaron requested a change from the number five he had been wearing, and in 1955 he began wearing number forty-four, the number he made famous.

Aaron performed well in 1955 and even better in 1956, when he hit .328 and won the National League batting title. Disappointment dominated his mood at season's end, however, when the Braves lost the pennant to the Dodgers in the final series. Determined to win the pennant his team had lost the previous year, Aaron had, arguably, his best year ever in 1957. Hitting a dramatic home run to win the pennant and playing solidly as the Braves defeated the New York Yankees to take the World Series, he won the National League's Most Valuable Player award.

Many observers wondered why Aaron, although the best hitter in baseball, was not regarded as an American superstar, as were Mickey Mantle and WILLIE MAYS. The issue is complex. Mantle's great popularity during the period might be attributed to his racial identity as a white man and to the greater opportunity for publicity afforded to those who played in New York. Mays enjoyed far greater adulation than Aaron, perhaps because of his more outgoing personality. At least part of the answer seems to lie in Aaron's personality: quiet, steady, workmanlike, balanced. Such steadfastness shouts no claims, calls no attention to itself. It exists; it endures.

Hank played well season after season and his home run totals accumulated, but the Braves suffered increasingly lean years following their glory days in Milwaukee, particularly after the club moved to Atlanta in 1966. Although Aaron experienced racist attitudes and behavior all his life, the tenor of abuse shifted once it was realized he had a chance to break Babe Ruth's career home run record. For some whites, the idea of a black man replacing Ruth as the home run king was too much to bear.

Pressures multiplied. Divorced from his first wife early in 1971, he married his second wife, Billye Williams, widow of the civil rights activist Dr. Sam Williams, late in 1973. During the 1973 season he hit a remarkable forty home runs in only 392 at bats, but threats on Aaron and his family increased. The FBI assigned agents to accompany Billye and the children. Aaron was often forced to eat by himself, and after he had received a particularly venomous death threat, he warned teammates not to sit next to him in the dugout. Somehow, though, he managed to concentrate on the game that he loved. Hank's friend Congressman JOHN LEWIS suggests that "Hank was shattering something. Sometimes I believe that maybe some force or some power gives you that extra ounce of grace" (Tolan, 169). Perhaps the example of his father and Jackie Robinson and the words of MARTIN LUTHER KING JR. gave Aaron the power to use his bat as his voice in overcoming racism in the United States.

Aaron broke Ruth's record on 8 April 1974, with his 715th home run. He increasingly used his place in the spotlight to press for greater equality, and in Atlanta he spoke his mind with increasing force. Buoyed when FRANK ROBINSON became the first black manager in Major League Baseball in 1975, Aaron stressed the need for more African American managers and executives. However, Atlanta's chilly reaction to his push for black front-office candidates led Aaron to endorse a trade to the American League Milwaukee Brewers in 1975. After two seasons, he retired with 755 home runs. Aaron's home run record would last for thirty-three years until August 2007, when BARRY BONDS of the San Francisco Giants struck his 756th home run.

In 1977 the Braves owner Ted Turner hired Aaron as an executive with responsibilities in the Braves farm system—the network of affiliated minor league teams that provides players for the major league team. As a Braves executive, Aaron served as an advocate for African American candidates and worked to eliminate racial barriers in sports, in part through partnerships with the NAACP, Operation PUSH, and Big Brothers/Big Sisters. He continued to work with such activists as ANDREW YOUNG and JESSE JACKSON in establishing baseball, as not only America's national pastime, but also as a leading force in creating a more just society.

FURTHER READING

Baseball-related documentation and clippings files relating to Hank Aaron's career are housed in the archives of the National Baseball Hall of Fame in Cooperstown, New York.

Aaron, Hank, with Furman Bisher. *Aaron, r.f.* (1968; rev. ed. as *Aaron*, 1974).

Aaron, Hank, with Lonnie Wheeler. *I Had a Hammer: The Hank Aaron Story* (1991).

Poling, Jerry. *A Summer Up North: Hank Aaron and the Legend of Eau Claire Baseball* (2002).

Tolan, Sandy. *Me and Hank: A Boy and His Hero, Twenty-Five Years Later* (2000).

PETER VALENTI

Aaron, Jesse (1887–1979), wood carver, sculptor, and folk artist, was born Jesse James Aaron in Lake City, Florida, to descendants of slaves and Seminole Indians. Aaron attended school for less than one year before he was sent to work as a contract laborer for local farms. Trained as a baker when he was twenty-one years old, he found he enjoyed the creativity it required. He opened several bakeries, worked as a cook at Gainesville's Hotel Thomas from 1933 to 1937, and then cooked for a variety of fraternities and hospitals in Florida. Aaron also worked as a cook aboard the Seaboard Air Line Railroad during this time.

Aaron married Leeanna Jenkins, and when the family settled in northwest Gainesville in the 1930s they opened a nursery. From this point until 1968, when Aaron became a folk artist at the age of eighty-one, it is difficult to determine what is fact and what has been embellished in his story. Some sources state that Aaron had carved since the 1940s, while others tell a story that involves an important turning point that opened the field of art to him. The latter, more dramatic account states that the family made a living with the nursery until 1968, when, unable to pay for a cataract operation for his wife, Jesse was forced to sell the nursery. This appears plausible, since the artist recounted to numerous interviewers that he was worried about his ability to pay for his wife's eye surgery. As Aaron told the story, he was awakened in the middle of the night on 4 July 1968 by a voice commanding him to "Carve wood!" And carve wood he did, until his death in 1979. He made wood sculptures at such a prodigious rate that, decades after his death, his carvings were still widely available for purchase.

Aaron was particular in his selection of the wood for his art. He said that his carving tools and chain saws brought out the forms and shapes that he saw inside the wood itself. He would hunt through swamps and forests for appropriate wood pieces for carving. He sculpted animal shapes and animal and human faces from Florida cypress, hardwoods, dogwood, and cedar. Aaron used both an abstract and a folk-inspired naturalistic style. Some of his works are humorous and include resin-molded noses and eyes attached to the wood pieces. Other works borrow totem pole motifs with animal figures stacked on top of one another. Some appear as if a child constructed the piece, including the use of animal legs extending from the center of the animal's anatomy. Aaron carved both large- and small-scale works. Most pieces average one to three feet in height, but he did smaller pieces as well as extremely large garden pieces. He displayed his finished carvings in his front yard, which doubled as his gallery, marked by the handmade sign on the lawn that read "Jesse J. Aaron Museum, Jesse J. Aaron, sculptor." Tourists as well as locals browsed

his property selecting wood sculptures for purchase. As Aaron's fame grew, so did his outdoor display area. He used a scarification technique on his trees, which involved cutting into the bark to allow later growth to create patterns and shapes in the treated areas. His home museum was featured on CBS News and in newspapers including the *Christian Science Monitor*.

"J. J.," as Aaron was known to his friends and fellow artists, worked in untreated hardwoods. The first cut he made used a chain saw, and the shaping and carving followed with hammers and woodworking tools. Many of Aaron's sculptures featured discovered objects such as old clothing, pipes, and special paints he would make from turpentine, brown tempera, and local mud. The paints were used for decoration while the overall wood remained unpainted. He also cast eyes and attachments for the wood from polyester resin.

Aaron's work was classified as folk art, sometimes called "outsider" or "intuitive" art. The critic Roger Cardinal used the term "outsider art" to describe works created by artists not recognized by the trained art community. This type of art is also called "self-taught" or "naive" art. Artists assigned to these categories have not been trained in art schools and tend to use nontraditional materials in their work; many turn to art late in life. Many outsider artists prefer natural and organic matter, and they attribute their creativity to spiritual and divine inspiration. The southern United States has a tradition of wood carving, and art historians have claimed that certain elements of Aaron's work suggest an intuitive borrowing of features found in native African woodcrafts.

Aaron was known as a practical man. Florida locals tell a story that Aaron found himself without a jack after having had a flat tire on his way to an art exhibition. Aaron purportedly took several of his wood sculptures and used them to lift the truck while he changed the tire. The story concludes with several drivers stopping to purchase the makeshift jacks before he had the tire changed.

Aaron continued to carve even when he could no longer search the swamps and forests for wood. As he grew older, he used assistants to collect wood, and many people brought their own choices of wood to his home. Aaron refused to carve most wood pieces, claiming he could not "interpret" them fully.

Despite the relatively short period of time in which he worked as an established artist, Aaron was recognized as an important carver and sculptor. He was awarded a grant from the National Endowment for the Arts, and from the 1970s on his works have been included in exhibits at Florida State University in Tallahassee, the Corcoran Gallery of Art in Washington, D.C., the New Orleans Museum of Art, and the High Museum of Art in Atlanta, Georgia. The University of Florida at Gainesville was the first to invite Aaron to display his work in a solo exhibition in 1970, and his carvings were displayed in 2003 at the Mennello Museum of American Folk Art in Orlando.

FURTHER READING

Arnett, Paul, and William Arnett, eds. *Souls Grown Deep: African American Vernacular Art of the South*, vol. 1: *The Tree Gave the Dove a Leaf* (2000).

Fine, Gary Alan. *Everyday Genius: Self-taught Art and the Culture of Authenticity* (2004).

Johnson, Jay, and William C. Ketchum Jr. *American Folk Art of the Twentieth Century* (1983).

Purser, Stuart R. *Jesse J. Aaron, Sculptor* (1975).

Ricco, Roger, Frank Maresca, and Julia Weissman. *American Primitive: Discoveries in Folk Sculpture* (1988).

Rosenak, Chuck, and Jan Rosenak. *Museum of American Folk Art Encyclopedia of Twentieth-century American Folk Art and Artists* (1990).

Russell, Charles, ed. *Self-Taught Art: The Culture and Aesthetics of American Vernacular Art* (2001).

Thomison, Dennis. *The Black Artist in America: An Index to Reproductions* (1991).

Yelen, Alice Rae, et al. *Passionate Visions of the American South: Self-Taught Artists from 1940 to the Present* (1993).

PAMELA LEE GRAY

Aarons, Charlie (1845 or 1847–?), slave, wagon driver, steamboat laborer, and sawmill worker, was born in Petersburg, Virginia, the son of Aaron and Louisa. Aarons had two siblings, but neither their names nor the surnames of his parents have been recorded. Considering that Charlie's father's first name was Aaron, Charlie probably adopted his father's first name as his own surname upon emancipation. The historian Eugene D. Genovese has argued that after the Civil War many former slaves rejected the surnames assigned to them when they were in bondage and adopted new ones, often choosing surnames—"entitles" the slaves called them—that connected them to their fathers or to other relatives. Some celebrated their newfound liberty by creating new surnames such as Freedman or Justice. Genovese notes that in the first decade of emancipation, freedmen and freedwomen changed their surnames frequently so that, as one freedwoman put it, if "the white folks get together and change their minds and don't let us be free anymore, then they have a hard time finding us" (447).

All that is known about Charlie Aarons's life can be found in the oral history interview of him recorded by the Federal Writers' Project, an agency of President Franklin Roosevelt's New Deal, in August 1937. At that time Aarons told an interviewer that he had been between eighteen and twenty—"a man able to do a man's work"—at the time of the surrender of the Confederacy in 1865. A number of historians have noted that the Federal Writers' Project interviews with former slaves should be used with caution. Oftentimes the respondents provided their white interviewers with inaccurately positive accounts of their time in bondage; African Americans in the Jim Crow South of the 1930s still had to tread carefully in their everyday dealings with white folks. White interviewers and Federal Writers' Project staff also on occasion rewrote parts of the interviews to conform to the white Southern contention that slavery had been a benign institution. The interview with Charlie Aarons, for example, is subtitled, "Ex-Slave Says He Loved Young Marster John."

Aarons did indeed recall his love for one of his masters, John Harris, and also noted that Harris loved him as well. The entire transcript of Aarons's interview, however, provides a more complex narrative of his life. When Charlie was ten years old, his first master, J. H. White, a store owner in Petersburg, sold him to a speculator in slaves named Jones, who brought the youngster to Mobile, Alabama, which at that time had a thriving trade in slaves. The cotton boom of the 1840s and 1850s resulted in a doubling of slave prices; children aged eight to twelve years old could fetch upwards of four hundred dollars in the slave markets. Charlie never saw his brother, sister, or parents again. In the interview eight decades later, he described his fear at being placed on a block at the Mobile slave mart and his anxiety at hearing various masters bid for him. Aarons was eventually purchased by Jason Harris, who ran a cotton slave-labor camp near Newton Station in Jasper County, Mississippi.

Harris was in Charlie Aarons's view a "pretty rough master" who provided miserly rations to his sixty or so male and female slaves, who worked in the fields from six in the morning until six at night. When asked if his master or mistress ever taught him to read or write, Aarons replied ruefully,

"No, madam, only to work." Punishments and beatings of slaves by Harris's white overseer and black drivers were also common. Although Aarons's duties included driving mule wagons filled with cotton long distances from his plantation home, he claimed that he never attempted to run away, such was his fear of being caught and beaten by patrollers and the "nigger dogs" sent to track down runaways.

When the Civil War began in 1861 Aarons went to the front with his master's son John Harris, whom he looked after while also caring for Harris's horses and tents. Both men survived the battle and siege of Vicksburg, Mississippi, unscathed, as did the Harris plantation. Aarons's white interviewer did not ask Aaron some direct questions that an African American interviewer might have—for example, how he felt upon being freed, or what he thought about Reconstruction. A clue to Aarons's political allegiances can be found, however, in his response to a question about having seen Jefferson Davis, the first and only president of the Confederacy, in Mobile. After replying that he had seen Davis in Mississippi after the war, Aarons's "face lit up," according to his interviewer, when he recalled that he had seen another president: "Yes, madam, I saw President [and former Union general Ulysses S.] Grant," who "came through Mobile from New Orleans, and my there was a big parade that day." When asked his opinion of another Republican president, Abraham Lincoln, Aarons, a longtime Baptist, replied that the Bible says "there was a time for slavery" when "people had to be punished for their sin, and then there was a time for it not to be, and the Lord had opened a good view to Mr. Lincoln, and he promoted a good idea."

Aarons's interview also revealed that he moved to Mobile, Alabama, after the war to work in a Yankee camp, where he drove wagons for the Union troops for a salary—his first ever—of fourteen dollars a month plus room and board. Aarons also worked as a laborer on steamboats on the Mississippi and, in his final working years, as a laborer in a sawmill at Oak Grove, Alabama. As of 1937 Aarons was a widower; he had been married four times, and he also survived his two sons, whose names are not known. Two of his daughters, Carrie Johnson of Kushla, Alabama, and Ella Aarons of Mobile, were still living at that time. In his late eighties Aarons expressed his view that "all people should be religious" and that "the present day folks are bad and wicked, and don't realize anything like the old folks." It is not known when Aarons died.

FURTHER READING

Genovese, Eugene D. *Roll Jordan Roll: The World the Slaves Made* (1974).

Interview of Charlie Aarons by Mary A. Poole, Oak Grove, Alabama, 4 Aug. 1937, in George P. Rawick, ed., *The American Slave: A Composite Autobiography*, supplement, series 1, vol. 1, *Alabama Narratives* (1977). Also available at http://memory.loc.gov/ammen/snhtml/mesnibibNarrators1.html#top.

Musher, Sharon Ann. "Contesting 'the Way the Almighty Wants It': Crafting Memories of Ex-Slaves in the Slave Narrative Collection," *American Quarterly* 53.1 (2001).

STEVEN J. NIVEN

Abbott, Anderson Ruffin (7 Apr. 1837–29 Dec. 1913), surgeon, was born in Toronto, Upper Canada (now Ontario), the son of Wilson Ruffin Abbott, a businessman and properties investor, and Mary Ellen Toyer. The Abbotts had arrived in Toronto around 1835, coming from Mobile, Alabama, via New Orleans and New York. Wilson Abbott became one of the wealthiest African Canadians in Toronto. Anderson received his primary education in Canadian public and private schools. Wilson Abbott moved his family to the Elgin Settlement in 1850, providing his children with a classical education at the famed Buxton Mission School. Anderson Abbott, a member of the school's first graduating class, continued his studies at the Toronto Academy, where he was one of only three African Americans. From 1856 to 1858 he attended the preparatory department at Oberlin College, afterward returning to Toronto to begin his medical training.

At age twenty-three Abbott graduated from the Toronto School of Medicine, having spent four years under the tutelage of ALEXANDER T. AUGUSTA, a black physician. Abbott became a licentiate of the Medical Board of Upper Canada in 1861, and in 1863 he petitioned U.S. Secretary of War Edwin Stanton and was commissioned as an assistant surgeon, assuming the rank of captain.

From 1863 to 1866 Abbott served in the Washington, D.C., area, first at Camp Barker, a "contraband camp" that accommodated runaway slaves, under the command of his former mentor, A. T. Augusta. The establishment of Freedmen's Hospital in Washington, D.C., in 1863, the first public hospital for African Americans in the United States, has been attributed to the work of these two doctors. When Augusta was transferred to another post, Abbott assumed the position of executive in charge of the contraband hospitals in Washington; these hospitals provided medical care to emancipated slaves and to soldiers. In 1864 he moved to Abbott's Hospital in the Freedmen's Village, the Union-controlled estate in northern Virginia seized from Robert E. Lee.

While in Washington, Abbott met Abraham Lincoln. In a memoir he described the stir that he and Augusta made during a White House reception in the winter of 1863–1864. After Lincoln's assassination in April 1865, Mary Todd Lincoln gave Abbott the plaid shawl that Lincoln had often worn about town.

At the end of the Civil War, Abbott signed a contract with the Freedmen's Bureau to serve at the Freedmen's Hospital in Washington, where he remained until his resignation on 5 April 1866.

Returning to Canada, Abbott resumed his medical studies at Toronto University, standing for the primary examination for the degree of medicine in 1867. In 1869 he was made a member of Ontario's College of Physicians and Surgeons. From 1869 to 1871 he continued to practice and for a time was acting resident at the Toronto General Hospital.

In 1871 Abbott married Mary Ann Casey, with whom he would have three sons and four daughters, five of whom survived infancy. He also moved that year to Chatham, Ontario, to practice medicine, remaining there until 1881. Abbott held numerous public positions in Chatham: he was president of the Wilberforce Educational Institute (1873–1880); coroner of the County of Kent (1874), possibly the first person of African descent to hold such a position in Canada; associate editor of the *Missionary Messenger*, the organ of the British Methodist Episcopal Church (1874); president of the Chatham Literary and Debating Society; president of the Chatham Medical Society (1878); and chief templar of the Masonic lodge.

For Abbott, intellect was the noblest part of human nature, an ideal that directed much of the remainder of his life and work. While continuing to practice medicine, he became known in North America and abroad as a champion of education and of the rights of African Americans, as well as a civic leader and orator. In Chatham, Abbott was active in the fight against segregated schools; at Wilberforce, a predominantly African Canadian school, he strove to ensure that the students received a good classical education.

In 1881 Abbott moved his family to Dundas, Ontario, where through his medical practice he continued to be involved in local educational and civic affairs, even though the population was primarily white. He served as an officer of the Dundas Mechanics' Institute as a high school trustee, as a warden for St. James Anglican Church, and as a registrar of the St. James Guild.

The Abbotts left Dundas in 1889, moving to Oakville, Ontario, where they remained for one year before returning to Toronto. In the spring of 1890 Abbott, though still residing in Toronto, was elected a member of the predominantly white James S. Knowlton Post No. 532 of the Grand Army of the Republic, New York State; he was made surgeon of the post in 1892 and appointed aide-de-camp to the commanding officer of the Department of New York. Abbott's appointment gave him the distinction of becoming the highest-ranking man of African descent in the organization (Henry S. Robinson).

When the renowned cardiologist DANIEL HALE WILLIAMS left Provident Hospital and Training School in Chicago in 1894, Abbott, who had been residing in Chicago with his family since 1891, was persuaded to come out of retirement and accept the position of medical superintendent for the facility. As a holder of medical licenses in both Illinois and Michigan, Abbott was able to practice in the United States. He remained at Provident for about three years, apparently resigning in the spring of 1897 for business reasons. An astute businessman like his father, Abbott had acquired several properties. The Abbotts remained in Chicago until they returned to Toronto around 1900.

An avid writer, lecturer, and poet, Abbott expounded on such topics as Darwinism, race, the medical profession, and the integration of schools. Over the years, in addition to writing for the *Missionary Messenger*, he contributed to such papers as the *Chatham Planet, Dundas Banner*, and *New York Age*. He died in Toronto, leaving a legacy in the field of medicine and in literary circles.

FURTHER READING
Abbott's papers are held in the Metropolitan Toronto Reference Library.
Hill, Daniel G. *The Freedom-Seekers: Blacks in Early Canada* (1981).
Robinson, Gwendolyn, and John W. Robinson. *Seek the Truth: A Story of Chatham's Black Community* (1989).
Robinson, Henry S. "Medical History: Anderson Ruffin Abbott, MD, 1837–1913," *Journal of the National Medical Association* 72 (1980): 713–716.

This entry is taken from the *American National Biography* and is published here with the permission of the American Council of Learned Societies.

DALYCE NEWBY

Abbott, Cleveland Leigh (9 Dec. 1894–16 April 1955), Tuskegee athletic coach, was born in Yankton, South Dakota, to Elbert B. Abbott, a stonemason, and Mollie (Brown) Abbott. Abbott grew up in Watertown, South Dakota, attending Watertown public schools, where he was a superior student and athlete. He graduated from high school in 1912 with an unheard-of sixteen Arrow letters in athletics.

Abbott entered South Dakota State College in Brookings, South Dakota, in the fall of 1912, selecting a dairy science major and joining the athletic program. His outstanding athletic and academic performance attracted the attention of the college president Ellwood Perisho, an acquaintance of BOOKER T. WASHINGTON. Washington promised Abbott a job at Tuskegee, contingent on his continued scholastic excellence. Abbott did not disappoint, maintaining his high marks and earning fourteen athletic letters in four years: in track, football, baseball, and basketball. In this last, he played center, captained the team, and was named All Northwestern Center. In football he helped the team to fifteen wins with only six losses in three seasons. He also anchored the track team.

Although Washington died during Abbott's junior year, his successor honored the memorandum of agreement for Abbott's employment. Abbott began at Tuskegee as an agricultural chemist under the direction of GEORGE WASHINGTON CARVER, and as assistant athletic coach in the fall of 1916. On leave from Tuskegee during World War I, he completed officers' training at Fort Des Moines, Iowa, in 1917 and served on the front lines in France, achieving the rank of major. After his discharge he took graduate work at Kansas State College and served briefly on the faculty of Kansas Vocational School in Topeka, where he coached and was commandant of cadets. Subsequently he took graduate work at Harvard. In 1919 Abbott married Jessie Scott of Iowa, whom he had met while representing South Dakota State College at the Drake College Relays in Des Moines; they would have no children. Abbott returned to Tuskegee in 1923 as the school's athletic director and head football coach, positions he would hold for thirty-two years.

During his long career at Tuskegee, Abbott built an outstanding men's athletic program, successful in all sports, bringing home many titles and honors. In 1954 he became the first coach in black college football to claim 200 victories. Perhaps his most important achievement, however, was his pioneering athletic program for women, especially in track and field. From 1935 until 1955 Abbott's Golden Tigers won fourteen national team outdoor titles in track and field, eight of them consecutively. Tuskegee's individual athletes won forty-nine indoor and outdoor titles, and six achieved membership on Olympic track-and-field teams.

Despite national discriminatory practices that separated black collegiate athletic programs from mainstream collegiate athletics, Abbott was widely respected and was frequently consulted by representatives of national programs. He served two times on the U.S. Olympic Track and Field Committee and was among the founders of the Southern Intercollegiate Athletic Conference Basketball Tournament. Many of Abbott's students became champions in their own right, including ALICE COACHMAN, the first African American woman to win a gold medal. (She won the 1948 Olympic Games high-jump title in London.) In 1956, Mildred McDaniel repeated that win at the Helsinki Olympics. Abbott's coaching style and care for his students influenced countless individuals and many coaches, including EDWARD S. TEMPLE, who coached the great WILMA RUDOLPH and patterned his program after Abbott's.

Beloved by his students, Major Abbott, as they called him, passed away on 16 April 1955 and was buried in Tuskegee, Alabama's University Cemetery. With the new appreciation of African American collegiate athletics, many posthumous honors came to Coach Abbott. In 1968, his South Dakota alma mater established its own Athletic Hall of Fame, and Cleveland Abbott was the second man inducted. His wife traveled to South Dakota to accept the honor. In 1992, Abbott was inducted into the SAIC Hall of Fame, and in 1994 to the Alabama Sports Hall of Fame. In 1996, he was inducted into the USA Track and Field Hall of Fame. Most recently, in 2007, he was nominated for admission to the South Dakota Hall of Fame, a statewide organization located in Chamberlain, South Dakota, that honors notable South Dakotans.

FURTHER READING

Dunkle, Amy, with V. J. Smith. *The College on the Hill: A Sense of South Dakota* (2003).

BETTI CAROL VANEPPS-TAYLOR

Abbott, Israel Braddock (11 May 1843–6 May 1887), carpenter, newspaper editor, and state representative during Reconstruction, was born free, of "unmixed African blood," in New Bern, North Carolina, to Israel B. Abbott and Gracie Maria Green. His father died in 1844, and Abbott was raised by his mother and maternal grandmother, Hannah, the wife of Bristow Rue (Rhew). His mother's second husband was Nelson Brown, with whom she had a daughter, Hannah Cora, and stepsons Samuel H. Brown and George M. Brown. She married her third husband, the Reverend Joseph Green, a Methodist Episcopal Zion Church minister, in 1854. When Abbott was four, his grandmother contributed one dollar toward his education, and he attended a school taught by Mrs. Jane Stevens. He went to school regularly until age ten, when he began serving two years as apprentice to a carpenter, completing his trade with his stepfather, Joseph Green. As the Civil War began in 1861, Abbott was required to work on constructing Confederate fortifications. Friends soon secured him work as a servant to a Confederate officer, Lieutenant Alexander Miller, of the Second North Carolina Infantry Regiment. Abbott escaped by forging a pass and running away. In December 1861 he reached New Bern, where he hid until the Union army arrived in spring 1862. His legendary escape made him a sought-after speaker in churches and other institutions in the black community.

The 1870 census erroneously lists Abbott as age thirty. He was, in fact, twenty-seven, a house carpenter residing in Ward 6, with real estate valued at $300 and a personal estate of $400. His wife, Susan, age twenty-four, is listed as "keeping house" for their four children. The 1880 census reveals that Abbott and his wife had seven children: James E. (16), Ann M. (14), Hannah C. M. (12), Gracy B. (10), Israel B. Jr. (7), Susan (4), and Dodge William (b. June 1880); all but the last two attended school that year. Abbott was active in Craven County's black community, where he was widely known and respected. He was a leader of the Abraham Lincoln and Frederick Douglass Equal Rights League and president of the New Bern Council, which had five hundred members. The black community embraced the Republicans, and significant numbers of black Republicans were elected to public office. In 1867 Abbott was appointed to a state Republican executive committee and campaigned for a constitutional convention and adoption of a constitution. In June 1868 the first state legislature under the new constitution convened, and Abbott

was elected assistant doorkeeper of the house of representatives—an important, nonlegislative position. On 1 January 1870, the seventh anniversary of the Emancipation Proclamation, he was chosen orator and, according to the *Daily Examiner* of 19 February 1874, delivered "an admirable and highly complimented address." In 1872 he helped to establish and became president of the Young Men's Intelligent and Enterprising Association, which promoted business opportunities, schools, and academies for the black population.

After the Civil War, the Ku Klux Klan and other secret societies seeking to reestablish white supremacy terrorized blacks and white Republicans. In 1870 North Carolina's General Assembly passed a law, named after the Republican senator T.M. Shoffner, enabling the governor to declare martial law and call out the militia against insurrections. That year the Republican governor William Woods Holden commissioned Abbott as second lieutenant in the state militia under the Shoffner Act. Abbott also represented Ward 6 of Craven County at Republican conventions. In 1870 he ran against Captain G.B. Willis for the North Carolina House of Representatives and lost by two votes. He then served as the county's deputy sheriff and a Superior Court crier. In 1871 he was an opposition candidate for the Republican convention. The following year he was elected to the North Carolina House of Representatives by a large majority, serving there for two years. When his term as state representative ended in 1874, he remained a force in party politics. In the mid-1870s he also served a term on New Bern's Board of Aldermen. He was a delegate in 1880 to the Republican National Convention that nominated James Garfield for president and was chair in 1884 of the Republication State Convention. Abbott was a passionate reformer, a good speaker, debater, and shrewd politician, and in his role as convention chair his executive abilities shone as he presided over "representatives disposed to be unruly" (*New Bern Daily Journal*, 7 May 1887, 1). He was praised by the *Daily Examiner* on 19 February 1874 for "getting votes where, seemingly, there are none to be had."

Abbott belonged to several black fraternal organizations, and in 1877 he joined the Good Samaritan Order. In October 1878 he was elected as the order's grand chief and subsequently was reelected five or six times. In 1880, with his friend GEORGE HENRY WHITE, a fellow Republican leader, Abbott began publishing and coediting *Good Samaritan*, a black weekly newspaper. In 1881 he led a strike for higher wages by black residents of James City who worked as servants and laborers—including in cotton fields across the river in New Bern, which meant the additional personal expense of taking private boats or ferries to work. The strike failed largely because New Bern's black population did not support the James City residents. In *James City: A Black Community in North Carolina*, Joe Mobley mentions a story by Abbott in the Good Samaritan urging black workers to join labor unions. On 18 September 1881 Abbott addressed the strikers in Red Church on West Street and was vilified in the white press. On 21 September, Abbott and E. E. Tucker founded a Laborers Union—which, notably, included women—to ensure that "each receives a reasonable compensation for his or her services" (Watson, 520). In 1886 Abbott ran for Congress as an Independent against the black Republican incumbent, JAMES EDWARD O'HARA. This split vote enabled the white Democratic challenger, Furnifold Simmons, to win.

The Interment Book for Greenwood Cemetery in New Bern records that Abbott died on Friday, 6 May 1887, at 6:00 A.M., five days short of age forty-four, of "Brites Disease Kidneys." Good Samaritan Lodge No. 18 appointed a committee of remembrance: FREDERICK DOUGLASS, Mary A. Green, S.S. Latham, and Merritt Whitley, who wrote an obituary describing Abbott as "indefatigable in his efforts to advance the Order in the State of North Carolina … a devout husband, a kind father, a good citizen, and a true Samaritan" (*New Bern Weekly Journal*, 26 May 1887). His tombstone inscription reads: "He was … a loyal and progressive leader of his race." Many years later, an obituary in the *Chicago Defender* (6 Nov. 1926, 2) for one of his sons states that Abbott was a man "whose name is among the pioneers of North Carolina."

FURTHER READING

Anderson, Eric. *Race and Politics in North Carolina, 1872–1902: The Black Second* (1981).

Foner, Eric. *Freedom's Lawmakers*, rev. ed. (1996).

Justesen, Benjamin R. *George Henry White: An Even Chance in the Race of Life* (2001).

Watson, Alan D. *A History of New Bern and Craven County* (1987).

ALICE BERNSTEIN

Abbott, Robert Sengstacke

Abbott, Robert Sengstacke (28 Nov. 1868–29 Feb. 1940), newspaper publisher, was born Robert Abbott in Fort Frederica, St. Simons Island, off the coast of Savannah, Georgia, the son of Thomas Abbott and Flora Butler, former slaves who operated a grocery store on St. Thomas Island. Thomas Abbott died the year after Robert was born, and Robert's mother moved to Savannah, where in 1874 she married John Herman Henry Sengstacke. Sengstacke was the son of a German father and a black American mother and, although born in the United States, was reared in Germany. He returned to the United States in 1869 and pursued careers in education, the clergy, and journalism. In the latter role Sengstacke became editor of the *Woodville Times*, a black community weekly newspaper that served Savannah-area residents. Abbott's admiration for his stepfather inspired him to add the name Sengstacke to his own and to attempt to become a publisher in his own right.

Abbott's first newspaper job was as a printer with the white-owned *Savannah Echo*. He soon decided to obtain a college education; after attending several other institutions, Abbott enrolled at Hampton Institute in Virginia in 1889 at the age of twenty-one. Hampton, founded by the Congregationalists and supported by northern philanthropists, was both a trade school and an academic institution for African Americans. Abbott completed training as a printer in 1893, then culminated his undergraduate career with a bachelor's degree in 1896, after nearly seven years at Hampton. His experience there included opportunities to hear two charismatic black speakers, FREDERICK DOUGLASS and IDA B. WELLS-BARNETT, who influenced him to seek a leadership role in the development of civil rights for black Americans. After graduating from Hampton, Abbott moved to Chicago, where in 1899 he earned a law degree from Kent College of Law, the only black in his class of seventy students. Abbott, however, was never admitted to the bar. For the next few years he tried to establish a career as a lawyer in several midwestern cities without success, eventually he returned to Woodville to teach in a local school.

In 1905, at the age of thirty-seven, Abbott returned to Chicago and began publication of his own newspaper, the *Chicago Defender*. He chose Chicago as the base for his paper because of its large black population (more than thirty thousand), though at the time the black newspaper field in Chicago was extremely crowded, with three established local weeklies and the availability of two other well-respected journals, the *Indiana Freeman* and the *New York Age*. The title "Defender" represented his pledge that the paper would defend his race against the ills of racism.

Abbott's first number of the *Defender* was virtually a one-man production operated from rented desk space in a real estate and insurance office with furnishings that included a folding card table and a borrowed kitchen chair. But with an initial investment of twenty-five cents (for paper and pencils) and the help of his landlady's teenage daughter, he was able to launch a publishing enterprise that became one of the most influential newspapers in the United States. Within ten years the *Defender* was the nation's leading black newspaper, with an estimated circulation of 230,000.

Despite his early exposure to the printing trade and newspaper publishing, Abbott was seen by many of his contemporaries as an unlikely candidate for success as a newspaperman. He was not an articulate speaker, but he had a strong talent for gathering rumor, hearsay, and other information and turning them into human-interest stories. Abbott also proved a master at upstaging his competitors. Proclaiming his paper to be "the only two-cent weekly in the city" and focusing front-page coverage on sensational and crime news, Abbott steadily increased his paper's readership. The *Defender's* most significant contribution, however, was perhaps its crusade to encourage black migration from the former slave states of the South to Chicago and other midwestern cities.

The campaign, launched during World War I, was instrumental in bringing thousands of blacks to the North in search of better jobs, housing, and educational opportunities. For Abbott the migration was part of a plan to increase the *Defender's* circulation and give him an opportunity to penetrate the black readership markets in the South. Several southern cities so resented the effectiveness of the *Defender's* campaign that they banned its distribution. The *Atlanta Constitution* wrote that the migration cost the South "her best labor" force and that the region's economy suffered greatly. It has been estimated that nearly thirty-five thousand blacks moved to Chicago from the founding of the *Defender* in 1905 to 1920, more than doubling the city's African American population.

An indirect result of the heavy influx of black migrants to Chicago was a race riot in 1919 that highlighted the tensions between whites and blacks in the city. Abbott was appointed to the Commission on Race Relations, charged with determining the causes of the riot. Although the commission's report implicated the *Defender's* strong stance for black civil rights as a contributing factor in the riots, Abbott signed the document.

The *Defender* was a fearless champion for the cause of racial equality for African Americans. Abbott enumerated his policies as the elimination of racial prejudice in the United States, the opening of trade union membership to blacks, black representation in the president's cabinet, equal employment opportunities for blacks in the public and private sectors, and black employment in all police forces nationally. He also sought the elimination of all school segregation and the passage of federal civil rights legislation to protect against breakdowns in desegregation laws at the state level as well as to extend full voting rights to all Americans. These policies found a ready market, and the *Defender's* growth during World War I allowed it to open and maintain branch offices in several major U.S. cities as well as one in London. During the war Abbott publicly asked why blacks should fight for the United States on foreign battlefields while being denied basic rights at home, a stance that provoked investigations by the federal government. In 1918, just two months short of his fiftieth birthday, Abbott married Helen Thornton Morrison; they had no children.

In the decade following World War I, the *Defender's* circulation began to fall with the arrival of a new competitor, the *Chicago Whip*, and the onset of the Depression years. The *Defender* generally supported Republican politics, although in 1928 Abbott opposed Herbert Hoover in favor of the Democratic candidate Alfred E. Smith. During the 1930s, perhaps because of the 1919 riots and the impact of the Depression, the *Defender* took a more moderate stance regarding racial matters. The period also took a personal toll on Abbott, and he suffered several financial reversals. By 1935 circulation had declined to seventy-three thousand. After his mother died in 1932, Abbott began to travel extensively and attempted during the mid-1930s an ill-fated venture into magazine publishing with *Abbott's Monthly*.

Following a costly divorce from his first wife in 1932, Abbott married Edna Brown Dennison in 1934 but soon fell into ill health. In 1939 he gave control of the *Defender* to his nephew John H. Sengstacke, son of his half brother Alexander. Abbott died at his home in Chicago the following year. He left behind a newspaper that had pioneered new territory for the black press, becoming the first national paper to have an integrated staff and to be unionized. In 1956, under John Sengstacke's leadership, the *Defender* became a daily newspaper, soon to become the flagship publication of the nation's largest black newspaper chain.

FURTHER READING

Abbott's papers are in the *Chicago Defender* Archives in Chicago.

Ottley, Roi. *The Lonely Warrior* (1955).

Wolseley, Roland E. *The Black Press U.S.A.* (1971; 2d ed., 1990).

This entry is taken from the *American National Biography* and is published here with the permission of the American Council of Learned Societies.

CLINT C. WILSON

Abd al-Rahman, Ibrahima (1760?–1829), a military leader in Africa, a slave in Mississippi, was born into the rising Bari family of the Fulbe people in the fabled but real African city of Timbuktu. His name is sometimes written as Abdul Rahahman and Abder Rahman. The Fulbe people were prominent leaders in West African jihads from the eighteenth to the twentieth centuries and, though enslaved, the most persistent adherents to Islam in the Americas. Abd al-Rahman's father and family had moved south to territory soon to be called Futa Jallon in the highlands of present-day Guinea after he and non-Muslim allies wrested power from their animist opposition between 1776 and 1778. Well into the twentieth century the military Bari-Soriya and religious Karamoko Alfiya families, usually peacefully, traded rule over their people and lands.

For about a century Futa Jallon was the strongest nation in the area. In its capital Timbo, Abd al-Rahman was educated in Fula-Muslim schools to read and write Arabic and to fight his people's enemies. The city's teachers instructed many important West African Muslim students, teachers, and leaders. At least three of the latter were stolen away to the New World and gained some renown there: BILALI, born in Timbo, became a de facto imam in Georgia; Samba, taken with Abd al-Rahman to Natchez, Mississippi, maintained his Muslim traditions and gave his children Muslim names; and the student-teacher LAMINE KEBE (a Serahule), was returned to Africa after enslavement in Georgia in 1835.

In 1788, in his early twenties, married, a father, and a respected cavalry officer, Abd al-Rahman commanded a troop charged with reopening trade to the coast. After an apparent victory, he and fifty of his men were ambushed and taken to the Gambia River where they were sold as slaves. Including a stop in Dominica, his six-month passage across the Atlantic Ocean ended in Spanish New Orleans. After a month there he was sold up the Mississippi to Thomas Foster of Spanish Natchez. Soon, however, Abd al-Rahman recovered his land legs and ran away. Weeks later he returned, presumably having not found allies or escape beyond the plantation. Nevertheless, though he was forced to adjust to his circumstances, Abd al-Rahman had his limits. He was called Prince by his master in deference, it seems, to his proud manner, antipathy to labor, and to his early, undoubtedly discounted argument that he was of royal blood.

Abd al-Rahman became a kind of slave foreman and was favorably noticed because of his seriousness, honesty, and religiosity. Though he listened politely to Christian preachers, he adhered to his Muslim obligations. Abd al-Rahman appreciated some Christian principles and practices, but declared, according to Cyrus Griffin, a sympathetic Natchez newspaper editor: "the [New] Testament very good law; you [Christians] no follow it; you no pray often enough; you greedy after money … you want more land, more neegurs; you make neegur work hard, make more cotton. Where you find dat in your law?" Not finding a Muslim to marry, he settled down with a recently purchased Baptist woman, Isabella, around 1794.

His own narrative of his place in Futa Jallon might have been forever overlooked but for the arrival in Natchez in 1807 of a medical doctor named John Coates Cox. Cox was the only European known to have sojourned in Abd al-Rahman's hometown of Timbo in the 1780s, and for six months as a patient he had even been within Abd al-Rahman's own family compound. The two men recognized one another at first sight. Cox corroborated the slave's high African status and emphasized it in his attempts to persuade his purchaser to free him.

After the doctor's death in 1816, his son also tried to free Abd al-Rahman. Both were unsuccessful. Abd al-Rahman's managerial skills (as well as his wife's obstetrical talents) had become indispensable to Foster and their growing plantation. Finally in 1826, having become something of a local celebrity, a father of nine children, and an old man by then relieved of his heavier duties, Abd al-Rahman decided to write home in Arabic—the only written language he knew. His letter was sent to Morocco—the only Muslim nation with which the United States had diplomatic relations. Cyrus Griffin sought the American Colonization Society's (ACS) assistance. Two years later, a surprising response came to the U.S. State Department asking for the Muslim man's freedom and transportation to Morocco. Foster agreed, providing the old man would leave the United States as soon as arrangements could be made. But he came up with a surprising caveat. Instead of quickly getting rid of Abd al-Rahman via a riverboat to New Orleans and out to sea, Foster wanted his proud African to be taken north and east so that he might be awed by and would report to his people about the urbanization, wealth, and productivity of the United States.

Abd al-Rahman was happy about being freed, but he was unhappy that no provision had been made for his wife and children. Showing something of their respect for him, sympathetic Natchezians raised enough money to redeem his wife. In late March 1828 he and Isabella were shipped up the Mississippi and Ohio rivers. From the time they arrived in Cincinnati to the time they left Virginia for Liberia on 7 February 1829, Abd al-Rahman, then aged sixty-four or sixty-five, a black man in a geographically extended, largely white world, was in constant motion. He was not awed by the cities, their prodigal materialism, or their mechanical progress. Instead, he became the chief campaigner in an attempt to redeem his children through donations in the North, comparable to the lesser campaign Natchez neighbors had completed to buy his wife.

In newspaper accounts composed in all the major coastal cities, Abd al-Rahman, though at some level begging, displayed a splendid dignity wherever he went. He appeared at the White House, Congress, the offices and homes of wealthy American Colonization Society members, street corner rallies, school campuses, and—most extraordinarily—public marches and meetings with African American leaders in opposition to the ACS. President John Quincy Adams donated to his cause, as did dignitaries and common people alike in Philadelphia, New York, New Haven, Hartford, Springfield, Worcester, Boston, and Providence. The Reverend Thomas Gallaudet, founder of the first school for the deaf, became one of his most ardent supporters. It was the Colonizationist Gallaudet who prevailed upon the artist Henry Inman to produce a wonderful crayon portrait of the remarkable freedman. JOHN RUSSWURM, one of the founders of *Freedom's Journal*, the first African American edited newspaper, met and soon followed Abd al-Rahman to Africa. DAVID WALKER, soon to be the author of the strongest and one of the earliest publications opposing slavery by an African American, toasted Abd al-Rahman in Boston. (This was in a time, 1828, at which William L. Garrison and other white abolitionists had not yet begun their fight against slavery. Indeed, Garrison donated to the ACS in that year.)

Commentators admired Abd al-Rahman's dignity, seriousness, and apparent spirituality as he sought money to purchase and free his children. Colonizationists assisting his travels hoped that he would increase interest in their plans to send other freed or troublesome people to Liberia. Businessmen hoped that he would improve African trade. Ministers hoped that their help and advice might convert him and other Muslims to Christianity. Abd al-Rahman's literacy led potential donors to seek samples of his writing. Some of his writings were presumed to be the Lord's Prayer but they were, in fact, variations on the first chapter of the Quran or were short autobiographical statements.

Abd al-Rahman became a kind of hero in the Northeast, but an anti-slavery villain in the old Southwest. Foster, his former owner, was incensed by his eloquent Prince's progress through cities that he had wanted his freed slave to be awed and dumbfounded by. In the election year of 1828 Foster and Natchez and New Orleans newsmen, former allies, and others, saw in Abd al-Rahman's travels a political rather than a charity-seeking campaign engineered by anti–Andrew Jackson (the incumbent's Democratic rival) and antislavery Adams supporters.

Ultimately Abd al-Rahman managed to raise only half of the exorbitant prices that Foster demanded for his children, but he was able to pay for passage for him and his wife to Africa. (Coincidentally, the future first president of Liberia, JOSEPH J. ROBERTS, crossed the Atlantic Ocean on the same ship. It is not known whether the two men met.) Immediately upon sighting the coast of Africa, Abd al-Rahman reconfirmed his adherence to the faith of his fathers.

Shortly after landing in mid-March 1829 Abd al-Rahman corresponded with his family in still-distant Timbo. Although he looked forward to revisiting his homeland with Isabella, his plans were cut short by his death in July. A year later, however, Isabella was able to greet the eight children and grandchildren whom her husband's heroic efforts had redeemed.

FURTHER READING

Alford, Terry. *Prince among Slaves* (1977).
Austin, Allan D. *African Muslims in Antebellum America: A Sourcebook* (1984).
Austin, Allan D. *African Muslims in Antebellum America: Transatlantic Stories and Spiritual Struggles* (1997).

ALLAN D. AUSTIN

Abdul, Raoul (7 Nov. 1929–15 Jan. 2010), classical singer, author, gay rights activist, and former literary assistant to writer LANGSTON HUGHES, was born in Cleveland, Ohio. Abdul's father, Hamid Abdul, was from Calcutta, India, and his mother, Bernice (Shreve) Abdul, was able to trace her ancestry back to the pre-Revolutionary War era. Abdul got his start in theater at a young age, participating in children's theater by age six. He attended John Hay High School and, after graduation, worked as a journalist for the *Cleveland Call and Post*. He would later go on to earn a diploma from the Vienna Academy of Music in 1962. He also studied at Harvard University, the New School for Social Research, the Cleveland Institute of Music, New York College of Music, and the Mannes College of Music.

In 1951, at age twenty-two, Abdul relocated to New York City. There he began studying music and was a singer in a number of classical and operatic performances with such notables as WILLIAM WARFIELD and MARIAN ANDERSON. He sang at Vermont's Marlboro Music Festival in 1956 and the Vienna Music Festival in 1962. He made his Carnegie Hall debut in 1967, in a recital of German lieder, with John Wustman accompanying on piano. He later had operatic roles in the first American stage productions of Carl Orff's *Die Kluge* and sang the title role in Darius Milhaud's *Les malheurs d'Orphée*. He also appeared in seventeen performances of Mozart's *Così fan tutte* and twelve performances of Gian Carlo Menotti's *Amahl and the Night Visitors* at Cleveland's Karamu House. He appeared in other concerts on tours in the United States, Canada, Austria, Netherlands, Hungary, and Germany.

In 1958 he organized the Coffeehouse Concerts, Harlem's first subscription series of chamber music concerts. He remained director of the series until 1963. Abdul began his most notable working relationship in 1961 with the poet and writer Langston Hughes. Abdul worked as a literary assistant to Hughes and became a close friend to the writer. He was Hughes's assistant until Hughes's death in 1967.

In the 1960s Abdul began working as a writer, editor, and critic, employing his wide knowledge of the arts in books and periodicals. In 1970 he published his first book, *3,000 Years of Black Poetry*, co-edited with Alan Lomax. Over the next few years he edited *The Magic of Black Poetry* (1972) and authored the volumes, *Famous Black Entertainers of Today* (1974) and *Blacks in Classical Music: A Personal History* (1977). His articles appeared in *Anthology of the American Negro in the Theatre* (1967) and *The Negro in Music and Art* (1967). He also wrote the column "The Cultural Scene" for *Associated Negro Press* and was cultural editor for the *New York Age*. He gave lectures and master classes at universities across the United States and abroad.

Abdul was also a gay rights pioneer. His lectures on famous gays in the African American community at Riverside Church and elsewhere became legendary. He was active for more than five decades in organizations devoted to gay rights, including the Stonewall Mattachine Society and One Incorporated. He was honored for his activism with several awards, including a Lift Every Voice Legacy Award and the New York organization Black Pride's Griot Award. Abdul's life companion, Richard Mayer Haber, was an attorney, writer, and philanthropist, and became a master's candidate in anthropology at Columbia University at age seventy-one. Haber died in 2001.

Abdul began giving private voice lessons in his home in New York in the 1970s, with a teaching method based on the Austrian singing technique he learned while studying in Vienna. He was for a time the entertainment editor for the *New York Amsterdam News*. He died in New York City at the age of eighty.

BRENNA SANCHEZ

Abdul-Jabbar, Kareem (16 Apr. 1947–), basketball player, was born Ferdinand Lewis Alcindor, the son of Ferdinand Lewis "Al" Alcindor, a police officer with the New York Transit Authority, and Cora Alcindor, a department-store price checker. The almost thirteen-pound baby arrived in Harlem one day after the major league debut of JACKIE ROBINSON in Brooklyn; as with Robinson, fiercely competitive athletics and the struggle against racial injustice would define much of his life.

From a young age, Alcindor was introspective and intense. He had an artistic sensibility, drawn in part from his father, a stern and silent cop who played jazz trombone and held a degree from Juilliard. An only child in a strictly Catholic household, he moved from Harlem at age three to the Dyckman Street projects on the northern tip of Manhattan, a racially mixed, middle-class community. In third grade he was startled to see a class photo that featured him not just towering over his classmates as expected, but standing out by the color of his skin. "Damn, I'm dark and everybody else is light!" Alcindor recalled thinking years later (Abdul-Jabbar, *Giant Steps*, 15). In fourth grade,

Kareem Abdul-Jabbar acknowledges cheering fans after setting a new NBA regular season scoring record of 31,421 points during the game with the Utah Jazz in Las Vegas, Nevada, 6 April 1984. (AP Images.)

his parents shipped him to an all-black boarding school outside Philadelphia, where he was taunted for his intellectual leanings. But in his one year at Holy Providence School, he developed street toughness and also launched his first hook shot, a weapon that would become his aesthetic and athletic trademark. Back in New York from fifth grade on, Alcindor began to grow into his coordination. By eighth grade, he was a sinewy six feet, eight inches; by tenth grade, he was a seven footer with astonishing agility. At Power Memorial, an all-boys Catholic school where his teams lost only one game in his final three years, Alcindor never fit neatly into the jock stereotype. He read widely, joined the debate team, and began to frequent New York's jazz clubs. On the court, though, the Renaissance man reigned. His game was at once graceful and ferocious. Coach Jack Donohue opened up the world for his sensitive star, bringing him to NBA games at Madison Square Garden. There the coach pointed with particular reverence to the inspired and unselfish play of the Celtics center BILL RUSSELL. Donohue's influence was not completely positive, however. At halftime of an unusually lethargic performance during Alcindor's junior year, the fiery coach tore into his prodigy, telling him he was acting "just like a nigger!" (*Sports Illustrated*, 27 Oct. 1969). The wound from that remark festered for many years.

That summer Alcindor's growing awareness of racism sharpened when he participated in the journalism workshop of the Harlem Youth Action Project. At one point he covered a press conference

by MARTIN LUTHER KING JR., a moment commemorated in a photograph in *Jet* magazine. He also witnessed five days of rioting in Harlem after a white policeman shot a black teenager. "Right then and there I knew who I was and who I had to be," he said in a *Sports Illustrated* profile (31 Mar. 1980). "I was going to be black rage personified, black power in the flesh."

The summer of 1964 also proved defining in his association with WILT CHAMBERLAIN. Eleven years Alcindor's senior and established (along with his rival Russell) as the dominant big man in the NBA, Chamberlain took the high school kid under his considerable wing. He loaned Alcindor jazz albums, invited him to his apartment to play hearts, and ferried him in his Bentley up to Saratoga to watch Chamberlain's prize thoroughbreds run. At one point the two played a memorable game of H-O-R-S-E, a matchup of trademark hook shots by Alcindor and fadeaways by Chamberlain that would have been captured on film in a better world.

After another scintillating high school season, Alcindor enrolled at the University of California, Los Angeles (UCLA), winner of the last two national championships. Although NCAA rules then forbade freshmen to play varsity sports, Alcindor served immediate notice by scoring thirty-one points and leading the freshman team to an emphatic fifteen-point victory over the storied varsity. The next year, under the dignified tutelage of the coaching legend John Wooden, Alcindor launched a collegiate career for the ages. In his very first game he broke the school scoring record with fifty-six points. He earned three consecutive All-America honors, leading the Bruins to three straight national titles and a glittering record of 88–2. Having reached his full height of seven feet, two inches, Alcindor had become a complete player. A menacing shot blocker, he intimidated on defense, and his devastating hook shot and ferocious inside moves were almost impossible to stop. So powerful was his impact on the game that the NCAA outlawed the dunk after his freshman year (though it was reinstated ten years later).

Never satisfied with a one-dimensional life, Alcindor broadened his horizons by studying martial arts with Bruce Lee and by reading *The Autobiography of Malcolm X*. Having dismissed what he considered to be the repressive Catholicism of his childhood, he developed a deep connection to Islam. After his junior year in the summer of 1968, he studied in a New York mosque and became a devout follower of Hamaas Abdul-Khaalis. That same summer, Alcindor decided to boycott the

Olympic Games, refusing to play for a country that, he felt, denied fundamental rights and respect to black people. He publicly supported the "black power" salutes of sprinters TOMMIE SMITH and John Carlos on the medal podium in Mexico City, earning him a mound of hate mail when he returned to UCLA for his senior year.

In 1969, shortly before he graduated with a B.A. in History, Alcindor polished off his college basketball career with a 37-point, 20-rebound performance in UCLA's victory over Purdue in the NCAA championship game. He became the first pick in the NBA draft, selected by the Milwaukee Bucks, an expansion team that had managed a grim 27–55 record in its first season. For six years he toiled in Milwaukee, a period marked by brilliance on the court and tumult off it. Averaging 28.8 points per game, he won Rookie of the Year honors in 1969–1970 and sparked the Bucks to a dramatic turnaround with a 56–26 record. Perhaps never before or since has one person's impact on a professional team been so profound. The next year, teaming with the newly acquired OSCAR ROBERTSON, Alcindor led his team to an NBA championship. Though criticized by the media as an aloof giant, his impact on the game was undeniable. He averaged 31.7 points and 16 rebounds per game, and earned the first of six Most Valuable Player (MVP) awards, a figure unmatched in NBA annals.

His connections to Islam and Abdul-Khaalis became increasingly public. The religious mentor chose Alcindor's bride in 1971 (Habiba Brown) and the name Kareem Abdul-Jabbar (meaning "generous and powerful servant of Allah"), which became legal a few months later. In one off-season, the NBA's most dominating player studied Arabic at Harvard; another year he traveled to the Middle East. In 1972–1973 he was followed by NBA security guards after six of Abdul-Khaalis's relatives, including four of his children, were murdered by Black Muslim extremists. (A few years later Abdul-Khaalis was sentenced to forty years in jail for his involvement in a hostage-taking incident, during which a reporter was killed.)

On the court Abdul-Jabbar's excellence was undiminished (MVP awards again in 1972 and 1974), but off-court strains were evident. He separated from his wife shortly after the birth of his first daughter in 1973, though they later had two more children. (He subsequently had two additional children with other women.) Abdul-Jabbar had a falling out with Chamberlain over the latter's claim in an autobiography that black women were sexually

inferior and his public support of President Richard Nixon. Then in the 1974–1975 season, Abdul-Jabbar got poked in the eye and responded by slamming his fist into a backboard support, breaking two bones in his hand, and taking him away from the game, his oasis. At year's end, the Bucks accommodated his demands for a trade, shipping him to the Los Angeles Lakers in return for four players.

Abdul-Jabbar's first years back in California were marked by more of the same: overpowering play (MVP awards in 1976 and 1977) coupled with a brooding court mien that earned him few friends. In the first game of the 1977–1978 season, he was widely criticized for responding to an elbow by Milwaukee's Kent Benson with a devastating punch that sidelined Benson with a concussion and Abdul-Jabbar with another fractured hand. Increasingly, the game's best player was regarded as an outcast. "No man is an island," opined the legendary *Los Angeles Times* columnist Jim Murray, "but Kareem gave it a shot."

In time, though, Abdul-Jabbar found his way back to shore, an American life that had a decided second act. In 1979–1980 the Lakers added the rookie point guard MAGIC JOHNSON, whose on-court exuberance was contagious. That year, with Abdul-Jabbar again earning MVP honors, the Lakers captured the NBA title. The Lakers became the dominant team of the 1980s, winning five titles with a stylish, fast-breaking brand of basketball known as "Showtime." In various ways Abdul-Jabbar seemed to soften. He displayed a deft comic touch in the 1980 movie *Airplane*, which opened up film and television roles for him in coming years. In 1983 he was visibly moved when fans around the country sent him jazz records after his treasured collection was destroyed in a house fire. Later that year he published *Giant Steps*, an unusually candid and cathartic autobiography. On the court he seemed almost impervious to age. In 1983–1984 he became the league's all-time leading scorer, eclipsing Chamberlain's record, appropriately enough, with his trademark shot, now widely known as a skyhook—"the most beautiful thing in sports," according to Bill Russell (*Time*, 20 Feb. 1989). Abdul-Jabbar seemed downright exuberant in 1984–1985 as the Lakers defeated the Celtics in the NBA Finals. Even pushing forty, bald and begoggled, he remained a force, helping the Lakers become the first repeat champions of the NBA in nineteen years in 1987 and 1988. So durable was he that when he played in his nineteenth and final All-Star game in 1989, he was older than seven of the twenty players in the accompanying NBA Legends

Classic. When he finally retired a few months later, he had played more games, scored more points, and blocked more shots than anyone in league history. "In my opinion," the regal John Wooden said, "he is the most valuable player in the history of the game."

In his retirement, Abdul-Jabbar took to writing, including a highly reflective account of his final season, *Kareem*, and a history book, *Black Profiles in Courage* (1996), written with Alan Steinberg. He started a jazz label and remained involved in television and motion pictures. He initially professed a desire to stay away from basketball, but in a variety of broadcasting and coaching roles, including one year as an assistant coach for a high school team on an Apache Indian reservation and a return to the Lakers as an assistant coach in 2005, he began another long, graceful arc to the hoop.

FURTHER READING
Abdul-Jabbar, Kareem, with Peter Knobler. *Giant Steps* (1983).
Abdul-Jabbar, Kareem, with Mignon McCarthy. *Kareem* (1990).
Abdul-Jabbar, Kareem, with Stephen Singular. *A Season on the Reservation* (2000).
Smith, Gary. "Now, More Than Ever, a Winner," *Sports Illustrated* (23 Dec. 1985).

MARTY DOBROW

Abele, Julian Francis (21 Apr. 1881–18 Apr. 1950), architect, was born in Philadelphia, Pennsylvania, the eighth of eleven children of Charles Sylvester Abele and Mary Jones, a washerwoman and milliner. Charles Able changed the spelling, although not the pronunciation, of his surname to Abele after mustering out of the Union army following the end of the Civil War. Charles, who worked as a carpenter and laborer at the U.S. Treasury Customs House, a sought-after patronage job, and as a porter, died when Julian was twelve. Mary Jones Able was a descendant of ABSALOM JONES, the first African American Protestant Episcopal priest. Julian and his siblings were fourth generation Philadelphians and were expected by their parents to achieve recognition, marry well, and assume their rightful place in Olde Philadelphia society. Julian's oldest brother, Robert, was one of the first African American graduates of Hahnemann Medical College and a cofounder in 1907 of Mercy Hospital, the only Philadelphia hospital which would accept African Americans. Julian's oldest sister, Elizabeth, was a calligrapher, and his sister Mary taught in a private

school prior to marrying. His brothers Charles Jr. and Joseph worked as a sign maker and electrical engineer, respectively. His brother Ernest was considered a ne'er-do-well inventor, and Frederick, according to his grand niece, was "a little off the bean." Another brother, Harry, died as an infant, while two other brothers, Harry II and Thomas, died in their twenties. Julian was raised in a home where the fine arts were appreciated and family members knew the difference between a finale and a finial. Although Charles Jr. was the wealthiest family member, Robert inherited leadership of the family after his father's death. He paid Julian's tuition so his younger brother could pursue his dream to become an architect.

Abele followed his sisters and brothers to the Institute for Colored Youth (ICY), a private, preparatory school founded and supported by Philadelphia Quakers. ICY's principal, Fanny Coppin, whose educational innovations included fostering close relationships between faculty and students, mentored Julian personally, encouraging his ambition to become an architect and counseling him to enroll in the recently organized Pennsylvania Museum School of Industrial Art (PMSIA) after his 1897 graduation from ICY. During a period when the Franklin Institute and the School of Design for Women, both in Philadelphia, refused to enroll African Americans, Abele was admitted to the PMSIA without objection, and in 1898 he became one of the school's first recipients of a certificate in architectural design. Abele continued his architectural training at the University of Pennsylvania School of Architecture, where he won the respect of his peers and several awards for design and rendering and was also elected president of the Architectural Society. In 1902 he graduated with a B.S. in Architecture, becoming the school's first African American graduate and the second African American to earn a degree in Architecture, following ROBERT ROBINSON TAYLOR, an 1898 graduate of the Massachusetts Institute of Technology.

Abele's training included a continuing relationship with Philadelphia's T-Square Club, a professional organization founded in 1883 by thirteen Philadelphia architects. Admitted while a student at the University of Pennsylvania, Abele was the club's only African American member. In 1901, while a fourth-year student at the University of Pennsylvania, he had been awarded the T-Square Club Prize for superior performance. Thereafter Abele consistently earned first-place mentions, beating out more experienced architects in the club's annual competitions, which were held until 1925. Abele also showed his work at the architecture clubs of Pittsburgh and Toronto and at the Architectural League of New York.

While still a student, Abele was listed as an architect in the Philadelphia city directory, and until 1903 he worked evenings for the noted Philadelphia architect Louis C. Hickman. Soon after graduation, Abele went to Spokane, Washington, to design a house for his sister, Elizabeth Abele Cook, and her husband, John F. Cook. Already one of the most formally educated architects in the Commonwealth of Pennsylvania, he took the evening architectural design course offered by the Philadelphia Academy of Fine Arts, receiving a certificate in May 1903. Abele spent the next few years in Europe. And while he was not, as has been claimed, a graduate of L'Ecole des Beaux-Arts in Paris, he did travel throughout France and Italy, later exhibiting sketches completed during his European sojourn. On his application for membership in the American Institute of Architects, Abele listed travel to England, France, Germany, Switzerland, Italy, and Spain.

Abele's ribbon-winning, pen-and-ink sketches revealed a talented draftsman who "could delineate shadows with a grease pencil in so subtle a way that the observer got the impression of far more detail than Abele had actually drawn" (Maher, 372). Deeply fearful that an injury to his right hand would destroy his livelihood, Abele taught himself to draw with his left hand. Abele was also a landscape painter.

In 1906 Horace Trumbauer, known for the design of elegant mansions, hired Abele as a junior architect, making Abele the first African American architect employed by a white-owned firm. When he was promoted to senior designer two years later, Abele became responsible for siting buildings, collaborating with Trumbauer in choosing architectural styles, and creating the "look" for all commissioned buildings. Abele remained with Trumbauer until 1950, contributing to the design of more than two hundred buildings, twenty-one of which are listed on the National Register of Historic Places. After Trumbauer's death in 1938, Abele became head of the firm and, for the first time, was able to sign his own name to his designs.

A lifelong Francophile, Abele was a smart dresser and a sports and symphony fan. He shunned the spotlight, preferring, either by temperament or necessity, to remain in the background. On 6 June 1925 Abele married the Parisian Marguerite Bulle, a graduate of the Paris Conservatoire of Music. After nine years of marriage and three children, Marguerite ran off with a Polish émigré singer.

Under Trumbauer, Abele designed lavish homes, including Whitemarsh Hall (1916), a 150-room limestone home for Edward Stotesbury, a banker and Philadelphia's wealthiest citizen; Shadow Lawn (1927), a West Long Beach, New Jersey, mansion for Hubert Parson, the president of F.W. Woolworth & Company; and Marly (1931) in Washington, D.C., for the Dodge Brothers Motor Company heiress Delphine Dodge Baker. Abele designed the New York mansion of James Buchanan Duke, president of both the American Tobacco Company and the Southern Power Company, a building that is now New York University's Graduate Institute of Fine Arts. The Trumbauer firm's largest and most important work was commissioned by Duke for Duke University; Abele designed eleven Georgian-style buildings on the east campus and thirty-eight Gothic-style buildings on the west campus. While this represented more buildings than Henry Ives Cobb designed for the University of Chicago, Ralph Adams Cram designed for Princeton University, or Robert Robinson Taylor designed for Tuskegee Institute, there is no evidence that Abele ever set foot on Duke University's campus.

Abele contributed to the design of the Philadelphia Museum of Art, and after Trumbauer's death, he played a key role in the completion of the building. Typically, until recently, histories of Widener Library at Harvard University, which was designed by the firm of Horace Trumbauer, made no mention of Abele, one of the building's chief architects.

Julian Abele died on 18 April 1950 after suffering his second heart attack. He was buried in Eden Cemetery in Collingdale, a suburb of Philadelphia, near the mausoleums for Charles Eishenlohr, Peter Widener, and Thomas Develon Jr. that Abele had designed. The Corinthian-colonnaded Free Library of Philadelphia, which Abele designed in 1917, can be seen from his gravesite.

FURTHER READING

Adams, Michael. "A Legacy of Shadows," *Progressive Architecture* (Feb. 1991): 85.

Bond, Max. "Still Here: Three Architects of Afro-America—Julian Francis Abele, Hilyard Robinson and Paul R. Williams," *Harvard Design Magazine* (Summer 1997).

Maher, James. *Twilight of Splendor* (1975).

Tatman, Sandra L., and Roger W. Moss, eds. *Biographical Dictionary of Philadelphia Architects: 1700–1930* (1985).

Wilson, Dreck Spurlock, ed. *African American Architects: A Biographical Dictionary 1865–1945* (2003).

DRECK SPURLOCK WILSON

Abernathy, Juanita Jones (24 Dec. 1929–), civil rights activist, educator, and businesswoman, was born Juanita Odessa Jones in Uniontown, Alabama, the youngest of eight children of Ella Gilmore Jones and Alex Jones Sr., an influential and prosperous black farmer in Perry County, Alabama. When Alabama telephone and electric companies refused to provide service to the Jones homestead, Alex Jones Sr. and his brothers installed their own telephone lines and wired their own homes for electricity. One consequence of the family's financial independence was that Juanita was able to attend boarding school from age five until she graduated from high school in Selma, Alabama, where she had older sisters in attendance at the historically black Selma University. After high school, in 1947 Jones enrolled in Tennessee State University in Nashville, Tennessee, where she majored in business education with a minor in history and social studies. She returned to Alabama after earning a B.S. in 1951 and taught high school business courses in Beatrice, Alabama, where she also became secretary for the local chapter of the NAACP.

As secretary for the NAACP, Jones participated in voter registration efforts in Monroe County, Alabama, but after two years she gave up her teaching position in Beatrice. In 1954 she began teaching business courses at Tuskegee Institute High School in Tuskegee, Alabama. With a social consciousness already developed by her family's civic and community service, however, she continued to resist both the overt and subtle forms of racism that characterized the Jim Crow South during the 1950s and 1960s. From individual acts of resistance such as refusing to purchase groceries after being denied the same carryout service as white patrons to later participation in virtually every major movement throughout the civil rights struggle, Jones continued to act on the belief, inculcated by her family, that she had a moral obligation to speak out against and challenge injustice.

Her work against racial discrimination and social injustice intensified after 1952, the year she married RALPH ABERNATHY, whom she had met when she was in the ninth grade. Four children— Juandalynn, Donzaleigh, Ralph David III, and Kwame Luthuli—were born to the marriage that lasted until Ralph Abernathy's death in 1990. As the wife of the minister who became one of the organizers of the Montgomery movement, top aide and confidant to MARTIN LUTHER KING JR., and successor to the presidency of both the Montgomery Improvement Association (MIA) and the Southern Christian Leadership Conference (SCLC), Juanita Jones Abernathy played important but often behind-the-scenes roles in the major movements organized by the SCLC after 1955. During the Montgomery bus boycott (1955–1956) she helped to organize and implement one of the first citizenship schools, conducting literacy classes before mass meetings. In 1956, like ROSA PARKS and SEPTIMA P. CLARK, she attended workshops at the Highlander Folk School in Monteagle, Tennessee.

In the early morning hours of 10 January 1957, while her husband was in Atlanta for the first meeting of the SCLC, the Abernathy home in Montgomery was bombed while she and her infant daughter Juandalynn were asleep. Fifteen minutes later she learned that her husband's church, First Baptist, had also been bombed. Before sunrise there were five bombings altogether in Montgomery, including the home of Robert Graetz, the white pastor of a black Lutheran congregation in the city. While police came to the Abernathy home after the bombing, they never entered the house and made no attempt to gather evidence.

As part of her continued civil rights activism, Abernathy faced violence again in the summer of 1966. As part of the Chicago Open Housing Movement, Abernathy and her husband, like Martin Luther King Jr. and CORETTA SCOTT KING, lived in an inner-city apartment building in the Lawndale section of that city. Both families not only lived in substandard housing to draw attention to the housing plight of blacks in that city, but also faced the violence of stone-throwing hecklers directed toward those who took part in peaceful demonstrations in Cicero, a predominantly white suburb of Chicago fiercely opposed to open housing legislation.

The Abernathy family moved to Atlanta in 1961. When Juanita Jones Abernathy was not participating in major national movements like Chicago in 1966, Memphis in 1967, and Charleston in 1968, she focused her energies on school desegregation, economic boycotts, and the integration of cultural organizations like the Atlanta Council for Visitors and events like the annual production of the Metropolitan Opera in Atlanta, which blacks were not allowed to attend. Over the next many years, using her business education background and acumen, she achieved a top sales position and an administrative position in Mary Kay Cosmetics and served as board member for a number of civic, educational, and business organizations.

A member of the founding board of directors for the Friends School of Atlanta, Abernathy went on to serve on the board of trustees for the Morehouse School of Religion, as secretary for the Metro Atlanta Rapid Transportation Authority (MARTA), as board member for the Fulton County Development Authority, the Atlanta Fulton County League of Women Voters League, and the Ralph David Abernathy Tower. As the widow of Ralph David Abernathy and CEO of the Ralph David Abernathy Foundation, she participated frequently in symposia and colloquia focused on issues of social justice, peace and human rights. In 2000, with DOROTHY HEIGHT and the civil rights attorney FRED D. GRAY, she served as panelist for a John F. Kennedy Jr. forum on the Montgomery bus boycott at Harvard University. Traveling nationally and internationally as a motivational speaker, she has addressed topics on religion, service, leadership, education, and the southern civil rights movement.

FURTHER READING

Abernathy, Donzaleigh. *Partners to History: Martin Luther King, Jr., Ralph David Abernathy, and the Civil Rights Movement* (2003).

Branch, Taylor. *At Canaan's Edge: America in the King Years, 1965–1968* (2006).

Hampton, Henry, and Steve Fayer. *Voices of Freedom: An Oral History of the Civil Rights Movement from the 1950s through the 1980s* (1990).

ALMA JEAN BILLINGSLEA BROWN

Abernathy, Ralph (11 Mar. 1926–17 Apr. 1990), clergyman and civil rights leader, was born David Abernathy near Linden, Alabama, the tenth of twelve children of farm owners Will L. Abernathy and Louivery Bell Abernathy. Abernathy spent his formative years on his family's five-hundred-acre farm in rural Marengo County in southwestern Alabama. His father's economic self-sufficiency and industry spared the family from most of the hardships of the Great Depression. "We didn't know that people were lining up at soup kitchens in cities all over the country," he would recall in his autobiography, *And the Walls Came Tumbling Down* (Abernathy, 6). Along with other family members, he attended Hopewell Baptist Church, where his father served as a deacon, and decided early to become a preacher, a commitment strengthened by a

Ralph Abernathy at National Press Club luncheon, 14 June 1968. (Library of Congress/U.S. News and World Report Collection/Warren K. Leffler, photographer.)

conversion experience at the age of seven. Abernathy attended high school at all-black Linden Academy, a Baptist-affiliated institution. Having little exposure to whites during his childhood, he remembered being "relatively unaware of racism or segregation" (Abernathy, 28).

In 1944 Abernathy was drafted into the armed services and enlisted as Ralph David Abernathy, a name given to him by his sister Manerva that he would use publicly for the rest of his life. Promoted to the rank of sergeant in the army, Abernathy served with his unit in France during the closing months of World War II, and he did not see combat before Germany's surrender. A bout of rheumatic fever prevented him from accompanying his unit to the Pacific theater, where, he later heard, nearly all of his comrades were killed in a battle on a Japanese-held island.

Returning to Alabama, Abernathy enrolled at Alabama State College in Montgomery. Elected president of the student council during his sophomore year, he led a strike against poor food in the student dining hall and the following year led another protest against substandard student housing. In 1948 Abernathy also chose the occasion of Mother's Day following his mother's death (his father had died several years earlier) to announce before the Hopewell congregation his call to the ministry. Soon afterward, he was ordained. He graduated from Alabama State College in 1950 with a B.S. in Mathematics. After serving briefly as a radio disc jockey during the summer of 1950, he spent a year in graduate studies in sociology at Atlanta University. While in Atlanta, Abernathy attended a service at Ebenezer Baptist Church, where he heard a sermon by MARTIN LUTHER KING JR., who was finishing his summer duties as his father's assistant before returning to his studies at Pennsylvania's Crozer Theological Seminar. "I stopped to shake his hand and comment on his sermon," Abernathy later wrote. "At that meeting we both recognized in one another a kindred spirit" (Abernathy, 89).

Abernathy returned to Montgomery to become dean of men at Alabama State, while also serving as minister of a small congregation at Eastern Star Baptist Church in Demopolis. Soon afterward, however, he accepted a call from Montgomery's hundred-year-old First Baptist Church. In 1952 Abernathy married Juanita Odessa Jones (JUANITA ABERNATHY) of Uniontown, Alabama, a teacher at the Monroe County Training School in Beatrice, Alabama. The following year, the first of the couple's four children was born.

In 1954 King moved to Montgomery to assume the pastorate of Dexter Avenue Baptist Church, and the Abernathys quickly formed ties with King and his wife, CORETTA SCOTT KING: "Because of Jim Crow we could only have dinner at home. So the four of us had dinner every night, with Coretta preparing the meal one evening, Juanita the next. And usually conversations among the four of us would last way beyond midnight" (Abernathy, 129). According to Abernathy, the two preachers and their wives discussed plans to turn Montgomery "into a model of social justice and racial amity," but they did not begin to implement these plans until ROSA PARKS was arrested on 1 December 1955 for refusing a bus driver's order to give up her bus seat to a white man (Abernathy, 129). The next day, E. D. NIXON, a local NAACP leader and a Pullman car porter, called Abernathy to seek his help in rallying support for a bus boycott initiated by JO ANN ROBINSON of the Women's Political Council in Montgomery. Abernathy took the lead in mobilizing the city's black clergy and other local residents.

After the boycott got off to a successful start on 5 December, Abernathy became program chairman of the newly organized Montgomery Improvement Association (MIA)—a name he later took credit for suggesting—and King was elected the MIA's president. As the boycott continued during the following year, Abernathy became a key figure in the movement. He often spoke at mass meetings, sometimes giving fulsome introductions of King, who would later describe Abernathy as "my closest associate and most trusted friend" (King, Autobiography [1998], 64). Abernathy was one of more than one hundred boycott leaders arrested in February 1956 for violating Alabama's antiboycott statute. The willingness of the indicted leaders to go to Montgomery's jail to be arrested demonstrated their resolve and proved to be a turning point in the boycott. After King's conviction in March was appealed, the trials of Abernathy and the other defendants were postponed by a continuance. In November the U.S. Supreme Court ruled that bus segregation in Montgomery was illegal, and in the following month Abernathy joined King in riding the city's first desegregated bus.

In January 1957 Abernathy was among a group of black ministers who gathered in Atlanta to organize a regional group to sustain and expand the bus protests that had occurred in Montgomery and other southern cities. Although he was called away from the meeting owing to the bombing of the First Baptist Church and his parsonage, he returned to form an organization that eventually became the Southern Christian Leadership Conference (SCLC). King became president and Abernathy secretary-treasurer of the new group.

Abernathy accompanied King to most of the subsequent major events of the southern civil rights struggle, joining him in jail during the key campaigns in Albany, Georgia, in 1961 and 1962 and Birmingham, Alabama, in 1963. A year after King moved from Montgomery to Atlanta in order to be closer to SCLC's headquarters in that city, Abernathy followed him and, at King's urging, became pastor of Atlanta's West Hunter Street Baptist Church in August 1961. Abernathy shared King's firm commitment to nonviolence and traveled with him to Oslo, Norway, in 1964 to attend King's Nobel Peace Prize acceptance ceremony. In 1965 Abernathy was named at King's request to the new position of vice president at large of SCLC, clarifying his status as King's successor.

Abernathy continued to work closely with King during the Poor People's Campaign of 1968 and was at the Loraine Motel in Memphis when an assassin killed King on 4 April. Abernathy was the first person at King's side. He knelt down and tried to comfort the dying King while cradling his head: "Martin. It's all right. Don't worry. This is Ralph. This is Ralph."

After the assassination, Abernathy assumed the presidency of SCLC and continued the Poor People's Campaign. He later admitted, however, that he lacked many of King's attributes: "I didn't have as many degrees as he did and I didn't have his polish. In addition, my skin was darker, a more important factor in dealing with the white press than anyone would dare admit" (Abernathy, 499). The Resurrection City encampment of antipoverty protesters in Washington, D.C., could be sustained only until July 1968, when Abernathy and the remaining protesters were arrested. He served twenty days in jail. After this setback, Abernathy continued as SCLC's president, but the group's effectiveness declined as many of King's former associates departed. In 1977 Abernathy left SCLC to make an unsuccessful run to represent an Atlanta district in the U.S. House of Representatives.

Abernathy's post-SCLC years were marked by continued outspokenness on civil rights issues and some controversy. In the 1980s, he broke ranks with most black leaders to support Ronald Reagan's presidential candidacy. "Reagan promised me that he would make a jobs program a top priority for his administration," he later explained. When Abernathy's autobiography was published in 1989, he again sparked controversy by confirming reports of King's "weakness for women" (Abernathy, 470). Abernathy denied rumors that King had interracial affairs, saying: "He was never attracted to white women and had nothing to do with them, despite the opportunities that may have presented themselves" (Abernathy, 472). But he suggested that on the night of King's assassination, King may have been involved in a sexual assignation and argued with another lover. Members of King's family and some of his former SCLC associates publicly rebuked Abernathy, who defended himself by insisting that King's dalliances had already been revealed. The year following the publication of his autobiography, Abernathy died at the age of sixty-four.

FURTHER READING

Some of Ralph Abernathy's papers are included in the Southern Christian Leadership Conference collection, Library and Archives of the Martin Luther King Jr. Center for Nonviolent Social Change, Atlanta, Georgia. Portions are available on microfilm.

Abernathy, Ralph David. *And the Walls Came Tumbling Down* (1989).

Branch, Taylor. *Parting the Waters: America in the King Years, 1954–63* (1988).

Branch, Taylor. *Pillar of Fire: America in the King Years, 1963–65* (1998).

Garrow, David J. *Bearing the Cross: Martin Luther King, Jr., and the Southern Christian Leadership Conference, 1955–1968* (1986).

Obituary: *New York Times*, 18 Apr. 1990.

CLAYBORNE CARSON

Abner, David, Sr. (Dec. 1820–14 May 1906), landowner, businessman, and state legislator, was born enslaved in Dallas County Alabama, to parents named Sarah and Pete, who had been born in South Carolina. David, like his parents, was the property of a family named Abner. There is some dispute as to his birth date—some giving 1826 and others 1838—but the most reliable date appears to be December 1820, as suggested by a letter from his youngest daughter. It is not known when David took the Abner surname for himself, a common but by no means universal practice for formerly enslaved persons. He was sent to Texas in 1843, driving a covered wagon for the newly married daughter (Thelma) of the man who held title to him.

Her father considered his new son-in-law unreliable and entrusted David to get his daughter safely to her new home and manage the farm (and slaves) he had bought for the newlyweds. At the time, the farm was part of Harrison County in the Republic of Texas, until the legislature of the newly annexed state carved out Upshur County in 1846. Upshur County was generally settled by slave owning immigrants from Alabama, in the eastern part, and in the western part by immigrants from Tennessee, who owned few or no slaves.

David Abner married three times. His first wife, whom he married in Alabama prior to 1843, was the property of a neighboring planter. When he drove a wagon back to Alabama with Thelma around 1845, he found that his wife had been sold to a man in Georgia and their two sons to South Carolina. He never saw his wife again, and his two sons were grown men when he was able to find them. He married a woman named Louisa in 1856, born in Alabama like Abner, with several grown and teenage children, all enslaved to a neighboring landowner in Texas. Their oldest sons, David Jr. and Peter, were born in 1860 and 1863, prior to emancipation. Daughter Fanny and sons Edward and Ben were born between 1866 and 1870.

Like most enslaved people in Texas, Abner was not freed until 19 June 1865, when federal troops arrived to announce and implement the Emancipation Proclamation; his freedom was later secured by the Thirteenth Amendment to the federal constitution. Within three days, Abner walked to Harrison County, lying a short distance west of Shreveport, Louisiana. There he obtained a loan from Mrs. Fannie Richardson, sister of his original owner in Alabama, of a mule and farm equipment, and forty acres rented on credit. He then moved wife Louisa and sons David and Peter, also freed in 1865, to join him in Harrison County. By December he made his first payment to buy the forty acres, and in 1870 he owned three hundred acres, harvesting a fifty-bale cotton crop. A founding member of Bethesda Baptist Church in 1867, Abner served as a deacon and also organized the first elementary school for colored children in Harrison County.

Abner was a leading Republican in what became, for a time, a strongly Republican county. By 1860, enslaved people of African descent were sixty percent of the population of Harrison County, compared to thirty percent in Texas generally and thirty-two percent in the southern states. Sixty percent of families in the county who thought of themselves as "white" owned slaves compared to twenty percent across Texas and twenty-five percent among all states with laws establishing slavery. The county elected a confederate army colonel and a former confederate congressman to the U.S. Congress in 1866, but produced overwhelming Republican majorities after adoption of the state constitution of 1869.

Abner served on the State Executive Committee of the Colored Men's Convention of 1873, was elected to a term in the state legislature in 1874, and served as a delegate to the state constitutional convention in 1875. This convention had only fifteen Republican delegates among ninety, crafting a constitution to undo Reconstruction. With a two-thirds African American majority by 1870, Harrison County remained Republican for some years afterward. Like Abner, most black legislators in Texas were formerly enslaved—there had been only 355 free colored residents of Texas immediately before the war. In 1876 Abner was elected vice president of the Republican state convention.

Adding business interests to his prosperous farm, Abner opened an ice plant and engaged in finance locally, signing notes, bonds, and securities for borrowers of both light and dark complexions. He later opened a brickyard. Louisa Abner died 23 November 1878 and was buried at Powder Mill Cemetery, where her husband was also buried twenty-eight years later. Before 1880, Abner married Mollie Price, a widow born in Kentucky in 1854, who brought into the family her grown sons, Coly, age thirty-four, and Manuel, age twenty-two, and a daughter Lucy, born in 1873. A daughter, Mae, was born in 1885 and son Clayton in 1891.

When Bishop College was founded 1881 in Marshall, Texas, by the American Baptist Home Mission Society, Abner was one of three African Americans among the eight incorporators and continued to serve as a trustee for the rest of his life. Abner helped to select and survey the site and offered the dedication prayer at the cornerstone of each campus building constructed during his lifetime. The southwest portion of the campus was land Abner sold to the college in 1891. Abner's son, David Jr., was Bishop's first graduate, having transferred from Fisk University to complete his senior year there.

At his death in 1906, Abner remained a resident of Harrison County, Texas, Justice Precinct No. 3, a farmer who owned his own land, clear of any mortgage. Between 1885 and 1900 the Abners adopted three children. His youngest daughter, Mrs. Mae Abner Moore, was still living in 1970.

Among his descendants are David Abner Jr., the first black professor at Bishop College, later president of Guadalupe and Conroe colleges, and grandchildren David Abner III, professor of business administration at Texas Southern University and Howard University, union mediator and United Auto Workers political action attorney Willoughby Abner, and Motown vice president Ewart G. Abner.

FURTHER READING

Some information on Abner's family background and early life appears in the Abner Family file at the Harrison County Historical Museum, Marshall, Texas.

Brewer, John Mason. *Negro Legislators of Texas and Their Descendants* (1970).

Campbell, Ralph B. *A Southern Community in Crisis: Harrison County, Texas, 1850–1880* (1983).

Simmons, William J., and Henry McNeal Turner. *Men of Mark: Eminent, Progressive and Rising* (1887).

CHARLES ROSENBERG

Abraham (fl. 1826–1845), also known as "Prophet," was a runaway slave who became a prominent leader among the Seminole. Nothing is known about his parents or childhood. Fleeing his master, Abraham escaped south into Florida, and was eventually adopted into the Seminole tribe, with whom he enjoyed considerable status. In 1826 he accompanied a tribal delegation to Washington, D.C., and became an influential counselor to Micanopy, a leading Seminole leader. The Seminole, or Florida Indians, once were a part both of the Muskogee (Creek) nation that had been driven out of Georgia by the early English colonists, and also of the Oconee and Yamasee tribes that had been driven out of the Carolinas following the Yamasee uprising of 1715. They had first settled among the Lower Creeks in the Florida Panhandle and created a haven for runaway slaves. Indeed, *Semino'le* is the Creek word for "runaway."

In 1818 Andrew Jackson led a command of American troops into Spanish Florida partly in an attempt to capture and return the runaway slaves to their masters. After the Florida purchase of 1819, southerners increased their demands for the return of their slaves, which the Seminole refused to do. Nonetheless, fugitive-slave hunters constantly raided

Negro Abraham

Abraham, a runaway slave who became a prominent counselor and interpreter among the Seminole in the early nineteenth century. (Library of Congress/Hughes & Meltzer.)

Seminole villages and clashed with Indian and black warriors. Federal officials attempted to force the Seminole to surrender the fugitives by withholding rations and annuities, but the Seminole insisted that the blacks were their private property or had been welcomed into the tribe as full members.

Two years after the passage of the Indian Removal Act of 1830, Abraham served as an interpreter during the negotiations between the Seminole and James Gadsden for the Treaty of Payne's Landing. The treaty called for the removal of the tribe to Indian Territory but not before an exploration party was sent west to examine the region. Abraham served as the party's interpreter. After touring Indian Territory the party signed another treaty at Fort Gibson, agreeing to removal. Returning to their homeland, however, the party reported that while the land was suitable, the location was unacceptably close to the Plains Indians; the tribe rejected the treaty. The federal government then dispatched troops to enforce removal. Abraham became a leader of the runaway slaves fighting alongside the Seminole. On 3 February 1837, Abraham was induced to surrender and appeared at the camp of General Thomas S. Jesup carrying a piece of white cloth attached to a stick. Abraham entered Jesup's camp and, maintaining his dignity, walked to the general's tent, where he stuck the staff into the ground and waited for Jesup to appear. According to the *Army and Navy Chronicle*, Abraham was "a cunning negro, of good consideration with the Seminoles." Although Abraham thought that he would be hanged for his part in the Seminole rebellion, federal officials realized that he could "do more than any other" to persuade those still fighting to surrender, and they used him as a peace mediator. On 6 March 1837 he served as the chief interpreter at a meeting held at Camp Dade at which the remaining leaders of the revolt, Jumper and Holahtochee, agreed to stop fighting and to report to Tampa Bay, Florida, for removal. Abraham continued to serve the government and in March 1838 was instrumental in convincing Alligator, one of the last warriors, to surrender. With Seminole resistance quelled, Abraham joined the other tribal members on their journey westward. On 25 February 1839 he, along with 195 other warriors, women, children, and former slaves, boarded the steamboat *Buckeye* for the trip to Indian Territory, where he continued to serve as an interpreter in negotiations between Seminole and U.S. officials.

As with his early life, little is known of Abraham's later life or his place of death. The Seminole were among the more isolated of the southeastern Indians, and they maintained less contact with non-Indians than did other tribes; therefore, Abraham's ability to serve as a translator between the Americans and the Seminole made him a valuable addition to the tribe.

FURTHER READING

Army and Navy Chronicle 4.

Foreman, Grant. *Indian Removal: The Emigration of the Five Civilized Tribes of Indians* (1932).

Mahon, John K. *History of the Second Seminole War, 1835–1842* (1967).

McKenney, Thomas L. *Memoirs with Sketches of Travels* (1846).

Porter, Kenneth W. "The Negro Abraham," *Florida Historical Quarterly* 25 (1946): 1–43.

This entry is taken from the *American National Biography* and is published here with the permission of the American Council of Learned Societies.

KENNY A. FRANKS

Abrams, Muhal Richard (19 Sept. 1930–), pianist and composer, was born in Chicago. He began studying piano at age seventeen and is largely self-taught, though in the late 1940s he studied briefly at Chicago Musical College and at Governors State University in Chicago. Abrams played his first professional gig in 1948, and during the early 1950s he wrote arrangements for the saxophonist King Fleming and other rhythm and blues groups. From 1957 to 1959 he was pianist, composer, and arranger for the hard-bop group MJT+3. Throughout the 1950s he also accompanied visiting soloists like MILES DAVIS, SONNY ROLLINS, Johnny Griffin, DEXTER KEITH GORDON, and MAX ROACH.

In the early 1960s Abrams and a group of young Chicagoans that included saxophonist EDDIE HARRIS and bassist Donald Garrett began to make plans for a rehearsal band. This initial attempt failed, but Abrams and Garrett revived the effort in 1961 and brought in the drummer Steve McCall and a cohort of adventurous players from Wilson Junior College—drummer Jack DeJohnette, saxophonists Roscoe Mitchell, Joseph Jarman, and Henry Threadgill, and bassist Malachi Favors. At first the music was quintessential hard bop; Abrams and Garrett had come from DuSable High School and cut their musical teeth playing with mainstream bop players like Harris and the saxophonist Johnny Griffin. But by 1963 they began to explore freer styles and, led by Abrams, established Experimental Band. There are no recordings

of this music; descriptions from the time suggest abrupt rhythmic and dynamic shifts and unusual instrumental combinations. Abrams emphasized group improvisation within written arrangements that privileged rhythm and melody over Eu-rooted harmony. An example of how this group might have sounded can be found in Joseph Jarman's "Song for Christopher" on *As If It Were the Seasons* (Delmark, 1968), as described by Alyn Shipton: "Delicate flue and bell sounds are superseded by the vast energetic ensemble of the entire group, but from which detailed moments, featuring the flute, trombone, and other individual soloists consistently emerge" (810).

Abrams also exerted a profound influence over the lives and careers of his fellow musicians by encouraging them to broaden their education and to explore the other arts, with the goal of heightening their self-awareness and self-respect. He also encouraged band members to develop their own styles in sessions at clubs like the Wonder Inn and Fifth Jack's and in private homes. In 1965 Abrams, along with Philip Cohran, Jodie Christian, and McCall, formed the Association for the Advancement of Creative Musicians (AACM), a cooperative group that offered training and education for young, inner-city musicians and sought to "set an example of high moral standards" and "uphold the tradition of elevated, cultured musicians handed down from the past." Central to this tradition was "the right of the individual to express the individual's unique and personal approach to the music" (Mandel, 37). To help achieve these goals, Abrams established the AACM School of Music at the Abraham Lincoln Center in Chicago. The AACM produced concerts and performances at bars and clubs and created a close-knit fraternity of more than fifty musicians.

Abrams began his own recording career at the relatively advanced age of thirty-seven, releasing *Level and Degree of Light* for Delmark Records, followed two years later by *Young at Heart, Wise in Time*. Both albums focus on structured ensembles with pieces that range from blues to hard bop and to free playing, rooted in the AACM's essential philosophy. Abrams moved to New York City in 1976, and from the mid-1970s to the mid-1990s he recorded a series of albums for the Italian Black Saint label, along with two 1978 efforts for Novus Records (*Lifea Blinec* and *Spiral Live at Montreux*). The Black Saint recordings comprise his most important musical statements. They include duets like 1990's *Duets and Solos* as well as medium-size groups from sextets to nonets. Each of these albums also contains pieces by smaller ensembles drawn from the larger group, and all contain expressive and often unexpected music that swings.

Most impressive, though, are Abrams's compositions for big bands. Two albums in particular reveal this music in all its brilliance. The *Hearinga Suite* (1989) contains horn arrangements, cello playing by Diedre Murray, and a trumpet solo reminiscent of LOUIS ARMSTRONG. *Blu Blu Blu* (1990) is a joyful, stomping tribute to the pre-swing era bands of FLETCHER HENDERSON, DON REDMAN, and Benny Carter. The title cut has a wonderful bluesy swagger, while "One for the Whistler" evokes a DUKE ELLINGTON-like melancholy. All of these recordings feature the constantly shifting structures of sound, with improvisations rising from the ensemble and falling back in again, that are hallmarks of Abrams's writing. These recordings feature many veterans of the Chicago scene and longtime associates of Abrams, such as Threadgill, Mitchell, and the trombonist GEORGE LEWIS. But they also highlight Abrams's role as a mentor to a wide range of younger musicians, such as saxophonists John Purcell, Patience Higgins, and Marty Ehrlich; trumpeters Eddie Allen and Baikida Carroll; and pianist Amina Claudine Myers. Between his work on these recordings and his efforts with the AACM, Abrams was a formative influence on dozens of the most creative artists in twentieth-century music, a role that has been widely recognized. In 1996 the Library of Congress chose his orchestra to open its concert season, and in 1990 Abrams was the first recipient of the prestigious Jazzpar Prize, awarded by the Danish government.

Abrams's compositions for classical orchestras and chamber groups represent an unjustifiably overlooked part of his career. These pieces have been performed by the Brooklyn Philharmonic Chamber Orchestra, the Kronos String Quartet, and the famed classical pianists Ursula Oppens and Frederic Rzewski. In 1991 the Friends of the Chicago Public Library and the Center for Black Music Research commissioned *What a Man*, in honor of the late Chicago mayor HAROLD WASHINGTON.

Abrams influenced the direction of jazz musically and institutionally. In addition to his seminal work in Chicago, he served as president of the New York chapter of the AACM, as a panelist for the National Endowment for the Arts and for the New York State Council on the Arts, and as a member of the board of directors of the National Jazz Service Organization and Meet the Composer. He taught at Columbia and Syracuse universities and served as a mentor for scores of important contemporary American musicians. His work for a wide variety of jazz ensembles is unsurpassed in its creative vision, and he refused to allow himself to be categorized, regarding himself not as a jazz or classical musician but simply as a musician. Abrams himself best summed up his musical philosophy: "Music has to touch you in some way and that thing that touches you is the thing that a performer went down into him or herself to get" (Mandel, 36).

FURTHER READING
Giddins, Gary. *Visions of Jazz: The First Century* (1998).
Jung, Fred. "A Fireside Chat with Muhal Richard Abrams," *Jazz Weekly*, available online at http:\\ www.jazzweekly.com.
Litweiler, John. *The Freedom Principle: Jazz after 1958* (1984).
Mandel, Howard. *Future Jazz* (1999).
Radano, Ronald M. *New Musical Figurations: Anthony Braxton's Cultural Critique* (1993).
Shipton, Alyn. *A New History of Jazz* (2001).
RONALD DUFOUR

Abron, Lilia Ann (8 Mar. 1945–), chemical engineer and environmental engineering entrepreneur, was born in Memphis, Tennessee, the second of four daughters of Ernest Buford Abron and Bernice Wise Abron, both educators. Abron was educated in Memphis public schools and was a member of the National Honor Society. Abron divorced and had three sons, Frederick, Ernest, and David; she is occasionally credited as Lilia Ann Abron-Robinson.

Abron stayed close to home when she attended LeMoyne College, a historically black college in Memphis, Tennessee. She considered medical school, but she was persuaded by her advisor, Dr. Beuler, to pursue a career in engineering instead. Her decision was a risky one. She did not know of any African Americans with engineering degrees who were actually working as engineers; instead, she once said in an interview, they were often working in post offices. In 1966 Abron received her B.S. in Chemistry from LeMoyne College.

Abron pursued her graduate education at Washington University in St. Louis, Missouri. At Washington University Abron faced a different environment than the nurturing one she had known at LeMoyne. She was away from home for the first time, and although she had outstanding professors, the general atmosphere was very different. Abron had to adjust to larger class sizes, less personal attention, and classmates who were predominately white men. During this time, Abron began a consulting firm as a side business. After just thirteen months, in 1968, she received her M.S. in Sanitary Engineering, a degree that allowed her to eventually become an environmental engineer.

When she could not find a job after she completed her master's degree, Abron pursued doctoral studies at the University of Iowa. Minorities were being actively recruited by the university, and efforts were made to help her feel at ease. Cecil Lue-Hing served as her advisor and mentor. Abron was not only the first African American woman to earn a Ph.D. in Chemical Engineering in 1971, but also the third woman to earn a doctorate in that department at the University of Iowa. After completing her doctorate, Abron worked as a professor at Tennessee State University, Vanderbilt University, Washington State University, and Howard University.

In 1978 Abron founded PEER Consultants, PC, an environmental and sanitary engineering consulting firm. PEER was awarded contracts from the Superfund program, the Boston Harbor cleanup, the Department of Defense for environmental policy work, and the Department of Energy through its Hazardous Waste Remedial Actions Program. *Engineering News-Record* magazine ranked PEER as a top engineering and design firm, its longevity remarkable in a field that saw many minority firms fail. PEER received the DoD Small Business/ Environmental Restoration Excellence Award for work done over many years for the U.S. Air Force and the Air National Guard. Headquartered in Rockville, Maryland, PEER had offices in seven U.S. cities and eventually had a staff of one hundred workers.

In 1995 Abron founded PEER Africa Pty (Ltd) with co-owner Douglas Guy in Johannesburg, South Africa. After the official end of apartheid in South Africa in 1994 houses were needed for millions of people. PEER Africa designed energy-efficient homes—40 to 50 percent more efficient than traditional homes—that could be built for less than $10,000. PEER Africa worked on projects elsewhere in Africa, including Mali, Uganda, and Nigeria, as well as the Caribbean islands. In 1997 the United Nations Framework Convention on Climate Change praised PEER Africa's trademarked methodology, known as the PEER Africa Energy and Environmentally Cost Optimized Human Settlement Development Model. Two years later the United Nations presented Abron with an award for creating the innovative, environmentally friendly design for these South African homes.

In 1993 she was honored with the Distinguished Alumni Award at the University of Iowa, and she won the Alumni Achievement Award from Washington University in 2001 in recognition of both her professional and personal achievements in environmental engineering and of her contributions to the people of South Africa. In 2004 she was inducted into the Academy of Arts and Sciences representing the field of Engineering Sciences and Technologies. Honorees were chosen from American and foreign applicants to honor achievement in science, scholarship, the arts, and public affairs.

An active member of many professional organizations, Abron received professional engineering registrations in environmental engineering and chemical engineering and served on the Board of Registration of Professional Engineers for the District of Columbia and on the Engineering Advisory Board for the National Science Foundation. She held memberships in the American Society of Civil Engineers, American Association of University Women, the American Water Works Association, the Society of Sigma Xi, and the Water Environmental Federation.

Community involvement was always a priority for Abron. She served as president of the Jack and Jill of America Inc. chapter based in Washington, D.C., and as a board member for the Baptist Home for Children. In addition to being a vocal advocate for science education, Abron and PEER sponsored science-fair projects. Her success as an engineer and entrepreneur and her dedication to public service and education made Abron a mentor and role model to women, minorities, and students.

FURTHER READING

Eversley, Shelly. "A True Renaissance Woman: Lilia Abron, Ph.D, P.E.," *AWIS: Association for Women in Science Magazine* (Jul.–Aug. 1995).

SHERRI J. NORRIS

Abu Bakr Al-Siddiq (c. 1794–1841?), Islamic scholar, Jamaican slave, and author, was born in Timbuktu, Mali. When he was two years old his family moved to Jenné in the western Sudan, another major center of Islamic learning and a renowned Sahelian trade city. Heir to a long tradition of Islamic saints and scholars claiming descent from the Prophet Muhammad, he was part of one of several dynasties designated as Sherifian or *Shurfaa*. Abu Bakr was trained and certified in Jenné by several *ulama*, the highly intellectual stratum of Islamic teachers. He was in the process of becoming a cleric when he was captured. As was true for many Islamized

Africans caught in the vortex of the Atlantic slave trade, Abu Bakr's itinerant life had pre-slave African and post-slave black Atlantic dimensions. His path shares the trajectory of many coreligionists from Muslim areas of the continent as well as of Christianized captives shipped to England, the Antilles, and North America. What is known about Abu Bakr comes to us through several autobiographical documents—in different English and Arabic versions—that he shared with contemporaries during and after his release from slavery in Jamaica. The first version came from a traveler to Jamaica, Richard Robert Madden, while others found their way to G.C. Renouard of Britain's Royal Geographical Society in 1836. A translation of another variant was rediscovered by the historian CHARLES HARRIS WESLEY, who published it in the *Journal of Negro History* in 1936. Each text is valuable in helping to reconstruct Abu Bakr's odyssey.

Abu Bakr claimed descent from a long line of literate and learned Muslim leaders. His father, Kara Muso (*Karamo* or *Karamoko* is Malinke for "learned man," from the Arabic *qalam*, or "pen"), was reputedly skilled in Koranic interpretation. Abu Bakr's paternal great-grandfather, 'Umar, was a *qa'id* (judge), and his maternal great-grandfather was designated as the king's witness (*shahid al-malik*) according to Ivor Wilks, possibly as a "jurisconsult." Abu Bakr frequently emphasized the critical importance that literacy had for him as a believer. This was clearly one of the cardinal virtues of his life.

His father died of fever soon after the family had moved to Jenné. Five years after his father's passing, with the sanction of his teacher, Abu Bakr traveled to visit his father's grave before journeying into the lands ruled by the Ashanti. At approximately age fourteen or fifteen, Abu Bakr was seized in the Asante (Ashanti) kingdom region of present-day Ghana and shipped to Jamaica in 1807 or 1808. He spent nearly three decades in slavery until he was emancipated in 1834.

During his captivity in Jamaica, Abu Bakr was the property of three owners. The first, a stonemason named Donellan, provided Abu Bakr's surname after he was bought by a man named Haynes, who baptized him as Edward Donellan. In 1823 he was purchased by Alexander Anderson, who so valued Abu Bakr's Arabic literacy that he engaged him as a bookkeeper for Anderson's business. Looking back in his narrative to his travails as a slave, Abu Bakr devoted special attention to reiterating the passionate piety that defined him as a believer, even as a chattel:

But for the bitterness of bondage, I have more to thank but those that brought me here. But praise be to God who has everything in his power to do as he thinks good, and no man can remove whatever burden he chooses to put on us. As he said, "Nothing shall fall on us except what he shall ordain, he is our Lord, and let all that believe in him put their trust in him" (Abu Bakr, "Life," 55).

Even in the depths of despair as a denizen of an island where life was short and days were long, Abu Bakr not only retained his faith but tenaciously hung on to the sacred language of the book, which remained inextricably linked in his consciousness with his ancestral lineage.

In 1834 Richard Madden, a sojourner in Jamaica, discovered that Abu Bakr was literate in Arabic and induced him to translate an autobiographical Arabic narrative of his life into phonetic spoken English, as Abu Bakr, now known as Edward Doulan (or Donellan) was not literate in the tongue of his overlord. Madden then incorporated the New World Muslim's memoir into his own compendium of reflections and letters treating the transformation of the economies and societies of Jamaica and Barbados from slavery to an apprenticeship system, a forerunner of what in the United States would be known as sharecropping and tenant farming. Madden negotiated Abu Bakr's sale and release from Anderson and also became persuaded that he should be repatriated to the western Sudan as soon as practicable. Prompted by Madden, John Davidson, a physician en route to Timbuktu, then began to explore this idea, actually going so far as to undertake a personal mission to western Sudan to make this possibility a reality. An auxiliary magistrate, Captain Oldrey, who had been involved in helping Abu Bakr earlier, continued to do so, and shortly thereafter, in 1835, Abu Bakr sailed to England under the guidance of Captain Oldrey, to whom he dictated another autobiographical account.

In late April 1836 the Reverend G. C. Renouard, foreign secretary of the Royal Geographical Society, stood before his colleagues to reveal several samples of Abu Bakr's thoughts, ranging from selections from the autobiographies to his geographical recollections of the regions of the western Sudan in which he had traveled and from which he had been taken in his youth. Those samples were later published in the Royal Society's journal as "Routes in North Africa." Meanwhile, Davidson sadly met his demise during a raid in West Africa, dying in

Timbuktu, momentarily complicating the process of Abu Bakr's African return. By 1841, however, Britain's deputy ambassador to Morocco reported that Abu Bakr was residing in Jenné. After this safe return, Abu Bakr disappeared from view yet lives on in print.

FURTHER READING

Abu Bakr al-Saddiq. "The History of Abon Becr Sadika, known in Jamaica by the name of Edward Doulan," in Richard Robert Madden, *Twelve Months' Residence in the West Indies, during the Transition from Slavery to Apprenticeship. With Incidental Notices of the State of Society, Prospects, and Natural Resources of Jamaica and Other Islands* (1835).

Abu Bakr al-Saddiq. "The Life and History of Abou Bekir Sadiki, Alias Edward Doulan," discovered by Dr. Charles H. Wesley, "Documents," *Journal of Negro History* 21, no. 1 (Jan. 1936).

Afroz, Sultana. "The Jihad of 1831–1832: The Misunderstood Baptist Rebellion in Jamaica," *Journal of Muslim Minority Affairs* 21, no. 2 (2001).

Diouf, Sylviane A. *Servants of Allah: African Muslims Enslaved in the Americas* (1998).

Renouard, Rev. G. C. "Routes in North Africa by Abu Bekr es Siddik," *Journal of the Royal Geographical Society* 6 (1836).

Singleton, Brent. "The Ummah Slowly Bled: A Select Bibliography of Enslaved African Muslims in the Americas and the Caribbean," *Journal of Muslim Minority Affairs* 22, no. 2 (2002).

Wilks, Ivor. "Abu Bakr al-Siddiq of Timbuktu," in *Africa Remembered: Narratives by West Africans from the Era of the Slave Trade*, ed. Philip D. Curtin (1967).

DAVID H. ANTHONY III

Abu-Jamal, Mumia (24 Apr. 1954–), a Philadelphia radio journalist who became an international icon in debates over race and the death penalty after he was convicted for the murder of a police officer, was born Wesley Cook to Edith and William Cook, migrants from the South. The family subsisted on welfare in the housing projects of North Philadelphia. As a boy Cook read avidly and sought enlightenment, attending services with his Baptist mother and Episcopalian father, then dabbling in Judaism, Catholicism, and the Nation of Islam. When he was about ten years old his father died of a heart attack, prompting him to assume a protective role toward his twin brother, Wayne, and younger brother, William.

The black liberation movement shaped Cook's coming of age. In a 1967 school class in Swahili, a

Mumia Abu-Jamal leaves Philadelphia's City Hall after a hearing on 12 July 1995. (AP Images.)

Kenyan teacher assigned him the first name Mumia. In 1968, at age fourteen, he and some friends protested at a South Philadelphia campaign rally of the Alabama segregationist and presidential candidate George Wallace. Attacked by racist whites, he appealed to a police officer for help, who "kicked me in the face" and "kicked me straight into the Black Panther Party" (*Live from Death Row*, 173). In 1969 Cook helped found the Philadelphia chapter of the Black Panther Party for Self-defense and became its lieutenant of information. Under FBI surveillance, he worked summers for the *Black Panther* newspaper in New York City and Oakland, California, as a street seller, and he witnessed the 1970 police raid on the Black Panther offices in Philadelphia. In 1971 his girlfriend Fran Hart, a Panther, gave birth to Jamal, a son, prompting Cook to adopt the Arabic surname "Father of Jamal." The metamorphosis was complete from Wesley Cook to Mumia Abu-Jamal.

Dismayed by infighting within the revolutionary left, Abu-Jamal in the 1970s was a "bored, slightly petit bourgeois, burnt-out ex-Black Panther who distrusted organizations and still simmered in a stew of generational rebellion" (*Live from Death Row*, 175).

Sympathetic teachers helped gain him admission to Goddard College in Vermont, where he volunteered on the campus radio station. There he married Hart, and they had a second child—Latifah, a daughter. But the relationship disintegrated, and he returned to Philadelphia without graduating from Goddard.

In 1974 Abu-Jamal began working on assignments for a variety of Philadelphia radio stations, sometimes using the name William Wellington Cole. In 1977 he married a schoolteacher who took the name Marilyn Cook; she gave birth to a son, Mazi. Abu-Jamal's reporting aired on National Public Radio, National Black Network, Mutual Black Network, and Associated Press Radio, and he was elected president of the Philadelphia Association of Black Journalists. In January 1981—by then living with a third wife, Mydiya Wadiya Jamal—he was included on a list of "People to Watch" by *Philadelphia Magazine*. It was as a reporter that Abu-Jamal came into contact with MOVE, a back-to-nature, armed, black nationalist religious group led by Vincent Leaphart, who had adopted the name John Africa. MOVE preached kindness and harmony while adopting a highly confrontational attitude toward police and the Philadelphia power structure—as well as neighbors irritated by MOVE's loudspeaker harangues and the stench of its many dogs' feces. Abu-Jamal increasingly viewed MOVE not as a deranged cult but as "idealistic, committed, strong, unshakable men and women who had a deep spirit-level aversion to everything this system represents" (Preface to *Death Blossoms*, 133). He was sharply critical of Mayor Frank Rizzo, a former police commissioner, and disputed Rizzo's account of the 1978 two-month police siege of MOVE's Powelton Village home, which led to convictions of nine MOVE members after an officer died during the conflict. Emulating MOVE, Abu-Jamal grew dreadlocks. He was impressed by Africa, who, representing himself, had won acquittal on bomb-building charges in a 1981 federal jury trial. However, Abu-Jamal lost his job at station WUHY when the station manager felt he was filing too many subjective reports about MOVE. Compelled to seek employment as a nightshift cabdriver, Abu-Jamal was robbed one night at gunpoint. He responded by purchasing a legally registered revolver.

At 3:55 A.M. on 9 December 1981, the twenty-five-year-old officer Daniel Faulkner, a Philadelphia policeman, stopped a Volkswagen Beetle driven by Abu-Jamal's younger brother, William Cook, on Locust Street in a downtown red-light district.

An altercation ensued. Cook may have punched Faulkner. Then Faulkner bludgeoned Cook with a heavy-duty, police-issue flashlight. A black man ran across the street from an adjacent parking lot. Faulkner was shot in the back once, then again in the face at point-blank range. Abu-Jamal, twenty-seven years old, was found sitting on the curb, bleeding from a gunshot wound, a few feet from Faulkner's dead body. His taxicab was in the adjacent parking lot. He wore an empty holster, and beside him was his .38 caliber handgun with spent cartridges in all five cylinders. Standing against the wall was William Cook, who told Robert Shoemaker, the first officer at scene, "I had nothing to do with it" (*Commonwealth v. Mumia Abu-Jamal*, 19 June 1982, 31). To many, the conclusion was inescapable: Abu-Jamal was a cop killer. After a 1982 trial presided over by Judge Albert F. Sabo, a panel of ten white and two black jurors convicted Abu-Jamal of first-degree murder and sentenced him to death.

Initially the case remained obscure as it wound its way through the courts. An appeal filed by a public defender was denied by the Pennsylvania Supreme Court in 1989, and the U.S. Supreme Court refused review. In 1995, when Pennsylvania's Republican governor Tom Ridge signed Abu-Jamal's death warrant, making imminent his execution by lethal injection, Abu-Jamal suddenly rocketed to international prominence. Rallies were held, his photograph adorned T-shirts and posters, celebrities took up his cause, and journalists scrutinized trial transcripts. A new team of lawyers headed by Leonard Weinglass filed for post conviction relief in Philadelphia.

One objection to the original trial's fairness was to the quality of the defense. Abu-Jamal and his family had hired Anthony E. Jackson, a young, progressive black lawyer. Since Abu-Jamal could not afford the bills, Jackson became, by consent, court appointed. However, Jackson had never been lead attorney in a capital case and had a reputation for substance abuse. Once it became apparent that he could not mount a compelling defense, he sought to withdraw, unsuccessfully. The court allowed Abu-Jamal to represent himself in jury selection but then ordered Jackson to resume as lead counsel because of the excessive time Abu-Jamal took to question potential jurors. Abu-Jamal persisted, demanding to represent himself and to have John Africa sit at his table. The court denied those requests. Abu-Jamal refused to cooperate with Jackson thereafter and engaged in disruptive outbursts, prompting his removal from the courtroom on multiple occasions. Jackson, with few funds and little experience, faced Joseph McGill, a seasoned assistant district attorney, and Judge Sabo, a former law enforcement official who at retirement had presided over thirty-one death sentences, more than any other judge in the country. Jackson did not place a single character witness for Abu-Jamal on the stand in the penalty phase. Critics consider his closing arguments feeble.

A second disputed area is the forensic evidence. Police did not test Abu-Jamal's gun to see if it had been fired recently. Nor did they run a standard test to see if his hands had fired a gun. A medical examiner's report stated incorrectly that the bullet removed from Faulkner's brain was .44 caliber, but Jackson failed to direct the jury's attention to this discrepancy. Finally, no fingerprints were found on the weapon (though it is unusual to find identifiable prints on guns).

Abu-Jamal's supporters frequently conjectured that he may have been framed by police resentful of his support of MOVE and journalistic criticism of police. Vulnerable witnesses, they suggest, may have been pressured to provide perjured testimony. Cynthia White's story changed dramatically across four sessions with detectives. Robert Chobert, whose account also changed, was a convicted arsonist on probation who was driving a cab despite a DWI-suspended license. McGill, however, has observed that saintly witnesses are rarely found at night in red-light districts, and others pointed out that Abu-Jamal was a cabdriver at the time of his arrest, hardly a major thorn in the side of police. The most dubious witness's testimony pertained to a supposed hospital confession by Abu-Jamal. Officer Gary Wakshul, who traveled with Abu-Jamal in the van and remained with him at the hospital, claimed in 1982 to have heard Abu-Jamal say, "I shot the motherfucker and I hope the motherfucker dies." But two months before, at the actual time of the shooting, Wakshul filed a report stating, "The negro male made no comments" (Lindorff, 196).

Many critics, finally, doubted that the killing was deliberate and premeditated, even if Abu-Jamal did shoot Faulkner. In his 1982 cross-examination McGill introduced a 1970 news article in which Abu-Jamal, then fifteen years old and still named Wesley Cook, quoted the Chinese Communist Party chairman Mao Tse-tung's dictum "Political power grows out of the barrel of a gun." Critics note that this reference was meant to illuminate why police were murdering Black Panthers, not justify

random attacks on police, and they find the introduction of the defendant's earlier political beliefs and affiliations into the trial to be prejudicial.

For twenty years Abu-Jamal maintained his innocence but refused to discuss the night of the shooting. In 2001 he claimed in a brief written account that he was shot by police while crossing the street to aid his brother, then lost consciousness. Meanwhile, his brother William Cook filed a 2001 affidavit stating that Kenneth Freeman, his business partner, who died in 1985, was in the Volkswagen but fled the scene, implying Freeman, rather than Abu-Jamal, may have shot Faulkner. Five witnesses told police in 1981 that they saw someone else fleeing, but critics point out that if someone other than Abu-Jamal was the killer, it strains credulity that Abu-Jamal and his brother would wait twenty years to mention it.

In 1995, just a few days before Abu-Jamal's scheduled execution, the death warrant was vacated. Judge Sabo, declining to recuse himself, presided over a 1995–1996 post-conviction relief hearing that the *Philadelphia Inquirer* described as overtly biased. When Governor Ridge signed a second death warrant in 1999, it, too, was vacated. Meanwhile, new revelations broke. In 2000 a court stenographer signed an affidavit that in 1982, on one of the first days of the trial, she overheard Judge Sabo (who died in 2002) say, "I'm going to help them fry the nigger" (Lindorff, 338).

In 1995 Abu-Jamal was housed at State Correctional Institute–Greene, a super-maximum death row prison in Waynesburg, Pennsylvania. Through distance learning he obtained a B.A. from Goddard College and an M.A. from California State University–Dominguez Hills. He published articles in the *Nation* and the *Yale Law Journal* and delivered recorded commencement addresses at several liberal arts colleges. In the early 1990s National Public Radio's *All Things Considered* canceled his scheduled commentaries, but they were published in *Live from Death Row* (1994), a book followed by *Death Blossoms: Reflections from a Prisoner of Conscience* (1997), *All Things Censored* (2000), *Faith of Our Fathers: An Examination of the Spiritual Life of African and African-American People* (2003), and *We Want Freedom: A Life in the Black Panther Party* (2004). In his writings Abu-Jamal maintains that mandatory exclusion of jurors who oppose capital punishment guarantees "pro-prosecution, pro-conviction, pro-death penalty" juries. He considers words like "corrections" and "penitentiaries" hypocritical, since prison is "a second-by-second assault on the soul, a day-to-day degradation of the self, an oppressive steel and brick umbrella" (*Live from Death Row*, 37, 64–65).

In 2001 the U.S. district judge William Yohn Jr. overturned Abu-Jamal's death sentence, saying jurors had been wrongly instructed. The Philadelphia district attorney appealed the ruling. Also in 2001 Abu-Jamal fired his legal team of Leonard Weinglass and Daniel Williams after Williams published a book that criticized "Free Mumia" supporters for insisting on his innocence rather than contesting the fairness of his trial. Eliot Lee Grossman and Marlene Kamish, his succeeding attorneys, required supporters to confirm Abu-Jamal's innocence and introduced the fantastic claim of Arnold Beverly, a man with an extensive criminal record and history of mental illness, that corrupt Philadelphia police hired him to kill Faulkner. In 2004 Abu-Jamal dropped Grossman and Kamish and made Robert Bryan lead attorney; the Beverly claim was abandoned.

In 2005 the Third Circuit Court of Appeals ruled that Abu-Jamal could appeal his case on three grounds: that jury selection was racially discriminatory; that improper comments to the jury by the prosecutor minimized the seriousness of returning a guilty verdict; and that Judge Sabo showed bias in the post-conviction relief hearings. The first two claims could lead to a new trial. The third could lead to a new evidentiary hearing. The court could also overturn Yohn's 2001 ruling, however, restoring Abu-Jamal's death sentence.

In 2006 the Parisian suburb of St. Denis named a street for Abu-Jamal, leading Congress to pass a resolution condemning the French city. Maureen Faulkner, the slain officer's widow, and Philadelphia's Fraternal Order of Police continued to insist upon Abu-Jamal's guilt and advocate his execution, but the public intellectual CORNEL WEST called Abu-Jamal "unjustly imprisoned for a crime he did not commit" (*Death Blossoms*, xii). Between these polarities of opinion fall critics of the trial's fairness who do not exonerate Abu-Jamal. The legal analyst Stuart Taylor has described Abu-Jamal as "guilty and framed," a killer subjected to a "grotesquely unfair" trial. The journalist Dave Lindorff hypothesized that Faulkner may have shot first or that Abu-Jamal might have fired in "a momentary paroxysm of anger and concern about his brother's safety," making the murder neither premeditated nor unprovoked (Lindorff, 61). Whether Abu-Jamal was the killer, whether his trial was fair, and whether he—or anyone else—deserves to be executed remained topics of sharp debate in the first decade of the 21st century. In April 2010 the Third Circuit Court of Appeals reaffirmed its 2008 ruling to vacate the death sentence because Abu-Jamal's sentencing hearing had been unfair. The Philadelphia District Attorney's office then petitioned the U.S. Supreme Court to resinstate the death penalty, but in October 2011 the highest court refused to hear that appeal. In December 2011, the District Attorney's office announced that it would abandon its effort to execute Abu-Jamal. He was released to the general prison population, where he will serve the rest of his life sentence.

FURTHER READING

Abu-Jamal, Mumia. *Death Blossoms: Reflections from a Prisoner of Conscience* (1997).

Abu-Jamal, Mumia. *Live from Death Row* (1995).

Amnesty International. *United States of America: A Life in the Balance: The Case of Mumia Abu-Jamal* (2000).

Bisson, Terry. *On a Move: The Story of Mumia Abu Jamal* (2001).

Commonwealth v. Mumia Abu-Jamal, a.k.a. Wesley Cook. Trail Transcripts, Court of Common Pleas, Philadelphia County, Criminal County Division (1982).

Lindorff, Dave. *Killing Time: An Investigation into the Death Row Case of Mumia Abu Jamal* (2003).

Taylor, Stuart, Jr. "Guilty and Framed," *American Lawyer*, Dec. 1995, 74–85.

Williams, Daniel R. *Executing Justice: An Inside Account of the Case of Mumia Abu-Jamal* (2001).

CHRISTOPHER PHELPS

Ace, Johnny (9 June 1929–25 Dec. 1954), musician, songwriter, and rhythm and blues star, was born John Marshall Alexander Jr. in Memphis, Tennessee, the son of John Marshall Alexander and Leslie Newsome. His father earned his living in Memphis as a packer, but his lifework was as a commuting minister to two rural Baptist churches in eastern Arkansas. At LaRose Grammar School in South Memphis, John Jr., as his family called him, displayed both musical and artistic talent. He mastered the piano at home but was allowed to play only religious music. Along with his mother and siblings, he sang in the choir at Bethel African Methodist Episcopal Church. Becoming restless at Booker T. Washington High School, John Jr. dropped out in the eleventh grade to join the navy and see the world. His sisters recalled military police coming to the house in search of their brother and thought of his brief period of enlistment in terms of weeks, ending in an "Undesirable Discharge" in 1947. His mother was furious. "I can't keep up with you," she scolded, "and *they* can't keep up with you."

It is possible that Alexander never had a job in the conventional sense, and he did not seek employment after his failed bit in the navy. He did, however, find kindred spirits on Beale Street, Memphis's famed nightlife center. Joe Hill Louis, "the Be-Bop Boy," may have started Alexander out as a professional musician, or the credit may belong to Dwight "Gatemouth" Moore, but by 1949 Alexander was the piano player with the Beale Street Blues Boys (later the Beale Streeters), a band that backed B. B. KING when he performed live. In 1950 Alexander wooed and married Lois Jean Palmer, a ninth-grader at Booker T. Washington High School, and moved her into his parents' home. A son was born to the couple that year and a daughter in 1952. Alexander's mother, who disapproved of his lifestyle and his occupation as a blues musician, embraced Alexander's wife and children but refused to let him sleep at the family home.

In 1952 David James Mattis, the program director at the Memphis all-black radio station WDIA (the "Mother Station of the Negroes"), founded Duke Records and changed Alexander's name to Johnny Ace. When Bobby "Blue" Bland could not sing a song scheduled for recording at the WDIA studio (it was subsequently revealed that Bland could not read), Mattis wrote new lyrics to an existing rhythm and blues hit, and Ace "faked out" a new melody. The result was "My Song," a "blues ballad" (*Billboard* called it a "heart ballad") that Ace sang in a vulnerable and innocent crooning style. Though the recording was poor, the charm of Ace's voice made it an immediate hit with its limited audience. "My Song" attracted the attention of the Houston entrepreneur Don D. Robey, a black man who owned Peacock Records and controlled a booking agency specializing in "chitlin circuit" venues. Robey became a partner and quickly the sole owner of Duke Records, moving the entire operation to Houston. He aggressively promoted Ace's "My Song" to the top of the rhythm and blues charts and groomed him as a national headlining rhythm and blues act, carefully cultivating the kind of polished, first-class, uptown image that BERRY GORDY JR. would later emulate at Motown.

Ace's career, which lasted less than two and a half years, produced eight rhythm and blues top-ten records, including three number one hits: "My Song" (1952), "The Clock" (1953), and "Pledging My Love" (1955). For the most part Ace lived the nomadic life of a road musician, with no permanent home or routine beyond a string of hotel stops, traveling coast to coast with a backup band and an opening act, the blues singer WILLIE MAE "BIG MAMA" THORNTON. In 1954 Ace may have performed as many as 350 one-nighters, sometimes driving as far as 800 miles between shows. According to Evelyn Johnson, the head of the Buffalo Booking Agency and the closest thing to a personal manager that Ace had, Ace was shy, childlike, and unassuming. "Sweetest thing since sugar," she recalled, "but he didn't care about nuttin', honey." At a pawnshop in Florida he purchased a .22 caliber pistol to amuse himself and to alleviate the boredom of the road. On Christmas night 1954, while backstage during intermission at a "Negro Christmas Dance" at Houston's City Auditorium, Ace began "snapping" his pistol at the heads of people in his dressing room. According to Thornton, Ace then put the pistol to his own head and uttered his last words: "I'll show you that it won't shoot." Authorities ruled the cause of death to be "playing russian roulette—self inflicted."

Ace's last record, "Pledging My Love," first advertised in *Billboard* on the day of his death, represented neither rhythm nor blues, but nevertheless the slow ballad became a rhythm and blues triple-crown hit (number one in retail sales, radio airplay, and jukebox action), was the most-played rhythm and blues record of 1955, and generated more than half a dozen tribute records to the romantic legend of Johnny Ace. In addition the record crossed over to the pop charts to become a hit there as well. For the first time in the postwar era, white record buyers (primarily teens) chose a ballad by a solo black male singer signed to an independent rhythm and blues label as the unique and definitive performance of a popular song against which all subsequent performances were ruthlessly judged. Arguably, "Pledging My Love" represents the transitional record between rhythm and blues and rock and roll.

Johnny Ace died a rhythm and blues star and was resurrected a rock and roll legend. He has been called rock's first "casualty," "the first fallen angel," and "the colored James Dean." For disc jockeys he remains "the Late Great Johnny Ace."

FURTHER READING

Gart, Galen, and Roy C. Ames. *Duke/Peacock Records: An Illustrated History with Discography* (1990).

Salem, James M. "Death and the Rhythm-and-Bluesman: The Life and Recordings of Johnny Ace," *American Music* (Fall 1993): 316–367.

Tosches, Nick. *Unsung Heroes of Rock 'n' Roll* (1984).

This entry is taken from the *American National Biography* and is published here with the permission of the American Council of Learned Societies.

JAMES M. SALEM

Adair, Thelma Cornelia (29 Aug. 1920–), Presbyterian educator and activist, was born Thelma Cornelia Davidson at Iron Station, North Carolina, one of five children of Robert James Davidson, a Baptist minister, schoolteacher, and principal, and Violet Wilson Davidson, a schoolteacher, mortician, and community organizer. Her grandfather, six uncles, and three brothers were all ministers, as would be her future husband. She grew up in Spindale, North Carolina, where her mother was a teacher and her father was principal and superintendent of Western Union Baptist Academy, and later in Kings Mountain, North Carolina, where her father served as a high school principal and as the pastor of several local churches. After her early years in public school, she enrolled in Lincoln Academy, a boarding school run by the American Missionary Society of the Congregational Church. Just before her thirteenth birthday, she enrolled in Barber-Scotia Junior College in Concord, North Carolina, a school of the "northern" United Presbyterian Church. She finished her college studies at the Methodist-affiliated Bennett College.

Adair's first full-time job was as a math, science, and history teacher at Mount Carmel Junior High School, a rural school located ten miles from Lancaster, South Carolina. She soon married Arthur Eugene Adair, a Presbyterian minister and missionary. Together they organized new churches and Sunday schools throughout North and South Carolina. The couple eventually had three children.

In 1942 the Adairs moved to New York City, where Eugene entered Union Theological Seminary and Thelma entered Columbia University Teachers College. At the request of Henry Sloane Coffin, president of Union Theological Seminary, Adair and her husband founded the Mount Morris Presbyterian Church in Harlem after a mostly white Presbyterian congregation had fled the neighborhood and abandoned its church building. The Adair family lived in an apartment in the church building for twenty-four years before they purchased a nearby brownstone. Adair eventually became one of the first women in that congregation to be ordained as an elder. She earned her M.A. from Columbia University Teachers College in 1945 and earned her Ed.D. in Curriculum and Teaching in 1959; in 1977 Adair received the Distinguished Alumni Award from Columbia University Teachers College.

Most of Adair's professional career was spent as a professor of education at Queens College at the City University of New York, even while she continued an active life of service to her church and her community. She also lectured or taught at Maryville College, the College of Wooster, Dubuque University, the College of Idaho, Macalester College, Lafayette College, and New York University. She served as adjunct professor at Colgate-Rochester Divinity School, Princeton Theological Seminary, and Union Theological Seminary in New York. After thirty-one years of service, she retired from Queens College as professor emerita of early childhood education.

Adair then went on to organize and direct a number of noteworthy programs. She helped initiate the federal Head Start program for at-risk children, and she directed several programs in conjunction with the United Nations Educational, Scientific, and Cultural Organization Year of Education and with Peace Corps training programs, traveling to observe or consult throughout the Caribbean, Western Europe, East Asia, the Far East, and many African countries, including Cameroon, Egypt, Ethiopia, Ghana, Ivory Coast, Kenya, Liberia, Nigeria, Senegal, Sierra Leone, Uganda, and Tanzania. In 1944 she established Mount Morris New Life as a day care facility. In 1966 Adair became the first African American trustee of the Orphan Asylum Society in the City of New York, which operated the Graham Home for Children, an integrated orphanage in Hastings-on-Hudson. That same year she helped begin an integrated day camp as a cooperative project of the Mount Morris church and the Huguenot Memorial Church of Pelham Manor, New York. Adair also wrote or cowrote several manuals for church schoolteachers, including *How to Make Church School Equipment: It's Easier Than You Think!* (1955), *When We Teach 4's and 5's* (1962), and *Parents and the Day Care Center* (1969).

Adair served on numerous Presbyterian Church agencies and boards. She served as president of the Black Presbyterian Caucus and on a national Special Committee on the Status of Women. Adair was vice president of the Board of

Christian Education and was coordinator of educational strategy for the Board of National Missions. In 1974 the General Assembly of the United Presbyterian Church appointed Adair the chairperson of a special Consulting Committee on the Needs and Rights of Children, a position she held until 1976, at which time she resigned to become the first African American woman, and only the second woman ever, to be elected moderator of the General Assembly of the United Presbyterian Church, the denomination's highest elected office. As moderator, she represented the denomination on every continent except Africa, including a trip to Australia to celebrate the merger of the Methodist, Congregational, and Presbyterian churches as they came together to form the Uniting Church in Australia. On 11 December 1979, at the age of sixty-three, her husband, Eugene, died of a heart attack he had suffered during a meeting of the Presbytery of New York City.

After her year as moderator concluded, Adair continued her activity in the national leadership of the Presbyterian Church and served as a member of the General Assembly Council, as chair of the Global Mission Ministry Unit, as a member of the Evangelism and Church Development Unit, and as chair of the Presbyterian Senior Services of New York. Adair was one of the featured Presbyterian speakers on the 1989 *Protestant Hour* series of radio broadcast sermons. In 1991 she was one of three honorees named as a *Woman of Faith*, an award given to Presbyterian leaders whose lives "exemplify faith in God and commitment to the mission of the Presbyterian Church (U.S.A.)." She was a featured speaker at many regional and national gatherings of Presbyterian Women, and when the Covenant Network of Presbyterians was founded to promote a socially progressive stance for the Presbyterian Church, Adair agreed to serve on its board of advisers.

Adair held several important leadership roles in Church Women United (CWU), a national ecumenical Christian women's movement organized in conjunction with the National Council of Churches. In 1974 she was a leader in the CWU Asian Causeway, and in 1975 she served as a consultant for its Caribbean Causeway. Adair twice served as vice president, and from 1980 to 1984 she served as president of CWU, just the second African American to hold that position. Long active in that organization, she frequently chaired national conferences and served as adviser to the group's national board.

Adair later became active in the World Council of Churches. She was a cochairperson of the U.S.

Committee on the Ecumenical Decade of Churches in Solidarity with Women, and in 1993 she was one of the planners and participants in the Reimagining Conference held in Minneapolis. In 1998 Adair and her daughter, Dr. Jeanne D. Adair, traveled to Zambia, and then on to Harare, Zimbabwe, where they served among the 125 U.S. delegates to the 1998 Ecumenical Decade Festival held 27–30 November in conjunction with the Eighth Assembly of the World Council of Churches. She also served on the advisory council of the National Council of Churches and was appointed to the International Board of Advisors of the United Nations Association of Haiti.

Adair became an advocate for health care and served on the Harlem Hospital Community Advisory Board. She worked with Harlem Hospital and the Columbia University School of Dental and Oral Surgery to establish a dental and medical clinic to serve the neighborhood's senior citizens, and in June 2002 the Thelma C. Davidson Adair Medical and Dental Center was opened in Harlem.

Adair served on the boards of the Frederick Douglass Creative Arts Center in New York City, Barber-Scotia College, Boggs Academy, Johnson C. Smith Seminary, the Inter-American University of Puerto Rico, and the Interdenominational Theological Center. Adair received numerous other honors, including an honorary degree and the Alumni Award for Meritorious Service in the Field of Education from Barber-Scotia College, an honorary degree from Middlebury College, and the United Negro College Fund Distinguished Award for Outstanding Service and Commitment to Higher Education.

FURTHER READING

The Presbyterian Historical Society in Philadelphia contains archival material related to Adair's service as moderator of the General Assembly, and Adair's work with Church Women United is documented in the Archives of the United Methodist Church at Drew University in Madison, New Jersey.

Basham, Beth, ed. *Women of Faith of the Presbyterian Church (U.S.A.), 1986 to 1996* (1997).

Cunningham, Sarah. "Thelma Adair: A Busy, Effective Moderator," *A.D. 1977: The Magazine for the United Presbyterian Family* 6:4 (Apr. 1977).

Wilson, Agnes T. "Four Black Moderators," in *Periscopes 2: Black Presbyterians—Yesterday, Today, and Tomorrow: 175 Years of Ministry, 1807–1982* (1982).

Wilson, Frank T., Sr., ed. "Thelma Cornelia Adair—For People, Love, and Light," in *Black Presbyterians in Ministry* (1979).

DAVID B. MCCARTHY

Adams, Alton Augustus, Sr. (4 Nov. 1889–23 Nov. 1987), flutist, composer, bandmaster, music educator, journalist, and hotelier, was born in Charlotte Amalie, St. Thomas, Danish West Indies (later U.S. Virgin Islands) and is remembered as the U.S. Navy's first African American bandmaster. Adams was the son of Jacob Henry Adams, a carpenter, and Petrina Evangeline Dinzey, a tailor; both his parents were members of the black artisan class centered around St. Thomas's port. This culture celebrated music and literature and instilled the young Adams with values of hard work and self-education. Although professional musicians were unknown in the Virgin Islands in his youth, Adams dreamt of a musical career inspired by his deeply held belief that music was not just entertainment, but vital to community health.

Adams attended elementary school and apprenticed as a carpenter and then a shoemaker, choosing his trade based on the musical abilities of his master. Adams learned solfége from a neighbor and taught himself piccolo. He joined the St. Thomas Municipal Band under the direction of Lionel Roberts in 1907, and he quickly rose to the position of assistant bandmaster. With no school of music on the islands, he took correspondence courses in music theory and composition with Dr. Hugh Clarke at the University of Pennsylvania (eventually earning a bachelor's degree in 1931 from the University Extension Conservatory in Chicago). Adams's first compositions were performed by the Municipal Band, but by late 1909 he had resigned to form his own ensemble called the Adams Juvenile Band. This new group soon became part of the local community fabric by performing at social and charitable events and giving regular concerts on the city's bandstand at Emancipation Garden. Adams's first musical publication, *Doux Rêve d'Amour* for solo piano, appeared in 1912; and beginning in 1916 he contributed a series of idealistic monthly columns for the widely distributed *Jacobs' Band Monthly* (Boston), which cemented his national reputation. He married Ella Eugenia Joseph on 6 October 1917, and the couple had eight children.

Following the United States' purchase of the Virgin Islands from Denmark on the eve of American entry into World War I, Adams and his bandsmen were inducted into the navy on 2 June 1917, thus becoming the first African Americans to receive official musical appointments in the U.S. Navy most likely since the War of 1812; and Adams became the navy's first known black bandmaster. The all-black ensemble was to serve as a bridge between the islands' all-white naval administration and the predominantly black population. While some local leaders chose instead to protest this "naval rule," Adams chose to join with the new administration. His decision was controversial, but through cooperation Adams not only fulfilled his artistic dreams by becoming a professional musician, but also used his newfound authority as chief petty officer to influence the new administration for the benefit of his fellow islanders.

Adams's influence soon began to expand in both the navy and the community. He served as an officer of the local chapter of the Red Cross, helped found Charlotte Amalie's public library in 1920, started the islands' first public school music program in 1920, and ran a local newspaper, the *St. Thomas Times*, from 1921 to 1923.

At the suggestion of a 1924 Congressional committee sent to investigate conditions on the islands, Adams's naval band toured the U.S. East Coast in the summer of 1924, including stops in Washington, D.C., Philadelphia, New York, and Boston, to enthusiastic applause from both white and black audiences and vociferous praise from the black press. While in New York, Adams conducted the all-white Goldman Band in Central Park. In 1931 when a civilian administration displaced the navy, Adams's ensemble was transferred to Guantánamo Bay, Cuba. This move signaled the end of the band, separating Adams and his bandsmen from family, friends, and their ensemble's social purpose. Still strictly segregated, the navy kept the black bandsmen apart from white musicians and the band languished in administrative isolation.

Tragically, a 1932 fire that destroyed Adams's home on St. Thomas also claimed many of his music manuscripts. Only about a dozen works survived. His best known compositions are the *Virgin Islands March* (1919), *The Governor's Own* (1921), and *Spirit of the U.S.N.*, which was written for President Calvin Coolidge during the 1924 tour. Adams's music has received little attention from scholars of black music, in part because his compositions, except for his arrangements of *bamboula* dances and spirituals, contain few characteristics traditionally associated with African American music. Rather, Adams's music is in the classic march idiom of John Philip Sousa, his musical idol, and communicates palpable energy along with a discernible sense of patriotism.

Adams retired from active duty and joined the U.S. Naval Fleet Reserves in 1933. He returned to St. Thomas, soon resuming his work in the music programs of the public schools. In 1940 he again took on a newspaper editorship, this time for the *Bulletin* in St. Thomas, but he was recalled to active duty after Pearl Harbor was attacked by the Japanese in 1941. Sent back to Guantánamo in 1942, Adams assumed command of an all-white ensemble and reinstated eight former bandsmen, thus creating the navy's first official racially integrated band. The next year Adams and the other Virgin Islanders returned to St. Thomas and were again segregated as an all-black unit. This band would be transferred once more in 1944, this time to Puerto Rico. In 1945 Adams retired from the navy permanently.

Returning again to St. Thomas in 1945 after his military discharge, Adams became chairman of the governing committee of the St. Thomas Power Authority and deepened his belief in the economic determinism of equality. In 1947 he answered a call to increase the number of local hotel rooms by opening his home as the Adams 1799 Guest House. By 1952 Adams had become a charter member of the Virgin Islands Hotel Association. He was soon elected president, a position he held until 1971, again functioning as a liaison between the mostly white hotel owners and their workers, who were mostly black. During the 1950s and 1960s, Adams also served as a reporter, working as a stringer for the Associated Press and Associated Negro Press and contributing regular articles to GEORGE SCHUYLER's *Pittsburgh Courier*. Although he eschewed public office, Adams was closely involved with island politics as an adviser and editorial commentator. Adams also maintained friendships with a number of black American leaders including Schuyler, MAUD CUNEY-HARE, and W. E. B. DuBois.

In 1963 the Virgin Islands' legislature officially accepted the rededication of his "Virgin Islands March" to the people of the Virgin Islands, since the composition had long served as a native anthem. In 1982 the "Virgin Islands March" became the official territorial anthem of the Virgin Islands. Around 1983 Adams closed his guesthouse; he died four years later, only a few weeks after his ninety-eighth birthday. Among his many awards were an honorary doctorate from Fisk University (1978) and the Virgin Islands Medal of Honor (1983). Originally refused admission because of his race, Adams was inducted into the American Bandmasters Association posthumously in 2006.

FURTHER READING

Adams, Alton. *The Memoirs of Alton Augustus Adams, First Black Bandmaster of the United States Navy* (2008).

Clague, Mark. "Instruments of Identity: Alton Augustus Adams, Sr., the Navy Band of the Virgin Islands, and the Sounds of Social Change," *Black Music Research Journal* (Spring/Fall 1998).

Clague, Mark. "Adams, Alton Augustus," *International Dictionary of Black Composers* (1999).

Floyd, Samuel. "Alton Augustus Adams: The First Black Bandmaster in the United States Navy," *The Black Perspective in Music* (Fall 1977).

MARK CLAGUE
JOHN H. ZIMMERMAN

Adams, Carolyn (1944–), dancer and arts administrator, was born in New York City, the daughter of Julius J. Adams, a journalist who rose to managing editor of the *New York Amsterdam News*, and Olive A. Adams, an accomplished pianist. Her parents cultivated in her a deep appreciation of the arts, as well as a legacy of social activism that stayed with Adams throughout her life—both during her career as a dancer and after her retirement from the stage, when she helped found community-based arts centers for children in Harlem. The dance writer Muriel Topaz described the Adamses' home as a "center of social and political activity," and noted that the Global News Syndicate, an organization of black newspapers, was founded in their small apartment (Topaz, 30).

When she was eight years old Adams entered New York's progressive Ethical Culture School, an institution dedicated to the moral as well as intellectual development of its students. There she began to study dance, also receiving extensive training in piano and violin. As a child she auditioned for the renowned School of American Ballet (the academy associated with the New York City Ballet) but chose not to attend for fear that it would interfere with her other activities, and she opted instead for private training. After an injury briefly curtailed her dancing, Adams resumed her training with Nelle Fisher at Carnegie Hall, where she studied movement for actors and jazz. At age fifteen she began taking classes at the Martha Graham School, furthering her knowledge of a technique she had already begun learning back in the Ethical Culture School. Following her graduation from high school, Adams enrolled in the dance program at Sarah Lawrence College, headed by the esteemed Bessie Schönberg, a legendary figure who nurtured the careers of countless dancers and choreographers. Schönberg taught Adams technique, composition, and dance history. Additionally, thanks to another of her teachers, Karin Waehner, it was also during this time that Adams enjoyed her first professional experience, touring with *Les Grands Ballets Contemporains*.

The defining moment of Adams's career, however, happened almost by accident during the last semester of her senior year, when she drove her friends to an audition for the company of the modern dance choreographer Paul Taylor. Although Adams originally had not intended to try out, at the last moment she changed her mind, and made a significant impression on Taylor. Adams finished her B.A. before officially joining the company in September 1965, becoming the first black dancer in the group.

Adams remained with Taylor for seventeen years, originating dozens of roles in dances ranging from plotless to dramatic and becoming a role model for African American dancers at a time when few performed in white modern dance or ballet companies. Like Adams, Taylor had a good grounding in both ballet and Graham techniques (he had danced with her company), so the elements of his movement style were already ingrained in her body. In an interview with the dance historian Brenda Dixon Gottschild, the choreographer Meredith Monk—a former classmate of Adams's at Sarah Lawrence—described Adams's dancing as so fluid it was like she had "no bones" (Gottschild, 49). Equally important, Taylor encouraged individuality among his performers, and he created a working situation in which Adams was never stereotyped, and one in which her best qualities—lyricism, lightness, a quicksilver quality of movement, and extraordinary musicality—were allowed to shine.

Among Adams's repertory was the beautiful *Esplanade* (1975), one of Taylor's signature pieces, which featured passages of dazzling, joyful runs and leaps; the daughter in the disturbing *Big Bertha* (1970), in which a mechanical carnival doll reveals the dark underside of an American family; *Airs* (1978); and the gangster mistress in his version of *Sacre du Printemps* (1980). In his autobiography, *Private Domain*, Taylor praised Adams as both a dancer and as a human being, calling her "unmannered and wondrous … an elegant nectar laced with warm delicacy, easy and effortless" (327).

Adams never lost the sense of social responsibility her parents had so carefully instilled in her. In an interview with *Dance Magazine* in November 1970, when she was still in her twenties and hitting the heights of her career, Adams spoke longingly of opening a performing arts center in Harlem. Three years later, she and her sister, Julie Strandburg (herself the head of Brown University's dance program), established the Harlem Dance Foundation. There, Adams not only trained students but also helped the most talented find much-needed scholarships. Her dedication to the community extended beyond choreography; she and the foundation fought vigorously to protect Harlem's architectural treasures, which were in danger of being demolished. In one instance Adams lay down in the street in front of bulldozers to prevent brownstones from being razed. She also went on to earn her realtor's license in order to combat destructive redlining.

Adams's concern for preserving dance history and for improving the quality of dance education led her—again with her sister—to bring another institution into being: the American Dance Legacy Institute, which they established in 1994. With the help of modern technology like the CD-ROM, as well as more traditional media like newspapers and video, she enlisted choreographers to document their dances so their knowledge could be disseminated to students and teachers throughout the country. In addition, the institute offered workshops and developed entire dance curricula for public school classrooms. In 1994 the American Dance Legacy Institute officially became a part of Brown University.

Adams became the director of the BFA program at the City College of New York, joined the faculty of the Juilliard School in 1983, and served as the director of both Jacob Pillow's education program and the New York State Education Department's summer program in modern dance. She and her sister also coauthored *American Education in the Arts: A Balancing of Visions for Cultural Transformation*, which was published in 1993.

In 1988 Adams married Robert Kahn, a former Paul Taylor dancer and Wall Street broker-turned-chef. The couple had two children, Sandra and Vitali. Through her inspirational dancing, widespread teaching, and social activism, Adams not only influenced a generation of dancers but has also helped affect the world beyond the stage.

FURTHER READING

Gottschild, Brenda Dixon. *The Black Dancing Body: A Geography from Coon to Cool* (2003).

Panel Discussion with Paul Taylor Dancers, on Paul Taylor Company Web site, available online at http://www.ptdc.org/dev/panel.php?id=51.

Taylor, Paul. *Private Domain* (1987).

Topaz, Muriel. "Carolyn Adams: A Lifelong Pursuit," *Dance Magazine* (July 1994).

KAREN BACKSTEIN

Adams, Cyrus Field (18 Jul. 1858–1940?), journalist and public official, was born in Louisville,
Kentucky, the younger son of the Reverend Henry
and Margaret Priscilla (Corbin) Adams. Their
father administered a respected school in Louisville.
Cyrus and his older brother, JOHN QUINCY ADAMS
(1848–1922), received excellent educations, Cyrus
graduating from preparatory school and college at
Oberlin College. In 1877 Cyrus began to teach in
the Louisville public schools, and soon pooled savings with his brother to open the weekly *Louisville
Bulletin*. They ran the newspaper until 1885, when
it was acquired by the *American Baptist* newspaper
owned by WILLIAM HENRY STEWARD, chairman
of trustees at State University, a black Baptist university in Louisville, where Cyrus taught German.
Already a dedicated traveler, Cyrus had spent much
of 1884 in Europe, and was also fluent in Italian,
French, and Spanish.

Both brothers had served as Louisville correspondents for the *Western Appeal*, a Saint Paul, Minnesota,
weekly with national aspirations. After John moved
to Saint Paul in 1886, Cyrus soon followed; by 1888
the brothers had acquired *the Appeal* and expanded
it on a national scale, printing regional editions in
Dallas, Louisville, Saint Louis, and its largest branch
in Chicago, which Cyrus managed. It was here that
he set down his strongest roots, for the next half-
century. Adams's light-colored complexion—so
light that few strangers realized he was African
American—was a mixed blessing. Darker-skinned
African Americans accused him of passing for
white, despite his rueful admission to REVERDY C.
RANSOM that "my trouble is, all my life I have been
trying to pass for colored" (Ransom, p. 83). The
National Journal (October 1908) compared the complexions of Adams and his boss, William T. Vernon,
saying Adams "could almost pass as a lily white in
any community, North or South."

Adams's early hopes for an appointment by
the Republican president William McKinley went
unfulfilled, in part because he set his sights so
high. "The prominent colored Chicago politician,
who wants to be Minister to Bolivia, spoke to the
President today about his case but received no assur-
ances. Adams speaks four languages and is one of
the most accomplished representatives of his race,"
wrote the Washington, DC, *Evening Star* (30 June
1897). Unwilling to settle for a lesser consulship,
Adams returned to Chicago empty-handed.

Adams now threw himself into Republican politics, as a publicist, Republican National Advisory
Committee member, and author of quadrennial
campaign textbooks (1908, 1912). In September
1898 he became general secretary of the new
National Afro-American Council, and later, its
executive committee secretary, until resigning in
1907. He claimed to be the first—perhaps only—life
member of the council before it dissolved in 1908,
and wrote the only contemporary history of the
council (1902). A self-styled "law and order" moderate on racial matters, he publicly distanced himself from intemperate remarks made before council
leaders by the militant suffrage leader James Hayes
(*Atlanta Constitution*, 31 Jan. 1903). Elected to three
terms as president of the National Afro-American
Press Association, he was also transportation agent
for the National Negro Business League.

His successful campaign for town clerk in
Chicago (1900) was attributed to his cultiva-
tion of ethnic voters in their own languages.
He corresponded sporadically with BOOKER T.
WASHINGTON, who recommended in 1901 that
President McKinley appoint him assistant register of the U.S. Treasury, with an annual salary of
$2,500, under Judson W. Lyons. Adams served for
a decade under Lyons and successors William T.
Vernon (1906) and James C. Napier (1911). His
concern over losing the position in 1906—when
S. Laing Williams of Chicago was briefly considered to replace Lyons—prompted further correspondence with Washington.

An active member of Washington's Pen and
Pencil Club, a public affairs group for black professionals, Adams also helped organize the mostly
white Washington Philatelic Society in 1905, serving as its first president. In 1907 a minor scandal
erupted over Adams's role in refusing club membership to African American schoolteacher Garnett
Wilkerson (*New York Times*, 11 June 1907).

In 1912 Adams resigned as assistant register,
returning to Chicago. After *the Appeal* closed its
Chicago branch in 1913, he became a special U.S.
customs inspector on daily salary, and later deputy
collector for Chicago, working in that capacity until
retirement in 1932. A lifelong traveler, particularly
to the Caribbean and Central and South America,
Adams never married. His death date is uncertain,
although family papers owned by his niece show
him to be alive as late as 1939.

FURTHER READING

Gatewood, Willard B. *Aristocrats of Color: The Black
    Elite, 1880–1920* (1990).
Ransom, Reverdy C. *The Pilgrimage of Harriet
    Ransom's Son* (1958).

Spear, Allan H. *Black Chicago: The Rise of the Ghetto, 1890–1915* (1967).

Taylor, David V. "John Quincy Adams: St. Paul Editor and Black Leader," *Minnesota History* (1973).

BENJAMIN R. JUSTESEN

Adams, Dock (1838–Sept. 1898), militia leader, was born in Georgia to parents whose names have not been recorded. Some sources list his name as Doc Adams. He was probably born a slave, as were the vast majority of African Americans in Augusta's cotton-rich hinterlands in the late 1830s; the 1840 U.S. census lists fewer than two hundred free blacks in Richmond County. As a carpenter Adams, like other slave artisans, may have been able to hire out his time, and he may have saved enough money to purchase his freedom. In any case Adams joined the Union army during the Civil War, and he acquired enough money to purchase five hundred acres of land—worth three thousand dollars—near Nashville, Georgia, where he lived for a time after hostilities ended in 1865. By 1872 he had returned to Augusta, where he earned good wages working as a boss carpenter. Adams was also involved in the political life of Richmond County, making an unsuccessful bid for local office in 1872, the same year that he founded a black militia company, the Grant Guard Infantry, named in honor of President Ulysses S. Grant. Similar armed clubs had begun to emerge in various Southern black communities as a response to the armed terrorism of the Ku Klux Klan and other white paramilitary groups.

After Klan violence helped to "redeem" Georgia from Republican rule in the early 1870s, white Democrats in the state legislature imposed a poll tax that greatly reduced the number of eligible black voters. With black Georgians "unable to exercise their political opinion as they wished" (Foner, 570) and unwilling to be oppressed, Adams moved in 1874 to Hamburg, South Carolina, a small community in Aiken County directly across the Savannah River from Augusta. Unlike in Georgia, the Republican Party remained in political control of South Carolina, which at that time had a majority black population. By 1874, however, the proliferation of white rifle clubs and other paramilitary organizations in Aiken County and in neighboring Edgefield and Barnwell counties signaled the growing determination of "straightout" Democrats in South Carolina to follow Georgia's lead by ending Republican rule, using violence if necessary.

In order to defend Hamburg's black residents against such violence, Adams resurrected the town's militia company, which had been founded in 1870 by the Republican governor Robert Scott and commanded initially by the Hamburg native PRINCE RIVERS. Since Rivers's appointment as Hamburg's trial justice the company had rarely mustered, but by 1876 Adams had enlisted around eighty militiamen, armed them with the best Winchester rifles, and had them perform drills on the streets of Hamburg on a regular basis. Local whites complained that Adams's men harassed them, prevented them from drinking at water fountains, and arrested them for trivial offenses. Most galling to Aiken County whites was Adams's demand that they give way on Hamburg's streets to allow his men to drill. Such behavior, one South Carolinian wrote, was an "insult [such] as no white people upon earth had ever to put up with before"— African Americans, of course, had been putting up with such behavior from whites for most of their lives prior to Reconstruction (Foner, 570).

Matters came to head on 4 July 1876 as Adams drilled his men on an abandoned street in Hamburg. Two young white farmers in a buggy approached them and ordered that they move aside to let their buggy through. Adams retorted that, at 150 feet wide, the street was wide enough for the men to pass without disrupting his drill; eventually, however, he ordered the militia to stand aside and let the buggy through. The following day one of the farmers submitted a complaint to Prince Rivers, demanding that the judge arrest Adams for obstruction of what the farmer called "his" road. Much to Adams's annoyance, Rivers did so, also charging Adams with contempt of court when he complained about the arrest at his arraignment. Rivers ordered Adams to stand trial on the following Saturday, 8 July.

In the meantime tensions escalated in Hamburg and the surrounding area, fueled by the intervention of the region's leading Democrat, the former Confederate general Matthew C. Butler, who also commanded an Edgefield County rifle club. On the day of Adams's trial Butler entered Hamburg at the head of a company of two hundred armed men and a cannon that he had procured in Augusta. Although he had no legal authority to do so, Butler demanded that the militia surrender its weapons and that Adams publicly apologize to the two white men. When Adams refused, the forty or so members of his militia retreated to their barracks, where Butler's men shot at them. The militia returned fire, killing one of the whites. Butler's troops responded by firing their cannon at the barracks, forcing the outnumbered black militiamen to flee. That night Butler's men killed Hamburg's black marshal and rounded up twenty-five African Americans, not all of them members of the militia. Although accounts differ in the details of what happened next, most agree that Butler's troops killed five of the prisoners in cold blood; eyewitnesses later testified that Butler personally selected the men to be killed. Later that night armed white mobs rode through Hamburg, attacking African Americans and setting fire to their homes and businesses. Dock Adams escaped unscathed.

The Hamburg massacre, as it came to be known, was a turning point in Reconstruction in South Carolina, and indeed in the South itself. In response President Grant, though reluctant to intervene militarily in the South, sent federal troops to South Carolina—an act that prevented widespread atrocities on the scale of those at Hamburg but did not entirely put an end to the violence. South Carolina blacks were outraged by events in Hamburg. Congressman ROBERT SMALLS viewed the incident as "a premeditated and predetermined … unwarranted slaughter," whose goal had been to "keep the negroes in their place" (Williamson, 271). Indeed, as Adams later testified to a U.S. Senate committee, the naked show of force by Butler's men at Hamburg had been overtly political: throughout the day they had repeatedly chanted, "This is the beginning of Redemption in South Carolina!" (Foner, 572). The Hamburg massacre also united nearly all South Carolina whites behind the Democrats in that year's election, which the Democrats won on the back of further acts of violence, fraud, and intimidation at the polls. The following year the redeemed South Carolina legislature elected Matthew Butler to the U.S. Senate. Charges against whites indicted for the Hamburg massacre were soon dropped.

After the end of Reconstruction, Adams lived out his final decades in relative obscurity. When he died peacefully in September 1898, one white newspaper used the occasion to place the blame for the violence of 1876 squarely on his shoulders: "Adams led his people against the whites, and they [Adams's militia] were shot down without mercy. … It was he who kept negroes constantly worked up, and he is responsible for so many of their lives being taken." A white Hamburg Republican offered a more accurate reading of Adams's role in the Hamburg massacre, namely that Adams's greatest fault was his skill in drilling his militia, which made him the target of Butler and his rifle clubs. Dock Adams's

determination to keep the peace by meeting violence with violence was ultimately futile, however, given the white rifle clubs' vast superiority in weaponry and the unwillingness of the federal government to intervene as an honest broker between the two armed factions.

FURTHER READING

Foner, Eric. *Reconstruction: America's Unfinished Revolution, 1863–1877* (1988).

Holt, Thomas. *Black over White: Negro Political Leadership in South Carolina during Reconstruction* (1977).

Williamson, Joel. *After Slavery: The Negro in South Carolina during Reconstruction, 1861–1877* (1965).

Obituary: *Columbia (South Carolina) State*, 9 Sept. 1898.

STEVEN J. NIVEN

Adams, Elizabeth Laura (9 Feb. 1909– ?), the first African American to publish an autobiography about conversion to Catholicism, was born in Santa Barbara, California, the only child of Lula Josephine Holden Adams, a painter, and Daniel Henderson Adams, a hotel headwaiter. Daniel and Lula Adams provided a comfortable, middle-class lifestyle for their daughter and raised her according to strict rules of courtesy, manners, and obedience. Shortly after Adams's birth the family moved to Los Angeles, where she attended an integrated primary school.

Adams and her parents fell victim to the influenza epidemic of 1918–1919. Mother and daughter returned to temperate Santa Barbara in 1920 at their doctor's recommendation and would suffer from chronic illness for the rest of their lives. Adams's father continued to work in Los Angeles for another four years and then died suddenly in 1924, shortly before he was to join the family in Santa Barbara. During this period friends of the family brought Adams and her mother to the Santa Barbara Mission, where "conversion came to me quickly and quietly—like the slumber that gently closes an infants eyes" (Adams, 106). Her parents, who raised her in the Methodist Episcopal Church, forbade her from joining the Catholic Church. She did not officially convert until 1928 or 1929, after graduating from high school and earning her mother's approval.

The family's financial standing plummeted after the death of Daniel Adams, and Adams had to give up her dream of going to college. During the 1930s she worked sporadically in domestic service and at secretarial jobs while caring for her ailing mother and struggling with her own health problems. She wanted to become a nun, but her obligation to her mother thwarted this ambition. Adams joined the Franciscan Tertiary instead, a secular "third order" that requires vows of moderation, temperance, and prayer and the commitment to remain in one's current marital state, whether married or unmarried (Kaplan, xix).

Adams published several poems, short stories, and autobiographical essays between 1930 and 1943. A shorter and slightly different version of *Dark Symphony* was serialized from October 1940 through March 1941 as "There Must Be a God … Somewhere" in the Catholic periodical *Torch*. The Catholic press's interest in Adams's work coincided with the church's attempt to convert African Americans in the 1930s and 1940s. Catholics viewed these efforts as domestic missionary work that could counter the growing radicalism in black communities (Kaplan, xlvi). The Catholic publisher Sheed & Ward released *Dark Symphony* in 1942; it sold ten thousand copies in its first four years and fifteen thousand copies total. White readers gave *Dark Symphony* high praise, commending its lack of bitterness and its educational value. Black critics, on the other hand, were skeptical of its optimism and its cautious handling of racism. For example, Theophilus Lewis, a writer for the radical black journal the *Messenger*, found Adams's descriptions of "petty discriminations" common and unremarkable, whereas a white reviewer found these same passages "uncommon and inspiring" (Kaplan, xxii).

Adams may have been attracted to the Catholic Church because paradoxically this patriarchal, antidemocratic institution gave her a forum for self-expression that was denied her at home and in the Sunday school classes of her youth. Whereas the "religious people" in the black churches she visited commanded, "Don't question God!" (Adams, 70), the Catholic confessional offered "an ideal place … to ask questions of God" (128). In *Dark Symphony*, Adams constructs her life as a search for voice—for the freedom to ask questions and to find her own answers. The opening scene locates the narrative in the African American tradition, which originated with slave narratives, of a dual quest for literacy and freedom. Upon discovering a school as a toddler, Adams experiences a thirst for knowledge that would be central to her identity: "I pondered. Questioned. The questions flew out, then circled back like a boomerang—unanswered" (8). Adams revises the conversion narrative formula by replacing cycles of sin and repentance with cycles of questioning and silencing. Her spiritual journey also involves cycles of interracial spiritual communion and segregation, situating race at the center of her narrative.

Although Adams structures her narrative around experiences of racism and expresses an impulse to fight, she ultimately endorses her parents' philosophy of forgiveness and forbearance in the face of racism. Each time Adams tells a story about an encounter with racism she mitigates the sting by incorporating a sympathetic white character. However, *Dark Symphony* may not be as conciliatory as it seems at first glance. In her introduction to the 1997 reprint of *Dark Symphony*, Carla Kaplan argues that although Adams represents herself as "submissive and frail," the text "participates in the African-American heritage of double-voicedness" (xviii). For example, Adams quotes Harlem Renaissance writers rather than espousing radical views herself, and her stories about racism and family conflict often challenge her professions of forgiveness and obedience.

Adams relied on royalties from *Dark Symphony* in the 1940s and 1950s as she moved from job to job, struggled with her health, and attempted to write. Between 1944 and 1955 Adams requested at least twelve emergency advances on her royalties from Sheed & Ward, indicating a life plagued by illness and economic instability (Kaplan, xxiii). When her mother died on 21 June 1952, Adams relinquished all future claims on *Dark Symphony* for a onetime royalty of $375. She planned to live with a family and work and write, but this arrangement did not work out. Adams contacted Sheed & Ward in desperation once more in 1953, but the editor rejected her request (Kaplan, xxv). Adams then virtually slips out of the historical record. Kaplan's research indicates that she was living in Santa Barbara in 1970, but her death date is unknown (xxii).

Dark Symphony fits into the tradition of African American autobiography by demonstrating the centrality of religious experience to personal identity. The narrative links a spiritual quest with the quest for racial justice, basing the notion of equality on divine authority. *Dark Symphony* invites comparison to African American autobiographies of the 1930s and 1940s, including RICHARD WRIGHT's *Black Boy* and *American Hunger* (1945) and ZORA NEALE HURSTON's *Dust Tracks on a Road* (1942). Twenty-first-century readers may be interested in the tensions between writer and patron and between Adams's social critique and her desire—or pragmatic need—to connect to a white Catholic readership.

FURTHER READING

Adams, Elizabeth Laura. *Dark Symphony and Other Works*, ed. Carla Kaplan (1997).

Barton, Rebecca Chalmers. *Witnesses for Freedom: Negro Americans in Autobiography* (1948).

Brignano, Russell C. *Black Americans in Autobiography* (1984).

David, Jay. *Growing Up Black* (1968).

Kaplan, Carla. "Introduction: 'I Wanna March,'" in *Dark Symphony* (1997).

Scally, Sister Mary Anthony, R.S.M. *Negro Catholic Writers, 1900–1943: A Bio-Bibliography* (1945).

ERIN ROYSTON BATTAT

Adams, George (c. 1847–29 Sept. 1939), cowboy and rancher, may have been born into slavery and escaped from bondage before the Civil War, though information about his life prior to his arrival in southwest Texas in the 1870s is limited. Based on stories he later told to his co-workers it seems likely that Adams spent his early adult life working as a cowboy in the brush country region of Texas, probably south and west of San Antonio. Given the circumstance of his birth and the times in which George came of age, he never received a formal education. As recent historical scholarship has made clear, black cowboys on the Texas plains enjoyed greater freedoms than did African Americans living in more settled regions of the state. However, their freedoms were always tainted by the persistent racism that prevailed during the late nineteenth and early twentieth centuries. George Adams's life was a vivid example of the common experiences of African American cowboys working in South Texas between the 1870s and 1930s.

In the 1870s Adams migrated to southwest Texas, where he found work in the Trans-Pecos region on the 7D Ranch, located on Comanche Creek four miles east of Fort Stockton, Texas. Adams worked for this outfit until the owners of the Western Union Beef Company, which had purchased the 7D in 1890, sold their operation to John T. McElroy, who owned a large cattle operation in Reeves County, in 1899. Adams next worked for the T5 Ranch, also known as the Independence Cattle Company, located on Independence Creek at Independence Spring. The T5 was the first big ranch established in what would later become Terrell County. Perhaps because of the company's problems in paying its employees Adams's stint with the T5 was short-lived. In 1902 he signed on with the C. F. Cox Ranch, located in present-day Brewster and Terrell counties. Coleman Cox, a native of Arkansas and staunch Republican who had moved to Texas in the 1870s, had moved from Throckmorton County in north-central Texas to his eighty-thousand-acre ranch shortly after purchasing it in 1900. Cox established the headquarters of the ranch in Sanderson, a town in Terrell County with a population of 112 citizens. Though meager in size Sanderson represented the only connection to the "outside world." Adams lived and worked on the ranch for the remainder of his life.

Adams and Cox developed a close relationship that lasted thirty-five years. Cox grew to respect Adams and eventually considered him a part of his family. Their friendship was firmly established during Adams's early days on the ranch when he took advantage of Texas homestead laws and claimed eight sections of land for Cox. Once Adams obtained free title to the land from the state, he sold it to his boss. In this way the Cox Ranch grew in size, and the two men became unofficial partners. During the Depression, Cox was unable to make his mortgage payments at the Sanderson bank. Just as the bank was ready to foreclose, Adams, who often received payment for his services in cattle and had managed over time to build up a sizable herd, put his own cattle up as collateral, and Cox's loan was renewed. Because of this act future generations of the Cox family were able to maintain ownership of the ranch.

For thirty-eight years Adams performed the same basic work and enjoyed the limited forms of entertainment offered by ranch life. He rode fence lines, pulled cattle out from the mud of drying stock ponds, joined in round-ups, doctored livestock, and trained horses. For these services George's boss often paid him in cattle. By modern standards George's entertainments were few. He participated in the annual ranch rodeo held in Sanderson. Every year he led the rodeo parade, and at the rodeo grounds he and his coworkers would show off their skills as professional cowboys. Throughout the year Adams often played cards and checkers with members of the Cox family and other ranch hands.

Adams first lived in an old bunkhouse at the ranch but later moved to an old storeroom that was previously used for storing horse tack after Coleman Cox's death in 1937. Generally speaking Adams's diet was simple and consisted primarily of meat, beans, and bread. Two of his favorite dishes were biscuits and "por jo," a kind of tomato dumpling. Adams enjoyed the freedom that ranch life offered black cowboys in the late nineteenth and early twentieth centuries, though he remained aware of the racial barriers present within the region. He never joined white cowboys at social functions, dinners, or in conversations, unless they invited him—though it is true that his presence was almost always requested. He believed that the best way to overcome the realities of racial prejudices was to perform his ranching duties better than his white counterparts. This emphasis on outworking whites served to make African American cowboys some of the best cowhands to ride the open range, and Adams was no exception. According to interviews with individuals who knew him personally, Adams gained recognition from the men who worked with him. Among his contemporaries, his abilities to use a lariat and to break wild horses were discussed at greater length than was the color of his skin.

Adams died of pneumonia. He had never married and had no known relatives, and so only the members of the Cox family and his friends were left to mourn his loss. In a kind of final testimony to his life he was laid to rest in the Cedar Grove Cemetery at Sanderson, in an era when African Americans and whites were almost always interred in segregated cemeteries. Adams, however, was laid to rest in a white cemetery near the grave of his long-time friend Coleman Cox. George Adams's life illustrates the African American cowboy experience in the Southwest, but his story was also exceptional in many ways. Unlike other black cowboys Adams became in many respects his own boss and for all practical purposes a partner with a white rancher. He was able to remain a cowboy all his life and continued working until the week before his death. Many black cowboys were forced into nonranching occupations when the cattle drives from Texas ended in the late 1800s. Adams had earned and retained the respect of the white population in Brewster and Terrell counties during his lifetime.

FURTHER READING

Barr, Alwyn. *The African Texans* (2004).

Downie, Alice E., ed. *Terrell County History: Its Past and Its People* (1978).

Howell, Kenneth W. "George Adams: A Cowboy All His Life," in *Black Cowboys of Texas*, ed. Sarah R. Massey (2000).

Obituary: *Sanderson Times*, 29 Sept. 1939.

KENNETH WAYNE HOWELL

Adams, Henry (16 Mar. 1843– ?), emigrationist leader, was born Henry Houston in Newton County, Georgia, to enslaved parents whose names are not now known. Most of what is known of Henry Adams's personal life is derived from testimony he offered in 1880 to the United States Senate during a government investigation of the causes of mass African American emigration from the former states of the Confederacy.

Henry was given the surname Adams when a planter of that name brought him and his family to Desoto Parish, Louisiana, in 1850. He used that surname for the rest of his life. Upon the planter's death eight years later ownership of Henry and his family was transferred to a teenage girl, Nancy Emily Adams, who hired the family out to various plantations near the Texas–Louisiana border. Laboring alongside his father on the plantation of a man named Ferguson in Logansport, Louisiana, Henry Adams was separated from his mother, who worked on a distant plantation owned by a brother of Nancy Adams. Like many couples torn apart by the slave system, Henry Adams' parents reunited shortly after the end of the Civil War and the general emancipation that followed. While still a slave in Louisiana, Henry Adams married a woman named Malinda, with whom he had four children: Lucy, Rena, Josephine, and Henry. That marriage was also ended by the economic dictates of slavery when Malinda's owner took Henry Adams's wife and children with him to Texas.

Like his father, an independent-minded lay preacher, Henry Adams "feared God but not man" (Hahn, 318). Having already amassed "three horses and a fine buggey, and a good deal of money" while still a slave, Adams was determined after his emancipation in June 1865 to receive due payment for his labors (Painter, 72). Most former slaveowners were, however, unwilling to bargain with him for the oats he cut, the cotton he baled, or the rails he split, and so Adams soon left for the city of Shreveport, Louisiana. There he made some money as a peddler on the road between Logansport and Shreveport, and witnessed the efforts of thousands of former slaves to reunite with their families and to try to make the best of freedom, in spite of harassment, violent intimidation, and unfair labor contracts and racist legislation—the notorious black codes—which threatened to return African Americans to a state of legal bondage. Adams attempted to eke out a living as a peddler, but was himself beaten and robbed.

Like other African Americans seeking to assert his newly-won right to a free and independent life,

Adams joined the institution most likely at that time to ensure it, the United States Army, in the fall of 1866. He served with the Thirty-Ninth and, later, the Twenty-Fifth Infantry divisions throughout Louisiana, rising eventually to the rank of quartermaster sergeant and learning to read and write in the process. Upon leaving the military in September 1869 he returned to Shreveport with enough money to invest in property, which, in true Jeffersonian fashion, provided him with the independence to speak his mind. Soon Adams and other literate veterans began helping black tenants throughout Caddo Parish to challenge the unfair labor contracts devised by many white landowners. Although these efforts invariably failed in courts that were controlled by those same landowners, Adams's forthright manner and his increasing wealth earned him the enmity and resentment of powerful whites in Shreveport, who threatened to kill him. Adams nonetheless prospered financially throughout the early 1870s. A prodigious rail-splitter—he reportedly could chop and stack as many as seven cords of wood a day—Adams also succeeded in managing plantations, lumber yards, and a cotton-oil mill. He also built a lucrative sideline as a faith healer and herbalist.

The same independent means and character that made Adams so threatening to whites made him a natural leader among the Louisiana freed people. Despite his protests that he was only a humble woodchopper and rail-splitter with no involvement in politics, Adams served as president of the Shreveport Republican club and was central to get-out-the-vote efforts in the early years of Reconstruction, a role that again brought him death threats from whites. In 1873 Adams served on Shreveport's grand jury, which had a majority of African-American members. Yet since all the lawyers, judges, and other court officials were white, he soon learned that justice in the post-emancipation South was almost as colorbound as it had been during slavery. Blacks received disproportionately harsher sentences than did whites for committing the same crimes, and the law provided little protection for African Americans who suffered from unfair labor contracts designed to enrich their former owners.

Increasingly aware of the limits of Reconstruction, and foreshadowing the progressive era methods of W. E. B. DuBois, Adams also formed a secret committee to "look into affairs and see the true condition of our race, to see whether it was possible we could stay under a people who held us under bondage" (Hahn, 319). After traveling throughout nine southern states, he found that the answer to his question was an unequivocal *no*. Adams met with hundreds of freedmen in these states between 1870 and 1874 and found examples of white intimidation of black voters, unfair labor contracts, and outright violence against African Americans similar to that he had witnessed in Louisiana.

The emergence in the summer of 1874 of the White League, a statewide organization dedicated to removing all African Americans from political office in Louisiana, spurred Adams and his committee to action, and to the belief that the promise of citizenship offered by Reconstruction could only be realized outside the South. The several hundred members of Adams's Colonization Council petitioned President Ulysses S. Grant to provide land in the United States, Liberia, or some other country since it had become "utterly impossible to live with the whites in Louisiana" (Hahn, 319). The White League also put pressure on employers to fire Republican activists, including Adams, who on purely political grounds was dismissed from his job managing a major plantation. Thereafter he devoted his energies to building the Colonization Council to a membership of 69,000 by August 1877, when it again petitioned the president, now Rutherford B. Hayes, to support a plan to aid the emigration of African Americans from the South. Hayes, like Grant, paid no heed to the request.

In November 1878 Adams helped launch in Shreveport the Negro Union Cooperative Aid Association, which appealed to the black laborers and farmers of Louisiana to form a political convention that drew on the grassroots networks of religious, fraternal, and political networks to form a specifically black-nationalist response to the problems of the freed people. Although his own preference was for emigration to Liberia or some other part of Africa, Adams also encouraged the many thousands of southern black "exodusters" who, led by Benjamin "Pap" Singleton, sought a better life in Kansas and Indiana. In spite of—or perhaps because of—his own experiences in the Republican Party, Adams opposed the involvement of prominent ministers and established politicians in the emigrationist cause, preferring that the organization be composed "entirely of laboring people" (Hahn, 343). Though this stance gave his emigrationist movement a more democratic character, it also ensured that the Colonization Council and similar groups throughout the South would struggle to find the money needed to execute their plans. A yellow fever epidemic that afflicted Adams and many others in Louisiana in 1878 did not help matters.

Although the Colonization Council had urged blacks after 1876 to protest by boycotting the political process, Adams returned to political activism in the Louisiana elections of 1878. Violent intimidation of black and white Republicans alike and vote-rigging by the White League intensified in that election, but in spite of Adams's vocal protests to the attorney general of the United States, it became apparent that the federal government had largely abandoned the South to the white supremacist Redemptionist arm of the Democratic Party. In December 1878 Adams traveled to New Orleans in the hope of testifying before federal authorities about the violence and other election abuses he had witnessed in the previous month's elections. He continued to promote the idea of emigration to Liberia and to the increasingly more popular destination of Kansas, but was cut off from the base of his movement in northern Louisiana as well as from the mainstream leadership of the emigrationist cause. Although he found work in New Orleans in a variety of minor federal positions, he lacked funds and was unable to join several Colonization Council members who left for Liberia in 1881.

Adams disappears from the historical record in 1884. It is not known when or how he died. His significance lies in his efforts to promote the emigrationist cause among working-class rural black southerners during Reconstruction, a legacy upon which later black emigrationists, notably MARCUS GARVEY, would successfully build in the 1920s.

FURTHER READING

Hahn, Steven. *A Nation under Our Feet: Black Political Struggles in the Rural South from Slavery to the Great Migration* (2003).

Painter, Nell. *Exodusters: Black Migration to Kansas after Reconstruction* (1976; repr. 1986).

STEVEN J. NIVEN

Adams, John Henry, Jr. (21 Aug. 1878–5 Sept. 1948), artist, was born in Colquitt County, Georgia, son of John Henry Adams, a former slave and preacher in the Methodist Church, and Mittie Rouse. Many questions surround Adams's early life. While he reported in an *Atlanta Constitution* article (23 June 1902) that he came from a humble background, his father served parishes throughout Georgia. According to the *History of the American Negro*

and His Institutions (1917), Adams Sr. was a man of accomplishment, leading black Georgians in a colony in Liberia for two years and receiving two honorary doctorates, from Bethany College and Morris Brown University. Educated in Atlanta schools, Adams claimed in the *Atlanta Constitution* article to have traveled to Philadelphia in the late 1890s to take art classes at the Drexel Institute of Art, Science, and Industry (later Drexel University). Drexel, established in 1891, opened its doors to a diverse student body. Even though the school's records do not show Adams's enrollment, it is likely that Adams reported the truth when he stated that he had studied under Howard Pyle, the famed illustrator and teacher who inspired a generation of American illustrators and who was at that time an instructor at Drexel. While the composition of Adams's drawings may have been inspired by Pyle's interest in dramatic narrative, the content of Adams's work is often closer in spirit to the socially progressive realist aesthetic of the Philadelphia newspaper illustrations of John Sloan, whose work, along with that of other artists, was dubbed by the press the Ashcan School and considered radical for its depiction of the working class.

There is greater certainty concerning Adams's life from 1901 to 1908, as he returned to Atlanta and established the art department of the African Methodist Episcopal (AME) Church's Morris Brown College in 1901. Listed as "professor of art," Adams designed a curriculum that guided both male and female students through various media disciplines, including mechanical drawing, oil painting, watercolors, and charcoal, pastel, and pencil drawing. According to course catalogs, the art department, among the first at a historically black college, balanced traditional figure studies from plaster casts, still life, and out-of-doors landscape painting. Studio classes were supplemented by lecture series conducted by leading black scholars, including JOHN HOPE, W. E. B. DUBOIS, and the Congregational clergyman the Reverend HENRY HUGH PROCTOR. Adams's first naturalistic religious paintings, completed in 1902, earned the praise of the city's major newspaper, the *Atlanta Constitution*. Its editors reproduced Adams's biblical painting, *The Accused Woman*, in the paper's pages that same year and urged readers to see his works in person.

During his tenure at Morris Brown, Adams also began his best-known works, illustrations for the major African American journal of the era, *The Voice of the Negro*. From 1904 until 1907 he produced more than sixty drawings and political cartoons, as well as articles and poems for the *Voice*. Adams's drawing style for the *Voice* was both conservative and modern, reflecting his admiration for both BOOKER T. WASHINGTON and DuBois. His drawings combined an interest in the Christian uplift and the Arts and Crafts–inspired aesthetics of Washington, as well as actively promoting positive images of African Americans based on self-determined ideas of beauty. In September 1906 the *Voice* began selling prints of his drawings, telling readers to place in their homes these "educative" works in order "to take the place of those meaningless white angels and black devils on our walls" (*Voice*, 622–623). One of these Adams prints, the editors of the *Voice* claimed, offered a black equivalent of the Gibson Girl, the favored motif of the popular white illustrator Charles Dana Gibson. Adams's political cartoons often recalled the vigorous marks of Thomas Nast's work. Those Adams drawings emphasizing moralizing racial uplift were quite similar to the work of Frank Beard. Not only was Beard a famous illustrator, but he was also widely known in the Atlanta black community for his drawings in Washington's first autobiography, *An Autobiography: The Story of My Life and Work* (1900).

In addition to teaching at Morris Brown, painting, and working for the *Voice*, Adams found time to work on other projects. In 1905 he collaborated with *The Voice* contributor SILAS XAVIER FLOYD to create *Floyd's Flowers*, a Christian moralizing guide for black parents for which Adams produced more than eighty drawings. Then, in 1906, Adams supplied DuBois with drawings for the short-lived *The Moon Illustrated Weekly*. The next phase of Adams's life as an artist, from 1908 to 1928, saw him leave Atlanta but continue to work for DuBois. The *Atlanta Constitution* announced in 1908 that Adams planned a trip to Paris to visit the painter HENRY OSSAWA TANNER. Instead Adams moved to Florida in 1908, living most of the time in Jacksonville until the early 1930s, although he lived in Tampa during the late 1920s. In Florida he worked as a newspaper writer and photographer and created drawings for DuBois's next publication, *The Horizon: A Journal of the Color Line*. The cover drawing for volume five of the 1909 *Horizon* showed Adams at his best, revealing how northern white patrons, in their refusal to see black progress, admired a white southern artist transforming a black man into a demeaning caricature. In 1910 Adams worked with DuBois on his new venture, the NAACP's *the Crisis*, to which Adams contributed cover illustrations as well as political cartoons. By the late 1920s, when Adams's

last drawings appeared in *The Crisis*, his style was considered old-fashioned and was replaced by the African-inspired modernism of artists such as AARON DOUGLAS.

In Adams's later years the Howard University artist and scholar JAMES AMOS PORTER stood almost alone in remembering Adams. Porter's important 1943 *Modern Negro Art* criticized the unevenness of Adams's style but recognized that he was an artist of considerable talent who deserved recognition. Porter seemed unaware that Adams was still alive. In 1948, twenty years after his last drawing appeared in *The Crisis*, Adams died quietly in a nursing home in Jacksonville, where he had returned two years earlier. Among the few places with Adams's works in their collections after his fame diminished were the Kenkeleba House in New York City, which had four oil portraits, and the Herndon Home in Atlanta, which had two Adams ink drawings.

Few modern artists experienced such fame and later obscurity as John Henry Adams Jr. During the first two decades of the twentieth century, Adams ranked high among the nation's leading African American artists, becoming perhaps the first nationally known black illustrator in America. Some thought his talent second only to Henry O. Tanner. Yet by the early 1930s Adams had vanished from the public eye.

FURTHER READING

Finding John Henry Adams's art and biographical information is challenging. The most accessible sources for seeing his art and reading his writings are microfilms of *The Voice of the Negro* (1904–1907) and *the Crisis* (Adams's drawings appear from 1910–1928).

Mellinger, Wayne Martin. "Ancestors: John Henry Adams and the Image of the New Negro," *International Review of Art* 14 (1997).

Porter, James Amos. *Modern Negro Art* (1943, repr. 1992).

Powell, Richard. *Black Art and Culture in the 20th Century* (1997).

MICHAEL BIEZE

Adams, John Hurst (27 Nov. 1927–), bishop, civil rights leader, and educator, was born in Columbia, South Carolina, to Rev. Eugene Avery Adams and Charity Nash Adams. He and his three siblings, Avery, Charity, and Lucy Rose, were raised in a spiritual and intellectually stimulating home. His father, an African Methodist Episcopal (AME) minister and social activist, in the 1920s organized the first African American bank in Columbia and the first modern statewide civil rights organization in South Carolina. None of these activities went unnoticed by young John and they helped to define his later focus and commitments. Adams was educated in the segregated Columbia school system and graduated from BOOKER T. WASHINGTON High School. His undergraduate work was completed at Johnson C. Smith University in Charlotte, North Carolina, where he earned an AB degree in History in 1947. After studying at Boston University School of Theology, he received a bachelor of sacred theology (STB) in 1950. In 1956 he received his master of sacred theology (MTB) there. While at the university he befriended MARTIN LUTHER KING JR., who was pursuing a Ph.D. in systematic theology. He became an apostle of King and his doctrine of nonviolence. Adams also did some study at Harvard University in 1951 and at Union Theological Seminary in 1956.

As a seminary student Adams was assigned to the pastorate of Bethel AME Church in Lynn, Massachusetts, from 1950 until 1952. He served on the faculty at Payne Theological Seminary at Wilberforce University in Ohio from 1952 until 1956. After that he became President of Paul Quinn College in Waco, Texas, and also served as campus pastor to all the students. Adams married Dollie Deselle of New Orleans in 1956; together they would have three daughters. His wife would also go on to become a prominent church leader and hold a doctor of education degree from Baylor University in Waco, Texas.

In 1962 Adams went to Seattle, Washington, as pastor of First AME Church and began his ascent as a national leader. The members of the church were at first dismayed by this fiery young man who spoke out so bluntly about social conditions in the city—the segregated housing, de facto segregated schools, and discriminatory hiring practices—as well as by the style of his ministry. The white community labeled him a troublemaker. Not long afterwards, however, he became a leader of the civil rights movement in Seattle and earned the respect of both the black and white communities. His articulate assessment of the race problems and his passionate belief in the potential of the city ignited one of the most successful movements in the country. He was the key spokesman for black people in Seattle during the height of the civil rights movement. He chaired the Central Area Civil Rights Committee, which included the heads of all the local civil rights organizations, ranging from the Congress of Racial Equality (CORE), led by Walter

Hundley; the NAACP, led by Charles Johnson and E. June Smith; and the Seattle Urban League, headed by Edwin T. Pratt, who in 1969 would be murdered on the doorstep of his home. The Committee was forceful and unique because it presented a unified front pressing for citywide racial reform and it determined the local civil rights agenda.

In 1965 Adams cofounded the Central Area Motivation Program, the country's first "war on poverty" agency. Two years earlier he led a march downtown for equal employment, led the fight for an open housing ordinance in 1964, and in 1966 spearheaded the school boycott to force integration of the Seattle Public Schools. He served on the Model Cities Planning Board and watched the agency become an exemplar for the rest of the nation. His influence spread even further during his five years in Seattle when he was appointed in 1965 to Governor Daniel Evans's Urban Affairs Committee, United Good Neighbors Planning Committee, and the boards of the Council of Churches and the YMCA. Among his many commendations during this period were the Man of the Year Award, given by the Seattle chapter of B'nai B'rith in 1964, and the Man of the Year award from the Seattle Urban League in 1965.

Adams became pastor of Grant AME Church in the Watts section of Los Angeles in 1968, three years after the riot. He was appointed by Bishop Howard Thomas Primm of the Fifth Episcopal District. There he again became involved in local NAACP activities and led a freedom patrol based on his Seattle experience. His design, however, was program, not protest. He launched the Education Growth Organization and Black Church Ethnic Schools with a published curriculum that spread to six other churches in the city. With the purpose of developing pride and academic excellence, the Grant AME School for middle school students was held every Saturday morning with free breakfast and lunch. The curriculum included mathematics, English, and African American history. In 1972 Adams was appointed bishop of the Tenth Episcopal District (Texas), a position from which he continued his civil rights activism by escorting a student to integrate the Waco Public Schools, and by supporting student protests to integrate all public facilities in Waco. Recognizing the need for establishing communication across denominational lines he was instrumental in the founding of the Congress of National Black Churches in 1978.

From 1980 until 1988 Adams served as bishop of the Second Episcopal District (comprising

Maryland, Washington, D.C., North Carolina, and Virginia) and began his pioneering efforts of expansion by facilitating the formation of thirty-five new congregations in his jurisdiction. His next four years were served as bishop of the Sixth Episcopal District (Georgia), where he welcomed four new congregations and continued his interest in civil rights. He resigned from the boards of the National Urban League and Southern Christian Leadership Conference in protest when the organizations' presidents supported the nomination of CLARENCE THOMAS to the U.S. Supreme Court.

Adams's final years in active ministry were spent in two southern AME districts. From 1992 until 2000 he was bishop of the Seventh Episcopal District (South Carolina), where he promoted the formation of ten new congregations and was a leader of the successful movement to remove the Confederate flag from the South Carolina State House. From 2000 to 2004 Adams served as bishop of the Eleventh Episcopal District (Florida, Barbados), where he encouraged the growth of eleven new congregations and oversaw the reorganization of fiscal affairs to eliminate indebtedness. He retired in 2005 and became adjunct professor at the Candler School of Theology at Emory University. His special and civic ministries comprised a vast array of social and educational activities, including membership on the boards of five colleges and universities and national boards of organizations dealing with racial, economic, and social problems. He was the recipient of over twenty-five awards for his service to the community.

FURTHER READING

Richardson, Larry Samuel. *Civil Rights in Seattle; a Rhetorical Analysis of a Social Movement* (1975).

Who's Who in America 2002, vol. 1 (c. 2001).

Who's Who in Religion, 1975–1976 (c. 1975).

MARY T. HENRY

Adams, John Quincy (4 May 1848–3 Sept. 1922), newspaper editor and publisher, civil rights leader, and Republican Party activist, was born in Louisville, Kentucky, the son of Henry Adams, a prominent minister and educator, and Margaret Corbin. Both of his parents were free persons of color. Following private schooling in Wisconsin and Ohio, Adams graduated from Oberlin College. After a brief teaching stint in Louisville, in 1870 he followed his uncle, Joseph C. Corbin, to work in Arkansas during Reconstruction. By 1874 Adams had risen from schoolteacher to assistant superintendent of public instruction. His lifelong activism in the Republican Party began in Arkansas; there he twice served as secretary to Republican state conventions, was elected as justice of the peace on the party ticket, and held the offices of engrossing clerk of the state senate and deputy commissioner of public works. The defeat of the Arkansas Republican Party in 1874 and the racial repression that followed led Adams to return to Louisville, where he again engaged in teaching.

Adams entered journalism in 1879 when he and his brother, CYRUS FIELD ADAMS, established the *Louisville Bulletin*, a weekly newspaper that served the Louisville African American community until 1885, when it was subsumed by the *American Baptist*. In 1880 Adams helped organize the National Afro-American Press Association, which held its first annual meeting in Louisville that year. Elected the organization's first president, he served from 1880 to 1882.

In 1886 Adams accepted an offer to join the staff of the St. Paul, Minnesota, *Western Appeal*, a black-owned weekly. Within a year he assumed the editorship and incorporated the Northwestern Publishing Company, which supported the expansion of the newspaper to include offices in Chicago, Louisville, Indianapolis, St. Louis, Dallas, and Washington, D.C. The *Western Appeal* prospered under his leadership; it was one of only nine African American newspapers established in the 1880s that survived until 1914. Its editorials consistently attacked racial discrimination and called for equal treatment both locally and nationally.

Adams helped organize resistance to racial discrimination in public accommodations and in the workplace in Minnesota through the establishment of the Minnesota Protective and Industrial League in 1887 and its successor, the Afro-American League of St. Paul, in 1889. He worked with T. THOMAS FORTUNE to found the National Afro-American League in 1890, serving on its first executive committee. The Afro-American Council, dominated by BOOKER T. WASHINGTON's accommodationist "Tuskegee machine," received his initial support in 1898. By 1903 the hostility of the council to civil rights activism in the North alienated Adams. Although he was not a leader in the National Association for the Advancement of Colored People (NAACP), he endorsed it by 1913 and broke with the Tuskegee faction. His editorials and civic activity continued to attack racial discrimination for the remainder of his life.

The other constant in Adams's public life was loyalty to the Republican Party. The *Western Appeal* consistently endorsed Republican candidates even as the party courted white southern votes by abandoning civil rights. Only President Warren G. Harding's acquiescence to segregation and lynching finally led Adams to question publicly his allegiance to the party.

Adams's influence peaked between 1890 and 1910. By 1913 the *Western Appeal* had closed its offices in Dallas, St. Louis, Louisville, Chicago, and Washington, D.C., and had shrunk to a local weekly. The paper and its editor remained influential in St. Paul, however, until his death. Adams was killed in an automobile accident in St. Paul. He was survived by his wife, Ella B. Smith, whom he had married in 1892; the couple had four children.

Even as he spent his life fighting the rising tide of racism during the Gilded Age, Adams demonstrated that the barriers to freedom were not insurmountable. His creation of a newspaper with offices in seven major cities, his leadership among African American journalists, and his advocacy of civil rights earned him a national reputation by 1900. He epitomized the African American middle class of the urban North. Light enough in complexion to pass for white, he edited a "race journal" supported by the African American community and dedicated to securing their civil rights.

FURTHER READING
No collection of Adams's papers exists, but the Minnesota Historical Society holds copies of his newspaper.
Spangler, Earl. *The Negro in Minnesota* (1961).
Suggs, Henry Lewis. "Democracy on Trial: The Black Press, Black Migration, and the Evolution of Culture and Community in Minnesota, 1865–1970," in *The Black Press in the Middle West, 1865–1985*, ed. Henry Lewis Suggs (1996).
Taylor, David V. "John Quincy Adams: St. Paul Editor and Black Leader," *Minnesota History* 43 (Winter 1973): 283–96.
Thornbrough, Emma Lou. "American Negro Newspapers, 1880–1914," *Business History Review* 40 (Winter 1966): 467–490.
Obituaries: *St. Paul Appeal*, 9 and 16 Sept. 1922.
This entry is taken from the *American National Biography* and is published here with the permission of the American Council of Learned Societies.

WILBERT H. AHERN

Adams, John Quincy (1845–?), author of an autobiographical slave narrative, was born near Winchester, Virginia, to slave parents whose names are now unknown. Adams and his family were owned by George F. Calomese, a member of a prominent planter family. John Quincy Adams and his twin brother were one of four pairs of twins born to their mother, who had twenty-five children.

What we know of Adams's life comes from his autobiography, *Narrative of the Life of John Quincy Adams* (1872), which briefly traces Adams's life as a slave and as a freeman. Written in simple, plain language, the *Narrative* captures the tragedy of slavery in powerful ways. The most poignant events in Adams's early life involve the sale of family members and friends. In 1857 the sale of his twin brother Aaron and his sister Sallie left Adams "very sad and heart-broken" (Adams, 28). Though crushed by the loss, he maintained contact with Aaron for a time through correspondence: "Two or three years after I heard from my dear brother. He had been sold seven times, and was bought every time for a house servant. The last time he was sold a gentleman bought him in Memphis, Tennessee. There he lived for some time, and when he got a chance he wrote to us" (Adams, 28–29). The two then lost contact. In 1868, after a friend of John's had encountered Aaron in Memphis, Tennessee, the brothers were reunited. Appreciating that freedom meant that they could visit each other at will, the brothers had their rejoicing tempered by their failure to locate Sallie Ann. "But still I sorrow yet," Adams wrote. "My dear sister, Sallie Ann Adams, who was sold with brother Aaron, has not been heard from yet, but we still hope that God will bless us with that opportunity to meet her on earth. If not, this is our hope in the last days" (Adams, 31).

Adams's parents had instilled a deep faith in him and his siblings, which he carried throughout his life. Sunday church gatherings and biblical readings that promised salvation for the poor and oppressed were comforting to slaves. Religion also served to make slaves, including John Quincy Adams, keenly aware of their illiteracy. Possessing a strong desire to read and write from an early age, Adams augmented whatever instruction he received from his father, who could read, by listening to the conversations of his owners and acquiring whatever learning he could by stealth. "The man who would deprive another of learning to read and write, and learn wisdom does not fear God," Adams concluded. "They [slave owners] took my labor to educate their children, and then laughed at me for being ignorant and poor, and had not sense enough to know that they were the cause of it" (Adams, 12).

That anger toward the institution of slavery spurred Adams and his family to escape their plantation on 27 June 1862. As the Union general John W. Geary's division approached the Calomese plantation, the Adams family fled. General Geary, however, had issued orders that no one—white or black, free or slave—could leave Winchester. But Adams's father implored Geary to let him and his family through. Geary not only allowed them to continue on, but provided them with a pass to Pennsylvania. John Quincy Adams and his relatives moved from town to town, eventually settling in Harrisburg, where his father bought property, an extraordinary act for anyone fresh from slavery. Though his parents returned to Winchester following the war, John remained in Harrisburg, where he worked as a house servant for several employers. One of the elite whites whom he encountered frequently was General Geary, who was elected governor of Pennsylvania in 1866.

Adams was deeply philosophical about his escape from slavery. He wrote, "I do not know that I ever stole anything very valuable but one thing, and I think that every just man will say that I done right. In 1862 I stole John Q. Adams from Mr. George F. Calomese, of Winchester, Va. They valued me at $2,000. At that rate I stole $2,000" (Adams, 47). The act of "stealing himself" allowed Adams to find employment in various hotels as a bellhop and waiter. Most important for him, his wages allowed him to purchase books and pursue his lifelong interest in learning to read and write.

At the conclusion of his narrative, Adams included several personal letters of recommendation written by employers, friends, and attorneys who vouched for his integrity and for the veracity of his life story. In addition, Adams included the first clause of the Declaration of Independence, undoubtedly to draw his readers' attention to the phrase, "all men are created equal." Likewise Adams inserted the text of the three Reconstruction amendments to the U.S. Constitution: the Thirteenth, which ended slavery; the Fourteenth, which granted citizenship to African Americans; and the Fifteenth, which extended suffrage to black men. *Narrative of the Life of John Quincy Adams* is an important example of the genre of the slave narrative. It demonstrates much of what modern-day historians have sought to capture about the experience of slavery. In Adams's work we see not only the cruelty of slavery, but the slaves' heroic efforts to maintain their families, acquire education, and resist an institution that sought to degrade them to the level of commodities. We see their unquenchable thirst for freedom; there are no "contented slaves" in the story of John Quincy Adams.

FURTHER READING

Adams, John Quincy. *Narrative of the Life of John Quincy Adams, When in Slavery, and Now as a Freeman* (1872).

KEVIN D. ROBERTS

Adams, Numa Pompilius Garfield (26 Feb. 1885–29 Aug. 1940), physician and medical educator, was born in Delaplane, Virginia. Little is known about Adams's family and early life. He attended a country school run by his uncle, Robert Adams. Numa received additional instruction and inspiration from his grandmother Amanda, a midwife who shared with him the secrets of herbal medicine. When Numa Adams was thirteen, his family moved to Steelton, Pennsylvania. Soon Adams taught himself how to read music and purchased a used cornet, which he taught himself how to play.

After graduating from high school in 1905, Adams spent a year as a substitute teacher in Steelton and another year teaching seventh grade in Carlisle, Pennsylvania. These jobs helped him earn sufficient money to pay for his college education, and in 1907 he left Pennsylvania to enter Howard University in Washington, D.C. He soon joined the Lyric Orchestra, a dance band composed mostly of medical and dental students, which performed three to five nights a week. On other nights Adams supplemented his earnings by appearing with Louis Brown's orchestra.

Adams received his undergraduate degree magna cum laude from Howard in 1911, and the following year he earned a master's degree in chemistry from Columbia University. He moved back to Washington, D.C., to take a post as an instructor of chemistry at Howard. He remained on the faculty of Howard's chemistry department until 1919, rising through the ranks and becoming first assistant and then associate professor of chemistry. In 1918 Adams was named head of the department, but he did not find chemistry sufficiently satisfying to continue his career in it. In addition he may have been concerned about the limited salary that a professor at that time could get; he had married OSCEOLA MACARTHY in 1915, and they had one child.

In the fall of 1919 Adams resigned the chair of the chemistry department to pursue a medical career. The following spring he moved to Chicago and entered Rush Medical College. Adams again turned to music to help finance his education, but tastes had changed, and playing the cornet was no longer a marketable skill. Adams then purchased a saxophone and within three weeks had become sufficiently expert to join the Charley Cooke Orchestra. Attending classes during the day and performing every night, Adams relegated most of his studying to the commute of an hour and a half from Chicago to the dance hall where the orchestra played. This grueling schedule did not stop him from winning Rush's Smiley scholarship nor from finishing second in his medical class. He graduated in 1924 and was elected to Alpha Omega Alpha, a medical scholastic fraternity.

After a year's internship at a city hospital in St. Louis, Adams returned to Chicago and opened a private practice. He also served as assistant medical director of the Victory Life Insurance Company. In 1927 he returned to teaching, this time as an instructor in neurology and psychiatry at Provident Hospital. In 1929 the quiet life he had established in Chicago ended when the president of Howard, MORDECAI JOHNSON, offered him the deanship of the university's medical school.

Even before Adams agreed to become the first African American dean of an approved medical school, he must have been aware of the difficulties that would face him. Although Howard had always been among the elite of the predominantly black medical schools, its budget was considerably smaller than that of many nonblack institutions. Howard had no endowment and subsisted entirely on tuition fees. Ten years earlier, Adams's predecessors had contemplated closing the school altogether.

Despite the obstacles and the mixed greetings that he received from the standing faculty—which included many white as well as black professors—Adams set to work charting a new path for Howard Medical School. Several of his actions in office proved controversial among the faculty. Traditionally the faculty members had worked their teaching schedules around other paid positions. Adams put an end to this system and enforced a daytime schedule of classes that would be more convenient for the students.

In another controversial move, Adams began a campaign to bring better-trained faculty to the medical school. In his first years he recruited a number of new faculty with doctorates in their disciplines. When interviewing new faculty members, Adams cared little for the reputation of the schools that a candidate had attended; rather, he paid particularly close attention to the candidate's course of study. Perhaps not surprisingly given his own background, he appeared to favor those who had a background in scientific research as well as in medicine. To attract the best candidates, Adams offered applicants a generous starting salary of $3,500, with a $500 increase each year up to $6,000. This move drew protest from the administrators at Nashville's Meharry Medical College, who argued that their school—then the only other black medical college in the country—would suffer because it could not match Howard's salaries.

Adams remained determined to provide Howard's medical students with the best possible education. Although the Depression forced him to withdraw his promise of raises, he continued his quest to mold Howard into an elite institution. During his ten years as dean, he steadily raised entrance requirements in the hope of improving the caliber of the student body. This policy, however, often resulted in fewer eligible students. One year, the school admitted a class of only twenty-six. Critics warned of loss of tuition revenues and reduction of opportunities for African Americans to enter the medical profession, but Adams's claim that this policy would produce better students was proven true toward the end of his tenure as dean. Previously, at least one student, and sometimes more, in each class had failed the annual board examinations, but the last four classes that Adams admitted while dean all passed.

In the final years of his deanship, Adams oversaw the integration of the Freedmen's Hospital with Howard University. Founded before the university, Freedmen's was operated by the U.S. Department of the Interior until the late 1930s. In 1937 the secretary of the department commissioned a study on the future of the hospital. On the basis of the study's recommendation, the department concluded that Howard Medical School should take over operation of the hospital. Even this change, which Adams oversaw, was not without its detractors; but despite protests, particularly from the city's Medico-Chirurgical Society, Freedmen's Hospital was transferred to Howard Medical School in 1940.

Adams died that same year in Chicago, after a long illness that many of his friends attributed at least in part to the strains of the deanship. He knew that he had antagonized many and endeared himself to few during his years as dean. Up to the end of his life, he continued to feel that his labors were unappreciated.

FURTHER READING

Cobb, William Montague. "Medical History," *Journal of the National Medical Association* 43 (1951).

Logan, Rayford. *Howard University: The First Hundred Years, 1867–1967* (1969).

Ludmerer, Kenneth M. *Learning to Heal: The Development of American Medical Education* (1985).

This entry is taken from the *American National Biography* and is published here with the permission of the American Council of Learned Societies.

SHARI RUDAVSKY

Adams, Ron (25 June 1934–), painter, graphic artist, printmaker, and publisher, was born in Detroit, Michigan, the son of Ned Adams, an electrician and occasional sign painter, and Laura. Adams first explored art making by mimicking his father, who, according to Adams, enjoyed drawing. After the divorce of his parents around 1944, Adams lived with his aunt and uncle, Claudia and Caleb Spivey. Although he sought to attend a program for gifted children at the Detroit Institute of Arts, his uncle vehemently prohibited it, preferring that Adams spend his free time working jobs such as delivering newspapers. Adams attended Northwestern High School in Detroit while continuing to live with the Spiveys until age fifteen, when he moved to his father's home.

After graduating from high school in 1951, Adams moved to Romeo, Michigan, a then rural town forty-one miles north of Detroit. There Adams worked at Graff Engineering, a small manufacturing company, and earned extra income on the weekends working on the farm of Victor Graff, the owner of Graff Engineering, during haying season. In 1951 Adams moved to Los Angeles; in 1955 he married Mary Black. The couple had a daughter, Rochelle Adams, and ultimately divorced in 1962. Adams worked on an assembly line for Mission Appliance Corporation and then for the Los Angeles Post Office while continuing his education; he studied graphic arts at the Los Angeles Trade Technical College (1955–1956), drafting at the Manual Arts Adult Night School in Los Angeles (1958), general engineering at Los Angeles City College (1959), and technical illustration and commercial art at Los Angeles Trade Technical College, where he received his certificate of trade proficiency in June 1963.

Adams had started working in 1962 as a technical illustrator for Hughes Aircraft Company in Los Angeles, and during his years there he continued his studies, this time in fine art, at the Otis Art Institute, Los Angeles, where he took courses in drawing, painting, and sculpture with Joseph Mugnaini and Arnold Meshes, who both became mentors for the young artist. In 1964 Adams was laid off from Hughes, whereupon he became a technical illustrator for Litton Industries in Woodland Hills, California. A year later Adams was laid off from Litton and was rehired by Hughes. In 1965 he also studied drawing at the University of California, Los Angeles. Subsequently he began to exhibit his art, first at the Watts Art Festival in 1965, followed by exhibitions at the Los Angeles Municipal Gallery, Brockman Gallery, and the Downey Museum.

An affinity for Mexican muralists, such as José Clemente Orozco and David Alfaro Siqueiros, led Adams to move in 1966 to Mexico City, where he studied lithography and metal engraving at the University of Mexico. The following year the International Olympic Committee selected Adams to design a wide variety of materials, including posters, signs, murals, and other illustrations, for the 1968 Olympics in Mexico City.

In 1969 Adams moved back to Los Angeles and began working for Gemini Graphic Editions Limited (GEL) under the tutelage of Kenneth E. Tyler, the founder and owner. Then in its fourth year of operation, Gemini was becoming one of the preeminent artists' workshops and publishers of limited edition prints and sculptures in the United States. While at Gemini, Adams advanced from assistant printer to master printer in four years. As a printmaker, Adams worked with a wide range of highly recognized artists at the time, including Jasper Johns, Robert Rauschenberg, Ellsworth Kelly, and Frank Stella.

In 1973 Adams began working as a master printer at Ernest De Soto's Editions Press in San Francisco while maintaining a residence in Los Angeles. The following year he married Hazel Jaramillo, and they moved to Santa Fe, New Mexico, where he opened his own graphic workshop, Hand Graphics Ltd., with his wife and Robert Arber. Adams attracted several artists of note during the thirteen years of the workshop's existence, including Judy Chicago, Luis Jiménez, Fritz Scholder, R. C. Gorman, and the African Americans JOHN BIGGERS and CHARLES WHITE—two seminal figures in the graphic arts in the later twentieth century. Adams separated from his wife in about 1981.

The desire to return to creating his own art full time led Adams in 1988 to sell Hand Graphics and accept an invitation from Hampton University, a historically black university in Virginia, to be an artist in residence for the 1989–1990 academic year. While an artist in his own right, Adams always recognized that printmaking, especially in the service of others, was a craft, albeit a highly skilled one. A pivotal work from this period was his large-scale color lithograph *Profile in Blue* (1988), which effectively summarized his life as a printmaker. In this work an African American printmaker—certainly a stand-in for the artist—sits on the bed of his press, ink roller in hand, and gazes into the distance.

The year 1987 marked the beginning of a long, intimate relationship between Adams and Arlene LewAllen and the foundation of LewAllen Contemporary, which became the preeminent modern and contemporary art gallery in Sante Fe. Four years after the beginning of his relationship with LewAllen, Adams divorced his wife, Hazel Jaramillo. Adam and LewAllen never married, and their relationship ended in 2002, the year LewAllen died of a brain aneurism. Two years later Adams moved to Atlanta, Georgia, where he continued to work as a professional artist.

Throughout Adams's career as an artist and printmaker, he was often engaged in a wide range of initiatives and projects that highlighted his long-standing role as an arts activist. These activities included his chairmanship of a committee he established in Sante Fe in 1985 to help provide artists with low-cost studios in a skyrocketing housing market.

Adams's career is also noted by numerous exhibitions that began in 1966 in venues that include, among others, the Museum of Fine Arts, Sante Fe (1987, 1992, 1995, 1996); Society of American Graphic Artists, New York (1986); Vanderbilt University Fine Arts Gallery in Nashville, Tennessee (2000); and the University of New Mexico Art Museum (1992). His art is in the collections of the Albuquerque Museum, New Mexico; the California Afro American Museum, Los Angeles; the Hampton University Museum, Virginia; and the Smithsonian Museum of American Art, Washington, D.C.

FURTHER READING

Kimbrough, Blake T., and Marshall, Melvin A. *From Challenge to Triumph: African American Prints and Printmaking 1867–2002* (2003).

Taha, Halima. *Collecting African American Art: Works on Paper and Canvas* (1998).

Western Michigan University. *Progressive Proof: Celebrating Forty Years of Collecting at Western Michigan University* (2003).

JOSEPH S. MELLA

Adams, Victoria Jackson Gray (5 Nov. 1926–12 Aug. 2006), civil rights activist, was born in Palmers Crossing, an all-black community in Hattiesburg, Mississippi, to Mack and Annie Mae Jackson. After the death of Adams's mother when she was three years old, she lived with her grandparents. Adams earned her high school diploma from Depriest Consolidated School in 1945 and subsequently enrolled at Wilberforce University, but was forced to leave school after one year because she lacked the money for tuition. She later studied at the Tuskegee Institute in Alabama and at Jackson State College (now Jackson State University) in Mississippi and eventually became a teacher. Adams also served as a campus minister at Virginia State University in Petersburg, Virginia. Her first marriage was to Tony West Gray and they had three children—Georgie, Tony Jr., and Cecil. Gray was in the U.S. Army and his military career took the family to Germany and Fort Mead, Maryland, during the 1950s. Adams later divorced Tony Gray and relocated back to Hattiesburg where she operated a successful cosmetic business. In 1966 she married Reuben Adams Jr. They had one child, Reuben Adams III.

Adams's civil rights work began coincidentally in 1962 when two Student Nonviolent Coordinating Committee (SNCC) field workers contacted Adams inquiring about a place to hold a mass meeting in Hattiesburg. That inquiry was the beginning of Adams's movement participation and soon after she attempted to register to vote. Mississippi had several barriers preventing African Americans from voting, including literacy requirements and white violence. By 1964 Adams sat on the Southern Christian Leadership Conference (SCLC) national board with Dr. MARTIN LUTHER KING JR., one of the few women to do so. She also organized the SNCC-sponsored economic boycott of Hattiesburg businesses that practiced discrimination. Adams's greatest passion was helping blacks to register to vote. After attending a citizenship school in Dorchester, Georgia, taught by SEPTIMA CLARK, Adams returned to Hattiesburg and organized voter education classes to teach blacks how to read, register to vote, and resist white supremacy. Her work made her the target of white violence, and there were several attempts made on her life. To encourage blacks to become active politically in the face of fear, Adams challenged the four-term incumbent U.S. Senator John C. Stennis (D-MS) in 1964. Although she had no chance of unseating Stennis, Adams's campaign galvanized a fearful

Victoria Jackson Gray Adams, center, talks to reporters at the University of Southern Mississippi about her 29 Feb. 2000, civil rights lecture, flanked by Raylawni Branch, left, of Hattiesburg, Missippi, and Elaine Chamberlain of Clinton, Maryland. (AP Images.)

black population and she made history as the first woman in Mississippi to run for the U.S. Senate.

In 1964, working with FANNIE LOU HAMER and Annie Devine, Adams founded the Mississippi Freedom Democratic Party (MFDP), a political party created to contest the exclusion of blacks from Mississippi's Democratic Party. She served as an MFDP delegate to the 1964 Democratic National Convention in Atlantic City, New Jersey, where she contested the all-white Mississippi delegation to the convention. Although MFDP delegates were not seated, their protest brought national attention to the disfranchisement and violence that governed black life in Mississippi and led to the Democratic National Party's commitment to integrated state delegations at all future conventions. Undeterred by the defeat of the Atlantic City challenge, the MFDP asserted that five Mississippi Congressmen were elected undemocratically in November 1964 since blacks were largely barred from voting. Adams, Hamer, and Devine challenged the seating of three of the white segregationists, making history as the first women from Mississippi to run

for U.S. Congress and the first black women to be seated as guests on the floor of the U.S. Senate.

Adams relocated to Thailand in 1968 with her second husband, Reuben Adams, where she continued to advocate on behalf of African American soldiers and their families who faced racism while in service to their country. Her contributions to society have made her the recipient of many honors including the Fannie Lou Hamer Humanitarian Award and the United Methodist Church's highest education award, the John Wesley Award. She is featured in numerous documentaries and books on the civil rights movement including the Academy Award–nominated *Freedom on My Mind* and Taylor Branch's Pulitzer Prize–winning trilogy on the African American freedom struggle.

On 12 August 2006, Adams succumbed to lung cancer in Baltimore, Maryland, at the home of her son Cecil Gray. At the time of her death, Mississippi had more black elected officials than any other state in the nation, a fact due in part to Adams's work to increase black political participation. According to her obituary in the *New York Times*, Adams once stated that in 1964 she learned that there were two kinds of people in grassroots politics, "those who are in the movement and those who have the movement in them. The movement is in me, and I know it will always be."

FURTHER READING

Victoria Gray Adams's papers are held at the McCain Library and Archives at the University of Southern Mississippi, Hattiesburg.

Franklin, V. P., and Bettye Collier-Thomas, eds. *Sisters in the Struggle: African American Women in the Civil Rights-Black Power Movement* (2001).

Houck, Davis, and David Dixon, eds. *Women in the Civil Rights Movement, 1954–1965* (2009).

Obituary: *New York Times*, 19 Aug. 2006.

CRYSTAL R. SANDERS

Adams-Ender, Clara (11 July 1939–), military leader, nurse, educator, and entrepreneur, was born Clara Mae Leach Adams in Willow Springs, North Carolina. Her parents, Otha Leach and Caretha Bell, were sharecroppers, and she was the fourth of ten children. Her parents were staunch supporters of education and made sure that all of their children knew this. Her parents further instilled in the children a sense of self-respect and a belief that with knowledge they could do anything.

As a child growing up in a family of sharecroppers, Adams-Ender realized early that she wanted more out of life. Her perseverance in continuing her education while missing school to work the farm with her family was evident when she graduated second in her class at the age of sixteen. Although she enrolled in a nursing program, her first career choice was to be a lawyer. However, in 1956 her father believed that women went into nursing, not into law. So Adams-Ender entered the nursing program at North Carolina A&T.

Because of circumstances beyond her control, she withdrew from school a year later. The family tobacco farm hit on hard times, and it became necessary for her to work. Nevertheless, she returned to the nursing program at North Carolina A&T and by the second semester found a way to pay for the rest of her training. She saw an army recruiting poster for nurses and met with the recruiters. She joined the army nursing corps, and the army paid for her junior and senior years of college. Just prior to graduating in 1961, Adams-Ender was commissioned as second lieutenant. After graduation she went to Fort Sam Houston in San Antonio, Texas, for basic military training.

Her duty station was Fort Dix, New Jersey, where she remained from 1961 to 1963, when she received a transfer to a base in the Republic of Korea. While Adams-Ender was in Korea her superiors came to recognize her natural skills as an administrator, a leader, and an instructor. In 1964 she was reassigned to the United States Army Training Center at Fort Sam Houston, where she took an advanced nursing course and served as a nursing instructor. Just prior to leaving Texas for the University of Minnesota to pursue a master of science degree in Nursing in 1967, she became the first woman in the army to receive an Expert Field Medical Badge.

After earning her degree in 1969, Adams-Ender was stationed at Walter Reed Army Medical Center in Washington, D.C., as an assistant professor. By this time she had attained the rank of captain. During her time at Walter Reed she moved quickly to the rank of major, soon followed by a promotion to lieutenant colonel. She then enrolled in the Army Command and General Staff College in Fort Leavenworth, Kansas. Completing her studies in 1976, she became the first African American woman and nurse to receive a master's degree in military art and science. After completing her studies, her next duty station was that of inspector general at Fort Sam Houston's Army Health Services Command.

In 1978 Adams-Ender was transferred to the Army Regional Medical Center in Germany. She worked tirelessly to run the intensive care unit (ICU), recruiting and training nurses for the unit and working to strengthen German–American relations among healthcare professionals. For her dedication and hard work Adams-Ender was promoted to the rank of full colonel in 1981. While stationed in Germany she met her husband, Heinz Ender, a German dentist; they married in 1981 and returned to the United States three months later.

Her next duty station took Adams-Ender to Fort Sheridan, Illinois, where she served as the chief of nurse recruiting and chief of the Army Nurse Corps division. Three years later Adams-Ender returned to Walter Reed Army Medical Center as chief of the department of nursing. By 1987 she was with the Surgeon General's Office as chief of the Army Nurse Corps and was promoted to brigadier general. In 1991 Adams-Ender became the deputy commander for the military district of Washington, D.C., and the commander of Fort Belvoir, Virginia.

Adams-Ender retired from military service in 1993 to become the CEO and president of CAPE (Caring for People with Enthusiasm), a management consulting firm in Lake Ridge, Virginia. Adams-Ender's military career spanned more than thirty years. She received numerous awards and honors, including the Distinguished Service Medal with oak-leaf cluster, the Legion of Merit, the Meritorious Service Medal with three oak-leaf clusters, the Army Commendation Medal, and Cross of Honor in Gold (from the German army).

FURTHER READING

Adams-Ender, Clara. *My Rise to the Stars: How a Sharecropper's Daughter Became an Army General* (2001).

Cheers, D. M. "Nurse Corps Chief," *Ebony* (June 1989).

TERI B. WEIL

Adderley, Cannonball (15 Sept. 1928–8 Aug. 1975), jazz saxophonist, was born Julian Edwin Adderley in Tampa, Florida, the son of Julian Carlyle Adderley, a high school guidance counselor and jazz cornet player, and Jessie Johnson, an elementary school teacher. The family moved to Tallahassee, Florida, where Adderley attended Florida Agricultural and Mechanical College High School from 1941 to 1944. He earned his bachelor's degree from Florida A&M in 1948, having studied reed and brass instruments with the band director Leander Kirksey and forming, with Kirksey, a school jazz ensemble. Adderley then worked as band director at Dillard High School in Fort Lauderdale, Florida, and jobbed with his own jazz group.

Adderley served in the army from 1950 until 1953, leading the Thirty-sixth Army Dance Band, to which his younger brother, the cornetist NATHANIEL "NAT" ADDERLEY, was also assigned. While stationed in Washington, D.C., in 1952, Adderley continued to play with his own group and furthered his musical studies at the U.S. Naval School of Music. Assigned to Fort Knox, Kentucky, he again led an army dance band. After his discharge, he returned to Fort Lauderdale to continue as the high school band director and as a jobbing musician.

Encouraged by the singer and saxophonist Eddie "Cleanhead" Vinson, Adderley moved to New York in 1955. After sitting in with OSCAR PETTIFORD at the Cafe Bohemia, he so impressed fellow musicians that he was asked to join Pettiford's band. Almost immediately, he signed a recording contract with EmArcy. These early recordings display the influence of the altoists CHARLIE PARKER and Benny Carter. Although the bebop influence led Adderley to play long and sometimes highly chromatic solo lines, his deeply rooted interest in gospel

and modern blues helped him create a distinctive voice. In January 1956 Nat and Cannonball formed a quintet that toured nationally until 1957, when Cannonball joined the MILES DAVIS quintet. When the tenor saxophonist JOHN COLTRANE was added, this ensemble of the trumpeter Davis, Adderley, Coltrane, the bassist PAUL CHAMBERS, the drummer PHILLY JOE JONES, and both BILL EVANS and RED GARLAND on piano became the most influential group in jazz. The spectacular recordings in which Adderley and Coltrane vie for dominance, such as 1958's "Dr. Jekyll," and the modal jazz improvisations of the *Kind of Blue* session of 1959, such as "So What?" are recognized jazz masterpieces. This latter session introduced a new style, establishing modal jazz, improvisation based on a succession of scales rather than a progression of harmonies, as one of the mainstream techniques in jazz from that time forward.

In late 1959 Adderley left Davis and re-formed a quintet with his brother Nat. This group, with changing rhythm section personnel and the occasional addition of a second saxophonist (first Yusef Lateef and later Charles Lloyd), continued until Adderley's death and enjoyed considerable popular and critical success. Influenced by the work of ORNETTE COLEMAN in the early 1960s and the technological advances of electronic instruments that became a part of jazz shortly thereafter, the

Julian "Cannonball" Adderley, jazz saxophonist and influential spokesperson for the black community, 1970. (AP Images.)

new Adderley brothers' ensemble played a fusion of bebop, modal jazz, rock, and free jazz elements, sometimes called "soul jazz," that carried them on the crest of one avant-garde jazz wave of the 1960s. Their *Jazz Workshop* sessions, recorded live in San Francisco in 1962, display an early stage of this development, and their 1966 live album *Mercy, Mercy, Mercy!* which reflects this style, became one of the best-selling jazz records to that time. Their music appealed to fans of rock 'n' roll as well as to those of modern jazz, and the ensemble's tours often drew huge crowds not only in the United States but also in Japan, East and West Europe, and Great Britain. Speaking of his music, Adderley was quoted in 1966 as saying, "I'm aware that jazz is changing, and I have listened to and absorbed many influences. I feel that Ornette Coleman was a most important force. However, what I play today is a logical development of my own style."

Adderley married the actress Olga James in 1962. In the late 1960s he added soprano saxophone as a regular solo instrument in his performances. His mature playing was a masterful combination of elements: lessons learned from Charlie Parker, associations with Miles Davis, John Coltrane, and the keyboardist Joe Zawinul, and a natural affinity for black soul and gospel music. His solo lines and incisive sound were charged with an unerring sense of direction, a dazzling improvisatory technique, and a sense of timbral exploration married to a "down-home" feel for the blues. While on tour before his forty-seventh birthday, he suffered a stroke and died several weeks later in a hospital in Gary, Indiana.

Adderley's legacy is twofold: as a creative and compelling jazz artist of the later 1950s through the mid-1970s and as an influential spokesperson for this music and the black community. He served as a committee member for the National Endowment for the Arts, was a member of the Black Academy of Arts and Letters, and served on the jazz advisory panel of the John F. Kennedy Center for the Performing Arts. He hosted thirteen weeks of a television series, *90 Minutes*; appeared in a few motion pictures, including *Play Misty for Me* (1971), *Soul to Soul* (1971), and *Save the Children* (1973); made guest playing appearances on several television shows; and participated in many college workshops and seminars.

Among Adderley's honors are the Julian Cannonball Adderley Artist in Residence Program at Harvard University and several *Down Beat*, *Playboy*, and Encyclopedia of Jazz All Star and Poll Awards. Among his important and representative recordings are *Presenting Cannonball Adderley* (1955), *Somethin' Else* (1958), Miles Davis's *Milestones* (1958) and *Kind of Blue* (1959), *Mercy, Mercy, Mercy!* (1966), *Country Preacher* (1969), and *Inside Straight* (1973). A posthumously issued recording, *Big Man* (1975), composed jointly with his brother Nat, was based on the legend of JOHN HENRY with the blues singer JOE WILLIAMS in the title role. Adderley considered this one of the major achievements of his career. Among his many jazz compositions, several have entered the repertoire as standards, including "Sack o' Woe," "Domination," "Sermonette," and "Them Dirty Blues."

Speaking of Cannonball Adderley in 1993, Nat Adderley reflected:

> I believe that a large part of what Cannonball did musically might have been missed or overlooked at the time he did it, because the concept of critical analysis of the music at that time was based more on alleged "European concepts" than on the total impact of what the music was. So it has only been in the last few years ... that there has been a lot more consideration, a lot more interest, in what Cannonball did as students now study the solos. It has become much more evident that Cannonball was far superior in many areas than he was originally given credit for ... many of the critics, I think, did not understand the infusion of Southern black gospel music and blues into what they considered a hallowed European classical tradition.

FURTHER READING

Adderley's papers, scores, and memorabilia are in the Black Archives Research Center of Florida Agricultural and Mechanical University in Tallahassee. Oral history material and recordings are preserved at the Institute of Jazz Studies of Rutgers University in Newark, New Jersey.

Baker, David. *The Jazz Style of Cannonball Adderley: A Musical and Historical Perspective* (1980).

Corey, Christiansen, and Tamara Danielsson. *In the Style of Cannonball Adderley, C Instruments Edition, Essential Jazz Lines Series* (2002).

Sheridan, Chris, comp. *Dis Here: A Bio-Discography of Julian "Cannonball" Adderley* (2000).

Obituary: *New York Times*, 9 Aug. 1975.

This entry is taken from the *American National Biography* and is published here with the permission of the American Council of Learned Societies.

FRANK TIRRO

Adderley, Nat (25 Nov. 1931–2 Jan. 2000), cornetist, trumpeter, bandleader, composer, arranger, and college educator, was born Nathaniel Adderley in Tampa, Florida, the second of two sons of Julian Adderley Sr. and Jessie Adderley. Julian Sr. was an educator who played trumpet and cornet, thus becoming Nat's first music teacher. Jessie was also a teacher. Nat's only sibling, JULIAN ADDERLEY JR., nicknamed "Cannonball" because of his rotund build, was three years older than his brother. The Adderleys moved from Tampa to Tallahassee, Florida, when Nat was a toddler so that Julian Sr. and Jessie could take teaching jobs at Florida A&M College (FAMC), a historically black school. The college changed its name to Florida A&M University (FAMU) in 1953.

Cannonball was the first of the two brothers to play trumpet. He later became more interested in the alto saxophone, leaving his trumpet to sit idle. Nat showed no interest in his brother's old horn and instead opted to develop his singing abilities. When Nat's voice began to change in 1946 as he matured, he decided to pick up and play his brother's trumpet, which he learned at an incredible pace. As a teenager he played with several music groups around Tallahassee and performed in his high school band. Around 1950 Nat decided to switch from trumpet to cornet, although he did not completely abandon the former instrument. Nat loved the way his father played the cornet, attracted to the fatter and much earthier sound of the cornet over the sometimes-piercing sound of the trumpet. Local musicians attempted to deter Nat from switching to the cornet because of its almost nonexistent status in jazz music of the era. He played both instruments on several of his early professional recordings, but the cornet defined his long career.

Following high school Nat enrolled at FAMC, where he became a member of the school's world-famous "Marching 100" band and the school's symphonic orchestra. Under the leadership of the bandmaster, Dr. William Foster, considered the ultimate creator of progressive and imaginative marching and music pageantry, Nat was chosen as the trumpet's section leader and rank sergeant for the high-and-fast-stepping aggregation. Prior to graduation Nat joined the U.S. Army, where he played cornet in the Thirty-Sixth Army Band. After a three-year stint in the military (1951–1953), Adderley returned to Tallahassee, where he reenrolled at what had by then become FAMU. He earned a B.A. in Sociology with a minor in Music in 1954.

After graduation Nat's mother, Jessie, urged him to go to law school. She felt Nat would be an outstanding lawyer because of his penchant for arguing. Nat had other plans as word began to circulate throughout jazz circles about his profound sound and style of playing. The jazz great LIONEL HAMPTON invited Nat to join him on an upcoming international tour. Against his mother's wishes Nat accepted Hampton's invitation and headed to Europe. Returning to the United States in 1955, he and Cannonball, an FAMC graduate, "Marching 100" alumnus, and by then high school music teacher, decided to play together in New York. The two brothers showed up at the famous Café Bohemia, where the jazz greats HORACE SILVER (piano), OSCAR PETTIFORD (bass), and KENNY CLARKE (drums) were performing. Nat and Cannonball, with horns in hands, asked to sit in with the legendary musicians. The two brothers were well received by the group and the audience as they displayed a fresh, hot, soulful, and funky brand of jazz. Nat and Cannonball were a hit, and they soon were in high demand for club and recording sessions around New York. Nat played a gritty but straight-ahead hard bop, sometimes laced with soft staccato, soul, and funk licks. Although his mentors and influences were the likes of DIZZY GILLESPIE, MILES DAVIS, and CLARK TERRY, Nat displayed his own distinctive style.

Nat's first solo album, *That's Nat* on Savoy, was released in 1955. He played both trumpet and cornet. Nat was joined on this recording by Kenny Clarke (drums), Hank Jones (piano), and Jerome Richardson (tenor saxophone and flute). Nat and Cannonball's debut recording together was on *Introducing Nat Adderley* in 1955 on the EmArcy label. Nat was the leader for the recording date; Cannonball was a sideman. Soon afterward Nat and Cannonball formed a short-lived band; following its demise Nat performed with Woody Herman's band and then joined forces with the trombone great J. J. JOHNSON.

Nat reconnected musically with his brother in 1959 to anchor the Cannonball Adderley Quintet. The group made such an impression on the jazz scene that Miles Davis called record executives about the brothers, which resulted in the sudden elevation of their recording and performance career. For the next sixteen years the Cannonball Adderley Quintet was one of the best and most successful jazz ensembles in the world. The group released dozens of albums on labels such as Savoy,

Blue Note, Riverside, Original Jazz Classics, Landmark, and Capitol. The jazz ensemble hit pay dirt in 1966 with the album *Mercy, Mercy, Mercy! Live at the Club*, which ushered in a new era of jazz, blending earthy sounds of soul, blues, funk, and gospel music. The album won a Grammy Award in 1968 for best instrumental jazz performance by a small group.

Nat was a major contributor to the success of the Cannonball Adderley Quintet. He composed or arranged many of its songs. His solos were uncanny, always painted with rich and soulful tones. Nat was also a shrewd businessman, often making the tough business decisions that kept the quintet on top. However, Nat never received the type of musical acclaim that his brother garnered. Sometimes jazz fans and critics took him for granted as he stood in his brother's musical shadow. During the Cannonball Adderley Quintet years Nat was leader for more than a dozen solo projects, but he always returned to play next to his brother. Perhaps Nat's greatest solo recording came in 1960, when he released the album *Work Song* on Riverside Records. The album's title song had a bluesy, hard-bop, call-and-response feel and featured the playing of the jazz guitarist WES MONTGOMERY. Through the years Nat wrote and arranged other compositions, including such classics as "Jive Samba," "Sermonette," and "The Old Country."

Nat performed with his brother until Cannonball's death in 1975. Nat then fronted his own jazz groups for more than two decades, which included work with the saxophonists Sonny Fortune and Victor Herring. He maintained a hectic national and international touring schedule that took his groups around the United States and to Europe, Japan, and Australia. He released several post-Cannonball albums, including *Don't Look Back, Hummin'*, and *A Little New York Midtown Music*.

In the mid-1990s Adderley was named as an artist-in-residence at Florida Southern College in Lakeland, Florida, where he taught a music theory class. He had performed numerous times at the school's annual Child of the Sun Jazz Festival. Nat occasionally performed with the late R&B and pop balladeer LUTHER VANDROSS; the cornetist's only son, Nat Adderley Jr., served as the singer's pianist and musical director.

Health issues began to take a toll on Nat's career, forcing him to curtail touring and recording sessions. His last two known recordings as a leader date from 1995, when he recorded a reprise of his

and his brother's classic album *Mercy, Mercy, Mercy!* on Evidence Records and released the album *Live on Planet Earth* on Westwind Records. In 1997 Nat Adderley was inducted into the Jazz Hall of Fame in Kansas City. One of his last live performances was also in 1997, at the Playboy Jazz Festival at Hollywood Bowl in Los Angeles. Nat's right leg was amputated that year as a result of diabetes, the disease that led to his death at age sixty-eight. He was survived by his wife, Ann; daughter, Alison; and son, Nat Adderley Jr.

Over his fifty-year music career Nat performed in more than twenty countries and can be heard on well over one hundred albums, of which he was leader on about thirty. His legacy as one of jazz's most talented and successful cornetists, trumpeters, composers, and arrangers is well documented.

FURTHER READING

Down Beat (Feb. 1994, Mar. 1994, Mar. 1996).
Erlewine, Michael. *All Music Guide to Jazz* (1996).
Feather, Leonard. *The Encyclopedia of Jazz in the '60s* (1966).

DISCOGRAPHY

Live on Planet Earth (WW2088).
Mercy, Mercy, Mercy, with Cannonball Adderley Quintet (Capitol Jazz 29915).
The Adderley Brothers: The Summer of '55 (SVY-17063).
Work Song (RISA-1167-6; OJCCD-363-2).

DONALD JAMES

Africa, John (26 July 1931–13 May 1985), founder of MOVE, an anarchist communal organization active primarily in the Philadelphia area, was born Vincent Leaphart in the Mantua section of West Philadelphia.

Africa served in the Korean War, though little else is known about his early life. In the early 1970s, while working as a neighborhood handyman and dog walker (nicknamed "the dog man"), he began to corral followers. With the assistance of Donald Glassey, a white graduate student in sociology at the University of Pennsylvania, Africa, a third-grade dropout, compiled the MOVE doctrine in a document known as "The Guidelines." His group was first known as the Christian Movement for Life, later the Movement, and finally MOVE. Numerous press reports stress the fact that MOVE is not an acronym and therefore the tenets of the group can only be vaguely delineated. Responding to this

Vincent Leaphart, known also as John Africa, smiles from a taxi as he leaves the federal courthouse in Philadelphia on 23 July 1981, after being acquitted on weapons and conspiracy charges. (AP Images.)

criticism, group member Delbert Africa quipped, "It means what it says. Move. Get active. Change. Revolution."

MOVE members—many of whom wore their hair in dreadlocks, deemed to be the hair's most natural state—considered themselves part of a naturalist "religion" that prohibited the killing of all animals and insects, including vermin, and prescribed a healthful lifestyle of exercise, raw food, and abstinence from tobacco, alcohol, and drugs. The organization eschewed organized government, big business, technology, and education, refusing to enroll their children in traditional schooling outside the home. A self-described "revolution," MOVE claimed to protect its members and others from the control and imposition of a capitalist system they felt was plagued by drugs, racism, crime, war, environmental ruin, and disease. Though predominately African American, the organization accepted members of all races. Additionally, all MOVE members took the surname Africa in homage to the continent's role as the birthplace of human beings.

As MOVE began to take shape, the group recruited new members around the Powelton Village neighborhood of Philadelphia at venues such as block parties. At its most prolific the group boasted approximately one hundred members. MOVE quickly became known for attending rallies and other events and drawing attention to themselves through their antigovernment, antitechnology, antizoo rhetoric (the group opposed caging animals) in loud tones, often employing profanity to illustrate the profane nature of the "system." From its inception in 1972 to the mid-1970s, MOVE members clashed with police countless times during public demonstrations. Throughout this time, over one hundred fifty misdemeanors and citations kept MOVE members constantly embroiled in legal dilemma.

Neighbors and historians maintain that in spite of its extremist views, MOVE remained approachable and nonviolent in its early years. As the decade waxed on, however, members of the organization became embittered from numerous arrests and alleged police brutality, incidents that no doubt contributed to the group's adoption of a more militant stance. In September 1976, legal efforts by the city to enter and inspect the MOVE house were rebuffed. Sending a message of preparedness to authorities, in May 1977, group members posed in uniform and wielded automatic weapons in a photograph taken on the porch of its communal home in Powelton Village. Concurrently, Donald Glassey turned federal informant in 1977, joining the Witness Protection Program and informing authorities about the group's stockpile of weapons, bombs, and bomb-making manuals. Arrest warrants were issued for several group members, though unsurprisingly they refused to leave the group's compound.

In April 1978 the Philadelphia police began to initiate around-the-clock surveillance of MOVE. A blockade was soon instituted, and authorities surrounding the house cut the compound off from all water, electricity, and gas. With the help of sympathizers smuggling goods in and out, the group was able to withstand the city's pressure; after fifty days, the cost of the siege was estimated at $1.2 million. Finally, under orders from Mayor Frank Rizzo, police attempted to enter the MOVE compound on 8 August 1978. Gunfire was exchanged with police, and Officer James J. Ramp was shot and killed in the crossfire.

Though the exact circumstances of Ramp's death remain in contention to this day, nine members of MOVE were tried, convicted, and given sentences of thirty to one hundred years for the killing. John Africa escaped charge in the incident as he was absent from the compound at the time. MOVE maintained its innocence, insisting that they could not have fired the shot that killed Ramp, who died from a gunshot wound to the back of the head, from their position. Obtaining evidence from the crime scene was impossible after the fact, as authorities razed the Powelton Avenue compound to the ground after the raid. From this point forward, MOVE focused much of its energy on freeing the "MOVE 9" from prison.

In 1981 John Africa and the remaining MOVE members took up quiet residency at 6221 Osage Avenue in the Cobbs Creek section of West Philadelphia, home to a mostly black middle class. The next year Africa was asked by Mumia Abu-Jamal to represent him at his trial for the murder of Philadelphia police officer Daniel Faulkner. Africa had since the early 1970s been an associate of Abu-Jamal, the activist, former Black Panther, and president of the Philadelphia Association of Black

Journalists. The presiding judge turned down the request, however, because Africa was not a trained lawyer. In explaining the appeal of Africa, who was barely literate, his sister Louise James said: "There's not one question, not one, that he couldn't answer. It was the first time in my life that somebody said things to me that I could absolutely not refute" (Gruson).

Within a few years the group resumed its habit of blasting propaganda over a loudspeaker several times a day—including death threats aimed at specific neighbors--and refused to remove the refuse accumulating on its compound. Unsurprisingly, relations with their Cobbs Creek neighborhood quickly degenerated. Efforts to negotiate with the group became locked in stalemate, and the neighborhood was forced to turn to the city for help. For the second time, the Philadelphia police were called to evict the group.

On 13 May 1985, after a five-month standoff, Philadelphia police evacuated residents from an entire city block of Osage Avenue, and closed in on the house at 6221 with a new batch of search and arrest warrants. MOVE members refused to leave, and the police once again placed a MOVE compound under siege. The police and fire department attempted to destroy the wood and steel bunker on the roof of the MOVE house with deluge pumps; after that failed, they fired tear gas at the house, which also failed to extricate the group. Finally, an "incendiary device" composed of "two 1 lb. tubes filled with a water-based gel explosive" was dropped by helicopter onto the roof. A fire was immediately sparked, which the fire department let burn without intervention; according to later testimony from Police Commissioner Gregore Sambor, the intent was to destroy the bunker. The unchecked fire quickly spread, leading to the decimation of the MOVE house along with fifty-six other homes on the block. Eleven people, including John Africa and five children died. One adult, Ramona Africa, and a child known at the time as "Birdie Africa," were the only survivors of the catastrophic raid.

Family members and supporters chanted "Long Live John Africa!" at Africa's burial in Ambler, Pennsylvania, on 5 December 1985, at which the Reverend Jesse Jackson served as a pallbearer.

FURTHER READING

Gruson, Lindsey. "The Philadelphia Siege: Ways of Life in Conflict." Special to the *New York Times*, 28 May 1985.

Pomer, Karen, and Jane Mancini. *MOVE: Confrontation in Philadelphia*. Documentary (1980).

Wagner-Pacifici, Robin Erica. *Discourse and Destruction: The City of Philadelphia versus MOVE* (1994).

CAMILLE A. COLLINS

Africa, Ramona (1955 June 8–), activist and sole adult survivor of a deadly bombing of a home of the MOVE organization, in one of Philadelphia's black neighborhoods, that killed 11 people and left over 250 people homeless. Africa was born Ramona Johnson in West Philadelphia, where she was raised by her mother, Eleanor Jones, and attended Catholic school from first through twelfth grade. She then attended Temple University, where she graduated with a bachelor's degree in Political Science and an associate's degree in Criminal Justice. In 1976, her last year at Temple, she was hired by Community Legal Services, the state-sponsored legal aid in Philadelphia. There she worked helping tenants with legal issues they had with their landlords, an experience that set the foundation for activism later in her life. "Prior to that I was not active in anything," Africa said. "I had a general idea about injustice by police brutality and wrongful imprisonment and racism in the system. I understood injustice in an academic sense. I had never personally experienced any of it so it wasn't very real to me."

After an arrest related to her work on behalf of tenants, she met a member of MOVE, an organization founded in 1972 by Vincent Leapheart, a Philadelphia handyman and Korean War veteran who had changed his name to JOHN AFRICA. Under Leapheart's leadership, the group grew dreadlocked hair, took on the adopted surname "Africa," and made reference to religion and beliefs as "Life." Vehemently back-to-nature, MOVE held protests at "the Zoo, the circus, furriers, Dow, du Pont, and unsafe boarding homes for the elderly." Ramona Africa explained, "[John Africa] gave us one common belief, in the all-importance of life" ("MOVE: An Oral History," *Philadelphia Magazine*, 2010, http://www.phillymag.com).

History would have a different take on the activists. "MOVE members believed in recycling trash outside in their yards, eating raw vegetables, and allowing children to go around naked," in order "to strengthen the immune system of their bodies." Group members would attend public events where government officials were speaking, holding signs freckled with profanity (Burroughs). Their appearance of uncombed and uncut hair was part of their overall philosophy to stay away from "the system's chemicals, cosmetics and disposable conveniences" (MOVE, 71). John Africa's system of beliefs, called "The Guidelines" by members of the family, emphasized a government of self, revolutionary acts, and consumption of raw food. Though almost illiterate, Africa recorded "The Guidelines"—which spanned three hundred pages—with the help of the white University of Pennsylvania graduate student and early MOVE member Donald Glassey.

While explicitly peaceful at its founding, the group's increasingly radical stance led to direct confrontation with police.

The first major incident occurred in 1978, when MOVE members began brandishing rifles and shouting speeches from the porch of their West Philadelphia compound. The group claimed it was protesting the incarceration of MOVE members. A blockade by the city failed to extract them, and in August the police moved in to dissolve the group. In the ensuing firefight, police officer James Ramp was killed. (However, controversy remains to this day over whether or not Ramp was killed by MOVE or by friendly fire.) In 1981 nine members of the organization went to jail in connection with Ramp's death. Three members of MOVE were convicted in connection with the police officer's death and given thirty- to one hundred–year sentences in one of the city's longest and most expensive trials. In December of that year, a close MOVE supporter, MUMIA ABU-JAMAL, was charged with the death of police officer Daniel Faulkner.

Undeterred, remaining group members created an illegal compound in one of Philadelphia's black communities on Osage Avenue. The group continued to protest the imprisonment of what came to be known as the MOVE 9 under the leadership of the city's new mayor, the African American WILSON GOODE. Neighbors complained about their presence and unorthodox lifestyle, and the police issued arrest warrants for four members, including Ramona. Group members refused to leave, however, and on 12 May 1985, police went in to shut down the compound.

The police tried multiple tactics to breach the compound, including water cannons, teargas, and boring into the side of the house, to no avail. The next morning, a ninety-minute gunfire exchange spent close to ten thousand rounds. His patience running out, police chief Gregore Sambor authorized drastic measures. Under his direction, a police helicopter dropped two 1-pound containers of explosive gel onto the roof of the compound, which, officials told reporters, was meant "to knock off a roof top bunker and allow police to pump tear gas and water into the house." The building quickly lit on fire, and in the ensuing blaze eleven members of MOVE were killed, including John Africa and five children. Ramona was the only adult survivor.

After being treated for her injuries, which included severe burns, Ramona was charged with riot and conspiracy, and sent to prison. The imprisoned activist Mumia Abu-Jamal, an intimate associate of MOVE, wrote that she could have been released from prison earlier if she had severed her ties with MOVE, but she refused. Ramona served her entire sentence, and was released in 1992.

In 1996 Ramona, along with relatives of MOVE members killed in the 1985 bombing, sued the city of Philadelphia. She served as her own lawyer and won a civil case against the city for $500,000. Abu-Jamal wrote of the verdict, "Only her naturalist faith, the teachings of John Africa, allowed her to competently defend herself, where she beat the majority of the charges. Ramona is 'free' today." Despite an exhaustive commission that included one thousand interviews and five weeks of televised hearings, no public official was ever charged for their role in the incident.

The *New York Times* excerpted parts of her tearful testimony in federal court in 1996, when she explained how MOVE members had gathered in the row house's garage before the bomb dropped. "The water in the basement was getting hot, real hot. And there was smoke that wasn't tear-gas smoke, it was thick," she said. "At this point, flames were starting to come into the garage area. I heard the gunfire and the ricochets. The last thing I remember was seeing the garage totally engulfed in flames.... It never leaves you. I can't believe they're gone and I can't believe the way they were taken."

As of 2011, Ramona Africa continued to speak on behalf of the release of the MOVE 9 and Mumia Abu-Jamal.

FURTHER READING

Abu-Jamal, Mumia. *All Things Censored* (2000).

Burroughs, Todd. *Encyclopedia of African American History, 1896 to the Present* (2008).

Rosebraugh, Craig, Jalil A. Muntaqim, and Jonathan Paul. *This Country Must Change: Essays on the Necessity of Revolution in the USA* (2009).

Various contributors. *25 Years on the Move* (1996).

JOSHUNDA SANDERS

Africanus, Scipio (fl. 1777–c. 1780), Revolutionary War sailor, is known for his service on the Continental navy sloop *Ranger* under Captain John Paul Jones. A story passing as truth has been written about Scipio Africanus stating that he was a slave owned by Jones and accompanied him on the ships he commanded. In fact virtually nothing is known about Africanus except for the fact that he was a free man when he enlisted to serve on board the eighteen-gun *Ranger* for one year while she was building at Portsmouth, New Hampshire, sometime between March and July 1777.

While we know little about Scipio Africanus the man, some guesses as to his servitude and character may be ventured. That he was a slave prior to his naval service, as suggested by his first name, is likely. Classical Roman names such as Scipio, Cato, and Caesar were commonly given at birth by owners to slaves in New England. The original names of those enslaved from Africa were seldom learned by their white masters, likely because they were considered barbaric. It was much easier to give the newly enslaved their master's surname, and classical Christian names were both easier to pronounce and perhaps even helped to lend an air of dignity to the institution of slavery. Even when slaves gained their freedom, they usually retained their former master's surname. Of interest is Scipio's surname of Africanus. Perhaps it was bestowed upon him by a more enlightened master, in recognition of the Roman leader that conquered Africa. However, this was not the norm for slave owners, and it can be speculated that instead Scipio himself chose this surname upon being freed, possibly in contempt of his former master and surely in proud recognition of his own African heritage.

Despite the images conjured up by the name Scipio Africanus, that of a stately and imposing figure, historians can only speculate as to Africanus's position aboard the *Ranger*. Black sailors serving in the Revolution, including his shipmate CATO CARLISLE and others such as JAMES FORTEN and CAESAR TARRANT, served in a wide variety of shipboard positions. These ranged from the lowly cabin boy, often a slave owned by the ship's captain, to ordinary seaman, able-bodied seaman, and even as marines and pilots. It was a common belief that Africanus was Captain Jones's personal cabin boy. While this is possible there is no evidence to suggest such a position except for the erroneous statement by earlier historians that Scipio Africanus was Jones's slave. It is just as likely that Scipio may instead have served in a more skilled position. Blacks were a common presence in New England's maritime trade well before the war so their service in the navy during the war in a variety of capacities was neither unusual nor controversial. In Massachusetts a number of blacks served on the Continental navy frigate *Boston* in 1777, with Cato Austin operating the number one gun on the larboard watch, and Scipio Brown and Caesar Fairweather serving as ammunition handlers. Even in the southern colonies, where blacks were effectively barred from serving in the army, their service in the Continental and state navies was both frequent and varied in scope.

In order to follow the service of Scipio Africanus during the war, we must follow the career of Captain John Paul Jones and the *Ranger*, as Scipio's specific actions are unknown. The *Ranger* departed Portsmouth, New Hampshire, on her maiden voyage, after many delays in taking on men and material, on 1 November 1777. The sloop of war arrived in France after a voyage of a month, capturing several prizes along the way. The *Ranger* and her crew dallied in French ports until April 1778, during which time Captain Jones expended much effort in trying to gain command of a larger and more prestigious ship. His crew, Scipio Africanus and Cato Carlisle included, were left behind in a rather boring port and were employed in a variety of everyday maintenance chores. By the time Captain Jones came back to his ship, his crew was an unhappy lot. During this time the only highlight was *Ranger*'s encounter with a French naval squadron at Quiberon Bay. Here, for the first time ever, the stars and stripes of America was recognized and saluted by a foreign power, and Scipio Africanus and his fellow crew were there to witness the event.

The *Ranger* and her crew finally sailed to glory, and into the history books, on 10 April 1778 when the ship departed France for the hostile waters off England. In a campaign that made Jones an American hero, and struck terror into the heart of England, the *Ranger* captured several prizes and marauded in the Irish Sea, raiding Whitehaven Harbor and St. Mary's Isle. The crowning achievement came when Jones and his men captured the British twenty-gun sloop of war *Drake* in a battle that lasted an hour. Following these engagements the *Ranger* returned to France, where troubles between Jones and his men came to the fore. Upset with Captain Jones's treatment of one of his officers, as well as their extended service time and a lack of prize money from the ships they captured, seventy-seven crewmembers, styling themselves "Jovial Tars," petitioned the American commissioners in France. Among these petitioners was Scipio Africanus and the ship's other black sailor, Cato Carlisle. Eventually, the dispute was settled, Captain Jones left the ship, and the *Ranger* returned home.

The final fate of Scipio Africanus is unknown. Perhaps he stayed aboard the *Ranger* for future cruises, or maybe he moved on to serve in the lucrative business of privateering. Whatever the case may be, his service in the Continental navy is indicative of the contribution made by black sailors who sailed the high seas during the American Revolution.

FURTHER READING
Knoblock, Glenn A. *"Strong and Brave Fellows"; New Hampshire's Black Soldiers and Sailors of the American Revolution, 1775–1784* (2003).
Morison, Samuel Eliot. *John Paul Jones; A Sailor's Biography* (1959).
Quarles, Benjamin. *The Negro in the American Revolution* (1961).
Sawtelle, Joseph G., ed. *John Paul Jones and the Ranger* (1994).

GLENN ALLEN KNOBLOCK

Agyeman, Jaramogi Abebe (13 June 1911–20 Feb. 2000), clergyman, community activist, denomination organizer, and black nationalist was born Albert Buford Cleage Jr., one of seven children of Pearl (whose maiden name is now unknown) and Albert Cleage Sr., in Indianapolis, Indiana. Shortly after Agyeman's birth, Cleage Sr., a medical doctor, relocated with his family to Detroit, Michigan, where the father helped to establish the city's first African American hospital. After an undergraduate education that included a stay at Fisk University in Tennessee, Agyeman received his B.A. in Sociology from Wayne State University in 1937, serving as a caseworker for the Department of Public Welfare from 1931 to 1938. Subsequently Agyeman felt the call to ministry and obtained a Bachelor of Divinity degree from Oberlin College Graduate School of Theology in 1943. Also in 1943 Agyeman married Doris Graham, to which union was born two children, Kris and the renowned author PEARL CLEAGE. The couple divorced in 1955. He received ordination to the Congregationalist ministry (1943); pastored a Congregationalist church in Lexington, Kentucky (1942–1943); led the Church for the Fellowship of All Peoples in San Francisco, an interracial congregation founded by HOWARD THURMAN (1943–1944); and served another Congregational church in Springfield, Massachusetts (1946–1951), where he was a strong supporter of the NAACP.

In 1951 Agyeman returned to Detroit to pastor the St. Mark's Community (Presbyterian) Church. In 1953 Agyeman and three hundred members seceded from St. Mark's to establish the Central

Congregational Church. Like his father, Agyeman continued his involvement in community and civic activities. He worked closely with MARTIN LUTHER KING JR. on civil rights issues in the city in 1963.

It was the influence of past and present black nationalist and separatist personalities, however, that eventually caused division in Cleage's congregation and prompted the founding of a new denomination. MARCUS GARVEY, the early twentieth-century black leader, and the Nation of Islam leaders MALCOLM X and ELIJAH MUHAMMAD all shared certain ideas. They all believed that the inherently racist political-economic status quo would not afford blacks the opportunity to achieve freedom and empowerment. They also expressed the need to envision God in terms applicable to the struggles of black people and highlighted the pressing necessity for the African American community to be economically self-sufficient. This move toward black nationalism prompted opponents in the Central Congregational Church to ask for the intervention of the denomination (United Church of Christ) to deny funding to the local church should Agyeman not conform his teachings to those of the larger group. Agyeman, however, rebuffed attempts by the denomination to discuss his black nationalism and its theological legitimacy. He raised the principle of congregational autonomy and suggested that the denomination itself was leveling the charges under the guise of anonymous complaints. The dissidents withdrew from Central, according de facto victory to Agyeman and his supporters.

By 1967 Agyeman's black Christian nationalist theology had achieved systematic form. During the Easter season the pastor placed an eighteen-foot Black Madonna and Child portrait in the sanctuary. Initiating the Black Christian Nationalist Movement, in 1967 Agyeman renamed the church the Shrine of the Black Madonna, and in the early 1970s he formed the Pan African Orthodox Christian Church (PAOCC) denomination. Also, the leader dropped the name Albert Buford Cleage Jr. in favor of Jaramogi Abebe Agyeman, which can be translated as "Liberator, Blessed Man, Savior of the Nation." The PAOCC was intended to be an overarching organization, including African American fellowships from various denominations united around the theme of black liberation. Agyeman's Black Christian Nationalism taught that Jesus was of African lineage and had descended from one of ancient Israel's darker tribes. Therefore, Jesus was the Black Messiah who led nonwhite Israelites in revolt against white Roman oppressors. Agyeman counseled that the power structure must be directly challenged by people who will not place their own individual desires over the well-being of the Black Nation and instead commit themselves to freeing black people throughout the world.

Agyeman shared with the major academic exponent of black theology, JAMES H. CONE, the basic understanding that a genuine embrace of Christianity required that people understand the indispensable necessity of standing in solidarity with the struggles of black people. Agyeman put forth his theology in two major books: *The Black Messiah* (1968) and *Black Christian Nationalism* (1972). Agyeman and his fellowship sponsored community-oriented programs, established a supermarket, and fostered other activities supporting black economic independence. In the political sphere they were instrumental in the use of the Black Slate to encourage black voting. They also assisted candidates in local and congressional races and helped to elect Detroit's first black mayor, COLEMAN YOUNG, and two members of the U.S. Congress.

The 1980s saw the decline of nationalist sentiment, religious or otherwise, in the African American community, adversely affecting membership in the PAOCC movement. Nonetheless, as of 2000 the PAOCC still had participating congregations in several cities, including Houston and Atlanta. Yet the influence of Agyeman and the Black Christian Movement extended beyond church membership. His teachings on the ethnic and political identities of ancient Israel influenced numerous scholars to ask piercing sociological questions regarding early Judaism and Christianity. Agyeman also stressed how important it is for theology and biblical studies to forthrightly address the concerns of blacks and others facing sociopolitical oppression.

Agyeman died in Calhoun Falls, South Carolina, in 2000.

FURTHER READING
Aaseng, Nathan. *African-American Religious Leaders* (2003).

McMickle, Marvin A. *An Encyclopedia of African American Christian Heritage* (2002).

Murphy, Larry G., J. Gordon Melton, and Gary L. Ward. *Encyclopedia of African American Religions* (1993).

Obituary: *New York Times*, 27 Feb. 2000.

SANDY DWAYNE MARTIN

Ailey, Alvin (5 Jan. 1931–1 Dec. 1989), actor, dancer, and choreographer, was born in Rogers, Texas, the son of Alvin Ailey, a laborer, and Lula Elizabeth Cliff, a cotton picker and domestic. Before Ailey was a year old, his father abandoned the family, leaving them homeless for close to six years. During that time Ailey and his mother made their way, often by foot, across the unforgiving terrain of the impoverished and bitterly racist Brazos Valley in southeastern Texas to seek shelter with relatives and find work in nearby fields. A bright, curious child, Ailey joined his mother in the cotton fields as soon as he could carry a sack. He reveled in the sights and sounds of the gospel

Alvin Ailey. In 1958, Ailey founded the Alvin Ailey American Dance Theatre in New York City. Ailey choreographed an important body of work, including such signature pieces as *Revelations* and *Blues Suite,* that celebrated black worship and music and other African American themes in dance. (New York Public Library.)

choirs and worshipers that he witnessed in the black Baptist churches of his youth. Ailey also became acquainted with the less pious side of life through those who spent Saturday nights dancing, drinking, and fighting in roadside bars and dance halls where blues musicians played over the constant drone of passing trains. Ailey had a photographic memory that allowed him to recall the body language of the people he saw in both bars and churches, memories he later drew on in his work.

In 1937 Ailey and his mother moved to Navasota, Texas, where they lived with Amos Alexander, a local black businessman. Alexander treated Ailey as a son and provided him with the only secure family environment he would experience. Ailey relished the stability of living in one place, eating regularly, going to the same school, and worshiping at the True Vine Baptist Church, but he developed a deep sense of obligation to Alexander and felt inferior to Alexander's own children. Ailey's 1961 autobiography, *Knoxville: Summer 1915*, is a moving account of his life in Navasota.

In 1942 Ailey's life changed dramatically. His mother moved to Los Angeles, determined to get one of the thousands of jobs being created by West Coast aircraft factories gearing up to handle the demands of World War II. Before his mother was hired as a night-shift worker for Lockheed, she and Ailey lived in a white section of the city, where she worked as a domestic and he attended a previously all-white school. Ailey's status as the only black student in the school reinforced his feelings of insecurity and inferiority. His love for dance was sparked by a class field trip to see Sergei Denham's Ballet Russe de Monte Carlo in 1943. Ailey had seen vaudeville shows, revues, and theater productions, but after seeing the Ballet Russe he attended as many dance events as he could. Among them was a presentation of the KATHERINE DUNHAM company. Dunham's spectacular productions of African and Caribbean dance styles had a tremendous influence on Ailey's concept of dance, theatricality, and the unique expressionism of ethnic dance.

In 1971, in his virtuoso solo *Cry*, Ailey immortalized his reaction to attending a white school and watching his mother scrubbing floors and hanging out laundry for white families. This piece, the first significant work created by Ailey for JUDITH JAMISON, was Ailey's tribute to his mother and "all black women—especially our mothers." Ailey always paid homage to his cultural heritage, and he created works based on experiences from different moments of his life. Of the seventy-nine works he created during his lifetime, his least successful dealt with subjects not drawn from his own experiences.

After moving to a racially mixed section of Los Angeles, Ailey attended Jefferson High School, which drew students of black and Hispanic heritage. He excelled in foreign language studies and distinguished himself as a gymnast. Intent on becoming a foreign language teacher, he entered the University of California, Los Angeles, in 1948 as a foreign language major.

By that time, however, he had started formal dance training under Lester Horton at the urging of his high school friend CARMEN DE LAVALLADE. A white man, Horton had founded the first multiracial dance company in America and developed his own modern dance technique. The breadth of movement and expression supported by the Horton technique appealed to Ailey. He also was intrigued by Horton's ability to fuse elements of theater and stagecraft in his works.

Ailey made his professional debut in Horton's company in 1950. He continued working toward his college degree until he decided to join Horton as a full-time dancer and teacher of the Horton technique. Late that year Horton died. With support from de Lavallade and the veteran Horton dancers James Truitte and Joyce Trisler, Ailey took over the artistic reins of the company, ran the school, and began to choreograph.

Ailey and de Lavallade were cast in the 1955 Twentieth Century Fox motion picture *Carmen Jones*, directed by Herbert Ross. After filming was completed in 1954, Ross paired them in the Broadway-bound Truman Capote show *House of Flowers*. Their Broadway debut catapulted Ailey and de Lavallade into the limelight, but they continued to appear with Horton's company. Until 1960, Ailey remained an integral part of the effort to keep the company alive.

Living in New York City, Ailey studied dance with, among others, Martha Graham, Doris Humphrey, Donald McKayle, Karel Shook, and Charles Weidman. He also studied acting under Stella Adler. As a dancer Ailey moved with the power and grace of a lion. His physical strength, riveting presence, and ability to make movement appear to spring from within rather than as a result of the choreography set him apart from his peers. His total immersion in the roles he performed defined his approach to choreography and attracted gifted dancers to his productions.

Ailey's success on Broadway as a dancer and actor garnered him numerous theater awards and a secure future in musicals and theater. During this period, in addition to *House of Flowers*, Ailey appeared in *The Carefree Tree* (1955), HARRY BELAFONTE's 1956 production of *Sing, Man, Sing*, and LENA HORNE's 1957 *Jamaica*, the latter choreographed by Jack Cole. In 1958 Ailey drew on his memories of Saturday nights at the roadside bars to create the dance *Blues Suite*, which captured the parade of emotions experienced by people unable to escape the drudgery of hapless lives. Two years later he brought the charismatic Baptist preachers, fire and-brimstone sermons, and gospel spirituals of his church to life in his signature masterpiece, *Revelations*. Noted for its spontaneity, *Revelations* has proven its universal appeal to audiences around the world. As a result, it remains the cornerstone of his company's outstanding repertoire. Ailey also appeared off-Broadway as an actor in *Call Me by My Rightful Name*, with Robert Duvall and Joan Hackett, and *Two by Saroyan*, and he made his Broadway debut in an acting role as CLAUDIA McNEIL's son in the 1962 production of *Tiger, Tiger, Burning Bright*.

Throughout his Broadway career Ailey never lost sight of his goal to establish a multiracial dance company with a repertoire representing the past and future of American modern dance and the unique qualities of black cultural expression. Ailey used the fees he earned on Broadway to fund his own company and recruited several Broadway dancers to join the Horton dancers he was assembling to create a concert group.

In 1958 Ailey presented the Alvin Ailey American Dance Theater in concert at New York City's Ninety-Second Street YM-YWHA. Public and critical response was excellent and inspired Ailey and his dancers to continue building the company. To keep his dancers together, Ailey provided food and shelter when they were unable to find work between concert engagements. He also ran the company by himself, getting bookings, taking care of production details, promoting the troupe, and handling the company finances out of a shoebox. As financially strapped as the company was, Ailey refused to limit the company and its audiences to an all-Ailey repertoire. He often crossed the color line to empower those who shared his dream of establishing a dance company without racial limitations.

In 1960 the premiere of Ailey's *Revelations* created a sensation in the dance world, and the company's future began to take shape. That year Robert Joffrey commissioned Ailey to create a work for his ballet company, which brought Ailey in touch with the Joffrey company's backer, Rebekah Harkness. Harkness established a nonprofit foundation to sponsor broadly diverse projects within the field and cooperated with the U.S. Department of State Cultural Exchange Program to generate international recognition of American cultural achievements. The success of Ailey's *Feast of Ashes*, inspired by Federico García Lorca's *The House of Bernarda Alba* and set to an original Carlos Surinach score, put him in good stead with Harkness. Impressed by Ailey's fusion of dance styles and aware of the financial gridlock his company was in, Harkness allocated foundation funds to send Ailey's company on its first foreign tour.

In 1963 Harkness established the Harkness Ballet under the artistic direction of George Skibine. Ailey was invited to restage *Feast of Ashes*, which remained the property of the new company, and he was commissioned to create a new work for the company's inaugural season. As usual, Ailey applied the fees he earned to his own company. Although Harkness's wealth reinforced Ailey's personal insecurities, his commitment to his own company enabled him to accept her largesse.

Ailey's company ran out of money during its appearance at the First World Festival of Negro Arts in Dakar, Senegal, in 1966. Ailey managed to get his dancers to Barcelona, Spain, where his *Macumba*, set to Harkness music, was scheduled to premiere. Within a few hours of their arrival in Barcelona, Ailey had arranged for his dancers to be absorbed into the Harkness Ballet for the remainder of its European tour.

Although several of Ailey's dancers immediately found jobs with other companies, several joined the Harkness company for its summer workshop in Rhode Island. Jamison and Morton "Tubby" Winston stayed on for its subsequent American tour, but only Winston remained with the ballet company after Ailey's company resumed operation following a brief period of reorganization.

Ailey's relationship with Harkness remained strong, and his company continued to receive support from her foundation. Ailey always credited her for giving his company the opportunity to survive long enough to gain an international following in the world of dance.

With the exception of its brief period of reorganization, the Alvin Ailey American Dance Theater continued to build audiences around the world and offer more performances a year than any other American dance company. According to Jamison, whom Ailey named his successor before his death,

the company covered most of its budget from almost year-round touring engagements in the United States and abroad.

Despite Ailey's achievements and enormous contributions to the world of dance, he remained unable to put aside his insecurities and accept his success. As a result, he felt undeserving of the many honors and awards that he received during his lifetime. His most significant awards included a Dance Magazine Award in 1975, the Spingarn Medal of the National Association for the Advancement of Colored People in 1976, the Capezio Award in 1979, the United Nations Peace Medal in 1982, the Samuel H. Scripps American Dance Festival Award in 1987, and a Kennedy Center award in 1988. The anxiety he felt over accepting awards often triggered long spells of depression and self-destructive behavior.

In 1980 Ailey was diagnosed as a severe manic-depressive during his hospitalization after he created a public disturbance. Although he continued to create significant new works for his company and others, Ailey began turning over his responsibilities for running the main company, its affiliated school, and a student repertory ensemble to others. However, he remained involved with developing an interactive, multidisciplinary summer workshop for inner-city children with interests in the arts.

Ailey, who never married, died in New York's Lenox Hill Hospital surrounded by his mother; Jamison; SYLVIA WATERS, director of the Alvin Ailey Repertory Ensemble; and Masazumi Chaya, assistant artistic director of the Alvin Ailey American Dance Theater.

FURTHER READING

Ailey's archive is housed at the Alvin Ailey American Dance Center in New York City.

Ailey, Alvin, with Peter Bailey. *Revelations* (1995).

Jamison, Judith, with Howard Kaplan. *Dancing Spirit* (1993).

West, Cynthia S'thembile. "Alvin Ailey: Signposts of an American Visionary." *African American Genius in Modern Dance* (1993).

Obituaries: *New York Times*, 2 Dec. 1989; *Dance Magazine*, Feb. 1990.

This entry is taken from the *American National Biography* and is published here with the permission of the American Council of Learned Societies.

LILI COCKERILLE LIVINGSTON

Al-Amin, Jamil Abdullah. *See* Brown, H. Rap.

Albert, Octavia Victoria Rogers (24 Dec. 1853–1890?), author and activist, was born in Oglethorpe, Georgia, the daughter of slaves. Details of her life are sketchy. Little is known of her parents or her childhood beyond the date and place of her birth and the fact that she was born into bondage; thus, it is particularly intriguing that in 1870, only five years after the Thirteenth Amendment abolished slavery and one year after Atlanta University opened, seventeen-year-old Octavia was among the 170 students enrolled at that institution. Most of the little we know of her life comes from *The House of Bondage* (1890), the book that made her famous. From that source we learn that in 1873 she was teaching in Montezuma, Georgia, when she met her fellow teacher A. E. P. Albert. They married in 1874 and had one daughter. Sometime around 1877 Albert's husband was ordained as a Methodist Episcopal minister, and the family moved to Houma, Louisiana, and later to New Orleans. It is not clear whether Octavia Albert ever worked professionally again. Most likely she did not, as it was rare for school systems, especially in the South, to employ married women, and because her husband quickly assumed a social prominence that would have discouraged her from being a wage earner.

Albert became a religious and political leader, held a degree in theology, was a trustee of New Orleans University, and served as editor of the *South-Western Christian Advocate*. As befitted her social position, Octavia Albert vacationed with her family at resorts such as the Bay St. Louis in Mississippi, attended lectures and receptions, and generally participated in the religious reform efforts deemed proper for a minister's wife. However, it is clear that she was not content with these activities, but she made her home a center of activity where people of all classes and conditions were welcome to study the Bible, learn to read and write, and discuss current events.

It was from just such community involvement that the idea was born for *The House of Bondage*. Albert's sympathies and interests had been increased by the frequent conversations she had with elderly former slaves, including Charlotte Brooks, who discussed with Albert her slavery experiences in Virginia and Louisiana. Albert announced that she intended to write Charlotte Brooks's story in—as closely as possible—Brooks's own words. Years later Albert stated, "My interest in, and conversations with, Aunt Charlotte, Aunt Sallie, Uncle John Goodwin, Uncle Stephen, and the other characters represented in this story led me to interview many other people [who gave] me additional facts and incidents about the colored people, in freedom as well as in slavery" (Albert, 120).

The full title of Albert's book reveals the grandness of her project: *The House of Bondage; or, Charlotte Brooks and Other Slaves: Original and Life-Like, as They Appeared in Their Old Plantation and City Slave Life; Together with Pen-Pictures of the Peculiar Institution, with Sights and Insights into Their New Relations as Freedmen, Freemen, and Citizens*. Some months after her death, Albert's *House of Bondage* was serialized in the *South-Western Christian Advocate*; it proved so popular that "letters poured in upon the editor from all directions, urging him to put it in book form" (Albert, v). The volume was published posthumously in 1890. The scope of Albert's project, covering rural and urban slavery and using oral testimonies, distinguishes her work from other studies of the period. In the 1880s slavery had once more become a popular topic for many writers, but most were of the so-called Plantation School, which considered the South a place of chivalry and slavery a benevolent, paternalistic institution. At the same time, many contemporary publications and politicians justified racial discrimination and increased violence against African Americans on the grounds that former slaves harbored deep hostility and plans for revenge and were without morals, self-discipline, or ambition. Declaring that "none but those who resided in the South during the time of slavery" (Albert, 1) could testify accurately to its horror, Albert set out to set the record straight by publishing interviews with former slaves, by describing their condition after slavery, and by celebrating the achievements they and their descendants had won despite great and increasing odds.

According to the historian John Blassingame, Albert was one of only a handful of experienced interviewers in the country and also "one of the most interesting" (Blassingame, lxi) in the country. Fascinating stories of slave life unfold in the dialogue between Albert and the interviewers. The major narrative is that of Charlotte Brooks; the half-dozen other extended accounts and the multitude of incidents in the lives of others they knew or had heard about serve primarily to supplement or emphasize the material that Brooks provides. Albert uses poetry, songs, speeches, and other material for documentation, for context, and for texture. Although she intended her work to combat negative stereotypes, Albert also emphasized another goal. It was vital, she argued, that the story of those who survived slavery and those who overcame racial oppression be treasured and transmitted to "our children's children," not only to set the record straight but to inspire African Americans. Her book posits "education, property, and character" as the "trinity of power" by which African Americans could gain their rightful places in society (Albert, 127).

FURTHER READING
Foster, Frances Smith. "Introduction to Octavia V. Rogers Albert," in *The House of Bondage* (1988).
Blassingame, John, ed. *Slave Testimony: Two Centuries of Letters, Speeches, Interviews, and Autobiographies* (1977).
Majors, Monroe. *Noted Negro Women* (1893).
This entry is taken from the *American National Biography* and is published here with the permission of the American Council of Learned Societies.

FRANCES SMITH FOSTER

Albrier, Frances Mary (21 Sept. 1898–21 Aug. 1987), civil rights activist and community leader, was born in Mount Vernon, New York, the daughter of Lewis Redgrey, a supervisor in a factory, and Laura (maiden name unknown), a cook. Following the death of their mother when Frances was three, Frances and her baby sister were reared by their paternal grandparents, Lewis Redgrey, a Blackfoot Indian, and Johanna Bowen, a freed slave, on their fifty-five-acre farm in Tuskegee, Alabama.

Frances attended Tuskegee Institute, where she studied botany under GEORGE WASHINGTON CARVER, who also advised her grandfather on productive farming techniques. In 1917 she enrolled at Howard University in Washington, D.C., studying nursing and social work. In 1920, following the death of her grandmother, Frances left college and moved to Berkeley, California, to join her father and stepmother. Two years later she married William Albert Jackson. They had three children. Jackson died in 1930, and in 1934 Frances married Willie Antoine Albrier, a Pullman Company club-car porter.

Because of precepts laid down by her grandmother and her teachers, Albrier was strongly motivated to improve the condition of black Americans. Imbued with the beliefs that education was essential in opening doors for African Americans and that those fortunate enough to become educated "owed something to the race," she made education a focus of all her activities. According to an oral history conducted in the 1970s, Albrier was admonished by her grandmother that "bitterness will kill you"

and that she had to "fight and earn what you got … earn respect." From this Albrier "developed a sense of retaliation and fighting through the system."

Albrier's social action began during the 1920s, when she joined MARCUS GARVEY's Universal Negro Improvement Association, serving with the association's Black Cross Nurses and as vice president of its women's auxiliary. From 1926 to 1931 she worked as a maid and manicurist on the Pullman Company's Sunset Limited, supporting A. PHILIP RANDOLPH's efforts to organize the Brotherhood of Sleeping Car Porters. During the 1930s and 1940s, as a member and then as president of the American Federation of Labor's Women's Auxiliary of the Dining Car Cooks and Waiters, Albrier worked actively to bring black men and women into the discriminatory mainstream labor unions.

In 1940, as president of the Citizens Employment Council, Albrier led a successful "Don't Buy Where You Can't Work" movement, and in 1955, as secretary of a church-sponsored employment committee, she pushed again for black employment. From 1938 to 1943 she lobbied to hire black teachers in the Berkeley school system, first organizing the East Bay Women's Welfare Club to do research and outreach and then running for the Berkeley city council in 1939 to publicize the color barriers in the schools and local government. In 1943 Berkeley hired its first black teacher.

During the 1930s and 1940s Albrier assisted the East Bay Women's Welfare Club, the Association of Colored Women's Clubs, and the National Association for the Advancement of Colored People (NAACP) in their eventually successful effort to admit black women into the county hospitals' nurses training program and to permit them to live in dormitories. Albrier's friendship with MARY CHURCH TERRELL and MARY McLEOD BETHUNE, both of whom taught her the value of black women's clubs, led Albrier to organize many such clubs, educating women on social and political issues and motivating them to community action.

During World War II Albrier broke other barriers. She was a pioneer in the Red Cross, qualified to drive in the motor corps and teach first aid classes. In 1942 she became the first black woman welder allowed to work in the Richmond Kaiser shipyards without a union card. African Americans were not allowed to become members of AFL unions, and because no separate black auxiliary existed in the Kaiser yards, Albrier complained directly to the manager, who permitted her to work without a union card. After an executive order was issued barring discrimination in union membership, a segregated auxiliary was organized, and in 1943 she joined the union. Suspecting that black postal employees suffered discrimination in work assignments, promotions, and general employee relations, Albrier left the shipyards in 1943 and went to work in the San Francisco post office. Shortly thereafter she organized the Postal Service Workers Club to deal with grievances related to discrimination.

Albrier saw Democratic Party politics as another way to fight for black rights. In 1938 she was the first woman elected to the Alameda County Democratic Central Committee, a position she held until 1962. She served as delegate to state party conventions and was a member of several local Democratic Party clubs, several of which she organized. She campaigned for state and national candidates, for fair employment and housing legislation, and for the election of black men and women to public office. An African American pharmacist from Berkeley, Byron Rumford, was elected to the California assembly in 1948, and in the 1960s blacks finally won seats on the Berkeley city council and school board.

Albrier's trip to Nigeria in 1960 to attend Nigerian independence ceremonies as a representative of the National Council of Negro Women was the crowning event of her life, symbolizing her commitment to the advancement of blacks worldwide. In line with her dedication to acknowledging black achievements, in 1958 and 1965 Albrier arranged the first window displays commemorating National Negro History Week in major downtown Oakland and San Francisco department stores. During the 1960s she spoke to schoolchildren on black history, and in 1968 she was president of the East Bay Negro Historical Society.

In the 1970s Albrier turned her attention to the elderly, taking a leading role in the development of Berkeley senior centers, speaking at seminars on aging, and serving as a delegate to the 1971 White House Conference on Aging. In 1967 the mayor of Berkeley appointed her to the seven-member Committee on Aging, and in 1972 she was named to the Herrick Hospital board of trustees, in each case becoming the first black appointee. In 1986 Albrier served as president of the Northern California Caucus on Black Aging.

From 1954 to 1978 Albrier received honors almost annually for her extraordinary community service, among them the NAACP West Coast Region "Fight for Freedom" Award (1954), the Woman of the Year Award (1966), the *Sun Reporter* Citizen of Merit Award (1967), a California assembly rules committee commendation for battling racial discrimination (1971), the California Congress of Parents and Teachers Honorary Service Award (1971), the National Congress of Negro Women's "Outstanding Woman of Northern California" Award (1973), the City of Berkeley Community Service Award (1976), and the Greyhound Corporation's "Woman of Tomorrow" Award (1978).

Albrier died in Berkeley, California. A soft-spoken but determined leader, she pioneered the cause of civil rights and participated actively in countless organizations aimed at encouraging African Americans to develop a sense of their own worth.

FURTHER READING
Albrier's papers are in the Bancroft Library, University of California, Berkeley.

Chall, Malca. "Determined Advocate for Racial Equality," in *The Black Women Oral History Project*, ed. Ruth Edmonds Hill, vol. 1 (1991).

Hill, Ruth Edmonds, and Judith Sedwick. *Women of Courage* (1984).

Painter, Charlotte, and Pamela Valoi. *Gifts of Age* (1985).

Obituaries: *San Francisco Chronicle* and *Daily Californian*, 28 Aug. 1987.

This entry is taken from the *American National Biography* and is published here with the permission of the American Council of Learned Societies.

MALCA CHALL

Albright, George Washington (1846–?), slave and state legislator, was born to unknown slave parents near Holly Springs in Marshall County, Mississippi, just south of that state's border with Tennessee. His parents were owned by different masters, and in 1857, when George was eleven, his father was sold and forced to move to Texas.

Later, when he was in his nineties, Albright recalled that he had learned to read and write as a child even though the state of Mississippi prohibited slaves from doing so. Historians have estimated that despite legal restrictions at least 5 percent of all slaves were literate on the eve of the Civil War, though literacy rates were probably lowest in rural, Black Belt communities like Holly Springs. In Albright's recollection, a state law required that any slave who broke this law be punished "with 500 lashes on the naked back, and [have his or her] thumb cut off above the second joint" (Rawick, 10). This somewhat exaggerated the actual statutory punishment, which as of 1856 required that slaves and free blacks who gathered in groups of five or more for the purpose of learning to read and write be given thirty-nine lashes. Because the state authorities did not monitor the punishment practices of individual owners, however, the number of lashes laid on—and any additional penalties, such as the severing of fingers—remained at the owner's discretion. Albright nonetheless learned to read and write, because his mother worked in the kitchen of her owner's house, where she listened as the white children of the plantation received their instruction; she in turn taught her own son, who later acquired a primer.

Albright recalled, however, that slave communication was greatly enhanced by what he called the "grapevine telegraph," through which slaves systematically conveyed news and information throughout the plantations. Despite the best efforts of planters to keep their slaves ignorant of the outside world, Albright and others learned, for instance, of John Brown's attack at Harpers Ferry and of the coming of the Civil War. Indeed, early in the war Albright's father ran away from his Texas plantation to join the Union forces but was killed at Vicksburg, Mississippi. At age fifteen, or perhaps a short while afterward, Albright himself joined "the fight for rights of my people," serving as runner for Lincoln's Legal Loyal League. The "4 Ls," as it was known, was a grassroots resistance movement that passed on information about the course of the war and President Lincoln's Emancipation Proclamation. Albright memorized various signals and passwords to ensure secrecy for the small gatherings in slave cabins that he addressed. Such acts of clandestine resistance worked to embolden slaves in Mississippi and elsewhere, who also learned how to assist the advancing Union army.

Active in this resistance network though he remained a slave, Albright continued his efforts to read and write. At nights he secretly read a copy of Harriet Beecher Stowe's *Uncle Tom's Cabin* that had been given to him by a white Northerner. After the war, in 1865, Albright attended a school founded in Marshall County by white Northerners, married one of his white teachers (whose name is not recorded), and trained to be a teacher himself. Albright's wartime resistance work and his literacy perhaps inevitably drew him into Reconstruction politics. In 1868 he worked to elect black delegates to Mississippi's constitutional convention, which established equal civil rights for both races and voting rights for black men, and in which an alliance of poor whites, blacks, and Republicans helped establish Mississippi's first system of publicly financed schooling for children of all races. Albright was among the state's first public school teachers for blacks. He taught at first under a shade tree, later in an old cabin, and finally in a church.

In 1873 Albright was elected to the Mississippi legislature on the Republican Party ticket headed by Adelbert Ames, a New England–born radical who became governor, and ALEXANDER K. DAVIS, a black lawyer who became lieutenant governor. The elections marked the high point of Reconstruction and black electoral power in Mississippi. Albright was, along with CHARLES CALDWELL, one of nine African Americans in the thirty-seven-member state senate, while fifty-five of the one hundred fifteen members of the House of Representatives were also black. The elections also marked the high point of biracial political activism in the entire South for more than a century. Unlike counties in the Yazoo-Mississippi Delta, where blacks outnumbered whites by ten to one or more, Marshall County had only a slim black majority, which meant that Albright needed to secure the votes of a significant minority of whites. It was this radical combination of blacks and poor whites working for the common good, Albright believed, that so incensed the state's rich white planters. "No wonder the rich folks hate the memory of those legislatures to this very day," Albright remarked in 1937 (Rawick, 13).

The legislative achievements of Albright and his fellow black Republicans were significant. The Republicans enacted a state civil rights law, modeled on the 1875 federal law, that gave all of Mississippi's citizens equal rights before the law. They also expanded educational opportunities for both races, but especially for the black majority, for whom there had been no previous state provision of education. Most scholars now agree with Albright's assessment that the 1874–1875 legislature was fiscally responsible. In the view of one historian, Albright and his fellow Republicans gave Mississippi "a government of greatly expanded functions at a cost that was low in comparison with that of almost any other state" (Vernon Lane Wharton, *The Negro in Mississippi, 1865–1890* [1947], 180). Prominent whites like John W. C. Watson, a Marshall County planter and former Whig, viewed the matter differently. Watson considered the Republican legislature corrupt and its black members unfit for public office. He described Albright as "very ignorant and wholly without qualifications" (*Mississippi in 1875*, 1003).

In 1875 a self-styled "taxpayers movement" formed throughout the state. Taking their cue from Watson and other so-called moderates, white Mississippians launched a campaign of violence and intimidation that left more than one hundred African Americans dead. In response Governor Ames attempted to establish and arm a biracial state militia to protect against marauding gangs of whites, and he appointed Albright to organize a militia in Marshall County. Though Ames called out these militias on only one occasion, the mere spectacle of armed blacks incensed white Mississippians. Albright recalled that his company "drilled frequently—and how the rich folks hated to see us, armed and ready to defend ourselves and our elected government!" (Rawick, 18). For his uncompromising attitude Albright was targeted by the Ku Klux Klan, who planned to kill him. He narrowly escaped with his life. Albright's colleague Charles Caldwell was not so lucky; he was executed by white vigilantes on Christmas Eve 1875, a few weeks after being reelected to the state senate.

Albright was also reelected to the senate, where he served until 1879. By then both houses of the legislature had been "redeemed" by conservative Democrats, who worked diligently to reassert white supremacy and curb black political power. That counterrevolution was cemented in Mississippi's constitution of 1890 that disfranchised all but a handful of blacks, as well as-many illiterate poor whites. It is not known if Albright was still resident in his home state at that time. Like many former Reconstruction legislators he disappeared—or was forced to disappear—from public life. He eventually settled in Colorado, and he was last heard of in June 1937 when he was profiled in the *Daily Worker*, a Communist Party newspaper. In that article Albright recalled his childhood and Reconstruction, and he made clear his continuing militancy and passionate support for a biracial coalition of workers. He announced that he—like many blacks at that time—had abandoned the Republican Party because it had "turned against the common fellow" and was no longer the party of Ames and Lincoln (Rawick, 9). He now supported the Communist Party and commended its nomination of JAMES W. FORD as a vice presidential candidate. Following that interview Albright once again disappeared from the historical record.

FURTHER READING
Albright's narrative appears in George P. Rawick, ed., *The American Slave: A Composite Autobiography*,

supplement, series 1, vol. 6, *Mississippi Narratives, Part 1* (1977), pp. 8–18. For information on Reconstruction in Marshall County, see *Mississippi in 1875: Report of the Select Committee to Inquire into the Mississippi Election of 1875* (1876).
Harris, William C. *The Day of the Carpetbagger: Republican Reconstruction in Mississippi* (1979).
                                   STEVEN J. NIVEN

Alcorn, George Edward, Jr. (22 Mar. 1940–), physicist, inventor, and educator, was born in Indianapolis, Indiana, the eldest of two sons of Arletta (Dixon) Alcorn and George Alcorn, an auto mechanic. Little is known of his early life. George Alcorn Jr. earned a B.A. in Physics in 1962 from Occidental College in Pasadena, California, where he excelled both academically and athletically, earning eight letters in football and baseball. His educational pursuits took him next to Howard University, where he received a master's degree in Nuclear Physics after only nine months of study. During the summers of 1962 and 1963 Alcorn worked as a research engineer at the space division of North American Rockwell, where he computed trajectories and orbital mechanics for missiles, including the Titan I and II, the Saturn IV, and the Nova.

From 1965 to 1967 Alcorn researched negative ion formation with funded support from the National Aeronautics and Space Administration (NASA). Alcorn furthered his higher education at Howard University, earning his Ph.D. in Molecular and Atomic Physics in 1967. He began working in the private sector soon after and by 1969 had married Maria DaVillier, with whom he had a son in 1979. His work in private industry sent him first to a position as a senior physicist at Philco-Ford and then to a position at PerkinElmer. Next Alcorn moved to IBM, where he worked as both an advisory engineer and an inventor. Meanwhile in 1973 Alcorn had begun teaching electrical engineering at Howard University, where he held teaching positions for several years, eventually rising to the rank of full professor. He held the same title at the University of the District of Columbia, again teaching electrical engineering.

In 1978 Alcorn's career path led him back to NASA. During his tenure there he invented the X-ray spectrometer. One of the best-known of his twenty inventions, this instrument is used to detect life on other planets and is said to have revolutionized radiology. The invention earned Alcorn the 1984 NASA–Goddard Space Flight Center (GSFC) award for inventor of the year. That same year Alcorn also received recognition from NASA's equal employment opportunity office both for recruiting minority women scientists and engineers and for helping minority businesses develop research programs. Although Alcorn's inventions may not be easily understandable or recognizable by the general public, his highly complex and extremely valuable technical contributions include:

- Method of fabricating an imaging x-ray spectrometer-GaAs Schottky barrier photo-responsive device and method of fabrication
- Dense dry-etched multilevel metallurgy with nonover-lapped vias
- Method for forming dense dry-etched multilevel metal-lurgy with nonoverlapped vias
- Hardened photoresist master image mask process

Among Alcorn's groundbreaking inventions is the fabrication of plasma semiconductor devices. The Institute of Electrical and Electronics Engineers called Alcorn's patent for the "Process for Controlling the Slope of a Via Hole" an important contribution to plasma etching, one that is now widely used by semiconductor manufacturing companies.

One of Alcorn's inventions while at NASA's GSFC brought him recognition in 1999 from *Government Executive* magazine. The magazine honored Alcorn with the Government Technology Award for developing the Airborne LIDAR Topographic Mapping System (ALTMS) in partnership with the Houston Advanced Research Center. The award was given to twenty-one programs out of the more than one hundred nominated, and only one other NASA facility received the honor that year. The ALTMS helps produce accurate elevation data and is used in such practical applications as floodplain mapping, highway design simulation, shoreline and erosion mapping, habitat assessments, and pipeline and utility surveys. Alcorn held numerous positions at NASA, including deputy project manager for advanced development, in which position he was in charge of developing new technologies for the space station Freedom; manager of advanced programs at NASA/GSFC from 1990 to 1992; and chief of Goddard's Office of Commercial Programs, which oversaw technology transfer, small business innovation research, and commercial use of space programs, from 1992 to 2005.

Alcorn's community service activities proved as wide ranging as his professional ones. A lifelong educator, Alcorn founded the Saturday Academy, a weekend honors program aimed at supplementing the science and math education of inner-city students. Howard University distinguished Alcorn in 1994 as a black achiever in science and technology at its Heritage of Greatness awards ceremony. Alcorn also worked with the Meyerhoff Foundation at the University of Maryland–Baltimore County (UMBC). Founded in 1988 by the UMBC president Freeman Hrabowski, the program encourages minorities to seek doctorates in science and engineering. In 2001 Congresswoman Donna M. Christian-Christensen recognized Alcorn for helping companies in the Virgin Islands apply NASA and other technological advances to their businesses. In 2005 Alcorn became assistant director of standards and excellence at the Applied Engineering and Technology Directorate.

FURTHER READING

Krapp, Kristine M. *Notable Black American Scientists* (1999).

"Physicists of the African Diaspora: George Edward Alcorn," accessible online at http://www.math. buffalo.edu/mad/physics/alcorn_georgeE.html.

PAMELA BLACKMON

Aldridge, Ira (24 July 1807–10 Aug. 1867), actor, was born Ira Frederick Aldridge, the son of Daniel Aldridge, a minister, and Lurona (maiden name unknown). Although certain historical accounts record that Aldridge was born in Senegal, Africa, and was the grandson of the Fulah tribal chieftain, modern biographical scholarship has established that he was born in New York City. It is possible that he could claim Fulah ancestry, but his lineal descent from tribal royalty is unconfirmed. Extant evidence concerning Aldridge's life is sketchy, conflicting, or exaggerated, possibly owing in part to the aggrandizements of theatrical publicity.

As a young boy, Aldridge attended the African Free School in New York City. Although Aldridge's father intended for him to join the clergy, Aldridge showed an early attraction to the stage, excelling at debate and declamation. Around 1821 Aldridge tried to perform at Brown's Theatre (also known as the African Theatre), but his father forced him from the stage. English playbills later stated that Aldridge came via the African Theatre, New York, so Aldridge must have circumvented his father's objections before the theater was closed in 1823. Recognizing the slim prospects for an African American actor in the United States at a time of strong prejudices against blacks, Aldridge made plans to immigrate to England.

Aldridge became a dresser to the English actor Henry Wallack, who was performing in New York.

Henry Wallack's brother, James, then employed Aldridge as a personal attendant while on passage to Liverpool. J. J. Sheahan, a friend of Aldridge's, wrote that James Wallack had planned to sponsor Aldridge and make money off his engagements, but when Wallack told a reporter that Aldridge was his servant, the two went their separate ways. (The often repeated account that Aldridge became the personal attendant of the British classical actor Edmund Kean and accompanied him back to England has been proved false.) Aldridge arrived in England in 1824, and although he announced his return to the United States a number of times throughout his career, he never went home.

Although it has been generally accepted that Aldridge made his debut in England in 1826 as Othello, playbills show that his first major engagement in London was at the Royal Coberg Theatre on 10 October 1825 under the name Mr. Keene. Aldridge, also dubbed the "African Roscius," acted under this name until around 1832. In his debut Aldridge played the royal slave Oroonoko in *The Revolt of Surinam*. During this engagement he also played in *The Ethiopian* and *The Libertine Defeated*. That the engagement was a success for Aldridge is evident in a playbill announcing his appearance in *The Negro's Curse*, a play written expressly for him. His biographers suggest that Aldridge rose to leading roles so quickly in part because of the novel appeal of having a "Man of Colour" in the cast. During the early part of Aldridge's career, many reviewers doubted the ability of a black actor, saying, for example, "Owing to the shape of his lips it is utterly impossible for him to pronounce English in such a manner as to satisfy the unfastidious ears of the gallery" (*The Times* [London], 11 Oct. 1825). Nonetheless, Aldridge was popular with audiences. The prejudiced criticism demonstrated in the London press made it difficult for Aldridge, despite his popularity with the public, to establish a career in the city. He turned, therefore, to the British provinces, where he developed his craft over the next twenty-five years. In his first provincial engagement at Brighton, he played Oroonoko and, for the first time on record, Othello, making no great impression. He toured Sheffield, Halifax, Manchester, Newcastle, Edinburgh, Lancaster, Liverpool, and Sunderland. His repertoire consisted of *Othello, Oroonoko, The Slave, The Castle Spectre, The Padlock*, and *The Revenge*. *Othello* and *The Padlock* remained in his repertoire until his death.

In 1829 Aldridge appeared in Belfast, with Charles Kean playing Iago to Aldridge's Othello and Oroonoko to his Aboan. In 1830 Aldridge played his first "white" role, Captain Hatteraick in *Guy Mannering*, using white makeup and a wig. Afterward, Aldridge regularly played white roles, such as Shylock in *The Merchant of Venice* and Rob MacGregor in *Rob Roy*. In 1833 Aldridge played Dublin and for the first time crossed paths with Edmund Kean. Playing in an overlapping engagement, Kean saw Aldridge in the role of Othello and afterward recommended him to the Royal Theatre at Bath, a prestigious provincial playhouse. Within three weeks Aldridge opened at Bath with his regular repertoire.

In 1833 Aldridge was invited to appear at the Theatre Royal Covent Garden, where he opened as Othello to Ellen Tree's Desdemona. The London press, however, was still unwilling, on the whole, to accept a black leading actor at its major theaters. A few critics found his performance commendable, but most agreed that Covent Garden was no place for a "curiosity" such as Aldridge. He had been scheduled to appear in two other roles at Covent Garden, but the performances were canceled for reasons that remain unclear. It is believed that the threats of critics perhaps convinced the Covent Garden manager, Pierre Laporte, that the "novelty" was not worth the financial risk. Whatever the reason for the cancellation, Aldridge's achievement is recorded by his biographers, who commented that his performance at Covent Garden "will forever be red-letter days in the history of world theatre and human progress, for ... a lone Negro from an enslaved people challenged the great white actors in the very heart of their Empire" (Marshall and Stock, 135).

Rejected by London for a second time, Aldridge returned to the provinces for many successful years. In 1852 he began his first tour of the Continent. His success in Europe was unequaled by any other in his career. His first tour through Belgium, Hungary, Germany, Austria, and Poland lasted three years. In 1857 he toured Sweden, and afterward he continually toured the Continent, including Russia, until his death, returning to England periodically to play the provinces. It was on his first tour that he added the roles of Macbeth, King Lear, and Richard III to his repertoire and received great honors from the princes of Europe. The king of Prussia awarded him the Gold Medal of the First Class for Art and Sciences; in Vienna the emperor presented him with the Medal of Ferdinand; and he was made an honorary member of the Hungarian Dramatic Conservatoire in Hungary, the Imperial and Archducal Order of Our Lady of the Manger in Austria, and the Imperial Academy of Beaux Arts in St. Petersburg. After he played the major cities of Europe to royalty and accolades, it is no wonder that Aldridge preferred to tour Europe rather than the small provincial theaters of England. The racism in the United States and, to a lesser extent, England, was not present in other European countries at the time. As a result, Aldridge thrived in continental Europe, which judged him by his ability on the boards rather than by the color of his skin. In 1858, however, Aldridge finally found success at the Lyceum Theatre in London and in 1863 was granted British citizenship.

His biographers credit Aldridge with being "the first to show that a black man could scale any heights in theatrical art reached by a white man—and recreate with equal artistry the greatest characters in world drama" (Marshall and Stock, 335). Known for his versatility, Aldridge played both the greatest tragic characters of Shakespeare and the melodramatic slave characters of his early career with dexterity. A physically impressive man, Aldridge was known for his strong, clear voice and a style more realistic than that used by his contemporaries—so realistic that accounts by actors mention that Aldridge caused them to forget that they were on a stage, and the play became "naked, shattering reality." He was known as well for personalizing his roles, especially Othello; he studied and interpreted his roles with little consideration for the traditional interpretation. When he was abroad, he acted in English, while his supporting cast used the native language. One Russian actor who worked with Aldridge, Davydov, said that "his mimicry, gestures, were so expressive that knowledge of the English language for the understanding of his acting was not needed at all" (V. N. Davydov, *Razkaz o Proshlom* [1930], 98).

Aldridge was married twice, although we know very little about his wives. His first wife, the Englishwoman Margaret Gill, whom he married in 1832, died in 1864. He married his second wife, the countess Amanda Paulina von Brandt of Sweden, in 1865. Aldridge and his second wife had five children, one of whom died in infancy. Aldridge died in Lodz, Poland, while on his way to perform in St. Petersburg.

FURTHER READING

Hill, Errol. *Shakespeare in Sable* (1990).

Malone, Mary. *Actor in Exile: The Life of Ira Aldridge* (1969).

Marshall, Herbert. *Further Research on Ira Aldridge: The Negro Tragedian* (1970).

Marshall, Herbert, and Mildred Stock. *Ira Aldridge: The Negro Tragedian* (1958).

Obituary: *The Times* (London), 18 July 1867.

This entry is taken from the *American National Biography* and is published here with the permission of the American Council of Learned Societies.

MELISSA VICKERY-BAREFORD

Alexander, Archer (c. 1813–8 Dec. 1879), fugitive slave, was born near Richmond, Virginia, on a plantation owned by the Delaney family. Despite his memories of being well treated, his father, Aleck, was sold to pay his master's debts and taken south. Rev. Delaney justified Aleck's sale by claiming that the literate slave had shared ideas about freedom with other slaves in the neighborhood. When Rev. Delaney died in 1831, Alexander's mother, Chloe, was left to Mrs. Delaney, and eighteen-year-old Alexander was left to the master's son, Thomas. Chloe Alexander died six months after Thomas Delaney took her son with him to Missouri.

Delaney settled in western St. Charles County, Missouri, where Alexander married a local slave woman named Louisa. He later sold Alexander to Louisa's master, Jim Hollman, when he moved from the state, and the couple spent the next twenty years living with their growing family on the Hollman farm. Alexander was trusted with the management of the farm and was treated well, he believed, because of his faithful service to his master. However, a number of his ten children were sold away because, as his biographer explained, they had "behaved badly" (Eliot, 41).

During the early months of the Civil War, Jim Hollman and a group of local secessionists burned bridges in an attempt to delay the progress of Union forces toward the state capital at Jefferson City. Alexander, like most of his fellow slaves, was aware of the tumultuous political situation in Missouri and understood that his freedom was at stake. One night in February 1863 he walked five miles to inform a local Unionist neighbor that secessionists had cut the timbers under a railroad bridge over which Union troops would be passing. Alexander fell under suspicion after the sabotage scheme was thwarted, and he was forced to flee. Though slave hunters quickly captured him, he escaped and made his way to St. Louis, where he found work on the estate of the prominent Unionists Rev. William Greenleaf Eliot and his wife, Abigail. Rev.

Eliot was a Unitarian minister and an important St. Louis civic leader, having helped found both Washington University and the Western Sanitary Commission. According to Eliot, Alexander immediately impressed him with his strong work ethic, deep Christian faith, and stoic demeanor (61). Eliot knew of his employee's fugitive status and sought a thirty-day military protection permit and at the same time offered to purchase Alexander from his master. Hollman rejected the proposal and instead sent slave catchers to abduct Alexander, but Eliot was able to use his Union military connections to obtain his freedom. Alexander is sometimes credited with being the last slave to be captured under the Fugitive Slave Act of 1850.

Alexander spent a brief time working in Illinois until the passage of Missouri's gradual emancipation law of 1863. He then arranged for Louisa and their youngest daughter, Nellie, to escape from Hollman and join him in St. Louis. Five of the Alexanders' children also fled to St. Louis and their son, Tom, enlisted and died in the Union army. Alexander worked intermittently for the Eliots for the remainder of his life. A year after the war Louisa Alexander died under suspicious circumstances when she returned to the Hollmans to collect her few personal belongings. Soon after, Alexander married a woman named Judy.

Archer Alexander achieved fame both through William Greenleaf Eliot's biography of him, *The Story of Archer Alexander. From Slavery to Freedom, March 30, 1863*, and because his image was used by the artist Thomas Ball in his Freedmen's Memorial to Abraham Lincoln. The monument's troubled history began soon after Lincoln's assassination, when a former slave named Charlotte Scott offered the first $5 she earned as a freedperson for the purpose of honoring the fallen president. A Union general learned of Scott's gesture and encouraged the Western Sanitary Commission of St. Louis to administer a fund to be raised through contributions from former slaves, many of who were Union soldiers. The tribute was conceptualized as a representation of the freedmen's gratitude toward the former president for his efforts on their behalf.

The Western Sanitary Commission erected a more modest monument after it failed to raise a larger sum of money through combined efforts with other memorial funds. As a member of the commission, William Eliot viewed a marble sculpture in Thomas Ball's Italian studio and arranged with the artist to use his work for the freedmen's tribute. Ball's original statue depicted Abraham Lincoln granting freedom to a half-naked man wearing a liberty cap and passively crouching amidst the broken shackles of his enslavement. However, because the emancipated slave figure closely resembled the idealized images of the slave man so often used in abolitionist literature, the commissioners requested that Ball instead substitute the image of an actual man. This one would be physically breaking the shackles of slavery, thus suggesting agency in his own emancipation. Bell was given a photograph of Archer Alexander to use as his model. The final bronze statue depicts a nearly naked Alexander with his arm outstretched and fist clenched, kneeling at the feet of his emancipator. In spite of these alterations, the arrangement still suggests Lincoln's centrality to emancipation, rather than portraying the reality that Alexander, like most former slaves, was largely responsible for securing his own freedom.

FREDERICK DOUGLASS refrained from mentioning the crouching man in his public remarks at the 1876 dedication of the Freedmen's Monument in Washington, D.C.'s Lincoln Park. Douglass is said to have privately commented that a standing figure would have better represented African American manhood. Erected at the end of Reconstruction, the Freedmen's Memorial quickly became one of the primary visual representations of emancipation in the nation's collective memory.

Archer Alexander died in St. Louis, Missouri. His well-attended funeral was presided over by William Greenleaf Eliot. Soon after, a monument was placed at the site of his capture as a fugitive; it read, "Archer Alexander. From Slavery to Freedom, March 30, 1863."

FURTHER READING

Eliot, William Greenleaf. *The Story of Archer Alexander. From Slavery to Freedom, March 30, 1863* (1885).

Savage, Kirk. *Standing Soldiers, Kneeling Slaves: Race, War, and Monument in Nineteenth-Century America* (1997).

DIANE MUTTI BURKE

Alexander, Archie Alphonso (14 May 1888–4 Jan. 1958), engineer, was born in Ottumwa, Iowa, the son of Price Alexander, a janitor and coachman, and Mary Hamilton. The Alexanders were members of a tiny African American minority both in the town of Archie's birth and in Des Moines, Iowa, where they moved when he was eleven years old. In Ottumwa the Alexanders lived in the section of town inhabited by the poor, both black and white. In Des Moines they lived on a small farm on the outskirts of town. Since Iowa's public schools were not segregated, Alexander attended school with whites, and he graduated from Des Moines's Oak Park High School in 1905. Then—uncommon for the son of a janitor, whether black or white—he went on to further study. By working hard at part-time jobs, and with some help from his parents, Alexander attended Highland Park College and the Cummins Art School, both in Des Moines, before enrolling in 1908 at the College of Engineering at the University of Iowa in Iowa City. He was the College of Engineering's only black student, and upon entering, he allegedly was warned, bluntly but not unkindly, by one official that a Negro could not hope to succeed as an engineer. Continuing to support himself through a variety of part-time jobs, Alexander did well academically, pledged a fraternity, Kappa Alpha Psi, and also was a star as the first black member of the varsity football team. On the gridiron as a tackle he earned the title "Alexander the Great."

Upon graduation in 1912 Alexander found his adviser's gloomy warning confirmed. Every construction firm in Des Moines rejected his application for employment as an engineer. So Alexander took a job, for twenty-five cents an hour, as a laborer in the steel shop of the Marsh Engineering Company. There his eagerness and his ambition were not denied. When he resigned two years later to found his own engineering company, he was earning seventy dollars a week as the engineer in charge of bridge construction in Iowa and Minnesota for the March Engineering Company.

Starting modestly, often at jobs that attracted few, if any, other bidders, Alexander soon took on a white partner, George F. Higbee, with whom he had worked earlier at the Marsh Engineering Company. The partnership lasted from 1917 until 1925, when Higbee was killed in a construction accident. For the next four years Alexander ran the company alone, building mostly bridges and viaducts, his specialty, but also apartment buildings and sewage systems. He also built a new heating plant, a new power plant, and a tunnel that went under the Iowa River on the campus of his alma mater in Iowa City. Alexander, who still encountered prejudice and occasional hostility despite his unblemished engineering record, served as president of the Des Moines chapter of the NAACP and of the local Interracial Commission.

In 1929 Alexander took on as a junior partner a white engineer, Maurice A. Repass, a former classmate at the University of Iowa. Under the firm name of Alexander & Repass, the partners went on to complete projects in nearly every state and to build what *Ebony* magazine called the "nation's most successful interracial business." The best-known, though not the biggest, projects completed by the firm of Alexander & Repass were in the nation's capital: the Tidal Basin Bridge and Seawall, the K Street elevated highway and underpass from Key Bridge to Twenty-Seventh Street, N.W., and the Whitehurst Freeway around Georgetown.

Alexander married Audra A. Linzy of Denver in 1913. The couple had one child, who died in early childhood.

Like many black Americans until the election of Franklin D. Roosevelt as president in 1932, Alexander supported the Republican Party. But unlike most black voters, Alexander remained a lifelong Republican, even though it might have been politically as well as economically astute for him to have supported the Democratic Party during its era of dominance, especially since his engineering company did so much public work. But his politics never seemed to hurt his business, and in fact, he was eventually rewarded for his loyalty. Alexander was not just a member of the Republican Party but he was also an active member who twice, in 1932 and in 1940, served as assistant chairman of the Iowa Republican State Committee. In 1952 he was an early supporter of Dwight D. Eisenhower for president. Alexander's long years of dedication to the party were rewarded by his appointment, in April 1954, as governor of the Virgin Islands. The appointment was a disaster for all concerned, though, and it may even have hastened Alexander's death. Dogmatic, paternalistic, undemocratic, and with an openly stated contempt for the easygoing Virgin Islanders, Alexander was sometimes described as a "Midwestern Babbitt" who brought all the values of small-town America to the Caribbean. He lasted a strife-torn and acrimonious sixteen months before he was pressured to resign in August 1955.

Less than three years later, Alexander died at his home in Des Moines. In his will he left a trust fund for the support of his wife, the corpus of which was to go, upon her death, to the University of Iowa, Tuskegee Institute in Alabama, and Howard University in Washington, D.C., for engineering scholarships. In 1975 each of the three institutions received $105,000.

FURTHER READING
Alexander's papers are located at the University of
Iowa, Iowa City.
Alexander, Archie Alphonso. "Engineering as a
Profession," *Opportunity* (Apr.–June 1946).
Boyer, William W. *America's Virgin Islands: A History
of Human Rights and Wrongs* (1983).
Wynes, Charles E. "'Alexander the Great,' Bridge
Builder," *Palimpsest* 66 (May–June 1985).
Obituary: *Des Moines Sunday Register*, 5 Jan. 1958.

This entry is taken from the *American National
Biography* and is published here with the permission of
the American Council of Learned Societies.

CHARLES E. WYNES

Alexander, Arthur (10 May 1940–9 June 1993), soul
and rhythm and blues singer and songwriter, was
born Arthur Alexander Jr. in Florence, Alabama,
to Arthur Alexander, a laborer and musician, and
Fannie Scott Spencer. He was exposed to music at
an early age by his mother and older sister, who
sang in church, and by his father, who played
weekend gigs as a bottleneck blues guitarist. After
high school Alexander was working as a bellhop
at the Sheffield Hotel when he met Tom Stafford,
a white R&B enthusiast who introduced him to
what would become the nucleus of the Muscle
Shoals–area studio scene: Dan Penn, Rick Hall,
Spooner Oldham, and Billy Sherrill. The men, all
then working for Rick Hall's Fame Music Stafford,
found Alexander's songwriting abilities every bit as
intriguing as his singing, and soon made sure that
Alexander became part of Fame's writing operation. In 1958 Alexander and Henry Lee Bennett
coauthored "She Wanna Rock," which was sold to
Decca and recorded by the country singer Arnie
Derksen. Two year later Alexander made his debut
on record, cutting the earthy "Sally Sue Brown" for
Judd Records under the pseudonym June (from
"Junior") Alexander.

By 1962 Alexander had become a star. Following
a short-lived separation from Fame, in 1961
Stafford convinced Hall to record Alexander singing the original "You Better Move On." This was the
first session of note at Hall's new studio in Muscle
Shoals, located in an old tobacco and candy ware-
house, which went on to become one of the most
productive (and hallowed) rooms in all of soul
music. "You Better Move On" was an appropriately
momentous beginning; its R&B–country hybrid
(as much a function of Alexander's tastes as his
white-backing band) laid the groundwork for the

sound that would define an era through Stax and
Atlantic recordings. Released on Dot, it proved
tremendously popular as well, reaching the top
twenty in the pop charts. Now under contract to
Dot, Alexander scored a minor hit with the commercially minded "Where Have You Been," and
then with "Anna (Go to Her)," a worthy follow-up
to "You Better Move On." But he failed to meet the
lofty expectations set by his debut and was released
by Dot in 1965.

While Alexander's performing career may have
been uneven, as a songwriter he was having far better luck. Steve Alaimo's 1963 version of "Every Day
I Have to Cry Some" sold well, and Alexander was
soon introduced to fans of the British Invasion by
the Rolling Stones' cover of "You Better Move On"
(1964) and the Beatles' early takes on "Anna" (1963).
Numerous other artists would eventually record
his compositions, including the Bee Gees, Dusty
Springfield, the Drifters, and TINA TURNER.

After a three-year absence, which has been
attributed to both illness and a variety of personal
problems, Alexander signed to Sound Stage 7 in
1965. But he managed only four singles for the label
between 1968 and 1970, further lending to his spec-
tral standing in the music world. In 1971 he became
a songwriter for Nashville's Combine Music, which
employed Kris Kristofferson and Tony Joe White,
and in 1972 he recorded a self-titled comeback
album at American Studios in Memphis, bolstered
by the support of many of his old Muscle Shoals colleagues. While considered a minor classic, neither
the album nor its singles (including the excellent
"Rainbow Road," Penn's telling of Alexander's story)
performed well on the charts. A version of "Every
Day I Have to Cry Some" provided Alexander with
a minor hit in 1975, but after a few other abortive
efforts he retired from music to drive a social services bus.

Alexander remained a cult figure to soul enthusiasts, however, as well as a songwriter's songwriter
whose body of work ranks among the finest in
American pop. It was this reputation that led the
Elektra/Nonesuch producer Ben Vaughn to recruit
Alexander for a nineties comeback. The result, 1993's
Lonely Just Like Me, was a mix of old and new material that played to Alexander's melancholic strengths;
like *Rainbow Road*, it featured contributions from
many of Alexander's longtime peers and admirers.
Tragically, Alexander passed away shortly after its
release, when he had just begun touring in support
of the well-received album. Alexander may have not
lived to reap the rewards of his efforts, but at least the

album served to remind audiences of a spectacular talent who had unjustly slipped into obscurity.

Penn, as sound an authority as there is on the history of southern soul, has said that "Arthur was the reason we all made it. He had the first Muscle Shoals hit and it was he that showed us anything was possible." Alexander's influence may have stretched well beyond his role in the genesis of one of the twentieth century's major musical movements. Alexander was a dazzling songwriter who refused to stay behind the scenes and a superb vocalist who insisted on interpreting his own material. Alexander's vision of the fully realized artist may have been his greatest gift to his acolytes in the British Invasion, his peers in the Muscle Shoals, and all of postwar American pop.

FURTHER READING

Guralnick, Peter. *Sweet Soul Music* (1986).

Younger, Richard. *Get a Shot of Rhythm and Blues* (2000).

DISCOGRAPHY

Rainbow Road: The Warner Brothers Recordings (Warner Brothers 45581).

The Ultimate Arthur Alexander (Razor & Tie 22014).

NATHANIEL FRIEDMAN

Alexander, Avery C. (29 June 1910–5 Mar. 1999), minister, civil rights leader, and member of the Louisiana House of Representatives, was born Avery Caesar Alexander in the town of Houma in Terrebonne Parish, Louisiana, to a family of sharecroppers. The names of his parents are not known. Seventeen years later, his family moved to New Orleans. Avery Alexander maintained an active life there and in Baton Rouge for the next seventy-two years.

Prior to his election to the Louisiana legislature, Alexander was employed as a longshoreman. At the same time, he pursued an education by taking night courses, receiving his high school diploma from Gilbert Academy in 1939. He became politically active by working as a labor union operative for a longshoreman's union, Local 1419. He also held the occupations of real estate broker and insurance agent.

Alexander received a degree in theology from Union Baptist Theological Seminary and became an ordained Baptist minister in 1944. As a minister, Avery joined the NAACP and became an activist in the civil rights movement. He was among the preachers present when the Southern Christian Leadership Conference (SCLC) was founded in New Orleans in 1957. He did not give up his loyalty

to the longshoreman's union, however, and managed the union's welfare system in the late 1950s and early 1960s.

During the 1950s, while riding segregated streetcars in New Orleans, Alexander was known to throw the wooden screens separating the white section from the black section into the street. He later became active on the issue of bus employment discrimination and led a boycott that forced the New Orleans Public Service to hire African American bus drivers for the first time.

Although Alexander accomplished much throughout his life, his most famous undertaking was his 1963 attempt to integrate the public cafeteria in the basement of New Orleans City Hall. With a cohort of staunch supporters, Alexander entered the basement cafeteria to stage a lunch-counter sit-in. The protestors declared they would not leave the premises until they had either been served a sandwich or placed under arrest. When the white

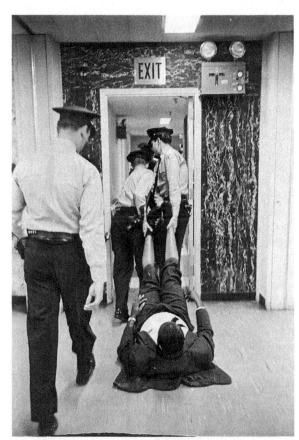

Reverend Avery C. Alexander, being dragged away from the City Hall cafeteria by the New Orleans police after he attempted to lead a sit-in in protest of the city's racial policy, 31 October 1963. (AP Images.)

cafeteria workers told Alexander that they could not serve him, he recalled in *A House Divided*, a 1984 documentary, he replied, "I understand everything. But that's food, I'm hungry, and I want to be served." For five hours Alexander and the other protestors refused to leave the lunch counter. Finally, white police officers pulled Alexander out of the cafeteria and, grabbing him by the heels, dragged him up the steps of city hall. Television footage showed Alexander's head banging on the staircase. As a whole, television coverage of the civil rights movement in New Orleans until this time had tended to ignore local police violence, concentrating instead on events in Birmingham, Montgomery, and Selma. The spectacle of Avery Alexander being dragged out of city hall, however, and the dramatic news coverage it spawned, galvanized the support of less engaged citizens in New Orleans for civil rights.

Around the same time, Alexander voiced support for an economic boycott against a commercial district located on Dryades Street, where white storeowners had historically refused to hire African Americans. While the storeowners maintained their resistance, the black community changed its shopping patterns to support a commercial district where the boycotts had succeeded. As a result many of the Dryades stores went out of business.

In 1975 Alexander was elected as a Democrat to represent the 93rd District in the Louisiana House of Representatives, a position he held for the remainder of his life. In 1977 Avery Alexander joined nine other state legislators to establish the Louisiana Legislative Black Caucus, a major goal of which was to increase the proportion of African Americans in the state legislature. In the late 1980s the caucus was successful in reapportioning or redrawing Louisiana's legislative boundaries to increase the number of districts that would send African Americans to the state capitol. In addition to being a founding member of the Louisiana Legislative Black Caucus, Alexander also served as its chaplain. (The fact that he was a minister as well as a politician led to his being affectionately known as "The Rev.")

Alexander remained active in religious affairs throughout his life. He established a nondenominational church, the Church of All People, in 1990. His political activism continued into the last few years of the twentieth century. When David Duke, a former member of the Ku Klux Klan, tried to hold a rally in New Orleans, Alexander protested the event and was restrained by the police. In 1996

Avery walked on a Baton Rouge picket line to protest proposed changes to Louisiana's state affirmative action laws. The following year he spoke out against racist killings and the brutality of police officers against African Americans.

Both a minister and a politician, Avery Alexander was instrumental in forming civil rights coalitions of both religious and political leaders. For example, in August 1997, he joined with DICK GREGORY, ministers, and politicians from Mississippi and Michigan to form a national coalition to protest the unfair legal treatment of poor and minority members of society. The resulting summit that Alexander co-hosted in Detroit was titled "Networking to Help the Hopeless to Obtain Equal Justice."

Though a protestor to the end, Alexander was also a statesman. He maintained his commitment to the Democratic Party and three times served as a delegate to the National Democratic Convention. Among his unfinished projects in the state legislature at the time of his death was a challenge to Louisiana's random drug-testing laws. When he died he was the most senior member of the Louisiana House of Representatives. A statue of Avery Alexander stands in a plaza across from the New Orleans city hall where he was arrested in 1963.

FURTHER READING

"In Memory of Louisiana State Representative Avery Alexander," *Congressional Record*, 11 Mar. 1999.

"Tribute to Reverend Avery C. Alexander," *Congressional Record*, 15 Mar. 1999.

Obituary: *New Orleans Times-Picayune*, 9 Mar. 1999.

NATHAN ZOOK

Alexander, Clifford Leopold, Jr. (21 Sept. 1933–), lawyer, businessman, and secretary of the army, was born in New York City, the only child of Clifford Leopold Sr. and Edith McAllister. Alexander's father, a Jamaican native, became an apartment building manager of Harlem's Young Christian Association. His mother was from Yonkers, New York, where she worked for a real estate firm. Later she headed the New York City welfare department. She was the first African American woman to get elected to the Democratic Party's Electoral College. In this position she became a prominent figure in the broader civil rights struggle. Both parents inspired Alexander's later work to end racial discrimination.

Alexander spent his childhood in New York City. He received his early education at the Ethical Cultural School and Fieldston Schools in the Bronx. After graduating from high school, Alexander went to Harvard University. Here he met McGeorge Bundy, Harvard's Dean of Arts and Science and later national security advisor to presidents John F. Kennedy and Lyndon Johnson. Bundy would prove an early influence on Alexander's career path. Following in the footsteps of his mother, Alexander became the first African American student-body president. In 1955 he graduated cum laude from Harvard and received the university's Ames Award, which recognized students who played important and positive roles in their communities. During much of the late 1950s Alexander worked for Mutual Life Insurance Company, directing the complaints division. He also enrolled at Yale Law School, where in 1958 he received an LLB degree.

After finishing law school in 1958 Alexander served until 1959 with the 369th Field Artillery Battalion at Fort Six, New Jersey. In July 1959 he married the former Adele Logan, a fellow Fieldston student and Pulitzer nominee. The couple had two children, ELIZABETH (ALEXANDER) and Mark. After becoming a member of the New York Bar in 1959 he was appointed assistant district attorney in New York County, remaining in the office until 1961. Shortly thereafter he became an executive director of Manhattanville Hamilton Grange Neighborhood Conservation District of New York, where he worked to improve housing conditions for rental homes. Alexander also served as the executive director of Harlem Youth Opportunities Unlimited from 1962 to 1963. The program's goal was to help inner city youth in Harlem.

Alexander's life took a dramatic turn in 1963, when LOUIS B. MARTIN, then deputy chairman for the Democratic National Committee, called him to Washington to work in the Kennedy Administration. Accepting this political position, Alexander served for the National Security Council as a foreign affairs officer under the presidential assistant McGeorge Bundy from 1963 to 1964. In the same year, Alexander's political career began to flourish when he was appointed deputy special assistant to President Lyndon B. Johnson in 1964, and later became associate special counsel to President Johnson in 1965. He accepted the office of a deputy special counsel on the White House staff in 1966. From 1967 to 1969, as a special representative of President Johnson, he worked on the Voting

Rights Act and headed the Equal Employment Opportunities Commission. He also led the delegation to ceremonies celebrating the independence of the Kingdom of Swaziland. Alexander stayed in the position of special representative until Senate Majority Leader Everett Dirksen accused him of pressuring employers to establish a work environment of equal opportunities for minorities and women. He resigned from his position in 1969.

Returning to his career as a lawyer, Alexander worked at the Washington law firm Arnold and Porter, LLP, from 1969 to 1975. Looking for new platforms to defeat white supremacy, Alexander in addition to his legal career was also a commentator, host, and co-producer on the TV program *Cliff Alexander: Black on White* from 1971 to 1976. Turning back to legal education, Alexander was for a short time a professor of law at Howard University from 1973 to 1974. In addition, he attempted unsuccessfully to win political office as the mayor of the District of Columbia in 1974. Alexander continued his legal career as a partner of the lobbying firm of Verner, Liipfert, Bernhard, McPherson, and Alexander in 1975.

In 1977 President Jimmy Carter appointed Alexander as the nation's first African American secretary of the army, a position in which he served until the end of Carter's term in 1981. The Department of the Army honored Alexander with the Outstanding Civilian Award in 1980. As secretary of the army, Alexander prioritized contracts to minority businesses and reemphasized the need for an all-volunteer army. After resigning from this position and receiving the Distinguished Public Service Award in 1981, he became the president of his own consulting firm, Alexander and Associates, which focused on increasing the number of minorities in major corporations. One of the firm's most important clients was Major League Baseball, which had a poor record of minority hiring in front office and other administrative roles.

Alexander served on the boards of directors of several companies. He sat on the board of American Home Products Corporations, MCI Worldcom, IMS Health, Mutual of America, Dreyfus Investment Funds, and Dun & Bradstreet. He also served on the board of several non-profit companies in addition to being a member of the Board of Governors of the American Stock Exchange. His accomplishments in the field of law were honored with the Washington Bar Association Award in 1969, followed by the FREDERICK DOUGLASS AWARD in 1970 for dedicating his life to fighting racism.

FURTHER READING

Alexander, Clifford Leopold. "Black Memoir of the White House," *American Visions* (Feb. 1995).

Christmas, Walter. *Negroes in Public Affairs and Government* (1966).

ANTJE DAUB

Alexander, Elizabeth (30 May 1962–), poet,- educator, and cultural critic, was born in Harlem, New York, to CLIFFORD LEOPOLD ALEXANDER JR., a lawyer, political adviser, and business consultant, and Adele (Logan) Alexander, a historian, educator, and writer, and was raised in Washington, D.C. Alexander's childhood was characterized by the privileges of the black professional elite, which included travel, education, and involvement in the ongoing struggle for civil rights. She later described her father as a "race man" who worked to make things better for blacks. He was, according to one of her poems, HAJJ BAHIYAH "BETTY" SHABAZZ's lawyer. Her mother published on African American history. Alexander's poems and essays about her childhood describe loving parents, a connected extended family, and the creation of an enduring sense of racial affiliation.

Alexander received her B.A. from Yale in 1984, an M.A. from Boston University in 1987, and a Ph.D. from the University of Pennsylvania in 1992. In Boston she studied with the poet and educator DEREK WALCOTT. Her first collection of poetry, *The Venus Hottentot* (1990), published in the *Callaloo* Poetry Series, attracted immediate acclaim. One of several creative works by African American women writers (including SUZAN-LORI PARKS and BARBARA CHASE-RIBAUD) to focus on the life and experiences of Saartjie Baartman—a South African (Xhosa) woman who was lured with false promises to Europe, where she was exhibited nude as a carnival freak, and whose genitals were subjected to scientific experiments—the volume also pays homage to a number of key black figures, including Alexander's West Indian paternal grandfather (Clifford L. Alexander Sr.), Nelson Mandela, ALBERT MURRAY, and JOHN WILLIAM COLTRANE, as well as to the figures named in the dedication: her parents and Derek Walcott.

Alexander began her academic career as an assistant professor of English at the University of Chicago (1991–1997). During this time Alexander won a National Endowment for the Arts creative writing fellowship (1992) and finished her Ph.D. dissertation, "Collage: An Approach to Reading African American Women's Literature" (1992). She also worked with the friends and family of MELVIN DIXON and Tia Chucha Press to publish a posthumous volume of his poems, *Love's Instruments* (1995), for which she penned an introduction. Alexander expressed in this project and in her second volume, *Body of Life* (1996), the immense impact of the AIDS crisis on her life and work and on the black intellectual and artistic community. The collection places the poet in a network of black experience, family, and friends, and generally charts her movement from relative innocence to experience, ending with the deaths of friends with AIDS and of two of her grandparents.

That same year Alexander's verse-play, *Diva Studies*, was produced at Yale. Alexander and an excerpt from *Diva Studies* were featured in the journal *Callaloo*'s Emerging Women Writers special issue in 1996, alongside other noteworthy young African American women writers such as EDWIDGE DANTICAT, NATASHA TRETHEWEY, and Suzan-Lori Parks, thus suggesting her significance as a black woman writer at the turn of the twenty-first century. Her work, and that of the others in the issue, is celebrated by TRUDIER HARRIS in the introduction as "consciously expand[ing] our notions of the concept of African Americanness. ... They are the descendants who have inherited a tradition, sifted through it for nourishment, and planted new seeds that will sprout new varieties of traditions" (*Callaloo*, Spring, 1996, 232–233).

In 1997 Alexander moved to Smith College, where she was the Grace Hazard Conkling poet-in-residence and the first director of the Poetry Center. She married Ficre Ghebreyesus in 1997; the couple had two sons. Upon leaving Smith in 1999 she moved to Yale University's African American studies department as an adjunct associate professor. She also began teaching at the Cave Canem Poetry Workshop for African American writers. During this productive period, she published her third volume of poetry, *Antebellum Dream Book* (2001), as well as a collection of essays, *The Black Interior* (2004), and a fourth book of poetry, *American Sublime* (2005). She also participated in the launching of the journal *Meridians* as a member of the founding editorial board (2002). *Antebellum Dream Book* was named by the *Village Voice* as one of its Twenty-five Favorite Books of 2001, and the poet and critic Edward Hirsch proclaimed it "her best yet." The volume used the trope of dreaming to explore the personal and cultural unconscious depths of motherhood, race, and history.

The Black Interior collected a number of essays that Alexander had published elsewhere between 1994 and 2000 and included three new pieces; the scope ranged from the role of *Jet* magazine as a conveyor of race pride to ANNA JULIA HAYWOOD COOPER as a black intellectual foremother. *American Sublime* was perhaps Alexander's most extended meditation on aesthetics, containing a section of *ars poetica* poems (that is, poetry on the art or nature of poetry itself), and sections invoking the blues, the story of the *Amistad* (the slave ship overtaken by the captive Africans in 1839), and American landscape painting. With this volume Alexander demonstrated her maturity as one of America's leading African American poets.

In the preface to her collection of essays *The Black Interior* Alexander wrote, "The work I do is culture work." Through her poetry, drama, and prose Alexander took the black civil rights legacy of her father and the black historical reclamation by her mother to the next level, imagining new possibilities for the black self, art, and African American culture. Recognition of the importance of her culture work came in 2005 when she was awarded a $50,000 Alphonse Fletcher Sr. Fellowship, for, according to the announcement, "work that contributes to improve race relations in American society and furthers the broad social goals of the U.S. Supreme Court's *Brown v. Board of Education* decision of 1954." Alexander's writing and teaching, deeply engaged in black history and culture and also inseparably interwined with America, continued to carry the struggle forward.

In 2007 she published a second set of essays, *Power and Possibility*, and won the first Jackson Prize for Poetry, awarded by *Poets & Writers*. Her other publications have included *Miss Crandall's School for Young Ladies and Little Misses of Color* (2008; co-authored with Marilyn Nelson) and *Crave Radiance: New and Selected Poems 1990-2010* (2010). The latter volume included the poem, "Praise Song for the Day" which she composed and delivered for the inauguration of President BARACK OBAMA in 2009. In 2011 she was chair of Yale's African American Studies Department.

FURTHER READING

Jones, Meta DuEwa. Interview, *Writer's Chronicle* 39.2 (2006–2007).

Keenan, Deborah, and Diane LeBlanc. Interview, *Water-Stone Review* (2003), available online at http://www.waterstonereview.com/pdf/6/Alexander.pdf.

Pereira, Malin. "The Poet in the World, the World in the Poet: Cyrus Cassells' and Elizabeth Alexander's Versions of Post-Soul Cosmopolitanism," *African American Review* 41.4 (Winter, 2007).

Phillip, Christine. "Interview." *Callaloo* 19.2 (Spring 1996).

MALIN PEREIRA

Alexander, Joyce London (1949–), magistrate judge, was born Joyce London in Cambridge, Massachusetts, to Oscar and Edna London. While attending Cambridge High and Latin School (now called Cambridge Rindge and Latin High School) Alexander was frequently elected as a class officer and eventually became the first African American president of the student council. After graduating from high school she entered Howard University in Washington, D.C., in the premedicine program. During her years at Howard the ongoing struggle for equality in the United States fueled Alexander's interest in the legal profession, and she decided to change her course of study from the medical to the political sciences, having also received an academic scholarship from the Boston NAACP.

While still at Howard, Alexander secured a job from the speaker of the U.S. House of Representatives Thomas P. "Tip" O'Neill. During her interview O'Neill informed Alexander that if hired she would learn a few things about political affairs, while earning a little extra spending money; Alexander assured O'Neill that she was there not "for fun or luxuries" but in order to pay for books and tuition. Impressed by her poise and candor, O'Neill hired her on the spot as his legislative aide.

Upon graduation from Howard University in 1969 Alexander enrolled in the New England School of Law in Boston, from which she graduated in 1972. She also took supplemental classes on federal jurisdiction and labor law at New York University. Her law school courses focused on political and community activism, and she was awarded the Reginald Heber Smith Community Lawyer Fellowship. The fellowship, lasting from 1972 to 1974, enabled Alexander to serve as a staff attorney with the Greater Boston Legal Assistance Project, where she dealt with cases involving juvenile defendants.

After completing her fellowship Alexander taught urban law and black politics at Tufts University and was legal counsel to the Youth Activities Commission of the City of Boston. She was active in many organizations, chairing the Massachusetts delegation for

President Jimmy Carter at the Democratic National Convention and serving as a cofounder, first female president, and president emeritus of the Urban League of Eastern Massachusetts.

As an accomplished public speaker, Alexander frequently was the spokesperson for various agencies and was sought after by the press for interviews. She became the first African American woman in the nation and the first woman in Massachusetts to act as an on-camera legal editor for a major network affiliate when she was hired at WBZ-TV (CBS) in Boston. At the same time she served as assistant vice chancellor and general counsel of the Massachusetts Board of Higher Education.

President Carter nominated Alexander for a federal judgeship at the U.S. District Court for Massachusetts, and on 6 August 1979 she was sworn in as the first African American female United States magistrate judge. Critics voiced their displeasure about the nomination, citing her race, age (she was only thirty years old at the time), and gender. In 1989 in the federal courts in Massachusetts she created Kids, Courts & Citizenship, which was the first school-based education project in the Massachusetts court. The program allowed fifth-grade students to visit her courtroom, attend trial proceedings, and engage her and other court officials in conversations regarding the legal system. The program also encouraged students to participate in mock trials. Still a judge, during this time Alexander also cofounded and served as president of the Urban League of Eastern Massachusetts. From 1987 to 1988 she served as chairperson of the Judicial Council of the National Bar Association, an organization of black judges with more than 800 members.

Once again making history, on 2 January 1996 Judge Alexander became the first African American woman chief United States magistrate judge on the federal bench, and the first African American chief judge of any court in Massachusetts. Among her many accolades and awards, several stand out. Judge Alexander has received honorary doctor of law degrees from Northeastern University, New England School of Law, Bridgewater State College, Suffolk University Law School, Cambridge College, and North Carolina Central University. Judge Alexander was honored as a "living legend" by the Museum of Afro-American History in February 2004, was recognized for twenty-five years of service by the Federal Bar Association in May 2004, and was given the THURGOOD MARSHALL AWARD by the Judicial Council of the National Bar

Association in August 2004. On 9 December 2006, Alexander married Johnny Ford, who served as mayor of Tuskegee, Alabama.

FURTHER READING

Reed, Pierce J. "Lady Justice: U.S. Magistrate Judge Joyce London Alexander," *New England Law Review* 38, no. 4 (2004).

KELLIE N. ADESINA

Alexander, Kelly Miller (18 Aug. 1915–2 Apr. 1985), funeral home director and civil rights leader, was born in Charlotte, North Carolina, the youngest of the five children of Zechariah Alexander, a funeral home director, and Louise B. McCullough. Zechariah Alexander, the son of slaves, was a graduate of Biddle University (later Johnson C. Smith University), fought for the North Carolina Volunteer regiment during the Spanish-American war, and had worked as the Charlotte branch manager of the nation's largest black-owned business, C. C. SPAULDING's North Carolina Life Insurance Company. He also helped found the Charlotte branch of the NAACP during World War I and ran, unsuccessfully, for Charlotte city council in 1937. The Alexander home was thus one that emphasized service to the nation and to the race, as well as the virtues of self-discipline, self-reliance, and Christian faith. Zechariah Alexander's political independence, rare in early-twentieth-century North Carolina, was largely a consequence of the freedom that came with running a business dependent primarily on black custom. Most black Tar Heels who worked for white employers in the Jim Crow era dared not be so outspoken.

From an early age it was clear that Kelly and his older brother Fred would follow in the Alexander family tradition of service and political activism. The young Kelly even practiced making speeches in front of a mirror. He also was a leader at Charlotte's Second Ward public high school, where he earned the nickname Shipwreck Kelly for his spirited, if sometimes reckless, performances as halfback on the football team. Upon his graduation from high school in 1933 Alexander studied first at the Tuskegee Institute in Alabama and then at the Renouard College of Embalming in New York City, where he trained to take over the family business alongside Fred. Before returning to Charlotte, however, Kelly worked as a jewelry salesman for a New York merchant. His travels throughout the South made him aware of the many indignities faced by African Americans who did not enjoy the economic protections of the Alexander Funeral Home or the Tuskegee Institute. Alexander and his white Jewish employer were barred from dining at most restaurants and hotels and were chased out of town by police officers on several occasions.

Alexander's experiences as a traveling salesman encouraged him to take an active role in the NAACP when in the mid-1930s he returned to North Carolina to work in the family funeral business. The Charlotte chapter—like most southern branches of the organization—had lain dormant since World War I. The coming of the New Deal, however, and particularly America's entry into World War II in late 1941 revived the NAACP's southern fortunes. At the forefront of these efforts in Charlotte, Kelly Alexander was elected president of both the city's branch and the statewide North Carolina Youth Council in 1940. The following year, while working as a reporter for a black Charlotte newspaper, Alexander met Margaret Gilreece, the May queen at Charlotte's Second Ward High School; the couple married five years later in April 1946 and had two sons, Kelly Jr. and Alfred.

The late 1940s and early 1950s marked a period of racial progress in North Carolina, at least in the large cities of the urban piedmont. Alexander was elected president of the North Carolina branch of the NAACP in 1948, and alongside several labor unions and crusading journalists like Durham's LOUIS AUSTIN he helped make the North Carolina chapter of the NAACP the nation's largest, with 120 branches and 30,000 members. As a result of the revitalized NAACP, black voter registration increased dramatically in Charlotte, Greensboro, Durham, and other cities. By 1954 there were six African American elected officials in the state, mostly on school boards, representing half of all blacks elected in the entire South. Kelly Alexander ran for Charlotte city council twice in the 1950s, though like his father two decades earlier he failed in both races. Alexander's civil rights work was recognized at a national level in 1950 when he was elected to the NAACP board of directors and again in 1954 when he became an NAACP life member.

Alexander also had his critics, notably ROBERT F. WILLIAMS, president of the Monroe, North Carolina, NAACP chapter. Williams, a blunt-spoken World War II veteran, believed that civil rights progress had stalled in North Carolina. This was certainly true of public school integration; Governor Luther Hodges had successfully circumvented the Supreme Court's 1954 *Brown* ruling by using a token integration plan. By 1959 only a handful of black students had been assigned to traditionally white schools in Charlotte, Greensboro, and Winston-Salem, though Kelly Alexander had led by example by seeking to admit his own children to these schools. Williams and Alexander also clashed over Monroe's notorious "kissing case" in 1958, when Monroe had worked closely with New York Trotskyites to publicize the arrest at gunpoint, imprisonment, and beating of two black children, Hanover Thompson, who was ten years old, and David Simpson, who was eight. The boys' alleged "crime" had been to kiss an eight-year-old white girl. Alexander sympathized with the children's plight, but as a cold war liberal and a staunch defender of the free enterprise system, he appears to have been even more opposed to Williams's involvement with northern Communists. On a practical level Alexander feared that such ties would jeopardize the NAACP's recent gains in North Carolina. The growing division between the two men came to a head in the summer of 1959 when Alexander, supported by the north Carolina NAACP and the national executive secretary ROY WILKINS, removed Williams from the presidency of the Monroe chapter for suggesting that blacks should prepare to arm and defend themselves against white supremacist attacks.

Alexander was somewhat more supportive of the student-led lunch counter sit-in movement, which began in Greensboro in February 1960 and quickly spread to other North Carolina cities, including Charlotte. The vigor and righteous commitment of the young demonstrators was not unlike that of Robert Williams, but their nonviolent philosophy and public expression of Christian faith was much more attractive to Alexander. Though there were some tensions between these younger activists and the mainline NAACP leadership, the period from 1960 to 1965 was one of relative success for a broad-based civil rights movement in North Carolina. In Charlotte, Alexander worked with both radical black student protestors and conservative white businessmen to integrate most of the city's public accommodations by 1963, a year before the national Civil Rights Act required them to do so. North Carolina also enjoyed by far the highest black voter registration rate in the South in the early 1960s: 40 percent. It would require the passage of the 1965 federal Voting Rights Act, however, to secure a decisive electoral breakthrough. That year Kelly's brother Fred became the first African American in the twentieth century to be elected to the Charlotte city council.

Such victories for the integrationist cause did not go unnoticed. On 22 November 1965, a few weeks after Fred Alexander's election victory, white supremacists firebombed the homes of four of Charlotte's leading civil rights activists: Kelly Alexander and his brother and neighbor Fred; the NAACP attorney JULIUS CHAMBERS; and Dr. Reginald Hawkins, a prominent dentist and long-time political campaigner. All four properties were badly damaged, but none of the occupants was injured. The bombings did, however, serve a positive purpose. A significant minority of whites in Charlotte, outraged at the damage to the city's reputation for tolerance, began to make common cause with Alexander and other black leaders. The city's leading white newspaper, the *Charlotte Observer*, condemned the violence and offered a reward for information about the perpetrators, though no one was ever arrested. White mayor Stan Brookshire organized a relief fund. Concern among the city's white businessmen was to some extent driven by a fear that violence would damage plans to attract new industries to Charlotte. Alexander understood this and began working closely with those leaders to ensure that African Americans, as well as whites, benefited from those new jobs.

The bombings also provided an opportunity for blacks and whites in the city to establish a school desegregation plan fully in the spirit of the 1954 *Brown* ruling. Led by Kelly Alexander and Julius Chambers, *Swann v. Charlotte-Mecklenburg Board of Education*, upheld by the U.S. Supreme Court in 1971, established an ambitious plan to achieve school desegregation through mandatory school busing. Throughout the 1970s and early 1980s the Charlotte school busing program was largely hailed as a success, particularly, as Kelly Alexander noted in an article in the *Crisis* in November 1975, compared to the violent white backlash in response to busing in northern cities like Boston. Alexander, who had been elected vice chair of the NAACP's national board in 1976, was elected chair in January 1984, at which point he stepped down as chair of the North Carolina conference of the NAACP, a position that he had held for thirty-six years. He was succeeded in that position by his son, Kelly M. Alexander Jr.

Kelly Alexander Sr. died at his Charlotte home, three days after giving a speech at a regional NAACP conference in West Virginia. In a statement announcing Alexander's passing, the NAACP executive director BENJAMIN HOOKS hailed him as a "fearless warrior who bowed to no foe." Although he was certainly a determined fighter for his cause, that assessment ascribes to Alexander a militancy that he rarely embraced or employed rhetorically. Rather, his work to end segregation in North Carolina was shaped primarily by the values that he shared with the white businessmen who ruled that state: belief in self-reliance and free enterprise; and faith in God and American patriotism. Kelly Alexander's skill lay in persuading whites that those values were fully compatible with racial equality.

FURTHER READING

The Kelly M. Alexander Papers (1915–1985) are held at the Special Collections Unit of the J. Murrey Atkins Library of the University of North Carolina at Charlotte.

Douglas, Davison M. *Reading, Writing, and Race: The Desegregation of the Charlotte Schools* (1995).

Gaillard, Frye. *The Dream Long Deferred* (1998).

Obituary:*New York Times*, 4 Apr. 1985.

STEVEN J. NIVEN

Alexander, Raymond Pace (13 Oct. 1897–25 Nov. 1974), lawyer and judge, was the third of five children born to Hillard Boone Alexander, a laborer from Mecklenburg County, Virginia, and Virginia Pace, from Essex County, Virginia. Alexander's parents were born slaves, but were freed by the Thirteenth Amendment following the Civil War. In 1880 they migrated to Philadelphia, Pennsylvania, where they lived in the Seventh Ward, a community that would later be made famous by W. E. B. DuBois's seminal 1899 study *The Philadelphia Negro*. In 1903 Alexander's mother died of pneumonia. Because his father worked long hours, Alexander and his siblings moved to North Philadelphia to live with his maternal aunt, Georgia Chandler Pace. From the age of seven Alexander attended school and worked at various jobs, including dockworker, newspaper boy, general helper at the Metropolitan Opera House in North Philadelphia, Pullman porter, and, when he was in his early twenties, teaching assistant in economics.

Alexander graduated from John Hancock Elementary School and then attended the prestigious all-boys Central High School in Philadelphia, the second oldest high school in America. Alexander went on to receive his B.S. degree with honors in economics in three and a half years from the University of Pennsylvania. His economics professors wanted him to pursue a doctorate in economics, but Alexander decided instead to attend Harvard Law School. Becoming a lawyer, he believed, would offer him the best opportunity to fight racism and segregation in Philadelphia. Alexander recalled that at Harvard his "sense of injustice to Negroes other than myself spilled to the point of public protest" (Alexander). Harvard Law had radicalized him.

Having passed the Pennsylvania bar exam in July 1923, Alexander worked for a short time with a white attorney in Philadelphia before establishing his own firm later that same year. Alexander litigated criminal cases, personal injury suits, and public accommodation desegregation cases. In 1924 he filed his first civil rights suit, against Charles Starkosh, the white manager of the Aldine Theatre located in downtown Philadelphia. Edward Green, an African American, had bought two tickets to *The Ten Commandments*, but when he presented the tickets Starkosh switched them and gave Green two old ticket stubs and prohibited him from entering. This case reached trial in April 1925. The white employees corroborated Starkosh's story, and after a thirty-minute deliberation the jury acquitted Starkosh. Despite this early setback Alexander went on to win a number of civil rights cases, and with each victory his reputation and status grew. In 1925 Alexander married SADIE TANNER MOSSELL ALEXANDER, a University of Pennsylvania graduate and member of the "old black" elite in Philadelphia. Sadie Alexander was the first black woman to earn a Ph.D. and J.D. from the University of Pennsylvania. The Alexanders had two daughters, Rae and Mary Elizabeth.

By the 1930s Alexander had begun to combine litigation with mass protests, and it was during that decade that he reached the apogee of his radicalism. In 1932 he litigated the Berwyn, Pennsylvania, school desegregation case. In March of that year the Berwyn school board built a new elementary school for white children; however, the black children's parents refused to send their children to a segregated school, so in June 1932 the black students initiated a school boycott that lasted for the next two years. In 1934 the boycott ended, and the schools desegregated.

Even though African Americans in northern cities voted in considerable numbers, the all-white power structure continued to deny them a fair share of city resources. From 1933 until 1937 Alexander mounted losing campaigns to become the first black judge in Philadelphia, defeats he blamed on both parties for refusing to support him. Between 1933 and 1948 Alexander switched parties three times, siding with whichever party gave him the best opportunity of becoming a judge and providing patronage to the black community. In this he was not alone; other black Philadelphia politicians, including CRYSTAL BYRD FAUSET, also switched between Republican and Democrat in those years. In 1948 a federal bench position in Philadelphia opened. Alexander campaigned hard for the position, but his opponent, WILLIAM HENRY HASTIE, a black attorney and longtime Democrat, had the advantage. Hastie was a lifelong Democrat and had more influence in the party. In spite of Alexander's civil rights work in Philadelphia and support from his peers, President Harry S. Truman appointed Hastie, because the Democratic Party was aware of Alexander's earlier party switching.

Though on the national level Alexander was not a major force, in Philadelphia he was instrumental in the 1951 Democratic Reform Movement. Alexander and white middle-class leaders formed a coalition to end the corrupt rule by the Republican Party, which had controlled Philadelphia politics since the Civil War. Alexander campaigned in the black sections of Philadelphia. In 1951 Alexander and the Democratic Party won the mayoral and city elections. Alexander was elected to the city council, upon which he served for the next eight years. In that role he was responsible for increasing the number of black city workers as well as improving public services for African Americans. Alexander enjoyed working as a city councilman, but he wanted to be a judge. As his political clout increased, in 1959 a Court of Common Pleas judge position became available and he was appointed by the Democrat George Leader to the position, becoming the second black judge in Philadelphia.

As a judicial activist Alexander sought to use his position to improve people's lives. In the late 1950s he noticed a rise in juvenile delinquency and black poverty. He created the Spiritual Rehabilitation Program (SRP) to stop juvenile delinquency. The SRP was designed to assist first-time offenders and help them find employment. A variety of Christian denominations and Jewish organizations were supposed to fund the SRP, but black churches provided most of the funding. In 1962 Alexander organized the Community Legal Services (CLS) to provide legal representation to poor people.

Alexander served as judge during the civil rights movement as younger activists and new leaders such as CECIL B. MOORE, a rhetorically militant attorney and president of the local NAACP branch, emerged in Philadelphia. Moore organized pickets and boycotts in Philadelphia to increase the number of black workers. Alexander supported demonstrations in the South, but believed that they were unnecessary in Philadelphia. Rather, he remained committed to litigation and to coalitions with sympathetic whites, a strategy that by the 1960s had failed to eradicate institutionalized racism in Philadelphia.

During the late 1960s and 1970s, Alexander commented on the devastating effect of black poverty in Philadelphia. Like MARTIN LUTHER KING JR., he advocated a guaranteed income for poor Americans. Alexander castigated middle-class whites in Philadelphia for not doing enough to battle injustice. Similar to King, during the late 1960s Alexander recognized the impact chronic poverty had on the black community. Unfortunately, a number of white liberals abandoned the movement when their voices were still needed to address institutionalized racism and poverty. Alexander died of a heart attack in his office at city hall.

FURTHER READING

Raymond Pace Alexander's papers are housed at the University Archives at the University of Pennsylvania in Philadelphia. See especially his "Legal Education and Formative Influences in the Law" (Raymond Pace Alexander, UPT 50 A 374 Box 1, Folder 15).

Canton, David A. "The Origins of a New Negro Lawyer: Raymond Pace Alexander, 1898–1923," *Western Journal of Black Studies* 27, no. 2 (2003).

Leonard, Walter J. *Black Lawyers, Training and Results, Then and Now* (1977).

Mack, Kenneth W. "Law and Mass Politics in the Making of the Civil Rights Lawyer, 1931–1941," *Journal of American History* 93 (June 2006).

Segal, Geraldine R. *Blacks in the Law: Philadelphia and the Nation* (1983).

Smith, J. Clay, Jr. *Emancipation: The Making of the Black Lawyer, 1844–1944* (1993).

Obituaries: *Philadelphia Inquirer*, 25 Nov. 1974; *Philadelphia Tribune* and *Congressional Record*, 26 Nov. 1974.

DAVID A. CANTON

Alexander, Sadie Tanner Mossell (2 Jan. 1898– 2 Nov. 1989), attorney and civil rights activist, was born Sadie Tanner Mossell in Philadelphia, Pennsylvania, the youngest of three children of Aaron Albert Mossell Jr., an attorney, and Mary Louise Tanner. In 1899 Mossell's father deserted the family and fled to Wales. During elementary school Sadie and her mother divided their time between

Mossell's grandparents' home in Philadelphia and an aunt and uncle's home on the campus of Howard University in Washington, D.C. When her mother returned to Pennsylvania, Mossell remained under the care of her aunt and uncle in Washington until she graduated from M Street High School.

Mossell entered the University of Pennsylvania in the fall of 1915 and majored in education. Her years as a student in an institution with so few women students and even fewer African Americans were extremely challenging. Yet, with her family's financial and emotional support, she prospered academically and graduated with honors in three years. In 1918 she received her B.S. from the University of Pennsylvania's School of Education. While her grades were high enough to gain her admittance to Phi Beta Kappa, the university did not select her for this honor for over fifty years.

Mossell completed her graduate work at the University of Pennsylvania, earning an M.A. in Economics in 1919 and being awarded the Frances Sargent Pepper Fellowship in Economics, one of five grants awarded to women in the Graduate School of Economics. On 15 June 1921 Mossell became the first African American woman in the United States to earn a Ph.D. in Economics. Despite her academic accomplishments, Mossell could find no suitable work as an educator, since even the Philadelphia high schools refused to employ African American teachers. She faced similar roadblocks in the business world. Mossell was forced to go to North Carolina, where she worked for the black-owned North Carolina Mutual Life Insurance Company in Durham as an assistant actuary.

Although she first met RAYMOND PACE ALEXANDER while they were both students at the University of Pennsylvania, she did not marry him until after he completed his education. In 1920 Raymond became the first black graduate of the University of Pennsylvania's Wharton School of Finance and Commerce and graduated from Harvard Law School in 1923. The two were married on 29 November 1923 at the Tanner home in North Philadelphia.

Feeling unsatisfied with a life of domesticity, Alexander decided to go to law school. In 1924 she became the first black woman to enroll at the University of Pennsylvania School of Law. As in previous years, Alexander continued to face challenges stemming from the racist and sexist attitudes harbored by the law school administration, students, and outside institutions. In 1926 she became one of the first two black student contributors and associate editors elected to the *University of Pennsylvania Law Review*. The dean of the law school, however, refused membership to any black woman. He eventually relented when Alexander received the support of a faculty member. In 1927 Alexander became the first black woman to graduate from the University of Pennsylvania School of Law, to gain admission to the Pennsylvania Bar, and to practice law in Pennsylvania. Alexander entered practice at her husband's law firm, making Raymond and Sadie Alexander one of the first husband and wife legal teams in the United States. Such a partnership afforded her a smoother transition into the profession than would have been possible on her own. At her husband's suggestion, Alexander arranged to be admitted to Orphans' Court in Philadelphia shortly after her admission to the Pennsylvania bar. Orphans' Court cases afforded Alexander the opportunity to gain more trial experience than most female lawyers, of any race, in Philadelphia. She argued appeals before the full Orphans' Court bench, the Pennsylvania Supreme Court, and the United States District Court. She developed expertise in probate law, divorce, and domestic relations matters and became the firm's expert on estate and family law. In addition to her legal work, Alexander served in local government. In 1928 she became the first black woman to be appointed assistant city solicitor in Philadelphia. She served until 1930 and again from 1934 to 1938. She continued to work even after she became pregnant, giving birth to two daughters, Mary Elizabeth in 1934 and Rae Pace in 1936.

Alexander was also active in the JOHN MERCER LANGSTON Law Club. The organization was formed in 1925 as an alternative to the Philadelphia Bar Association, which prohibited any significant participation by African Americans. In 1932 Alexander, the only woman in the law club, helped to form a legal aid bureau to assist African Americans who could not afford to hire lawyers.

For years Alexander worked with her husband—who specialized in civil rights and criminal defense cases—to combat racial discrimination and segregation in Philadelphia movie theaters, hotels, and restaurants. They helped to draft the 1935 Pennsylvania state public accommodations law, which prohibited discrimination in public places. Later Alexander advocated for the integration of the University of Pennsylvania's faculty and the U.S. military.

Alexander was instrumental in the development of the National Bar Association (NBA), formed in 1925 as an alternative to the American Bar Association, which excluded blacks from membership. As one of the few female members of the organization, Alexander labored to highlight the role of black women in the law. She published a study on the status of African American women lawyers and found that the overwhelming majority of black women admitted to practice at the time were actively engaged in the law. Alexander was elected national secretary of the NBA on 26 November 1943 and remained in office until 1947.

Alexander became the first black woman appointed to a presidential commission when President Harry S. Truman selected her as a member of his Committee on Civil Rights in 1946. In 1948 the committee issued *To Secure These Rights*, a report on the need for more adequate means to protect civil rights. The report provided recommendations for increasing civil rights protections for all Americans, regardless of race, religion, or national origin. These recommendations became the basis for future civil rights policies and legislation, including the desegregation of the armed forces.

In addition to her duties as assistant city solicitor, Alexander played an active role in Philadelphia civic affairs. She served as a member of the Philadelphia Fellowship Commission from 1949 to 1965 and as its chairperson from 1965 until 1968. Alexander also chaired a special subcommittee charged with ensuring that a new version of the city's charter would contain provisions to safeguard equal opportunity and fair treatment in the city's administration. In 1952 Alexander drafted a portion of the charter that provided for the formation of the Philadelphia Human Relations Commission (HRC) and was subsequently appointed to be one of the nine commissioners on the HRC, which investigated allegations of employment discrimination in Philadelphia.

In 1959 Alexander opened her own law practice soon after her husband was appointed Philadelphia's first black judge. She continued to specialize in domestic relations and often took on clients who could not afford to pay her, considering such pro bono work "as much my duty as I consider it the duty of a physician to serve a dying patient" (Nier, 59). She worked diligently in her solo practice until 1974, when she joined the Philadelphia firm of Atkinson, Myers, and Archie as counsel.

In 1979 President Jimmy Carter appointed Alexander chair of the White House Conference on Aging. Throughout her life she remained active with a number of civil rights and social action organizations. She continued contributing to public life until 1983, when she was diagnosed with Alzheimer's disease. Alexander succumbed to this and other maladies at the age of ninety-one.

For over half a century, Alexander excelled as a pioneering lawyer, feminist, and civil rights activist by opening many of the doors of opportunity that were closed to African American women of her era. She "knew well that the only way [to] get that door open was to knock it down" (Hill, 80). In doing so, she dismantled racial and gender constructs of her time and created a new identity for women and African Americans by using the law as a tool for social change.

FURTHER READING

Sadie Alexander's papers are housed in the University of Pennsylvania Archives and Records Center in Philadelphia, Pennsylvania.

Hill, Ruth Edmonds. *The Black Women Oral History Project* (1991).

Mack, Kenneth W. "A Social History of Everyday Practice: Sadie T. M. Alexander and the Incorporation of Black Women into the American Legal Profession, 1925–1960," *Cornell Law Review* 87, no. 1405 (2002).

Nier, Charles Lewis. "Sweet Are the Uses of Adversity: The Civil Rights Activism of Sadie Tanner Mossell Alexander," *Temple Political and Civil Rights Law Review* 8, no. 59 (1998).

Segal, Geraldine R. *Blacks in the Law: Philadelphia and the Nation* (1983).

Smith, J. Clay, Jr. *Emancipation: The Making of the Black Lawyer 1844–1944* (1993).

Obituaries: *New York Times* and *Philadelphia Inquirer*, 3 Nov. 1989.

LIA B. EPPERSON

Alexander, Virginia Margaret (4 Feb. 1900–24 July 1949), physician and public health provider, was born in Philadelphia, Pennsylvania, the fourth of five children of Hillard Boone Alexander, a horse trainer, and Virginia Pace Alexander. Born enslaved in 1856 to James and Ellen Alexander in Mecklenburg, Virginia, Alexander's father migrated to Philadelphia in 1880. Alexander's mother was born enslaved in 1854 to Thomas and Jenne Pace in Essex County, Virginia. She and her brother migrated to Philadelphia in 1880. In 1882 Hillard and Virginia were married. A working-class but respectable family, the Alexanders lived in the city's Seventh Ward with their three boys, Raymond Pace Alexander, Milliard, and Schollie, and two girls, Irene and Virginia. Strong family values were instilled in the Alexander children at an early age. Church, education, and a solid work ethic were emphasized in the home. Shortly after the birth of the youngest child in 1903, Alexander's mother died of pneumonia. Faced with financial hardship, Alexander's father moved the family to North Philadelphia to reside with their maternal aunt. The Alexanders soon joined Zion Baptist Church, Philadelphia's third largest African American church at the time.

The Alexander children persevered after the loss of their mother and excelled in school. The eldest, Raymond, began working on fishing docks after school to help support the family. Later, Alexander's father lost his livery stable business, placing an even greater economic strain on the family. Thirteen-year-old Virginia decided to leave school in order to work. Her father, determined that education would provide a better life for his children, refused to allow Virginia to relinquish her studies. She remained in school and graduated from high school in 1918 with an outstanding academic record. Following graduation she enrolled in the University of Pennsylvania, where she joined her brother Raymond as one of a few African American students.

In the early twentieth century, students of color at the University of Pennsylvania and at other predominantly white northern colleges experienced racism, discrimination, and isolation. Black students were not allowed to reside in dormitories, eat in cafeterias, or visit many of the social gathering places on campus. African American students at the university established their own support network, often through clubs and organizations. At the university Alexander joined Delta Sigma Theta Sorority, a public service organization for African American women that provided its members with social, cultural, and intellectual fellowship in the midst of an unreceptive racial environment. Because of her father's business failure, Alexander was responsible for her own educational expenses and worked as a clerk, maid, and waitress. In 1920 she was awarded a B.A. in education.

After college Alexander attended the Woman's Medical College of Pennsylvania, aided by a philanthropic friend. Alexander excelled in her studies and ranked second highest among medical aptitude test examinees. As one of only a handful of African American students, she faced myriad racially motivated incidents, such as professors who exhibited bigoted attitudes during class lectures. Nonetheless, she overcame these challenges and, once her studies were complete, sought entrance into the Philadelphia General Hospital internship program. The director of health at the hospital refused her admittance and indicated that he would continue to do so in spite of Alexander's impeccable credentials. Determined to succeed, Alexander instead sought entrance and was reluctantly accepted into the Kansas City General Hospital internship program. After completing the program in 1923, she returned to Philadelphia to begin diagnostic medical practice.

Armed with a desire to elevate the African American community through improved health conditions, she founded the Aspiranto Health Home in 1931. The private practice was established in her own home, where she cared for Philadelphia's poorest African Americans. In 1935 Dr. Helen Dickens, a fellow African American physician, joined Alexander's practice. Together they delivered babies and administered general medical care and emergency treatment. The clinic also offered parenting classes and postnatal recuperation to patients who often could not afford the services. Alexander did not allow her patients' inability to pay influence her decision to serve them. Never one to rest, Alexander pursued graduate study at Yale University School of Medicine, where she earned a master's degree in public health in 1937. Afterward she was appointed physician in charge of women's studies at Howard University in Washington, D.C. In this role she established a student health program and served as a medical adviser to the female students at the university until 1941.

When the United States entered World War II, Alexander became a medical volunteer. She was assigned by the U.S. Public Health Service in 1941 to treat poverty-stricken African American coal and iron miners in Birmingham, Alabama. The difficult conditions under which Alexander worked caused her to develop lupus, an autoimmune disease. After the war Alexander returned to her private practice in her Philadelphia home, where she specialized in obstetrics and gynecology. She delivered countless numbers of babies in Philadelphia, including Yolande DuBois Williams, the granddaughter of W. E. B. DuBois. She worked tirelessly to aid families most in need. As a staff member of the Woman's Medical College Hospital, Pennsylvania Hospital, and Mercy-Douglass Hospital, Alexander remained a constant advocate for African American health. She once noted:

If we can reduce the incidence of death at both ends of Negro life in the United States, we can add greatly to the overall contribution which our group can make to the Nation as a whole. To do this, we will have to send physicians into sections which have no bright lights and little social enterprise, take public health information across the railroad tracks and, above all, give knowledge to Negro women who are going to become mothers (Philadelphia Inquirer, 31 July 1933).

Finding time to contribute to professional and civic associations, Alexander was a member of the Philadelphia County Medical Society, American Medical Society, and the YWCA Board of Directors. She was also a member of the Germantown Meeting, Society of Friends. She was a much-sought-after speaker on health issues in Philadelphia's African American community. She dedicated her life to improving medical care for African American women, children, and families, many of whom otherwise would have been neglected. She died in 1949 in Philadelphia from acute lupus.

FURTHER READING

The Virginia Margaret Alexander Papers are located in the University of Pennsylvania Archives.

Baker, Joseph. "Dr. Alexander's Work in Public Health Hailed," *Philadelphia Inquirer*, 31 July 1949.

"Can a Colored Woman Be a Physician?," *Crisis* (Feb. 1933).

Canton, David A. "The Origins of a New Negro Lawyer: Raymond Pace Alexander, 1898–1923," *Western Journal of Black Studies* 27, no. 2 (2003).

"Dr. Virginia M. Alexander," *National Library of Medicine: Changing the Face of Medicine*, available online at http://www.nil.gov/changingthefaceofmedicine.

Lyon, Marvin P., Jr. "Blacks at Penn, Then and Now," in *A Pennsylvania Album: Undergraduate Essays on the 250th Anniversary*, ed. Richard Slator Dunn and Mark Frazier Lloyd (1990).

Obituary: *Philadelphia Inquirer*, 25 July 1949.

LANESHA DEBARDELABEN

Alexander-Ralston, Elreta (21 Mar. 1919–14 Mar. 1998), lawyer and judge, was born in Smithfield, North Carolina, the youngest of the three children of Reverend Joseph C. Melton, a Baptist minister and teacher, and Alian A. Reynolds Melton. She received her early education in the public school system of Danville, Virginia, and at the age of fifteen graduated from James B. Dudley High School in

Greensboro, North Carolina. In 1937 she graduated from the neighboring North Carolina Agricultural and Technical College with a bachelor's degree in music. The following year, at the age of eighteen, she married Girardeau Alexander, a surgeon, and had a son, Girardeau Alexander III.

Alexander worked as a mathematics and history teacher and directed music in South Carolina and North Carolina for four years before deciding that music would not be her lifelong vocation. Instead she longed for a career in law, despite the profession's being largely a bastion of privileged white men. She enrolled in the Columbia University School of Law and was awarded an LLB in 1945, which gave her the distinction of being the first black woman accepted at Columbia law school and the first to graduate.

Alexander became the first black woman licensed to practice law in North Carolina, the first black woman to try a case—which she won—in the North Carolina Supreme Court, and the first black woman elected as a judge in the United States. During her twenty-one-year legal career she was actively involved in a myriad of cases that brought her wide acclaim. She once represented a group of citizens who brought suit against the Greensboro City Council for its attempt to block the rezoning of a tract of land that would have permitted a private housing project for African Americans. The consequences of this suit also led to the election of the first black member to the Greensboro City Council and energized the movement to create more federal housing projects for low-income people. Alexander also served as the attorney for the incorporation of the first city-owned golf course in Greensboro that catered to African Americans.

In 1966 she wrote a book of poems, *When Is a Man Free?* In 1968 she was elected district court judge for Guilford County, a position she held until 1981. Alexander was the only Republican woman elected in her district and the only black elected in the state. While on the bench she earned the nickname "Judge A" and was an early pioneer in what became known as first-offender programs and in applying community service in her various judgments. She also instituted what she called Judgment Day, a program in which youthful offenders were offered an opportunity a few weeks after a conviction to convince the judge of their progress toward rehabilitation. If the offender had stayed out of trouble, then the charges were dropped; if not, the offender suffered the consequences of his or her actions.

Alexander's brand of justice earned her many accolades and recognition by various national publications, but it also generated much resentment and prompted calls for her ouster. Each time she was successful in being elected and even switched her party affiliation from Democratic to Republican to win her seat. Having been elected to four consecutive terms, she retired from the bench, but she remained a highly respected jurist and attorney who was selected several times by Guys and Dolls, Inc., a public service organization that donates funds for scholarships for needy African American students, as the most admired black citizen of Greensboro, North Carolina.

In 1976 the Greensboro chapter of the National Conference of Christians and Jews awarded Alexander the Brotherhood Citation, and in 1977 the North Carolina Federation of Women's Clubs selected her as one of the twenty-five most distinguished women in the state. After the death of her husband in 1979, she married John D. Ralston, who had retired from the IRS appellate division. In 1981 she formed the law firm Alexander-Ralston, Pell & Speckhard. There she served as a successful trial attorney and senior partner in the firm.

Judge Alexander was an active participant in the affairs of her city and served as a member of the board of the Governor's School; the board of management of Hayes-Taylor YMCA; the advisory boards of the Henry Wiseman Kendall Center and the University of North Carolina at Greensboro; and the boards of visitors of Appalachian State University and Guilford College. She was a member of the American Bar Association, the American Judicature Society, the American Trial Lawyers Association, and the Greensboro Chamber of Commerce, and she was twice a conferee of the President's Committee on Equal Employment and served as legal advisor for The Links, Inc., a nonprofit organization of women of color, from 1958 until 1966. Alexander Ralston died in 1998.

FURTHER READING
"Elreta Alexander-Ralston," in *Paths toward Freedom* (1976).
Smith, Jessie Carney, ed. "Elreta Alexander-Ralston," in *Notable Black American Women* (1992).
ANDRE D. VANN

Ali, Muhammad (17 Jan. 1942–), world champion boxer and political activist, was born Cassius Marcellus Clay Jr. in Louisville, Kentucky, the eldest of two sons raised by Cassius Clay Sr., a sign painter and something of a frustrated artist, and Odessa Grady, a domestic. Young Clay began to take boxing lessons at the age of twelve because someone had stolen his bicycle and he was determined to exact revenge against the perpetrators. He never discovered who stole his bike, but he did blossom as a young fighter, taking instruction from the Louisville policeman Joe Martin. His brother, Rudolph Arnette Clay (Rudolph Valentino Clay in some sources and later Rahaman Ali), also took up boxing, but, lacking his brother's talent, never became a significant presence in the sport.

Clay became a gym rat, feeling that he could succeed in boxing as he never could in school. Although he showed no special ability in his first few years, he was extraordinarily determined. He was indeed a poor student, graduating from Central High School with a D-minus average, ranking 376 in a class of 391. But he became one of the most impressive amateur boxers in the country, winning six Kentucky Golden Gloves championships. He was the National Amateur Athletic Union (AAU) champion in 1959 and 1960 and won a gold medal as a light heavyweight in the 1960 Rome Olympics, although he almost did not go to the Olympics because he was afraid to fly.

His boyish good looks and his outgoing personality, combined with the gimmicks of his poetry and his good-natured bragging, made Clay famous after the Olympics, and he received a great deal more media attention than most amateur fighters. He turned professional immediately after returning from Rome and was managed by a syndicate of seven Louisville businessmen. He was skillfully guided by the wily veteran trainer Angelo Dundee, who did not try to change Clay's unorthodox style, which had always infuriated most of the old heads of boxing. Clay, like most highly touted young fighters, won all of his early fights against either second- or third-rate opponents or noted fighters whose skills had deteriorated, like ARCHIE MOORE. His most difficult fight of this "contender" stage was against Doug Jones, in which Clay won a ten-round decision, although many at ringside thought he lost the fight. With his constant bragging, his poetry, and his zany antics, he won a national following, even appearing briefly in the 1962 film version of Rod Serling's *Requiem for a Heavyweight*. At six feet three inches tall and over two hundred pounds, Clay astonished sportswriters with his hand and foot speed, his reluctance to punch to the body, his ability to defend himself while holding his hands at his waist, and his insistence on avoiding punches

by moving his head backward instead of to the side. Clay modeled much of his style after his idol, the welterweight and middleweight champion SUGAR RAY ROBINSON. No heavyweight before Clay ever possessed such speed, quickness, or grace, and he attracted many people to boxing who would normally have had little interest in the sport, simply because they were enthralled with his style.

On 25 February 1964 in Miami, Clay fought as an underdog for the heavyweight title against SONNY LISTON, a former convict. Liston was thought to be virtually invincible because of his devastating one-round knockouts of the former champion FLOYD PATTERSON, the last heavyweight champion to weigh less than two hundred pounds. So few thought that the bragging Clay had a chance that rumors circulated that he would not even show up for the fight. Most thought the young braggart had no punch and no chin and would barely be able to withstand the hard-punching Liston. Clay, for his part, had been harassing Liston during most of the period before the fight, taunting him by calling him "the Bear" and "ugly" and banging on Liston's front door in the early morning hours, demanding that he fight him then and there. The weigh-in ceremony the morning of the fight was part theater of the absurd and part screwball comedy. Clay, wearing a robe that said "Bear Hunting," seemed as if he wanted to attack Liston and gave the appearance of being completely out of control. It was all an act on Clay's part to gain a psychological edge over his opponent.

More ominous, from the perspective of the fight's promoters and most of the general public, were rumors coming out of Miami that Clay was being seen with MALCOLM X, the charismatic minister of the Nation of Islam (NOI). This was probably the most feared and misunderstood religious sect of the time and certainly one of the most militant black organizations to emerge since the Depression. Clay had already joined the controversial group, but he did not announce his membership until after the fight with Liston. In part this was because he did not want the fight cancelled as the result of his religious conversion and in part because the Muslims did not want to be overly embarrassed by his defeat, which nearly all in the organization thought would happen, including the group's leader, ELIJAH MUHAMMAD. Malcolm X, however, was confident that Clay would win. He convinced the young boxer that the fight was a jihad, a symbolic war, both political and religious, between the crescent and the cross or between the black man who was for his people and the black

Muhammad Ali defeats Sonny Liston for the heavyweight title in a first round knockout, 1965. (Library of Congress.)

man who represented white interests. The jihad image was a psychological device that Clay (and in many cases, his opponents) used to dramatize virtually all the major fights of his career, turning them into contesting forms of black political propaganda.

Clay stunned the sporting world by defeating the aging Liston fairly easily in seven rounds. After the fight Clay announced that he had not only joined the NOI but that he also had a new name, Muhammad Ali. The response from the boxing establishment, the sporting press, and the white public generally was hostile, even vitriolic. The NOI was largely seen, mistakenly, as an anti-white hate group, something analogous to the Ku Klux Klan. Although there had been a few black jazz musicians who had converted to Islam, most of the public, black and white, knew little about the religion, and the NOI's highly racialized version of Islam further distorted the perceptions of most Americans. Never was an athlete so pilloried by the

public as Ali was. Most sports journalists ridiculed his religion and refused to call him by his new name. The former champion Floyd Patterson went on a personal crusade against the NOI in his fight with Ali on 22 November 1965, which Patterson lost. Patterson later became one of the few fighters to defend Ali publicly during his years of exile. No black athlete since the reign of JACK JOHNSON (1908–1915), the first black heavyweight champion, so enraged most whites and not a few blacks with his opinions and the way he chose to live his life.

He won a rematch with Sonny Liston in Lewiston, Maine, on 25 May 1965 in a bizarre first-round knockout, just two months after Malcolm X was gunned down in Harlem; however, these were soul-wrenching times for Ali because a scandal surrounding Elijah Muhammad had separated Ali from Malcolm X at the time of his mentor's assassination. Ali, probably one of the most unpopular fighters in history, spent most of the next year beating George Chuvalo in Toronto, Henry Cooper in London, and Karl Mildenberger in Germany. He also defeated ERNIE TERRELL in Houston, one of his few American fights during this period.

While Ali was abroad, the Selective Service changed his draft status from 1-Y (unfit for military service because of his low score on army intelligence tests) to 1-A (qualified for induction). Many saw this change as a direct response to intense negative public opinion concerning Ali's political views and the result of the escalation of the Vietnam War. In fact, after the Gulf of Tonkin incident, the passing score on the army intelligence tests was lowered, so that many other men besides Ali were affected. Ali refused to serve in the military on the grounds that it violated his religious beliefs. (Elijah Muhammad had served time in prison during World War II for refusing to enter the armed services and for sympathizing with the Japanese. WARITH DEEN MUHAMMAD, son of Elijah, also served time for refusing military service.)

In 1967 Ali was convicted in federal court of violation of the Selective Service Act and sentenced to five years in prison. He was immediately stripped of his boxing title, and every state athletic commission stripped him of his boxing license. For the next three and a half years, Ali, free on bond while appealing his case (which he eventually won on appeal to the U.S. Supreme Court on a technicality), was prohibited from boxing. He spoke on college campuses, became a darling of the antiwar movement, and inspired black athletes and activists such as the sports sociologist HARRY EDWARDS, who tried to organize a black boycott of the 1968 Olympics. The medal-winning track stars TOMMIE SMITH and John Carlos gave clenched-fist salutes during the playing of the National Anthem at those Games and were promptly sent home.

In 1970, with public opinion strongly against the Vietnam War and aided by growing black political power in several southern state governments, Ali was given a license to fight in Georgia. He returned to the ring on 26 October and defeated Jerry Quarry in three rounds. Although he was still a brilliant fighter, the long layoff had eroded his skills to some degree. He took far more punishment in the ring when he returned than he had before his hiatus. This was to have dire consequences for him as he grew older.

Ali had his biggest, most competitive and commercially successful fights in the 1970s. On 8 March 1971 he lost to the undefeated Philadelphian JOE FRAZIER in a close fifteen-round decision at Madison Square Garden in New York City, in what was the richest, most publicized sporting event in American history. The fight was so brutal that both men were hospitalized afterward, Frazier for several days. It was Ali's first defeat. He won the North American Boxing Federation title, a significant but lesser honor than the world's championship, in July 1971. He lost again in March 1973 against the former marine KEN NORTON in a twelve-round decision in which Ali's jaw was broken. Ali regained his North American Boxing Federation title from Norton in a highly disputed twelve-round decision six months later.

In January 1974 he fought Frazier again at Madison Square Garden. It was a nontitle match, as Frazier had lost his title to GEORGE FOREMAN. This time Ali won a close twelve-round decision. Ali finally regained the title in Kinshasa, Zaire, on 30 October 1974, when he knocked out Foreman in the eighth round of a fight where he was a decided underdog, most of the public thinking that Ali, at thirty-two, had passed his prime. Ali used a technique he called "Rope-a-Dope," where he leaned against the ropes and permitted Foreman to punch away at him; this approach, punctuated by Ali's punishing flurries at the end of each round, eventually fatigued the heavy-fisted younger champion. Ali was to use the technique in later fights, when he was too lazy to train, thus taking increasingly great punishment in the ring.

After regaining the title, Ali was lionized in the United States and enjoyed incredible popularity around the world. He became not only the most famous American Muslim but also the most famous Muslim anywhere and was the most photographed and publicized black man in history. He appeared in a film version of his life—*The Greatest* (1977)—based on his 1975 autobiography (edited by TONI MORRISON), joining JACKIE ROBINSON and JOE LOUIS as black athletes who starred in versions of their life stories on the screen. Ali also appeared on television programs and commercials. He even beat Superman in a special 1978 oversized issue of that comic. Part of this adulation and acceptance stemmed from the fact there was a general shift in attitude on the part of white sportswriters and the white public, but Ali himself tended to be less doctrinaire in his political and religious views as he grew older. And he was always gregarious and funny, something that lessened some of the white public's venom against him even when Ali was most demonized. Sometimes, his denigration of black opponents and his bragging seemed shrill and tasteless, as if he himself had grown weary of the act. He eventually embraced Wallace D. Muhammad's more ecumenical form of Islam when the NOI split into two factions following the death of Elijah Muhammad in 1975.

On 15 February 1978 an out-of-shape, uninspired Ali lost his title again to a young former marine and Olympic champion from St. Louis named Leon Spinks. Ali, however, managed to regain his title by beating Spinks on 15 September of the same year. In 1979, weary of the ring wars, his reflexes shot, his legs gone, and his appetite for competition slaked, Ali retired from the ring, only to do what so many great, aged champions do: come back. On 2 October 1980 Ali unsuccessfully challenged the heavyweight champion and his former sparring partner Larry Holmes, enduring a savage beating over ten rounds. His next fight was a ten-round decision loss to Trevor Berbick on 11 December 1981. After the Berbick fight, Ali retired for good, with a professional record of fifty-six wins, thirty-seven by knockout, and five losses. He was elected to the Boxing Hall of Fame in 1987.

Even before his retirement from the ring, Ali's speech was becoming slurred. After retirement he seemed to age, moving slowly and speaking with a thick tongue, his speech almost incomprehensible. He also suffered bouts of palsy. There is some debate as to whether Ali has Parkinson's disease or a Parkinson-like deterioration of his neurological system. Was this condition caused by the punishment he took in the ring in the later years of his career? It can certainly be safely said that his illness was aggravated by his ring career. By the end of the twentieth century, although Ali led a very active life, doing magic tricks, signing autographs, giving out copies of the Koran, traveling, and appearing at various public events, including, most famously, the lighting of the Olympic flame at the 1996 Games in Atlanta, he walked slowly and rarely talked.

Ali's private life was turbulent. He has married four times: to Sonji Roi (1964–1965), Belinda Boyd Ali (1967–1976), Veronica Porsche Ali (1977–1986), and Lonnie Ali, whom he married in 1986. He also had numerous affairs when he was younger. He has nine children, including one adopted son. Interest in Ali has been rekindled in recent years thanks to the Academy Award–winning documentary *When We Were Kings* (1996) and *Ali*, a Hollywood feature film released in 2001. Books continue to be written about him, and he has probably been the subject of more photographic books than any athlete in the twentieth century.

It is impossible to overestimate Ali's importance not only as a gifted athlete who dominated his sport for nearly two decades and helped make sports a multimillion-dollar television enterprise but also as a religious and political presence in American popular culture. He clearly made white America more aware not only of Islam but also of the growing militancy of black people who were discontent with the status quo. Ali clearly symbolized in the 1960s and 1970s the fact that blacks were redefining their relationship with whites as they were redefining themselves. Ali came to represent racial pride, strong religious principles, and youthful exuberance. In November 2005 Ali received the Presidential Medal of Freedom, the nation's highest civilian award.

FURTHER READING

Early, Gerald, ed. *The Muhammad Ali Reader* (1998).

Hauser, Thomas. *Muhammad Ali: His Life and Times* (1991).

Kram, Mark. *Ghosts of Manila: The Fateful Blood Feud between Muhammad Ali and Joe Frazier* (2001).

Mailer, Norman. *The Fight* (1975).

Oates, Joyce Carol. *On Boxing* (1987).

Olsen, Jack. *Black Is Best: The Riddle of Cassius Clay* (1965).

Plimpton, George. *Shadow Box* (1977).

Remnick, David. *King of the World: Muhammad Ali and the Rise of an American Hero* (1998).

Sheed, Wilfred. *Muhammad Ali* (1975).

Torres, Jose. *Sting like a Bee: The Muhammad Ali Story* (1971).

GERALD EARLY

Ali, Noble Drew (8 Jan. 1886–20 Jul. 1929), religious leader and founder of the Moorish Science Temple, was born Timothy Drew, the son of former slaves, in North Carolina. Much of his life is shrouded in mystery that he and his followers helped to create. He was apparently orphaned and claimed at various times that he was raised by Cherokee Indians and that he was a descendant of Bilali Mohammed, a heroic African Muslim Sufi who had been enslaved in the United States. Without parents and with little formal education, Drew may have joined a traveling circus and been influenced by such extravaganzas as the Barnum and Bailey pageant "The Wizard Prince of Arabia." He further claimed that at the age of sixteen he was taken by a gypsy woman to North Africa and there studied with a Moroccan mystic in the Essene Schools. As a test of his wisdom and worthiness, he was placed inside an Egyptian pyramid and miraculously found his way out, proving to all that he was a prophet. Having passed this test, he relates that he embarked on a pilgrimage to Mecca, where the sultan Abdul ibn Said gave him the name "Ali" and the sheiks presented him with a charter to teach Islam in America to those people of African descent who had been robbed of their true identity.

While much of Ali's biography may be fabricated, the story contains clues to his actual development and the origin of the ideas he would eventually propagate. His tale of exotic world travels, in fact, may describe an intellectual journey; the books he read and the people he encountered supplied the content of his eclectic ideology. Since he was born in the South after Reconstruction, it is reasonable to assume that his lot was similar to that of the 4 million black people of the period: poor and uneducated, with little opportunity for improvement. Thus, at an early age, Ali came to believe that the way to change one's future is to change one's past. In this way, Ali set the stage for future black cultural movements to reinterpret history as a means of racial empowerment.

The evidence suggests that Ali migrated north—as did nearly half the black population of the South between 1890 and 1930. He settled in Newark, New Jersey, where he worked as a railway expressman, attended Masonic lodges, worshipped with proselytes of a new Islamic sect called the Ahmadiyya Muslim Community, and joined the Theosophical Society, which included Mohammed Alexander Russell Webb, a prominent American convert to Islam and a proponent of Eastern religious thought. In 1913 Noble Drew Ali founded a congregation,

Noble Drew Ali (first row, standing in white jacket), in the cultural garb that he pioneered, standing before the Moorish Science Temple of America. (Schomburg Center.)

the Canaanite Temple, in Newark. He claimed that before starting this organization he had met with Theodore Roosevelt at the White House, informed the president of his plan to convert "the Negro," and assured him that black Muslims would be loyal American citizens. According to Ali, Roosevelt responded by saying "Getting Negroes to accept Islam will be about as easy as getting horses to wear pants" (Evanzz, 62–63). There is no independent record that such a meeting ever took place.

By the 1920s the essential elements of Ali's doctrine had begun to coalesce. From the Judeo-Christian tradition, he emphasized the importance of Ruth, a Moabite woman who converted to Judaism and became a maternal ancestor of Jesus Christ. Morocco, Ali argued, was the ancient land of the Moabites, who, he believed, had olive skin tones like the blacks of America. Therefore, he proposed the term "Moorish American" as a

replacement for "Negro," which did not connect a people with any particular land, language, religion, or history. "Asiatic Blackman," which he also coined, expanded the presumed ancestral homeland of black people from sub-Saharan Africa to include lands and peoples from the Middle East to India. From his limited knowledge of Islam, Ali found a god for the Moorish people in Allah.

The garb and ceremonies that Ali developed for his movement were influenced by the black Masonic tradition in America begun by PRINCE HALL in 1784. Modern observers who did not understand the historical context or cultural importance of these innovations often ridiculed the ceremonial dress, headwear, handshakes, passwords, and symbols that Ali used. Actually, such practices were quite common in both white and black lodges and secret societies. African Americans often took these organizations seriously, believing that such groups held the answers to questions about their true identity. Ali's experimentation with garb and culture prefigures the Black Power movement's adoption of African garb in the 1960s as a form of political expression.

In 1927 Ali codified his basic beliefs and published them as *The Holy Koran of the Moorish Science Temple*, also known as the *Circle Seven Koran*. While most of this text is derived from other wisdom literature, he introduced a number of practices, such as a diet that excluded meat and prohibitions on smoking and alcohol, that distinguished his movement from others of the time.

After several splits, power struggles, and doctrinal differences, Ali moved his headquarters to Chicago in 1925 and began referring to his growing organization as the Moorish Holy Temple of Science. In 1928 it was renamed the Moorish Science Temple of America (MSTA); by that time it had more than thirty thousand members with seventeen branches in fifteen states and operated many small businesses. The addition of "America" in the title indicated that members of this group were trying to forge a kind of patriotic black nationalism that incorporated their American identity. Those who joined the organization were issued identity cards that described the bearer's nationality as "Moorish American." The card also read, "I am a citizen of U.S.A." There are reports of MSTA members who brandished these cards at white people as if to say, "I know who I am." Noble Drew Ali taught that black people in America had had an intact Moorish culture, complete with a flag and tribal appellations. He claimed that these cultural markers were taken away after the American Revolution in order to subordinate black slaves to their white masters. Allegedly, Ali confronted President Woodrow Wilson with this information and demanded the return of the Moorish flag and the right of black people in America to add Bey and El to their surnames.

Ali's appointment of women to leadership positions within the organization was remarkably progressive. During the restructuring of the MSTA in 1928, M. Whitehead-El (also known as Dove-El) was made a "grand sheikess" over one congregation in Chicago and then elevated to the position of governor of several temples under her jurisdiction. Black women of this time were rarely given similar positions within black Christian denominations, and women within Islamic sects were traditionally excluded from such roles. Ali also supported changes that made the MSTA a more democratic organization and ultimately led to the local election of certain officers, many of whom were women.

By the late 1920s the MSTA had become a political force in Chicago and played an important role in the election of OSCAR DE PRIEST to the U.S. House of Representatives in 1928, the first African American elected from a northern state.

Ali's demise and the subsequent decline of the MSTA coincided with the murder of Sheik Claude Greene. When Sheik Greene, who had publicly challenged Ali's management of the organization, was found murdered in his office at Unity Hall in March of 1929, Ali was immediately indicted as an accomplice to the crime—even though he and his wife, Pearl Jones Ali, were not in the city at the time of the assassination. Shortly after being released from police custody, Noble Drew Ali died at his home. While newspapers reported the cause of death as tuberculosis, members of the MSTA speculated that he had succumbed to injuries inflicted by the police or that MSTA members loyal to Greene had killed him.

Noble Drew Ali did not have any known heirs, but he left a legacy of African American interest in Islam that survived in the MSTA, in orthodox Sunni Muslim sects, and in other black nationalist organizations. He had a profound influence on W. D. Fard and ELIJAH MUHAMMAD, who were both members of the MSTA before they established the more militant Nation of Islam. Today, African Americans constitute one of the largest segments of the Muslim population in the United States.

FURTHER READING

The MSTA maintains a private archive of its material at its headquarters in Chicago. Primary documents about Noble Drew Ali also can be found in the files on the MSTA at the headquarters of the Federal Bureau of Investigation (also called the "Noble Drew Ali" file).

Clegg, Claude Andrew, III. *An Original Man: The Life and Times of Elijah Muhammad* (1997).

Evanzz, Karl. *The Messenger: The Rise and Fall of Elijah Muhammad* (1999).

Lincoln, C. Eric. *The Black Muslims in America* (1961).

Marsh, Clifton. *From Black Muslims to Muslims* (1996).

Turner, Richard Brent. *Islam in the African-American Experience* (1997).

Wilson, Peter Lamborn. *Sacred Drift: Essays on the Margins of Islam* (1993).

SHOLOMO B. LEVY

Ali, Rashied (1 July 1935–12 Aug. 2009), jazz drummer, was born Robert Patterson in Philadelphia, Pennsylvania, the son of Poston Patterson. His talented pianist aunt was asked by the famous band-leader LIONEL LEO HAMPTON to tour with him, but as she was not yet finished with school her grandmother would not allow it. However, Ali liked what he heard emanating from his aunt's living-room rehearsals with a local group, especially the sounds from the drummer. Although he did not graduate, Ali's high school dances provided him the opportunity to hear such luminaries as the saxophonist CHARLIE PARKER and the big bands of Woody Herman and Stan Kenton. The young Rashied listened to the jazz drummers MAX ROACH and ART BLAKEY, but his earliest influences were his father's first cousins, the drummers Bernard and Charlie Rice. Upon returning to Philadelphia after beginning his drumming career in the U.S. Army, Ali briefly studied at the Granoff School of Music.

Ali picked up invaluable experience learning to play strict-time backbeats and "grooves" behind Philadelphia "chitlin' circuit" rhythm and blues bands and the blues singers Big Maybelle and Dick Hart and the Heartaches. Ali gradually progressed to the Philadelphia/Wilmington, Delaware/Camden-Trenton, New Jersey, jazz scene with the organists Don Patterson and Jimmy Smith and the trumpeter LEE MORGAN. After touring Japan with the saxophone colossus SONNY ROLLINS in 1963 Ali moved to New York City and quickly became ensconced in the jazz capital's burgeoning avant-garde movement.

Variously referred to by music critics as "free jazz," "new wave," or "The New Thing," New York's downtown experimental music of the 1960s and early 1970s reflected the political, social, and cultural changes happening in America, especially within the African American community. As the title of Frank Kofsky's 1970 book *Black Nationalism and the Revolution in Music* implies, some writers of the time were attempting to conflate racial unrest with musicians such as the trumpeter DON CHERRY, the saxophonists PHAROAH SANDERS, ERIC DOLPHY, ORNETTE COLEMAN, MARION BROWN, and ALBERT AYLER, the keyboardists/composers Paul Bley and SUN RA, and the drummers Sunny Murray, Beaver Harris, Andrew Cyrille, and Milford Graves, all of whom were radically challenging traditional melodic, harmonic, and rhythmic boundaries. This may have been for reasons more musical than political, however. Just as the bebop musicians of the 1940s deliberately crafted a technically complicated methodology to separate themselves from the preceding "swing" generation, the 1960s artists were determined to distance their style from its inherent 1950s post-bop or hard-bop

roots in order to make their own distinctive statements and forge their own identifiable voices.

The champion of this movement was the saxophonist JOHN WILLIAM COLTRANE, whose successful sales at Impulse Records enabled him to recommend up-and-coming artists to the label. One of these was another Philadelphian, the saxophonist ARCHIE VERNON SHEPP, who provided Rashied Ali with his first major album release, *On This Night*, in 1965. Subsequently, Ali began working with John Coltrane in November 1965, and after a few engagements as a quintet together with Coltrane's legendary drummer Elvin Jones (documented on the 1965 album *Meditations*), Coltrane began his own "free jazz" period with his wife, ALICE MCLEOD COLTRANE, on piano, the mainstay bassist Jimmy Garrison, and Rashied Ali.

The relatively obscure Ali was now the drummer for arguably the premier group in jazz, and during the next two years, from 1965 to 1967, he toured the nation and the globe, recording and sharing Coltrane's passionate quest for new ways of making music, answering the leader's ongoing evolution with his own exceptionally idiosyncratic version of drum set playing. The final period of exploration for Coltrane with Rashied Ali produced the 1966 recordings *Live at the Village Vanguard Again* and *Cosmic Music*; the 1967 recordings *Stellar Regions, Interstellar Space, Expression*, and the last recorded live performance, in April 1967, *The Olatunji Concert*. *Interstellar Space* was perhaps the most controversial release from their collaboration, consisting of four saxophone and drum set duets, each titled for a planet. Unfortunately this multidirectional rhythmic approach could not be further pursued because of Coltrane's untimely passing later that year. Still in his early thirties, Ali worked for a while with Alice Coltrane, then expatriated to Europe, where he performed in Copenhagen, Germany, and Sweden. He had always admired the drummer PHILLY JOE JONES, and studied with him in England. Upon his return to New York in the early 1970s, Ali worked and recorded with the saxophonists JACKIE MCLEAN, GARY LEE BARTZ, and Dewey Redman. While developing his leadership and organizational skills, he helped coordinate the New York Musicians Festival in 1972.

Finding the New York scene somewhat depressed, he wasted no time opening his own venue, Ali's Alley, in 1973. Originally a performance loft with a decidedly noncommercial booking policy concentrating on the avant-garde, his space eventually became a showcase for jazz across the stylistic spectrum. The club closed in 1979.

Ali's other trailblazing venture was his own artist-run label, Survival Records, which he founded at the same time as Ali's Alley. With this unusual amount of independence and control, he built a fine catalog of his own projects as a leader, along with some worthwhile releases from other artists. One important recording from Ali during this period was his own *Duo Exchange* with the saxophonist Frank Lowe. Survival's output was later rereleased on the Knitting Factory Classics imprint.

During the 1980s Ali performed with the saxophonists Makanda Ken McIntyre and David Murray. He recorded with the guitarist James "Blood" Ulmer, the tenor saxophonist George Adams, and the bassist Sirone in 1987. *Touchin' on Trane* with the bassist William Parker was recorded in 1991 and merited high praise from critics. Since the 1990s Ali has led a side project, Prima Materia, dedicated to preserving the spirit of Coltrane's music. Additionally, Ali was instrumental in encouraging young artists, including the respective saxophone and bass-playing sons of his mentors John Coltrane and Jimmy Garrison.

In addition to performing with his own Rashied Ali Quartet, he began performing duo concerts with the saxophonist Sonny Fortune, another fellow Philadelphian, in the 2000s. The pair sometimes played ninety minutes to a full two hours in exploration of a single composition. Festival organizer, promoter, independent label entrepreneur, club owner, and teacher by example, Rashied Ali devoted his life to pushing the envelope of jazz drumming. He died in New York City at the age of seventy-six.

FURTHER READING

Pareles, Jon. "Rashied Ali Quartet," *New York Times*, 6 Jan. 1988.

Patel, Mark. "Rashied Ali: 10 Questions," *One Final Note: The Jazz and Improvised Music Webzine* (6 June 2005).

Shteamer, Hank. "Rashied Ali," *All About Jazz/New York* 18 (Oct. 2003).

JIM MILLER

Ali, Salimah (Dec. 1954–), photographer, was born Joyce Allen at Harlem Hospital in New York, the oldest of four children, all of whose names were changed after her father converted to Islam in the late 1950s. In 1972 Ali graduated from Jamaica High School in Queens. Although a guidance counselor told Ali that as a young African American woman she would never attend college, she enrolled in LaGuardia Community College that fall. She concentrated on liberal arts until she took her first black

and white photography course. Impressed by her negatives, Ali decided to pursue a degree in photography. At the time colleges and universities had only recently begun offering graduate and undergraduate degrees in photography. Ali applied to the Fashion Institute of Technology (FIT) in New York City in 1975. Although she possessed an exceptional portfolio and passed a required entrance exam three times, she was refused entry to the program because the administration did not believe a young African American woman was capable of producing such work. Ali was finally accepted when Dean Mentor of LaGuardia, also an African American woman, called FIT on her former student's behalf. Before she matriculated, Ali had given birth to Jamilah Aisha Allen. As a single mother, Ali had to balance raising her daughter, attending school, and supporting the household by working odd jobs. Her instructors provided a tremendous amount of support by allowing Ali to bring her daughter to class when she could not find a babysitter. In 1977 Ali graduated with an A.A. degree in Photography.

Ali's career began at a time when African American photographers were either "creating works purely for exhibition as fine art" (Willis, 171) or using photography to document the era's prevalent social issues such as the Black Power Movement. Few African Americans were involved in fashion and entertainment photography, and the number of African American women in these fields was even smaller. Understanding the limitations faced by African American women in the fashion industry, both in front of and behind the camera, Ali still chose to concentrate on entertainment photography. There she found many creative influences to sustain her drive, among them Ozier Mohammed, GORDON PARKS, JAMES VANDERZEE, and her own father. From the mid-1970s to the mid-1980s she photographed numerous celebrities, including Earth, Wind & Fire, GRACE JONES, EARTHA KITT, PATTI LABELLE, BOB MARLEY, and STEVIE WONDER. During this time she also worked as the photo editor for *Encore*, a national black news and entertainment magazine.

In the mid-1980s Ali continued to freelance as a photojournalist and documentary photographer, publishing in weekly newspapers like the *Amsterdam News* and magazines such as *Essence* and *Ms.* The caliber of Ali's work was such that the photographic historian Jean Moutoussamy-Ashe profiled her in the biographical anthology *Viewfinders: Black Women Photographers* (1993). In the late 1990s Chris Hatch, the photo editor for *Newsday*, gave

Ali her first of many assignments for daily news-papers; soon she would also contribute to the *New York Times* and *USA Today*. Aside from shooting for print publications, Ali also worked as the still photographer for the African American vampire movie *Def by Temptation* (1990) and *A Litany for Survival: The Life and Work of Audre Lorde* (1995), the critically acclaimed documentary about the poet, teacher, and activist. While on the film set, Ali shot the portrait of Lorde that would decorate the cover of her book, *Sister Outsider* (1984). During this time Ali also worked as an artist educator at the Jamaica Center for Arts & Learning, which was founded in 1972 to provide cultural programs for Queens' underserved communities. While there she taught the basics of black and white photography and darkroom techniques to at-risk youth.

During the course of her thirty-year career Ali exhibited extensively in many prestigious museums and galleries, including the Museum of Fine Arts in Boston; the Brooklyn Museum of Art, for its 2001 show Committed to the Image: Contemporary Black Photographers; the Black Enterprise Gallery in New York and the Studio Museum of Harlem for Self-Portrait, an exhibi-tion sponsored by *Black Enterprise Magazine* in 1980 as a tribute to its black photographers; and the Bronx Borough President's Art Gallery for Speaking of the Bronx, a project completed in 2006 by Image Griots, a Bronx-based photog-raphy collective that documents various Bronx neighborhoods. In addition the Schomburg Center for Research in Black Culture commis-sioned her and the photographer Jules Allen to shoot the Twentieth-Century African Americans series, which became part of the center's perma-nent collection in 1999.

Ali's work has been featured in a number of books about photography and women artists, including *Patchwork of Dreams: Voices from the Heart of New America* (1996), a book that celebrates the cultural and artistic diversity of Queens-based artists; *The Face of Our Past: Images of Black Women from Colonial America to the Present* (1999); and *Committed to the Image: Contemporary Black Photographers* (2001).

Ali's professional affiliations include the National Association for Black Journalists (NABJ), the larg-est organization of journalists of color, which provides programs and services to and advocates on behalf of black journalists; Kamoinge Inc., an artists' group founded by the photographer Roy DeCarava in 1963 as a response to the negative and biased representation of African Americans in mainstream media; and Image Griots.

FURTHER READING
Hine, Darlene Clark. *Black Women in America* (2005).
Hine, Darlene Clark, and Kathleen Thompson. *A Shining Thread of Hope* (1999).
Moutoussamy-Ashe, Jeanne. *Viewfinders: Black Women Photographers* (1993).
Willis-Thomas, Deborah. *A Bio-Bibliography of Black Photographers, 1940–1988* (1989).
Willis, Deborah. *Reflections in Black: A History of Black Photographers, 1840 to the Present* (2000).

CRYSTAL AM NELSON

Alice B. *See* Speed, Ella.

Alice of Dunk's Ferry (c. 1686–1802), oral historian and centenarian, was born a slave in Philadelphia, Pennsylvania, to parents who were slaves brought to the United States from Barbados. She was moved to Dunk's Ferry in Bucks County, Pennsylvania, when she was ten years old to be with her master, of whom no information is available. There Alice lived as a slave, collecting ferry fares for forty years of her life.

Alice was a spirited and intelligent woman. She loved to hear the Bible read to her, but like most other enslaved people she could not read or write. She also held the truth in high esteem and was con-sidered trustworthy. Her reliable memory served her well throughout her long life.

Many notable people of the time are said to have made her acquaintance, like Thomas Story (founder of the Association of Medical Superintendents of American Institutions for the Insane, which was the precursor to the American Psychiatric Association) and James Logan (a statesman and scholar). She is even said to have lit the pipe of William Penn, the man considered to be the founder of Pennsylvania. Alice would comment on issues pertinent to the times as she collected ferry fees from travelers. After a time she came to be seen as a sensible, intelligent, and Christian woman, and not just a functionary to be ignored. People stopped to speak with her dur-ing their travels. She became a human storehouse for local information. As she aged she told per-sonal anecdotes of the people, events, and places of young Philadelphia. Her early recollections told of Philadelphia when it was still wilderness and Native Americans hunted wild animals in the woodland. Her later recollections told of the early settlement of

Philadelphia and other nearby areas. People loved to hear her stories as they were usually about their own family members, people of local note, and others who were responsible for building up Philadelphia and its surrounding areas. Because she lived such a long life Alice personally experienced a momentous time in American history and was still alive to tell the tales to subsequent generations. Her stories helped to form a true history and folklore of Pennsylvania from the point of view of an honest common person.

Alice rode her horse from Dunk's Ferry to Christ Church in Philadelphia until she lost her sight at the age of 96. An excellent fisherwoman she still rowed her own boat and caught fish while blind. Her sight miraculously returned at the age of 100 or 102. There is no record of her having married or borne children. She died at Bristol in Bucks County at the age of 116. She remained a slave her entire life.

Alice was one of the first respected African American oral historians. A centenarian, she lived to see the birth and growth of an historic American city. As an oral historian she lived to tell generations of Americans about one of the birthplaces of modern day America. Her stories were not written down verbatim but rather passed from one generation to another. She herself is written about in many histories of Pennsylvania.

FURTHER READING

Cima, Gay Gibson. *Early American Women Critics* (2006).

Davis, W. W. H. *The History of Bucks County, Pennsylvania* (1905).

Gale Research. "Alice of Dunk's Ferry," in *Notable Black American Women Book 2* (1996).

Kaplan, Sidney. *The Black Presence in the Era of the American Revolution, 1770–1800* (1975).

Mott, Abigail. *Biographical Sketches and Interesting Anecdotes of Persons of Colour* (1826).

Stephens, Robert. "Part I," in *Six Part Investigation Into a Family of Slavers, Traders & Thieves; Quakers & Anglicans; Colonialists, Royalists & Warmongers* (2003).

Watson. *Watson's Annals of Philadelphia and Pennsylvania*, vol. 1 (1857).

DARSHELL SILVA

Allain, Théophile T. (1 Oct. 1846–2 Feb. 1917), businessman and politician, was born a slave in West Baton Rouge, Louisiana, to Sosthene Allain, a wealthy white planter, and one of Allain's slave mistresses, whose name is not recorded. Sosthene Allain appears to have favored his son, to whom he gave the nickname "Sologue," after a Haitian dictator of the 1840s and 1850s. In 1856, when Théophile was ten, his father called him to France to attend the christening of the son of Louis Napoleon III in Paris and also to travel with him to Spain and Britain. Théophile returned to the United States in 1859, where he studied with private tutors in New Orleans and at a private college in New Brunswick, New Jersey.

Although Allain had been born a slave, his education and foreign travel prepared him well for a leadership position in Louisiana business and politics after the Civil War. So, too, did his inheritance of the family plantation around that time. Upon returning to Louisiana from New Jersey in 1869, he began a lifelong interest in education by establishing schools for both blacks and whites. He also opened grocery businesses in West Baton Rouge and Iberville parishes and began cultivating and exporting rice and sugar, employing thirty-five laborers on his eight-hundred-acre plantation. Allain also secured a contract from the state of Louisiana to construct 150,000 yards of levees on the Mississippi River. By the early 1870s Allain's various business interests, including a cattle ranch, had secured him an annual income in excess of $15,000, making him one of the wealthiest people of color in Louisiana during Reconstruction.

Allain's burgeoning business ventures and his interest in expanding educational opportunities perhaps inevitably brought him to a career in politics. An active Republican, he won a seat in the Louisiana House of Representatives from West Baton Rouge Parish in 1870, but he was prevented from taking his seat because of alleged voting irregularities in his district. Allain won election to the house in 1872 and in 1874, was seated, and served with some distinction. Alongside his fellow Republicans and as chairman of the house appropriations committee he attempted to ease the burden of Louisiana taxpayers, while still maintaining state aid to education and other matters of government that had been neglected during slavery. Achieving that balance proved difficult, particularly in the wake of the worldwide depression that began in 1873 and greatly restricted the spending plans of all of the Southern state legislatures.

Allain also earned a reputation as something of a peacemaker in the Louisiana legislature, which was arguably the most contentious in the nation. The 1872 elections resulted in rival state legislatures in New Orleans—one Republican, supported by Allain and most African Americans, the other an alliance of white supremacist Democrats and conservative Republicans. The intensification of White League opposition to Republican rule also precipitated the infamous Colfax riot on Easter Sunday 1873, the single bloodiest episode during Reconstruction, which resulted in the death of more than a hundred African Americans in Louisiana's Red River Valley. In response to the Colfax riot and to the bitter divisions in the state legislature in 1873, Allain emerged as one of the most prominent black advocates of the unification movement, an effort by moderate white New Orleans businessmen and a few prominent people of color to seek a middle ground in Louisiana politics. The unification movement hoped to weaken both Northern Radical Republicans and the more extreme White League Democrats and to encourage an alliance of black and white businessmen to-govern the state. The philosophy of black unificationists—most of whom were, like Allain, wealthy and of mixed race—prefigured that of BOOKER T. WASHINGTON in its emphasis on economic self-help and political moderation. The unification movement was short-lived, however, because the majority of black Louisianans, particularly the former slaves, distrusted the unification movement's white leaders and their mixed-race allies and because whites, particularly in rural and northern Louisiana, were in no mood to compromise. Although the Republicans narrowly won the 1874 elections—with Allain securing a seat in the state senate—the Colfax riot, among other atrocities, persuaded white Louisianans that violence and intimidation would eventually reclaim the state government from Republican rule.

Allain served in the Louisiana Senate from 1874 to 1876, the final two years of narrow Republican rule, during which his efforts to reform local government, build better roads and bridges, and repair levees on the Mississippi were defeated by Democrats and conservative Republicans determined to cut spending. He chaired the senate standing committee on elections, one of the more important assignments given the state's problems with voter fraud and intimidation, but he could do little to solve the problem of another contested state election in 1876. On that occasion the federal commission in Washington, D.C., brokered a compromise that secured the presidency for the Republican Rutherford B. Hayes, while allowing the Democrats to regain control of the contested Southern legislatures, including Louisiana's.

The end of Reconstruction did not end Allain's involvement in Louisiana politics, though the changed tenor of the times was made clear to him in 1879 when a barman on a steamer called the senator a "nigger" and refused to serve him a glass of water (Blassingame, 193). Allain participated in the Louisiana constitutional convention of 1879, where, along with P. B. S. PINCHBACK, he helped to establish Southern University, a state-funded institution for blacks only, which started in New Orleans and later moved to Baton Rouge. Some of Allain's fellow black politicians opposed the university's segregated status, but the senator, who served as vice president of the board of trustees, believed that Southern's free tuition would benefit African Americans of all backgrounds, not just the traditional Creole elite. In 1880 Allain left the senate but returned to the house, where he represented West Baton Rouge until 1890 and helped secure an appropriation of fourteen thousand dollars for Southern University. He displayed his pragmatism and political independence in 1886 by supporting a Democrat for Congress, for which he was briefly expelled from the Republican Party.

After Allain left the house in 1890 his financial resources went into decline. Some sources suggest that he lost his plantation, and others that he moved to Chicago to work for the Illinois Fish and Conservation Commission. Little is known about his personal life. He married Aline Coleman, a Louisianan who owned some property, and had six children, all of whom attended Straight University (later Dillard University) in New Orleans. By the time of Allain's death in February 1917, constitutional amendments had removed all African Americans from the state legislature and all but a handful from minor public offices. The educational establishments that Allain had helped to found and support in the 1870s and 1880s proved more durable, however, and the graduates of Straight, Southern, Leland, and other colleges eventually played a central role in restoring democracy to Louisiana in the second half of the twentieth century.

FURTHER READING

Information on Théophile T. Allain can be found in the Turnbull-Allain Family Papers, Manuscripts 4261, Louisiana and Mississippi Valley Collections, Louisiana State University, Baton Rouge, Louisiana.

Blassingame, John. *Black New Orleans, 1860–1880* (1973).

Vincent, Charles. *Black Legislators in Louisiana during Reconstruction* (1978).

STEVEN J. NIVEN

Allen, Anthony D. (15 June 1772–31 Dec. 1835), explorer and businessman, was born a slave in German Flats, New York. He was owned by the Dougal family and spent his youth in Schenectady. It is very likely his mother was a slave (New York did not abolish slavery until 1827); his father was a freeman and a mariner. Following the death of his master, he was purchased by another owner. After gaining his freedom in 1796, Allen arrived in Boston in 1800 and went to sea just as his father had done. Indeed, many African Americans living in Boston had ties to the maritime industry in some way. Like other black mariners, Allen faced the risk of reenslavement when he traveled to Southern ports. Once he was saved from imprisonment by one of the ship's owners, who paid $300 for his release.

Allen's years at sea between 1800 and 1810 provided him with unique experiences. He traveled to France where he saw Toussaint-Louverture, the black liberator of Haiti, and the Englishman Lord Nelson. He also traveled to China, India, Indonesia, Santo Domingo, Cuba, Jamaica, and Hawaii. He decided to leave ship while on the Hawaiian island of Oahu, and for a brief time he served as a steward to King Kamehameha I. In 1811 he was awarded a land grant by the high priest Hewahewa, a great honor since land grants were made only to chiefs and people who were highly respected in the kingdom. In 1812 Allen returned to sea, sailed to China, and then came back to Oahu to settle there permanently. Called "Alani" by the Hawaiian people, he was widely respected not only because of the land grant he had received but also because of his generosity—he supplied fresh meat and vegetables to the missionaries and befriended sailors who became sick aboard ship by providing them a place for rest and rehabilitation. He eventually married a Hawaiian woman who gave birth to three children: Peggy, Anthony Jr., and George Caldwell. There is evidence that Allen may have married a second wife, which was a common practice in Hawaii at the time. It is very likely that his second wife's name was Pehu, since this woman was mentioned twice in accounts by Stephan Reynolds, a missionary and Allen's friend. Much of what we know about Anthony D. Allen can be attributed to the diaries and journals that were kept by missionaries like Reynolds (Scruggs, 42). For example, Maria S. Loomis wrote the following in 1820: "Among the residents of this island is a Black man native of Schenectady named Allen. He has been our constant friend … (and) he lives on a beautiful plain called Wyeta (Waikiki)."

By the time the first missionaries arrived in Hawaii in 1820 Allen was well established. Allen's developments on his six acres of land in Waikiki included a compound with eight or ten buildings. Some of the buildings were used for sleeping quarters, dining, cooking, storage, and for housing seamen who became ill on their journeys. According to missionary reports, Allen operated what could be considered the first Hawaiian hospital for American seamen. Many of the patients were brought to Allen's hospital for treatment and recuperation (Scruggs, 38–39); evidently he had learned some medical skills from Dr. Dougal in Schenectady.

Allen turned out to be an astute businessman and entrepreneur. Among his most successful ventures was as a farmer. He supplied fresh vegetables, eggs, milk, fowl, and meats. He also provided boarding for other people's cattle and horses. Another important part of his business was providing supplies for newly arrived ships in Honolulu's port. Reynolds reveals that Allen also ran a successful tavern that was popular among seamen. In the tavern could also be found the Hawaiian Islands' first bowling alley. Bowling, it seems, was a very popular recreational activity, as Reynolds stated in his journal in 1824 that "all the village is rolling at Allen's." In B. O. Wist's *A Century of Public Education in Hawaii*, Allen is recognized as the first individual to build a schoolhouse in Hawaii. Allen was literate and taught his own children to read and write at an early age.

Allen's daughter Peggy married Robert Moffet, a European American shoemaker in Honolulu. His other children went on to marry Hawaiian women and make lives for themselves in various enterprises. Anthony Allen Jr. moved to the island of Hawaii, and he became known as an expert catcher of wild bullock. He was also a valued friend of Prince Lot Kamehameha of Honolulu. George Caldwell Allen married Maria Lahilahi, the daughter of a Hawaiian woman and Don Francisco Marin, a Spanish adventurer and confidant of the king. Today, very little is known of what happened to subsequent descendants of Anthony D. Allen. Scruggs has stated that it is possible that "many do not even know they are of African ancestry" (Scruggs, 46).

Allen suffered a stroke in December 1835 and died on 31 December. Not only did Allen play a significant role in Hawaii's history, but he is also considered to have been the best-documented person of African ancestry who lived in Hawaii during the early nineteenth century.

FURTHER READING

Scruggs, Marc. "Anthony D. Allen: A Prosperous American of African Descent in Early 19th Century Hawaii," *Hawaiian Journal of History* (1992).

Scruggs, Marc. "There Is One Black Man, Anthony D. Allen," in *They Followed the Trade Winds: African Americans in Hawaii* (2005).

MILES M. JACKSON

Allen, Aris Tee (27 Dec. 1910–8 Feb. 1991), physician and state legislator, was born in Beeville, Texas, the son of James and Mary Etta Whitby Allen. His parents separated when he was an infant. When Allen was six years old, his mother, feeling that he needed male guidance and discipline, sent him to San Antonio to be reared by his father, a hotel bellman. Even while attending elementary school, he was expected to earn his keep, selling newspapers, delivering clothes for a local tailor, and, at the age of twelve, serving as a hotel washroom attendant. Allen excelled in the classroom through primary and junior high schools. But apparently in his final year of junior high he left school after a classmate harassed him for wearing his father's clothing. He was soon hired as a busboy in a hotel dining room and within two years found employment as a waiter at a San Antonio hotel. By the spring of 1928 Allen had moved to Houston and found seasonal employment on the docks loading cotton bales onto freighters and found odd jobs as a domestic worker, chauffeur, waiter, and assistant to a clothing salesman. Becoming restless again, he moved north, where he had long heard that blacks had better opportunities.

Allen arrived in Chicago in the middle of the Great Depression but was fortunate to find work as a janitor's assistant, busboy, and chauffeur. By the spring of 1932 he was sweeping floors and making deliveries for a drugstore on Chicago's South Side. That fall he enrolled in night school in pursuit of his long-postponed high school diploma. Ever anxious to improve himself, Allen began taking every civil service examination that he could until he was informed of an opening in Washington, D.C., as an elevator operator. In the spring of 1934 he began the long drive to the nation's capital. In Washington he was assigned to the U.S. Department of Agriculture, where he worked days and attended high school night classes, completing two courses with good grades. In mid-August he transferred to the night shift and enrolled as a full-time high school day student.

In May 1938, at the age of twenty-seven, Allen finally earned his high school diploma, and the following fall he entered Howard University as a premedical student. During his third year at Howard, the U.S. entry into the war that had erupted in Europe was imminent. Enrolled as a reserve officer training candidate and accepted for preflight training, Allen considered joining the Ninety-ninth Pursuit Squadron, a black military air unit forming in Tuskegee, Alabama. But a friend convinced him that if the United States entered the war, physicians would be needed as well as pilots. Allen entered Howard Medical School, where, after the U.S. entry into the war, the curriculum was condensed to three years.

Before the war ended, Allen was released from his military obligation early when he agreed to practice medicine in Annapolis, Maryland, where there was a shortage of physicians. Once his practice was established, Allen married Faye Watson, a nurse in the Howard University medical clinic whom he had met while he was a student. She enrolled in medical school, and they became partners in their Annapolis medical office. Allen's medical practice was interrupted during the Korean conflict when he was called back into the air force to serve in the Flight Surgeon's Office at Vance Air Base near Enid, Oklahoma. Following his service he returned to Annapolis, resumed the practice of medicine, and became involved in community activities, including serving as president of the Parent Teacher Association at his children's school.

Allen was appointed by the governor of Maryland to the Anne Arundel County school board in the 1950s after the Supreme Court ordered the desegregation of public schools. He was often at odds with the county school superintendent, who favored gradual school desegregation. Allen was anxious to change the deplorable conditions of the black schools, particularly one that had no running water, where children wanting a drink or to wash their hands had to go to a nearby stream and get down on their hands and knees.

In 1966 Allen was elected to the Maryland House of Delegates as a Republican in a jurisdiction where Democrats outnumbered Republicans three to one. After two four-year terms in the house, he ran for a seat in the Maryland Senate but was defeated by 125 votes. He was subsequently elected chairman of the Maryland Republican Party, becoming the only black Republican state chairman in any of the fifty states, and in 1978 he was the first black to run for lieutenant governor of Maryland. Though he was defeated in his bid for state office, he was chosen to fill a vacancy in the state senate. Two years later he became the first African American in modern history to preside as secretary of the Republican National Convention.

In 1981 Allen resigned his seat in the Maryland Senate when President Ronald Reagan named him to serve as the director of the Bureau of Health Standards in the Health Care Financing Agency of the U.S. Department of Health and Human Services. While serving there, Allen, who had completed his medical school curriculum without finishing his bachelor's degree requirements, enrolled in night classes at Howard University. In the spring of 1985 the seventy-four-year-old Allen, who graduated from high school at twenty-seven, accepted his bachelor's degree. In 1990 Allen again won a seat in the house of delegates, where at the age of eighty he was its oldest member. Three months after his election Allen learned that he had terminal cancer and took his own life.

FURTHER READING

Bentley, Helen Delich. "The Death of a Pioneer," *Congressional Record*, 11 Apr. 1991.

May, Jude Thomas. *Achieving the American Dream: The Life of the Honorable Aris T. Allen, M.D.* (1990).

"The Odyssey of Aris Allen," *Annapolitan* (Apr. 1990).

HAROLD N. BURDETT

Allen, Debbie (16 Jan. 1950–), dancer, choreographer and actress, was born Deborrah Kaye Allen in Houston, Texas, to Andrew Allen, a dentist, and Vivian Ayers-Allen, a poet and librarian; her parents had two other children, the actress Phylicia Rashad, and Hugh Allen, better known as Tex. Although she exhibited an early interest in dance and desired to join the Houston Foundation for Ballet, she was denied admission when she applied in the 1950s in what her mother saw as a clear example of discrimination. Her parents were able to pay for private ballet lessons with the Ballet Russes. She later traveled and trained in Mexico City with the Ballet Nacional de Mexico. In 1964 she returned to Houston where she once again auditioned for the Houston Foundation for Ballet. This time she was not only accepted to the prestigious organization but was awarded a scholarship. Her talent won her the high school appelation of "Miss Versatile." After graduation she traveled to Washington, D.C., to attend Howard University, her sister Phylicia's alma mater. She graduated from Howard in 1971 with a B.A. in Classical Greek Literature, Speech, and Theater. During her time at Howard, she continued to develop as a dancer, working with the Michael Malone dance troupe.

In 1971 Allen moved to New York City, where she roomed with her sister while they both worked in a variety of acting roles. She performed in a wide variety of roles including Purlie in OSSIE DAVIS's *Purlie Victorious* and Beneatha in *A Raisin in the Sun*. In 1972 she became a principal dancer in GEORGE FAISON's Universal Dance Experience. In 1980 she earned a Tony Award nomination for the role of Anita in *West Side Story*; although she did not win the Tony, she did earn a Drama Desk Award for the role in that year. In the early 1980s Allen achieved her greatest recognition when she undertook the role of dance teacher Lydia Grant in the Broadway production of *Fame*. She later reprised the role in the television program of the same name, which ran from 1984 to 1987. The television role eventually earned her two Emmy Awards and a Golden Globe.

Despite her commitment to dance and acting, she eventually succumbed to the allure of direction and production. During Allen's tenure as Lydia Grant on Broadway and television, her sister earned a role on the popular situation comedy *The Cosby Show*. The show's originator and star, BILL COSBY, wanted Allen to direct an episode of the Cosby spin-off *A Different World*, based on the experiences of one *Cosby Show*–daughter attending a historically black college. Initially Allen resisted but in 1988 she accepted Cosby's offer and directed the series off and on throughout its duration. In the interim, she performed as Charity in *Sweet Charity* (1986) and was once again nominated for a Tony. She also performed in several specials, including *The Debbie Allen Show* and *Polly* (1989) and *Polly One More Time* (1990). Her tenure as director for *A Different World* eventually led to opportunities in the 1990s to direct other television shows such as *The Fresh Prince of Bel-Air* and *Quantum Leap*. She also choreographed the Academy Awards at least five times during the 1990s, and produced and directed *Stomping at the Savoy* at the Kennedy Center.

Among Allen's other television work are children's shows like *Brothers of the Knight* and *Dancing in the Wing* (2000) as well as programs such as *Cool Women* and *The Old Settlers*, which she directed and co-produced. She also directed episodes of series such as *Girlfriends, All of Us*, and *The Parkers*, and produced the film Amistad (1997). She had been inspired by William Owens's *Black Mutiny*, which told the story of the mutiny and trial of slaves captured after their mutiny aboard the schooner *La Amistad*. Working with acclaimed director Steven Spielberg and an all-star cast headed by Sir Anthony Hopkins and MORGAN FREEMAN, she served as executive producer of the film. During filming, the production encountered a series of problems, one of which was a lawsuit by writer BARBARA CHASE-RIBOUD, who claimed that the project plagiarized her own work on the subject.

Allen's first marriage was to record executive William Wilford, whom she divorced. She met husband Norm Nixon during the filming of *The Fish that Saved Philadelphia*; they married in 1984 and have two children, Vivian Nicole and Norm Jr., whom they call Thump.

Allen's work garnered her awards beyond Tony, Emmy, and Golden Globes. She was the first ever honoree of the Lena Horne Award for Career Achievement in 1995, and was also the recipient of a 1992 Essence Award and a 1995 Soul Train Lady of Soul Award. A member of the Black Filmmakers Hall of Fame, she has been given honorary doctorates from North Carolina School of the Arts and Howard University. Allen also served on the President's Committee on Arts and Humanities as well as the American Film Institute and the UCLA School of Theatre and Film. Allen opened The Debbie Allen Dance Academy in East Los Angeles with a design to teach dance as a cultural meaning. Students at the academy learn twelve different dance forms in what is meant to serve as a youth outreach opportunity as well as an educational one. The program also offers students the opportunity to study dance as a serious career.

FURTHER READING

"Allen, Debbie," *Encyclopedia of African American Cultural History*, vol. 5 (1996).
"Debbie Allen: On Power, Pain, Prime Time," *Ebony* (March 1991).
Hine, Darlene Clark, ed. *Black Women in America: An Historical Encyclopedia* (1994).

DONNA WALLER HARPER

Allen, Elise Ford (29 July 1921–), editor and publisher, was born in Peoria, Illinois, to Dr. Cecil Bruce Ford and Florence Henderson Ford. She was the granddaughter of Major George Ford and a great-great-granddaughter of WEST FORD, who may have been the African American son of George Washington. Cecil Bruce Ford, a graduate of Meharry Medical College, was Peoria's first African American dentist, while Elise's mother, Florence, was a well-known seamstress. Elise Ford was baptized at the age of three at Bethel Methodist Church and attended the Peoria public school system with her siblings Bruce, Florence, and Harrison. Later Ford acted as her grandfather's secretary when he was the president of the Springfield chapter of the National Association for the Advancement of Colored People (NAACP), and wrote his correspondence as his eyesight failed in his later years.

The Ford oral history, which held that she was the three-times great-granddaughter of George Washington, was relayed to Elise by her grandfather at annual family reunions at Camp Butler. She was admonished not to discuss her heritage outside of the immediate family for fear of racial reprisals. She became the Ford family chronicler upon the death of Major Ford.

Elise Ford married James O. Allen in 1937, and the couple had eleven children. Her husband, a printer and inventor, started the Allen Printing Company in 1946, the first African American–owned printing establishment in Peoria.

During the early years of Allen's marriage, the civil rights movement swung into full force, with equal education at the forefront. This period would begin her long involvement as an advocate for the rights of the disenfranchised. In May 1954 the U.S. Supreme Court in its landmark *Brown v. Board of Education* decision declared segregation in public schools unconstitutional; the Allen children attended a neighborhood school with a student body that was 80 percent minority. They had yet to be bused to the city's all-white neighborhoods. A firm believer that inequality could be fought through education, Allen became an active PTA member. She served as the first African American president of the PTA at McKinley Elementary and Roosevelt Junior High schools. This presidency would head the list of her numerous firsts as an African American.

In 1960 the Allen Printing Company became the Traveler Printing and Publishing Company. In 1966 Allen launched the *Traveler Weekly Newspaper*, becoming the first African American woman to edit and publish a newspaper in the state of Illinois. The newspaper started out as a single 8.5x11 sheet of paper with local news items and Allen's editorials but grew to tabloid size the following year. For the next four decades Allen would remain an important and influential voice for freedom and equality.

She also continued her civic work. From 1968 to 1973 she was the first African American to serve on the board of the Peoria Girl Scouts, receiving a certificate for "uplifting young black girls in the inner city of Peoria." She organized the first 4-H Club for black girls in the state. Discrimination was still a barrier for many African Americans trying to fight their way out of poverty and into a decent life, and, with this in mind, Allen ran for mayor in 1973. Much of the white populace considered her candidacy a joke, but many voters changed their minds after they heard Allen speak in debate, during which she demonstrated her understanding of the issues confronting the city and laid out solid, workable solutions that many of the other candidates lacked. Though Allen did indeed lose her bid as mayor, her run made her a household name, and the *Traveler Weekly's* circulation went statewide. A year later, in 1974, Allen was named Citizen of the Year by the Magnificent Gentlemen, Inc., a big brother organization, for her outstanding service to the community. Other awards came that same year: the Certificate of Achievement from the Peoria Commission on Human Rights, a commendation from the Peoria chapter of the National Organization for Women (NOW), and the Outstanding Business Women Award by the National Association of University Women.

That same year Allen continued her pursuit of equal protection under the law for all Americans, without regard to race, color, or creed. An African American mother of eleven had been sentenced to life in prison for killing her husband in self-defense. Allen reviewed the case with the public defender, interviewed witnesses, and began writing editorials in the *Traveler Weekly*, charging that the woman had not received a fair trail. The governor of Illinois, Dan Walker, read her editorials and later paroled the condemned woman. The power of Allen's insightful writing would lead to many more commendations from all over the state of Illinois.

As Allen knew, unchecked poverty kept the poor out of the mainstream society and made them easy targets for discrimination. To honor Allen's pursuit of quality education for minorities, a scholarship was established in her name in 1985, at the Roosevelt Magnet School. Her newspaper, the *Traveler Weekly*, has earned dozens of awards in the field of excellence in journalism. In humanitarian circles, she was presented numerous awards including the prestigious Martin Luther King Jr. Commemorative Leadership Award (1989). Elise Ford Allen's passion for equality for African Americans has earned her a place of honor in the realms of civil rights activists.

FURTHER READING
Allen-Bryant, Linda. *I Cannot Tell a Lie: The True Story of George Washington's African American Descendants* (2004).
Burton, Judith Saunders. "A History of Gum Springs, Virginia: A Report of a Case Study of Leadership in a Black Enclave," Ph.D. diss. (1986).

LINDA ALLEN-BRYANT

Allen, Ethel D. (8 May 1929–16 Dec. 1981), physician and politician, was one of three children born in Philadelphia, Pennsylvania, to Sidney S. Allen Sr., a Georgia native, Democratic committeeperson, and tailor with a seventh-grade education whose dream of becoming a doctor was realized by his daughter. Ethel's mother, the former Effie Jean Goodall, was a Democratic committeeperson born in Maryland who operated a tailoring business with her husband for many years. Ethel Allen became fascinated by medicine and the mysteries of life and death as a child while living in North Philadelphia, and she began to move toward medicine while studying at a Catholic institution, the then mostly white John W. Hallahan Girls Catholic High School, although her parents were Baptists.

Allen's intellectual curiosity led to intense scientific and medical inquiry, prompted by a visit to an uncle's dental practice as well as by visits to a local physician who kept animal specimens in jars. Sheltered by her parents and an avid reader of political novels, Allen found refuge in the local library not far from her home near Twenty-third Street and Ridge Avenue. After attending national conventions in Philadelphia relating to her parents' political activities, Allen began to pattern herself after the famed black educator and activist MARY MCLEOD BETHUNE, who advised President Franklin Roosevelt. Allen later told the *Philadelphia Inquirer Today* magazine, "Like most people thought about movie stars, I thought about politicians." She even managed the presidential campaign of a fellow student in high school, where she also learned how to play the piano and trumpet. By 1952, in fact, she had become involved in Dwight Eisenhower's presidential campaign by "scheduling appointments for the Philadelphia area," she said in the *Today* interview, likely a precursor to her gravitating toward the Republican Party.

Those experiences prepared her for local and state politics, but not before her medical career flourished once she enrolled in an all-black school, West Virginia State College (later West Virginia State University), where she hungered to learn more about African American culture. There she became a lifelong friend of the student Augusta A. Clark, who later became the second black woman on the Philadelphia City Council, with Allen's urging and support. Allen also excelled in Latin and drama. After graduation in 1946 with a bachelor's degree in biology, she was employed over the next dozen years as a research assistant for the pharmaceutical firm Rohm and Haas, as a chemist for the Atomic Energy Commission, and as an adviser to the Cheyney State College chapter of Delta Sigma Theta sorority, helping to find scholarships for college-bound students. Meanwhile, as she took graduate courses at Temple University from 1952 to 1954 and at the University of Pennsylvania in 1959, Allen applied to medical schools hoping to fulfill her lifelong dream of becoming a physician—just as the civil rights movement expanded.

Allen said that her father was initially ambivalent about her planned medical career because of the sexism and racism that a black woman would have to endure. In fact she spent more than five years applying to medical schools before the Philadelphia College of Osteopathic Medicine (PCOM) accepted her in 1959. There she encountered bigotry and chauvinism—particularly from white males in the student body—before graduating with a doctor of osteopathy degree in 1963.

By 1964 the quick-witted Allen had completed an internship at Grand Rapids Osteopathic Hospital in Grand Rapids, Michigan, after having been rejected at a number of institutions for an internship. She opened an office in Philadelphia at Fifteenth Street and Columbia Avenue, in the heart of black North Philadelphia. Once, while she was on a house call, thugs attempted to rob her at gunpoint, but she pulled her own handgun and forced them to exit the building naked.

Allen gained a reputation as a gritty, no-nonsense doctor and attracted the attention of community activists, some of whom were her patients. Several asked her to run for city council. Because of her political upbringing, her sensitivities related to racism and sexism, and her ambitions, she accepted the offer, defeating the three-term Democratic councilman Thomas McIntosh in November 1971 for the Fifth District seat. Allen had successfully switched aisles and became a powerful Republican with mayoral aspirations in a city known for its dominant Democratic base, often confronting the Democratic mayor Frank L. Rizzo (who later became a Republican) over such issues as funding to combat street gangs, rent control, affordable housing for her constituents, children's public health care, and even protecting the rights of street vendors.

Allen's initial foray into politics and primarily antipoverty stances during nearly two terms as a councilperson were especially noteworthy because she was a black Republican as well as an osteopathic physician, characteristics that media and political observers found fascinating. She sometimes joked about her uniqueness, calling herself a "BFR" or black female Republican. She was particularly concerned about issues that affected women, and in 1977 she traveled to China to monitor women's rights advances, an issue close to her heart in the United States.

A self-proclaimed practitioner of "ghetto medicine" who had a searing sense of humor, Allen contemplated national office after winning an at-large council seat, even giving President Gerald Ford a seconding speech at the National Republican Convention. Rising politically to become Secretary of the Commonwealth of Pennsylvania in 1979, Allen had already been named by *Esquire* magazine in 1975 as one of the nation's twelve outstanding women politicians, along with Representative SHIRLEY CHISHOLM, the first African American to run for president, an office that Allen briefly contemplated.

Allen's tenure as Pennsylvania's secretary—which followed the brief term of another black woman, C. DELORES TUCKER, who left the office amid controversy—lasted just nine months, because of charges that Allen had given speeches and received payment while she was supposed to be performing duties for the state. The Republican governor Richard Thornburgh dismissed her amid objections from civil rights groups claiming that his action was politically motivated. Though disappointed, Allen rebounded to take a position as a Philadelphia school district doctor with management responsibilities. She fought her own heart disease and cancer, which resulted in a mastectomy in 1975. She died at age fifty-two from heart disease. She was memorialized as the first black woman Philadelphia councilperson, as Secretary of the Commonwealth of Pennsylvania, and as a women's rights advocate and community activist. She was a tenacious fighter for the powerless, always mindful of racial and gender rights, despite the size and ferocity of her opposition.

FURTHER READING
Files of newspaper articles about Allen from the
    Philadelphia Bulletin, Philadelphia Inquirer, and

Philadelphia Daily News are at Temple University's Urban Archives Center in Philadelphia.

Burkart, Kathryn W. "A Minority of One," *Philadelphia Inquirer Today,* 9 Sept. 1973.

Sims, Patsy. "I've Learned to Survive …," *Philadelphia Inquirer,* 25 Jan. 1976.

Obituary: *Philadelphia Bulletin,* 18 Dec. 1981.

DONALD SCOTT SR.

Allen, Geri Antoinette (12 June 1957–   ), pianist and composer, was born in Detroit, Michigan, the daughter of Mount Vernell Allen Jr. She began studying classical piano at age seven but was also exposed to jazz at an early age. She met the trumpeter Marcus Belgrave when he was an artist-in-residence at her high school, Cass Technical; she studied jazz piano with him, and he became an important mentor, appearing on several of her later recordings. Allen also studied at the Jazz Development Workshop, a community-based organization.

After graduating from high school, Allen attended Howard University, where she was captivated by the music of THELONIOUS MONK and studied with John Malachi. In 1979 she earned a B.A. in Jazz Studies and taught briefly at Howard before moving to New York City, where she studied with the pianist Kenny Barron. She also met the jazz educator Nathan Davis, who invited her to enroll at the University of Pittsburgh; there she wrote a thesis on ERIC DOLPHY and earned an M.A. in Ethnomusicology in 1982. During her time in Pittsburgh she played in a trio led by the drummer Roy Brooks.

Allen returned to New York in 1982 and resumed her studies with Barron, rapidly making a name for herself among the more progressive young jazz leaders. She was a member of Oliver Lake's group Jump Up from 1982 to 1987, and between 1982 and 1984 she toured with a variety of prominent artists, including Brooks, the trumpeter LESTER BOWIE, the vibraphonist Jay Hoggard, the saxophonist Joseph Jarman, the flutist James Newton, and the singer Nancy Wilson. In 1984 she toured Europe with her own quartet and recorded *The Printmakers,* her first album as a bandleader, with Anthony Cox on bass and Andrew Cyrille on drums. The recording cemented her growing reputation among the jazz avant-garde. In 1985 she recorded *Home Grown,* featuring six of her own compositions, as well as a pair of Monk covers. Allen regularly featured her own writing, penning all of the compositions on *Open on All Sides in the Middle* (1986). This album

had a funkier, more up-tempo feel than some of her later work, perhaps reflecting her contemporaneous involvement in the M-Base Collective, founded by the saxophonist STEVE COLEMAN. Allen appeared on two of that group's albums in 1985 and 1986, fitting easily into the dense ensembles and funky grooves.

Allen also freelanced widely throughout the late 1980s, playing with artists such as the saxophonists ARTHUR BLYTHE and Chico Freeman, the trumpeter WOODY SHAW, and the vibraphonist Hoggard. In 1987 she began a lengthy relationship with the bassist Charlie Haden and the drummer Paul Motian. The trio recorded several highly praised albums, including *Etudes* (1987), *Segments* (1989), *Live at the Village Vanguard* (1991), and *In the Year of the Dragon* (1991), all while touring extensively in the United States and Europe. These recordings contain many moments of breathtaking melodic beauty, as well as more experimental playing that helped showcase Allen's technical and stylistic range. She also played in a more conventional trio with the drummer Ralph Peterson and the bassist Essiet Essiet in the late 1980s; together these groups demonstrate Allen's ability to both play and compose across the entire spectrum of modern jazz piano, from post-bop to free jazz.

Allen's profile continued to rise with a string of acclaimed recordings in the 1990s. *The Nurturer* (1990) featured Belgrave on trumpet and Kenny Garrett on saxophone, and *Maroons* (1992) contained thirteen of Allen's own compositions. One of her former students, the trumpeter Wallace Roney, also appeared on *Maroons.* They were married in 1995 and had three children. In the fall of 1993 Allen toured Europe as a member of the singer BETTY CARTER's group, joining the drummer Jack DeJohnette and the bassist Dave Holland in the rhythm section and appearing on Carter's 1993 recording *Feed the Fire.* Also in 1993 Jazz at Lincoln Center commissioned a suite, *Sister Leola, an American Portrait.* In 1994 Allen appeared with the saxophonist ORNETTE COLEMAN's New Quartet at the San Francisco Jazz Festival, and she played on both versions of Coleman's *Sound Museum* recordings. She was, in fact, the first acoustic pianist that the iconoclastic Coleman had worked with in thirty-five years, and her appearances provided still further evidence of her remarkable stylistic range. That same year she recorded *Twenty-One* with the bassist Ron Carter and the drummer TONY WILLIAMS, perhaps the most accomplished rhythm section in modern jazz. The recording again showcased her mastery of a broad range of the modern jazz piano vocabulary. In addition to several of her own compositions, it features the up-tempo "Lullaby of the Leaves," the gorgeous ballad "A Beautiful Love," and Monk's "Introspection."

In 1996 Allen appeared as MARY LOU WILLIAMS in Robert Altman's film *Kansas City*, and she was the first woman to win the Danish Jazzpar Prize. Under the auspices of this award she recorded a 1996 session, *Some Aspects of Water*, consisting of several trio pieces and larger selections accompanied by a Danish nonet, most notably the nineteen-minute title piece. Her 1997 session *Eyes in the Back of Your Head* is a mixture of solo pieces and duets with Roney or Coleman. *The Gathering* (1998) is a collection of atmospheric originals showcasing Allen's highly individual playing—a melodic, lightly percussive bridge between a fleet-fingered bop style and the more abrasive percussive approach of the avant-garde; it is a masterpiece of relaxed phrasing and intense feeling.

At the peak of her powers Allen suddenly found herself without a recording contract until the fall of 2004, when Telarc Records released *The Life of a Song*, a trio with the bassist Dave Holland and the drummer DeJohnette. The recording covers a wide stylistic range, from the slightly dissonant "LWB's House (The Remix)," a musical portrait of her family, to "In Appreciation: A Celebration Song," which has flavors of gospel and Motown and is dedicated to ROSA PARKS. "The Experimental Movement" is a tribute to the dancer and choreographer Jacquelyn Hillsman, and "Black Bottom" pays homage to Paradise Valley, the black neighborhood that was the center of Detroit's jazz community during Allen's formative years. Allen's imaginative rearrangements of BILLY STRAYHORN's "Lush Life" and of BUD POWELL's "Dance of the Infidels" are exclamation points to one of the great albums of the new millennium.

Allen has received broad recognition from her peers as a composer, soloist, and educator. In the early 1990s she taught at the New England Conservatory, and in 1995 she became a faculty member at Howard University. She received many awards and honors, including the EUBIE BLAKE Award from Cultural Crossroads. Allen's playing clearly reflects the boppish influences of Bud Powell and the quirky rhythms and phrasing of Thelonious Monk, and even a bit of CECIL PERCIVAL TAYLOR, but she also embraces the lyricism of HERBIE HANCOCK and Bill Evans, the conceptual freedom of Ornette Coleman, and even the more populist experiments of the M-Base

Collective. She worked as an arranger for the singer Andy Bey on his album *American Song* (2003) and wrote and arranged material for the vocalist Mary Stallings. With BERNICE JOHNSON REAGON and Toshi Reagon she scored the HBO movie *Beah: A Black Woman Speaks*, a documentary of the life of the actress and civil rights activist Beah Richards. In "Time Line," Allen employs electric keyboards, synthesizers, and other electronic devices other electronic devices to explore the historical continuity of African music. Finally, the "Mary Lou Williams Project" is a trio effort with the drummer BILLY HART and the bassist Buster Williams. The group performed Williams's *Zodiac Suite* at Jazz at Lincoln Center in 2004 and performed excerpts from the suite at the Kennedy Center for the Mary Lou Williams Women in Jazz Festival. The suite was recorded and released on Mary Records in 2006. That same year Allen released a trio album with Ron Carter on bass and Jimmy Cobb on drums, along with the Atlanta Jazz Chorus, titled *Timeless Portraits and Dreams*, structured around a series of musical portraits of African American figures such as MARTIN LUTHER KING JR. and BILLIE HOLIDAY. In 2004 Allen was appointed director of jazz combos at the University of Michigan's department of jazz and contemporary improvisation.

FURTHER READING

Gourse, Leslie. *Madame Jazz: Contemporary Women Instrumentalists* (1995).

Holley, Eugene, Jr. "Geri Allen: Full Circle," *JazzTimes* (Jan. 1995).

Murph, John. "Mothership Connection," *JazzTimes* (Sept. 2004).

Palmer, D. "Geri Allen: Real Life Music Comes to Town," *Down Beat* 4, 6 (1988).

RONALD P. DUFOUR

Allen, James Latimer (7 Feb. 1907–1977), photographer, was born in New York City to Virginia Allen, a dressmaker who migrated from the British Virgin Islands in 1900, and an unidentified father. James attended Dewitt Clinton High School, where he discovered photography through the school's camera club, the Amateur Cinema League. The school was fertile ground for several members of the upcoming Harlem Renaissance, including the poet COUNTEE CULLEN, whose first published piece appeared in the school magazine, the *Magpie*. The artist CHARLES ALSTON also developed his talents as the art editor for the *Magpie* and leader of the art club. In 1923 Allen began a four-year apprenticeship at Stone, Van Dresser and Company, a white-owned illustration firm, where he received additional instruction in photography. Louis Collins Stone, the firm's owner and a portrait painter, and his wife seem to have taken a personal interest in Allen and in nurturing black talent. The writer and artist Richard Bruce Nugent also spent part of his adolescence in New York City, attended Dewitt Clinton, and was employed by this firm.

Following graduation from high school in 1925 Allen embarked on a career as an artist-photographer. With the support of patrons like ALAIN LEROY LOCKE and Carl Van Vechten, Allen opened a portrait studio at 213 West 121st Street in 1927 and quickly became the photographer of choice for the luminaries of the Harlem Renaissance. With subjects including Alston, Cullen, AARON DOUGLAS, W. E. B. DuBois, LANGSTON HUGHES, NELLA LARSEN, Locke, HAROLD JACKMAN, CHARLES SPURGEON JOHNSON, HALL JOHNSON, JAMES WELDON JOHNSON, JACOB LAWRENCE, NORMAN LEWIS, ROSE McCLENDON, CLAUDE McKAY, LOUISE THOMPSON PATTERSON, PAUL ROBESON, JOEL AUGUSTUS ROGERS, ARTHUR ALFONSO SCHOMBURG, EDNA LEWIS THOMAS, Van Vechten, and A'LELIA WALKER, Allen's roster of clients makes up the most comprehensive visual record of Harlem's cultural elite by an African American photographer. Carl Van Vechten, who was white, began his extensive body of photographs in 1932.

Allen created a visual image of the New Negro—the modern, urban, sophisticated, well-educated African American who exemplified the best that the race had to offer and refuted the claims of black inferiority that sustained white supremacist beliefs and Jim Crow policy. In his images well-groomed, well-dressed African American men and women posed in front of a simple gray backdrop are elegantly displayed as testaments to African American talent and achievement. Inscriptions on many of the photographic prints indicate that these portraits not only were meant for private display but also were exchanged between members of Harlem's social circles. The photographs seemed to have functioned as mutually reaffirming talismans of shared ideals and purpose in a world hostile to African American equality. This compelling vision was also deployed to promote the New Negro ideal among a national audience. Allen's portraits and his commercial images were consistently published in the leading Negro periodicals of the day, such as the *Crisis*, *Opportunity*, and the *Messenger*.

Opportunity, the magazine of the National Urban League, featured Allen's photographs on their cover sixteen times between 1934 and 1942. His images provided a model of the New Negro that black leaders encouraged all African Americans to emulate.

Allen also enjoyed considerable recognition as a fine artist. He was one of four photographers who competed for the William E. Harmon Foundation Awards for Distinguished Achievement among Negroes established in 1926. The annual exhibition (1927–1931, 1933, and 1935) of submissions in the fine arts category was the chief venue open to African American artists. In 1930 Allen was awarded the Commission on Race Relations Prize for Photographic Work from the Harmon Foundation. This was a special award established that year specifically to honor photography. Allen won this prize again in 1931 and 1933. He was the only photographer included in the film *A Study of Negro Artists* produced by the foundation in 1934. Allen was featured in other key exhibitions, including the Exhibition of Young Negro Artists in 1927, An Exhibition of Negro Art in 1935 at the Harlem YMCA, and the Exhibition of Fine Arts Productions by American Negroes, Hall of Negro Life, Texas Centennial in 1936 in Dallas. In 1930 he received a solo show, An Exhibition of Portraits by James L. Allen (A Group of New Portraits) at the Hobby Horse, a Harlem bookstore and café located at 113 West 136th Street.

With the onset of the Great Depression, Allen supplemented his income by taking photographs for the Harmon Foundation and the Harlem Art Workshop, thus producing an important archive of artworks and portraits of artists at work in their studios. He was employed as an instructor at the WPA-funded Harlem Community Art Center founded by the sculptor AUGUSTA SAVAGE in 1937. His documentation of activities there allowed Allen to work exclusively as a photographer and to maintain a studio, which he relocated to 2138 Seventh Avenue and then to 1858 Seventh Avenue until 1944.

Allen appears to have enlisted in World War II and was assigned to the Office of Strategic Services in Washington, D.C., where because of his prior experience he was tasked with processing film taken for intelligence purposes. Allen married around this time and never resumed his career as a photographer. He remained in Washington, working as a civil servant. When he died his personal archive was destroyed by his wife, who did not approve of his early profession. Surviving photographs by Allen can be found in the Moorland-Spingarn Research Center at Howard University, the Beinecke Rare

Book and Manuscript Library at Yale University, the Schomburg Center for Research in Black Culture in New York, and the Harmon Foundation Collection at the National Archives and the Library of Congress. Allen, along with other photographers of his generation, reinvented the iconography of blackness and established a modern black aesthetic that symbolized the racial pride that African Americans felt during the interwar period.

FURTHER READING

Holloway, Camara Dia. *Portraiture and the Harlem Renaissance: The Photographs of James L. Allen* (1999).

Willis, Deborah. *Reflections in Black: A History of Black Photographers 1840 to the Present* (2000).

Wright, Beryl, and Gary Reynolds. *Against the Odds: African-American Artists and the Harmon Foundation* (1989).

CAMARA DIA HOLLOWAY

Allen, Macon Bolling (1816–15 Oct. 1894), lawyer and judge, was born A. Macon Bolling in Indiana; the names of his parents and the exact date of his birth are unknown. He changed his name to Macon Bolling Allen by an act of the Massachusetts legislature on 26 January 1844. Details of Allen's early life and education are sparse and contradictory. His birth name is given in some sources as Malcolm B. Allen, and his birthplace as South Carolina. Evidence suggests that he lived in Maine and Massachusetts as a young man. Maine denied his initial application to the Maine bar because of allegations that he was not a state citizen, but he purportedly ran a Portland business before 1844. It is known that he read law in the Maine offices of two white abolitionist lawyers, Samuel E. Sewell and General Samuel Fessenden, and that Fessenden promoted his admission to the Maine bar in 1844.

Allen became a member of the Maine bar later in 1844 after passing the law examination required of all nonresidents. He thus became the first African American licensed to practice law in the United States. When he was admitted to the Massachusetts bar in 1845, a Boston abolitionist newspaper, the *Liberator*, stated on 9 May 1845 that Allen had received a classical education and that he was a brilliant and energetic young man of exceptional character and deportment. Allen never practiced law in Maine, possibly because of its small African American population (only 1,335 in 1844); instead, after being admitted to the bar, he immediately moved (or perhaps returned) to Massachusetts.

Allen began practicing law in Massachusetts after his admission to the Suffolk County bar on 3 May 1845, making him the first African American admitted to that state's bar as well. He apparently experienced some difficulty in obtaining clients during the first year of his practice. In November 1845 Allen wrote the New Yorker John Jay Jr. (the chief justice's grandson) that New Englanders supported only famous, wealthy, or long-established attorneys; he wondered whether New York's lack of such a tradition and its large African American population offered better opportunities for a black lawyer. Undoubtedly some of Allen's difficulty stemmed from Boston abolitionists' public denunciation of Allen's refusal to support their petition pledging nonsupport for the government during the Mexican War. A bitter 1846 letter from Allen to the radical abolitionist William Lloyd Garrison explained both his strong sympathy with enslaved African Americans and his private and independent approach to the problem.

Allen's fortunes soon changed. He was appointed a justice of the peace by Massachusetts's Whig governors in 1847 and 1854; the first appointment made him the nation's first appointed African American judicial official. He remained in Charlestown, near Boston, where he practiced law and served as justice of the peace until after the Civil War.

In the late 1860s Allen joined a small cadre of northern African American lawyers and activists who migrated to the South—in Allen's case, to Charleston, South Carolina. There, in 1868, he joined ROBERT BROWN ELLIOT and WILLIAM J. WHIPPER, two African American lawyer-politicians, to form a law firm that attracted clients of both races. With offices at 91 Broad Street in Charleston, Whipper, Elliot, and Allen was the first known African American law firm in the United States. The firm's combination of legal talents and political influence enabled it to hire and train many other African American lawyers. Allen never gained high political office, as his law partners did—both were elected to the South Carolina legislature, and Elliot to the U.S. Congress in 1870 and 1872—though he ran for secretary of state as a Republican in 1872 and for the same position on MARTIN DELANEY's 1874 fusion ticket. In February 1873 the South Carolina legislature elected him a judge of the Inferior Court, to fill a vacancy left by George Lee, with whom Allen had competed for the original appointment. Allen was elected to probate court in 1876 and served with distinction through 1878.

Allen returned to law practice in Charleston, and little is known of his life after that. He died in Washington, D.C., leaving a widow (whose name is unknown) and a son, Arthur W. Macon.

Allen left a legacy as a pioneer in African American legal history that transcended time, space, and, to a large extent, racism—and which placed him in the forefront of the black struggle. His accomplishments in New England and South Carolina paved the way for the generations of black lawyers and activists who followed.

FURTHER READING

Carter, George E., and C. Peter Ripley, eds. *Black Abolitionist Papers, 1830–1865* (1981).

Finkelman, Paul. "Not Only the Judge's Robes Were Black: African-American Lawyers as Social Engineers during and after Slavery," *Stanford Law Review* 47 (1994): 161–209.

Smith, J. Clay. *Emancipation: The Making of the Black Lawyer, 1844–1944* (1993).

Obituaries: Charleston *Daily News and Courier,* 17 Oct. 1894.

This entry is taken from the *American National Biography* and is published here with the permission of the American Council of Learned Societies.

JOHNIE D. SMITH

Allen, Marcus (26 Mar. 1960–), professional football player and sports analyst, was born in San Diego, California, to Harold "Red" Allen, a carpenter and general contractor, and Gwen Allen, a registered nurse. Developing an interest in football at the age of ten, Allen began to utilize the work ethic stressed by his parents, who sought to instill in their children a strict understanding of dignity, courage, and self-reliance. Allen's parents believed that for their children to become successful they must adhere to far-reaching tenets of character and faith by first actively demonstrating an understanding of hard work, team work, and unyielding discipline. Allen understood at an early age the significance of working hard and the possibility of achieving unforeseeable dividends. This ingrained ability would propel him beyond his own notions of success on the football field and into a realm of stardom as a national and international sports figure. At Lincoln High School in San Diego, several of Allen's teachers and coaches supported the charismatic teen, choosing to influence and encourage the high school prep star to excel beyond his own expectations. Allen's personal drive and dedication to the details of his performances, both on the playing field and in the classroom, would be definitive of his four-year collegiate and sixteen-year professional career.

In 1978 the highly recruited Parade All American chose to stay close to home, agreeing to attend the University of Southern California (USC) on a football scholarship. Recruited as a defensive back, the very talented Allen was switched to running back during his freshman year. Amassing a mere 171 yards as a freshman, Allen gained close to 700 yards in his sophomore year after being converted to a fullback. Spending his first two seasons in relative silence backing up and blocking for Charles White—the 1979 Heisman Trophy winner—Allen became a mainstay in the Trojan backfield during his junior season. During his first two seasons as a reserve back, Allen took advantage of his opportunities to hone his skills of blocking, catching out of the backfield, and reading defenses, all of which would become significant features of his long, illustrious career.

It was during his junior year at USC that Allen, with the help of head coach John Robinson and running backs coach John Jackson, began his assault on the record books of college football. Over the course of two seasons Allen set twelve National Collegiate Athletic Association records, including the single-season rushing record, by gaining 2,342 yards during his senior year, shattering the mark once held by the University of Pittsburgh's Tony Dorsett, a future National Football League (NFL) Hall of Fame running back of the Dallas Cowboys and Denver Broncos. In 1981, Allen shone as the nation's most exciting player in college football, winning praise and tribute from several of football's most prestigious institutions, including the Walter Camp Award for his exemplary adherence to the character traits his parents, coaches, and teachers stressed, as well as exceptional athletic ability; the Maxwell Award as the outstanding college football player of the year; major Football News First Team All America honors and awards; and college football's most significant award for individual achievement, the Heisman Trophy. In winning the Heisman, Allen became just the fourth USC running back to claim the award, placing his name amid those of past winners including former teammate and College Football Hall of Famer Charles White, NFL Hall of Famer O. J. Simpson, and College Football Hall of Famer Mike Garrett.

Indeed, in April 1982 the six foot two inch, two hundred pound Allen became the tenth overall pick in the NFL Draft, a first-round selection by the Los Angeles Raiders. In his inaugural season, shortened by the professional football players' labor strike, Allen led the American Football Conference (AFC) with fourteen touchdowns and all running backs with thirty-eight receptions, netting the twenty-two-year-old Rookie of the Year honors and an invitation to his first Pro Bowl. In 1983 in only his second year in the NFL, Allen enjoyed the success of competing at the top of his game by contributing to one of the Los Angeles Raiders' finest seasons, which culminated in a trip to Super Bowl XVIII. In a dazzling exhibition of athleticism and confidence, Allen scored three touchdowns while rushing for 191 yards against the National Football Conference Champion Washington Redskins. The Los Angeles Raiders' 38–9 victory over the Washington Redskins and Allen's outstanding performance won him the Most Valuable Player Award for the Super Bowl, but what will be most remembered about this particular game will be one particular display of skill and determination, which would punctuate the Hall of Fame running back's career. In the third quarter of the game, Raiders' quarterback Jim Plunkett pitched the ball to Allen, who ran into several waiting Redskin defenders. Thinking quickly on his feet, Allen reversed the field, running in the opposite direction, outmaneuvering the entire Redskins' defense. Allen culminated his amazing seventy-four-yard run by scoring a touchdown.

Allen's magnificent effort in Super Bowl XVIII was a promise of things to come for the sometimes underrated self-proclaimed overachiever. From 1982 to 1992, Allen rushed for more than 8,500 yards, scoring ninety-eight touchdowns and setting several records in the process. However, by the end of the 1991 NFL season, contract disputes with the Los Angeles Raiders majority owner, Al Davis, would relegate Allen to a part-time starter and backup role to the two-sport phenomenon Bo Jackson. In 1993 Allen regained his confident stride when he joined the Kansas City Chiefs, scoring an AFC-leading fifteen touchdowns, which helped the organization achieve a 13–3 record and an appearance in the 1994 AFC Championship game. After five seasons with the Chiefs, during three of which he led the team in rushing and all-purpose yards, Allen retired in 1997 as the all-time touchdown leader with 123 touchdowns. His many awards included the NFL Most Valuable Player in 1985, appearances in six Pro Bowls (1983, 1985–1988, and 1994), and NFL Comeback Player of the Year in 1993. Marcus Allen was inducted into the College Football Hall of Fame in 2000 and into the Pro Football Hall of Fame in 2003.

FURTHER READING
Allen, Marcus. *Marcus: The Autobiography of Marcus Allen* (1997).
Cobbs, Chris. *Marcus Allen: Super Raider* (1984).
Fulks, Matt. *Road to Canton* (2003).

PELLOM MCDANIELS III

Allen, Mary Rice Hayes (2 Mar. 1875–10 Oct. 1935), college president, activist for the National Association for the Advancement of Colored People (NAACP) and Young Women's Christian Association (YWCA). Born Mary Rice in Harrisonburg, Virginia, she was the acknowledged daughter of confederate general John R. Jones and Malinda Rice, who was hired as a servant in his household at the age of seventeen in 1873. There appears to have been some enduring affection between Jones and Rice. He acknowledged paternity of Mary and her brother William, and his first wife, Sarah, ill and often confined to bed, asked to see the children and gave them presents. Mary Rice was raised in part by John Rice, Malinda's brother, and his wife, Dolly. She also spent time in Jones's household, and after Sarah Jones died in 1879 the general bought a house for Malinda and her children. The immediate neighborhood was racially mixed; the next door neighbors had been born in Ireland.

Mary Rice entered a free public school in Harrisonburg in 1881 and in 1883 transferred to the newly built Effinger Street School. Both were separate schools for children classified as "colored," but at the time the city government took pride in their progress. In 1891 Rice's father sent her to Hartshorn Memorial College in Richmond, Virginia, where she was an honor student. In 1894 she met visiting speaker Gregory Willis Hayes, whom she married 3 May 1895. In eleven years of marriage they had seven children, five of whom survived infancy.

Hayes was the second president of Virginia Seminary and College in Lynchburg. With his young wife's active support, he fought a determined battle to retain a curriculum of higher mathematics, ethics, economics, foreign languages, classics such as the work of Cicero and Horace and the *Iliad*, and history, including that of Greece and Rome. The board of the American Baptist Home Mission Society, which provided substantial funding to the college, sought to limit courses to industrial and vocational subjects. This was a fashionable emphasis at the time among "white friends of the Negro." Promoting self-reliance, doing a great deal of fundraising around the country and abroad, and obtaining support from local black churches, Hayes survived the withdrawal of American Baptist funding, winning renewal of his contract as president in close-fought battles in 1895 and 1898. After Hayes died on 22 December 1906, his wife stepped forward to serve as interim President of the seminary from 1906 to 1908.

In 1911 she married William Patterson Allen, a lawyer from Danville, Virginia. They had three daughters, Rosemary, born in 1912, Carrie in 1913, and Dolly in 1915. The middle daughter, CARRIE ALLEN MCCRAY (who married South Carolina civil rights leader JOHN H. MCCRAY), would pen a well-received memoir of her mother, *Freedom's Child: The Life of a Confederate General's Black Daughter* (1998). Mary Allen continued to live in Lynchburg, joined by her husband on weekends, and was elected secretary of the Lynchburg NAACP when it was first organized in 1913 by JAMES WELDON JOHNSON. She frequently gave lawn parties as fundraisers to save the land of black families threatened with foreclosure. Allen sent a series of letters to President Woodrow Wilson, pointing out the contradiction between offering a "New Freedom" and his policy of segregating federal civil service employees who had previously not been subject to separation by race. "If Wilson had kept his promises," was a frequent comment in political conversations (McCray, 132).

In 1920 the Allens moved to Montclair, New Jersey, where Mary Allen served as president of the colored YWCA for nine years, was a member of the Montclair Interracial Committee, and renewed her participation in the NAACP, which elected her as president of the Montclair branch in 1930. She kept up extensive correspondence with W. E. B. DuBois, James Weldon Johnson WALTER WHITE, Joel and Arthur Spingarn, and WILLIAM PICKENS. During the 1920s Rice championed the cause of Italian immigrants, writing a letter to the judge hearing the trial of Nicolo Sacco and Bartolomeo Vanzetti to admonish his evident prejudice against Italians.

When Warren G. Harding was elected president in 1920 Allen sent him a letter of congratulations, firmly calling on him to present a federal antilynching bill to Congress. That was the first in a series of frequent letters to President Harding on the subject. In matters of racially motivated injustice, Allen had a policy of confronting people again and again, over matters large and small, never giving up. When her friend ANNE SPENCER's daughter Alroy needed a haircut, Allen took her to a salon in Newark known to find "no appointments are open" if anyone of color walked in the door. She told Alroy not to cut her hair until the place gave her an appointment, which, after many attempts and a meeting by Allen with the manager, they did.

Hearing that a newly built Montclair theater had a policy of seating Negroes to one side, she gathered her children, went to see a movie, and sat right in the center. After conversations with two ushers and the manager, her money was refunded and she was asked to leave; she began a several-year battle to end the practice. In the meantime, she was successful, with a combination of public protests and eventual support from the mayor, in stopping the theater from showing the movie "Birth of a Nation," based on Thomas Dixon's ahistorical novel *The Clansman*, both of which glorified the Ku Klux Klan and rendered a false portrait of Reconstruction. Throughout this work, she reminded her children that "angels and devils come in all colors" (McCray, 161, 184).

Rice died in 1935 shortly after planting tulip and daffodil bulbs in her garden from an infection that had seemed to be a slight cold, but grew rapidly worse. Mary Rice Hayes Allen was a persistent and consistent advocate for racial equality. Her lifelong friend, the poet Anne Spencer, observed in the 1960s, "Young people today think they're the original protesters. They didn't know Mary" (McCray, 6).

FURTHER READING
The Crisis, Dec. 1935, p. 377.
McCray, Carrie Allen. *Freedom's Child: The Life of a Confederate General's Black Daughter* (1998).
Potter, Clifton W., and Dorothy. *Lynchburg: A City Set on Seven Hills* (2004).

CHARLES ROSENBERG

Allen, Newt (19 May 1901–9 June 1988), infielder for the Kansas City Monarchs Negro Leagues baseball team, was born Newton Henry Allen in Austin, Texas. The names and occupations of his parents are unknown. Allen attended Lincoln High School, Kansas City, Missouri, and played ball for the Kansas City Tigers while still in school, before leaving to play for the Omaha Federals in 1921. While handling the middle of the infield for the Federals, Monarchs owner J. L. Wilkinson saw the youngster play and signed him to his All-Nations ball club. After only one season with the All-Nations, Allen was promoted to the Monarchs in 1923.

Allen played for twenty-three seasons in the Negro Leagues. Most of his playing time was spent at either second base or shortstop for the Kansas City Monarchs, one of the original teams in the Negro National League established in 1920. In addition to playing for Kansas City, Allen played in the California Winter League for six seasons and played two seasons in Cuba.

Allen's baseball career in the Negro Leagues began in 1923 when he was signed by the Monarchs. He also served as the player-manager for the Monarchs beginning in 1937. Over the course of the next six years he helped guide the ball club to five Negro American League titles. The only time Allen did not play for the Monarchs was in 1931 and 1932 when the original Negro National League folded because of the Great Depression. At that time, Allen signed with the St. Louis Stars and then the Homestead Grays. In 1933 with the revival of the Negro National League, Allen was able to rejoin the Monarchs through the 1944 season. He returned to play in 1947 with the Indianapolis Clowns, playing in only two games before retiring. He hit .287 over the course of his career, which ended in 1947.

One of the highlights of Allen's career came with his four selections to the East–West All Star team. Allen was selected by the fans to play in 1936, 1937, 1938, and 1941. The East–West Classic was held each year at Comiskey Park in Chicago, starting in 1933, and was the lifeblood of the Negro Leagues because it attracted thousands of fans to the game and helped many teams stay afloat financially from year to year.

Allen played with the Monarchs in the first Negro League World Series in 1924, helping the club beat the Hilldale Daisies from Pennsylvania. The World Series began after the creation of a second Negro League in 1923 led by Ed Bolden of Philadelphia. Because of the expenses of travel, Bolden decided to create a league that was closer to home for the East Coast teams. This new league gave all the teams a chance to see who really was the best and in 1924 Bolden and RUBE FOSTER, president of the Negro National League, agreed to stage the first World Series. The Monarchs returned to the Series in 1925 and then again in 1942, when they triumphed over the Homestead Grays with Allen at the helm. In postseason play Allen played in thirty-nine games and hit .266, with forty-one hits and nine walks. Even when Allen did not hit for a high average, he managed to get on base to make things happen on offense.

During the off season most players either found another job or played baseball where the weather was warmer. Players were not paid enough to be able to take the winter off. Newt Allen played for six seasons in California in an integrated league that began in 1912. One or two black teams usually played in the league each season, which ran from October through February. Allen played in 135 games, led the league twice in doubles, and hit .324 over the course of six seasons.

Allen also ventured to Cuba for two winters. In 1924 he hit .313 in 48 at-bats for Almendares; when he returned in 1937 he hit only .269 in 175 at-bats for the Havana ball club. Allen found Cuba to be a great place to play baseball because the fans loved the game and he was treated like a ball player, rather than as a black man as he was in the United States. For many Negro Leaguers that was the big draw of playing south of the border: they were treated to a world that was not segregated. Allen also spent time playing in Mexico, Puerto Rico, and Venezuela.

Although he was a pretty good hitter, Allen never displayed much power. He only hit eighteen homeruns over the course of his entire career, with three more added in the postseason. He walked over three hundred times and stole 126 bases. He ranks among the leaders in the Negro Leagues with over one thousand hits. He had two nineteen-game hitting streaks during his career and on fourteen different occasions he had four hits in a game.

Allen's real strength lay in his great defensive play. He made turning the double play look easy and he had a strong arm, which made it possible for him to play either second base or shortstop. His teammates also recognized his leadership qualities and he was often the team captain before becoming the player-manager. He worked well with younger players, teaching them the fundamentals of the game.

After he retired from playing Allen got involved in local politics and then moved to Cincinnati, where he died in 1988. Allen was among a select group of players considered for selection into the National Baseball Hall of Fame in 2006. Although he was not one of the final seventeen selected, his career accomplishments were significant.

FURTHER READING
Allen, Newt. Interview by John Holway (n.d.).
Kleinknecht, Merl F. "Allen, Newton Henry 'Newt,'" in *Biographical Dictionary of American Sports, Baseball*, ed. David L. Porter (2000).
"Newt Allen." In *Baseball, The Biographical Encyclopedia*, ed. David Pietrusza, Matthew Silverman, and Michael Gershman (2000).

LESLIE HEAPHY

Allen, Red (7 Jan. 1908–17 Apr. 1967), trumpeter, was born Henry James Allen Jr. in Algiers, Louisiana, the son of Henry James Allen Sr., a trumpeter and leader of a brass band, and Juretta (maiden name unknown). Red Allen received instruction from his father and his two uncles, who were also trumpeters. Rehearsals were held at home, giving Allen the opportunity to hear New Orleans greats like LOUIS ARMSTRONG, BUDDY BOLDEN, OSCAR CELESTIN, BUNK JOHNSON, KING OLIVER, SAM MORGAN, and Kid Rena. Though surrounded by trumpet players, Allen played the violin and the alto horn before he settled on the trumpet. Soon after his tenth birthday he felt secure enough on the trumpet to become a member of his father's brass band. Allen learned to improvise by playing along with recordings. He varied the speed to change the pitch, thereby developing keen pitch perception.

In addition to playing with his father's band, Allen played riverboat gigs and freelanced until his nineteenth birthday in 1927, when he accompanied King Oliver's band to New York for an engagement at the Savoy Ballroom and for recordings for RCA Victor (*King Oliver, Vols. 1 & 2*). Allen returned to New Orleans for a stint with FATE MARABLE's riverboat bands (1928–1929), returning to New York again in July 1929 to record *It Should Be You/ Biffly Blues* (Victor 38073) and to work as sideman with Louis Armstrong on *I Ain't Got Nobody* (Okeh 8756). Allen worked in 1930 as sideman with JELLY ROLL MORTON on *Jelly Roll Morton and His Red Hot Peppers, 1927–1930, Vol. 1* for RCA Victor, and he recorded as leader on *Sugar Hill Function* (Victor 38140).

Other early recordings as lead trumpet, on such tunes as "It Should Be You," "Feeling Drowsy," "Dancing Dave," "Doctor Blues," and "Louisiana Swing," were made with members of the LUIS RUSSELL band from 1929 to 1932, which at the time included Albert Nichols, Charlie Holmes, J. C. HIGGINBOTHAM, and blues vocalist VICTORIA SPIVEY. Allen's work can be heard on *Luis Russell & His Louisiana Swing Orchestra* (1930, Columbia), *The Luis Russell Story* (1929, Parlophone), and *Song of the Swanee* (1930, Okeh 8780).

Allen's early improvisational style was characterized by sudden, odd turns of phrase, asymmetrical rhythmic construction, mixing of double-time flurries, long-held notes, contrasting dynamics, alternate fingerings of a single note, and a love of fast octave jumps (Schuller, 618–619). Although his style was heavily influenced by Louis Armstrong's, Allen's idiosyncratic rhythmic flexibility, glissandi, smears,

tonguing, emotional conveyance, and technical fluency were unparalleled. Like Armstrong he challenged two- and four-bar phrasing, thinking more of playing through the changes. Several recordings made with Luis Russell—including "Saratoga Shout," "Doctor Blues," "Jersey Lightning," and "Song of the Swanee" on *The Luis Russell Story*, and "It Should Be You" and "Feeling Drowsy" on *Henry "Red" Allen, Vol. 1*—showcase Allen's style.

Allen's brilliance continued with his tenure in FLETCHER HENDERSON's band from 1932 to 1934 on tunes such as "Wrappin' It Up" and "Rug Cutter's Stomp" on *Fletcher Henderson* (1934), "Queer Notions" and "King Porter Stomp" on *The Fletcher Story, Vol. 4* (1933, Columbia), and *Wrappin' It Up* (1934, Decca 157). In 1935 Allen recorded *Ride, Red, Ride* (Columbia 30870) with the Mills Blue Rhythm Band, with whom he played from 1934 to 1937, and *Body and Soul* (Vocalion 38080). In 1937 he returned to Luis Russell's band, which was then accompanying Louis Armstrong, and found himself playing second to ROY ELDRIDGE. Eldridge had replaced Allen in Fletcher Henderson's band as well.

Allen left Russell's band in 1940 and went on to perform and record with musicians such as SIDNEY BECHET (*Egyptian Fantasy*, 1941, Victor 27337), Spike Hughes (*Spike Hughes and His All American Orchestra*, London Records), COLEMAN HAWKINS (1930–1941, CBS records), BILLIE HOLIDAY (*Billie Holiday: The Golden Years, Vol. 2*, Columbia), BUSTER BAILEY, Higginbotham, JAMES P. JOHNSON, KID ORY, and LIONEL HAMPTON. Allen also served as leader on *Get the Mop* (1946, Victor 201808). Other releases of the 1940s and 1950s include the compilation *Henry "Red" Allen, Vols. 1–4*. Gunther Schuller further states, "Allen's stints with Coleman Hawkins in 1957 and Kid Ory in 1959, provided evidence of his growth as a trumpet soloist. Specifically, on 'I Cover the Waterfront' and 'I Got Rhythm,' one can hear creative and contrasting ideas and a rich and singing tone" (Schuller, 630). Allen himself described his experience of playing: it is "as if somebody [is] making your lip speak, making it say things he thinks" (Balliett, 13). In addition to his recordings, Allen appeared in three important TV jazz specials toward the end of his life: "Chicago and All That Jazz," "The Sound of Jazz," and "Profile of the Art." His career ended with the recording of two celebrated albums, *The Henry Allen Memorial Album/Mr. Allen—Henry Red Allen* and *Feeling Good*. He died of cancer in New York City.

Like many trumpeters of his time, Allen was influenced by Louis Armstrong. Unlike most of his peers, however, he developed a personal repertoire of performance concepts and effects that freed him from the musical constraints of the styles of both New Orleans and swing. That repertoire included a smooth legato articulation, a rhythm that was not tied to the fixed pulse, a wide range of dynamics, and a host of glissandi, growls, lip trills, rips, smears, and spattered notes. Allen thereby presaged the later avant-garde or free jazz movement, which extensively featured the performance techniques that Allen pioneered. His ability to transcend his immediate musical environment, as well as his originality and innovativeness on his chosen instrument, raised Allen to the stature of one of the best jazz performers of his era.

FURTHER READING

Balliett, Whitney. *Improvising* (1977).

Chilton, John. *Ride, Red, Ride: The Life of Henry "Red" Allen* (1999).

Evensmo, Jan. *The Trumpet and Vocal of Henry Red Allen, 1927–1942* (1977).

Hester, M. L. "Henry 'Red' Allen," *Mississippi Rag* 12, no. 1 (1984).

Schuller, Gunther. *The Swing Era: The Development of Jazz, 1930–1945* (1989).

This entry is taken from the *American National Biography* and is published here with the permission of the American Council of Learned Societies.

EDDIE S. MEADOWS

Allen, Richard (10 June 1830–16 May 1909), politician, was born a slave in Richmond, Virginia. His parents' names are not known. In 1837 Allen was taken to Harris County in Texas and was owned by J. J. Cain until the end of the Civil War in 1865. Allen married soon after the notification of his emancipation. He and his wife Nancy went on to have one son and four daughters. As a slave Allen was known to be a skilled carpenter; he is credited with designing and building a Houston mansion occupied by Mayor Joseph R. Morris. In 1867 Allen entered the political world as a federal voter registrar, and in 1868 he served as an agent for the Freedmen's Bureau and as a supervisor of voter registration for the Fourteenth District of Texas. Although he had not received a formal education, he was literate by 1870.

After attending several Republican Party meetings and, in 1869, being elected to the Texas legislature, Richard Allen evolved into one of the first and most engaged African American legislators. As a legislator Allen focused on the issues of education, law enforcement, and civil rights. In 1870 he unsuccessfully sought the Republican nomination for U.S. Congress. In 1873 he was reelected to the legislature, but the house instead seated his Democratic challenger, who had contested the election. In 1878 the Republican Party nominated Allen for lieutenant governor, making him the first African American to seek statewide office in Texas.

From 1881 to 1882 Allen served as quartermaster for the black regiment of the Texas militia, and from 1882 to 1885 he was storekeeper and then inspector and deputy collector of U.S. customs in Houston. As a political leader Allen took some unpopular positions, including his 1879 support for the Exoduster Movement, which encouraged African Americans to leave Texas and other Southern states for Kansas.

From 1872 to 1879 Allen served as a delegate to the National Colored Men's Convention. He served as a vice president in 1873 and as a chairman in 1879 of the African American state conventions that addressed concerns about civil rights, education, and economics. By 1883 African American politicians had consolidated their Republican power base; African Americans made up 90 percent of the party's membership. Allen became one of four delegates to attend the Republican National Convention in 1884.

Allen's achievements were not just political. In 1875 he presided over a Prince Hall Masonic lodge in Texas, and in 1877 he became the grand master for the state of Texas. He was also active in the labor movement, playing a key role in an 1890 labor dispute at the port of Houston. A civic leader, Allen spearheaded emancipation celebrations and served at Antioch Baptist Church as the superintendent of the Sunday school. He also served on the board of directors at Gregory Institute, Houston's first African American secondary school. Allen died in Houston and was buried in the city cemetery.

FURTHER READING

Barr, Alwyn. *Black Texans: A History of African Americans in Texas*, 1528–1995 (1973).

Rice, Lawrence D. *The Negro in Texas 1874–1900* (1971).

Smallwood, James M. *Time of Hope, Time of Despair: Black Texans during Reconstruction* (1981).

This entry is taken from the *American National Biography* and is published here with the permission of the American Council of Learned Societies.

WANDA F. FERNANDOPULLE

Allen, Richard (14 Feb. 1760–26 Mar. 1831), American Methodist preacher and founder of the African Methodist Episcopal church, was born into slavery to parents who were the property of Benjamin Chew of Philadelphia. He and his parents and three additional children were sold in 1777 to Stokely Sturgis, who lived near Dover, Delaware. There he attended Methodist preaching events and experienced a spiritual awakening. Allen, his older brother, and a sister were retained by Sturgis, but his parents and younger siblings were sold. Through the ministry of Freeborn Garretson, a Methodist itinerant preacher, Sturgis was converted to Methodism and became convinced that slavery was wrong. Subsequently, Allen and his brother were permitted to work to purchase their freedom, which they did in 1780. For the next six years Allen worked as a wagon driver, woodcutter, and bricklayer while serving as a Methodist preacher to both blacks and whites in towns and rural areas in Maryland, Delaware, Pennsylvania, and New Jersey. By attending Methodist instructional meetings between 1777 and 1780, Allen became an exhorter and then a licentiate as early as 1780. After the American War of Independence, he traveled extensively in Delaware, Maryland, New Jersey, and Pennsylvania. In December 1784 he and HARRY HOSIER were the only two black preachers to attend the Christmas Conference in Baltimore, where the Methodist Episcopal Church was organized. He probably saw the Methodist leaders Thomas Coke, Bishop Francis Asbury, Richard Whatcoat, and Thomas Vasey at the conference. During 1785 he traveled the Baltimore circuit with Whatcoat.

At one point Asbury, the leader of American Methodism, invited Allen to become his traveling companion, an offer Allen accepted. In 1786 he preached to interracial groups of Methodists in Radnor, Pennsylvania, and at St. George's Church, Philadelphia. Assigned to preach at predawn meetings, Allen often preached four or five times a day and organized evening prayer groups. Unpaid by the church, he supported himself and later his family as a shoemaker. He married Flora (maiden name unknown) in 1791 and, after his first wife's death, was married a second time, in 1805, to Sarah (maiden name unknown). Allen and his second wife had six children.

In February 1786, while he was in Philadelphia, Allen organized a prayer-meeting society of forty-two members. His concern was to find and instruct "his African brethren," few of whom attended public worship. Noting the need for a place of worship for African Americans, he and his colleagues ABSALOM JONES, William White, and Dorus Ginnings found their efforts to meet this need opposed by the leadership of St. George's Church. In November 1787 black members of St. George's Church were pulled away from prayer and asked to leave, so Allen and Jones and their associates withdrew. Renting an unused store, Allen and Jones, with the help of Benjamin Rush and Robert Ralston, raised funds for a new building, which in 1794 became the St. Thomas African Episcopal Church of Philadelphia, the first independent black church in North America.

Allen, who remained a Methodist, purchased an abandoned blacksmith shop, moved it to Sixth Street near Lombard, and had it renovated. On 29 June 1794 Bishop Asbury dedicated the building as a church. For years Allen and his congregation thought the property, called Bethel Church, was theirs, only to be informed by successive elders at St. George's that Bethel Church was within their charge. In 1816, however, the Pennsylvania Supreme Court confirmed the independent existence of Bethel, and official contact between the two churches ceased.

Aware of friction between black and white Methodists in other places, Allen sent invitations to African churches to form an ecclesiastical organization. On 9 April 1816 sixty delegates from five black congregations met at Bethel Church and agreed to confederate. The result was the formation of the African Methodist Episcopal (AME) Church. Allen, who had been ordained deacon by Bishop Asbury in 1799, was ordained elder on 10 April 1816 and the next day was consecrated as bishop. The first *Discipline* was published in 1817, and the new organization's first General Conference was held in Philadelphia on 9 July 1820, with Bishop Allen presiding. For Allen, the Methodist emphasis on the simplicity of the Gospel, expressed through discipline and community, pointed the way to freedom from sin and physical slavery as well. His life and career, and the founding of Bethel Church, embodied this development and confirmed his role as a leader in the forefront of the black church movement.

Early in 1797 Allen, Jones, and JAMES FORTEN Sr. led black Philadelphians to petition the national government for the first time to revoke the Fugitive Slave Act of 1793 and to end slavery. In 1814, when it was feared that Philadelphia would be attacked by the British, Allen, Jones, and Forten raised the Black Legion of 2,500 men. Although Allen did not initially oppose voluntary emigration of blacks, as promoted by the American Colonization Society (formed in 1817), he came to see that large-scale emigration of free blacks would result in the abandonment of their brethren to slavery. In *Freedom's Journal* (2 Nov. 1827), Allen declared colonization a mistake. In 1830 he presided over the first meeting of the National Negro Convention Movement, which provided a structure for black abolitionism and organized the American Society of Free Persons of Color.

Allen led and participated in the formation of many organizations for the betterment of his people. The Free African Society established 12 April 1787 was the first black institution with the characteristics of a benevolent and reform organization. In 1795 a day school was operational in Bethel Church, and on 26 October 1796 the founding of a First Day school, or Sunday school, and a night school was reported. In 1804 Allen led in the creation of the Society for Free People of Color for Promoting the Instruction and School Education of Children of African Descent. From 1818 to 1820 he served as book steward of the Book Concern of the AME church. The creation of the Free Produce Society of Philadelphia, on 20 December 1830, was also his work. He chaired the first National Negro Convention from 20 to 24 September 1830, which was held at Bethel Church. In 1831 the address to the First Annual Convention of the People of Colour was signed by the Reverend Allen, in his role as president and senior bishop of the AME Church. In 1794 Allen and Jones had been cited by the mayor of Philadelphia for their services to the sick and dying during the yellow fever epidemic of 1793. Allen died in Philadelphia, but his contributions to religion, education, and culture live on in such institutions as the Allen Temple, Cincinnati, Ohio; Allen University, Columbia, South Carolina; and the Richard Allen Center for Culture and Art, opposite Lincoln Center, New York City.

FURTHER READING

Allen, Richard. *The Life, Experience and Gospel Labors of the Rt. Rev. Richard Allen* (1833, 1983).

George, Carol V. R. *Segregated Sabbaths: Richard Allen and the Emergence of Independent Black Churches 1760–1840* (1973).

Nash, Gary B. *Forging Freedom: The Formation of Philadelphia's Black Community, 1720–1840* (1988).

Raboteau, Albert J. "Richard Allen and the African Church Movement," in *Black Leaders of the Nineteenth Century* (1988).

Wesley, Charles H. *Richard Allen, Apostle of Freedom* (1935).

FREDERICK V. MILLS

Allen, Sarah and Flora Allen (1764?–16 July 1849) and (?–11 March 1801), churchwomen and reformers, were, respectively, the second and first wives of RICHARD ALLEN, a bishop and founder of the African Methodist Episcopal (AME) Church. Although little is known of Flora Allen, she had probably met Richard Allen while attending Methodist class meetings and services at St. George's Methodist Church in Philadelphia. Known as a pious and respectable woman, Flora Allen helped her husband purchase a home at 150 Spruce Street in 1791 (as well as other properties, including those used by Allen's new church) and inaugurate the Bethel AME church in July 1794. White as well as black preachers celebrated her dedication to charity and hospitality. She died in Philadelphia after a long illness but is remembered as an early advocate of the independent black church. Sarah Allen was born Sarah Bass, a slave in Isle of Wight County, Virginia. She probably remained in bondage until the 1780s or 1790s, by which time she had moved to Pennsylvania. By the early 1790s, Sarah Bass's name appeared on the membership rolls of class meetings, the weekly preparation meetings required for those seeking membership in the Methodist Episcopal Church, nominally under the leadership of white preachers from St. George's Methodist Church in Philadelphia. Class lists also included Richard Allen and his first wife, Flora. Bass likely followed them out of the segregated white church and into Allen's fledgling AME organization. She also served an important role as a nurse and caregiver during Philadelphia's yellow fever epidemic, which claimed several thousand lives (including those of hundreds of African Americans) during the fall of 1793. The following year, when Richard Allen and ABSALOM JONES published their history of black involvement in yellow fever charity work, *A Narrative of the Proceedings of Black People during the Awful Calamity in Philadelphia*—which became the first copyrighted pamphlet by black writers in America—Sarah Bass's reform activities garnered special mention.

Bass married Richard Allen on 11 March 1801, after the death of his first wife. Bass had apparently been part of the AME congregation during the 1790s, although membership rolls are no longer extant. The couple had six children over the next two decades—Richard Jr., James, John,

Peter, Sara, and Ann—and lived in Allen's home on Spruce Street (between present-day Fourth and Fifth streets). Sarah Allen also helped tend home at the Allen family's country property located in Delaware County, Pennsylvania, and purchased in 1808. Like Flora, Sarah became Richard's helpmeet, keeping a respectable home befitting her husband's stature as one of the leading black reformers of the age. She also cosigned property deeds with her husband, including a grant of property to the AME church. Finally, she was active in church and community benevolent activities, and helped found the Daughters of Conference, a group that aided black ministers attending AME conferences, and the Bethel Benevolent Society, a charitable organization that raised funds for AME families. Allen also supported women preachers, including JARENA LEE, who became the first black woman to preach at Bethel Church. According to Lee herself, Sarah Allen purchased the very first copy of Lee's autobiography, titled *Religious Experience and Journal of Mrs. Jarena Lee*, in 1836.

In one sense, both Sarah Allen and Flora Allen represented the African American equivalent of the "Republican Mother." According to eighteenth-century theorists of American republicanism, women served a key role in the nation's moral life, inculcating the virtues of piety, sacrifice, and virtue in young men. Both of Richard Allen's wives were regarded as pillars of community and institution-building efforts among Northern free blacks, for they worked alongside their husbands to emphasize the significance of piety, moral uplift, and racial redemption. Nineteenth-century AME minister James Handy referred to Sarah Allen as a "matron"—someone who always sacrificed herself for the greater good of the black church and the free black community as a whole. Not until the era following the War of 1812 did a new generation of Bethel women, including Jarena Lee and Mary Still, chart new directions as public figures, seeking to become preachers, activists, and (later still) even ministers.

The great example of Sarah Allen's "matronly" self-sacrifice occurred before one of the AME churches' early conferences in Philadelphia. As ministers arrived at the Allens' house, Sarah expressed concern about their shabby appearance, with bare elbows showing through many of the men's garments. She quickly gathered together a sewing brigade of Bethel women, working all night to produce dignified clothing fit for leaders of the community. In another sense, Sarah Allen, like Flora Allen

before her, represented the reality of most free black women's existence during the early national period. Unlike the idealized white Republican mother, free black women often worked both in and beyond the home to garner extra wages, particularly during the Bethel Church's earliest years. Indeed, although Richard Allen's many investment properties and personal savings later allowed Sarah Allen to live a comfortable existence as a free black woman, she still collected monies from Allen family rental properties following her husband's death. She was not, in other words, above working outside of the home. This image fit well with Bethel Church congregants, who before the 1830s comprised mostly day laborers and unskilled workers, with women as well as men helping their families survive the vicissitudes of life in northern cities. Jarena Lee was attracted to the AME church, she recalled, because of her acquaintance with a black female cook who spoke well of Richard Allen's church. For all of these reasons, subsequent generations of AME ministers, reformers and even bishops would hail Sarah Allen in particular as a founding mother of the black church. After Richard Allen died (26 Mar. 1831), she remained active in Bethel reform activities and aided fugitive slaves traveling through Philadelphia. After her own death, she was interred in the basement of Bethel Church with Richard Allen.

FURTHER READING
The Richard Allen Museum, Mother Bethel AME Church, Philadelphia has many exhibits and documents about the lives of Richard and Sarah Allen. An introduction is available online at http://www.motherbethel.org/museum/.
Jones, Absalom, and Richard Allen. "A Narrative of the Proceedings of Black People During the Awful Calamity in Philadelphia," (1794), reprinted in Richard S. Newman et al. *Pamphlets of Protest* (2000).
Handy, James A. *Scraps of African Methodist Episcopal History* (1902).
Johnson, Charles Richard, and Patricia Smith, eds. *Africans in America* (1999)
Lee, Jarena. *Religious Experience and Journal of Mrs. Jarena Lee* (1836).
Newman, Richard S. *Black Founder: Richard Allen, African Americans and the Early Republic* (2008).
RICHARD S. NEWMAN

Allen, Thomas Cox (2 Apr. 1907–11 Sept. 1989), aviation mechanic and pilot, was born in Quitman, Wood County, Texas, the youngest of three children;

both of his parents were teachers. Allen's father died when Thomas was three months old. His mother, Polly, continued to teach school and to run the family farm.

Allen became interested in flying in 1918, when an airplane made a forced landing in a pasture. The pilots paid the two young Allen brothers to guard the plane overnight so that its fabric and glue would not be eaten by cows. From this experience, Thomas Allen decided to become either an aviator or a mechanic.

In 1919, when Allen was twelve, the family moved to Oklahoma City, where his mother resumed teaching school. Allen often bicycled to a nearby airfield. In his teens, he persuaded the field owner to take a $100 saxophone as partial trade for flying lessons. He worked off the rest of the fee by helping the airplane mechanics. Eventually he earned enough to fly for five hours but could not afford the $500 bond needed to fly alone.

When Allen was seventeen, the ground crew dared him to fly solo while the instructor was away. The instructor saw the plane in the air and returned to the field in a rage as Allen landed. However, he was persuaded that the feat would be good advertising, in the racist belief that if he could teach a "Negro boy" to fly, he could teach anyone.

Soon after he had soloed, Allen hitchhiked to San Antonio, hoping to become an army aviator. He soon was made aware of the military's ban against African Americans. Instead, he became a mechanic's assistant at San Antonio's Stinson Field and subsequently held various jobs related to aviation mechanics in Texas and Kansas. By 1927 he had returned to Oklahoma City, where he joined Tulsa-Oklahoma Airline, later known as Braniff.

In the spring of 1929 Allen met several of the organizers of the BESSIE COLEMAN AERO CLUB, founded in memory of the first black woman aviator, who had died in 1926. He moved to the Los Angeles area to join the group as a mechanic. Later that year he married Celine Smith; the couple had two sons.

In the late 1920s and early 1930s many pilots sought financial backing for transcontinental flights. White pilots found it easier to receive corporate backing than did African Americans, although there was a rumor of a $1,000 prize for the first black pilots to fly cross-country. With unemployment high during the Great Depression, Allen worked at whatever aviation job he could find. Over time he gained a reputation as a gifted mechanic, although his relations with the Aero Club's founder William J. Powell and other club members were often stormy.

Late in the summer of 1932, Allen was approached by JAMES HERMAN BANNING, the lead pilot for the Bessie Coleman Aero Club and the first black pilot to receive an American aviation license. Banning had access to a World War I surplus Eagle Rock aircraft with a fourteen-year-old engine, owned by Sam Moore and Arthur Dennis. He planned a transcontinental attempt, but he needed a mechanic and an additional investment of about $125 for fuel. Allen provided both the investment and the expertise.

With barely $100 left, Banning and Allen left Los Angeles on 18 September 1932. The team became known as the "Flying Hoboes." They planned to "hobo," begging for their meals and beds, which they hoped would raise enough money at each stop to continue across the country. Those who assisted them were asked to sign the "Gold Book" on the airplane's lower left-wing tip. They crossed the Rockies by a southern route over Arizona, New Mexico, and Texas. In Tulsa, Oklahoma, the oil company owner William Skully arranged credit for fuel from Tulsa to St. Louis. In St. Louis, trade school students provided needed repairs. In Pittsburgh the team agreed to drop fifteen thousand flyers for Franklin Delano Roosevelt's presidential campaign en route to New York. The Democratic Party financed that segment of the flight and rebuilt the plane in New York.

The Flying Hoboes landed in Valley Stream, Long Island, on 9 October 1932. Their flight time over three weeks totaled forty-one hours and twenty-seven minutes. They were feted by the New York mayor Jimmie Walker and in Harlem, but they were unable to locate the putative donor of the thousand-dollar prize.

On 10 November 1932 Allen and Banning started west. However, the plane was severely damaged when they were forced to land in a snowstorm not far from Pittsburgh. The *Pittsburgh Courier* financed their trip to Los Angeles by bus. They were unable to raise funds to retrieve the airplane before it was sold for scrap, with the "Gold Book" signatures eventually painted over. Banning and Allen dissolved their partnership in January 1933. Banning was killed in an air-show crash in February of that year.

Allen remained in Alhambra, California, and continued to work in the aviation industry. In the fall of 1939 he incorporated the Thomas C. Allen Aviation School in Los Angeles. According to a press release, the school planned to provide instruction in aviation mechanics "based on democratic principles" and was to accept students regardless of "race, creed or color." The emphasis was to be on safety and on training African Americans to join the aviation industry. It is likely that the outbreak of World War II subsumed the resources of the proposed school. During World War II, Allen ferried bombers for Douglas Aircraft. In 1949 Allen announced plans to become the first African American to make an around-the-world flight. Called the "People's Project," the flight was proposed without any corporate sponsorship and failed to raise sufficient backing.

Retiring from Douglas Aircraft in the 1960s, Allen moved back to Oklahoma City, where he was active as a volunteer with the Oklahoma Air and Space Museum in the 1980s. He died in Oklahoma City in 1989.

In 1992 Allen was inducted into the Oklahoma Aviation and Space Hall of Fame at the Kirkpatrick Science and Air Space Museum in Oklahoma City.

FURTHER READING

The Sam Moore Papers (1931–1936) at the Seaver Center, Natural History Museum of Los Angeles County, includes materials relating to the transcontinental flight.

Lynn, Jack. *The Hallelujah Flight* (1989).

Powell, William J. *Black Aviator: The Story of William J. Powell* (repr. 1994).

Obituary: *New York Times*, 13 Sept. 1989.

CAROLINE M. BROWN

Allen, William G. (c. 1820–?), abolitionist and educator, was born in Virginia, the son of a Welshman and a free mixed-race mother. After the death of both parents, a young Allen was adopted by a free African American family in Fortress Monroe, Virginia. Allen soon caught the eye of the Reverend William Hall, a New Yorker who conducted a black elementary school in Norfolk. Hall wrote Gerrit Smith, the well-known philanthropist and abolitionist from Madison County, New York, asking him to sponsor Allen's education. With Smith's support, Allen studied at the Oneida Institute, an interracial and abolitionist school in Whitesboro, New York, presided over by the abolitionist Beriah Green. In a letter written to Smith, Green mentioned Allen's good conduct, his accomplishments on the flute, and his service as clerk to Reuben Hough, the institute's superintendent and treasurer.

While attending the institute, Allen spent the summer of 1841 teaching in a school that Hiram Wilson, an Oneida Institute alumnus, had established among fugitive slaves in Upper Canada (Ontario). Allen supported the Liberty Party and the political abolitionists centered in upstate New York. Allen also participated in the black national convention movement,

annual meetings organized by African Americans to discuss their common problems. Allen graduated from the Oneida Institute in 1844 and moved to Troy, New York, where he taught school and assisted HENRY HIGHLAND GARNET in editing the *National Watchman*, an abolitionist and temperance paper for African Americans. Three years later he moved to Boston, where he was employed as a law clerk by Ellis Gray Loring. While in Boston, Allen lectured on African American history, wrote *Wheatley, Banneker, and Horton* (1849), a collection of brief biographical sketches of PHILLIS WHEATLEY, BENJAMIN BANNEKER, and GEORGE MOSES HORTON, and served as secretary of the Boston Colored Citizens Association.

In 1850 Allen was appointed professor of Greek and of rhetoric and belles lettres at New York Central College in McGrawville, Cortland County. This interracial and coeducational institution, chartered in 1849 by the American Baptist Free Mission Society, was the only college in the country then employing African American faculty. In 1852 Allen became engaged to one of the white students, Mary King, the daughter of a former trustee. The engagement incensed the residents of Fulton, New York, King's hometown, and the couple, fearing mob violence, went to New York City, where they were secretly married in 1853.

Because of the racial antagonisms that their marriage had sparked, Allen resigned from the faculty of New York Central College, and he and his wife traveled to England in the spring of 1853. Allen attempted to earn a living in England by writing and lecturing on various literary and philosophical subjects. In 1854 Lady Byron engaged him to speak on behalf of penal reform. Allen also advocated moral reformatory schools and lectured against American slavery and prejudice. In 1853 his account of the problems caused by his marriage appeared under the title *The American Prejudice Against Color: An Authentic Narrative, Showing How Easily the Nation Got into an Uproar*. Because of the warm reception he had received on a speaking trip to Ireland, Allen brought his family to Dublin in 1856; three of his seven children were born there. He published *A Short Personal Narrative* there in 1860.

The same year, Allen moved his family back to London, where he continued to lecture on Africa, educational reform, and abolitionism. In 1863 he became principal of the Caledonian Training School in Islington, established by the British abolitionist and philanthropist Harper Twelvetrees to meet the educational needs of the poor. The school closed after five years. Allen found it difficult to support his large family and appealed to friends of the abolitionist cause, such as Gerrit Smith, for assistance. The struggle to survive compounded the bitterness that he felt toward the American prejudice exhibited at the time of his marriage. About 1878 the Allens were living in a boardinghouse in Notting Hill, dependent on the charity of friends. Little is known of the circumstances of Allen's last years or of his death.

William G. Allen belongs to that cohort of nineteenth-century African Americans who, although free of slavery's yoke, encountered many obstacles in the North. Allen used the vehicle of education, first as a student and later as an instructor, to fight against racial restrictions in the United States. After moving to England, he continued to attack American slavery and racism, and his personal life was beset by many difficulties. Though he never achieved the public notoriety of FREDERICK DOUGLASS nor was as actively involved in the American abolitionist movement as some other African Americans of his time, Allen's most notable contribution lay in his efforts to expose the connections between the institution of slavery and American prejudice.

FURTHER READING

Letters from Allen to Gerrit Smith are in the Gerrit Smith papers, George Arents Research Library, Syracuse University.

Blackett, R. J. M. "William G. Allen: The Forgotten Professor," *Civil War History* 26 (Mar. 1980).

Ripley, C. Peter, ed. *The Black Abolitionist Papers*, vol. 1 (1985).

This entry is taken from the *American National Biography* and is published here with the permission of the American Council of Learned Societies.

MILTON C. SERNETT

Allen-Noble, Rosie (22 June 1938–), professor and educational administrator, was born Rosie Elizabeth Allen in Americus, Georgia, to Ulysses Grant Allen and Velma Douglas Allen. After completing a B.S. in Biology at Albany State College in Georgia, Allen-Noble taught in three Georgia high schools: the Vienna High and Industrial School (1960–1961), West Point High School (1962–1963), and Carver High School in Columbus (1963–1964). She also served as chairperson of the biology department at Columbia High School in Decatur, Georgia, from 1965 to 1970. Allen-Noble and Daniel Bernard Noble married in April 1964

and divorced in April 1968. They have one child, Antoinette Celine Noble-Webb.

While working on a master's degree in zoology at Atlanta University, Allen-Noble taught courses in biology, anatomy, and physiology at Spelman College, also in Atlanta (1965–1966). She completed the M.S. in 1967. From 1970 to 1976 she was an instructor of general biology and general physiology at Rutgers University in New Jersey, and from 1972 to 1978 she stood as visiting assistant professor of anatomy and physiology at Seton Hall University in South Orange, New Jersey. Allen-Noble completed her second M.S., in Physiology, at Rutgers in 1974. Allen-Noble taught medical embryology, genetics, and physiology at New Jersey's College of Medicine and Dentistry from 1972 to 1987, and as an assistant professor she taught anatomy, physiology, microtechniques, and microscopic anatomy (histology) from 1976 to 1980.

In addition to teaching, Allen-Noble served as director of several science programs. In 1976 she led the science enrichment program (USEP) at Upsala College in East Orange, New Jersey. From 1978 to 1980 she acted as coordinator of medical technology programs at Fairleigh Dickinson University in Madison, New Jersey. Beginning in 1978 Allen-Noble directed the health careers programs at Montclair State College in Upper Montclair, New Jersey. She received awards for outstanding service from both Fairleigh Dickinson and Montclair State in 1982, and again from Montclair State in 1984–1985 and 1987. Moreover, she served on the President's Commission on Affirmative Action from 1980 to 1987.

Allen-Noble increasingly focused her efforts in the field of education, earning a doctor of education degree in 1991 from Rutgers's Graduate Program in Science Education. After completing this degree Allen-Noble joined the faculty at the Medical College of Georgia (MCG), where she taught in the Department of Cellular Biology and Anatomy and served as associate dean for Special Academic Programs. She continues to work with the school's educational outreach programs, in an effort to attract underrepresented minority and disadvantaged students to careers in the health and medical sciences and to ensure their success in undergraduate programs and on their medical school applications.

Beginning in 1996 Allen-Noble worked with the Health Professions Partnership Initiative, which teams MCG with nearby high schools, colleges, and universities that are generally attended by minority students. The program aims to strengthen students' science education and create a pipeline of well-qualified students to feed into medical schools and the health professions, as well as provide professional development resources for faculty members. The program has increased in size and has been successful in creating and sustaining educational diversity. It is particularly relevant in the wake of the Supreme Court's 1996 Hopwood decision, which declared affirmative action policies unlawful, and after which the MCG revoked scholarships specifically for minorities.

FURTHER READING

"Fewer Minorities Entering Medical Schools," *Shawnee News-Star*, 2 Nov. 1997.

Fincher, Ruth-Marie E., Wilma Sykes-Brown, and Rosie Allen-Noble. "Health Science Learning Academy: A Successful 'Pipeline' Educational Program for High School Students," *Academic Medicine* 77 (July 2002): 737–738.

GINNY CROSTHWAIT

Allensworth, Allen (7 Apr. 1842–14 Sept. 1914), soldier, minister, and social activist, was born in Louisville, Kentucky, the youngest of the six children of Levi Allensworth and Phyllis (maiden name unknown), slaves of the Starbird family. The Starbirds were respected members of the community and were partners in Wilson, Starbird, and Smith, a wholesale drug company based in Louisville. Levi died when Allen was an infant. Phyllis's other five children either had been sold down the Mississippi River or had escaped to Canada. Phyllis hoped that Allen could "even if partly educated, win his freedom" (Alexander, 9). Believing that God would play a role in his redemption as well, Phyllis named Allen after RICHARD ALLEN, the founder and first bishop of the African Methodist Episcopal (AME) Church. In Allen Allensworth's early years he was given to Thomas Starbird, Mrs. Starbird's son, as a companion.

When Thomas was sent to school, Allensworth's mother saw an opportunity for her son to become educated, even though it was a crime for a slave to do so. She instructed him to get "your 'Marse' Tom to play school with you every day he comes home; then you can learn to read and write like him" (Alexander, 8). Allensworth convinced Tom to do this, and the boys turned Tom's nursery into a classroom. Tom diligently relayed his school lessons to Allensworth every day. When this practice was revealed to Starbird, another home was found for Allensworth: he was put in the custody of Mr. and Mrs. Talbot, Quakers. This change was fortuitous for Allensworth, who was sent to the Sunday afternoon slave school at the St. Paul Protestant Episcopal Church, where slaves were taught the Ten Commandments, the Lord's Prayer, and to obey their masters. Furthermore, Mrs. Talbot also instructed him in spelling and reading. When Mrs. Starbird discovered that the boy was being taught to read, he was sold to John J. Smith, the owner of a large plantation in Henderson County, Kentucky. After saying goodbye to his mother, Allensworth left Louisville in the spring of 1854 aboard the steamer *Rainbow*. Before boarding the steamer he managed to purchase a copy of Noah Webster's blue-back spelling book, a book second in popularity only to the Bible among slaves who could get either.

A short time after arriving Allensworth was discovered studying his book by Smith's wife and was punished. He also became friends with Eddie, a young orphan white boy. Ironically, Eddie was routinely punished for not completing his lessons. The two quickly formed an alliance and studied together whenever circumstances allowed.

Allensworth was not caught studying again; however, he was not able to avoid trouble altogether. When the Smiths left to visit their brother in Louisville, an overseer beat him severely. This inspired Allensworth to escape to Canada. Allensworth, thirteen years old, made it only a few miles away from the Smith farm before being caught. When the Smiths returned, Allensworth was sold downriver to New Orleans, where he was offered for sale at the auction house of Poindexter & Little with more than a thousand other slaves. In New Orleans, Allensworth was bought by Fred Scruggs, a horse racer. He became a jockey and returned to Louisville, Kentucky, where he remained the property of Scruggs until 1861, when the Civil War erupted.

In spring 1861 Scruggs made a business trip to Mobile, Alabama. He was unable to return because of the war, and Allensworth was shuffled between several masters over the next year. When the Confederate general Braxton Bragg's advance reached Louisville, Allensworth was invited to become a member of the hospital corps of the Forty-fourth Illinois and became a freeman. Soon after this, General William S. Rosecrans's Union forces moved on Bragg's position and forced a retreat. Nurse Allensworth reported for duty in Nashville, Tennessee, under Dr. Gordon of Georgetown, Ohio. On Dr. Gordon's advice, Allensworth enlisted in the navy in April 1863.

Immediately after reporting for duty aboard the gunboat *Queen City*, Allensworth was selected as a wardroom steward and was given thirty dollars a month. This was his first paid job as a freeman, and he advanced quickly thanks to his loyal service. For example, when two other African American members of the crew deserted, Allensworth decided to remain behind. As a direct result he became the captain's steward and was given a raise of five dollars a month. He was honorably discharged on 4 April 1865, days before the official end of the Civil War.

Two years later Allensworth and his brother William opened two restaurants in St. Louis, Missouri. This venture proved successful, and they attempted to expand their business. However, after being falsely accused of passing counterfeit currency, they sold both restaurants and left St. Louis. Allensworth returned to Louisville, where he found his mother and began supporting her. In addition he became both janitor and pupil at the Ely Normal School for freemen, organized by the American Missionary Society of New York. Allensworth remained at this school until the Freedmen's Bureau applied to the principal for a young man to go to Christmasville, five miles south of Louisville, to teach. Allensworth accepted the position and in 1868 took over this school.

Allensworth's congregation, the Fifth Street Baptist Church in Louisville, ordained him as its minister on 9 April 1871. Realizing his lack of biblical expertise, he enrolled in the Theological Institute at Nashville. From this point on Allensworth combined his skills as a teacher, preacher, and disciplinarian to develop churches, schools, and corporations with a view toward providing African Americans the moral and intellectual tools that he considered necessary for success as freemen. He built not only institutions but also an irreproachable reputation for integrity and intelligence. Allensworth had notable achievements in the Kentucky towns of Franklin, Georgetown, Elizabethtown, Louisville, and Bowling Green. Before accepting a post in Bowling Green he married Josephine Leavell (JOSEPHINE LEAVELL ALLENSWORTH) on 20 September 1877. They had one boy, who died shortly after birth, and two girls, who survived to adulthood.

While in Bowling Green, Reverend Allensworth became politically active. He was a Republican elector in 1880 and was a delegate to the Republican National Convention in 1880 and again in 1884. He further increased his public stature by authoring five lectures: "Five Manly Virtues," "Humbugs

and How They Live," "The Battle of Life and How to Fight It," "America," and "Character and How to Read It." Temporarily leaving his congregation, he embarked upon a tour of New England, supported by the Williams Lecture Bureau of Boston, Massachusetts. His lectures were hailed as extraordinary by newspapers from Kentucky to Boston.

Shortly after his mother died in 1878, Allensworth left Bowling Green and accepted a post as pastor of a Baptist church in Cincinnati, Ohio. There in 1882 an African American soldier brought it to Allensworth's attention that African American regiments were served by white chaplains. After learning that the chaplain of the Twenty-fourth Infantry was to retire in four years, Allensworth mobilized his friends to help him gain the chaplaincy. As a result, both Charles P. Jacob and Senator Joseph E. Brown met with President Grover Cleveland about the new chaplaincy. He became Chaplain Allensworth of the Twenty-Fourth Infantry on 3 June 1886.

Allensworth served as chaplain until 1906. During this time he strove for the advancement and improvement of all enlisted men by designing an educational curriculum for servicemen at all levels of rank and responsibility. This curriculum was so successful that it was adopted throughout the U.S. Army. Through his powers of oration he won other smaller victories, such as convincing white officers to salute him. Allensworth emphasized that he would go out of his way to avoid a salute from a man who, having sworn to obey army regulations, would violate this oath. Allensworth called upon influential friends such as Congressman JOHN MERCER LANGSTON to draw attention to inequalities in the system of army deployment and appointment that made it impossible for an African American to be promoted from an African American regiment. His actions made promotion an official possibility for African American enlisted men. Allensworth's military career began winding down in 1900 when he injured his knee serving in the Philippines. Allensworth reinjured this knee in January 1901 and requested a transfer to Fort McDowell, California, where he had been recuperating. This transfer was granted. He served until 1906, when he was retired at his own request with the rank of lieutenant colonel, then the highest rank ever achieved by an African American in the U.S. Army.

After retiring, Allensworth and his family settled in Los Angeles. Though retired, Allensworth never ceased working for the advancement of African Americans. With the professor William Payne, the minister William Peck, and the real estate agent

Harry Mitchell, Allensworth created an all-black community in Tulare County, California. The town was called Allensworth and in 1914 reached a peak population of approximately two hundred. As the community he founded reached its apex in prosperity, Allensworth's life ended suddenly when he stepped off a streetcar and was struck by a motorcycle.

Allen Allensworth began life with no advantages but worked tirelessly to succeed. Having illicitly obtained an education, he came to believe that inequality was a result of limited opportunity and nothing else, a belief reinforced by his success as a teacher, preacher, and chaplain. This attitude was embodied in the creation of California's first all-black community.

After Allen Allensworth's death, his town, Allensworth, prospered for a short time. However, when the Pacific Farming Company refused to provide water as promised, economic activity slowed. With the water table falling and the economy failing, the community began to collapse. After the Great Depression and World War II, Allensworth never recovered. In 1971 the town became Colonel Allensworth State Park, and many of the original buildings were restored. The park stands not only as a testament to Allensworth's life and lasting achievements but also as a reminder of the struggle of African Americans to create positive social environments during the nadir of race relations in the United States.

FURTHER READING

Alexander, Charles. *Battles and Victories of Allen Allensworth* (1914).

Radcliffe, Evelyn. *Out of Darkness: The Story of Allen Allensworth* (1998).

Wheeler, B. Gordon. "Allensworth: California's African American Community," *Wild West* (Feb. 2000).

JACOB ANDREW FREEDMAN

Allensworth, Josephine Leavell (3 May 1855–27 Mar. 1939), pianist, educator, and philanthropist, was born a slave in Trenton, Kentucky, to Mary Dickinson, also a slave, and Mr. Leavell, likely a scion of the white Benjamin Leavell family, pioneers of Trenton. According to family history, Josephine's father wanted to send her and her sister to Canada on the Underground Railroad, but their mother objected because of the danger and distance. Sometime between 1868 and 1875 Josephine attended the Nashville Normal and Theological Institute (also known as the Baptist Institute), a college for African

Americans that was later renamed Roger Williams University. Daniel W. Phillips, a white Baptist minister, had started the school in 1864, teaching Bible classes to freed people in his home. The school was later acquired by Vanderbilt University and incorporated into its George Peabody campus, a teachers' college.

While at the Baptist Institute, Josephine studied music, particularly piano, and trained as a teacher. At the school she also met her fellow student ALLEN ALLENSWORTH, a traveling minister with the First District Baptist Association, who pastored several churches in southern Kentucky. Though Allen was thirteen years Josephine's senior, both had been born and raised in Kentucky and felt they had similar experiences. Allen was a former slave who as an adolescent had escaped bondage and joined Union soldiers during the Civil War. Josephine and Allen married on 20 September 1877 in Trenton, just as Allen accepted a pastorate with the State Street Baptist Church in Bowling Green, Kentucky.

Josephine was her husband's collaborator and partner as he moved from one church to the next, developing church-based Sunday schools and grade schools from Bowling Green, Kentucky, to Cincinnati, Ohio, for African American children who did not have access to public grade schools. The Allensworths firmly believed that churches had a responsibility to educate African Americans coming out of the era of slavery, and that uplifting the race was possible through a holistic approach to moral, spiritual, and academic education. In 1878 the Allensworths had their first child, Alpha, a son who died in infancy. They had two more children, Eva, born in 1880, and Nella, born in 1882.

That same year Allen learned that black regiments in the U.S. Army did not have black chaplains to serve their spiritual needs. He became aware of an opening with the 24th Infantry, an African American regiment, and began a personal campaign to get the job, soliciting support from prominent political friends. The U.S. Army offered him the position on 1 April 1886, giving him the rank of captain. On 1 July, his first day of duty, he reported to Fort Supply, the western Oklahoma base then responsible for policing and protecting grazing lands leased by cattlemen on Indian territories. Josephine, their two daughters, and her niece joined him two months later.

With children in tow, Josephine followed her husband to each station, including Fort Bayard in New Mexico, Fort Douglas near Salt Lake City, Fort Harrison in Montana, Fort Huachuca in

Arizona, and the Presidio and Fort McDowell in San Francisco. While her husband served in the Philippines in 1899, she and their children stayed on the Presidio. Josephine helped Allen teach and develop Sunday school lessons, and she played the organ and piano during worship services. Her daughters later accompanied on violin and organ.

Many of the military stations were isolated from nearby towns, and when soldiers visited while off duty, they often garnered bad reputations for heavy drinking, carousing, and disrupting the peace. African American soldiers had won a probably undeserved reputation as the worst offenders. The Allensworths made it their cause to provide enlisted men and their families in the 24th Infantry with wholesome entertainment on base, so as to maintain good relations with the surrounding communities and keep a good image of the African American troops. Josephine often performed piano recitals for the men and their families. While at Fort Douglas, she also took on a job as telegrapher, the first African American in Salt Lake City to hold the position.

Josephine was revered and respected by the wives of enlisted men, though she and her husband made it a rule not to socialize with enlisted families, nor to let their children socialize with those of enlisted men. Because Allen was the sole black officer in the 24th Infantry, his family often could not socialize with the families of white officers, leaving Josephine and her children sometimes feeling isolated and alone (African American Museum and Library at Oakland vertical file, c. 1975).

When the 24th Infantry was stationed in the Philippines, Josephine served as a treasurer of sorts for the wives of the enlisted men, collecting and distributing money the soldiers sent home to their families. The Reverend Allen Allensworth retired from the army with the rank of lieutenant colonel in April 1906, and the couple and their grown children settled in Pasadena, Los Angeles County, California. The Allensworths soon found that Southern California did not fully meet their expectations as a place free of racial discrimination. In 1908 Lieutenant Colonel Allensworth founded Allensworth, a black farming colony, with four other African American men. The town, located in California's San Joaquin Valley, prospered for several years, boasting its own elected government, law enforcement, and school district. Josephine served as the president of the town's first school board in 1910, and she organized the Women's Improvement Club, which developed a playground for the children of the colony.

Education was a cornerstone of the colony, and one of the first public buildings erected was a schoolhouse. In 1914 the townspeople approved a $5,000 bond to build a permanent school. Once the new school was completed, the original building was donated to Josephine. She then purchased a plot of land near the school and had the old schoolhouse moved there to house the town library. She named it the Mary Dickinson Memorial Library, after her mother. She, her husband, and other prominent townspeople donated books for the collection.

Josephine died at the age of eighty-three in Los Angeles County after living with her daughter Eva's family for about a decade. Though most of her work is overshadowed by the achievements of her husband, Josephine's contributions illustrate the essential role of women as partners of race-conscious men who pursued a vision of racial equity.

FURTHER READING
The African American Museum and Library at Oakland has a small but significant collection of papers related to Josephine Allensworth. See Vertical Files, B2, F1, F6 for an interview with Allensworth's granddaughters Josephine B. Smith and Louise Skanks Collier (c.1975).
Alexander, Charles. *Battles and Victories of Allen Allensworth* (1914).
Beasley, Delilah Leantium. *The Negro Trail Blazers of California* (1919).
Ramsey, Eleanor Mason. *Allensworth—A Study in Social Change* (1977).
Robinson, Jini M. *Allensworth Town Is Born Again* (1975).

VENISE WAGNER

Allison, Luther (17 Aug. 1939–12 Aug. 1997), blues musician, was born Luther Allison in Widener, Arkansas, the fourteenth of fifteen children born to his parents (names unknown), who were cotton farmers. He grew up with an interest in music; playing the organ in church, singing gospel, and listening to the Grand Ole Opry from Nashville, Tennessee, over the radio. Allison was exposed early to blues; from the music his father played on the family radio to hearing blues musicians like B.B. King, broadcast from Memphis on WDIA.

By the age of ten, Allison had begun to show interest in the guitar. In 1951, at the age of twelve, he moved with his family, in search of better opportunities, to the Westside of Chicago. After high school, Allison studied the craft of shoemaking. Meanwhile, several of his siblings were members of a gospel group; and one of his older brothers, Ollie, had become a popular guitarist on the Southside of Chicago, where the blues scene was flourishing. Observing his brother and admiring the guitar, Allison sensed his own desire to become a blues musician. He studied the guitar seriously, taking basic lessons from his brother; and was soon adept enough to play with his band and eventually behind the blues guitarist, Jimmy Dawkins. Dawkins grew up in the same neighborhood as Allison, where other blues musicians like OTIS RUSH, FREDDIE KING, and MAGIC SAM (SAMUEL GENE MAGHETT) also lived. When Allison moved with his family to the Southside of Chicago, a new world of opportunities on the blues circuit became available to him. Only a few blocks from his new home lived the established blues musician MUDDY WATERS. Allison became friends with his son Charles and was soon performing with Waters and eventually with blues artists like HOWLIN' WOLF and ELMORE JAMES.

In 1957, Allison formed the original Rolling Stones, a band named for a song by Waters; his brother Grant was a member. Soon thereafter he changed the band's name to The Four Jivers, the moniker for which they became known on the Southside blues circuit. Allison was recognized for his explosive guitar performances and was invited to perform as sideman by blues musicians on the Southside and artists like Magic Sam and Freddie King on the Westside. Freddie King had encouraged Allison to sing, and when he began his national tour bequeathed his band and Westside gig to him. Allison soon became popular on the Westside, a familiar frontier from his early years. His career flourished throughout the late 1950s and the 1960s. In 1969 Allison was invited by Bob Koester to record an album on his label, Delmark Records, and released *Love Me Mama*. Allison had received national attention when two years earlier he performed on a Delmark Records compilation album, *Sweet Home Chicago*.

After the release of his album, Allison was deemed the next star to emerge from the Westside blues scene, which included BUDDY GUY and Otis Rush. Allison, like Guy and Rush, had begun to incorporate rock and roll into his music without surrendering the sanctity of the time-honored blues sound. During this period he began to take his band outside of Chicago in order to promote his album, sometimes touring with the harmonica player Shakey Jake. Allison delivered outstanding performances in 1969, 1970, and 1971 at the Ann Arbor Blues Festival in Ann Arbor, Michigan. His

fan base increased as he garnered the attention of rock and roll aficionados, and his vibrant performances often lasted up to four hours. By 1972 Allison had caught the attention of the recorder, producer, and founder of the Motown label, BERRY GORDY JR., and was signed to Motown Records, where he was one of a few blues musicians on the label. Allison traveled to Japan and throughout Europe with Motown; however, his record sales were poor due to the label's unfamiliarity with promotion of the genre. He recorded three albums for the label: *Bad News Is Coming* in 1972, *Luther's Blues* in 1974, and *Night Life* in 1976.

In 1977, Allison recorded *Love Me Papa*, for the French label Black and Blue. In 1979, Allison recorded four live albums: *Gonna Be a Live One in Here Tonight* and *Power Wire Blues*, both in Peoria, Illinois, on the Rumble label; and *Live in Paris* and *Live*, also in Paris, for the Paris Album/Blue Sky/ Buda label. In 1980 he recorded the album *Time* for Paris Album/Buda. Allison moved to Paris, France, in 1983 and continued to perform throughout Europe. In 1984 he relocated to a home just outside of Paris, where he could continue to take advantage of his popularity as an artist in France and Germany; his performances in the United States were intermittent and based on sporadic bookings. Allison had become one the most celebrated blues musicians in Europe.

In 1984 and 1985 Allison had two releases on the French label Encore!/ Melodie: *Life Is a Bitch*, which was rereleased in 1987 in the United States on the label Blind Pig as *Serious*; and *Here I Come*. He released *Rich Man* on Ruf in 1987, and a performance recorded in Berlin in 1989 was released in 1991 on the label East West titled *More from Berlin*. In 1994, Allison released his first U.S. album in twenty years, *The Soul Fixin' Man*, on the Alligator label. In 1995, he released *Blue Streak*, which earned him five W.C. Handy Awards, highly regarded recognition for blues entertainers. The same year, back on native ground, Allison performed at the world renowned Chicago Blues Festival and other blues festivals like King Biscuit, the Mississippi Valley Blues Festival, the San Francisco Blues Festival, and in the Poconos. This period had marked a resurgence in his music career. In 1996 two live albums were released on Ruf; one in Berlin and the other in Montreux. Two years later, in 1997, Allison released *Reckless* and began touring. During a July 1997 tour performance Allison suddenly left the stage after experiencing dizziness and loss of coordination. At the hospital it was discovered that Allison had developed lung cancer and brain tumors; his condition was inoperable and ultimately terminal. On 12 August 1997, just three days before his fifty-eighth birthday, Allison died in a hospital in Madison, Wisconsin. Allison was buried at Washington Memory Gardens Cemetery in Homewood, Illinois.

Allison was married to Fannie Mae; together they had two sons, Bernard and Luther T; the couple later separated. Allison also has seven stepchildren. Bernard Allison had performed with his father's band and also achieved a career as a solo artist. In 1996 and 1997 the W.C. Handy Blues Awards had named Allison "entertainer of the year." From 1999 through 2009 there were eight posthumous releases—six audio and two video. In 1998, Allison was posthumously inducted into the Blues Hall of Fame.

FURTHER READING

Dahl, Bill. "Luther Allison, 57, Popular Blues Guitarist," *Chicago Tribune*, 13 Aug. 1997.

Reger, Rick. "Luther Allison: Attending a Luther Allison Show One Knows …," *Chicago Tribune*, 19 May 1997.

Watrous, Peter. "Exploring, Improvising and Remembering," *New York Times*, 22 Oct. 1996.

SAFIYA DALILAH HOSKINS

Alou, Felipe (12 May 1935–), baseball player and manager, was born Felipe Rojas Alou, in Haina, Dominican Republic, to Jose Rojas, a carpenter/blacksmith and grandson of a slave, and Virginia Alou, a homemaker and Caucasian daughter of a Spanish migrant. The second Dominican-born player in major league baseball, Alou was one of three baseball-playing brothers and became the first Dominican to manage in the big leagues.

Alou grew up with five younger siblings in a fifteen-by-fifteen-foot house his father had built in the village of Haina. For much of his childhood, food came from where Alou and his family could scavenge it: using bamboo poles and construction wire to fish in the Haina River or climbing coconut trees and scouring for other fruit. Baseball equipment was scarce in the poor village, and Alou and his brothers would play with lemons or coconut husks for balls and their hands for bats.

Alou traveled to Santo Domingo for his education and joined the track and field team in high school. During his senior year Alou traveled to Mexico City for the Central American Games, where he competed in dashes, the discus, and javelin. Having enrolled at Santo Domingo University in 1954, Alou played baseball and was a premed student, harboring dreams of becoming a doctor.

The following summer, Alou returned to Mexico City for the games, batting cleanup for the baseball team. Scouts from major league baseball expressed interest, but the team's coach barred them from talking with Alou. When his father and uncle lost their jobs because of political trouble with the dictator Rafael Trujillo, Alou dropped out of school and signed with the New York Giants in December 1955 for a deferred bonus of $200. Through a misunderstanding in the Dominican name system, Felipe was signed as "Alou," although "Rojas" was his official family surname.

The following spring, Alou was assigned to a Giants affiliate in Lake Charles, Louisiana. Because a new Louisiana law prohibited "colored people participating in athletic contests with or against whites," Alou was forced to relocate to the Cocoa Indians, a team in the Florida State League. The young Dominican soon learned the entrenched Jim Crow laws of the South, when he was barred from restaurants and hotels where his white teammates were served. Although placid in his personal comport, Alou's frustration came out against the baseball—he led his league in batting that year with a .380 mark.

In 1957 Alou was promoted to Minneapolis and in 1958 to Phoenix, where he lived with future Hall-of-Famer Willie McCovey. That season Alou debuted with the Giants and over the next couple of years became a semiregular, until his breakout season of 1962, when he batted .316 and made the All-Star team.

A vocal proponent for Latin American ballplayers and critic of the racism he perceived in the game, Alou argued for the creation of a post in major league baseball to address Latin Americans' needs. He was also part of a new wave of devoutly religious Latin players and became a prominent Christian speaker at San Francisco businesses and churches.

In December 1963 Alou was traded to the Milwaukee Braves (soon to move to Atlanta), where he remained for six seasons, including his career year of 1966, when he led the league in hits and was the runner-up in batting average with a .327 mark. Alou played partial seasons with the Oakland Athletics, New York Yankees, and Montreal Expos before retiring in 1974, following his release from the Milwaukee Brewers. He finished his career with 2,101 hits, 206 home runs, and three All-Star appearances.

Alou's second life in baseball began in 1976, when he was hired as a spring training instructor for the Expos. For the next sixteen seasons, Alou spent time as a manager in three levels of Montreal's minor league system and as a first- and third-base coach for the major league club. Although rumored and interviewed for other major league positions throughout the 1980s, Alou finally became the Expos manager in May 1992, becoming the first Dominican and just the fourth Latin to helm a big-league team.

Despite working for a team that continually faced budgetary constraints, Alou had a successful tenure in Montreal, leading the team to first place during the strike-shortened season of 1994. After being replaced in 2001, Alou served as a Detroit Tigers bench coach in 2002 and returned to the Giants when he was hired to manage the team in 2003. Alou was fired following the 2006 season and joined the Giants' front office in January 2007 as a special assistant to the general manager. Alou managed the Dominican team in the World Baseball Classic in 2009 but saw his team ousted in the first round.

The Alou name became synonymous with baseball; while playing for the Giants, Alou was joined on the team by his brothers Matty and Jesus in 1963, and in September of that year the three siblings all started in the outfield together. Of Alou's ten children with four wives, three sons played professional baseball, including the All-Star Moises, whom his father managed on the mid-1990s Expos and the mid-2000s Giants.

FURTHER READING
Alou, Felipe, with Herm Weiskopf. *My Life and Baseball* (1966).
Regaldo, Samuel O. *Viva Baseball!* 3rd ed. (2008).
ADAM W. GREEN

Al-Rahman, Ibrahmia Abd. *See* Abd al-Rahman Ibrahima.

Alston, Charles Henry (26 or 28 Nov. 1907–27 Apr. 1977), artist and teacher, was born in Charlotte, North Carolina, the youngest of five children of the prominent Episcopalian minister Primus Priss Alston and his second wife, Anna (Miller) Alston. Nicknamed "Spinky" by his father, Charles showed his artistic bent as a child by sculpting animals out of the red clay around his home. His father died suddenly when Charles was just three. In 1913 his mother married a former classmate, Harry Pierce

Bearden (uncle of ROMARE BEARDEN), and the family moved to New York City. Charles's stepfather worked at the Bretton Hotel as the supervisor of elevator operators and newsstand personnel, and over the years the family lived in comfortable brownstones in better neighborhoods.

Alston attended DeWitt Clinton High School, where he was art editor of the student newspaper the *Magpie* during the week, and he studied at the National Academy of Art on Saturdays. He turned down a scholarship to the Yale School of Fine Arts, choosing instead to work as a bellhop at Pennsylvania Station and attend Columbia University in New York. At Columbia he became a member of Phi Alpha Phi, the prestigious black fraternity whose members included at various times ADAM CLAYTON POWELL JR. and PAUL ROBESON. He also worked on the student newspaper the *Spectator* and drew cartoons for the *Jester*, the students' humor magazine. Alston also frequented nightclubs like Pod's and Jerry's or Mike's, turning his artistic eye on the energy of the jazz clubbers. *Opportunity* used his portrait of the popular dancer Lenore Cox for its cover. After he completed his undergraduate studies at Columbia, Alston became director of the boys' program at Utopian House, a community center that provided care for the children of working mothers, where one of his pupils was the young JACOB LAWRENCE.

In 1929 when he received a Dow Fellowship to pursue his graduate studies, Alston left Utopian House and its children's program to the management of GEORGE GREGORY. After earning his M.A. at Columbia in 1930, he became director of the library school at the Carnegie Art Workshop located at the 135th Street branch of the New York Public Library, which is now the Schomburg Center for Research in Black Culture. There Alston worked with the program supervisor and sculptor AUGUSTA SAVAGE as well as with the author GWENDOLYN BENNETT and the artist AARON DOUGLAS. When the school lost its Carnegie funding, the New Deal's Works Progress Administration (WPA) sponsored its new quarters in part of an old stable that Alston had found for his own studio at 306 West 141st Street. Known simply as "306," it became a center for creative minds, black and white. The success of that center led to the formation of the Harlem Artists Guild in 1935, after 306 closed.

In the mid-1930s not only did Alston become the first African American supervisor of the WPA Federal Art Project Commission but he also established his reputation as an artist. His 1934 *Girl in a*

Red Dress demonstrated his engagement with the cutting edge of art. As the art historian Richard J. Powell noted, the woman is "defiantly black, beautiful and feminine, yet also unsettled, mysterious and utterly modern" (Powell, 19). The two murals that Alston executed in 1936—*Magic and Medicine* and *Modern Medicine*—were exhibited at the Museum of Modern Art before they were moved, after a controversy quelled only by community support, to their permanent location in Harlem Hospital. The controversy stemmed from white reaction to Alston's portrayal of African magic alongside modern medicine. As NATHAN IRVIN HUGGINS noted in *Harlem Renaissance*, the panel *Magic and Medicine* depicted the artist's conception of African magic. It has strong elemental and natural emphasis: animals, lightening, and the sun share the scene with dancing and conjuring Africans. Alston employed these obvious symbols—for example, dancing, drums, fetishes—to embody the mural's message: modern medicine is better than primitive medicine. Nevertheless, the African panel was more effective—more romantic and magical—than those that depicted modern doctors in white smocks (Huggins, 169).

Two Rosenwald Fellowships (1938–1939 and 1940–1941) enabled Alston to travel and work extensively in the southern United States, spending studio time at Atlanta University with HALE WOODRUFF. Alston's return to New York brought him back to commercial art as an illustrator for magazines such as *Mademoiselle, Fortune, Scribner's, Red Book*, and *Collier's*. The draft in World War II kept him stateside, and in 1942 Alston began working for the U.S. Office of War Information as an illustrator for a weekly series, "Negro Achievement," carried by 225 black newspapers. He married Myra Adala Logan in New York on 8 April 1944. He decided to pursue his prospering commercial art career and produced magazine covers and book jackets. While attending Pratt Institute under the GI Bill, Alston studied fine arts under the artist Charles Martin, who introduced Alston to the postimpressionist sculptor Alexander Kostellow, who introduced him to abstract expressionism. Alston continued his graduate studies at New York University.

In 1950 Alston became the first African American instructor to teach at New York's Art Students League. The 1950s brought Alston commissions for several murals: in Los Angeles, the Golden State Mutual Life Insurance Company, with Hale Woodruff; in New York, the Abraham Lincoln High School (Brooklyn) and the Museum of Natural History (Manhattan).

He painted his abstract *Configuration* (1952) and the racially ambiguous couple of *Adam and Eve* (1954). During this period his work was exhibited in galleries throughout New York. Alston also taught at the Museum of Modern Art (1956–1957) and participated in the MOMA art educator Victor D'Amico's teaching project at the World's Fair in Brussels. Alston's painting *The Family* was purchased and presented to the Whitney Museum of American Art.

In the 1960s Alston continued to produce signature work on African American families: figurative, colorful, and heavily sculptural in form. But as Beryl Wright pointed out in *African-American Art: 20th-Century Masterworks*, the catalog produced for a 1994 exhibit at New York's Michael Rosenfeld Gallery, Alston's oeuvre encompassed much more: his work "ranges from caricatures of Harlem nightclubbers, absorbing abstractions like *Untitled* (1952), paintings of protest and large public murals" (Wright, 63). Indeed, the turmoil of the early 1960s led Alston and other artists in 1963 to form the Spiral Group in New York, an attempt by African American artists to define their relationship to the civil rights struggles of students in the South. That group dissolved, but not before it produced the Spiral Black and White Exhibit on 5 June 1965 of work done only in black and white.

Alston's career continued to prosper throughout the 1960s and 1970s, from murals for several New York buildings to a bronze bust of MARTIN LUTHER KING JR. now in the permanent collection of the National Portrait Gallery of the Smithsonian. Alston was appointed full professor at the City College of New York in 1973, and in 1975 he received the first Distinguished Alumni Award from Columbia University. His final years were difficult: Alston's wife, Myra, battled cancer for several years, succumbing in January 1977. Three months later, on 27 April 1977, Alston himself died of the disease. His lifelong friend George Gregory eulogized Alston as a "man for all seasons: genteel and friendly, wise and with the power of perception—to see and feel things, people, his surroundings. Added to perspective and understanding, he lived his life by that Arista motto of character, service, and excellence" (Henderson, 26).

FURTHER READING

Henderson, Harry. "Remembering Charles Alston," in *Charles Alston: Artist and Teacher* (1990).

Huggins, Nathan Irvin. *Harlem Renaissance* (1973).

Michael Rosenfeld Gallery. *African-American Art: 20th-Century Masterworks*, essay by Beryl Wright (1993).

Powell, Richard J. "Re/Birth of a Nation," in *Rhapsodies in Black: Art of the Harlem Renaissance* (1997).

MARY ANNE BOELCSKEVY

Alston, Melvin Ovenus (7 Oct. 1911–30 Dec. 1985), educator and civil rights litigant, was born in Norfolk, Virginia, the son of William Henry "Sonnie" Alston, a drayman, and Mary Elizabeth "Lizzie" Smith, a laundress. The Alstons owned their home, and Melvin grew up in a middle-class environment. After attending Norfolk's segregated black public schools and graduating from Booker T. Washington High School, he graduated in 1935 from Virginia State College, where he was honored for his debating and for excellence in scholarship. Following graduation he began teaching math at Booker T. Washington High School. Beginning in 1937 he served as president of the Norfolk Teachers Association, and he also held local leadership positions in the Young Men's Christian Association and the First Calvary Baptist Church.

Alston played a key role in an effort by black teachers in the Norfolk city public schools to challenge racial discrimination in their salaries. In 1937 the Virginia Teachers Association (VTA) and its local branch, the Norfolk Teachers Association, representing black teachers in the public schools, joined forces with the NAACP to organize a joint committee to pursue salary equalization—by which was meant that all teachers would be paid according to the white teachers' salary schedule rather than according to the lower black teachers' schedule. The NAACP supplied legal assistance, and the VTA established a fund of one thousand dollars to indemnify the lost salary of any teacher who was fired in retaliation for serving as plaintiff in a court case. In 1939 Alston's colleague Aline Elizabeth Black initiated but lost a case in state court to achieve salary equalization. Before her case could be appealed to the Virginia Supreme Court of Appeals, the school board declined to renew her contract, and when she lost her job, her lawyers concluded that she no longer had standing to sue. The joint committee paid Black her salary for the school year, and she went to New York, where she taught school and took classes toward a doctorate at New York University. With some reluctance Alston took her place in the litigation, guaranteed a similar indemnity of a year's salary if he lost his job as a consequence.

Alston's lawyers were the NAACP's big guns—THURGOOD MARSHALL, LEON A. RANSOM, and WILLIAM HENRY HASTIE—together with the

Virginia attorneys OLIVER W. HILL and J. Thomas Hewin Jr. As a teacher, Alston sought a permanent injunction against the school board's racial discrimination in its salary schedule, and as a taxpayer he also challenged the city's discriminatory allocation of the state school fund. He and his attorneys lost the case in February 1940 in federal district court, but in June they won on appeal in the Fourth Circuit Court of Appeals, *Alston v. Board of Education of the City of Norfolk*. Pending a final resolution of the case, the court directed the school board not to distribute contracts for the coming year until July, so Alston could not be denied his job and no teachers could be required to waive their rights for that year.

The appeals court determined that the Norfolk school board had denied equal protection of the laws by paying, solely on the basis of race, black teachers lower salaries than white teachers. The court rejected the school board's contention that teachers, having signed contracts for the year, could not contest the terms to which they had agreed and, if they failed to sign, had no standing to sue. The court ruled that such waivers could not extend beyond the single year of the contract. Moreover, the appeals court overruled the district judge in the matter of whether the case concerned only Alston; rather, the court said, the case was a class action suit that affected all black teachers in the Norfolk system.

In October 1940 the United States Supreme Court let the decision stand. Alston's case proved to be one of the NAACP's more important victories in its campaign in the courts for equalization of salaries because it supplied a powerful precedent, both in law and in strategy, for similar suits in Virginia and in other southern states over the next ten years. The NAACP immediately altered its approach to a case then in progress in Florida, for example, and a 1942 out-of-court settlement in Richmond, Virginia, called for salary equalization in five annual increments. The Alston case led to litigation designed to achieve progress on other fronts, too—equal busing, equal facilities, and equal curricula—in the public schools of the South, and black Virginians achieved victories regarding each of those in the 1940s.

After two years away and no longer a litigant, Black retrieved her old job in 1941, while Alston undertook graduate work at Columbia University in New York. He earned an M.S. in Mathematics Education in 1942 and an Ed.D. in the same field in 1945 with a dissertation on "Vitalized Verbal Problem Material in Algebra." During 1945 and 1946 Alston was perhaps the only teacher in the

Virginia public schools, black or white, with a doctoral degree. In 1945 he married Doris Ruby Newsome. They had five children and an adopted daughter.

In 1946 Alston moved to Tallahassee, Florida, to take a position as professor of mathematics and head of the math department at Florida's black land-grant school, Florida Agricultural and Mechanical College. People who knew him there recalled him with great respect as someone with prodigious industry; his wife remembered him as a "workaholic." He served as college registrar from 1947 to 1948 and as dean of the School of Education from 1948 to 1953. Reflecting its new status as a university, the school changed its name in 1953 to Florida Agricultural and Mechanical University and reorganized its divisions into eight colleges. Alston served for a time as acting dean of the graduate school, and he was dean of the College of Education from its establishment in 1953 until he retired in 1969.

Alston then took a position at Southern Illinois University. From 1969 to 1974 he taught courses in secondary education and conducted research in local school systems. In declining health, he retired again and returned to Tallahassee, where he died.

FURTHER READING

The NAACP Papers in the Library of Congress include relevant material.

Lewis, Earl. *In Their Own Interests: Race, Class, and Power in Twentieth-Century Norfolk, Virginia* (1991).

Neyland, Leedell W., and John W. Riley. *The History of Florida Agricultural and Mechanical University* (1963).

Tushnet, Mark V. *The NAACP's Legal Strategy against Segregated Education, 1925–1950* (1987).

Obituary: *Tallahassee Democrat,* 1 Jan. 1986.

This entry is taken from the *American National Biography* and is published here with the permission of the American Council of Learned Societies.

PETER WALLENSTEIN

Amaki, Amalia (8 July 1949–), artist, art historian, curator, critic, and educator, was born Lynda Faye Peek in Atlanta, Georgia. Amaki, who legally changed her name in 1978, is the fourth of six surviving daughters of Mary Lee Hill, a homemaker, gardener, and quilter, and Norman Vance Peek, a landscape designer and gardener during the summer, and a cake and candy caterer during the winter. Early in her life and throughout her artistic career

Amaki was influenced by her parents' penchant for recycling materials into creative forms.

Amaki's parents supported and encouraged her early artistic pursuits. Her mother enthusiastically showed Amaki's drawings to family friends and members of the community. Aware of Amaki's interest, the Reverend William Holmes Borders, a friend of the family and pastor of the Wheat Street Baptist Church where the Peek family worshipped, introduced ten-year-old Amaki to HALE ASPACIO WOODRUFF, a prominent painter who had taught at Spelman College in Atlanta between 1931 and 1946, and had painted a mural for the church.

When she was thirteen Amaki created a series of still lifes from burlap bags and yarn. Originally her father used burlap to make shopping and tote bags, and her mother used yarn in her sewn fabrics and quilts. Amaki's yarn and burlap wall hangings were framed and became part of a furniture display at Rich's Department Store in downtown Atlanta. A customer not only purchased the furniture but also bought Amaki's artwork.

Amaki attended David T. Howard High School in Atlanta where, while continuing to make art, she also studied journalism. In 1967 she enrolled at Georgia State University, where she received a B.A. in 1971 with a dual degree in Journalism and Psychology. During her tenure at the university she interned as a meteorologist and was a feature writer for the student newspaper, the *Signal.* In 1970 she won the prestigious Sigma Delta Chi Award for Outstanding Journalism from the Society of Professional Journalism.

In the 1970s, while employed as a reservations agent at the later defunct Southern Airways in Atlanta, Amaki traveled extensively throughout the United States, South America, Africa, and Europe. Her exposure to various cultures influenced her notions about American marginalization of racial and gender identities in her later positions as artist, curator, and teacher.

During this period Amaki continued to paint and take photographs. For years she was the family photographer at gatherings. Cognizant of Amaki's interest in both photography and painting, BENNY ANDREWS, a renowned painter and close friend, encouraged her to pursue a career in photography. He suggested that she "stop trying to paint photographs and learn something about photography." His comments persuaded her to decline offers to study painting at both Yale University and the University of California, Berkeley. Instead in 1976 she matriculated into the photography program at the University of New Mexico. Never completely relinquishing her interest in painting, Amaki was attracted to New Mexico, largely because of her admiration for the painter Georgia O'Keeffe, who resided in Abiquiu and whom Amaki would cite as an influence throughout her career.

At the University of New Mexico, Amaki's instructors included Betty Hahn, who taught Amaki the non-silver process, particularly cyanotype; Beaumont Newhall, who taught her the history of photography; and Garo Zareh Antreasian, an internationally renowned printmaker of lithographs, who taught Amaki drawing and critiqued her paintings. While in New Mexico, Amaki met eminent artists such as the painter Agnes Martin and the photographers Paul Caponigro, Ansel Adams, Linda Connor, and Minor White. In 1980 Amaki graduated with a B.A. in Photography and the History of Art.

In the spring of 1982, after residing in New Mexico and New York City as a freelance artist the previous year, Amaki returned to Atlanta. During the summer of 1982 she had a fortuitous meeting with Paul R. Jones, an Atlanta-based African American art collector. Amaki was introduced to Jones by Dan Moore, the founder and president of the Collections of Life and Heritage, Inc. (later the APEX Museum), to assist in cataloging Jones's collection. Jones had agreed to loan Moore part of his collection for an art exhibition at the main branch of the Atlanta-Fulton County Public Library, with the stipulation that Moore provide assistants to catalog Jones's extensive collection. Moore sent Amaki and two other recruits to Jones's home. Of the three recruits, only Amaki had a background in art and the stamina to tackle organizing Jones's massive collection, which at the time included artworks by African American, African, Southeast Asian, and South American artists. For the remainder of the summer Amaki alone completed the task, photographing and researching the artworks. This initial encounter between Jones and Amaki spawned a continuing professional relationship.

In the 1980s Amaki supplemented her art career with other jobs. She worked as an investigator for a bank, an employee for the Environmental Protection Agency, a contributing writer for *Art Papers*, an art critic for the Atlanta entertainment paper *Creative Loafing*, and an instructor of art history at Spelman and Morehouse colleges. During this period she was also enrolled in Emory University's Institute of Liberal Arts; she received an M.A. in Modern European and American Art in 1992 and a Ph.D. in Twentieth-century American Art and Culture in 1994.

During the 1990s Amaki taught art history in Greater Atlanta-area institutions, including Morehouse College, Kennesaw State University, Spelman College, Atlanta College of Art, and North Georgia College and State University. She also curated exhibitions on African American art, received numerous commissions to create art, published articles and essays on artists, and exhibited in numerous national group and solo exhibitions. Prior to her retrospective exhibition, in 2001 Amaki was appointed curator of the Paul R. Jones Collection at the University of Delaware and assistant professor of art, art history, and black American studies. In 2004 she curated an annual inaugural exhibition of Jones's African American art collection donated to the university and edited a book of the same title, *A Century of African American Art: The Paul R. Jones Collection*. The exhibition traveled to Spelman College, Montana State University, North Carolina A&T University, and the University of Louisiana at Lafayette. In addition to her curatorial role at the University of Delaware, Amaki was a professor of black American studies and taught art history courses. In the summer of 2004 Amaki was a visiting scholar at the Student Art Centers International (SACI) in Florence, Italy, where she taught photography.

In the summer of 2005, showcasing the art she had produced over thirty years, Amaki held a mid-career retrospective exhibition, *Amalia Amaki: Boxes, Buttons and the Blues*, at the National Museum for Women in the Arts. The exhibition was accompanied by a catalog of the same title and traveled to Spelman College Museum of Fine Art in the spring of 2006. By combining photography (including the cyanotype and digital techniques), painting, and found objects, Amaki created a multimedia array of commentaries about changing realities and perceptions. She reconstructed familiar and popular items—including boxes, buttons, beads, fans, quilts, replicas of the American flag, postcards, reproductions of women from magazine cosmetic ads, and photographs of African Americans, particularly female blues singers—into memorabilia embodying human emotions, identities, and concepts about beauty, gender, and race in American culture.

During the academic year 2005–2006 Amaki was scholar-in-residence at Spelman College, where she researched and coedited the book *Hale Woodruff, Nancy Elizabeth Prophet and the Academy*, published in 2007. In 2006 Amaki was promoted to full professor in the black American studies program at the University of Delaware while maintaining her position as curator of the Paul R. Jones Collection.

For her service and progressive contributions to enriching the community with African American art, Amaki received a 2002 Alumni Award of Distinction from Emory University, a 2006 Christi Award from Christina Cultural Art Center, and a 2006 Commendation from Governor Sonny Perdue of the state of Georgia.

FURTHER READING

Some of the information for this article was acquired during a telephone interview with Amaki on 2 August 2006 and in an e-mail dated 24 April 2007.

Barnwell, Andrea, Gloria Wade-Gayles, and Leslie King-Hammond. *Amalia Amaki: Boxes, Buttons and the Blues* (2005).

Fox, Catherine. "Visual Arts: Accentuating Positivity," *Atlanta Journal-Constitution*, 19 Feb. 2006.

Lewis, Samella Saunders. *African American Art and Artists* (2003).

Robinson, Jontyle, et al. *Bearing Witness: Contemporary African American Artists* (1996).

SHARON PRUITT

America, Richard F. (c. 1940–), author, educator, and economist, was born Richard Franklin America Jr. in Philadelphia, Pennsylvania, to Richard Franklin America Sr. and Arline America. In 1960 America received a B.S. in Economics from Pennsylvania State University and in 1965 an MBA from the Graduate School of Business at Harvard University. Afterward, he joined the Stanford Research Institute in Menlo Park, California, where he worked for the next four years as a Development Economist in the Urban and Regional Economics Group.

In April 1969 America published "What Do You People Want?" in the *Harvard Business Review*. In it he advocated major federal subsidies to facilitate economic equality and large-scale participation of blacks in the corporate world, and made suggestions as to how these goals might be accomplished, including the transfer of corporations to black shareholders and managers. The article offered a radical approach to policy pertaining to reparations and the economic development in the black community. However, America's unique suggestions for the most part went unnoticed in the mainstream reparations debate.

From 1968 to 1972 America served as a lecturer and director of Urban Programs at the Haas School of Business Administration at the University of California, Berkeley. Later he moved to Washington, D.C., to work in consulting and then in the federal government.

During this time America wrote extensively on the economic development of "Afro-America," a term that described a "social, political, and economic system" inclusive of every facet of the black community in the United States. In 1977 America expanded on this theme in *Developing the Afro-American Economy*, again addressing issues of economic equality and how to manage the development process. He discussed the idea of a "social debt" that whites owed blacks because of the benefits the former received directly or indirectly from slavery and discrimination. The resulting disparity between black and white median incomes was to be reduced through redistribution methods such as progressive taxation and development in the black community. America described the economic situation as one of "social monopoly" and suggested ways to apply antitrust laws to industries in which whites held an overconcentration of market power. He also addressed the major barriers to development such as crime and underfunded social services and other noncommercial activities, discussing how blacks could volunteer the funds needed to overcome these difficulties.

In the early 1980s the idea of "social debt" became an important issue within the National Economic Association (NEA). In 1969 Richard America, Marcus Alexis, Bernard E. Anderson, Robert S. Browne, Karl Gregory, Thaddeus Spratlen, Charles Z. Wilson, and others had founded the NEA, formerly called the Caucus of Black Economists. Its purpose was to increase blacks' participation in the field of economics and develop policy to address economic problems experienced in the black community. In addition the NEA published the *Review of Black Political Economy*, a journal previously published by the Black Economic Research Center, to advance policy that would "reduce racial economic inequality" around the world. America remained involved with the organization by writing for the Review, participating in the NEA conferences, and serving as president in 1985.

In 1990 America edited *The Wealth of Races: The Present Value of Benefits from Past Injustices*, a volume that incorporated many of the papers presented at NEA annual meetings in sessions organized and chaired by America. Included were estimates of the benefits whites received from slavery and discrimination as well as contributions to the discussions on reparations and other methods of achieving racial equality. This book was followed by *Paying the Social Debt: What White America Owes Black America* (1993), which again stressed the restitution that whites owed to blacks. Adding to his previous discussion on development, America examined issues such as drug use and crime that hindered economic advancement within the black community.

America continued on the theme of restitution in "Reparations and Public Policy," which appeared in the Winter 1999 issue of the *Review of Black Political Economy*. He wrote that, from 1619 to the present, whites had benefited economically from the unjust treatment of blacks. According to America, the majority of these benefits were enjoyed by those whose income lay in the top 30 percent of the income distribution for whites, and restitution was primarily owed to low-income blacks. The repayment of this debt was necessary to improve not only the economic conditions of many blacks but also for the overall health of the economy, as America argued in "Reparations and Higher Education," published in *Black Issues in Higher Education* (January 2000).

As a Professor of the Practice, Director of the Africa Initiative, and Director of Community Reinvestment, America taught courses in community reinvestment and economic development at the McDonough School of Business at Georgetown University in Washington, D.C. He also worked with business schools in Africa to improve education in management and development. America was an active member in Omega Psi Phi, the fraternity formed in 1911 by Frank Coleman, Oscar J. Cooper, Edgar A. Love, and ERNEST EVERETT JUST at Howard University in Washington, D.C. He continued to write on reparations, economic development, community reinvestment, and public policy, and later broadened his focus to include Africa, Latin America, and the Caribbean.

FURTHER READING
This essay is based on information drawn from personal interviews with the author.

JENNIFER VAUGHN

Amini, Johari (13 Jan. 1935–), poet, writer, educator, and chiropractor, was born Jewel Christine McLawler in Philadelphia, Pennsylvania. She was the oldest of six children born to William McLawler, a minister, and Alma Bazel McLawler, a gospel songwriter. During her childhood, Jewel McLawler's elders, especially the religious poet Frances Theresa Smith, her grandmother on her mother's side, encouraged her to cultivate her precocious intelligence. As a preschooler Jewel learned to read, memorize poetry, and excel in math. The *Pittsburgh Courier*, a leading black newspaper, reported on her rapid progression through school.

At age twelve, Jewel graduated from McCosh Elementary School on Chicago's South Side. At sixteen she finished Englewood High School and married her first husband. She had two children with him: a son, Kim Allan, and a daughter, Marcianna, called Marci. She returned to school at age thirty-two, when she found herself the widowed mother of teens. A student of psychology, she earned an A.A. (City Colleges of Chicago, 1968), a B.A. (Chicago State College, now University, 1970), and an M.A. (University of Chicago, 1972). Her master's thesis was "Some Effects of Acculturation on the Ashanti Nation."

During her first year at City Colleges, she met Don Luther Lee, later HAKI R. MADHUBUTI, a fellow student and an emerging poet, who encouraged her to write poetry as well. She began to publish under the name Jewel C. Latimore. She married Lee in 1963 and had one son with him, Don. They were divorced before Madhubuti's marriage to his second wife in 1974. However, their personal and professional partnership was decisive for both of them as writers and for the black literary world as a whole.

During summer 1967, the couple teamed up with the poet Carolyn M. Rodgers to create Third World Press. Eventually one of African America's most enduring and influential publishers and a guiding spirit of the Black Arts Movement, the press started out in a South Side Chicago basement apartment with only $400 and a secondhand mimeograph machine. It published Latimore's poetry collections *Images in Black* (1967) and *Black Essence* (1968). Like other poets of the Black Arts Movement, she wrote in colloquial African American speech and expressed political protest and other values defined as Afrocentric. Latimore was deeply involved in the early days of other important cultural institutions, such as the Organization of Black American Culture (OBAC), its literary journal *NOMMO*, the Gwendolyn Brooks Writer's Workshop, and the Institute of Positive Education (IPE). She was writer-in-residence with the Kuumba Performing Arts Company of Chicago.

By 1969 Latimore changed her name to Johari Amini, Swahili for "faithful jewel." Later, she was known as Johari Amini-Kunjufu, following her marriage to Jawanza Kunjufu, and as Johari Amini-Hudson. As Johari Amini, she published two more poetry books on Third World Press, *A Folk Fabel* [sic] (For My People) (1969) and *Let's Go Some Where* (1970), as well as *A Hip Tale in the Death Style* (1972) on DUDLEY RANDALL's Broadside Press. IPE reprinted a cultural critique by Amini from *Black World/Negro Digest* as *An African Frame of Reference* (1972) and issued her call to vegetarianism, *A Commonsense Approach to Eating* (1972/1975).

During the early 1970s, Amini was employed as an editor at Third World Press and as an OBAC and IPE officer. She taught psychology and African American literature at Kennedy-King, one of Chicago City Colleges (1970–1972), and at the University of Illinois at Chicago Circle (1972–1976). She became intensely interested in alternative health practices as means of community renewal. Haki Madhubuti credits her for his switch to a vegetarian lifestyle. Amini earned a B.S. and a Ph.D. from the National College of Chiropractic. She practiced as a chiropractor in both the Chicago and Atlanta, Georgia, areas.

As of 2011, Johari Amini had long devoted most of her energies to pursuits other than poetry, although she continued to write. She had not received much critical attention for her literary work, even though it had appeared in at least eighteen anthologies. Yet at the height of the Black Arts Movement, Gwendolyn Brooks praised her as exemplifying the finest qualities of its poets, namely "this constructive impudence, this endorsement of chainlessness, this singular blend of confidence and awe" (in Guzman, xxii). Brooks also described her as "armed with understanding and with assistance for her people. She is diligent revolt. A salted frenzy. A freedom. Even the most exquisite freedom needs an anonymous spine of discipline, and this may be found in Johari's poetry. Music is here. But it is … relevant to Johari's blacktime" (in Brown, 1985).

FURTHER READING

Amini, Johari. "a poet I knew," "positives," and "signals." In *The Poetry of Black America*, ed. Arnold Adoff with an introduction by Gwendolyn Brooks (1973).

Brown, Fahamisha Patricia. "Johari M. Amini (Jewel Christine McLawler Latimore/Johari M. Kunjufu)." *Dictionary of Literary Biography*, Vol. 41: Afro-American Writers after 1955, ed. Thadious M. Davis and Trudier Harris (1985).

Guzman, Richard, ed. *Black Writing from Chicago: In the World, Not of It?* (2006).

Reid, Margaret Ann. "Johari Amini." In *The Concise Oxford Companion to African American Literature*, ed. William L. Andrews, Frances Smith Foster, and Trudier Harris (2001).

MARY KRANE DERR

Ammi, Ben (12 Oct. 1939–), Hebraic scholar, author, anointed spiritual leader of the African Hebrew Israelites of Jerusalem, was born Ben Carter in Chicago, Illinois, the youngest of six children of Rena and Levi Carter. Little is known about Ben's mother and father.

As a young teenager, Carter was a gregarious person, very communicative, and he knew how to vocally motivate people. Growing up, he worked a variety of odd jobs, dusting chairs, collecting garbage, running errands, delivering groceries, and shining shoes.

Around 1959 he married Patricia Price, but nothing more has been documented about his wife or possible children. As things began to intensify during the Vietnam War, Carter joined the U.S. Army. By 1960, after serving about a year and a half of military duty, he was assigned to an army missile base in Chicago. Becoming more perceptive and grown-up, Carter began to display a working knowledge of world affairs. During these years the consciousness of African Americans began to change. African Americans nationwide began preaching Black Power and advocating African American solutions to African American problems.

In 1964 Carter worked as a metallurgist at Howard Foundry in Chicago. While working at the foundry, he studied Hebrew history with an individual by the name of Elder Buie. He learned about men who spoke of the connection between African Americans and the land of Israel, such as Prophet WILLIAM SAUNDERS CROWDY, who in 1896 founded the Church of God and Saints of Christ group. At this time Ben changed his name to Ben Ammi Ben Israel. Ammi felt that God had chosen a special people (African Americans) to be an example and guide for all people to follow. He explained that African Americans had indeed forced the anger of God as a direct result of walking opposite to his established order, which to him explained the unfortunate social conditions suffered by African Americans.

The Hebrew classes that Ammi attended began to grow in numbers. The classes were then moved to the second floor of an office building on 47th Street and Cottage Grove in Chicago. The new location was called Abeta Hebrew Culture Center. It was at this time that Ammi and everyone attending these classes began to refer to themselves as African Hebrew Israelites. In 1965, as his biblical knowledge continued to grow, Ammi split from Elder Buie's teachings and started instructing others at the Abeta Hebrew Culture Center. He spoke to the other members of Abeta about repatriation back into the Holy Land of Israel. He believed that African Americans could not stay true to the biblical scriptures while living in America and began his own quest to lead his followers. Thus, he started to lead a "back to Africa" movement among the members of Abeta. Even with this knowledge, leaving the confines of modern America seemed to be easier said than done. Many of his followers at first hesitated to leave their homes and jobs.

Despite the doubts and questions, Ammi stayed very positive and encouraging to the rest of the members of Abeta. As their date of departure grew near in 1967, he and his followers began to stock various supplies that they might need to survive in the jungle, activities that attracted police attention. During these volatile civil rights years, many organizations and African American individuals, such as the Black Panthers, the Student Nonviolent Coordinating Committee, and H. RAP BROWN and other activists were on the FBI's list as potential suspects. The FBI and the riots in Detroit in 1967 led the Chicago police to become wary of Ammi and the Hebrew Israelites of Abeta. Ammi and his followers were harrassed by whites and other African Americans regarding their plan to leave America.

Ammi claimed to have had a vision in which the archangel Gabriel revealed to him that African Americans descended from the biblical tribe of Judah. He led others to believe that the time had come for the biblical Israelites among the African Americans to return to Israel. As a result, in 1967 about 350 people from Chicago, along with Ammi, traveled to Liberia, West Africa, on their way to Israel. The reason for Ammi's decision to stop in Liberia was because in 1822 the West African country had already been chosen as a safe haven for African Americans escaping slavery. Their first settlement was about 100 miles from the capital city of Monrovia. Initially it was extremely difficult for them to adjust to living without Western comforts. Two years later only 39 of the original 350 people were still there.

Then, in 1969, the group finally settled in the southern region of Israel in a town called Arad and another small town in the Negev Desert called Dimona. By 1971 they had their immigrant status revoked and suffered many attempts at deportation, as they were not accepted into Israel because of the reason they gave for being there (to reclaim their homeland) and who they claimed to be (original Jews).

In 1973 the African Hebrew Israelites officially became the Original African Hebrew Israelite Community at Jerusalem. Into the early twenty-first century Ammi was the leader of twelve princes, ministers, and crowned brothers and sisters who administered the direction of the community. The group's children attended the Kingdom School in Holiness, and upon graduation, they continued study at an institute of higher learning called the School of the Prophets. The African Hebrew Israelites were completely vegan, abstaining from any meat or dairy products. Mothers delivered their babies at the House of Life, a communal clinic with its own medical staff. The community produced tofu, established health food restaurants, and operated an ice cream factory that manufactured non-dairy ice cream. By 1977 the community had grown to 2,500 members. In 1986 forty-six members were deported on charges of living and working illegally in Israel, but in 1990 the Israeli government accorded the community legal recognition.

Ammi was responsible in the early 2000s for resettling more than five thousand individuals in Israel from Liberia, Ghana, Zaire, Benin, Zimbabwe, and Kenya, as well as the United States, St. Croix, and Bermuda. In 2005 he and members of the Southern Christian Leadership Conference inaugurated the Institute for a New Humanity from Chaos to Community, a conflict resolution center in Dimona, Israel. Making a guest appearance at the Million Family March in Washington, D.C., in 2000, Ammi was invited to speak at countless community centers, colleges, and universities. He was also the author of a collection of writings called the Resurrection Series. This included the books *God, the Black Man, and Truth* (1982); *God and the Law of Relativity* (1991); *The Messiah and the End of This World* (1991); *Everlasting Life ... from Thought to Reality* (1994); *Yeshua the Hebrew Messiah or Jesus the Christian Christ?* (1996); and *An Imitation of Life* (1999).

FURTHER READING

Ahtur Yatsiliel Ben Nasik Immanuel. *Tree of Life: African Hebrew Israelites of Jerusalem, Absorbtion Manual* (2003).
Ben Ammi. Available online at http://www. kingdomofyah.com/Ben%20Ammi.htm.

HaGadol, Prince Gavriel, and Odehyah B. Israel.
The Impregnable People: An Exodus of African Americans Back to Africa (1993).

WILLIAM E. BANKSTON

Ammons, Albert C. (23 Sept. 1907–2 Dec. 1949), jazz pianist, was born in Chicago. His parents' names are unknown; both were pianists. Albert was a teenage friend of MEADE LUX LEWIS. The two learned to play by following the key action of player pianos and by imitating more experienced musicians, including Hersal Thomas and Jimmy Yancey. Albert, having access to his parents' instrument, developed his skills faster than Lewis. Both men were particularly influenced by a tune called "The Fives," a blues tune involving strong, repetitive, percussive patterns in the left hand set against equally strong and percussive but less rigorously repetitive counterrhythmic patterns in the right. This piano blues style came to be known as boogie-woogie.

In 1924 Ammons joined a band in South Bend, Indiana. He married around this time, although details about his wife are unknown. His ultimately more famous and talented son, the tenor saxophonist GENE AMMONS, was born in 1925. At some point Ammons left for Chicago and then returned to South Bend to play in a big band at a whorehouse, the Paradise Inn. By 1927 he was playing in Detroit, and then he went back to Chicago. He continued to perform regularly while working as a driver at the Silver Taxi Cab company, where Lewis also was employed. They lived in the same rooming house as their fellow pianist PINE TOP SMITH, who taught Ammons "Pine Top's Boogie Woogie," the piece that named the style.

At some unspecified point Ammons led a band at the Dusty Bottom club in Chicago. He joined François Moseley's Louisiana Stompers in the summer of 1929 and played with William Barbee and His Headquarters from 1930 until 1931. Barbee, also a pianist, gave Ammons valuable lessons that expanded his stylistic range, and Ammons became somewhat comfortable playing in swing groups in the 1930s, although his repertoire remained limited by comparison with many other jazz pianists. He joined the drummer Louis P. Banks's Chesterfield Orchestra from 1931 until 1934, playing in clubs in Chicago and on a theatrical tour. He led a five-piece band, including the trumpeter Punch Miller, which played for weekend excursions to the South on the Illinois Central Railroad. In 1934 Ammons formed Rhythm Kings, which toward year's end began a two-year stand at the Club DeLisa. The group made recordings in February 1936, including "Nagasaki," on which Ammons broke away from the boogie-woogie style, and "Boogie Woogie Stomp," an arrangement of "Pine Top's Boogie Woogie" without Smith's vocal chatter and with the six-piece group rather than the piano alone. In April 1936 the Rhythm Kings' bassist, Israel Crosby, left to join the FLETCHER HENDERSON band. Soon thereafter the Club DeLisa began to present more complicated floorshows, and the music proved too difficult for Ammons. He was fired, and the job was given to his saxophonist, Delbert Bright.

Ammons played alone at the It Club, and in 1938 he led a band at the Claremont Club before traveling to New York to take part in the "Spirituals to Swing" concert at Carnegie Hall on 23 December. There he accompanied BIG BILL BROONZY on two numbers, including "Louise, Louise," and he formed a boogie-woogie piano trio with Lewis and PETE JOHNSON. Their enthusiastic reception furthered the public's developing passion for the boogie-woogie style, and the three pianists were catapulted to fame. With BIG JOE TURNER, the trio worked at Café Society in New York and the Hotel Sherman in Chicago, and they broadcast nationally. Ammons remained at the uptown location of Café Society in a duo with Johnson until 1942, when the two men began touring together.

In 1939 Ammons recorded a solo version of "Boogie Woogie Stomp" and his finest solo, "Shout for Joy," which the critic Jimmy Hopes commends for the rhythmic power of Ammons's left hand, Ammons's sense of structure, and the unusual final choruses, which are surprising within the context of the often predictable boogie-woogie style. A recording session that same year with the Port of Harlem Jazzmen, including the trumpeter FRANKIE NEWTON, produced "Port of Harlem Blues," for which Ammons improvised an uncharacteristically delicate, high-pitched, tuneful, and nonpercussive blues melody. In 1941 he recorded with Johnson and the drummer Jimmy Hoskins, and he performed in the movie short *Boogie Woogie Dream*. The following year he recorded "Suitcase Blues" in memory of his early influence Thomas, who had recorded a version of it in 1925. "Bass Goin' Crazy," a playful performance also recorded in 1941, was equally percussive but altogether freer and more dissonant than Ammons's usual boogie-woogie style. Although he revived the name Rhythm Kings for recordings in 1944 that featured eminent swing musicians, the results were dull.

Sometime in the mid-1940s Ammons suffered a temporary paralysis of both hands. He resumed playing, mainly in Chicago, and in 1947 he recorded under the leadership of his saxophonist son. Ammons joined LIONEL HAMPTON at the beginning of 1949 and recorded "Chicken Shack Boogie." Having long suffered from alcoholism, he died in Chicago before year's end. His death date is commonly given as 2 December, but the brief and not necessarily reliable *Chicago Tribune* obituary of 4 December reports his death "yesterday."

Ammons was a somewhat more versatile pianist than his close friend Lewis and hence worked regularly with jazz groups. But he was never more than competent in this area and was no match for his colleague Johnson. Ammons's specific significance lies within the confines of the boogie-woogie piano style, in which Lewis and he are rated as the finest practitioners after Yancey. Later and indirectly Ammons's music reached a vast audience when the rhythm and blues, urban blues, and rock and roll styles adopted boogie-woogie piano patterns as part of their basic vocabulary.

FURTHER READING

Harrison, Max. "Boogie Woogie," in *Jazz*, ed. Nat Hentoff and Albert J. McCarthy (1959).

Hopes, Jimmy. "Boogie Woogie Man: A Bio-Discography of Albert Ammons," *Jazz and Blues* 1, no. 6 (1971): 4–7.

Newberger, Eli H. "Archetypes and Antecedents of Piano Blues and Boogie Woogie Style," *Journal of Jazz Studies* (Fall 1976): 84–109.

Page, Christopher I. *Boogie Woogie Stomp: Albert Ammons and His Music* (1997).

Pease, Sharon A. "'Pine Top' Smith Influenced Early Piano Style of Swingin' Ammons," *Down Beat* (July 1937).

Travis, Dempsey J. *An Autobiography of Black Jazz* (1983).

Obituary: *Chicago Tribune*, 4 Dec. 1949.

This entry is taken from the *American National Biography* and is published here with the permission of the American Council of Learned Societies.

BARRY KERNFELD

Ammons, Gene (14 Apr. 1925–6 Aug. 1974), jazz tenor saxophonist, was born Eugene Ammons in Chicago, Illinois, the son of ALBERT AMMONS, a boogie-woogie pianist; his mother's name is unknown. Like several other prominent jazzmen, Gene studied music at Du Sable High School under Captain Walter Dyett. Initially he idolized LESTER YOUNG's improvising and even imitated Young's manner of playing with head and horn at a grotesquely tilted angle. During his third year in high school Gene began playing locally with the trumpeter King Kolax's band. At the semester's end he embarked on a cross-country tour with Kolax that included performances at the Savoy Ballroom in New York.

In 1944 the singer BILLY ECKSTINE formed a big band that included the tenor saxophonist CHARLIE ROUSE and the alto saxophonist CHARLIE PARKER. According to the group's pianist, John Malachi, Rouse was so smitten by Parker's playing that he was unable to concentrate on his own parts. Around August 1944 Rouse was fired. Ammons took Rouse's place on the recommendation of a friend, the Eckstine trumpeter Gail Brockman, who later participated in Ammons's early recordings as a leader. The group mainly recorded ballads featuring Eckstine's romantic voice, but it was also known as the first bop big band. That aspect of its musical personality is best preserved on two takes of "Blowin' the Blues Away," in which Ammons engages with the tenor saxophonist DEXTER GORDON in a magnificent battle of fast-paced blues improvisation. (Both men win.) Playing such as this exemplified Ammons's (and Gordon's) ability to draw a perfect balance between smooth tunefulness, a heady linear expression of harmony, and earthy honking and riffing.

While with Eckstine, Ammons acquired his nickname, "Jug." Evidently he had difficulty finding a straw hat big enough to fit, and the singer said, "You've got a head like a jug." From late 1944 onward Ammons was the principal instrumental soloist in a band teeming with up-and-coming bop musicians. He is featured on several records, including "I Love the Rhythm in a Riff" (1945), "Second Balcony Jump," "Cool Breeze," and "Oop Bop Sh'bam" (all from 1946), and in the movie *Rhythm in a Riff* (1946).

In Chicago in the first part of 1947, Ammons was featured alongside the trumpeter MILES DAVIS and the alto saxophonist SONNY STITT in jam sessions at the Jumptown Club, and he played in Stitt's octet at the Twin Terrace Café in March. Around May 1947, if not a couple of months before that, the Eckstine group split up. Ammons led small groups from mid-1947 onward. He had immediate success with the tuneful blues "Red Top" (1947), which had a second life when it was rereleased with lyrics overdubbed in 1953, but apart from this title his recordings of the late 1940s, including a session with his father on piano, are not among his best.

Ammons interrupted his band leading in late March or early April 1949 to replace Stan Getz in Woody Herman's Second Herd, with which he figured most prominently in "More Moon." Ammons left Herman at the beginning of September 1949, his place taken by the tenor saxophonist Billy Mitchell. Following directly in the tradition of "Blowin' the Blues Away," Ammons then formalized the saxophone battle in a quintet co-led by Stitt, who was now focusing on tenor as well as alto saxophone. They worked mainly at Birdland in New York from 1950 to 1951. Their finest recordings, made for the Prestige label, are two takes of "You Can Depend on Me" and three of "Blues Up and Down" (1950). The group continued intermittently until 1955. Around 1955 Ammons married Geraldine (maiden name unknown). They had two children. From 1955 to 1958 he led a number of ad hoc all-star blues and bop sessions for Prestige, one of which resulted in the outstanding album *Blue Gene* (1958).

Ammons has been rumored to be the composer of the blues theme "Walkin'," popularized by Miles Davis in 1954. Legally, "Walkin'" is credited to Ammons's manager, Richard Carpenter. There is no firm evidence that Carpenter appropriated it, although such actions have been commonplace in jazz. In any event, Ammons was not a significant jazz composer.

Ammons started using heroin sometime in the early 1950s (by his own account) and perhaps before that time; several of Herman's sidemen were notorious junkies. In 1958 he was convicted for possession of narcotics and sent to the Statesville Penitentiary near Joliet, Illinois. Paroled in June 1960, he recorded the album *Boss Tenor* but then returned to prison for violation of the condition of his parole that forbade him to perform in nightclubs. He served out the remainder of his sentence and in January 1961 resumed his career, recording the album *Boss Tenors* as coleader with Stitt in August of that year. For engagements at McKie's Lounge in Chicago, Ammons was joined by Gordon in September and by Stitt and the saxophonist James Moody from late that year into February 1962.

During this period, 1960 to 1962, Ammons modified his style, placing less emphasis on his abilities as a bop improviser and more emphasis on African American gospel-influenced melodic gestures that were becoming popular in soul music. This reorientation led to a few modest hit singles, including his soulful instrumental rendering of the songs "Canadian Sunset" (from the Prestige *Boss Tenor* disk) and "Ca' Purange" (from the 1962 LP issued as *Bad! Bossa Nova* and also as *Jungle Soul*).

In June 1962 Ammons began using narcotics again and in September he was arrested. For this second conviction he spent seven years at Statesville, where, as previously, he kept his career alive by directing the prison band and playing every day. Meanwhile Bob Weinstock of Prestige, having recorded many sessions with Ammons from 1961–1962, released these gradually throughout the decade, effectively keeping Ammons's name before the public. Ammons was paroled in October 1969 and resumed his career with an engagement at the Plugged Nickel in Chicago, with Kolax playing trumpet. The following month a two-day recording session yielded two new albums, *The Boss Is Back* and *Brother Jug!*, the latter including a new hit single, Ammons's romantic instrumental rendering of "Didn't We." In March 1970 the New York State Liquor Board ruled against his performing in New York City, but he was able to work elsewhere and held a noted engagement in Chicago with the tenor saxophonists DON BYAS and Gordon in September 1970. He worked alongside EDDIE "LOCKJAW" DAVIS in Chicago in May 1973. Ammons performed at the Ahus Jazz Festival in Sweden on 14 July 1974. Nine days later he entered Michael Reese Hospital in Chicago, where he died of bone cancer and pneumonia.

FURTHER READING

Burns, Jim. "Gene Ammons," *Jazz Journal* (23 Apr. 1970).

Feather, Leonard. "The Rebirth of Gene Ammons," *Down Beat* (25 June 1970).

Obituaries: *Chicago Tribune*, 7 Aug. 1974; *New York Times*, 8 Aug. 1974; *Chicago Defender*, 10 Aug. 1974; *Down Beat*, 10 Oct. 1974.

DISCOGRAPHY

Porter, Bob, and Frank Gibson. "Gene Ammons: A Discography." *Discographical Forum* 6 (May 1968): 11–14; 7 (July 1968): 10–12.

This entry is taken from the *American National Biography* and is published here with the permission of the American Council of Learned Societies.

BARRY KERNFELD

Amos, Emma Veoria (1938–), painter and printmaker, was born in Atlanta, Georgia, to a family with a long line of educated and powerful women. Her grandmother, Emma, was a college-educated university professor in the 1890s, and her mother, India, was a similarly educated partner in the family drugstore with her father, Miles. Her paternal lineage included a grandfather who was the first black pharmacist in the state of Georgia. The family's social circle included such figures as BOOKER T. WASHINGTON and ZORA NEALE HURSTON. Along with her older brother, Larry, Amos attended schools in Atlanta's then-segregated public school system—first E.R. Carter Elementary and then Booker T. Washington High School.

Amos remembered wishing to be an artist from an early age, and eventually she enrolled in Ohio's Antioch College with a firm interest in the visual arts. She earned a B.A. from Antioch in Fine Arts as well as an etching diploma from London Central School of Art in 1959. After finishing her program in London, Amos returned to the United States, arriving in New York City in 1960. There she spent a year teaching at the prestigious Dalton School before she began working for the textile designer, Dorothy Liebes. From 1964 to 1966, Amos completed her MFA in Art Education at New York University (NYU), studying lithography with ROBERT BLACKBURN, and abandoning abstraction for figurative painting. At NYU, Amos also resumed her acquaintance with faculty member HALE WOODRUFF who invited her to join Spiral—a historic group of black male artists including Norman Lewis, ROMARE BEARDEN, CHARLES HENRY ALSTON, and Merton Simpson with whom Amos exhibited until the group's dissolution in 1967.

Amos married Bobby Levine, an advertising director, in 1965. The birth of their first child, Nicholas, in 1967 prompted her to redirect her energies into printmaking rather than painting. In 1970, when her daughter India was born, and after suffering a near-miscarriage brought on by exposure to toxic printing inks and solvents, Amos turned full time to nontoxic pursuits such as quilting, illustration, and, in particular, weaving. Amos's interest in so-called craft and traditional "feminine" arts culminated in her co-production of *A Show of Hands*, a 1977–1978 "how-to" television show on crafts produced by WGBH in Boston.

As her children grew older, Amos returned to painting in the late 1970s, holding her first solo show at New York's Art Salon in 1979. The following year she began teaching at Rutgers' Mason Gross School of Art in New Jersey where she would become a full professor as well as chair of the Art Department. The 1980s, an enormously productive period for Amos, also marked her involvement in writing for and editing feminist publications such as *Heresies* and *M/E/A/N/I/N/G*. Her paintings

from these years reveal both her shift to acrylic paint and her signature incorporation of either her own weavings, or African fabrics such as Kente cloth, into vibrant canvases that depict athletic figures running, dancing, and diving. By the late 1980s and through the mid-1990s these dynamic figures became completely freed from their terrestrial grounding, and they began to fall or fly through an unmoored, often fantastical space which continued to be edged with African fabrics—and thus literally and figuratively framed by Amos's interest in African cultures.

Along with her interest in African arts, Amos's career was distinguished by her longtime attention to the political dimensions of making images. Her art invariably treated subjects such as African American history and the visual representations of blacks, especially black women, within Western art. She also wrote and spoke extensively about issues of race and gender, as well as the obstacles facing black women artists.

Amos's interest in examining the objectionable ways in which nonwhite peoples were represented in the Euro-American visual tradition led her to include more collaged historical photographs or icons of Western art history within her canvases. She would appropriate these iconic images of art history only to deconstruct their racist and sexist meanings. She accomplished this deconstructive effect by highlighting the contemporary primitivism of German Neo-Expressionist painters such as A.R. Penck and Georg Baselitz in her *A.R. Pink Discovers Black* (1992) and *Which Way Is Up Georg Baseless?* (1992). Amos also repainted Paul Gauguin's primitivistic Tahitian nudes, endowing them with agency, or revealing the racist stereotyping of the nonwhite body that occurs throughout Gauguin's oeuvre. In *Models* (1995), Amos considered the culturally specific norms of Western beauty and the exoticization of the non-Western body: Gauguin's model Te He Amana was whitened and juxtaposed with the figures of an African woman and a Greek *kouros*, the sculptural embodiment of Classical beauty—yet a sculptural form which was, ironically, closely related to West African sculpture. Here, as in her other paintings, Amos employed a bold, painterly *X* as a way to both invoke the repressive erasure of minority histories and to signal the remaking of identity in positive terms—a project that informed many of Amos's powerful and celebratory images.

Amos's work was shown in a major midcareer retrospective organized by the Ohio's College of Wooster in 1993, and this show was followed by a smaller 1994 exhibition at the New York gallery Art in General. The artist's paintings are held in the collections of the Museum of Modern Art, the Studio Museum in Harlem, and the Wadsworth Athenaeum.

FURTHER READING

Gouma-Peterson, Thalia. *Emma Amos: Paintings and Prints 1982–92* (1993).

hooks, bell. *Emma Amos: Changing the Subject. Paintings and Prints 1992–1994* (1994).

Murray, Al. "Interview with Emma Amos," *Smithsonian Archives of American Art* (1968). Available at http://www.aaa.si.edu/collections/oralhistories/transcripts/amos68.htm#top.

Patton, Sharon F. "Emma Amos: Art Matters," *Nka: Journal of Contemporary African Art* (Fall–Winter 2002).

LEORA MALTZ LECA

Amos, Harold (7 Sept. 1918–26 Feb. 2003), scientist and educator, was born in Pennsauken, New Jersey, the second of nine children, to Howard R. Amos Sr., a Philadelphia postman, and Iola Johnson, who had been adopted by and worked for a prominent

Harold Amos, a microbiologist who was Harvard Medical School's first black department chair and a mentor to hundreds of aspiring physicians, 1994. (AP Images.)

Philadelphia Quaker family who schooled her with their own children at home. This family remained lifelong friends of Iola and kept the young Amos family well supplied with books, including a biography of Louis Pasteur, which piqued Harold's interest in science in the fourth grade. Both Howard and Iola expected their children to be serious about their education and to excel academically. Harold, along with his siblings, took piano lessons and remained a competent amateur pianist. He also gained a reputation as an excellent tennis player.

Harold received his early education in a segregated school in Pennsauken, then graduated first in his class from Camden High School, in New Jersey. He later recalled that his love of teaching was awakened by the "wonderful teachers" that he had from first through twelfth grade. After graduation in 1936, Harold attended Springfield College in Springfield, Massachusetts, on a full academic scholarship at a time when few such scholarships were offered to African Americans. Amos graduated summa cum laude in 1941, with a major in biology and a minor in chemistry. The following year he worked as a graduate assistant in the biology department at Springfield College, until he was drafted into the U.S. Army, where he served in the Quartermaster Corps as a warrant officer, personnel. He spent close to two years in England before the invasion of France and then served on the Continent until he was discharged in February 1946. In the fall of 1946 Amos enrolled in the biological sciences graduate program at Harvard Medical School (Division of Medical Sciences), earning an M.A. in 1947 and a Ph.D. in Bacteriology and Immunology in 1952, becoming the first African American to earn a Ph.D. from the division. After spending a year as a Fulbright Fellow at the renowned Pasteur Institute in Paris, where he worked with the molecular biologist Georges Cohen, Amos returned to Harvard Medical School. With the exception of three subsequent sabbatical periods in France, he remained at Harvard for close to fifty years, rising through the ranks as a faculty member in the Department of Bacteriology and Immunology (now Microbiology and Molecular Genetics). Amos was made a full professor in 1969, named the Maude and Lillian Presley Professor of Microbiology and Molecular Genetics in 1975, and became professor emeritus in 1988. As chair of his department from 1968 to 1971 and again from 1975 to 1978, Amos was the first African American to head a department at Harvard Medical School. He was known particularly for his interest in and encouragement of students and young faculty.

In his role as chairman of the Division of Medical Sciences at Harvard Medical School from 1971 to 1975 and from 1978 to 1988, Amos provided creative, forward-looking leadership with fairness and diplomacy. The door to his office was almost always open, and he welcomed drop-in visitors. For decades, students and faculty found Amos personified the Division of Medical Sciences. He was an effective, inspiring, and inexhaustible supporter of all students, especially minorities, in science and medicine, and served, often in leadership positions, on numerous boards and advisory committees dedicated to these interests. Among others, Amos sat on the board of directors of the Josiah Macy Jr. Foundation, the Minority Medical Faculty Development Program Advisory Committee of the Robert Wood Johnson Foundation, the National Cancer Advisory Board, the President's Cancer Panel, and the Massachusetts Division of the American Cancer Society. As part of his interest in expanding the participation of minorities in research, he was an early advocate of the National Institute of Health's programs for minority college students.

Early in his career Amos intended to pursue research as an *E. coli* microbiologist, but, upon realizing that it was a field already crowded with competent senior scientists, he decided to study animal viruses and animal cells in culture. He was particularly interested in cells that could become malignant when infected with animal viruses and in sugar metabolism in cells. The body of scientific work that Amos carried out was eclectic in its scope and in the questions he asked, but it can be characterized as uncovering many facets of metabolism and of understanding how cells function and influence organisms. Amos pioneered approaches to studying how proteins and RNA in cells are affected by nutrients, including glucose, and hormones, such as insulin, from outside the cell.

Amos used cells in culture to understand how molecules get into cells and how entry is regulated during cell starvation or in plentiful conditions. He was particularly interested in how these influences controlled metabolism of RNA, work he did at an early time in the history of RNA biology. His work provided valuable information to other investigators, who studied the normal and abnormal control of cell division and how this could provide insights into understanding cancer. Major laboratories around the world were influenced by the careful and dependable work that he published. Between 1953 and the mid-1980s he was an author on over seventy scientific papers.

Amos was legendary for the continual contributions that he made to the work of his colleagues, his own students, and to untold numbers of other students with whom he talked and worked. He had a prodigious memory and an unusually creative approach, and he always asked insightful questions and offered clear suggestions to a myriad of other scientists who were fortunate enough to cross his path. In this way he created an aura of old-fashioned intellectualism in its best sense, and he contributed, behind the scenes, to literally thousands of scientific papers by other authors who directly benefited from his input. By reaching such a broad group of scientists—in terms of their levels of training or profession, their institutions, and the types of biological science they pursued—Amos helped usher in modern biology and modern biologists.

Amos described teaching as one of his primary responsibilities, and he was always accessible, quick to offer words of praise and encouragement, advice, and support. Even during his graduate school days, Amos was praised for his devotion to and competence as both a teacher and a mentor. He followed his students' careers and personal lives with enthusiasm, regularly communicating with countless medical and graduate students, many of whom held important positions in a broad range of fields, long after they had graduated. He had an unusual ability to capture people's strengths and to help develop them.

Amos never married but had a large circle of devoted friends, drawn from all walks of life and representing many phases and interests of his own life. He was well known as an enthusiastic Francophile, enjoyed using his fluent French, and appreciated French literature, music, and cuisine. Amos was a gracious and attentive host, organizing dinners at interesting restaurants or at his farm near Kezar Falls, Maine, to which he invited people whom he thought would enjoy meeting each other.

Amos was the recipient of numerous awards, including several honorary doctoral degrees, the Centennial Medal of the Harvard Graduate School of Arts and Sciences (2000), the first Charles Drew World Medical Prize from Howard University (1989), and the National Academy of Sciences' highest honor, the Public Welfare Medal (1995). He was named a Fellow of the American Academy of Arts and Sciences (1974), and elected to the American Association for the Advancement of Science (1991) and the Institute of Medicine of the National Academy of Sciences (1991). A modest man, few of his colleagues were aware of the full range of honors he had received.

Upon the occasion of his retirement from Harvard Medical School at the age of seventy, he noted that he "had to get back to work to try to do something useful with these few remaining years" (letter, October 1989). He accepted the position as the first national director of the Minority Medical Faculty Development Program (MMFDP) of the Robert Wood Johnson Foundation, serving until 1994. He developed a reputation for keeping in contact with and encouraging the MMFDP Fellows and their family members long after their tenure in the program, and for seeking alternative positions for applicants who were not awarded fellowships. Amos wrote to a friend less than a year before his death that he was "still working full-time in the lab and writing two manuscripts" on glycerol metabolism in mammalian cells (letter, March 2002). Amos died in Boston on 26 February 2003, shortly after suffering a stroke.

Harold Amos broke many barriers during his lifetime, in the scientific insights he directly and indirectly made possible, in his teaching and mentoring, and in his administrative contributions. Wherever he served, he was chosen because of his superior credentials. Amos's personable and accessible style in all aspects of his life and work succeeded in blending highly competitive academic work with the highest level of cultural appreciation and enjoyment, all with a profound degree of attention to collegiality and friendship.

FURTHER READING

Amos's 1972–2003 papers are housed at the Countway Library of Medicine, Harvard Depository of Rare Books.

Beecher, H. K. *Medicine at Harvard: The First Three Hundred Years* (1977).

Obituaries: *Boston Globe*, 4 Mar. 2003; *Harvard University Gazette*, 6 Mar. 2003.

THOMAS O. FOX AND JOCELYN SPRAGG

Amos, John (27 Dec. 1939–), actor, athlete, singer, and producer, was born in Newark, New Jersey, to Annabelle Patricia West and John Allen Amos Sr., a self-taught diesel auto mechanic and tractor trailer driver. Shortly after his second birthday, the family moved to East Orange, New Jersey, where they lived while John Sr. served in the military during World War II. His father left after the war, and his mother struggled to support her family by working as a domestic and then as a certified dietician. Amos recalled that "the only time [he] ever saw his mother

concede to possible failure was one time when she could not find any food in the cupboards. She had to ask him to go to the next-door neighbor to borrow food" (interview with John Amos by the author, 2010). Amos first joined the Metropolitan Baptist Church in Newark, New Jersey, at about the age of ten, when it became clear to him that his mother's faith in God sustained her as a single mother.

Called "Sonny" by his family, Amos enjoyed pick-up games of football and, along with three other black students, integrated Stockton Grade School and Columbia Junior High School. He spent alternating summers with relatives in Birmingham, Alabama, and Library, Pennsylvania. He recalled that when the train arrived in Washington, D.C., he would glimpse the Washington Memorial and then be forced to move to the back of the train. In Birmingham, he worked for his aunt and her husband, prominent members of the black community who owned a block of businesses. Other summers he spent with his coalmining relatives in Library, Pennsylvania. There, Amos discovered his latent acting abilities by entertaining his family with storytelling, which gave him the confidence he would later demonstrate as a performer (interview with author, 2010).

Following the examples of his hard-working mother and relatives, Amos entered the National Guard during the last year of junior high, when he was fifteen. He joined the 50th Armored Division (now called the 50th Military Brigade) of the New Jersey National Guard. Designated as an N-7 tank driver, he was shot during training maneuvers and honorably discharged. He returned to East Orange and graduated from East Orange High School in 1958.

Amos then pursued his love of football by attempting a career in professional sports. He went to Long Beach City College in California to hone his skills; there he met his father for the first time. He then transferred to Colorado State University, and in 1964 was signed as a free agent with the Denver Broncos, though an injured hamstring cost him his contract. For the next few years, he moved from team to team in the United States and Canada, including a short but inspiring experience with the Kansas City Chiefs. He even became a Golden Gloves competitor, but gave up boxing after being soundly thrashed by his first opponent (interview with author, 2010).

In between football contracts, he married Noel Mickelson in 1965 and became a father to daughter Shannon and son K. C. He performed stand-up comedy in Greenwich Village, performing at the Café Wha? with other newcomers such as BILL COSBY, RICHARD PRYOR, and Robert Kline, and also worked for juvenile offenders as a social worker at the Vera Institute of Justice and at the Brooklyn House of Detention. During this era, he participated in the civil rights movement in protests and marches, and even briefly joined the Nation of Islam before becoming disenchanted with its philosophies and returning to his original church (interview with author, 2010).

He then pursued writing, first as an advertising copywriter in Los Angeles and then as a comedy writer for the *Lohman and Barkley Show* and the *Leslie Uggams Show* in 1969, which he left when he was not allowed to audition for a role on the show even though white writers were able to both write and act. At this point, Amos landed the role of the weatherman Gordy Howard on the enormously popular *Mary Tyler Moore Show*, which he played from 1970 until 1973. His imposing figure, passion, and integrity earned praise, and he parlayed this into more dramatic work. In 1971 he earned a best actor nomination from the Los Angeles Drama Critics Circle for *Norman, Is That You?* A small role on the sitcom *Maude* led to a spin-off, *Good Times*, about a struggling black family in the Chicago ghetto. As James Evans Sr., Amos tried to create a strong image of black family life while dramatizing the problems of chronic unemployment and ghetto life, but was fired after fifty-seven episodes because he objected to the increasing trivialization of scripts (interview with author, 2010).

This led to his participation in television history in 1977, when he portrayed the adult Kunta Kinte in the miniseries *Roots*, based on the book by ALEX HALEY. *Roots* was one of the first mainstream presentations of the history of African Americans and earned Amos an Emmy nomination for best actor in a television series. Since then, while he has fought to bring equality in the industry to black performers, he has maintained a steady career in television, theater, and film, including dozens of television guest performances, recurring roles in *The West Wing* (1999–2004) and *Men in Trees* (2006–2008), and has appeared in the films *The Beastmaster* (1982), *Coming to America* (1988), and *Die Hard 2* (1990). He has acted and directed on the stage, performing on Broadway and at England's Old Vic, and earned the NAACP Award as Best Actor for his performance in the 1985 play *Split Second*. He is the writer and producer of the one-man play *Halley's Comet* (1990) and the documentary *Gangs at Sea* (2010); in 2009 he released a country album, *We Were Hippies* (2009).

For his work as an actor, activist, and humanitarian, John Amos was awarded the New Jersey Education Association's (NJEA) 2009 Award for Excellence, for public school graduates who have demonstrated exceptional leadership in their fields of expertise. He is also Honorary Master Chief of the U.S. Coast Guard. Divorced four times, Amos has two children, Shannon and K. C., and two grandchildren, Quiera and Jhazz.

FURTHER READING

Amos, John. 2010. Interview by the author. Transcript of interview in author's possession.
Contemporary Black Biography, vol. 6 (1994).
Contemporary Theatre, Film, and Television, vol. 4 (1987).

JILL SILOS-ROONEY

Amos, Wally (1 July 1936–), entrepreneur, author, and inspirational speaker, was born Wallace Amos Jr. in Tallahassee, Florida, to Ruby (maiden name unknown), a domestic worker, and Wallace Amos, a laborer at the local gasoline plant. Hard work, discipline, and religion were the cornerstones of Wally's strict childhood. The Christian faith was important to his parents, and they took him to church regularly.

Wally Amos posing with cookies at a Tallahassee luncheon, 17 March 1983. (AP Images.)

By the age of eight Wally had learned all the books of the Bible. In their tight-knit black community, Friday nights were reserved for community dinners where hearty southern fare was served: fried chicken, potato salad, black-eyed peas, and collard greens. Schooling options for black children were less abundant, however, so Ruby and several of her Methodist church members started a school, which Wally began attending at age ten. Wally's entrepreneurial spirit surfaced in his childhood when he started a roving shoeshine stand and delivered newspapers for the local *Tallahassee Democrat*.

In 1948 Wally's parents divorced, and his mother sent him to live with her sister Della in New York City. New York made a striking impression on Wally, who after coming from the segregated South was fascinated by the rich cultural diversity of his new classmates. In contrast to Wally's serious mother, Aunt Della was lighthearted and instilled the joy of laughter into Wally. Ruby eventually followed her son to New York, and they shared a two-bedroom apartment in Harlem. Deciding that he wanted to become a cook, Amos enrolled at the Food Trades Vocational High School. He split his time between his vocational training and his academic subjects. Amos's training included part-time work in food services at the Essex House Hotel in Manhattan. Despite working hard and being qualified, Amos was passed over for a promotion, as were his black colleagues. Discouraged by the racism he had encountered, Amos dropped out of school to join the U.S. Air Force. He earned his GED High School Equivalency Diploma while in the Air Force, and he returned to New York four years later after being honorably discharged. In 1957 Amos started a new job as a stock clerk in the supply department at Saks Fifth Avenue, a New York department store. He worked hard and was promoted to manage the department, and the company paid for him to take retail and merchandising classes at New York University. In 1958 Amos married Maria (maiden name unknown); they had a son, Michael Anthony. Despite being given increasing responsibility, Amos felt that he was not being compensated adequately by Saks and decided to leave the company in 1961 with his wife expecting a second child.

Amos quickly found another job as a clerk in the mailroom of the William Morris Agency. Within a year of demonstrating his work ethic and managerial potential, he became the company's first black talent agent, in charge of the new rock-and-roll division. During his tenure at William Morris, Amos brought in Simon and Garfunkel and promoted clients including the Supremes, the Temptations, and MARVIN GAYE. In the shadow of his successful career and extramarital affairs, his marriage was faltering, and he divorced Maria and left their two children, Michael Anthony and Gregory, in her custody.

In 1967 Amos left William Morris and ventured out to Los Angeles with his new wife, Shirlee Ellis, and son, Shawn, to start his own talent agency. His startup did not fare well, but his next venture proved more successful. Using his Aunt Della's recipe, Amos started baking chocolate-chip cookies. His cookies quickly became legendary, and inspired by a friend's suggestion, Wally started the Famous Amos Chocolate Chip Company in March 1975 with funds invested by Marvin Gaye, United Artists CEO Artie Mogull, and other friends. The first store was located on the Sunset Strip in Hollywood, and the demand for the company's cookies spread nationwide. Amos expanded the company over the next nine years, but managing the enterprise proved challenging. Outside investors infused cash into the ailing company on several occasions and retained a stake in the company, eventually leaving its founder with a minority share. In 1985 Amos's share had dwindled to 17 percent; after the company changed ownership a few more times, his stake in the company had eroded to zero, and he reluctantly agreed to disassociate himself from the company altogether. He signed a noncompete clause, effectively barring him from the cookie industry.

In 1977, his second marriage having ended, Amos moved to Hawaii and married for the third time, to his long-term girlfriend Christine (maiden name unknown); they had a daughter, Sarah. In 1979 he became the national spokesperson for Literacy Volunteers of America and became more involved in nonprofit organizations, including Cities in Schools, the Aloha United Way, and the Napoleon Hill Foundation. In November 1991, with the expiration of the noncompete clause, Amos started the Chip & Cookie Company. The owners of the Famous Amos Company launched a lawsuit charging that he had reneged on his previous agreement not to compete or use his likeness in association with food products. In 1993 an agreement was reached in which Amos would own his name for businesses not related to food and the rights of publicity to his name, and the Famous Amos Company would own the trademark rights to his name in association with foods. Amos had invested most of his financial resources into fighting the lawsuit and was burdened by debt. In spite of his financial woes he decided to start another cookie venture, the Uncle Noname Cookie Company. According to Amos, "The greater the pain, the harder the shock, the more hopeless the crisis, the more miraculous the outcome. Not only is every crisis resolved eventually; it is always resolved in the best possible way."

Amos has been a recurring guest on television shows, a product spokesman for corporations including Hush Puppies and United Airlines, and an inspirational speaker. His numerous awards include an honorary doctorate in education from Johnson and Wales University, the President's Award for Entrepreneurial Excellence, and the National Literacy Honors Award. He has also published several books, including his autobiography, and coauthored a self-help book with his son Gregory.

FURTHER READING

Amos, Wally, with Leroy Robinson. *The Famous Amos Story: The Face That Launched a Thousand Chips* (1983).

AYESHA KANJI

Anderson, Aaron (18??–?), sailor, was one of eight African American seamen to earn the Medal of Honor during the Civil War. Likely in his early twenties when he enlisted as a landsman (for which he was tasked with the simplest sail-handling and duties like manning the yardarm) in the Union navy from Pennsylvania, Anderson was probably born a free black and, because he was rated a landsman, had little or no prior seafaring experience.

Though few details of Aaron Anderson's military service are known, and virtually nothing of his private life, his exemplary service nonetheless serves to highlight the importance of the African American contribution to the Union navy in what was, up to that time, the nation's bloodiest war. Along with such men as JOACHIM PEASE, ROBERT SMALLS, and JOHN LAWSON, Aaron Anderson was one of approximately eighteen thousand African Americans (eleven of them women) to serve in the Union navy from 1861 to 1865. Accounting for approximately 20 percent of the navy's enlisted force, these men and women came from such predominantly coastal states as Maryland, Massachusetts, New York, Pennsylvania, and New Jersey. Twenty-three hundred men alone came from Maryland, many of them experienced Chesapeake Bay sailors. Even inland states, such as Ohio and Kentucky, provided a healthy number of men with experience as river boatmen. When the war began, African Americans

made up only 8 percent of the navy's strength. This number would peak at 23 percent from 1863–1864.

While segregation was the rule in the Union army for African American soldiers, the navy was less restrictive when it came to race relations. There had always been a tradition of black service in the navy, dating back to the days of the American Revolution, and the Civil War proved to be no different. Because of this, sailors like Aaron Anderson ate and slept with their white shipmates and were subject to the same naval code of discipline. Although conflicts between African American and white sailors aboard ship were not uncommon, records indicate that white sailors who took part in such fights were often disciplined on an equal basis with black sailors. Though instances of abuse of African American sailors at the hands of their white officers were not unknown, they do not seem to have been the norm. As to the positions held by African American sailors, most, like Anderson, served as landsmen. Black sailors also filled a wide variety of other ratings, including "ship's boy," coal-passer, fireman, steward, able-seaman, and ordinary seaman. One important aspect of African American naval service was the significant use of those men, such as ROBERT BLAKE, who were formerly enslaved. Referred to as contrabands, these men often acted as pilots and served to guide the Union navy through the small creeks and rivers in the South to attack Confederate positions. A major complaint of those blacks serving in the navy, however, was the inability to gain promotion to petty officer status. Despite their fine and in many cases heroic service, only a small number of men achieved such a promotion, in stark contrast to the men serving ashore as noncommissioned officers in the army's black regiments.

Whatever their rating, it is almost certain that every ship in the Union navy had at least one African American crewman. The majority of black sailors served on colliers, store ships, and other support vessels. Research has shown that anywhere from 63 to 100 percent of the men serving on these types of ships were of African American descent (Reidy, 5). The black presence in other ships, such as sloops of war, was considerably less. Examples of Union vessels crewed primarily by African Americans include the store-ship *Valparaiso* (43 of 46 men), the receiving ship *Vermont* (143 of 144 men), the paddle-wheel steamer *Stepping Stones* (32 of 34 men), and the gunboat *Glide* (30 of 38 men). In all of these cases, the few whites in each crew served as masters and in other officer positions.

Despite the perceptions of whites regarding their heritage, black sailors were in fact a welcome addition to the ships of the Union navy, always in competition with the army when it came to manpower needs. To be sure, navy admirals always preferred white crewmen. However, they also recognized the quality of their black enlistees and, unlike the army, utilized African Americans from the beginning of the war. Rear Admiral David Porter wrote to Rear Admiral A. H. Foote on 3 January 1863, "Don't be astonished at the lists of niggers I send you. I could get no men. They do first-rate," while Rear Admiral Samuel Du Pont wrote Secretary of the Navy Gideon Welles later that year that contrabands were "very useful, particularly as there is difficulty in obtaining men in the North ports" (Quarles, 229).

In regards to the service of Aaron Anderson, we know little of the details except for the act of bravery that made him the last African American naval Medal of Honor winner in the Civil War. Indeed it is because so little is known of Anderson that he is often the forgotten recipient among the African Americans who earned this high honor. While serving as a landsman on the store ship *Wyandank*, on 17 March 1865 he was part of a small boat crew sent on an expedition to clear Confederate positions in Mattox Creek, Virginia. According to his citation, Anderson "carried out his duties courageously in face of a devastating fire which cut away half the oars, pierced the launch in many places and cut the barrel off a musket being fired at the enemy" (*Medal of Honor*, 13). Earning the Medal of Honor alongside Anderson during the engagement was the *Wyandank's* white boatswain's mate, Patrick Mullin.

After winning the Medal of Honor, Aaron Anderson disappears from history; his common name and a lack of naval records have made it impossible for historians to trace his whereabouts with any certainty. His meritorious naval service, however, dictates that he should always be remembered as a true American hero.

FURTHER READING

King, Lisa Y. "They Called Us Bluejackets,"
    International Journal of Naval History 1.1 (Apr. 2002).
Quarles, Benjamin. *The Negro in the Civil War* (1953).
Reidy, Joseph P. "Black Men in Navy Blue during the Civil War," *Prologue Magazine* 33.3 (Fall 2001).
United States Navy. *Medal of Honor, 1861–1949: The Navy* (1950).

GLENN ALLEN KNOBLOCK

Anderson, Ada C. (2 Oct. 1921–), grande dame of Austin's African American community and cultural doyenne, was born Ada Collins on a family farm in Travis County, Texas, the fourth of nine children of Walter Collins and Cecilia Rucker Collins. She was a fifth-generation Texan, descended from two prominent African American families.

Anderson's middle-class immediate and extended family included African and African American slaves, white slaveholders, midwives, and Buffalo soldiers. One of her great-grandfathers was David Rucker, who was born a slave in Tennessee and freed when he was ten. Her other great-grandfather, NEWTON ISAAC COLLINS, was born to a slave mother and an Irish slaveholder in Alabama but purchased his freedom only to be reenslaved in Texas when he arrived there in the 1820s.

Anderson inherited a rich legacy from her ancestors of defying odds and fighting for freedom. She graduated from L.C. Anderson High School when it was still segregated. She wanted to study at the University of Texas, but the school wasn't integrated yet, so she attended Austin's predominantly black colleges, Samuel Huston and Tillotson (later called Huston–Tillotson University).

In 1941, she received her bachelor's degree in home economics. She met her future husband, Marcellus J. "Andy" Anderson, a teacher at Samuel Huston College. They were married in 1943, and she traveled with him to his army post in Princeton, New Jersey. There, she worked in civil service until the couple returned to Austin after World War II. Marcellus Anderson was admitted to the Austin Board of Realtors upon their return. He is the first known African American admitted to membership in the Board of Realtors in Texas, the seventeen Southern states, and the District of Columbia. He founded Anderson Wormley Real Estate in 1953 assisted by Ada, who later became a full partner. When Marcellus Anderson died in 2004, the two had been married for sixty-one years.

The couple raised two children, Sandra and Jack. A segregated Austin skating rink that barred the participation of their children became the catalyst for Anderson's community activism and engagement.

When the Ice Palace rink opened in 1962, black children weren't allowed to skate there. Anderson organized a yearlong boycott that gained national media attention when passersby shot at protestors who were on a picket line from a car. No one was hurt, but after the incident letters from black and white segments of the community flooded the Anderson household. Eventually, the ice rink went bankrupt and closed. But a meeting in the

Anderson home afterward, on 6 February 1963, to discuss creating more open accommodations for blacks in Austin would eventually lead to the creation of the City of Austin Human Relations Commission. The group helped push city leaders to create more integrated hotels, restaurants, and theaters in the 1960s.

Anderson later became one of the first African Americans to be admitted to graduate school at the University of Texas. Her first choice of a degree, educational psychology, was off limits to her at the time, so she enrolled in the School of Library Science. She would not be permitted to enroll in the educational psychology program until the 1960s, and she earned her master's degree in 1965.

She worked as a teacher and psychometrist in Austin, assisted the Austin Community College Board and the University of Texas, and served on the board of the Laguna Gloria Art Museum for fifteen years.

Anderson went on to become associated with the family of former president Lyndon Baines Johnson and the LBJ Library. She has served on several boards and influential committees including the Governor's Commission on the Status of Women and the Governor's Committee on Human Relations. She has served as Regional Director and National Secretary for Jack and Jill of America and on the board of directors for the Girl Scouts of America and president of the Austin-Travis County Mental Health Association.

She established the Leadership Enrichment in the Arts Program, a nonprofit outreach program of the Austin Lyric Opera (she was a founding member of the city's Opera in 1986), meant to educate and develop leaders in the African American community using opera, in 1989. She raised funds for the construction of Austin's Long Center, which opened in 2008. She was elected to the Texas Black Women's Hall of Fame, received the leadership award from the Austin Chamber of Commerce Business Committee on the Arts, and was the recipient of a commemorative resolution adopted by the Texas House of Representatives in 2005. In 2006, she was awarded a Distinguished Alumni Award from the University of Texas.

FURTHER READING

Briscoe Center for American History at the University of Texas. "A Guide to the Anderson (Ada Collins and Marcellus J. "Andy") Papers, 1924–2001." Available online at http://www.lib.utexas.edu/taro/utcah/00513/00513-P.html.

Hamilton-Lynne, Deborah. "A Historic Moment 40 Years in the Making." *Austin Woman Magazine*, 1 January 2009.

JOSHUNDA SAUNDERS

Anderson, Bruce (19 June 1845–22 Aug. 1922), Civil War soldier and Medal of Honor winner, was born in Mexico, Oswego County, New York. Unrecorded in the 1850 federal census, the names of Anderson's parents are confirmed to be unknown. However, likely candidates are Samuel and Mary Anderson, the only black or "mulatto" family recorded living in Oswego County in the 1840 (town of Granby) and 1850 (town of West Oswego) censuses. Samuel Anderson was a native of Bermuda, and his wife, Mary, was a New York native. Bruce Anderson does appear in the 1860 census, listed as a fourteen-year-old "mulatto" residing in Johnstown, New York, on the farm of Henry Adams and his daughter Margaret; he was likely a simple laborer. How he came to live with the Adams family is unknown, but Anderson would remain a resident in the area—except during the time of his Civil War service—for the remainder of his life.

While some African Americans served in units formed in Kansas, South Carolina, and Louisiana late in 1862, until adoption of the Emancipation Proclamation, the Lincoln administration refused to recruit black soldiers. Although a very small number of blacks such as Anderson and H. FORD DOUGLAS did serve in white units, northern racial prejudice precluded the general recruitment of black soldiers. But with falling recruitment rates and ballooning causality lists, the federal government was compelled to change course, recognize black patriotism, and recruit black troops. By mid-1863 black regiments had been formed in Massachusetts, Pennsylvania, and Ohio, but New York lagged behind and did not begin to form its own black units until the next year.

Sometime in 1863 or 1864 Bruce Anderson decided to enlist in the Union army. While military records do not give the date, his place of enlistment as a private in Company K of the 142nd New York Infantry Regiment was at Ephratah, New York, a short distance west of Johnstown. Although census records describe Anderson as "Mulatto" or "Black," he must have been rather light-skinned to have been allowed to assimilate into a white regiment; otherwise his recruitment would have been rejected, or he would have been immediately transferred to one of New York's all-black regiments, which began forming in 1864. By establishing himself in the 142nd, Anderson became a rare exception to Northern recruitment patterns. He also joined the nearly 180,000 African American troops fighting for the Union, and symbolized their exceptional valor.

Because it is unknown when Anderson joined his regiment, the full extent of his service remains a mystery. He might have taken part in the regiment's most notable actions at Cold Harbor, Petersburg, and New Market Heights from May to October 1864. He could have been enlisted as a replacement for casualties suffered in these battles, but he was a confirmed member of the regiment by November 1864 during its trench duty before the Confederate capital of Richmond, Virginia. In any case, Anderson became a private in the 142nd when it was assigned to the First Brigade, Second Division of General Alfred Terry's Provisional Corps in the Department of North Carolina in early December 1864 to aid in the reduction of Fort Fisher, one of the few remaining Confederate strongholds in the South.

Located at the mouth of the Cape Fear River, Fort Fisher stood guard over the Confederacy's sole remaining port of Wilmington, North Carolina. Made of earth and sand and armed with forty-seven cannons, twenty-five of them facing land and twenty-two pointed seaward, the fort proved formidable. In the first Union assault, conducted by General Benjamin Butler from 24 to 26 December 1864, Union forces were thwarted. The second attempt was led by General Terry, who well understood that a coordinated naval and ground attack was required to achieve victory. Union troops, including Anderson and the men of the 142nd, landed before the fort on 13 January 1864. Two days later an intense bombardment by Union naval forces knocked out nearly all of the fort's guns, while marine forces undertook an assault at the point where the sea and river sides of the forts met. Although the assault was unorganized and costly, it did serve to divert forces away from the main infantry assault on the river side of Fort Fisher. This assault began at 2:00 P.M. when an advance guard composed of men from the 142nd and other units in the Second Brigade armed themselves with axes and cut through the wooden palisades and abatis guarding the fort's outer works. Then they stormed the fort in the first assault wave, suffering heavy casualties. Among the men in this advance guard—a group sometimes referred to as a "forlorn hope" because their chances of returning alive were slim—was Anderson. Bravely volunteering to serve in the advance guard, Anderson not only exhibited supreme heroism but lived to tell about it. The fight for Fort Fisher lasted for nearly eight hours before the Confederates surrendered just before ten o'clock that evening. Casualties for the Union numbered just over thirteen hundred, while the Confederacy's were nearly double that number.

Anderson continued his service with the 142nd until the end of the war, participating in actions during the capture of Wilmington and Raleigh, North Carolina, and the surrender of General Joseph Johnston's Confederate army before leaving the service on 7 June 1865. Anderson's activities immediately after the Civil War are unknown, but it is likely he returned to New York. By 1880 Bruce Anderson was working as a farm laborer in Amsterdam, New York, living as a boarder at the house of a black family, John (b. 1840) and Alida (b. 1843) James, along with their son Edward (b. 1861) and grandson Harvey Howard (b. 1879). There he met his future wife, Julia James (b. 1855), and married her in 1884. By 1900 the couple had four children: Grace (b. 1886), Elizabeth (b. 1888), Edward (b. 1890), and Lena (b. 1893). Alida James, Julia's stepmother, also lived with the Anderson family.

Anderson remained in Amsterdam, living a quiet but respectable life. His heroism in the Civil War was not entirely forgotten; on 28 December 1914, at the age of sixty-nine, he received the Medal of Honor for his actions with the advance guard at Fort Fisher in January 1865. How the medal came to be awarded to Anderson at such a late date is unknown, but it was likely because of efforts by fellow townsmen, veterans, and local or state politicians. Anderson was not alone in receiving his medal so late; even WILLIAM HARVEY CARNEY, the "first" black Medal of Honor winner, did not actually receive his award until years after the close of the war. Racial discrimination likely played a role in the delays, but so did simple oversight and bureaucratic delays during the confusion that reigned at the war's end. For Anderson, however, the Medal of Honor, sadly, came just after the death of his wife, Julia; Anderson himself would die eight years later. Perhaps the least known of any decorated African American Civil War soldier, a Medal of Honor gravestone marks Anderson's burial site in Amsterdam's Green Hill Cemetery to ensure that his heroism will not be forgotten.

FURTHER READING
Quarles, Benjamin Arthur. *The Negro in the Civil War* (1989).

GLENN ALLEN KNOBLOCK

Anderson, Caroline Virginia Still Wiley (1 Nov. 1848–2 June 1919), physician, educator, and community worker, was born in Philadelphia, Pennsylvania. She was the eldest daughter of the abolitionist movement leaders WILLIAM STILL and Letitia George Still. In 1850 William Still became the head of the Philadelphia Underground Railroad and Vigilance Committee. He would later chronicle his experiences in the best-selling 1872 account, *The Underground Railroad.*

After completing primary and secondary education at Mrs. Henry Gordon's Private School, the Friends Raspberry Alley School, and the Institute for Colored Youth, Anderson entered Oberlin College. Although she was the youngest member of the graduating class of 1868, Anderson presided over the annual Ladies' Literary Society, a singular honor that had never been awarded to a student of African ancestry.

After graduating from Oberlin, Anderson returned home to teach drawing and elocution, and on 28 December 1869 she married Edward A. Wiley, a former slave and fellow Oberlin student. The ceremony took place in her parents' home, and the celebration that followed was in effect a reunion of former workers in the antislavery movement. ELIZABETH TAYLOR GREENFIELD, the first major American concert artist of African descent, performed music for sixty or seventy guests including ROBERT PURVIS, Dilwyn Parrish, H. M. Laing, SARAH MAPPS DOUGLASS, WILLIAM WHIPPER, and Lucretia Mott.

Edward Wiley died prematurely in 1874, and in the following year Anderson left Philadelphia with their two children, William and Letitia, to matriculate at Howard University College of Medicine in Washington, D.C. To support her young family, she also taught drawing and elocution at Howard.

There is sufficient evidence to indicate that Anderson had entertained thoughts of becoming a physician long before the death of her husband; possibly, as a student at the Institute for Colored Youth, where Sarah Mapps Douglass headed the girls' department. Douglass, a member of the Philadelphia Female Anti-Slavery Society and the first black woman to complete a medical course in the United States, believed that women should be educated for more than domesticity and made science, particularly physiology, an integral part of the curriculum for her female students. At Oberlin, Anderson had selected courses in chemistry, physiology, and anatomy. Back home in Philadelphia, she had attended lectures in physiology at the Woman's

Medical College of Pennsylvania during the 1872–1873 winter sessions. Others who might have influenced Anderson's decision to pursue a career in medicine were her father's brother, JAMES STILL, a well-known medical practitioner in Medford, New Jersey, and his son, James Thomas Still, one of the first black graduates from Harvard Medical School who by 1874 had established an extensive practice in Boston.

At the end of her first year at Howard's medical school, Anderson returned to Philadelphia and matriculated at the Woman's Medical College of Pennsylvania, which had been founded by the Quakers in 1850. With philosophical underpinnings of liberalism and humanitarianism, this first American medical school for women would educate more black and Native American female doctors than any other predominantly white medical college in nineteenth-century America. Anderson graduated in the class of 1878 with one other student of African ancestry, Georgianna E. Young. They were the first black students to graduate from the school since 1867, when REBECCA COLE, the first black graduate from Woman's Medical College, was awarded an MD.

In 1879, after a yearlong internship at Boston's New England Hospital for Women and Children, Anderson established a practice in Philadelphia. A year later, on 17 August 1880, she married MATTHEW ANDERSON, a Presbyterian minister from Greencastle, Pennsylvania, who had studied at Oberlin College and seminaries at both Yale and Princeton. As a student at Princeton, he had been the first black student to live "in-residence." The couple had three daughters: Helen, Maude, and Margaret.

Less than a year after the marriage, on 10 June 1881, the Reverend Anderson organized the Berean Presbyterian Church, which spawned several enterprises, and his wife, "Dr. C. V.," as she was fondly called by the parishioners, played a major role in the development and operation of all of them, particularly the Berean Institute, established in 1899. In his groundbreaking sociological study of blacks in Philadelphia, W. E. B. DuBois observed that the church also conducted "a successful Building and Loan Association, a kindergarten, a medical dispensary, and a seaside home" and cited the Berean Presbyterian Church as one of two churches that were working "for the social betterment of the Negro" (DuBois, 216–217). Later a bureau of mutual help, a type of placement service for students who had completed courses at the Berean Institute, was also created. As part of a continuing education program, each year the church sponsored two conferences that were held at the church and cottage and featured prominent speakers, both black and white, including BOOKER T. WASHINGTON, ALEXANDER CRUMMELL, Grover Cleveland, FRANCIS JAMES GRIMKÉ, and CHARLOTTE FORTEN GRIMKÉ. Occasionally, Anderson herself would present a paper.

Anderson was assistant principal, instructor of elocution, physiology, and hygiene, and supervisor of the dispensary at the Berean Institute. She was also manager of the seaside cottage and the bureau of mutual help, as well as the head of the Berean Woman's Christian Temperance Union. But her activities were not limited to those directly associated with the work that she and her husband had established. Anderson was often asked, and usually consented, to assume leadership for community projects such as organizing a Young Women's Christian Association for blacks or serving on the editorial board for *Who's Who in Philadelphia*, a collection of biographical sketches that was published in 1912. One contemporary described her as the "most intellectual woman" he had ever met.

In spite of commitments to church, community, and family, Anderson managed to maintain a private practice that was "evenly divided between white and colored people" (Richings, 412). She also treated patients at the City District and the Home for the Aged and Infirm Colored Persons, an institution established in 1864 and principally funded by prominent blacks and Quakers of Philadelphia. To meet the challenge of keeping informed of the rapidly changing developments in late-nineteenth- and early-twentieth-century medicine, Anderson assiduously retained her relationship with professional colleagues and participated in the meetings of the alumni association of the Woman's Medical College of Pennsylvania, serving as treasurer in 1888.

Anderson practiced medicine for more than thirty years, becoming a member of an elite group of American women: the first to demonstrate that gender and race prejudice in medicine need not be deterrents for black women who want to become physicians. Following a series of progressively debilitating strokes, she died at her home in Philadelphia.

FURTHER READING

Papers on Caroline Virginia Still Wiley Anderson are on file in the Archives and Special Collections/Black Women Physicians at Drexel University College of Medicine.

DuBois, W. E. B. *The Philadelphia Negro: A Social Study* (1899, repr. 1967).

Hine, Darlene Clark. "Co-laborers in the Work of the Lord," in *"Send Us a Lady Physician": Women Doctors in America*, ed. Ruth Abrams (1985).

Peitzman, Steven J. *A New and Untried Course: Woman's Medical College and Medical College of Pennsylvania, 1850–1998* (2000).

Richings, G. F. *Evidences of Progress among Colored People* (1902).

GERALDINE RHOADES BECKFORD

Anderson, Cat (12 Sept. 1916–29 Apr. 1981), jazz trumpeter, was born William Alonzo Anderson Jr. in Greenville, South Carolina. Nothing is known of his parents, who died when he was four. Anderson grew up in Jenkins' Orphanage in Charleston, where as a boy he received the nickname "Cat" after scratching and tearing in a fight with a bully. He played in the orphanage's renowned bands, beginning on trombone and playing other brass and percussion instruments before taking up trumpet. From 1929 onward he participated in orphanage band tours, and in Florida in 1933 he formed the cooperative Carolina Cotton Pickers with fellow orphanage musicians. Returning to Charleston in 1934, they continued playing as the Carolina Cotton Pickers and then resumed touring.

Independent of the orphanage, Anderson held his first lasting affiliation with the Sunset Royals (c. 1936–1942). From 1942 to 1944 he worked in the big bands of LUCKY MILLINDER; the trumpeter ERSKINE HAWKINS, from which Anderson was quickly dismissed for upstaging Hawkins with his high-note trumpeting; LIONEL HAMPTON; Sabby Lewis; and Hampton again. In September 1944 Anderson joined DUKE ELLINGTON's orchestra. Anderson followed in the path of established trumpeting roles in the group, contributing an intense but understated and muted solo on his own composition "Teardrops in the Rain" (1945) and a vocalized plunger-muted solo on "A Gatherin' in a Clearin'" (1946). But his personal trademark was his ability to play in an astonishingly high range, of which the finest example is certainly "Trumpet No End" (1946).

Leaving Ellington in February 1947, Anderson led his own band until he rejoined Lewis briefly in 1949 and then Ellington in December 1950. Apart from a long absence in 1951, he remained with Ellington until November 1959. Notable recordings from this period include a plunger-muted solo on his own blues composition "Cat Walk" (1951) with the Coronets, a septet spun off from the big band; an improvised trumpet battle with CLARK TERRY and Willie Cook on "Duke's Jam" on the alto saxophonist JOHNNY HODGES's album *Ellingtonia '56* (1956); and a featured solo on "Madness in Great Ones" on Ellington's album *Such Sweet Thunder* (1957).

After leading another band and freelancing in Philadelphia, Anderson rejoined Ellington once again in April 1961. He is seen and heard in the film short *Duke Ellington and His Orchestra* (1962). In 1967 Ellington held a lengthy engagement at the Rainbow Grill in New York City with an eight-piece band that afforded Anderson an opportunity to demonstrate much more versatile trumpeting skills than his role as a high-note player normally allowed. Anderson remained in the orchestra until January 1971.

In 1971, finally tiring of incessant touring, Anderson became a freelancer on the West Coast, where he worked extensively as a studio musician. But he continued playing with jazz bands. He was a guest soloist with the bassist CHARLES MINGUS's group at the Newport Jazz Festival in July 1972, and on a European tour in the fall, Mingus featured Anderson in lengthy, plunger-muted solos on "Perdido." Anderson later played with the trumpeter Bill Berry's big band, and he participated in a few reunions with Ellington's band and with Hampton's, including the album *Lionel Hampton and His Jazz Giants '77* (1977) and some European tours with Hampton until 1979. Anderson also recorded his own album, *Cat Speaks* (1977). He died of cancer in Norwalk, California.

Before the Canadian trumpeter Maynard Ferguson emerged during the 1950s, Anderson was the undisputed master of freakish high-note trumpeting. Many Ellington aficionados prefer his stylistically derivative work, after the manner of LOUIS ARMSTRONG, COOTIE WILLIAMS, and others, to his personalized high-note displays, which were often sloppy, out-of-tune, and tasteless (for example, numerous versions of "Jam with Sam"). But on those occasions when it worked, as in the last minute of "Trumpet No End," Anderson's exhilarating trumpeting was nothing short of spectacular.

FURTHER READING

Chilton, John. *A Jazz Nursery: The Story of the Jenkins' Orphanage Bands of Charleston, South Carolina* (1980).

Dance, Stanley. *The World of Duke Ellington* (1970; repr. 1981).

Lambert, Eddie. "Cat Anderson: A Résumé of His Recorded Work," *Jazz Journal International* 35 (June 1982).

Obituaries: *New York Times*, 2 May 1981; *Jazz Journal International* 34 (July 1981).

This entry is taken from the *American National Biography* and is published here with the permission of the American Council of Learned Societies.

BARRY KERNFELD

Anderson, Charles Alfred "Chief" (9 Feb. 1907–13 Apr. 1996), aviator and instructor of the Tuskegee Airmen, was born in Bryn Mawr, Pennsylvania, to Janie and Iverson Anderson, of whom little else is known. During his early childhood, he lived with his grandmother in Staunton, Virginia. There Anderson longed for an airplane so he could fly to see what was on the other side of the mountains that surrounded Staunton and the Shenandoah Valley. He frequently left home in search of airplanes that were rumored to have crashed in the valley. His constant disappearances frustrated his grandmother, and she sent him back to his parents. Once back in Pennsylvania, however, he continued leaving home in search of airplanes.

At the age of thirteen Anderson applied to aviation school, but was denied admission because he was African American. In 1926, at the age of nineteen, he used his savings and borrowed money from friends and relatives to purchase a used Velie Monocoupe, one of the first airplanes manufactured for private pilots. He appealed to white flight instructors and flight schools to teach him to fly, but no program would accept an African American student, but, persevering, he eventually found a school that would teach him basic ground school subjects and elementary aircraft maintenance. Anderson learned about aviation at the airport by listening to the pilots talk and watching airplanes take off and land. He spent six weeks practicing in his airplane learning on his own until he developed the courage to take off. On one of his early flights, Anderson hit a tree but remained undaunted and was successful in teaching himself to fly. In August 1929 he earned his private pilot's license, and in 1932 he earned his air transport license—becoming the first African American to do so.

Earning the coveted air transport license, however, was not the means to productive employment in aviation that Anderson had anticipated. No airline or aviation company would hire him. Instead of using his piloting skills, he had to take a series of menial jobs, including caretaker for a boarding school and ditch digger.

It was while Anderson was employed as a ditch digger that he met Dr. ALBERT E. FORSYTHE, a prominent African American doctor who practiced in Newark and Atlantic City, New Jersey, and a pilot in his own right. Forsythe approached Anderson with the idea of using their mutual expertise in aviation to showcase African American potential in the burgeoning field of aviation. In July 1933 Anderson and Forsythe flew from Atlantic City, New Jersey, to Los Angeles, California, and back, making them the first African Americans to complete a round trip, transcontinental flight across the United States. This flight was accomplished without the aid of landing lights, parachutes, air-to-ground radios, or other modern instrumentation. In fact the only instruments they had were a compass and an altimeter, and they navigated the route using a road map.

The aviation duo also flew to Montreal, Canada, making them the first African Americans to fly internationally. In 1934 they promoted their "Pan American Goodwill Tour" of the Caribbean and South America in Forsythe's Fairchild 24, "The Spirit of Booker T. Washington" which he had purchased earlier that year. They first flew from Miami to the Bahamas, making them the first pilots to land an airplane in Nassau, which had no airport. Later in the tour, the plane crashed in Trinidad. Even with the unfortunate end of the airplane, the tour received worldwide attention and upon their return to the United States, the pair was honored in Newark, New Jersey, with a parade with more than 15,000 onlookers. Anderson would later recreate this historic flight on his eighty-sixth birthday.

Anderson married his childhood sweetheart, Gertrude Elizabeth Nelson, in 1933. The couple would have two sons, Alfred and Charles.

In the late 1930s Anderson offered flight instruction to African American youth and adults in Pennsylvania, and in 1939 he initiated the Civilian Pilot Training Program at Howard University in Washington, D.C. In 1940 he became an instructor in the Civilian Pilot Training Program at Tuskegee Institute (later Tuskegee University) in Alabama. He was the first pilot to fly an airplane into Tuskegee.

On 19 April 1941 First Lady Eleanor Roosevelt, wife of President Franklin Delano Roosevelt, visited Tuskegee Institute to learn more about infantile paralysis on behalf of her husband, who suffered with the disease. A Tuskegee Institute physician told her about the aviation program, and she requested a tour. She was introduced to Anderson and asked if he would give her a ride in his airplane.

Against the adamant advice of her Secret Service staff, Anderson gave Eleanor Roosevelt a successful, forty-minute ride in his two-seater airplane.

The First Lady's flight with Chief Anderson was quite likely the first time a black man flew a plane with a white woman as his passenger. The publicity from the event greatly assisted the campaign to integrate the US Army Air Force. This campaign had been initiated by MARY McLEOD BETHUNE, a member of Roosevelt's "Black Cabinet," and promoted by aviatrix WILLA BROWN in the black press. Both women had lobbied Eleanor Roosevelt to give her support to Tuskegee's pilot-training program.

In 1941 the first class of aviation cadets arrived at Tuskegee Institute to begin flight training. "Chief" Anderson was the key flight instructor for the primary phase of flight training for the Tuskegee Airmen, who became the first African Americans to serve as pilots in the U.S. military. His students included General BENJAMIN O. DAVIS, General DANIEL "CHAPPIE" JAMES, and the over 1,000 African American men who received flight instruction at Tuskegee Institute's Moton Field.

Anderson was a founding member of Tuskegee Airmen, Inc., an organization dedicated to remembering and honoring those first pilots, and Negro Airmen International. In 1988 he was awarded an honorary doctor of science degree from Tuskegee University. Known as the father of black aviation Charles Alfred "Chief" Anderson is noted for his persevering spirit in the field of aviation and his innumerable contributions to the legacy of the Tuskegee Airmen. Anderson died of cancer at his home in Tuskegee.

FURTHER READING
Cooper, Charlie. *Tuskegee Heroes* (1996).
Dryden, Charles. *A-Train: Memoirs of a Tuskegee Airman* (1997).
Obituary: *New York Times*, 17 Apr. 1996.

LISA M. BRATTON

Anderson, Charles W., Jr. (26 May 1907–14 June 1960), attorney, politician, and diplomat, was born in Louisville, Kentucky. He was the youngest of two children and the only son of Charles W. Anderson Sr., a physician, and Tabitha L. Murphy, a teacher.

Motivated by the high value that his parents placed on education, Charles W. Anderson Jr. entered Kentucky State College at age fifteen and attended from 1922 to 1925. He then transferred to Wilberforce University, one of the earliest universities established for African Americans. Although the reason for Anderson's transfer to Wilberforce University during the penultimate year of his undergraduate career is unclear, it is likely that he, like other black Kentuckians, was forced to pursue higher education outside of the state because of the still-standing *Plessy v. Ferguson* decision of 1896 authorizing separate but equal educational facilities. Higher educational institutions for blacks did not exist in Kentucky, and rather than wait for them to be created Anderson moved to where the opportunities existed. After graduating from Wilberforce, Anderson attended Howard University's law school in Washington, D.C., and graduated with an LLB in 1930, at the age of twenty-three.

Anderson returned to Kentucky after graduation and passed the bar in 1932. Four years later, while working as a partner in his own firm of Anderson, Thomas & Walker, he helped to prepare the appeal of RAINEY BETHEA, a black man who was accused of robbing, raping, and murdering Lischia Edwards, a white woman, on 7 June 1936. Bethea's conviction was based on a variety of evidence, including fingerprints, possession of stolen goods, and no fewer than five confessions. He was convicted of rape and sentenced to death by hanging in accordance with Kentucky law. Although Bethea was initially accused of raping and murdering Edwards, the latter being a crime punishable by death in an electric chair, the Daviess County commonwealth attorney decided to drop the murder charges against Bethea and charge him solely with the crime of rape. By taking this step, the attorney all but eliminated the risk of having to decide between the competing punishments of death by hanging and death by electrocution in the case of a conviction.

Anderson and his legal team were not part of their client's initial defense, but they did volunteer to work on his appeal and lobbied to have the case overturned. The request was denied by the circuit court, led by the Daviess County commonwealth attorney, on the false grounds that Anderson and his team had inaccurately submitted Bethea's paperwork to the clerk of court. In anticipation of the court's negative response, Anderson and his team filed a writ of habeas corpus, which would allow them to petition the Daviess commonwealth for a new trial by arguing that the lower court had ruled against Bethea in error. This request was also denied. Bethea was hanged on 14 August 1936 in a public spectacle.

Unable to prevent Bethea's death through litigation, Anderson sought legislatively to end all future deaths by hanging. Later that year Anderson won a seat in the Kentucky House of Representatives as a Republican.

One of Anderson's first missions as state representative was to sponsor a bill that would repeal Kentucky's law mandating hanging for the crime of rape. The bill, which passed into law, stipulated that rape would carry the same sentence as other capital felonies, death by electrocution.

During his five two-year terms, Anderson succeeded in sponsoring many bills that became laws. For example, in an effort to combat his state's school segregation statute, one of Anderson's bills mandated that rural school districts offer secondary education to their black students. Moreover, the districts were required to pay each student $100, as well as transportation costs to a neighboring district in the event that students were unable to attend schools in their own home districts. Anderson similarly sponsored legislation entitling black students to $5,000 each if they were forced to enroll in a graduate degree program outside of Kentucky because one did not exist for them in the state. Finally, and perhaps as a tribute to his mother, Anderson helped to ensure that teachers were no longer required to forfeit their jobs upon marriage.

In 1946 Anderson resigned his seat in the Kentucky House of Representatives and accepted a position as Jefferson County's first black commonwealth assistant attorney. Unlike attorneys at the city and county levels, the new position gave Anderson the power he had lacked years earlier when defending Bethea. Among his duties was the ability to prosecute rape felonies and grant legal appeals. Anderson held the position until 1952.

It is not known whether Anderson was married or had any children. His life was cut short ten months after Dwight D. Eisenhower appointed him as an alternate U.S. delegate to the General Assembly of the United Nations on 21 August 1959. He died in Shelby County, Kentucky, when his car was struck by a train.

FURTHER READING

Kentucky Personnel Cabinet. *History of the Anderson Laureate*, available online at http://personnel. ky.gov/eeo/laureate.htm.

Ryan, Perry T. *The Last Public Execution in America*, available online at www.geocities.com/lastpublichang.

Wright, George C. *Life behind a Veil: Blacks in Louisville, Kentucky, 1865–1930* (1985).

Wright, George C. *Racial Violence in Kentucky, 1865–1940: Lynchings, Mob Rule, and "Legal Lynchings"* (1990).

Wright, George C. A. *History of Blacks in Kentucky: In Pursuit of Equality, 1890–1980*, vol. 2 (1992).

TERESA A. BOOKER

Anderson, Charles William (28 Apr. 1866–28 Jan. 1938), politician and public official, was born in Oxford, Ohio, the son of Charles W. Anderson and Serena (maiden name unknown). After a public school education in his hometown and in Middletown, Ohio, Charles studied at Spencerian Business College in Cleveland and at the Berlitz School of Languages in Worcester, Massachusetts. Anderson's schooling continued informally as he matured into an intellectually accomplished and engaging man. His friend JAMES WELDON JOHNSON noted Anderson's versatility, which included acute powers of observation and an ability to converse on many subjects, including "the English poets, the Irish patriots, [and] the contemporary leaders of the British Parliament" (Johnson, 219).

Anderson put these talents to good use after moving to New York City in 1886. He grabbed whatever opportunities that Republican Party politics offered ambitious black men, and he developed a ward heeler's capacity for keeping close track of voters, loaves, and fishes. By 1890 he had entered upon a succession of party and patronage positions that kept him busy through much of the rest of his life. Also in 1890 Anderson became president of the Young Men's Colored Republican Club of New York County and was appointed a gauger at the Internal Revenue Service. He served in that position until 1893, when he became private secretary to the New York State treasurer. In 1895 Anderson was named chief clerk of the state treasury, and in 1898 he became supervisor of accounts for the state racing commission, holding that post until 1905. In 1904 Anderson organized the New York City Colored Republican Club and worked for the reelection of Theodore Roosevelt. By then he had married Emma Lee Bonaparte.

Anderson's rise through the ranks seems to have been not simply because of party loyalty and personal charisma but also because he performed his jobs quite well. Theodore Roosevelt, one-time governor of New York, praised the "splendid efficiency" of Anderson's work for the racing commission and, in 1905, named him collector of internal revenue for the Second New York District. Explaining Anderson's appointment to this most visible position, BOOKER T. WASHINGTON contended that, given the widespread resistance to black officeholding, Roosevelt was "determined to set the example by placing a coloured man in a high office in his own home city, so that the country might see that he did not want other parts of the country to accept that which he himself was not willing to receive" (Harlan and Smock, vol. 1, 442). But the collectorship was not a position that could have been well

served by any mere token appointee. The Second District included the financial heart of New York (and, consequently, of the nation), as well as the Manhattan docks. Anderson had charge of scores of deputy collectors, inspectors, and clerks, and he annually collected millions of dollars in revenue, eventually including income taxes. Anderson did good work, earning considerable support among the Wall Street elite. During this and his second collectorship, Anderson always kept his eye out for openings that might be filled by African Americans in the Internal Revenue Service, in other federal, state, and municipal agencies, and in the Republican Party. For instance, he helped arrange James Weldon Johnson's appointment to the consular service.

Though he had a hand in the passage of a state civil rights statute in 1895, Anderson's interest in developing practical opportunity and material reward for African Americans, rather than in more forthrightly agitating for racial justice, put him in sympathy with Booker T. Washington. The two were close allies as well as ideological soul mates. Washington helped secure the collectorship for Anderson, and Anderson became one of the most important cogs in the "Tuskegee Machine," the vehicle of patronage and discreet influence that Washington operated from his Alabama base, even as he counseled African Americans to put aside politics. As the machine's man in New York, Anderson traded political intelligence, gossip, and favors with Washington, who periodically forwarded an opossum from Alabama for Anderson's dinner table. Anderson egged Washington on in his struggles with critics like W. E. B. DuBois, recommending that Washington administer "a good thrashing" to "these young upstarts" (Harlan, 78). Indeed, Anderson did what he could to have Washington's adversaries dismissed from federal jobs, monitored the progress of the NAACP, and even played dirty tricks on NAACP supporters, such as planting stories of race mixing in white newspapers.

Anderson's excellent reputation as collector, which moved even DuBois to recommend him for a diplomatic post, and his strong ties to the New York business community apparently kept him from immediately falling victim to Woodrow Wilson's hostility to black Republican officeholders. Anderson was not required to step down until March 1915, two years into Wilson's term as president. Anderson thereupon returned to state and party employ to wait out the interregnum. In 1915 he went to work for the New York State agriculture department, supervising inspectors and marketing operations in New York City. In 1916 and 1920 he was active among black voters during the GOP national campaigns. He returned to the higher reaches of federal patronage in 1923, when he was appointed collector of internal revenue for the newly created Third New York District. The district included his own neighborhood of Harlem. By 1928 the ailing Anderson had become less active in the day-to-day operations of the collectorship. He retired in 1934 and died in New York City four years later.

Anderson was the first important black politician in New York City and was certainly among the most powerful African American officeholders anywhere in the United States during the first decades of the twentieth century. His influence illustrated the growing importance of northern city-dwellers in black politics, as African Americans migrated out of the South and those that remained were marginalized by disfranchisement and the rise of "lily white" Republicanism. Anderson's career symbolizes, too, the significance in that era of the federal government and of the Republican Party to African Americans not simply as guarantors, though inconstant, of civil rights but also as providers of professional opportunity.

FURTHER READING

Harlan, Louis. *Booker T. Washington: The Wizard of Tuskegee, 1901–1915* (1983).

Harlan, Louis, and Raymond Smock, eds. *The Booker T. Washington Papers*, 14 vols. (1972–1989).

Johnson, James Weldon. *Along This Way: The Autobiography of James Weldon Johnson* (1933).

Meier, August. *Negro Thought in America, 1880–1915: Racial Ideologies in the Age of Booker T. Washington* (1963).

Osofsky, Gilbert. *Harlem: The Making of a Ghetto* (1966).

Obituary: *New York Times*, 29 Jan. 1938.

This entry is taken from the *American National Biography* and is published here with the permission of the American Council of Learned Societies.

PATRICK G. WILLIAMS

Anderson, Eddie "Rochester" (18 Sept. 1905–28 Feb. 1977), radio and movie actor, was born Edward Lincoln Anderson in Oakland, California. Anderson was from a show business family. His father, "Big Ed" Anderson, was a vaudevillian, and his mother, Ella Mae (maiden name unknown), was a circus tightrope walker. As a youngster Eddie sold newspapers on the streets of Oakland, a job that, according to his own account, injured his voice and gave it the rasping quality that was long his trademark on radio.

Between 1923 and 1933 Anderson's older brother Cornelius had a career in vaudeville as a song and dance man, and Eddie, who had little formal education, joined him occasionally. With vaudeville dying, however, Eddie drifted toward Hollywood. In the depths of the Depression, pickings were slim. His first movie appearance was in 1932 in *What Price Hollywood?* For a few years he had only bit parts, but then he secured a major role in the movie *Green Pastures* (1936), playing the part of Noah, an old southern preacher. *Green Pastures* was a movie adaptation of a Marc Connelly play from stories by Roark Bradford. A rather lavish version of a simple Negro interpretation of the Bible, with heaven a giant "fish fry," the movie was considered to be the first since *Hallelujah* (1929) to treat with sympathy issues of concern to blacks.

After his performance in *Green Pastures*, Anderson was continually employed in Hollywood and made a great many movies. Very often he played minor roles, usually black stereotypes, but there were enough of them to provide a handsome living. For example, he had minor roles in *Show Boat* (1936) and *Gone with the Wind* (1939), in which he was so elaborately made up that few people recognized him. His talent for both comic and serious roles was readily apparent to the movie industry. In the year 1937 alone he appeared in six movies.

Anderson's rise to fame came through the role of Rochester on the *Jack Benny Show*. This radio program had been on the air since 1932, and Jack Benny had tried numerous comic personae—always purporting to be himself and not a fictional character—before settling on "the thirty-nine-year-old skinflint." Anderson joined the show in 1937. According to numerous scripts of later years, Benny "found" Rochester working as a Pullman porter and hired him as his personal valet. The truth was slightly different. Anderson was engaged for one show in which he played a train porter, and the sketch was so successful that five weeks later Benny decided to put in another porter scene featuring Rochester. These two shows worked so well that Benny decided to make Rochester a permanent part of his radio team. Rochester became his butler, valet, and general factotum.

By the early 1940s Anderson was earning more than $100,000 a year, making him the highest-paid African American in show business until Sidney Poitier began acting in the 1950s. A superb comic actor with exquisite timing, Anderson owed much of his success to his highly distinctive voice, often described as rasping or wheezing. Whatever the description, it was one of the classic voices of radio, instantly recognizable after two words—perhaps even after one syllable. Someone once suggested to Anderson that he have an operation to remove the "frog" in his throat, to which Anderson responded that if he had a frog in his throat he had no intention of having it operated on since it was a "gold-plated frog."

Because all the characters played themselves on the Benny show, many listeners came to believe that Rochester (as he was now called by everyone, even members of his own family) really was Benny's much-harried servant. Several listeners wrote in to complain about the low wages that Rochester was receiving and about the other intolerable burdens that he had to endure. Benny was forced to write back to many of these people and tell them that Rochester was really a well-paid actor named Eddie Anderson. During these years Anderson and his family lived in a mansion with a ballroom and were waited on by servants of their own. (He had married Mamie Sophie Wiggins in 1932; they had three children.) Anderson collected custom-built sports cars and raised thoroughbred horses. One of these ran in the Kentucky Derby in 1945.

Benny was, in fact, sensitive to the problem of using a "stock colored butler character," and to its racial implications. In the early 1940s he made an effort to eliminate any of Rochester's traits or habits that might appear to be racial stereotypes. For example, he removed all references to Rochester's eating watermelon or drinking gin. The racial issue was seldom raised in these years, least of all by Eddie Anderson, probably in part because it was always Benny, and not Rochester, who was the butt of the jokes.

Anderson stayed with the Benny radio program until it ended in 1955. He also appeared on Benny's television show until it ended in 1965; but in Benny's later television specials he was not a regular. By this time, feelings were running high against black stereotypes. When asked in a 1970 television appearance to recreate his old role as butler, he said, "Massa Benny, we don' do dat no mo'" (Leslie Halliwell, *The Filmgoer's Companion* [4th ed., 1974], 22).

Throughout the radio years and beyond, Anderson continued his film appearances. In 1943 he had the lead in the successful movie version of the Harold Arlen and E. Y. Harburg stage musical *Cabin in the Sky*, which also featured ETHEL WATERS and LOUIS ARMSTRONG.

Directed by Vincente Minnelli, this film was considered notable for its humanized version of black American life. Anderson continued to have movie roles in the 1960s and had a splendid part as a taxi driver in Stanley Kramer's visual farce *It's a Mad, Mad, Mad, Mad World* (1963). On television he had a role in *Bachelor Father* (1962) and *Love, American Style* (1969). He also did a cartoon voice for the Harlem Globetrotters' television program.

Anderson's first wife died in 1954; his second marriage was to Eva Simon, but it ended in divorce. He died in Los Angeles.

FURTHER READING

Bogle, Donald. *Blacks in American Films and Television* (1988).

Harmon, Jim. *The Great Radio Comedians* (1970).

Landy, Eileen. *Black Film Stars* (1973).

Watkins, Mel. *On the Real Side: Laughing, Lying, and Signifying* (1994).

Obituary: *New York Times*, 1 Mar. 1977.

This entry is taken from the *American National Biography* and is published here with the permission of the American Council of Learned Societies.

GEORGE H. DOUGLAS

Anderson, Garland (1886–31 May 1939), playwright and minister, was born in Wichita, Kansas. Little is known about his parents, although his mother is said to have been an active reformer and a poet. Anderson completed four years of school (the only formal education that he ever received) before his father moved the family to California to take a job as a janitor in the post office. The following year Anderson's mother died, and at age twelve he left home to become a newsboy, selling the *Telegraph Press* on the corner of Third and Market streets in San Francisco.

After working as a porter on the railroad, Anderson worked for the next fifteen years as a bellhop in various San Francisco hotels. During this period he also became a temporary convert to Christian Science. One afternoon in 1924 he saw a performance of Channing Pollack's moralistic drama *The Fool* and knew immediately that he had found the medium for his message to the world: He would write a play. He later said:

At first the idea seemed absurd. … No one realized more than myself that though I wanted to write this play, I had no training in the technique of dramatic construction; but I also realized that to shirk what I wanted to do could be likened to the outer shell of the acorn after it was planted in the ground saying to the inner stir of life for expression, "What are you stirring for? Surely you don't expect to become a great oak tree?" With this firm conviction I determined to write a play.

In three weeks of writing, between phone calls summoning him at the hotel where he worked, he completed *Don't Judge by Appearances* (later shortened to *Appearances*), the story of a black bellhop falsely accused of rape by a white woman—a bold topic in 1924 for a black author. At the play's denouement, however, the woman is revealed to be a mulatto who has been passing as white; this denouement was the only possible one in a year in which riots had threatened the Provincetown Playhouse in New York City because the black actor PAUL ROBESON had kissed onstage the hand of a white actress playing his wife in Eugene O'Neill's drama *All God's Chillun Got Wings*.

With the encouragement of the residents at the hotel where he worked, Anderson sent his play to the popular performer Al Jolson, who provided Anderson with the means to travel to New York City to seek his fortune. At a backers' audition at the Waldorf-Astoria Hotel, six hundred guests applauded the reading of the play by actor Richard B. Harrison, but they donated only $140 toward the production of *Appearances*.

Believing that "you can have what you want if you want it hard enough," Anderson wrote President Calvin Coolidge and persuaded Coolidge's secretary to grant him a meeting at the White House. Possibly as a result of the publicity surrounding that meeting, producer Lester W. Sagar took over Anderson's script in June 1925 and put the play into rehearsal with three African Americans in the cast of seventeen. Immediately, the white actress Nedda Harrigan resigned, refusing to perform on the same stage with a black actor (in previous Broadway shows, the black characters had been played by whites in blackface). Nevertheless, on 13 October 1925 at the Frolic Theater, *Appearances* opened. It was the first full-length play by a black playwright to be presented on the Broadway stage and the first Broadway play to incorporate both black and white cast members. Although it received tepid notices, the reviewers praised Anderson's entrepreneurial spirit. The drama ran for twenty-three performances, then toured major American cities until, on 1 April 1929, it returned to the Hudson Theatre in New York City to prepare for its opening at the Royale Theatre in London the following March.

In London the play became a *succès de curiosité*. Apparently Anderson's impeccable manners coupled with his unrelenting optimism attracted the British press, and he became somewhat of a celebrity. He was introduced to Queen Mary and was invited by the author John Galsworthy to speak at a meeting of PEN, the most prestigious literary club in London. Anderson also undertook a business venture, with the backing of a British industrialist, by establishing a chain of milk bars called Andy's Nu-Snack, thus introducing to Londoners cold malted milk. During his stay in England, Anderson met a white Englishwoman named Doris (maiden name unknown), whom he married in 1935 in Vancouver, Washington, one of the few states at that time to allow racially mixed marriages. She later published, under the name Doris Garland Anderson, her own account of the interracial marriage, the provocatively titled *Nigger Lover* (1938).

Although Anderson is said to have written two or three other plays, none was produced, and in his middle years he turned his energies to religion. In 1933 he published *Uncommon Sense: The Law of Life in Action*, a text extolling the virtues of religious faith. In 1935 he became a minister in the New Thought movement at the Seattle Center of Constructive Thinking. During the last five years of his life he toured the United States, Canada, and England, lecturing on the topic, "You Can Do What You Want to Do If You Believe You Can Do It." Following his free lecture he offered—in the optimistic tradition of Elbert Hubbard, and later Dale Carnegie—a series of eight lessons (for fifteen dollars) on how faith in self and God can lead to good fortune. In 1936 a newspaper in Regina, Canada, observed: "He is the first Negro since BOOKER T. WASHINGTON to tour the country speaking to white people only. Seldom, he admitted, does a Negro ever appear to hear him. 'They are not interested,' he said rather sadly." He died in New York City.

Anderson sold a second script entitled *Extortion* to David Belasco in 1929, but it was never produced. Nor was his first play ever produced again. According to JAMES WELDON JOHNSON, *Appearances* "may not be an altogether convincing argument for the theories it advances, but the author himself is." Nonetheless, Anderson left his stamp on the Broadway stage. Because no New York critic complained about black and white actors appearing together on stage, within four months of the opening of Anderson's most notable play, Belasco produced *Lulu Belle* (1926), with ninety-seven black actors and seventeen white actors. Hence, the production of

Appearances marked the beginning of an integrated Broadway stage.

FURTHER READING

Anderson, Garland. *From Newsboy and Bellhop to Playwright* (1929).

Abramson, Doris. *Negro Playwrights in the American Theatre, 1925–1959* (1969).

Hatch, James V., and Omanii Abdullah. *Black Playwrights, 1823–1977: An Annotated Bibliography of Plays* (1977).

Hatch, James V., and Ted Shine, eds. *Black Theatre USA* (1974).

Peterson, Bernard L., Jr. *Early Black American Playwrights and Dramatic Writers* (1990).

This entry is taken from the *American National Biography* and is published here with the permission of the American Council of Learned Societies.

JAMES V. HATCH

Anderson, Gloria Long (5 Nov. 1938–), physical organic chemist and pioneer F-19 synthetic organic chemist, was born in Altheimer, Arkansas, one of six children of parents who were sharecroppers. Her father, Charlie Long, had a third-grade education and her mother, Elsie Lee Foggie Long, a tenth-grade education. Gloria entered school at age four already able to read. She attended the segregated schools in Arkansas, which had all-black faculty who encouraged the students to succeed.

Anderson graduated from Altheimer Training (High) School in 1954 at the age of sixteen. She had no choice as to where to attend college, as going to college out of state was financially impossible, and at this time there were no affirmative action admissions to college so in-state student admissions would have taken precedence over out-of-state black student admissions. At the time, Arkansas A&M, now called the University of Arkansas at Pine Bluff, was the only college in the state that accepted black students. For her freshman year, she received a partial scholarship from Arkansas A&M and her parents paid the difference; for her sophomore year she received a full Rockefeller scholarship on the condition that she maintain an A average. She got her only two Bs during that year, one in chemistry, a course she took on a dare. That she received even a B is remarkable because chemistry was not taught in her high school. Anderson then received a Rockefeller scholarship to complete her education. She majored in chemistry and in 1958 graduated first in her class of 237, with a grade point average of 2.96 out of 3.0. She did not want to teach after graduation, so she

applied to graduate school and was accepted by Stanford University; she could not attend, however, because the school declined to offer any financial support. Instead she applied for an industrial job at the Ralston Purina Company but was not hired, possibly because of her race. As a result Anderson taught seventh grade for six months at Altheimer Training (High) School, but she disliked teaching young children.

Fortunately for her, the Russians launched *Sputnik* in 1957. The resulting panic compelled the federal government to invest heavily in science education. Kimuel Alonzo Huggins, chair of the chemistry department at Atlanta University, asked her to apply for admission to a master's degree program there for high school science teachers. She almost dropped out of the program when she married a high school teacher, Leonard Sinclair Anderson, on 4 June 1960 (the couple divorced in 1977) and because of the financial hardship that full-time study presented. She was encouraged by her thesis adviser and mentor Huggins to remain in the program, and he found financial support for her until she completed her degree in 1961. Her master's thesis, "Studies on 1-(4-Methylphenyl)-1,3-Butadiene," described a new three-step synthesis of butadiene, a gaseous hydrocarbon. That same year she gave birth to her son, Gerald. After graduation she taught at South Carolina State University in 1961–1962.

Anderson was encouraged to continue her graduate education by her next mentor, HENRY CECIL RANSOM McBAY. McBay was instrumental in the lives of many black chemists from the 1930s to the 1990s. He hired her as a research assistant and chemistry instructor at Morehouse College, where she stayed from 1962 to 1964. She was then awarded a research teaching assistantship at the University of Chicago in 1965 to pursue a Ph.D. Thomas Cole, a black teaching assistant, became her role model, and she completed her degree in 1968. A portion of her dissertation, "F-19 Chemical Shifts for Aromatic Molecules," appeared in a 1968 issue of the *Journal of the American Chemical Society*.

McBay encouraged Anderson to apply for the position of chair of the chemistry department at Atlanta's Morris Brown College, where she had been appointed an associate professor of chemistry, even though she was just out of graduate school. She got the position. While in Atlanta she did postdoctoral research with Charles L. Liotta at the Georgia Institute of Technology, and in 1984 she received a faculty research fellowship at the Rocket Propulsion Laboratory at Edwards Air Force Base in California.

Throughout her career Anderson successfully supported her research through grants from organizations like the National Science Foundation. She was a tireless proposal writer for her research and was able to obtain $271,614 for various research projects between 1969 and 1985. She was also able to obtain grants for Morris Brown for precollege programs and science improvement programs. Even though she was an avid researcher who spent most of her personal salary on supplementing her research, Anderson chose to remain at Morris Brown College, turning down offers to work at mainstream white universities.

She was eventually appointed Fuller E. Callaway Professor of Chemistry, an endowed professorship sponsored by the Callaway Trust to bring the salaries of Georgia professors up to the national average. Anderson continued her service to Morris Brown as a dean and acting president. She also improved the chemistry department at Morris Brown by hiring five chemistry professors with PhDs and by upgrading the program so it would be approved by the American Chemical Society, which included introducing modern scientific instrumentation to the chemistry labs.

During the 1980s Anderson focused her research on amantadienes, antiviral drugs, under the Minority Biomedical Support Program of the National Institutes of Health. In 1985 she investigated the synthesis of potential antiviral drugs as a United Negro College Fund Distinguished Scholar. She was also affiliated with BioSPECS of The Hague, Netherlands, as a research consultant.

Anderson was a member of the American Association for the Advancement of Science, the American Chemical Society, the National Science Teachers Association, the National Institute of Science, the Georgia Academy of Science, the New York Academy of Science, the American Association of University Professors, and Beta Kappa Chi, a scientific honor society.

FURTHER READING

Anderson, Gloria L., and Leon M. Stock. "Chemical Shifts for Bicyclic Fluorides," *Journal of the American Chemical Society* 90, no. 1 (3 Jan. 1968).

Sammons, Vivian Ovelton. *Blacks in Science and Medicine* (1990).

Warren, Wini. *Black Women Scientists in the United States* (1999).

JEANETTE ELIZABETH BROWN

Anderson, Hallie L. (5 Jan. 1882?–9 Nov. 1927), multi-instrumental musician, teacher, and orchestra conductor, was born in Lynchburg, Virginia. Some sources give her birth year as 1885; however, according to U.S. census data, it was most likely 1882. Her mother, Betty Anderson, was born March 1849 in Virginia. Little is known about Hallie Anderson's father except that he was also a Virginia native. When Hallie was three, the family migrated to New York City. As a child, Hallie took public school and private music lessons. She received classical training at the New York German Conservatory of Music. Although it did not record her occupation, the 1900 census noted that Hallie's mother was a widow who could neither read nor write, and who had seven living children. Betty Anderson was then living with three of her children, all of whom could read and write: Charles (born Sept. 1872), a waiter; John (born Jan. 1875), also a waiter; and Hallie, already a music teacher at the age of eighteen.

As the twentieth century opened, Hallie Anderson became known as a bass player and vocalist. She moved rapidly into conducting and managing the business of her own protean musical outfit. In the pages of the African American newspaper *New York Age*, Anderson advertised her "orchestra for all occasions" (quoted in W. Antoinette Handy, *Black Women in American Bands and Orchestras*, 2d edition, 1998, 37). In 1905, JAMES WELDON JOHNSON included Anderson's among the "several good orchestras" run and staffed by blacks. Johnson also noted that Anderson and her Harlem colleague Walter Craig "have led large mixed orchestras" ("The Negro of Today in Music," in *The Negro in the Cities of the North*, ed. Charities Publication Committee, 1905, 59). "Mixed" apparently referred to gender as well as race. However, when Anderson conducted for riverboat parties, picnics, festivals, and dances, she probably employed single-sex (all-male or all-female) bands most of the time. She gained fame for her Ladies Orchestra, one of several women's society orchestras in Harlem at the time. The Ladies Orchestra even ventured to Albany, New York, to celebrate Ladies Day at the Hamilton Street Church, once an Underground Railroad stop. From 1905 to 1912 or 1913, the Orchestra held an Annual Reception and Ball.

Anderson and her ensemble gave concerts under the auspices of the New Amsterdam Musical Association, which originated as a response to the exclusion of African Americans from the American Federation of Musicians' New York City local. Anderson and her group also shared the bill with JAMES REESE EUROPE and his Clef Club Orchestra. An advertisement for the Clef Club's "Musical

Melange and Dancefest" conveys the exuberance of the Harlem musical scene at the time: "Sensation of the Season! First Funny Festival!" The event boasted no fewer than twenty-six acts, starting with "one hundred musicians, dancers, and singers" under Europe's direction and culminating with a contest between Anderson's and Walter Craig's orchestras "supplying Popular Tunes for our Patrons. AND THEN ON WITH THE DANCE. AND LET JOY BE UNCONFINED" (*New York Age*, 26 May 1910).

Around 1905, Anderson wed Hoffer Richardson. Their daughter Marguerite Richardson was born in New York around 1907. The 1910 national census labeled all three family members "mulatto." Like his wife and both of his parents, Hoffer Richardson (born around 1871) was a Virginia native. He worked in a "moving picture" theater, at that time a new, glamorous, often extravagantly presented type of entertainment venue. The couple also took in a number of lodgers. Although Hallie Anderson is listed in this particular census as Hallie Richardson, she continued to conduct and perform under her birth surname.

By the early 1910s, dance and society orchestras waned in popularity. From that time up through the 1920s, Anderson worked as an in–house musician at two well-known theaters in Harlem. She played the organ at the Douglas, on 142d Street at Lenox Avenue, later the original location of the Cotton Club. At the Lafayette, she conducted both a "lady band" and a five-piece all-male orchestra. The 1920 Census found Anderson divorced from her husband and living with the 12-year-old Marguerite as well as a cook and a lodger. Her employment of a live-in household servant may indicate that she earned a comfortable living from her theater work. It also appears that at some time she taught dance. Thaddeus "Teddy" Drayton recounted that his pioneering "class act" dance duo with RUFUS GREENLEE started after they "met at Hallie Anderson's dancing school" (Marshall Winslow Stearns, *Jazz Dance: The Story of American Vernacular Dance*, 2d rev. ed., 1994, 291).

Little else is known about Hallie Anderson except her death at age forty-two. Her career ended as it began—at a relatively young age. It is unknown whether she ever capitalized on the then-new and ascendant technology of sound recording. Because information about her is sparse and scattered, Anderson's legacy is difficult to assess precisely. Nevertheless, it is clear that her contemporaries respected her talent and influence, just as later scholars of African American music history did. Eleven years after her death, the WPA (Works Progress Administration) volume on New York City honored Anderson as a "capable singer and music director," and one of the "Negroes in the North [who] carried on their work in the popular music field" at the same time that "W. C. Handy was notating the blues and New Orleans composers were participating in the development of the still nascent jazz strain" (Federal Writers' Project New York, *New York Panorama: A Comprehensive View of the Metropolis*, 1938, 247). Eileen Southern identifies Anderson as "perhaps the first woman conductor to attract wide attention" (*The Music of Black Americans: A History*, 3d edition, 1997, 349). W. Antoinette Handy observes that Anderson was one of several prominent black, female "musical pacesetters for all-male, all-female, sexually integrated, and . . . racially integrated ensembles." Throughout all her musical enterprises, says Handy, "Hallie Anderson always wielded the baton" (*Black Women in American Bands and Orchestras*, 2d ed., 1998, 37).

FURTHER READING
Kellner, Bruce. *The Harlem Renaissance: A Historical Dictionary for the Era* (1984).
Southern, Eileen. *Biographical Dictionary of Afro-American and African Musicians* (1982).

MARY KRANE DERR

Anderson, Ivie (10 July 1905–27 or 28 Dec. 1949), jazz singer, was born in Gilroy, California, the daughter of Jobe Smith. Her mother's name is unknown. Anderson's given name is sometimes spelled "Ivy." She studied voice at Saint Mary's Convent from age nine to age thirteen, and she sang in the glee club and choral society at Gilroy grammar and high school. While spending two years at the Nunnie H. Burroughs Institution in Washington, D.C., she studied voice under Sara Ritt.

Anderson performed in Los Angeles, California, around 1921, and in 1922 or 1923 she joined a touring version of the pioneering African American musical revue *Shuffle Along*, which brought her to New York City. She performed in Cuba in 1924, at the Cotton Club in New York City in 1925, and then in Los Angeles, where she was accompanied by the bands of Paul Howard, CURTIS MOSBY, and SONNY CLAY. In 1928 she sang with Clay's group in Australia. She starred at Frank Sebastian's Cotton Club in Los Angeles in April 1928 and then toured the United States as a solo singer.

Anderson spent twenty weeks with the pianist EARL HINES's big band at the Grand Terrace in Chicago, Illinois, from 1930 into early 1931. In February 1931 she joined DUKE ELLINGTON's orchestra, and during the next dozen years her career followed Ellington's incessant touring, mainly in America, but also for his first appearance in Europe in 1933. With Ellington she recorded "It Don't Mean a Thing (If It Ain't Got That Swing)" (1932), "Raisin' the Rent," "Stormy Weather," and "I'm Satisfied" (all 1933), and in 1933 she also performed "Stormy Weather" in a film short, *Bundle of Blues*. In 1937 she sang "All God's Chillun Got Rhythm" in the Marx Brothers' movie *A Day at the Races* (1937). Further significant recordings with Ellington include vocal versions of his instrumental themes "Solitude" and "Mood Indigo" (both 1940), "I Got It Bad and That Ain't Good" (1941)—also on a soundie (a film short for a video jukebox) of the same name, released in 1943—and "Rocks in My Bed" (1941). She left Ellington's band in 1942.

Anderson married Marque Neal, with whom she opened Ivie's Chicken Shack in Los Angeles. After divorcing Neal and selling the business, she married Walter Collins. The dates of the marriages are unknown. Having suffered for years from asthma, she died in Los Angeles. In what is evidently the most detailed and earliest obituary (its source unidentified), her date of death is given as 27 December 1949; all other sources give 28 December. Anderson was probably Ellington's most versatile singer and perhaps, after the extraordinary Swedish vocalist Alice Babs, his finest as well. She was a scat singer who imitated instrumental sounds, including the growling, trumpet-like vocalizations that ADELAIDE HALL had earlier introduced into Ellington's repertoire; she sang lively pop tunes, clearly enunciating lyrics that she delivered in a piercingly bright voice; and she sang ballads, in which setting her voice became full-bodied and took on a sultry quality. With her joyful delivery of "It Don't Mean a Thing," Anderson gave the forthcoming swing era its name and rhythmic spirit. Her affiliation with Ellington is also remembered especially for her understated but emotionally powerful rendition of the ballad "I Got It Bad and That Ain't Good." Ellington wrote of Anderson in his *Music Is My Mistress* (1973):

Although Ivie was not well known at that time [early 1930s], I soon found that she was really an extraordinary artist and an extraordinary person as well. She had great dignity, and she was greatly admired by everybody everywhere we went, at home and abroad.... She stopped the show cold at the Palladium in London in 1933. Her routine normally consisted of four songs, but while she was singing "Stormy Weather," the audience and all the management brass broke down crying and applauding (124).

FURTHER READING

Collier, James Lincoln. *Duke Ellington* (1987).

Miller, Paul Eduard. "Ivie Joined the Duke for Four Weeks, Stays with Band for 12 Years," *Down Beat* (15 July 1942).

Placksin, Sally. *American Women in Jazz, 1900 to the Present: Their Words, Lives, and Music* (1982).

Schuller, Gunther. *The Swing Era: The Development of Jazz, 1930–1945* (1989).

Walker, Herbert E. "Ivy Anderson Quit Typing to Sing; She's a Star Now," *Chicago Defender*, 9 Feb. 1935.

Obituaries: *New York Times*, 30 Dec. 1949; *Pittsburgh Courier*, 7 Jan. 1950; *Metronome* 66 (Feb. 1950).

This entry is taken from the *American National Biography* and is published here with the permission of the American Council of Learned Societies.

BARRY KERNFELD

Anderson, James, Jr. (22 Jan. 1947–28 Feb. 1967), U.S. Marine and Medal of Honor Recipient, was born in Los Angeles, California, the son of Mr. and Mrs. James Anderson Sr. Anderson attended and graduated from Carver Elementary School, located in Los Angeles, in 1958. After moving to Compton, he graduated from Willowbrook Junior and Centennial Senior High School. Anderson went on to attend Los Angeles Harbor College for approximately a year and a half.

Anderson left college and enlisted in the U. S. Marine Corps on 17 February 1966. He participated in recruit training with the First Recruit Training Battalion at the Marine Corps Recruit Depot in San Diego, California. After graduating from recruit training, Anderson was promoted to Private First Class in August 1966. Transferring to Camp Pendleton, California, Anderson attended infantry training with the Second Battalion of the Second Infantry Training Regiment.

Private Anderson arrived in Vietnam in December of 1966. There he served as a rifleman with Company F of the Second Battalion, Third Marines, Third Marine Division operating in Quang Tri Province. While engaged in a savage firefight with the Viet Cong on 28 February 1967 Private Anderson shielded his platoon mates from certain death by sacrificing his own life to smother a grenade blast. In an official statement, Anderson's comrade Private First Class Larry C. Herring commented, "I was trying to get my weapon to function when the next grenade came in. It fell about a foot in front of Anderson and he reached out and pulled the grenade into himself.... I feel that this man saved my life through his action of bravery and also the lives of the men around him." As a result of his actions in Quang Tri Province, Private First Class James Anderson Jr. was posthumously awarded the Congressional Medal of Honor for conspicuous gallantry, the highest decoration awarded in the U.S. military. He was also awarded the Purple Heart, the National Defense Service Medal, the Vietnam Service Medal with one bronze star, the Vietnamese Military Merit Medal, the Vietnamese Gallantry Cross with Palm, and the Republic of Vietnam Campaign Medal. He was survived by his parents, five sisters, and one brother.

FURTHER READING

The information in this biographical sketch was obtained courtesy of the U.S. Marine Corps History and Museums Division through the primary source documents present in James Anderson Jr.'s personal file. Documents were provided by the historian Annette Amerman per the author's request of 3 October 2006.

U.S. Marine Corps History Division biography of Anderson. Available at http://hqinet001.hqmc.usmc.mil/HD/Historical/Whos_Who/Anderson_J.htm

CHARLES EDWARD WILES, IV

Anderson, Jervis (1 Oct. 1932–7 Jan. 2000), writer, was born Jervis Beresford Anderson in the rural village of Chatham, Jamaica, in the British West Indies, to Peter Anderson, a building contractor, and Ethlyn Allen, a homemaker. Peter Anderson enforced a strict Baptist upbringing on his son. Having passed a series of rigorous qualifying exams, within days after graduating from Kingston Technical School, a high school affiliated with the University of the West Indies, Jervis was hired as a trainee journalist at the *Daily Gleaner*, the most revered and influential newspaper on the island. He left its employ after a year—uncomfortable with the newspaper's conservatism and acquiescence to the colonial regime—and joined the writers' staff at *Public Opinion*, a weekly that advocated self-rule and was closely allied with the People's National Party. Having rejected the stern religion of his father and the unquestioning allegiance to the British Crown manifested by his school's headmaster, at his new position Anderson wrote numerous articles reflecting his maturing socialist, pro-independence stance.

During the two years he was at *Public Opinion*, from 1956 to 1958, he crossed paths with the future Nobel laureate poet DEREK WALCOTT, the South African novelist Peter Abraham, the future Jamaican prime minister Michael Manley, and others who composed the region's literary and political avant-garde.

Seeking to expand his intellectual horizons, in 1958 Anderson left Jamaica to study literature at New York University (NYU). At NYU he was influenced by the pragmatist philosophy professor Sidney Hook, and earned a bachelor's degree in 1963 and a master's degree in 1966. While attending the university Anderson mingled in New York City's intellectual circles and managed to remain on friendly terms with feuding editors Norman Podhoretz at *Commentary* and Irving Howe at *Dissent*, to whose magazines he contributed articles mainly about African American culture and the black cultural elite. He later wrote articles and reviews for *the New Republic, the American Scholar, the New York Times, the New Leader*, and *the New York Review of Books*, among others. Anderson had worked for several months as director of research at the A. Philip Randolph Institute and was employed as a copy editor for the publisher John Wiley when editor William Shawn hired him in 1968 to write sketches for "The Talk of the Town" section of *the New Yorker*. For the next thirty years he worked as a staff writer there. Though for most of those years he was the only black staff writer at the magazine, he was appreciative of the fact that his editors did not restrict him to writing only about matters pertaining to lives of African Americans. In 1969 Anderson wed Eugenia Kemble, who worked in various positions as a trade union administrator; the marriage that ended in divorce ten years later. A member of the Authors Guild and the Society of American Historians, he was the recipient of a Guggenheim Fellowship in 1978.

Anderson's first bylined piece appeared in *the New Yorker* in 1972, followed later that year with a three-part series that profiled the life and times of trade unionist and civil rights activist A. PHILIP RANDOLPH, who in the 1920s and 1930s successfully organized African American railroad employees into the Brotherhood of Sleeping Car Porters. The series formed the basis of Anderson's critically acclaimed first book, *A. Philip Randolph: A Biographical Portrait* (1973), which earned him the Sidney Hillman Foundation Award. Similarly, the text of most of his next book, *This Was Harlem: A Cultural Portrait, 1900–1950* (1982), which tried to capture the spirit of the Upper Manhattan district in its heyday, was initially serialized in *The New Yorker* and mostly touted by reviewers. His attempt to demonstrate the relationship between crime and the availability of firearms that resulted in the 132-page *Guns in American Life* (1984), though not as widely received was, nonetheless, praised as a sobering reflection of a dark aspect of American culture. Anderson was intrigued by the interplay of external societal forces and what he called the "human character" of a resilient and vital African American culture, particularly those individuals who had a lasting impact on it.

In the 1980s and 1990s he wrote essays and profiles of persons for *the New Yorker*, most notably philosophy professor CORNEL WEST, poet COUNTEE CULLEN, jazz musician WYNTON MARSALIS, Episcopal bishop Paul Moore Jr., and writer DEREK WALCOTT. A grant from the National Endowment for the Humanities in 1992 facilitated the publication of Anderson's last book, BAYARD RUSTIN: TROUBLES I'VE SEEN (1997), a biography of the talented civil rights activist and close lieutenant of A. Philip Randolph, and to whom MARTIN LUTHER KING JR. entrusted the responsibility of organizing the 1963 March on Washington. The book promptly ascended to the *New York Times* best-seller list.

Anderson retired from *The New Yorker* in 1998. With his reputation as a prominent intellectual firmly established, he chose to remain an active writer and scholar. In summarizing Anderson's professional achievements, a then senior editor of the magazine and longtime friend, Hendrik Hertzberg, tried to convey a bit about his personality, observing that "he was courtly, a little solemn (except when he exploded in laughter, as he did frequently), deliberate, precise, and exceptionally tweedy" (Hertzberg, 28). One of his final works was a memoir of his life in Jamaica titled "England in Jamaica," published shortly after his death in *the American Scholar*, in which he related experiences that helped to shape the course of his career. His last-known project was a book-length biography on the early life of RALPH ELLISON, the celebrated novelist, whom he had interviewed in depth and profiled in *the New Yorker* in 1976, and whose writings he discussed in a public television documentary. Anderson's body was found in his New York City apartment nearly two weeks after he had died there, according to the attending medical examiner, of natural causes.

FURTHER READING

Anderson, Jervis. "England in Jamaica," *the American Scholar* (Spring 2000).

Hertzberg, Hendrik. "Postscript," *the New Yorker* (24 Jan. 2000).

Obituary: *New York Times*, 12 Jan. 2000.

ROBERT FIKES JR.

Anderson, John (c. 1831–?), fugitive slave and abolitionist, was originally named Jack Burton after his enslaver, a Missouri planter. His parents are unknown. Raised in his master's household, Anderson (the name he used in later life) eventually supervised other slaves and farmed his own small plot. In 1850 he married Maria Tomlin, a fellow slave from a nearby farm, and devoted himself to buying their freedom. In the meantime he had become accustomed to visiting Maria at her plantation and was growing impatient with the restrictions of slavery. His master tried to curb his wandering, but Anderson refused to submit to the lash. When this resulted in his sale to a planter on the far side of the Missouri River, Anderson resolved to run off.

On 3 September 1853, the third day of his escape, he encountered a planter, Seneca Digges, and four of his slaves. By Missouri law Digges had the legal authority to arrest any fugitive. When Digges ordered Anderson to come along to his house, the latter suddenly broke away. During the course of the pursuit Anderson encountered Digges and fatally stabbed him with a knife. With the help of the Underground Railroad, Anderson eventually made good his escape to Canada. Missouri authorities, outraged that a slave had murdered a white man, hired bounty hunters, who made several unsuccessful attempts to recover him. For the next seven years he lived quietly in Canada and took up the trade of mason and plasterer.

Then in April 1860 William Mathews, a Brantford, Ontario, magistrate, had Anderson charged with murder after a fellow fugitive named Wynnes, who had quarreled with Anderson, told the local sheriff that he was a wanted man in Missouri. However, no Missouri charges were presented and Anderson was released on a legal technicality. When the Canadian authorities finally had the paperwork, a warrant was issued and Anderson was rearrested that September. His case began to attract support, and Canadian abolitionists retained the services of a lawyer. At the hearing the only direct evidence that Anderson had murdered Digges came from a slave named Phil, whose testimony was given by way of a sworn deposition, as Phil would have been free as soon as he reached Canadian soil. Phil was the only eyewitness to the stabbing available to the prosecution. Anderson's lawyer, Samuel Black Freeman, should have objected to the deposition being admitted, but he did not, and shortly after the hearing he was criticized in the press for this tactical error. The facts of the assault were proven as was Digges's authority to apprehend the fugitive. Anderson was committed to be extradited to Missouri.

"The fate of Anderson is the general topic of conversation," wrote a correspondent to the leading provincial newspaper the Toronto *Globe* on 10 December 1860. "Should Anderson be given up, there will be such a burst of indignation as was never before heard in Canada." Canadians were, by and large, proud of their role in providing a haven for escaped slaves, and the prospect of sending Anderson to trial and almost certain death was politically abhorrent. Antislavery forces had warned that Article 10 of the Webster-Ashburton Treaty of 1842, which had normalized relations between Great Britain and the United States and provided for the extradition of criminals, could be used by Southern slaveholders to regain their lost property. By November 1860 the province's attorney general, John A. Macdonald, had artfully moved the issue into the courts by agreeing to fund a habeas corpus hearing. For the first time the interpretation of this clause would be directly before a court.

There was nervous expectation on 15 December 1860 when Anderson, described in the press as a short, powerful man with "an intelligent looking countenance," appeared before the Court of Queen's Bench to receive the verdict. Fifty Toronto police, nearly the entire force, were present and armed with muskets and bayonets to ensure that Anderson would not be freed by force. While one judge gave a ringing denunciation of slavery and denied that slave laws could ever be enforced in British territories, the majority, including the provincial chief justice, concluded that Anderson had resisted and killed a man who had legal authority to detain him. Therefore, by the terms of the treaty, he should be returned to Missouri.

The decision in the Anderson case, coming only days before South Carolina seceded from the Union, alarmed many abolitionists, as Canada had been seen as a safety valve, the one place where fugitives could be safe; now it seemed that not even Canada was safe. Slaveholders, of course, were delighted with it. The Southern press seized on it as evidence that Britain would accommodate itself to the Confederacy. More thoughtful Northern writers noted that the case had sparked mass rallies across Canada in support of Anderson and that popular sympathy in British territories lay with the antislavery cause. A leading American abolitionist, Gerrit Smith, spoke in Toronto in January 1861 and asked if Canadians would permit Anderson to be returned to Missouri where he would be "seized by a mob and amidst fiendish exultations be burnt at the stake" (Toronto *Globe*, 19 Jan. 1861). Would Canadians act in the same spineless manner as did the Buchanan administration in Washington and accommodate slave owners? The overwhelming response from Smith's audience was "no."

So upset were abolitionist forces that British sympathizers, particularly the British and Foreign Anti-Slavery Society under the direction of Louis Alexis Chamerovzow, obtained a writ from a court in London ordering Anderson's attendance there. This imperial interference created indignation in Canada but was ultimately resolved when the writ was taken by a London bailiff to Toronto and served on the sheriff of Toronto. He ignored it, pending the next decision from the Canadian Court of Common Pleas, which ordered that Anderson be released. The English writ became a nullity. In order to ensure that he would not be subject to any more hearings, Anderson became the ward of British abolitionists and members of a new English organization, the London Emancipation Society, a group associated with William Lloyd Garrison, who invited him to come to England. His Canadian supporters, who were anti-Garrisonians, urged him to leave for his own safety. Anderson himself did not seem to notice that he had passed from one abolitionist faction to another. He was given a major reception in London on 2 July 1861 at Exeter Hall. Thereafter he traveled around England giving speeches.

Once there John Anderson was finally able to escape his unwanted role as a silent figure in the drama and express his own feelings, especially because for most of the period of his notoriety he was in jail and unable to talk with the press. He spoke at more than twenty-five rallies across southern England at which he described the repellent nature of Southern slavery. The antislavery movement in Britain, which had become moribund by 1860, was reinvigorated by the appearance of this personification of resistance to bondage. Under the direction of the Reverend Harper Twelvetrees, Anderson wrote an account of his life, his escape, and his legal tribulations in Canada. After some educational training, the London Emancipation Society decided to send

Anderson to Liberia, and he took ship for Monrovia on 24 December 1862. The details of his life from this point onward are unknown.

During its brief notoriety, the John Anderson case focused attention in Britain, the United States, and Canada on the question of how far non-slave-holding states would recognize the laws of slavery. The public indignation stirred up by the case illustrated the depth of moral repugnance felt outside the South toward slavery and suggested that public opinion in other countries would show little sympathy toward the nascent Confederacy.

FURTHER READING
Brode, Patrick. *The Odyssey of John Anderson* (1984).
Reinders, Robert C. *The John Anderson Case, 1860–1861: A Study in Anglo-Canadian Imperial Relations* (1975).
Twelvetrees, Harper, ed. *The Story of the Life of John Anderson, the Fugitive Slave* (1863, repr. 1971).

PATRICK BRODE

Anderson, Leafy (c. 1887–Dec. 1927), religious leader, was born in Wisconsin. The names of her parents are not known, but there is evidence that she was of mixed African American and Native American heritage. "Mother Leafy Anderson," as she was known to her followers, claimed Mohawk as well as African American ancestry. Little is known of her childhood, but she already had become heavily involved in the Spiritualist movement by the time she reached her twenties. In 1913 Anderson established her first congregation, the Church of the Redemption, on State Street in Chicago. It was also known as the Eternal Life Christian Spiritualist Church, a name shared by many of her churches and by the first recorded organization of Spiritualist churches, also founded by Anderson.

Spiritualist churches were known for healing, prophecy, and especially for conveying messages from important spirits of the dead. The spirits that Anderson claimed to have contacted most often were Father John (or Jones), a prominent healer who she said had taught her to master evil; Queen Esther, a courageous woman of the Old Testament who had dared to petition the king on behalf of her people; and Black Hawk, a leader of the Sauk (Sac) Indians, whom she identified as the saint for the South, as White Hawk was for the North. Whether an actual person served as a model for White Hawk is not known, but Black Hawk, Queen Esther, and Father John were all real persons known to history.

Black Hawk was, by far, the most prominent of Anderson's spirit guides. The black Spiritual movement that Anderson promoted had some roots in-nineteenth-century white Spiritualism with its séances and psychic arts. Indeed, nineteenth-century Spiritualists frequently contacted the spirits of American Indians, and Anderson quite possibly learned of Black Hawk and White Hawk from this earlier Spiritualist tradition. Anderson's churches, however, were not occult centers, and she vehemently denied connections between her movement and any form of "magic," especially voodoo. Anderson saw voodoo (or hoodoo) as an instrument for evil or a form of witchcraft. She viewed herself and the leaders of her churches as instruments of God.

Anderson and followers of her movement—as well as other similar black congregations—called themselves Spiritual, rather than Spiritualist, to disavow any connection to the occult. In the *Encyclopedia of African and African-American Religions* (2001), however, Claude F. Jacobs makes it clear that the more important reason was to distance themselves from racist white Spiritualists, who not only excluded black Spiritualists, but had begun to denounce them as frauds. Anderson combined elements of Spiritualism and Pentecostalism in her movement and also drew heavily on Roman Catholicism. Some congregations added elements from Quaker and Shaker doctrine, Judaism, Ethiopianism, astrology, and nineteenth-century scientific ideas, especially about disease. Anderson's theology was conservative in comparison with other early Spiritual congregations. She used familiar Protestant hymns and lessons based on biblical passages, especially the description of God as spirit from John 4:24, and the enumeration of spiritual gifts from 1 Corinthians 12.

Despite her conservative theological bent, reports associating her Spiritual churches with hoodoo and witchcraft resulted in occasional legal trouble for Anderson. It was sometimes difficult for her to obtain official recognition from cities and states where she tried to obtain charters for her churches and for the Eternal Life Christian Spiritualist Association, which she chartered in New Orleans in October 1920. There are unconfirmed reports of Anderson's arrest in New Orleans on charges related to occult practices, as well as a widely circulated, but perhaps apocryphal, story that her legal troubles ended when she gave a reading for the judge in her case and told him a number of things about his life that were not generally known.

Anderson's Spiritual movement, particularly because of its syncretistic nature, found especially fertile ground in New Orleans. When Anderson arrived there in 1920, she found a diverse population and religious traditions that already contained African, French, Spanish, and Caribbean influences. The Spiritualist churches that already existed in New Orleans were located primarily among French-speaking Creoles. Anderson introduced Spiritualism to New Orleans's non-Creole population, attracting people of all ethnicities and classes and both genders for worship, readings, training in healing and prophecy, and calling up spirits. This was true also for her Chicago congregations, as well as for other Spiritual churches she founded in Little Rock, Memphis, Pensacola (Florida), Biloxi (Mississippi), and Houston. The churches themselves were located in black neighborhoods, but the congregations were ethnically mixed, largely eliminating racial barriers.

The Spiritual movement also constituted one important way for black women to be freed from the male dominance in most black churches. Central beliefs in Anderson's Spiritualism included a democratic concept of equality among spirits, which must have been attractive to marginalized persons. Additionally, in the aftermath of the Civil War—as well as in the midst of the high incidence of fatal diseases and violent deaths common among blacks in the South at the turn of the twentieth century—Spiritualism provided a form of comfort that traditional religions could not offer to the bereaved. Communication with spirits provided proof of a life beyond the grave.

Skilled at fund-raising, Anderson charged hefty fees of those who could afford them, but she offered her services to the poor without charge, so she never amassed a fortune. When she died of a respiratory ailment in New Orleans in December 1927 at the age of forty, her estate consisted of only $36, two pianos, and six city lots with a total value of $8,800. Her niece, the Reverend A. Price Bennett, inherited—and in 1930 mortgaged and lost—Anderson's big three-story Eternal Life Christian Spiritual Church Number 12. That well-known institution on Amelia Street is no more, but Spiritual leaders actually trained by Anderson continued to operate churches and missionary societies into the 1980s.

In the early twenty-first century the black Spiritualist movement remained most prominent in New Orleans, but in 2007 there were records of black Spiritualist congregations in twenty-seven states and the District of Columbia. The Spiritual church sanctuaries resembled those in Catholic churches, and a number of the church's rituals celebrated Catholic saints. Séances were rare, but the spirit message session was an important part of worship, especially the "bless service" or "prophecy service." As of 2007, Black Hawk services were still common in contemporary black Spiritual churches, whose leaders also sometimes contacted Anderson's spirit.

FURTHER READING

Baer, Hans A. *The Black Spiritual Movement: A Religious Response to Racism* (1984).

Baer, Hans A., and Merrill Singer. *African-American Religion in the Twentieth Century: Varieties of Protest and Accommodation* (1992).

Jacobs, Claude F. "Black Spiritual Churches," in *Encyclopedia of African and African-American Religions*, ed. Stephen D. Glazier (2001).

Jacobs, Claude F., and Andrew J. Kaslow. *The Spiritual Churches of New Orleans: Origins, Beliefs, and Rituals of an African-American Religion* (1991).

SHERRY WRIGHT

Anderson, Marian (17 Feb. 1897–8 Apr. 1993), contralto, was born in Philadelphia, Pennsylvania, the daughter of John Berkeley Anderson, a refrigerator room employee at the Reading Terminal Market, an ice and coal dealer, and a barber, and Anne (also seen as "Annie" and "Anna," maiden name unknown), a former schoolteacher. John Anderson's various jobs provided only a meager income, and after his death, before Marian was a teenager, her mother's income as a laundress and laborer at Wanamaker's Department Store was even less. Still, as Anderson later recalled, neither she nor her two younger sisters thought of themselves as poor. When Marian was about eight, her father purchased a piano from his brother; she proceeded to teach herself how to play it and became good enough to accompany herself. Also as a youngster, having seen a violin in a pawnshop window, she became determined to purchase it and earned the requisite four dollars by scrubbing her neighbors' steps. When she attempted to teach herself this instrument as well, she discovered that she had little aptitude for it.

Anderson joined the children's choir of Union Baptist Church at age six. Noticing her beautiful voice and her ability to sing all the parts, the choir director selected her to sing a duet for Sunday school and later at the regular morning service; this was her first public appearance. Later she joined the senior choir and her high school chorus, where occasionally she was given a solo.

While she was still in high school, Anderson attempted to enroll at a local music school but was rejected with the curt statement, "We don't take Colored." She applied and was accepted to the Yale University School of Music, but a lack of finances prevented her from enrolling. Although she was not the product of a conservatory, Anderson was vocally prepared by Mary Saunders Patterson, Agnes Reifsnyder, Giuseppe Boghetti, and Frank La Forge. Over the years she was coached by Michael Raucheisen and Raimond von zur Mühlen, and she also worked briefly (in London) with Amanda Aldridge, daughter of the famous black Shakespearean actor IRA ALDRIDGE. Boghetti, however, had the greatest pedagogical influence.

Anderson's accompanists (with whom she enjoyed excellent relationships) were the African Americans Marie Holland and William "Billy" King (who, for a period, doubled as her agent), the Finnish pianist Kosti Vehanen, and the German pianist Franz Rupp. Between 1932 and 1935 she was represented by the Arthur Judson Agency and from 1935 through the remainder of her professional life by the great impresario Sol Hurok.

One of the happiest days of Anderson's life was when she called Wanamaker's to notify her mother's supervisor that Anne Anderson would not be returning to work. On another very happy occasion, in the late 1920s, she was able to assist in purchasing a little house for her mother in Philadelphia. Her sister Alyce shared the house; her other sister, Ethel, lived next door with her son JAMES DE PREIST, who became a distinguished conductor.

For many, including critics, an accurate description of Anderson's singing voice presented challenges. Because it was nontraditional, many simply resorted to the narrowly descriptive "Negroid sound." Others, however, tried to be more precise. Rosalyn Story, for example, has described Anderson's voice as "earthy darkness at the bottom ... clarinet-like purity in the middle, and ... piercing vibrancy at the top. Her range was expansive—from a full-bodied D in the bass clef to a brilliant high C" (Story, 38). Kosti Vehanen, recalling the first time he heard Anderson's "mysterious" voice, wrote, "It was as though the room had begun to vibrate, as though the sound came from under the earth.... The sound I heard swelled to majestic power, the flower opened its petals to full brilliance; and I was enthralled by one of nature's rare wonders" (Vehanen, 22). Reacting to his first encounter with Anderson's voice, Sol Hurok wrote, "Chills danced up my spine. ... I was shaken to my very shoes" (Story, 47).

In 1921 Anderson, who was by then a well-known singer at church-related events, won the National Association of Negro Musicians competition. Believing that she was ready for greater public exposure, she made her Town Hall (New York City) debut in 1924. Disappointed by the poor attendance and by her own performance, she considered giving up her aspirations for a professional career. The following year, however, she bested three hundred other singers to win the National Music League competition, earning a solo appearance with the New York Philharmonic at Lewisohn Stadium.

In 1926, with financial assistance from the Julius Rosenwald Fund, Anderson departed for Europe for further musical study. After returning to the United States, she gave her first concert at New York City's Carnegie Hall in 1930. That same year she gave her first European concert, in Berlin, and toured Scandinavia. In 1931 alone she gave twenty-six concerts in fifteen states. Between 1933 and 1935 she toured Europe; one of her appearances was at the Mozarteum in Salzburg, where the renowned conductor Arturo Toscanini uttered the memorable line "Yours is a voice such as one hears once in a hundred years" (Anderson, 158). Another exciting experience took place in the home of the noted composer Jean Sibelius in Finland. After hearing Anderson sing, he uttered, "My roof is too low for you," and then canceled the previously ordered coffee and requested champagne. Sibelius also honored Anderson by dedicating his composition *Solitude* to her.

Anderson's second Town Hall concert, arranged by Hurok and performed on 30 December 1935, was a huge success. A one-month tour of the Soviet Union was planned for the following year but ended up lasting three months. Anderson was a box-office sensation as well in Europe, Africa, and South America. Her seventy U.S. concerts in 1938 still stand as the longest and most extensive tour for a singer in concert history. Between November 1939 and June 1940 she appeared in more than seventy cities, giving ninety-two concerts. Her native Philadelphia presented her with the Bok Award in 1941, accompanied by $10,000. She used the funds to establish the Marian Anderson Award, which sponsors "young talented men and women in pursuit of their musical and educational goals."

During 1943 Anderson made her eighth transcontinental tour and married the architect Orpheus

H. Fisher of Wilmington, Delaware. The marriage was childless. In 1944 she appeared at the Hollywood Bowl, where she broke a ten-year attendance record. In 1946, six hundred editors in the United States and Canada, polled by *Musical America*, named Anderson radio's foremost woman singer for the sixth consecutive year. Anderson completed a South American tour in 1951 and made her television debut on the *Ed Sullivan Show* the following year. Her first tour of Japan was completed in 1953, the same year that she also toured the Caribbean, Central America, Israel, Morocco, Tunisia, France, and Spain.

Anderson sang the national anthem at the inauguration of President Dwight D. Eisenhower in 1957, and between 14 September and 2 December of that year she traveled thirty-nine thousand miles in Asia, performing twenty-four concerts under the auspices of the American National Theater and Academy and the U.S. State Department. Accompanying Anderson was the journalist Edward R. Murrow, who filmed the trip for his *See It Now* television series. The program, which aired on 30 December, was released by RCA Records under the title *The Lady from Philadelphia*. In 1958 Anderson served as a member of the U.S. delegation to the General Assembly of the United Nations. Three years later she sang the national anthem at the inauguration of President John F. Kennedy, appeared in the new State Department auditorium, and gave another concert tour of Europe. Her first tour of Australia was a highlight of 1962.

In early 1964 Hurok announced Marian Anderson's Farewell Tour, beginning at Constitution Hall on 24 October 1964 and ending on Easter Sunday 1965 at Carnegie Hall. The momentousness of the event was reflected in Hurok's publicity: "In any century only a handful of extraordinary men and women are known to countless millions around the globe as great artists and great persons. ... In our time there is Marian Anderson." After the tour she made several appearances as narrator of Aaron Copland's *Lincoln Portrait*, often with her nephew James DePreist at the podium.

Although in her own lifetime Anderson was described as one of the world's greatest living contraltos, her career nonetheless was hindered by the limitations placed on it because of racial prejudice. Two events, in particular, that illustrate the pervasiveness of white exclusiveness and African American exclusion—even when it came to someone of Anderson's renown—serve as historical markers not only of her vocal contributions but also of the magnificence of her bearing, which in both instances turned two potential negatives into resounding positives.

In 1938, following Anderson's numerous international and national successes, Hurok believed that it was time for her to appear in the nation's capital at a major hall. She previously had appeared in Washington, D.C., at churches, schools, and civic organization meetings and at Howard University, but she had not performed at the district's premier auditorium, Constitution Hall. At that time, when negotiations began for a Marian Anderson concert to be given in 1939 at the hall owned by the Daughters of the American Revolution, a clause appeared in all contracts that restricted the hall to "a concert by white artists only, and for no other purpose." Thus, in February 1939 the American who had represented her country with honor across the globe was denied the right to sing at Constitution Hall simply because she was not white. A great furor ensued, and thanks to the efforts of First Lady Eleanor Roosevelt and Secretary of the Interior Harold Ickes, the great contralto appeared the following Easter Sunday (9 April 1939) on the steps of the Lincoln Memorial before an appreciative audience of seventy-five thousand. She began the concert by singing "America" and then proceeded to sing an Italian aria, Franz Schubert's "Ave Maria," and three Negro spirituals—"Gospel Train," "Trampin'," and "My Soul Is Anchored in the Lord." Notably, she also sang "Nobody Knows the Trouble I've Seen." Commemorating the 1939 Lincoln Memorial concert is a mural at the Interior Department; it was formally presented in 1943, the year that Anderson made her first appearance in Constitution Hall, by invitation of the Daughters of the American Revolution and benefiting United China Relief.

The second history-making event came on 7 January 1955, when Anderson made her debut at the Metropolitan Opera House in New York, becoming the first black American to appear there. Opera had always interested Anderson, who tells the story in her autobiography of a visit with the noted African American baritone Harry Burleigh, during which she was introduced to and sang for an Italian gentleman. When she climbed the scale to high C, the man said to Burleigh, "Why sure she can do Aida," a traditionally black role. On her first trip to England, Anderson had visited a teacher who suggested that Anderson study with her, guaranteeing that she would have her singing Aida within six months. "But I was not interested in singing Aida,"

Anderson wrote. "I knew perfectly well that I was a contralto, not a soprano. Why Aida?"

The international press announced Anderson's pending debut at the Met in October 1954. As the educator and composer Wallace Cheatham later noted, the occasion called for the most excellent pioneer, "an artist with impeccable international credentials, someone highly respected and admired by all segments of the music community" (Cheatham, 6). At the time there was only one such person, Marian Anderson. About Anderson's debut, as Ulrica in Giuseppe Verdi's *Un Ballo in Maschera, Time* magazine (17 Jan. 1955) reported that there were eight curtain calls. "She acted with the dignity and reserve that she has always presented to the public…. Her unique voice—black velvet that can be at once soft and dramatic, menacing and mourning—stirring the heart as always."

Anderson was a recipient of the Spingarn Medal (from the NAACP), the Handel Medallion (from New York City), the Page One Award (from the Philadelphia Newspaper Guild), and the Brotherhood Award (from the National Conference of Christians and Jews). She was awarded twenty-four honorary doctorates and was cited by the governments of France, Finland, Japan, Liberia, Haiti, Sweden, and the Philippines. She was a member of the National Council on the Arts and a recipient of the National Medal of Arts; in 1978 she was among the first five performers to receive the Kennedy Center Honors for lifetime achievement.

Several tributes were held in the last years of Anderson's life. In February 1977 the musical world turned out to recognize Anderson's seventy-fifth (actually her eightieth) birthday at Carnegie Hall. On 13 August 1989 a gala celebration concert took place in Danbury, Connecticut, to benefit the *Marian Anderson* Award. The concert featured the recitalist and Metropolitan Opera star JESSYE NORMAN, the violinist Isaac Stern, and the maestro Julius Rudel, conducting the Ives Symphony Orchestra. Because Anderson's residence, Marianna, was just two miles from the Charles Ives Center, where the concert was held, the ninety-two-year-old grand "lady from Philadelphia" was in attendance. The Public Broadcasting Service (PBS) television station affiliate WETA prepared a one-hour documentary, Marian Anderson, which aired nationally on PBS on 8 May 1991. Anderson died two years later in Portland, Oregon, where she had moved to live with her nephew, her only living relative.

Many actions were taken posthumously to keep Anderson's memory alive and to memorialize her many accomplishments. The 750-seat theater in the Aaron Davis Arts Complex at City College of New York was named in her honor on 3 February 1994. The University of Pennsylvania, as the recipient of her papers and memorabilia, created the Marian Anderson Music Study Center at the Van Pelt–Dietrich Library. Of course, her greatest legacy is the singers who followed her. As the concert and opera soprano LEONTYNE PRICE, one of the many beneficiaries of Anderson's efforts, said after her death, "Her example of professionalism, uncompromising standards, overcoming obstacles, persistence, resiliency and undaunted spirit inspired me to believe that I could achieve goals that otherwise would have been unthought of" (*New York Times*, 9 Apr. 1993).

FURTHER READING
Anderson's papers and memorabilia are housed at the Van Pelt–Dietrich Library at the University of Pennsylvania.
Anderson, Marian. *My Lord, What a Morning* (1956).
Bogle, Donald. *Brown Sugar: Eighty Years of America's Black Female Superstars* (1980).
Cheatham, Wallace. "Black Male Singers at the Metropolitan Opera," *Black Perspective in Music* 16, no. 1 (Spring 1988): 3–19.
Sims, Janet. *Marian Anderson: An Annotated Bibliography and Discography* (1981).
Southern, Eileen, ed. *Biographical Dictionary of Afro-American and African Musicians* (1982).
Southern, Eileen, ed. *The Music of Black Americans: A History*. 2d ed. (1983).
Story, Rosalyn. *And So I Sing* (1990).
Vehanen, Kosti. *Marian Anderson: A Portrait* (1941; repr. 1970).
Obituaries: *New York Times* and *Washington Post*, 9 Apr. 1993.
This entry is taken from the *American National Biography* and is published here with the permission of the American Council of Learned Societies.

ANTOINETTE HANDY

Anderson, Matthew (25 Jan. 1845–11 Jan. 1928), Presbyterian pastor, educator, and social reformer, was born in Greencastle, Pennsylvania, the son of Timothy Anderson and Mary Croog. One of fourteen children, he was raised in the comforts of a rural, middle-class home, less than thirty miles from historic Gettysburg. On a typical day of his youth, Matthew faced both the physical demands of farm life and the movement back and forth between two cultures. One, dominated by commerce and materialism, was uncharacteristically open to the

Andersons, who owned lumber mills and real estate at a time when most black Americans were dehumanized and disenfranchised by chattel slavery. The other was a culture defined by close family ties and Presbyterian piety. At home Matthew heard Bible stories and dramatic tales of runaway slaves; indeed, religious piety and the pursuit of racial freedom were dominant themes in his life. These early experiences inspired Matthew so deeply that, by the time he left Greencastle in 1863, he had decided on the ministry as his vocation. Study at Oberlin College in Ohio was the first step toward serving his religious faith and his vision of social and racial justice.

Shortly after graduation from Oberlin in 1874, Anderson entered Princeton Theological Seminary. He became the seminary's first African American in residence after he refused to live off-campus, which at that time was the custom for black seminarians. This refusal to accommodate himself to segregationist practices was the first of many assertive acts against unjust social and church practices. Anderson completed his theological studies in 1877 and then spent two years in part-time pastoral assignments in New Haven, Connecticut, where he took courses at Yale Divinity School. Anderson's time in New Haven marked the end of his "supply" (temporary) work and formal academic training.

While traveling to the South to do missionary work in October 1879, Anderson stopped in Philadelphia, Pennsylvania, to visit friends. It became, however, a permanent stop. On 17 August 1880 he married CAROLINE VIRGINIA STILL WILEY, daughter of the civic leader WILLIAM STILL and later the mother of their two children. Caroline, known as "Carrie" to friends, distinguished herself professionally by becoming one of the first black women to graduate from the Women's Medical College of Philadelphia in 1878. Together, Matthew and Caroline raised a family, were active in church and civic affairs, and collaborated on many programs until she died in 1919. Anderson was remarried the following year to Blanche Williams, a longtime associate.

In 1880 Anderson founded the Berean Presbyterian Church. In 1884 he established the Berean Building and Loan Association, a bank that has never—not even during the 1929 stock market crash—closed its doors. In 1899 he opened the Berean Manual Training and Industrial School. Each institution grew out of a need to provide services, skills, and support systems for the black community

of Philadelphia during Reconstruction, when the country was being transformed from a slaveholding nation to a more pluralistic one. In addition, each institution bore the imprint of Caroline Anderson's medical training, whether in prenatal and vocational classes for women or in the establishment of the nurseries that she supervised within the Berean complex. Each of these institutions continued to thrive throughout the twentieth century.

Through the "Berean enterprise"—Anderson's general name for the complex of institutions that he established—Anderson continued a clergy tradition of activism within the African American community in Philadelphia, a tradition that had been established by the African Methodist Episcopal bishop RICHARD ALLEN and Reverend ABSALOM JONES in the late eighteenth century. Like them, Anderson formulated ideas and plans for improving the lives of blacks in particular but without excluding others. The name "Berean" represented two known references in Anderson's life and work. One came from studying Christian history and the early importance of the ancient city of Berea in northern Syria. The other reference was to Berea, Ohio, where in 1872 Anderson, then an uncredentialed but self-proclaimed evangelist, was confronted by church people who rejected his spiritual enthusiasm. Anderson was also known for his civic and intellectual leadership, for example, as an active member from 1901 to 1910 in the Universal Peace Movement, a Quaker organization opposed to slavery and war, and in the Afro-American Presbyterian Council, an organization started in 1893 for social fellowship and inspiration among black Presbyterians.

Anderson's Berean enterprise stood out like a signpost at a time when the course of Reconstruction presented savage attacks on black Americans. Anderson's initiatives bore added significance because they were taken at a time when the social order was undeniably antiblack and fervently racist. Moreover, the struggle for freedom, as Anderson saw it, was not simply the struggle for removing sinful barriers of racial discrimination; it also meant replacing the barriers with the pieties of religious, specifically Presbyterian, devotions. This was the ideal for Anderson, and the title of his only published book, *Presbyterianism: Its Relation to the Negro* (1899), symbolized his view of the interrelatedness of self and religion—in particular, the racial "self" as it defined the experiences of the black American. In the book's preface, Anderson outlined his work as a goal that would benefit all. He saw the doctrines of Presbyterianism as leading the oppressed black person into a state of "independence and decision of character necessary to enable him to act nobly and well his part as a man and a citizen of our great republic."

Another important illustration of Anderson's views is found in "A Private Investigation of Prevalent Conditions on the Panama Canal Zone," a report written in his seventy-fifth year in which Anderson continued to make personal statements about life events that, dominated by racial bigotry, contradicted positive (Presbyterian, he would say) human values. Anderson wrote the report while visiting the Canal Zone and traveling through much of the West Indies and Latin America in 1921. It was addressed to his Princeton seminary classmate and lifetime friend, the Reverend FRANCIS GRIMKÉ, informing him of the pattern of color prejudice that he saw in the zone. Anderson characterized these discriminatory policies as a "prodigious blunder" that diminished the great technical achievement of the Panama Canal. It was not always secular prejudice, however, that Anderson witnessed and protested against.

Anderson became increasingly involved in the Presbyterian Church's struggle to remain united after the Civil War, when some church policies toward the freed person threatened to divide blacks and whites, particularly in the church's debate over whether the Board of Home Missions and the Freedman's Board should remain separate organizations. Anderson believed that not enough money was being given to the Freedman's Board, and he eventually concluded that the two boards should be merged. Anderson's account of his role in this struggle is preserved in his book, in which he presents a record of his service as chairman of the Philadelphia Council of the Freedman's Board (1889–1890). In his account Anderson describes how he continually tried to raise the consciousness of the church's power structure, not just once, but over a period of time, through written appeals and involvement in the church's regional and national meetings. Several subsequent publications funded by the Presbyterian Church offer additional examples of Anderson's writing as the regional leader of Presbyterian clergy, most of whom were serving predominantly black congregations. By that time Anderson was no longer just a local leader; he was spokesman for the protest against a national Presbyterian Church policy that he and others believed violated the principles of the church's mission to the poor and believed diminished its potential for closing the gap between the races. Anderson died in Philadelphia.

Through the development of the Berean Presbyterian Church, the Berean Bank, and the Berean School, and through other reform activities, Matthew Anderson, defender of his Presbyterian faith and an articulate witness for social justice, created a legacy of hope and opportunity while leaving a permanent mark on community development in Philadelphia and the nation.

FURTHER READING

Anderson, Matthew. *Presbyterianism: Its Relation to the Negro* (1899).

Trotman, C. James. "Matthew Anderson." *American Presbyterians* 66, no. 1 (1988).

Trotman, C. James. "Matthew Anderson." *Princeton Seminary Bulletin* 9, no. 2 (1988).

Obituary: *Crisis* 35, no. 4 (Apr. 1928).

This entry is taken from the *American National Biography* and is published here with the permission of the American Council of Learned Societies.

C. JAMES TROTMAN

Anderson, Michael (25 Dec. 1959–1 Feb. 2003), astronaut, was born Michael Phillip Anderson in Plattsburgh, New York, to Barbara and Andy "Bobby" Anderson. Because his father was a member of the United States Air Force, young Anderson moved regularly until the family settled in Spokane, Washington, in the 1960s. It was there that he attended public schools and became fascinated with America's space race. Michael would wear goggles when cutting lawns because he knew that he needed to protect his eyes in order to be an astronaut.

After high school Anderson went to the University of Washington, where in 1981 he received a bachelor of science degree in Physics and Astronomy, and then went to Creighton University, where he received a master of science degree in Physics in 1990. As an undergraduate he received pilot training at Vance Air Force Base in Oklahoma, and as a postgraduate he piloted KC-130 and T-38 transport and training aircraft and became a second lieutenant by the time he had more than four thousand hours of flight training. Anderson graduated from technical training at Keesler Air Force Base, Mississippi, in 1982, and completed his undergraduate pilot training at Vance Air Force Base, Oklahoma, in 1986. From 1988 to 1990 he was assigned to the Second Airborne

Command and Control Squadron at Offut Air Force Base in Nebraska, where he became a KC-130 pilot. Anderson went on to serve as an aircraft commander and flight instructor pilot in the 920th Air Refueling Squadron at Wurthsmith Air Force Base in Michigan; this assignment lasted from January 1991 to September 1992. He then was an instructor pilot and tactics officer in the 380th Refueling Wing of Plattsburgh Air Force Base in New York, from September 1992 through February 1995.

In 1987 Anderson married his high school sweetheart, Sandra "Sandy" Hawkins. Michael and Sandy's first daughter, Sydney Anderson, was born in 1991, and their second daughter, Kaycee Anderson, was born in 1993. In 1994 the National Aeronautics and Space Administration (NASA) selected Anderson for astronaut training, and four years later on 16 January 1998 he was part of STS-89 (Space Transport System 89) aboard the space shuttle *Endeavor*. During its nine-day mission his vehicle docked with the Russian space station *MIR*, making Major Anderson the first and only African American to do so, because his was the fifth and final mission that docked with *MIR* before the Russian government decided to abandon the station. Shortly after that mission Anderson was promoted to the rank of lieutenant colonel and became the first and only African American ever to sit on the board of NASA that selects which candidates become astronauts.

NASA selected Anderson to be part of STS-107 (the 107th space shuttle mission), but the August 2002 mission was delayed when cracks were found in one of the shuttle's external fuel tanks. NASA grounded the entire fleet until all the shuttles were checked. On 16 January 2003 the space shuttle *Columbia* blasted off in what was considered a picture-perfect launch. Aboard were Payload Commander and Mission Specialist Michael Anderson (USAF), Commander Rick Husband (USAF), Pilot William McCool (USN), Mission Specialist Kalpana Chawla (USAF), Laurel Clark, MD (USN), Mission Specialist David Brown, MD (captain, USN), and Payload Specialist Colonel Ilan Ramon (Israeli Air Force). Eighty seconds into the launch NASA cameras picked up what appeared to be a foam tile coming off one of the solid rocket boosters, hitting the left wing. It appeared to be nothing out of the ordinary, and the sixteen-day mission continued, conducting more than eighty experiments.

After passing through the earth's atmosphere on the morning of Saturday, 1 February 2003, it became vividly clear to NASA that something had gone wrong. As *Columbia* blazed a preset descent from space over California and Texas, witnesses on the ground saw pieces of the shuttle streaking from it while NASA picked up *Columbia's* onboard computers attempting to correct some sort of problem centered on the left wing. Television news cameras then recorded and broadcast around the world the fiery breakup of the spaceship over the skies of Texas. All seven astronauts perished.

Tributes, accolades, and memorial services abounded. The first official memorial service was on 4 February 2003, while Grace Community Church in Houston—the church of both Anderson and Rick Husband—held a nationally televised service on 5 February. At the National Cathedral in Washington, D.C., a memorial service was held the following day, at which the singer PATTI LABELLE sang "Way Up There," a song written especially for the fallen seven of *Columbia*. The Washington State Transportation Commission honored Anderson by renaming state route 904 in his name, while Creighton University honored him with a seven-foot statue. Arlington National Cemetery held another official memorial service on 7 March and dedicated a permanent plaque in honor of the courageous astronauts on 2 February 2004. NASA's Jet Propulsion Laboratory in Pasadena, California, proposed the idea of naming celestial bodies in the astronauts' honor, and on 6 August, after approval by the International Astronomical Union (the official clearinghouse for asteroid data), it honored the seven by naming after them seven asteroids that orbit the sun between Mars and Jupiter.

FURTHER READING

The main sources for this entry were personal interviews with the subject and his family by the author.

"Anderson Gave his Life to his Dream," *St. Louis American* (6–12 Feb. 2003).

"Creighton University Honors Black Astronaut," *Jet* (5 July 2004).

"DeClue Family Member Is in Space," *St. Louis American* (Jan. 29–4 Feb. 1998).

"Returning Astronaut Has Pizza on Order," *St. Louis Post-Dispatch*, 31 January 1998.

"Shuttle Probe Locating Left Wing's Breach," *Associated Press*, 30 April 2003.

"Silence, Then Shock: 7 Astronauts Are Killed When *Columbia* Disintegrates" and "He'd Go Up Every Day If You'd Let Him," *St. Louis Post-Dispatch*, 2 February 2003.

DAVID DE CLUE

Anderson, Osborne Perry (27 July 1830–13 Dec. 1872), abolitionist, was born in West Fallowfield Township in Chester County, Pennsylvania, the son of Vincent Anderson, a free black man. Both Osborne and his father are listed in the U.S. census as "mulatto." Osborne's mother, according to family lore, was a white woman of Irish or Scottish descent. Osborne Anderson attended the public schools of Chester County and may have studied at Oberlin College in Ohio in the 1850s, although the university has no official record of him doing so.

The most significant development in Anderson's early life was the passage by the U.S. Congress in 1850 of the Fugitive Slave Act, which made it a federal offense to harbor escaped slaves. Many free blacks in the North, as well as slaves who had escaped bondage and sought refuge in the free states, immediately made plans to flee to Canada, fearing that they would be captured by slave catchers and sold in the South. Anderson was among the forty thousand African Americans who fled to Canada in the decade following passage of the act. He settled in the community of Chatham, in the present-day province of Ontario, a popular destination for black emigrants. Among the nearly two thousand black settlers in Chatham at that time were Anderson's friend and former neighbor in Pennsylvania, MARY ANN SHADD (CARY). Anderson at first managed Shadd's uncle's farm, but by 1856 he was working with the Quaker-educated Shadd, who in 1853 had founded the *Provincial Freedman*, a newspaper for Ontario's black émigré community. He was employed at first as a subscription salesman, then as a printer, and he also wrote articles for the paper condemning both slavery and black emigration to Africa.

The *Provincial Freedman's* uncompromising abolitionism and the militancy of Chatham's black community did not go unnoticed by John Brown, the radical white abolitionist who supported direct action tactics, including violence if necessary, to end slavery. In May 1858 Brown organized a direct action convention in Chatham at which Anderson served as one of two recording secretaries. Several prominent abolitionists invited to the meeting, notably FREDERICK DOUGLASS and HARRIET TUBMAN, did not attend, though others, including MARTIN DELANY, did. At the convention Delany and forty-five other delegates—thirty-four black and twelve white— elected Anderson as one of two members of congress for a future black state to be established in the southern Appalachians after the abolition of slavery. Some accounts suggest that Brown first discussed his plans for an armed raid on the federal arsenal at Harpers Ferry, Virginia (later West Virginia), at the Chatham meeting.

On 13 September 1859 Anderson left Canada to assist Brown in his planned attack on Harpers Ferry, which both men believed would help foment a general slave uprising in Virginia and the rest of the South. He was met by Brown himself on the Pennsylvania-Maryland border and traveled with him to a farm four miles from the federal arsenal where Brown and his allies had secretly been preparing for the raid for more than two months. Anderson, among the last of the conspirators to arrive, proved crucial to Brown's plans by thwarting a last-minute mutiny among twenty or so of Brown's followers, who were concerned that promised reinforcements had not yet arrived from Canada or other posts on the Underground Railroad. On 16 October 1859 "Chatham" Anderson, as he was known to Brown's men, chaired the final meeting of the insurrectionists before seventeen of them, including Anderson, DANGERFIELD NEWBY, and three other African Americans, set out for Harpers Ferry. That evening the raiding party captured the town's armory, arsenal, and rifle works with relative ease. Brown then sent Anderson and five other men to capture and hold as hostage Colonel Lewis W. Washington, a prominent local landowner and a descendant of President George Washington. Perhaps as many as 150 slaves in the nearby area were aware of the plot, and Anderson armed around thirty of them with pikes, spears, and muskets. Other slaves in the region assisted the revolt by burning and destroying their owners' property. Anderson's role in encouraging slaves to rebel resulted in his being named as the leader of the revolt in many of the first reports of the insurrection.

In spite of these early successes it quickly became apparent—as Frederick Douglass, among others, had warned—that Brown's forces were no match for the fifteen hundred members of the local militia and for federal troops led by Colonel Robert E. Lee. By the evening of Monday, 17 October, these forces had surrounded the firehouse at Harpers Ferry, where Brown was holding several hostages. Anderson, aided by Albert Hazlett and a fugitive slave named Shields Green, was in charge of guarding the arsenal. Green chose to join Brown in the firehouse, where he and eight of his comrades met the martyr's death that many of them had anticipated and welcomed. Six others, including Brown, were captured, tried, and executed.

Since Anderson was the sole survivor among the main participants of the raid, his account remains the best inside account that we have of those events. His seventy-two-page *A Voice from Harpers Ferry* is, however, misleading on some matters. Anderson suggests, for example, that he and Hazlett made their escape on the Monday afternoon, after seeing that Brown had been captured and in the hope of later securing his release. Most other accounts suggest that Brown was captured on the Tuesday, the morning after Hazlett and Anderson abandoned the arsenal. Most historians nonetheless accept as accurate Anderson's description of his perilous escape with Hazlett along the Shenandoah and Potomac rivers to Pennsylvania. Ten miles south of Chambersburg, Pennsylvania, the two men split up. Shortly afterward Hazlett, injured and exhausted, was captured, extradited to Virginia, and executed in January 1860. Anderson remained undetected and reached York, Pennsylvania, where he was assisted by WILLIAM GOODRIDGE, a veteran of the Underground Railroad—and also the owner of an actual railroad line—who helped him to reach Philadelphia. From there Anderson made his way to Cleveland, Ohio, and then back to Chatham.

The sole survivor of the Harpers Ferry raid, Anderson became instantly both a fugitive from federal justice and a hero to radical abolitionists. On 4 July 1860 he addressed a thousand people at a memorial service for the Harpers Ferry martyrs at Brown's farm in North Elba, New York, and devoted the rest of that year to writing *A Voice from Harpers Ferry*. Anderson's main reason for writing the volume was to counter the erroneous statements of journalists and government officials who claimed that all slaves in the vicinity of Harpers Ferry had opposed the insurrection. Following the outbreak of the Civil War in 1861 Anderson recruited black Canadians to fight for the Union cause, and he may also have fought in the Union army himself. After the war he moved to Washington, D.C., where he remained an active public speaker and worked as a messenger until his death in that city in 1872, aged forty-two. Like all of the Harpers Ferry rebels other than John Brown, Osborne Perry Anderson was largely forgotten in the century following his death. In 2000, however, Anderson's *Voice from Harpers Ferry* was made available to a new generation when it was republished with commentaries by the death-row prisoner MUMIA ABU-JAMAL, among others.

FURTHER READING

Anderson, Osborne Perry. *A Voice from Harpers Ferry* (1861).

Libby, Jean. *Black Voices from Harpers Ferry: Osborne Anderson and the John Brown Raid* (1979).

Stauffer, John. *The Black Hearts of Men: Radical Abolitionists and the Transformation of Race* (2002).

STEVEN J. NIVEN

Anderson, Peter (c. 1822–1879), tailor, store owner, and newspaper editor, was born in Pennsylvania, to parents whose names and occupations are now unknown. Little is known about Anderson's early life except that he was a member of the Masonic Fraternity, ultimately gaining appointment as Deputy Grand Master of the Grand Lodge for the State of Pennsylvania. Anderson migrated west in the waning days of the California gold rush and in 1854 set up a tailor shop and clothing store in San Francisco. There he plunged into the city's small but energetic black community, a community linked by both the mining economy and by shared protest against injustices in the new state of California.

Anderson soon became a regular contributor to political discussions at the recently organized Atheneum Institute, a reading room and cultural center for black Californians. In January 1855 he and other prominent African Americans joined together to call for a Colored Citizens' Convention to protest racial discrimination in the state. Eventually Anderson would participate in every Colored Citizens' Convention held in California between 1855 and 1865.

Many African Americans profited from the state's mining economy, usually through small businesses such as barbershops, restaurants, or laundries. The money earned from such ventures allowed these pioneers to send for the wives and children they had temporarily left behind, and the state's black population quickly expanded. Despite California's status as a free state some Southern white migrants openly brought slaves to work in the gold fields. State law denied blacks the right to vote, send their children to public schools, or even testify in court, a prohibition upheld (and extended to Chinese immigrants) by the California supreme court in 1854 in *People v. Hall*.

During an 1855 meeting called to protest such discrimination Peter Anderson broached the idea of mass emigration to Sonora, Mexico. But when delegates gathered at the first State Convention of Colored Citizens in November 1855 they refused Anderson's call to endorse such a plan, instead focusing on testimony rights and public education demands. They also called for the development of a newspaper to help foster and sustain black political activism, an idea Anderson enthusiastically promoted to black San Franciscans after the conference. The first issue of the *Mirror of the Times* (1856–1858) appeared shortly before the second California Colored Convention, under the ownership of MIFFLIN WISTAR GIBBS and others.

During the turbulent years of the late 1850s Anderson established himself as a prominent voice in black politics. African Americans increasingly saw California as a hostile environment both because of the continued ban on black testimony and the infamous ARCHY LEE case. In 1858 the California State supreme court overturned a lower court's decision freeing Lee, a Mississippi-born slave, despite his residence in the state for over a year. African Americans rallied to his cause and after much legal wrangling, Lee eventually gained his freedom. In the midst of this conflict Anderson once again publicly endorsed emigration to Mexico, and though by this time there was greater interest in such ideas, the debate was cut short when news of a gold strike in Vancouver, Canada, reached California. Hundreds of African Americans headed north, including Archy Lee and Mifflin Gibbs, one of the editors of the struggling *Mirror of the Times*, which had ceased publication.

Anderson, meanwhile, remained in California, participating in continuing efforts to pressure the California legislature to reform its testimony laws and provide other civic opportunities to African Americans. In a letter to the *Weekly Anglo-African* (17 Dec. 1859) he complained that few remaining California blacks demonstrated an interest in politics. He noted that a restaurant occupied the old Atheneum Institute and that minstrel shows were being put on in the abandoned St. Cyprian African Methodist Episcopal (AME) Church of San Francisco. In 1859 Anderson and several allies created the Savings and Land Association, optimistically suggesting that with enough stockholders, blacks could acquire land for their own republic or state, but the arrival of the Civil War again dampened any real interest in Anderson's emigration plans.

For his part, Anderson recognized the political opportunities of the Civil War era and in 1862, after a stint as a reporter for the *Lunar Visitor*, a newspaper briefly published by the AME minister JOHN J. MOORE, he began publishing the *Pacific Appeal* under the slogan, "He who would be free, himself must strike the blow." Testimony rights emerged as the immediate focus of this weekly journal. By 1863 African Americans had finally gained the right to testify in California's courts and Anderson turned his political attention to education. He served on a San Francisco committee to press city officials for black children's schooling rights and regularly publicized other such efforts around northern California in the *Pacific Appeal*.

Anderson shared editorship of the *Pacific Appeal* with PHILIP A. BELL, an experienced abolitionist and journalist from New York who migrated west during the Civil War years. Bell used his significant political connections with African American leaders in the East to ensure that the *Pacific Appeal* maintained a national perspective on black politics. The newspaper also published social and business news from around the northern California region, creating an important network for black Californians.

Peter Anderson and Philip Bell increasingly quarreled however, and in 1865 Bell launched his own weekly newspaper, the *Elevator*, under the slogan "Equality before the Law." Through their rival newspapers the editors regularly clashed over political strategy and partisan loyalty. Initially suspicious of the Republican Party, Anderson later came to insist that only strict Republican allegiance would ensure civil rights reforms. Regarded by some as arrogant he alienated other black leaders in northern California's political circles and soon his influence was eclipsed by Bell's. As early as the late 1860s Anderson was struggling to maintain regular publication of the *Pacific Appeal*. When he died in San Francisco the newspaper closed. Ultimately Anderson's commitment to civil rights protest and his rivalry with Bell demonstrates the political vitality of northern California's nineteenth-century black community.

FURTHER READING

Beasley, Delilah. *The Negro Trail Blazers of California* (1919).

Daniels, Douglas Henry. *Pioneer Urbanites: a Social and Cultural History of Black San Francisco* (1980).

Fisher, James Adolphus. "A History of the Political and Social Development of the Black Community in California, 1850–1950." Ph.D. diss., State University of New York at Stony Brook, 1971.

Lapp, Rudolph M. *Blacks in Gold Rush California* (1977).

SUSAN BRAGG

Anderson, Regina (21 May 1901–5 Feb. 1993), librarian, Harlem Renaissance cultural worker, and playwright, was born in Chicago, the daughter of Margaret (Simons) Anderson, an artist, and William Grant Anderson, a prominent criminal attorney. She was reared in a black Victorian household in Chicago's Hyde Park district, amply provided for by a father who counted W. E. B. DuBois, Theodore Roosevelt, and Adlai Stevenson among his friends and clients. Regina attended normal school and high school in Hyde Park, studying later at Wilberforce University and the University of Chicago, and eventually receiving a degree in Library Science from Columbia University's School of Library Science.

The Chicago of her youth and early adulthood struck her as provincial, yet it was flavored by migrants from the deep South and enlivened by the voice of IDA B. WELLS, whose writings on lynching gave Anderson an understanding of the link between race and violence, a subject of one of her Harlem Renaissance plays, *Climbing Jacobs Ladder* (1931). While the young woman scorned her parents' adherence to the genteel tradition, she inherited from their household a firm sense of self and a *savoir-vivre* that enabled her to move through different levels of society with ease and confidence. Following her parents' divorce, Anderson lived for a short time with her grandmother, then moved to New York in 1923, joining other "new women" and "new Negro women," who, empowered by their new voting rights, flocked to New York in search of personal emancipation. Anderson first settled in downtown Manhattan, living at a YWCA, and applied for a library position in the vast New York Public Library system. At the time without a degree, but with some experience working in libraries in Chicago, Anderson was placed in Harlem, at the 135th Street branch as assistant to the enlightened Ernestine Rose, a white woman who would make the branch an intellectual center for Renaissance Harlem.

Realizing that she herself was a victim of an educational system that had disregarded black contributions to America, and having never taken even a single course in black history, Anderson began to study African American history and culture in order to accommodate the interests of the library's black patrons. She perfectly understood the historical significance of her appointment and with inexhaustible energy set about building the collection of books, organizing groups for literary discussions featuring the younger generation of writers and artists, and the likes of LANGSTON HUGHES and COUNTEE CULLEN, who were hosted by an impressive volunteer corps that included

ETHEL RAY NANCE, Regina's roommate. Nance later recalled her roommate's late-night reading activity, which produced notes on new and promising books, and her roommate's vigilant lookout for new and promising authors to bring to the library. Within a year of her residency in Harlem, she was instrumental in convincing CHARLES S. JOHNSON to organize the now-famous March 1924 Civic Club dinner which launched the Harlem Renaissance, a turning point in African American history and culture. If, as NATHAN HUGGINS suggested, Anderson had taken on the mission of getting to know herself through her race, it can also be said that she shared ARTHUR SCHOMBURG's mission of educating African Americans about themselves.

Recognizing the value of drama as a pedagogical tool, Anderson opened the basement of the library in 1924 for community theater, joining DuBois in establishing the Crigwa (later Krigwa) Players, which would employ the theater as an extension of the aims of the *Crisis* Magazine. The Crigwa Players offered more serious fare than that provided by Harlem's Lafayette Theatre and, influenced by THOMAS MONTGOMERY GREGORY's Howard University Players and the revolutionary design of new Irish drama, it created additional outlets for writers and performers and attracted a loyal Harlem audience. With the demise of Krigwa, in 1928 Anderson herself spearheaded the founding of the Harlem Experimental Theatre, which opened the way for the founding of the American Negro Theatre (ANT). Relocated to St. Philip's Episcopal Church Parish House, the ANT established a tradition of theater-going that continued even into the early twenty-first century in the form of the community-based H.A.D.L.E.Y players, led by the octogenarian Gertrude Jeannette, a former member of the now-defunct American Negro Theatre, which also included SYDNEY POITIER and HARRY BELAFONTE as members. Working full time at the library, raising funds, and helping run the Harlem Experimental Theatre, under her pen name Ursula Trelling, Anderson composed a number of plays which saw production by the company, beginning with *Climbing Jacob's Ladder* in 1931.

The apartment that Anderson shared with Ethel Ray Nance and Luella Tucker at 580 St. Nicholas Avenue became an important salon, its significance captured in its alternate name, "Dream Haven." Firm believers in the importance of dialogue, the residents of Dream Haven brought together members of the younger generation, JEAN TOOMER, ERIC WALROND, AARON DOUGLAS, and

ZORA NEALE HURSTON and the older custodians of culture, CHARLES S. JOHNSON, ALAIN LOCKE, and DuBois. Located in a newly integrated building, 580, where ETHEL WATERS also lived, faced the beautiful St. Nicholas Park and its roof, affording a splendid view of Harlem, the Mecca of the black world that all had come to love so much. "Dream Haven" embodied the wonderful friendship between Anderson and Nance that was to last many years after 1926, when Nance left New York and Anderson married William T. Andrews, an attorney and New York state assemblyman. They would have one daughter, Regina Ann.

A letter from DuBois proved instrumental in helping Anderson secure a permanent position in the library after graduating from library school. Career advancement propelled the move from the 135th Street to downtown branches until 1936, when she began work at the Columbia branch, located on 115th Street near the university. In 1947 Anderson became supervisor of the Washington Heights branch and instituted discussion groups and a "Family Night" program that brought international and national notables to the neighborhood's mostly East European immigrant population. As responsive to the Washington Heights neighborhood as she had been to her Harlem clientele, Anderson established English as a second language classes in order to help immigrants make the transition to American life.

A cosmopolitan who enjoyed travel Anderson visited many countries in Europe, Asia, and Africa on behalf of women and human rights, while serving as vice president of the National Council of Women and the Urban League's representative to the United Nations Educational, Scientific, and Cultural Organization (UNESCO). In 1967 Anderson retired to her country home in Mahopac, New York, an area she and her family integrated, bringing large numbers of guests of color who received a warm welcome in the area. From their penthouse apartment atop 409 Edgecombe Avenue, home base over the years to WALTER WHITE, DuBois, THURGOOD MARSHALL, and Aaron Douglas, she and Andrews remained important figures in Harlem's social and political life. With long memory, she was mindful of the radical thrust of her own aims for black theater and welcomed the revolutionary Black Arts Movement of the 1960s and 1970s. She was a consultant to New York Metropolitan Museum's controversial 1968 retrospective exhibition, *Harlem on My Mind*, a project that brought back vivid memories of "Dream Haven" and the Harlem of her earlier days The rediscovery of the *Harlem Renaissance* in the 1970s provided additional opportunities for Anderson to share her own memories of the period. She was a source for Huggins's important study, Harlem Renaissance (1971), which initiated the modern reappraisal of the period.

In 1971 Anderson and her former Dream Haven mate, Ethel Ray Nance, completed a manuscript, *A Chronology of African-Americans in New York, 1621–1966*, a reflection of the "power of pride" in heritage that had energized 580 St. Nicholas Ave. Unpublished at the time of her death in 1993 the manuscript was foundational to the millennium exhibition and book, *The Black New Yorkers: The Schomburg Illustrated Chronology*, produced by the New York Public Library's Schomburg Center for Research in Black Culture, the successor to the 135th Street branch which Regina Anderson had nurtured.

FURTHER READING

The Schomburg Center in New York has a five-videocassette interview with Anderson conducted by Jean Blackwell Hutson in 1986 and a large photo collection covering the subject's personal, professional, and civic activities. It also holds committee reports she compiled for the Human Relations Committee of the National Council of Women of the United States.

Huggins, Nathan. *Harlem Renaissance* (1971).

Hull, Gloria. *Color, Sex, and Poetry: Three Women Writers of the Harlem Renaissance* (1987).

Levering Lewis, David. *When Harlem Was in Vogue* (1979).

Marks, Carol, and Diana Edkins. *The Power of Pride* (1999).

Roses, Lorraine Elena, and Ruth Elizabeth Randolph. *Harlem's Glory: Black Women Writing, 1900–1950* (1997).

ONITA ESTES-HICKS

Anderson, T. J. (17 Aug. 1928–), musician, composer, arranger, teacher, scholar, and humanitarian, was born Thomas Jefferson Anderson in Coatesville, Pennsylvania, the only son and eldest of three children born to Thomas Jefferson Anderson Sr., a college professor and school principal, and Anita Turpeau Anderson, a teacher. Anderson's early years were spent in Washington, D.C., and Cincinnati, Ohio. His mother was a pianist who accompanied singers in church. She was his first musical mentor, providing encouragement from a very early age through music lessons on violin and trumpet.

Anderson attended James Monroe Elementary School in Washington, D.C., where he conducted a rhythm band and impressed Esther Ballou, a city supervisor of music, who told his mother, "the musical world will hear from your son." He later attended Benjamin Banneker Junior High in Washington, D.C. It was during his time in Washington that he discovered the Howard Theatre and the big bands of the likes of TINY BRADSHAW, LUCKY MILLINDER, FATS WALLER, JIMMIE LUNCEFORD, ERSKINE HAWKINS, DUKE ELLINGTON, and COUNT BASIE. Anderson also studied violin for six years with Louis van Jones, a member of the Howard University music faculty.

He later moved to Cincinnati to live with his maternal grandparents. His grandfather, the Reverend DAVID DEWITT TURPEAU, was a member of the Ohio House of Representatives, and his grandmother was a social activist. While in Cincinnati, Anderson attended Harriet Beecher Stowe Junior High School. He credits his music teacher Charles Keys as being very important in his training. He also continued to hear big bands and regularly attended several churches, including Methodist, Episcopal, and African Methodist Episcopal (AME), all chosen for the music.

In 1946 Anderson graduated from Horace Scott High School in Coatesville, Pennsylvania, where he was a member of the orchestra and the band. He performed on trumpet at the commencement ceremony, and his jazz band was honored. From 1946 to 1950, Anderson pursued undergraduate studies at West Virginia State College, graduating with a bachelor's degree in music in 1950. Two of his professors, Dr. Edward C. Lewis and Dr. Ahmed Williams, had great influence on him. In 1950 Anderson entered a graduate program in music education at Pennsylvania State University. He took composition courses with Professor George Ciega, whose encouragement prompted him to become a composer. He graduated in 1951 with a master's in music education.

Anderson began a teaching career at the secondary level as an instrumental music instructor for the High Point, North Carolina, public schools from 1951 to 1954. He also performed in the area with school groups and in a trio with JACKIE MCLEAN and DANNIE RICHMOND. Anderson spent the summer of 1954 studying composition with Dr. T. Scott Huston at the Cincinnati Conservatory of Music.

From 1954 to 1958, Anderson pursued doctoral studies in composition at the University of Iowa, graduating in 1958 with a Ph.D. in music composition. His teachers at Iowa were Dr. Philip Bezanson and Dr. Richard Hervig, both of whom were important in his musical development. While pursuing his doctoral studies, Anderson continued his career as an educator, moving to historically black institutions of higher education. He taught at West Virginia State College in 1955–1956. On 16 June 1956 in Cincinnati, Ohio, Anderson married Lois Ann Fields. They went on to have three children. Upon completion of his doctoral studies, Anderson was appointed professor and chair of music at Langston University in Langston, Oklahoma, in 1958, and held that position until 1963. He then moved to Tennessee State University in Nashville, where he was a professor of music from 1963 to 1969.

In the summer of 1964, Anderson studied composition with the French composer Darius Milhaud at the Aspen School of Music. From 1969 to 1972, while serving as composer-in-residence for the Atlanta Symphony Orchestra, he orchestrated SCOTT JOPLIN's opera *Treemonisha*, which brought him worldwide recognition. During this same period, he was the Danforth Visiting Professor at Morehouse College.

In 1972, he moved to Tufts University in Medford, Massachusetts, as professor and chair of the music department, where in 1978 he was named Austin Fletcher Professor of Music, a position he held until 1990. In that year he retired from Tufts to devote his time to composing.

Anderson's teaching career in secondary and higher education spanned more than five decades, during which time he had an impact on thousands of students. When queried about his purposes in teaching, Anderson said:

Basically, my teaching focused on the personality of the student—what they were listening to and what they wanted to do. Those two things in particular. That's why … if you look over my students who are out there now, a variety of styles are represented. I believe in the freedom for them to choose and at the same time to incorporate skills as a composer. So those two things were the main focal points. (telephone interview between author and Anderson, 6 July 2005)

Anderson's career as a composer spanned more than forty years, during which time he created more than eighty compositions that included music for instrumental solos, small ensembles, combinations, chamber orchestra, full orchestra, orchestra (chamber and full) with soloists or chorus, band, solo voice, voice with instrumental ensemble, vocal duet, choral music, and dramatic music. His works include "Pyknon Overture" (1958), "In Memoriam Malcolm X" (1974), "Soldier Boy, Soldier" (1982), "Thomas Jefferson Anderson's Orbiting Minstrels and Contraband" (1984), "Dear John, Dear Coltrane" (1989), "Bahia, Bahia" (1990), "Walker" (1992), "Huh! (What did you say?)" (1997), "Slip Knot" (2000), and "A Song for Elma Lewis" (2004).

Anderson has received more than thirty commissions, including those from the National Endowment for the Arts, the Fromm Foundation, ASCAP, Yo-Yo Ma, Meet the Composer, Robert Shaw, Symphony of the New World, and the Berkshire Music Center. He has been the recipient of numerous honors and awards, including those from the Rockefeller Foundation, the National Black Music Caucus, the John Simon Guggenheim Foundation, the National Association of Negro Musicians, the Mellon Foundation, the American Music Center, and the National Humanities Center. Anderson also received six honorary doctorates. In 2005 he was inducted into the American Academy of Arts and Letters, the highest formal recognition of artistic merit in the United States.

Anderson's compositional legacy is profound and eclectic, reflecting a deep mastery of African and African American musical aesthetics, traditions, and approaches as well as musical traditions from the East and the West. Regarding his intent as a composer, Anderson says:

Each piece has a different message, and what I try to do is write the best piece, technically and spiritually, that I can. And I don't mean spiritual in the religious sense. I mean spiritually in terms of roots to integrity and truth. That's what I'm talking about. So they are my children, so to speak. And what I try to do is bring forth what I knew. Let me put it this way: the goal is not to, say, incorporate. The goal is to use music as a part of—as an extension of my own personality. So if I have a piece that is influenced by jazz, I'm not trying to write a jazz piece, I'm writing a piece that is influenced by jazz but I'm trying to write a T. J. Anderson piece. (telephone interview between author and Anderson, 6 July 2005)

Anderson's legacy is multidimensional, encompassing musical composition and arranging, teaching, and mentoring. He has served as an outstanding educator, as a leading spokesperson for issues related to black composers and scholars, and has been a major composer.

FURTHER READING

For additional biographical information, a list of compositions, commissions, reviews, memberships, awards, and honors information, see *The International Dictionary of Black Composers*, vol. 1, ed. Samuel A. Floyd Jr. (1999), 35–42.

"Black Composers and the Avant Garde: T. J. Anderson, Jr., Hale Smith, and Olly Wilson," in *Black Music in Our Culture: Curricular Ideas on the Subjects, Materials, and Problems*, ed. Dominique-René De Lerma (1970).

"The Composer and His Relationship to Society: T. J. Anderson, David N. Baker, John Cater, John E. Price, and Herndon Spillman," in *Reflections on Afro-American Music*, ed. Dominique-René De Lerma (1973).

Hunt, Joseph. "Conversation with Thomas J. Anderson: Blacks and the Classics," *Black Perspective in Music* 1, no. 2 (1973): 156–165.

DISCOGRAPHY

b Bop in 2 (Arizona University Recordings Contemporary Composer and Performer Series).

The Black Composers Series (The College Music Society CBS Special Products P19425–P19433).

Chamber Concerto (Remembrance) (Albany Records, Troy 303).*Chamber Symphony* (Composers' Recordings, Inc. CRI-SD258).

"Don't Panic: 60 Seconds for Piano," on *Watermelon Revisited* (Wergo WER6649 2).

"Intermezzi," on *A City Called Heaven* (ACA Digital Recordings).

"It Won't Be the Same River," on *7 Cabaret Songs* (Capstone CPS8684).

Patterson, Willis C., ed. *The Second Anthology of Art Songs by African American Composers* (2002). Contains score and recording of *Words My Mother Taught Me*.

Songs of Illumination. Works by Hale Smith, Camille Nickerson, Thomas Kerr, Adolphus Hailstork, Stephen Newby, Howard Swanson, William Banfield, Evelyn Simpson-Curenton, and T.J. Anderson (Centaur CRC2357).

Variations on a Theme by M. B. Tolson New American Music, vol. 5, (Nonesuch Records, H-71303).

Videmus: Works by T. J. Anderson, David Baker, Donal Fox, Olly Wilson (New World Records, 80423-2).

LEONARD L. BROWN

Anderson, Violette Neatley (16 July 1882–24 Dec. 1937), activist, lawyer, and the first woman of color to be admitted to practice before the U.S. Supreme Court (active in women's clubs and the Chicago

Urban League), was born Violette Neatley in London, England, to Marie Jordi Neatley, a thirty-two-year-old German-Swiss woman, and Richard E. Neatley (sometimes spelled Neatly), a thirty-four-year-old Jamaican of African descent. She moved with her parents to America in 1885, settling in Chicago, where her father worked as a day laborer. Violette Neatley graduated from North Division High School in 1899, leaving her parents' apartment on Wells Street in North Town to marry Amos Preston Blackwell. They remained in North Town, at 473 Park Avenue. Her husband worked as a valet and in 1900 informed the census (which recorded him as black) that he was born in Canada, as were his parents. However, a divorced man of the same name, working as a railway porter in 1910, reported he was born in Virginia to parents born in Kentucky. Violette attended Chicago Athenaeum from 1902 to 1903. Her mother was widowed before 1910.

Neatley's marriage to Blackwell lasted seven years, ending in divorce in 1906 on grounds of cruelty. The same year, in December, she married Dr. Daniel H. Anderson, a general practice physician, recorded by the census as mulatto, born in Wisconsin to an Irish immigrant mother and a father born in Ohio. Beginning work as a court reporter in 1905, she developed her own business, also offering stenography and shorthand services. The *Crisis* reported that "all the colored lawyers and many noted white lawyers" employed her. During this period of her life, she served as president of the Elite Social Charity Club and as secretary of the Alba Rose Club. She joined St. Thomas Episcopal Church, spiritual home to the more socially and financially prominent black families in Chicago. Violette Anderson enrolled in the Chicago Seminar of Sciences (1912–1915), then entered Chicago Law School in 1917, graduating in 1920 with an LL degree, and passed the Illinois state bar exam. The only woman in her graduating class, Anderson was also the first woman of color to graduate from any law school in Illinois.

The circumstances of her separation from Dr. Anderson are not well known, but by 1920 they were divorced, and he was living with his older brother Thomas, a newspaper editor. That summer, she married for a third time, to the pharmacist Albert E. Johnson, but continued to use the name Anderson professionally for the rest of her life. Opening a private law practice after graduation, Anderson was the first African American woman admitted to practice in the U.S. District Court for what was then called the Eastern Division of Illinois. She served as assistant state's attorney in Chicago in 1922–1923, the first woman to do so. Anderson was a member of the Cook County Bar Association, formed in 1915 by attorneys excluded from the Chicago Bar Association on account of their color—although nondiscriminatory in its own membership policies. She was elected vice president of the association between 1920 and 1926.

Anderson was admitted to practice before the U.S. Supreme Court on 29 January 1926; there is no clear record of when or whether she argued a case before the court. Her admission was sponsored by Washington, D.C., municipal judge James A. Cobb, who ten years later made sensational charges that Howard University president MORDECAI W. JOHNSON "has publicly advocated the doctrines of communism." *Time* magazine covered the landmark in patronizing language, referring to Anderson as a "Negress," prompting D. C. Chisolm of Wichita, Kansas, to cancel the family's subscription, admonishing "We do not care for a paper of any kind who call the Women of the Colored Race a 'NEGRESS'" (*Time*, Letters, 15 Mar. 1926).

Continuing her participation in civic clubs, Anderson held membership in the Federal Colored Women's Clubs and was president of the Friendly Big Sisters League of Chicago (which sustained homeless black women and children in a residential building known simply as "The Home"), secretary of the Idlewild Lot Owner's Association (the wealthiest summer resort for people of African descent north of the Ohio River), and a member of the Chicago Council of Social Agencies executive board. Zeta Phi Beta Sorority elected her as its eighth Grand Basileus (equivalent to national president) and has continued since her death to observe Violette Anderson Day each April. Anderson was also a member of the Special Shelters Committee, Chicago Urban League.

Responding to the Depression, Anderson lobbied the Illinois congressional delegation in support of the Bankhead-Jones Farm Tenant Act, introduced in 1936 and passed into law in July 1937, a few months before she died. The original draft of the legislation would have authorized a billion-dollar bond issue for government purchase of land, to be resold to tenant farmers and sharecroppers at affordable rates of interest. Ultimately, the bill approved by both houses of Congress allocated $10 million for 1938, rising to $50 million in fiscal year 1940, and gave preference to the most prosperous tenants, who owned farm equipment and could make down payments—as well as requiring approval by local committees and assessment of whether the applicant could prove a "viable family unit." Anderson encouraged all Zeta Phi Beta chapters to advocate for the bill, but supporters were fighting a rising conservative backlash against the New Deal. Anderson died of colon cancer on 24 December 1937 at Provident Hospital in Chicago.

FURTHER READING

Schultz, Rima Lunin. *Women Building Chicago, 1790–1990: A Biographical Dictionary* (2001).

Smith, Jessie Carney, and Shirelle Phelps. *Notable Black American Women* (2003).

Smith, John C. *Emancipation: The Making of the Black Lawyer, 1844–1944* (1993).

CHARLES ROSENBERG

Anderson, Webster (15 July 1933–30 Aug. 2003), Korean and Vietnam War veteran and Medal of Honor winner, was born in Winnboro, South Carolina, the son of Frizell Anderson, a carpenter, and Blanche Rabb Anderson, a homemaker. Webster's parents had seven children, daughters Frances, Alberta, Marjorie, and Marie and sons Frizell Jr., Webster, Billy, and Larry.

In 1953, Anderson was drafted by the Army to serve in the Korean War. Although racism suffused the armed forces despite President Harry Truman's executive order to integrate the military, Anderson's initial Army experiences were largely positive. He would later tell his son Davis that joining the Army was "a good thing for him." He believed that his white commanding officers as much as his fellow soldiers "helped pave the way" for his military career (Anderson). Webster enjoyed a happy private life too, marrying Ida Davis in 1959. In their thirty-two years of marriage, before Ida's death in 1991, the couple had four children: daughters Vonnie and Tanetta, and sons Webster II and Davis. His children remember him as a good father even if, as son Davis laughingly recalls, "My father was always going to be a drill sergeant."

Following the Korean War, Anderson continued in the United States Army, serving in Battery A, 2d Battalion, 320th Field Artillery of the distinguished 101st Airborne Division as a staff sergeant and section chief. It was while his unit was operating at Tam Ky, Republic of Vietnam, on 15 October 1967, that Battery A's position was attacked by North Vietnamese infantry supported by automatic weapons, heavy mortars, and rocket propelled grenade launchers. When the enemy breached Battery A's position,

Anderson, with complete disregard for his personal safety, mounted the exposed parapet of his howitzer position and became the mainstay of the defense of the battery position. Sfc. Anderson directed devastating direct howitzer fire on the assaulting enemy while providing rifle and grenade defensive fire against enemy soldiers attempting to overrun his section gun position. While protecting his crew and directing their fire against the enemy from his exposed position, two enemy grenades exploded at his feet knocking him down and severely wounding him in the legs. Despite the excruciating pain and though not able to stand, Sfc. Anderson valorously propped himself on the parapet and continued to direct howitzer fire upon the closing enemy and to encourage his men to fight on. Seeing an enemy grenade land within the gun pit near a wounded member of his gun crew, Sfc. Anderson, heedless of his own safety, seized the grenade and attempted to throw it over the parapet to save his men. As the grenade was thrown from the position it exploded and Sfc. Anderson was again grievously wounded. Although only partially conscious and severely wounded, Sfc. Anderson refused medical evacuation and continued to encourage his men in the defense of the position. (Medal of Honor Citation, 1968)

After this action, Anderson was evacuated by helicopter for medical treatment by Colonel Patrick Brady. He would subsequently suffer the amputation of both legs and the loss of a portion of one arm. For his "inspirational leadership, professionalism, devotion to duty … gallantry and extraordinary heroism at the risk of his life above and beyond the call of duty" (Medal of Honor Citation) at Tam Ky, Anderson received the Medal of Honor. He and Brady, himself a Medal of Honor winner, became lifelong friends from that day forth.

Anderson's honorable service in two wars is worthy of recognition; in the Korean War Anderson learned the ways of a soldier, while in the Vietnam War he put all his experience to the best possible use and became a true leader of men. He would later tell his family that Vietnam was "a war we couldn't win," but that "it was my job" to fight wherever his country sent him. Anderson deserves continued recognition today not only as a Medal of Honor winner, but also as a man representative of the fine service rendered in the Vietnam War by African American career soldiers; too often black soldiers in the Vietnam War have been unfairly portrayed as men who "chose" to serve in Vietnam only as a means of avoiding a prison sentence back home.

While Webster Anderson endured the considerable difficulties involved in fighting in Vietnam, the obstacles he faced after the war were equally daunting; having lost both legs and part of an arm, his recovery and rehabilitation would be long and arduous, lasting from late 1967 into the early 1970s. A quiet and modest man, Anderson persevered through his rehabilitation period and, with the help of prosthetics, recovered to live a long and productive life, operating a successful television repair business. As his son Davis recalls, "You name it, he did it … he walked five times a week on his prosthetics, could load and unload his own pontoon boat on his own, and, well, hell, would take off his prosthetics and crawl under the house to make repairs. He was six feet, four inches, but he could be as tall or short as he wanted to be and there wasn't anything he couldn't do." Indeed, Anderson's older children saw no change in their father's attitude; Vonnie remembered him "as the same father, only he was shorter," while Webster II recalls that "he was different physically, but still the same daddy." Ironically, Anderson's war-induced disabilities would also serve as an example to Webster and Ida's youngest son, Davis Anderson. Born in 1970, Davis was diagnosed with ligament cancer before he was a year old, forcing the amputation of a leg and its replacement with a prosthesis; in his father he found a role model to help him overcome his disability from the very beginning, providing love, discipline, and encouragement whenever it was needed.

Following his military career, Webster Anderson lived the rest of his life in Winnsboro, South Carolina, as one of its most distinguished citizens. After the death of his first wife Ida in 1991, he married his second wife Vickie in 1996. When not at work, he and his family traveled all around the world to Medal of Honor conventions, and he often spoke to veterans' organizations and at veteran hospitals before succumbing to cancer at the age of seventy.

FURTHER READING

All of the personal quotations reproduced above are from an interview conducted with Davis Anderson, the son of Webster Anderson, by the author on 2 February 2007.

Hane, Bobb. "Farewell the Hero," *Herald Independent*, Winnsboro, South Carolina (4 September 2003).

Medal of Honor. *Vietnam War Medal of Honor Recipient Webster Anderson*, http://www.medalofhonor.com/WebsterAnderson.htm.

GLENN KNOBLOCK

Anderson, William T. (20 Aug. 1859–21 Aug. 1934), clergyman, army chaplain, and physician, was born a slave in Seguin, Texas. Little is known about his parents except that his mother was a slave, and during the Civil War she and William fled to Galveston, Texas. As a young boy, he joined the African Methodist Episcopal (AME) Church, which took on both local and national responsibility for the religious, intellectual, and social uplift of African Americans, often taking a leading role in promoting both secular and religious education. The AME Church, in fact, sponsored Anderson's education for three years at Wilberforce University in Ohio. The remainder of Anderson's education was financed by an Ohio sponsor, Stephen Watson, who was then the vice president of the London Exchange Bank of Madison County. In 1886 Anderson received a theology certificate from Howard University and two years later graduated from the Homeopathic Medical College of Cleveland. Much later, he served as pastor for AME churches in Toledo, Ohio, Urbana, Illinois, Lima, Ohio, and Cleveland, Ohio, where he ministered to his largest congregation, St. John's.

A congressional act of 2 March 1867 had given the president of the United States the right to commission army chaplains. HENRY VINTON PLUMMER, in 1884, became the first black clergyman to be commissioned a chaplain to the Ninth Cavalry regiment, one of the units popularly known as Buffalo Soldiers. It was not until thirteen years later, in November 1897, that President William McKinley appointed Anderson to be a chaplain. He entered with the rank of captain into the Tenth Cavalry, another unit of Buffalo Soldiers. He was soon stationed at the Assinniboine headquarters in Montana. His religious programs were always well attended, and he organized a reading group, which sometimes discussed essays written by members of the group. His ministry at Fort Assinniboine ended in April 1898 when the Tenth Calvary departed for Camp Chickamauga in Georgia to prepare for the invasion of Cuba during the Spanish-American War.

For reasons that are unclear, Anderson failed to depart with his unit and did not rejoin his men until 25 July 1898 near Santiago, Cuba, where he cared for those who had contracted fever and dysentery.

Immediately after his short stay in Cuba, Anderson and his regiment spent some months along the Gulf Coast of Alabama and Texas.

While languishing on the shores of the gulf, Anderson and his fellow troopers Herschel Cashin, Charles Alexander, HORACE W. BIVINS, and ARTHUR McKINNON BROWN published *Under Fire with the Tenth Cavalry* (1899). Based on eyewitness accounts, this book traced the history of the unit's action and the steadfastness and bravery of black soldiers—both commissioned officers and enlisted men. *Under Fire with the Tenth Cavalry* revealed that in a private letter to JOHN EDWARD BRUCE of Albany, New York, Colonel Theodore Roosevelt praised the Ninth and Tenth Cavalry regiments for their courage during operations in Cuba.

Anderson and his regiment returned to Manzanillo, Cuba, in mid-1899, where they served as part of the army of occupation until April 1902. He spent the next five years at Fort Mackintosh, Texas, and he also had a stint in Nebraska. In Cuba—and later in Nebraska—Anderson helped the enlisted men organize a regimental Young Men's Christian Association (YMCA) as a way for them to engage in self-help programs and to address issues such as racial inequality. In April 1907 Anderson's regiment was relocated to Fort William McKinley, near Manila in the Philippines, where he commanded the United States Morgue. Shortly after this assignment, he returned to the United States and was stationed at Fort Ethan Allen in Vermont. On 10 January 1910 he retired because of a disability that resulted from a fever he had contracted during his stay in Cuba.

Anderson returned to his home in Wilberforce and worked as an accountant and secretary to the bishop in the Third Episcopal District. In September 1916 he became the minister of Warren Chapel in Toledo, a church he had served for a short time in 1896 and 1897. He resigned from his ministry in September 1918 to offer his services to the Quartermaster Corps of the army. After the close of World War I, he led a drive to raise money for the defense of Dr. Leroy Bundy, a prominent leader of the East St. Louis black community who was charged with murder during the East St. Louis riot of 2 July 1917. He died in Cleveland in 1934, survived by his wife, Sada J. Anderson, who was also an active member of the AME Church and held several offices in the Women's Parent Mite Missionary Society. In the Cleveland area, an American Legion post was named for him.

FURTHER READING
Cashin, Herschel V., Charles Alexander, William T. Anderson, Arthur M. Brown, and Horace W. Bivins. *Under Fire with the Tenth U.S. Cavalry: Being a Brief, Comprehensive Review of the Negro's Participation in the Wars of the United States. Especially Showing the Valor and Heroism of the Negro Soldiers of the Ninth and Tenth Cavalries, and the Twenty-Fourth and Twenty-Fifth Infantries of the Regular Army* ... (1899, repr.1969).
Rudwick, Elliott. *Race Riots in East St. Louis, July 2, 1917* (1980).

SHERROW O. PINDER

Andrews, Benny (13 Nov. 1930–10 Nov. 2006), artist, was born in Madison, Georgia, the second of ten children of Viola Perryman and George Andrews, sharecroppers. Benny Andrews grew up in a household where creativity was encouraged. With what little money they had, his parents bought pens and paper for their children and encouraged them to draw and tell stories. Although not formally trained as an artist, George Andrews painted throughout his life and received considerable recognition in his later years. As a teenager Benny Andrews attended Burney Street High School only sporadically, when weather conditions excused him from his work picking cotton in the fields. In 1948 he became the first member of his family to graduate from high school.

In 1948 Andrews moved to Atlanta and was awarded a 4-H club scholarship to attend one of Georgia's three black colleges. He entered Fort Valley State College in Fort Valley, Georgia, but dropped out two years later when his scholarship ran out. He joined the United States Air Force and fought in the Korean War until 1954, when he was honorably discharged. After hearing about the Art Institute of Chicago from an army artist, he applied, and with the help of the GI Bill he enrolled in September 1954. It was in Chicago that Andrews visited a museum for the first time. In Georgia, African Americans were prohibited from entering museums.

Although Andrews attended the Art Institute of Chicago at the height of Abstract Expressionism, his real interest lay in realism, particularly the American narrative tradition of artists like Norman Rockwell, Raphael Soyer, Thomas Hart Benton, and Andrew Wyeth. While attending art school and spending time in the streets of Chicago, Andrews developed the subject matter that would occupy him throughout his life: everyday people with ordinary jobs. He carefully recorded their clothes, gestures, and expressions, and though he was particularly interested in the African American experience, he was not limited to it. While at the Art Institute of Chicago, Andrews created *Janitors at Rest*, a milestone in his development, combining collage and painting. Andrews was, however, rejected by every show, organization, and club at the institute. While in Chicago he met and began living with Mary Ellen Jones Smith, a secretary.

In 1958, after graduating from the Art Institute of Chicago, Andrews moved to New York to try his hand as a professional artist. One week after arriving in New York City he and Mary Ellen Smith had a son, Christopher. Andrews painted at home while taking care of his son while Mary Ellen went off to work as a secretary. In New York he found support for his approach to realistic subject matter and collage, as well as inspiration in the concurrent trends in abstraction and figuration. Andrews was influenced by the pop art scene and by two southerners, Jasper Johns and Robert Rauschenberg, who incorporated found objects into their paintings. *Beggar Man* (1959) exemplifies his style in this period; it portrays a beggar holding out his hand asking for money. Andrews used torn, ragged paper in the painting to symbolize urban debris. The abstract, painted collage of a beggar is a metaphor for the difference between poverty in the rural South and in New York City. Andrews also regularly sketched and painted people on the streets and jazz musicians throughout the Bowery and Greenwich Village. In August 1959 he and Smith had another son, Thomas. They married that same year, and Andrews remained the children's primary caregiver.

Andrews began to show in 1959 at group exhibitions such as the Detroit Institute's Thirteenth Biennial of Painting and Sculpture. At a New York art fair that same year he met Paul Kessler, who offered him his first one-man show at Kessler's gallery in Provincetown, Massachusetts, in 1960. Andrews eventually made his way into the New York art scene, meeting and befriending other young, aspiring artists, and he was included in contemporary exhibitions, especially many abstract expressionist shows. But his connection with older artists such as Raphael Soyer, JACOB ARMSTEAD LAWRENCE, and Chaim Gross, social realists from the 1930s and 1940s, also had an impact. He became a member of the Forum Gallery, where he met many of these older artists and eventually had a one-man show, which was well received. Andrews continued

his unique style and defied categorization; neither a realist nor an abstractionist, he drew on elements of both styles.

In the mid-1960s Andrews became increasingly interested in surrealism, particularly because of his own experience of trying to balance his life with his art and realism with abstraction. A third child, Julia, was born in June 1964, and the family moved into a five-thousand-square-foot loft. In 1965 Andrews's work was selected for the New York World's Fair. He was also awarded a John Hay Whitney Fellowship, which he used to travel back to his childhood home. His research there led to his Autobiographical Series, which focused on his black southern roots, a subject that he continued to explore throughout his life.

In the 1960s Andrews began to apply the lessons of the civil rights movement to his own world—the New York art scene. He was particularly upset that his gallery seemed to favor his use of white subject matter over black subject matter. Following the protests of black artists angry about the exclusion of African American curators and artists from Harlem on My Mind: Cultural Capital of Black America, 1900–1968—a 1969 exhibition at the Metropolitan Museum of Art—Andrews, along with Ed Taylor and Henri Ghent, formed the Black Emergency Cultural Coalition. The group protested the lack of black representation in major New York art institutions, such as the Metropolitan Museum of Art and the Whitney Museum of American Art. During this period Andrews emerged as a leader and spokesperson for social and artistic causes. Some critics labeled him a militant, which caused many galleries and collectors to turn away from his art well into the 1970s. Andrews himself pulled his work from commercial galleries and began a period of lecturing at universities and showing mainly in college and university galleries. He became a professor at Queens College in 1969. His efforts did eventually pay off; more black artists began to be shown in major New York City museums and galleries, and some black curators were hired in the 1970s. But Andrews also began to feel pigeonholed as a black artist who exhibited mainly in black art shows. However, he maintained his commitment to works with specific themes. Throughout the 1970s he worked mainly on a series titled The Bicentennial Series, portraying two hundred years of African American life. Although many artists in the 1970s were exploring the boundaries of art and experimenting with different styles, such as minimalism and earth art, Andrews continued in his personal style of painting, drawing, and collage. He also began to illustrate the novels of his brother, RAYMOND ANDREWS.

The 1980s brought new recognition to Andrews; America's artistic boundaries broadened to include more cultures and styles, and his work began to sell well, a development that experts credit to the growth of the black middle class in the 1980s. Andrews turned away from his political activism. His collages gained acceptance by a wider audience. In 1980 he was commissioned to paint a mural for the Hartsfield International Airport in Atlanta, and from 1982 to 1984 he served as the director of the visual arts program at the National Endowment for the Arts. As director he instituted programs to help young artists, including a prison program in which he brought art lessons to prisoners. In 1986, following a ten-year separation, Andrews and his wife divorced. He then married his fellow artist Nene Humphrey. Several series—Portraits of America, Revival, and Music—occupied him into the 1990s.

During the 1990s Andrews turned his attention to exhibiting with members of his family. In 1990 he showed with his father in an exhibit called Folk: The Art of Benny and George Andrews, mounted by the Memphis Brooks Museum of Art in Tennessee. He also continued his interest in helping African American art institutions and young artists by starting a foundation that finds African American artists willing to donate their work. The foundation also runs workshops for young artists, teaching them how to break into the art world. In 2001 the Ogden Museum of Southern Art in New Orleans offered Benny Andrews and his family—his wife, Nene Humphrey; his father, George; and other family members—a permanent gallery within the facility.

Benny Andrews traveled far in his life, from a sharecropper in the rural South to an established artist in New York City. His combinations of painting, drawing, and collage reflected his journey, capturing rural southern life, religious beliefs, and everyday people on the streets of New York. He brought his extraordinary penmanship and his deep sensitivity and humanity to each artwork. He died in New York City at the age of seventy-five.

FURTHER READING

Brenson, Michael. "The Collages of Benny Andrews," *New York Times*, 4 Nov. 1988.

Fox, Catherine. "A Sharecropper's Son Goes the Distance," *Atlanta Constitution*, 20 May 1982.

Gruber, Richard J. *American Icons: From Madison to Manhattan, the Art of Benny Andrews, 1948–1997* (1997).

Tully, Judd. "Benny Andrews," *American Artist* 52 (Apr. 1988).

SARAH WOLOZIN

Andrews, Ludie (1875–1943?), nursing educator and administrator, was born in Milledgeville, Georgia, the daughter of a poor family about whom nothing is known. In 1901 Andrews applied to Spelman College's MacVicar Hospital School of Nursing. On her application, she asked for financial assistance, explaining that her family could not help her pay. Her mother had a large family to support and "an old flicted husband," who was not Andrews's father. Andrews also said that she had been married but did not currently live with her husband and expected no support from him. Letters praising Andrews and talking about her "good moral character" that came from the pillars of Milledgeville society proved instrumental in securing Andrews's admission.

In 1906 Andrews received her diploma from Spelman and set upon her life's work. During her training she resolved "that I wanted to work for my people, how or where this was to be done I did not know." She did not have to wait long to find out. After caring for only two private cases—the bread and butter of black nurses in that time period—Andrews was offered the position of superintendent of Lula Grove Hospital and Training School for Colored Nurses and Patients.

Located in Atlanta, the school, which was run by a group of white physicians who served on the faculty of the Atlanta School of Medicine, was one of the few health facilities in the area open to African Americans. Andrews quickly developed a reputation for excellence both in administration and on the surgical floor. Howard Kelly, an internationally known surgeon and professor from Johns Hopkins University, helped cement that reputation after Andrews assisted him on an operation. At the end of the procedure, he proclaimed, "I have never been better served even by nurses that I myself have trained."

Knowing that white and black nurses had equal skills, Andrews started a crusade to allow black nurses to take the same state medical exam as white nurses in 1909. Some proposed that black nurses take a different test than their white counterparts. Andrews did not accept that suggestion, pointing out that this scenario would make it difficult for graduates of black nursing schools in Georgia to find jobs in other states. The state board then offered to issue her a license. Again Andrews refused, saying she wanted that opportunity for all black nurses. When the state board refused to change its policy, Andrews instituted legal proceedings, a case she eventually won.

When the city of Atlanta opened the 250-bed Grady Hospital in 1914, Andrews was a natural choice to serve as superintendent of colored nurses for the facility. Always cognizant of opportunities for women like herself, Andrews spearheaded the establishment of Grady Hospital's Municipal Training School for Colored Nurses in 1917. Grady had a nursing school, founded in 1892, but that institution allowed only white women to apply.

Once more, Andrews earned kudos from her physician colleagues. One doctor, W. B. Symmerall, said "her services were of the highest character; she showed ability in organization and in administration. I always found her thoroughly devoted to her duties; she had high ideals in regard to the work of her people and the nursing profession."

In 1920 Andrews not only won her case against the state medical board but she also received one of the more coveted positions in black nursing, the superintendency of Morehouse College's infirmary. As a faculty member, Andrews also taught home and community hygiene in the summer program for teachers and the school of social work. She did not restrict her message to students enrolled at Morehouse. A frequent lecturer on public health throughout the community, Andrews delivered a variant on that lecture in the Neighborhood Union. Her efforts in public health went beyond the theoretical. She served on the Tuberculosis Association, chairing its relief committee and helping to raise money for patients. She also was a member of an interracial committee that worked with troubled women who had ended up in prisons or in medical wards. Andrews continued to champion the cause of black nurses throughout her life. She served on the committee of several nursing organizations as a representative of the National Association of Colored Graduate Nurses. In that capacity she lobbied for equal treatment of black nurses before the American Nursing Association, the National League of Nursing Education, and the National Organization for Public Health Nursing. In 1926 Andrews suggested to the American Nursing Association that it allow black nurses who could not join their local chapters because of discrimination to join the national group. Her lifetime of hard work on behalf of black nurses made Andrews a natural choice for the Colored Nursing Association's Mary Mahoney Award in 1943, which she received shortly before she died.

FURTHER READING

Carnegie, Mary Elizabeth. *The Path We Tread: Blacks in Nursing Worldwide, 1854–1994* (1995).

Hine, Darlene Clark. *Black Women in White: Racial Conflict and Cooperation in the Nursing Profession, 1890–1950* (1989).

Staupers, Mabel Keaton. *No Time for Prejudice: A Story of the Integration of Negroes in Nursing in the United States* (1961).

Thoms, Adah B. *Pathfinders: A History of the Progress of Colored Graduate Nurses* (1929).

This entry is taken from the *American National Biography* and is published here with the permission of the American Council of Learned Societies.

SHARI RUDAVSKY

Andrews, Raymond (6 June 1934–26 Nov. 1991), writer, was born in Plainview, Georgia, in Morgan County, the fourth of ten children of George Cleveland Andrews, a sharecropper and self-taught folk artist, and Viola (Perryman) Andrews, also a sharecropper and, later, a newspaper columnist and the author of published short stories and an unpublished autobiography. Raymond's older brother, BENNY ANDREWS, would become an internationally known painter and printmaker. Raymond Andrews's paternal grandmother, Jessie Rose Lee Wildcat Tennessee, was the daughter of an African American mother and a Native American father. Although she married Eddie Andrews, an African American who died in 1917, Raymond Andrews's paternal grandfather was James Orr, a plantation owner's son.

In 1935 Andrews and his family moved to a small house near his grandmother's home on land owned by Orr. Then in 1943 the Andrews family moved to the nearby Barnett Farm to work as sharecroppers. The family endured the hardships of sharecropping, yet the Andrewses, unlike most of their neighbors, read newspapers and magazines and owned a radio.

Andrews started school in 1939; the first through the seventh grades for African American children were taught at Plainview Lower Church. Like most of the other students at Plainview, he only attended school when he did not have to work in the fields. Attending school also meant that Andrews and his schoolmates had to walk to and from school because Georgia did not provide school buses for black children. Andrews discovered that African Americans wrote books after reading about RICHARD WRIGHT's *Black Boy* in an issue of *Life* magazine, and became an avid sports fan after being inspired by JOE LOUIS's status as one of the nation's first African American celebrities. After completing seventh grade at Plainview Elementary, Andrews attended Burney Street High School, the African American secondary institution in the nearby city of Madison.

On 4 December 1949 Andrews, then fifteen, moved to Atlanta, for the first time riding a Greyhound bus and traveling more than five miles from home. Andrews resided at Atlanta's Butler Street YMCA, where another older brother, Harvey, also lived. During the day Andrews was employed as a hospital orderly; at night he attended Booker T. Washington High School and earned his diploma.

From 1952 to 1956 Andrews served in the U.S. Air Force, stationed in Korea. Following his discharge he attended Michigan State University for one year before moving to New York in 1957. The next year his brother Benny also moved to New York. Raymond Andrews held a variety of jobs while living in New York, including working as a reservations agent for KLM Royal Dutch Airlines. His position with the airline allowed him to travel to such European locations as the Netherlands and Switzerland. Andrews worked for the airline for eight years, quitting on his thirty-second birthday in 1966 in order to pursue his dream of becoming a professional writer. That same year Andrews's article about football in Plainview, "Yesterday: A Football Rebellion in Backwoods Georgia," was published in the 7 November issue of *Sports Illustrated*. One month later, on 28 December 1966 in New York City, he married Adelheid "Heidi" Wenger, who was also an airline agent. The couple divorced in 1980.

Although Andrews continued to work various jobs from 1967 to 1984, writing remained his priority. In addition to *Sports Illustrated*, his work appeared in magazines such as *Athens Magazine*, *Atlanta Review*, *Ataraxia*, *Catalyst*, and *Harper's* and in newspapers like the *Atlanta Journal-Constitution*. In 1978 his first novel, *Appalachee Red* (originally titled *Red, White, and Blue*), was published. The novel received Dial Press's first JAMES BALDWIN Prize for Fiction at a ceremony attended by Baldwin himself. After Andrews's impressive debut as a novelist, a number of literary critics hailed him as one of America's most promising novelists. Starting

with *Appalachee Red*, Andrews published five books in a thirteen-year period, each illustrated by his brother, Benny Andrews. *Appalachee Red* was the beginning of his Muskhogean County trilogy, which included *Rosiebelle Lee Wildcat Tennessee* in 1980 and *Baby Sweet's* in 1983. His 1990 memoir *The Last Radio Baby* and two novellas, *Jessie and Jesus and Cousin Claire* in 1991, followed. A second memoir was published posthumously in the *Chattahoochee Review* in 1998.

Andrews left New York for Georgia in 1984, settling near Athens. In 1991, one month after the publication of his two novellas, Andrews, who was fifty-seven years old and in poor health, committed suicide. At the time of his death, he was writing another novel, *99 Years and a Dark Day*. He devoted his literary career to paying homage to his rural Georgia roots and providing glimpses into African American life in the South during the twentieth century.

From 28 September 2001 to 12 January 2002, the Robert W. Woodruff Library at Emory University in Atlanta mounted the exhibit "The Mother is Like a Vine in Thy Blood: Viola P. Andrews and the Andrews Family," which documented the family's history via their written and visual works.

FURTHER READING

Raymond Andrews's papers are housed in Emory University's Manuscript, Archives, and Rare Book Library, in Atlanta, Georgia.

Andrews, Raymond. *The Last Radio Baby: A Memoir* (1990).

Andrews, Raymond. "Once Upon a Time in Atlanta," *Chattahoochee Review* 18.2 (Winter 1998).

Camp, Lynn Robinson. *Morgan County, Georgia* (2004).

LINDA M. CARTER

Angelou, Maya (4 Apr. 1928–), writer, poet, and performer, was born Marguerite Annie Johnson in St. Louis, Missouri, the second of two children of Bailey Johnson, a doorman and a naval dietician, and Vivian Baxter Johnson, a card dealer who later became a registered nurse. Her parents called her "Rita," but her brother, Bailey, who was only a year older, called her "My Sister," which was eventually contracted to "Maya." When Maya was three years old, she and Bailey were sent to Stamps, Arkansas, to live with their paternal grandmother, Annie Henderson, whom Maya often referred to as "Mother." Mrs. Henderson was a strong, independent black woman who owned a

Maya Angelou at an interview in her New York apartment, 29 January 2002. (AP Images.)

country store, in which Maya lived and worked. Maya was a bright student and an avid reader; she absorbed the contradictory messages of love emanating from the Christian Methodist Episcopal Church and of hatred, revealed in the pervasive mistreatment of blacks by their white neighbors. In 1935 Maya returned to live with her mother in Chicago, until it was discovered that the eight-year-old had been raped by her mother's lover, Mr. Freeman, in whose care she was often left. Freeman was murdered, probably by Maya's uncles, after she testified in court. The trauma of the attack, the trial, and the misplaced guilt she felt for the death of the man who had abused her trust caused Maya to withdraw into an almost complete silence. She was sent back to Arkansas, where for the next four years she rarely spoke. By reading literature and poetry to her, Mrs. Bertha Flowers, a local, sophisticated black woman with impressive elocution, helped renew a love of language in a girl many believed to be mute.

At the age of thirteen Maya was at the top of her class when she and Bailey went again to live with their mother, who had by then moved to San Francisco.

She attended George Washington High School and studied dance and drama at the California Labor School. She spent a summer with her father, but violent quarrels with his girlfriend compelled Maya to run away, preferring to live in an abandoned van for a month. In 1944 she temporarily dropped out of school and got a job as a streetcar conductor (becoming the first black woman in San Francisco to hold that position). As an adolescent she was almost six feet tall, insecure, desperate for affection, and confused about her sexuality. In this emotional state, she began an intimate relationship with a male acquaintance and became pregnant at the age of sixteen. Yet with indomitable determination she returned to school and graduated one month before giving birth to her only child, Clyde.

Angelou's journey to adulthood became the basis of her first and most celebrated autobiographical novel, *I Know Why the Caged Bird Sings* (1970), which was nominated for a National Book Award and named from a line in the poem "Sympathy," by PAUL LAURENCE DUNBAR. This book was soon followed by *Gather Together in My Name* (1974), which continues her odyssey. Angelou takes the reader through her postwar years as a single mother working as a cook at a Creole café in San Diego. She attempted to join the army and tried to retreat to Arkansas, the place of past comfort, only to learn that as an adult her lack of racial deference endangered her and those she loved. In 1947 her early efforts to become an entertainer led her into a world of drug use. During this period she became a madam for two lesbian demimondaines, and an abusive relationship with a man briefly plunged her into a life of prostitution. The narrative ends at the close of the 1940s with Angelou pulling her life together, as the religiously inspired title implies.

In 1950 Angelou began a three-year marriage to a former Greek sailor, Tosh Angelos ("Angelou" is a variant of his name), recounted in her third autobiographical volume, *Singin' and Swingin' and Gettin' Merry Like Christmas* (1976). Her singing and dancing career began to show promise when she became a calypso performer at the Purple Onion in San Francisco. This led to bookings in Chicago and ultimately at the Village Vanguard in New York. She moved to New York to study dance with PEARL PRIMUS and in 1954 landed a role in the George Gershwin opera *Porgy and Bess*, which toured Europe until 1955. When she returned to the United States, her career was progressing, but her failed marriage and frequent separations from her son evoked troubling memories of her own childhood. The book ends on a note of reconciliation and redemption as she sets out with her son on a Hawaiian cruise.

A fourth volume, *The Heart of a Woman* (1981), begins shortly after her return from Europe, when an old friend brings BILLIE HOLIDAY to Angelou's small San Francisco apartment for lunch. In this passage Angelou's skills as a writer are particularly evident. She recalls events with astonishing detail and relates them in an authentic and compelling style as her prose shifts between Standard English and the black vernacular she summons when its effect is most appropriate. Her ear for the particular speech patterns of her characters is evident in her re-creation of Billie Holiday's sassy and salty manner. These lively narrative qualities are sustained as the scene shifts to Brooklyn, where she moved in 1957 to appear in the off-Broadway play *Calypso Heatwave*. While in New York she joined the Harlem Writers Guild, whose members included JAMES BALDWIN, PAULE MARSHALL, and JOHN HENRIK CLARKE. This intellectual environment nurtured her literary interests and shaped her political activism. In 1960 she played a leading role in staging *Freedom Cabaret*, a revue she wrote to raise money to help MARTIN LUTHER KING JR. and the civil rights movement.

A few months later BAYARD RUSTIN nominated her to become the northern coordinator for the Southern Christian Leadership Conference. She held this position for a few months, but in May 1961 she was offered the role of White Queen in Jean Genet's Obie Award–winning play *The Blacks*, which had a cast that included JAMES EARL JONES and CICELY TYSON. However, soon after the production began, she left because of a monetary dispute with the director. Angelou's common-law husband at the time, the South African freedom fighter Vusumzi Make, did not want his wife to work, insisting that "no wife of an African leader can go on the stage" (Angelou, *The Heart of a Woman*, 205). Angelou found out that Make could not support the family without her income shortly before their move to Cairo, Egypt, in late 1961, when she discovered that they were being evicted from their Manhattan apartment.

In Cairo, Angelou became disillusioned by the chauvinism of black nationalists and defied her controlling, philandering husband by taking a job as the associate editor of the *Arab Observer*, an English-language newspaper. In 1963 she left Make and moved to Accra, Ghana, where she worked for the University of Ghana and became an editor of the *African Review* and a contributor to the *Ghanaian Times* and the Ghanaian Broadcasting Company. She arranged the itinerary for her friend MALCOLM X during his visit to Ghana, and she enjoyed a close relationship with the family of W. E. B. DuBois, who had expatriated from the United States to live in Ghana some years earlier. Angelou returned to the United States in 1966 to continue her career in the theater; however, James Baldwin urged her to pursue her writing. Angelou's penultimate final autobiographical volume, *All God's Children Need Traveling Shoes* (1986), recounts her sojourn in Africa. Her final autobiography, *A Song Flung Up to Heaven* (2002), documents the tumultuous events after Angelou returned to America to help Malcolm X and the Organization of African-American Unity. Angelou describes in vivid detail the period between the assassinations of Malcolm X and Martin Luther King Jr., and brings us to the verge of her literary stardom.

David Levering Lewis has argued that Angelou's work is prominent within a grand tradition of African American autobiography extending from the slave narratives of FREDERICK DOUGLASS and HARRIET JACOBS, through the early modern memoirs of BOOKER T. WASHINGTON and the somewhat fictionalized autobiography of ZORA NEALE HURSTON, to the contemporary *Autobiography of Malcolm X*. While she incorporates the elements of triumphalism that one typically finds in the slave narratives and some of the determined individualism of the Horatio Alger genre, Angelou mingles Brer Rabbit savvy with resilient love to produce books that reveal harsh realities about race and gender in American life.

Most of her literary acclaim focuses on her autobiographies, but Angelou has also published nine volumes of poetry, including *Just Give Me a Cool Drink of Water 'fore I Diiie* (1971), which was nominated for a Pulitzer Prize, and the noteworthy *And Still I Rise* (1978), which contains the very popular title poem and the often recited "Phenomenal Woman." In addition, she received a Tony Award nomination for her role in the Broadway play *Look Away* in 1973 and an Emmy Award nomination for her performance in ALEX HALEY's *Roots* in 1977. She became the first woman and the only African American to read a poem at a presidential inauguration when President Bill Clinton invited her to read "On the Pulse of Morning" in 1993. Two years later she was one of the few women to speak at LOUIS FARRAKHAN's Million Man March, where—despite her own unhappy relationships—she affirmed her hope for the black family.

When her eight-year marriage to the British builder Paul Du Fue ended in divorce in 1981, Angelou moved to North Carolina, where she became the Reynolds Professor of American Studies at Wake Forest University. She has remained a prolific writer, performer, and speaker well into her eighties.

In the 2008 Democratic presidential primary, Angelou was a prominent supporter of her long time friend, Senator Hillary Clinton (D-NY), but enthusiastically endorsed Clinton's opponent, BARACK OBAMA (D-IL), once he became the party's nominee. In 2008 she was honored with the Ford's Theatre Society Lincoln Medal. Her cultural output continued, working with scholar MOLEFI K. ASANTE on a film, *The Black Candle: A Kwanzaa Celebration* (2008), which she narrated and for which she composed several new poems. She has also published *Letter to My Daughter,* (2009) a poignant volume dedicated to the daughter she never had, and a cookbook, *Great Food, All Day Long: Cook Splendidly, Eat Smart* (2010). Angelou, who in 2010 donated her personal papers to New York's Schomburg Collection, was the recipient of

the nation's highest civilian award, the Presidential Medal of Freedom, in 2011.

FURTHER READING
Angelou, Maya. *All God's Children Need Traveling Shoes* (1986).
Angelou, Maya. *Gather Together in My Name* (1974).
Angelou, Maya. *The Heart of a Woman* (1981).
Angelou, Maya. *I Know Why the Caged Bird Sings* (1970).
Angelou, Maya. *Singin' and Swingin' and Gettin' Merry Like Christmas* (1976).
Bloom, Harold, ed. *Modern Critical Views: Maya Angelou* (1999).
Lupton, Mary Jane. *Maya Angelou: A Critical Companion* (1998).

SHOLOMO B. LEVY

Ansa, Tina McElroy (18 Nov. 1949–), novelist, journalist, and educator, was born in Macon, Georgia, the youngest child of Walter J. McElroy, an entrepreneur and business owner, and Nellie Lee McElroy, a teaching assistant. Ansa grew up surrounded by storytellers. Her grandfather was one, and the patrons of her father's neighborhood juke joint often shared the tales of their seedy lives.

This love of storytelling remained with Ansa as she pursued a B.A. in English at the historically black Spelman College in Atlanta. There, Ansa was introduced to the writing of ZORA NEALE HURSTON by her professor GLORIA WADE-GAYLES, an introduction that continued to shape Ansa's appreciation for the art of storytelling and folk tradition in the African American community, and one that would influence her own writing style tremendously. After completing her degree in 1971 Ansa became the first African American woman hired to work for the *Atlanta Constitution* (later the *Atlanta Journal-Constitution*). Ansa occupied several different positions during her years of employment with Georgia's most prominent newspaper, including copyeditor, makeup editor, layout editor, features editor, news reporter, and entertainment writer. Her work at the paper was the beginning of her career as a professional writer.

On 1 May 1978 Tina McElroy married Joneé Ansa, a cinematographer and graduate of the American Film Institute. After completing eight years at the Atlanta paper, Ansa accepted a position as an editor for the *Charlotte Observer* in North Carolina. In 1982 Ansa decided to market herself as a freelance journalist in order to free enough time to pursue a career in creative writing. She began to attend writing workshops and to submit her short fiction for publication, only to receive many rejection letters. Ansa returned to Georgia two years later and took residence on St. Simons Island, one of Georgia's famous Golden Isles.

Ansa published her first book-length project, *Not Soon Forgotten: Cotton Planters and Plantations of the Golden Isles of Georgia, 1784–1812*, for the Georgia Historical Society in 1987. The project piqued Ansa's interest in the history and legacy of her surroundings. Taking pride in the black folk life and history of the region, Ansa and her husband produced and directed the first of a now decades-old event in 1989; the Georgia Sea Island Festival is an attempt to preserve the cultural life and lore of the enslaved African communities that inhabited the rice, indigo, and cotton plantations along the Georgia coast.

Ansa's career as a novelist began to take shape shortly after attending a writing workshop in Macon with JOHN OLIVER KILLENS. Writers with Roots in Georgia, a local program that sponsored writers native to the state on the college lecture circuit, recruited Killens as a writer-in-residence at Mercer College. Ansa had long claimed Killens as her mentor, though she had never met him. Killens and Ansa's father attended high school together and graduated in the same class, so Ansa had known of Killens and his writing from a young age. Ansa revised a short story titled "Mamie" in the workshop with Killens; that story later became a chapter in her debut novel, *Baby of the Family* (1989).

Baby of the Family centers on the trials of young Lena McPherson, who is born with a caul, or thin membrane of the amniotic sac, over her face, an occurrence that according to African American folk beliefs signifies a connection to the supernatural. Ansa herself was born with a caul over her face and grew up hearing much of the lore surrounding the peculiarity of such a birth. In the book she explores the loss and disregard of tradition and the repercussions of such actions. The novel was named a Notable Book of the Year by the *New York Times* and also won the 1989 Georgia Authors Series Award.

In the fall of 1990 Ansa returned to Spelman as a writer-in-residence. She taught creative writing courses and continued to teach and supervise writing workshops at Emory University and Brunswick College. She also taught courses on mass media and communications. In 1993 Ansa published *Ugly Ways*, a novel that challenges the sanctity of motherhood by questioning what it means and what happens when women like Esther "Mudear" Lovejoy bring unorthodox convictions to the art of childrearing. Ansa and the actress Alfre Woodard negotiated a deal to bring *Ugly Ways* to the screen. Another work, *The Hand I Fan With* (1996), is the playful journey into the adult life of Lena McPherson, who continues to clash with the spirit world. In order to reconcile her mother's mishandling of her birth caul, and thus Lena's spiritual prowess, Herman—a hundred-year-old ghost—is sent to help Lena find her way. *The Hand I Fan With* received the 1996 Georgia Authors Series Award; Ansa is the only author to win the award twice. *You Know Better* (2002) confronts the divide between parents and children in the contemporary world, taking up the issue of what might be termed failed parenting in the African American community. All of Ansa's novels are set in the fictional town of Mulberry, Georgia, which is modeled after her beloved Macon. In a similar vein as TONI MORRISON, ALICE MALSENIOR WALKER, and Zora Neale Hurston, Ansa incorporates African American vernacular traditions and folklore as primary elements in her work. She calls her work "blackfolkcentric," asserting that her stories begin and end with black folks (Ansa, 26).

Ansa's work has garnered critical attention at the Schomburg Center, the Richard Wright/Zora Neale Hurston Foundation, and the Smithsonian's African American Center. Ansa's feature articles, reviews, and editorials have appeared in the *Atlanta Journal-Constitution*, the *Los Angeles Times*, and other newspapers. Her essays, "Postcards from Georgia," have been featured on CBS' *Sunday Morning*. Interweaving the land, legends, and heritage of Georgia, Ansa's novels situate her not only as one of Georgia's most prominent women writers next to Flannery O'Connor and Alice Walker but also as a valuable link in a chain of African American literary women who infuse and thus preserve the ways of the folk in their writing.

FURTHER READING

Ansa, Tina McElroy. "Tina McElroy Ansa," in *I Know What the Red Clay Looks Like: The Voice and Vision of Black Women Writers*, ed. Rebecca Carroll (1994).

Cherry, Joyce L. "Tina McElroy Ansa," in *Contemporary African American Novelists: A Bio-bibliographical Critical Source Book*, ed. Emmanuel Nelson (1999).

Jordan, Shirley Marie. *Broken Silences: Interviews with Black and White Women Writers* (1993).

Mosby, Charmaine Allmon. "Tina McElroy Ansa," in *Contemporary Southern Writers*, ed. Roger Matuz (1999).

KAMEELAH L. MARTIN

Antoine, Caesar Carpetier (1836–Sept. 1921), Union army officer and politician, was born in New Orleans, the son of a West Indian midwife and a free black soldier who had served in the Corps d'Afrique with General Andrew Jackson in the War of 1812. His parents' names are not recorded. Family lore had it that Caesar's maternal grandfather, an African chief, had been enslaved and taken to America and that his paternal grandmother, Rose Antoine, had earned enough money from her work as a midwife to purchase her freedom. Rose Antoine also left each of her seven sons twenty thousand dollars in her will.

As a free black child in New Orleans, Antoine attended private schools—the public schools of the city were closed to blacks—and became fluent in both English and French. Upon leaving school as a teenager in the early 1850s he then apprenticed and worked as a barber, one of the more lucrative trades open to free blacks, until Union forces entered Louisiana in winter 1862. Within forty-eight hours of a Confederate move on Union positions, Antoine closed his barber shop to organize a company of black federal troops, Company I of the Seventh Regiment, Louisiana Militia. The company, in which Antoine served as captain, was also known as the Corps d'Afrique, perhaps in honor of his father's regiment. Antoine earned a reputation as one of the most accomplished black combat officers, though that did not prevent the Union general Nathaniel Banks from attempting to dismiss all black commissioned officers in Louisiana in mid-1864. C. C. Antoine, his brother Felix Antoine, and his friend P. B. S. PINCHBACK were among several black officers who resigned their commissions in protest.

Antoine's interest in political affairs appears to have begun at this time, and in January 1865 he was one of fifty delegates to the Convention of Colored Men of Louisiana, which met in New Orleans to demand political rights for the freedmen. Antoine also helped to launch a short-lived newspaper, the *New Orleans Black Republican*, which—perhaps surprisingly given Antoine's earlier resignation—was supportive of General Banks's tenure as Louisiana's military governor.

After the war and the failure of the *Black Republican*, Antoine moved to Shreveport, Louisiana, where he established a grocery and was elected as a delegate from Caddo Parish to the Louisiana constitutional convention, which met from 1867 to 1868. In the elections that followed in 1868 Antoine was elected to the state senate from Caddo Parish and quickly emerged as one of the leading black Republicans in the Louisiana legislature. Antoine's brother Felix was elected to the Louisiana House of Representatives the same year. In the senate Antoine worked to increase spending on higher education and to expand the powers of local government. His skills as a legislator were recognized in 1872 when he was elected lieutenant governor of Louisiana. He served briefly as acting governor and along with state representative THÉOPHILE ALLAIN was prominent in the unification movement of 1873, a doomed effort to forge a new moderate political coalition between wealthy white and black businessmen.

While he was lieutenant governor Antoine studied for and received a law degree at Straight University (later Dillard) in New Orleans and was appointed to the Caddo Parish school board in 1875. It is quite possible that Antoine again received the majority of Louisiana's votes for lieutenant governor in the controversial 1876 elections, which effectively left the state with two rival governments. Antoine and Stephen Packard, the Republican candidate for governor, were removed from office in 1877, however, as part of the compromise that elected the Republican Rutherford B. Hayes as U.S. president and ended Republican rule in Louisiana and other Southern states.

While serving in the senate and as lieutenant governor, Antoine's business interests prospered. In partnership with Pinchback he owned a newspaper, the *New Orleans Louisianian*, and a prosperous cotton brokerage. He also raised several racehorses, which he entered, with varying degrees of success, in several contests. After Reconstruction, Antoine fell on hard times, forcing his wife, whose name is not known, to petition President Hayes to find a federal position for her husband. She did not succeed, but in 1882 Antoine found work as president of the Cosmopolitan Insurance Association in New Orleans. Yet this company also fared poorly, no doubt in part because its officers no longer carried the political clout that they had enjoyed during Reconstruction.

In the 1890s Antoine returned to political prominence as vice president of the Comité de Citoyens, an organization opposed to Louisiana's newly enacted segregation and antimiscegenation laws. In 1892 the Comité raised funds to assist HOMER PLESSY's ultimately unsuccessful legal challenge to the constitutionality of the segregation laws. In 1896, the same year that the U.S. Supreme Court upheld the doctrine of "separate but equal" in *Plessy v. Ferguson*, Antoine attended the Republican National Convention.

Caesar Carpetier Antoine died in Shreveport, the owner of a small plantation and some real estate. His wealth and renown was greater than that of most African Americans in Louisiana at that time, but much less, surely, than he might have enjoyed had not Reconstruction—and Antoine's political career—ended so abruptly four decades earlier.

FURTHER READING

Information on Antoine can be found in The Honorable C. C. Antoine Scrapbook, Black Heritage Room, Southern University, Baton Rouge.

Blassingame, John. *Black New Orleans, 1860–1880* (1973).

Vincent, Charles. *Black Legislators in Louisiana during Reconstruction* (1976).

STEVEN J. NIVEN

Antoine, Felix C. (1839–Apr. 1917), a Civil War soldier and veterans leader and Reconstruction-era legislator, was born and lived all of his life in Louisiana. Felix Antoine was born into the distinct community of gens de couleur libre, free persons of color, which existed in the New Orleans area and some other parts of Louisiana since French colonial times. His father was a veteran of the War of 1812, who fought under General Andrew Jackson at the Battle of New Orleans, and his mother was a native of the West Indies. His paternal grandmother was reputed to have been the daughter of an African prince, who purchased her freedom from slavery; she saved $150,000 as a free woman (*Shreveport Journal* obituary of C.C. Antoine, 14 Sept. 1921). Antoine was the younger brother of Louisiana Lt. Governor CAESAR C. ANTOINE, who moved from New Orleans to Shreveport prior to his first election to the legislature.

In 1860 twenty-two-year-old Antoine lived in Orleans Parish with his eighteen-year-old wife (1860 Census), born Elizabeth Hutchinson, whose father was from Scotland and mother from Maryland (1900 Census, although the 1880 Census says they were both native to Louisiana). They lived in a neighborhood of skilled tradesmen (a shoemaker, bricklayer, carpenter, and butcher, plus a wine merchant and two laborers) who were recorded as "white." About half, like the "mulatto" Antoines, were native to Louisiana. The rest had

immigrated from France, Germany, and Ireland or moved from Pennsylvania, New York, and South Carolina. Antoine owned $800 in real property and $200 in personal property—at least three of his neighbors owned more, but most owned no real property at all.

He enlisted in Company B, Seventh Louisiana Infantry, on 3 July 1863, with the rank of lieutenant, while his older brother organized Company I of the same regiment, serving as captain. The duration and extent of their military service are clouded by incomplete information and shifting policies. Louisiana had a history of free colored regiments dating to 1729, which were reconstituted for Confederate service in 1861, supplying their own uniforms, weapons, horses, and ammunition. There is no record that either of the Antoine brothers volunteered for the Native Guards, but many did; the confederate government refused to accept them. When the United States recovered control of New Orleans in April 1862, the First, Second, and Third Native Guards immediately offered to serve in the federal army. Unlike the later United States Colored Troops, the Louisiana regiments all had commissioned officers of color. Regiments formed in 1863, including the Seventh, also had colored officers.

The Seventh Louisiana Infantry was initially enrolled for sixty days on 19 July 1863. Although General Benjamin Butler accepted colored officers, his successor, General Nathaniel Banks, worked aggressively to remove them, in favor of officers deemed to be "white." Felix C. Antoine resigned his commission in protest, along with many others, before being dismissed by Banks. It is not clear whether he served in the reconstituted Seventh Infantry, organized 1 December 1863, in the Memphis area. His name does not appear in the muster rolls of the Sixty-Fourth United States Colored Troops, formed from the Seventh Infantry on 11 March 1864, but the record of his wife's widow's pension of 21 May 1917 does show service in the Sixty-Fourth. Existing records show induction and discharge, both with the rank of lieutenant (USNA, Civil War Service, Box 387, Extraction 1, Record 287) and second lieutenant (USNA, Civil War Service, Box 589, Extraction 3, Record 411).

Federal officers and administrators refused to consider free people of color as a distinct class. When the first restored Louisiana government attempted to perpetuate slavery in all but name by adoption of "Black Codes," it likewise replaced enslavement with general racial designation as the legal standard. Felix C. Antoine shared the determination of gens de couleur libre that if classed with the freedmen, they would provide political and social leadership, being the most educated property owners among those now universally designated colored, black, or Negro. Of twenty-four colored state senators during Reconstruction, only three had formerly been enslaved, and a similar proportion of state representatives existed. Antoine served in the Louisiana state house of representatives from 1868 to 1872, one of nine colored representatives from Orleans Parish.

Antoine chaired the Committee of Elections and Qualifications in the 1871 session with seven members, of which two others shared his complexion and social background. Four weeks into the session, he was the only house committee chair of color, after a tumultuous struggle over the speakership; initially, nine of thirty committee chairs had been colored. Later, he served for a time as recorder of births and deaths, but was dismissed from this post in 1874 by Governor William Kellogg, the state's last Reconstruction governor. Kellogg's reasons are not clear, but a rally was organized in New Orleans to protest the action. This was the same year that the "White League" organized a violent takeover of the state government, which was reversed only by the intervention of federal troops to restore Kellogg, a weak Republican who was later elected to the U.S. senate by his former Democratic opponents.

When Reconstruction came to an end in Louisiana, as in most of the states that had at one time adhered to the failed confederate government, Antoine obtained a job as a nighttime customs house inspector, which he held for the rest of his life. The customs house had been a political base for a faction in the Republican Party, which supported President Ulysses S. Grant, and included Caesar Antoine, as well as Kellogg. Their rivals included Governor Henry Warmoth and state senator and lieutenant governor Pinchback, although Pinchback was a friend and business partner of Caesar Antoine. Felix Antoine's family had grown in 1880 to include four children, from newborn Felix, Jr. to sixteen-year-old Louis. Living in the household were a washerwoman and a laborer, who may have been either boarders or house servants.

In 1900 Antoine served as commander of the Department of Mississippi and Louisiana, Grand Army of the Republic (GAR), an organization of U.S. armed forces veterans who served in the Civil War. The GAR officially was color-blind in membership, although many local posts were segregated.

As department commander, Antoine supervised all posts in both states. A previous commander of the same department, George T. Hodges, had advocated racially segregated departments for southern GAR members, saying it would ease membership for veterans who were thought of as "white," surrounded by larger numbers of confederate veterans. The 1891 national encampment in Detroit refused to endorse the proposal. The ambivalence of even the GAR on race was reflected in the statement by Edward R. Salomon, commander of the Department of California, at the national encampment in St. Louis in 1887, that "I would rather shake hands with the darkest nigger in the land if he was a true and honest man, than with a traitor" (Shaffer, 146–148). It was taken as faint praise by the comrades he referred to. Antoine, whose son Louis, a daughter-in-law, granddaughter, and three nieces shared his house in 1910, died in 1917, survived by his wife, Elizabeth.

FURTHER READING

Blassingame, John W. *Black New Orleans, 1860–1880* (1973).

Brasseaux, Carl A. *Creoles of Color in the Bayou Country* (1996).

Ripley, C. Peter. *Slaves and Freedmen in Civil War Louisiana* (1976).

Shaffer, Donald Robert. *After the Glory: The Struggles of Black Civil War Veterans* (2004).

Vincent, Charles. *Black Legislators in Louisiana during Reconstruction* (1976).

CHARLES ROSENBERG

Appiah, Kwame Anthony (8 May 1954–), novelist, philosopher, and scholar was born in London, England, to Joe Appiah, a Ghanaian barrister and statesman, and Peggy Cripps, novelist and daughter of Sir Stafford Cripps, a British statesman. Not long after Appiah's birth, his family relocated to Ghana, where he attended primary school. After the political imprisonment of his father by then-president Kwame Nkrumah, Appiah returned to England. There he completed his secondary education at Bryanston, a British boarding school.

Influenced by his mother's affinity for the literary arts, Appiah read works of authors such as Chinua Achebe, D. H. Lawrence, and Leo Tolstoy. Visitors to the Appiah residence included the Pan-Africanist authors and theorists C. L. R. JAMES and RICHARD WRIGHT. Appiah's multiethnic family and early fascination with literature helped shape his identity and his worldview. In 1972 he entered

Cambridge University, where he earned both a B.A. and a Ph.D. in Philosophy in 1975 and 1982, respectively, becoming the first person of African descent to have earned a Ph.D. in Philosophy from the university. As an undergraduate he met HENRY LOUIS GATES JR., with whom he would later collaborate on a number of projects.

In 1985 Cambridge University Press published Appiah's first book, his revised dissertation *Assertion and Conditionals*, which explores the idea that assertion is simply the articulation of belief systems, and an understanding of an assertion implies the understanding of the belief systems it expresses. Though his earlier work focused on semantics and logic, Appiah's later efforts were grounded in cultural identity and race. Published in 1992, *In My Father's House: Africa in the Philosophy of Culture*, a compilation of racially motivated and charged essays that explore notions of identity, race, and culture, is regarded as a philosophical classic on multiculturalism. A semi-autobiography together with cultural criticism and postcolonial theory, *In My Father's House*, is a well-known and respected book among most Africana Studies circles. Written in the 1980s, a time when race-based dialogue was uncommon and much less acceptable, *In My Father's House* explores African identity in the context of globalization. The book was honored by the the Modern Language Association and awarded the Annisfeld-Wolf Book Award and the African Studies Association's Herskovits Award.

Appiah, along with Amy Gutmann, a Princeton colleague, was awarded the North American Society Annual Book Award for Social Philosophy (1996), the American Political Science Association's Ralph J. Bunche Award (1997), and the Gustavus Myers Award for the Study of Human Rights (1998) for their collaboration, *Color Conscious: The Political Morality of Race*, published in 1996. The foremost argument of *Color Conscious* is the social construction of race. Appiah and Gutmann emphasize that race is not a reputable biological construct. Despite its flawed foundations, however, racial identities are perfectly real and can be of legitimate significance—especially in racist societies.

Appiah's work includes book reviews, short essays, articles, poetic volumes, scholarly books, and mystery novels, most of which address issues of ethics and politics, personal and political identity, gender, nationalism, race, religion, and sexual orientation. Additionally Appiah co-authored a number of African American resource guides, including *The Dictionary of Global Culture Africana: The Encyclopedia of the African and African-American*

Experience and the website Africana.com, both of which are collaborations with his long-time colleague and friend, Henry Louis Gates Jr.

Appiah held appointments at the University of Ghana, Cambridge University, and numerous institutions in the United States, including Yale (1981–1986), Cornell (1986–1989), Duke (1990–1991), Harvard (1999–2002), and Princeton (beginning in 2002). Appiah was named the Laurance S. Rockefeller University Professor of Philosophy at Princeton University in 2002. Additionally, he has taught courses ranging from epistemology to African American history. At Harvard, Appiah was on the board of the W. E. B. DuBois Institute for African and African American Research. There he became an integral part of Harvard's black studies "Dream Team," which included Henry Louis Gates Jr., EVELYN BROOKS HIGGINBOTHAM, CORNEL WEST, and WILLIAM JULIUS WILSON.

Asserting that all people are teachers and students of each other, Appiah argues that, "through teaching I learn; I learn all the time. So it's as much for my sake as for the sake of my students (perhaps, even more for my sake, I don't know!) that I teach" (Dienst 2005). Correct answers, like identities, Appiah believed, are not fixed variables but rather fluid, complex realities that shift as much as they remain rooted and distinct. Instead of offering his students ready-made answers Appiah presented them with the necessary tools to allow them to make conscious decisions. Without telling them what to think he taught them how to reason critically. This, he believed, was the responsibility of an intellectual: to deepen understanding without dictating its application.

Kwame Anthony Appiah was an internationally renowned scholar who provided a wealth of intellectual resources for generations yet to come. With family ties that span the globe, Appiah was a cosmopolitan philosopher who specialized in identity, race, and culture. Reflected in his personal and professional life choices, Appiah was a man of converging identities. Born in London, raised in Ghana, and a citizen of the United States, he was personified the "citizen of the world."

Appiah's prolific output continued into the first decade of the twenty-first century. His most important publications included *Bu Me Bé: Proverbs of the Akan* (2003; co-authored); *Ethics of Identity* (Princeton University Press, 2005); *Cosmopolitanism: Ethics in a World of Strangers* (Norton, 2006), which won the 2007 Arthur Ross Award of the Council on Foreign Relations; *Experiments in Ethics* (Harvard

University Press, 2008), and *The Honor Code: How Moral Revolutions Happen* (Norton, 2010). In 2009 he became President of the PEN American Center. Appiah lives with his partner, Henry Finder, Editorial Director of the *New Yorker*, in New York City and Pennington, New Jersey.

FURTHER READING

Appiah, K. Anthony. *Color Conscious: The Political Morality of Race* (1996).

Appiah, K. Anthony. *In My Father's House: Africa in the Philosophy of Culture* (1992).

Attiyeh, Jenny. "In Defense of the Ivory Tower," *Christian Science Monitor* (22 August 2002).

Dienst, Karin. "Deepening the Conversation about Identity," *Princeton Weekly Bulletin*, vol. 94, no. 17 (21 February 2005).

Henry, Tanu T. "A Dream Team Defection: A Chat with K. Anthony Appiah," *AOL BlackVoices* (2002).

Poste, Danny. "Is Race Real? How Does Identity Matter?" *Chronicle of Higher Education*, vol. 48, issue 30 (5 April 2002).

NICOLE SEALEY

Applegate, Joseph R. (4 Dec. 1925–18 Oct. 2003), linguist, educator, early computer language translator, Africanist, and scholar of Arabic and Berber, was born in Wildwood, New Jersey, to Joseph Henry Applegate and Nancy Berkley Applegate. His father was a second-generation New Jersey resident, whose father was a Native American from Maine. Applegate's mother, whose father was also Native American, migrated from Virginia to Philadelphia, where Applegate's parents met around the time of World War I. Neither parent had more than an elementary school education. Hardworking and ambitious, they held high aspirations for their children. Applegate and his sister enjoyed the advantages of a small-town working-class upbringing, along with direct contact with black artists and entertainers who frequented the seaside summer boarding house their parents operated in Wildwood, New Jersey. Although the family was not affluent, Applegate's environment was sophisticated and urbane. He recalled awakening to the sounds of Louis Armstrong and Duke Ellington in the parlor composing music for their next performances. In the off-season, Applegate's father supported the family in small building contracting, especially plastering and bricklaying.

When Applegate was eleven or twelve, the family moved to Philadelphia, where he completed high school. A gifted language learner, he studied Latin in school and learned Yiddish and Italian from his friends in the diverse South Philadelphia community. Along the way, he picked up French without formal study. In 1941, at age sixteen, he received several academic scholarships and entered Temple University, majoring in Spanish education, with double minors in German and English.

By the time he graduated with a bachelor of science in Education in 1945, he had achieved an almost perfect score on the National Teacher's Examination. In February 1946, Applegate accepted a teaching position at Vaux Junior High School. By January 1947, he became the first African American to teach Spanish in the high schools of Philadelphia. Assigned to Bok Vocational-Technical School, a commercial high school for girls, Applegate found himself carefully scrutinized because of both his age and gender. "I got annoyed … and I think that was part of the reason that I worked with the teacher's union and helped unionize … the public schools in Philadelphia" (Williams, 116). In September 1947, he transferred to William Penn Senior High School, where he taught until 1955.

Soon after beginning his teaching career, Applegate enrolled in the University of Pennsylvania part time. He also became involved in labor union organizing, encouraged by his parents' interest in politics. During their active participation in Republican Party organizational activities in Applegate's and his sister's formative years, their parents had taken both children to numerous political events. At the University of Pennsylvania, Hillary Putnam, the son of Samuel Putnam, the Communist Party activist and editor of *New Masses*, became one of Applegate's close friends. They both participated in campus politics. After completing his master's in Linguistics in 1948, Applegate continued at the University of Pennsylvania working toward a Ph.D. in Linguistics. During his years at the university the Ford Foundation provided funds for the study of Asian and Near Eastern languages. As the language classifications were modified, the Afro-Asiatic group came to include the languages of North Africa, among them Arabic and Berber. The Ford Foundation, realizing the need for more analysis of the languages of North Africa, encouraged the Linguistics Department in that direction. Applegate, consequently, studied one of the Berber languages of Morocco. By 1955, he had completed his dissertation on *Shilha: A Descriptive Grammar with Vocabulary and Texts*. He was the first American to write on Berber. His study became the basis for later work on the Berber language group.

As graduation neared, the linguist Zellig Harris wrote the linguist Mark Hanna Watkins at Howard University to inquire about a position for Applegate (5 Jan. 1954, Watkins Archive). None was available. Therefore, in July 1955, Applegate and Noam Chomsky, who were both students of Harris, were invited to join the MIT machine translation project in the Research Laboratory of Electronics. At MIT, Applegate provided a mathematical description of the noun phrase and Chomsky the verb phrase, descriptions that continue to define the major structure of the English sentence in transformational generative grammar. They collaborated for four years. Chomsky remained at MIT, writing *Syntactic Structures* (1957), the defining text for transformational generative grammar.

By July 1956, Applegate had been appointed as assistant professor of Modern Languages, to teach German to American students and English to foreign students. He assisted MIT in setting up its first language laboratory or "electronic classroom." According to Applegate, "I did not know until Clarence Williams contacted me that I was the first full-time black faculty member at MIT—and I was not offered tenure" (interview with author, 6 June 2002, Washington, D.C.).

Applegate was, however, offered another opportunity that served as the pivotal juncture of his career. There were two factors that combined to change his life. One was the realization that machine translation of languages was less practical than expected and the second was that when Russia launched the space vehicle *Sputnik*, on 4 October 1957, the priorities of the American government changed. "The U.S. realized that it had fallen behind in part because of the lack of linguistic specialists." Congress then passed the National Defense Education Act, and the mastery of "critical languages" became a priority (interview with author, 26 June 1986, Washington, D.C.).

By July 1960, Applegate had accepted a grant from the U.S. Office of Education to continue research on the Berber languages. Until 1966, his university base was the Department of Near Eastern and African Languages at the University of California, Los Angeles (UCLA). There he became the first American to write on the Berber languages and to teach courses on them. Applegate's expertise allowed UCLA to become the only university in the United States where Berber languages could be studied. Almost immediately, though, Applegate traveled to Morocco, settling among the Riff cultural group in the mountains to study their language for almost a year (Williams, 120). He adapted quickly, finding the experience "rich," learning not only the language but also many cultural practices and principles, including how to ride camels, survive in the desert, and migrate yearly for agricultural and traditional reasons. Applegate's *The Structure of Riff* (1964) was the first analysis of the language. The same year, he wrote *The Structure of Kabyle* (1964), on the Berber language of Algeria, and compiled *The Berber Languages: A Selected and Annotated Bibliography* (1964). The following year, he published *A Reference Grammar of Kabyle* (1965), followed by *Spoken Kabyle* (1966), a textbook with tapes and visual materials, all for the Office of Education. Within several years, Applegate had produced a basic *Manual of Libyan Arabic* (1968) and a basic *Manual of Tamachek* (1968), both for the Peace Corps. He spent a summer with the Tuaregs, as they migrated from Northern Niger to Libya, in order to prepare instructional material on their language, Tamazight/Tamachek, for the Peace Corps.

By 1966, the position that had not been available at Howard University in 1955 had become available. Frank Snowden, the Dean of Arts and Sciences, invited Applegate to become an associate professor of Linguistics and to establish a language laboratory. He accepted. In 1967, however, he was invited to become director of the African Studies and Research Program, a position he held until 1969, by which time student nationalism called for a more African-centered approach (interview with author, 26 June 1986, Washington, D.C.). Beginning in 1969, Applegate served as a graduate professor of African Studies until his retirement in 2002. Modest about his own accomplishments, he is credited with the development of the Ph.D. Program in African Studies, the first in the nation. At Howard, Applegate was seldom far from his labor organizing interests. For many years, he served as president of the Faculty Senate, and as a member of the Faculty Grievance and Ethics Committee. Well respected on and off campus, he did not hesitate to take Howard to court in support of faculty issues.

A major theme in Applegate's life was the importance of the use of technology for educational purposes. For many years, he produced a video series, *The African World*, to fill some of the gaps left by the series *The Africans*. After his retirement, he joined a laboratory where he continued to experiment with innovative methods of translating and teaching languages. Applegate authored eight books and more than eighteen articles. He could function in seventeen languages, eight of them from the Berber family. Among the others were Egyptian,

Moroccan, Libyan, Modern Standard Arabic, Portuguese, Italian, and Greek. Well traveled in Africa and the Arabic world, he served as a positive ambassador for the United States. One of the highlights of his life was receiving a personal letter from CONDOLEEZZA RICE, the National Security Advisor, in 2002, in the aftermath of the destruction of the World Trade Center on 11 September 2001, requesting that he serve as a translator of Arabic documents for the American government (interview with author, 6 June 2002, Washington, D.C.). The opportunity of a lifetime was within reach, but never to be grasped. In a few short months, his health had declined. Near the end, he was placed in the Washington Home Hospice, where he died of pneumonia. There was no widow and no heirs.

FURTHER READING

"The African American Linguist Who Broke the Faculty Barrier at MIT," *Journal of Blacks in Higher Education*, 17 (Autumn 1997).

Bernstein, Adam. "Professor Joseph Applegate Dies," *Washington Post*, 22 Oct. 2003.

Slater, Robert Bruce. "First Black Faculty Members at the Nation's Highest-Ranked Universities," *Journal of Blacks in Highest Education*, 22 (Winter 1998–1999).

Unpublished interview with author, 26 June 1986, Washington, D.C.

Unpublished interview with author, 2 June 2002, Washington, D.C.

Williams, Clarence G., ed. "Joseph R. Applegate," *Technology and the Dream: Reflections on the Black Experience a MIT, 1941–1999* (2003).

MARGARET WADE-LEWIS

Arbor, Jesse Walter (26 Dec. 1914–11 Jan. 2000), pioneer black naval officer, was born in Cotton Plant, Arkansas, a predominantly black community, one of twelve children of Tecora and Alexander Arbor. He had two sisters and nine brothers, and his ancestors had received land in the area when slavery ended. Outgoing, humorous, and loquacious by nature, Arbor possessed a typically rural southern sense of place. During an oral history interview in the mid-1980s, he described Cotton Plant as, "A little place that only me and the Good Lord knows [with a population of] 1,661 up until the day I left, and there's never been that many since." Like his siblings, Arbor received a private school education. During his years in Arkansas he attended Arkadelphia–Cotton Plant Academy. Around 1930 the family left the farm area and moved to Chicago

as part of a northerly migration of blacks seeking employment opportunities. Arbor's father worked as a carpenter, and his siblings attended Catholic schools. Because of his athletic prowess, several colleges sought to recruit Arbor in the early 1930s. He accepted a football scholarship at the all-black Arkansas Agricultural, Mechanical & Normal (AM&N) College, now, the University of Arkansas at Pine Bluff. A large, solidly built man, Arbor played right tackle on the football team and majored in the social sciences. He left school one semester short of a degree, after his football eligibility expired.

In 1935 Arbor observed that black professionals were not well paid, so he returned to Illinois and took a job at the Chicago Beach Hotel as doorman and receiving clerk. As he explained, he preferred pay to prestige. In 1939 he became a Pullman porter on trains that traveled widely about the country, then returned to Chicago to become a tailor. In September 1942—shortly before he would have been drafted into the Army—Arbor enlisted in the Navy. He went through recruit training at all-black Camp Robert Smalls, part of the large naval training station complex at Great Lakes, Illinois, north of Chicago. During World War II, Arbor advanced to quartermaster second class with responsibilities involving navigation, log keeping, and visual signaling. He was among the first blacks rated in that specialty. Arbor was stationed in the Boston area, where he served on board two coastal minesweepers and took an advanced navigation course in a Navy facility at Harvard University. In late 1943 Arbor's life changed dramatically when he was ordered to report back to Camp Robert Smalls to take part in the Navy's first officer training course for African Americans. Of the approximately one hundred thousand black sailors then in the Navy, Arbor and fifteen other men were chosen to begin the training in January 1944. The service-wide selection process included FBI background checks and recommendations on leadership ability. Almost all in the group had college experience, and a few had advanced degrees. In two and a half months, they went through a cram course that included training in such areas as navigation, communications, gunnery, propulsion machinery, seamanship, naval history, and the Navy disciplinary system.

The members of the training class concluded that they were part of a Navy experiment and they were determined to succeed or fail as a group, rather than compete with each other. Thus they pooled their knowledge in after-hours sessions. The men were not only in segregated Camp Robert Smalls but also separated from all other black trainees. At times the constant togetherness and the novelty of much of the material led to frayed nerves. Arbor and Dennis Nelson, one of the other officer candidates, often defused the tension with humor. The group did exceptionally well on exams. All sixteen passed the course in March 1944, but the Navy chose to commission Arbor and eleven others as ensigns; one man in the course, Charles Lear, became a warrant officer. The other three remained as enlisted men. Years later the pioneer officers received a distinctive group identity when they were retroactively named the Golden Thirteen.

Once they became officers, Arbor and Lear received assignments to the supply depot in Pearl Harbor, Hawaii; they were the first two black naval officers to be assigned overseas. The executive officer of the depot paved the way for their arrival by specifying that they should be treated with respect and no discrimination. Arbor's duties included an assignment as shore patrol officer and he delighted in wearing a .45-caliber automatic pistol on his hip as a badge of authority. Subsequently Arbor and Lear transferred to the island of Guam, which was gearing up for the planned invasion of Japan in 1945. The two served as troubleshooters in supply and logistics. As the senior black officer in the area, Arbor also served essentially as an unofficial adviser for black sailors. Once the war ended, Arbor left the service and returned to Chicago's South Side, where he resumed his work in the clothing business. He set up his own dry cleaning and tailor shop and in 1948 married Autry Brown, a schoolteacher in Memphis, Tennessee, whom Arbor had met during a trip there and who already knew other members of his family. They had three children: Jesse Jr., Deborah, and Brenda. Arbor's work in his shop continued until 1968, when a combination of urban renewal and concerns about his health led him to seek other employment. He applied to the Chicago Board of Education and was asked what he could do. As he did so often in life, Arbor gave a flip answer: "Run my mouth and boss like hell" (Stillwell, 188). He took a job running heating systems in various schools and performing administrative duties. He finally retired in 1984 at age seventy, but devoted much of his time to helping the Navy recruit minorities and met with later generations of black naval officers. He summed up his achievements by saying of the Golden Thirteen: "Having been one of the guinea pigs, I'm glad I had the endurance and fortitude to withstand the challenges we faced.... The black officers today express

their appreciation when they see us" (Stillwell, 191). Arbor died in 2000.

FURTHER READING

Stillwell, Paul, ed. *The Golden Thirteen: Recollections of the First Black Naval Officers* (1993).
Obituary: *Chicago Tribune*, 14 Jan. 2000.

PAUL STILLWELL

Archer, Osceola Macarthy (Adams) (13 June 1890–20 Nov. 1983), actor, director, educator, and artist advocate, was born Osceola Marie Macarthy in Albany, Georgia, of black, white, and Native American racial heritage. The daughter of a life insurance executive, Archer attended Fisk University Preparatory School in Nashville, Tennessee. She then enrolled at Howard University in Washington, D.C., in 1909, where she was a pupil of ALAIN LOCKE and the sociologist KELLY MILLER. Self-defined as a suffragette, in 1913, her senior year at Howard, Archer and twenty-one fellow female students cofounded one of the largest black fraternal organizations in the United States, Delta Sigma Theta, a sorority dedicated to community service and the mutual support of African American women. That same year Archer began to pursue her interest in drama by performing the title role in the Howard University Dramatics Club production of *The Lady of Lyon*, a Victorian romantic comedy known as a showcase for actors like Ellen Terry.

As a young actor, Archer entered a theatrical community that offered limited choices for African American women. Marrying her chemistry professor, NUMA P. G. ADAMS (who later became the first African American dean of the Howard Medical School), in 1915, Archer chose to put her artistic dreams on hold while she raised her only child, Charles Macarthy Adams. In 1919 Archer followed her husband to Chicago as he pursued his medical studies at the University of Chicago, and supported the family by working as a dress designer under her own label, Mrs. Adams. In 1932, as her son approached college age, Archer was encouraged by her husband to renew her professional dreams of a career on the stage as an actor and director.

During the time between Archer's university days and her return to acting, opportunities for blacks on the dramatic stage had begun to change. In 1917 Ridgeley Torrence's *Three Plays for a Negro Theater* opened the door for blacks on Broadway in nonmusical roles. The emergence of the Lafayette Players, Anita Bush's company dedicated to the creation of a legitimate African American theater, set a precedent for a self-produced Negro Theater. And the heated debates between Alain Locke and W. E. B. DuBois over aesthetics served to redefine what African Americans might achieve in the theatrical arts. Half a generation after the first wave of African American actresses like FLORENCE MILLS, ADA WALKER, and DORA DEAN, Archer avoided having to take roles as a chorus girl in order to pursue the dramatic stage, and sought institutional training in dramatics.

Upon her arrival to New York City in 1932, however, Archer was refused admission to the Academy of Dramatic Arts because of her race. Searching for a theater school that accepted African American students, Archer enrolled in the Repertory Playhouse Associations' American Theater Wing School of Drama, founded by former members of the Moscow Art School. Graduating in 1934 at the age of forty-four, she adopted the stage name Osceola Archer. Archer soon received her first professional role in the avant-garde production of Dana Bernett's *Strange House*.

Setting her sights on the Broadway stage, Archer turned down two roles in her first season of auditioning, including John Houseman's *4 Saints in 3 Acts*, because she wanted her debut to be as a dramatic, rather than as a musical, actress. Soon, Archer won a role in Elmer Rice's *Between Two Worlds*, with Joseph Schildkraut. In 1935 Archer again found herself of Broadway, in Archibald MacLeish's *Panic*, with John O'Shaughnessy and Orson Welles. That same year, she toured with PAUL ROBESON in *The Emperor Jones*.

Although fortunate enough to have received two roles on Broadway during her first two years as a professional actress, Archer soon faced a slump in her career. Like many educated women of her time, Archer relied on her options in the field of education as fallbacks to the unstable world of the theater. In 1937 Archer completed a master's degree in Dramatic Art from New York University's School of Education, taking a position teaching drama and directing at Bennett College in North Carolina, where she also began to work on her next dream of being a director with her own theater company.

In 1939 Archer left Bennett College to again appear in *The Emperor Jones*, as well as to lay the foundations for her own company; her ambitions for a company ended, however, with the death of her husband in 1940. That same year, Archer relocated to New York City and began teaching and directing at the American Negro Theater, where she remained until 1949, training the next great generation of black theater professionals such as HARRY BELAFONTE, RUBY DEE, SIDNEY POITIER, OSSIE DAVIS, and Hilda Haines. Archer also taught at the American Theater Wing and the Harlem School of the Arts.

Archer was an actor, director, and teacher who forged strong careers in both the performing arts and in education. As a director she staged numerous plays for the American Negro Theater, the Putnam County Playhouse (where she is remembered as the first African American director of Summer Stock theater), and for various groups in and around New York City. As an actress she performed in five Broadway plays, numerous Off-Broadway productions, and at university and regional playhouses. She also appeared on the radio, as well as in television, commercials, and film, most notably in the made-for-television film *Rashomon* (1960) and in *An Affair of the Skin* (1963).

Dedicated to performing and directing the classics, Archer created a balance in her career that reflected both her artistic vision and her personal politics. She played roles in integrated casts at traditional white theaters, in addition to working with many African American companies and playwrights. Self-described as "a humanist against any separatism, especially on the stage," she was a staunch advocate for minorities' rights in the theater (interview, 1972). A member of four theatrical unions, she held positions on the equal rights committees of Actors Equity, the American Federation of Television and Radio Artists (AFTRA), Screen Actors Guild (SAG), and the Director and Writers Guild. In 1943, she was a member of the Executive Committee for the Stage Door Canteen, a New York City supper club that entertained military personnel during WWII. She also held positions of leadership with her sorority to continue her lifetime relationship to service and advocacy. In 1973, Delta Sigma Theta established the Osceola Award, which used her name to recognize distinguished achievements in the arts. In 1978 the Audience Development Committee (Audelco), an organization devoted to stimulating the arts in black communities, awarded Archer (along with the composer and pianist EUBIE BLAKE) an Outstanding Pioneer Award for a lifetime of service through art. Continuing her work until she was eighty-eight, Osceola Macarthy Adams Archer died at the age of ninety three.

FURTHER READING
Recording and transcript of 21 Feb. 1972 interview with
  Osceola Archer by James Hatch and Paula Singer

is located at the Hatch-Billops Collection in New York City.

Obituary: *New York Times,* 24 Nov. 1983.

SUZI TAKAHASHI

Archer, Dennis (1 Jan. 1942–), lawyer, State Supreme Court Justice, mayor of Detroit, Michigan, and president of the American Bar Association, was born in Detroit to Ernest and Frances Archer, and was raised in Cassopolis, Michigan. Determined to raise himself from poverty, and encouraged by his parents to value education, Archer was steadfast in his studies. He graduated from Cassopolis High School in 1959 and entered Western Michigan University that fall. While attending Western Michigan he pledged Alpha Phi Alpha Fraternity, the first black collegiate fraternal organization. He graduated in 1965.

Archer had a desire to teach, so he relocated to Detroit and took a position in the Detroit schools teaching and assisting emotionally disturbed students. He met Trudy Duncombe, another young teacher, during this tenure, and they married on 17 June 1967. Although dedicated to education, Archer began to prepare himself for another level of public service when he entered law school at Detroit College of Law, taking courses in the evening while continuing to teach during the day. After his graduation in 1970 he passed the Michigan State Bar and began working for the Detroit-based firm of Gragg & Gardner. Within a year he was invited to join the firm of Hall, Stone, Allen, Archer & Glenn, ultimately becoming a partner. Despite having young children, Archer encouraged and supported his wife as she, too, pursued a law degree.

Archer and his wife became active in the southeastern Michigan Democratic Party and worked to help many African American and Democratic

Dennis Archer, the first black president of the American Bar Association, San Francisco, 7 August 2003. (AP Images.)

candidates win political office in the 1970s and 1980s. He assisted in the election of many Democrats, including Governor James Blanchard. Most notably, Archer served on the committee that assisted in the successful reelection of COLEMAN A. YOUNG as mayor of Detroit in 1977. He continued to practice law until 1986 when he was appointed by Governor James Blanchard as the first African American to sit on the Michigan State Supreme Court. Archer remained in that role for four years. When Coleman Young announced his intention to retire, Archer decided to step down from his seat on the Supreme Court and return to private practice in the hope of launching a campaign to run for the office. This move allowed the outgoing governor to appoint another African American, Conrad Mallet, to replace him, maintaining both an African American and a Democratic presence on the Court while Archer focused on becoming mayor of Detroit.

Criticized by African American residents of Detroit for courting the white and suburban vote during the 1993 mayoral election, Archer's personal appeal and broader message of change, unity, and hope gave him a 57–43 percent win over his opponent, Sharon McPhail, who had been handpicked by Coleman Young as his successor. The results of the election appeared to indicate that residents were prepared for a change from the type of government Coleman Young represented—one heavily dependent on local union and African American residential support. After his inauguration Archer began working to reunite the city internally and to reestablish ties with suburban leaders previously estranged by his predecessor's political methods. This was a stark departure from the polemic politics of Young, who launched verbal attacks at suburban leaders such as Prosecutor Brooks Patterson and, near the end of his term, Governor Blanchard and others. Archer represented a corporate shift that, if used wisely, could transform the image of Detroit from a murder capital to a commerce capital. At this time Detroit had a national reputation for high crime, especially around Halloween, when random arson fires plagued the city for almost a week each year. Among his initiatives was a drive to increase police presence on city streets, decrease the number of fires, and reunite the metropolitan area. Archer used the force of his position to begin a transformation of the city and its reputation. Under his leadership, business and commerce began to return to the city. The establishment of three casinos and the decision of the Compuware

Corporation to relocate its headquarters to downtown Detroit gave rise to the new baseball and football stadiums, Comerica Park and Ford Field, which were funded by Comerica Bank, the Ilich Family and the Ford family, respectively, a new city center, Campus Martius, and a successful bid to host Super Bowl XL. The Campus Martius project represented a shift in the city center and established a base for corporate headquarters, retail shops such as Ben and Jerry's Ice Cream, Border's Bookstores, and the Hard Rock Café, as well as activities such as ice-skating in winter and concerts in the summer. While serving as mayor, Archer held the position of president of the U.S. Conference of Mayors and was well respected by his peers.

After making his mark on the city's political and economic landscape, Archer expressed his longing for a more private life by not running for re-election in 2000. He left office in 2001 and was immediately-appointed to the Board of Directors of Compuware—the first African American ever to hold this post. Archer later accepted the chairmanship of the Dickinson Wright law firm and was elected to a term as president of the American Bar Association. A tribute to his desire to help others and another testament of his credibility, Archer was appointed in 2004 as independent guardian to ROSA PARKS as her health began to decline, a role he held until her death in 2005.

FURTHER READING
"Dennis Archer," *Newsmakers* (1994).
Doyle, Jack. *Taken for a Ride: Detroit's Big Three and the Politics of Pollution* (2000).
Greenberg, Michael R. *Restoring America's Neighborhoods: How Local People Make a Difference* (1999).

SIBYL COLLINS WILSON

Archey, Jimmy (12 Oct. 1902–16 Nov. 1967), jazz trombonist, was born James H. Archey in Norfolk, Virginia. Nothing is known of his parents. He started playing the trombone in 1912, and from 1915 to 1919 he studied music at the Hampton Institute, spending his summers playing in a band led by the pianist Lillian Jones. After working in Quentin Redd's band on the Atlantic City boardwalk around 1922, Archey moved to New York City in 1923 and played with the trumpeter Lionel Howard's band at the Saratoga Club and the Capitol Palace. The next year he worked at Ed Small's, and from 1925 to mid-1926 he spent a year touring with the Lucky Sambo Revue and another few months with the Tan Town Topics.

Starting in late 1926 he worked with the bands of John C. Smith and Arthur Gibbs and began a residency at the Bamboo Inn with Ed Campbell. In 1927 he played in the pianist Edgar Hayes's pit band at the Alhambra Theater, briefly toured with KING OLIVER in early June, and continued working at the Bamboo Inn with Campbell and then with Henri Saparo. In 1928 the pianist Joe Steele took over leadership of the Bamboo Inn band, and Archey remained with him into 1929. After leaving Steele he filled out the remainder of the year working with the bands of Charlie Skeete and Bill Benford. In April 1930 he once again toured with Oliver, and in June he joined LUIS RUSSELL's band for long engagements at the Saratoga Club, Connie's Inn, the Arcadia Ballroom, and other venues.

In early 1931 Archey worked for six months with Bingie Madison at the Broadway Danceland. But then he rejoined and remained with Russell's band—from October 1935 under the leadership of LOUIS ARMSTRONG—until early 1937, at which time he joined the singer Willie Bryant for regular appearances at the Apollo Theater. Archey stayed with Bryant until March 1939, when he left to begin a long residency at the Savoy Ballroom with Benny Carter. Carter's band was a favorite at the Savoy, but it occasionally played at other locations as well, among them the Apollo, Roseland Ballroom, Howard Theater, and Golden Gate Ballroom. In June 1940 Archey left Carter to work in the bands of ELLA FITZGERALD and Coleman Hawkins at the Savoy, but he was back with Carter in late January 1941 for a month-long engagement at Nick's in Greenwich Village. After a series of tours from March through September, Carter's group split up and Archey began a three-year period of freelancing, during which time he occasionally worked with CAB CALLOWAY and DUKE ELLINGTON. In 1944 and 1945 he was at the Zanzibar with CLAUDE HOPKINS, and from 1946 through 1948 he played sporadically at Billy Rose's Diamond Horseshoe with NOBLE SISSLE.

For almost twenty years Archey had found regular employment in big bands, usually playing lead trombone but rarely having the opportunity to establish a reputation as a jazz soloist. All that changed, however, in June 1947 when Rudi Blesh, producer of the *This Is Jazz* radio series, hired Archey as a permanent replacement for George Brunies. The half-hour broadcasts were aired weekly through 7 October, and Archey appeared on all the shows alongside widely respected jazzmen such as Wild Bill Davison, ALBERT NICHOLAS, SIDNEY BECHET,

JAMES P. JOHNSON, Danny Barker, POPS FOSTER, and BABY DODDS. For part of the summer of 1947 Archey also took part in "Jazz on the River," Blesh's weekend chartered boat trips up the Hudson River. In February 1948 Archey made his first trip to Europe to play at the Nice Jazz Festival with Mezz Mezzrow in a band that also included the trumpeter Henry Goodwin, the pianist SAMMY PRICE, Foster, Dodds, and a young disciple of Bechet's, the clarinetist and soprano saxophonist Bob Wilber. After they returned home, Wilber decided to build a band of his own around Goodwin and Archey. In December 1948 Archey, Goodwin, and Foster, along with the young stride pianist Dick Wellstood and the drummer Tommy Benford, joined Wilber at the Savoy Café in Boston. Playing in a style associated with Bechet's New Orleans Feetwarmers, the personnel of Wilber's band remained intact until April 1950, when Wilber himself left the group to form another band to open George Wein's new Storyville Club in Boston.

The leadership of the Savoy band was turned over to Archey, who replaced Wilber with the veteran Harlem clarinetist and saxophonist Benny Waters, whom both Archey and Goodwin had known since the 1920s. After their departure from the Savoy, Archey's band began a residency at Jimmy Ryan's on Fifty-second Street, where they remained until the spring of 1952, alternating with WILBUR DE PARIS's recently formed Rampart Street Paraders. After leaving Ryan's, Archey's band embarked on a European tour, but when that folded because of poor management, the band broke up. The men returned home, but Archey stayed on to play with EARL HINES's sextet, which was then also on tour. Back in New York, Archey resumed freelancing, frequently appearing at the Central Plaza, where, with Jimmy McPartland, Pee Wee Russell, and others, he was filmed for the 1954 documentary film *Jazz Dance*. From late 1954 to early 1955 Archey toured Europe again, this time as a sideman with Mezzrow, and from September 1955 through December 1962 he played with an all-star sextet under the alternate leadership of Muggsy Spanier and Hines. In 1963 he led his own bands on dates in the United States and Canada, and in February 1966 he toured Europe once more with the New Orleans All Stars, a stellar group assembled by the British trumpeter Keith Smith. Archey remained active professionally until his death in Amityville, New York.

Even from the beginning of his recording career, Archey was considered a reliable and forthright soloist, as is evidenced by the space accorded him by King Oliver, FATS WALLER, Joe Steele, James P. Johnson, and RED ALLEN on recordings made between 1927 and 1929. On the earlier of these his brash, blues-intoned style reflects that of KID ORY, whom he replaced in Oliver's band, but by late 1929 he had come under the influence of the more technically assured, rhythmically propulsive J. C. HIGGINBOTHAM, then the trombonist with Luis Russell's exciting new orchestra. Though lacking Higginbotham's inventiveness, Archey continued to play with a sprightly, robust earthiness for the remainder of his career. Between 1934 and 1939 he recorded with the Russell/Armstrong orchestra, Willie Bryant, and Benny Carter, but almost exclusively in the capacity of a sectionman. Starting in 1947, though, Archey was heard to advantage on small-band sessions led by MUTT CAREY, Wild Bill Davison, Punch Miller, and Tony Parenti and from 1949 through 1953 as a sideman with Sidney Bechet, Bob Wilber, SIDNEY DE PARIS, George Wettling, and WILLIE "THE LION" SMITH. Between 1954 and 1961 he worked and recorded with Muggsy Spanier and Earl Hines at Los Angeles clubs such as the Hangover and the Crescendo, and in 1966 he appeared on several albums by the touring New Orleans All Stars. Additionally, a number of Archey's band's weekly radio broadcasts from Jimmy Ryan's in 1952 have since appeared on record as well as on audio checks of Blesh's *This Is Jazz* series.

Nothing can be ascertained about Archey's private life, including whether he ever married or had children.

FURTHER READING
McCarthy, Albert. *Big Band Jazz* (1974).
Wright, Laurie, ed. *King Oliver* (1987).

DISCOGRAPHY
Bruyninckx, Walter. *Swing Discography, 1920–1988* (12 vols., 1986–1989).
Bruyninckx, Walter. *Traditional Jazz Discography, 1897–1988* (6 vols., 1985–1988).
Rust, Brian. *Jazz Records, 1897–1942* (1982).
This entry is taken from the *American National Biography* and is published here with the permission of the American Council of Learned Societies.

JACK SOHMER

Archibald, Nathaniel (2 Sept. 1948–), professional basketball player, was born in New York City. He was commonly known as "Tiny." Some say he was nicknamed after his father, "Big Tiny," while others believe that he was given that label because he was small in comparison with the other players on the basketball court. He was the oldest of seven children and was raised in the South Bronx's Patterson Housing Projects. At age fourteen, his father left the family and Archibald effectively became head of the household. His mother worked at a neighborhood supermarket called Alexander's to make enough money to care for the family. Basketball became Archibald's sanctuary from drugs and violence, which were rampant in his neighborhood and among his friends. Still, it wasn't easy for him to get himself on a team, as he was small, painfully shy, and lacked confidence on the basketball court. He tried out and failed to make his high school basketball team at DeWitt Clinton High School in his sophomore year and considered dropping out of school. However, Floyd Layne, a community sports director, later to be the head basketball coach for City College of Manhattan, knew the DeWitt Clinton coach and convinced him to give Archibald another chance. He made the team in his junior year, and by his senior year he had been named to the All-City team.

His grades were not good enough for him to attract scholarship offers from major college basketball programs, so Archibald went to Arizona Western Community College. After one year at Arizona Western, he was offered and accepted a scholarship to the University of Texas at El Paso, where he earned a bachelor of science degree and became a star for the school's basketball team. He averaged twenty points a game over three seasons. He won Honorable Mention All-American and WAC MVP in 1970. He continued to build his reputation during the postseason collegiate All-Star games in 1970, scoring 51 points in the Aloha Classic and averaging close to 40 points a game in five postseason exhibitions.

The NBA's Cincinnati Royals selected him in the second round of the 1970 draft. He became a starter in his rookie season when the veteran guard Flynn Robinson held out in a contract dispute. In his first season Archibald averaged 16 points a game. He became the floor leader in his second season, averaging 28.2 points a game, and was selected to the All-NBA Second Team at the end of the season.

Before the 1972–1973 season the Royals moved to Kansas City/Omaha and became the Kings. It was in his first season as a King that Archibald established himself. In 80 games, he averaged 34 points and 11.4 assists a game, becoming the only player in history to lead the league in both average points scored and assists in a single season. He was named to the All-NBA First Team at the end of that season.

Archibald played only 35 games in the 1973–1974 season because of an injured Achilles tendon, averaging 17.6 points a game. However, he played in all 82 games for the Kings in 1974–1975 and led the team to its first winning season since 1966. He averaged 26.5 points and 6.8 assists a game and was named to the All-NBA First Team at the end of the season. Moreover, the Kings made the playoffs that season but lost the Western Conference semifinals in six games to the Chicago Bulls. The following season Archibald averaged 24.8 points and 7.9 assists in 78 games and was again selected to the All-NBA First Team. The Kings suffered through a losing 1975–1976 season, and Archibald was traded to the New York Nets prior to the 1976–1977 season. However, he suffered a severe foot injury and missed most of the season. He was traded to the Buffalo Braves the next year, but tore an Achilles tendon and never played for the Braves. He was traded to the Boston Celtics before the 1978–1979 season. In the 1979–1980 season the Celtics had a 61-21 regular-season record, making the playoffs, but lost to Philadelphia in the Eastern Conference finals. Archibald led the league with 910 assists and was again named an NBA All-Star. In the 1980–1981 season Archibald directed the Celtics offense to a 62-20 record. He was named the All-Star Game MVP and was selected to the All-NBA Second Team at the end of the season, while leading the Celtics to the NBA championship. Archibald helped to get the Celtics back into the playoffs during the 1981–1982 season. He had eight assists per game, which was fourth best in the league. However, the Celtics lost to the Philadelphia 76ers in the Eastern Conference finals.

In the 1982–1983 season Archibald, who was now thirty-four years old, experienced a decline in his play. In 66 games he averaged only 27.4 minutes of playing time and had only 6.2 assists. He was cut by the Celtics at the end of the season and signed with the Milwaukee Bucks as a free agent for the 1983–1984 season. He retired after playing only 46 games for the Bucks.

In a fourteen-year career with the NBA, Archibald garnered 16,481 points, 6,476 assists, and was selected to six NBA All-Star games. He was elected to the Naismith Memorial Basketball Hall of Fame in 1991 and five years later was named to the NBA 50th Anniversary All-Time Team. After his retirement, Archibald returned to New York City, where he ran basketball schools for underprivileged children and earned a master of science degree in Adult Education from Fordham University in 1990. He also worked as athletic director at the Harlem Armory homeless shelter until it closed in 1991. He served as both a physical education and health education teacher and career development counselor at PS 175/IS 275 in Manhattan, as executive director for the New York Urban Summer Career and Sports Academy, participated in numerous basketball clinics throughout the United States, and headed the Nate "Tiny" Archibald Basketball Camp at Riverbank State Park in New York. He was honored by Mayor DAVID N. DINKINS in 1993 for his work in New York City. He also served as the head basketball coach of the ABA Long Beach (California) Jam in 2004.

FURTHER READING

Devaney, John. *Tiny!: The Story of Nate Archibald* (1977).

Goldaper, Sam. *Hot Shots: Havlicek, Barry, Monroe, Archibald* (1975).

Greenfield, Jeff. *Tiny Giant: Nate Archibald* (1976).

ROBERT JANIS

Armstead, Robert "Bob" (8 Dec. 1927–9 Dec. 1998), coal miner who wrote the first published memoir of an African American coal miner, was born Robert Lee Armstead in Watson, West Virginia, to Queen Esther Armstead and James Henry Armstead. James worked in Alabama and West Virginia coal mines for fifty years. Bob received his formal education in all-black schools. The eighth of eleven children born and reared in coal camps, he learned early on that the family's well-being depended on his parents' extraordinary ability to feed and clothe so many on his father's meager income. His religious mother and authoritarian father instilled in their children a strong sense of responsibility, dedication to the family, and solid work ethic.

In 1929, when Bob was two years old, the family moved to Grays Flats, a segregated coal camp on the edge of Grant Town, West Virginia. In the late 1920s the Grant Town mine employed 2,200 men, 500 of whom were black. Armstead watched his father, a horse driver, collapse from exhaustion after working twelve- to fourteen-hour shifts for two dollars a day. His father's suffering, the use of mine guards on horseback to intimidate miners, and policies designed to keep miners poor left young Armstead with contempt for coal mine operators. Deeply aware of his poverty, he made sure to always carry change in his pockets and to keep what little money he had well hidden. Armstead wasn't paid for doing boyhood chores like carrying water, splitting wood, hunting and fishing for food, picking berries, and hoeing the family cornfield, so he solicited additional work from other coal camp residents. As a boy he loved camp life and kept his coal camp memories alive by telling and retelling stories from that time.

To cut labor costs and weaken the United Mine Workers of America (UMWA) in the mid-1930s, coal companies began to replace human labor with mining machines. The mechanization of the Grant Town mine left a disproportionate number of blacks without jobs. By 1941 James Armstead had lost his job and the company-owned family home. He found work driving horses in the deep Dakota mine outside Fairmont, while Bob Armstead attended one of the most notable black schools in West Virginia. Dunbar School, named for the poet PAUL LAWRENCE DUNBAR, included the only black high school in Marion County and had a K–12 enrollment of 600 students.

Although Bob Armstead worked various paying jobs as a teenager, he enjoyed boxing and dedicated himself to training as if it were one of his jobs. He left school in the eleventh grade and married the woman who was expecting his child. Following two years of low-paying jobs, he reconsidered working as a miner and, with the help of his father, joined the hundreds of men at the Consolidation Coal Company's Barnesville Shaft in Fairmont. Armstead's first day underground exhausted and thrilled him. Every coal mining process fascinated him. Above ground he continued to train as an amateur lightweight boxer, and from 1948 to 1951, scored thirty-three wins and only three losses; however, traveling mountain roads to tournaments, working, and trying to be supportive of his growing family proved too demanding. Although he quit boxing when he was twenty-four, Armstead served as a local referee for another six years. From 1950 to 1959 shutdowns and layoffs forced him to work at five different mines. During this difficult period his wife left the crowded Armstead home and relinquished care of their three children to Armstead and his family. On 24 December 1959 he married Zelda Gay Holloway. They lived apart from the family and reared two boys, Michael and Anthony.

From 1948 until his retirement in 1987 Armstead witnessed tragedy and death in the mines, but he never suffered a lost-time injury. He remained employed even as mechanization cut the workforce drastically. In addition to Barnesville Shaft, he worked at several West Virginia mines, including Everettville, Jordan, Grant Town, Loveridge, Four States, and Robinson Run. In a forty-year career, he was furloughed nearly five years due to layoffs, strikes, and mine shutdowns.

In 1968 while at Loveridge mine, Bob earned his mine certification and joined a short list of African Americans in management. As a foreman he guided all-white crews in coal production. Just as he had earned a reputation for being an excellent machine operator on any equipment he tried, his crews also earned recognition as excellent coal producers. His closest encounter with death occurred in 1980 at Four States mine, when he rescued a machine operator who was buried under rock from a roof fall with his heavy tool belt snagged on a continuous mining machine lever. Armstead went in, cut the belt, and pulled the man out and away. Seconds later, tons of rock fell where they had been struggling. That second rock fall would have killed them both had Armstead not acted quickly.

Armstead retired from coal mining at the age of fifty-nine and, between part-time jobs, settled down to write his life story. His goal was to tell young people about camp life and to take readers underground to see how coal was mined through the years. What he did not realize was that he was writing a detailed history of sixty years of underground coal mining in northern West Virginia.

In May 1998 he approached the Fairmont writer S. L. Gardner when her feature on the Dakota mine appeared in the Fairmont *Times West Virginian*. Armstead impressed Gardner, an avid student of coal mining, with his never-before-published coal camp stories. Aware that no published memoir of a black coal miner existed, Gardner proposed a book project. The two worked closely with his writings and taped interviews until Armstead died of lung cancer in Morgantown, West Virginia. Assisted by the Armstead family, Gardner finished the book. *Black Days, Black Dust: The Memories of an African American Coal Miner* was published by the University of Tennessee Press in 2002 and was lauded as "an important historical work" (Pack, Lexington, Kentucky, *Herald Leader*, May 2002).

Bob Armstead's memoir has been adopted as required reading by black studies, Appalachian studies, and labor studies departments in colleges and universities nationwide. The success of *Black Days, Black Dust* honors two generations of hardworking African American men and establishes their place in history. It is also a testimonial to one man with a great gift for storytelling and teaching.

FURTHER READING
Armstead, Robert. *Black Days, Black Dust: The Memories of an African American Coal Miner*, as told to S. L. Gardner (2002).

Gardner, S. L. "Black Days, Black Dust: An Oral History of Life in the Coalfields," *Traditions: A Journal of West Virginia Folk Culture and Educational Awareness*, vol. 9, no. 1 (2004).

S. L. GARDNER

Armstrong, Anton (26 Apr. 1956–), choral director, was born Anton Eugene Armstrong in New York City, the third son of William B. Armstrong, a tailor, and Esther Holder, a nurse. Esther embraced music and passed that love on to her son. She sang in the church choir and encouraged him to do the same. His maternal uncle, Herbert, played the saxophone, organ, and piano and urged his nephew to play an instrument.

Armstrong's musical development was nurtured and encouraged. As his penchant toward music became more apparent, his mom engaged his first piano teacher. She taught him meticulously, crafting the development of his musical discipline. During the middle school years, Armstrong's musical journey led him to the prestigious American Boychoir School in Princeton, New Jersey; there he laid the foundation for his craft. He was taught the fundamentals of choral singing by being immersed in the genre, and he developed a profound love for this musical style. He traveled the world with the American Boychoir, setting the stage for what was yet to come.

A pivotal experience that would unwittingly hold a hint of what Armstrong's future would bring came during high school. When offered tickets to a rock concert, Armstrong jumped at the chance to attend. It also happened that his pastor had tickets for a concert that same evening at New York's Avery Fisher Hall. When given the choice to attend the performance featuring the St. Olaf's Choir or the rock concert, Armstrong politely declined the pastor's offer and selected the rock concert. However, being the ever present force of nature that she was, Armstrong's mother thought that the opportunity to hear St. Olaf's Choir perform was substantially more rewarding. So, despite his decision to the contrary, off to Lincoln Center he went. That performance made an indelible mark on Armstrong's musical psyche and August 1974 found Armstrong as a freshman at St. Olaf College in Northfield, Minnesota. He became a member of its acclaimed choir and would spend the next four years honing his choral skills. After graduating with a bachelor's degree in music from St. Olaf College in 1978 Armstrong went on to earn his master's of Music in 1980 from the University of Illinois and his Doctorate of Musical Arts from Michigan State University in 1987. Armstrong's first teaching position was with Calvin College in Grand Rapids, Michigan, where he also conducted the Campus Choir, the Alumni Choir, and the Grand Rapids Symphony Chorus.

In December 1989 Armstrong received an intriguing proposal from St. Olaf College, his alma mater, which led to him becoming the Harry R. and Thora H. Tosdal Professor of Music and taking over the reigns as its choir's fourth conductor. He was the first African American in the school's history to hold that position. With Armstrong at the helm, the choir not only sustained its prominence, but began to take on a new flair of diversity. While maintaining its esteemed musical history, what was once an extremely traditional classical choir now began to rock and sway with motion to African spirituals, hymns, and psalms. In the sacred halls of the most cloistered churches and concert halls the beat of the conga drum stirred the soul. Hands clapped, feet tapped, and a new era was under way. Under Armstrong's tutelage the choir produced a savory, rich sound. Crooning songs that reached deep into the core of the listener purveying the soulful heritage from whence they came, St. Olaf's choir was irrevocably transformed.

Between 1981 and 1990 Armstrong conducted the St. Cecilia Youth Chorale, a treble chorus in Grand Rapids, Michigan, and in 1991 he began conducting The Troubadours, a boys' ensemble in Northfield, Minnesota. Armstrong made his European conducting debut the following year at the International Band and Choir Festival in Brussels, Belgium; in 2000 he conducted the twenty-fifth anniversary concerts of that same festival in Austria. Under Armstrong's direction the St. Olaf Choir have toured Denmark, Norway (including a performance at the Bergen International Festival), New Zealand, Australia, and Central Europe.

In 1998 Armstrong began his tenure as founding conductor of the Oregon Bach Festival Stangeland Family Youth Choral Academy. During 2001 Armstrong conducted the World Youth Choir in Venezuela and the United States. In 2005 he and the St. Olaf choir returned to tour Norway and performed for Queen Sonja. Also in 2005, Armstrong and the choir performed at the White House for President George W. Bush, Mrs. Laura Bush, and their guests in celebration of The National Day of Prayer.

Armstrong has been featured at the fourth, sixth, and eighth World Symposiums on Choral Music. He has stood before choirs with conductor's baton in hand throughout North America, Europe, Scandinavia, Korea, Singapore, Australia, New Zealand, Venezuela, and the Caribbean. He served as the first Peter Godfrey Visiting Professor of Choral Music at the University of Auckland, New Zealand in 2003. Armstrong has guest conducted such musical greats as the Utah Symphony and Symphony Chorus, the Mormon Tabernacle Choir, the Westminster Choir, the American Boychoir, and the St. Paul Chamber Orchestra.

In 2006 Armstrong was selected to receive Baylor University's Robert Foster Cherry Award for Great Teaching (118 outstanding teachers were nominated). He also functions as editor of a multicultural choral series for Earthsongs Publications and coeditor of the revised St. Olaf Choral Series (Augsburg Fortress Publishers). He collaborated with André Thomas on the instructional video *Body, Mind, Spirit, Voice*. He is a contributing writer for *Teaching Music through Performance in Choir (Volume I)* and for *Way Over in Beulah Lan': Understanding and Performing the Negro Spiritual* (André Thomas). Armstrong, who has served on the Board of Trustees of the American Boychoir School since 1994, was honored with that organization's Distinguished Alumnus Award in 2007.

With unwavering passion he sets the musical bar at a lofty height. His requirement for his students is akin to perfection. His results are angel-like voices joined in meticulous melodious unity. He possesses the ability to reach within the musical novice and draw out a budding connoisseur. Celebrated and revered across the globe, he has appeared before kings, queens, and high-ranking dignitaries allowing them to experience the talent, creativity, and musical diversity God generously imparts to this world through him.

FURTHER READING

"Armstrong Named Cherry Award Winner" *Baylor Magazine,* Spring 2006 Volume 4, Number 4.

"Body, Mind, Spirit Voice" *Baylor Magazine,* Summer 2007 Volume 6, Number 1.

Shaw, Joseph. *The St. Olaf Choir: A Narrative* (St. Olaf College June 1997).

St. Olaf College, St. Olaf Choir "Anton Armstrong, Conductor," http://www.stolaf.edu/music/stolaf_choir/conductor.html. *Baylor Magazine,* A publication of Baylor University- http://www.baylormag.com.

Discography

Harmony: American Voices of Faith. The American Boychoir conducted by Fernando Malvar-Ruiz with The St. Olaf Choir conducted by Anton Armstrong and The Alumni Chorus of The American Boychoir School conducted by James Litton (2007).

Great Hymns of Faith Vol. 2. The St. Olaf Choir, Anton Armstrong, Conductor (2004).

Charles Ives—The Celestial Country. The St. Olaf Choir and the St. Olaf Chamber Ensemble, Anton Armstrong, Conductor (2002).

My Soul's Been Anchored in the Lord. The St. Olaf Choir, Anton Armstrong, Conductor (2001).

Great Hymns of Faith Vol. 1. The St. Olaf Choir, Anton Armstrong, Conductor (1999).

The Spirituals of William Dawson. The St. Olaf Choir, Anton Armstrong, Conductor with Marvis Martin, Soprano (1997).

Worthy To Be Praised. The St. Olaf Choir, Anton Armstrong, Conductor (1997).

A Choral Tapestry. The St. Olaf Choir, Anton Armstrong, Conductor (1994).

O Yule Full of Gladness: Songs of Christmas from around the World. The St. Olaf Choir, Anton Armstrong, Conductor (1993).

HALLELUJAH We Sing Your Praises. The St. Olaf Choir, Anton Armstrong, Conductor (1992).

JANELLE F. H. WINSTON

Armstrong, Henry (12 Dec. 1912–22 Oct. 1988), boxer, was born Henry Jackson Jr. near Columbus, Mississippi, the son of Henry Jackson. His mother, whose name is unknown, was a full-blooded Iroquois, and his father was of mixed Indian, Irish, and black ancestry. He was the eleventh child in a family of sharecroppers. When he was four years old his family moved to St. Louis, Missouri, where his father and older brothers worked in the food-processing industry. His mother died a few years later, after which he was reared by his paternal grandmother. Jackson graduated from Toussaint L'Ouverture Grammar School and Vashon High School, working during his school years as a pin boy at a bowling alley and becoming the inter-alley bowling champion in midtown St. Louis. He gained his first boxing experience by winning a competition among the pin boys.

Lacking funds to attend college, Jackson worked at a series of unskilled jobs. At the "colored" Young

Henry Armstrong, boxer and Baptist minister, 15 July 1937. (Library of Congress/Carl Van Vechten.)

Men's Christian Association he came under the tutelage of a former boxer, Harry Armstrong, who gave him the ring name of "Melody Jackson" after hearing him singing in the shower. He had several amateur fights in St. Louis and then left with Harry for Pittsburgh, where he trained to become a professional. Ill-nourished and badly trained, Jackson was knocked out in his first professional fight in July 1931, but he won his second on points. He returned to St. Louis and then with Harry went (probably in the fall of 1931) to Los Angeles, where he fought as an amateur boxer, using the name "Henry Armstrong." Managed by Tom Cox, Henry Armstrong had almost a hundred amateur fights in California and won nearly all of them. Meanwhile, he set up a shoeshine stand and from 1931 to 1934 mainly earned his living by shining shoes. In 1932 Cox sold Armstrong's contract to Wirt Ross; the boxer became a professional again, losing his first two battles on points before becoming a consistent winner. A featherweight at five feet five and a half inches, Armstrong fought mostly in Los Angeles, with occasional trips to other California cities. In November 1934 he had his first major fight, losing a close decision in Mexico City to Baby Arizmendi,

who claimed the world featherweight championship. In January 1935 Armstrong fought Arizmendi for the California-Mexico version of the featherweight title, but he lost. Later that year he beat the former flyweight champion Midget Wolgast in Oakland, California, and in August 1936 he defeated Arizmendi to claim the featherweight title. Armstrong won his last twelve fights in 1936, including a victory over Mike Belloise, another featherweight contender. Late that year Ross sold his contract to the New York manager Eddie Mead; the actual cash for the sale was supplied by the entertainers Al Jolson and George Raft.

In 1937 Armstrong had twenty-seven fights and won them all, twenty-six by knockout, including several matches in New York City. On 29 October he knocked out Petey Sarron to win the world featherweight title at Madison Square Garden. This remarkable series of victories was followed in 1938 by fourteen consecutive wins, ten by knockout, and the acquisition of two more world titles. Armstrong challenged the lightweight champion Lou Ambers to a title fight, but Ambers's manager refused the match. Then, in an audacious move, Armstrong challenged the welterweight champion Barney Ross, and they met in Long Island City on 31 May. Armstrong trounced Ross on points in fifteen rounds and won the world welterweight title despite weighing only 133.5 pounds (less than the lightweight division limit). On 17 August at Madison Square Garden he defeated Ambers in fifteen rounds and won the lightweight title. Armstrong held the championship of three divisions until November, when he voluntarily relinquished the featherweight title, which he had never defended. He successfully defended his welterweight title twice that year against Ceferino Garcia and Al Manfredo. Armstrong's manner of fighting was aptly described by the sportswriter and cartoonist Ted Carroll:

> Armstrong's hurricane style ... has amazed veteran ring observers for many reasons. Although he is forever pressing forward, he sheds punches with a peculiar movement of head and shoulders like the proverbial duck sheds water. His energy and endurance seem limitless as he ... forces his opponents to break ground with a ceaseless barrage of punches tossed with power and precision from all angles.

Armstrong's style invariably resulted in action-filled, exciting fights.

Armstrong frequently was handicapped by the loss of points or rounds because of fouling. His head-down windmill style often resulted in low blows, butts, and other infractions. This problem cost him the lightweight title in his second fight with Ambers at Yankee Stadium on 22 August 1939, when the referee Arthur Donovan deducted five rounds for fouls. However, Armstrong successfully defended his welterweight title eleven times in 1939, including victories over Arizmendi, Davey Day, Lew Feldman, and Ernie Roderick.

Armstrong's amazing series of successes continued in 1940, including six more successful defenses of the welterweight title. Furthermore, he fought a draw with Ceferino Garcia for the middleweight title—160-pound weight limit—in Los Angeles on 1 March, although he weighed only 142 pounds. Had he not been penalized two rounds by the referee George Blake for "rough tactics," Armstrong would have held a fourth world title.

At last, on 4 October 1941 at Madison Square Garden, Fritzie Zivic found the answer to overcoming Armstrong's style and captured the welterweight title. Zivic won decisively by throwing right uppercuts as Armstrong advanced, dramatically flooring the champion at the final bell, as the arena lights suddenly failed. In a return match on 17 January 1941, before a record crowd at the Garden, Zivic pummeled Armstrong even worse, stopping him in twelve rounds. Armstrong made a financially successful comeback in 1942 and continued boxing until 1945; although he won many fights, he was never again a serious title contender.

Armstrong lost his earnings to high living and excessive generosity. He served a brief stint in the army near the end of World War II and managed other fighters. Then he began to drink excessively before experiencing a religious conversion in 1949 and becoming a Baptist minister shortly afterward. He spent the remaining years of his life as an evangelist and founded and directed the Henry Armstrong Youth Foundation in Los Angeles. He had married Willa Mae Shandy in 1934; the couple had one child. Later, he married a second time, but his wife's name and the date of their marriage are unrecorded. In his later years Armstrong suffered from many medical problems, some of them boxing-related, such as cataracts and mental impairment. He died in Los Angeles. He was an inaugural inductee into the International Boxing Hall of Fame in 1990.

FURTHER READING
Armstrong, Henry. *Gloves, Glory, and God: An Autobiography* (1956).
Fleischer, Nat. *Black Dynamite*, vol. 2 (1938).
Obituary: *New York Times*, 25 Oct. 1988.
This entry is taken from the *American National Biography* and is published here with the permission of the American Council of Learned Societies.

LUCKETT V. DAVIS

Armstrong, Lil (3 Feb. 1898–27 Aug. 1971), jazz pianist, composer, and singer, was born Lillian Hardin in Memphis, Tennessee, the daughter of Dempsey Hardin, a strict, churchgoing woman who disapproved of blues music. Nothing is known of her father. At age six Lil began playing organ at home, and at eight she started studying piano. In 1914 she enrolled in the music school of Fisk University in Nashville, taking academic courses and studying piano and music theory. After earning her diploma, around 1917 she joined her mother in Chicago, where she found work demonstrating songs in Jones' Music Store. Prompted by her employer, in 1918 Hardin became house pianist for the clarinetist Lawrence Duhé's band at Bill Bottoms's Dreamland Ballroom, where she played with the cornetists "Sugar Johnny" Smith, FREDDIE KEPPARD, and KING OLIVER; the trombonist Roy Palmer; and other New Orleans musicians. Because she was still a minor, her mother picked her up every night after work.

In January 1920 Hardin joined a second Oliver-led band, and in May 1921 she went to San Francisco with Oliver's Creole Jazz Band for a six-month job at the Pergola Dance Pavilion. Hardin then went back to Chicago and a job at the Dreamland, resuming her former position with Oliver in the summer of 1922. In late August, LOUIS ARMSTRONG joined Oliver's group as second cornetist. Shortly thereafter Armstrong and Hardin began courting. However, while working at the Dreamland, she had married a singer named Jimmie Johnson, whose infidelities soon proved grounds for divorce. Eager to help free Armstrong from his own ill-advised first marriage, Hardin arranged divorces for both of them in 1923, and they were married in February 1924. They had no children. In 1923 King Oliver's Creole Jazz Band recorded thirty-seven performances, on which the pianist was limited to a strictly subordinate role in the rhythm section.

Even before they were married, Lil had begun trying to make Louis more sophisticated in his manners and dress, as well as urging him to leave Oliver. Louis, however, remained adamantly loyal to Oliver until mid-1924, when the band broke up following a long midwestern tour. Months of Lil's prodding had taken their toll, and, finally convinced that he should seek better avenues to showcase his own talent and reap its reward, Louis gave Oliver notice. In September he was offered a featured position in FLETCHER HENDERSON's orchestra at the Roseland Ballroom in New York. In October, Lil followed her husband east but soon returned to Chicago to lead her own band at the Dreamland. During this period, Louis Armstrong's reputation grew far beyond what it had been in Chicago, but by early November 1925 he was ready to leave New York, primarily because Lil wanted him to come home. By this time she was enjoying a successful run with her Dreamland Syncopators and encouraged the owners to pay a higher salary than usual to bring in Louis as a featured attraction.

Between November 1925 and December 1927 Lil Armstrong appeared on all of the Louis Armstrong Hot Five and Hot Seven recordings, forty-four titles in all. She also led one Hot Five date under her own name (as Lil's Hot Shots) in May 1926 and participated, along with Louis, on sessions with Butterbeans (JODIE EDWARDS) and Susie, ALBERTA HUNTER, and the Red Onion Jazz Babies. In July 1926 she also recorded with the New Orleans Bootblacks and the New Orleans Wanderers. In early 1929 she recorded with JOHNNY DODDS in both trio and sextet settings.

Although her command of the piano was marred by limited technique, swift, unswinging time, and a paucity of melodic ideas, Lil Armstrong was nevertheless a highly productive composer of jazz songs. It is difficult to ascertain exactly which songs she wrote independently of Louis Armstrong, but it can be assumed that she played an important role in transcribing and arranging certain melodic themes that he invented. Among the Hot Five and Hot Seven numbers for which she is given full or partial credit are "I'm Gonna Gitcha," "Droppin' Shucks," "King of the Zulus," "Jazz Lips," "Struttin' with Some Barbecue," "Hotter than That," and "Knee Drops." She also contributed "Gate Mouth," "Too Tight Blues," "I Can't Say," "Perdido Street Blues," "Papa Dip," and "Mixed Salad" to the 1926 Bootblacks and Wanderers sessions as well as "Pencil Papa," "Heah Me Talkin'," and "Goober Dance" to Dodds's 1929 dates. However, it must be said that her own contributions on piano,

whether as soloist or accompanist, are invariably the least interesting elements of these recordings.

During the late 1920s Lil bought an eleven-room home in Chicago and real estate on Lake Michigan's Idlewild resort, properties she retained throughout her life. When Lil's job at the Dreamland ended in the spring of 1926, Louis joined CARROLL DICKERSON's orchestra at the Sunset Café while Lil worked in Hugh Swift's band and later toured with Freddie Keppard. During this time Lil also studied at the Chicago Musical College, and, after earning a degree in teaching, she studied at the New York College of Music, where she received her postgraduate degree in 1929.

Louis, who had started philandering while he was in New York, was beginning to tire of Lil's constant jealousy and pressure for him to better himself commercially. He began a serious relationship with another woman, Alpha Smith, around 1928. After numerous arguments with her husband, who had at last become successful, Lil finally sued for legal separation in August 1931, retaining her properties and receiving a considerable cash allowance. She eventually granted him a divorce and also won a suit against him for the rights to the songs they had co-composed. Lil never remarried, and she kept all relevant Louis Armstrong memorabilia, including letters, photos, and his old cornet, until her death.

Through the mid-1930s Lil Armstrong led both all-female and all-male bands of varying sizes in the Midwest, sometimes under the billing of Mrs. Louis Armstrong and Her Orchestra. She also broadcast regularly and appeared as a soloist in the *Hot Chocolates* and *Shuffle Along* revues. From 1936 Lil Armstrong lived in New York and worked as a house pianist for Decca Records, between 1936 and 1940 leading small jazz groups with such featured sidemen as JOE THOMAS, J. C. HIGGINBOTHAM, BUSTER BAILEY, and CHU BERRY. She also provided the accompaniments for the singers Blue Lu Barker, Rosetta Howard, Alberta Hunter, Frankie "Half Pint" Jaxon, PEETIE WHEATSTRAW, and others and participated in jazz dates under the leadership of RED ALLEN, Johnny Dodds, and ZUTTY SINGLETON. She emerges as a vivacious and entertaining singer on her own Decca recordings of 1936–1940. Among her compositions from this period are "My Hi-De-Ho Man," "Brown Gal," "Just for a Thrill," "Born to Swing," "Let's Get Happy Together," and "Everything's Wrong, Ain't Nothing Right." In late 1940 Armstrong returned to Chicago, where she worked throughout the next decade as a soloist in many local venues.

In early 1952 Armstrong went to Paris, where she recorded in a trio with SIDNEY BECHET and Zutty Singleton and also under her own name in 1953 and 1954. She worked primarily as a soloist in Paris but also spent some time in London before returning in the late 1950s to Chicago. In December 1960 she recorded with Franz Jackson's band and in September 1961 led her own group for an album in the Riverside label's *Chicago: The Living Legends* series. In late October 1961 she participated in the telecast of *Chicago and All That Jazz*, an all-star jazz concert segment of NBC's *Dupont Show of the Week*. Little is known of Armstrong's activities after this point, but she probably continued appearing in clubs in Chicago and environs. Following Louis Armstrong's death in July 1971, a memorial concert was staged in his honor on 27 August at Chicago's Civic Center, and it was during her performance at this event that Lil Armstrong suffered a fatal coronary.

FURTHER READING

In 1960 or 1961 an oral interview with Lil Armstrong titled *Satchmo and Me* was released as Riverside RLP12–120.

Dahl, Linda. *Stormy Weather* (1984).

Giddins, Gary. *Satchmo* (1988).

Jones, Max, and John Chilton. *Louis: The Louis Armstrong Story 1900–1971* (1971; rev. ed., 1988).

Placksin, Sally. *American Women in Jazz* (1982).

Unterbrink, Mary. *Jazz Women at the Keyboard* (1983).

Obituary: *New York Times*, 28 Aug. 1971.

DISCOGRAPHY

Bruyninckx, Walter. *Swing Discography, 1920–1988* (12 vols., 1985–1989).

Rust, Brian. *Jazz Records, 1897–1942* (1982).

This entry is taken from the *American National Biography* and is published here with the permission of the American Council of Learned Societies.

JACK SOHMER

Armstrong, Louis (4 Aug. 1901–6 Jul. 1971), jazz trumpeter and singer, known universally as "Satchmo" and later as "Pops," was born in New Orleans, Louisiana, the son of William Armstrong, a boiler stoker in a turpentine plant, and Mary Est "Mayann" Albert, a laundress. Abandoned by his father shortly after birth, Armstrong was raised by his paternal grandmother, Josephine, until he was returned to his mother's care at age five. Mother and son moved from Jane Alley, in a violence-torn slum, to an only slightly better area, Franklyn and Perdido streets, where nearby cheap cabarets gave the boy his first introduction to the new kind of music, jazz, that was developing in New Orleans. Although Armstrong claims to have heard the early jazz cornetist BUDDY BOLDEN when he was about age five, this incident may be apocryphal. As a child, he worked odd jobs, sang in a vocal quartet, and around 1911 bought a used cornet with his savings. He dropped out of school and got into trouble; in 1913 he was placed in the New Orleans Colored Waifs' Home for Boys, where Peter Davis, the music instructor, gave Armstrong his first formal music instruction. He left the home in June 1914. Although he was remanded to the custody of his father, he soon went to live with his mother and younger sister, Beatrice, whom Armstrong affectionately called "Mama Lucy." As a teenager, Armstrong played street parades, associated with the older musicians, and held various jobs, including delivering coal with a mule-drawn coal wagon. In his second autobiography, *My Life in New Orleans*, he relates the importance of these years in his development, particularly the influence of KING OLIVER:

> At that time I did not know the other great musicians such as JELLY ROLL MORTON, FREDDY KEPPARD, … and Eddy Atkins. All of them had left New Orleans long before the red-light district was closed by the Navy and the law [1917]. Of course I met most of them in later years, but Papa Joe Oliver, God bless him, was my man. I often did errands for Stella Oliver, his wife, and Joe would give me lessons for my pay. I could not have asked for anything I wanted more. It was my ambition to play as he did. I still think that if it had not been for Joe Oliver jazz would not be what it is today. (99)

In 1918 Armstrong married Daisy Parker and began his life as a professional musician. Between November 1918 and August 1922 he played cornet at Tom Anderson's club as well as in the Tuxedo Brass Band, in FATE MARABLE's band on Mississippi River excursion paddle-wheel steamers, and incidentally in several New Orleans cabarets. His musical associates during these years were Oliver, Warren "BABY" DODDS, JOHNNY DODDS, JOHNNY ST. CYR, HONORE DUTREY, George "POPS" FOSTER, and EDWARD "KID" ORY.

Armstrong's rise to prominence began with his move to Chicago in August 1922, when Oliver invited him to come to the Lincoln Garden's Cafe

Louis Armstrong, preeminent jazz musician, playing the trumpet, 1953. (Library of Congress.)

as second cornet in Oliver's Creole Jazz Band. This group defined jazz for the local Chicago musicians and stimulated the development of this music in profound ways. Armstrong's first recordings were made with Oliver in 1923 and 1924; "Riverside Blues," "Snake Rag," "Mabel's Dream," "Chattanooga Stomp," and "Dipper Mouth Blues" are some of the performances that preserve and display his early mature work.

In 1924 Armstrong divorced his first wife and that same year married the pianist in Oliver's band, Lillian Hardin (LIL ARMSTRONG). She encouraged him to accept an invitation to play with the FLETCHER HENDERSON orchestra at the Roseland Ballroom in New York City. Armstrong's impact on this prominent name band was phenomenal. His solo style brought to the East a tonal power, creative virtuosity, and rhythmic drive that had not been a regular aspect of the Henderson band's performance practice. Armstrong's influence on Henderson, himself an arranger and pianist, and

two of his fellow band members, in particular, the arranger and saxophonist DON REDMAN and the saxophone virtuoso COLEMAN HAWKINS, was partially responsible for the development of a new jazz idiom or style—swing. During his fourteen months with Henderson, Armstrong participated in more than twenty recording sessions and left memorable solos on "One of These Days," "Copenhagen," and "Everybody Loves My Baby," on which he cut his first, brief, vocal chorus. While in New York, Armstrong also recorded with CLARENCE WILLIAMS's Blue Five, a small combo that included the already famous saxophonist SIDNEY BECHET, and with the star blues singers MA RAINEY and BESSIE SMITH. With Henderson, Armstrong played trumpet, but in these small-group sessions he returned to cornet. For another two years he continued to use both instruments but finally retired his cornet for the brighter, more focused sound of the trumpet.

Despite his growing stature among the jazz community, Armstrong was still but a sideman when he returned to Chicago in 1925. He immediately became the star of his wife's band at the Dreamland Cafe and soon joined Erskine Tate's orchestra at the Vendome Theater. In November 1925 he made his first recordings as a leader with a pickup group of old associates he called the "Hot Five"—his wife, Lil, on piano; Kid Ory on trombone; Johnny Dodds on clarinet; and St. Cyr on banjo. These recordings of the Hot Five and the Hot Seven (with the addition of bass and drums) are towering monuments of traditional jazz. "Cornet Chop," "Gut Bucket Blues," "Heebie Jeebies," "Skid-Dat-De-Dat," "Big Butter and Egg Man," "Struttin' with Some Barbecue," "Hotter Than That," and several others are numbered among the classics of this style, have entered the standard repertoire, and continue to be studied and performed regularly. In these recordings Armstrong established his eminence as a cornet and trumpet virtuoso and an unparalleled improviser, composer, and jazz vocalist. Melrose Brothers published notated transcriptions of some of his solos in 1927 immediately after the appearance of these recordings; these may be the first transcriptions from recorded performances ever published. The significance of this series of recordings is summarized by Gunther Schuller in his study *Early Jazz*:

> The smooth rhythms of the earlier improvisations give way to stronger, contrasting, harder swinging rhythms. Double-time breaks abound. Melodic line and rhythm combine to produce more striking contours. This was, of course, the result not only of Armstrong's increasing technical skill, but also of his maturing musicality, which saw the jazz solo in terms not of a pop-tune more or less embellished, but of a chord progression generating a maximum of creative originality…. His later solos all but ignored the original tune and started with only the chord changes given. (Schuller, 102–103)

Armstrong's association with EARL "FATHA" HINES in 1927 led to another series of pathbreaking recordings in 1928, most notably "West End Blues," with a reconstituted Hot Five, and "Weather Bird," a trumpet and piano duet. In "West End Blues," Armstrong not only achieves an unprecedented level of virtuosity but also displays the beginnings of motivic development in jazz solos. In "Weather Bird," Hines and Armstrong partake in a rapid exchange of antecedent-consequent improvised phrases that set a pattern for future jazz improvisers who "trade fours and twos."

In 1929 Armstrong moved with his band from Chicago to New York for an engagement at Connie's Inn in Harlem. The floor show used a score by FATS WALLER that became a Broadway success as *Hot Chocolates* and featured an onstage Armstrong trumpet solo on "Ain't Misbehavin'." He also pursued many other endeavors, going into the recording studio to front his own band with Jack Teagarden and playing and singing in LUIS RUSSELL's group, which also featured the Chicago banjoist and guitar player Eddie Condon. Armstrong's singing style was unique in American popular music, especially when it was first presented to listeners on a broad scale through recordings of the 1920s.

One of his first vocal accomplishments was to introduce an improvisatory vocal-instrumental mode of singing called "scat singing" in his recordings of "Heebie Jeebies" and "Gully Low Blues" of 1926 and 1927, respectively. Although this method of singing nonsense syllables was common in New Orleans and had been used by others, it was Armstrong's recordings that were credited with the invention of this new device and that influenced hosts of later jazz singers. Contrasting with the classically oriented popular-song vocalists of the day, with the shouting-and-dancing stage singers of ragtime and minstrelsy, and with the loud and lusty belters of the classic blues, Armstrong's natural technique brought a relaxed but exuberant jazz style and a gravelly personal tone to popular singing. His 1929 recordings of "I Can't Give You Anything but Love" and "Ain't Misbehavin'" achieved great popular success. Armstrong continued to sing throughout his career and reached a pinnacle of popular success in 1964 when his recording of "Hello Dolly" became the best-selling record in America, moving to number one on the popular music charts.

From 1930 to the mid-1940s Armstrong was usually featured with a big band. In 1935 he joined forces with Joe Glaser, a tough-minded businessman who guided his career until 1969. Armstrong divorced Lil Hardin, marrying Alpha Smith in 1938. He later divorced her and was married a fourth and final time in 1942 to Lucille Wilson. He had no children with any of his wives. After World War II, Armstrong returned to performing with a small ensemble and played a concert in New York's Town Hall, with "Peanuts" Hucko (clarinet), Bobby Hackett (trumpet), Jack Teagarden (trombone), Dick Cary (piano), Bob Haggart (bass), and BIG SID CATLETT (drums), that inaugurated a new phase in his career. After the success of this "formal concert," Armstrong began to tour with a band labeled his "All Stars," ensembles of approximately the same size but with varying personnel selected from the ranks of established, well-known jazz musicians. Through Glaser's efforts, Armstrong and his All Stars became the highest-paid jazz band in the world. They toured successfully, sparking a renewed interest in Armstrong's recordings and earning him a place on the cover of *Time* magazine on 21 February 1949.

Throughout his long career Armstrong, as trumpeter, remained the leading figure among classic jazz musicians and rode many waves of public and financial success, but his historical impact as a jazz instrumentalist lessened as new styles developed and younger musicians looked elsewhere for leadership. Still, his solo trumpet playing remained superlative while other phases of his career, such as singing, acting, writing, and enjoying the fruits of his celebrity, gained prominence as time passed. Between 1932 and 1965 he appeared in almost fifty motion pictures, including *Rhapsody in Black and Blue* (1932), *Pennies from Heaven* (1936), *Every Day's a Holiday* (1937), *Doctor Rhythm* (1938), *Jam Session* (1944), *New Orleans* (1946), *The Strip* (1951), *High Society* (1956), *Satchmo the Great* (1957), *The Beat Generation* (1959), *When the Boys Meet the Girls* (1965), and *Hello, Dolly!* (1969). Beginning with broadcasts in April 1937, he was the first black performer to be featured in a network radio series, and he appeared as a guest on dozens of television shows starting in the 1950s.

Often unjustly criticized for pandering to the racist attitudes that prevailed in the venues where he performed, Armstrong was, in fact, a significant leader in the struggle for racial equality in America. He was a black artist whose work blossomed contemporaneously with the other artistic and intellectual achievements of the Harlem Renaissance and an important personage who spoke publicly in protest and canceled a U.S. State Department tour in 1957 when Governor Orval Faubus of Arkansas refused to let black children attend a public school. Armstrong firmly believed in equal opportunity as a right and in personal merit as the only measure of worth, and he was one of the first black jazz musicians to perform and record with white musicians (Hoagy Carmichael, Tommy Dorsey, Jack Teagarden, Bud Freeman, and Bing Crosby, among others). His artistry was such that he became a role model not only for black musicians but also for numerous aspiring young white musicians, most notably Bix Beiderbecke, Jimmy McPartland, Bobby Hackett, and Gil Evans.

Informally he became known as an "Ambassador of Goodwill," and Ambassador "Satch" toured Europe and Africa under the sponsorship of the Department of State during the 1950s. Armstrong amassed many honors in his lifetime—medals, stamps in his honor from foreign countries, invitations from royalty and heads of state, and critical awards such as the annual *Down Beat* Musicians Poll—but none seemed to hold greater significance for him than returning to his birthplace, New Orleans, in 1949 as King of the Zulus for the annual Mardi Gras celebration. Even though ill health plagued him in his last few years, Armstrong continued to work, appearing on television and playing an engagement at the Waldorf-Astoria Hotel in New York City during the last year of his life. He died in his home in Corona, Queens, New York.

Louis Armstrong and but three or four others are preeminent in the history of jazz. His importance in the development of this art form has gained greater, almost universal recognition in the years since his death as scholars and musicians reevaluate his contributions as a soloist, composer, bandleader, and role model. The measure of his impact on the social history of twentieth-century America also seems to be greater now as he gains recognition for his contributions to the Harlem Renaissance, for his actions as a thoughtful spokesperson for black Americans, as a significant writer of autobiography, as an entertainer of stature, and as a singer responsible for the development of major trends in American popular and jazz singing. His most accomplished biographer, Gary Giddins, wrote in *Satchmo*: "Genius is the transforming agent. Nothing else can explain Louis Armstrong's ascendancy. He had no formal training, yet he alchemized the cabaret music of an outcast minority into an art that has expanded in ever-widening orbits, with no sign of collapse" (26).

FURTHER READING

The papers of Louis Armstrong are preserved in the Louis Armstrong Archive at Queens College of the City University of New York, and virtually all of his recordings, some oral history material, and other related documents are at the Institute of Jazz Studies at Rutgers University in Newark, New Jersey.

Armstrong, Louis. *Satchmo: My Life in New Orleans* (1954).

Armstrong, Louis. *Swing That Music* (1936).

Collier, James Lincoln. *Louis Armstrong: An American Genius* (1983).

Friedwald, Will. *Jazz Singing: America's Great Voices from Bessie Smith to Bebop and Beyond* (1990).

Giddins, Gary. *Satchmo* (1988).

Gourse, Leslie. *Louis' Children: American Jazz Singers* (1984).

Jones, Max, and John Chilton. *Louis: The Louis Armstrong Story 1900–1971* (1971; rev. ed., 1988).

Schuller, Gunther. *Early Jazz: Its Roots and Musical Development* (1968).

Schuller, Gunther. *The Swing Era: The Development of Jazz 1930–1945* (1989).

Obituary: *New York Times*, 7 July 1971.

DISCOGRAPHY

Westerberg, Hans. *Boy from New Orleans: A Discography of Louis "Satchmo" Armstrong* (1981).

This entry is taken from the *American National Biography* and is published here with the permission of the American Council of Learned Societies.

FRANK TIRRO

Armwood, Blanche (23 Jan. 1890–16 Oct. 1939), educator and activist, was the youngest of five children born to Levin and Maggie Armwood in Tampa, Florida. Armwood's father was born a slave in Thomas County, Georgia, in 1855 and in the late 1870s became the first African American police officer in Tampa, Florida, and in 1895 became a deputy sheriff.

Armwood started her education at St. Peter Claver's Catholic School. She completed her studies in 1902 at the age of twelve and passed the Florida State Uniform Teachers' Examination. Since Tampa did not have a continuing education school for African Americans, the Armwoods sent Blanche to Spelman Seminary (later Spelman College), an all-female prep school for black women, in Atlanta, Georgia. There she studied English, Latin, and home economics, courses that would later prove an asset to her. Graduating from Spelman Seminary in 1906 with honors, summa cum laude, after four years of study, Armwood was the youngest in her class and began looking forward to attending college. However, because of her father's illness, she returned to Tampa. She immediately passed the Florida teacher's examination and started teaching first grade in the city's African American public schools. She quickly moved from teaching the primary grades to high school and took several summer classes in home economics from Florida Agricultural and Mechanical College, Columbia University, and the New York School of Social Sciences.

At age twenty-three Armwood married Daniel Webster Perkins, an attorney, on 23 November 1913. She resigned her position, having served seven and a half years in the school system and advancing from teacher to principal of the College Hill School in Tampa, and moved with her husband to his hometown of Knoxville, Tennessee. Within a few months, however, she discovered that her husband had an illegitimate son. History does not document her personal relationship with Perkins, but her religious beliefs and attitudes about marriage would not allow her to remain married. She eventually had the marriage annulled and in late 1914 returned to Tampa. That same year she was approached by the Tampa Gas Company and the Hillsborough County Board of Education to organize an industrial arts school that would specialize in domestic science. The school opened in January 1915, largely funded by the Tampa Gas Company. The Tampa School of Household Arts sought to help African American women properly perform their domestic duties by teaching them how to operate modern gas appliances. The school was such a success that more than two hundred women completed the training the first year. Armwood served as principal and head instructor for three years and was instrumental in the successful training of several hundred African American women and girls. She went on to open and organize a number of similar schools in other southern states. In the summer of 1917 New Orleans Gas and Light Company asked Tampa Gas Company to release Armwood to come to New Orleans to organize and operate its new school.

Armwood traveled throughout Louisiana, overseeing home demonstration agents. On 15 October 1917 she opened the largest school of domestic science in New Orleans for African American women and girls, New Orleans School of Domestic Science. She made numerous food demonstrations and in May 1918 published a cookbook called *Food Conservation in the Home*. In 1919, when she was twenty-nine years old, she met and married Dr. John C. Beatty, a dentist and graduate of Howard University Dental College, and four months later she resigned her position as supervisor of home economics. From 1919 until 1922 Armwood took on several projects, serving as-spokesperson on women's voting rights, anti-lynching, and other civil rights issues. She joined the Republican Party, was recommended to serve as a national campaign speaker for the party, and went on to help create Republican clubs to teach African American women about politics and the voting process. She served on the presidential campaign for Warren G. Harding. Because of her dedication to the campaign, she was invited to the Marion, Ohio, home of Senator Harding to celebrate a Social Justice and Woman's Day affair.

In 1922 Armwood and her husband returned to Tampa, where she became the first executive secretary of the Tampa Urban League (TUL), a social welfare organization designed to help African Americans adjust to urban life. That same year the Hillsborough County school board appointed Armwood the first supervisor of African American schools, a position she held for eight years. During her tenure she purchased new school buildings, increased teachers' salaries, and extended the school year from six to nine months. She was influential in the 1926 opening of Booker T. Washington High School, which after four years became the first accredited African American school in the county. Armwood also held leadership positions in two major African American organizations, the Home Economics Department for the National Association of Colored Women (NACW) and the Louisiana chapter of the National Association for the Advancement of Colored People (NAACP). She also served as the state director of Florida's Anti-Lynching Crusades. During her time as executive secretary, Armwood assisted in opening the first library in an African American community, the Busy Merrymakers Women's Club, Helping Hand Day Nursery and Kindergarten for working mothers, and the Booker T. Washington Tampa chapter of the American Red Cross.

In the late 1920s Armwood's second husband was murdered by the family chauffeur amid unfounded rumors that she was involved in an affair with the driver. Devastated by the murder, Armwood threw herself into church work, where she met Edward T. Washington, a supervisor for the Interstate Commerce Commission. They were married in 1931, and soon afterward the couple relocated to Washington, D.C. Throughout the 1930s she labored for the NACW and NAACP. In 1934 Armwood enrolled in Howard University School of Law, earning her law degree in 1937 and graduating in 1938 with her juris doctorate degree, becoming the first African American woman born in Florida to earn a law degree. Her decision to become a lawyer was based on her commitment to the suffrage movement and the antilynching campaign. Her law degree helped divert her attention from activities having to do with racial uplift to the legal issues and fight against racism.

Armwood died suddenly at the age of forty-nine during a speaking engagement in the Northeast. It is not certain exactly what her illness was, but it was documented that she died from complications of many ailments, including phlebitis and exhaustion. Her life ended just when her career was starting a new phase. She was buried in the Armwood family plot at L'Unione Italiana Cemetery in Tampa, Florida. She was eulogized by Dr. BENJAMIN E. MAYS, then president of Morehouse College at the John Wesley AME Church in Washington, D.C. Having no children or dependants, she left a scholarship trust fund to her alma mater, Spelman College. Nearly a half century after her death, congressmen from Tampa and Tampa city officials paid tribute to her and in 1984 the Blanche Armwood Comprehensive High School opened in Seffner, Florida.

FURTHER READING

Alishahi, Michele. "'For Peace and Civic Righteousness': Blanche Armwood and the Struggle for Freedom and Racial Equality in Tampa, Florida," M.A. thesis, University of South Florida (2003).

Bilirakis, Michael. "Blanche Armwood: Tribute to the Late Blanche Armwood," *Congressional Record*, 2 Oct. 1984.

Burke, Mary. "The Success of Blanche Armwood," *Sunland Tribune*, Nov. 1989.

Davis, Elizabeth Lindsay. "Blanche Armwood," in *Lifting as They Climb* (1933).

Durham, John R. "Blanche Armwood: The Early Years," M.A. thesis, University of South Florida (1988).

LINDA WILSON-JONES

Arnett, Benjamin William (6 Mar. 1838–9 Oct. 1906), African American religious, educational, and political leader, was born in Brownsville, Pennsylvania, the son of Samuel G. Arnett and Mary Louisa (maiden name unknown). Benjamin Arnett was a man of "mixed Irish, Indian, Scots, and African ancestry" (Wright, *Eighty-Seven Years*, 79). He was educated in a one-room schoolhouse in Bridgeport, Pennsylvania. Arnett worked as a longshoreman along the Ohio and Mississippi rivers and worked briefly as a hotel waiter. His career as a longshoreman and waiter ended abruptly in 1858 when a cancerous tumor necessitated the amputation of his left leg. He turned to teaching and was granted a certificate on 19 December 1863. At that time he was the only African American schoolteacher licensed in Fayette County, Pennsylvania. For ten months during the academic year 1884–1885, Arnett served as a school principal in Washington, D.C. He returned to Brownsville in 1885, teaching there until 1887. Although largely self-educated, he also attended classes at Lane Theological Seminary in Cincinnati (later affiliated with McCormick Theological Seminary in Chicago). A man of many interests, Arnett was an occasional lecturer in ethics and psychology at the Payne Theological Seminary at Wilberforce University, a historian of the African Methodist Episcopal (AME) Church, a trustee of the Archaeological and Historical Society of Ohio, a member of the executive committee of the National Sociological Society, and was statistical secretary of the Ecumenical Conference of Methodism for the western section from 1891 to 1901.

Arnett's formal association with the AME Church began in February 1856. He was licensed to preach on 30 March 1865 and was ordained a deacon on 30 April 1868 in Columbus, Ohio. He became an elder on 12 May 1870 in Xenia, Ohio. As a delegate from the Ohio Annual Conference, Arnett attended the General AME Conference in 1872. He was appointed assistant secretary of the General Conference in 1876 and became general secretary in 1880. He was also elected financial secretary of the General Conference in 1880 and again in 1884. As financial secretary, he had primary responsibility for the publication of the annual *Budget* of the AME Church. Arnett's budgets contain not only detailed financial records but also personal observations and historical information. He continued as an editor of the AME *Budget* until 1904.

At the General Conference of 1888, Arnett was elected a bishop of the AME Church, the church's seventeenth bishop. He served the seventh episcopal district (South Carolina and Florida) from 1888 to 1892, the fourth episcopal district (Indiana, Illinois, and Iowa) from 1892 to 1900, the third episcopal district (Ohio, California, and Pittsburgh) from 1900 to 1904, and the first episcopal district (Philadelphia, New York, and New England) from 1904 to 1906.

An ardent Republican and active in party politics, Arnett was chaplain to the Ohio legislature in 1879 and to the Republican State Convention in Ohio in 1880. His most notable political accomplishment was his election (by eight votes) to the Ohio legislature to represent predominantly white Greene County in 1886. Arnett was the first African American legislator in Ohio to represent a predominantly white constituency. During his term in office he drafted a bill to abolish Ohio's discriminatory Black Laws and introduced bills to secure state funding for Wilberforce University, which at the time was near bankruptcy. While in the Ohio legislature, Arnett also established an enduring friendship with William McKinley Jr., and on behalf of the AME Church presented McKinley with the Bible used when he took the oath of office of the presidency in 1897. Arnett maintained close ties with McKinley and is said to have exerted considerable influence in Washington during the McKinley administration (1897–1901). He served as chaplain to the Republican National Convention in St. Louis in 1896.

Arnett enjoyed a considerable and deserved reputation as a public speaker and parliamentarian. He addressed the Republican State Convention in Denver in 1886 and the Centennial Celebration of the First Settlement of the Northwest Territory in Mariti, Ohio, in 1888; he was invited to give commencement addresses at Wilberforce University in 1887 and at Claflin College, South Carolina, in 1889; and he presented the keynote address at the meeting of the Grand Army of the Republic in Chicago in 1900. He presided at the Parliament of Religion held at Chicago in September 1893 and at the Ecumenical Conference of Methodists held in London in September 1901. Arnett was vice president of the Anti-Saloon League of America and an active member of FREDERICK DOUGLASS's National Equal Rights League. Arnett was also active in the Masons and worked diligently on behalf of the Young Men's Christian Association.

Arnett married Mary Louise Gordon in 1858. The couple had seven children. Two of their sons, Benjamin William Arnett Jr. and Henry Y. Arnett, became ministers in the AME Church. Benjamin Jr. became president of Edward Waters College and Allen University. Henry became a pastor and presiding elder in the AME Church's Philadelphia and Delaware Conferences.

During Arnett's term in the Third Episcopal District (1900–1904), he established a ten-acre estate near Wilberforce University, called Tawawa Chimney Corner, where he hosted numerous visitors and amassed a large collection of African American literature. A number of volumes from Arnett's personal library were later acquired by W. E. B. DuBois; other volumes from Arnett's library are now a part of the Arthur A. Schomburg collection of the New York Public Library. Arnett died of uremia in Wilberforce, Ohio.

Richard R. Wright Jr., in *Eighty-Seven Years behind the Black Curtain*, describes his initial encounter with Arnett: "I was greatly impressed. Bishop Arnett, a handsome, clean-shaven man, was Northern born, very intelligent, unusually witty, an expert in church financing, author of half a dozen books and pamphlets, a distinguished and convincing orator, and a 'soul-stirring' preacher" (Wright, 92–94). This assessment was echoed by not a few of Arnett's contemporaries.

Arnett served as a bishop for more than eighteen years and had a considerable influence on church affairs. Perhaps his greatest contributions stem from his ability to mediate among various factions within the church and from his ability to successfully transcend racial, ethnic, and class boundaries. His published lectures, notably his 1888 centennial address "The Northwest Territory," show careful scholarship and a keen intellect.

FURTHER READING

Arnett's papers are in the Carnegie Library, Wilberforce University.

Coleman, Lucretia H. Newman. *Poor Ben: A Study of Real Life* (1890).

Wright, Richard R., Jr. *The Bishops of the African Methodist Episcopal Church* (1963).

Wright, Richard R., Jr. *Eighty-Seven Years behind the Black Curtain* (1965).

Obituary: *New York Times*, 9 Oct. 1906.

This entry is taken from the *American National Biography* and is published here with the permission of the American Council of Learned Societies.

STEPHEN D. GLAZIER

Arnold, Hendrick (?–1849), scout and pioneer of the West, was one of the free blacks in Texas who experienced some degree of freedom under four different governing entities—Spain, Mexico, the Republic of Texas, and the United States. Free blacks never constituted a large population in Texas in the eighteenth and nineteenth centuries. For example, a census in 1860 put the number of free blacks at four hundred, but later estimates by historians suggest that their numbers approached eight hundred. Despite their small numbers free blacks made a significant contribution to the early history of Texas. Hendrick Arnold played a pivotal role in the Texas Revolution (1835–1836) and beyond.

The date of Arnold's birth is not known. He emigrated from Mississippi with his parents, Daniel and Rachel Arnold, in the winter of 1826. His father was likely white, while his mother was black; nothing else is known about them. The family joined the existing Stephen F. Austin colony of approximately three hundred families on the Brazos River and migrated with an additional nine hundred families

between 1825 and 1829. Historical records indicate that by the fall of 1835 Hendrick Arnold had moved to the area of San Antonio, where he married a Tejana (Mexican) woman named Martina. She was the stepdaughter of Erastus "Deaf" Smith, another noteworthy figure in Texas history. Arnold had a daughter named Harriet in 1827, whose mother was one of his father's slaves. A second daughter named Juanita was born later, although the exact date is not known, likely from his marriage with Martina.

By the fall of 1835 Arnold was operating a gristmill in San Antonio. The social and political realities leading up to the Texas Revolution are summarized succinctly by the historian Harold Schoen: "It was as easy for the Negro as for the white man to place all his grievances, real and imaginary, at the door of the Mexican government, and when the outbreak of hostilities threatened his life and property and the safety of his family, all of which he held as dearly as his neighbors, he was willing to risk his life in their preservation" (Schoen, 26).

While Arnold and Deaf Smith (his father-in-law) were hunting buffalo in a frontier region north of present-day Austin, Mexican military forces successfully occupied San Antonio. On their journey home, when they were about five miles east of San Antonio, Smith and Arnold came upon a military encampment of Texans at Salado Creek commanded by Stephen F. Austin. Smith and Arnold volunteered as guides. A council of Texan officers met in December 1835 to consider moving on San Antonio, but they decided to postpone the attack.

When another Texan leader, Benjamin Milam, arrived at the encampment, he called for an immediate attack on San Antonio, an attack referred to by historians as the Siege of Bexar. Arnold was among the few known to have served as guides for Milam's military division. The start of the battle, however, was delayed because of Arnold's absence. It was only upon his return (from a hunting trip) that Milam's army of some three hundred expressed willingness to proceed with the attack. The Siege of Bexar was successful militarily, but Milam was killed. A leader of another military division, Francis Johnson, wrote the official report of the battle and specifically cited Arnold for his meritorious service. The Siege of Bexar was one of four major engagements of the war for Texas's independence. Later engagements involving the fall of the Alamo and Goliad were followed by final victory and Texas's independence after the Battle of San Jacinto on 21 April 1836. Arnold also served in the Battle of San Antonio, probably in a similar role as a scout. Historical records note that he was wounded sometime during his military service.

In 1836 Arnold petitioned the general council of the Texas provisional government for relief for his family, a common practice of Texas Revolution war veterans. He received a land grant a few miles northwest of the present site of Bandera, a relatively unexplored area less highly valued by others seeking land grants. Arnold successfully secured adjacent land for his grandmother, his father, and his brother. His brother appears to have been the only family member to settle on the land. Arnold died in a cholera epidemic in Bexar County in 1849 and was buried on the banks of the Medina River near his homestead.

Arnold's military service and his financial success are noteworthy given that the status of blacks deteriorated sharply under the Republic of Texas, whose constitution did not grant them full rights as citizens and allowed the practice of slavery. The Hendrick Arnold–Bertha Tryon Cemetery in Bandera, Texas, is named in his honor. A Texas state historical marker in San Antonio commemorates the Siege of Bexar and notes the contribution of Arnold, "free Negro & scout," to the Texas Revolution. The present-day Landmark Inn State Historical Site near Castroville, Texas, is located near the area where Arnold is believed to have settled near the Medina River.

FURTHER READING

Barr, Alwyn. *Black Texans: A History of African Americans in Texas, 1528–1995* (1996).

Jenkins, John, ed. *The Papers of the Texas Revolution, 1835–1836* (1973).

Schoen, Harold. "Free Negro in the Republic of Texas: The Free Negro and the Texas Revolution," *Southwestern Historical Quarterly* 40, no. 1 (July 1936).

Willett, Donald, and Stephen Curley. *Invisible Texans: Women and Minorities in Texas History* (2005).

JACK BORDEN WATSON

Arnold, James (15 Feb. 1901–8 Nov. 1968), singer and guitarist known as "Kokomo," was born in Lovejoy Station, Georgia, a small railroad town in Clayton County, approximately twenty-five miles south of Atlanta. He was raised on a farm and learned some guitar from a relative named John Wigges, who was an accomplished knife-style guitarist. In 1919 Arnold moved to Buffalo, New York, where he worked in a steel mill. After stops and similar jobs in Pittsburgh, Pennsylvania, and Gary, Indiana, Arnold moved to the Mississippi Delta in the late 1920s. He reportedly made a living as a bootlegger and throughout his life regarded his music as a sideline. He lived for a while in Glen Allan, Mississippi, and played with a partner named Willie Morris.

In 1930 Arnold made his recording debut as "Gitfiddle Jim" in a Memphis recording session for Victor. The two songs, "Rainy Night Blues" and "Paddlin' Madeline Blues," displayed the kinetic and speedy style for which he became known. "Rainy Night Blues," with its characteristic riff, presaged the classic "Dust My Broom." Arnold was a left-handed guitarist and often hummed while executing his manic slide runs.

Arnold settled in Chicago in the early 1930s, again taking jobs in steel mills. "Kansas" Joe McCoy recommended him to the Decca producer Mayo Williams. Arnold's first Decca recordings in 1934 produced a rare occurrence in blues: a double-sided hit. "Milk Cow Blues" and "Old Original Kokomo Blues" became Decca's first significant blues successes since 1930. Both songs were immeasurable influences on many blues and country artists who followed. A few of the most notable examples were ROBERT JOHNSON in his "Milk Cow Calf Blues," and Elvis Presley in his cover of the same piece in his original Sun Records sessions. Robert Johnson also adapted "Kokomo Blues" into his "Sweet Home Chicago."

Arnold's records sold very well and were widely heard throughout the South. Previously the recordings of important male blues singers such as SKIP JAMES and SON HOUSE enjoyed only modest and mostly regional success and were not appreciated on a wide scale until many years later. By comparison, Arnold's records were wildly successful immediately. His style was informed partly by the jazz music of the 1920s, with his deft slide guitar flourishes hinting at melodies from the great female singers and trumpeters of that era. Arnold was also influenced by the popular hokum bands of the time, and his slide playing could impart humor and a kazoo-like characteristic. It is probably no coincidence that there are similarities in his guitar playing to that of Hudson Whitaker, better known as TAMPA RED, who was also born and raised in Georgia.

Arnold made many records and tended to repeat themes and styles, as did many blues artists with great bodies of work. His living in several locales in the North allowed him to absorb the sophisticated jazz stylings of the cities and develop an articulation and wordplay in his singing not usually heard in blues singers in the South. His move to the Delta added grit and depth to his music before he finally settled in Chicago.

Arnold's influence on the great blues singers who followed cannot be overstated. Though he is largely unknown by many of today's blues fans, Arnold was a major influence on many great artists and provided both musical and lyrical archetypes. The "Dust My Broom" lick alone shaped the career of ELMORE JAMES, who adapted it from Robert Johnson, who borrowed it from Arnold. Such borrowing was one of the great traditions in the blues. A version of "Kokomo Blues" was first recorded by Scrapper Blackwell in the late 1920s. For his own hit version of the song, Arnold supposedly adopted "Kokomo" from the brand of coffee; "Kokomo" also became Arnold's nickname. Arnold was strongly influenced by the singer and guitarist TOMMY JOHNSON.

Lyrically, there are many themes and word combinations heard in Arnold's songs that have made their way into the blues lexicon. A few examples are "I believe I'll dust my broom," asking for water and getting gasoline, and rolling and tumbling. Perhaps the most startling is the "Smokestack Lightning" reference heard in his version of "Stop, Look, and Listen," which also features a kind of yodeling. Certainly these topics and tactics were not lost on subsequent blues legends such as Robert Johnson, HOWLIN' WOLF, MUDDY WATERS, Elmore James, and MISSISSIPPI FRED McDOWELL. Arnold's lyrics could be quite wry, and he adapted his "Dirty Dozens" from the traditional put-down songs called the "twelves." In addition to deep blues and novelty songs Arnold also recorded the interesting "Sissy Man Blues," in which the singer laments his willingness to settle for a "sissy man" if no woman can be found. This was surely a topic not often sung about.

Arnold's music was also widely heard by white country and hillbilly artists in the 1930s and influenced the burgeoning western swing style. The Decca recording artist Johnny Lee Wills, brother of Bob Wills, may have been the first to cover "Milk Cow Blues." Bob Wills himself later went on to cover the song, and his composition "Brain Cloudy Blues" owed much to the song. "Milk Cow Blues" became a staple in the hillbilly and rockabilly canon and has been recorded by many famous artists, including Presley, Ricky Nelson, and rock groups like the Kinks and Aerosmith, to name but a few.

Mayo Williams proceeded to record Arnold's catalog over the next four years, from 1934 to 1938. Arnold became embittered after recording some eighty-nine titles for Decca for very low fees. Thirty-eight songs were released, and Arnold received little in the way of royalty payments even though his records generated significant revenue for Decca. He left the label in 1938 and never recorded again. He played off and on in Chicago clubs until the late 1940s. When French researchers tracked him down in 1959, Arnold was working as a janitor at a steel mill and was reluctant to discuss his blues past. Arnold had never really wanted to make records and sought to live a simple life. He understood the temporal nature of the world and was not interested in the glitter and glamour. There are reports of his playing sporadically into the 1960s in Chicago. Kokomo Arnold's fast and rhythmic slide guitar playing, exuberant vocal styles, and prodigious output of recordings from 1934 to 1938 strongly contributed to the foundations of many of the giants of blues, country, and rock and roll who followed. This music would be strikingly different without his deep influence.

FURTHER READING

Calt, Stephen. Liner notes for *Bottleneck Guitar Trendsetters of the 1930s* (1992).
Harris, Sheldon. *Blues Who's Who* (1979).
Killian, Klaus. Liner notes for *Old Original Kokomo Blues* (1999).
Palmer, Robert. *Deep Blues* (1981).
Russell, Tony. *Blacks, Whites, and Blues* (1970).

DISCOGRAPHY

Bottleneck Guitar Trendsetters of the 1930s (Yazoo Records L-1049).
Old Original Kokomo Blues (Wolf Records BC001).

MARK S. MAULUCCI

Arnold, Juanita Delores Burnett (27 July 1909–21 March 2005), schoolteacher and activist, was born in Tulsa, Oklahoma, the daughter of Eugene Lawrence Burnett, an oil worker, and Mary Jane McGowan Burnett, a seamstress. As a youth, Burnett survived the Tulsa Race Riot of 1921 and was a plaintiff in the subsequent legal case, *Alexander v. State of Oklahoma*. Burnett grew up in the Greenwood neighborhood of Tulsa, Oklahoma. In the early twentieth century, as Tulsa's economy boomed thanks to oil recently discovered in Oklahoma, Greenwood was a thriving enclave of African American businesses, schools, and churches. Her grandparents lived in Tulsa; her grandfather owned a grocery store and his family home. In a span of just a night and a day, from 31 May to 1 June 1921, the lives and livelihood of the Burnett family and the Greenwood community were threatened when the Greenwood section of Tulsa was devastated by the Tulsa Race Riot.

Racial tension within Tulsa had been building for many years before the riot. Although the city's prosperity had earned it the nickname "Oil Capital of the World," Tulsa was rife with conflict surrounding the influx of immigrants and uneasy relations between prosperous African American business owners and poor white laborers. As in many cities across the United States during this period, the Ku Klux Klan was active in Tulsa, and African American residents of Greenwood were well aware of the constant threat of violence and retaliation. The riot was sparked by the publication of a front-page editorial in the *Tulsa Tribune*. The editorial accused a nineteen-year-old black shoeshine boy named Dick Rowland of assaulting Sarah Page, a white teenage girl, in the elevator of a building in downtown Tulsa—charges that were later dropped. Although the *Tribune* editors removed the article after the paper had run a few hundred copies, the inflammatory headline, "Nab Negro for Attacking Girl in Elevator," had already done its damage. When Tulsa police arrested Dick Rowland, a mob of thousands of white people thronged the courthouse ready to lynch the accused. A group of armed African American men gathered to protect Rowland from mob vigilantism, a shot was fired, and the riot began.

In her oral account of the riots, recorded in 1999 by Eddie Faye Gates, an activist and member of the Tulsa Reparations Committee, Arnold recalled the growing anger and fear among African Americans in Greenwood as armed white men began to roam up and down her street. Many carried torches made from oil-soaked rags, which they used to set fire to homes and businesses. These men, Arnold believed, were "especially jealous of men like my father and grandfather who had nice homes and businesses." Her father was among the group of men who armed himself, ready to defend his family and his home. One white man whom Eugene Burnett had ordered off his property returned the next day, ready for further confrontation—but by that time, the Burnett family, along with many others, had fled northward to safety. As they did so, her parents assisted wounded and elderly black men and women who had fallen behind. Her grandfather's grocery store was spared with the help of several white salespeople who were also regular customers of the store. On 1 June 1921, they came to the store intending to guard it, warning the mob as it approached to stay away. According to Arnold's recollection, the men warned, "The man who owns this store is a good man. He worked hard for his property. He has done you and no one else any harm. You *will not* destroy the efforts of this man's hard work" (Gates, 1999).

Arnold's grandfather was one of the few lucky ones. The mob destroyed more than a thousand homes and business in the Greenwood area during the riot, leaving thousands homeless. The Burnett family home was among those destroyed. Estimates of the death toll from this, one of the worst race riots in U.S. history, have varied; once conservatively estimated at around one hundred, some historians now believe that at least several hundred people, mostly African American, were killed. Many of the victims were buried in unmarked mass graves.

After the riot, victims' attempts to seek legal justice met with stiff resistance from Tulsa's government, and the Ku Klux Klan further stifled any dissent. It was not until 1997, with the creation of the Tulsa Race Riot Commission, that the Oklahoma State government began to investigate the riot. The Commission gave its final report to the Tulsa City government and the Oklahoma governor and state legislature in 2001. The report recommended that five reparations be granted to the community of Greenwood, the survivors of the riot, and their descendants. These included reparation payments to survivors; reparation payments to survivors' descendants; the establishment of a scholarship fund for students affected by the riot; the creation of an economic development enterprise zone in the Greenwood District; and finally, the creation of a memorial and the reburial of human remains found in unmarked graves.

The Tulsa Reparations Coalition (TRC), an activist group that formed in 2001, took up the cause on behalf of the survivors to ensure that reparations would indeed be granted. On 24 February 2003, Juanita Arnold—along with more than one hundred other survivors—served as a plaintiff in *Alexander vs. State of Oklahoma*, a suit filed against the state of Oklahoma, the city of Tulsa, the chief of police of the city of Tulsa, and the City of Tulsa Police Department. However, despite the efforts of the TRC legal team, headed by Harvard Law professor Charles Ogletree, the drive to secure reparations was an uphill battle. On 9 March 2005, after a series of failed appeals and subsequent state court dismissals made on the grounds that the statute of limitations for filing complaints about the riot had passed, the TRC submitted a petition to the U.S. Supreme Court. On 16 May 2005, the U.S. Supreme Court dismissed their suit without comment.

Despite these setbacks, the fight has continued. In March 2007, Charles Ogletree appeared before the Inter-American Commission on Human Rights to file a petition on behalf of the survivors. The City of Tulsa, which had by this time established a Human Rights Commission, was also debating whether to build a Tulsa Race Riot museum. Greenwood itself experienced a slow economic rebirth, evidenced by several commercial establishments and churches, but the district has not recaptured its former economic success. However, with the help of people like Juanita Delores Burnett Arnold and other survivors of the Tulsa Race Riot, the Greenwood Cultural Center, built in the early 1970s, now helps preserve the memories of the place once known as the "Negro Wall Street of America."

FURTHER READING

Brophy, Alfred. *Reconstructing the Dreamland: The Tulsa Race Riot of 1921, Race Reparations, and Reconciliation* (2002).

Ellsworth, Scott. *Death in a Promised Land: The Tulsa Race Riot of 1921* (1982).

Gates, Eddie Faye. *Oral History Accounts of the Tulsa Race Riot of 1921 by Black Survivors*, available online at http://www.tulsareparations.org/JArnold.htm (1999).

Madigan, Tim. *The Burning: Massacre, Destruction, and the Tulsa Race Riot of 1921* (2001).

ANDREA A. BURNS

Arrieta, Saturnino Orestes Armas Miñoso ("Minnie Miñoso") (29 Nov. 1925–), baseball player, was born in El Perico, Cuba, the son of Carlos Arrieta, a sugarcane worker, and Cecilia Armas, a divorced homemaker. Armas had four older children from her previous husband, Julian Miñoso; when the family's new arrival began tagging along with his two older brothers, he was referred to by neighbors as one of the Miñoso brothers, a name by which he was known into his adult years. Growing up on a ranch near a sugarcane factory, Miñoso became enamored of baseball at a young age, idolizing the Negro Leagues star MARTIN DIHIGO. After his mother died when he was ten years old, Miñoso shuttled between Havana and El Perico, cared for by his older siblings.

While in Havana, Miñoso played semipro baseball for a cigar factory, candy factory, and a team in the Oriente Province, before being offered a job in 1944, on his nineteenth birthday, by the Marianao Tigers of the Cuban Professional League. Miñoso quickly became a young star in the league, hitting .301 in his rookie year, and drawing the attention of the Mexican League owner Jorge Pasquel, who offered him $10,000 to play in Mexico. Miñoso declined, his eyes set on America and the Negro Leagues. He didn't wait long: Following the season, the New York Cuban Giants' owner, Alex Pompez, offered Miñoso a contract.

Miñoso spent three and a half seasons with the Cuban Giants, playing at the rented-out Polo Grounds and Yankee Stadium, and gradually learning English. The day after the 1948 Negro League All-Star Game, his contract was purchased by the Cleveland Indians, under the direction of the owner Bill Veeck, with whom Miñoso would enjoy a long friendship.

The only black player on the Indians' Single-A affiliate in Dayton, Ohio, Miñoso was forced to stay apart from his team, either at a black hotel or with a black host family. In the spring of 1949, Miñoso became Major League Baseball's first black-Latin player before being sent down to the team's Triple-A affiliate, San Diego.

Miñoso was traded two springs later, and became the first black player in Chicago White Sox history on 1 May 1951. He accentuated his arrival with a homerun off New York Yankees' ace Vic Raschi in his debut game. Miñoso finished the season second in the league in batting average. Though he was the runner-up in Rookie of the Year voting, he bested the winner, Gil McDougald, in most offensive categories, and finished ahead of him in MVP voting, prompting speculations of bias on the part of Eastern sportswriters.

Miñoso's charm endeared him to Chicago fans and the media, earning him two nicknames: "The Cuban Comet," for his speed on the basepaths, and "Minnie," by which he would forever be known. Miñoso enjoyed seven productive seasons with the White Sox, making the All-Star team five times, including his best offensive year of 1954, in which he led the league in total bases and triples. Along with his exciting speed, Miñoso also routinely led the league in a dubious category—most times hit by a pitch. Though he would mostly attribute the plunkings to his aggressive batting stance, some saw racial undertones in the statistic: Miñoso himself once suggested that "a bucket of white paint" would stop the beanings.

In December 1957, Miñoso was traded back to the Indians, where he batted .302 for two seasons, before the new White Sox owner Veeck reacquired him for Chicago. Miñoso played parts of seasons with the Cardinals, the new Washington Senators, and the White Sox again before being released at the end of 1964.

In January 1961, Miñoso married Edelia Delgado, with whom he had a daughter, Marilyn, in 1964 to add to the two children he already had, Orestes Jr. and Cecilia, born to Julia Perez. In 1965 Miñoso accepted an opportunity to play and manage in the Mexican League, where he soon won a new nickname: El Charro Negro (The Black Cowboy).

In December 1975, Veeck, who had since relinquished and repurchased the White Sox, offered Miñoso the job of first-base coach, and introduced him to the Chicago press during a banquet. At the end of his first season, Miñoso was put on the White Sox' active roster, and became the fourth player to play in four different decades. On 12 September 1976, Miñoso hit a single, becoming the second-oldest player to hit safely in a major league game.

Miñoso eventually moved from the field to the public relations office; but in 1980, Veeck activated Miñoso for two at-bats, enabling the fifty-four-year-old to become the second ballplayer in history to play in five different decades. Miñoso took the field again in 1993 and 2003, both for the independent St. Paul Saints of the Northern League. The Saints' partial owner, Mike Veeck, son of the late White Sox mastermind, orchestrated Miñoso's return to the field, resulting in his status as the game's only six- and seven-decade player.

Miñoso married Sharon Rice in November 1984, and had a son, Charlie Orestes, four years later at the age of sixty-two. In the decades that followed he continued to work in public and community relations with the White Sox, had his number retired in May 1983, and was immortalized with a statue at the team's stadium, Cellular Field.

FURTHER READING

Miñoso, Minnie, with Herb Fagen. *Just Call Me Minnie: My Six Decades in Baseball* (1994).

Regalado, Samuel O. *Viva Baseball: Latin Baseball Players and Their Special Hunger* (1998).

ADAM W. GREEN

Arrington, Richard, Jr. (19 Oct. 1934–), mayor and educator, was born in rural Livingston, Alabama, to Richard Arrington Sr. and Ernestine Bell, sharecroppers. In 1940, when his father found work in a steel mill, the family moved to Fairfield, a suburb of Birmingham, Alabama. At Fairfield Industrial High School, Arrington took an interest in the study of history and also learned dry cleaning, a practical skill that he later used to finance his college education. In 1952, during his sophomore year at Miles College in

Birmingham, he married his high school sweetheart, the former Barbara Jean Watts. Two influential professors persuaded him to major in biology, and he graduated with a bachelor's degree in 1955. He went on to earn his master's degree in Biology in 1957 at the University of Detroit and in 1966 completed his Ph.D. dissertation, "Comparative Morphology of Some Dryopoid Beetles," at the University of Oklahoma, where his popularity among zoology students and faculty, as well as his academic excellence, earned him the Ortenburger Award. He began teaching biology at Miles College in 1957 and became chairman of the department of natural science and academic dean. He also had part-time teaching appointments at the University of Oklahoma and the University of Alabama. From 1970 to 1979 Arrington was director of the Alabama Center for Higher Education (ACHE), an organization funded by the Ford Foundation that sought to enhance educational programs at the state's eight historically black colleges and universities.

Social reforms pushed by protesting blacks, as well as legislative measures like the 1965 Voting Rights Act to redress past discrimination, set the stage in Birmingham—the largest southern city where white resistance to desegregation seemed fiercest—for a black to attempt to become the city's first African American mayor. Arrington's high visibility in the black community, his record of accomplishment at Miles College and at ACHE, and his involvement in civic organizations moved his name to the top of the list of potential political candidates to represent the large and growing black population of Birmingham. These blacks, along with many whites, wanted to shed Birmingham's tarnished image and refashion the city as a modern urban place where opportunities in its expanding healthcare, education, telecommunications, banking, and finance sectors pointed to a brighter future.

Initially contacted by a group of young men hopeful that he would agree to run for mayor, Arrington flatly rejected their proposal but later decided that a run for a seat on the city council was more feasible. Capitalizing on the voters' desire for a new generation of black leaders not handpicked by the white power structure, Arrington was easily elected to the city council in 1971 as its second black member and was reelected to a second four-year term in 1975. Arrington championed affirmative action in government hiring and contracts, as well as efforts to check police brutality—issues of greatest priority to his black constituency. Perceiving that he had a more realistic chance of capturing the mayor's office, in 1979 he won an extremely close election, thanks in part to carrying ten percent of the city's white vote. Thus Arrington became Birmingham's first African American mayor.

Over the next two decades, from 1979 to 1999, Arrington presided as mayor of Birmingham, a city's whose population grew increasingly black as whites retreated to the suburbs. He won reelections by delivering on his promise to increase substantially the number of blacks employed in city government—by the mid-1990s twelve of his twenty-three department heads were black, as were half of all city employees—and to ease tensions between the black community and the police. Throughout his tenure as mayor Arrington enjoyed good relations with the city's predominantly white business community, which also helped to facilitate Birmingham's makeover as a progressive "New South" metropolis with a diverse and balanced economy, a far cry from the bygone era of dingy steel mills, shotgun houses, stifling racial segregation, and white racial hegemony.

There was, however, a low point in Arrington's twenty-year reign as mayor. Repeatedly accused of corruption and cronyism, in 1992 he was investigated for allegedly receiving a kickback of five thousand dollars from a Georgia architect and spent a night in jail for temporarily refusing to provide records related to the case. His critics also contended that Arrington failed to bridge the racial divide between blacks and whites in the city and that he was unable to attract businesses to its long-suffering downtown.

Arrington's 1985 address at the honors convocation at the University of Alabama at Birmingham (UAB) confirmed his appreciation of the history of-the region and revealed his ambitious vision of the city's role in the New South. Reflecting on the strides that the city had made since the church bombings and street demonstrations of the 1960s, he told his audience, "We have tried never to move forward on a particular issue without being mindful of the lessons of our past.... The shifting and sharing of political power among all the people of this community has been a remarkable story in itself" (Arrington, 9).

Eventually the majority of city council seats were held by people loyal to Arrington. Hoping to ensure that his handpicked ally William Bell would succeed him as mayor—and with the endorsement of the Jefferson County Citizens Coalition (JCCC), the once-powerful local organization of black Democrats that he created in 1977—Arrington resigned in July 1999, three months before his term

as mayor was due to expire. Bell, however, lost his bid to replace the long-serving mayor, and a new generation of black leaders—not as dependent on bloc voting and racial solidarity—began to take control of the city.

In the fall of 1999 Arrington commenced teaching as a visiting professor at UAB and worked on metropolitan planning and service projects at the university's Center for Urban Affairs. Perhaps to revitalize his faltering political machine (the JCCC) and to sway upcoming city council elections, in the summer of 2001 Arrington announced his intention to run for a sixth term as mayor, but shortly thereafter he dropped out of the race and quietly retired from the political scene.

FURTHER READING
Arrington, Richard, Jr. *Birmingham: The Reality of a New South Experience* (1985).
Franklin, Jimmy Lee. *Back to Birmingham: Richard Arrington, Jr., and His Times* (1989).
ROBERT FIKES JR.

Arroyo, Martina (2 Apr. 1936–), opera singer and college professor, was born in New York, the second child of Demetrio Arroyo, a mechanical engineer who moved to the United States from Puerto Rico at eleven years of age, and Lucille Washington Arroyo, a Charleston, South Carolina native. Her father studied engineering at the University of Florida and worked at the Brooklyn Navy Yard. With the exception of piano lessons from her mother and occasional singing at church, Arroyo received very little musical training during her childhood. Her family, however, ensured that films, concerts, plays, and other performances were a part of her upbringing.

After completing junior high school, Arroyo attended the Hunter College–operated special high school for gifted children. Her interest in opera, which took root during those years, developed from her experience with the Hunter College Opera Workshop. Upon listening to her performance of the "Jewel Song," a piece from Gounod's *Faust*, the workshop's director, Joseph Turnau, recognized potential in Arroyo. He introduced her to Thea Dispeker, who later became her manager, and Madame Marinka Gurewich, who would become and remain her voice teacher.

After graduating from Hunter High School, Arroyo proceeded to Hunter College, where she majored in romance languages and comparative literature. She graduated in 1954. Through the work of a guidance counselor and Turnau, Arroyo received special permission to enroll in Hunter's opera workshop, an opportunity not generally accorded undergraduates. During this time she began to attend Metropolitan Opera performances, particularly those of her favorite soprano, Renata Tebaldi.

Realizing that opportunities for African Americans in opera were limited, Arroyo prepared to be a teacher. Her musical aspirations, however, continued. While teaching high school in the Bronx, she took graduate courses at New York University, and continued her musical studies in the Hunter College Workshop and with Gurewich. Finding her schedule overwhelming, Arroyo, after one year of teaching, became, for two years, a caseworker for the New York City Welfare Department.

Arroyo had two careers at the Metropolitan Opera. The first one began on 14 March 1959, and ended on 2 January 1962; her second began on 6 February 1965. During her first career she sang comprimario and minor roles beginning with the offstage celestial voice in Verdi's *Don Carlo*. Other comprimario and minor roles were the third Norm and Woglinde in Wagner's *Götterdämmerung*, Woglinde in Wagner's *Das Rheingold*, Orltinde in Wagner's *Die Walküre*, and Forest Bird in Wagner's *Siegfried*. Arroyo's second career at the Metropolitan began when Rudolf Bing asked her, on two days' notice, to replace an ailing Birgit Nilsson in the title role of Verdi's *Aida*. Arroyo's success in this performance secured for her, the next day, a contract to perform major roles at the house. Thanks to this classification, after *Aida*, she did thirteen major roles: Elisabetta in Verdi's *Don Carlo*; Cio-Cio-San in Puccini's *Madame Butterfly*; Leonora in Verdi's *Il Trovatore*; Elsa in Wagner's *Lohengrin*; Amelia in Verdi's *Un ballo in maschera*; Donna Anna in Mozart's *Don Giovanni*; Liu in Puccini's *Turandot*; Santuzza in Mascagni's *Cavalleria rusticana*; Elvira in Verdi's *Ernani*; Leonoro in Verdi's *La forza del destino*; Lady Macbeth in Verdi's *Macbeth*; Gioconda in Ponchelli's *La Gioconda*; and Maddalena in Giordano's *Andrea Chénier*.

Arroyo has also performed with the Vienna State Opera, Hamburg State Opera, Covent Garden, Teatro Colón in Buenos Aires, Argentina, Deutsche Oper Berlin, San Francisco Opera, Paris Opera, Lyric Opera of Chicago, San Diego Opera, Pretoria Opera in South Africa, Miami Opera, La Scala, and Canadian Opera Company. Roles performed away from the Metropolitan included Amelia in Verdi's Simon Boccanegra, Elena in Verdi's *I vespri siciliani*, Magna in Puccini's *La Rondine*, and the title roles in Puccini's *Tosca* and *Turandot*.

Arroyo performed in concert with the world's great orchestras and conductors. She was soloist with the New York Philharmonic for the world premiere of Samuel Barber's *Andromache's Farewell*, a work she subsequently introduced in Europe. She performed Karlheinz Stockhausen's *Momente* in Cologne and again with the Buffalo Philharmonic, Stockhausen conducting. She also premiered William Balcom's *Simple Stories*, performed in recital both nationally and internationally, and did master classes at the Salzburg Mozarteum and the Music Academy of the West.

Arroyo not only helped to open doors for other African Americans in opera, she became one of the first African American women to attain a high level of visibility in the lyric theater. While the social and political upheaval of the civil rights movement produced a community of African American women singers in opera, the movement did not produce a similar community of African American male singers who attained a high level of visibility in opera. Unlike that of their female counterparts, the African American male experience in opera is a story of individuals.

Arroyo was a six-term member, appointed by President Gerald Ford, of the National Endowment of the Arts and a member of the Carnegie Hall Board of Trustees. She remained a trustee emeritus of the Hunter College Foundation. She was inducted, in 2002, as a fellow of the American Academy of Arts and Sciences, and in 2004 London's Amici di Verdi awarded her the Verdi Medal in recognition of her many appearances in the United Kingdom. In the early years of the twenty-first century, Arroyo maintained studios at Indiana University, where she was a distinguished professor of voice, and in New York, where she taught the study and preparation of operatic roles under the auspices of the Martina Arroyo Foundation.

FURTHER READING

Abdul, Raoul. *Blacks in Classical Music* (1977).

Cheatham, Wallace McClain. "African American Women Singers at the Metropolitan Opera before Leontyne Price," *Journal of Negro History* 84 (Spring 1999).

Gray, John. *Blacks in Classical Music* (1988).

Smith, Eric Ledell. *Blacks in Opera* (1995).

Southern, Eileen. *Biographical Dictionary of Afro-American and African Musicians* (1962).

Story, Rosalyn. *And So I Sing* (1990).

Turner, Patricia. *Afro-American Singers, an Index and Preliminary Discography of Opera, Choral Music and Song* (1977).

Turner, Patricia. *Dictionary of Afro-American Performers, 78 RPM and Cylinder Recordings of Opera, Choral Music and Song, c. 1900–1949* (1990).
WALLACE MCCLAIN CHEATHAM

Artemus, John C. (1885–1964), carpenter, insurance agent, contractor, and activist, was born in Edgefield, South Carolina, in 1885. As a young boy, Artemus saw that discrimination and oppression was still very much alive in the South, even following Emancipation in 1865. His parents were sharecroppers; thus, they were subject to subordination through this system because it ultimately favored the owners of the land, not the workers. Although there were many important benefits to this agricultural arrangement, the sharecropping system was ultimately oppressive. Landlords exploited their positions by extending credit to the workers during times of bad weather and poor quality of crop and market price. The interest rates were often so high that workers were unable to pay them. Often, this meant landlords and sharecroppers were in much the same relationship as master and slave had been. It was precisely for this reason that Artemus grew up determined to fight for his family's welfare. However, when he confronted their landlord over unfair wages, he was evicted from his home.

Artemus moved to Columbia, South Carolina. Here, he worked a day job as a sales clerk while attending Benedict College at night. Benedict was founded in 1870 by the American Baptist Home Mission Society to provide an education to recently freed black Americans. While at Benedict College, Artemus learned the construction trade, specializing in carpentry and contracting. Artemus spent many years repairing homes and rental properties. He worked in neighborhoods across South Carolina—and across racial lines. He was one of the first black carpenters to work in white neighborhoods repairing homes.

Artemus eventually found a job as an insurance agent and assistant manager for North Carolina Mutual Life Insurance Company and stayed there for twelve years. However, after the Great Depression, he had cause to rethink his career. The numerous building projects undertaken under the auspices of the New Deal gave Artemus the chance to use his carpentry training. Artemus decided to try contracting in hopes that he could organize his own building projects. But, more importantly, he intended to hire other blacks as skilled labor. Unfortunately, black contractors were not eligible to compete for these new building projects. The exclusion of blacks in the job bidding process prompted Artemus to become one of the first black labor organizers.

Artemus, among others, organized Local 2260 of the United Brotherhood of Carpenters and Joiners to unionize blacks in the building trades in central South Carolina. First on Artemus's agenda was to fight for the rights of other black contractors. They fought for and won the inclusion of black union contractors and workers on major South Carolina construction projects. As the union's business agent and representative from 1939 to 1954 Artemus made sure that major companies, including DuPont, Fort Jackson, and other numerous housing contractors employed the skilled labor of black Americans.

While active in union organizing, Artemus also pursued a political agenda. A South Carolina court decision in 1947 opened up the primaries to black voters. In 1950 Artemus was the first elected treasurer of the Progressive Democratic Party, which was organized to enable blacks to participate in state and national elections. Artemus never stopped educating black voters on issues central to the elections. From 1952 until his death, he spent time as a poll manager helping acquaint black voters to the issues involved in voting.

His civil rights activism did not stop there. From 1951 to 1959 Artemus represented the black community as vice president at large of the South Carolina Federation of Labor Executive Board. His role was to oversee union actions and to maintain these actions under principles of justice and fairness. During this time there was still opposition to the integration of local union chapters. The responsibility of the Federation of Labor was to oversee this integration and ensure that black workers were offered the same choices as white workers. In 1963 Artemus's Local 2260 was responsible for breaking down many institutionalized racial barriers, eventually winning the integration of union locals. He died in 1964.

Throughout his life, Artemus fought for the civil liberties of black Americans. He never tired of teaching and proving that it was possible to overcome injustices. It was precisely because of the actions of individuals such as Artemus that the working environment in the South opened up to and incorporated contributions by black Americans.

FURTHER READING
African American Registry, retrieved from http://www.aaregistry.com/african_american_history/1787/

John_Artemus_an_ally_of_blue_collar_workers on August 12, 2007.

CHRISTINE SCHNEIDER

Arter, Jared (27 Jan. 1850–1928), college president, educator, and minister, was born Jared Maurice Arter in Jefferson County, West Virginia, the son of Jeremiah Arter, a slave and a miller by trade, and Hannah Frances Stephenson, a slave. When Arter was seven years old his father died in an accident at the mill. The plantation on which the family lived, the Little plantation, was located four miles from Harpers Ferry. In 1859 Arter witnessed the hanging of four men who participated in John Brown's raid at that city. This childhood memory sparked in him the desire to fight for equality; the schoolroom would be his battleground.

As a teenager Arter applied for a position as a bellboy, for which he would have to pass a test demonstrating his ability to read numbers. With help from his brother-in-law he mastered the skill sufficiently in one evening to pass the test. This accomplishment reinforced for Arter the notion that education would be his key to success. His desire to learn grew, and his mother seized the opportunity for Arter to receive an education and learn a trade by hiring him out to Mr. Ayers, a white businessman from New York, on the condition that her son receive academic instruction. Arter spent the next three and a half years working on a farm and learning basic skills in English. Within two years of completing his service, Arter had earned enough money to buy a house near Harpers Ferry for his mother, stepfather, and eight siblings.

In October 1873 Arter entered Storer College in Harpers Ferry (later part of Virginia Union University). The college was established under the Freewill Baptist doctrine and the Freedmen's Aid societies; it was the first African American college in West Virginia and had as its mission the training of African American teachers. While at Storer, Arter vowed to live a clean Christian life, abstaining from cigarettes, alcohol, and profanity. Shortly thereafter he received a license to preach. Arter spent the next six years at Storer teaching and studying. In 1879 he entered Pennsylvania State College as a freshman with William Adger; they were the institution's first African American students. In 1882 he entered Hillsdale College in Hillsdale, Michigan, as a sophomore and received a bachelor of philosophy degree in 1885. There he led a successful prohibition campaign to close a saloon

in town and preached frequently on the subject of temperance. In 1887 Arter became an ordained gospel minister—which permitted him to complete the ecclesiastical duties of the Missionary Baptist denomination—and was hired as a teacher and minister at his alma mater back in Harpers Ferry. Arter stayed at Storer College for four years, setting the foundation for quality education. He married Emily Carter, a teacher, in 1890; they had three children.

In 1891 Arter entered the Chicago Theological Seminary and in 1894 graduated with a bachelor of divinity. He stayed in Illinois to pastor two Baptist churches, and in January 1895 he taught Latin, civil government, physics, and rhetoric at the American Baptist Home Mission Society. In 1900 Arter was asked to open a Bible school at the Cairo Mission, chartered as the J. S. Manning Bible School in Cairo, Illinois. The purpose of the school was to train men and women for missionary service. Emily Arter worked as an assistant teacher at the school.

In 1907 Arter experienced tragedies that tested his faith. His brother William died of pneumonia, two months later Emily Arter died after a long illness, and several months after her death their son Jared Jr. died from blood poisoning at the age of seven. Experiencing the deaths of three loved ones in such a short time caused Arter to reflect on his mission in life. In October 1907 Arter accepted the presidency of the West Virginia Industrial School Seminary and College in Hill Top.

From the beginning Arter motivated and inspired students and faculty. His leadership proved to be invaluable when the main building of the college burned in 1908. When Arter was asked what they should do, he replied, "Let us rise and build better" (Arter, 45). The day after the fire Arter gathered students, family, trustees, and the citizens of Hill Top for prayer, and they pledged that they would all persevere. In the interim, classes were held in a school that was once used to teach white children. A year after the fire Arter had procured fifty acres of land deeded to the college and $5,000 to begin reconstruction. In 1910 he married his second wife, the teacher Maggie Wall.

Arter oversaw the completion of a four-story brick structure before resigning in 1914. He stayed in the area to pastor the Baptist Church of Sun and to serve as principal of Fayetteville graded school until he was asked to return to Storer College Church, becoming pastor again in 1917. The church grew in membership, activity, and dues. Feeling that he had accomplished all he could, Arter retired on

9 October 1921. Shortly thereafter he was afflicted with a serious urinary tract infection, and although doctors told him that he needed surgery Arter recovered and continued his works for education and benevolence until the end of his life.

FURTHER READING
Arter, Jared Maurice. *Echoes of a Pioneer Life* (1922).
Mitchell, Henry H. *Black Church Beginnings: The Long-Hidden Realities of the First Years* (2004).
Sernett, Milton C., ed. *African American Religious History: A Documentary Witness*, 2d ed. (1999).
VALERIE A. GRAY

Artis, William Ellisworth (2 Feb. 1914–1977), sculptor, ceramicist, and educator, was one of America's most prolific and respected three-dimensional artists in the mid-twentieth century. Born in Washington, North Carolina, to Elizabeth Davis and Thomas Miggett, he lived primarily with his father until the fall of 1926 when he relocated to Harlem and began living with his mother and her husband, George Artis. In New York he assumed the surname of his stepfather. He attended Haaren High School and went on to study sculpture and pottery at the Augusta Savage Studio of Arts and Crafts in the early 1930s, joining the ranks of Jacob Armstead Lawrence, Gwendolyn Knight, Romare Bearden, Norman Lewis, and other notable artists whose initial studies included instruction under Savage. Artis was also a contemporary of his fellow sculptors Selma Hortense Burke and Richmond Barthé, the latter the most exhibited and honored three-dimensional artist associated with the Harmon Foundation.

Artis won the John Hope Prize affiliated with the Harmon Foundation exhibition of 1933 for the terra-cotta *Head of a Girl*, which contributed to his receiving the Metropolitan Scholarship Award for Creative Sculpture to attend the Art Students League of New York in 1933–1934. At the league he studied with the French-born cubist sculptor Robert Laurent, a close colleague of the famed sculptor William Zorach, who also taught there. In 1935 Artis received a second John Hope Prize and went on to study at the Crafts Students League with Roberta Laber and at the Greenwich House Ceramic Center under Maude Robinson between 1936 and 1938. He was among the artists featured at the 1936 Texas Centennial exhibitions. Artis entered the New York State College of Ceramics in Alfred, New York, in 1940 for a year of instruction under Charles M. Harder and Marion L. Fosdick,

after whom the Alfred University School of Art and Design Gallery was later renamed. Audrey McMahon of the College Art Association, who also served as regional director of the New York Works Project Administration/Federal Art Project, subsequently hired Artis to teach modeling and ceramics at the 135th Street branch of the YMCA in Harlem. He was later appointed director of the Boys' Work Department and instructed arts and crafts classes between 1937 and 1941; he also participated in a citywide mural project that targeted community centers and churches.

During World War II Artis served as a technical sergeant in the army, winning first prize in sculpture at the 1944 Atlanta University Annual Exhibition of Paintings, Sculpture, and Prints by Negro Artists of America while still enlisted. The prizewinning piece, *Woman with a Kerchief*, embodied the characteristics of the style for which he became well known—an elegantly executed head or bust of an unidentified subject with smooth, clean lines and serene expression. He received the prestigious Purchase Award from the International Print Society for his sculpture titled *African Youth* in 1945. Upon the completion of his military commitment, Artis received a Harmon Foundation Fellowship that subsidized brief residencies at six of the member institutions of the Historically Black Colleges and Universities (Spelman, Tuskegee, Talladega, Hampton, Fisk, and North Carolina Central) in the early months of 1946 to hold workshops demonstrating his ceramics techniques. That fall he reentered the ceramics program at New York State College for another year of study under Fosdick and Harder.

In 1947 Artis was awarded a Julius Rosenwald Fellowship to work at Tuskegee Institute and explore the use of Alabama clays in his ceramic work and to hold periodic open-studio sessions for student observation. He declined the opportunity, opting to briefly attend classes at Alfred University before enrolling at Syracuse University on the GI Bill. At Syracuse he came under the tutelage of the acclaimed Yugoslavian-born sculptor Ivan Meštrović and began to more vigorously explore abstract forms and functional adaptations in his work. Meštrović exposed him to Modernist techniques and composition and challenged him to investigate a range of visual stimuli, most notably contemporary documentary films. Artis moved away from production of busts and began creating works that referenced the entire human form, though not in an upright pose. He earned a BFA in 1950 and an MFA in Sculpture from Syracuse in 1951.

In the spring of 1947 he had received a second Atlanta University Art Annual Purchase Prize for a terra-cotta piece done in his signature style titled *Head*. Professional recognition continued in 1951 with his receipt of the National Sculpture Society Award and the Atlanta University Purchase Prize in Sculpture for a dramatic marble work of a crouched boy titled *Quiet One*. He spent a summer teaching on a South Dakota Native American reservation followed by one semester at Tuskegee Institute before matriculating at Nebraska State Teachers College, earning a second B.A. in art education in 1955. He did graduate study at Pennsylvania State University between 1956 and 1959, working concurrently during a portion of that time as associate professor of ceramics at Nebraska State Teachers College at Chadron from 1956 to 1965. His reputation continued to mount, and Artis won four additional Purchase prizes at Atlanta University over this period of time for *Head of Boy* in 1952, *Head of Young Lady* in 1959, *Young Mother* in 1962, and *Young Mother's Love* in 1963. In 1965 he received second prize in sculpture for *We Have Seen His Face*. Additionally, he won the annual Purchase Prize for a piece that was included in a group exhibition held at the Joslyn Museum of Art in Omaha, Nebraska, in 1962.

In the summer of 1965 Artis was hired by the metals specialist Alvin Pine to work at California State University, Long Beach, as assistant to the sculptor and Modernist jeweler Claire Falkenstein and the French sculptor of Polish origin Piotr Kowalski, two of the eight artists-in-residence awardees whose work was featured at that year's International Sculpture Symposium. Artis remained through the fall, continuing to assist both artists. The next fall he took a position as professor of art at Mankato State College in Minnesota, working there from 1966 until 1975. For his dedication and effectiveness as an instructor, he was named Outstanding Educator of America by the University of Minnesota in 1970, adding to the National Conference of Artists' Outstanding Afro-American Artist Award earned the same year. He was also presented with the Smith-Mason Gallery Award in 1971.

Over the course of his career, Artis received more than one hundred distinguished awards, commissions, and honors and had his work reviewed in *Time, Sculpture Review,* and the *Christian Science Monitor*. He was a member of several national professional organizations, including the American Ceramic Society, National Sculpture Society, National Art Educators Association, New York Society of Arts and Crafts, and College Art Association. His work appeared in more than thirty exhibitions including at the Museum of Modern Art, Whitney Museum of American Art, and High Museum of Art in Atlanta. Artis's work is in the permanent collections of many of the major art museums and galleries in the United States.

Artis was described by the artist Mary Parks Washington, a Spelman College student during the time Artis visited the campus and who was the subject of a bust he created around 1945, as hard-working, reclusive, quiet, and devoted to a male friend living in Paris. Artis died in 1977 of unknown causes.

FURTHER READING

Driskell, David Clyde. *Paintings by Ellis Wilson, Ceramics and Sculpture by William E. Artis* (1971).

Pendergraft, Norman E. *Heralds of Life: Artis, Bearden and Burke* (1977).

Reynolds, Gary A., and Beryl J. Wright. *Against the Odds: African-American Artists and the Harmon Foundation* (1989).

AMALIA K. AMAKI

Artrell, William Middleton (1836–28 Mar. 1903), temperance reformer, federal customs official, and educator, was born William Middleton Artrell, of one quarter African and three quarters European ancestry, at Nassau in the Bahamas. There Artrell benefited from a basic education on the British model, acquired experience as a schoolteacher, and became a staunch Episcopalian.

During the American Civil War the Bahamas prospered as a result of services to blockade runners, who transported British cargo in the short but dangerous voyage between the Bahamas and the Confederate coast. When the war ended, however, economic depression forced many Bahamians to seek work in the United States. In 1870 Artrell migrated to Key West, at that time a major port in Florida. Unlike most African Americans in the South, he had never been a slave. In 1870 Key West opened the Douglass School for African American children. Artrell became its first principal, and as a result he was sometimes called Professor Artrell. He was elected a Key West alderman in 1875 and received a patronage job as an inspector at the federal customs office in the following year.

From 1876 to 1885 Artrell received a series of promotions at the Key West customs office. In 1880 fellow Bahamians in Key West helped organize a petition against him, arguing that he was unpopular with local Republicans (this libelous charge was simply a tactic of his enemies). The Key West collector of customs indignantly rejected the charge against Artrell, saying it was "as false as it is malicious." Moreover, he stated, Artrell was "the peer of any colored man in Florida." Three days later, leading African Americans in Key West convened at the Good Templar hall, with the Reverend Thomas Darley in the chair, to declare their "esteem" for the embattled Artrell (National Archives, Wicker to Lamphere, with attached report of the Darley meeting and cover letter). As a statistical and marine clerk in the customs office, Artrell's salary was $1,200. Later he was promoted to impost clerk at $1,500 per year.

Artrell is best known as a temperance reformer. A moderate drinker until late in 1874, he became a teetotaler and a prohibitionist. He came to believe that alcohol robbed black people of the opportunity for self-improvement and that the temperance movement offered them the possibility of escape from poverty and subjugation. He argues in a letter to the editor of the Philadelphia *Christian Recorder* that "the colored man cannot *afford* to waste his *time* and his *money* with drink…. It is highly necessary that the colored man should try and obtain riches in this world. It is a power for good, a lever that removes all obstacles." He adds, "There is no swifter way of obtaining it than by a temperate life" (10 Oct. 1878).

In 1875 Artrell applied to a fraternal temperance society called the Good Templars for a charter to organize a local lodge. Though blacks could always join Templar organizations in the northern states and overseas, Atrell was rejected by the southern white Templars because of his race. Reluctantly he instead organized a True Reformer fountain, a Jim Crow fraternal temperance society. Although he took office as assistant grand master of the grand fountain of Florida, Artrell rejected segregation in principle. In 1876, when a schism broke out in the international Good Templar organization, a British faction provided Artrell with a Templar charter. Liberated from the subordination to the southern white Templars, he appealed to biblical analogy to express his outrage: "Southern whites remind me forcibly of Pharaoh of old" (Artrell to J. G. Thrower, 15 Oct. 1876, in [Birmingham, England] *Good Templar's Watchword*, 27 Dec. 1876, quoted in Fahey, *Temperance & Racism*, 120). He did not exonerate the northern Templars. "The south, it seems, is willing to do all the dirty work, while the north quietly acquiesces." He added: "prejudice against the colored

man is the great sin of the United States of America" (Artrell to editor, 16 Sept. 1878, in [Philadelphia] *Christian Recorder*, 10 Oct. 1878).

In 1878, having established a sufficient number of local lodges, African Americans organized a grand lodge of Florida, affiliated with the British faction of the Good Templar order. Although white Floridians were eligible to join, none did, so the grand lodge was segregated in practice, if not in theory. Artrell was elected grand worthy secretary, an office he occupied until 1884. The grand lodge was a small but durable organization with about a thousand members, equally divided between women and men, plus a small auxiliary for children. Most members lived at Jacksonville in the northeast, or at Key West in the far south of the state. In the latter city, Cubans organized a Spanish-speaking lodge. In 1883 Artrell represented Florida at an international Templar convention held in Canada. In 1884 Florida's *Journal of Proceedings* declared: "when our Grand Lodge has not been in session [Artrell] has been the Grand Lodge himself" (7–8). In that year Artrell's secretarial salary was $150.

When a Democrat entered the White House in 1885, Artrell lost his federal patronage job. As a result he left Key West for Jacksonville, where he taught and served as principal at a black school alternately called a graded school and Stanton Institute. While principal, he added an eighth grade. JAMES WELDON JOHNSON, one of his pupils, became well known as an African American intellectual. In his autobiography, he praised Artrell: "despite the fact that his education was not extensive, he actually knew what he was supposed to know and teach" (62). The job could not have paid much. Artrell concurrently worked as a tailor. During the yellow fever epidemic in 1888, he headed the Jacksonville relief society that aided African Americans. The general agent of the Slater fund said that Artrell "has done heroic service & won universal praise" (Garrison, 241).

After he moved to Jacksonville, Artrell headed the Templar grand lodge from 1885 to 1889. His election led to controversy with the supporters of his predecessor, Joseph E. Lee, a Republican politician, Jacksonville lawyer, and Baptist minister. In 1886 Artrell participated in the negotiations at Boston that reunited the British and American based Good Templar factions. He reluctantly accepted terms for reunion that included racial segregation. In the same year he served as director of the *Florida Templar* of Jacksonville, the only black-run temperance newspaper in the United States. Prestigious titles mattered less to Artrell than did the opportunity to recruit new members into his moral reform society. On one occasion he and wife endured a rain-soaked journey by steam ferry and mule-drawn dray to organize a small rural lodge at a Baptist church near Jacksonville, a winery expedition that ended with their return home at 2 A.M., only four hours before the Artrells began their next workday.

In 1894 James Weldon Johnson succeeded Artrell as Stanton's principal. At some point—the date is unclear, but 1897, when a new Republican president assumed office, seems likely—Artrell returned to Key West, where he resumed his career at the customs office. He held the office of deputy collector of the revenue until his death in 1903. He supplemented his government salary by working as a merchant tailor. His wife, Alexandrina Victoria Artrell, outlived him, and there is no record that they had any children.

FURTHER READING

Brown, Canter. *Florida's Black Public Officials, 1867– 1924* (1998).

Fahey, David M. *Temperance & Racism: John Bull, Johnny Reb, and the Good Templars* (1996).

Fahey, David M. "The Good Templars and the African American Temperance Movement: W. M. Artrell of Florida," *Social History of Alcohol Review* 28.39 (1984).

Garrison, Curtis W. "Slater Fund Beginnings: Letters from General Agent Atticus G. Haywood to Rutherford B. Hayes," *Journal of Southern History*, vol. 5, no. 2 (May 1939).

Johnson, James Weldon. *Along this Way: The Autobiography of James Weldon Johnson* (1933).

DAVID M. FAHEY

Asante, Molefi Kete (14 Aug. 1942–), scholar and author, was born Arthur Lee Smith Jr. in Valdosta, Georgia. He was the first son of Lillie Wilkson, a domestic worker, and Arthur L. Smith, a railroad worker. The family grew over the years and eventually included sixteen children.

Valdosta, a small southern town also known as the Azalea City, was the arena in which young Arthur first saw the abuses and injustices suffered by black people under segregation. He picked cotton during the summer to help his family, a task representing for him not only the injustices of the present but also the awful, backbreaking conditions that his ancestors had to endure for hundreds of years during slavery. While shining shoes at age eleven, he was spat upon by a white man, an experience he would later recall in describing his growing determination to fight against racism.

Identified early in life as possessing exceptional intellectual capabilities, Arthur could read at age four and was sought after by many parents in his neighborhood to tutor their children. His intellectual gift created the opportunity for him to leave Valdosta at age eleven to attend the Nashville Christian Institute, one of few black boarding schools in the United States at the time. Upon finishing high school in 1960 he attended Southwestern Christian College for two years before graduating from Oklahoma Christian College in 1964 with a B.A. in Communication. He received an M.A. in Communication from Pepperdine University in 1965 and a Ph.D. in the same field from the University of California at Los Angeles in 1968. The title of his dissertation was "Samuel Adams' Rhetoric of Agitation during the American Revolution." While still in college, in 1964, Smith published his first book, *Break of Dawn*, a collection of poetry. In 1966 he married Ngena Scarber, with whom he had one daughter, Kasina Eka. The marriage, however, ended in divorce in 1979.

In 1968 Smith embarked on his academic career, with his first appointment at Purdue University as an assistant professor of communication. He was there only a short time before being lured back to UCLA, where he became associate professor of communication and director of the Center for Afro-American Studies between 1969 and 1973. It was during those critical years that Smith cofounded the *Journal of Black Studies*, created the African American Library, and wrote the curriculum for UCLA's M.A. program in African American studies. In 1973 Arthur Smith legally changed his name to Molefi Kete Asante. Molefi, a Suto name, means "One who remains to keep the traditions after a great disaster." Kete ("One who loves music and dance") and Asante (a common West African name, which typically means "I told you to leave me alone but you would not"), on the other hand, were given to him personally by the late Asantehene of Ghana, Opoku Wari II. That same year Asante left UCLA to join the faculty at SUNY Buffalo, where he served as professor and chair of the department of communication until 1982. From 1977 to 1979 he chaired SUNY's department of black studies. While in Buffalo, Asante met his second wife, the dancer, choreographer, and scholar Kariamu Welsh, with whom he had one son, Molefi Khumalo. After twenty years, their marriage ended in divorce in 2001.

Asante's next academic appointment, to Temple University as chair of its department of African American studies in 1984, provided him with the space to develop and implement fully his vision for the study of African people, culminating in 1988 with the creation of the world's first Ph.D. program in African American studies. Such an initiative represented enormous progress, because the field's academic legitimacy had faced constant challenges since its inception in the late 1960s. Temple's Ph.D. program in African American studies became an instant success, attracting hundreds of students from within the United States and around the world.

The program owed much of its success to Asante's paradigmatic vision. In 1980 Asante had published *Afrocentricity*, the first formulation of a theory that made him both famous and controversial. Afrocentricity's most fundamental concern is the conceptual disenfranchisement and invisibility of African people worldwide as a result of European intellectual hegemony and racism. At the heart of the Afrocentric idea lies the assertion that African people must operate as self-conscious cultural agents, no longer satisfied to be defined and manipulated from without, but more in control of their destinies through a positive and assertive self-definition. The criteria for this self-definition must be drawn from African culture. At its core Afrocentricity is a theory concerned with African epistemological relevance.

This first book on the topic was followed by two major theoretical works, *The Afrocentric Idea* (1987) and *Kemet, Afrocentricity, and Knowledge* (1990), in which Asante further expanded his theory on the centrality of the African experience for the proper study of African people. In addition to these key works of Afrocentric scholarship, Asante authored or edited more than sixty books, including the first *Encyclopedia of Black Studies* (2005), as well as hundreds of articles and chapters in books. In 1997 Asante decided, both because of personal reasons and because of growing intradepartmental conflict and pressure from an administration eager to change the philosophical orientation of the department, not to seek reelection as chair of the department of African American studies at Temple University.

A popular lecturer, Asante spoke at more than 130 university campuses in the United States. His work has been translated into several languages, including French, Portuguese, and Spanish, and he lectured in England, France, Japan, China, Malaysia, Brazil, the Caribbean, and Africa. In 2003 Asante was the special guest of the South African president

Thabo Mbeki. In addition to being an extraordinarily prolific scholar, Asante was also active in the black community as both activist and educator. Consistent with his deep belief in the importance of children's textbooks, Asante authored *African American History: A Journey of Liberation* (1995), the first African American high school text written by a black person. Asante also served as an Afrocentric educational consultant for school districts across the United States, as well as sitting on the boards of several Pan-African organizations. In 1993 he was honored as a traditional king in Ghana: Nana Okru Asante Peasah, Kyidomhene of Tafo. In 2002 Asante married Ana Yenenga, an African Costa Rican. During the first part of the twenty-first century he became the preeminent mentor of graduate students in African American studies when he supervised more than seventy-five doctoral dissertations. In 2003 he was appointed to the African Union's Steering Committee for the Conference of Intellectuals of Africa and Its Diaspora. In 2004 he was inducted into the Literary Hall of Fame for Writers of African Descent.

FURTHER READING

Molefi Kete Asante's papers are housed in the Amistad Research Center, Tulane University.

Mazama, Ama, ed. *The Afrocentric Paradigm* (2003).

Ziegler, Diana, ed. *Molefi Kete Asante and Afrocentricity: In Praise and in Criticism* (1995).

AMA MAZAMA

Asberry, Nettie J. (15 July 1865–17 Nov. 1968), classical pianist, civil rights activist, and social worker, was born Nettie Craig in Leavenworth, Kansas, the daughter of William P. Wallingford, an immigrant farmer from England, and Viola, his former slave. In 1837, prior to Nettie's birth, Wallingford moved his family from Kentucky and settled on the Platte purchase in Missouri. He was married three times and fathered seventeen children including six by Viola. Nettie, the youngest of these, was the only one born free. Information is scarce about Viola. After she was emancipated she rejected Wallingford's name and adopted Craig as her surname, likely because she was born on the Craig plantation in Kentucky. She took her children to Leavenworth, Kansas, where she married Taylor Turner. Her occupation was listed as a domestic. She died in Denver, Colorado, on 29 September 1906 at the age of seventy-six.

Nettie Craig began studying the piano at eight years of age, showing remarkable ability, and later composed her own music. At thirteen she served as secretary for a Susan B. Anthony woman's suffrage and abolitionist club. Few women of any race were attending college when Nettie attended the University of Kansas: "It was virtually unheard of for a black girl to do so in the reconstruction era following the Civil War" (*Tacoma News Tribune*, 1977). Believed possibly to be the first black woman in the nation's history to receive a Ph.D. in any field, Nettie was granted a doctorate of music from the Kansas Conservatory of Music and Elocution in Leavenworth, Kansas, on 12 June 1883. In the 1880s, after working as a music teacher, choir director, and organist in Kansas City, Missouri, and Denver, Colorado, Nettie and her family were among the early settlers in the black town of Nicodemus, Kansas, where she was a music and school teacher.

In 1890, during her work in Kansas, she met and married Albert Jones, about whom little is known. They traveled by train to Seattle, Washington, where she was the first organist and musical director for the First African Methodist Episcopal (AME) Church. At the age of ninety-six, Nettie recalled their arrival in Seattle: "News of the great Seattle fire in 1889 aroused a lot of interest in the Midwest. Many disposed of their belongings and moved to Seattle. We arrived amid much bustle and excitement. It was a good time of friendship and good neighborliness" (*Tacoma News Tribune*, 1963). In 1893, after three years in Seattle, Jones tragically died, although the details of his death are unknown. She returned to her old hometown of Leavenworth, Kansas, where she was organist and musical director of Bethel AME Church. She taught music to students in Kansas City. After a few years of residence in Leavenworth, Nettie moved to Tacoma, Washington, where she continued her activities as organist and musical director for Tacoma's First AME Church. She then married Henry J. Asberry, a well-known businessman and proprietor of the Tacoma Hotel Barbershop.

Asberry was active in the NAACP, establishing branches in Tacoma, Seattle, and Spokane, Washington, Portland, Oregon, and other cities in Canada and Alaska. Asberry submitted the Tacoma charter application to the New York office and in 1913 her group became the first NAACP auxiliary established west of the Rocky Mountains. For a time she served as regional field secretary and later as the local branch secretary.

In 1916, in response to the film "Birth of a Nation," Asberry drafted a letter to the Tacoma newspapers protesting the movie's release and its racist portrayal of African Americans. "My blood was at the white-heat point. Instantly I began to hiss in my feeling of resentment at the series of infamous lies. People turned around and stared at me, but I had lost my equilibrium; I was in a fighting mood.... No one can witness the production of this movie and be the same as before he saw it. No city can afford to have the equilibrium of its people disturbed" (*Tacoma Ledger*, 1916).

Asberry was well known for her ambitious participation in statewide women's clubs. In 1908, she helped organize the Cloverleaf Club, an art club for the exhibition of needlecraft and artwork of black women in Tacoma and the surrounding county. These women were determined to be a part of the 1909 Alaska-Yukon-Pacific Exposition in Seattle, where the club's exhibition earned them a gold medal. A handmade Battenburg lace opera coat Asberry and her sister Martha Craig Johnson made for the exhibit won a bronze medal, as did ceramics and paintings contributed by Mrs. Hiram Moore-Baker. In 1917, she started a number of clubs, all of which became charter members of the Washington State Federation of Colored Women's Organizations. The preamble to the organization's constitution declared: "We, the colored women of the State of Washington and Jurisdiction, feeling the need of united and systematic effort along moral, physical, and intellectual lines, in order to elevate our race, do hereby unite into a State Federation" (Bragg, 123). Asberry served as president of the Federation and was also a member of the Progressive Mother's Club of Tacoma and the Tacoma Inter-Racial Council. In 1918, Asberry served as auxiliary chairman of the Allen African Methodist Episcopal Red Cross Auxiliary. She devoted much of her senior life to social causes and volunteered countless hours of social work to those who needed assistance. When the United States entered the World War, her auxiliary did a lot of work for the men overseas. After the armistice was signed at the close of the war Asberry received a badge with two crosses for her services. She did not intend to devote her life to teaching. Later in life she answered the call to the endless need for social work. She said that although many people think of social workers as highly paid, many social workers gave countless volunteer hours.

Asberry was a member of the Baha'i faith for twenty-five years, an organization devoted to the unity of humanity. In this spirit she pursued "harmony between the races" (*Tacoma News Tribune*, 18 April 1976). She applied the principals of music, including beauty of form, harmony, and expression of emotion, and used them in a broader sense to heal the world's ills. Asberry died at the age of 103. A year later, in memory of her musical accomplishments and community work, the mayor of Tacoma, A. L. Rasmussen, proclaimed 11 May Dr. Nettie J. Asberry Day. In November 2004, the Asberry Cultural Club celebrated its fiftieth anniversary.

FURTHER READING

The Nettie J. Asberry Papers are in Special Collections at the University of Washington Libraries in Seattle. These contain correspondence, bulletins, notes, and minutes kept by her various organizations.

Bragg, L. E. *More Than Petticoats: Remarkable Washington Women* (1998).

Mumford, Esther Hall. *Seattle's Black Victorians 1852–1901* (1980).

Taylor, Quintard, and Moore, Shirley Ann Wilson. *African American Women Confront The West, 1600–2000* (2003).

Obituary: *Tacoma News Tribune,* 18 Nov. 1968.

ANTOINETTE BROUSSARD FARMER

Ashby, Irving C. (29 Dec. 1920–22 Apr. 1987), jazz guitarist, was born in Somerville, Massachusetts, near Boston, the son of an apartment superintendent. His parents' names are unknown. The family was musical and closely in touch with the world of entertainment: "FATS WALLER used to come by the house all the time," Ashby told the writer James Haskins. Ashby taught himself to play guitar. At age fifteen he joined a band that played sophisticated arrangements for college dances, and, deeply embarrassed by his inability to read music, he began to learn chordal notation. He performed at a nightclub at Revere Beach while attending Roxbury Memorial High School. Ashby's abilities as a classical guitarist won him a scholarship at an open audition for the New England Conservatory of Music in Boston, but the school had no guitar teacher and thus the award went to the runner-up: "So that's the extent of my conservatory background—in and out the same day," he told the writer Harvey Siders (10). Having made his own ukulele at age twelve, Ashby helped to manufacture guitars at the Stromberg factory in Boston during a period when he was performing on a radio show on station WNAC.

When the guitarist CHARLIE CHRISTIAN came to prominence in 1939, he became the strongest influence on Ashby, who memorized all of Christian's recorded solos. While performing in Provincetown, Massachusetts, and planning to enter Boston

University to study art and writing, Ashby accepted an offer to join LIONEL HAMPTON's band in California in fall 1940. Late in life Ashby regretted the move. He needed the money, but music was not his first choice for a career, and he felt—correctly, despite his considerable talent—that he never ranked with the greatest jazz guitarists. His recordings with Hampton include "Altitude" and "Fiddle-Dee-Dee," both from 1941. Sometime before the middle of that year he had an opportunity to play informally with Christian when the Hampton and Benny Goodman bands were staying at the same hotel in Chicago. Ashby left Hampton's band in 1942.

In Hollywood in January 1943 Ashby played in the group that accompanied Waller in the celebrated film *Stormy Weather.* Drafted, Ashby served in an army band. In 1946 he returned to Los Angeles, where he worked with the pianist Eddie Beal and participated in recording sessions as a sideman with the tenor saxophonist LESTER YOUNG, with the pianist André Previn (toward the start of Previn's career in jazz), with the bassist CHARLES MINGUS, and with the singers IVIE ANDERSON, LENA HORNE, and HELEN HUMES. He also sometimes participated as a leader. Around this time Ashby married Pauline (maiden name unknown), a schoolteacher; they had two daughters. He performed with the pianist ERROLL GARNER and the tenor saxophonist WARDELL GRAY at Gene Norman's Just Jazz concert in Hollywood in April 1947.

On 27 September 1947 Ashby replaced Oscar Moore in the singer and pianist NAT KING COLE's trio. After enjoying more than a year of touring, he encountered musical and personal problems early in 1949, when the conga and bongo player Jack Constanzo joined Cole's group. Ashby's best-known recording, "Bop Kick," is from this period, but unfortunately Costanzo's incongruous playing and Cole's new fascination with bop—a style to which Cole was unsuited—made this performance unsatisfying. Ashby nonetheless continued to admire Cole's talent greatly, and he stayed in the quartet through a European tour and the making of the film short *King Cole and His Trio,* both in 1950. Finally, around March 1951, Cole's gambling and tax problems provoked Ashby's resignation.

Ashby joined the bassist RAY BROWN in the pianist OSCAR PETERSON's trio for live performances, but Barney Kessel—who soon replaced Ashby in the trio—made studio recordings with Peterson late in 1951. Ashby recorded only a single session as Peterson's guitarist in January 1952. Among his work from this date is a solo in "Blue

Moon." The highlight of Ashby's career came later the same year, when he joined Peterson, Young, ELLA FITZGERALD, and other stars for a European tour with Jazz at the Philharmonic: "That's what spoiled me; that's what ruined all other music for me" (Siders, 30).

Ashby then dropped out of the international and national jazz scene, with the exception of intermittent recordings—including sessions with the tenor saxophonist Illinois Jacquet (1955), the alto saxophonists EARL BOSTIC (1957) and WILLIE SMITH (1965), Peterson (1972), the pianist COUNT BASIE and the singer BIG JOE TURNER (1973), and the guitarist Mundell Lowe (1974)—and his own album *Memoirs* (1976). Ashby taught guitar in the Los Angeles area, worked in landscape design, and after moving to Perris, California, in 1969, delivered newspapers. His *Guitar Work Book* was self-published sometime in the early 1970s. He died at home in Perris.

Despite his doubts about his career, Ashby was a significant jazz guitarist who closely adhered to the model of Christian's innovative, single-note improvisational style—though unlike Christian, he also excelled as a chordal, rhythmic player.

FURTHER READING
Britt, Stan. *The Jazz Guitarists* (1984).
Siders, Harvey. "Irving Ashby: Playing with the Greats," *Guitar Player* 8 (Sept. 1974): 10, 27, 29–30.
Summerfield, Maurice J. *The Jazz Guitar: Its Evolution and Its Players*, 2d ed. (1980).
Obituary: *Los Angeles Times*, 2 May 1987.
This entry is taken from the *American National Biography* and is published here with the permission of the American Council of Learned Societies.

BARRY KERNFELD

Ashe, Arthur (10 Jul. 1943–6 Feb. 1993), tennis player, author, and political activist, was born Arthur Robert Ashe Jr. in Richmond, Virginia, the son of Arthur Ashe Sr., a police officer, and Mattie Cunningham. Tall and slim as a young boy, Ashe was forbidden by his father to play football; he took up tennis instead on the segregated playground courts at Brookfield Park, near his home. By the time he was ten years old he came under the tutelage of a local tennis fan and physician from Lynchburg, R. Walter Johnson. Johnson had previously nurtured the talents of ALTHEA GIBSON, who became the first African American to win Wimbledon, in 1957 and 1958, and his second protégé would prove no less successful.

Arthur Ashe, an amateur tennis player, works his way into the quarter finals as he defeats defending champion John Newcombe, an Australian pro, in the Wimbledon Tennis championships, 1 July 1968. (AP Images.)

Johnson was an exacting coach; he had his charges practice hitting tennis balls with broom handles to develop their hand-eye coordination. But his lessons extended beyond tennis; he also helped the young Ashe navigate an often hostile, segregated South. Johnson and Ashe's father (his mother died when he was six) instructed Arthur in the manners, discipline, and grace that would mark his carriage within and without the nearly all-white tennis world. When Arthur was fifteen, Johnson tried to enter him in an all-white junior tournament sponsored by the Middle Atlantic Lawn Tennis Association and held at Richmond's Country Club of Virginia, but the club refused his application. As a result, Ashe, who was ranked fifth in his age group in the country, was unable to earn a ranking from his own region.

In 1958 Ashe reached the semifinals in the under-fifteen division of the junior national championships.

Soon afterward a tennis coach from St. Louis, Richard Hudlin, offered to take Ashe under his wing, and after completing his junior year in high school in Richmond, Ashe accepted. He moved in with Hudlin and his family and completed his schooling at Sumner High School in St. Louis, the alma mater of the African American comedian and activist DICK GREGORY. In 1960 and 1961 Ashe won the U.S. junior indoor singles title.

After graduating from high school, Ashe accepted a tennis scholarship to the University of California at Los Angeles (UCLA), where he became an All-American, led his college team to the National Collegiate Athletic Association championship, won the U.S. Hard Court Championship, and was named to the U.S. Davis Cup team. While at UCLA, he also spent time training with the tennis legends Pancho Segura and Pancho Gonzalez, who helped him develop the powerful serve and volley game that would become, along with his sheer athleticism, Ashe's trademark.

In 1965, while still in college, Ashe was ranked third in the world, and he beat the Australian Roy Emerson in five sets to win the Queensland championships at Brisbane, Australia. Graduating from UCLA in 1966 with a degree in Business Administration, Ashe entered a Reserve Officer Training Corps camp and finished second in his platoon for overall achievement at the end of the six-week course. He attained the rank of first lieutenant, serving in the military from 1967 to 1969. During this time he continued playing tennis, winning the U.S. Clay Court Championships in 1967. In 1968, while still an amateur and still in the U.S. Army, he defeated Tom Okker to win the first U.S. Open, one of the two most prestigious tennis tournaments in the world; with this victory he was ranked first in the world. Numerous wins followed, including three Davis Cups, the World Championships of Tennis in 1975 (a year in which he again became the world's highest-ranked player), and two additional Grand Slam championships—the Australian Open in 1970 and Wimbledon in 1975. At Wimbledon he became the first African American man to win at the All-England Club, beating Jimmy Connors. Ashe also won the doubles titles at the French, Australian, and Wimbledon championships.

John McPhee, whose book *Levels of the Game* (1969) chronicled Ashe's match with Clark Graebner, his opponent in the semifinal of the 1968 U.S. Open, considered Ashe a competitive genius. "Even in very tight moments, other players thought he was toying with them," McPhee wrote later in an appreciation piece in the *New Yorker* after Ashe's death. He continues:

> They rarely knew what he was thinking. They could not tell if he was angry. It was maddening, sometimes, to play against him. Never less than candid, he said that what he liked best about himself on a tennis court was his demeanor: "What it is is controlled cool, in a way. Always have the situation under control, even if losing. Never betray an inward sense of defeat." And of course he never did—not in the height of his athletic power, not in the statesmanship of the years that followed, and not in the endgame of his existence.

Over the course of his career Ashe earned more than $1.5 million, becoming the sport's first black millionaire and one of his era's most visible African American athletes. Several companies, including Coca-Cola and Philip Morris, hired him to promote their products, and he worked for ABC television and HBO as a sports commentator. Ashe married Jeanne Marie Moutoussamy in 1977, and they had one daughter, Camera Elizabeth. In 1979, at the age of thirty-six, Ashe suffered a heart attack, which forced him to undergo bypass surgery and retire from playing competitive tennis. Still, one year after his operation he became the first and only African American to be named captain of the U.S. Davis Cup team, a position he held until 1985. Under his leadership the team won the international competition in 1981. In 1985 he became the first African American man elected to the International Tennis Hall of Fame.

Throughout his career and afterward Ashe spent considerable time and energy working for civil and human rights. He wrote eloquently about his complex position as a world-renowned success in a field dominated by whites; even as his moderation appealed to whites, he was occasionally criticized by more vocal black activists. "There were times, in fact, when I felt a burning sense of shame that I was not with other blacks—and whites—standing up to the fire hoses and the police dogs, the truncheons, bullets and bombs that cut down such martyrs as Chaney, Schwerner, and Goodman, Viola Liuzzo, MARTIN LUTHER KING JR., MEDGAR EVERS and the little girls in that bombed church in Birmingham, Ala.," he was quoted as saying in *The Black 100: A Ranking of the Most Influential African Americans, Past and Present* ([1993], 363). "As my fame increased, so did my anguish. I knew that many blacks were proud of my accomplishments on the tennis court. But I also knew that many others, especially many of my own age or younger, did not bother to hide their indifference to me and my trophies or even their disdain and contempt for me."

In 1973, after three years of trying, Ashe had received an invitation to play in the previously all white South African Open; twelve years later Ashe, the longtime friend of the still imprisoned Nelson Mandela, was arrested in South Africa for protesting apartheid. In 1992 he joined a group of protesters who were arrested in Washington, D.C., for objecting to the treatment of Haitian refugees by the George H. W. Bush Administration. Ashe's concern for fairness and human dignity extended beyond race. In 1974 he helped found the Association of Tennis Professionals, a players' union, and served as president until 1979. He later became a board member of the United States Tennis Association, chairman of the American Heart Association, and a board member for the National Foundation for Infectious Diseases.

Always a bookish, thoughtful man, Ashe cultivated a second career as a writer and sports historian. Through his research, he managed to trace his own roots back ten generations on his father's side to a woman who, in 1735, was brought from West Africa to Yorktown, Virginia, on the slave ship *Doddington*. Ashe's benchmark three-volume history of black athletes in America, *A Hard Road to Glory*, was published in 1988.

Ashe suffered a number of serious health problems that ended his playing career but barely seemed to slow him down. He had a second heart attack in 1983, followed by emergency brain surgery in 1988; after the last operation rumors began to spread about his infection with HIV, the virus that causes AIDS. Although he kept his illness secret for nearly a decade, Ashe was forced to admit his diagnosis publicly when, on 7 April 1992, the newspaper *USA Today* threatened to print the story as soon as it could be confirmed. Because Ashe did not officially acknowledge his illness to the newspaper, he was able to put off publication of the story for a day and to inform friends, family members, and health officials of his condition. On 8 April, the day after *USA Today*'s initial phone call, Ashe held a press conference to break the news himself, reporting that the virus had been transmitted during blood transfusions associated with his second heart operation in 1983. The event prompted a worldwide outpouring of grief and a squall of commentary about the conflict between the press's responsibility to report the news and an individual's right to privacy. That year he helped raise $15 million for the Arthur Ashe Foundation for the Defeat of AIDS, and in part for

this work he was named Sportsman of the Year by *Sports Illustrated*.

Ashe's death in New York City provoked a sense of loss that extended far beyond the boundaries of the tennis world or the borders of the United States. A memorial service held at the Richmond governor's mansion of DOUGLAS WILDER, the first African American governor of Virginia, attracted thousands of admirers from around the world. Wilder said that Ashe's "leadership may not be confined to athletics and sports alone, for he was totally committed to improving the lives of those yet to enjoy the full fruition of rights and opportunities in this country" (*New York Times*, 7 Feb. 1993).

Ashe's passing was mourned by many who saw in his example an unusual dignity and elegance, even in the face of a terrible disease. "Why, when we knew Arthur Ashe's health was precarious, did the news of his death from pneumonia last Saturday hit us like a ball peen hammer between the eyes?" wrote Kenny Moore in a cover story in *Sports Illustrated*. "Why did the announcement of this gentle man's passing force even the raucous Madison Square Garden crowd at the RIDDICK BOWE–Michael Dokes fight into unwonted reflection, never quite to return to the fray? In part, surely, we reel because, even with AIDS and a history of heart attacks, Ashe didn't seem to be sick. He, of all men, hid things well. His gentility shielded us from appreciating his risk" (15 Feb. 1993, 12).

FURTHER READING
Ashe, Arthur, with Frank Deford. *Arthur Ashe: Portrait in Motion* (1975).
Ashe, Arthur, with Arnold Rampersad. *Days of Grace* (1993).
Ashe, Arthur, with Neil Amdur. *Off the Court* (1981).
This entry is taken from the *American National Biography* and is published here with the permission of the American Council of Learned Societies.

MCKAY JENKINS

Asher, Jeremiah (13 Oct. 1812–27 July 1865), Civil War army chaplain and Baptist minister, was born in North Branford, near New Haven, Connecticut, to Ruel and Jereusha Asher. His paternal grandfather had been captured in the Guinea region of Africa at the age of four and was brought to America as a slave. Young Jeremiah grew up hearing fascinating tales of his grandfather's life, which included military service during the American Revolutionary War. Those stories would later inspire Asher in his own life.

Asher's father was a shoemaker who married a Native American woman from Hartford, Connecticut. Jeremiah grew up as a member of the only African American family in North Branford and was permitted to attend school along with white children. At the age of twelve he left school to help out his family financially, and over the next several years he worked as a farmhand, servant, and coachman. In 1833 he married Abigail Stewart of Glastonbury, Connecticut.

The young couple began their married life with much promise and soon joined the local Baptist church. After moving around Connecticut they eventually ended up in the Hartford area in 1839. His home church, the First Baptist Church of Hartford, was predominantly white and, as was the custom of the day, compelled African Americans to sit in segregated "Negro pews" during the worship service. White members had built a new pew for the congregation's black members, which Asher described as "the most objectionable one I had ever seen" (Asher, 44). The pew had high sides, about six feet tall, so that blacks sitting in it could not see, and perhaps more important, could not be seen. The black members were resentful but seemed reluctantly resolved to endure the new form of discrimination.

Asher, on the other hand, protested by boycotting church services, which encouraged other black members to do the same. That led the church to inquire why the black members were, in their words, "getting quite out of their place" (Asher, 45). Asher countered that they were not getting out of their place nor were they hard to please. Instead, they simply objected to the new pew and wished to sit in the gallery of the church. Writing later, he said, "I did not of course presume that black Christians had a right to sit below in their Father's house" (Asher, 45). Asher and other black members boycotted the church and, finally, after much going back and forth, the white pastor and deacons met with Asher and black members in the private home of a black member. After hearing arguments from the blacks, the white pastor and deacons agreed to allow the blacks to sit "where they pleased in the galleries, and that was the end of this revolution" (Asher, 47).

Asher's experience in protesting the Negro pew led him to a deeper spiritual conviction and brought to light his leadership abilities. He went on to become a Baptist minister and helped to form a new church in Providence, Rhode Island. He served as pastor of that church for nine years, until he was called to Shiloh Baptist Church in Philadelphia. Shiloh was struggling financially, and so he determined to travel to England to raise money. With letters of support from other churches as well as the mayor's office, he set sail for Britain in 1849. Asher traveled across Britain, meeting with limited success initially, but eventually he was able to obtain support from local Baptist pastors. His British supporters encouraged him to publish an account of his life in order to raise more money, as well as to highlight racial prejudice in the United States. *Incidents in the Life of the Rev. J. Asher*, his autobiography, was published in London in 1850.

Asher's trip was a success, and he returned from England with enough money to pay off the church's debt. For the next eleven years he continued his work as pastor of Shiloh and served in various positions at the National Baptist Convention level. When the American Civil War broke out, Asher became interested in serving his country, much like his grandfather had done during the American Revolution. After Abraham Lincoln's Emancipation Proclamation went into effect on 1 January 1863, African Americans were permitted to join the Union army. No regular black officers were authorized, but provision was soon made for blacks to serve as chaplains. Although technically they were officers, they had no command authority and thus no possibility to serve over whites. Asher volunteered and was assigned to the Sixth United States Colored Infantry (USCT), one of only fourteen black chaplains to serve in the Union army.

The Sixth was sent to join the Army of the James in Virginia on 14 October 1863 and was put to work building fortifications around Yorktown. "The last month has been one of constant excitement and fatigue," Asher wrote. "The men having been working on the fortifications day and night, not excepting the Sabbath" (Redkey, 337). The Sixth eventually went on to see combat around Petersburg and Richmond. From an army hospital at Portsmouth, he noted, "There are in the hospitals here about five hundred sick and wounded colored soldiers … some few are without arms and legs." Wounded himself at the Battle of the Wilderness in May 1864, he spent time in the hospital recuperating.

Asher and the men of the Sixth were deployed to North Carolina and took part in the successful capture of Fort Fisher and the key port of Wilmington. From Wilmington they advanced into the interior of the state, joining forces with General William T. Sherman and participating in the capture of Raleigh and the surrender of General Joseph Johnston on 26 April 1865. In the aftermath of the war Asher and the men of the Sixth were assigned to occupation duty in the Wilmington area. He continued his chaplain duties and also helped the freedmen's schools teach the former slaves. Unfortunately, Asher soon fell victim to disease and died on 27 July 1865, the only black chaplain to die on duty. His remains were brought to Philadelphia, and he was buried at Olive Cemetery near Shiloh.

FURTHER READING

Asher, Jeremiah. *Incidents in the Life of the Rev. J. Asher* (1850).

Lamm, Alan K. *Five Black Preachers in Army Blue, 1884–1901: The Buffalo Soldier Chaplains* (1998).

Paradis, James M. *Strike the Blow for Freedom: The 6th United States Colored Infantry in the Civil War* (1998).

Redkey, Edwin S. "Black Chaplains in the Union Army," *Civil War History*, vol. 33, no. 4 (1987).

ALAN K. LAMM

Ashford, Emmett Littleton (23 Nov. 1914–1 Mar. 1980), baseball umpire, was born in Los Angeles, California, the son of Littleton Ashford, a truck driver, and Adele Bain. Ashford was two or three years old when his father abandoned the family, so he grew up under the strong influence of his mother, a secretary for the *California Eagle*, an African American newspaper published in Los Angeles. As a youth, Ashford exhibited the traits that marked him in adult life as a gregarious extrovert. At Jefferson High School he was a sprinter on the track team, a member of the scholastic honor society, and the first African American to serve as president of the student body and as editor of the school newspaper. He graduated from Los Angeles City College and attended Chapman College in nearby Orange from 1940 to 1941. From 1944 until 1947 he served in the U.S. Navy.

Ashford began his umpiring career in 1941 by working recreation league, high school, college, and semiprofessional games. While in the navy in 1946, after hearing that JACKIE ROBINSON had broken the modern color line in organized baseball, Ashford first thought about an umpiring career and the possibility of reaching the major leagues. After the war Ashford added softball to his umpiring schedule and twice worked the National Softball Congress World Tournament. After the 1948 tournament—in which the team from Georgia initially opposed his presence on racial grounds but wound up insisting that he umpire the plate in the final game—he decided to give up his administrative job in the payroll and finance division of the Los Angeles post office to explore professional umpiring. With the assistance of the major league scout Rosey Gilhousen and after a four-game tryout in Mexico, Ashford was hired in July 1951 by the Class C Southwest International League, thereby becoming the first African American umpire in minor league baseball. He spent two seasons in Class C, advanced in 1953 to the Class A Western International League, and in 1954 he reached the Class AAA Pacific Coast League (PCL), thanks to the support of the league president Clarence "Pants" Rowland, a former major league manager. Ashford spent twelve years in the PCL, three as umpire in chief (1963–1965), quickly becoming a favorite with fans because of his effervescent personality and flamboyant style. During the off-season he became the first African American to referee high school and college football and basketball games in southern California. He also conducted an umpiring clinic in Japan in 1958 under the auspices of the U.S. Air Force, and he umpired in the Dominican Republic winter league in 1959 and 1964.

After fifteen years in the minors, Ashford reached the major leagues at age fifty-one, when he was hired in September 1965 by the American League for the 1966 season. During a brief career terminated by the league's mandatory retirement of umpires at age fifty-five, he umpired the 1967 all-star game and the 1970 World Series. He retired in 1970, but he continued his umpiring activities by working Pacific Coast Conference college games, by serving as commissioner and umpire in chief of the professional-amateur Alaskan League, and by conducting clinics in Canada, Europe, and Korea. He also served from his retirement until his death as a special assistant to the commissioner of baseball, Bowie Kuhn, performing public relations duties on the West Coast. Married four times (1937, 1950, 1966, and 1979) and detached from his three children, Ashford never experienced the familial intimacy that he missed as a child.

Controversy dogged Ashford throughout his major league career. As the first African American to reach the major leagues in a capacity other than as a player, he received numerous threats and endured racial epithets. In addition, some fellow umpires criticized his flamboyant officiating style and resented his popularity with fans and sportswriters. Ashford's jocularity, his booming voice, and his exaggerated motions when making calls led many people to regard him as a clown who sacrificed judgment and accuracy for self-promoting showmanship. Others, especially some African Americans, considered his showboating to be a manifestation of a degrading STEPIN FETCHIT–like behavior that perpetuated negative stereotypes. Still others considered his elegant use of language, cultural interest in the arts and opera, and fashionable wardrobe (he wore cufflinks when umpiring) to be affectations intended to impress whites. Most pervasive were the charges that Ashford was a poor umpire who reached the majors solely to satisfy the civil rights advocates who championed his promotion.

The criticisms of Ashford, while not unfounded, were exaggerated. By the time that he reached the majors his umpiring skills had diminished, particularly when he called balls and strikes and when he followed batted balls into the outfield. But as some fellow umpires and Dewey Soriano, president of the PCL who had urged Ashford's promotion, argued, Ashford was a hard-working, competent, thorough professional who was neither the best nor the worst in the league. Ashford's jovial demeanor, especially pronounced during arguments with players and managers, occasionally called to mind uncomplimentary racial stereotypes, but his personality was authentic, and his wit and charm facilitated his acceptance as a racial pioneer in sports officiating. His unconventional style clashed with the traditional conservative demeanor of veteran umpires, but it was natural rather than deliberate and presaged the more aggressive bearing and emphatic gestures that soon became the norm. Political pressures and the exigencies of the civil rights movement did boost his promotion, but his hiring had been long delayed by racist attitudes.

When asked why he gave up fifteen years of seniority with the U.S. Postal Service to become the first black umpire in minor and major league baseball, Ashford replied simply: "How many men go to their graves without ever doing what's in their hearts?" He was a courageous and determined man whose pioneering achievements spurred the racial integration of sports officiating at all levels of athletic competition. Even after his death in Los Angeles, Ashford, who always considered himself "an *umpire*, not a black umpire," achieved a historic first: his was the initial burial in the section of a cemetery in Cooperstown, New York, owned by the National Baseball Hall of Fame. In 1982 a Little League field in Los Angeles was named in his honor.

FURTHER READING

Gerlach, Larry R. *The Men in Blue: Conversations with Umpires* (1980).

Margulies, Alan. "The Entertainer," *Referee* (Sept. 1992).

Rust, Art. *"Get That Nigger Off the Field!": A Sparkling, Informal History of the Black Man in Baseball* (1976).

Obituaries: *Los Angeles Sentinel*, 6 Mar. 1980; *Los Angeles Times*, 7 Mar. 1980; *New York Times*, 4 Mar. 1980.

This entry is taken from the *American National Biography* and is published here with the permission of the American Council of Learned Societies.

LARRY R. GERLACH

Ashford, Evelyn (15 Apr. 1957–), sprinter, was born in Shreveport, Louisiana, the eldest of five children of Samuel Ashford, a non-commissioned U.S. Air Force officer, and Vietta Ashford, a homemaker. Because of her father's service assignments, the family lived a nomadic lifestyle before settling

Evelyn Ashford defends her title in the women's 100-meter dash at the USA/Mobil Outdoor Track Championships in Indianapolis on Saturday, 18 June 1983, which she won in 11.24 seconds. (AP Images.)

in Roseville, California, where Ashford was the only girl on Roseville High's boys track team. She earned her spot by beating the school's fastest boys. Ashford's precocious world-class speed was obvious by her senior year, when she recorded times of 11.5 and 24.2 seconds, respectively, in the 100 and 200 meter dashes.

Ashford entered UCLA in September 1975 with an athletic scholarship. She soon qualified for the 1976 Olympic Games in Montreal, Canada, and there, at nineteen, she qualified for the finals and was the top U.S. finisher in the 100 meters, finishing fifth in 11.24 seconds. Ashford was a collegiate all-American in 1977 and 1978. She won individual AIAW (Association for Intercollegiate Athletics for Women) national championships in the 100 and 200 meters, and was part of UCLA's first-place 4 × 200 meter relay team, in 1977, and repeated as AIAW 200 meter champion in 1978.

Ashford left UCLA in 1978 to train full-time. That same year she married Ray Washington. Ashford had been disappointed with her results after finishing fifth in the 100 meters in the 1977 World Cup (won by new world record holder Marlies Göhr of East Germany), and fourth in the 200 meters. She lowered her personal best in the 100 to 11.18 seconds in 1978, the fastest time in the United States and the fourth best in the world that year. She also had the top U.S. time in the 200, and was third in the world, at 22.66 seconds.

Ashford won her first world champions in 1979, when she finished first in the 100 and 200 meters at the TAC Championships, Pan-American Games, and World Cup. Her 10.97 second time in the TAC semifinals was the first by an American woman under 11 seconds. At the World Cup in Montreal, she defeated East Germany's Marita Koch to win the 200 in a US record time of 21.83, then defeated Göhr in the 100 with an 11.06.

A hamstring injury and the U.S. boycott of the Moscow Olympic Games cut short Ashford's 1980 season but after a period of self-evaluation during which she considered retirement and decided to take on the responsibility of coaching herself, she returned in 1981 to win seventeen of eighteen outdoor sprint finals, including the 100 and 200 at the TAC Championships and the World Cup. She lowered the U.S. record in the 100 to 10.90, only 0.02 behind Göhr's 1977 world record, was named female Athlete of the Year by *Track & Field News*, and finished the year ranked first in the world in both sprints.

Ashford set her first world record, 10.79 seconds in the 100, at the U.S. National Sports Festival in Colorado in June 1983. In 1983, she ran twenty of the twenty-three then-fastest times ever recorded by a woman in the 100 meters. Later that year she reinjured her hamstring at the inaugural World Championships in Helsinki, which proved to be a blessing in disguise as her recovery period gave her an opportunity to work out marital problems and rest in preparation for the Olympic year of 1984.

Ashford dominated the first two rounds of the 100 at the U.S. Olympic Trials in June 1984, but then felt a twinge in her right hamstring while warming up for the semifinals the next day and struggled to a third-place finish. For the final, Ashford wore skin-tight leggings. Her right leg was bandaged and taped from the knee up. That worked well enough for her to win the 100 final in 11.18 seconds. Ashford then withdrew from the 200 to avoid further injury. The Los Angeles Games proved less challenging. Ashford's leg had healed, and East Germany was boycotting the Games. She breezed through the 100 with an Olympic record of 10.97 in the final, and earned a second gold medal as anchor of the American 4 × 100 meter relay team.

The year 1984 presented Ashford with one more challenge: East Germany's Göhr. Ashford had not beaten her since 1979, and she had been dominating European meets. Ashford answered that challenge by bettering her world record. The much-awaited showdown took place on August 22 at Zurich's *Weltklasse* meet. Göhr had a slight lead after sixty meters, then Ashford flew by her to finish in a record 10.76 seconds. Ashford was named *Track & Field News* Athlete of the Year again, and her race in Zurich was named Performance of the Year.

Ashford took a break from competition in 1985, when her daughter, Raina Ashley Washington, was born. When she returned in 1986, she quickly became a world champion again. Ashford won the 100 meter final in the 1986 Goodwill Games in Moscow, edging East Germany's Heike Drechsler with both athletes finishing in 10.91 seconds, then was undefeated in the 100 for the remainder of 1986 and had the year's fastest time of 10.88. In the 200 meters Ashford won eight of nine finals, including one over Drechsler, by then the co-world record holder. She finished the year ranked first in the world in the 100 and fourth in the 200, receiving the Vitalis Award for excellence in track and field.

Hamstring problems forced Ashford's withdrawal from the U.S. Olympic Sports Festival and World Championship Games in 1987, but she once again qualified for the U.S. Olympic team in 1988, at age thirty-one, and was the U.S. team's flag bearer at Seoul. Ashford bettered her Olympic record time of 10.97 seconds with a 10.83 finish in the 100 meter final, but finished in second place behind FLORENCE GRIFFITH-JOYNER, who won in 10.54 seconds. Ashford won her third gold medal in the 4×100 relay, one of the most exciting races of the Seoul Games. Starting her anchor leg three meters behind East Germany's Göhr, Ashford passed her before the finish line to earn gold for the U.S. team.

Ashford's track career still was not finished. She received the FLO HYMAN Trophy from the Women's Sports Foundation in 1989 for support of women's advancements in sports, placed third in the 100 meters at the U.S. Championships in 1991, and at thirty-five qualified for the 1992 Olympic Games in Barcelona. There she was eliminated by 0.001 seconds in her 100-meter semifinal but won her fourth gold medal, and became the oldest woman to earn an Olympic gold medal in track, as the starting runner on the American first-place 4 × 100 relay team.

After retiring from competition, Ashford went into business in Southern California. She was elected to the USA Track & Field Hall of Fame in 1997, the U.S. Olympic Hall of Fame in 2006, and the new Sacramento Sports Hall of Fame in 2007.

FURTHER READING

Connolly, Pat. *Coaching Evelyn: Fast, Faster, Fastest Woman in the World* (1991).

Hendershott, Jon. *Track's Greatest Women* (1987).

Woolum, Janet. *Outstanding Woman Athletes: Who They Are and How They Influenced Sports in America* (1992).

WILLIAM A. JACOBSON
STEVEN B. JACOBSON

Ashley, Eugene, Jr. (12 Oct. 1930–7 Feb. 1968), Special Forces soldier in the Vietnam War and Medal of Honor winner, was born in Wilmington, North Carolina, the son of Eugene and Cornelia Ashley. Within a short time after the younger Eugene's birth, the family moved to New York City, likely to take advantage of greater opportunities for employment during the Depression years. Ashley graduated from Alexander Hamilton High School in 1948. With employment opportunities limited in the post–World War II era and meaningful jobs hard to come by, Ashley joined the United States Army on 7 December 1950.

During World War II black soldiers had fought in both the Pacific and European theaters in segregated units commanded by white officers. President Truman's 1947 Executive Order 9981, however,

officially ended segregation practices in all branches of the U.S. armed forces. The tradition-bound services proved slow to change, and several years passed before actual practices were to comply with Truman's order. Even during the Korean War, African American soldiers like CORNELIUS CHARLTON fought for a time in segregated units. Indeed, Vietnam War soldiers, men like WEBSTER ANDERSON, Eugene Ashley, and thousands of other black enlisted men who entered the service in the 1950s would benefit from the social and racial changes made within the army at the very same time that the civil rights era was in full swing. African Americans gradually began to perceive service in the army as a desirable career choice.

Ashley's service in the army was varied both geographically and in the tasks he performed. Serving in Korea, Germany, Okinawa, and at several bases stateside, Ashley saw duty as an ambulance driver and infantryman. As he rose through the ranks, gained more training, and honed his skills, he worked as an antiaircraft gunner and later as a heavy weapons specialist, with experience in armor and airborne operations. In January 1968, his seventeenth year in the army, Ashley was sent to Vietnam as a sergeant first class, trained in operations and intelligence duties, and as operations sergeant in Special Forces (popularly known as the Green Berets) Airborne Detachment A-101, Company C, Fifth Special Forces Group, stationed at Camp Lang Vei under the command of Captain Frank Willoughby.

By the time Ashley arrived at Camp Lang Vei, the Americans' situation in Quan Tri province in South Vietnam had become perilous. Camp Lang Vei was located on Route 9 near the Laotian border, about six miles west of the marine base at Khe Sanh. A frontier outpost largely rebuilt by Captain Willoughby and his Special Forces detachment, it was first established in December 1966 and was said to have been ill-fated from the beginning. During the North Vietnamese assault and subsequent seventy-seven-day siege on the marine base at Khe Sanh, beginning on 21 January, Camp Lang Vei was in imminent danger, and subjected to mortar attack on 24 January 1968. By 6 February 1968, the camp was manned by twenty-four American Special Forces soldiers, with Sergeant First Class Eugene Ashley Jr. as lead intelligence sergeant, as well as fourteen South Vietnamese Special Forces (LLDB), a 161-man mobile strike force, nearly 300 Civilian Irregular Defense Group (CIDG) troops, and approximately 500 Laotian troops and civilians.

The CIDG and Laotian troops often proved unreliable in battle, with the added danger that CIDG units were sometimes infiltrated by the North Vietnamese. The defense of Camp Lang Vei would fall primarily on the shoulders of the Green Berets, none more so than Eugene Ashley Jr.

Just after midnight on 7 February 1968, North Vietnamese Army (NVA) infantry and tank units began their assault on the outer perimeter of Camp Lang Vei—the NVA's first use of armor in the war. Despite a fierce defense on the outer perimeter by the mobile strike force and the destruction of three Soviet-built tanks, the NVA overwhelmed the perimeter defenders. Employing satchel charges, thermite and tear gas grenades, and flamethrowers, the NVA decimated the CIDG troops and within hours captured both ends of the camp. Outside the camp, Eugene Ashley lent support by directing mortar attacks, and when camp communications were cut, took on the added duty of directing air strikes on enemy positions using portable radio communications equipment. The NVA nearly succeeded in overtaking the underground command bunker using grenades and satchel charges. They also tried to bluff Captain Willoughby and the other defenders into surrendering by threatening to blow up the bunker; a number of LLDB men fell for this ruse, surrendered, and were summarily executed. The Americans remained and held the post. The defense of the camp was further imperiled when the Laotian troops refused to fight. Continuing to lead support efforts, Eugene Ashley mustered two Americans, Sergeant Richard Allen and Specialist Joel Johnson, and sixty Laotian troops to counterattack, but the effort failed when the Laotian troops bolted at the sound of NVA machine-gun fire. Joined by sergeants William Craig and Peter Tiroch, Ashley demonstrated determined leadership when he was able to muster more defenders who were retreating down Route 9, and attempted three more counterattacks on the command bunker. Each time, Ashley and his men were subjected to heavy machine-gun and automatic weapons fire, grenades, and satchel charges. Now close to his objective, Ashley led a fifth assault against the NVA; reflecting the legacy of the World War II Medal of Honor recipient Lieutenant JOHN FOX, Ashley directed air strikes against enemy forces very near to his own position. This final assault, combined with Ashley's directed air strikes, succeeded in driving the enemy off the high ground and thwarting the NVA attack. Later in the day, Special Forces commandos from Khe Sanh led a mission to reinforce Camp Lang Vei. The battle was over by late afternoon, with many of the wounded evacuated by marine helicopters. Sergeant First Class Eugene Ashley Jr., however, would not survive the attack. Severely wounded during his final assault, he was killed while being carried from the battlefield when an enemy mortar round landed nearby.

Ten Americans were killed or went missing and eleven were wounded in the battle that would later become known in Special Forces lore as "the night of the Silver Stars," so named because of the many Silver Star medals awarded to those who fought at Camp Lang Vei. However, the Silver Star was not the highest award earned for action at Lang Vei. Ashley was awarded the Medal of Honor for his resolute valor and the gallant charges that led to his death, and for saving many of his fellow soldiers. The Medal of Honor was presented by Vice President Spiro Agnew to Ashley's wife, Barbara, in a White House ceremony on 2 December 1969. Ashley is buried at Rockfish Memorial Park in Fayetteville, North Carolina. On 13 August 2001 the Eugene Ashley Jr. Memorial High School was dedicated in his honor in Wilmington, North Carolina.

FURTHER READING

Eugene Ashley High School. "About Ashley," http://www.nhcs.net/ashley.

Medal of Honor Citation. "Eugene Ashley, Jr.," http://www.aavw.org/served/homepage_ashley.html.

Phillips, William. *Night of the Silver Stars: the Battle of Lang Vei* (1997).

POW Network. *Bio, Hanna, Kenneth*, http://www.pownetwork.org/bios/h/h015.htm.

GLENN ALLEN KNOBLOCK

Askin, Luther B. (26 Dec. 1843–6 Apr. 1929), the first African American to integrate baseball, was born in Pittsfield, Massachusetts, the second son of Nelson Askin and Sarah Lloyd. In 1844 Nelson Askin moved to Florence, a mill village in Northampton, Massachusetts, to open a livery. Across the road was the Northampton Association of Education and Industry, a utopian community whose ideals and practices ensured an integrated membership. Although the association disbanded in 1846, many members stayed in Florence, including SOJOURNER TRUTH and DAVID RUGGLES; their influence marked the village as a "sanctuary" for all, regardless of religion, class, or race. But in 1849, when Sarah Askin arrived in Florence with her six children, Nelson had already sold off parts of his property, and shortly thereafter the livery was seized by creditors. By 1850 Nelson had abandoned Sarah. From then on, Sarah took in washing to support her children, who at the earliest opportunity left school to find work.

Luther Askin worked for more than fifty years in a brush shop, rising to foreman, in itself an accomplishment. He was also a stonecutter, carpenter, fireman, and musician. But his principal accomplishment was to play first base, from 1865 to 1866, for the Florence Eagle Base Ball Club. In 1872 Askin married Alice Lattimore of Moreau, New York. The couple remained in Florence for fifty-six years, raising five children. After Alice's death in 1928, Askin moved to Brooklyn to be with his daughters, where he died in 1929.

By every account, Askin led an unassuming life; the attention he received came about not from his own desire for recognition, but from an abiding need on the part of the people of Florence to celebrate the Eagle Base Ball Club. That Askin took pride in his seasons as an Eagle is evident, for his obituary lists his membership in the club before any other association. Yet no reference is made to his integration of the "Eagle nine." References to Askin's race can be found only in birth and census records or in accounts that address subjects other than the Eagles.

The papers of the Eagles' captain, Arthur G. Hill, show that he regarded Askin as "colored" (Hill, 1916). Although Askin's skin was light enough for his race to go unnoticed beyond the village, it is safe to assume that his teammates knew Askin's racial identify, as did most of Florence. Yet even in Florence the subject of Askin's integration of the Eagles went unmentioned for over a century. The reasons for this silence may be found in the shifting identity of the Askin family, some of whom were variously referred to as "colored," "black," "mulatto," and one of whom, by the 1900s, identified himself as "white." The drawing of the color line in baseball had its roots in the game's origins. In the 1840s, when amateur clubs were formed in New York City, baseball was a gentlemanly activity engaged in by professional men of the upper middle class. In time, the dockworkers of Brooklyn formed their own ball clubs and introduced a greater degree of competition, often offending the older clubs, who regarded "rough play" with distaste. Before the Civil War, blacks and whites had little social contact, and therefore no overt effort was required to segregate ball clubs. Blacks were playing baseball "as early as whites," along separate, "roughly parallel lines" (Seymour, *People's*, 532).

After the Civil War, "base ball fever" swept down upon the northeastern United States, and hundreds of amateur "nines" were formed. The limited pool of talent in Florence, with a population of only 1,400, partly explains why Catholics and Protestants, Irish mill workers, and Ivy League graduates played side by side. Also, the village's communitarian heritage, especially the Northampton Association, accounts for the heterogeneity of the Eagles. Even so, it would have been highly unusual for a black player to appear in "match games" arranged through invitations by clubs of adult white males. Yet this is what happened when Askin played for the Eagles.

The Eagles made their debut on 1 August 1865, defeating a team of Civil War veterans who called themselves champions of the "Army of the Potomac." In this, the Eagles' first official match, Askin played first base, qualifying him as "one of the original nine," and in most sources he is recognized as such.

The Eagles went undefeated from August 1865 to June 1866, and in each game Askin started at first base. The people of Florence had set their sights on winning the silver ball, a trophy symbolic of the championship of western Massachusetts. Crowds up to five thousand turned out; a pair of "sporting men" won seven hundred dollars at a single match, twice the annual salary of a millworker. The Eagles, who only the season before had taken the field barefooted and without uniforms, were altogether transformed. The club now wore fine uniforms, ordered balls for $3.50 apiece from New York, and had one hundred members, all of whom paid dues even if they did not play. It was as if the evolution of baseball had been compressed into the Eagles' first two seasons, transforming the game from a leisurely recreational activity to an intensely competitive sport.

On 9 June 1866, in the aftermath of the Eagles' first defeat (against the silver ball–champion Hampdens of Chicopee, no less), Askin was summarily dropped from the lineup. Whether the drive to win the silver ball brought about his demotion is difficult to say. All along, Askin was highly regarded for his fielding. In 1895 an anonymous player reminisced about Askin, calling him "Old Bushel Basket" because "the balls seemed to drop into his fingers and stay there as if a basket had held them" (Sheffeld, 186). In that reminiscence, there is a perplexing reference to a "sickness" that had, in some unspecified fashion, impaired Askin's performance. Yet a few weeks after his demotion, Askin scored seven runs for the Eagles' "second nine," so he was not so sick that he could not play.

In 1867, the year after Askin was dropped from the Eagles, the Pythians, a black team from Philadelphia, tested the baseball color line by applying for membership in the National Association of Amateur Base Ball Players. The National Association responded by putting in place a written ban against blacks, thus codifying the separate racial lines along which amateur ball clubs had evolved. Professional baseball, beginning with the National League in 1876, made little effort to address this situation. With rare exceptions, most notably the Walker brothers (MOSES FLEETWOOD WALKER and WELDY WALKER), who played in the American Association in 1884, segregation in professional baseball was the norm.

For years to come, local fans cited the Eagles as the amateur ideal, for compared to the Florence lads, it was said that all professional teams fell short. Some Eagles were well placed to cultivate their legend, having prospered as businessmen, politicians, journalists, and judges. Celebrations were staged in 1915 and 1916, the golden anniversaries of the club's founding and reign as champions. On both occasions Askin, then in his seventies, spoke on the evolution of baseball to a more "scientific" game. His remarks were reported, but no mention was made of the anomaly of his inclusion at reunions of an all-white team, nor did Askin pose for photographs. Like many African Americans of his era, Askin may have been deferential to the point of invisibility; or he may have chosen not to risk calling attention to his son, Luther Benjamin Askin, a bandleader in Lowville, New York, who had been passing for white for years.

Askin remained an unacknowledged pioneer of baseball integration until 1999, when Jim Ryan, a Florence centenarian, in the course of contributing to a local baseball history, recalled that he and Askin had "talked baseball" during the 1920s. During these encounters, Askin, then in his eighties, spoke to Ryan of his days with the Eagles. In reporting this, Ryan did not hesitate to identify the Askin family as black, for that was how the people of Florence had long regarded them. Other instances of integration in early baseball may yet be discovered, but finding them could be difficult, especially if a veil was drawn over the evidence, as with the Florence Eagles and Askin.

FURTHER READING

Papers that clarify the racial identity of the Askin family, especially the writings of Arthur G. Hill, are housed in the archives of the Florence Civic and Business Association, in Florence, Massachusetts.

Seymour, Harold. *Baseball: The Early Years* (1960).
Seymour, Harold. *Baseball: The People's Game* (1990).
Sheffeld, Charles A. *History of Florence Massachusetts* (1895).
Turner, Brian. "America's Earliest Integrated Team?" in *The National Pastime* (2002): 81–90.
Turner, Brian, and John S. Bowman. *The Hurrah Game: Baseball in Northampton 1823–1953* (2002).

BRIAN TURNER

Atkins, Charles "Cholly" (13 Sept. 1913–19 Apr. 2003), tap dancer and choreographer, was born Charles Atkinson in Pratt City, Alabama, the son of Sylvan Atkinson, a construction and steel worker, and Christine Woods. At age seven Atkins moved with his mother to Buffalo, New York. Woods, herself an avid social dancer, encouraged her children to dance, and Atkins won his first local contest at age ten doing the Charleston. As a teenager Atkins made his first money as a dancer by busking at rest stops while working as a bus line porter between Buffalo and Albany. His dancing caught the attention of a talent scout for the Alhambra on the Lake, a Lake Erie nightclub, who booked Atkins as a regular act. There he learned to tap from William "Red" Porter, a dancing waiter who became Atkins's first dance partner.

In 1929 Atkins joined a traveling revue produced by Sammy Lewis and toured through the Midwest and the South. Returning home to Buffalo, he reconnected with Porter and formed The Rhythm Pals. In 1933 Atkins had his first experience as a choreographer when he arranged a soft-shoe routine (a tap style performed in "soft" footwear without metal) for four chorus girls at Buffalo's Moonglow nightclub. Atkins married Catherine Williams, a dancer and singer, in 1936. That year Atkins went to California to dance in a show featuring the jazz vibraphonist Lionel Hampton and began recording soundtracks for tap sequences in Hollywood films, including *The Big Broadcast of 1938* and *Broadway Melody of 1938*. During this time he was the tap dancer and film star Eleanor Powell's personal choreographer.

After returning to New York in 1939 Atkins began dancing with and doing choreography for the Cotton Club Boys during their appearance with BILL "BOJANGLES" ROBINSON in *The Hot Mikado*, which was being performed at the New York World's Fair. At this time Atkins reconnected with the tap dancer CHARLES "HONI" COLES, and the two developed a friendship and partnership that would endure for decades. The two joined together

Cholly Atkins, choreographer, with members of the Four Tops—Lawrence Payton, Abdul "Duke" Fakir, Renaldo "Obie" Benson, and Levi Stubbs Jr.—in the basement of the Apollo Theater in 1964. (Photofest.)

on a 1942 tour with Cab Calloway, and each was drafted into the army the following year. In 1944 Atkins's first marriage ended in divorce, and he married Dotty Saulters, also a dancer. Following their service discharge in 1946, Coles and Atkins formed their now legendary "Class Act" duo and toured internationally for the next three years, appearing with LOUIS ARMSTRONG, COUNT BASIE, CAB CALLOWAY, BILLY ECKSTINE, and LIONEL HAMPTON. Coles and Atkins were noted for their elegance, precision, refined hand and body movements, and intricate syncopations. After three years of performing in the Broadway musical *Gentlemen Prefer Blondes*, Coles and Atkins took a hiatus from "Class Act" in 1952; Atkins ran the tap program at the Katherine Dunham School of Arts and Research in New York City and taught at the International School of Dance at Carnegie Hall. During the 1950s he began choreographing for vocal groups such as the Cadillacs, Little Anthony and the Imperials, and Gladys Knight and the Pips. After his wife's death in 1962, Atkins met his third wife, Maye Harrison Anderson, and married her the following year; they remained together until his death.

In 1965 Atkins became staff choreographer for the record label Motown's Artist Development wing, also known as "Motown U." In his six years at Motown, Atkins developed choreography for the decade's most popular soul and R&B vocal groups, including the Miracles, the Temptations, and the Supremes and also for the solo singer MARVIN GAYE. This "vocal choreography," as Atkins called it, was rooted in traditions of African American chorus line dancing and incorporated classic tap and vernacular jazz movements, often simplified to accommodate performers' skill levels and the demands of vocal performance. At Motown, Atkins developed many unique routines that featured the personalities and talents of each group's members. His choreographies displayed significant rhythmic contrast with the music as he drew from his experience in the heavily syncopated genre of tap dancing.

Atkins left Motown in 1971, though he continued working with Motown acts as well as with SAMMY DAVIS JR., ARETHA FRANKLIN, and the O'Jays. He moved in 1975 to Las Vegas, Nevada, where he worked for the remainder of his life as a freelance choreographer. In 1989 Atkins won a Tony Award for best choreography for the Broadway musical *Black and Blue* along with Frank Manning, FAYARD NICHOLAS, and HENRY LETANG. He also became heavily involved with the tap dance revival, teaching and lecturing internationally and earning a National Endowment for the Arts fellowship in 1993. Atkins died of pancreatic cancer in Las Vegas in 2003.

FURTHER READING

Atkins, Charles "Cholly," and Jacqui Malone. *Class Act: The Jazz Life of Choreographer Cholly Atkins* (2001).

Malone, Jacqui. *Steppin' on the Blues: The Visible Rhythms of African American Dance* (1996).

Stearns, Marshall Winslow, and Jean Stearns. *Jazz Dance: The Story of American Vernacular Dance* (1964, repr. 1994).

Valis-Hill, Constance. *Tap Dancing America: A Cultural History* (2010).

Obituary: *Los Angeles Times*, 23 Apr. 2003; *New York Times*, 23 Apr. 2003.

CHRISTOPHER J. WELLS

Atkins, Charles Nathaniel (11 Oct. 1911–27 Dec. 1988), first African American member of the Oklahoma City Council, family physician, and civic leader, was born in Trinidad, West Indies, to Gertrude St. John, a domestic worker, and John Atkins. He had one younger sister. Charles Atkins immigrated to the United States, arriving at Ellis Island in March 1929. He was required to attend Dewitt Clinton High School in the Bronx, New York City, because the United States did not accept his education credentials from Trinidad. One of the first black students at DeWitt, he graduated in 1933. Aided by the Urban League, he worked as a summer counselor to earn money for college. Although he took some classes at City College of New York, he moved to North Carolina to attend St. Augustine's, an Episcopalian historically black college in Raleigh. He graduated in 1941 with a bachelor's degree in Chemistry. On 27 March 1943 Atkins became a naturalized citizen. He married Hannah Mariah Diggs in North Carolina on 24 May 1943. The couple had two sons and one daughter. Atkins then served in the U.S. Army from 7 January 1944 to 12 April 1946, attaining the rank of staff sergeant.

In 1950 Atkins received his medical degree from Meharry Medical College in Nashville, Tennessee, having interned at the Kate Bitting Reynolds Memorial Hospital in Winston-Salem, North Carolina. The hospital was established to provide medical care for the black community, which was barred from other facilities in Winston-Salem. Atkins moved with his family to Oklahoma City and did his residency at Edwards Memorial Hospital in 1951 and 1952. One reason Atkins moved to Oklahoma City was to work at Edwards, the only racially integrated medical hospital at that time in the southern United States.

A photograph from 7 November 1955 shows Atkins, holding his infant son Charles, with Hannah and son Edmund at his side, looking up at a sign that reads "Negro Waiting Room" at the Santa Fe Train Station in Oklahoma City, commemorating the Interstate Commerce Commission's ruling against segregated buses. In 1960, as president of the Urban League of Oklahoma, Atkins fought against Jim Crow laws to desegregate the state parks in Oklahoma. Atkins served as vice chair of the Oklahoma City Human Relations Commission in 1965, and received an award for service from the Oklahoma City Youth Council. That same year, Atkins was a delegate to the White House Council of Aging. In 1966 Atkins helped bring Opportunities Industrialization Center (OIC), a nonprofit, self-help organization devoted to academic and career training, using volunteers and partnering with businesses, to Oklahoma City. From 1973 to 1987 Atkins was professor of Clinical Medicine, teaching family practice, community medicine, and dentistry at the University of Oklahoma Medical Center. From 1974 to 1987 he chaired the department of Family Practice at the Baptist Medical Center and was a member of its Executive Board.

In 1985 the OIC senior housing complex in Oklahoma City was named the Atkins Opportunities Garden. Atkins also served on the Oklahoma City Planning Commission from 1967 to 1969. He was a member of the National Business League, and the Board of Corrections. Atkins became the first black to serve on the Oklahoma City Council in 1967 when he was appointed a fill a vacancy, but he lost a bid for election.

Atkins belonged to numerous medical societies. He was president of the Oklahoma City Med-De-Phar Society and the Oklahoma Heart Association. In 1972 Atkins was elected Doctor of the Year by the Medical Service Society of Oklahoma City. In 1973 he helped found the Medical Center State Bank in Oklahoma City, the first racially mixed minority bank chartered in Oklahoma. He also served as its chairman. Atkins was a licensed Lay Reader for the Episcopal Diocese of Oklahoma, a Shriner, and a 33rd Degree Mason. He also served on the Oklahoma City mayor's Commission on Civil Rights.

In 1986 Atkins was elected to the Oklahoma African-American Hall of Fame, one of only thirty-nine people chosen between 1983 and 2010, for "significant contributions to the local community or the state of Oklahoma."

In 1988 Dr. Atkins died of acute cardiac arrest. A funeral was held at St. Paul's Episcopal Cathedral in Oklahoma City.

FURTHER READING

Franklin, Jimmie Lewis. *Journey toward Hope: A History of Blacks in Oklahoma* (1982).
"Head of Urban League Urges Legislation Now on Civil Rights." *New York Times*, 9 Sept. 1959.
Janson, Donald. "Equality Asked in All Oklahoma." *New York Times*, 7 June 1964.
"NAACP Youth on the Move." *Crisis*, Dec. 1965.
Tolson, Arthur L. *The Black Oklahomans: A History 1541–1972* (1974).
Obituaries: *Oklahoman*, 29 Dec. 1988; *Daily Oklahoman*, 30 Dec. 1988.

JANE BRODSKY FITZPATRICK

Atkins, Daniel (18 Nov. 1866–11 May 1923), United States Navy enlisted man, Spanish-American War combatant, and Medal of Honor recipient, was born in Brunswick, Virginia. Though nothing is known of his early life, it is likely that he was born to parents who had been formerly enslaved and who gained their freedom during the Civil War years. Perhaps because of his childhood proximity to the Atlantic Ocean and the major naval base at Norfolk, Virginia, Daniel Atkins joined the United States Navy around 1886.

The navy that Atkins joined in the 1880s was one in which opportunities for African Americans were steadily declining. In the years between the American Revolution and the close of the Civil War, black sailors served in a variety of shipboard posts, rated anywhere from cabin boy, cook, and steward to such higher positions as able-bodied seaman and gunner. In 1842 Senator John C. Calhoun attempted to have blacks banned from the navy altogether, but was unsuccessful. During the Civil War black sailors played a vital role in manning the Union navy, and a number of men, including JOACHIM PEASE, JOHN LAWSON, AARON ANDERSON, and ROBERT SMALLS were awarded the Medal of Honor for their courage under fire. However, in the postwar navy the situation of blacks in the service began to erode drastically, as the Reconstruction period came to an end and white supremacy reasserted itself in many of the nation's institutions. Because many of

the navy's primary bases were located in the South and many naval officers were white southerners, black seamen began to experience the restrictions of a Jim Crow navy. While many white officers attempted to retain the accomplished black sailors in their charges, the restriction of blacks to steward- and commissary-related ratings had become unofficial U.S. Navy policy by the mid-1890s.

With regard to Daniel Atkins's naval service, few details are known. By early 1898 he was rated as ship's cook first class, a sure indicator of his years of service, as his next promotion would make him a petty officer. Atkins's shipboard duties would have included, as his rating suggests, not only preparation of food for his ship's crew but also additional duties, such as procuring food supplies while the ship was in port and possibly assisting the captain's personal steward. As with all crew members of a ship of war, Daniel Atkins also had a battle station position (general quarters or GQ) during military operations, and he might have been employed as an ammunition passer, member of a gun crew, or lookout, to name a few possibilities. Though little is known about Atkins's service, one thing is clear: after years in the service, he was a respected and valued crew member, and subsequent events would bring that experience to bear to the utmost.

The month of February 1898 found Daniel Atkins aboard USS *Cushing* (TB-1) heading for Havana, Cuba. Relations between Spain and America had deteriorated in the wake of Spanish efforts to crush an independence movement in its Cuban colony, prompting the United States to send vessels to patrol the waters of Cuba and the Florida Straits. The *Cushing* was the navy's first torpedo boat; commissioned in 1890, the ship weighed 116 tons and measured 140 feet long, was manned by twenty-two men, and carried three six-pound cannons. With Daniel Atkins aboard, the ship was assigned to the North Atlantic Fleet Blockading Force in late 1897, performing picket duty and also serving as a courier boat. On 11 February 1898 the *Cushing* was steaming toward Havana in heavy seas when Ensign Joseph Breckinridge was washed overboard. Rushing to his aid and showing gallant conduct, Daniel Atkins and Gunner's Mate Third Class John Everetts attempted to save the officer in the stormy seas. While the efforts to save Breckinridge from drowning in the mounting seas were unsuccessful, Atkins's and Everetts's efforts did not go unheralded; both men were awarded the Medal of Honor for their actions aboard the *Cushing*. Daniel Atkins was one of eight African Americans to win the Medal of Honor in peacetime; in 1942, the award was restricted to valor shown in combat operations.

Following these heroics, Atkins probably stayed aboard his ship during the Spanish-American War and took part when it captured four small Spanish vessels in the Cays, and possibly served in an armed boat crew that helped capture and burn another small craft. The *Cushing* subsequently returned north in August 1898 to be stationed out of Newport, Rhode Island, before being sent to the Reserve Flotilla at Norfolk, Virginia, in 1901. As for Atkins, the remainder of his career is largely unknown. He would ultimately rise to the rank of chief commissary steward (CCS) and was probably still in the service in 1908 when blacks in the navy were once and for all restricted to the role of steward in preparation for the aptly named Great White Fleet's naval voyage around the world. From that time until 1920, and again from 1933 to 1942, African Americans joining the navy were restricted to the Steward's Branch, and from 1920 to 1933 they were banned from enlisting entirely.

Chief Commissary Steward Daniel Atkins, USN (Retired), died in Portsmouth, Virginia, and is buried in the Captain Ted Conaway Memorial Naval Cemetery in that town. A Medal of Honor gravestone marks his resting place.

FURTHER READING

Naval Historical Center. "Chief Commissary Steward Daniel Atkins, USN, (1866–1923)," available online at http://www.history.navy.mil/photos/pers-us/uspers-a/d-atkins.htm.

GLENN ALLEN KNOBLOCK

Atkins, Hannah Diggs (1 Nov. 1923–17 Jun. 2010), first African American woman legislator in Oklahoma, librarian, teacher and activist, was the fifth of six children born in Winston-Salem, North Carolina, to Mabel Kennedy and James Thackeray Diggs Sr., a contractor for Gulf Oil Company.

Both Atkins's parents graduated from Slater Industrial Academy. Her parents encouraged the children, four of whom were girls, to attend college. Her brother Edward O. Diggs was the first black to attend the University of North Carolina Medical School (1961). Atkins attended segregated public schools in Winston-Salem, and graduated as valedictorian of Atkins High School at age fifteen. She enrolled in St. Augustine's, an Episcopalian college in Raleigh, North Carolina, where she met and married Charles Nathaniel Atkins on 24 May 1943.

A few days later she graduated with a B.A. in French and Biology. She was an honors student, whose advisor was the historian JOHN HOPE FRANKLIN. In 1948 Atkins and her husband moved to Nashville, where Hannah worked as a reference librarian at Fisk University and was a biochemical researcher. They moved to Chicago in 1949 where she earned a B.S. in Library Studies from the University of Chicago. They had three children.

In 1952 they moved to Oklahoma, a segregated state, where both she and her husband were involved in civil rights causes (Charles was the first black elected to the Oklahoma City Council, and president of the Urban League). Hannah was a branch librarian in the Oklahoma City Public Libraries from 1953 to 1956. At the Oklahoma State library she rose from reference librarian to chief of the General Reference Division (1962–1968). Atkins taught courses in law, political science, and library science at the University of Oklahoma, where she had taken law courses. She also taught at Oklahoma State and Oklahoma City Universities.

Growing up in the segregated south, Atkins saw her father beaten for trying to vote, and from an early age she was determined to improve the lives of blacks. Motivated by MARTIN LUTHER KING JR.'s assassination, she ran for the Oklahoma House of Representatives with a grassroots campaign called "Hannah's Helpers," mostly young friends of her children. She ran and won six times, serving from 1969 to 1980, the first black woman elected to Oklahoma state government. She was the first woman to chair a house committee, the Public and Mental Health committee, and was an active legislator, promoting mental health, children's health, education reform, elder care, and prison reform. She supported passage of the Equal Rights Amendment. In 1980 President Jimmy Carter appointed her to the 35th United States delegation to the United Nations.

Charles Atkins died in 1988, and Atkins married Everett Patton O'Neal, a retired businessman from Missouri, on 12 June 1993. They divorced in January 1996.

From 1983 to 1987 Atkins was the assistant director of human services for the state of Oklahoma. In 1987 the Republican governor Henry Bellmon appointed Atkins as both secretary of human resources and secretary of state, although Atkins was a lifelong Democrat, and in 1989 she became secretary of the cabinet of human services. That same year, Atkins was selected to attend a program for senior executives at the John F. Kennedy School of Government at Harvard University. In 1989 she earned an M.A. in Public Administration from the University of Oklahoma and was elected to the Phi Beta Kappa honor society.

Atkins retired from public service in 1991. In addition to her government service, Atkins was active in and served on the boards of many organizations, including the Democratic National Committee Oklahoma chapter, the U.S Commission on Civil Rights, the National Women's Education Fund, and Women Executives in State Government.

Atkins was elected to the Oklahoma Hall of Fame and the Oklahoma Afro-American Hall of Fame in 1983. Among the many honors Atkins received are the National Public Citizen of the Year (1975) and the Oklahoma American Civil Liberties Union's (ACLU) Angie Debo annual award for a helping "to preserve individual freedom in Oklahoma" (1980). She received honorary doctorates from Benedict College in South Carolina (1983), the University of Oklahoma (1998), and Oklahoma State University (2000), which established an endowed chair in Political Science and Government in her honor. She was a member of the African American Alpha Kappa Alpha sorority, and a licensed lay reader in the Episcopal Church.

A teacher, political activist, librarian, and legislator, Atkins died of cancer in a hospice in Kensington, Maryland. Having overcome racism and sexism, her cool determination made her an effective activist and politician. Her body laid in state at the Oklahoma State House Rotunda on 24 June 2010, and flags were flown at half-mast in her honor.

FURTHER READING

An interview with Atkins was conducted for the Women of the Oklahoma Legislature Oral History Project on 22 June, 2007 by Tanya Finchum. A transcript and audio excerpts are available at http://dc.library. okstate.edu/cdm4/document.php?CISOROOT=/wo men&CISOPTR=1711&CISOSHOW=1706.

Atkins's personal and government papers are in both the Oklahoma Historical Society and the Hannah Diggs Atkins Collection at Oklahoma State University.

Franklin, Jimmie Lewis. *Journey toward Hope: A History of Blacks in Oklahoma* (1982).

Tolson, Arthur L. *The Black Oklahomans: A History 1541–1972* (1974).

Obituaries: *Oklahoman*, 24 June 2010; *Winston-Salem Journal*, 1 July 2010.

JANE BRODSKY FITZPATRICK

Atkins, Jasper Alston (8 Aug. 1898–28 June 1982), civil rights lawyer, community activist, editor, and publisher, was born in Winston, North Carolina, the sixth and last son of nine children of Simon Green and Oleona Pegram Atkins. His father was the founder and first president of the Slater Industrial Academy, later known as Winston-Salem State University. Atkins graduated from the Slater Academy in 1915 and then went to Fisk University in Nashville, Tennessee, graduating magna cum laude in chemistry in 1919.

When Atkins obtained his LLB cum laude at Yale University in 1922, he was the first African American to graduate with honors from that institution. While there, Atkins was a member of the debate team and served as a monitor of the Yale Law Library, where he oversaw the indexing of thirty-one volumes of the *Yale Law Journal*. In 1921 he was the first African American elected to the editorial board of the *Yale Law Journal*. Upon graduation, he was also the first black elected to the National Honorary Law Society, Order of the Coif.

In 1922 Atkins joined former Fisk schoolmate Carter Walker Wesley to form the law firm of Wesley & Atkins in Muskogee, Oklahoma, focusing primarily on the construction and brokerage business. Three years later he expanded his practice, relocating to Houston, Texas. There he continued in the firm of Wesley & Atkins, and then in 1931 added a third member, JAMES MADISON NABRIT JR., forming the new firm of Nabrit, Atkins & Wesley. Not satisfied to stay within the courts, Atkins joined Wesley in making an investment of $5,000 in the newly formed Webster-Richardson Publishing Co.; Clifton F. Richardson, publisher since 1919 of the Houston Informer, brought the paper into the new company as his investment. In 1931, Wesley forced Richardson out, merging the Informer with the Texas Freedman, which had begun publishing in 1893. Atkins served as editor of the newly combined paper. Wesley and Atkins expanded readership across the state with calls for the repeal of Jim Crow laws, the hiring of blacks in the postal services, and the establishment of equal pay for black teachers, among other actions in support of the growing black communities. With the paper's growing appeal, Wesley expanded the initial publication into a chain of *Informer* papers published in towns across the state.

For five years, Atkins and Wesley, and later Nabrit, Atkins & Wesley worked with the NAACP on suits filed against the Houston Democratic Party for its practices preventing blacks from the voting in primary elections. Atkins and Wesley were often at odds with the national NAACP office, and with a substantial portion of the local NAACP chapter in Houston. Two successive lawsuits filed by the national NAACP legal staff on behalf of Dr. LAWRENCE A. NIXON went to the Supreme Court, establishing that state law may not limit the Democratic party primary to "white" voters (*Nixon v. Herndon*, 1927), and that state law may not authorize the Democratic party to choose to limit its primary to "white" voters (*Nixon v. Condon*, 1932). In both decisions, the Supreme Court agreed that black voters were being barred from voting in the primary by action of state law, which was banned by the Fifteenth Amendment. Atkins and Wesley denounced the fact that local black attorneys, particularly themselves, did not have a more prominent role, and that white attorneys such as A.B. Spingarn had the primary role of arguing in the Supreme Court.

Atkins and many other black lawyers began actively proselytizing for the permission to file briefs and join the NAACP in oral arguments. Texas civic leaders joined in the campaign, singling out Atkins as a prime candidate. William White, then head of the NAACP, received letters from Charles Houston and other Texas civic leaders, pointing out that "a man of Atkins's ability should be employed, since he is 'of our own nationality and from that fact, is more vitally interested in that which Negroes of the South desire'" (Meier, 936). Atkins's 1932 book *The Texas Negro and His Political Rights: A History of the Fight of Negroes to Enter the Democratic Primaries of Texas* details the long fight to gain voting rights in Texas and the vital roles played by black lawyers.

When the Texas state Democratic Party chose to limit its primary to "white" voters without any sanction of state law, Atkins and Wesley, against the advice of the national NAACP, took a case to court themselves with Richard Grovey, president of the Third Ward Civic Club, as plaintiff. The result was disastrous; in 1935 the Supreme Court ruled in *Grovey v. Townsend* that acting entirely as a private organization, the state Democratic Party could adopt any rules it wished for itself, without violating the Fifteenth Amendment. (LaVergne, Gary M., *Before Brown: Heman Marion Sweatt, Thurgood Marshall, and the Long Road to Justice*, p. 52). Wesley and Atkins argued that their failure in the Grovey case was really a failure of the NAACP to develop a case using black attorneys. The two eventually acquiesced to allowing the NAACP to take control of development of future cases. The NAACP recognized that Wesley, Atkins and Nabrit were ten percent of all black attorneys in Texas, as well as running the *Informer*. In

the subsequent NAACP-led case, *Hollins v. State of Oklahoma*, the NAACP leadership allowed the black lawyer and Howard Law School Dean CHARLES HAMILTON HOUSTON to argue its case before the court. Atkins noted, "Now that the NAACP has had a Negro lawyer for the first time in its history ... before the Supreme Court, I trust that this will be the beginning of a new policy" (Meier, 942).

In 1936 Atkins left his law practice in Texas to help his brother, Frank, then president of Winston-Salem Teachers College, who had fallen ill. He took on the position of Executive Secretary for the College, a position he held until 1960. But Atkins's return to Winston-Salem did not signal a retreat from his long legacy of serving the community. He was a member of the Winston-Salem Housing Authority Board from its inception in 1941 until he resigned in 1958. He was a member of the Winston-Salem draft board from the outbreak of World War II until the Korean War. Then, after his retirement from Winston-Salem Teachers College in 1960, he returned to publishing as the executive editor of the Freedmen's Publishing company.

Nor did Atkins' legal work cease. Initially focusing on voting rights, he now turned his attention to discrimination in other arenas. In 1959 Atkins returned to the U.S. Supreme Court, where he led the successful prosecution of the *Wolfe v. State of North Carolina* case against racial discrimination on publicly owned golf courses. Atkins's legal expertise was sought again in 1968 and 1970. Initially serving as a plaintiff in *Atkins, Pro Se v. State Board of Higher Education of North Carolina* (1966–1970), and then as part of *Allen v. State Board of Higher Education of North Carolina* (1966–1973), Atkins helped dismantle segregated public education in North Carolina. Though the consent decree was not signed until 1985, three years after his death, it was a testament to Atkins's lifelong commitment to equality and opportunity.

Atkins died at the age of eighty-four. In 2003 the Lillian Goldman Law Library at Yale Law School welcomed the addition of his papers to its collection.

FURTHER READING

Jasper Alston Atkins' papers are housed in the Lillian Goldman Law Library of Yale University in New Haven, Connecticut. See "Guide to the Jasper Alston Atkins Papers (1922–1997): Manuscript Group 1811," comp. Mike Strom (2003).

Atkins, Jasper Alston. *The Texas Negro and His Political Rights: A History of the Fight of Negroes to Enter the Democratic Primaries of Texas* (1932).

Smith, J. Clay, Jr. *The Making of the Black Lawyer, 1844–1944* (1999).

Meier, August, and Elliot Rudwick. "Attorneys Black and White: A Case Study of Race Relations in the NAACP," *Journal of American History* 62.4 (Mar. 1976).

Finkelman, Paul. "Not Only the Judges' Robes Were Black: African-American Lawyers as Social Engineers," *Stanford Law Review* 47.1 (Nov. 1994).

Hine, Darlene Clark. "Blacks and the Destruction of the Democratic White Primary, 1935–1944," *Journal of American History* 62.1 (Jan. 1977).

JOY GLEASON CAREW

Atkins, Thomas Irving (2 March 1939–27 June 2008), civil rights leader, lawyer, and Boston city councilman, was born in Elkhart, Indiana, the son of Lillie Curry, a domestic, and Norse Pierce Atkins, a Pentecostal minister. At the age of five, he contracted polio. Despite a doctor's insistence that he would require crutches for the rest of his life, three years later he was walking unassisted. He attended a segregated school for the first and second grades until the derelict building collapsed. The City of Elkhart could not afford to replace it. As a result, the city's schools were integrated by default. Despite his infirmity, Atkins was elected student body president at Elkhart High School, played saxophone in the school band, and was chosen for the all-state orchestra. There he met Sharon Soash, whom he married in December 1960. As a result of Indiana's anti-miscegenation laws, they traveled to Michigan to wed. At Indiana University, he held twelve scholarships, was elected to Phi Beta Kappa, and became the school's first African American student body president and the first black student body president of a Big Ten school. The Atkins Living Learning Center at the university is named in his honor.

After graduating from Indiana University, Atkins entered Harvard in 1961 to pursue a graduate degree in Middle Eastern studies, obtaining a master's in 1963 with the assistance of fellowships from the Ford Foundation. In the last semester of his work for the master's, he undertook a project that changed the course of his intellectual, political, and professional life. To fulfill a course requirement, he wrote a fifty-page paper that was highly critical of the NAACP generally, and specifically of the Association's Boston branch. He gave a copy of the paper to Kenneth Guscott, the President of the Boston branch, who offered him the job of acting executive secretary. The Boston branch collected funds to support his employment, and he began working there on the day he was to collect his Master's degree from Harvard.

The summer of 1963 was a momentous period for the civil rights movement. In Boston, it marked the early stages of a long battle over de facto segregation in the public schools. On a national level, major demonstrations were organized throughout the South, notably in Birmingham, Alabama, culminating in the historic March on Washington. Atkins remained with the NAACP's Boston branch for the next two years, and then took a position as general manager of the business enterprises of Bill Russell, the professional basketball player. After one year, however, he entered Harvard Law School. Concluding that Boston city government was not interested in responding to problems in the black community, he chose to run for the city council while a full-time law student and was elected. He was the first African American to serve in city government in sixteen years.

Atkins served two terms on the Boston City Council, becoming Chairman of the Council's Urban Renewal Committee where he worked to prevent the dislocation of African Americans undertaken to satisfy the residential or commercial needs of middle-class whites. His efforts prompted the City Council to establish an elected body of residents drawn from an urban renewal area who would have the power to make decisions about the urban renewal program in Boston. Atkins also gained a reputation as an effective mediator, notably during the unrest in the city following the assassination of MARTIN LUTHER KING JR. His role in persuading Mayor Kevin White to allow James Brown, the entertainer, to perform a scheduled concert on the night of King's death was crucial in preventing Boston from experiencing the explosive rioting that scarred most major American cities.

As an elected official, he advocated "the development of a black political awareness that eventually leads to black political organization that creates a kind of strength that can make black people politically accountable. The key to black success in politics" he maintained, "is accountability" (Interview, August 28, 1970, 622–29, *Ralph J. Bunche Oral History Collection*, Moorland-Spingarn Research Center, Howard University).

In 1971, Atkins chose to run against Mayor Kevin White and lost by a wide margin. Later that year, as a Democrat, he became the first black cabinet official in Massachusetts history when Governor Francis Sargent, a Republican, named him Secretary of Communities and Development, a position in which he remained until 1974 when he returned to the NAACP's Boston branch to serve as President. He also opened a law practice, concentrating on civil rights cases. He served as President of the Boston branch for six years.

In 1980, the National NAACP board hired Atkins as the organization's general counsel. It proved to be a tumultuous tenure, marked by internal dissension within the board, and, ultimately, the ouster of its Chairwoman, Margaret Bush Wilson. Atkins resigned as general counsel, and a lingering dispute erupted between Atkins and the board over the right to legal fees for work performed by Atkins while in private practice. Numerous lawsuits followed and were eventually settled.

After leaving the NAACP national office, Atkins opened a law practice in Brooklyn, New York, specializing in civil rights cases, but the pressures of living a life of unrelieved intensity took its toll. In 1984, he separated from his wife, Sharon, and four years later they divorced, although remaining on friendly terms. In 1998, he was diagnosed with Amyotrophic Lateral Sclerosis, also known as Lou Gehrig's disease, which ultimately left him unable to speak or care for himself.

In spite of the relentless pace of his life, he and his wife raised three children, two boys and a girl, making a point to have dinner together every night. His love of fishing was legendary. He was known to sit in a boat in a three piece suit for hours waiting for a nibble.

Atkins was the most dynamic black leader in Boston during the 1960s and 1970s. Driven, politically astute, and a brilliant strategist, he moved easily from the world of protest, to electoral politics, then to the courtroom. In Boston's raw, unyielding racial climate, he stood out as a man of principle.

For the last eight years of his life, his son, Thomas Jr., cared for him. He died on June 27, 2008 at age sixty-nine. In addition to his son, Thomas Jr., he also leaves a son, Todd, and his former wife, Sharon. His only daughter, Trena, died in 2006.

FURTHER READING

Boston Sunday Globe, November 9, 1997.

"Interview with Thomas I. Atkins, August 28, 1970," Ralph J. Bunche Oral History Collection, Moorland-Spingarn Research Center, Howard University.

Obituaries: *Boston Globe*, 29 June 2008; *The Truth Newspaper*, 1 July 2008; *Bay State Banner*, 10 July 2008.

JULIAN HOUSTON

Attaway, William Alexander (19 Nov. 1911–17 June 1986), writer, was born in Greenville, Mississippi, the son of William S. Attaway, a medical doctor, and Florence Parry, a teacher. His family moved to Chicago when Attaway was six years old, following the arc of the Great Migration, that thirty-year period beginning in the last decade of the nineteenth century during which more than two million African Americans left the South for the burgeoning industrial centers of the North. Unlike many of these emigrants, who traded the field for the factory and the sharecropper's shack for the ghetto, the Attaways were professionals at the outset, with high ambitions for themselves and their children in their new homeland.

Attaway attended public schools in Chicago, showing no great interest in his studies until, as a high school student, he encountered the work of LANGSTON HUGHES. He became, from that point on, a more serious student and even tried his hand at writing, composing scripts for his older sister's amateur drama club. After completing high school he enrolled at the University of Illinois, where he initially flourished not only academically but also athletically, becoming a collegiate tennis player.

His father's death while Attaway was still at college, however, derailed his academic career. As the Great Depression descended over America, Attaway dropped out of the university to wander the country, working as a seaman, à la Langston Hughes and CLAUDE MCKAY, a salesman, and a labor organizer, as well as in a variety of other odd jobs. He writes that "in Chicago I had all the advantages that a self-made man imagines are good for an only son. But after my father's death I rebelled and spent my time hoboing" (Bone, 132). After two years away from the university, he returned to finish his degree. During this period he experimented with one-act plays and short stories, publishing some of this work in newspapers and literary magazines. His first published short story, "Tale of the Blackamoor," appeared in 1936 in the little magazine *Challenge*, formed in 1934 to give another literary outlet for the new generation of African American writers. A drama, *Carnival*, was written and produced about the same time.

In the mid-1930s Attaway became involved in the Federal Writers' Project (FWP), a government initiative that provided work opportunities for unemployed writers during the Depression that was administered through the Works Projects Administration. Attaway helped write the Illinois section of the FWP's chief project, an American

Guide Series, profiling the then forty-eight states. His work brought him into contact with some of the luminaries of contemporary African American literature also employed by the FWP, including RICHARD WRIGHT, Claude McKay, ARNA WENDELL BONTEMPS, MARGARET WALKER, RALPH WALDO ELLISON, and FRANK YERBY.

Moving to New York, Attaway entered the theater world with the assistance of his sister Ruth, who by now had achieved something of a reputation as a stage actress. He performed in several productions, including a 1939 traveling production of George S. Kaufman's *You Can't Take It with You*. In that year, he learned that his first novel, *Let Me Breathe Thunder*, had been accepted for publication by Doubleday. The novel, heavily influenced by John Steinbeck's *Of Mice and Men*, focuses on the adventures of two white hoboes during the Depression. It received limited critical attention and that mainly negative. It was generally thought to be too derivative and too heavily dependent upon mere reportage drawn from Attaway's own wanderings to be a successful work of literature.

His efforts did earn Attaway a two-year grant from the Julius Rosenwald Fund, which enabled him to work on a second novel. He completed and published in 1941 *Blood on the Forge*. This is a novel of an altogether different scope than his first, incisively portraying the collapse of traditional black folk culture in the relentlessly dehumanizing ghettos of the industrial, urbanized North. *Blood on the Forge* was well received critically but did not sell profitably, perhaps owing to the publication at about the same time of Richard Wright's *Native Son*, a novel that garnered immense critical and popular attention. The lack of commercial success of his second novel led Attaway to find new directions for his creative energy, most notably in writing songs and books about music and, eventually, scriptwriting for stage, screen, and television.

Attaway's songwriting was heavily influenced by calypso rhythms, and in 1957 he published the *Calypso Song Book*, containing many of the songs from which he drew inspiration. In the 1950s he made the acquaintance of HARRY BELAFONTE and collaborated with him and others in writing songs, authoring or coauthoring more than five hundred in his lifetime. Perhaps his most famous collaboration led to one of Belafonte's most popular hits, the "Banana Boat Song." Then, in 1967, Attaway published for children a compilation of representative popular music in America, including historical commentary, *Hear America Singing*.

Also, beginning in the 1950s, Attaway turned to writing for radio, film, and television, one of the first African American writers to do so. His work was featured in such television series as *Wide Wide World* and the *Colgate Comedy Hour*. He was one of the writers for an hour-long television special, airing in 1964, *One Hundred Years of Laughter*, showcasing, among the others, the African American comedians REDD FOXX, MOMS MABLEY, and FLIP WILSON in their first appearances on the small screen.

In 1962, at the age of fifty-one, Attaway married Frances Settele, from New York, at a ceremony held in his friend Belafonte's home. The couple had two children—a son, Bill, born in 1964, and a daughter Noelle, born in 1966. In the year of his daughter's birth, Attaway took his family to Barbados for a vacation and wound up staying eleven years among the people and the music he loved. Upon their return to America, the family settled in California, where Attaway spent the remaining years of his life writing screenplays.

FURTHER READING

Bone, Robert A. *The Negro Novel in America* (1965).

Gayle, Addison, Jr. *The Way of the New World: The Black Novel in America* (1975).

Gloster, Hugh Morris *Negro Voices in American Fiction* (1948).

Hughes, Carl M. *The Negro Novelist* (1953).

Margolies, Edward. "Migration: William Attaway and *Blood on the Forge*," in *Native Sons: A Critical Study of Twentieth-century Negro American Authors* (1968).

Redding, J. Saunders. "The Negro Writer and American Literature," in *Anger and Beyond: The Negro Writer in the United States* (1966).

GEORGE P. WEICK

Attucks, Crispus (c. 1723–5 Mar. 1770), probably a sailor, was the first to be killed in the Boston Massacre of 5 March 1770. Generally regarded to have been of mixed ancestry (African, Indian, and white), Attucks seems to have hailed from a Natick Indian settlement, Mashpee (incorporated as a district in 1763, near Framingham, Massachusetts). While Attucks's life and background before the tragic event are uncertain, two reasonable conjectures stand out. First, he was a descendant of those Natick Indians converted to Christianity in the seventeenth century. One tribesman, John Attuck, was hanged on 22 June 1676 for allegedly conspiring with the Indian insurrection of that year. Second,

The Boston Massacre. "The massacre perpetrated in King Street Boston on March 5th 1770, in which Messrs Saml. Gray, Saml. Maverick, James Caldwell, Crispus Attucks, Patrick Carr were killed, six other wounded, two of them mortally." Engraving by Paul Revere, 1770. (Library of Congress.)

it appears that Attucks may have once been a slave. The *Boston Gazette* of 2 October 1750 printed this notice: "Ran away from his Master, William Brown of Framingham on the 30th of September last, a mulatto Fellow, about twenty-seven years of age, named Crispus, 6 feet 2 inches high, short curled hair, his knees nearer together than common."

J. B. Fisher, who argues that Attucks had Indian blood, also claims that he became a crewman on a Nantucket whaler, owned by a Captain Folger, which was docked at the time of the Massacre in Boston harbor. A sailor, James Bailey, testified that the assaulting group, which Attucks headed, "appeared to be sailors." John Adams (1735–1826) said that Attucks "was seen about eight minutes before the firing at the head of twenty or thirty sailors in Cornhill…. He was a stout fellow, whose very looks were enough to terrify any person…. He was about forty-seven years old."

The Bostonians' wrath had long been building against the stationing of the Fourteenth and Twenty-Ninth British regiments in the town. On the evening of 5 March, Attucks dined at Thomas Symmonds's victualing house and, learning of the commotion taking place at the customshouse on King Street, joined a group headed in that direction. It is said that he and others had earlier threatened British soldiers at Murray's barracks. Attucks and his gang gathered cordwood sticks and wooden pieces from butchers' stalls, carrying these makeshift weapons over their heads as they approached the scene of the disturbance. John Adams, in remarks before the jury that tried the British soldiers for their role in the Massacre, stated that "Attucks appears to have undertaken to be the hero of the night, and to lead this army with banners." In his summation, Adams also said that "it is in this manner, this town has been often treated; a Carr from Ireland, and an Attucks from Framingham, happening to be here" to "sally out upon their thoughtless enterprises, at the head of such a rabble of negroes, &c., as they can collect together." Testimony at the soldiers' trial differed over whether Attucks had grabbed for the bayonet of Private Hugh Montgomery, causing a struggle that resulted in the shooting. John Adams tried to portray Attucks as the instigator, "to whose mad behavior, in all probability, the dreadful carnage of that night is chiefly ascribed." Adams added that Attucks's group was a "mob whistling, screaming, and rending like an Indian yell." Some witnesses, however, testified that Attucks was killed while leaning on his cordwood stick. Two shots to his breast caused the fatality.

After the massacre, the bodies of Attucks and James Caldwell, the two nonresident victims, were brought to Faneuil Hall. On 8 March a funeral procession of ten to twelve thousand people and numerous coaches accompanied the hearses of Attucks and three other victims to Granary burial ground, where all four coffins were buried in one grave.

Captain Thomas Preston, the British officer of the day who commanded the squad that fired upon the civilians, and eight soldiers were tried before the Suffolk Superior Court in Boston from 27 November to 5 December 1770. Preston and six of his men were acquitted, including William Warren, who was charged specifically with killing Attucks; two others were found guilty of manslaughter and were branded on the thumb after pleading benefit of clergy.

Crispus Attucks, apparently of African and Indian ancestry, was the first martyr of the American

Revolution. Years later, in response to adoption of a new Federal Fugitive Slave Law in 1850, Attucks became a powerful symbol of black resistance to slavery and racism. His name was repeatedly invoked during the Civil War to recruit soldiers for the famed Fifty-Fourth Massachusetts Regiment. Other black military companies were named for him. In 1888 the city of Boston and the state of Massachusetts erected on Boston Common a memorial to Attucks and the other massacre victims.

FURTHER READING

Fisher, J. B. "Who Was Crispus Attucks?" *American Historical Record* 1 (1872): 531–533.

Quarles, Benjamin. *The Negro in the American Revolution* (1961).

Temple, Josiah H. *History of Framingham, Massachusetts, 1640–1885* (1887).

Wroth, L. Kinvin, and Hiller B. Zobel, eds. *Legal Papers of John Adams* (3 vols., 1965).

Zobel, Hiller B. *The Boston Massacre* (1970).

This entry is taken from the *American National Biography* and is published here with the permission of the American Council of Learned Societies.

HARRY M. WARD

Atwater, Ann (1 July 1935–), community activist, was born in Columbus County, North Carolina, the youngest of nine children of William Randolph George and Emma Jane Shaw, sharecroppers. While she was still quite young, Ann started working on the farm, where her parents taught her the values of hard work, discipline, and Christian compassion. When Ann was six, her mother died, but her father took on extra work at a nearby sawmill and managed to build an eight-room house for the family.

Ann attended Farmers Union High School in Whiteville, North Carolina, until the tenth grade. When she was fourteen she became pregnant and married the baby's father, French Wilson, who disappeared a month after the wedding. He reappeared shortly before the birth, but Ann lost the child. In 1952 the couple had a baby girl named Lydia. In 1953 Wilson secured a job at Central Leaf Tobacco Company in Durham and Ann and the baby soon followed. Despite Durham's reputation as "the capital of the black middle class," most blacks in the city remained poor, and Ann and French struggled with serious financial and emotional problems resulting from domestic violence.

Ann gave birth to another daughter, Marilyn, in 1956, but Wilson again disappeared. He soon surfaced with a better-paying job in Richmond,

Virginia, but Ann refused to follow him, and the couple soon divorced. It was at this point that she dropped Wilson's name and adopted "Atwater," the surname of a man she had dated. Atwater continued working as a domestic for white families, supporting her two young daughters in a run-down section of Durham's Hayti neighborhood. In 1975 she married Willie Pettiford, a sanitation worker in nearby Wake Forest.

Although Atwater did not participate directly in Durham's early civil rights movement, she occasionally staged individual protests that at times had dire consequences. For example, shortly after learning of ROSA PARKS's refusal to move from a Montgomery bus seat in 1955, Atwater overheard her white employer making disparaging comments about blacks. Enraged, she confronted her boss and ended her tirade with a suggestion that black cooks might be spitting in the pots of their white employers. Unable to recall whether she quit or was fired, Atwater spent the next years working part-time jobs and struggling to support her two young daughters. By 1965 Atwater was forced to rely on welfare benefits after a doctor ordered her to quit domestic work because of her diabetes. That same year, HOWARD FULLER, a Louisiana native raised in Milwaukee and one of the most talented black community organizers in North Carolina, successfully recruited Atwater to a new antipoverty effort begun by the North Carolina governor Terry Sanford in 1963, a year before President Lyndon Johnson launched his national War on Poverty. Howard Fuller had made Atwater's acquaintance as a result of community organizing drives conducted in low-income neighborhoods, under the auspices of Durham's antipoverty agency, Operation Breakthrough (OBT). Atwater quickly became one of the most effective and well-respected grassroots organizers in Durham and was widely recognized as a veritable expert on welfare and housing regulations. She worked with OBT and then for United Organizations for Community Improvement, a majority-female federation of low-income black neighborhood councils, which set the tone and agenda of black protest in Durham from the middle of the 1960s to the end of the decade.

In 1967 the *Carolina Times*, Durham's black weekly, named Atwater Woman of the Year. In 1968 she became the first black woman elected as vice president of the local Democratic Party. Although she embraced the tenets of nonviolent protest, she hinted that she was an expert at making the kinds of Molotov cocktails that exploded throughout

Ann Atwater (left) and C. P. Ellis, (right) waiting to see the premiere screening of the video documentary *An Unlikely Friendship* on 9 November 2001 in Chapel Hill, North Carolina. The documentary recounts the friendship that formed between Atwater, a poor civil rights organizer, and Ellis, a Ku Klux Klan member, in Durham during a racially charged period in the early 1970s. (AP Images.)

Durham in the wake of MARTIN LUTHER KING JR.'s assassination in 1968. That same year she also joined Women-in-Action for the Prevention of Violence and Its Causes, a biracial women's organization established by Elna Spaulding to ease racial tensions in the city. Atwater was a key participant in the Black Solidarity Committee's seven-month boycott of Durham's white downtown merchants from 1968 to 1969. She also publicly supported Malcolm X Liberation University, a community-based black nationalist school founded in Durham after the black student takeover of the administration building at Duke University in 1969.

In 1971 Atwater and the Durham Ku Klux Klan leader Claiborne "C. P." Ellis formed an unlikely alliance. Wilbur Hobby, a white Durham labor leader, had secured a grant to establish a ten-day Save Our Schools community forum known as a "charrette" in order to ease a court-ordered school desegregation plan, and Ellis and Atwater reluctantly agreed to head the charrette. Ellis, a white

maintenance worker and son of a textile worker, was initially quite hostile to Atwater, showing her the gun he carried in his car trunk. However, Ellis soon realized that he and Atwater shared similar problems of poverty and disempowerment. He left the Klan, became a union leader at Duke University, and the odd couple remained friends for more than three decades. The militant black activist and former Klansman attracted national attention and were featured in the award-winning book *The Best of Enemies* (1996) and the award-winning documentary film *An Unlikely Friendship* (2003). When Ellis died of Alzheimer's disease in 2005, his children called Atwater to speak at his funeral, which she did. Upon learning of his death, Atwater commented on their enduring friendship: "At the end of 10 days, him and I fell in love, and we've been in love ever since until he closed his eyes on Thursday" (*News and Observer*). Atwater and Ellis did not have a romantic relationship, but had remained close friends throughout the years.

During the 1970s and 1980s Atwater worked at Head Start and at the Durham Housing Authority before declining health and a workplace injury forced her to retire in the early 1990s. Even in retirement and into her seventies, she continued her community work, teaching Bible classes at the local homeless shelter, securing funds to reopen a local recreation center, and assisting Durham's poor, who still called on her for assistance. She also remained active in local organizations, including the Durham Committee on the Affairs of Black People (one of the oldest black political machines in the South), the NAACP, and Mount Calvary United Church of Christ, where she served as deacon.

For more than four decades the issue of housing remained one of Atwater's central concerns. In the 1960s she took on the Durham Housing Authority director Carvie Oldham, earning the nickname "Roughhouse Annie," and managing to reverse regulations that excluded single mothers from public housing. One of her greatest triumphs was in the late 1960s, when she prevented the illegal eviction of thirty-five families that stood in the way of the construction of the Durham Expressway. She also served as president of the Birchwood Heights Homeowners Association, an innovative community of 200 homes created by the Durham Housing Authority in the 1970s, which allowed residents to make payments as rent until they became homeowners. However, the Birchwood Heights area was isolated, with no schools or community facilities nearby, and was plagued by drugs and violence. After the violent deaths of seven young adults during the period 1995–1996 Atwater and Reverend Paul Godshall founded the Birchwood Learning Center in 1996, which targeted unemployed teenage high school dropouts. Atwater also participated in New Hope, a ten-year project designed to end homelessness in Durham. In 2002 a charter school, the Ann Atwater Community School, was named after her, and one of New Hope's apartment buildings was also named after her in 2005.

Over the years Atwater has received countless awards and honors that filled an entire wall of her modest home. These included the Rosa Parks Award from the Durham Women in Community Service, the MARY MCLEOD BETHUNE Award from the National Council of Negro Women, numerous Durham Mayor's and Human Relations Commission Awards, the Distinguished Service Award from the Durham NAACP, and the Martin Luther King Jr. Keep Your Dream Alive Award. Like so many low-income black women activists, Atwater received little monetary compensation for her work. Impoverished and in deteriorating health, Atwater, one of the city's most dedicated activists who never forgot the plight of the poor, was herself given assistance from several local and national church and community groups.

FURTHER READING

Much of the information for this entry was acquired during two interviews with Ann Atwater on 12 Jan. 1993 and 20 Feb. 2007.

Bloom, Diane. Producer and director, *An Unlikely Friendship*, thirty-five minute documentary video/ DVD (2003).

Davidson, Osha Gray. *The Best of Enemies: Race and Redemption in the New South* (1996).

Greene, Christina. *Our Separate Ways: Women and the Black Freedom Movement in Durham, North Carolina* (2005).

Rochman, Bonnie. "Activist Mourns Ex-KKK Leader," *News and Observer*, 8 Nov. 2005.

Terkel, Studs. *Race: How Blacks and Whites Think and Feel about the American Obsession* (1992).

CHRISTINA GREENE

Augusta, Alexander Thomas (8 Mar. 1825–21 Dec. 1890), physician, Civil War surgeon, and medical educator, was born free in Norfolk, Virginia, to parents whose names and occupations are unknown. Augusta received his early education from a Bishop Payne, defying a law that forbade African Americans to read or write. He continued to improve his reading skills while working as an apprentice to a barber. His interest in medicine led him to relocate to Baltimore, where he studied with private tutors. Eventually, Augusta moved to Philadelphia, Pennsylvania, to serve an apprenticeship. Although he was denied entry to the University of Pennsylvania, Augusta caught the attention of Professor William Gibson, who allowed the young man to study in his office.

In January 1847 Augusta married Mary O. Burgoin in Baltimore. They lived in California for three years before returning to the East Coast so that Augusta could pursue a medical degree. Denied access, despite his prior training in medicine, to the medical schools in both Philadelphia and Chicago, he applied to study in Canada. He was accepted by Trinity Medical College in Toronto, from which he graduated in 1856 with a bachelor of medicine degree. While studying in Toronto, Augusta supported himself and his wife by operating a store that offered services such as cupping and bleeding, as well as medicines. Mary Augusta worked as a dressmaker, and her skills were much sought after.

Records of Augusta's activities for the years between 1856 and 1861 are incomplete. He apparently ran the City Hospital and acted as a physician at Toronto's poorhouse, while possibly managing a private practice. There is further speculation that he was in charge of an industrial school for two years. He may also have spent some of this period in the West Indies, eventually returning to Canada.

With the onset of the Civil War, Augusta was eager to use his talents. In 1862 he journeyed to Washington, D.C., to take the examination for the volunteer medical service. Impatience prompted him to petition both President Abraham Lincoln and Secretary of War Edwin M. Stanton on 7 January 1863 with respect to a surgical appointment. In March he received a reply from the Army Medical Board denying his petition on the grounds that, first, he was of African descent and that, second, accepting him into the service would be a direct violation of Queen Victoria's Proclamation of Neutrality because as a Canadian resident he was "an alien and a British subject." In a letter to Lincoln and the Army Medical Board dated 30 March 1863, Augusta argued that the officials had misinterpreted his case. He explained that he had expected to serve the colored regiments, and that he was still a U.S. citizen despite having obtained his medical credentials in Canada.

On 1 April 1863 the board overturned its decision, finding Augusta "qualified for the position of surgeon in the Negro regiment now being raised." On 14 April 1863 Augusta was appointed a surgeon with the Seventh U.S. Colored Infantry, making him the first African American to receive a medical commission in the U.S. Army. Only seven other African Americans received such an appointment during the Civil War.

Serving from 1863 to 1864 as chief executive officer of Freedmen's Hospital, formerly called Camp Barker, Augusta was the first African American to head a U.S. hospital. In February 1864 several white physicians at the hospital petitioned the president to have Augusta permanently reassigned, because they refused to be subordinate to an African American. Augusta was then assigned to a recruiting office in Baltimore. When the Seventh U.S. Colored Troops were sent to Beaufort, South Carolina, Augusta went with them. He remained there until the end of the war.

Throughout most of Augusta's war service, the army paid him at the level of an enlisted Negro soldier, despite his holding the rank of major. This insult continued until Senator Henry Wilson of Massachusetts intervened on Augusta's behalf. The indignities that Augusta suffered during the war were not limited to the military, however. Average citizens were enraged at the sight of an African American in an officer's uniform. While journeying to Baltimore at one point during the war, Augusta was assaulted by a group of men and had to be rescued by police. When Augusta and his protégé, ANDERSON RUFFIN ABBOTT, attended the White House levee of 1863–1864, Abbott recorded that in full-dress regalia the two were "the synosure of all eyes."

Augusta's obstinacy scored a major victory for all African Americans residing in Washington, D.C., however. On his way to testify in a court-martial case on 1 February 1864, he was ejected from a streetcar when he refused to sit in the "Negroes Only" section. When he was forced to give an explanation for his tardiness to the judge advocate, the incident drew the attention of the Senate and became the subject of a debate resulting in the integration of all Washington streetcars.

On 13 March 1865 Augusta was brevetted lieutenant colonel in the U.S. Volunteer Corps "for meritorious and faithful service." He was the first African American to be awarded such rank. Following the war his services were retained by the medical division of the Bureau of Refugees, Freedmen, and Abandoned Lands, where he served as an assistant surgeon responsible for the Freedmen's Hospital in Savannah, Georgia.

Augusta, the highest ranking African American to serve in the U.S. Civil War, mustered out of the army on 13 October 1866, returning to Washington, where he opened a medical practice. On 21 September 1868 he was appointed demonstrator of anatomy at the newly formed medical department at Howard University, making him the first African American to hold a faculty position at a U.S. medical school. While at Howard, Augusta held several professorships in anatomy. He was one of three faculty members to retain their positions in the medical department, despite severe salary cuts, when the nation and the university faced financial collapse in 1873. In 1877, after the medical faculty recommended to the trustees that Augusta switch positions with Dr. Daniel Lamb and become chair of materia medica rather than of anatomy, Augusta resigned and returned to private practice.

In 1869 Augusta and two other African American doctors were denied membership in the Medical Society of the District of Columbia, an association responsible for licensing and professional development. Frustrated with racist admission policies, Augusta helped found in 1884 the Medical-Chirurgical Society of D.C., the first African American medical society in the United States.

In 1870 Augusta became the attending physician at a smallpox hospital in Washington, also renewing his involvement with Freedmen's Hospital. By this time Freedmen's Hospital had become the teaching facility for Howard University's medical department. From 1870 to 1875 he served as a staff physician for the urino-genital diseases division, and from October 1875 to July 1877 he was the ward physician at the hospital. In 1888 he assumed the position of clinical lecturer on diseases of the skin. Augusta died in Washington, D.C.

FURTHER READING
Relevant material is available in the papers of Anderson Ruffin Abbott, the Abbott Collection, Metropolitan Toronto Reference Library.

Cobb, William Montague. "Medical History: Alexander Thomas Augusta," *Journal of the National Medical Association* 44, no. 4 (July 1952).

Greene, Robert Ewell. "Alexander T. Augusta," in *Black Defenders of America, 1775–1973: A Reference and Pictorial History* (1974).

Lamb, Daniel Smith. "Alexander Thomas Augusta, A.M., M.D.," in *Howard University Medical Department Washington, D.C.: A Historical, Biographical, and Statistical Souvenir* (1971).

Morais, Herbert M. *The History of the Negro in Medicine* (1967).

This entry is taken from the *American National Biography* and is published here with the permission of the American Council of Learned Societies.

DALYCE NEWBY

Aunt Clara. *See* Brown, Clara (Aunt Clara).

Aunt Sally. *See* Campbell, Sarah (Aunt Sally) *or* Williams, Sally Isaac (Aunt Sally).

Austin, Doris Jean (1949–Sept. 1994), novelist and columnist, was born in Mobile, Alabama. Raised primarily by her mother, Tommie Letitia Austin, and her grandmother, Rebecca Stallworth, Doris Jean was five years old when her family moved to Jersey City, New Jersey. Reverend Ercell Webb, her high school teacher, encouraged Austin to write, and Austin's early life in New Jersey provided a geographical and temporal backdrop for her only novel, *After the Garden* (1987).

Austin transformed the trials of her young adulthood into fodder for her writing. Before she was thirty, Austin's mother and grandmother had died of cancer, she had lived through two divorces, she had been diagnosed with and overcome cancer herself, and she had struggled with alcoholism. She also recovered the memory of the rape that she had survived when she was a child. Austin drew on these sources of pain for both her fiction and her nonfiction; in her-contributions to *Essence* magazine, including "Holisitic Healing," "The 30-year Rape," and "The Men in My Life," Austin uses autobiographical writing as a way to begin discussions of larger issues, such as women's health and coping with sexual violence.

Published in 1987, Austin's novel *After the Garden* focuses on the narrative of the protagonist Elzina Tompkins, a young woman from an affluent neighborhood in Jersey City. In an interview with *Essence*, Austin described the text as not autobiographical, but explained that "I consciously wrote about *my* people—those who nurtured me—though the characters are composites, straight out of my imagination" (Guy-Sheftall, 28). In the novel, Elzina falls in love with Jesse James, a high school athletic star. Elzina becomes pregnant during her senior year of high school, dashing the hope of her grandmother Rosalie that Elzina will attend Tuskegee University. Jesse and Elzina marry and move in with Rosalie, and Austin's novel studies the dynamic of this intergenerational household.

An investigation of the workings of family, class, race, gender, and history, *After the Garden* met with generally positive reviews. Described as "a powerful first novel" in the *Library Journal*, *After the Garden* also received the praise of the *New York Times Book Review* critic Robert G. O'Meally, who lauded Austin's "courageous confrontation of character" (16 August 1987, 20).

In addition to contributing to *Essence*, Austin published articles in the *Amsterdam News* and the *New York Times Book Review*. Her short story "Room 1023" was published in the anthology *Streetlights: Illuminating Tales of the Urban Black Experience*, which Austin edited with Martin Simmons; the anthology was published in 1996, after Austin's death.

Austin was named a MacDowell Colony fellow and was awarded the DeWitt Wallace–Reader's Digest Award for Literary Excellence. She was known by some as a "writer's writer," and she was a good friend of the novelists ELIZABETH NUNEZ and TERRY MCMILLAN. Austin was a member of the

Harlem Writer's Guild. She also cofounded (with others, including A. R. Flowers and B. J. Ashanti) the New Renaissance Writer's Guild in New York and subsequently served as its executive director.

From 1989 to 1994 Austin taught fiction workshops at Columbia University. She was living in New York and had begun work on a second novel when she died of liver cancer in 1994. After her death Terry McMillan established the Doris Jean Austin Writers Fellowship Award Program at the Frederick Douglass Creative Arts Center. Although her work is largely unstudied, Austin continues to be recognized as a talented novelist.

FURTHER READING

Andrews, William L., Frances Smith Foster, and Trudier Harris, eds. *The Oxford Companion to African American Literature* (1997).

Guy-Sheftall, Beverly. "Word Star," *Essence* (Oct. 1987).

Jones, Evora. "Doris Jean Austin," in *Contemporary African American Novelists*, ed. Emmanuel S. Nelson (1999).

King, Christine. Review of *After the Garden, Library Journal* (July 1987).

SARA E. HOSEY

Austin, H. Elsie (10 May 1908–26 Oct. 2004), lawyer, diplomat, and activist, was born Helen Elsie Austin in Cincinnati, Ohio, the daughter of George J. Austin and Mary Louise Dotson Austin. Elsie Austin grew up in a family with a history of standing up for justice and equality. Her role model was her great-grandmother, the wife of one of the first black U.S. congressional representatives elected after the Civil War, who, when she was taunted by racist terror and threat of death by the Ku Klux Klan in Alabama because of her husband's role in politics, defied the Klan.

Austin expressed this courage and spirit as a child in Cincinnati's public schools; when she was eight years old and one of only two African American children in her class, she pointed out textbook errors that degraded the role of Africans in world history, and she listed many of the contributions made by Africans. After she spoke, she remembered later, there was an "electric silence" in the classroom. Her teacher, however, agreed with Austin and went on to discuss contributions made by African Americans and Africans.

Austin was one of six African Americans who integrated the undergraduate program at the University of Cincinnati in 1927, and in 1930 she became the first African American woman to graduate from the University of Cincinnati College of Law. After law school Austin practiced law in Ohio and Indiana and was the first black woman to serve as assistant attorney general in the state of Ohio and the first woman lawyer in the federal government's Senior Attorney Office of Emergency Management. In 1937 Elsie Austin received an honorary LLD degree from Wilberforce University in Ohio.

From 1939 to 1944 Austin served as president of Delta Sigma Theta, a service-based sorority of college-educated African American women. With more than nine hundred chapters worldwide, the sorority provides support and assistance in local communities in the United States and throughout the world, such as building and maintaining a maternity hospital in Kenya and in the United States operating Delta Academy, in which local Delta sororities work tutoring and mentoring African American students. In 1945 Austin wrote a play for high school students that went on to be produced in various communities through the Young Women's Christian Association (YWCA). The play, *Blood Doesn't Tell*, confronts the prejudicial thinking that African American blood is different and not suitable for blood donations. The drama portrays prejudice among schoolchildren and the community, discusses that prejudice, and educates students that all blood is the same.

In 1934 Elsie Austin joined the Baha'i community in Cincinnati. Founded in Iran in 1844, the worldwide Baha'i faith focuses on the principles of unity of God and humankind and denounces and works to abolish racism and prejudice. The community is led not by clergy but by a democratically elected spiritual assembly. In 1944 Austin was elected to the nine-member national governing body of the U.S. Baha'i community. In 1953 Austin met the head of the faith, Shoghi Effendi, on a pilgrimage to the Holy Land. Responding to a call among the community to establish new Baha'i communities, Austin resigned from the national board in the United States and settled in Tangier, Morocco. She lived there for five years, teaching school and traveling throughout Africa. From 1953 to 1958 she served on the Baha'i spiritual assembly in North and West Africa. During her membership in the Baha'i community, Austin served local spiritual assemblies in the United States, Nigeria, Kenya, and the Bahamas. She wrote numerous articles and pamphlets and reported on the 1957 Kenya Conference for the *Baha'i News*. She penned a pamphlet on the life of the Baha'i spiritual leader LOUIS GEORGE GREGORY, who was her mentor.

In 1960 Austin joined the U.S. State Department, and for the next ten years served as a cultural attaché with the United States Information Agency (USIA). She initiated the first USIA women's programs in Africa. These programs targeted women leaders and organizations in thirteen African countries. Austin received the Federal Women's Award in 1968 for her work, and in 1969 the University of Cincinnati honored her with a doctor of humanities degree.

Austin retired from the State Department in 1970, settled in Silver Spring, Maryland, and worked as a consultant in human relations and law. She worked with the Phelps Stokes Fund, which strives to build bridges of intercultural, interracial, and international understanding through educational initiatives. In 1974 Austin founded the African and American Women's Association, a nonprofit organization devoted to better understanding among the women of Africa and the Americas. While working with the Stokes Fund she lived and worked in Nigeria and helped the Nigerian government to build a nationwide judiciary system. In 1977 Austin attended the Baha'i International Teaching Conference in Kenya, and in 1975 she chaired the Baha'i delegation to the 1975 International Women's Conference in Mexico City. In 1982 Austin traveled to the People's Republic of China for the Stokes Fund. As part of a study team, she inspected schools and community educational services, and researched the education of minority groups in China.

The Baha'i World News Service's obituary of Dr. Austin cites a speech she gave during a 1998 gathering of Baha'is, in which Austin continued to urge action: "If we go about with faith, with intelligent protest, standing up and demonstrating what the right attitude and motivation is for human progress, we can cause progress," she said. In 2000 the University of Cincinnati named a scholarship in her honor. Austin died in San Antonio, Texas, at the age of ninety-six.

FURTHER READING

Burkett, Randal K., Nancy Hall, and Henry Louis Gates Jr., eds. *Black Biography, 1790–1950. A Cumulative Index*, vol. 1 (1991).
Hatcher, William S., and J. Douglas Martin. *The Baha'i Faith: The Emerging Global Religion* (1984).
Obituary: *Washington Post*, 26 Nov. 2004.

LINDA SPENCER

Austin, Louis Ernest (24 Jan. 1898–12 June 1971), journalist, was born in Enfield, North Carolina, the year of the infamous Wilmington Race Massacre. His parents were William Louis Austin, owner of a barbershop, and Carrie Johnson. Louis Austin graduated from the Joseph K. Brick High School. His father, who never let any of his children work for whites, taught him in word and deed that no person was superior to him.

In Durham, Austin attended and graduated from the National Training School (later North Carolina Central University), which had been founded in 1910 by JAMES E. SHEPARD. Following graduation Austin sold life insurance for the North Carolina Mutual Life Insurance Company, founded in Durham in 1898 by black entrepreneurs. Austin also served as sports editor for Durham's black newspaper, the *Standard Advertiser*, founded in 1921 by Charles Arrant. In 1927, with the help of a loan from the Mutual affiliate Mechanics and Farmers Bank, Austin bought the paper, which was then known as the *Carolina Times*. Austin married Stella Louise Walker, and they had one daughter, Vivian, who after the death of her father took over as editor and publisher of the *Carolina Times*.

Austin's Christianity and his egalitarianism formed the foundation for his editorial positions. A longtime trustee of Saint Joseph's African Methodist Episcopal (AME) Church in Durham, Austin believed that it was his moral duty to speak the truth about the suffering and injustice inflicted upon African Americans. For twenty-seven years Austin served as president of the Interdenominational Ushers of North Carolina.

From the beginning Austin's editorials were forthright and resolute—the paper's motto was "The Truth Unbridled." For more than four decades Austin fought courageously against economic injustice, police brutality, racial segregation, and white supremacy. When in 1929 he published editorials in support of a black family under attack for purchasing a home in a white neighborhood, Austin received threatening phone calls, some promising to burn his house down. The Ku Klux Klan threw rocks and bottles at his house and burned a cross on his lawn. Austin once told an interviewer of an occasion when he was "ordered out of town" (he did not say by whom). Undaunted, Austin visited the man who had threatened him, "just to let him know that I would still be here any time he wanted me." That night a group of Austin's friends "gathered to stand guard and defend" him (Walker, p. 167). But Austin was not deterred by the threats of white racists—neither then nor later. Because Austin was so dismissive of whites' notions of racial etiquette, many whites viewed him as an anomaly and a radical who had little black support, but the truth was that his words and deeds made him a hero to many African Americans. Austin's outspokenness alienated advertisers, however, which meant that the newspaper struggled to remain solvent.

In 1933 Austin joined with the attorneys CONRAD PEARSON and Cecil McCoy in backing Thomas Raymond Hocutt's lawsuit against the white-only policy of the University of North Carolina at Chapel Hill. The NAACP lawyer WILLIAM HASTIE joined Pearson and McCoy in representing Hocutt. Because of a legal technicality and because of the refusal of North Carolina College president James Shepard to submit Hocutt's transcript, the suit failed in state court. Nonetheless, the case served as the beginning of the NAACP's legal battle to overturn segregated public education, culminating in 1954 with the *Brown v. Board of Education* decision.

Two years later in 1935 Austin helped found the Durham Committee on Negro Affairs to register black voters and increase black political influence in the city and the state. One of the original members of the executive committee, Austin worked for the Durham Committee for decades in various capacities. In 1953 he handled public relations for Rencher N. Harris's successful campaign to become the first black member of the Durham city council. Austin himself had unsuccessfully run for Durham city council in 1945.

During World War II, Austin capitalized on the nature of the war to press for equal rights for African Americans. In North Carolina, Austin was the leading proponent of the "Double V" strategy, coined by the *Pittsburgh Courier*, which encouraged blacks to fight for victory abroad while fighting for victory at home against the forces of white supremacy and racial oppression. Austin voiced the views of many African Americans when he spoke out against racial segregation and racial discrimination by the state and federal governments and by private businesses. After the outbreak of war in Europe in 1939 Austin—an avowed anti-imperialist—joined the chorus of black editors and columnists who saw little difference between German Nazism and British imperialism and thus urged the United States to stay out of the war. Austin demanded that the United States insist that Britain free its colonies: "We cannot fight a war on one hand to preserve the rights of free people while denying those rights to others" (*Carolina Times*, 14 Mar. 1942).

The *Carolina Times* joined other black newspapers to attack racial discrimination by the nation's armed forces and to fight for equal access for blacks in all service branches. In September 1940 Austin urged Congress to ensure that blacks would be included in all branches of the armed forces in the selective service bill then being debated.

After the Japanese attack on Pearl Harbor and America's entrance into the war, Austin regularly illuminated the contradictions between American policies to defeat the racist Nazis and racist violence at home against blacks. Austin renewed his criticism of segregation in the wake of violence that erupted in North Carolina as a result of racist discrimination by whites against black soldiers. In 1941 Austin backed A. PHILIP RANDOLPH's March on Washington movement, which succeeded in pressuring President Franklin D. Roosevelt to issue an executive order banning racial discrimination in hiring by defense contractors.

As president of the Durham branch of the NAACP, Austin helped establish the North Carolina State Conference of NAACP Branches, which provided a stronger and more united base to press forward in the fight for equal rights. During the war the North Carolina NAACP doubled the number of local branches and increased its membership to almost ten thousand.

Unlike some older black activists Austin sustained his position at the forefront of the movement for justice and equal opportunity during the modern civil rights movement of the 1950s and 1960s. He joined with a new generation of activists in supporting desegregation of public schools, lunch counters, and restaurants; equal access to employment opportunities; and voting rights. He continued to support litigation but also supported civil disobedience. After the *Brown* decision, Austin courageously criticized the White Citizens' Council as a latter-day KKK. He advocated boycotts of stores that refused to hire blacks. In 1963 he chastised black businessmen who failed to join picket lines in support of a boycott of white-owned stores. Moreover, the *Carolina Times* published the names of businesses that were being boycotted by the black community. Austin spoke out in favor of striking workers at Duke University, and he supported black citizens' rent strikes and actions against the city housing authority, which failed to address racial discrimination in public housing. He encouraged Howard Fuller, who led a local antipoverty agency in Durham called Operation Breakthrough, to confront a recalcitrant black upper class while battling powerful white leaders.

For more than half a century Louis Austin played an important role in African Americans' struggle for freedom. Courageous and forthright local leaders like Austin laid the foundation for the important victories produced by the postwar civil rights movement. Bridging the years before and after the landmark Supreme Court decision in *Brown v. Board of Education*, this intrepid journalist led voter registration campaigns, advocated integration of public education, lobbied for equal pay for black teachers and equal funding for black schools, publicized police brutality, and demanded equal employment opportunity for African Americans. Even in the year of his death, Austin was still speaking out for equity in education by challenging the policy wherein the boards of desegregating schools replaced black principals with whites.

FURTHER READING

The best primary sources regarding Austin are his editorials in the *Carolina Times*. The newspaper is available on microfilm from Duke University's Perkins Library.

Boyd, Harold Kent. "Louis Austin and the Carolina Times," M.A. thesis, North Carolina College at Durham, 1966.

Gershenhorn, Jerry. "Double V in North Carolina: The *Carolina Times* and the Struggle for Racial Equality during World War II," *Journalism History* 32 (Fall 2006).

Gershenhorn, Jerry. "*Hocutt v. Wilson* and Race Relations in Durham, North Carolina, during the 1930s," *North Carolina Historical Review* 78 (July 2001).

Walker, Harry J. "Changes in Race Accommodation in a Southern Community," Ph.D. diss., University of Chicago, 1945.

Weare, Walter B. *Black Business in the New South: A Social History of the North Carolina Mutual Life Insurance Company* (1973).

Obituary: *New York Times*, 26 July 1971.

JERRY GERSHENHORN

Austin, Lovie (19 Sept. 1887–10 July 1972), jazz singer, was born Cora Calhoun in Chattanooga, Tennessee. Nothing is known about her parents. In a 1950 article on Austin in *Down Beat*, the journalist George Hoefer wrote that "Lovie" was a nickname given to her by her grandmother. Hoefer further claimed that her grandmother "also brought up another little girl a few years younger then Lovie. Her name was BESSIE SMITH, and the two little playmates were parted before either of them began to get the blues."

Lovie studied music theory and piano at Roger Williams University in Nashville and Knoxville College in Knoxville. Her career was launched in 1912, when she began touring the vaudeville circuit. At about this time she married a Detroit movie house operator, a union that lasted briefly. She then married the vaudeville performer Austin of the team Austin and Delaney. Lovie worked the vaudeville circuit as the piano accompanist of her husband's act. She then traveled with Irving Miller's *Blue Babies* revue. Other revues with which she was associated as director or producer were *The Sunflower Girls* and *The Lovie Austin Revue*. The latter had a long and successful run at New York City's Club Alabam. The former was a part of her experiences with the Theater Owners Booking Association (TOBA), a group of influential theater owners organized in 1920.

In the early 1920s Austin settled in Chicago, where she remained until the end of her life. She worked as house pianist for Paramount Records, accompanying such classic blues singers as IDA COX, MA RAINEY, ALBERTA HUNTER, and ETHEL WATERS. She was the pianist on Cox's first record and Rainey's first release. Other blues singers with whom she performed or recorded with were Bessie Smith, CHIPPIE HILL, Edmonia Henderson, Edna Hicks, HATTIE MCDANIEL, Priscilla Stewart, Viola Bartlette, and Ozzie McPherson. As for her collaborating instrumentalists, the list includes the trumpeters LOUIS ARMSTRONG, LEE COLLINS, and Tommy Ladnier; the saxophonist WILLIAM "BUSTER" BAILEY; the clarinetist JOHNNY DODDS; the trombonist KID ORY; and the drummer BABY DODDS. She also recorded under her own name, Lovie Austin and Her Blues Serenaders. Her accompaniments were described as "sturdy and even-pulsed, yet rolling and rhythmic."

During the 1920s the piano was a vital rhythm accompaniment instrument. Not a solo improviser, Austin believed in collective improvisation. Although she often led small supporting ensembles (generally three members) for accompaniments, there was always a fullness of sound. Of her individual playing, a *Chicago Defender* journalist wrote, "percussive, pushing the beat along, filling in the bass parts with her right hand maintaining a steady flow of counter/melody." Austin's distinguishing features were "considerable skill and musical sophistication." Her many recordings with the Blues Serenaders are classics.

The pianist, composer, and arranger MARY LOU WILLIAMS throughout her career consistently recalled her impression of an early exposure to Austin's genius. Williams indicated that as a child she visited a Pittsburgh theater and was fascinated and inspired by the female at the keyboard, Austin, who was writing down music with her right hand while accompanying the performance with her swinging left. Austin had done all of the orchestrations for the show. Behind schedule, she was at the same time arranging the music for the next act. In a later interview Williams recalled: "During this period, we didn't have very many readers and this woman was a master reader. I haven't seen a man yet that can compare with that woman" (*Black Perspective in Music*, Fall 1980).

In Chicago, Austin worked as musical director for the Monogram Theater, where the leading black performers appeared. She remained in the post for twenty years and accompanied acts by Waters, McDaniel, BILL "BOJANGLES" ROBINSON, and others. Subsequently she worked in a similar capacity at both the Gem and the Joy theaters. Austin shared composition credits with Hunter on "Nobody Knows You When You're Down and Out" and "Down Hearted Blues." Other Austin compositions include "Bad Luck Blues," "Barrel House Blues," "Travelin' Blues," "Steppin' on the Blues," and "Frog Tongue Stomp." But there was little copyright protection, and she was deprived of many royalties.

As her New Orleans–style playing fell out of vogue, Austin worked as a security inspector at a naval defense plant during World War II. When Hoefer wrote his 1950 feature article on Austin, she was pianist for the Penthouse Studios at the Jimmy Payne School of Dance in Chicago. She recorded with Hill for Capitol Records in 1946 and with Hunter for Riverside Records in 1961, although her longest recording association was with the Paramount label. Austin officially retired in 1962 and died ten years later in Chicago. Her musical contributions remained overlooked until the revived interest in women in jazz in the 1970s and the subsequent publication of three books on women in the early days of jazz.

FURTHER READING

Handy, D. Antoinette. *Black Women in American Bands and Orchestras* (1981).

Hoefer, George. "Lovie Austin Still Active as a Pianist in Chicago," *Down Beat* (16 June 1950).

Shapiro, Nat, and Nat Hentoff, eds. *Hear Me Talkin' to Ya* (1955).

Obituaries: *Chicago Tribune*, 9 July 1972; *Living Blues*, Summer 1972; *Down Beat*, 12 Oct. 1972.

This entry is taken from the *American National Biography* and is published here with the permission of the American Council of Learned Societies.

ANTOINETTE HANDY

Austin, Oscar Palmer (15 Jan. 1948–23 Feb. 1969), Marine Corps soldier in the Vietnam War and Medal of Honor winner, was born in Nacogdoches, Texas, the son of Frank and Mildred Austin, and was raised in Phoenix, Arizona. A graduate of Phoenix Union High School, Austin was inducted for service in the U.S. Marine Corps during the height of the Vietnam War on 22 April 1968. Upon joining the marines, he was sent to boot camp at the Marine Corps Recruit Depot in San Diego, California, and served as a member of the Third Recruit Training Battalion through July 1968. Austin subsequently received individual combat and infantryman training at Camp Pendleton, California, from August to September 1968 as part of the Second Infantry Training Regiment, following which, in October 1968, he was promoted to private first class. Later that month, on 15 October, he was sent to the Republic of Vietnam for his first tour of duty as a combat soldier as a member of Company E, Second Battalion, Seventh Marines, in the First Marine Division.

The role played by blacks in the marine corps during the Vietnam War was vital, and the conditions under which their service was performed mirrored in general the racial conditions that then existed in America. As marine corps historians have noted, "From the first commitment of troops until the last, black Marines were always present in Vietnam" (Shaw and Donnelly, 78). Unlike other wars, where blacks fought in segregated units, black marines fought side by side with their fellow marines who were white, and "the color of a man's skin was of no import to his role as a combat Marine" (Shaw and Donnelly, 78). Despite the fact that serious racial tensions between white and black marines often flared up at marine bases, especially at Camp Lejeune in North Carolina, and "that bigotry and prejudice were practiced in the Corps" (Shaw and Donnelly, 72), these issues often faded into the background in combat situations. Indeed, black marine corps combatants, numbering nearly 41,000 during the war, performed to such a high level that five soldiers would win the Medal of Honor. Among these men were JAMES ANDERSON JR., RODNEY MAXWELL DAVIS, Ralph Johnson, and Robert Jenkins Jr. Also in this class was Oscar Austin who, like his fellow

Medal of Honor winners, died in the service of his country.

The month of February 1969 found Oscar Austin and the Seventh Marines stationed in vicinity of Da Nang in South Vietnam, an area noted for many hard-fought battles between the Americans and the Communist North Vietnamese. On the evening of 22 February, Austin's company was stationed six and a half miles west of Da Nang, where he served as an assistant machine gunner. In the early hours of 23 February, Austin's observation post came under severe fire from a ground attack by a large North Vietnamese army force. Grenade and small-arms fire predominated, and Austin's company was in a dangerous position. When Private First Class Oscar Austin observed that one of his fellow soldiers was wounded and in an exposed position, he unhesitatingly left the security of his fighting hole and, with a complete disregard for his own safety, raced across the fire-swept terrain to assist the Marine to a covered location. As he neared the casualty, he observed an enemy grenade land nearby and, reacting instantly, leaped between the injured Marine and the lethal object, absorbing the effects of its detonation. As he ignored his painful injuries and turned to examine the wounded man, he saw a North Vietnamese Army soldier aiming a weapon at his unconscious companion. With full knowledge of the probable consequences and thinking only to protect the Marine, Private First Class Austin resolutely threw himself between the casualty and the hostile soldier and, in doing so, was mortally wounded. (Shaw and Donnelly, 100)

For his "indomitable courage ... and selfless devotion to duty" on that Sunday morning in February 1969, Oscar Palmer Austin was posthumously awarded the Medal of Honor, the fourth black marine so honored in the war to that date (Shaw and Donnelly, 100). The medal was issued to Austin's parents in April 1970 at the White House in Washington, D.C., by Vice President Spiro Agnew.

Just like American soldiers in the nation's wars from the American Revolution through the Korean War, many of those fighting in Vietnam showed courage under extremely difficult circumstances, and Austin's heroism serves to exemplify their sacrifice. Oscar Austin has not been forgotten; not only was his name etched on the Vietnam Veterans Memorial Wall (panel 32W, row 088), but he was further memorialized when the *Arleigh Burke*–class Aegis destroyer *Oscar Austin* (DDG-79) was named in his honor and commissioned in 2000 by the United States Navy.

FURTHER READING

Leatherwood, Art. "Oscar P. Austin," in *The Handbook of Texas Online*, http://www.tsha.utexas.edu/ handbook/online/article/AA/fause.html.

Shaw, Henry, Jr., and Ralph Donnelly. *Blacks in the Marine Corps* (2002).

GLENN ALLEN KNOBLOCK

Avery, Byllye (20 Oct. 1937–), women's health advocate, was born Byllye Yvonne Reddick in Waynesville, Georgia, the daughter of L. Alyce M. Ingram, a schoolteacher. The name and occupation of her father is unknown. Although Byllye was born in Georgia, her family eventually settled in Deland, Florida, a town of five thousand people near Daytona Beach. Her mother, a graduate of Bethune-Cookman College, was a schoolteacher in nearby Perry, Florida. When Byllye was a teenager, her mother enrolled in a graduate program at New York University to earn a master's degree in education. Consequently, Avery's mother spent her summers in New York, away from her daughter, which was the only time in which she could take courses. Avery's father died during the last year of her mother's graduate studies.

Byllye attended Talladega College in Alabama and graduated in 1959 with a B.A. in Psychology. She soon married Wesley Avery, whom she had met at Talladega, in 1960. Byllye Avery eventually earned an MEd in Special Education from the University of Florida in 1969 and began working as head teacher in a children's mental health unit at the teaching hospital at the University of Florida in Gainesville.

Avery is often credited with starting the contemporary African American women's health movement in the United States. Given that she had no formal training or background in medicine or health care, Avery attributed her success to her personal experiences and her commitment to health issues. One major moment was the abrupt death of her husband from a massive heart attack in 1970 at the age of thirty-three, after which Avery was left with the responsibility of rearing their two children alone. The traumatic event forced her to think critically about preventive care and maintaining a healthy lifestyle.

Avery became active in health issues in the early 1970s. After a petition to open a Planned Parenthood clinic in Gainesville was rejected, Avery and four colleagues decided to establish and operate a clinic of their own. In 1974 they opened the Gainesville Women's Health Center, which was the first abortion and gynecological care clinic in the city. Continuing her interest in providing quality health care to women, in 1978 Avery helped found Birthplace, an alternative birthing center in Gainesville, where certified nurse-midwives assisted women with deliveries. Avery personally assisted in more than one hundred births at the center before her departure.

Recalling the negative attitudes toward sex that she encountered from her mother, Avery decided that she would not repeat the cycle with her own daughter. For her daughter's eleventh birthday Avery decided to celebrate it as a rite of passage marking her daughter's first menstruation, giving her a cake that read "Happy Birthday, Happy Menstruation!" Soon thereafter Avery conducted a workshop on menstruation and childbearing for students at her daughter's elementary school. Taking this public education project a step further, in 1987 Avery produced a video for the National Black Women's Health Project. The video, *On Becoming a Woman: Mothers and Daughters Talking Together*, encouraged open communication between mothers and daughters about the physical and emotional changes that occur during adolescence.

Avery's interest in the health of African American women developed at the most unlikely of places, the Comprehensive Employment Training Program (CETA), a job-training program for young women at Santa Fe Community College in Gainesville. While serving as the program's director, she observed and became increasingly concerned about the level of high absenteeism among the young African American women participants. She soon learned that many of the women were dealing with a multitude of issues, including hypertension, diabetes, raising many children, domestic violence, and sexual abuse. This realization spurred Avery to collect as much health information and statistics as she could possibly find. She was astounded by the health disparities between African American and white women and concluded that there is a "conspiracy of silence" concerning the poor health status of African American women (White, 6).

While serving on the board of directors for the National Women's Health Network in 1981, Avery conceived and started a two-year project called the Black Women's Health Project that focused on the health of African American women. Under the auspices of the project, Avery and twenty-two colleagues met to plan the Conference on Black Women's Health Issues, which was held in June 1983 at Spelman College in Atlanta. More than two thousand women attended the three-day event. Participants openly discussed pressing issues such as domestic violence, sexual abuse, obesity, diabetes, sexuality, childbirth, mental health, and overall well-being. The conference promoted a holistic, self-help approach to health that encouraged women to take charge of their own health through consciousness-raising groups and self-examination; it also emphasized the integration of physical wellness with spiritual and emotional well-being.

Prompted by the enthusiasm that was sparked among the conference's participants, the project officially became a free-standing organization based in Atlanta and was renamed the National Black Women's Health Project (NBWHP). The organization grew exponentially with the immediate founding of seventy-five self-help groups. By 1991 chapters had been formed in twenty-five states. The organization also began working with women in other countries, such as Belize, Jamaica, Brazil, Nigeria, and South Africa, through its SisteReach program. In 1990 the NBWHP opened an office in Washington, D.C., that focused on public policy advocacy.

In 1989 Avery was one of twenty prominent African American leaders, including DOROTHY HEIGHT, SHIRLEY CHISHOLM, FAYE WATTLETON, and MAXINE WATERS, who issued and signed a public statement entitled "We Remember: African American Women for Reproductive Freedom." The statement declared the group's support of reproductive freedom, broadening its very definition to include the right to have children; the right of access to contraceptive services, reproductive health information, and health care; and the right to safe and legal abortions. The statement addressed the effects of racism, poverty, and violence on the reproductive health of African American women. After many requests for reprints 250,000 copies of the brochure were subsequently circulated nationwide. The influential statement continues to appear in anthologies on women's rights and activism.

The recipient of many awards, Avery won a MacArthur Foundation Fellowship in 1989, as well as several honorary doctorates. Avery served as the first president of the National Black Women's Health Project until 1990. (In 2003 the organization changed its name to the Black Women's Health Imperative.) After stepping down as the NBWHP's president, Avery pursued other projects, including publishing a small book of inspirational affirmations, *An Altar of Words: Wisdom, Comfort, and Inspiration for African American Women*. In 2002 she founded the Avery Institute for Social Change in New York City, which focused on the health of people of color, with a special focus on affordable health care.

By showing the connections among race, ethnicity, economic circumstances, and health, Avery helped to create a viable health movement that addresses the pressing concerns of women of color. Her vision paved the way for other women's health activists of other racial and ethnic backgrounds, and the National Black Women's Health Project served as the model for other groups such as the National Latina Health Organization and the National Asian Women's Health Organization. Other African American groups, such as African American Women Evolving, built on the NBWHP's pioneering work. All of these groups fully embraced Avery's philosophy that women and people of color need not be experts in order to take charge of their health and well-being.

FURTHER READING

Silliman, Jael, Marlene Fried, Loretta Ross, and Elena Gutierrez. *Undivided Rights: Women of Color Organize for Reproductive Justice* (2004).

Simurda, Stephen J. "Byllye Avery: Guardian of Black Women's Health," *American Health* (March 1993).

Solinger, Rickie, ed. *Abortion Wars: A Half Century of Struggle, 1950–2000* (1998).

Springer, Kimberly, ed. *Still Lifting, Still Climbing: African American Women's Contemporary Activism* (1999).

White, Evelyn C., ed. *The Black Women's Health Book: Speaking for Ourselves* (1994).

KIMALA PRICE

Avery, Margaret (c. 1950–), singer and actor, was born in Mangum, Oklahoma. Neither the exact date of her birth nor her parents' names are known. An only child, Margaret quickly developed a sense of independence that provided the foundation for a number of the strong characters she later played in her career as an actor. Her father's naval career took the family to San Diego, where Avery attended high school and performed in several drama competitions.

Upon graduation she enrolled in San Francisco State University, where she was inspired by Dr. MARTIN LUTHER KING JR.'s commitment to cultivating and mentoring the next generation of black leaders. She fostered King's notion of preparing African American youth for a brighter future by attaining her goal of becoming an elementary school teacher. Her interest in the stage never

waned, however, despite the scarcity of roles for African American women, and she continued pursuing performance opportunities as a singer and drama student.

Eventually Avery moved to Los Angeles, where she worked as a substitute teacher while auditioning for television commercials. Pitching products such as mouthwash led to various stage roles and parts in several so-called black exploitation, or "blaxploitation," films, one of the few cinematic prospects available to black actors during the early 1970s. At this time Avery had her debut in television with roles in *Something Evil* (1972) and *Louis Armstrong—Chicago Style* (1976). She continued to be cast in feature films, including *Magnum Force* (1973) with Clint Eastwood and *Which Way Is Up?* (1977) with RICHARD PRYOR. Roles in the television series *A. E. S. Hudson Street* (1978) and in the made-for-TV movies *The Sky Is Gray* (1980), *The Lathe of Heaven* (1980), and *For Us, the Living* (1983) honed her skills before the camera and increased her visibility to American audiences.

In 1985 the director Steven Spielberg brought ALICE WALKER's novel *The Color Purple* to the big screen. The film featured several performers who were newcomers to movies, including WHOOPI GOLDBERG and OPRAH WINFREY. Spielberg, who had directed Avery in a commercial years before, tapped her to play the role of Shug Avery, a chanteuse and mistress to DANNY GLOVER's character, known only as Mister. The part, reportedly turned down by the singer TINA TURNER, called for Avery to showcase the character's independent streak by standing toe-to-toe with Mister, while revealing the character's romantic streak by intimately kissing Goldberg's Celie. Avery's passionate performance earned her an Academy Award nomination for Best Supporting Actress.

In addition to subsequent appearances as a guest star in TV series including *The Cosby Show*, *JAG*, and *Walker, Texas Ranger*, as well as made-for-TV movies, Avery performed in various feature films, including *White Man's Burden* (1995), *Waitin' to Live* (2002), and *Second to Die* (2002). She also appeared as herself in the documentary *The Collaboration of Spirits: Casting and Acting "The Color Purple"* (2003).

FURTHER READING

Collier, Aldore. "Margaret Avery Says She 'Couldn't Buy a Job' before *The Color Purple*," *Jet* (10 Mar. 1986).

"Margaret Avery: Anatomy of an Actress." *Black Stars* (Apr. 1976).

"Margaret 'Shug' Avery, Beyond *The Color Purple!*"
Essence (May 1986).
"What a Sweet Role! The Role of 'Shug' in *The Color
Purple* Brings Margaret Avery's Illustrious Career
Back to Life." *Right On!* (May 1986): 46–47.

ROXANNE Y. SCHWAB

Ayler, Albert (12 July 1936–c. 5 Nov. 1970), composer
and musician, was born in Cleveland, Ohio, the
son of Edward Ayler, a semiprofessional violinist
and tenor saxophonist, and Myrtle Hunter. Albert
and his brother Donald, who later became a professional jazz trumpet player, received musical training early in life from their father. In second grade
Albert performed alto saxophone recitals in school.
He performed duets with his father (who also
played alto saxophone) in church. Together they
listened to a great deal of swing and bebop music,
both on recordings and at jazz concerts.

From age ten to age eighteen Ayler attended
Cleveland's Academy of Music, taking jazz lessons from Benny Miller. Throughout his mid-
teenage years Ayler performed in young jazz and
rhythm and blues bands. He also was a captain of
his high school golf team; at the time, Cleveland's
golf courses were largely segregated. While in high
school Ayler spent two summers on the blues circuit, performing with LITTLE WALTER JACOBS.
According to John Litweiler, the noted avant-garde
jazz historian and critic, Ayler's knowledge of jazz
standards and his mastery of bebop style gained
him the nickname of "Little Bird" after the great
CHARLIE PARKER.

Ayler entered the army in 1958, where he
switched to tenor saxophone and traveled throughout Europe with a Special Services band based in
France. Among the musicians with whom Ayler
came into contact during this period were the
bebop tenor saxophonists DON BYAS and DEXTER
GORDON as well as the KING OLIVER reedman
ALBERT NICHOLAS. Europe in the late 1950s and
early 1960s was a hotbed of activity in the fledgling
free-jazz movement. Innovations such as abandoning chord changes, exploring sound for its own sake,
and collective improvising—all recalling music's
true roots—were ways of approaching free jazz's
goal of "spiritual transcendence." Ayler's proximity
to jazz clubs in Copenhagen and Paris allowed him
to listen to and practice this emerging style when
off duty.

Ayler remained in Europe immediately following his discharge in 1961, performing throughout

Sweden with a bebop trio that was recorded live
in 1962. That year he returned to Copenhagen,
where he experienced his first studio recording
date; the recordings that resulted from this session
were released as *The First Recordings*, or *Something
Different*, on Bird Notes. From that point on Ayler
performed only his own music. He sat in with the
avant-garde pianist CECIL TAYLOR's group at the
Club Montmartre in the winter of 1962–1963. Ayler
soon felt constrained by what he termed the "simplicity" of bebop and gravitated toward free performance. Ayler moved to New York in 1964, where he
occasionally performed with Taylor and recorded
an album in the winter of 1963–1964. He formed
a quartet in New York in the summer of 1964 with
the bassist Gary Peacock and the drummer Sunny
Murray, picking up the trumpeter DON CHERRY in
Europe. The quartet toured Sweden and Holland.
Ayler married Arlene Benton in 1964; they had one
daughter.

Ayler possessed a big, soulful sound very much in
the style of rhythm and blues music. Wailing, bray-
ing, growling, buzzing—these are just a few terms
that have been used to describe his playing. A thorough master of his instrument, Ayler was noted for
bringing out multiple overtones in his sound through
overblowing and manipulation. Characteristic of his
playing were split tones, loud honks in the lower
register, shrieks in the upper register, wide harsh
vibrato, and extreme interval leaps.

Ayler used modes and scales, as well as sound
for its own sake, in his emotional improvisation,
which often featured simple motivic repetition
based upon initially stated thematic material that
would suddenly deviate from the established harmonic changes to collective improvisation. He
played anything that came to his mind that possessed a connection with the material, developing
relationships within a free context that were somewhat analogous to free association in psychology
and stream-of-consciousness writing in literature.
The social and philosophical aspects of his music
assumed greater importance for Ayler than strict
musical interpretation did. He once stated that
his goal was to provide an atmosphere of spiritual
transcendence for the audience (and for his fellow
musicians) that would combine the collective cohe-
siveness of a New Orleans jazz band with a formal
freedom arrived at individually.

Although Ayler received acclaim from critics,
he was unable to gain a steady audience for his
music, leaving him with a meager personal income.
He performed and toured sporadically with his

group throughout the 1960s, both in Europe and in the United States. Ayler played in studios and clubs in New York from 1965 to 1968. A member of the short-lived Jazz Composers Guild, Ayler performed his first major United States concert at New York's Town Hall in 1965 with his brother Donald. An appearance at the 1966 Newport Jazz Festival and a European Tour in November of that year highlighted the group's accomplishments.

A 1967 European tour included Ayler and his brother Donald, the violinist Michel Sampson, the bassist Bill Folwell, and the drummer Beaver Harris. Ayler performed college concerts with such musicians as Gary Peacock or HENRY GRIMES on bass; Beaver Harris, Sonny Murray, or Milford Graves on drums; and Cal Cobbs on piano or harpsichord. Ayler also occasionally performed on instruments such as alto and soprano saxophone, and even the bagpipes.

After returning from a European tour with his quintet in 1970, Ayler was reported missing in New York City. According to his companion, Ayler, in despair over family strife involving his brother Donald, had boarded the ferry to the Statue of Liberty and jumped off before the ferry reached Liberty Island. His body was found on 25 November in the East River near the Congress Street Pier in Brooklyn. The exact cause of death was unconfirmed.

Ayler, together with JOHN COLTRANE, ARCHIE SHEPP, and PHAROAH SANDERS, expanded the definition of jazz that was initiated by ORNETTE COLEMAN in the late 1950s, creating for future jazz musicians and audiences a much broader concept of improvised music.

FURTHER READING

Litweiler, John. *The Freedom Principle: Jazz after 1958* (1984).

Lyons, Len, and Don Perlo. *Jazz Portraits: The Lives and Music of the Jazz Masters* (1989).

Wilmer, Valerie. *As Serious as Your Life: The Story of the New Jazz* (1980).

Obituary: *New York Times*, 4 Dec. 1970.

DISCOGRAPHY

Litweiler, John. "The Legacy of Albert Ayler," *Down Beat* 38, no. 7 (1971): 14–15, 29.

This entry is taken from the *American National Biography* and is published here with the permission of the American Council of Learned Societies.

DAVID E. SPIES

Babb, Valerie Melissa (6 May 1955–), writer, editor, and scholar, was born in New York City to Dorothy L. Babb and Lionel S. Duncan, both of whom were immigrants from the Republic of Panama. Her parents were part of the larger West Indian community, the "diggers" as many were called, who built the Panama Canal. Babb shared a close relationship with her mother, who instilled in her the value of an education.

Babb attended the Bronx High School of Science, a high school specializing in math and sciences and with some of the best English teachers, whose influence Babb credits for choosing this profession. After graduating from high school in 1973, she enrolled in Queens College of the City University of New York. She graduated with honors in 1977, earning a bachelor's degree in English with a minor concentration in Romance Languages. Babb went on to attend graduate school at the State University of New York at Buffalo, where she majored in English and pursued linguistics as a minor field of study. She earned a master's degree in 1979 and remained at SUNY Buffalo to earn her Ph.D. in English in 1981. Babb's dissertation, "The Evolution of an American Literary Language," examined ways in which American writers used dialect, vernacular, and linguistic racial symbolism to create a literary language more appropriate for a national multicultural literature.

Babb accepted a tenure-track position as an assistant professor of English at Georgetown University in Washington, D.C., in 1981. In 1983 she published her first work of fiction, "A Panama Story," a short story that appeared in *Sargasso*. In 1987 she earned tenure, thus cementing her professional credentials. That same year, she gave birth to her first and only child, a son, Jaren.

At Georgetown, Babb produced *Black Georgetown Remembered*, a video documentary compiling the oral histories of members of the black Georgetown community. Intrigued by stories of this underrepresented community, Babb collaborated with the local historian and journalist Carroll Gibbs, who had developed a walking tour of Georgetown's black community. Based on her work with Gibbs, Babb outlined a preliminary script for a film on the history of black Georgetown. With Babb and Gibbs as narrators, the half-hour documentary premiered at the university in February 1989, in conjunction with Black History Month.

During the next two years, Babb served as associate professor of English at Georgetown, while extending the material in the video into her first published book, *Black Georgetown Remembered: A History of Georgetown's Black Community*. This documentary was published in 1991 and compiles the oral histories documenting the story of black presence in Georgetown from the first half of the twentieth century to the beginning of the twenty-first century.

Babb completed *Ernest Gaines* in 1991. Part of Twayne Publishers' United States Authors Series, the book reviewed Gaines's work and examined his use of communal narrative to capture the oral storytelling in his native Louisiana. In doing so Babb revealed her own ongoing concern for the complexities of language, storytelling, and American culture. In 1994 her essay "Old-Fashioned Modernism: 'The

Changing Same' in Ernest Gaines's *A Lesson before Dying*," an excerpt from her book, appeared in *Critical Reflection on the Fiction of Ernest J. Gaines*, edited by David C. Estes.

In collaboration with Gay Gibson Cima, Babb co-authored the article "Questioning the Canon in a Multicultural Classroom," which appeared in *New Theatre Quarterly* in 1995. It is one of her many articles to appear in refereed journals and the only one specifically to demonstrate Babb's pedagogical approach to literature. That same year, she published her first of six book reviews, a critique of Sara Lawrence-Lightfoot's *I've Known Rivers: Lives of Loss and Liberation*, which appeared in *America*, and she earned a Keck fellowship from the Georgetown University American Studies Program.

In 1998, while teaching courses in American literature, women's studies, and American studies at Georgetown, Babb published her third book, the one that would anchor her position as a theorist of note, *Whiteness Visible: The Meaning of Whiteness In American Literature and Culture*. In it Babb investigated the language of "whiteness," not as a theory of race but as a social, political, and economic construct. Acting as both literary and cultural theorist, Babb deconstructed the idea of whiteness as necessarily representative of American culture. She combined cultural theory and material theory with close textual analysis to develop her own theory, namely that the term "America" has become synonymous with the concept of whiteness. Babb guided readers on a journey through the development of the American literary canon, concluding that America's propensity to conflate whiteness with being American is not only dangerous but also antithetical to the foundation of American literature. From literature of the seventeenth and eighteenth centuries, in which white voices dominate American literature, to literature of the early twentieth century, in which immigrants' voices emerge and challenge the implicit whiteness of American culture, Babb offered a new approach to reading and comprehending the language of the American literary canon.

Babb achieved the rank of full professor at Georgetown in 1998. During this time Babb also joined the faculty of the Bread Loaf School of English at Middlebury College in Vermont, where she devoted her summers to building the English curriculum. In 1999 Babb assumed the position of director of undergraduate studies at Georgetown.

In 2000 Babb left Georgetown University and accepted a position as professor in the English department at the University of Georgia. In this capacity Babb taught a variety of courses and served as editor of the Langston Hughes Review, the official publication of the Langston Hughes Society. In 2005 she earned a fellowship to participate in the Scholars-in-Residence Program at the Schomburg Center for Research in Black Culture. Upon her return to the University of Georgia in 2007 Babb became the first African American woman to hold the position of head of the English department.

FURTHER READING

Kazensky, Michelle, ed. "Valerie Babb," in *The Writers Directory* (2007).

Klebba, Caryn, ed. "Valerie Babb," in *Directory of American Scholars*, 10th ed. (2002).

Mallegg, Kristen, ed. "Valerie Babb," in *Who's Who among African Americans* (2006).

ONDRA KROUSE DISMUKES

Baby Laurence (24 Feb. 1921–2 Apr. 1974), jazz tap dancer, was born Laurence Donald Jackson in Baltimore, Maryland. His parents' names and occupations are unknown. He was a boy soprano at age twelve, singing with McKinney's Cotton Pickers. When the bandleader DON REDMAN came to town, he heard Laurence and asked his mother if he could take the boy on the road. She agreed, provided that her son was supplied with a tutor. Touring on the Loew's circuit, Laurence's first time in New York was marked by a visit to the Hoofers Club in Harlem, where he saw the tap dancing of HONI COLES, Raymond Winfield, Roland Holder, and Harold Mablin. Laurence returned home sometime later to a sudden tragedy; both of his parents had died in a fire. "I don't think I ever got used to the idea," he told Marshall Stearns in Jazz Dance in 1968. "They always took such good care of me."

Laurence and a brother formed a vocal group called The Four Buds and tried to establish themselves in New York. He worked in the Harlem nightclub owned by DICKIE WELLS—the retired dancer from the group Wells, Mordecai, and Taylor—who nicknamed him "Baby" and encouraged his dancing. Laurence frequented the Hoofers Club, absorbing ideas and picking up steps from EDDIE RECTOR, Pete Nugent, Toots Davis, Jack Wiggins, and Teddy Hale, who became his chief dancing rival. "I saw a fellow dance and his feet never touched the floor," the tap dancer Bunny Briggs said, recalling when he first saw Laurence dance in the 1930s. Laurence worked after-hours sessions, gigged around Harlem, Washington, D.C., and Cincinnati, and began playing theaters such as Harlem's Apollo in the late 1930s. He performed with a group called The Six Merry Scotchmen (in some billings, the Harlem Highlanders), who dressed in kilts, danced, and sang JIMMIE LUNCEFORD arrangements in five-part harmony.

Around 1940 Laurence focused on tap dancing and became a soloist. Through the 1940s he danced with the big bands of DUKE ELLINGTON, COUNT BASIE, and Woody Herman, and in the 1950s he danced in small Harlem jazz clubs. Under the influence of the jazz saxophonist CHARLIE PARKER and other bebop musicians, Laurence expanded tap technique into jazz dancing. He performed with the jazz pianist ART TATUM, duplicating with his feet what Tatum played with his fingers. Through listening hard to Parker, DIZZY GILLESPIE, and BUD POWELL as well as jazz drummers such as MAX ROACH, Laurence developed a way of improvising solo lines and variations as much like a horn man as a percussionist. "He was more a drummer than a dancer," Whitney Balliett wrote in *New York Notes* (1976). "He did little with the top half of his torso. But his legs and feet were speed and thunder and surprise … a succession of explosions, machine-gun rattles and jarring thumps." Like musicians in a jazz combo, Laurence was also a fluent improviser who took solos, traded breaks, and built on motifs that were suggested by previous horn men. He was a master of dynamics who would start a thirty-two-bar chorus with light heel-and-toe figures, then drop in heavy offbeat accents and sprays of rapid toe beats that gave way to double-time bursts of rhythm.

Beset by drugs, alcohol, and financial troubles, Laurence stopped performing in the late 1950s. After a long illness he returned to Harlem in the early 1960s to work again in small jazz clubs. In 1960 he began a longtime engagement with CHARLIE MINGUS at the Showplace and that summer danced with Roach and Mingus in Newport, Rhode Island. Laurence was a sensation at the Newport Jazz Festival in 1962 in a legendary concert that included Nugent, Coles, and Briggs and marked the revival of tap dancing.

Laurence drifted into near oblivion in the late 1960s, dancing weekends in a restaurant in Gaithersburg, Maryland, with an excellent trio headed by the drummer Eddie Phyfe. By 1973 he reappeared in New York City, heading up the successful Sunday afternoon tap dancing sessions at the Jazz Museum. During this time he took in students, danced at the Palace with JOSEPHINE BAKER, did some television work, and gave one of his last triumphant performances at the Newport–New York Jazz Festival.

Laurence is regarded as an authentic jazz dancer who further developed the art of tap dancing by treating the body as a percussive instrument. "In the consistency and fluidity of his beat, the bending melodic lines of his phrasing, and his overall instrumentalized conception, Baby is a jazz musician," Nat Hentoff wrote in the album notes for *Baby Laurence—Dance Master*, a 1959 recording of Laurence's rhythmic virtuosity that demonstrates the inextricable tie between jazz tap dancing and jazz music.

FURTHER READING

Balliett, Whitney. *New York Notes: A Journal of Jazz, 1972–1975* (1976).

Stearns, Marshall, and Jean Stearns. *Jazz Dance: The Story of American Vernacular Dance* (1968).

DISCOGRAPHY

Baby Laurence—*Dance Master* (Classic Jazz CJ30, recorded 1959, released 1977).

This entry is taken from the *American National Biography* and is published here with the permission of the American Council of Learned Societies.

CONSTANCE VALIS HILL

Bacon-Bercey, June (23 Oct. 1932–), meteorologist, was born June Esther Griffin in Wichita, Kansas, the only child of James Griffin, an auto mechanic who put himself through law school and eventually became an attorney, and Cherrie MacSalles, a music teacher. The name she is known by, Bacon-Bercey, is a combination of the last names of her first two husbands. She was married to Walker Bacon, a doctor, from 1956 to 1967 and to John Bercey, a businessman, from 1968 to 1980. Encouraged by her parents, Bacon-Bercey became interested in science at a very young age, and in high school a physics teacher steered her toward a career in meteorology. Bacon-Bercey attended the University of California at Los Angeles, where she earned a B.S. in Mathematics and Meteorology in 1954 despite the attitude of many of her professors who felt that a woman was better suited to studying home economics. She continued on at UCLA and earned an M.S. in Mathematics and Meteorology in 1955, and, armed with her degrees and her love of science and mathematics, she became the first black female professional meteorologist in the United States.

Bacon-Bercey joined the National Meteorological Center (NMC) as a meteorologist in 1956. In 1962 she left the NMC to work as a consultant for the Sperry Rand Corporation. As a Sperry Rand consultant she worked at the Atomic Energy Commission, where she monitored the effects of nuclear explosions in the atmosphere. It was also at the Atomic Energy Commission that she met her future husband, George W. Brewer, an atomic scientist.

From 1970 to 1973 Bacon-Bercey worked as a roving reporter for NBC in New York City and Buffalo, thus becoming the first black woman television meteorologist for the NBC affiliate in Buffalo, New York. Bacon-Bercey had predicted a heat wave, and when it happened as predicted, she was offered the job of meteorologist. The job served as a stepping-stone to other weather-related endeavors, including becoming the station's chief meteorologist and ultimately working with federal and state governments. In 1975 Bacon-Bercey left NBC to lecture on meteorology, speaking across the country. From 1975 to 1978 she worked for the National Weather Service (NWS) in Washington, D.C., as a meteorologist and broadcaster.

In 1979 she completed a master of public administration degree at the University of Southern California and joined the National Oceanic and Atmospheric Agency (NOAA) as a public affairs specialist, later becoming chief of television services. Bacon-Bercey's duties at NOAA included conducting weather briefings for ocean survey researchers, weather forecasters, and business and government officials, as well as the U.S. media. While working at NOAA in 1977 she won the top prize on the television game show the *$128,000 Question* and used most of the prize money to establish a scholarship fund, administered by the American Geophysical Union, for women who want to become meteorologists. In 1976 Bacon-Bercey rejoined the National Weather Service and moved to Redwood City, near San Francisco, where she worked primarily with pilots and air traffic controllers, did weather forecasting, and served as a training officer. She remained at the NWS for the rest of her career before retiring in 1989.

Not one to sit idly, Bacon-Bercey began working as a substitute teacher in the San Mateo public school system in 1990. She also continued to work as a consultant with private foundations, universities, various professional associations, and NOAA. In addition to other publications before and after retiring from meteorology, Bacon-Bercey contributed a lesson on weather titled "Weather Watch" to the Harcourt-Brace CD-ROM *Science AnyTime*. She has also taught in San Francisco Bay–area schools.

Throughout her career Bacon-Bercey was active in a variety of professional organizations, including the American Meteorological Association, Women in Science and Engineering, the American Geophysical Union, the American Association of Public Administrators, and the New York Academy of the Sciences. As a member of the American Geophysical Union she served on the Committee on Women and Minorities in Atmospheric Sciences. According to the American Meteorological Society, Bacon-Bercey was a founding member of the Board of Women and Minorities. The board's responsibilities include "increasing the participation of women and minorities in the atmospheric and related oceanic and hydrologic sciences; to recommend and develop programs and ideas for educational and professional opportunities for women and minorities; and to survey periodically the membership and report on the society's character, demographics, and professional needs."

Bacon-Bercey was also actively involved in science and engineering fairs, believing that they are a wonderful way to encourage schoolchildren's interest in science and engineering and to recognize the students' accomplishments. She received a number of awards, including the 1972 Seal of Approval for Excellence in Television Weathercasting from the American Meteorological Society—she was the award's first female recipient. In 1984 Bacon-Bercey received NOAA's Certificate for Sustained Superior Performance; she later won an award for Outstanding Contribution to Furthering the Mission of NOAA from 1984 to 1992. In 2000 she was one of ten people recognized by the National Science Foundation and the National Aeronautics and Space Administration (NASA); she was recognized as a pioneer and role model in science and as a minority pioneer in atmospheric sciences.

FURTHER READING

Hall, Paula Quick. *A Day's Work?—A Life's Work!: A Visit with Some Women Whose Careers Began with Chemical, Civil, Electrical, Industrial, and Nuclear Engineering* (1987).

Workman, Bill. "Substitute Science Teacher Is a Meteorology Legend: Weather Pioneer June Bacon-Bercey Given More Honors," *San Francisco Chronicle,* 23 Mar. 2000.

ANNE K. DRISCOLL

Badger, Roderick (4 July 1834–Dec. 1890), dentist, was born a slave in the Panthersville District of Dekalb County, Georgia. His mother (name unknown) was a slave, and his father, J. D. Badger, was a white dentist and also his master. Roderick had several brothers, including Robert and Ralph, all of whom had the same white father but different mothers. In many ways his life story can be seen as an example of the complex relationships between the races in the antebellum and postbellum South, where the black and white societies were supposed to be separate but where mixed-race children were common, growing ever more numerous in the decade leading up to the Civil War. As the son of his owner, Badger enjoyed the privileges associated with that status, including his eventual freedom and prosperity. However, his status as a mulatto and as a professional man did not protect him from many of the disadvantages of being a black man in the antebellum South.

Roderick learned the art of dentistry from his father. While working for his father during the week he was able to set aside Sundays as a day that he could work for himself. Saving the money he made on Sundays, he was able to obtain his freedom, although it is unclear whether his father liberated him or if he purchased his freedom. Some accounts indicate that his working on Sundays was not to buy his freedom but was to purchase his own tools to practice his trade. That his brothers also eventually became freemen implies that they were manumitted, not forced to buy their freedom. In any case, well before the advent of the Civil War, Badger was a free man of color. He married Mary A. Murphey, who was the daughter of a wealthy Georgia lawyer and was one of the black gentry. They had eight children between 1856 and 1879, two daughters and six sons, seven of whom lived beyond childhood, their first child Zora having died when she was one year old.

Badger and his family moved to Atlanta in 1856 where he set up his practice, becoming the first black dentist in the city. His practice was by all accounts highly successful, to the degree that he was the object of a hostile petition from white Atlanta businessmen in 1859. The petition, presented to the city council, named Badger as a "negro" businessman who unfairly took customers away from white businessmen. In response to the petition the council passed a rule that free blacks in the city of Atlanta would have to pay a fee of two hundred dollars to stay within the city limits. They were also imprisoned for five days, during which time they could be hired out to raise money to pay their fee. Every day that the fee was not paid the free person of color was to receive thirty-nine lashes. A second petition protesting Badger's prominence and practice was presented to the Atlanta ordinance committee in February 1861, though no record exists that the punitive ordinance was ever enforced.

With the onset of the Civil War, Badger served as an aide to a Confederate army colonel. When the colonel lost his watch during the campaign and Badger managed to retrieve it for him, the colonel gave the watch to Badger. It became a family heirloom. There is no indication in the record of whether or not he was pressed into this service with the colonel or entered it voluntarily. That he was a free man before the war and that he escaped from this service in 1864 with the arrival of the Union army in Georgia seem to indicate that he was an unwilling participant in the Confederate cause. Badger and his family fled to Chicago, where they waited out the rest of the war.

After the war Badger and his family returned to Atlanta, where he reestablished his practice, which included many prominent blacks in Atlanta. He also became active in assisting the freed people and joined the Republican Party. He served as a tutor at a school established for blacks at one of the local churches, and he was appointed an election official by Governor Bullock to help monitor the polls and make certain that blacks were allowed to practice their newly acquired right to vote. In 1879 he was elected for a three-year term to the board of trustees of Clark College (later Clark Atlanta University), making him the first black trustee of the college. Badger was able to amass considerable property in Atlanta, owning at least five other properties besides his office on Peachtree Street. He died on 27 December 1890 and is interred in the black section of the historic Oakland Cemetery in Atlanta.

FURTHER READING

Hornsby, Anne R. "The Accumulation of Wealth by Black Georgians, 1890–1915," *Journal of Negro History* 74, no. 1 (1989).

Howard, W. P. "Atlanta as Left by the Enemy," *Charleston Mercury* (19 Dec. 1864).

Robinson, Henry S. "Robert and Roderick Badger, Pioneer Georgia Dentists," *Negro History Bulletin* 24, no. 1 (1961).

Sammons, Vivian Ovelton. *Blacks in Science and Medicine* (1990).

United States Congress Joint Select Committee on the Affairs in the Late Insurrectionary States. *Report of the Joint Select Committee appointed to inquire into the conditions of affairs in the late insurrectionary states, so far as regards the execution of laws and the safety of the lives and property of the citizens of the United States and Testimony Taken* (1892).

M. COOKIE E. NEWSOM

Bagneris, Vernel Martin (31 July 1949–), playwright, actor, director, singer, and dancer, was born in New Orleans, Louisiana, the third child of Gloria Diaz Bagneris and Lawrence Bagneris Sr. Bagneris's mother was a housewife and deeply religious woman who "quietly outclassed most people," and his father was a playful, creative man, a World War II veteran, and lifelong postal clerk. Bagneris grew up in the tightly knit, predominantly Creole Seventh Ward to a family of free people of color that had been in New Orleans since 1750. From the age of six he had a knack for winning popular dance contests, and during christenings and jazz funerals he learned more traditional music and dance. By the mid-1960s the once-beautiful, tree-lined neighborhood in which he was raised fell victim to the U.S. government's program of urban renewal, known colloquially as "Negro removal." A freeway overpass was constructed over a thriving neighborhood, inviting crime and eventually shuttering businesses and community. Trees were uprooted, homes were razed, the promenade was destroyed, and a neighborhood diaspora was in effect. Bagneris describes it thus: "Imagine the Champs-Elysées minus all trees, with a brooding highway held up by concrete poles and bare, unplanted dirt as its walkways." The Bagneris family moved to Gentilly, along with many other residents of the Seventh Ward.

Bagneris was in the advanced-placement track at St. Augustine High School, an institution committed to teaching dignity and respect to its young men, despite segregation in nearly every aspect of their lives in New Orleans. At fifteen years old, he and his compatriots were encouraged by the school leaders to quietly protest segregation at bowling alleys and drugstore counters citywide. Bagneris

graduated in 1967, when overt instances of Jim Crow had diminished but seating was still segregated on public transportation, in restaurants and restrooms, and at water fountains. In the fall of 1967 he headed directly to a seminary to study for the priesthood where he stayed for three long days. "I didn't go there to meditate," said Bagneris. "I went to be of service. That was the confusion."

Fortunately, Xavier University, his older siblings' alma mater and one of the few predominantly black Catholic universities in the country, scrambled to enroll him. He declared sociology as his major, but during his sophomore year Bagneris was dragged to a theater audition by his girlfriend who was afraid to go alone. Bagneris was cast as Gremio in *The Taming of the Shrew*. His girlfriend was not cast. He was a naturally adept actor and made up his mind to pursue a career on the stage. Though he'd never even attended the theater before this audition, by his junior year he was writing, directing, and producing his own plays. The Free Southern Theatre, which began by touring rural, underprivileged areas in the South and eventually basing itself in New Orleans, performed two of Bagneris's plays before he had even graduated.

Bagneris was curious about avant-garde theater methods and, upon his graduation in 1972, traveled to Amsterdam to learn more about the Bread and Love experimental theater group. He returned to New Orleans and worked day jobs. He'd brought with him highly experimental European scripts and staged them in his hometown. He produced and directed Samuel Beckett's *Endgame* on a double bill with Eugène Ionesco's *The Lesson* in a photo gallery, was awarded an artist-in-residence grant by the Arts Council of New Orleans, and made a foray into a daring, wholly integrated theater company in the French Quarter called Gallery Circle. By 1972 he had won two Best Actor awards in New Orleans.

In 1976 Bagneris saw a play in New York City that would change his life: Will Holt's *Me and Bessie*, a one-woman show about the blues legend BESSIE SMITH. After seeing the show, Bagneris realized that there was a way to put New Orleans on the stage. It would require a year of research, oral histories, and interviews with his grandmother, all between gigs playing voodoo priests in independent movies and producing and starring in Edward Albee plays.

For six months Bagneris and his troupe prepared for a one-night-only production of *One Mo' Time*, a musical he had written based on black vaudeville performers in New Orleans. Their limited-run show quickly turned into three nights a week at the Toulouse Theatre in the French Quarter, with JAMES CARROLL BOOKER III playing piano in the lobby before each show. Then, by chance, a New York producer saw it and promised to move it to the city. In October 1979 *One Mo' Time* went to the Village Gate in New York, where it played for three and a half years, spinning a host of internationally touring companies, including a royal command performance in Britain for Queen Elizabeth II. The show earned a Grammy nomination for Best Cast Album in 1980 and was nominated for Society of West End Theatres (SWET) awards for Outstanding Achievement in a Musical, Best Musical, and Best Actress in a Musical in 1982.

Through *One Mo' Time* Bagneris met the dance masters HONI COLES and Charles "Cookie" Cook; however, he cites Pepsi Bethel of the P.B. Authentic Dance Ensemble, who had worked in independent black films during 1930s and 1940s, as his dance mentor. After their meeting, Bethel choreographed every show Bagneris directed. "My interest was not in preserving traditional musical theater. It just so happens that my culture has a lot of music and dance in it." It was Bagneris's father who, after seeing *One Mo' Time*, encouraged Bagneris to work on Creole themes. "I'm always being asked what I am. Even ALLEN TOUSSAINT asked me once, 'Where do you come from—Mars?' No, Allen, I'm from the 7th Ward."

After the success of *One Mo' Time*, Bagneris continued stage explorations with *Staggerlee* in 1985; *Further Mo'*, the sequel to *One Mo' Time*, in 1990; and Cy Coleman's *The Life* on Broadway in 1998. In 1995 Bagneris received an Obie Award for *Jelly Roll!*, his portrait of jazz pioneer JELLY ROLL MORTON. Other notable performances include a 2004 revival of *Bubbling Brown Sugar* in which Bagneris starred with DIAHANN CARROLL. During this time he also worked in film, including *Pennies from Heaven* (1981), *Down by Law* (1986), and *Ray* (2004), the award-winning film adaptation of RAY CHARLES's life. In this film, Bagneris worked as choreographer and played the character Dancin' Al. Bagneris also played opposite OSSIE DAVIS in what was to be Davis's last film, the independent feature *Proud* (2004). *One Mo' Time* was revived on Broadway in 2002 and again in New Orleans in 2006.

Bagneris acted as the voice of numerous jazz figures on Public Radio International's *Riverwalk Jazz* program in 1993, recreating the lives of BUNK JOHNSON, DANNY BARKER, Jelly Roll Morton, and others. In the program for a special performance in the new auditorium at the Library of Congress, Bagneris was proclaimed "a master of the American vernacular."

In October 2005, just two months after the devastation caused by Hurricane Katrina, Bagneris returned to live in New Orleans, ultimately settling in the French Quarter. He said:

It was an emotional choice to return to New Orleans. The whole thing was about feeling needed, to assure that certain things about your cultural history would be preserved. Besides, my heart has always been in New Orleans. Once you're dipped in it, you're *it*.

When Bagneris remounted *One Mo' Time* in New Orleans in December 2006, the three female cast members returned nightly to FEMA trailers that stood next to their damaged homes. But they performed brilliantly, as if there had been no devastation at all. "At times you think that performance—theater—is such a light, unnecessary thing but then you realize that it's not dessert, that it's an integral part of the meal after all."

FURTHER READING

Unless otherwise indicated, quotations are drawn from an interview between the author and Vernel Bagneris, 2 March 2007.

Bagneris, Vernel, and Leo Touchet. *Rejoice When You Die: The New Orleans Jazz Funerals* (1998).

Hay, Samuel A. *African American Theatre* (1994).

Woll, Allen L. *Black Musical Theatre: From Coontown to "Dreamgirls"* (1989).

WENDI BERMAN

Bailey, Beryl Isadore Loftman (15 Jan. 1920–18 Apr. 1977), the first African American female linguist, early theorist in Pidgin and Creole linguistics, and educator, was born Beryl Isadore Loftman in Black River, Jamaica, West Indies. Her mother, Eliza Isadore Smith Loftman, was a teacher, and her father, James Henry Loftman, was an educator who became an inspector of schools. Because she was of the middle class, Beryl Loftman was expected to converse in Standard Jamaican English. Nevertheless, she valued the rhythm, music, and style of Creole: "Though I was forbidden to speak Jamaican Creole in the home during my childhood, my use of Standard Jamaican English was restricted to the earshot of my parents, teachers. … With my playmates, brothers and sisters, household help, and the country folk, I conversed always in Creole" (Bailey, "Creole Languages," 3).

Loftman was the eldest of six children, and she and her siblings, Lucille, Myrtle, Kenneth, Seymour, and Howard (who died at six months), grew up valuing education. As an honor student at Wolmer's Girls School, in Kingston, Jamaica, Loftman continued her forays into Creole, prompting one of her teachers to question whether she "intended to go through life talking mathematics" (Bailey, *Jamaican Creole Syntax*, xiii). Loftman soon endeavored to become bi-dialectal, embracing Metropolitan English as a necessity for upward mobility, one of the factors that resulted in her placing first in Jamaica, with near-perfect scores, on both her junior and senior Cambridge examinations. These tests were sent from Great Britain to Jamaica, which was a British colony at the time, and their passage was required to complete one's education.

After completing Wolmer's with distinction in 1942, Loftman was qualified to accept teaching positions. (Wolmer's was the equivalent of an American community college, and provided the education needed to become a teacher in Jamaica.) Immediately she accepted an appointment to teach English composition and literature at the Bethlehem Training College in Malvern, Jamaica, a women's school operated by the Moravian Church. In 1946 she left Wolmer's to become an English teacher at Ardenne High School in Kingston, Jamaica. As a teacher, she became more aware of the complications her students faced attempting to maintain Jamaican Creole (their home language), while simultaneously mastering Metropolitan English; these issues prompted her interest in linguistics (Bailey, *Jamaican Creole Syntax*, xiii).

Loftman moved to New York City in 1948 and accepted a position as a secretary. That same year, she enrolled in the Columbia University School of General Studies, completing a bachelor's degree in History in February 1952, graduating summa cum laude. She then enrolled in the Graduate School of Arts and Sciences to begin her master's in linguistics, encouraged by Allen Walker Read, an American etymologist, lexicographer, and professor of linguistics at Columbia. She was also influenced by André Martinet, a French linguist who taught at Columbia from 1947 to 1955. Martinet suggested that she consider researching a comparative analysis of creoles for her master's thesis.

On 20 January 1952 Loftman married Neville Huntley Bailey, also of Jamaica, and had two daughters, Stephanie Abiodoun Bailey and Jennifer Ayaba Bailey. Neville Bailey, finding life in New York unfulfilling, returned to Jamaica to live in 1965. In December 1953 Beryl Bailey completed her master's degree in Linguistics, with the thesis "Creole Languages of the Caribbean Area: A Comparison of the Grammar of Jamaican Creole with Those of the Creole Languages of Haiti, the Antilles, the Guianas, the Virgin Islands, and the Dutch West Indies." Her work represented a breakthrough in Creole studies, as Bailey was the first to maintain with strong evidence the notion of "sister Creoles." First, Bailey maintained that the Caribbean Creoles she analyzed in her thesis were genetically related, having as their African roots the Niger-Congo languages. Second, she classified them as having been lexified by (having gained the vocabularies of) either Germanic languages, principally English and Dutch, or Romance languages, principally French and Spanish. Third, Bailey advocated abandoning the term "Creole," utilizing instead "Afro-European languages" to describe those languages comprising the features of both African and Indo-European languages.

Although linguists have not embraced Bailey's "Afro-European" concept, many of the ideas she advanced have been accepted in the field. Because her thesis remains unpublished, linguists are generally unaware of the range of her ideas that are important to Pidgin and Creole linguistics. Over time, many of her ideas have become associated with the work of others. According to the Creolist William Stewart, "Creole Languages of the Caribbean Area" was Bailey's most significant contribution because of the range of its important theories, and its publication was overdue.

Devoutly religious, Bailey accepted employment with the American Bible Society as she continued her education toward the Ph.D. in Linguistics from Columbia University. Although she spent the remainder of her life in the United States, she returned to Jamaica to conduct fieldwork in 1956 on a grant from the Research Institute for the Study of Man. From 1960 to 1962 she returned on a Junior Research Fellowship provided by the University of the West Indies. On a second fellowship from the Research Institute for the Study of Man, she gathered data for the *Language Guide to Jamaica*, the first full-length grammar of Jamaican Creole, prepared for Peace Corps volunteers and published in 1962. During the summer of 1963, she returned to Jamaica for a third time, completing the fieldwork stage of her dissertation project. While in Jamaica, she assisted Frederic G. Cassidy and Robert B. LePage as they collected data for their *Dictionary of Jamaican English.* Bailey received a Founder's Fellowship from the American Association of University Women (from 1962 to 1963) and a Senior Graduate Fellowship from the American Council of Learned Societies (from 1963 to 1964) in support of her research. In May 1964 Bailey completed her Ph.D., with the dissertation "Jamaican Creole Syntax: A Transformational Approach."

Among Bailey's major assets was her ability to communicate effectively across social class lines and the advantage of having native-speaker competency. Her most recognized contribution is her dissertation, published by Cambridge University Press in 1966. It was the first full-length description of the syntax of a Creole language and the first study to utilize the generative grammatical format outlined by the linguist Noam Chomsky in his 1957 book *Syntactic Structures.* Bailey became an assistant professor in the linguistics and behavioral program of Yeshiva University, New York, teaching there from 1964 to 1968. In 1966 she prepared a second book, *Jamaican Creole Language Course,* for the Peace Corps. After four years at Yeshiva she joined the linguistics program at Hunter College in 1968. When black studies became a university discipline, Hunter College initiated a department of black and Puerto Rican studies, selecting Bailey as the founding chair. She served in this position until 1977, when she contracted lung cancer; she died a few months later in New York City, at the age of fifty-seven.

During her brief career, Bailey published three books and twelve articles focusing on three issues: the structure of Creole languages spoken by African people in the Caribbean and the United States, second-language learning, and the development of processes for teaching "Metropolitan" English to speakers of Creole languages. Six of her articles focused on Black English as she connected the Caribbean Creoles and Black English to their African-language sources. Bailey emphasized through her research that Creoles and Black English were correct and independent linguistic systems and not "mistakes" within English. During the final decade of her career, Bailey also served as a consultant to the Department of Health, Education, and Welfare; Brooklyn College; the Ford Foundation; the American Bible Society; and the National Council of Churches.

At the end of her life, Bailey was dismayed that many citizens from her homeland opposed the promotion of the systematic analysis of Jamaican Creole. Likewise, many in the United States opposed the systematic analysis of Black English. She was a "foremother" whose research laid the groundwork for the expanded interest in both specialties after her death. Bailey continues to be regarded as one of the significant voices in developing both the theory and practice that has brought Pidgin and Creole studies and Black English/Ebonics studies to the center of linguist interest. In 1991 Marcyliena Morgan, a linguistic anthropologist at Stanford University, organized a panel called Racism, Linguistics, and Language in African America: Papers in Honor of Beryl Loftman Bailey, at the annual conference of the American Anthropological Association in Chicago.

FURTHER READING
Bailey, Beryl Loftman. "Creole Languages of the Caribbean Area," master's thesis, Columbia University (1953).
Bailey, Beryl Loftman. *Jamaican Creole Syntax: A Transformational Approach* (1966).
Holm, John. "Focus on Creolists (3): Beryl Loftman Bailey," *Carrier Pidgin* 10:3 (Sept. 1982).
Wade-Lewis, Margaret. "Beryl Bailey," in *African American Women: A Biographical Dictionary*, ed. Dorothy C. Salem (1993).
Wade-Lewis, Margaret. "Beryl Loftman Bailey: Africanist Woman Linguist in New York State," *Afro-Americans in New York Life and History* 17:1 (Spring, 1993).
Wade-Lewis, Margaret. "Beryl Bailey," in *Lexicon Grammaticorum: Who's Who in the History of World Linguistics*, ed. Harro Stammerjohann (1996).
Obituary: *New York Times*, 21 Apr. 1977.

MARGARET WADE-LEWIS

Bailey, Buster (19 July 1902–12 Apr. 1967), jazz clarinetist and saxophonist, was born William C. Bailey in Memphis, Tennessee. Nothing is known of his parents. He attended the Clay Street School in Memphis, where he began studying clarinet at age thirteen. In 1917 he turned professional after joining the touring band of the famed blues composer W. C. HANDY, and it was during a trip to New Orleans with Handy that he first heard authentic jazz. In early 1919 he left Handy to move to Chicago, where he studied with Franz Schoepp, first clarinetist with the Chicago Symphony, and worked in Erskine Tate's Vendome Theatre Orchestra and doubled in FREDDIE KEPPARDS's small jazz band at the Lorraine Gardens. In late 1923 or early 1924 Bailey replaced JOHNNY DODDS in KING OLIVER's Creole Jazz Band

Buster Bailey, with John Kirby (left) at the Brown Derby in Washington, D.C., c. May 1946. (© William P. Gottlieb; www. jazzphotos.com.)

for an extensive tour that concluded with its return to the Lincoln Gardens in June 1924. In August 1922, while working with CARROLL DICKERSON at the Sunset Cafe, Bailey first met LOUIS ARMSTRONG, who had just come up from New Orleans to join the Oliver band. Following Armstrong by one week, on 6 October 1924 Bailey left Oliver and joined Armstrong in the FLETCHER HENDERSON Orchestra at New York's prestigious Roseland Ballroom. Bailey and Armstrong both made their first records with Henderson the next day, and on or about 16 October they backed up the blues singer MA RAINEY with a small contingent of Henderson men.

Bailey also recorded as a freelancer from the mid-1920s on; his most enduring association was with CLARENCE WILLIAMS's studio groups sporadically from 1925 to 1937. One of the most active jazz clarinetists of his time, Bailey appeared on hundreds of records throughout the prewar years as an accompanist to blues and vaudeville singers such as BESSIE SMITH, SIPPIE WALLACE, Maggie Jones, TRIXIE SMITH, ALBERTA HUNTER, EVA TAYLOR, and Cool Grant as well as to jazz singers such as BILLIE HOLIDAY, Mildred Bailey, MAXINE SULLIVAN, UNA MAE CARLISLE, Jerry Kruger, Midge Williams, and Teddy Grace.

Although working with Henderson enabled Bailey to play with the best jazzmen of the day, including the trumpeters JOE SMITH and Tommy Ladnier, the trombonists Charlie Green and Jimmy Harrison, and the tenor saxophonist COLEMAN HAWKINS, Bailey increasingly took time off for engagements with other bands. In April 1929 he left Henderson, and in early May he embarked on a European tour with the singer and band leader NOBLE SISSLE. After Bailey returned to the United States in late 1929, he worked in the bands of Edgar Hayes and Dave Nelson, rejoined Sissle for two years starting in 1931, and then returned to the Henderson fold in January 1934, leaving once more in November to join the Mills Blue Rhythm Band. Bailey stayed with that organization from December 1934 to October 1935, at which time he went back to Henderson and remained until February 1937, when he left permanently to begin a long and fruitful association with the former Henderson bassist JOHN KIRBY in Kirby's newly formed swing sextet. Unquestionably because of his formal training, Bailey had developed a fluent clarinet technique early in his career. Indeed, had it not been for the racial temperament of the times, he might very well have gone on to perform in symphony orchestras. As he said many years later in an interview reprinted in *Hear Me Talkin' to Ya*:

> One thing I'm happy to see is the integration that's been happening among musicians. … Years ago, if it had been like this when I came up I would be able to play with some symphony orchestra. I would have had more of an incentive to study because there would have been more of a prospect of my making a living the way I wanted to. Sure, we played concerts and overtures and numbers like that in the theatres, but when I started you couldn't even think, if you were a Negro, of making symphony orchestras.

On the evidence of his early jazz recordings, Bailey displayed a commendable technical assurance but lacked the passion and improvisatory skills of the foremost New Orleans clarinetists—SIDNEY BECHET, JOHNNY DODDS, and Jimmie Noone. He progressed rapidly, however, and his best performances of this early period are on the Henderson records of the late 1920s and mid-1930s. Bailey also appeared on scores of records with other bands—most notably the Red Onion Jazz Babies and the bands of Erskine Tate and Dave Nelson—and with a number of small groups in sessions organized by the prolific Clarence Williams. As busy as he was in the 1930s, Bailey always found time to participate in the small-band swing sessions that were common. Thus much of his characteristic work in those years can be found on the records of HENRY "RED" ALLEN, LIL ARMSTRONG, LEON "CHU" BERRY, ROY ELDRIDGE, LIONEL HAMPTON, Wingy Manone, Red Norvo, STUFF SMITH, WILLIE "THE LION" SMITH, and a host of others, including those under his own leadership.

It was with the John Kirby band, though, that Bailey finally found his most symbiotic musical setting. Except for Benny Goodman, perhaps no other jazz clarinetist could have executed the technically demanding parts written by Kirby and his trumpeter CHARLIE SHAVERS. The unique style of this group was well suited to Bailey's particular skills as a reader, technician, and the possessor of a legitimately trained tone. Alternating swing versions of operatic arias and familiar classical themes with exotic original compositions and jazz standards, the Kirby sextet enjoyed successful engagements at many venues in New York, Chicago, and Los Angeles, as well as recording extensively for both commercial labels and for the Lang-Worth Radio Transcription Service. For the first time in his long career, the peripatetic, bustling nature of Bailey's earlier years with the big bands was now a thing of the past. Bailey remained a regular member of the Kirby band from 1937 through 1944 and occasionally appeared with the group for brief engagements in 1945 and 1946.

Buster Bailey spent most of his later years playing in and around New York. He worked with WILBUR DE PARIS from September 1947 to April 1949, and after a brief try at leading his own quartet he went with the trumpeter Red Allen in 1950 and with the trombonist "Big Chief" Russell Moore in 1952. A rare opportunity to perform theater music again presented itself in late 1953, when he joined the pit orchestra of *Porgy and Bess*. In 1954 he rejoined Allen for a job at the Metropole, but during this period he also started receiving calls for symphony rehearsals and concerts. Jazz festivals were becoming frequent venues in the late 1950s and early 1960s, and Bailey performed at several of them, often in the company of Allen. In 1961 he participated in the film *Splendor in the Grass* and began working with Wild Bill Davison (1961–1963) and then with Red Richards's Saints and Sinners (1963–1964). Bailey joined Louis Armstrong's All Stars in July 1965 and was still with them at the time of his death in Brooklyn.

From the 1940s on, Bailey's most representative recordings were made with Red Allen, Armstrong, the Capitol Jazzmen, BUCK CLAYTON, Wild Bill Davison, Bobby Donaldson, Pee Wee Erwin, Leonard Gaskin, Coleman Hawkins, CLAUDE HOPKINS, Jonah Jones, Billy Kyle, Red Richards, REX STEWART, JOE THOMAS, and TRUMMY YOUNG. Also significant is the one album he made under his own name, *All About Memphis* (1958).

FURTHER READING
Bruyninckx, Walter. *Swing Discography, 1920–1988* (12 vols., 1985–1989).
Bruyninckx, Walter. *Traditional Jazz Discography, 1897–1988* (6 vols., 1985–1989).
Charters, Samuel B., and Leonard Kunstadt. *Jazz: A History of the New York Scene* (1962).
Dance, Stanley. *The World of Swing* (1974).
Rust, Brian. *Jazz Records, 1897–1942* (1982).
Schuller, Gunther. *Early Jazz* (1968).
Schuller, Gunther. *The Swing Era* (1989).
Shapiro, Nat, and Nat Hentoff, eds. *Hear Me Talkin' to Ya: The Story of Jazz by the Men Who Made It* (1955).
This entry is taken from the *American National Biography* and is published here with the permission of the American Council of Learned Societies.

JACK SOHMER

Bailey, DeFord (14 Dec. 1899–2 July 1982), musician, was born in Bellwood, Smith County, Tennessee, the son of John Henry Bailey and Mary Reedy, farmers. Bailey grew up in the rolling hills east of Nashville and as a child listened to what he later called the "black hillbilly music" played by his family. His grandfather Lewis Bailey was a skilled fiddler who won numerous local championships, and a family string band often appeared at local fairs and dances. DeFord's fascination with the harmonica, an instrument that was especially popular in Middle Tennessee, resulted from a childhood illness. When he was three he was stricken with polio and was bedridden for several years; to amuse himself he practiced the harmonica. Lying in bed and listening to the distant sound of trains, hunting dogs, and barnyard animals, DeFord became adept at working imitations of these into his playing, creating unorthodox "bent" notes and mouthing patterns into what would become a unique musical style. DeFord survived his illness, but it left him stunted and frail.

By 1918 Bailey had moved to Nashville, where he worked at a variety of jobs for wealthy white families. In his spare time he went to local theaters, where for the first time he heard professional entertainers, including the blues singers BESSIE SMITH and MA RAINEY. He soon adapted their songs to his harmonica, and in 1925 he entered a harmonica contest broadcast over a local radio station, WDAD. He won first place, embarrassing the management and forcing them to award two prizes, one for "each race." A short time later he met Humphrey Bate, a white harmonica player who was leading a string band that played for a large new Nashville radio station, WSM. Impressed with Bailey's playing, Bate recommended him to the station manager, George D. Hay, who invited Bailey to appear on the new Saturday night *Barn Dance* (later called the *Grand Ole Opry*). In June 1926 Bailey made his first documented appearance on the show.

Bailey, playing his solo nonchromatic harmonica, quickly became one of the most popular stars on the show. Radio fans, many of whom were unaware that Bailey was black, wrote hundreds of letters requesting his specialties, such as "The Fox Chase" and "Pan American Blues," in which he imitated a train. Hay made big plans for Bailey and told him that he was "nothing but a gold mine walking around on earth." Hay set up dates with several record companies, and Bailey did sides for Columbia (1927), Brunswick (1927), and Victor (1928). Surprisingly, the records did not sell well, and some were never even released to the public. The surviving eleven sides preserve the only documentation of Bailey playing in his prime.

Bailey became a familiar figure around Nashville, riding a custom-designed bicycle back and forth to work. In 1929 he married Ida Lee Jones; they had three children.

In 1932 the Grand Ole Opry started an Artists Service Bureau to help its radio entertainers set up tours and personal appearances. Bailey overcame his nervousness about traveling and went on tours with such Opry stars as the Delmore Brothers, the Fruit Jar Drinkers, Uncle Dave Macon, Robert Lunn, and later Bill Monroe and Roy Acuff. Though he continued to be a favorite on live shows—he had to play his harmonica through a big megaphone to be heard over primitive public address systems—Bailey often had trouble finding lodging in the segregated South. Hotels that welcomed the other Opry musicians often refused Bailey a room, forcing him to seek accommodation in the private homes of local blacks.

At about the time that the Opry started winning a national audience on network radio, Bailey left the show. In 1941 he was fired; the official reason was that he refused to learn any new tunes. In truth it was a complex dispute involving a struggle between two song-publishing organizations, ASCAP and BMI. In the 1920s Bailey had allowed his producer to publish and copyright his songs with ASCAP, and in 1941 ASCAP songs were banned from the airwaves as a result of a licensing disagreement between ASCAP and the major radio networks. Bailey was told that he could not play his old favorites such as "John Henry" and "Fox Chase," songs with which he had made his reputation. Confused, bitter, and angered by the new styles of music that he heard on the show, Bailey did not fight the firing, instead dropping entirely out of music. During this time he operated a shoeshine parlor in downtown Nashville, occasionally playing for friends but refusing to talk to journalists or historians about his early days.

By the late 1960s a new generation of fans began to see Bailey as a folk music hero. One of them, the Vanderbilt student Dick Hulan, coaxed Bailey into playing at local coffeehouses and festivals. He refused offers to record again, however, and turned down chances to go to the Newport Folk Festival and to appear in films like Burt Reynolds's *W. W. and the Dixie Dancekings* (1975). In 1974 another young friend, David Morton, who worked with the Nashville Housing Authority, talked Bailey into returning to the Opry stage for an "Old Timers' Reunion." He returned to the Opry several other times before his death in Nashville.

Fans of country and folk music speak of Bailey as the genre's finest harmonica virtuoso. His songs are part of the standard repertoire, serving as an important link between rural nineteenth-century folk music and the more commercial music of the twentieth century. His struggle as the first black star in the nearly all-white world of country music has won the respect of generations.

FURTHER READING

Morton, David, and Charles Wolfe. *DeFord Bailey: A Black Star in Early Country Music* (1991).

Wolfe, Charles. *Grand Ole Opry: The Early Years* (1975).

This entry is taken from the *American National Biography* and is published here with the permission of the American Council of Learned Societies.

CHARLES K. WOLFE

Bailey, Herman "Kofi" (1931–1981), graphic artist, painter, printmaker, and political activist, was born in Chicago in 1931. An only child, he attended Chicago public schools, moving briefly to Washington, D.C., to study at Howard University with ALAIN LEROY LOCKE, STERLING ALLEN BROWN, and JAMES AMOS PORTER. After one year he then enrolled at Alabama State College (later Alabama State University) to study under the sculptor, painter, and printmaker Hayward Louis Oubre, and he received a bachelor of arts degree. Bailey continued study at the University of Southern California (USC) as a student of CHARLES WHITE and the Hungarian-born Francis de Erdely. He earned the bachelor of fine arts degree in 1958 and the master of fine arts degree in 1960. At USC he worked as a graduate assistant for two years, introducing the students MEL EDWARDS and CALVIN BURNETT to the work of JOHN BIGGERS and other established African American graphic artists. Major influences on Bailey's career were Charles White, JACOB ARMSTEAD LAWRENCE, El Greco, Goya, and the Mexican muralists.

Bailey was mentored by W. E. B. DU BOIS, who shared his Pan-African ideology and penchant for experiencing the people and societies of the continent of Africa firsthand. Before embarking on numerous international travels, Bailey taught at Florida Agricultural and Mechanical University and Clark College (renamed Clark Atlanta University). He then continued studying and working in France, Switzerland, Mexico, Guyana, Nigeria, and finally Ghana, where he resided from 1962 to 1966. He was the official artist for the nation of Ghana before serving three years as the chair of the art department at the Kwame Nkrumah Ideological Institute, and he left the country when Nkrumah, the first prime minister and later president, was deposed.

Returning to Atlanta in 1967 as an artist-in-residence at Spelman College, Bailey worked with the MARTIN LUTHER KING JR.'s Poor People's Campaign, designing the poster that became the symbol of the 1968 March on Washington, as well as creating the Southern Christian Leadership Conference (SCLC) Hunger Poster. Convinced that representational art and noble depiction of "true Black life" were the best approaches to serving the African masses worldwide, Bailey was a prolific producer of drawings, paintings, and prints of portraits and figure-based works ranging from famous faces to cultural narratives. Epitomizing his sociopolitical consciousness, the imagery frequently contained a single figure that through personal or character reference emerged as a statement of the struggle against adversity, while also being an image of pride and solidarity. While he explored numerous materials—including inks, charcoal, graphite, pastels, oils, acrylics, watercolor, and mixed media—conté crayon became his signature drafting material, and lithography was his most common printmaking type.

Bailey's work has been shown in exhibitions at the Los Angeles County Museum of Art, the University of Southern California, the University of Ghana, the Ghana Institute of Art and Culture, Spelman College, the University of Delaware, Montana State University, Boston's National Center of Afro-American Artists, and Clark Atlanta University; and he has exhibited in Mexico, England, Canada, Brazil, Japan, Ivory Coast, Benin, Zaire, Uganda, and Nigeria. His work is in the permanent collections of the Paul R. Jones Collection at the University of Delaware, Spelman College Museum of Fine Art, and Clark Atlanta University Art Galleries, and in public and private collections in Algeria, Congo, Ghana, Nigeria, Guinea, Kenya, Tanzania, Uganda, Ivory Coast, France, England, Poland, Puerto Rico, Chile, Spain, Italy, Indonesia, and Hungary, as well as throughout the United States.

FURTHER READING
Lewis, Samella Saunders. *African American Art and Artists* (2003).

AMALIA K. AMAKI

Bailey, John B. (fl. 1840s), skilled daguerrean, practiced photography in Massachusetts and in White Sulphur Springs, West Virginia. Little is known about his early life, other than that he was from Boston, Massachusetts, and was most likely a freeman. He was a pioneer of the daguerreotype. The daguerreotype process is exceedingly laborious and includes polishing the daguerreotype plate, buffing it, coating it with iodine and bromine, exposing the plate in the camera, positioning both the subject and the camera, and then developing it, exposing it to mercury, removing the coating, gilding the image, and then coloring the image as necessary. This process requires highly skilled artists to get a clean image.

While little is known about Bailey, his importance stems from his role in teaching JAMES PRESLEY BALL the art of daguerreotyping in the 1840s. Bailey most likely taught Ball in White Sulphur Springs, West Virginia. Ball was a renowned abolitionist who published pamphlets and held photo exhibitions in order to show the misery of slavery. Ball later became fairly famous and much of his work is known. In 1847, Bailey's most famous work, "Unidentified woman seated in chair, with hand resting on table," was created. This work can be found in the Library of Congress Daguerreotype Collection. Bailey is listed as a lieutenant in the Massachusetts guards in August 1855.

Bailey's importance is fairly subjective. As an African American daguerrean he was able to begin a legacy of African American photography that continues today. He was able to overcome slavery, persecution, and discrimination to become an independent businessman. By his presence alone, he was able to fight against racism and aid the abolitionists. He was one of the first African American artist–photographers, and he set a precedent for all that followed him. John B. Bailey created the foundation for African American art and photography by taking advantage of a new technology and the growing demand for it. The use of the daguerreotype allowed for both his artistic expression and skill to be used.

FURTHER READING

Library of Congress has a daguerreotype by John B. Bailey, "Unidentified woman seated in chair, with hand resting on table," available at http://hdl.loc. gov/loc.pnp/cph.3g10577.

Craig, John S. http://www.daguerreotype.com/b_table. htm#E-Mail.

Cuthbert, John A. *Early Art and Artists in West Virginia: An Introduction and Biographical Directory* (2000).

Willis, Deborah, ed. *J.P. Ball: Daguerrean and Studio Photographer* (1993).

Willis–Thomas, Deborah. *Black Photographers, 1840–1940: An Illustrated Bio-Bibliography* (1985).

Willis, Deborah. *Reflections in Black: A History of Black Photographers 1840 to the Present* (2000).

KIMBERLY L. MALINOWSKI

Bailey, Pearl (29 Mar. 1918–17 Aug. 1990), actress, singer, and entertainer, was born Pearl Mae Bailey in Newport News, Virginia, the daughter of the Reverend Joseph James Bailey and Ella Mae (maiden name unknown). Her brother, Bill Bailey, was at one time a well-known tap dancer.

While still in high school, Bailey launched her show business career in Philadelphia, where her mother had relocated the family after separating from Reverend Bailey. In 1933, at age fifteen, she won the first of three amateur talent contests, with a song-and-dance routine at the Pearl Theatre in Philadelphia, which awarded her a five dollar prize. In a second contest at the Jungle Inn in Washington, D.C., she received a twelve dollar prize for a buck-and-wing dancing act. After winning a third contest at the famed Apollo Theater in Harlem, she began performing professionally— first as a specialty dancer or chorus girl with several small bands, including Noble Sissle's band, on the vaudeville circuits in Pennsylvania, Maryland, and Washington during the 1930s, then as a vocalist with COOTIE WILLIAMS and COUNT BASIE at such smart New York clubs as La Vie en Rose and the Blue Angel, and on the World War II USO circuit, during the 1940s.

Bailey made her Broadway debut as a saloon barmaid named Butterfly in the black-authored musical *St. Louis Woman*, which opened at the Martin Beck Theatre, 30 March 1946, and ran for 113 performances. Although the show was only modestly successful, she was praised for her singing of two hit numbers, "Legalize My Name" and "(It's) A Woman's Prerogative (to Change Her Mind)." For her performance, she won a Donaldson Award as the best Broadway newcomer. After several failed marriages, one to comedian SLAPPY WHITE, Bailey married the legendary white jazz drummer Louis Bellson Jr., in 1952; they adopted two children. Their marriage was reportedly a happy one. In later years, she frequently sang with her husband's band, and at one time toured with CAB CALLOWAY and his band.

After appearing in supporting roles in two predominantly white shows in 1950–1951, Bailey's first Broadway starring vehicle was *House of Flowers* (1954), a Caribbean-inspired musical. Bailey played the part of Mme. Fleur, a resourceful bordello madam, whose house of prostitution in the French West Indies is facing hard times, forcing her to resort to desperate measures to save it. The show opened at the Alvin Theatre, 30 December 1954, and had a run of 165 performances. Despite what the *New York Times* (30 Dec. 1954) called "feeble material," she was credited with "an amusing style" and the ability to "[throw] away songs with smart hauteur."

Bailey's most important Broadway role was as the irrepressible Dolly Levi (a marriage broker who arranges a lucrative marriage for herself) in the all-black version of *Hello, Dolly!*, which opened at the St. James Theatre in November 1967 for a long run, sharing the stage with the original

1964 Carol Channing version. The black version provided tangible evidence that roles originally created by white actors could be redefined and given new vitality from the perspective of the African American experience. Lyndon Johnson, who had used the show's title song as his campaign theme song in 1964, changing the words to "Hello, Lyndon!," saw the show when it came to Washington and was invited, along with his wife, Lady Bird, to join Bailey onstage for a rousing finale. For her performance, Bailey won a special Tony Award in 1968.

Bailey's most important film roles included *Carmen Jones* (1954), as one of Carmen's friends; *St. Louis Blues* (1958), as the composer W. C. HANDY's Aunt Hagar; *Porgy and Bess* (1959), as Maria, the cookshop woman; *All the Fine Young Cannibals* (1960), as a boozing, over-the-hill blues singer; and *Norman ... Is That You?* (1976), opposite the comedian REDD FOXX, as estranged parents of a gay son. Her voice was also used for Big Mama, the owl, in the Disney animated film *The Fox and the Hound* (1981).

A frequent performer and guest on television talk shows beginning in the 1950s, Bailey also hosted her own variety series on ABC, *The Pearl Bailey Show* (Jan.–May 1971), for which her husband directed the orchestra while she entertained an assortment of celebrity guests. She also appeared on television in "An Evening with Pearl" (1975) and in a remake of *The Member of the Wedding* (1982), in the role of Berenice. Bailey released numerous albums and was also the author of several books, including two autobiographies, *The Raw Pearl* (1968) and *Talking to Myself* (1971), and *Pearl's Kitchen* (1973), a cookbook.

In 1975 Bailey was appointed as a U.S. delegate to the United Nations. Other honors and awards included a citation from the New York City mayor John V. Lindsay; *Cue* magazine entertainer of the year (1969); the First Order in Arts and Sciences from the Egyptian president Anwar Sadat; the Screen Actors Guild Award for outstanding achievement in fostering the finest ideals of the acting profession; and an honorary Doctor of Humane Letters from Georgetown University (1977). She later earned a degree in theology from Georgetown.

During the later years of her life, Bailey was hospitalized several times for a heart ailment. She also suffered from an arthritic knee, which was replaced with an artificial one just prior to her death. She collapsed, apparently from a heart attack, at the Philadelphia hotel where she was staying (her home was in Havasu, Arizona); she died soon after at Thomas Jefferson University Hospital in Philadelphia.

Bailey was best known for her lazy, comical, half-singing, half-chatting style, expressive hands, tired feet, and folksy, congenial philosophy of life, which endeared her to audiences both black and white. The *New York Times* obituary (18 Aug. 1990) called her "a trouper in the old theatrical sense," who had "enraptured theater and nightclub audiences for a quarter-century by the languorous sexuality of her throaty voice as well as by the directness of her personality." At her funeral, Cab Calloway, who had starred with her in *Hello, Dolly!*, said that "Pearl was love, pure and simple love"; and her husband called her "a person of love," who believed that "show business" meant to "show love."

FURTHER READING

Bailey, Pearl. *The Raw Pearl* (1968).

Bailey, Pearl. *Talking to Myself* (1971).

Bogle, Donald. *Blacks in American Films and Television: An Illustrated Encyclopedia* (1988).

Bogle, Donald. *Brown Sugar: Eighty Years of America's Black Female Superstars* (1980).

Peterson, Bernard L., Jr. *A Century of Musicals in Black and White: An Encyclopedia of Musical Stage Works by, about, or Involving African Americans* (1993).

Obituaries: *New York Times*, 18, 24, and 25 Aug. 1990.

This entry is taken from the *American National Biography* and is published here with the permission of the American Council of Learned Societies.

BERNARD L. PETERSON

Bailey, Walter T. (11 Jan. 1882–Feb. 1941), architect, was born Walter Thomas Bailey in Kewanee, Illinois, to Emanuel Bailey and Lucy Reynolds. After attending Kewanee High School, Walter enrolled at the University of Illinois at Urbana-Champaign in 1900. There he studied in the architecture program, which was then part of the College of Engineering. The program at Illinois differed from those at most other architecture schools in the country: many schools followed in the tradition of the École des Beaux-Arts, emphasizing classical modes and principles of architecture, but the program at Illinois was influenced largely by German polytechnic methods of teaching. At Illinois, Bailey received an extensive education in the science of construction and in the history of architecture. Construction courses gave students both theoretical and practical training, while courses in the history of architecture taught them periods and styles such as Egyptian and Islamic, as well as classical.

As a student Bailey was active in various student groups on campus, including the Architects Club and the Twentieth Century Club. In October 1903 Bailey married Josephine L. McCurdy of Champaign, Illinois. The following spring he received a B.S. in Architecture, becoming the first African American to graduate from the architecture program at the University of Illinois and the first registered African American architect in the state of Illinois.

After graduating Bailey worked briefly as a draftsman for Henry Eckland, an architect in Kewanee, Illinois. In February 1904 Bailey moved back to Champaign to work as a draftsman in the firm of Spencer & Temple. The firm's principals, Nelson Strong Spencer and Harry R. Temple, were graduates of the architecture program at the University of Illinois. Bailey's obituary from the *Urbana Courier* states that Bailey assisted in the planning of the Colonel Wolfe School in Champaign, designed by Spencer & Temple and built in 1905. On 8 March 1905 Bailey's daughter Edyth Hazel was born. His second child, Alberta Josephine Bailey, was born on 16 August 1913. In September 1905 Bailey left Spencer & Temple to take on the position as head of the department of architecture at the Tuskegee Institute in Alabama.

From 1905 to 1914 Bailey oversaw the architecture program at Tuskegee while also undertaking his first independent commissions. Among his responsibilities were supervising the planning, design, and construction of all new buildings on campus and taking charge of the repairing and remodeling of older structures. During his tenure he designed White Hall, a girls' dormitory on campus, in 1908. He also designed two churches in nearby Montgomery, Alabama: St. John's African Methodist Episcopal Church in 1910 and the Old Ship African Methodist Episcopal Zion Church in 1912. Also in 1910 Bailey was awarded an honorary master's degree in architecture from the University of Illinois. He served as head of the department of architecture at Tuskegee until 1914, when he left to practice architecture full-time.

Bailey and his family moved from Tuskegee to Memphis, Tennessee, where he set up his own office and from which he undertook some of his largest and most important commissions. In 1923–1924 he designed the Fraternal Savings Bank and Trust Company building located on Beale Street, an affluent African American area of Memphis. Upon its completion Bailey moved his office to the building. In Little Rock, Arkansas, he designed the Mosaic State Temple building in 1922 and the Pythian Theater building in 1922–1923. In Hot Springs, Arkansas, a popular resort town, he designed the Pythian Bathhouse and Sanitarium in 1922–1923 and the Woodmen of the Union Bathhouse in 1924. In Nashville, Tennessee, he designed the Tennessee State Pythian building in 1924–1925.

In 1926 Bailey began plans for the National Pythian Temple to be located in Chicago, Illinois. Shortly before the National Pythian Temple was completed in 1928, Bailey moved his practice to Chicago, where he remained for the rest of his life. In Chicago, Bailey also designed an expansion of the First Church of Deliverance in 1939 and was hired by the Chicago Housing Authority to work as one of the architects on the Ida B. Wells Housing Project, completed in 1941. Early that year Bailey completed plans for the rebuilding of the interior of the Olivet Baptist Church. In February 1941 Bailey died as a result of complications developed from pneumonia.

Throughout his career Bailey designed buildings for an African American clientele. The Pythian Theater, Pythian Bathhouse and Sanitarium, Tennessee State Pythian building, and the National Pythian Temple were all structures commissioned by the Colored Knights of Pythias, a large, national African American fraternal order that grew to national prominence in the black community in the early twentieth-century. The buildings that they commissioned served as places of African American social retreat or business. Additionally, the First Church of Deliverance and the Olivet Baptist Church were situated in an affluent African American part of Chicago and were both strong institutions of faith and community. These buildings, among others, exist as examples of architecture by African Americans for African Americans.

FURTHER READING

Portions of Bailey's correspondence are held by the Hot Springs National Park Administrative Archives, Hot Springs, Arkansas, and by the University of Illinois at Urbana-Champaign University Archives.

Taussig, Meredith, Timothy Barton, the Commission on Chicago Landmarks, and the Chicago Department of Planning and Development. *First Church of Deliverance, 4315 S. Wabash Avenue: Preliminary Staff Summary of Information* (1994).

Wilson, Dreck Spurlock, ed. *African-American Architects: A Biographical Dictionary, 1865–1945* (2004).

Obituary: *Urbana Courier*, 3 Feb. 1941.

MIKAEL D. KRIZ

Baker, Anita (26 Jan. 1958–), singer and performer, was born in Toledo, Ohio, but relocated with her family at an early age to Detroit, Michigan, where she was raised and attended school. Unfortunately, reliable details concerning her early life are difficult to come by, and Baker herself has sometimes offered contradictory information (even the exact date of her birth is subject to some debate). What is known is that Baker's birth mother—only sixteen years old at the time—gave her up to a woman named Mary Lewis, who may or may not have been a blood relative but who later went on to become Baker's legal foster mother. After Lewis died when Baker was only thirteen, Baker was raised by an adoptive sister named Lois Landry. Growing up in a religious family, she sang in the church choir. Sometime later, her talent brought her to the attention of David Washington, whose rhythm and blues group Chapter 8 was a local favorite. Baker dropped out of high school to join the ensemble, which eventually landed a recording contract with Ariola Records. Chapter 8 had a pair of modest hits with their 1980 debut, but shortly thereafter Ariola went under and was bought by Arista Records, which was highly critical of Baker's singing voice and refused to offer Chapter 8 a contract.

Dispirited, Baker returned to Detroit, where she worked a number of odd jobs, including as a waitress and office receptionist. In 1982 she was contacted by a former executive and producer from the defunct Ariola, Otis Smith. Smith was forming his own label, Beverly Glenn, and he wanted to enlist Baker, promising he could turn her into a recording star. Baker, for her part, was dubious. For one thing, she recalled keenly the sting of her rejection at the hands of Arista. For another, she had finally landed a job with decent pay and good benefits. Smith promised to match her salary, however, and Baker at last agreed to sign a contract with the fledgling venture.

Baker's first album with Beverly Glenn, *The Songstress*, appeared in 1983. Coproduced by Smith himself, the album proved a small hit on the rhythm and blues charts, sold fairly well for an album from an unknown label, and (no doubt most importantly) brought Baker and her talent to the attention of the broader recording industry. Soon, however, her relationship with Beverly Glenn soured, and Baker left the label, singing with Elektra Records in 1985. For her second album, she enlisted a former Chapter 8 bandmate as producer and mixed contemporary rhythm and blues with gospel and jazz to produce what would become her signature sound. The album, *Rapture*, yielded numerous hits (including the Top-Ten "Sweet Love"), sold eight million copies, and brought Baker a pair of 1987 Grammy Awards, including one for Best Rhythm & Blues Song for "Sweet Love." The following year, 1988, Baker married an admirer, Walter Bridgforth, whom she'd met on one of her frequent trips to and from Detroit. The couple had two children but divorced in 2007.

Her next album, 1988's *Giving You the Best That I Got*, likewise became a hit, selling five million copies worldwide and yielding numerous hit singles. Bolstered by confidence and now a reliable hit-maker, Baker took a more active role in her next album, 1990's *Compositions*. Though Michael Powell remained producer, Baker oversaw the

Anita Baker performs during the 2009 Essence Music Festival at the Louisiana Superdome in New Orleans. (AP Images.)

album's production and wrote many of its songs. Compositions brought Baker her seventh Grammy Award. Exhausted from her touring and performing schedule and having suffered a pair of miscarriages, Baker went on professional hiatus. She did not reappear until 1994 with her album *Rhythm of Love* (this one produced without her long-time associate Powell). The record hit number three on the Billboard Top 200 and won Baker her eighth Grammy, this one for Best Female Rhythm and Blues Vocal Performance.

A dispute with Elektra led to her departure. She signed with Atlantic Records in 1996 but failed to produce an album and was released from her contract. Again on hiatus, Baker remained more or less out of the public eye until 2004, when she signed with the Blue Note label to record a pair of albums. *My Everything*, her first album in a decade, appeared that same year. The album went gold and landed in the Top 200 at number four. The next year, 2005, she recorded an album of Christmas songs.

FURTHER READING

Floyd, Samuel A., Jr. *The Power of Black Music: Interpreting Its History from Africa to the United States* (1995).

Southern, Eileen. *The Music of Black Americans: A History* (1997).

JASON PHILIP MILLER

Baker, Augusta Braxton (1 Apr. 1911–23 Feb. 1998), storyteller, librarian, and author, was born Augusta Braxton in Baltimore, Maryland, the only child of two educators, Winford J. and Mabel Braxton. Her father later became a wood craftsman, and her mother retired from formal teaching to raise her daughter. Baker skipped at least two grades in elementary school and might have skipped more—she explained later in an interview with Robert V. Williams—if her father hadn't insisted that she be educated among her peers. Baker's maternal grandmother, Augusta Fax Gough, was an integral part of Baker's childhood and found that the only means of quieting the young Baker was to entertain her through storytelling. These beloved experiences with storytelling would become the catalysts for a career in storytelling and would inspire Baker to write children's literature.

At age sixteen Baker was admitted to the University of Pittsburgh. She did well with the academic material, despite the death of her father during her freshman year, but struggled with personal relationships since she was much younger than many of her peers. Raised in segregated Baltimore, Baker had difficulty establishing and maintaining relationships with white students. She met and married her first husband, James Baker, a graduate student in social work at the University of Pittsburgh. He was a fellow of the Urban League and assigned to establish the Albany Interracial Council in New York. Baker transferred to the Albany State Teacher's College, first pursuing a degree in education and later in library sciences.

Her experiences in confronting racial boundaries began at Albany State Teacher's College, where during her admission interview Baker was informed that she would do her practicum not at the affiliated high school attended by the professors' children, but instead at a local black elementary school. Clearly, Baker thought, Albany State Teacher's College was hesitant to admit her. In response she wrote to the administrative body at the University of Pittsburgh about the situation. Her husband, James Baker, also informed his supervisor, Eleanor Roosevelt, Franklin Delano Roosevelt's wife, about the college's decision to place Baker at a black elementary school, as opposed to the prestigious high school. The wife of then New York governor, Mrs. Roosevelt was able to pressure Albany State Teacher's College to admit Baker on the same terms that they admitted all other students. In addition, the University of Pittsburgh wrote a letter on Baker's behalf, demanding that she be admitted and receive the same treatment as the college's white students.

After graduating in 1933 with BAs in both Education and Library Science, she applied for a position with the New York Public Library (NYPL) system. As the Depression still gripped the country and few jobs existed, Baker's husband discouraged her from taking a job that might deny support from families in greater need. He believed that his well-paying job with the Urban League afforded his family a decent lifestyle during the harsh economic times. So for the next three years Baker labored at home as a devoted wife and mother of her only son, James H. Baker III. In February 1937 she received a letter from Anne Carroll Moore, head of the Children's Division at NYPL. Moore offered Baker a position as a children's librarian at the Harlem branch.

At the time, libraries were the cultural hubs in their communities, hosting plays, literary events, and community gatherings, and serving as a safe harbor for young adults who wished to escape the rough streets of Harlem. Baker was working closely with ARTHUR ALFONSO SCHOMBURG to establish and maintain black materials that were housed on the third floor of the library (Schomburg Collection). During these times Baker became acquainted with a young JAMES BALDWIN, who naturally gravitated to this section of library. He was often found among the stacks of black literature and culture; Baker was immediately notified. She was considered the authority on children in this unique environment, and was, in fact, called several times a day to collect children from other sections of the library. Admiring Baldwin's interests in African American history and literature, she became an advocate on the child's behalf. Though Dr. Schomburg was fairly permissive, the administration discouraged children in those sections reserved for adults, particularly in areas housing research material. Nevertheless, from time to time Baldwin was permitted to peruse the collection.

In 1953 Baker began working for the NYPL in an administrative capacity. She became the first black administrator as storytelling specialist and assistant coordinator of Children's Services of the NYPL. That same year she advised and helped establish the Children's Library Service for the Trinidad Public Library. Within a few years she began to publish her first set of children's books. She also began to promote her philosophies about negative versus positive images of African Americans in children's literature to a number of children's authors and book publishers, expressing her concerns about the psychological impact of such literature and advocating for it to be removed from the children's section of public libraries. Soon the types of books Baker encouraged began to be published widely. In addition to adding to her own collection, she began to compile a bibliography titled *Books about Negro Life for Children*, still widely used in many library systems around the world. She also organized and established the JAMES WELDON JOHNSON Memorial Collection at the Countée Cullen Regional Branch of the NYPL. In 1961 she was promoted to coordinator of children's services for the entire NYPL system, where she became one of the first to incorporate audiovisual materials into general circulation. She became a consultant for the children's program *Sesame Street* and in 1971 began broadcasting a weekly series, *The World of Children's Literature*, for WNYC Radio. Later she taught a number of courses in storytelling and children's literature at Syracuse University. She retired from the NYPL in

1974 and lived in Queens, New York, with her second husband, Gordon Alexander.

After serving fifteen years as a visiting lecturer for the state and local levels of the public school systems in South Carolina and the university, Baker conceded and, in 1980, accepted an appointment as storyteller-in-residence at the University of South Carolina. It was the first position of its kind at any university. She served on various advisory boards at the University of South Carolina and other institutions in the state in order to serve students of historically black colleges and universities, South Carolina State University, and Bennett College. Baker's honors include the Parents Magazine Medal, the Constance Lindsay Skinner Award from the Women's National Book Association, and a Distinguished Services Award from the Association of Library Services to Children of the American Library Association.

FURTHER READING

Augusta Braxton Baker's papers are housed in South Caroliniana Library, University South Caroliniana Society Manuscripts Collections, University of South Carolina, Columbia, South Carolina.

"Augusta Baker," in *Notable Black American Women*, book 1 (1992).

Williams, Robert V. "Interview with: Augusta Baker (AB)," University of South Carolina, Columbia South Carolina (7 May 1989).

DAMARIS B. HILL

Baker, Bertram L. (10 Jan. 1898–8 Mar. 1985), first African American elected to political office in Brooklyn, New York, and a leader in the mid-twentieth century effort to integrate American tennis, was born on the Caribbean island of Nevis, then part of the British West Indies. His mother was Lillian de Grasse Baker, whose family had successful retail businesses on the island; his father was the Reverend Alfred B. Baker, a Wesleyan Methodist minister.

Tragedy struck in 1900 when Lillian Baker died of consumption. Bertram, an only child, would find comfort in the care of his maternal grandmother, Eliza de Grasse. In 1905 Baker's father left Nevis, accepting an offer to become founding pastor of the Ebenezer Wesleyan Methodist Church in Brooklyn. The Reverend Baker would later also found the Beulah Wesleyan Methodist Church in Manhattan.

In 1915 the Reverend Baker returned to Nevis to pick up his seventeen-year-old son Bertram, who had been working in a family-owned store and taking college preparatory courses on the neighboring island of St. Kitts. The father and son sailed together to Brooklyn, where the younger Baker apparently harbored lingering resentments over his father's decision years earlier to leave him in Nevis. Despite his father's strong ties to the Wesleyan Methodist Church, Bertram began making plans to become an Episcopalian priest; but he was soon pulled in other directions.

Baker studied accounting with LaSalle Extension University, which offered correspondence courses, and was eventually hired as a bookkeeper with a Brooklyn chandelier-manufacturing firm. In 1920 he married Irene Louise Baker, a relative, who sacrificed her ambitions of becoming an artist to labor for decades as a homemaker and supportive wife. The couple would have two daughters, Lilian (who married and became Lilian Bemus) and Marian (who became Marian Howell). In 1924 Baker was naturalized as a U.S. citizen.

Believing that blacks in Brooklyn could only advance if they attained political power, Baker, in 1932, organized the United Action Democratic Association. Later in the decade he was appointed deputy collector of Internal Revenue, serving in Brooklyn's income tax audit section. In 1944, he was named confidential aide to the Brooklyn borough president John Cashmore.

Then came the accomplishment for which he would be recognized in local newspapers. In 1948 Baker won a seat on the New York State Assembly, becoming the first African American elected to office in Brooklyn. His victory set the stage for an explosive growth of black political power, which would occur later in the century as tens of thousands of blacks continued to migrate to Brooklyn from the Caribbean, Latin America, and Africa, as well as from other parts of the United States. Baker held his Assembly seat for 22 years.

Among Baker's notable legislative accomplishments was the passage in 1955 of the Baker-Metcalf law, which news articles described as the first piece of legislation in the country to bar housing discrimination. The act outlawed racial discrimination in the sale or rental of federally insured houses. Baker co-authored the bill along with George R. Metcalf, a white liberal Republican state senator from upstate New York. As chair of the Assembly's Education Committee in the 1960s, he withstood slanderous attacks from white conservatives who were angered by his support for school desegregation measures.

Baker practiced politics the old-fashioned way, dispensing patronage and aggressively fighting those who dared to challenge him. At the same time, he groomed the borough's first black judges and representatives to the city council and state senate, all nurtured by his United Action Democratic club.

Outside of New York party politics, Baker devoted much of his time to leading the American Tennis Association, the national organization of black tennis players, for which he served as executive secretary for three decades, until 1966. In that capacity he spearheaded the drive to desegregate American and international tennis competitions. ALTHEA GIBSON, who broke down the racial barrier in tennis in the 1950s, credited Baker with helping initiate the process that enabled her to compete at Wimbledon. Gibson won the Wimbledon Singles Championship in 1957 and, upon her return to New York, celebrated at Baker's home in the Bedford-Stuyvesant section of Brooklyn and rode with him in a ticker-tape parade in Manhattan.

As for his métier of politics, Baker was one of a number of West Indian immigrants who made breakthroughs in the early 1900s. Among the other notable figures were Harlem politicians such as J. Raymond Jones, who emigrated from the Virgin Islands in 1918 and became the first black leader of the Manhattan Democratic Party in 1964, and Hulan Jack, who emigrated from St. Lucia in 1923 and became the first black borough president of Manhattan in 1954.

A number of scholars have postulated reasons for the political successes of Baker and other early immigrants. One possible explanation is rooted in New York political history. Many native-born blacks, from the mid-nineteenth century and into the twentieth century, remained loyal to the anti-slavery Republican Party of Abraham Lincoln. But in New York City, government was controlled by European immigrants in the Democratic Party, and black immigrants carried less psychological baggage related to the Civil War and thus were more easily able to form alliances with the white Democrats. The loyalty of native-born blacks to the Republican Party did not seriously begin to erode until the 1930s, when the Democratic president Franklin Delano Roosevelt pushed through New Deal social reforms that benefited urban blacks.

The twilight of Baker's career came in the late 1960s as he and other so-called Democratic machine politicians fell victim to the reform politics of the era. The grassroots movements of the 1960s spawned a new generation of activists in federally funded and other neighborhood organizations, which diluted Baker's power. Seeing the handwriting on the wall, he announced his retirement in 1970 and settled into a life of collecting books.

Baker was seen from a broad historical perspective, and his tenure was the first stage in a major demographic transformation of Brooklyn. In 1940, as he was ratcheting up the pressure on white Democratic bosses, blacks made up only 4 percent of Brooklyn's 2.6 million residents. By 2000 blacks were 34 percent of the total population, including tens of thousands of immigrants from the Caribbean, Africa, and Latin America. Moreover, by 2000 there were dozens of black elected officials representing Brooklyn in the U.S. Congress, in local, state, and federal courts, and in the city and state legislative bodies. Baker is thus regarded by whites and blacks as a "pioneer in Brooklyn politics" (Gerson, 22). During his retirement there was one piece of trivia in particular that Baker enjoyed relating. He would tell audiences, whether small ones at his home or larger ones at the Long Island Historical Society, that there was only one other person to have been born on the island of Nevis and to have served in the New York State Assembly: Alexander Hamilton.

In 1983, almost 60 years after becoming a U.S. citizen, Baker returned to his native island, which gained its independence from Great Britain. Weak and emotionally overwhelmed at being in the land of his birth, he gave a speech at a dedication of the rebuilt Alexander Hamilton House. He then went back to New York to live out his remaining months, pleased with the honors that came his way. In 1984 Baker received an honorary Ph.D. from St. John's University.

FURTHER READING

Connolly, Harold X. *A Ghetto Grows in Brooklyn* (1977).

Gerson, Jeffrey. "Bertram L. Baker, the United Action Democratic Association, and the First Black Democratic Succession in Brooklyn, 1933–1954," *Afro-Americans in New York Life and History*, vol. 16, no. 2 (1992).

Gray, Frances Clayton, and Yanick Rice Lamb. *Born to Win: The Authorized Biography of Althea Gibson* (2004).

Holder, Calvin. "The Rise and Fall of West Indian Politicians," in *Political Behavior and Social Interaction: Caribbean and African American Residents in New York* (1970).

Kasinitz, Philip. *Caribbean New York* (1992).

Lewinson, Edwin R. *Black Politics in New York City* (1974).

Obituary: *New York Times*, 10 Mar. 1985.

RON HOWELL

Baker, Ella (13 Dec. 1903–13 Dec. 1986), civil rights organizer, was born Ella Josephine Baker in Norfolk, Virginia, the daughter of Blake Baker, a waiter on the ferry between Norfolk and Washington, D.C., and Georgianna Ross. In rural North Carolina where Ella Baker grew up, she experienced a strong sense of black community. Her grandfather, who had been a slave, acquired the land in Littleton on which he had slaved. He raised fruit, vegetables, and cattle, which he shared with the community. He also served as the local Baptist minister. Baker's mother took care of the sick and needy.

After graduating in 1927 from Shaw University in Raleigh, North Carolina, Baker moved to New York City. She had dreamed of doing graduate work in sociology at the University of Chicago, but it was 1929, and times were hard. Few jobs were open to black women except teaching, which Baker refused to do because "this was the thing that everybody figures you could do" (Cantarow and O'Malley, 62). To survive, Baker waitressed and worked in a factory. During 1929–1930 she was an editorial staff

Ella Baker, speaking at the Jeannette Rankin news conference, 3 January 1968. [AP Images.]

member of the *American West Indian News* and in 1932 became an editorial assistant for GEORGE SCHUYLER's *Negro National News*, for which she also worked as office manager. In 1930 she was on the board of directors of Harlem's Own Cooperative and worked with the Dunbar Housewives' League on tenant and consumer rights. In 1930 she helped organize and in 1931 became the national executive director of the Young Negroes' Cooperative League, a consumer cooperative. Baker also taught consumer education for the Works Progress Administration in the 1930s and, according to a letter written in 1936, divided her time between consumer education and working at the public library at 135th Street. She married Thomas J. Roberts in 1940 or 1941; they had no children.

Beginning in 1938 Baker worked with the National Association for the Advancement of Colored People (NAACP), and from 1941 to 1946 she traveled throughout the country but especially in the South for the NAACP, first as field secretary and then as a highly successful director of branches to recruit members, raise money, and organize local campaigns. Among the issues in which she was involved were the-antilynching campaign, the equal-pay-for-black-teachers movement, and job training for black workers. Baker's strength was the ability to evoke in people a feeling of common need and the belief that people together can change the conditions under which they live. Her philosophy of organizing was "you start where the people are" and "strong people don't need strong leaders." In her years with the NAACP, Baker formed a network of people involved with civil rights throughout the South that proved invaluable in the struggles of the 1950s and 1960s. Among the more significant of her protégés was the Alabama seamstress ROSA PARKS. Baker resigned from her leadership role in the national NAACP in 1946 because she felt it was too bureaucratic. She also had agreed to take responsibility for raising her niece. Back in New York City, she worked with the NAACP on school desegregation, sat on the Commission on Integration for the New York City Board of Education, and in 1952 became president of the New York City NAACP chapter. In 1953 she resigned from the NAACP presidency to run unsuccessfully for the New York City Council on the Liberal Party ticket. To support herself, she worked as director of the Harlem Division of the New York City Committee of the American Cancer Society.

In January 1958 BAYARD RUSTIN and Stanley Levison persuaded Baker to go to Atlanta to set up the office of the Southern Christian Leadership Conference (SCLC) to organize the Crusade for Citizenship, a voter registration program in the South. Baker agreed to go for six weeks and stayed for two and a half years. She was named acting director of the SCLC and set about organizing the crusade to open simultaneously in twenty-one cities. She was concerned, however, that the SCLC board of preachers did not sufficiently support voter registration. Baker had increasing difficulty working with MARTIN LUTHER KING JR., whom she described as "too self-centered and cautious" (Weisbrot, 33). Because she thought that she would never be appointed executive director, Baker persuaded her friend the Reverend John L. Tilley to assume the post in April, and she became associate director. After King fired Tilley in January 1959, he asked Baker once again to be executive director, but his board insisted that her position must be in an acting capacity. Baker, however, functioned as executive director and signed her name accordingly. In April 1960 the executive director post of SCLC was accepted by the Reverend WYATT TEE WALKER. After hundreds of students sat in at segregated lunch counters in early 1960, Baker persuaded the SCLC to invite them to the Southwide Youth Leadership Conference at Shaw University on Easter weekend. From this meeting the Student Nonviolent Coordinating Committee (SNCC) was eventually formed. Although the SCLC leadership pressured Baker to influence the students to become a youth chapter of the SCLC, she refused and encouraged the students to beware of the SCLC's "leader-centered orientation." She felt that the students had a right to decide their own structure. Baker's speech "More than a hamburger," which followed King's and JAMES LAWSON's speeches, urged the students to broaden their social vision of discrimination to include more than integrating lunch counters. JULIAN BOND described the speech as "an eye opener" and probably the best of the three. "She didn't say, 'Don't let Martin Luther King tell you what to do,'" Bond remembers, "but you got the real feeling that that's what she meant" (Hampton and Fayer, 63). JAMES FORMAN, who became director of SNCC a few months later, said Baker felt the SCLC "was depending too much on the press and on the promotion of Martin King, and was not developing enough indigenous leadership across the South" (Forman, 216).

After the Easter conference weekend, Baker resigned from the SCLC, and after having helped Walker learn his job she went to work for SNCC in August. To support herself she worked as a human relations consultant for the Young Women's Christian Association in Atlanta. Baker continued as a mentor to SNCC civil rights workers, most notably ROBERT P. MOSES. At a rancorous SNCC meeting at Highlander Folk School in Tennessee in August 1961, Baker mediated between one faction advocating political action through voter registration and another faction advocating nonviolent direct action. She suggested that voter registration would necessitate confrontation that would involve them in direct action. Baker believed that voting was necessary but did not believe that the franchise would cure all problems. She also understood the appeal of nonviolence as a tactic, but she did not believe in it personally: "I have not seen anything in the nonviolent technique that can dissuade me from challenging somebody who wants to step on my neck. If necessary, if they hit me, I might hit them back" (Cantarow and O'Malley, 82).

After the 1964 Mississippi summer in which northern students went south to work in voter registration, SNCC decided to organize the Mississippi Freedom Democratic Party (MFDP) as an alternative to the regular Democratic Party in Mississippi. Thousands of people registered to vote in beauty parlors and barbershops, churches, or wherever a registration booth could be set up. Baker set up the Washington, D.C., office of the MFDP and delivered the keynote speech at its Jackson, Mississippi, state convention. The MFDP delegates were not seated at the Democratic National Convention in Washington, D.C., but their influence helped to elect many local black leaders in Mississippi in the following years and forced a rules change in the Democratic Party to include more women and minorities as delegates to the national convention.

From 1962 to 1967 Baker worked on the staff of the Southern Conference Education Fund (SCEF), dedicated to helping black and white people work together. During that time she organized a civil liberties conference in Washington, D.C., and worked with Carl Braden on a mock civil rights commission hearing in Chapel Hill, North Carolina. In her later years in New York City she served on the board of the Puerto Rican Solidarity Committee, founded and was president of the Fund for Education and Legal Defense, which raised money primarily for scholarships for civil rights activists to return to college, and was vice chair of the Mass Party Organizing Committee. She was also a sponsor of the National United Committee to Free ANGELA DAVIS and All Political Prisoners, a consultant to both the Executive Council and the Commission for Social and Racial Justice of the Episcopal Church, and a member of the Charter Group for a Pledge of Conscience and the Coalition of Concerned Black Americans. Until her death in New York City she continued to inspire, nurture, scold, and advise the many young people who had worked with her during her career of political activism.

Ella Baker's ideas and careful organizing helped to shape the civil rights movement from the 1930s through the 1960s. She had the ability to listen to people and to inspire them to organize around issues that would empower their lives. At a time when there were no women in leadership in the SCLC, Baker served as its executive director. Hundreds of young people became politically active because of her respect and concern for them.

FURTHER READING

Ella Baker's papers are in the Schomburg Center for Research in Black Culture of the New York Public Library.

Cantarow, Ellen, and Susan Gushee O'Malley. *Moving the Mountain* (1980).

Forman, James. *The Making of Black Revolutionaries* (1972).

Hampton, Henry, and Steve Fayer. *Voices of Freedom* (1991).

Ransby, Barbara. *Ella Baker and the Black Freedom Movement* (2003).

Weisbrot, Robert. *Freedom Bound* (1990).

Obituary: *New York Times*, 17 Dec. 1986.

This entry is taken from the *American National Biography* and is published here with the permission of the American Council of Learned Societies.

SUSAN GUSHEE O'MALLEY

Baker, Etta (31 Mar. 1913–23 Sept. 2006), Piedmont-style guitarist, was born near Collettsville in the African American community of Franklin, an Appalachian hollow not far from the John's River in upper Caldwell County, North Carolina. Her grandfather Alexander Reid and father Boone Reid, both born in Franklin, played the banjo in the old-time clawhammer manner, with Boone going on to become an accomplished musician who also played fiddle, harmonica, and guitar, on which he used a two-finger-style approach. Boone Reid had absorbed many kinds of music of the mid-to-late nineteenth century, including Anglo-American dance tunes, lyric folksongs, ballads, rags, religious music, and published pieces that had drifted into folk tradition—popular Tin Pan Alley songs, old minstrel tunes, and Victorian parlor music. Boone and his wife Sallie, who sang, instilled their love of music in their eight children, a process that led eventually to the formation of a Reid family string band that played after supper and at local social events.

In January 1916 Reid moved his family to Chase City, Virginia, to farm tobacco. It is likely that he sometimes sold his crops in Durham, North Carolina, a tobacco-market center about 60 miles south. The storage warehouses there also served as a center of remarkable musical activity, and Reid probably ingested a great deal of music, perhaps even the finger-picked rags and reels of Reverend GARY DAVIS and BLIND BOY FULLER, as well as the newer form called blues. Around the time of this move Reid began teaching his barely three-year-old daughter Etta, perhaps his most persistent pupil, to play finger-style guitar. He found in her an eager student, expertly assimilating her father's instrumental styles and repertoire, although she was never able to master Reid's "fisting" clawhammer method on the banjo; she did in later years, however, begin to play a few of her father's banjo songs in a thumb-lead, finger-uppicking style.

The guitar technique that Etta learned from her father was to become known as "Piedmont blues," "East Coast blues," and more accurately, "the Piedmont style," since a great many musicians in the region had adopted the same method. This style consisted of a soft, syncopated melody produced by the index finger, and a relentless alternating bass pattern played with the thumb, which was also used to brush chords on the afterbeat. This style was particularly well suited to marches, cakewalks, reels, open-tuned parlor pieces, and, especially, ragtime tunes, but it did not lend itself whatsoever to the primary blues form. Indeed, roughly 85 percent of Etta Baker's repertoire consisted of "reels," named for an ancient Scottish dance and defined primarily on the basis of its rapid tempo (at least 120 beats per minute). Reels, also called "breakdowns" or "hoedowns," became an umbrella term for any kind of song played to a brisk, danceable tempo, subsuming other generic classifications in the process. When musicians began to insert partially flatted thirds and sevenths into these reels, many people—including Pink Anderson, FRED MCDOWELL, and BUKKA WHITE —came to think of them as "blues," which of course they were not. Consequently the term "Piedmont blues" is a misnomer; indeed the Piedmont style is an instrumental technique that has little to do with such genres as lyric folksongs, ballads, or religious music, all of which Etta played using it, or blues, which she did not, due to the form's requisite "slow-drag" tempo. Labels aside, Etta would later become an exemplar of both African American and Anglo American folk-musical traditions that existed in the mountains and Piedmont at least as far back as the Reconstruction era, if not before.

In 1923 the family moved back to Franklin, where Etta continued to play her music with her family and friends, especially her sister Cora, who also finger-picked the guitar, and her sister-in-law and first cousin Babe Reid, still another finger-style guitarist, and Babe's husband Fred (Boone's brother), who picked two-finger-style banjo. When Cora in 1931 married Theopolis ("The") Phillips, who played both guitar and banjo, an equally impressive extended family of musicians joined with the Reids, resulting in highly talented ensembles that played for "entertainments"—family get-togethers, house parties, and square dances—often alongside white mountain musicians who had for years been playing the same kinds of music in the same basic styles. Vocals were not a strong component of these events, which tended to focus on music for dancing, so Etta had few opportunities to develop her singing, although she did sing a handful of blues tunes now and then.

Etta married Lee Baker in 1936 and moved down the mountain to Morganton, where she worked in a textile mill. She kept up with music during the next many years, often jamming with her nine children and of course with Cora, The, Fred, and Babe. She also began experimenting with songs from outside the family tradition, for example RAY CHARLES's "But On the Other Hand, Baby" and "One Mint Julep," but she always insisted that she'd learned most of her music from her father.

During a trip to Blowing Rock in early 1956 the Bakers attended a performance by the folksong revivalist Paul Clayton, who became impressed with Etta's playing after Lee persuaded his wife to pick a couple of tunes for the folks. Shortly thereafter, Clayton returned to the region to record Etta, her brother-in-law The, and her father Boone, the result of which was the seminal album *Instrumental Music of the Southern Appalachians* that influenced a great many revivalist guitar players.

Baker retired from her day-job in 1962 and began to devote time to her family, her gardening, at which she was also a master, and her music. After her husband Lee died in 1967 she became a semi-professional musician, taking her regional style to schools, colleges, and innumerable concerts and festivals, including Wolf Trap, the 1982 Worlds' Fair, the John Henry Memorial Festival, and Merlefest.

In 1991 Baker was awarded an National Endowment for the Arts National Folk Heritage Fellowship, officially declaring her an American national treasure.

FURTHER READING

Biographical information on Etta Baker is based primarily on several tape-recorded interviews with the author, especially during 1980–1985.

Lightfoot, William E. "The Three Doc(k)s: White Blues in Appalachia," *Black Music Research Journal* (2005).

Lightfoot, William E. "Etta Baker: One Dime Blues," *North Carolina Folklore Journal* (1995).

Lightfoot, William E. "Eight-Hand Sets and Holy Steps," *North Carolina Folklore Journal* (1990).

Lightfoot, William E. "Etta Baker and Cora Phillips," [Brown-Hudson Award Citation] *North Carolina Folklore Journal* (1982).

Wilson, Emily Herring. "One Dime Blues: Elizabeth Moore Reid, Cora Reid Phillips, Etta Reid Baker," in *Hope and Dignity: Older Black Women of the South* (1983).

WILLIAM E. LIGHTFOOT

Baker, Frankie (30 May 1876–6 Jan. 1952), the inspiration for the "Frankie and Johnny" song, was born and raised in St. Louis, Missouri. Her parents were Cedric Baker and his wife Margaret (maiden name unknown), and she had three brothers: Charles, Arthur, and James. Charles, who was younger than Frankie, lived with her on Targee Street in 1900. In 1899 Baker shot and killed her seventeen-year-old "mack" (pimp), Allen "Al" Britt. St. Louis pianists and singers were soon thumping and belting out what would become one of America's most famous folk ballads and popular songs, "Frankie and Johnny," also known as "Frankie and Albert," "Frankie Baker," and "Frankie."

At age sixteen or seventeen Baker fell in love with a man who, unknown to her, was living off the earnings of a prostitute (this kind of man was known as an "easy rider," a term made famous by W. C. HANDY in his "Yellow Dog Blues"). When the prostitute, who had romantic relations with this man, discovered that he was also seeing Baker, she came to Baker's home one night and sliced the left side of her face. Baker received thirty-eight stitches and was left with a long scar.

Baker, emotionally broken by finding out her lover was involved with another woman, joined the "sporting life": that of pimps and whores, "hustlers and gamblers, brothels and taverns, musicians and other entertainers, and allied people and institutions." According to reports, she was quite successful. She dressed in fine clothes and jewelry and became a "queen sport" (Huston, 105) of the African American district around Targee Street:

Frankie was a sporting lady
A red light hung over her door
She always paid fifty or sixty dollars
For every suit that Johnny wore.
He was her man
But he done her wrong.
(usual refrain, sometimes varied)
(Buckley, 40)

After Baker met Al, a pianist, at the Orange Blossom's Ball at Stolle's Hall, he moved in with her at 212 Targee Street, where she roomed and did business. On occasion he beat her.

Problems arose when Baker found out that Al had another girl, an eighteen-year-old prostitute named Alice Pryor:

Johnny says, "Listen now Frankie
Don't want to tell you no lies
I've lost my heart to another queen
Her name is Nellie Bly."
(Buckley, 52)

When he didn't come home on Saturday night, 14 October 1899, Baker went out and found him with Alice at the Phoenix Hotel.

Frankie says to the barkeep
"Have you seen my Albert nigh"
The barkeep says to Frankie
"He's with a woman called Alice Bly."
(Buckley, 57)

After an argument, Baker returned home. Feeling ill she went to bed in the front bedroom, where she thought there was "more air" than in her customary room (David, 214). Al came in the next morning around 3:00 A.M., very angry, and their quarrel renewed. Claiming to be outraged that she was in the wrong room, he grabbed a lamp. She jumped up and stood by the bed. As he started after her with a knife, she pulled a pistol from under her pillow and shot him, the bullet going through his liver. He staggered to his parents' house at 32 Targee Street and was taken to City Hospital, where he died in the early morning of 19 October:

Frankie shot him once
She shot him thru and thru
"Please don't kill me, Frankie
"You've shot me, that will do."
(Buckley, 75)

A coroner's jury ruled that the killing was self-defense and justifiable homicide. On 13 November 1899 Baker was tried before Judge Willis B. Clark, Court of Criminal Correction, and acquitted.

Baker remained in St. Louis for about a year, drifted around some, and then settled in Omaha, Nebraska, where she was living in the early 1920s. Having heard about a "great flower show, the Rose Festival" (David, 216), in Portland, Oregon, she accepted an invitation from friends there to visit. By 1930 she was living in Portland and had "quit playing the game" (Terrett, *The World*), though she never married. She opened a shoe-shine parlor on Flanders Street and later worked as a chambermaid at the Royal Palm Hotel.

Illness struck in the 1930s, and within a few years Baker was unable to work. It appears that she spent much of her time playing solitaire in her home at 22 North Clackamas. She also collected items related to "Frankie and Albert/Johnny."

The 1933 release of the Paramount movie *She Done Him Wrong*, starring Mae West, stirred deep resentment in Baker, who thought it wrong that someone could profit from her story without paying her anything. She filed suit on 1 March 1935, but her lawyers decided that she could not win and withdrew the complaint.

Another opportunity came with the release in 1936 of Republic's movie, *Frankie and Johnnie*, starring Helen Morgan as Baker in an all-white cast. Baker's attorneys filed suit for $200,000 damages against Republic and others in April 1938. Depositions began in October 1939, but the trial itself was not held until February 1942.

One of the important witnesses was the famous radio personality and author Sigmund Spaeth, who was also known as the "Tune Detective" and the "Song Sleuth" because he had made a profession of tracking down song histories. Spaeth "lectured" the court for "nearly two days" (David, 228–229), severely damaging Baker's case. In *Read 'Em and Weep* (1926) he had written, "It is generally agreed that the beautifully honest story is a true one, and that the locale was St. Louis." Even though he had

reaffirmed this belief in 1934, he testified otherwise as an expert witness in 1942, saying, "I've changed my mind" (David, 230). "Perhaps he had been mesmerized by money" (Harris, 38). It was believed that he had received $2,000 for his testimony.

Having a weak case and facing all-white defense witnesses and defense lawyers, as well as a white jury and judge, Baker lost. She was left penniless. Unable to work, she was on relief by 1949, when she was made the "first life member of Portland's Urban League," to which she had given "unfailing support" (David, 234).

Baker was found by a court to be mentally ill. She had a poor memory and a persecution complex, and she was belligerent—hallmark signs of Alzheimer's disease (though whether she suffered from this disease is not confirmed). Baker was committed to Eastern Oregon Hospital and Training Center, Pendleton, and was admitted there in April 1950. In less than two years she was dead. When she died in Pendleton, her body was sent to Los Angeles for burial.

Before 1912 the folk ballad was about Frankie and "Albert," which is easily understood as a mishearing of "Al Britt." The ballad may have been written by Bill Dooley, "one of the 'barroom bards' who collaborated with piano men in writing 'the topical, gay and ribald songs which emanated from the Negro quarter'" (David, 228). In 1912 a Tin Pan Alley version, "Frankie and Johnny," was published, music by Ren Shields and lyrics by the Leighton Brothers (Bert, Frank, William), who may have thought "Albert" dull and "Johnny" catchy. Since then "Johnny" has dominated. Shields's tune differs from the one usually sung, which was first published in 1912 as part of the tune for an unrelated song, "You're My Baby," music by Nat D. Ayer.

Bawdy elements, colorful incidents (often historically incorrect), the raggy blues tune, and a refrain that lends itself to dramatic, seriocomic renderings have all helped make "Frankie" immensely popular. Even so, the ballad's most important quality may be that it captures the spirit of a proud woman.

FURTHER READING

Buckley, Bruce Redfern. "Frankie and Her Men: A Study of the Interrelationships of Popular and Folk Traditions," Ph.D. diss., Indiana University (1961).

David, John Russell. "Tragedy in Ragtime: Black Folktales from St. Louis," Ph.D. diss., St. Louis University (1976).

Harris, Ellen. "They Done Her Wrong," *St. Louis*, Nov. 1999.

Huston, John. *Frankie and Johnny* (1930).

Terrett, Courtenay. "Frankie Still Mourns Her Man," *The World* (New York), 8 June 1930.

JOHN GARST

Baker, General (6 Sept. 1941–), automobile worker and activist, was born General Gordon Baker Jr. in Detroit, Michigan, one of five children of General Gordon Baker Sr., an automobile worker, and Clara Baker, a housewife. Baker attended Southwestern High School in Detroit and went on to take classes at Highland Park Community College and Wayne State University. In the early 1960s he took a job with Ford Motor Company and continued to work in the automobile industry for almost forty years. In 1941 Baker's father had moved his family to Detroit from Georgia in search of a job in the booming war-production industries, taking part in the massive migration of African Americans from the rural South to cities in the North during the first half of the twentieth century. Becoming an autoworker allowed Baker Sr. to dramatically improve his family's standard of living, especially in comparison to his prospects in the poverty-stricken South.

While his father sought a better life for his family through the relatively high pay of auto work, Baker Jr. demanded social and racial equality along with a fair wage. By the late 1950s he was involved in the civil rights movement, which grew rapidly among Detroit's large black population. He joined a group of black Wayne State University students organizing protests against businesses that practiced discrimination against African Americans and took its name, Uhuru, from a Swahili word for "freedom." Baker attended several speeches by MALCOLM X and participated in the July 1963 Walk to Freedom, led by MARTIN LUTHER KING JR., which brought 200,000 people to downtown Detroit. Baker also traveled to the August 1963 March on Washington. In 1965 he met the civil rights activist Marian Kramer. They worked together on many campaigns for social and economic justice, and continued to do so after their marriage in September 1978. They had eight children of their own and helped raise several of their nieces and nephews.

Baker was committed to a more confrontational and uncompromising approach to racial politics than the nonviolent civil rights movement associated with King. He was attracted to the philosophy of armed self-defense advocated by the NAACP activist ROBERT FRANKLIN WILLIAMS. Baker would gather with friends to listen to Williams's radio program, *Radio Free Dixie*, which Williams produced from exile in Cuba. He joined the Revolutionary Action Movement (RAM), a small but influential network of African American students and activists that adopted Williams's philosophy. In 1964 he made a clandestine trip to Cuba with a group of about eighty American university students in defiance of the travel ban declared by the United States. There he met Fidel Castro, Che Guevara, Williams, and other students and revolutionaries from Latin America, the Caribbean, Africa, and Asia. Baker returned committed to anti-imperialism and cognizant of the global impact of race on national and class divisions.

Baker's trip to Cuba would not be the only instance in which he openly defied the federal government. In 1965 Baker was drafted into the army and refused to serve in the Vietnam conflict, which he considered a justified struggle for national liberation. He responded to the draft board with a scathing letter denouncing the American military's repressive actions abroad and the role of American corporations in the exploitation of workers in Africa, Asia, and Latin America, which he linked to the treatment of African Americans within the United States. On his draft day, he passed a physical to prove that he was fit for service because he did not want to be mistaken for a pacifist or conscientious objector. Baker and others organized a simultaneous protest which, combined with his political beliefs, resulted in his dismissal as a security risk.

Baker's activism for civil rights and against imperialism converged with the workplace issues of the auto industry. He was particularly concerned with working conditions and racial injustice on the shop floor, where he felt black workers were unable to gain access to higher-paid skilled jobs and supervisory positions. In May 1968 a wildcat strike occurred at the Dodge motor company's main plant. Management fired seven workers accused of leading this strike, which the United Auto Workers (UAW) had not authorized. The five white workers involved were rehired, while Baker and another black worker were not. Baker and others used this as an opportunity to form the Dodge Revolutionary Union Movement (DRUM), a black workers' organization that fought for better working conditions, the desegregation of job classifications, and more blacks in the leadership structure of the UAW and the Chrysler Corporation. In 1969 DRUM became one part of the League of Revolutionary Black Workers, a conglomeration of several Revolutionary Union movements in the city that were committed to black nationalism, workplace rights, and a revolutionary anticapitalist perspective. The league emphasized the global nature of the struggle for racial equality and proclaimed the black working class the vanguard of revolutionary change. This movement incorporated economic and workers' rights issues into the local and national debate concerning civil rights for African Americans, linking the issues of race and class on the shop floor.

Baker's activism was not confined only to the 1960s. In 1976 he campaigned for state representative for his district on the Communist Labor Party ticket, garnering more votes than the Republican candidate but losing to the Democrat. Baker placed second in the Democratic primary of 1978 for the same position. Despite his open opposition to the UAW in the 1960s and 1970s, he saw the union as a means to make a difference on the shop floor. In 1986 he was elected unit president in UAW Local 600 and later worked for the local's staff. In 1990 he gave up his position with the union to return to work until he retired in August 2003. He continued to organize against racism and economic injustice, campaigning for homeless rights, working for the Midwest Labor Library and Resource Center in Detroit, and traveling to give speeches about his experiences at union-sponsored conferences and on college campuses.

FURTHER READING

General Baker's papers were collected on microfilm by LexisNexis and published as *The Black Power Movement: Part 4, The League of Revolutionary Black Workers, 1965–1976*, ed. Ernie Allen Jr. (2004).

Georgakas, Dan, and Marvin Surkin. *Detroit: I Do Mind Dying*, rev. ed. (1998).

MICHAEL J. MURPHY

Baker, George. *See* Father Divine.

Baker, Harriet Ann (Aug. 1829–4 Mar. 1913), evangelist and African Methodist Episcopal (AME) minister, was born a freewoman near Havre de Grace, Harford County, Maryland. One of seven children of William and Harriet Lego Cole, she was descended from a family that included a Native American maternal great-grandmother married to an Englishman, a maternal grandfather born in Guinea, and a paternal grandmother reputedly freed from slavery by a Baltimore court after enduring an unwarranted and savage beating while pregnant. In October 1845, when she was sixteen

years of age, Harriet married William Baker, ten years her senior and a slave on the Edward Gallop plantation in Michaelsville, a nearby Maryland hamlet.

In 1847, when the couple learned of Gallop's plan to sell William to a slave dealer in Georgia, they fled north with their infant daughter. After a forty-eight-mile flight along the western bank of the Susquehanna River, they crossed into Columbia, Pennsylvania, a Lancaster County center of Underground Railroad activity. Despite being beset with racial tensions as manumitted and runaway blacks crowded into the commercially oriented town, Columbia, with its successful black population, nevertheless provided reasonable protection and numerous economic opportunities for ambitious workers and would-be entrepreneurs. The Bakers quickly found work, built a home, and settled into Columbia's vibrant black community, which at the time constituted 21 percent of the town's 4,100 residents.

Passage of the Fugitive Slave Act of 1850 dramatically altered life for the Bakers and other blacks throughout the southernmost free states. Emboldened slave catchers and owners promptly descended on Columbia to reclaim their property, and scores of black residents hurried north for increased safety. Baker's husband escaped to Boston for several months, but returned in December. In January the local magistrate committed him to jail as a runaway, wrongly accusing him of being involved in a riot in Lancaster City. His arrest purportedly made him the first victim of the act. An angry crowd of white abolitionists and irate blacks from the town's segregated Tow Hill area protested as officials transported William to Philadelphia, where a hearing ruled that he was to return with Gallop to Maryland. Harriet, with the help of white supporters, obtained an unsecured loan for $750 to purchase her husband's freedom. Over the next thirty years William Baker became a prominent figure in the economic and political life of Columbia's African American community.

Married life proved difficult for Baker. In twenty-six years she bore twelve children and saw seven die. To repay the debt incurred to free William, the Bakers had to refinance the house they had built in 1848. In 1863, soon after redeeming this second mortgage, a fire thought to be the work of Southern sympathizers completely destroyed the home. In the spring of 1872, her daughters Hannah Rebecca and Rulletta Stephen, ages fifteen and thirteen, died within two weeks of each other. Nine years later a neighboring businessman was charged with raping eleven-year-old Eva, Baker's youngest child. Periodic bouts of assorted ailments, including heart, kidney, and liver illness, and even an accidental poisoning, plagued her.

Baker had experienced personal salvation in 1842, when at twelve or thirteen years of age, her mother tricked her into attending a prayer gathering at a vacant estate several miles outside Havre de Grace. The heartfelt and highly emotional prayers, songs, and praises of the assembled women combined with the extreme heat in the small building to overwhelm the skepticism of the youthful Harriet, who left believing that the heretofore unknown Jesus had saved her soul. During the subsequent decades, as Baker taught herself to read the Bible, she concluded that the Lord willed her to undertake a life of evangelism. Her husband, family, pastor, friends, and members of the church responded with vehement disapproval of a wife, mother, and a woman pursuing a life of evangelical activity. Baker, however, experienced a series of vivid dreams that deepened her feelings and intensified her prayers to abate the universal resistance she endured.

The death in 1872 of two of her daughters, Baker held, was providential and convinced her of the need to act. That winter she poured out her beliefs at a church meeting and boldly announced her intention to set forth in search of souls. The sincerity of her statement so disarmed the opposition that she began preparations for a new life, despite the lack of formal church approval. At the time Baker was forty-three years of age with an aging husband and three minor children at home, the youngest of whom was only two years old. During the following quarter century, while maintaining her residence in Columbia, Baker traveled throughout Pennsylvania and much of the Northeast. Affiliated with the Philadelphia Conference of the African Methodist Episcopal Church, which in the mid-1870s authorized her to preach, Baker labored in towns, small cities, and even such urban centers as New York, Baltimore, and Philadelphia. White and black churches of numerous evangelical denominations sought her out. These included Methodist Episcopal, Primitive Methodist, United Brethren, Baptist, Methodist Protestant, and AME Zion churches. She preached from pulpits, participated in camp meetings, conducted revivals, wrote hymns, led song services, and assisted at Sabbath schools. A highly effective and energetic minister of the gospel, she converted thousands of individuals, raised impressive sums of money, and aided pastors with the varied responsibilities of missionary work. In 1889 she became the pastor of a struggling church in Lebanon, Pennsylvania, the first woman to hold this position in the AME Church.

Harriet Baker's religious concepts were largely typical of conventional evangelical preachers of the day. Her printed sermons, an 1892 biography, and published letters of commendation from pastors stress her belief in standard biblical truths and of the need for personal conversion and sanctification through the workings of the Holy Spirit. The historian Bettye Collier-Thomas contends, moreover, that Baker's fundamentally orthodox sermons also subtly revealed a social message regarding the status of blacks and women. She maintains that Baker, particularly in "Behold the Man" and "Jesus Weeping over Jerusalem," used the story of Christ's rejection and passion in an autobiographical manner to assert the need for sinners to lead lives of holiness, no matter the pain caused by social alienation and opposition from earthly and church leaders.

Baker left Columbia following the death of her husband in the late 1880s and lived alternately with daughters in Bethlehem and Allentown, Pennsylvania. In 1900, at age seventy-one, she built at her own expense a two-story structure whose first-floor auditorium served as the Gospel Union or Bethel Mission (later St. James AME Zion Church), while the second story became her residence. For the next thirteen years Baker conducted weekly and Sunday services while continuing to travel throughout the region preaching special sermons, giving lectures, and leading revivals. These activities helped raise funds to support her and assist in paying the mortgage. The proceeds from the Reverend John H. Acornley's 1892 biography, *The Colored Lady Evangelist*, also served this purpose. Baker died at her Allentown home at eighty-three years of age, having labored for three decades to convert thousands to Jesus Christ. Evangelists whose lives and careers loosely paralleled those of Harriet Baker include AMANDA BERRY SMITH, JULIA A. J. FOOTE, MARY JANE BLAIR SMALL, and FANNY JACKSON COPPIN.

FURTHER READING

Harriet Baker seems not to have left any papers. The only thorough account of her life, written with her assistance, is a period biography by the Reverend John H. Acornley, *The Colored Lady Evangelist, Being the Life, Labors, and Experiences of Mrs. Harriet A. Baker* (1892). Period accounts of some of

Mrs. Baker's activities in Columbia and during her years as an evangelist appear in *the Columbia Spy* and the *Christian Recorder*, the official organ of the AME church.

Collier-Thomas, Bettye. *Daughters of Thunder: Black Women Preachers and Their Sermons, 1850–1979* (1998).

Obituaries: Allentown *Democrat*, 3 Mar. 1913; Allentown *Morning Call*, 3 Mar. 1913.

JAMES CHRISMER

Baker, Henry Edwin (18 Sept. 1859?–28 Oct. 1928), first African American Patent Examiner, a lawyer, and author of *The Colored Inventor: A Record of Fifty Years* (Crisis Publishing Co., 1913) and other works on black inventors and scientists of the nineteenth and early twentieth century, was born in Columbus, Mississippi. Little is known of his parents or his early life in Columbus, except that he attended public schools and the Columbus Union Academy. Toward the end of Reconstruction, in June 1874, he was selected to attend the Annapolis, Maryland, naval academy by white Congressman Henry W. Barry (R-Mississippi), who had commanded black troops for the union Army during the Civil War. Despite government and naval policies during this period directing the military to integrate, the first two African American cadets failed to survive intense hazing, taunting, assaults, and social isolation from classmates and left before graduation. Still, Congressman Barry, originally from New York and a former agent of the Freedman's Bureau, remained intent on integrating the academy.

Therefore, Baker, after passing a rigorous entrance exam, became the third African American to attend the prestigious officers' training school as a cadet midshipman. His tenure there was marked by aggressive hazing and occasional violence because of his race. Although he was able to overcome the academic challenges, Baker continued to defy classmates' attacks. The first was recorded only a month after his arrival. Numerous incidents followed. At times, an escort was assigned to take Baker to and from meals. He left the academy around 1876 and returned briefly to Columbus. Determined to get a formal education, however, in 1877 he relocated to Washington, D.C., where he began work as a copyist for the U.S. Patent Office, thus beginning a government career of more than fifty years. That same year, he enrolled in the Ben-Hyde Benton School of Technology, where

he remained until 1879, when he entered Howard University's law school and graduated at the head of his class in 1881. Baker capped his formal education with postgraduate law studies at Howard that he completed in 1883. In May 1893 Baker married Violetta Clarke of Detroit, daughter of fugitive slave, abolitionist, and author LEWIS G. CLARKE and his wife, Emily Walker.

Although Baker and his wife had no children, they were known for their encouragement and support for black youth and for their many civic activities. They supported the college education of Violetta's niece, Virginia Clarke, who came from Washington state to live with them in 1920 at their home on Sixth Street NW to attend Howard University across the street. Many others benefited from the couples' encouragement, including ALAIN LOCKE, noted philosopher and a professor at Howard, and inventor SHELBY DAVIDSON. Baker was especially supportive of black entrepreneurs.

The Bakers were among the mainstays of their Howard University neighborhood, one of the most fertile communities for African American intellectual, cultural, and business life, where the couple often associated with African American leaders and thinkers of the day. The neighborhood was home to notables such as poet PAUL LAWRENCE DUNBAR and wife ALICE RUTH MOORE, who lived nearby on Fourth Street NW. They were members of the Howard Park Citizens Association. Along with Davidson and inventor ROBERT A. PELHAM, Baker was a core member of the Bethel Literary and Historical Association formed to enhance the cultural interests of its members. He served as secretary of the Industrial Building and Savings Company and director of the Capital Savings Bank and was a longtime treasurer of the Berean Baptist Church. Violetta, herself a former teacher who worked for many years at the Library of Congress, also organized groups devoted to books and to commenting on or correcting news stories of African Americans in the press. Before she died in 1923 she undertook her most ambitious project: compiling the most complete index of literary works by and about African American women with the intention to publish the collection, showing the complexities of these women's lives along with a record of their works.

Around the turn of the century, along with the Industrial Revolution, interest in black inventors grew. Requests for information on black inventors and their inventions from sponsors of national exhibits and fairs like the Cotton Centennial at

New Orleans (1884), the World's Fair in Chicago (1893), and the Southern Exposition in Atlanta (1895) began filtering in to the Patent Office. It was the inquiry from the Paris Exhibit of 1900, however, that prompted Baker's groundbreaking research. The Patent Office had little information on black inventors for at least two reasons: the cost of applying for patents was often prohibitive for many blacks and racist attitudes of the day. African American inventors often feared identifying themselves as black or Negro because doing so would discourage sales and distribution of their invention or possibly bring harm to themselves and their families. Therefore, many named whites as inventors of their product.

Patents were and are important because they protect the rights of people who invent or improve inventions. With that protection comes not only official credit but also remuneration because no one else is allowed to profit from the development. Therefore, patent examiners make decisions that effect society's economic well-being and also confer status on applicants.

Armed with this knowledge and the determination to uplift the race, Baker approached his research as a mission; he undertook what became the first known attempt to compile information on black inventors. With the support of the Patent Commissioner, Baker sent letters around the country to patent lawyers, large manufacturing companies, black newspaper editors, and anyone else he thought could provide information. Respondents to his initial survey letters resulted in information on more than four hundred patents being granted to "colored" inventors.

Beginning in 1834 with Henry Blair, credited with inventing a corn harvester and believed to have been free because the law prohibited slaves from taking out patents, Baker's survey revealed more than dates, numbers, and names. He discovered that although most black inventors received no royalties, many did and some possessed several patents. ELIJAH McCOY, for example, held twenty-eight patents, the most on record at the time. Most of McCoy's were related to lubricating appliances for engines. W. B. Purvis held sixteen patents related to the paper bag machinery. GRANVILLE WOODS, an assistant to Thomas Edison, also held several patents related to electricity. At least two women appeared on that first list: SARAH BOONE, who patented an ironing board in 1892, and Miriam E. Benjamin, who invented a device used by the House of Representatives to signal pages.

Eventually, Baker amassed more than two thousand original patents or patents for improvements by African Americans and bound them into four volumes originally titled *Patents by Negroes: 1834–1900* for the Patent Office and later called *The Colored Inventor: A Record of Fifty Years* (Crisis Publishing Co., 1913). A few years later, he also published "Benjamin Banneker: The Negro Mathematician and Astronomer" in the *Journal of Negro History* (Vol. 111, No. 2, April 1918, pp. 99–118).

Before Baker died in 1928, he sold the volumes to prominent black architect, John A. Lankford of Washington, D.C., whose surviving family donated them to Howard University in 1950. The well-known historian of African American history, William Loren Katz, ordered a reprint, in which he provides a preface to Henry Baker and his early work.

FURTHER READING

Culp, D.W., ed. "The Negro as an Inventor," in *Twentieth Century Negro Literature* (1902).

Fouche, Rayvon. *Black Inventors in the Age of Segregation: Granville T. Woods, Lewis H. Latimer, and Shelby J. Davidson* (2003).

Schneller, Robert J., Jr. *Breaking the Color Barrier: The U.S. Naval Academy's First Black Mid-Shipmen and the Struggle for Racial Equality* (2005).

Sluby, Patricia Carter. *The Inventive Spirit of African Americans: Patented Ingenuity* (2004).

Sullivan, O. R. *Black American Inventors (Black Stars)* (1998).

JANICE L. GREENE

Baker, Josephine (3 Jun. 1906–10 Apr. 1975), dancer, singer, and entertainer, was born in the slums of East St. Louis, Missouri, the daughter of Eddie Carson, a drummer, who abandoned Baker and her mother after the birth of a second child, and Carrie McDonald, a onetime entertainer who supported what became a family of four by doing laundry. Poverty, dislocation, and mistreatment permeated Baker's childhood. By the age of eight she was earning her keep and contributing to the family's support by doing domestic labor. By the time Baker was fourteen, she had left home and its discord and drudgery; mastered such popular dances as the Mess Around and the Itch, which sprang up in the black urban centers of the day; briefly married Willie Wells and then divorced him; and begun her career in the theater. She left East St. Louis behind and traveled with the Dixie Steppers

Josephine Baker, at the Winter Garden Theater in New York, 11 February 1936. (AP Images.)

on the black vaudeville circuit, already dreaming of performing on Broadway. Baker's dream coincided with the creation of one of the greatest musical comedies in American theater, *Shuffle Along*, with music by EUBIE BLAKE and lyrics by NOBLE SISSLE. A constant crowd-pleaser with her crazy antics and frantic dancing as a comic, eye-crossing chorus girl, Baker auditioned for a role in the musical in Philadelphia in April 1921, only to be rejected as "too young, too thin, too small, and too dark." With characteristic determination, she bought a one-way ticket to New York, auditioned again, and was rejected again, but she secured a job as a dresser in the touring company. On the road she learned the routines, and, when a member of the chorus line fell ill, she stepped in and became an immediate sensation. More than five hundred performances later, in the fall of 1923, the *Shuffle Along* tour ended, and Baker was cast in Sissle and Blake's new show, *Bamville*, later retitled and better known as *The Chocolate Dandies*. When the musical opened in New York in March 1924, Baker not only played Topsy Anna, a comic role straight out of the racist minstrel tradition, but also appeared as an elegantly dressed "deserted female" in the show's "Wedding Finale," foreshadowing the poised and

polished performer of world renown she would become.

In the summer of 1925 Baker's dancing at the Plantation Club at Fiftieth Street and Broadway caught the eye of Caroline Dudley Reagan, a young socialite planning to stage a black revue in Paris in the vein of *Shuffle Along* or *Runnin' Wild*, the revue that introduced the Charleston in 1924. The company that came to be known as La Revue Nègre was long on talent, with such now legendary figures as the composer Spencer Williams, the bandleader and pianist CLAUDE HOPKINS, and the clarinetist SIDNEY BECHET, the dancer and choreographer LOUIS DOUGLAS, and the set designer Miguel Covarrubias. Baker joined the troupe as lead dancer, singer, and comic. When the performers arrived in Paris in late September 1925, opening night at the Théâtre des Champs Elysées was ten days away. During that brief time the revue was transformed from a vaudeville show, replete with the stereotypes expected by a white American public, into a music-hall spectacle filled with colonialist fantasies that appealed to the largely male, voyeuristic Parisian audience.

When La Revue Nègre opened to a packed house on 2 October 1925, it was an instantaneous *succès de scandale*. First, Baker stunned the rapt onlookers with her blackface comic routine, in which, seemingly part animal, part human, she shimmied, contorted her torso, writhed like a snake, and vibrated her behind with astonishing speed. Then she provoked boos and hisses as well as wild applause when, in the closing "Dance sauvage," wearing only feathers about her hips, she entered the stage upside down in a full split on the shoulders of Joe Alex. Janet Flanner recorded the moment in the *New Yorker*: "Midstage, he paused, and with his long fingers holding her basket-wise around the waist, swung her in a slow cartwheel to the stage floor, where she stood like his magnificent discarded burden, in an instant of complete silence. She was an unforgettable female ebony statue." Called the "black Venus" and likened to African sculpture in motion, Baker was seen both as a threat to "civilization" and, like *le jazz hot*, as a new life force capable of energizing a weary France mired down in tradition and in need of renewal.

Paris made "la Baker" a celebrity, embracing both her erotic yet comic stage persona and her embodiment of Parisian chic as she strolled the city's boulevards beautifully dressed in Paul Poiret's creations. Beginning in 1926 Baker starred at the oldest and most venerated of French music halls, the Folies-Bergère. Once again, she was a shocking sensation. Instead of the customary bare-breasted, light-skinned women standing in frozen poses onstage at the Folies, Baker presented the Parisian audience with a dark-skinned, athletic form clad in a snicker-producing girdle of drooping bananas, dancing the wildest, most electrifying Charleston anyone had ever witnessed. As the young African savage Fatou, she captured the sexual imagination of Paris.

In 1928, sensing that her public was beginning to tire of her frenetic antics, Baker left Paris. During an extended tour of European and South American cities with her manager and lover, Giuseppe "Pepito" Abatino, she studied voice, disciplined her dancing, and learned to speak French. However, Baker's reception in such cities as Vienna, Budapest, Prague, and Munich was not what it had been in Paris. Protests broke out in hostile reaction to her nudity, to jazz music, and to her foreignness. Baker also encountered for the first time the racism she thought she had left behind in America, the racism against which she would campaign onstage and off for the rest of her life. By the time she made her triumphal return to Paris two and a half years later, she had transformed herself into a sophisticated, elegantly attired French star.

In the 1930s Baker's career branched out in new directions. Singing took on new importance in her performances, and in her 1930–1931 revue at the Casino de Paris she perfected her signature song, "J'ai deux amours," proclaiming that her two loves were her country and Paris. She began recording for Columbia Records in 1930. She starred in two films, *Zou-Zou* (1934) and *Princesse Tam-Tam* (1935), whose story lines paralleled her rags-to-riches life. In the first film she is transformed from a poor laundress to a glamorous music-hall star and in the second from a Tunisian goat girl to an exotic princess. In the fall of 1934 she successfully tackled light opera in the starring role of Offenbach's operetta *La Créole*.

One year later, hoping to enjoy the success at home she had earned abroad, Baker sailed with Pepito to New York and began four months of preparation for the Ziegfeld Follies of 1936. The reviews of the New York opening in January took hateful aim at Baker's performance. Belittling her success abroad with the explanation that in France "a Negro wench always has a head start," the reporter remarked that "to Manhattan theatergoers last week she was just a slightly buck-toothed Negro woman whose figure might be matched in any night-club show, and whose dancing and singing might be topped practically anywhere outside of Paris." Critics, black and white, resented her performing only French cabaret material rather than "Harlem songs." Newspapers also reported that Baker personally was snubbed, refused entrance to hotels and nightclubs. Reactions to this discrimination varied, with some condemning her for "trying to be white." The columnist ROI OTTLEY of the *Amsterdam News*, on the other hand, praised her efforts to overcome Jim Crowism, saying that "she was just trying to live ignoring color." He recommended that "Harlem … should rally to the side of this courageous Negro woman. We should make her insults our insults."

Disappointed by her reception in her homeland and saddened by the death from cancer of Pepito, Baker returned to Paris and to the nude revues at the Folies-Bergère. By then thirty years old, she wanted to marry and have children. She realized the first desire on 30 November 1937, when she wed Jean Lion, a rich and handsome Jewish playboy and sugar broker. After fourteen months of marriage, during which Baker did not become pregnant and Lion continued his wild ways, she filed for divorce, which was granted in 1942.

In June of 1940 German troops invaded Paris. Baker, who refused to perform either for racist Nazis or for their French sympathizers, fled to Les Milandes, her fifteenth-century château in the Dordogne, with her maid, a Belgian refugee couple, and her beloved dogs. Since September 1939 Baker had served as an "honorable correspondent," gathering information about German troop locations for French military intelligence at embassy and ministry parties in Paris. Once Charles de Gaulle had declared himself leader of Free France in a radio broadcast from London and called for the French to resist their German occupiers, Baker joined "*résistance*" and was active in it throughout World War II, working mostly in North Africa. For her heroic work she was awarded the Croix de Guerre, and de Gaulle himself gave her a gold cross of Lorraine, the symbol of the Fighting French, when he established headquarters in Algiers in the spring of 1943. Baker was a tireless ambassador for the Free France movement and for de Gaulle, performing for British, American, and French soldiers in North Africa and touring the Middle East to raise money for the cause. In recognition of the propaganda services she performed during this tour, she was made a sublieutenant of the Women's Auxiliary of the French Air Force. After the war de Gaulle awarded Baker the coveted Medal of Resistance.

Moving into the 1950s Baker harnessed her formidable energies behind two causes. The first was her own pursuit of racial harmony and human tolerance in the form of her "Rainbow Tribe." To demonstrate the viability of world brotherhood, with the orchestra leader Jo Bouillon, whom she had married in 1947, Baker adopted children of many nationalities, races, and religions and installed them at Les Milandes. In order to support the family that eventually numbered thirteen and to finance the massive renovation of the château and related construction projects, Baker returned to the stage. A quick trip to the United States in 1948 was as unsuccessful as the one twelve years earlier and left her convinced that, if possible, race relations there were even worse than before. This realization prompted Baker's second cause, the pursuit of civil rights for black Americans through the desegregation of hotels, restaurants, and nightclubs.

Traveling with a $250,000 Parisian wardrobe; singing in French, Spanish, English, Italian, and Portuguese; and performing with masterly showmanship, in 1951 Baker began an American tour in Cuba. When word of her success in Havana reached Miami, Copa City moved to book the star for a splashy engagement. Contract negotiations were long and difficult. Initiating what would become her standard demand with nightclubs, Baker insisted on a nondiscrimination clause. If management would not admit black patrons, she would not perform. The integrated audience for Baker's show at Copa City was the first in the city's history. Baker took her tour and her campaign against color lines from city to city—New York, Boston, Atlanta, Las Vegas, and Hollywood. And audiences loved her. *Variety* wrote, "The showmanship that is Josephine Baker's … is something that doesn't happen synthetically or overnight. It's of the same tradition that accounts for the durability of almost every show biz standard still on top after many years."

The pinnacle of Baker's civil rights efforts was reached in August 1963 when she was invited to the great March on Washington. Dressed in her World War II uniform, Baker stood on the platform in front of the Lincoln Memorial and spoke to the crowd of thousands, blacks and whites, demonstrating for justice and equality: "You are on the eve of victory. You can't go wrong. The world is behind you." Baker was among those arrayed around MARTIN LUTHER KING JR. as he delivered his "I

Have a Dream" speech. Certainly, for Josephine Baker, that day was a dream come true.

The remaining years of Baker's life were not tranquil. Given her extravagant spending and generosity, financial problems continued to plague her. Jo Bouillon finally despaired of trying to raise so many children or to impose any fiscal responsibility and left Baker. In 1968 Les Milandes was sold, and Baker, who barricaded herself in the house with her children, was evicted. Such setbacks notwithstanding, she continued to give comeback performances, astonishing crowds with her ability to rejuvenate herself the moment she stepped on stage, the consummate star. Her final performance in Paris to a sold-out house on 9 April 1975 was no exception. The following day, just two months shy of her sixty-ninth birthday, Baker died of a cerebral hemorrhage brought on by a stroke. All of France mourned the passing of "la Joséphine." National television broadcast the procession of her flag-draped coffin through the streets of Paris and the funeral service at the Church of the Madeleine, where twenty thousand Parisians gathered to pay their respects.

In *Jazz Cleopatra: Josephine Baker in Her Time*, Phyllis Rose writes of Baker's "cabaret internationalism" as her "way of expressing a political position." A performer of consummate skill, Baker enthralled audiences for more than a half century. But personal adulation was not enough. Like PAUL ROBESON, HARRY BELAFONTE, LENA HORNE, BILL COSBY, and others, Baker put her prestige and popularity in the service of civil rights, racial harmony, and equality for all humanity.

FURTHER READING

Baker, Josephine, and Marcel Sauvage. *Les mémoires de Joséphine Baker* (1927).

Baker, Josephine, and Marcel Sauvage. *Les mémoires de Joséphine Baker* (1949).

Baker, Josephine, and Jo Bouillon. *Joséphine* (1976).

Colin, Paul. *Le tumulte noir* (1927).

Hammond, Bryan, and Patrick O'Connor. *Josephine Baker* (1988).

Rose, Phyllis. *Jazz Cleopatra: Josephine Baker in Her Time* (1989).

Obituary: *New York Times*, 13 April 1975.

KAREN C. C. DALTON

Baker, LaVern (11 Nov. 1929–10 Mar. 1997), singer, was born in Chicago as Delores Williams. Nothing is known about her parents. Raised by her aunt,

Merline Baker, also known as the blues singer MEMPHIS MINNIE, Baker started singing almost as soon as she could walk, both in her Baptist church and in the street. She grew up in poverty and sang for change on the downtown Chicago streets from the age of three. She started singing professionally as a teenager at the Club Delisa, decked out in down-home clothes and billed as "Little Miss Sharecropper." The "Sharecropper" sobriquet was a takeoff on the popular blues shouter "Little Miss Cornshucks," and although it garnered her attention at the time, she was embarrassed by it later in her life. She also appeared at different venues as Bea Baker.

At the age of seventeen, Baker moved to Detroit. By 1947 she was appearing regularly at the city's legendary Flame Show Bar. She was first heard on a commercial recording in 1949, singing with the Eddie Penigar Band for RCA Records. Over the next several years she recorded on different labels with two separate groups; with HOT LIPS PAGE and Red Sanders she recorded (as "Little Miss Sharecropper") on Columbia and on Okeh Records (as Bea Baker) with Maurice King and his Wolverines. Baker joined the Todd Rhodes Orchestra in 1952, taking the name LaVern Baker, and toured the national "chitlin' circuit" while recording with Rhodes for King Records.

Baker signed on with Ahmet Ertegun and Atlantic Records in 1953. At that point Atlantic was a strictly R&B and blues label whose other female star, RUTH BROWN, had a completely different voice and style from Baker's. Brown's hits like "Mama, He Treats Your Daughter Mean" and "Teardrops from My Eyes" were like most of Atlantic's successes of the era: black records made for black adults and strictly aimed at the R&B market, eschewing any attempt at gaining a white audience. Ertegun and the producer Jerry Wexler apparently had different designs for Baker.

Her first important Atlantic recording, "Soul On Fire," was a rewrite by Ertegun, Baker, and Wexler of the gospel standard "Journey to the Sky." Baker's simmering delivery and the record's gospel-tinged tension and release presaged the metaphorical fire to come. It served as a precursor of the crossover from rhythm and blues to rock and roll, a phenomenon that was to transform popular music in the 1950s.

Baker's first crossover pop hit was "Tweedle Dee" in 1955. An early example of the "white cover" phenomena, which reflected the pernicious racism of the era, "Tweedle Dee" was quickly covered and released by the white singer Georgia Gibb. Gibb's version was the bigger pop hit since it received massive airplay on the pop radio stations of the day. While Baker did appear singing the song on the Ed Sullivan Show, the "cover" practice (Gibbs later covered other Baker songs and ETTA JAMES's early hits as well) seriously curtailed some of the momentum of Baker and other R&B acts like FATS DOMINO and BIG JOE TURNER. Baker even unsuccessfully attempted to get Congress to change the copyright law to prevent the identical copying of arrangements. Two rhythm and blues hits, "Bop-Ting-a-Ling" (1955) and "Play it Fair" (1956) followed her first smash, but the release of "Jim Dandy" (1956) confirmed Baker's status as a rock and roll star.

Baker's crossover success brought her to the attention of pioneering deejay Alan Freed, who not only popularized the use of the term "rock and roll" on his New York radio show, but also became identified with the "new" music through the national multi-artist tours he promoted and the movies he produced and in which he starred. Baker's records epitomized his "big beat" sound, and she joined CHUCK BERRY, the Everly Brothers, Buddy Holly, Fats Domino, and LITTLE RICHARD on Freed's all-star shows throughout the country. She also starred in Freed's films *Rock, Rock, Rock* (1956) and *Mister Rock & Roll* (1957). The biggest hit of her career was the blues ballad "I Cried a Tear" (1958), which reached number three on the pop chart.

In a change of pace from her hits, Baker sang on what is arguably the best "BESSIE SMITH" album ever recorded: *LaVern Baker Sings Bessie Smith*. Produced by Nesuhi Ertegun and engineered by Tom Dowd, the album paired Baker with the hippest jazz musicians of the era, such as BUCK CLAYTON, Jerome Richardson, DANNY BARKER, and VIC DICKENSON, and she belted Bessie's tunes in her own inimitable style over the swinging arrangements of ERNIE WILKINS, Phil Moore, and Nat Pierce. While Bessie Smith was undoubtedly the greatest of blues singers, she lived in a time with limited recording resources; this was the album she might have made had she lived into the 1950s.

A television special from this period on the music of Harold Arlen showed some of the depth and breadth of Baker's talent and reflected her desire to broaden her range. She starred with Peggy Lee, Vic Damone, and Arlen in the *DuPont Show of the Week, Happy with the Blues: The Music of Harold Arlen*, broadcast on 24 September 1961.

After sitting through the absurdity of a jungle set, the viewer was treated to Baker's seminal takes on "I've Got a Right to Sing the Blues" and "Stormy Weather," as well as Lee's sultry "The Man That Got Away" and the definitive "I've Got the World on a String." She soon joined LOUIS ARMSTRONG's band as featured female singer and toured the world with him for the next two years.

Baker left Atlantic in 1964 and signed with Brunswick the following year. There she recorded more R&B hits, the last of which was a funky duet with JACKIE WILSON, released in 1966, called "Think Twice." She joined a USO tour of Vietnam and the Far East in 1967. While on tour in 1969, she became ill and convalesced at a hospital on Subic Bay in the Philippines. The commander of the base was a fan and offered her a job running the Non-Commissioned Officers Club. She took the job and sang at the club for the next twenty years, completely dropping out of the music business in the United States.

Baker returned to the States for the first time in 1988 to sing at the Atlantic Records fortieth anniversary celebration, and once back in the country, she became active in the music business once more. In 1990 she recorded a song for the *Dick Tracy* soundtrack album, played dynamic gigs in New York and Washington, D.C., and was awarded a Career Achievement Award by the Rhythm and Blues Foundation. The offer of a lead role in the Broadway hit *Black and Blue* brought her back for good; she performed in the show for nine months in 1990. Tours of the United States and Europe followed in 1991, capped by an appearance with B. B. KING and Ruth Brown at the Montreux Jazz Festival in July. Her comeback was complete.

Baker suffered formidable health setbacks in 1993–1994, culminating in the loss of both her legs due to diabetic complications. She then embarked on what can only be described as one of the most inspiring comebacks in recent show business history. She relearned her material and started singing from a wheelchair. By 1995 she was back to captivating audiences, and in 1996 she made a triumphant performance before 10,000 people at the Newport Rhythm and Blues Festival. She had just learned to walk with artificial legs when she succumbed to heart failure in 1997. She was the second woman (after ARETHA FRANKLIN) inducted into the Rock and Roll Hall of Fame in 1991.

FURTHER READING

Ertegun, Ahmet, et al. *What'd I Say: The Atlantic Story, 50 Years of Music* (2001).

Wade, Dorothy, and Justine Picardie. *Music Man: Ahmet Ertegun, Atlantic Records, and the Triumph of Rock 'n' Roll* (1990).

Wexler, Jerry, and David Ritz. *Rhythm and the Blues: A Life in American Music* (1993).

DISCOGRAPHY

LaVern Baker Sings Bessie Smith, Atlantic Records (1958).

LaVern Baker Live in Hollywood '91, Rhino (1991).

Soul on Fire: The Best of LaVern Baker, Atlantic (1991).

Obituary: *New York Times*, 12 Mar. 1997.

BARRY MARSHALL

Baker, Lena (8 June 1900–5 Mar. 1945), the first woman executed by electric chair in Georgia, was born in Cuthbert, Georgia, to Queenie Baker, a sharecropper, and a father whose name is unknown. Little is known about her early life. If typical of the African American experience in southwestern Georgia in the early 1900s Baker's

Lena Baker, at the Georgia State Prison in Reidsville, Georgia, 23 February 1945. (AP Images/Georgia Department of Corrections File.)

childhood was probably one of long working hours and low expectations. Indeed, it was in the debt-ridden and desperate Georgia black belt of the early 1900s that W. E. B. DU BOIS discovered the "Negro problem in its naked dirt and penury" (Litwack, 114). In an attempt to escape from that world of debt and desperation, Baker began working at an early age, at first helping her mother chop cotton for a neighboring white family, the Coxes. Like other black women in the community, she also worked as a laundress and occasional domestic for white families in town. Despite the legacy of Cuthbert's most famous black educator, RICHARD R. WRIGHT, Baker attended school sporadically, when her labor was not needed by the her family or by the-Coxes, and she did not return to school after the sixth grade.

Baker would also have been aware of the ever-present undercurrent of racial violence in Jim Crow-era Georgia. In addition to the notorious public lynching of SAM HOSE in 1899, more than four hundred other African Americans were lynched by white mobs in that state between 1882 and 1920. Five black men were lynched in tiny Randolph County alone in that period, including a double lynching in Cuthbert in September 1916, when Baker was sixteen years old and which she may well have known about. Baker regularly attended Cuthbert's Mount Vernon Baptist Church, where she sang in the choir, but she may also have been familiar with the region's many taverns, juke joints, and tent shows, which produced the likes of Columbus, Georgia's MA RAINEY, among others in their heyday before World War I. Some time in the mid-1920s, Baker and another black woman began to operate a small brothel in Cuthbert, catering to both black and white customers. After being arrested for prostitution and sentenced to several months in the workhouse, Baker returned to Cuthbert to work as a domestic and to raise three children, apparently without the assistance of their father, of whom nothing is known. Though she remained active in her church and choir, she was shunned by many in the black community who were unwilling to forgive her transgressions.

Isolated, she turned increasingly to alcohol. By the early 1940s her steady drinking had led Baker into the company of a fellow alcoholic, Ernest B. Knight, a white gristmill owner in his sixties with a reputation for casual violence. After Knight broke his leg in a fall, Baker began working for him, ostensibly to help him around his home. When rumors spread throughout Cuthbert that the couple were having a sexual affair—illegal under Georgia law—they were visited by the local sheriff, but not arrested. Knight's son also tried to end the affair by savagely beating Baker and later by threatening to kill her when Baker and Ernest Knight moved briefly to Tallahassee, Florida.

By early 1943 both Baker and Knight had returned to Cuthbert. Their relationship—violent, chaotic, and fueled by alcohol—continued. According to Baker's trial testimony, matters came to a head on the evening of 30 April 1943, when Knight forced her at gunpoint to come to his gristmill to drink and have sex. Baker resisted, but Knight threatened to beat and kill her. At some point during the following day Knight attempted to rape Baker, who resisted and managed to grab the pistol that he always wore strapped to his chest. Fearing for her life and seeing Knight holding an iron bar, Baker told a Randolph County court at her trial that she then fired the pistol in self-defense, killing Knight. Baker admitted her crime to the county coroner—a member of the white Cox family—was promptly arrested, and on 14 August 1944, an all-white, all-male jury found her guilty of the capital murder of Ernest Knight. The trial lasted only a few hours. Baker's attorney's appeals for clemency were swiftly dismissed, probably because the prosecution had made much of Baker's unsavory reputation and her conviction for prostitution.

On 5 March 1945 Lena Baker became the first woman to die in Georgia's electric chair. In her final statement she continued to insist that she had acted in self-defense and that she was ready to meet her God. The local white newspaper headlined the event "Baker Burns." To a considerable extent Lena Baker was a victim of unfortunate timing, as well as Georgia's racist criminal legal system. Two years after Baker's execution Rosa Lee Ingram, another African American woman from the southwest Georgia black belt, was also given the death sentence for her role in killing a white man in self-defense. In Ingram's case, however, pressure from the Civil Rights Congress, the Communist Party, the NAACP, and the *Pittsburgh Courier* persuaded the authorities to reduce her sentence to a life prison term and, eventually, to release her on parole. Five years later the U.S. Supreme Court ruled against the application of the death penalty in cases such as Baker's and Ingram's where there was such a clear element of self-defense.

Outside her own family Lena Baker's life and early death remained largely forgotten and ignored until the late 1990s, when some of her relatives, members of Mount Vernon Baptist Church, and anti–death penalty activists in Randolph County erected a permanent marker for her unmarked grave in Cuthbert Cemetery. They also began a campaign seeking a posthumous pardon for Baker from the state of Georgia, on the grounds that she had been a victim of abuse who had killed in self-defense. The campaign succeeded in August 2005, when the Georgia Board of Pardons and Paroles apologized for the state's refusal to grant Lena Baker clemency sixty years earlier.

FURTHER READING

Litwack, Leon. *Trouble in Mind: Black Southerners in the Age of Jim Crow* (1998).

Phillips, Lena Bond. *The Lena Baker Story* (2001).

STEVEN J. NIVEN

Baker, Ruth Baytop (6 Nov. 1908–22 Oct. 2006), voice teacher, mezzo-soprano, pianist, educator, was one of four children born to Dr. THOMAS NELSON BAKER SR. and ELIZABETH BAYTOP BAKER in Pittsfield, Massachusetts. Her father's parents were slaves. Dr. Thomas Nelson Baker was born a slave on 11 August 1860 and worked on the farm until he was twenty-one years old. He was one of five children and was the first African American to earn and receive a Ph in Philosophy from Yale University in 1906. In 1890 he received a B from Boston University and a Bachelor's in Divinity from Yale University and studied psychology and philosophy from 1896 to 1900 at Yale Graduate School. He was minister of the Dixwell Congregational Church in New Haven, Connecticut, from 1896 to 1900. He was listed in *Who's Who in New England, 1908–1909*, and his writings paved the way for the Harlem Renaissance era, which lasted from 1917 to 1935. He married Elizabeth (Lizzie) Baytop in 1901, a graduate of Hampton Institute. They had four children: Ruth, Harry, Edith and Thomas Jr. All of them graduated from Oberlin College in Ohio. Ruth received a B.A. in 1933 and a B.S. in 1934 from Oberlin Conservatory. Edith graduated from Oberlin Conservatory in 1928. Edith and Ruth specialized in voice and piano, Harry in piano and organ, and Dr. Thomas Nelson Baker Jr. in chemistry. Dr. Thomas Nelson Baker Jr. became head of the Chemistry Department at Virginia State University.

Ruth B. Baker was trained as a concert singer and had a beautiful mezzo-soprano voice. However, she chose to teach vocal technique instead. Later, she and her sister, Edith Baker, came to New York City and settled in Harlem. Their aim was to uplift the people. Ruth attended Columbia University, where she received a master's degree in Music Education in 1988. She was a member of the New York Music Teacher's League and was listed in *Who's Who among American Women*. She worked first as an administrative assistant and later as a supervisor for the Department of Social Service in New York City in the Division of Child Welfare and taught voice and piano after work.

For many years, Ruth and her sister, Edith, were associates of Reverend A. Merral Willis and his cultural center, which was located in a loft building on West 125th Street in the heart of the African American business district in Harlem. Reverend Willis was one of the first officers of Omega Psi Phi fraternity, established in 1919. After his demise, Ruth and Edith Baker established the A. Merral Willis Cultural Center and Foundation. In her studio at the A. Merral Willis headquarters, she taught hundreds of vocal students of all races and never charged more than twenty-five dollars a lesson or whatever they could afford. Edith and Ruth shared the music studio until Edith's demise. Four times a year, at her own expense, Ruth Baker would rent a hall in Harlem and present her students in recital, giving them the experience of performing before a large audience.

Ruth and Edith Baker were associated with the renowned African American tenor ROLAND HAYES, who sponsored African American singers in recitals at Carnegie Hall. Ruth Baker continued that tradition for more than forty years. This gave aspiring singers a chance to perform at Carnegie Hall. Ms. Baker paid most of the expenses out of her own pocket. Ruth and Edith Baker were also involved with the National Negro Opera Company headed by the first female African American opera conductor, Ms. Mary Cardwell Dawson.

Ruth Baker was the mentor and sponsor of the great African American scientist, Solomon B. Harper, who was listed in *Who's Who in American Science*. She was also associated with the well-known African American New York assistant district attorney Joseph A. Bailey, who was a frequent keynote speaker at her monthly cultural programs. Ms. Baker was also a friend of Dr. JOHN HENRIK CLARK, a well-known African American historian. He was a frequent speaker at her monthly cultural events. Ruth Baker and her sister Edith founded the Colonel Young Memorial Foundation in honor of Colonel CHARLES YOUNG, one of the first African

Americans to graduate from West Point. Yearly programs were presented in his memory.

Ruth and Edith never married. Their brother, Dr. Thomas Nelson Baker Jr., married and had two sons, Dr. Thomas Nelson Baker III and Newman Taylor Baker, both musicians.

FURTHER READING

Ruth Baytop Baker's papers are housed in the Oberlin College and Conservatory Archives in Oberlin, Ohio and Teacher's College, Columbia University, New York, New York.

LOIS BELLAMY

Baker, Thomas Nelson, Sr. (11 Aug. 1860–25 Feb. 1940), philosopher and first African American to receive a Ph.D. in Philosophy in the United States, was born enslaved of enslaved parents, Thomas Chadwick Baker, a Civil War veteran, and Edith (Nottingham) Baker, on Robert Nottingham's

Thomas Nelson Baker, Sr., a former slave who became the first African American to earn a doctorate in philosophy in the United States, in an undated photograph. (University of Massachusetts, Amherst.)

plantation in Northampton County, Virginia. Edith was the daughter of Southey and Sarah Nottingham of Northampton County. Thomas Nelson Baker was one of five children.

Describing the influences on his early intellectual life, Baker remembered:

My mother taught me my letters, although I well remember when she learned them herself. My first reading lesson was the second chapter of Matthew, the Bible being the only book we had. I never read a bad book in my life which is one of the blessings I got by being poor. I began to attend the common schools at eight and learned to love books passionately. I used to read through my recesses. Evenings I read the Bible to my parents and grandparents, while they listened with weeping eyes, thankful that I had received the great blessing of being able to read (untitled newspaper, Hampton University Archives).

In 1872, when Baker was twelve, his father removed him from school so that he could work to help meet rent payments for the house that the family occupied. Baker worked for ten years as a farmhand, which led him to break all connections with books and schoolmates. However, once he came of age, his burning desire to get an education returned.

In 1881 Baker entered Hampton Institute in Virginia, where he studied for the next four years. During his first year Baker worked during the day and attended Hampton Institute's night school. During the last three years he attended the day school. After leaving, Baker taught for a year at schools in the Dismal Swamp, a region in southeast Virginia and northeast North Carolina.

In May 1886 Baker entered Mount Hermon School in Massachusetts (also known as the Reverend Dwight L. Moody's Boys' School), where he received training for entrance to college. Baker was one of only two black students there, but during his first year he acted as drillmaster. He graduated in June 1889.

Around 1890 Baker entered Boston University's liberal arts school, graduating with a B.A. in 1893. That year he went on to attend the Yale Divinity School, where he completed a bachelor of divinity degree in three years. Following this degree Baker studied philosophy and psychology from 1896 to 1900 at the Yale graduate school. Coupled with pastoral duties—for from 1896 to 1901 he was the minister of the Dixwell Avenue Congregational Church in New Haven, Connecticut, and was ordained there in 1897—he completed his Ph.D. in Philosophy at Yale in 1903, becoming the first African American in the United States to receive a Ph.D. in Philosophy.

Baker probably wrote much of his dissertation, "The Ethical Significance of the Connection between Mind and Body," while living in Pittsfield, Massachusetts, because in 1901 he had become the minister of the town's Second Congregational Church (the second minister in the church's history). He held this position until 1939, when he was made minister emeritus from 1939 to 1940. He was also the dean of clergymen in Pittsfield. In keeping with his high standing, in 1926 Baker had the honor of being the only black pastor to deliver an address at the mound of the unknown dead in Pittsfield Cemetery on Memorial Day.

On 18 September 1901, while he was still working on his dissertation, Baker married Elizabeth Baytop, an alumna of Hampton Institute and the daughter of Harry and Millie (Bright) Baytop, in Capahosic, Virginia. They had four children: Edith, Harry, Ruth, and Thomas Jr. All four excelled academically, with all four earning bachelor's degrees and some earning higher degrees.

Baker wrote various significant philosophical articles dealing with black values and ideals. Indeed, Baker's views concerning black aesthetics and black cultural identity constitute an early and significant philosophical precursor to the Harlem Renaissance and the 1960s Black Arts Movement. As early as May 1906, even before ALAIN LEROY LOCKE's *The New Negro* (1925), Baker, in *Alexander's Magazine*, forged a philosophical critique of racism and advanced an aesthetic alternative to the reigning white aesthetic of beauty. He argued, "not where we are, but what we are is the great and final question that should concern us" ("Not Pity but Respect," 111). For Baker, "It is the perversion of the aesthetical sense of physical beauty that the American Negro has struck his lowest depths of racial degradation" ("Ideals," 28). And in 1908, in the *Southern Workman*, Baker suggested a critical pedagogy that could create representational and semiotic diversity: "The pictures of the boys and girls in school are just what the Negro child needs to see. If there is to be any real race love, the Negro child must be taught to see beauty in the Negro type."

Baker was acutely aware of colonial hegemony and its inhumane manifestations. He maintained:

Everywhere the colored man sees built into the steamboats, trains and waiting rooms the teachings of Nietzsche: "All that is best is for my folk and for myself. If it is not given us, we take it. The best land, the purest sky, the best food, the most beautiful thoughts and the most beautiful women" (*Berkshire Eagle*, 1919).

Baker was also concerned with the symbolic reorientation of black consciousness. He argued that the watchword of black people should be "Not Pity but Respect." In short, by stripping away the identity of helplessness as imposed from the outside, black people could say to their oppressors in unequivocal terms that the "Jim Crow Negro" personality is dead, that they as black people stand within the domain of their own self-worth and self-value. Baker clearly understood the seriousness of the issue of black aesthetic symbolization; it was an issue of black survival within a racist, cultural, and institutional symbolic space designed to create a destructive black double consciousness, self-alienation, and somatic malediction.

Through his philosophical efforts to create a discourse of race pride and race identity, Thomas Nelson Baker became an important philosophical figure of the twentieth-century black intellectual vanguard. Baker died accidentally as a result of poisoning from illuminating gas and was buried at the Pittsfield Cemetery.

FURTHER READING
Materials by and about Thomas Nelson Baker can be found in the Baker file at the Hampton University Archives, Hampton, Virginia.
Baker, Thomas N. "Ideals," *Alexander's Magazine* (2 parts, Sept. and Oct. 1906).
Baker, Thomas N. "Not Pity but Respect," *Alexander's Magazine* (May 1906).
Yancy, George. "On the Power of Black Aesthetic Ideals: Thomas Nelson Baker as Preacher and Philosopher," *A.M.E. Church Review* (Oct.–Dec. 2001).
Obituaries: *Berkshire Eagle* 49, no. 207 (n.d.); *Yale University Alumni Records, 1940–1941* (1942).

GEORGE YANCY

Baker, Vernon Joseph (17 Dec. 1919–13 July 2010), soldier and Medal of Honor recipient, was born in Cheyenne, Wyoming, to Manuel Caldera and Beulah Baker. After the deaths of his parents, Vernon and his sisters, Irma and Katherine, were raised by their maternal grandparents, Joseph Samuel Baker, a retired brakeman for the Union Pacific Railroad, and Dora Lucas. Although his grandparents never officially adopted him, Vernon took the surname Baker and did not know his original surname until later in life. Baker was educated at various elementary and secondary schools, including two years at Father Flanagan's Boys Home in Omaha, Nebraska. Baker finally earned his high school diploma at Clarinda, Iowa, in 1939.

After graduation, Baker returned to Cheyenne, where he found work at the army depot at night doing maintenance, repair, and cleaning jobs. Baker was rejected on his first attempt to join the army. Finally in June 1942 he enlisted and was shipped to Fort Walters, Texas. While in Texas, Baker worked as the company supply clerk and was promoted from private first class to sergeant. His commanding officer noticed Baker's ability as a supply sergeant and assigned him to Officer Candidate School in Fort Benning, Georgia.

Following officer training, Baker was sent to the 370th Infantry Regiment as a second lieutenant and rifle platoon leader and was stationed at Fort Huachuca, Arizona. In October 1943 Baker was reassigned to the 360th Regimental Combat Team of the 92nd Infantry Division and was sent to Italy. In August 1944 his unit joined General Mark Clark's Fifth Army and engaged a veteran German army in fierce combat. Lacking proper equipment and training, the typical enlisted man held only a fourth-grade education, and the 92nd Infantry Division suffered a casualty rate of almost 25 percent from August 1944 until the final German surrender in Italy on 2 May 1945.

After nearly eighteen months of duty in Italy, Baker's platoon was ordered to assault Hill X and Castle Aghinolfi nearly three miles behind the vaunted German Gothic Line on 5 April 1945. During this action the platoon suffered a nearly 60 percent casualty rate. Baker was ordered to withdraw his battered platoon but was unable to do so because of intense German bombardment. Rather, he chose to fight the Germans almost single-handedly in order to save as many of his men as possible, and in the process he destroyed one machine-gun nest and a German observation tower. Along with another platoon member, Baker smashed two more gun emplacements and drew enemy fire away from attempts to withdraw his decimated unit.

The following morning, on 6 April 1945, Baker led the 360th and 361st Regimental Combat Teams through mine fields near Viareggio, Italy, to capture both of the original objectives of the mission. For these actions and the injuries he suffered while undertaking them Baker was awarded the Purple Heart, the Bronze Star, and the Distinguished Service Cross.

The 92nd Infantry Division pulled out of Italy in late 1945, but Baker remained there, staying in the army despite losing his officer's commission because he lacked a college degree. By the time Baker returned to Lincoln, Nebraska, in 1947 he had attained the rank of master sergeant and worked as a recruiting photographer. While in Lincoln he considered using the GI Bill to attend the University of Nebraska but instead chose to join the Eleventh Airborne, an all-black division. Baker trained at Fort Bragg, North Carolina, where he earned his jump wings and completed the army's noncommissioned officer school. Baker was promoted to first sergeant and assigned to Company K, 505th Infantry of the famed 82nd Airborne Division.

With the outbreak of hostilities in Korea in 1950, Baker volunteered for a tour of duty. He was denied because of his status as a Distinguished Service Cross winner but was later repromoted to lieutenant because of the wartime demand for officers. President Harry Truman had ordered the military desegregated in 1948, and Baker became one of the first black officers to command an integrated company. With the Korean armistice in 1953, Baker was mustered out of the airborne to the signal corps with his officer status revoked again.

After the war Baker was stationed in Tucson, Arizona, where he met Fern V. Brown, whom he married in June 1953. Brown was divorced and had twin four-year-old daughters, and she and Baker had one daughter, LaVerne, in December 1954 and adopted another daughter, Larise, in Korea in 1955. After returning from Korea, Baker was stationed at Fort Ord, California, where he served until he was transferred to Germany in 1967. Baker retired from the army in August 1968.

After retiring, Baker worked as a loan officer and an assistant field director with the American Red Cross. He was sent to Vietnam in 1969, where he worked in the field at Pleiku and Da Nang. Baker continued to work for the Red Cross until 1986. He retired after the death of his wife and moved to Spokane, Washington, so that he could pursue his lifelong love of big-game hunting. Baker was married a second time in 1993 to Heidy Pawlik, a German immigrant.

For his actions in Italy, Baker was awarded the Medal of Honor, the nation's highest award for military service, on 17 January 1997 by President Bill Clinton. Baker was one of only seven African

Americans to receive this honor for their World War II service. At the time of the ceremony, Baker was the only recipient still living. The six other African Americans posthumously awarded the Medal of Honor were Private George Watson, Sergeant Edward A. Carter Jr., Private Willy F. James Jr., Sergeant Ruben Rivers, First Lieutenant Charles L. Thomas, and First Lieutenant JOHN FOX.

Baker died of brain cancer at the age of nintey, outside of St. Maries, Idaho.

FURTHER READING

Baker, Vernon J., and Ken Olsen. *Lasting Valor* (1997).

Gibran, Daniel K. *The 92nd Infantry Division and the Italian Campaign in World War II* (2001).

Hargrove, Hondon B. *Buffalo Soldiers in Italy: Black Americans in World War II* (1985).

Motley, Mary Penick, ed. *The Invisible Soldier: The Experience of the Black Soldier, World War II* (1987).

Obituary: *Washington Post*, 15 July 2010.

JEFFERY OTHELE MAHAN

Baldwin, James (2 Aug. 1924–1 Dec. 1987), author, was born James Arthur Baldwin in Harlem, in New York City, the illegitimate son of Emma Berdis Jones, who married the author's stepfather, David Baldwin, in 1927. David Baldwin was a laborer and weekend storefront preacher who had an enormous influence on the author's childhood; his mother was a domestic who had eight more children after he was born. Baldwin was singled out early in school for his intelligence, and at least one white teacher, Orrin Miller, took a special interest in him. At P.S. 139, Frederick Douglass Junior High School, Baldwin met black poet COUNTÉE CULLEN, a teacher and literary club adviser there. Cullen saw some of Baldwin's early poems and warned him against trying to write like LANGSTON HUGHES, so Baldwin turned from poetry to focus more on writing fiction. In 1938 he experienced a profound religious conversion at the hands of a female evangelist/pastor of Mount Cavalry of the Pentecostal Faith, which he later wrote about in his first novel, *Go Tell It on the Mountain* (1953), in his play *The Amen Corner* (1968), and in an essay in *The Fire Next Time* (1963). Saved, Baldwin became a Sunday preacher at the nearby Fireside Pentecostal Assembly.

In 1938 Baldwin entered De Witt Clinton High School in the Bronx; he graduated in 1942. There Baldwin was challenged intellectually and was able to escape home and Harlem. He wrote for the school magazine, the *Magpie*, and began to frequent Greenwich Village, where he met the black artist BEAUFORD DELANEY, an important early influence. Torn between the dual influences of the church and his intellectual and artistic private life, Baldwin finally made a choice. At age sixteen he began a homosexual relationship with a Harlem racketeer and later said he was grateful to the older man throughout his life for the love and self-validation he brought to the tormented and self-conscious teenager. As a preacher, Baldwin considered himself a hypocrite. At this same time, he discovered that David Baldwin was not, in fact, his real father and began to understand why he had felt deeply rejected as a child and had hated and feared his father. Fearing gossip about his homosexual relationship would reach his family and church, Baldwin broke with both the racketeer and the church. Now eighteen, he also moved away from home, taking a series of odd jobs in New Jersey and spending free time in the Village with artists and writers, trying to establish himself. He returned home in 1943 to care for the family while his stepfather was dying of tuberculosis. A few hours after his father's death, his youngest sister was born, named by James Baldwin, the head of the family. The Harlem riot of 1943 broke out in the midst of this family upheaval, all of which Baldwin described eloquently in *Notes of a Native Son* (1955).

After his stepfather's funeral Baldwin left home for the last time, determined to become a writer. In 1944 he met RICHARD WRIGHT, who helped him get a Eugene F. Saxon Fellowship to work on his first novel, then titled "In My Father's House." He gave part of the $500 grant to his mother and tried to start his literary career. Although Baldwin's first novel was rejected by two publishers, he began to have some success publishing book reviews and essays, establishing a name and a reputation. At the same time, he had difficulty extracting himself from the influence of Richard Wright, who became for Baldwin the literary father that he had to reject, as David Baldwin had been the punishing stepfather to be overcome. With what was left of the Rosenwald Fellowship he had received in 1948, Baldwin, frustrated by the fits and starts of his writing career and tired of America's racism, bought a one-way air ticket to Paris and left the United States on 11 November.

In Paris, Baldwin met writers such as Jean-Paul Sartre, Jean Genet, and Saul Bellow. He garnered notice as a critic with the essay "Everybody's Protest Novel," which came out in *Partisan Review* in 1949. Although mostly a critique of Harriet Beecher Stowe's *Uncle Tom's Cabin*, this was the first of a series of three essays in which Baldwin attacked his literary mentor, Wright. Baldwin followed with "Many Thousand Gone" in 1951 and, after Wright's death, "Alas Poor Richard" in 1961. But not until he took himself, his typewriter, and his BESSIE SMITH records to a tiny hamlet high in the Swiss Alps in 1951 did Baldwin begin to work in earnest on his first and best novel, *Go Tell It on the Mountain*. In this autobiographical family novel, fourteen-year-old John Grimes undergoes an emotional-psychological-religious crisis of adolescence and is "saved." *Go Tell It on the Mountain* explores the histories and internal lives of John's stepfather Gabriel, mother Elizabeth, and Aunt Florence, spanning the years from 1875 to the Depression and including "the Great Migration" from the South to Harlem. It was well received and was nominated for the National Book Award in 1954; Baldwin said in an interview with QUINCY TROUPE that he was told it did not win because RALPH ELLISON's *Invisible Man* had won in 1953 and America was not ready to give this award to two black writers in a row.

Baldwin won a Guggenheim grant to work on a second novel, published in 1956 as *Giovanni's Room*, about a homosexual relationship and with all-white characters in a European setting. Baldwin's American publisher turned it down for its honesty, so Baldwin had to publish *Giovanni's Room* first in London. It was a book Baldwin had to write, he said in an interview with Richard Goldstein, "to clarify something for myself." Baldwin went on to say, "The question of human affection, of integrity, in my case, the question of trying to become a writer, are all linked with the question of sexuality." The central character, David, a young American living in Paris, is forced to choose between his fiancée, Hella, and his male lover Giovanni. David rejects Giovanni, who is later tried and executed for the murder of an aging homosexual. Racked with guilt, David reveals his true homosexual nature and breaks his engagement, making Giovanni the injured martyr and moral pole in the novel.

Baldwin's first collection of essays, *Notes of a Native Son*, appeared in 1955. These autobiographical and political pieces made Baldwin famous as an eloquent and experienced commentator on race and culture in America. Here he says on his stepfather's funeral:

This was his legacy: nothing is ever escaped. That bleakly memorable morning I hated the unbelievable streets and the Negroes and whites who had, equally, made them that way. But I knew that it was folly, as my father would have said,

this bitterness was folly. It was necessary to hold on to the things that mattered. The dead man mattered, the new life mattered; blackness and whiteness did not matter; to believe that they did was to acquiesce in one's own destruction. Hatred, which could destroy so much, never failed to destroy the man who hated and this was an immutable law (Bantam ed. [1968], 94–95).

Baldwin returned periodically to the United States throughout the 1950s and 1960s, but never to stay. He first visited the South in 1957 and met MARTIN LUTHER KING JR. In 1961 he published the collection of essays *Nobody Knows My Name: More Notes of a Native Son*. By 1963 he was prominent enough to be featured on the cover of *Time* magazine as a major spokesman for the early civil rights movement after another collection of essays, *The Fire Next Time*, arguably Baldwin's most influential work, appeared. His first play, *Blues for Mr. Charlie* (1964), a fictionalized account of the 1955 Mississippi murder of fourteen-year-old EMMETT TILL, followed. In *The Fire Next Time* Baldwin effectively honed his prophetic, even apocalyptic rhetoric about racial tensions in America, fusing his themes of protest and love. During this period Baldwin had also published his third novel, *Another Country*, in 1962. His influence in national politics and American literature had reached a peak.

Another Country took Baldwin six years to complete; it eventually sold 4 million copies after a slow start with negative reviews. It is considered to be Baldwin's second-best novel. In it Baldwin portrays multiple relationships involving interracial and bisexual love through a third-person point of view. Again he looks for resolutions to racial and sexual tensions through the power of love. The characters, however, often have trouble distinguishing sex from love and sorting through their attitudes toward sex, race, and class. Though successful, the novel is somewhat unwieldy with nine major characters, dominated by the black jazz drummer Rufus Scott, who commits suicide at the end of the first chapter. The conclusion leaves readers with the hope that some of these troubled characters can achieve levels of self-understanding that will allow them to continue searching for "another country" within flawed and racist America. As the Nigerian writer Wole Soyinka wrote in 1989:

In the ambiguities of Baldwin's expression of social, sexual, even racial and political conflicts will be found that insistent modality of conduct, and even resolution, celebrated or lamented as a tragic omission—love. … James Baldwin's was—to stress the obvious—a different cast of intellect and creative sensibility from a Ralph Ellison's, a SONIA SANCHEZ's, a Richard Wright's, an AMIRI BARAKA's, or an ED BULLINS's. He was, till the end, too deeply fascinated by the ambiguities of moral choices in human relations to posit them in raw conflict terms. His penetrating eyes saw the oppressor as *also* the oppressed. Hate as a revelation of self-hatred, never unambiguously outward-directed. Contempt as thwarted love, yearning for expression. Violence as inner fear, insecurity. Cruelty as an inward-turned knife. His was an optimistic, grey-toned vision of humanity in which the domain of mob law and lynch culture is turned inside out to reveal a landscape of scarecrows, an inner content of straws that await the compassionate breath of human love (Troupe, 11, 17–18).

With the death of Martin Luther King Jr., and the change in the civil rights movement of the late 1960s from integrationist to separatist, Baldwin's writing, according to many critics, lost direction. The last two decades of his life he spent mostly abroad, particularly in France, which may have increased his distance from America in his work. In the essay collection *No Name in the Street* (1972), Baldwin discussed his sadness over the movement's waning. At the same time, he found himself the subject of attacks by new black writers such as ELDRIDGE CLEAVER, much like his own rejection of Richard Wright in the 1950s. *The Devil Finds Work* (1976) is Baldwin's reading of racial stereotypes in American movies, and *The Evidence of Things Not Seen* (1985), an account of the Atlanta child murder trials, was unsuccessful, although the French translation of this book was very well received. Baldwin also wrote a series of problematic novels in his later years: *Tell Me How Long the Train's Been Gone* (1968), *If Beale Street Could Talk* (1974), and *Just above My Head* (1979). In these novels Baldwin seems to go over the familiar ground of the first three novels: racial, familial, and sexual conflicts in flawed, autobiographical plots. He never again achieved the mastery of his first novel, *Go Tell It on the Mountain*, one of the key texts in all of African American literature and of American literature as a whole.

After Baldwin died on the French Riviera, his funeral was celebrated on 8 December 1987 at the Cathedral of St. John the Divine in New York, where MAYA ANGELOU, TONI MORRISON, Amiri Baraka,

the French ambassador Emmanuel de Margerie, and other notables spoke and performed. Baldwin has generally been considered to be strongest as an essayist, though he published one outstanding novel, and weakest as a playwright because he became too didactic at the expense of dramatic art. His achievements and influence tended to get lost in the sheer productivity of his career, especially as his later work was judged not to measure up to his earlier work. After his death scholars were able to look at Baldwin's contribution with perspective and a sense of closure, and his literary stature grew accordingly.

FURTHER READING
Baldwin's personal papers and manuscripts are in the James Weldon Johnson Collection, Beinecke Rare Book and Manuscript Library, Yale University; the Berg collection at the New York Public Library; and the Schomburg Center for Research in Black Culture of the New York Public Library, among other repositories.
Books by Baldwin not mentioned here include *Going to Meet the Man* (1965), *A Dialogue: James Baldwin and Nikki Giovanni* (1971), *One Day When I Was Lost: A Scenario Based on* Alex Haley's "*The Autobiography of* Malcolm X" (1972), *A Rap on Race* (with Margaret Mead [1973]), *Little Man, Little Man: A Story of Childhood* (1976), *Jimmy's Blues: Selected Poems* (1983), *The Price of the Ticket: Collected Nonfiction* (1985), and *Perspectives: Angles of African Art*, ed. James Baldwin et al. (1987).
Campbell, James. *Taking at the Gates: A Life of James Baldwin* (1991).
Gates, Henry Louis, Jr. "The Welcome Table [James Baldwin]," in *Thirteen Ways of Looking at a Black Man* (1997).
Leeming, David Adams. *James Baldwin: A Biography* (1994).
Porter, Horace A. *Stealing the Fire: The Art and Protest of James Baldwin* (1989).
Standley, Fred L., and Nancy V. Burt, eds. *Critical Essays on James Baldwin* (1988).
Standley, Fred L., and Louis H. Pratt, eds. *Conversations with James Baldwin* (1989).
Troupe, Quincy, ed. *James Baldwin: The Legacy* (1989).
Weatherby, W. J. *James Baldwin: Artist on Fire* (1989).
Obituaries: *New York Times*, 2 Dec. 1987; *Washington Post*, 5 Dec. 1987; *New York Review of Books* 34 (Jan. 1988).
This entry is taken from the *American National Biography* and is published here with the permission of the American Council of Learned Societies.
ANN RAYSON

Baldwin, Maria Louise (13 Sept. 1856–9 Jan. 1922), educator, lecturer, and activist, was born in Cambridge, Massachusetts, the oldest daughter of Peter L. Baldwin, a Haitian mariner who became a Boston postman, and Mary E. Baldwin, a Baltimore native whose maiden name is now unknown. Baldwin was educated in Cambridge public schools, attending Sargent Primary School, Allston Grammar School, and Cambridge High School. After graduating from high school in 1874 she attended the Cambridge Teachers' Training School. Initially refused a job by the Cambridge school district, she looked elsewhere for employment and eventually took a position teaching elementary school in Chestertown, Maryland. Within a few years, however, she was back in Cambridge. Reportedly under pressure from the African American community, the Cambridge school district decided to offer her a job. In 1881 Baldwin accepted a teaching position at the Agassiz Grammar School on Oxford Street, where she would spend the remainder of her career.

As the only African American teacher at a school that was 98 percent white, Baldwin faced considerable challenges, but she soon earned the respect of the school community. She was especially beloved by her students, many of them the children of Harvard professors and other influential Cambridge residents. In 1889 she was appointed principal, and in 1916 she was promoted to "master" of the school, overseeing twelve white teachers and over 500 students. At the time Baldwin was the only African American in New England to hold such a position, and one of only two women masters in the Cambridge school district. Throughout her long career Baldwin was an educational innovator. She organized Cambridge's first Parent-Teacher Association, added art classes to the curriculum, and experimented with new methods of teaching math. Interested in the physical as well as the mental well-being of her students, she was the first master to hire a school nurse.

Though Baldwin worked primarily within a white world she remained deeply involved in Cambridge's African American community. She hosted a weekly reading group for black Harvard students in her home at 196 Prospect Street. One of these students, W. E. B. Du Bois, remained a life-long admirer of her work. Baldwin later served on the board of the Boston branch of the NAACP and lectured widely on issues relating to race and education.

Baldwin was also active in Cambridge and Boston civic life more generally. She audited classes at Harvard, was a founder and president of the League of Women for Community Service, and participated in local organizations including the Twentieth Century Club, the Boston Ethical Society, the Cantabriga Club, and the Unitarian Universalist Church. She socialized with members of the local elite including Elizabeth Agassiz, Edward Everett Hale, Thomas Wentworth Higginson, and Alice Longfellow. By the time of her death Baldwin had become a beloved local institution and widely acknowledged as one of the most distinguished educators of her era. Baldwin's most important legacy was her students, but she was memorialized in more tangible ways as well. In 1951 a dormitory at Howard University was named in her honor, and in 2002 the Cambridge School Committee renamed the Agassiz School the Maria L. Baldwin School.

FURTHER READING
Porter, Dorothy B. "Maria Louise Baldwin, 1856–1922," *Journal of Negro Education* (1952).
Wilds, Mary. *I Dare Not Fail: Notable African American Women Educators* (2004).

BRIALLEN HOPPER

Ball, Alice Augusta (24 July 1892–31 Dec. 1916), pharmacist, chemist, researcher, and instructor, was born in Seattle, Washington, one of four children of James P. Ball Jr., an attorney and photographer, and Laura Howard, a photographer and cosmetologist. Alice grew up in a remarkable family. Her grandfather, JAMES PRESLEY "J. P." BALL SR., a photographer, was one of the first blacks in the country to master the new art of the daguerreotype. His famous daguerreotype gallery in Cincinnati, Ohio, displayed a well-publicized six-hundred-yard panorama of pictures and paintings depicting the horrors of slavery. Later he opened photography galleries in Minneapolis, in Helena, Montana, in Seattle, and in Honolulu. Alice Ball's father, in addition to being a photographer, also was a newspaper editor and lawyer and was credited with having a lasting effect on Montana history. The Balls lived in Montana for several years before moving to Seattle, and Ball's newspaper, the *Colored Citizen*, had "campaigned vigorously on Helena's behalf" during the battle between Helena and Anaconda for designation as the state capital. When Montana voters, including many blacks, selected Helena, "Ball claimed no small part in the result" (William L. Lang, "The Nearly Forgotten Blacks on Last Chance Gulch 1900–1912," *Pacific Northwest Quarterly* 70, no. 2 [April 1979]: 52).

Little is known of Alice Ball's early life except that she lived in Seattle and probably helped out in the busy family's Globe Photo Studio. Her grandfather, J. P. Ball Sr., suffered from rheumatism and sought relief in the warmer climate of Hawaii, where he died in 1904. The Honolulu city directory indicates that the Balls lived at two different residences between 1903 and 1905 and lists Alice's father's occupation as attorney at law, her mother's as photographer, and her two brothers', Robert and William, as stenographer and collector, respectively. Alice Ball attended the Central Grammar School in Honolulu and made a lasting impression on an eighth-grade classmate, John Pratt. Sixty years later he wrote in his memoir that "Alice Ball was brilliant, and later went far in chemistry" (John Scott Boyd Pratt, *The Hawaii I Remember* [1965], 18).

After graduating from Broadway High School in Seattle in June 1909, Alice Ball earned two degrees from the University of Washington: a pharmaceutical chemist (PhC) degree in 1912 and a bachelor of science in Pharmacy on 17 June 1914. A November 1914 alumni newsletter reported that Alice A. Ball was working on her master's degree in the department of chemistry at the College of Hawaii (later the University of Hawaii). On 1 June 1915 she graduated with her master of science in Chemistry as the first—and only—woman to do so in the history of the college (*Honolulu Star-Bulletin*, 1 Mar. 2000, p. A3). She also was the first black woman instructor at the college's chemistry department, where she taught from 1915 to 1916. Her college graduation photograph shows a beautiful, soft-featured woman with an air of seriousness. She could have easily been mistaken as Hawaiian, and in fact a 1925 *Honolulu Advertiser* article announced in bold front-page headlines: "Hawaiian Girl Heroine First Made Possible the Chaulmoogra Leprosy Cure."

Because of its disfiguring, stigmatizing, and incurable traits, few diseases have terrified mankind more than Hansen's disease. Once called leprosy, Hansen's disease was renamed for Dr. Gerharad Armauer Hansen, a Norwegian physician who identified the causative microorganism. For many centuries desperate physicians and patients had tried numerous treatments to combat the disease, including surgery, diet, x-rays, mercury, dyes, strychnine, and many other esoteric concoctions. All failed to cure the terrible disease, and most—except for one—offered little relief. Since the fourteenth century in China and even earlier in India, one substance had been used with moderate success to reduce the effects of Hansen's: chaulmoogra oil. Plain chaulmoogra, however, has a disagreeable taste and upsets the stomach, preventing patients from taking it long-term. For hundreds of years scientists had searched diligently for a way to administer chaulmoogra oil as an injection, but these early attempts failed because the virtually insoluble drug created painful muscle abscesses.

In 1916 Ball, then a twenty-four-year-old pharmacist and chemist, tackled the problem that had thwarted innumerable chemists, pharmacologists, and researchers working in some of the world's most sophisticated and well-equipped laboratories, and she accomplished what no other scientist had. She isolated an injectable ethyl ester of chaulmoogra oil. As a result she changed the lives of millions of Hansen's disease sufferers for almost a quarter of a century.

Perhaps it was Ball's chemical wizardry in analyzing the active principles of kava root for her master's thesis that impressed Dr. Harry T. Hollmann, acting assistant surgeon at the Kalihi Hospital and former medical assistant at the federal Leprosy Investigation Station on Kalaupapa, an isolation settlement on the island of Molokai. Hollmann related in a 1922 article in a leading medical journal how he had sought Ball's help: "I interested Miss Alice Ball, M.S., an instructress in chemistry at the College of Hawaii in the chemical problem of obtaining for me the active agents in the oil of chaulmoogra."

Tragically, Ball became ill, returned home to Seattle, and died at the age of twenty-four. After her untimely death, Arthur Dean, a Ph.D. chemist, Alice's former thesis adviser, and then dean of the College of Hawaii, continued her work. However, by 1920 the chaulmoogra process became labeled in the professional literature as the "Dean Method." Unlike Dean, Hollmann did acknowledge Alice Ball's significant work in his 1922 article, which he gave a subheading: "Ball's Method of Making Ethyl Esters of the Fatty Acids of Chaulmoogra Oil." The article restored Alice Ball's name and achievements to the pages of history for the outstanding work that she had accomplished for Hansen's disease patients around the world.

Eighty-four years later, on 29 February 2000, Alice Ball was formally recognized for her breakthrough research in treating Hansen's disease when the governor of Hawaii proclaimed 29 February as Alice Ball Day in the state. A bronze plaque honoring Ball and her achievements was placed near a chaulmoogra tree on the University of Hawaii campus. In December 2006 the board of regents of the University of Hawaii honored Alice Ball by posthumously awarding her the Regents' Medal of Distinction, which is presented to individuals of exceptional accomplishment and distinction who have made significant contributions to the university, state, region, or nation or within their field of endeavor.

FURTHER READING

Hollmann, Harry T. "The Fatty Acids of Chaulmoogra Oil in the Treatment of Leprosy and Other Diseases," *Archives of Dermatology and Syphilology* 2 (1922).

Law, Anwei V. Skinsnes, and Richard A. Wisniewski, eds. *Kalaupapa National Historical Park and the Legacy of Father Damien: A Pictorial History* (1988).

Wermager, Paul. "Healing the Sick," in *They Followed the Trade Winds: African Americans in Hawaii*, ed. Miles M. Jackson (2004).

PAUL WERMAGER

Ball, Charles (1781?–?), fugitive slave, soldier, and slave narrative author, was born on a tobacco plantation in Calvert County, Maryland, the son of slave parents whose names are unknown. When Charles was four years old, his mother and siblings were sold to slave traders to settle their late master's debts; he never saw them again. Charles was sold to John Cox, a local slave owner, and continued to live near his father and grandfather. After the sale of Charles's mother, his father sank into a deep depression, eventually escaping from slavery on the eve of his purchase by a slave trader. Charles grew close to his octogenarian grandfather, a former African warrior who had arrived in Maryland about 1730.

Cox died when Charles Ball was twelve, and the young slave worked for his late master's father until he was twenty years old. During this time Ball married a slave named Judah who worked on a neighboring plantation as a chambermaid. Ball was the subject of a two-year lawsuit between a Mr. Gibson, who purchased him from the senior Cox, and Levin Ballard, who purchased him from Cox's children. Ball eventually worked for Ballard for three years before being sold to a slave trader from Georgia. Ball was separated from his wife and children without being allowed to say goodbye to them. He and fifty-one other slaves, bound by neck irons, handcuffs, and chains, were forced to travel on foot for more than a month from Maryland to Columbia, South Carolina. Ball recalled in his

memoir, *Slavery in the United States: A Narrative of the Life and Adventures of Charles Ball* (1836), "I felt indifferent to my fate. It appeared to me that the worst had come, that could come, and that no change of fortune could harm me."

In South Carolina, Ball was auctioned to the owner of a large cotton plantation. Upon the marriage of his master's daughter, Ball moved to Georgia to serve her and her new husband in September 1806. After the death of his new master in a duel, however, the Georgia estate, along with its slaves, was leased in January 1807 for seven years to another man. Ball seems to have enjoyed an unusually close relationship with his new master, traveling with him to purchase cattle and horses from the Cherokee and to Savannah, Georgia, to buy supplies for the plantation, as well as exerting authority on the plantation as overseer. After his master died around May 1807, Ball was severely beaten by his mistress's visiting brothers. He made his first escape from slavery in August of that year.

Despite being caught and imprisoned in Virginia, where he escaped from jail, Ball successfully walked from Georgia to Maryland in a year, traveling by night and foraging for food. Reunited with his wife and children about May 1808, he worked as a freeman in Maryland then enlisted as a seaman and cook under Commodore Barney in December 1813. Ball was dispatched by the United States to negotiate with several hundred slaves who had escaped from slavery under British protection. Unsuccessful, Ball himself was given the opportunity to travel to Trinidad with the other "contraband." He declined on the basis that he was already free. Discharged in 1814 and widowed in 1816, Ball worked in Maryland and Washington, D.C. In 1820 he invested his savings in a farm and dairy near Baltimore. He married—this wife's name is unknown—and fathered four more children.

Ball's domestic happiness was destroyed in June 1830 when he was captured and returned to slavery by his former mistress's brother. In Milledgeville, Georgia, at the residence of his new master, Ball unsuccessfully sued for his freedom. Finally he managed to escape, only to be recaptured and sold. After a week Ball once again escaped, this time heading east instead of north, to Savannah. While loading cotton on a Philadelphia-bound ship, Ball persuaded a free black sailor to allow him to stow away on the ship. Hidden among bales of cotton and equipped with only a jug of water, bread, and molasses, Ball safely made the journey to Philadelphia, emerging, undetected, free once again. Upon his arrival he was assisted by an unnamed Quaker who provided him with clothing and lodging. After a few weeks Ball returned to his home in Baltimore, only to find that his wife and children, all of whom were legally free, had been captured and sold into slavery. He never saw them again. Afraid of being enslaved again, Ball moved to Pennsylvania, where he composed his memoirs.

Ball is best known as the subject of a popular and controversial slave narrative that was printed at least six times before the Civil War, including in an unauthorized, unattributed, abridged version, Fifty Years in Chains (1859). This novel-like account of slavery was popular not only for its subject's sensational adventures and its detailed descriptions of life in the South but also for its restraint. Acknowledging "the bitterness of heart that is engendered by a remembrance of unatoned injuries," Ball's ghostwriter, the Pennsylvania attorney Isaac Fischer, was careful to exclude "every sentiment of this kind" from his rendering of Ball's life. This editorial censorship, combined with Fischer's inclusion of anecdotes from sources other than Ball in the narrative, led both contemporary critics and recent scholars to question the authenticity of the text, and even the existence of its subject. Most agree, however, that despite its embroidery and its silences, the narrative tells the true story of a courageous man who refused to be broken by an inhuman system.

FURTHER READING

Ball, Charles. *Slavery in the United States: A Narrative of the Life and Adventures of Charles Ball* (1836).

Andrews, William L. *To Tell a Free Story: The First Century of Afro-American Autobiography, 1760–1865* (1986).

Davis, Charles T., and Henry Louis Gates Jr., eds. *The Slave's Narrative* (1985).

Starling, Marion Wilson. *The Slave Narrative: Its Place in American History* (1981).

This entry is taken from the *American National Biography* and is published here with the permission of the American Council of Learned Societies.

JEANNINE DELOMBARD

Ball, James Presley (J. P. Ball) (1825–4 May 1904), daguerreotypist, photographer, and entrepreneur, was born in Virginia, the second of four children of William Ball and Susan Ball, who were free blacks. In his youth Ball was a stevedore who worked along the Ohio River. He may have learned daguerreotypy around 1840 from a Boston-based African

American photographer named John B. Bailey in White Sulphur Springs, West Virginia. Ball settled in Cincinnati, a busy river town that was growing dramatically. One of Ball's earliest known works (early1840s) is an outdoor scene, a half-plate daguerreotype of the Myers & Co. Confectioners in Cincinnati. It is a remarkably clear image featuring a horse and cart standing in the dirt street and a group of top-hatted men standing in front of the company building. This piece, like many of Ball's daguerreotypes, is enclosed in a brass mat and embossed "J. P. Ball/Cincinnati." Such works were frequently housed in navy- or red-velvet-lined leather or Union cases, a type of hinged case made of thermoplastic.

Between short-lived attempts at business in Cincinnati in 1845, 1847 (Ball's first Daguerrean Gallery of the West), and 1849, Ball was an itinerant artist in Pennsylvania and Richmond, Virginia, opening his first successful studio in Cincinnati on New Year's Day in 1851, about two years after he married Virginia Thomas. The business employed Ball's father, his brothers, Tom and Robert G., and his brother-in-law, Alexander Thomas, as well as the landscapist ROBERT S. DUNCANSON, who hand-tinted photographs at the studio, from the early to mid-1850s. In 1852 Ball's work was included in the Ohio Mechanics Institute Annual Exhibition in Cincinnati, and again in 1854, 1855, and 1857. By 1854 Ball employed nine men (including a white man) and averaged $100 a day in sales in his new Great Daguerrean Gallery of the West. That year Ball's first child, James Presley Ball Jr., was born, and an engraving of his studio was featured with a full-length article in *Gleason's Pictorial*. Ball's portrait daguerreotypes often featured frontal, three-quarter-length poses of husbands and wives, sisters, or a single subject against a plain background.

In 1855 Ball, an ardent abolitionist, commissioned a team of unknown African American artists to paint an enormous, 2,400-square-yard panorama, *Ball's Splendid Mammoth Pictorial Tour of the United States Comprising Views of the African Slave Trade; of Northern and Southern Cities; of Cotton and Sugar Plantations; of the Mississippi, Ohio, and Susquehanna Rivers, Niagara Falls, &C.* No longer in existence, the work depicted the slave trade from its inception in Nigeria to its height in the American South to freedom in Canada. Achilles Pugh, a Quaker, published a pamphlet describing each of the fifty-three scenes in detail. Thousands paid to see the work at the Ohio Mechanics Institute and Boston's Amory Hall, and Ball reportedly gave part of the proceeds to benefit children's schools.

After touring Europe and opening establishments in London (where his daughter Estella was born), Liverpool, and Paris, in 1856 Ball exhibited his European pictures in a new gallery he co-owned with another African American photographer, ROBERT JAMES HARLAN. Harlan had made a fortune in the Gold Rush in the West and used the funds to underwrite their business venture. Together the two won a bronze medal for a photograph and a diploma for a daguerreotype from the Ohio Mechanics Institute exhibition of 1857. The partnership dissolved after eighteen months, yet Ball continued to flourish as a portraitist. While few of his images of identified African Americans (such as FREDERICK DOUGLASS and Congressman JOHN ROY LYNCH) survived, a family album was found that contained sensitive *cartes-des-visite* of his mother, brothers, and brother- and sister-in-law and their children, as well as portraits of unidentified women and children.

In 1860 a tornado destroyed Ball's studio, but numerous white families contributed funds to set him up again in business, which achieved its greatest success during the Civil War. Ball photographed many Union soldiers and their families, using such features from conventional British painted portraits as the three-quarters pose for sitters and distinguishing props such as a Doric column, an elaborately carved Victorian chair, and theatrical drapery. Notable patrons included the singer Jenny Lind, the family of Ulysses S. Grant, General William Lytle, Congressman Timothy C. Day, the entrepreneur Samuel Pike, the artist Thomas D. Jones, the civil engineer R. C. Phillips, and the reverends Max Lilienthal and Moncure D. Conway.

In October 1862 Ball's wife, Virginia, violently attacked him because she suspected him of having an affair. She was arrested, and the couple divorced. In 1864 Ball married Fannie Cage. By the end of the war, Ball probably lost much of his business in the face of increased competition from other photographers as well as the declining patronage of former abolitionists.

Around 1871 he and his family moved south in search of greater opportunities for his photography business. They lived in Greenville, Mississippi, until 1875. From 1880 until 1886 he lived in Vidalia, Louisiana, and had a brisk real estate business. Ball and his children bought thirty-six plots of land and sold thirty-one of them between 1878 and 1889. Ball's son edited and published the weekly *Concordia Eagle* in Vidalia in the late 1870s and early 1880s. His granddaughters worked as dressmakers and milliners.

Ball next moved to Minneapolis. There he married Annie E. Ewing in July 1887 (it is not known what happened to his second wife) and was the official photographer for a celebration of the twenty-fifth anniversary of the Emancipation Proclamation in September of that year. A month later he served as delegate for a civil rights convention, then moved to Helena, Montana. There he and his son produced numerous cabinet cards, small photographic prints about the size of a postcard, of white civic and infantry groups, families, business partners, infants in their baptismal gowns, and children, women, and men with props such as cloth-covered tables, wooden gates, books, broken columns, hay bales, and bicycles. Some of these portraits feature painted backdrops of parlors or pastoral scenes, or frames with scroll or shell motifs. Notable sitters included the Montana senator Lee Mantle; Joe (a Chinese cook); an African American porter, William Irvin, in his Masonic uniform; and William Biggerstaff (a former slave), before and after his hanging for murder and in his coffin.

While most of Ball's images were studio work, he also photographed outdoor scenes, such as the Old Helena Library, a group portrait of the congregation of St. Paul's Church, and the cornerstone-laying ceremony of the state capitol. A popular citizen, in 1894 Ball served as a black delegate to the state Republican Party convention and as president of the Afro-American Club in Montana. That same year he also declined a nomination for the position of coroner.

Around 1900 Ball, with his daughter-in-law Laura and his son, who also worked as a lawyer, opened the Globe Photo Studio in Seattle and continued to practice commercial photography. Ball also sold advertisements for the *Seattle Republican* newspaper and organized Shriners' lodges in Seattle and Portland before seeking relief from crippling rheumatism in Hawaii around 1902. He died there two years later. He was cremated, and his remains were interred in Cincinnati.

FURTHER READING

Ball's work is in the collections of the Cincinnati Historical Society; the Cincinnati Art Museum; the International Museum of Photography and Film at George Eastman House, Rochester, New York; Montana Historical Society, Helena; Ohio State University, Columbus; Schomburg Center, New

York Public Library; the University of Washington, Seattle; Library of Congress; Smithsonian Institution, National Underground Railroad Freedom Center; Haverford College; and Texas African American Photography Archive in Dallas, Texas.

Ball, James Presley. *Ball's Splendid, Mammoth Pictorial Tour of the United States* (1855).

Thompson, Lucille Smith, and Alma Smith Jacobs. *The Negro in Montana, 1800–1945: A Selective Bibliography* (1970).

Willis, Deborah. *J. P. Ball, Daguerrean and Studio Photographer* (1993).

Willis, Deborah. *Reflections in Black: A History of Black Photographers, 1840 to the Present* (2000).

Willis, Deborah, and Howard Dodson. *Black Photographers Bear Witness: 100 Years of Social Protest* (1989).

THERESA LEININGER-MILLER

Ball, William (fl. 1781), servant of Lieutenant Colonel William Washington (1752–1810), hero of the Battle of Cowpens in 1781, is a figure largely lost to history, known exclusively for a single act of heroism for which he has been sometimes celebrated as an early black American patriot and hero of the Revolutionary War.

Though slavery had been slow to find a foothold in Great Britain's New World holdings, by 1776 the practice had become widespread and existed in all thirteen colonies. Despite this—and despite the paradox of slaves who were noncitizens fighting in a war for national independence—black people were quick to join the national debate about the direction in which Americans ought to go. Sensing advantage, the British sought to exploit this moment by offering freedom to the slaves of the rebels in the southern colonies—hoping to arouse fears among slaveholders of slave revolts. Thousands of black men, however, joined the Patriots, even if their leaders did not always want them, and many fought in units alongside whites. When the British opened their southern campaign in May 1780, they hoped at once to appeal to what they considered a Loyalist stronghold and to again raise fears of the chaos of mass slave revolts. Perhaps the most important battle of the campaign was fought at Cowpens, South Carolina, on 17 January 1781, between Patriot forces under General Daniel Morgan (1736–1802) and an elite unit of redcoats commanded by the widely reviled and feared Colonel Banastre Tarleton (1754–1833).

Some dozen or more black men fought at Cowpens, but William Ball (his name may not even have been Ball, but rather Collin or Collins)

was not a soldier. He is sometimes described as an orderly, a waiter, a servant, or a bugler, and even his race is an assumption based on his position. What little is known of him is this: sometime during the battle Ball's master, Lieutenant Colonel William Washington, rode out to meet Tarleton and his men. As Washington, a relative of George Washington's (1732–1799), searched for the British colonel, he was attacked and surrounded by Tarleton and two of his officers. Just as one of these raised his sword to strike, Ball appeared, fired his pistol, and wounded the officer. Tarleton and his fellows galloped away, and Washington was saved. This event was immortalized by John Marshall (1755–1835) in his multivolume biography of George Washington and by William Ranney (1813–1857) in a highly romanticized painting in 1845. On 17 January 1981 the United States Post Office issued a stamp to commemorate Ball's valor.

FURTHER READING

Babits, Lawrence E. *A Devil of a Whipping: The Battle of Cowpens* (1998).

Fleming, Thomas J. *Downright Fighting: The Story of Cowpens* (1988).

Greene, Robert Ewell. *Black Courage, 1775–1783: Documentation of Black Participation in the American Revolution* (1984).

Marshall, John. *The Life of George Washington* (1804–1807).

JASON PHILIP MILLER

Ballance, Frank Winston, Jr. (15 Feb. 1942–), United States congressman, was the third child born to Frank Winston Ballance, a sharecropper, and Alice Eason Ballance, a homemaker and care worker. Ballance was born and raised on a farm in Windsor, eastern North Carolina, part of the rural tobacco farming communities of the impoverished and segregated Bertie County. Ballance learned at an early age the import of fighting for civil rights; his mother was heavily involved in black voter registration drives when he was a child. After graduating W.S. Etheridge High School in 1959, he moved to attend North Carolina Central University in Durham.

In college, Ballance became involved in marches and sit-ins in the city, including ones aimed at larger department stores like Woolworth's. After receiving his B in 1963, he remained at the university to study law. In 1965 he taught law at South Carolina State College, but the following year moved to Warrenton in his home state to practice at the firm of

Theaoseus T. (T. T.) Clayton, a preeminent African American lawyer in eastern North Carolina.

Ballance became the youth director for the NAACP in the late 1960s, and began attending rallies for school integration with Clayton's wife, the future U.S. congresswoman, EVA CLAYTON. One protest resulted in blows from a Warren County deputy sheriff, leaving a permanent scar he would bear for the rest of his life. After being tear-gassed during a protest in 1970 for leading a demonstration, Ballance filed a countersuit against a police officer for assault. The late 1960s also marked the beginning of Ballance's career in public service: He served in the National Guard in 1968, and remained a reserve member through 1971. He also ran unsuccessfully for district judge in 1968 for Warren County Commission in 1970.

In the 1970s, Ballance became a full partner in the law firm before opening his own in Warrenton, Frank W. Ballance Jr. & Associates. After switching briefly to the Republican Party—a not-uncommon strategic political maneuver in the 1970s—he shifted back to the Democratic Party in 1979, and in 1982, was elected to the North Carolina House of Representatives. The first African American from the eastern part of the state elected to the House in almost a century, Ballance served for four years in the State House before winning a 1988 North Carolina State Senate bid.

In keeping with his pro-labor, pro-education initiatives in state government, Ballance proposed a four-year education plan that raised teachers' salaries, and a fund that would pay for state community colleges with local bonds.

When the North Carolina legislature adjusted the federal congressional districts in 1990, a new black-majority Congressional seat was created. Though Ballance at first considered running, he deferred to his longtime friend Eva Clayton, serving as campaign manager for her successful candidacy.

While Ballance remained in the State Senate through 2002, he was the recipient of numerous state awards for his legal practice and public service: In 1996 he was selected Lawyer of the Year by the North Carolina Academy of Trial Lawyers; in 1998 the state chapter of the ACLU honored him with the Frank Porter Graham Award, named after the former liberal governor of the state.

Clayton announced her impending retirement in 2001 from the U.S. Congress, and despite initial hesitation, Ballance declared his candidacy through the advice and support of Clayton. In September 2002 he defeated a county commissioner, former U.S. attorney, and chairwoman of a local school board to win the Democratic primary. Two months later he easily defeated his Republican opponent, Greg Dority, a security consultant, in the heavily Democratic district.

Loyal to his district's interests in tobacco, cotton, and peanut farming, Ballance was named to the Agriculture Committee and Small Business Committee; he was also named the spokesperson for the incoming freshman class of Democratic representatives.

Just a few months into his term, Ballance became the subject of an FBI investigation over the finances of the John A. Hyman Memorial Foundation, a substance-abuse nonprofit he helped start in 1985. During his time in the North Carolina Senate, he had helped arrange more than two million dollars in state funding for the foundation while also serving on its board. Investigations revealed that a portion of the state funding had been funneled to Ballance's relatives, political allies, and campaign staff, and the foundation had neglected to file state and federal taxes.

With charges pending and his health deteriorating due to myasthenia gravis, a neuromuscular disease, Ballance resigned from Congress in June 2004, and ended his reelection bid. Five months later, Ballance pled guilty to one count of conspiracy to commit mail fraud and launder money. His son, Garey, by then a state district judge, had also pled guilty in April for failing to file an income tax return in 2000. The following October, Ballance was sentenced to four years in prison, disbarred, and commanded to pay back nearly $62,000, along with $203,000 from his foundation's escrow account. Ballance was released from prison in 2009.

Along with his son Garey, Frank and his wife, Bernadine Smallwood, had two daughters, Angela and Valerie.

FURTHER READING
"N.C.'s Ballance Pleads Guilty to Conspiracy." *Washington Post*, 10 Nov. 2004.

ADAM W. GREEN

Ballard, Butch (12 Dec. 1918–), jazz drummer, was born George Edward Ballard in Camden, New Jersey, the son of Asbury Ballard and Ada Brooks. Ballard was the oldest of seven children; at a year old he was brought to the Frankford section of Philadelphia, Pennsylvania, to live. For much of his life Ballard remained in the same neighborhood that he grew up in as a boy. Ballard's father was originally from Princess Anne, Somerset County, Maryland, before migrating to Philadelphia. The town of Princess Anne was established in 1733 and the family of Jarvis Ballard had a strong influence there. A number of the Ballard family slaves were listed on the Manokin Hundred poll tax list in the early 1700s. The poll tax lists were the record of the poll taxes levied on free males over the age of fifteen and slaves of both sexes over fifteen. During the colonial period, Maryland county officials collected taxes to cover the costs of government, the established church, and various county expenses such as maintenance of indigent residents, payment of jurymen, and the expenses for judges. It is unknown if Asbury Ballard is a descendant of the slaves of this family, but the possibility is strong. Ballard's mother, Ada Brooks, was from Philadelphia. Asbury Ballard worked his entire life for the Philadelphia water department; Ada remained at home with the children.

Butch Ballard was educated in the Philadelphia public school system, attended Northeast High School, and was a member of the school band. Ballard was about fifteen years old when he began taking drum lessons from Professor Coles, bandmaster of the O.V. Catto Elks Lodge at 16th and Fitzwater streets in Philadelphia. Lessons cost seventy-five cents. O.V. Catto's was a popular spot for African American teen and adult dances in the 1930s, and was named for the Philadelphian OCTAVIUS V. CATTO.

When Ballard was about sixteen years old, the Philadelphia band leader Herb Thornton had a job playing at a club near the drummer's church, the Second Baptist Church of Frankford. Butch Ballard snuck into the club and his friends goaded him into sitting in with the band on drums. Ballard said, "I was scared to death," but Thornton invited him to join his band a few weeks later (cited in Cloud Tapper, Ph.D. diss.). Because the band practiced in South Philadelphia, Ballard had to haul all of his drums once a week to the station, take the train to Center City, then hop a trolley to the rehearsal. After high school Ballard and some of his other young musician friends in 1938 formed a band called the Celebrated Youth Band/Dukes Orchestra. In 1941 Butch Ballard married a native of Gary, Indiana, Jesse Davis, who had just moved to Frankford. That same year they both moved to Manhattan so Ballard could play with EDDIE "LOCKJAW" DAVIS at the celebrated and legendary Minton's Playhouse, at West 118th Street, and later with the COOTIE WILLIAMS's big band. With Williams's band, Ballard played the Apollo Theater and the famed Savoy Ballroom and took his first tour of the Deep South.

Having been raised in Philadelphia it never dawned on Ballard to check for signs that said "No Colored Served Here" when he reached a Mobile, Alabama, restaurant. Ballard said, "I'm trying to find bacon and eggs for how much it's gonna cost me, and someone says, 'Look up over your head and look at that sign.' Well, I noticed everyone around me was being served except me, and the waitress kept passing me by" (cited in Cloud Tapper, Ph.D. diss.).

In 1943, while playing at the Earle Theatre in Philadelphia, Butch Ballard learned that the selective service was looking for him. He had been touring so much he had not gotten his draft notice. Signing on with the U.S. Navy, Ballard spent World War II with his ship's company band in the South Pacific until he was honorably discharged in 1945. As soon as the war ended, Ballard's music career soared into high gear with stints playing in LOUIS ARMSTRONG's band in 1946, ILLINOIS JACQUET's in 1947, and with the COUNT BASIE Orchestra in 1949. Big bands traveled mostly in Greyhound buses with the names of the bandleaders emblazoned on the sides of the bus; sometimes the band members rode in "nine-seater Chryslers or DeSoto's," Ballard remembered. "When you pulled into town, everybody would run to the hotel and say, 'Hey, the band's here!'" (cited in Cloud Tapper, Ph.D. diss.). But racism was everywhere in the South; dances in the Carolinas were sometimes held in tobacco warehouses and African Americans were roped off from whites. In an Arizona theater Count Basie and Ballard were sitting in a practically empty movie theater trying to catch an afternoon matinee. An usher, not recognizing the famous band leader, asked them both to move to the balcony section reserved for blacks. Basie and Ballard received refunds and left.

In 1950 Ballard got a call from DUKE ELLINGTON, who wanted Ballard to go to Europe with him to back up SONNY GREER, Ellington's longtime drummer, whose drinking problem made him undependable. This three-month tour was a great opportunity. In 1953 Ballard became the Ellington Band's main drummer, making some classic recordings. Butch Ballard is one of the few men to have worked in both the Count Basie Orchestra and the Duke Ellington Band.

During the late 1950s Ballard led his own band in the Philadelphia area with noted local musicians.

From 1960 to 1962 Ballard led the band that backed the singer EVELYN SIMMS in a nightclub called the Underground, at Broad and Spruce in downtown Philadelphia. The band included an up-and-coming young drummer-turned-comic named BILL COSBY. That same decade Ballard would back up NINA SIMONE, DINAH WASHINGTON, SONNY STITT, and many others at the famed Philadelphia jazz spot the Showboat.

In 1989 Butch Ballard toured Europe with the trumpeter Clark Terry's Spacemen and continued to play Europe every year, despite his advanced age (Ballard turned eighty-seven years old in December 2005). Ballard continued also to teach and lecture in public schools and was the drummer for the big band the Philadelphia Legends of Jazz Orchestra.

Ballard's wife, Jesse, died of Alzheimer's disease in 1999 after fifty-eight years of marriage. They had no children. Aside from his musical career Butch Ballard served as the Democratic ward leader in his district, a neighborhood civil rights activist, and a dedicated trustee of his church. He lived on Plum Street, just a few blocks from where he grew up. Ballard said, "I've been very well blessed because I've been doing this all my life. I'm still doing it, and I'm going to keep on doing it until you come to my funeral. Getting up on stage and performing on my drums. I just love it" (Larry King, "Jazzman Keeps Up the Beat," *Philadelphia Inquirer*, 6 June 1990: NO4).

On 1 December 2006 Ballard was given the Mellon Bank Community Jazz Award at the Kimmel Center, sharing the stage with the saxophonist SONNY ROLLINS.

FURTHER READING

Cloud Tapper, Suzanne. *Children of the Earle Theater: The Philadelphia Jazz Community and the Jazz Aesthetic*. Ph.D. diss., University of Pennsylvania (2003).

Hunter, Al, Jr. "Philly and All that Jazz. When Ellington Looked for Musicians, He Often Looked Here," *Philadelphia Daily News*, 26 Apr. 1999: p. 41.

King, Larry. "Jazzman Keeps Up the Beat," *Philadelphia Inquirer*, 6 June 1990: NO4.

Schermer, Victor L. "Butch Ballard: Legendary Philadelphia Jazz Drummer," 9 Jan. 2007. Available at http://www.allaboutjazz.com/php/article.php?id=24210.

DISCOGRAPHY

Cootie Williams and His Orchestra (Classic Capitol Jazz Sessions, Jan., July, Sept. 1946).

Louis Armstrong and His Orchestra (SNAFU Victor LPM, 27 Apr. 1946).
Eddie "Lockjaw" Davis Quartet with Red Garland, (NYC, 1947).
Count Basie "Shoutin' Blues" (RCA, no date).
Johnny Hodges and His Orchestra (Paris sessions, Apr. and June, 1950).
Duke Ellington Orchestra. "I Got It Bad and that Ain't Good" (Raretone, NYC, 9 Feb. 1953); "Duke Ellington Plays Duke Ellington" (13–14 Apr. 1953).
Shirley Scott with Count Basie. "On the Street Where You Live" (NYC, 18 Dec. 1957).
The Complete Capitol Recordings of Duke Ellington 1953–1955 (Mosaic). Duke Ellington "Piano Reflections" (Capitol).
The Clark Terry Spacemen. "Squeeze Me" with Phil Woods. (13 Feb. 1989) (Chiaroscuro).

SUZANNE CLOUD

Ballard, Florence (30 June 1943–22 Feb. 1976), singer and member of the Supremes, was born in Rosetta, Mississippi, the eighth child of Jessie and Lurlee Ballard. In 1953 the Ballards, following the Great Migration path taken by millions of African Americans, moved to Detroit, Michigan, where Jessie Ballard worked in an automobile factory until his death in 1959. The family lived in the Brewster-Douglass Projects, and Ballard's powerful singing voice distinguished her both in school and around the neighborhood. Two of her neighbors, EDDIE KENDRICKS and Paul Williams, who were members of the local singing group the Primes, told their manager, Milton Jenkins, about Ballard, and Jenkins was impressed enough to book Ballard—still in her teens—as a solo act at the Primes' performances.

This early connection between Ballard and the Primes is vitally important, both to Ballard's career and to the history of American popular music, for two reasons. First, the Primes would be renamed the Temptations in 1961 and go on to become one of the most popular groups in the country while recording for Detroit's then fledgling Motown Records. Second, under Jenkins's encouragement, Ballard put together a singing group of her own, initially a female counterpart to the Primes called the Primettes, formed in 1960. Ballard asked her friend MARY WILSON to join, and Wilson in turn recruited Diane Earle, soon to be known as DIANA ROSS. (Early versions of the group had a fourth member, first Betty McGlown and then Barbara Martin.) Ballard was the group's first lead singer, and the Primettes began rehearsals in the spring of 1959. Their performances, usually in conjunction with the Primes, soon gained them a local following, even though they were not consistently paid and the group's family and school obligations proved an obstacle to regular rehearsal.

In 1960 Diana Ross contacted her neighbor, WILLIAM "SMOKEY" ROBINSON, then working as a performer and songwriter at Motown Records, in hope of getting the Primettes a recording contract. The Motown chief BERRY GORDY JR., on the cusp of his label's reign at the top of popular music, liked the group, but he passed on signing them until they graduated from high school. Undeterred, the Primettes began visiting the Motown studios regularly, eventually recording background vocal accompaniment for several tracks. Later in 1960 they recorded a commercially unsuccessful single, "Tears of Sorrow," for Lupine Records.

In 1961 Gordy signed the Primettes to Motown. Their first single was "I Want a Guy," and soon after its release, Barbara Martin left the group. Remaining a trio, the Primettes, who changed their name in 1963 to the Supremes—Ballard's suggestion—cut several singles for Motown, none of which made any significant dent on the charts or on the radio. On these early recordings, Ross shared lead duties with both Wilson and Ballard, both of whom had arguably stronger voices. Gordy, however, chose to promote Ross as the group's lead singer, believing that her sweet vocals provided a better opportunity for success in a white marketplace.

In June 1965, after two years of little commercial success, "Where Did Our Love Go?" became the Supremes' first number one record, signaling the beginning of a run of chart dominance that put them on the highest plateau of success. Marked by the expert playing of the Motown house band the Funk Brothers and the spirited, gospel-based arrangements favored by the songwriting/production team Holland-LAMONT DOZIER-Holland, these mid-1960s singles, including "You Can't Hurry Love" and "You Keep Me Hangin' On," are definitive examples of the hugely successful "Motown Sound," and Gordy's strategy of success among white audiences found its perfect vehicle in the sophisticated, nonthreatening trio. Like the rest of Motown's roster, the Supremes were sent through Motown's Department of Artist Development, a kind of charm school run by the Motown label and housed in the company offices, where etiquette and fashion instructors helped craft Motown performers into polished performers capable of entertaining any sector of the public. Endorsements and

television appearances followed, and the Supremes went from also-rans to perhaps Motown's primary success story.

Unfortunately, despite their success, serious divisions were brewing within the group. Both Wilson and (especially) Ballard resented Gordy's push of Ross as the star of the group, and Ballard also expressed concern over the fact that, as the Supremes racked up hit after hit, the group members remained relatively underpaid. Ballard's dissatisfaction with both the artistic direction and financial inequity of the Supremes' situation, plus the torrid pace of the Supremes' touring, began taking a toll on her, and she started to drink heavily and miss scheduled appearances. A somewhat ambiguous combination of these factors led to her forced removal from the group in 1967.

Ballard's post-Supremes life was marked by tragedy. She began a protracted legal battle in 1968, first against Motown and then against her attorney, which would bring her a large settlement only in 1975. She married the former Motown chauffeur Thomas Chapman in February 1968. This was a turbulent relationship that produced three daughters—Michelle, Nicole, and Lisa—and that temporarily fell apart in 1972. Musically, Ballard remained active, opening for BILL COSBY and WILSON PICKETT, and even singing at Richard Nixon's 1969 inauguration. She signed with ABC Records in 1968, producing an album's worth of Motown-esque performances, but her ABC tenure would be a short-lived commercial failure, a failure that Ballard felt Motown exacerbated through the ABC label head Larry Newton's long friendship with Berry Gordy (George, 166). By the early 1970s Ballard was abusing pills and alcohol, and she was in such serious financial straits that she and her family were forced to go on welfare and move into public housing, only five years after she left the Supremes.

In 1975 she finally received money from her lawsuits, reconciled with Thomas Chapman, moved into a new house in Detroit, and made appearances around the city, including a performance at the Ford Auditorium that received a standing ovation. Just as it appeared that the story of the original Supreme would turn away from tragedy, Ballard suddenly took ill and was rushed to the hospital. A day later, Ballard, her system weakened by years of drug abuse and hard times, died of cardiac arrest. Her ultimate legacy is twofold. On the one hand, she is a symbol of the great hope provided by Great Migration–era shifts in black socioeconomics. But on the other hand, the painful tragedy of her later life is a reminder of the limitations of even the brightest dreams of uplift and opportunity.

FURTHER READING

George, Nelson. *Where Did Our Love Go?: The Rise and Fall of the Motown Sound* (1985).

Hamilton, Andrew. "Florence Ballard," in *All Music Guide to Soul: The Definitive Guide to R&B and Soul*, ed. Vladimir Bogdanov (2003).

Posner, Gerald. *Motown: Music, Money, Sex and Power* (2002).

Whitall, Susan. *Women of Motown: An Oral History* (1998).

Obituary: *New York Times*, 23 Feb. 1976.

DISCOGRAPHY

Florence Ballard. *The Supreme* (Spectrum Records 544517).

The Supremes. *Ultimate Collection* (Motown Records 530827).

CHARLES L. HUGHES

Ballard, Hank (18 Nov. 1927–2 Mar. 2003), singer and songwriter, was born John Henry Kendricks in Detroit, Michigan, to Dove Ballard, a truck diver, and Sie Bell Hendricks, about whom little is known. The story goes that Dove drove Sie Bell away from the household with a shotgun, but whatever the truth, Ballard's mother abandoned the family when he was just a boy. His father died in 1934 in a car accident, when Ballard was seven, and he was sent to Alabama to live with relatives.

The upbringing was strict. Ballard's paternal aunt and her husband were religious disciplinarians who discouraged the young man's growing affection for popular music. Even country music star Gene Autry—a youthful favorite and inspiration—was forbidden. Ballard was allowed, at least, to sing in the church choir, and he soon developed a talent for singing. When he was fifteen, he could take the repressive atmosphere no more. He left Alabama and returned to Detroit, where he worked on an assembly line in a Ford auto plant. His cousin, FLORENCE BALLARD, was an early member of the Motown family and a founding member of the Supremes vocal group. She offered Ballard guidance and encouragement.

Around 1951 Ballard met Sonny Woods, who also worked at the Ford plant and how had a doo-wop group called the Royals. When one of the band members was drafted into the military, Ballard leapt at the chance to try out. He was successful, and his professional singing career was underway. Soon, the Royals and Ballard came to the attention of Johnny Otis, the bandleader, at a contest he'd organized in the city. Otis signed the Royals to a recording contract, but the band soon changed its name to the Midnighters to avoid confusion with a currently popular act.

Ballard quickly moved from backup singing duties to lead singer and songwriter. He also changed the Midnighters' style. Whereas they had been known for soothing, sentimental rhythm and blues, Ballard brought a harder-edged style, driving, and with an explicitly sexualized mood. His 1953 "Get It" was a top-ten hit and brought the Midnighters to a broader listening audience. A year later, the group cut the smash "Work With Me Annie," which became a number-one hit on the R&B charts despite being banned by the FCC from radio play due to its "explicit" lyrics (for the day, at any rate; it's hard to imagine anything in "Work With Me Annie" raising an eyebrow today). The success of the single inspired attempts to replicate its success: "Annie Had a Baby," "Annie Kicked the Bucket," and "Annie's Aunt Fanny" soon followed. Each sold incredibly well, and each was banned by the FCC. So popular were the tunes that a tamer (and deracinated) version of "Work With Me Annie" was produced for white audiences, "Dance With Me Henry."

The origins of what would become Ballard's greatest contribution to popular music are difficult to ascertain. It's possible that "The Twist" grew out of an earlier song by Ballard, or that he was inspired by a Gospel number from his youth, or that the idea of the song came to him while watching young people dance and groove during a Midnighters' show. The popular group the Drifters have also been linked to the song, as some have surmised that Ballard was inspired by their 1955 hit "Whatcha Gonna Do?" Whatever the case, Ballard penned "The Twist" sometime in 1959, and it was released that year as the b-side of the sentimental "Teardrops on Your Letter." "Teardrops" was the bigger hit, at least at first, but "The Twist" soon came to the attention of Dick Clark, who wished to spotlight it on his smash *American Bandstand* television show. He invited Ballard on the show to sing. What happened next is uncertain. According to some reports, Clark didn't want to pay the entire Midnighters outfit to appear for what amounted to a lip-syncing. According to others, he got cold feet because of Ballard's bawdy reputation. Whichever,

Ballard's invitation was eventually withdrawn, but Clark was determined. DJs had begun spinning the b-side more and more often, and the song was picking up steam into what Clark guessed might be a major hit. He settled on CHUBBY CHECKER, who appeared on the show and turned "The Twist" into one of the most famous rock numbers in history. Indeed, the song leapt out to number one on the pop charts in 1960 and then returned to that spot in 1962, a heretofore unheard-of accomplishment.

Hits in the mold of "The Twist" followed. Ballard wrote and recorded with the Midnighters "Let's Go, Let's Go, Let's Go" in 1960. 1961 saw the "Hoochi Coochi Coo," "The Continental Walk," and "The Switch-a-Roo." All were hits. Nevertheless, Ballard had grown anxious to strike out on his own and start a solo career. The Midnighters had been known as Hank Ballard and the Midnighters for some time, but Ballard no longer wanted to share the headline. He disbanded the group either in 1962 or 1963.

Rock and roll, however, was changing rapidly. The British Invasion brought a new sound to American listeners, and Ballard found himself in the waning years of his career. For a time, he played with JAMES BROWN, but his smash-making days were behind him. He played small venues and clubs. "From the Love Side" appeared in 1972 and "Let's Go Streaking" two years later, but they were minor hits.

Sometime in the early 1980s he met and married Theresa McNeil, a fan and frequent audience member. McNeil took over Ballard's career and was bringing him back to the public eye. He reformed versions of the Midnighters and recorded a well-regarded double album, *Hank Ballard Live at the Palais* (1987). In 1990, however, McNeil was killed in a hit-and-run accident. Ballard was devastated by the loss. Shortly thereafter, he was inducted into the Rock & Roll Hall of Fame. He died in 2003 of throat cancer at his home in Los Angeles.

FURTHER READING

Shannon, Bob, and John Javna. *Behind the Hits: Inside Stories of Classic Pop and Rock and Roll* (1986).

Obituaries: *Los Angeles Times*, 4 Mar. 2003.

The Independent, 4 Mar. 2003.

JASON PHILIP MILLER

Ballard, John (June 1829–19 Aug. 1905), pioneer settler in Los Angeles County, California, in the 1850s, blacksmith, teamster, firewood salesman, and landowner, was born in Kentucky around 1827. Although it is commonly assumed that he had been enslaved there, he arrived in California a free man prior to the Civil War, and nothing has been established about his previous life.

He was married on 6 November 1859 to a woman named Amanda, born in Texas, by Jesse Hamilton, the earliest pastor of First African Methodist Episcopal church, Los Angeles. Their first two children, Dora and Julia, were born in 1857 and 1859. In 1860 the household included a laborer named Juan Jose, recorded by the census as being of Indian ancestry. Another man of African descent, Oscar Smith from Mississippi, lived next door, and no race was specified for the other neighbors, who had either English or Hispanic names. Common occupations included laborer, farmer, teamster, ropemaker, and seamstress.

Ten years later the family had grown. Sons John, Willie, Henry, and Freddie had been born, and daughter Alice was one year old. Ballard had had been saving money to buy property in the city, and by 1870 had acquired both real estate and personal property worth $1000 each, which was about median among his neighbors. There was another family of African descent a few doors away, Lewis G. Green with his wife, Maria, and son, John. The rest of the neighbors were from Mexico, Ireland, England, or states farther east, all recorded in the census as "white." Typical occupations included barber, carpenter, farmer, bricklayer, teamster, and laborer, and most wives stayed home to keep house.

Ballard was one of seven trustees of the First AME Church in Los Angeles, named in the deed for the church's first permanent house of worship, purchased 13 March 1869 for $1,860. Services had previously been held at the home of another founding member, Biddy Mason. Ballard's neighbor in 1870 was probably the Louis Green also serving as a trustee, despite the difference in spelling.

In 1871 Amanda Ballard died in childbirth, along with the couple's eighth child. Eight years later, in 1879, Ballard remarried, to a woman named Francis. A land boom in the 1880s, which could have been good for his business, instead brought a heightened sensitivity to racial distinctions, which excluded Ballard from community life. In 1888 he moved about fifty miles outside of Los Angeles, settling at a location subsequently named "Nigger Ballard Hill," then "Niggerhead Mountain." In a clumsy attempt at racial sensitivity, in 1964 it was officially renamed "Negrohead Mountain," and finally, at the request of people living in the area in 2010, Ballard Mountain. The area is now known as Seminole

Hot Springs; the mountain sits above Tunnel 3 on Kanan-Dume Road between Malibu and Agoura Hills in the now intensely urbanized county.

In addition to farming his new land, Ballard went several miles through Triunfo Canyon to do blacksmithing work at Russell Ranch, near the present-day Westlake Village. J. H. Russell, a child growing up on the ranch who often rode to Ballard's cabin, provided one of the few published contemporary accounts of the man. He was described as powerfully built, able to hoist 100-pound bags with one hand, traveling in a wagon pulled by five mules, sometimes with a cow or horse added in. Ballard continued to make trips into the city to sell charcoal and firewood.

An old mountaineer, quoted in Frederick Hastings Rindge's reminiscent *Happy Days in Southern California* (1898/1972, p. 136) referred to his "old colored neighbor" (believed to have been Ballard), whose cabin was set on fire by would-be claim-jumpers "with white faces and black hearts." Ballard did not take the hint and depart. "This was not the material the good old gentleman was constructed of, and, as a shame to his tormentors, he put up a sign over the ruins of his cabin which read: 'This was the work of the Devil.'"

Francis Ballard died in 1896. County records show that it was not until 1900 that Ballard was able to claim a homestead of 160 acres. Ballard's youngest daughter, Alice, claimed 160 acres adjoining her father's property. In 1900 Ballard's household consisted of himself, Alice, now age twenty-nine, and two grandsons, Lyman L. Ballard and George W. Ballard. Alice Ballard worked as a nurse, in addition to owning land. All of their neighbors were classified by the census as "white," a little less than half born in California, the rest from states as varied as Iowa, Illinois, Arkansas, Texas, and New York. Farming, stock raising, and woodchopping were the most common occupations. The variety of census terms used to denote African descent in 1860, "black," "mulatto," and "colored," had been collapsed into the general designation, "Negro."

Ballard died at Los Angeles County Hospital, and was buried at Rosedale Cemetery in Los Angeles. Ballard's identity was brought to light in 2006 by Patty R. Colman, history professor at Moorpark College, whose research was cited by residents requesting that the mountain be named for Ballard, as a person, rather than for a racial identity. Among many descendants are Claudius Ballard, awarded the French Croix de Guerre for bravery during World War I; his son Reginald Ballard, retired in 1978 from the Los Angeles Fire Department; and Ryan Ballard, a Los Angeles school teacher.

FURTHER READING
Russell, J. H. *Heads and Tails—and Odds and Ends* (1963).
Pool, Bob. "Heightened Profile for a Black Pioneer." *Los Angeles Times*, 24 Feb. 2009.

CHARLES ROSENBERG

Baltimore, Jeremiah Daniel (15 Apr. 1852–29 July 1929), engineer, machinist, and inventor, was born in Washington, D.C., the son of the free blacks Thomas and Hannah Baltimore. Though his father was a Catholic, Jeremiah followed his mother's influence and adopted the Methodist religion. As a child Jeremiah was fascinated with engineering and science. He was known to have experimented often with such utilitarian things as tin cans, coffeepots, stovepipes, and brass bucket hoops.

Jeremiah was educated at the Sabbath School of the Wesley Zion Church in Washington, D.C., which was located on Fourth Street near Virginia Avenue and was founded in 1839 after black members left the Ebenezer Church. As part of his education Jeremiah also attended the school of Enoch Ambush, which had begun operation in about 1833 in the basement of the Israel Bethel Church and remained open until 1864. Despite his attendance, Jeremiah left unable either to read or to write his own name.

Jeremiah experimented on his own and achieved his first major design in a steam boiler made out of stovepipes and old brass bucket hoops. The design was displayed at the Wesley Zion Sabbath School by the Reverend William P. Ryder. Jeremiah continued to improve upon his steam boiler, and his second design effort proved to be even more successful and was submitted to the United States Patent Office by Anthony Bowen. Bowen, a former slave, was born around 1805 in Prince George's County, Maryland, and moved to Washington, D.C., in 1826, where he became legally free four years later.

As a result of the exhibition of his second steam boiler an article about Baltimore appeared in the *Washington Sunday Chronicle* entitled "Extraordinary Mechanical Genius of a Colored Boy." Understanding the significance of this article, Baltimore sent a copy of the paper to President Ulysses S. Grant, who later gave him a card with the following words:

Will the Secretary of the Navy please see the bearer, J.-D.-Baltimore? I think it would be well to give him employment in one of the Navy Yards, where he can be employed on machinery. Please see statement of what he has done without instructions.

U. S. Grant Once Baltimore presented the card to the secretary of the navy, George M. Roberson, he was immediately appointed as an apprentice in the department of steam engineering at the Washington navy yards. He encountered much unfair treatment and racial discrimination and after complaining was transferred to the Philadelphia navy yard.

While in Philadelphia, Baltimore attended the Franklin Institute and upon graduating was detailed to go to the naval station at League Island on the Delaware River, where he assisted in repairing four United States Monitors, which were iron, Civil War–era vessels. In Philadelphia he applied for positions at the Crump & Sons yard, a ship and engine building manufacturer, and also at Sellers & Brothers, a wire working manufacturer. Although denied employment at both yards because of his race, Baltimore persisted and applied for a position with Sellers & Brothers at least five more times until he was finally given a job. Unfortunately, ill health cut short his time there, and he soon returned to Washington, D.C. On 29 May 1872, not long after his return to Washington, he married Ella V. Waters, the daughter of Richard and Margaret Waters of Washington, D.C. After his marriage he opened a general repair shop in Washington.

Baltimore went on to have an extraordinary career. On 2 April 1880 he was appointed chief engineer and mechanician at the Freedman's Hospital in Washington, D.C. Established by the government after the abolition of slavery, the Freedman's Hospital later became the Howard University Medical School and Hospital. He also served as an instructor in metalwork at the Colored Manual Training School in Washington, D.C., and was a member of the Mechanic's Union in Washington, D.C. Furthering his own learning, Baltimore studied at the navy yard in Boston and at the government ordnance and armor-plate works at Bethlehem, Pennsylvania. He invented the pyrometer, a device used for measuring high temperatures, which was exhibited at the 1884 World's Fair in New Orleans. Baltimore died on 29 July 1929 of kidney failure and was buried on 1 August 1929 at the Columbian Harmony Cemetery in Washington, D.C.

FURTHER READING

"J. D. Baltimore, Esq.: Chief Engineer and Mechanician at the Freedman's Hospital—Engineer—Machinist—Inventor," *Freedman*, 20 Apr. 1889.

"A Leader of His Race: Interesting Career of Engineer J.-D. Baltimore, a Protégé of President Grant," *Philadelphia Times*, 28 July 1892.

"A Negro Metallurgist," *Philadelphia Times*, 25 Nov. 1893.

Simmons, William J. *Men of Mark: Eminent, Progressive, and Rising* (1887).

KENYATTA D. BERRY

Baltimore, Priscilla (13 May 1801?–28 Nov. 1882), former slave, entrepreneur, steamboat worker, nurse, and church founder, was born in Bourbon County, Kentucky, in 1801 or 1804. Although her father was a white man and also her master, his name is unknown. Her mother, Lydia, was his slave. While she was still a child, Baltimore's father sold her to a trader who carried her to the St. Louis area. Over the next few years, she passed among several masters, including the New Orleans judge Joachim Bermudez, working as a house servant for French, Spanish, and Anglo-American households in Louisiana and eastern Missouri.

In New Orleans, Baltimore joined the Methodist Church. Her piety so impressed one preacher that he purchased her, then allowed her to hire her own time and buy her freedom. Baltimore worked as a chambermaid on steamboats and as a lying-in nurse. According to tradition, it took her seven years to earn the sum required. Her master returned part of the money along with her freedom papers.

Like many slaves sold away from their families, Baltimore immediately set out to find her mother. She found both her father and her mother, who was still his slave, not in Kentucky, where she had left them, but in Fredericktown, Missouri, not far from where she had once lived. It is reported that after upbraiding her father for his heartlessness, Baltimore purchased her mother's freedom. The two women moved to St. Louis, where Baltimore worked as a nurse and on steamboats. In 1833 she married a free African American named Lewis Coonce, but he died of cholera just three weeks later. The small estate Baltimore inherited from her husband included an eight-year-old boy. His inclusion in the inventory suggests that he was born to an enslaved mother and had been purchased by his father but never formally manumitted. He became the first of Baltimore's foster children.

The following year, Baltimore purchased a house and lot on Seventh Street in St. Louis and went to work for John Daggett, a steamboat operator. There she met a boat hand named John Baltimore, and they married in 1835. It is unclear whether the Baltimores ever had children together, but in future years, their home was sometimes full of children. In 1835 a free African American woman sued Baltimore, claiming to own part of the property she had purchased. By 1840 the costs of the suit and her husband's debts had caused her to lose her home. In 1836 a mob murdered a free black boatman, Francis McIntosh, by chaining him to a tree and burning him alive about two blocks from Baltimore's house. These events contributed to the Baltimores' decision to move to the free state of Illinois. By 1840 the couple had joined a handful of free African Americans living in the American Bottom district of St. Clair County, just across the Mississippi River. They soon become substantial property owners in what grew to-be Brooklyn, a black-majority village with a-reputation as a refuge for fugitive slaves. One of-Baltimore's foster children, Milton Carper, was the-orphaned son of a neighbor murdered by slave catchers.

Baltimore expanded her entrepreneurial activities in Illinois, where she raised and sold vegetables and livestock and continued to work as a steamboat chambermaid, carrying on a side trade of selling pickles and preserves to passengers. She invested in house lots in nearby Belleville and contracted with carpenters to build houses, which she then sold. During this period, John Baltimore worked as a boat hand and sometimes as a butcher in the stockyards of East St. Louis.

In 1840 Baltimore met WILLIAM PAUL QUINN, a traveling evangelist and future bishop of the African Methodist Episcopal (AME) Church. When he sought lodging, she invited him to stay and preach. According to Bishop A. W. Wayman, the first AME Church in the West was organized in her home the following evening. This may also have been the occasion when, according to several reports, she crossed the Mississippi River to St. Louis one Sunday and recruited a few hundred slaves to hear Quinn preach. When the ferry operator balked at transporting slaves, demanding, "What security shall I have that you will return to your masters?" Baltimore answered, "I'll be their security" (*St. Louis Daily Globe Democrat*, 4 Dec. 1882). She was so well known and trusted that her word was enough.

Over the next years Baltimore became an important patron of the AME Church. The legal difficulties faced by free African Americans visiting the slave state of Missouri made her home a refuge. Quinn stayed with her whenever he came to St. Louis, relying on Baltimore to row him back to free soil at dusk. When authorities in St. Louis attempted to imprison Bishop DANIEL ALEXANDER PAYNE in 1856 for illegal preaching, he, too, fled to Baltimore's home, sure of her protection. The 1850s, however, brought new tragedy to her life. Her husband raped a young girl living in their household, and when the girl found herself pregnant, she became his mistress. By 1856 John had decided to elope with the girl, who was expecting his second child. He began selling off livestock and other property and appropriated some $700 in cash from his wife's savings. She sued for divorce, asking the court to restore the property John had sold. She claimed she had earned all of it through her own labor, and John had no right to dispose of it. The court agreed, but it is unclear how much property she recovered.

With the outbreak of the Civil War, Baltimore, now divorced, returned to St. Louis. She worked as a nurse and devoted herself to St. Paul's AME Church. At one point, she single-handedly retired the church's five-thousand-dollar mortgage. Her devotion to the black community reached far beyond the church. She collected donations for Wilberforce University and joined the Daughters of the Tabernacle, one of the new fraternal organizations taking a leading role in postwar black civil society.

Vigorous and active to her last days, Baltimore outlived all of her kin and died quietly at home of old age. Her funeral drew enormous crowds and was among the largest St. Louis had ever witnessed. Mourners remembered her as "Mother" Baltimore, beloved for her generosity, kindness, and especially for her work building up the African American community.

FURTHER READING

Manuscript court case files: *Kitty Dickerson v. Priscilla Baltimore, John Baltimore, and Wilson Primm*, St. Louis Circuit Court–Chancery (Nov. 1835), Missouri State Archives, St. Louis; *Priscilla Baltimore v. John Baltimore*, St. Clair County Circuit Court (Aug. 1856), Illinois Regional Archives Depository, Carbondale.

Buchanan, Thomas C. *Black Life on the Mississippi: Slaves, Free Blacks, and the Western Steamboat World* (2004).

Clamorgan, Cyprian. *The Colored Aristocracy of St. Louis*, ed. with an introd. by Julie Winch (1999).

Obituaries: *St. Louis Daily Globe Democrat*, 30 Nov. 1882 and 4 Dec. 1882.

SHARON E. WOOD

Bambaataa Aasim, Afrika (10 Apr. 1960–), disc jockey, master of ceremonies, community leader, and rapper, was born Kevin Donovan in South Bronx, New York City. (No information on his parents is available.) Bambaataa, an early developer of hip-hop music, is credited with being the first rapper. In introducing hip-hop culture to a worldwide audience during the 1970s, he gained the reputation as one of the godfathers of the genre.

In his early years, Donovan organized the Savage Seven, a Bronx River Projects–area street gang, which eventually became known as the Black Spades. After observing the negative impact of gang activities on his community, he endeavored to promote positive gang activities. In 1974 he established The Organization, later known as the Zulu Nation, a group of racially and politically aware rappers, B-boys (break dancers), graffiti artists, and others dedicated to peace, unity, and the pursuit of knowledge through music and hip-hop culture. Zulu Nation members came to include QUEEN LATIFAH, Monie Love, and the band De La Soul. Eventually rechristened the Universal Zulu Nation, the group established chapters in many countries and focused on numerous community initiatives, including designating the month of November as Hip-Hop History month. Donovan visited Africa in the late 1970s, in part inspired by the TV mini-series Roots (1977), based on ALEX HALEY's epic book. Later he changed his name to Afrika Bambaataa Aasim,

which means "affectionate leader," as depicted in the movie *Shaka Zulu* (1986). On his return from Africa he continued to try to convince friends involved in gang life and violence to channel that energy into community uplift.

In emphasizing community involvement, Bambaataa focused on initiating block parties, informal gatherings that introduced break dancing contests, a dynamic feature of emergent hip-hop culture. Bambaataa maintained that offering young people an alternative and viable activity helped curtail gang violence in New York neighborhoods. The block parties also provided Bambaataa a reputation as one of the best DJs in the business. He owned a vast record collection, which he began while DJing at house parties in high school. Later, he used his broad knowledge of music to experiment with drum machines and computer sounds, which yielded "Planet Rock" in 1982, the first 12-inch single to fuse the burgeoning electro sound with the funk-based beats of hip-hop.

Bambaatta's expertise in DJing generated a following of artists, writers, and other musicians who attended his parties. By 1976 the popularity of DJing instigated DJ contests, and Bambaataa was instrumental in developing guidelines to choose the winners. His turntable techniques and musical proficiency garnered him a reputation as being one of the best DJs in hip-hop. His record debut as a producer came in 1980 with his band, Soul Sonic Force, recording "Zulu Nation Throwdown." The single became a rallying cry for the Zulu Nation, which by the late 1980s had become widely known. He received production credit on other singles in the early 1980s and became a recording artist himself in 1982, when he signed with Tommy Boy records and released "Jazzy Sensation." He followed that with "Planet Rock," a single that became a hit on R&B charts that same year. The song combined electronic hip-hop beats with the main melody of "Trans-Europe Express," by Germany's Kraftwerk. It also included portions of other songs from records by Ennio Morricone and Captain Sky, thereby creating a new style of music, electro funk. "Planet Rock" went to number four on the R&B charts and joined the Sugarhill Gang's "Rapper's Delight" as one of the early classics of hip-hop. Bambaataa repeated his own success with the release later in 1982 of "Looking for the Perfect Beat" (with Soul Sonic Force).

With his newfound popularity, Afrika Bambaataa began branching out and working with musicians from other genres. In 1984, he recorded

Afrika Aasim Bambaataa, speaking at a press conference in New York, 28 February 2006. (AP Images.)

"Unity," with help from JAMES BROWN, and "World Destruction," featuring former Sex Pistol John Lydon (as *Time Zone*). That same year, he debuted an album, *Shango Funk Theology*, recorded as Shango, with Material personnel Bill Laswell and Michael Beinhorn. An LP-length single titled "Funk You!" appeared in 1985, after which Bambaataa recorded a second album, *Beware (The Funk Is Everywhere)* in 1986. He left Tommy Boy records in 1986 and signed with Capitol Records. His first album release for the label, in 1988, was *The Light*, recorded by Afrika Bambaataa & the Family, which included contributions from GEORGE CLINTON, UB40, Bootsy Collins, and Boy George. Three years later, Capitol released his next album, *1990–2000: Decade of Darkness*. It coincided with his career retrospective, Time Zone, released on his own Planet Rock Records. Bambaataa recorded sporadically during the 1990s but returned to the mainstream in 1997 with *Zulu Groove*. The new millennium brought the release of *Hydraulic Funk on Strictly Hype* (2000), and *Electro Funk Breakdown* followed in early 2001.

Bambaataa was a driving force in hip-hop. Frequently recognized as a pioneer at such venues as the annual Hip-Hop Music Awards, he also worked as a social activist. In 1991 he traveled around the world promoting hip-hop and giving concerts in England with Hip Hop Artists Against Apartheid to benefit the African National Congress. He also helped raise money for the Ansar (Muslim sect) community. Bambaataa's activities reflect the influence of people he admires, such as MALCOLM X and James Brown. He constantly stressed the importance of knowledge and enlightenment, and his ability to reach out and convey his art through music won him a devoted following.

FURTHER READING

Mitchell, Gail. "Afrika Bambaataa," *Billboard* (Aug. 2002).

Murphy, Bill. "Return of the Funk: Renegade," *Remix* (Nov. 2004).

Powell, Kevin. "Dead? Hip-Hop Culture Has Been Murdered," *Ebony* (June 2007).

JULIETTE BARTLETT PACK

Bambara, Toni Cade (25 Mar. 1939–9 Dec. 1995), writer, activist, screenwriter, and educator, was born Miltona Mirkin Cade to Walter and Helen Cade in New York City. Originally named for her father's employer, she renamed herself Toni in kindergarten, revealing an independent and imaginative streak at an early age. She took the surname Bambara after discovering it signed on a sketchbook in her great-grandmother's trunk in the attic; who this original Bambara was is now unknown. She legally changed her name in 1970. Bambara spent her childhood exploring Harlem, Bedford-Stuyvesant, Queens, and Jersey City with her brother, Walter. Through exploring these areas she developed her sharp eye for political activism and the power of the word, the tones of blues and jazz that she would translate into her written work (particularly through going to the Apollo Theater with her father), and listening to the stories told by those in her community. Raised in a family with few extended relatives, as a child she would often "adopt" the people she met in her neighborhood, including numerous "grandmothers."

Bambara worked for the Department of Social Welfare in New York City in the late 1950s as a social investigator with a goal of improving the living conditions of minority residents, and then went on to be the director of recreation in the psychiatry department of Metropolitan Hospital in New York City. After earning a B.A. in Theater Arts and English from Queens College in 1959 she studied acting and mime at the University of Florence in Italy and Ecole de pantomime Etienne Decroux in Paris in 1961. She then earned an M.A. in Modern American Literature from the City University of New York in 1964 while working as the program director of the Colony House Community Center. She served at the Venice, Italy, Ministry of Museums, pursued filmmaking in the United Kingdom, conducted doctoral work at the State University of New York in Buffalo, studied at the Commedia del' Arte in Milan, and attended KATHERINE MARY DUNHAM's Dance Studio. After teaching English at the City College of the City University of New York in the late 1960s she went on to teach at Rutgers University, Duke University, Spelman College, Barnard College, Atlanta University, Stephens College, and the School of Social Work. Bambara wrote her first story, "Sweet Town," as an undergraduate, and the piece won the John Golden Award for fiction. In 1970 she edited the path-breaking anthology *The Black Woman*, which featured the work of NIKKI GIOVANNI, AUDRE LORDE, ALICE WALKER, PAULE MARSHALL, and Bambara's own writing. The anthology, published during the Black Arts Movement, helped to signal a body of feminist work by black women writers who would emerge during the 1970s and 1980s. In 1971 she published her second anthology, *Tales* and *Stories for Black Folks*, focused on African American folk heritage, with an emphasis on storytelling, and featuring tales that Bambara reportedly wished had been available to her when she was growing up. She then published two short story collections of her own work, *Gorilla, My Love* in 1972, which featured the renowned stories "My Man Bovanne," "The Lesson," "Black English," and "Raymond's Run," and *The Sea Birds Are Still Alive* in 1977, which featured the stories "The Organizer's Wife" and "The Apprentice." Bambara realized the political power of writing, and her work often featured strong black women as protagonists and a powerful sense of orality, urbanity, and musicality.

Traveling to Cuba, Vietnam, Brazil, and Guinea-Bissau in 1973 and 1975 with the North American Academic Marxist-Leninist Anti-Imperialist Feminist Women gave Bambara a deeper understanding of women's movements and grassroots organizing on an international level. Upon her return to the United States, she lectured extensively throughout the nation on political issues and founded the Southern Collective of African American Writers and the Pamoja Writers Collective after moving to Atlanta.

Although she was best known for her work in the short story genre, Bambara published a novel, *The Salt Eaters*, in 1980. Her mother's influence is illustrated by Bambara's dedication of the book to: "Mama, Helen Brent Henderson Cade Brehon, who in 1948, having come upon me daydreaming in the middle of the kitchen floor, mopped around me." Set in Claybourne, Georgia, the novel focuses on Velma Henry, a dispirited social and political activist who has attempted suicide, who finds herself in the hospital being cared for by Minnie Ransom, a traditional healer who works with people to mend their physical and psychical pain. This complex novel featured an experimental nonlinear writing style (which garnered mixed reviews), and focused on healing, spirituality, political and social change, personal empowerment, and environmental issues related to nuclear waste, all told with Bambara's signature bravura when dealing with matters of working-class struggle and race.

She also wrote screenplays, arguing that mainstream films, particularly those about people of color, were often racist. She wrote more than ten scripts and screenplays, many based on her own short stories: "Zora" in 1971; "Gorilla, My Love" and "The Johnson Girls" in 1972 (the latter produced in 1996); "Transactions" in 1979; "The Long Night" in 1981; "Epitaph for Willie" in 1982; "Tar Baby,"

based on TONI MORRISON's novel of the same title, in 1984; "Raymond's Run" in 1985; and "If Blessing Comes" in 1987.

She also collaborated with JULIE DASH and BELL HOOKS on *Daughters of the Dust: The Making of an African American Woman's Film* (1991), and then wrote an article on the film for Black American Cinema in 1993. In moving toward film Bambara took her political ideals with her, something made evident in her narrating and writing *The Bombing of Osage Avenue* in 1986, a film directed by LOUIS MASSIAH about the city of Philadelphia's police force shooting and then bombing the headquarters of MOVE, a black organization, which resulted in the destruction of sixty-one homes and the loss of eleven lives in May 1985. Bambara won an Academy Award for Best Documentary Film for this work, which was. Bambara and Massiah collaborated again on *W. E. B. Du Bois: A Biography in Four Voices*, which was released in early 1995. Each of the four acts was written and narrated by an African American author: Bambara, Wesley Brown, THULANI DAVIS, and AMIRI BARAKA. She also provided commentary for an American Experience documentary, *Midnight Ramble: Oscar Micheaux and the Story of Race Movies,* which aired on PBS in 1994.

After battling colon cancer Bambara died in Philadelphia at the age of fifty-six, survived by her daughter, Karma Bene Bambara. *Deep Sightings and Rescue Missions*, a collection of Bambara's published and unpublished short stories, essays, and conversations, was published in 1996, and *Those Bones Are Not My Child*, a novel by Bambara based on the more than forty child abductions and murders that took place in Atlanta in the early 1980s, was published in 1999. Bambara, who was living in Atlanta at the time of the murders, had researched them for twelve years. Both books were edited and published after Bambara's death by Toni Morrison, who had long been a close friend.

While Bambara explored diverse media and genres, she never strayed from her portrayal of the sociopolitical aspects of black culture and communities, and continued to raise awareness of racial and feminist causes. Bambara was a major figure in twentieth-century African American literature, and her strongly held beliefs regarding the importance of political activism were evident in her immersion in civil rights issues around the world and her ability to translate her passion for this work onto the page and screen.

FURTHER READING

The Toni Cade Bambara papers are located at Spelman College in Atlanta.

Deck, Alice. "Toni Cade Bambara," in *Dictionary of Literary Biography*, eds. Thadious M. Davis and Trudier Harris (1985).

Guy-Sheftall, Beverly. "Commitment: Toni Cade Bambara Speaks," in *Sturdy Black Bridges: Visions of Black Women in Literature*, eds. Roseann P. Bell, Bettye J. Parker, and Beverly Guy-Sheftall (1979).

Tate, Claudia. *Black Women Writers at Work* (1983).

Obituaries: *New York Times*, 11 Dec. 1995; *Guardian* (London), 12 Dec. 1995; *Washington Post*, 13 Dec. 1995.

JENNIFER WOOD

Bankhead, Sam (18 Sept. 1905–24 July 1976), baseball player-manager, was the eldest of five Negro Baseball League playing brothers born to Garnett Bankhead, a coal miner, and Ara Armstrong, a housewife, in Empire, Alabama. Before becoming one of the Negro Leagues' most popular players, Samuel "Sam" Howard Bankhead spent his youth playing in sandlots around his hometown when he wasn't working the coal mines. In 1929, his professional baseball-playing days began with the Birmingham Black Barons, but he would move from team to team.

A five-tool ballplayer, Bankhead's Negro League Baseball career spanned two decades. The five foot eight inch, 175-pound dynamo consistently hit for average, hit with power, possessed a rifle-like throwing arm, excelled at fielding, and was a leading base stealer throughout the 1930s and 1940s. His lifetime batting average of .318 and versatile abilities earned him seven East—West All Star berths at five different positions (second base, shortstop, left field, center field, and right field).

In 1930 Bankhead joined the Nashville Elite Giants. The following season, he returned to the Black Barons, where he established himself as an all-around utility man, playing infield, outfield, and catcher. Touted as having one of the best fielding throwing arms in the Negro Leagues, during the 1932 season he pitched for several Negro League teams including the Black Barons, the Elite Giants, and the Louisville Black Caps. Pitching, however, did not become his forte; records indicate two wins and six losses for the year. Eventually, shortstop and right field became Bankhead's dominant positions. In the 1932–1933 California winter leagues he hit .371 and .344, respectively, and was a top-ranking base stealer. With the Elite Giants in 1934 he hit .338 and garnered the first of his All Star outings.

In 1935 the Pittsburgh Crawfords snared Bankhead, who became a member of their infamous powerhouse lineup, which included Hall of Famers JOSH GIBSON, OSCAR CHARLESTON, COOL PAPA BELL, JUDY JOHNSON, and SATCHEL PAIGE. A feared clutch hitter, Bankhead lent an intimidating presence to what many baseball historians consider one of the greatest black teams of all time. Belting .336 and .324 for the 1935 and 1936 seasons, Bankhead helped propel the Crawfords to win back-to-back world championships.

On 3 March 1936 Sam married Helen Hall in Homestead, Pennsylvania. The couple had three children, two girls and a boy.

Now a Negro League star, Bankhead was recruited by Satchel Paige (along with several other big-name Negro League stars including Josh Gibson) to play in the Dominican Republic for the 1937 season. Paid handsomely by team owner and Dominican Republic dictator Rafael Leónidas Trujillo, the squad was composed of renowned Negro League and Dominican players. In the island's series finale, Bankhead hit the go-ahead homerun, giving the dictator his much desired championship trophy.

After returning stateside to the Crawfords for the 1938 season, Bankhead's batting average dipped sharply to .200. The following season found him traded to the Homestead Grays, where he would regain his stride by hitting .333.

He helped the Grays win three World Series titles (1943, 1944, and 1948) and developed a close friendship with fellow teammate Josh Gibson. Seeing an opportunity for better pay and less exposure to racism, the duo decided to play in the Mexican Leagues in 1940 and 1941. In 1940 with the Monterrey Industriales, Bankhead batted .318 and led the Mexican League in stolen bases with thirty-two swipes. In 1941 he averaged .351 and knocked in eighty-five runs. The twosome also became good drinking buddies.

Bankhead and Gibson returned stateside to the Grays for the 1942 season. In five of his first seasons back in a Grays' uniform, Bankhead was voted into four All Star games. In thirty-one overall plate appearances he averaged .346. In various exhibition games against white major leaguers, he is credited with a .342 average.

Although a mainstay with the Grays for the next nine seasons, Bankhead could not resist his love affair with Latin American baseball. Throughout

1937 to 1941 he appeared in Cuba's winter league. In his first season with the Santa Clara team he led the league with forty-seven runs and a .366 average. His lifetime average in Cuba was .297. In 1942 and 1944–1946 Bankhead played in Puerto Rico, earning averages of .351, .271, and .290. He also played in Venezuela (1946) and Panama (1948).

In 1948 Bankhead helped the Homestead Grays win their final Negro League pennant. The Negro National League folded that same season because of dwindling business and integration in the Majors, forcing the Grays to become an independent barnstorming team. Bankhead served as player-manager until the Grays disbanded in 1950.

After the untimely death of his friend Josh Gibson, Bankhead became a surrogate father to Gibson's eldest son, Josh Gibson, Jr. Eventually he even signed Gibson, Jr. to a Gray's contract while he was the team manager.

Although "Sam" was the most well-known of the ball-playing Bankheads, his brother Dan overshadowed Sam's fame. On 26 August 1947, Dan was recruited and signed by Branch Rickey, becoming baseball's first black major league pitcher with Rickey's Brooklyn Dodgers.

Sam Bankhead would also be tapped by Rickey, albeit not until 1951. Having taken over the reins as General Manager for the Pittsburgh Pirates, Rickey assigned Sam as the first Black manager of a Minor League team—the Pirates' Farmham, Quebec, affiliate in Canada's Provincial League. With Bankhead as a player-manager, the team finished the season in seventh place with an unimpressive .423 winning percentage. Bankhead, at age forty-seven, hit a .274 average. He was released from his managerial duties. Another ten years passed before the minors hired another black manager (Gene Baker).

After retiring from baseball in 1952, Bankhead took a job as a sanitation worker in Pittsburgh. Some historians contend that he inspired the lead character of Troy Maxson in August Wilson's Pulitzer Prize–winning play Fences.

In his final years Bankhead worked as a porter at the William Penn Hotel in Pittsburgh. Continuing to drink heavily, he was shot in the back and killed at the hotel after provoking an argument with a friend in a drunken quarrel.

FURTHER READING
Peterson, Robert. Only the Ball Was White (1970).
Tygiel, Jules. Baseball's Great Experiment (1983).
Riley, James A. The Biographical Encyclopedia of The Negro Baseball Leagues (1994).
Loverro, Thom. The Encyclopedia of Negro League Baseball (2003).
Lanctot, Neil. Negro League Baseball: The Rise and Ruin of a Black Institution (2004).

BYRON MOTLEY

Banks, Charles (25 Mar. 1873–1923), banker and businessman, was born in a log cabin in Clarksdale, Mississippi, the son of Daniel Banks and Sallie Ann (maiden name unknown), poor farmers. Banks grew up in extreme poverty but was educated in the local public schools and later attended Rust University in nearby Holly Springs, Mississippi. Returning to Clarksdale, he speculated in land and cotton. After marrying Trenna A. Booze of Natchez, Mississippi, in 1893 Banks engaged her brother, Eugene P. Booze, as his apprentice, teaching Booze how to trade cotton and work his general store, Banks & Co. In 1904 Banks and Booze resettled in the black-owned town of Mound Bayou, Mississippi. Temporarily leaving the merchandising business, Banks established the Bank of Mound Bayou, owning roughly two-thirds of its stock and serving as cashier as well as operating head. Several years later, in 1909, Banks and Booze founded the Farmer's Cooperative Mercantile Company. Capitalized at $10,000, the firm, which Booze managed, sold reasonably priced goods to area farmers until, for a variety of demographic as well as economic reasons, it closed its doors in 1922.

Located about halfway between Memphis and Vicksburg in the Mississippi delta, Mound Bayou was then one of the most promising examples of a new phenomenon in early twentieth-century American history: a town founded, run, and largely governed by African Americans. Established in 1886 by ISAIAH T. MONTGOMERY, Mound Bayou stood for two decades of economic and civic opportunity for black Americans. Though situated in the Deep South, the town epitomized BOOKER T. WASHINGTON's vision of self-help, and the bank of Mound Bayou—itself sufficiently unusual, since relatively few black-owned banks had been established in the United States by that time—enabled local residents to become economically independent of the larger white community. In 1907 Washington wrote a lengthy article in World's Work in which he praised Mound Bayou, the Bank of Mound Bayou, and Charles Banks in particular for the example and potential they demonstrated for all African Americans. Despite the bank's early success—by 1910 it had more than $100,000 in assets and was housed in a two-story building—the

Bank of Mound Bayou failed in the recession of 1914. Within eighteen months Banks and Montgomery started a second bank, called Mound Bayou State Bank. This lending institution remained solvent for a decade but only partially met the community's demand for credit.

Banks and Montgomery, the wealthiest and most powerful figures in Mound Bayou, were principal spokesmen for Washington's policies and were instrumental in the founding and for many years the operation of Washington's National Negro Business League, established in 1900. Banks served as third vice president of the league from 1901 to 1905 and as first vice president from 1907 until his death. Banks was also organizer and president of the league's Mississippi branch and was politically active with the so-called Black and Tan Republicans in Mississippi.

Another of Banks's economic ventures was the Mound Bayou Loan and Investment Company, which he established and ran with WILLIAM THORNTON MONTGOMERY, Isaiah Montgomery's older brother. This chartered financial institution, which was capitalized at $50,000 and sold shares to the public, was founded to turn a profit but also to help keep the ownership of area farmland in the hands of African Americans. This was to be accomplished by covering defaulted mortgages of area farmers with capital raised locally, thus obviating the need to seek financial help elsewhere.

The most significant of Banks's ventures in Mound Bayou was the Mound Bayou Oil Mill and Manufacturing Company, an ambitious but ill-fated project whose failure crippled Banks financially and had a devastating effect on the town. Arguing that a cottonseed-oil mill operation would further the Washingtonian goal of helping southern blacks become economically independent, Banks convinced the Mississippi chapter of the National Negro Business League to sponsor the venture, an apparently winning proposition given that the town's principal economic activity was growing cotton. The mill would thus enable Mound Bayou to become a producer of cotton products as well as cotton. Banks and Isaiah Montgomery began selling shares of stock in 1908, and construction of the plant began two years later. Unfortunately, there were serious problems from the outset. For one thing, Banks and Montgomery were unable to raise sufficient investment capital from local blacks and had only limited success in securing funds from wealthy white philanthropists. Banks ultimately convinced Julius Rosenwald, head of Sears, Roebuck &

Company, to purchase $5,000 of oil mill bonds and to promise to lend the venture up to $250,000. This left the mill short of operating capital but with enough to finish construction. The mill was dedicated in November 1912. Banks's hope that the opening of the mill would increase the prospect of stock sales was realized, but still the operation was plagued by production problems. The economic recession of 1913–1914 exacerbated an already difficult situation and forced the partners to bring in B. B. Harvey, who invested in and then ran the mill. This turned out to be a death knell. Harvey, a white mill owner from Memphis, embezzled the profits and reneged on interest payments on a corporate loan from Rosenwald. Banks was unable to save the firm. Investors lost $100,000, and the virtually new factory building remained vacant for decades.

High cotton prices caused by World War I resulted in an upsurge of business activity, but after prices returned to prewar levels, the town's economic situation was in decline. Making matters worse was the dissolution of the partnership between Banks and Isaiah Montgomery in 1917 as a result of a political dispute. The town and Banks's fortunes were intimately connected. After he and Montgomery ceased to be partners, Montgomery consolidated his holdings and no longer supported broader town ventures. Banks, who had always been more concerned with racial solidarity than had Montgomery, continued his efforts to boost the town and thus saw his fortune plummet as the town's vitality flagged. In 1923, the year after the Farmer's Cooperative Mercantile Company, the town's largest retail outlet, failed, Banks died in virtual poverty. Little is known of his personal life or of the circumstances of his death.

Charles Banks was an important figure in post-Reconstruction America, and his career exemplified the interconnectedness of African American politics and black capitalism. Taking their cue from Booker T. Washington, African Americans in the South pursued the ideals of uplift and black capitalism. Mound Bayou, one of the most successful of a series of all-black towns on the frontier of the Trans-Appalachian West, was a prime example of this type of enterprise. Banks and Montgomery brought about this growth and development by skillfully attracting new settlers and outside financial assistance through an effective boosterism laced with black nationalism. As the historian Kenneth Hamilton has noted, Banks and Montgomery's joint speculative endeavors "made money, heightened racial pride, and built a black town."

FURTHER READING

Hamilton, Kenneth M. *Black Towns and Profit: Promotion and Development in the Trans-Appalachian West, 1877–1915* (1991).

Ingham, John N., and Lynne B. Feldman. *African-American Business Leaders* (1944).

Jackson, David H., Jr. *A Chief Lieutenant of the Tuskegee Machine: Charles Banks of Mississippi* (2002).

Mollison, W. E. "What Banks Managed by Colored Men Are Doing for Their Communities," *Colored America*, 12 Aug. 1907.

This entry is taken from the *American National Biography* and is published here with the permission of the American Council of Learned Societies.

JOHN N. INGHAM

Banks, Ernie (31 Jan. 1931–), Major League Baseball player and sports marketing executive, was born Ernest Banks in Dallas, Texas, to Eddie, a semi-professional baseball player, WPA worker, and wholesale grocery employee, and Essie Banks, a homemaker. Raised in Dallas as the second child and first boy of twelve children, his mother said he "was a blessing to us all" (*Contemporary Black Biography*, 2002, 17). Ernie graduated from Booker T. Washington High School in Dallas in 1950 and later took courses at the University of Chicago, Northwestern University, and other colleges.

At Washington High, Banks excelled in baseball, basketball, and track and field (high jumping 5'11", broad jumping 19 feet). Once batboy for his dad's semipro team and on the Washington softball team, during high school summers he played in a barnstorming "summer time baseball troupe," the Amarillo Colts, earning $15 a game (*Current Biography*, 1959). After graduating from Washington in 1950, he was signed by Negro League star COOL PAPA BELL to play with the Kansas City Monarchs of the Negro American League for a $2,000 bonus. At season's end, JACKIE ROBINSON invited Banks to play with major league all-stars including ROY CAMPANELLA and LARRY DOBY. After serving in, and playing baseball for, the U.S. Army from March 1951 to 1953 in Europe during the Korean War, he finished the 1953 season with the Monarchs.

In 1953, Banks signed a contract with the Chicago Cubs, becoming their second black player (after Gene Baker), and the first to take the field, which he did on 14 September 1953. He and second baseman Baker became "the first black double-play combination in the majors" (Ashe, 19). "The

major leagues, recently integrated, were eager to take advantage of the wealth of talent in the Negro leagues" (*Encyclopedia Britannica*, 2003). He was the second to last Negro League player, before HANK AARON, to go to the majors from the Negro Leagues. In his first short Cubs season, he played ten games, hit two home runs, and batted .314; in 1954, he hit nineteen homers.

After becoming one of the first players to switch to a lighter bat, better for the slightly built, wrist-hitting six-foot one-inch right hander to whip around quickly, Banks's hitting improved significantly in 1955. From 1954 to August 1956 he also set a new-player record by playing 424 consecutive games. Starting for the Cubs at short in 1955, Banks hit forty-four home runs, a major league record for a shortstop; he also set a major league record by hitting five grand-slam home runs. In 1958, he broke his mark with forty-seven home runs, a twentieth-century record for the position. For four consecutive years (1957–1960) he hit over forty home runs, hitting his five hundredth homer (and sixteen hundredth RBI) on 12 May 1970 (*Contemporary Black Biography*, 2002, 18). He is regarded as "one of the finest power hitters in the history of the game" (*Encyclopedia Britannica*, 2003).

Banks was also one of the best defensive players, setting a record for highest fielding average (.985) for a shortstop in 1959, and winning the Gold Glove in 1960. "Informed baseball men are agreed that Banks is unquestionably the best shortstop in the business right now. He's a graceful, flowing fielder with wide range, strong arm, and good speed" (*Current Biography*, 1959). In 1962, at age thirty-one, he moved to first base because of leg injuries, and in 1969 he led National League first basemen in fielding average. He also played third base and the outfield occasionally.

In 1958 and 1959 Banks became the first National League player named Most Valuable Player two years in a row, achieving stats of 47 and 45 home runs, 129 and 143 RBIs, batting averages of .313 and .304, and slugging averages of .614 and .596 respectively. He was on the National League All Star teams thirteen times between 1957 and 1970. On retiring in 1971, he held most Cubs offensive records. Banks's accomplishments are more impressive because he played his entire career for the long-suffering Cubs and never appeared in a World Series.

Popular among fans for his performances and "an infectious enthusiasm for the game," including an unusual willingness to sign autographs, he was "known for his favorite saying: 'Let's play two today!'" (*Encarta Africana*, 1998), declared on a blistering hot day in July 1969 before the Cubs faded. His enthusiasm and professional demeanor earned admiration of players and fans alike. For those reasons and playing all nineteen of his major league seasons (1953–1971) with the Chicago National League ball club in the "friendly confines of beautiful Wrigley Field," he earned the nickname "Mr. Cub."

He ended his career with 512 home runs (the eighth highest career total at that time), 2,583 hits, 1,636 RBIs, and a .274 lifetime batting average. Between 1955 and 1960, he hit more home runs than any other player, including Hank Aaron, WILLIE MAYS, and Mickey Mantle, though his highest salary was $65,000 (*Contemporary Black Biography*, 18). Banks's power hitting also improved Cubs attendance, from 750,000 in 1954 to over 1 million in 1958 (*Contemporary Biography*, 1959).

In 1977, Banks became only the third black player (after Jackie Robinson and Roy Campanella) elected to the Baseball Hall of Fame. He was only the eighth player elected in his first year of eligibility, and one of few elected without "ever playing in a post season game" (*Encyclopedia Britannica*, 2004). Known as "Number 14, Ernie Banks," his jersey number was the first the Cubs retired in 1982.

In 1963 Banks ran for Alderman in Chicago as an Independent but came in third after the machine Democrat and a Republican. In 1967, another alderman suggested replacing a Picasso sculpture in downtown Chicago with one of Banks instead. In the fall of 1968 he visited U.S. troops in South Vietnam for the United Service Organizations. In 1969 Chicago fans selected him the "Greatest Cubs Player" ever and he was named Chicagoan of the Year.

After his 1971 retirement as a player, Banks worked for the Cubs as coach, minor league instructor, "goodwill ambassador" for the team and for baseball, Cubs community relations consultant, and spokesman. In May 1973 the Cubs manager was thrown out of a game, and coach Banks briefly became the first black to manage a team, three years before FRANK ROBINSON managed the Cleveland Indians. When Cubs ownership changed from the Wrigley family to the Chicago Tribune company in 1981, Banks "was offered a lesser post" (*US News*, 20 Apr. 1987, 12). "I paid my dues to baseball, and its hurts to be out of the game," he noted, lamenting also the lack of progress in getting "blacks in top management." Yet he continued as an occasional Cubs goodwill ambassador.

Since 1945 the Cubs "hadn't won much ... except accolades for their lovely if anachronistic old ballpark, where ivy clutters up the outfield wall and no light towers impale the sky" (*Christian Science Monitor*, 26 Sept. 1984). But in 1984, when the Cubs finally won their first divisional title in 40 years, they invited Banks to sit in the dugout for the playoffs (and again in 1989).

In the 1990s, he opened Ernie Banks International, a sports and events marketing firm. As a motivational speaker, he also established the Live Above and Beyond Foundation, a nonprofit organization that "assists children and senior citizens in building self-esteem" (*Contemporary Black Biography*, 19). In 1998 he received a Doctorate in Humanities from Missouri Valley College, in 1999 he was chosen among the hundred "Greatest Chicagoans of the Century" (*Jet*, 14 June 1999), and in 2001 he was named an Illinoisian of the Year.

Banks has served on the boards of Jackson Park Hospital, Big Brothers, Chicago YMCA, and Chicago Transit Authority. In retirement, he "might serve as a model for other players, as he carved out goals and interests of his own independent from the world of baseball" (*Contemporary Black Biography*, 19).

In 1958 Banks married Eloyce Johnson and had three children. In 1993, they divorced, and in a settlement Ernie lost eighty-five trophies, which sold together at auction for $82,000. In 1997 he married Liz Elizey of Chicago, president of Ernie Banks International.

Banks's inspiration to a generation of fans and future baseball players continued to be remembered fondly in Chicago and the nation at the beginning of the twenty-first century. This was particularly so in 2003, when the Cubs let another pennant slip away.

FURTHER READING

Banks, Ernie, and Jim Enright. *Mr. Cub* (1971).
Ashe, Arthur. *Hard Road to Glory: A History of the Afro-American Athlete since 1946* (1988).
Libby, Bill. *Ernie Banks: Mr. Cub* (1971).
Salzman, Jack, David L. Smith, and Cornel West. *Encyclopedia of African-American Culture and History* (1996).
Smith, Jessie Carney. *Black Heroes of the Twentieth Century* (1998).

RICHARD SOBEL

Banks, Tyra (4 Dec. 1973–), media mogul, model, and actress, was born Tyra Lynne Banks and grew up in Inglewood, California. Her father, Donald

Tyra Banks attends the 2008 Glamour Women of the Year Awards at Carnegie Hall in New York. (AP Images.)

Banks, was a computer consultant, and her mother, Carolyn London, was a medical photographer and business manager. The couple divorced when Tyra was six years old, in 1980.

Banks attended Immaculate Heart Middle and High School, an all-girl's private school. She credited her mother's photography business and friends' encouragement with her ability to overcome a self-consciousness during her awkward adolescence that almost made her pursue another path.

"I grew three inches and lost 40 pounds in 90 days," she told the *Black Collegian* in an interview about her teen years. "It was just this crazy growth spurt. I felt like a freak: people would stare at me in the grocery store."

A friend encouraged her to try modeling during her senior year. At the time, several agencies told her she was too ethnic. She was accepted to attend Loyola Marymount University, but when she was offered a modeling contract with Elite Model Management, she went to Paris instead.

She was booked for twenty-five fashion shows during her time in Paris working for the agency. She also branched out into music videos in the 1990s, appearing in MICHAEL JACKSON's "Black or White" and George Michael's "Too Funky" video. She also appeared as Will Smith's girlfriend on *The Fresh Prince of Bel-Air* (Schweitzer, p. 15).

She was dating the director JOHN SINGLETON the year that she appeared in the movie he directed, *Higher Learning* (1995), which was her big-screen debut. In 1995 she also landed a lucrative contract with CoverGirl cosmetics and became the first African American model to appear by herself on the cover of the *Sports Illustrated* swimsuit issue in 1997. When, in the same year, she appeared on the covers of *GQ* and the Victoria's Secret catalog—both firsts for an African American model—she quickly gained more recognition. In 1997 she received the industry's prestigious Michael Award for Supermodel of the Year.

People Magazine listed her one of the "50 Most Beautiful People in the World" in 1994 and 1996. In *Time* magazine, Banks is one of only four African Americans (and seven women) to have repeatedly ranked among the world's most influential people. In 1999, she established TYInc., and around the same time she established Bankable Productions, her television company.

As she achieved greater success, Banks established T-Zone, a self-esteem-building organization for young women. She became a mainstay on channels like VH1 and red carpet specials. In 2003, she created *America's Next Top Model*, a successful reality TV show featuring aspiring young models that quickly became a standard by which all other reality shows were measured. Two years later, her own daytime program, *The Tyra Banks Show*, premiered.

In popular culture, she was sometimes scrutinized for her weight. In 2007, for example, she was shooting a segment for *America's Next Top Model* when an unflattering photo of her in a one-piece bathing suit made headlines suggesting that she had gained too much weight and calling her "Tyra Porkchop," according to *Shape* Magazine. She lambasted the press by going on her own show in a bathing suit to compare herself with the photos, which she claimed had probably been digitally altered.

While Tyra used her talk show platform to encourage women to have a positive self-image, her behavior gave some academics pause. Tulane University professor Shayne Lee wrote in *Erotic Revolutionaries: Black Women, Sexuality, and Popular Culture* (2010), that the show is just one example of how Banks "places sexuality at the forefront of her life, message and career as a talk show host and executive. She develops *The Tyra Banks Show* as a safe space for female lust and sexual power, which at times means relegating men to the female gaze."

Lee describes an exchange between Tyra and some of her male guests that include long, sensual hugs, other unnecessary touching, and sexual innuendo. "This interplay reflects her fondness for controlling and objectifying male guests," Lee wrote. "It's worth noting that she is fully clothed while her male guest is almost naked during his subjection to her lustful banter. As host, Tyra is very physical and pushes the envelope of sexual suggestiveness with many of her male guests."

In 2007 and 2008, respectively, she won Teen Choice awards, and she won a 2008 Daytime Emmy Award for her talk show. She announced in 2010 that she planned to end the show after the spring 2010 season to focus on her film production company, Bankable Studios, the reporter Pearl Stewart wrote in the *Black Collegian*.

FURTHER READING

Lee, Shayne. *Erotic Revolutionaries: Black Women, Sexuality, and Popular Culture* (2010).

Schweitzer, Karen. *Modern Role Models: Tyra Banks* (2009).

JOSHUNDA SANDERS

Banks, William Venoid (6 May 1903–24 Aug. 1985), radio and television pioneer, Masonic Christian Order founder, ordained Baptist minister, lawyer, community advocate, and business leader, was born on a sharecroppers' farm in Geneva, Kentucky, the son of Richard and Clara Banks, both tenant farmers. In June 1922 Banks graduated from the Lincoln Institute of Kentucky and moved to Detroit, Michigan, where he secured a job at the Dodge automobile main plant. He graduated from Wayne State University in 1926 and the Detroit College of Law in 1929. He briefly opened a criminal law practice, but after two years he discontinued his criminal work and invested in property during the Depression, while helping elect liberal Democrat and future Supreme Court justice Frank Murphy as Detroit's mayor in 1930.

In 1931 Banks was the head of the International Labor Defense League (ILDL), a legal organization known for defending numerous labor unions, which at that time were a hotbed for Communist activities. A year later he married a young, white, Jewish secretary named Rose Glassman. His wife's family disowned her, and she was often shunned by other whites because she had married a black man.

As the leader of the ILDL, Banks was considered a Communist sympathizer because he defended members of the Communist Party. In the late 1930s Banks resigned from his position but continued to practice law. In 1939, when war broke out in Europe, Banks purchased the Mackinaw Hotel in Mackinaw City, Michigan.

Banks's heart remained in serving others, and in 1948 he graduated from the Detroit Baptist Seminary and became an ordained Baptist minister in 1949. This same year Banks divorced Glassman. She was granted custody of their three children, Alterio, Harumi, and Tenicia, aged twelve, fourteen, and fifteen, respectively.

In 1950, realizing that the fraternal movement was an ideal vehicle with which to raise the economic status of blacks, Banks sold the Mackinaw Hotel and the thirty-two-story David Broderick Towers, which he owned as well. With a significant amount of the proceeds and some personal financing, Banks founded the International Free and Accepted Modern Masons (IFAMM) in Detroit. Banks served for thirty-five years as president and supreme grand master of IFAMM until the time of his death.

In 1957, acting upon his commitment to help black people, Banks organized and established several enterprises for young people, including the Universal Barber College, the Industrial College, and the International School of Cosmetology. Banks married Ruth Brown Dade, a Detroit schoolteacher, in August 1958; this second marriage was brief. In 1961 he married his law office secretary, Ivy Bird Morris.

In 1964 Banks led IFAMM to purchase a small radio station, whose call letters were changed to WGPR (or "Where God's Presence Radiates") on 107.5 FM. WGPR was the first black-owned and -operated radio station located in the city of Detroit. During the Detroit race riots of 1967, Banks witnessed majority-owned stations controlling the information that was provided and often airing misleading information for and about blacks.

By 1970 Banks had founded lodges in every state in the United States. By 1978 IFAMM had set up more than two thousand lodges in various states and countries, including in Africa, the West Indies, and South America.

By 1975 WGPR was generating more than $1 million in annual revenues. Although Banks realized television was a major force in the lives of blacks, he also knew there were no television stations owned and operated by blacks. So Banks pursued $2.5 million in assets needed to request a television broadcasting permit. When President Nixon heard about this request, he invited Banks to the White House and said that he would be watching Banks's progress. At the next WGPR board meeting, the board agreed to liquidate enough assets to gain approval of the license and begin construction of a station. One problem that arose was that the location for the proposed station would violate an international treaty regarding the spread of the signal into Canada. But U.S. congressmen Charles Coles Diggs Jr. and JOHN CONYERS JR. had the treaty altered to allow the signal intrusion. President Ford helped the station obtain FCC approval by helping Banks override Pentagon priority in transmitter tower construction. Banks enlisted the help of his eldest daughter, Tenicia Banks Gregory. She left her teaching position of twenty years to help him manage the TV station and became the first black female station manager in the United States. Later she became vice president of operations and remained in that capacity until after Banks died.

TV-62 went on the air on 29 September 1975, becoming the first black-owned and -operated television station in the United States. Making the necessary one-year advertising commitments for the FCC license were the following: the three major U.S. automobile manufacturers; Atlantic, CBS, and Warner Brothers recording studios; a few Fortune 500 companies; and several small black businesses. WGPR TV-62 was the first Detroit television station to offer twenty-four-hour programming. Many persons who trained at WGPR TV-62 moved on to lucrative positions at CNN, ABC, NBC, CBS, PBS, and other networks.

Banks received an honorary doctorate from Shaw University and a key to the City of Detroit from Mayor COLEMAN YOUNG. Dr. Banks helped bridge the gap between the generations, and in the October/November 1986 edition of *Dollars and Sense*, a little more than a year after his death, Banks was honored as a Distinguished American and Television Pioneer. Many people mentioned that he taught by example and left a legacy of dreams.

On 23 September 1994 the Masons announced the purchase of WGPR TV-62 by CBS for $24 million. Several black leaders and businesses that had supported Banks and WGPR TV-62 challenged the sale of the station to CBS and the transfer of the FCC license because of its historical significance in the community. The sale, however, was approved,

and many viewed it as the end of an era in Detroit for all those who supported community-based programs in the interest of black people.

FURTHER READING

"Distinguished American: William V. Banks, Television Pioneer," *Dollars and Sense* (Oct./Nov. 1986).
Gregory, Sheila T. *A Legacy of Dreams: The Life and Contributions of Dr. William Venoid Banks* (1999).
SHEILA T. GREGORY

Banks, Willie (11 Mar. 1956–), track-and-field athlete, was born William Augustus Banks III at Travis Air Force Base in northern California, the son of Georgia Corinthian, who worked in various factories and the school cafeteria, and William Augustus Banks II, a U.S. Marine. He attended Jefferson Junior High School (now Jefferson Middle School) and Oceanside High School, both in Oceanside, California. While at the latter institution, he was first recognized for his talent in both the high jump and the long jump events. However, it was not until his junior year—when the state decided to add the triple jump (sometimes referred to as the hop, step, and jump) to its competitions—that he found the area in which he most excelled. It turned out that his history teacher, Bill Christopher, was a former U.S. champion in the event himself. With his assistance, Banks quickly became a dominant triple jumper.

After graduating from high school in 1974, Banks attended the University of California, Los Angeles (UCLA). Two years into his collegiate career he was considered one of the favorites to compete for the United States at the Olympics in Montreal, but he finished fourth in the qualifiers in Eugene, Oregon—one place away from making the national team.

Banks finished his undergraduate degree at UCLA in 1978, having twice been the runner-up at the NCAA championships. He then began law school at UCLA. He earned the nickname the "Bouncing Barrister" for balancing his graduate studies while continuing to compete athletically.

In 1980 Banks secured a slot in the Olympics in Moscow, but the United States boycotted the games in protest of the Soviet Union's invasion of Afghanistan the previous year. He overcame the disappointment of not being to compete on track and field's biggest stage, and in 1981 he set the U.S. record in the triple jump at 56 feet 7.75 inches—a mark he later increased 6 additional times. He also began to build his legend as a transcendent performer. At event in Stockholm, Sweden, in 1981 he instructed the spectators to clap their hands in unison as he began to make his jump; the crowd clapped faster and faster, in rhythm to his movement. The crowd loved this participation, and it seemed to help Banks. He set the European allcomers record. The drama of this accomplishment was heightened because his event had been long dominated by Soviet and Eastern European athletes. With his success and charm, Banks gained a special place among the world's most recognized amateur athletes, and his clapping tactic was imitated by many others in the years to come.

In 1984 Banks had another chance at Olympic glory—this time in the familiar environment of Los Angeles, but he suffered another setback, finishing sixth. A year later Banks not only rose above that frustrating result but achieved his greatest athletic success, setting the triple jump world record at 58 feet and 11.5 inches. His mark stood for nearly a decade. In recognition of his feat, that year he was given USA Track and Field's highest honor—the JESSE OWENS Award. In 1988 Banks made the Olympic team for the third time but again finished sixth after struggling to overcome an injury.

After his athletic career was over, Banks remained involved with USA Track and Field by serving stints as president of its alumni association, beginning in 2002, and chair of its athletes advisory committee. He also pursued business ventures under the name HSJ, Inc.—which stands for hop, skip, jump—including selling artificial athletic turf in Japan. In 2002 he founded the San Diego Sports Institute, a nonprofit organization that provides academic tutoring and athletic training to young boys and girls.

In 1986 he married for the first time. The couple had two children, Erin and Cori, and later divorced. In 1995 he married Hitomi Kamiya and adopted her two children, Yoshihiro and Yuki. Though he never achieved an Olympic medal, Banks is still remembered as one of the greatest triple jumpers in history. More than just a brilliant physical competitor, his charisma and personality made him an ambassador for American athletics abroad. Near the end of the cold war, at a time of global political unrest, he excelled in an event often dominated by the USSR. His reputation among track-and-field fans extended even farther than his world record.

FURTHER READING

Ashe, Arthur. *A Hard Road to Glory: A History of the African American Athlete: Track and Field* (1988).

Concannon, Joe. "Jumping Back to the Fore: 'Ambassador' Banks Returns for His Run at a Festival Crown," *Boston Globe* (July 1985).

Litsky, Frank. "Goals Keep Banks Jumping," *New York Times* (June 1985).

GERARD SLOAN

Banneker, Benjamin (9 Nov. 1731–19 Oct. 1806), farmer and astronomer, was born near the Patapsco River in Baltimore County in what became the community of Oella, Maryland, the son of Robert, a freed slave, and Mary Banneky, a daughter of a freed slave named Bannka and Molly Welsh, a freed English indentured servant who had been transported to Maryland. Banneker was taught by his white grandmother to read and write from a Bible. He had no formal education other than a brief attendance at a Quaker one-room school during winter months. He was a voracious reader, informing himself in his spare time in literature, history, religion, and mathematics with whatever books he could borrow. From an early age he demonstrated a talent for mathematics and for creating and solving mathematical puzzles. With his three sisters he grew up on his father's tobacco farm, and for the rest of his life Banneker continued to live in a log house built by his father.

At about the age of twenty Banneker constructed a striking clock without ever having seen one, although tradition states he may once have examined a watch movement. He approached the project as a mathematical challenge, calculating the proper sizes and ratios of the teeth of the wheels, gears, and pinions, each of which he carved from wood with a pocket knife, possibly using a piece of metal or glass for a bell. The clock became a subject of popular interest throughout the region and many came to see and admire it. The timepiece operated successfully for more than forty years, until his death.

After his father's death in 1759, Banneker continued to farm tobacco, living with his mother until she died some time after 1775. Thereafter he lived alone, his sisters having one by one married and settled in the region. They attended to his major household needs. His life was limited almost entirely to his farm, remote from community life and potential persecution because of his color, until the advent of new neighbors.

In about 1771 five Ellicott brothers of Bucks County, Pennsylvania, purchased large tracts of land adjacent to the Banneker farm and began to develop a major industrial community called

Ellicott's Lower Mills (now Ellicott City, Maryland). They initiated the large-scale cultivation of wheat in the state, built flour mills, sawmills, an iron foundry, and a general store that served not only their own needs but also those of the region. They marketed their flour by shipping it from the port of Baltimore. Banneker met members of the Ellicott family and often visited the building sites to watch each structure as it was being erected, intrigued particularly by the mechanisms of the mills.

George Ellicott, a son of one of the brothers, who built a stone house near the Patapsco River, often spent his leisure time in the evenings pursuing his hobby of astronomy. As he searched the skies with his telescope, he would explain what he saw to neighbors who came to watch. Banneker was frequently among them, fascinated by the new world in the skies opened up by the telescope. Noting his interest, in 1789 young Ellicott lent him a telescope, several astronomy books, and an old gateleg table on which to use them. Ellicott promised to visit Banneker as soon as he could to explain the rudiments of the science. Before he found time for his visit, however, Banneker had absorbed the contents of the texts and had taught himself enough through trial and error to calculate an ephemeris for an almanac for the next year and to make projections of lunar and solar eclipses.

Banneker, now age fifty-nine, suffered from rheumatism or arthritis and abandoned farming. He subsequently devoted his evening and night hours to searching the skies; he slept during the day, a practice that gained him a reputation for laziness and slothfulness from his neighbors.

Early in 1791 Banneker's new skills came to the attention of Major Andrew Ellicott, George's cousin, who had been appointed by President George Washington to survey a ten-mile square of land in Virginia and Maryland to become the new site of the national capital. Major Ellicott needed an assistant capable of using astronomical instruments for the first several months of the survey until his two brothers, who generally worked with him, became available. He visited Ellicott's Lower Mills to ask George to assist him for the interim, but George was unable to do so and recommended Banneker.

At the beginning of February 1791 Banneker accompanied Major Ellicott to Alexandria, Virginia, the beginning point of the survey, and was installed in the field observatory tent where he was to maintain the astronomical field clock and use other instruments. Using the large zenith sector, his responsibility was to observe and record stars near the zenith as they crossed the meridian at different times during the night; the observations were to be repeated a number of nights over a period of time. After he had corrected the data he collected for refraction, aberration, and nutation and compared it with data in published star catalogs, Banneker determined latitude based on each of the stars observed. He also used the transit and equal altitude instrument to take equal altitudes of the sun, by which the astronomical clock was periodically checked and rated.

Banneker had the use of Major Ellicott's texts and notes, from which he continued to learn, and spent his leisure hours calculating the ephemeris for an almanac for 1792. In April, with the arrival of Major Ellicott's brothers, Banneker returned to his home. He was paid the sum of sixty dollars for his services and travel. Ellicott was paid five dollars a day exclusive of room and board while his assistant surveyors were paid two dollars a day. Banneker still supported himself primarily with proceeds from his farm.

Shortly after his return home, with the assistance of George Ellicott and family, Banneker's calculations for an almanac were purchased and published by Baltimore printers Goddard & Angell as *Benjamin Banneker's Pennsylvania, Delaware, Maryland and Virginia Almanack and Ephemeris, for the Year of Our Lord, 1792* …; a second edition was produced by the Philadelphia printer William Young. The almanac contained a biographical sketch of Banneker written by Senator James McHenry, who presented Banneker's achievement as new evidence supporting arguments against slavery.

Shortly before the almanac's publication, Banneker sent a manuscript copy of his calculations to Thomas Jefferson, secretary of state, with a covering letter urging the abolition of slavery. Jefferson replied, "No body wishes more than I do to see such proofs as you exhibit, that nature has given to our black brethren, talents equal to those of the other colors of men, and that the appearance of a want of them is owing merely to the degraded condition of their existence. … No body wishes more ardently to see a good system commenced for raising the condition both of their body & mind to what it ought to be." The exchange of letters between Banneker and Jefferson was published as a pamphlet by the Philadelphia printer David Lawrence and distributed widely at the same time that the almanac appeared. Promoted by the abolitionist societies of Pennsylvania and Maryland, the almanac sold in great numbers.

Encouraged by his first success, Banneker continued to calculate ephemerides for almanacs that were published for the succeeding five years and sold widely in the United States and England. A total of at least twenty-eight editions of his almanacs were published, largely supported by the abolitionist societies. Although he continued to calculate ephemerides each year until 1804 for his own pleasure, diminishing interest in the abolitionist movement failed to find a publisher for them after the 1797 almanac.

Although he was not associated with any particular religion, Banneker was deeply religious and attended services of various denominations whenever ministers or speakers visited the region, preferring meetings of the Society of Friends. He was described as having "a most benign and thoughtful expression," as being of erect posture despite his age, scrupulously neat in dress. Another who knew him noted, "He was very precise in conversation and exhibited deep reflection." Banneker died in his sleep during a nap after having taken a walk early one Sunday morning a month short of his seventy-fifth birthday. He had arranged that immediately after his death, all of his borrowed texts and instruments were to be returned to George Ellicott, which was done before his burial two days later. During his burial in the family graveyard on his farm, his house burst into flames and was destroyed. All that survived were a few letters he had written, his astronomical journal, his commonplace book, and the books he had borrowed.

The publication of Banneker's almanacs brought him international fame in his time, and modern studies have confirmed that his figures compared favorably with those of other contemporary men of science who calculated ephemerides for almanacs. Long thought lost, the sites of Banneker's house and outbuilding have been the subjects of an archaeological excavation from which various artifacts have been recovered. Banneker has been memorialized in the naming of several institutes and secondary schools. Without the limitation of opportunity because of his regional location and the state of science in his time, Banneker would undoubtedly have emerged as a far more important figure in early American science than merely as the first black man of science.

FURTHER READING

Most of Banneker's personal papers, correspondence, and manuscripts are privately owned.

Bedini, Silvio A. *The Life of Benjamin Banneker* (1972).

Tyson, Martha Ellicott. *Banneker, the Afric-American Astronomer: From the Posthumous Papers of Martha E. Tyson* (1884).

This entry is taken from the *American National Biography* and is published here with the permission of the American Council of Learned Societies.

SILVIO A. BEDINI

Banning, James Herman (5 Nov. 1899–5 Feb. 1933), aviator, was born in Oklahoma, the younger of the two children and only son of Riley and Cora Banning, of whom little else is known. In 1919 the family settled in Ames, Iowa, where Banning attended Iowa State College to study electrical engineering but soon became fascinated with the idea of flying and of gaining his pilot's license. After a year of college, Banning left and learned to fly in Des Moines, Iowa, where he was taught by an army aviator at Raymond Fisher's Flying Field. Banning did so well that he became the first black pilot to gain a pilot's license, CAA #1324, issued by the U.S. Department of Commerce.

To earn a living—and to support his interest in flying—Banning formed and operated the J. H. Banning Auto Repair Shop in Ames from 1922 to 1928. In 1929 Banning was named the chief pilot of the BESSIE COLEMAN Aero Club, which was named for the pioneering black pilot, and which had been formed to encourage blacks to enter aviation. As chief pilot, he moved to Los Angeles, where Banning became a demonstration pilot, flying a 1926 two-seater Hummingbird biplane named "Miss Ames," after his hometown of Ames, Iowa, and advertising "FLY WITH BANNING" on the side. The Hummingbird was a small plane by today's standards, with a wingspan of just over thirty-three feet and an overall length of twenty-three feet six inches. Banning flew whenever and wherever he could, performing as a barnstormer or a stunt pilot, in air circuses, and even as a charter pilot, flying politicians to their various speaking stops during their campaigns for office. One of his most famous political passengers was the Illinois representative OSCAR STANTON DE PRIEST, who was the first African American elected to the U.S. Congress from a northern state.

Throughout the 1920s and 1930s aviators were trying to complete longer flights and set endurance records. Charles Lindbergh's solo flight across the Atlantic in 1927 was an inspiration for many pilots. In 1932 Banning and his mechanic, THOMAS COX ALLEN, an African American pilot in his own right, set off to fly from Los Angeles to New York. The plane they used, an Alexander Eaglerock biplane, was several years old and had been pieced together by the two men with spare parts, some of them from the junkyard. The Eaglerock, built by the Alexander Aircraft Company of Colorado, had been made famous during the 1920s as the preferred aircraft of barnstormers, who prized its relative stability. Banning and Allen's flight became known good-naturedly as that of the "Flying Hobos," since flying non-stop was beyond the technology of aviation at that time, and they needed to raise money for fuel and food for each new step of their trip every time they stopped. "The Flying Hobos" completed their coast-to-coast flight of 3,300 miles in forty-one hours and twenty-seven minutes of air time. However with all those stops to refuel, rest, and raise money, the entire trip actually took twenty-one days. Now Banning was well-known and popular as an aviator.

Banning's life ended in tragedy the following year, during an air show in San Diego. Banning had planned to perform a number of stunts and then take the stuntwoman Marion Daugherty up to 4,000 feet. From there she was to have made a parachute jump. But the flight school instructor at the Airtech Flying School denied him use of a plane, believing that Banning, as an African American, could not be a qualified pilot. Thus he was forced to be a passenger in a Travelair biplane, a two-seater with the passenger compartment in the plane's front and with no controls. The Travelair was—and still is—a fairly reliable aircraft; many from that era still exist. But it was being flown by a white navy pilot named Albert Burghardt, aviation machinist mate, second class, from San Diego Naval Air Station, who lacked flight experience. His only qualification for the assignment appears to have been his race. Burghardt, apparently trying to show off to his passenger, pulled the plane into a steep climb. It then stalled at approximately 400 feet and fell into a spin from which the pilot was unable to recover. To the horror of the thousands of spectators, the plane crashed. Banning was rushed to a hospital but never regained consciousness. He died an hour later and was buried in Evergreen Cemetery, in Los Angeles. Although Banning's life ended tragically, he left a bright legacy for African American aviators.

FURTHER READING

de Vries, Col. John A. *Alexander Eaglerock: A History of Alexander Aircraft Company* (1985).
Hart, Philip S. *Flying Free: America's First Black Aviators* (1996).
Haskins, Jim. *Black Eagles: African Americans in Aviation* (1997).
Lynn, Jack. *The Hallelujah Flight* (1989).

JOSEPHA SHERMAN

Bannister, Edward Mitchell (c. 1826–9 Jan. 1901), painter, was born in St. Andrews, New Brunswick, Canada, the son of Hannah Alexander, a native of New Brunswick, and Edward Bannister, from Barbados. While his birth date has generally been given as 1828, recent research has suggested that he was born several years earlier. After the death of his father in 1832, Edward was raised by his mother, whom he later credited with encouraging his artistic aspirations: "The love of art in some form came to me from my mother. … She it was who encouraged and fostered my childhood propensities for drawing and coloring" (Holland, *Edward Mitchell Bannister*, 17). His mother died in 1844, and Edward and his younger brother, William, were sent to work for a wealthy local family, where he was exposed to classical literature, music, and painting. Edward's interest in art continued, and an early biography of the artist reported that "the results of his pen might be seen on the fences and barn doors or wherever else he could charcoal or crayon out rude likenesses of men or things about him" (Hartigan, 71).

In the early 1850s Bannister settled in Boston, where he supported himself by working as a hairdresser. By 1853 he was employed by Madame Christiana Carteaux, a successful black entrepreneur who operated several beauty salons and sold her own line of hair products and who would later become his wife. Unable to persuade any of the local established artists to take a black man on as a pupil, Bannister studied art independently during this period. Despite these obstacles, he achieved some local recognition as a landscapist and portrait painter. In 1854 Dr. JOHN V. DEGRASSE, the first black doctor admitted to the Massachusetts Medical Society, gave Bannister his first commission, a harbor scene entitled *The Ship Outward Bound* (location unknown). On 10 June 1857 Bannister and Carteaux were married, and by the following year Bannister had established himself as a full-time artist. His wife's financial and emotional support was critical to his success. As he recalled in later years, "I would have made out very poorly had it not been for her, and my greatest successes have come through her, either through her criticisms of my pictures, or the advice she would give me in the matter of placing them in public" (Holland, *Edward Mitchell Bannister*, 8). The couple was active in Boston's African American arts community and in the abolitionist movement. Bannister served as an officer of the Union Progressive Society and the Colored Citizens of Boston and was a delegate to the New England Colored Citizens Convention in 1859 and 1865.

In the 1860s Bannister began his professional artistic career in earnest. A listing in the Boston city directory identifies him as a portrait painter, and in 1862 he traveled to New York to study photography in order to enter into the lucrative daguerreotype business. Bannister advertised his services as a daguerreotypist in 1863 and 1864, but none of his photographs has been identified. During these years he also undertook his only formal art training, taking life-drawing classes at the Lowell Institute between 1863 and 1865 with the sculptor and anatomist Dr. William Rimmer. Few works survive from this period of Bannister's career, but his portraits of *Prudence Nelson Bell* (1864, private collection) and of *Robert Gould Shaw* (c. 1864, location unknown), the latter raffled to raise money for the families of black soldiers killed in the Civil War, are evidence both of his success as a portraitist and his ties to Boston's abolitionist and activist communities.

In 1869 Bannister left Boston and settled in Providence, Rhode Island, perhaps because of his wife's family ties to the area. He announced his professional arrival in the city by exhibiting two paintings, a portrait of the famous Boston abolitionist *William Lloyd Garrison* (location unknown) and *Newspaper Boy* (1869, National Museum of American Art [NMAA]), a sensitive portrait of one of the many young boys who sold papers on the streets of Boston. Although the racial identity of the fair-skinned child is uncertain, the painting is often discussed as one of Bannister's few known works dealing directly with African American subjects.

Upon moving to Providence, Bannister began to paint fewer portraits and more landscapes and sea scenes, the work for which he is primarily known today. While he never traveled to Europe, his work—like the work of many American painters—was strongly influenced by European art, particularly the landscape paintings of the Barbizon school. These loosely handled scenes of peasants and farm animals working in bucolic harmony touched a chord among many American landscape painters, and in works such as *Driving Home the Cows* (1881, NMAA) and *Hauling Rails* (1891, NMAA), Bannister created similarly idyllic images of pastoral landscapes. In *Haygatherers* (c. 1893, private collection), Bannister extended this poetic vision of rural life to a specifically American context, depicting African American women and children loading a cart with hay. The artist also painted many scenes of Rhode Island's coastline, which he observed from the decks of his small yacht, the *Fanchon*. In addition to his finished oil paintings completed in the studio, Bannister did many sensitively handled oil sketches and drawings, and these small works are among the freshest and most attractive of his works.

Like many nineteenth-century artists, Bannister viewed the depiction of the natural world as a spiritual endeavor. In a lecture delivered in 1886, he described the artist's role as "the interpreter of the infinite, subtle qualities of the spiritual idea centreing [sic] in all created things, expounding for us the laws of beauty, and so far as finite mind and executive ability can, revealing to us glimpses of the absolute idea of perfect harmony" (Hartigan, 77).

Bannister came to national attention when his painting *Under the Oaks* (location unknown) was awarded a first-prize medal at the Centennial Exhibition in Philadelphia in 1876. The only other African American artist represented at the exhibition was EDMONIA LEWIS, whose life-sized sculpture, *Death of Cleopatra*, caused quite a sensation. Bannister had submitted his work without any biographical detail, and he later recalled the surprise of the awards committee upon learning of his racial identity: "Finally when I succeeded in reaching the desk where inquiries were made, I endeavored to gain the attention of the official in change. He was very insolent. ... I was not an artist to them, simply an inquisitive colored man; controlling myself, I said deliberately, 'I am interested in the report that *Under the Oaks* has received a prize; I painted the picture.' An explosion could not have made a more marked impression. Without hesitation he apologized, and soon every one in the room was bowing and scraping to me" (Hartigan, 70). A Boston collector, John Duff, purchased the painting for fifteen hundred dollars, a substantial sum of money at the time.

This success led to increased demand for his work and to his visibility and prominence in the local Providence art world. Bannister served on the first board of the new Rhode Island School of Design (RISD) and was a founding member of the Providence Art Club. Officially chartered in 1880, the club served as a center for Providence's artistic community, hosting lectures and social events and mounting regular exhibitions in the spring and fall. Bannister showed his work at the club's exhibitions for the remainder of his career and served regularly on the executive committee. His work was purchased both by African American patrons, such as JOHN HOPE, George Downing Jr., and Madame SISSIERETTA JONES, and by local white collectors, such as Isaac Bates and Joseph Ely.

While landscape and sea scenes remained Bannister's specialty, he made occasional forays into religious and history painting throughout his career. An account of Bannister's studio in the 1860s mentions a painting of *Cleopatra Waiting to Receive Marc Antony* (location unknown), and in the 1890s he painted several literary compositions, including a small oil sketch of *Leucothea Rescuing Ulysses* (1891, Newport Hospital, Rhode Island) and scenes from Edmund Spenser's *Faerie Queen*. Bannister's figure paintings are less confident in their execution than his landscapes, perhaps because of his lack of formal artistic training, but he continued to experiment artistically throughout his career. The late work *Street Scene* (late 1890s, Museum of Art, RISD), a brightly colored impressionist view of an urban thoroughfare, demonstrates Bannister's continued interest in experimenting with new styles and subjects even in the final years of his career.

Bannister died of a heart attack on 9 January 1901, while attending a prayer meeting at the Elmwood Street Baptist Church in Providence. In May of that year a memorial exhibition of his work, including 101 paintings, was mounted at the Providence Art Club. In the catalog the artist John Arnold recalled, "His gentle disposition, his urbanity of manner and his generous appreciation of the work of others made him a welcome guest in all artistic circles. ... He was par excellence a landscape painter, the best our state has ever produced. He painted with profound feeling, not for pecuniary results, but to leave upon the canvas his impression of natural scenery, and to express his delight in the wondrous beauty of land, sea, and sky" (*Painters of Rhode Island*, 1996, 13).

FURTHER READING

Bannister's papers are at the Archives of American Art at the Smithsonian Institution, Washington, D.C.

Hartigan, Lynda Roscoe. *Sharing Traditions: Five Black Artists in Nineteenth-Century America* (1985).

Holland, Juanita. *Edward Mitchell Bannister, 1828–1901* (1992).

Holland, Juanita. "To Be Free, Gifted and Black: African American Artist, Edward Mitchell Bannister," *International Review of African American Art* 12.1 (1995).

PAMELA M. FLETCHER

Baquaqua, Mahommah Gardo (c. 1824–?), abolitionist and slave-narrative author, was born in the commercial center of Djougou, West Africa, inland from the Bight of Benin in what would later be the republic of Benin. He was a younger son of a Muslim merchant from Borgu and his wife, who was from Katsina, the Hausa city in northern Nigeria—then known as the Sokoto Caliphate; his parents' names are now unknown. His home town, Djougou, was located on one of the most important caravan routes in West Africa in the nineteenth century, connecting Asante, the indigenous African state that controlled much of the territory that would become Ghana, and the Sokoto Caliphate. After a childhood in which he attended a Koranic school and learned a craft from his uncle, who was also a merchant and a Muslim scholar, Baquaqua followed his brother to Dagomba, a province of Asante. There he was captured in war in the early 1840s, but he was released when his ransom was paid. However, back home in Djougou, he was again taken captive, apparently kidnapped, in 1845, at about age twenty or twenty-one. Baquaqua was then sold south to Dahomey and eventually to a Portuguese ship trading at Ouidah and Popo and taken to Brazil.

In Brazil he was initially sold to a baker in Pernambuco, probably in the city of Olinda, near Recife. Because he attempted to escape and even plotted the assassination of his master, he was sold south to Rio de Janeiro, where a ship captain purchased him for employment as a cabin boy on various trading expeditions to southern Brazil and then in 1847 on a voyage to New York City, where his master was taking a consignment of coffee. Upon arrival in New York in June 1847, Baquaqua became the object of a legal dispute between abolitionist members of the New York Committee of Vigilance, who helped him jump ship, and his Brazilian master, who attempted to recover him through legal means. When two judges refused to free Baquaqua and declared that he was a foreign sailor who had deserted, Baquaqua's abolitionist supporters helped him to escape from jail in lower Manhattan and make his way to Boston, via Springfield, Massachusetts, on the Underground Railroad. From Boston he was sent to Haiti to avoid being arrested again.

Upon arrival in Port-au-Prince, Baquaqua became associated with the American Free Will

Baptist mission. He remained under their patronage until he was in danger of being drafted into the Haitian army, which was involved in an abortive invasion of the Spanish colony to the east of Haiti on the island of Hispaniola. In late 1849 Baquaqua returned to the United States and enrolled in New York Central College, south of Syracuse, where he was a student until 1853. Baquaqua was one of the first Africans to be educated at an American institution of higher education.

Baquaqua knew most of the key abolitionists in upstate New York in the early 1850s, initially through his Baptist connections and then through his association with Gerrit Smith, the wealthy radical abolitionist who was elected to Congress in 1854 and subsequently ran for President of the United States on the Liberty Party ticket. Unlike most other abolitionists Baquaqua was preoccupied with returning to Africa. In pursuit of this goal he served as a member of the Baptists' Africa Mission, which in fact never sent a mission to Africa, despite Baquaqua's willingness to go and his speaking tours that were intended to raise funds for the mission. Baquaqua also tried to join the Mendi Mission of the Congregationalists, but was also unsuccessful in securing an appointment.

In 1854 Baquaqua traveled to Ontario, then known as Canada West, where he finished a fifty-six-page pamphlet about his life in Africa and his relatively brief experiences of slavery in Africa and Brazil. He wrote his autobiography in Chatham, Canada West, and published it in Detroit as *An Interesting Narrative. Biography of Mahommah G. Baquaqua, A Native of Zoogoo, in the Interior of Africa (A Convert to Christianity,) with a Description of That Part of the World; including the Manners and Customs of the Inhabitants* (1854). George Pomeroy, owner of the *Detroit Free Press* and founder of Wells Fargo, helped him to write and edit the manuscript.

His autobiography differs from the other "slave narratives" written in the United States and Canada in the 1840s and 1850s because of his description of Africa, the notorious "Middle Passage," and his captivity in Brazil. His account is valuable because it was one of the most detailed and fully authenticated accounts of Africa and the Atlantic crossing on a slave ship. Despite his conversion to Christianity, Baquaqua chose to keep his Muslim name and his cultural identification with the families of his father and mother, whose association with the Hausa and Dendi commercial networks of the African interior beckoned him to return to his homeland. Despite

Baquaqua's speaking tours on the abolitionist circuits of New York and Pennsylvania, sales of his autobiography were not sufficient to enable him to secure passage to Africa. In early 1855, however, he was able to sail for Liverpool and remained in England until at least 1857, at which point he drops from the historical record. How and where he died, whether he married and had a family, are all unknown today.

FURTHER READING
Law, Robin, and Paul E. Lovejoy, eds. *The Biography of Mahommah Gardo Baquaqua: His Passage from Slavery to Freedom in Africa and America* (2006).
                                    PAUL E. LOVEJOY

Baquet, Achille (15 Nov. 1885–20 Nov. 1956), jazz clarinetist, was born in New Orleans, Louisiana, the son of Theogene V. Baquet, a cornetist, music teacher, and leader of the Excelsior Brass Band of New Orleans, and Leocadie Mary Martinez. Achille was the younger brother of the clarinetist GEORGE BAQUET. No information exists about the extent of Achille Baquet's formal education; however, he was probably exposed to some musical instruction at an early age by virtue of his musical family. Nevertheless, like so many other New Orleans musicians of that period, he was initially an "ear" musician before he began lessons with Santo Juiffre at the Orpheum Theater in New Orleans.

Later, while still a young man, Baquet developed a reputation of his own as a teacher of music fundamentals. Achille Baquet was both a successful teacher and an instrumentalist and was known to have been active both in early jazz bands and in brass bands when jazz was first developing in New Orleans. Although Baquet was a Creole, his light skin color allowed him to pass for white. Consequently, he was known to have performed with both black and white bands, including with "Papa" Jack Laine's, with Ernest Giardina's Ragtime Band, and with members of the Original Dixieland Jazz Band before it left New Orleans in 1916. In *Brass Bands and New Orleans Jazz* (1977), William J. Schafer maintains that Baquet, along with another Creole, the trombonist Dave Perkins, worked with Laine's bands to impose order on the members' ear playing, and in the process they taught many musicians to read music.

Baquet's most significant professional move came in 1918 when he answered the summons of the pianist Jimmy Durante to join him in New York City for an engagement at the Alamo Cafe on West 125th Street in Harlem. Durante, a ragtime pianist and singer, was assembling a New Orleans–style jazz band and had learned of Baquet from Nick La Rocca of the Original Dixieland Jazz Band. Durante's new group, known as the Original New Orleans Jazz Band, was a five-piece band that played at the College Inn on Coney Island and continued on at the Alamo for some years after Baquet left. In November 1918 the band recorded for the Okeh label and subsequently for the Gennett label in 1919 and 1920. Unlike his older brother, Baquet is not well represented on recordings; only a relatively small number have survived. But from his investigation of the Baquet brothers and of Achille's 1919 recordings for Gennett, Alan Barrell (*Footnote*, 1986) concludes that Achille possessed "an exceptional clarinet technique—beautifully mobile and accurate in hitting the notes."

Although Achille Baquet lived into his early seventies, whatever contributions he made as a jazz musician occurred during the formative years of his career. Durante's Original New Orleans Jazz Band was one of the earliest jazz bands to play New York, and contemporaries compared the band very favorably with La Rocca's Original Dixieland Jazz Band of that same period. Yet for reasons unknown, fame smiled on one and eluded the other. In addition, little is known of Baquet in his later years, other than that he moved to Los Angeles in 1920, where he became a member of Local 47 of the American Federation of Musicians. It is unknown whether he ever married or ever had children.

The recognition that was bestowed on some of his contemporaries from New Orleans somehow escaped Baquet, and he died in Los Angeles, one of the many largely uncelebrated early jazz musicians who failed to attain more than a parochial reputation. Still, enough evidence exists through his recordings—and from the testimony of those who knew both him and his playing—to place him among the founding generation of Creole musicians from New Orleans. By virtue of their participation as early performers at a time when few models existed, they, like Baquet, are regarded as pioneers in the development of early jazz.

FURTHER READING

Averty, Jean-Christophe. "A Look at Lizana," *Storyville* 146 (June 1991).

Barrell, Alan. "Back to Baquet," *Footnote* 17, no. 4 (Apr.–May 1986).

Barrell, Alan. "The Baquets—Some Concluding Notes," *Footnote* 18, no. 2 (Dec.–Jan. 1987).

Barrell, Alan. "B Is for … Baquet," *Footnote* 17, no. 3 (Feb.–Mar. 1986).

This entry is taken from the *American National Biography* and is published here with the permission of the American Council of Learned Societies.

CHARLES BLANCQ

Baquet, Dean P. (21 Sept. 1956–), journalist and the first African American editor of the *Los Angeles Times*, was born in New Orleans, Louisiana, one of five sons of Myrtle Baquet and Eddie Baquet Sr., prominent restaurant and bar owners. After years as a mail carrier, Baquet's father retired from the postal service, sold the family home, and opened a restaurant and bar, Eddie's Place, in 1966. At first the family moved into the restaurant's back rooms, with the brothers sharing one bed. The restaurant became famous for its authentic Creole cuisine, attracting such celebrities as BILL COSBY while still catering to the discriminating tastes of local residents. The Baquets, in fact, had long-established roots in the New Orleans community dating back 200 years, and many family members were local jazz musicians of note.

After graduating from the Catholic all-boys St. Augustine High School, Baquet attended Columbia University in New York City from 1975 to 1978, majoring in English literature. His first time outside of Louisiana, Baquet was homesick and returned during summers to New Orleans, where he interned at the *States-Item*. Baquet later told Joe Strupp, "Journalism was just an accident. It just happened, and I fell in love with it" (*Editor and Publisher*, 13 Dec. 2006). In 1978, after three years of college, he quit Columbia and joined the paper's staff full time.

Baquet began as a police reporter on the afternoon paper, working from five in the morning to the early afternoon and gathering news at city hall and the courts. Later Baquet and the reporter Jim Amoss served as the two members of the newspaper's investigative unit. Working to uncover corruption, Baquet revealed his talent as a journalist. Amoss said that Baquet would bite down on a story like a pit bull and not let go (*Editor and Publisher*, 13 Dec. 2006). His investigations exposed police shakedowns of prostitutes, organized crime, and racial discrimination in the New Orleans housing market. New Orleans' two newspapers merged in 1980, and Banquet continued with the New Orleans *Times-Picayune*, where he met Dylan Landis, his future wife and a noted author.

In 1984 Baquet started at the *Chicago Tribune*, where he continued as an investigative reporter. The paper elevated him to the position of associate metropolitan editor for investigation. Within four years Baquet had earned the Pulitzer Prize when he directed a team of three in a ten-month examination of corruption in Chicago's city council. The series of articles exposed a broad array of devices by which city aldermen exploited their offices for private gain.

From the *Tribune*, Baquet moved to the *New York Times* in 1990. Starting as a metropolitan reporter, he was assigned to the business desk as a special projects editor in 1992. He was soon back to in-depth investigations, and in 1994 he was again nominated for a Pulitzer for a fact-finding exposé of fraud and mismanagement at the health insurer Empire Blue Cross and Blue Shield.

The *New York Times* executive editor Joseph Lelyveld appointed Baquet as deputy metro editor on a one-year trial basis. In 1995 Baquet became chief of the *Times'* national desk and ran a bureau noted for its open, collegial atmosphere and contented staff in a business often marred by hostility and resentment. In subsequent years at the *Times* and later the *Los Angeles Times*, Baquet showed himself consistently able to raise newsroom morale, get results, and maintain warm relations with reporters.

In 2000 John S. Carroll, the new executive editor at the *Los Angeles Times*, recruited Baquet from the *New York Times*, offering him the post of managing editor. Carroll was seeking to repair the paper's languishing reputation and credibility. Together Carroll and Baquet recruited top investigative reporters from across the country, and during the next five years the *L.A. Times* garnered a remarkable thirteen Pulitzers, including five in 2004. Critics claimed, however, that the paper was filled with long, tedious stories and focused more on the national and international beat while failing to report adequately on Los Angeles itself and its myriad cultural, ethnic, and minority enclaves.

The Tribune Company owned the *L.A. Times*, and as a publicly traded media corporation, its overriding concern was maintaining its profit margins. The *L.A. Times* consistently earned profits in the 15–20 percent range, which was insufficient for its owners, who were also preoccupied with the paper's loss of readers and advertising revenues, part of a nationwide trend. Between 2000 and 2005 the Tribune repeatedly ordered cuts, and the editorial staff was reduced from 1,200 to 960. Confronting demands for additional layoffs, Carroll resigned in 2005, citing his unwillingness to undermine the quality of journalism practiced by the paper.

Carroll handed the mantel of leadership to Baquet, making Baquet the first African American editor of a top U.S. newspaper. He was celebrated in the media and applauded by the *L.A. Times* editorial staff, who appreciated his management skills and his commitment to upholding the quality of the paper's journalism. The conflict with the Tribune Company, however, was not resolved. Over the next fifteen months Baquet, along with the paper's publisher Jeffrey M. Johnson, became increasingly vocal about resisting the Tribune's demands for deeper cuts in bureaus and staff, and on 5 October 2006 Johnson was fired. Baquet stayed on, hoping to defend the paper. On 26 October 2006, at the convention of the Associated Press Managing Editors, he called upon his fellow editors to fight excessive demands for profits and cuts by newspaper owners. Such an appeal enhanced Baquet's reputation but was intolerable from the point of view of the *L.A. Times'* owners. Baquet was forced to resign on 7 November 2006. The *New York Times* quickly hired Baquet back, appointing him Washington bureau chief in March 2007.

FURTHER READING
Auletta, Ken. "Fault Line," *New Yorker* (10 Oct. 2005).
Strupp, Joe. "How Baquet Brothers Survived Setbacks in L.A. and NOLA," *Editor and Publisher*, 13 Dec. 2006.

RICHARD L. KAPLAN

Baquet, George (1883–14 Jan. 1949), jazz clarinetist, was born in New Orleans, Louisiana, the son of Theogene V. Baquet, a music teacher and the leader of the Excelsior Brass Band of New Orleans, and Leocadie Mary Martinez. Baquet and his younger brother, ACHILLE BAQUET, were descendants of "downtown" Creoles, whose musical training was closely allied to the traditions of the French musical conservatory—a musical tradition held at that time to be far superior to that of the "uptown" jazz musicians. At age fourteen, Baquet was already playing E-flat clarinet with the Lyre Club Symphony Orchestra, a Creole ensemble with twenty to thirty pieces, directed by his father. Baquet later received additional training from the legendary Mexican-born clarinetist Luis "Papa" Tio, who, with his nephew LORENZO TIO JR., was among the founding members of the New Orleans school of clarinetists, a group that included JOHNNY DODDS, ALBERT NICHOLAS, OMER SIMEON, and BARNEY BIGARD.

Baquet is known to have played with the Onward Brass Band in 1900, with MANUEL PEREZ's Imperial Orchestra between 1901 and 1902, and with BUDDY BOLDEN and Frankie Dusen sometime before 1905. In 1902 he left New Orleans to tour with P. T. Wright's Nashville Student Minstrels, but he returned around 1905 to join the orchestra of John Robichaux, an uptown Creole and a rival of Buddy Bolden's, who led one of the most popular and successful pre-jazz ensembles of that period. During the years 1905 to 1914 Baquet was in great demand as a member of the Magnolia, Olympia, and Superior orchestras. He departed for Los Angeles in 1914 to join the Original Creole Orchestra—perhaps the first New Orleanians to expose a national audience to early jazz. Their music was jazz only in an embryonic sense. The element of ragtime was still strong, improvisation was minimal, and the feeling of rhythmic swing—so important in later jazz—was only partially developed. The group, which included the cornetist FREDDIE KEPPARD, played more vaudeville than dance venues; in Los Angeles they were even featured during the intermissions of prizefights. They toured extensively on the Orpheum Circuit, a chain of vaudeville theaters whose hub was the Orpheum in San Francisco. Fearing that their material would be copied and objecting to the low pay, Keppard supposedly refused Victor's offer to record them while in New York, thus allowing the Original Dixieland Jazz Band the distinction, a few months later, of becoming the first band to make a jazz recording.

Baquet moved to Philadelphia, Pennsylvania, in 1923 for an engagement with the Lafayette Players at the Dunbar Theater. He lived in Philadelphia for the next twenty-nine years, performing regularly for fourteen years at Wilson's Café on Walnut Street and also as a member of the Earle Theater Pit Orchestra. He was a venerated jazz senior among local musicians, but one who, on occasion, still recorded with nationally known artists. During this period Baquet appeared on recordings with the vocalists BESSIE SMITH and CLARA SMITH, and in July 1929 he recorded at least nine titles with JELLY ROLL MORTON's Red Hot Peppers during their sessions for RCA at RCA's Camden, New Jersey, plant.

A stroke in 1945 prompted Baquet's return to New Orleans, where he lived with his sister. Contrary to some earlier accounts, a second stroke occurred in New Orleans, not in Philadelphia, and he died there at Flint Goodridge Hospital.

Like his younger brother Achille, George Baquet became the focus of considerable legend over the years. He personally confirmed the assertion that he was one of the two clarinetists on the fabled Buddy Bolden cylinder, supposedly made in the early years of the century. Were it located, the much sought after cylinder might shed an entirely new light on the nature of early jazz, since it would predate the recordings of the Original Dixieland Jazz Band by more than twenty years. Baquet is also reputed to have been a teacher of SIDNEY BECHET and to have been the first to play the clarinet obligato in the New Orleans classic "High Society."

Baquet's contemporaries generally remember him as the possessor of a full, round tone and a legato style of playing associated with the first generation of jazz clarinetists from New Orleans. In his informative article in *Footnote*, Alan Barrell identifies Baquet and his generation as the progenitors of the modern reed sound of the 1930s ("B Is for ... Baquet"). Barrell credits the New Orleanian Jimmie Noone (whose similar tone and full, legato style made him Baquet's replacement in the Original Creole Orchestra) with being the model for the young Benny Goodman, and he says that later reed players (among them Irving Fazola, Eddie Miller, and BARNEY BIGARD—all from New Orleans) were heavily influenced by Baquet's reed jazz style as they developed the new saxophone sound in orchestras led by DUKE ELLINGTON, Glenn Miller, Benny Goodman, and Bob Crosby.

FURTHER READING

Barrell, Alan. "Back to Baquet," *Footnote* 17, no. 4 (Apr.–May 1986).

Barrell, Alan. "The Baquets—Some Concluding Notes," *Footnote* 18, no. 2 (Dec.–Jan. 1987).

Barrell, Alan. "B Is for ... Baquet," *Footnote* 17, no. 3 (Feb.–Mar. 1986).

Ramsey, Fred. "Vet Tells Story of the Original Creole Orchestra," *Downbeat* (15 Dec. 1940).

This entry is taken from the *American National Biography* and is published here with the permission of the American Council of Learned Societies.

CHARLES BLANCQ

Baraka, Amiri (/ Oct. 1934–), poet, playwright, educator, and activist, was born Everett Leroy Jones in Newark, New Jersey, the eldest of two children to Coyette Leroy Jones, a postal supervisor,

Amiri Baraka, speaking at the Newark Public Library in Newark, New Jersey, 2 October 2002. (AP Images.)

they "teach you to pretend to be white" (Watts, 22). With his college ambitions dashed, Jones joined the air force in 1954, where he trained as a weatherman. He graduated at the top of his class and was stationed at Ramey Air Force Base in Puerto Rico. There he became an avid reader of Proust, Hemingway, Dostoyevsky, Sartre, and Camus. He subscribed to literary journals such as the *Partisan Review* and began to send his poems to publishers, who promptly rejected them. Jones claimed that his possession of left-leaning reading material was responsible for his dishonorable discharge from the military in 1957. Working as a stock clerk at the Gotham Book Mart in Manhattan, he resumed a friendship with Steve Korret, an aspiring writer in New York's Greenwich Village.

Through Korret, Jones was introduced to an avant-garde literary scene and a bohemian culture that profoundly altered his life. Allen Ginsberg, the doyen of the beat poets of the 1950s, became a mentor after Jones wrote him a letter on toilet paper to show how hip he was. Charles Olson, a leader of the ultramodern Black Mountain poets, influenced his writing, and even LANGSTON HUGHES, who occasionally gave readings in the Village accompanied by the bassist CHARLES MINGUS, encouraged him and nurtured a friendship that Jones cherished deeply. In 1958 Jones married, in a Buddhist temple, a white, Jewish woman, Hettie Cohen, the secretary of *The Record Changer*, a jazz magazine where Jones worked as the shipping manager. Together they had two children and published *Yugen*, a chic, though short-lived, literary magazine.

By the late 1950s Jones's poetry began to appear in such periodicals as *Naked Ear, Evergreen Review*, and *Big Table*, and in 1959 he founded a publishing company, Totem Press, which issued his first collection of poems, *Preface to a Twenty-Volume Suicide Note* (1961). Though his poetry at this point had a distinct blues idiom, it was not yet overtly political. That transformation was prompted by a visit to Cuba in 1960, where he saw artists as revolutionaries who advanced Cuban nationalism. This experience led him to view his own situation more critically. Soon after returning he began to write polemical essays such as "Cuba Libre," he became a street activist, and he urged his beat peers to strive for greater political relevance in their work. Jones then demonstrated that he was a serious student of history and music with the publication of *Blues People: Negro Music in White America* (1963). RALPH ELLISON remarked that "the tremendous burden of sociology which Jones would place upon

and Anna Lois Russ, a social worker. Jones's lineage included teachers, preachers, and shop owners who elevated his family into Newark's modest, though ambitious, black middle class. His own neighborhood was black, but the Newark of Jones's youth was mostly white and largely Italian. He felt isolated and embattled at McKinley Junior High and Barringer High School, yet he excelled in his studies, played the trumpet, ran track, and wrote comic strips.

Graduating from high school with honors at age fifteen, Jones entered the Newark branch of Rutgers University on a science scholarship. In 1952, after his first year, he transferred to Howard University, hoping to find a sense of purpose at a black college that had eluded him at the white institution. It was at this point that a long process of reinventing himself first became evident; he changed the spelling of his name to "LeRoi" and told anyone who asked that he was going to become a doctor. Yet, he was more interested in pledging fraternities than getting good grades. In retrospect Jones blamed the college's "petty bourgeois Negro mentality" (*Autobiography*, 113) for his academic failure and came to regard black colleges as places where this body of music is enough to give even the blues the blues" (Justin Driver, *New Republic*, 25 Apr. 2002), but most critics regarded the book as an important contribution.

In 1963 Jones tried his hand at playwriting and discovered that here, too, he had the Midas touch. *Dutchman*, a play about a "black boy with a phony English accent" who has a fatal encounter with an attractive white woman on a New York City subway, won an Obie in 1964, and became a sensation in many circles; it continues to be performed, and established Jones's new persona as an American firebrand. The following year, while at a book party surrounded by his cohorts from the Village, Jones received word that MALCOLM X had been assassinated up in Harlem. He later remembered this moment as an epiphany in which he realized that he was in the wrong crowd: "I felt that I had been dominated by white ideas, even down to my choice of wife" (*Village Voice*, 12 Dec. 1980). He left his wife and moved to Harlem, where he established the Black Arts Repertory Theater-School and soon became a leading black nationalist.

Jones's only novel, *The System of Dante's Hell*, was published in 1965, and much of the poetry he wrote during this period was a repudiation of his earlier life and career. In "Black Dada Nihilismus" he wrote, "Rape the white girls. Rape / their fathers … choke my friends," and in "The Liar" he reasoned, "What I thought was love / in me, I find a thousand instances / as fear." In "Black Art" he lays out his criteria for black poetry in lines such as "Poems are bullshit unless they are / teeth. … We want poems / like fists beating niggers out of Jocks / or dagger poems in the slimy bellies / of the owner-jews," and he speaks of his verses as a "poem cracking steel knuckles in a jewlady's mouth." Later, in an essay entitled "Confessions of a Former Anti-Semite," he acknowledged that during his "personal trek through the wasteland of anti-Semitism," his need to make an intellectual and political break with American liberals was unfortunately expressed as a venomous attack on Jews—who had earlier been his greatest liberal influences—and was often motivated by an unresolved anger toward his ex-wife. "Anti-Semitism," he wrote, "is as ugly an idea and as deadly as white racism" (*Village Voice*, 12 Dec. 1980).

The treatment of gays and homosexuality in Jones's work is highly problematic, as it is both complex and contradictory. Two of his early plays, *The Baptism*, set in a church, and *The Toilet*, set in a men's room, feature gay characters who can be interpreted sympathetically. According to Werner Sollors, "Homosexuality is viewed positively by Baraka both as an outsider-situation analogous to, though now also in conflict with, that of Blackness, and as a possibility for the realization of 'love' and 'beauty' against the racial gang code of a hostile society" (Sollors, 108). Ron Simmons argues that the gay tension is present in his work because Jones "never reconciled his homosexual past," a past that Jones alludes to in *The System of Dante's Hell* and ruminates about in "Tone Poem": "Blood spoiled in the air, caked and anonymous. Arms opening, opened last night, we sat up howling and kissing. Men who loved each other. Will that be understood? That we could, and still move under cold nights with clenched-fists" (Simmons, 318). Jones concludes that race-conscious men could not safely sleep with men and be credible black nationalists. Yet, unlike ELDRIDGE CLEAVER, Jones did not see a contradiction in JAMES BALDWIN, who was explicit and unapologetic about his homosexuality. In "Jimmy!," a stirring eulogy to Baldwin he read at Baldwin's funeral in 1987, he credits Baldwin with starting the Black Arts Movement and pleads, "Let us one day be able to celebrate him like he must be celebrated if we are ever to be truly self determining. For Jimmy was God's black revolutionary mouth."

In 1966 Jones married Sylvia Robinson, a fellow poet. The following year he adopted the Swahili Muslim name Imamu Amiri Baraka (which means "spiritual leader, prince, blessed"), and she became Amina ("faithful") Baraka. Together they had five children. Baraka never fully embraced Islam as a religion and later dropped Imamu from his name. Rather he practiced "Kawaida," a form of cultural black nationalism that is an eclectic blend of Islamic, Egyptian, West African, and other traditions synthesized by MAULANA KARENGA, Baraka's mentor from about 1967 until Baraka became a Marxist in 1974. With the publication of Home (1966), especially the seminal essay "The Myth of 'Negro Literature," Baraka profoundly influenced a new generation of writers, including AUGUST WILSON, HAKI MADHUBUTI, and SONIA SANCHEZ. As a political organizer in 1970, Baraka helped Kenneth Gibson to become the first black mayor of Newark, New Jersey, where Baraka had returned to live, and he was a principal organizer of the National Black Political Convention in Gary, Indiana, in 1972.

While serving a forty-eight week sentence in a Harlem halfway house in 1979, following a domestic dispute and a conviction for resisting arrest,

Baraka began writing his autobiography, in which he characterizes some of the earlier sexist, racist, and specious ideological reasoning of the Black Power movement as little more than "nuttiness disguised as revolution" (*Autobiography*, 387). After becoming a Third World Marxist, the pace of both his writing and his activism slowed over the next two decades, during which he taught at several colleges, including Yale University, Rutgers University (where he was denied tenure), and at Stony Brook University, where he retired as Professor Emeritus in 1999. He received the American Book Awards' Lifetime Achievement Award in 1989, and in 2002 he was named Poet Laureate of New Jersey.

Yet controversy continued to dog him as the governor and state legislature introduced legislation to remove Baraka as laureate in reaction to his poem "Somebody Blew Up America," which questions whether Israel and President George W. Bush had foreknowledge of the 11 September 2001 terrorist attack on the World Trade Center in New York City. After months of legal wrangling, with Baraka refusing to rescind his comments, the state abolished the position of poet laureate in order to force his dismissal.

In 2006 Baraka published a collection of his short stories, *Tales of the Out & the Gone*.

FURTHER READING

Baraka, Amiri. *The Autobiography of Leroi Jones* (1984, repr. 1997).

Simmons, Ron. "Baraka's Dilemma: To Be or Not To Be?," in *Black Men on Race, Gender, and Sexuality*, ed. Devon Carbado (1999).

Sollors, Werner. *Amiri Baraka/LeRoi Jones: The Quest for a "Populist Modernism"* (1978).

Watts, Jerry Gafio. *Amiri Baraka: The Politics and Art of a Black Intellectual* (2001).

SHOLOMO B. LEVY

Barbadoes, James G. (c. 1796–22 June 1841) was an abolitionist and community activist. Nothing is known of the circumstances of his birth, early life, or education, although his surname may indicate West Indian origins.

Barbadoes emerged as an important figure in the small but influential African American community in Boston's West End by the mid-1820s. From 1821 to 1840 he operated a barbershop in Boston. He was a prominent member of the African Baptist Church and of African Lodge #459, the preeminent black fraternal organization in the nation. An amateur musician applauded for both his vocal and his instrumental talents, he performed regularly before local audiences. But he was best known as an "indefatigable political organizer."

In 1826 Barbadoes joined with the controversial essayist DAVID WALKER and several others to organize the Massachusetts General Colored Association (MGCA), which over the next few years led local protests, corresponded with race leaders throughout the North, supported the emerging African American press, and petitioned the U.S. Congress for an end to slavery in the nation's capital. Barbadoes served as secretary of the organization. He continued to hold a prominent place among Boston blacks in the 1830s. He was one of the founders and officers of the Boston Colored Temperance Society, which sought to convert local blacks to total abstinence from alcoholic beverages as a means of deflecting white criticisms and conserving community resources. He also represented Boston blacks at the 1833 and 1834 black national conventions.

After the conversion of William Lloyd Garrison to the cause of immediate abolition in 1830, Barbadoes became a devoted supporter and colleague of the Boston editor. He was one of the first African Americans to gain a prominent place in the new interracial antislavery movement that Garrison helped create. One of three blacks who attended the 1833 founding convention of the American Anti-Slavery Society (AASS) in Philadelphia, Pennsylvania, Barbadoes enthusiastically signed the organization's Declaration of Sentiments. He served on the board of managers of the AASS during its first four years. But he proved even more important to the movement at the local and regional levels. In 1833 Barbadoes helped bring the membership of the MGCA into the New England Anti-Slavery Society (NEASS), making the AASS affiliate a racially mixed body.

Barbadoes used this new forum to publicize the kidnapping and incarceration of free black sailors in southern ports, making his white colleagues aware of the problem for the first time. Barbadoes knew about the problem firsthand. His brother Robert had been imprisoned in New Orleans for five months in 1815 until word reached family and friends in Boston. In 1834 Barbadoes was named to the board of counselors of the NEASS. He remained active in the movement through the end of the decade. When the antislavery movement began to fracture in 1839–1840 over questions of political action and women's role, with many abolitionists viewing the Garrisonian positions as too extreme,

Barbadoes emerged as one of Garrison's strongest defenders.

Throughout the 1830s Barbadoes, like Garrison, was a vocal critic of African colonization schemes, including the American Colonization Society's plan to resettle American blacks in Liberia. Yet in 1840, disillusioned by a lack of progress in the struggle for emancipation and equality in the United States, Barbadoes began to explore the possibility of migrating to a more hospitable location in the Caribbean. At first he promoted a venture in British Guiana (now Guyana), acting as secretary to a group of Boston blacks authorized by the colonial government to recruit African American settlers. Later in the year, contrary to the advice of many of his friends, Barbadoes and his family were among thirty Bostonians who migrated to St. Ann's Parish in Jamaica to participate in a venture devoted to the culture and manufacture of silk. It was sponsored by the Jamaica Silk Company, which had recently been organized by the Boston entrepreneur Samuel Whitmarsh. Barbadoes joined the enterprise "hoping to better his condition." But the venture developed slowly, and Barbadoes soon perceived that he had been duped by the flattering representations of company agents. Even worse, two of his children died of malaria, and Barbadoes himself soon succumbed to the disease. His widow, Rebecca, and their surviving children returned broken and destitute to their Boston home.

FURTHER READING

Dozens of documents relevant to Barbadoes's careers as an abolitionist and as an African American community activist are in issues of the *Liberator*, 1831–1841.

Child, David Lee. *The Despotism of Freedom; or, The Tyranny and Cruelty of American Republican Slave-Masters* (1971).

Hall, Douglas. *Free Jamaica, 1838–1865: An Economic History* (1959).

Logan, Rayford W., and Michael R. Winston, eds. *Dictionary of American Negro Biography* (1982).

Ripley, C. Peter, ed. *The Black Abolitionist Papers*, vol. 3, *The United States 1830–1846* (1991).

Obituaries: *Liberator*, 20 Aug. 1841; *Tenth Annual Report of the Massachusetts Anti-Slavery Society* (1842).

This entry is taken from the *American National Biography* and is published here with the permission of the American Council of Learned Societies.

ROY E. FINKENBINE

Barbarin, Paul (5 May 1899–17 Feb. 1969), jazz drummer, was born Adolphe Paul Barbarin in New Orleans, Louisiana, the son of Isidore John Barbarin, a coachman for undertakers, and Josephine Arthidore. The Barbarins were a distinguished musical family. Paul's father played alto horn with the Onward, Excelsior, and Tuxedo brass bands and recorded with Bunk Johnson in 1945. Paul's brothers were Louis, a drummer in New Orleans long associated with Papa Celestin; Lucien, also a drummer; and Willie, a cornetist. Barbarin's nephew was the jazz musician Danny Barker.

Having begun to play by using two forks on kitchen chairs, Barbarin was later arrested for drumming his sticks too loudly on the neighbor's steps; such was his skill that on his performing in court the judge dismissed the case, paid him fifty cents (his first professional income), and sent him home. Around 1915 he began working as a freight elevator operator to earn money for a drum set, and this purchase led to his accompanying Buddy Petit, SIDNEY BECHET, and Jimmie Noone. An astute observer, Barbarin retained and later recounted engaging memories of these early years of New Orleans jazz.

Going north to Chicago in 1917, he worked in the stockyards by day and as a musician by night. He joined the bassist BILL JOHNSON at the Royal Gardens early in 1918. The band included KING OLIVER and Noone. FREDDIE KEPPARD and Bechet also joined for a time. Barbarin toured into Canada with the Tennessee Ten, a musical comedy show, and he led a band in Connecticut before returning to Chicago to join Keppard briefly, then Noone. Barbarin and Noone married sisters. By his own account, Barbarin married Onelia Thomas in September 1922 while playing with King Oliver, although at that time Oliver's drummer was BABY DODDS. In any event Barbarin and his wife returned to New Orleans in 1923, initially staying with BARNEY BIGARD while the two men joined a band including LUIS RUSSELL and ALBERT NICHOLAS at Tom Anderson's Cabaret. Barbarin also began playing with the Onward and Excelsior brass bands, in which he marched with a snare drum before switching to bass drum. He later joined the Tuxedo Brass Band.

Nicholas, Bigard, Barbarin, and Russell left for Chicago late in 1924. All but Russell were to join Oliver at Lincoln Gardens, but the dance hall burned down and they began working only in February when Oliver introduced his Dixie Syncopators, now including Russell, at the Plantation Café.

Bigard recalled that during this period Barbarin began using a gimmick of New Orleans drumming: he would pick up the snare drum during the last part of "Tiger Rag" and shout, "Hold that tiger" through the drum skins. Barbarin's drumming with the Dixie Syncopators was not well recorded except for a consistently prominent cymbal on many titles and clomping sounds from the temple blocks on "Wa-wa-wa" (1926). His contribution was nonetheless crucial. This is nowhere more evident than in "Deep Henderson" (1926), when Barbarin, with a single chunky cymbal stroke, pulls the band back into place after Russell had allowed the rhythm to go astray in his piano solo.

Barbarin remained with Oliver until mid-1927, eventually touring to New York and then to Baltimore, where the band broke up. Barbarin and RED ALLEN went home to join the pianist WALTER PICHON at the Pelican Café in New Orleans. Later that same year Barbarin returned to New York to join Russell at the Nest Club. He remained in the band until early in 1932, in the process making recordings under Russell's own name (including "Muggin' Lightly," 1930); he also recorded under the leadership of LOUIS ARMSTRONG (including "St. Louis Blues," 1929), Oliver, Allen, and J. C. HIGGINBOTHAM, the last two being members of Russell's orchestra. Allen remembered the Russell band as "the most fiery band I ever heard. … It had the finest rhythm section, with POPS FOSTER on bass and Paul Barbarin on drums especially inspiring to the soloists."

After working in New York with lesser-known bands, including Pichon's and his own, Barbarin returned home to lead his Jump Rhythm Boys. He recorded with Russell again in New York in 1934 and then rejoined Russell's big band, with Armstrong taking over its leadership in 1935. Armstrong, "when discussing drummers, singled out Barbarin as an exceptional timekeeper." Recordings from this period capture Barbarin's drumming better than before. Additionally, on several titles from 1938, a decision evidently was made to feature Barbarin, whose musicality had generally been kept from the spotlight. Among these "Jubilee" offers solos based on military snare drum rudiments, juxtaposed with a conventional swing rhythm accompaniment, while "I Double Dare You" includes a classic example of syncopated New Orleans parade drumming in support of solos by the trombonist Higginbotham and the tenor saxophonist Bingie Madison. Ironically, this same year Barbarin was fired, his job given to BIG SID CATLETT.

At home once again, he led bands, joined Joe Robichaux's New Orleans Rhythm Boys, and worked with Pichon and Red Allen before leaving with Allen for a year in Chicago and on the West Coast (1942–1943). In Springfield, Illinois, he led a band in 1943, and he worked with Bechet in 1944, when his wife's illness brought him back home. Thereafter he was based in New Orleans, leading bands, playing in parades, and teaching at the Grunewald School of Music. He also worked with Art Hodes in Chicago in 1953 and performed in New York, Los Angeles, and Toronto. As a member of brass bands he was celebrated for the manner in which he danced while playing bass drum. He died while leading the Onward Brass Band in a carnival parade on Saint Charles Avenue in New Orleans.

The leading figure in one of the most distinguished musical families in New Orleans, Barbarin had a modest career as a composer. "Bourbon Street Parade" became a part of the standard repertoire in the revival of New Orleans jazz; he originally recorded it as a sideman with GEORGE LEWIS in 1951 and later on numerous occasions. As a leader, he recorded a number of his other compositions, including "The Second Line." His significance, though, was as a drummer, and he approached his own sessions as he would any other, filling a supportive, subsidiary role. In this manner he made his impact on jazz, particularly in affiliations involving Luis Russell.

FURTHER READING
Barker, Danny, and Alyn Shipton. *A Life in Jazz* (1986).
Bolton, Clint. "All Gone Now," *New Orleans Magazine* 5, no. 8 (1971).
Charters, Samuel Barclay. *Jazz: New Orleans, 1885–1963* (1963).
Norris, John. "Paul Barbarin," *Eureka* 1, no. 1 (1960).
Stagg, Tom, and Charlie Crump. *New Orleans: The Revival* (1973).
This entry is taken from the *American National Biography* and is published here with the permission of the American Council of Learned Societies.

BARRY KERNFELD

Barber, Jesse Max (5 July 1878–23? Sept. 1949), journalist, dentist, and civil rights activist, was born in Blackstock, South Carolina, the son of Jesse Max Barber and Susan Crawford, former slaves. Barber studied in public schools for African American students and at Friendship Institute in Rock Hill, South Carolina, where he graduated as valedictorian. In

1901 he completed the normal school course for teachers at Benedict College in Columbia, South Carolina, and afterward entered Virginia Union University in Richmond. There Barber was president of the literary society and edited the *University Journal*. In 1903 Barber earned a bachelor's degree and spent the summer after graduation as a teacher and traveling agent for an industrial school in Charleston, South Carolina.

By November 1903, Barber had moved to Atlanta to accept an offer from a white publisher, Austin N. Jenkins, to assist in launching a new literary journal, the *Voice of the Negro*, which was addressed to a national audience of African Americans. Initially listed as the journal's managing editor, Barber joined J. W. E. BOWEN of Gammon Theological Seminary as coeditor by March 1904. Bowen was a senior figurehead, however, and Barber served as the operative editor. Peter James Bryant, JOSEPH SIMEON FLIPPER, and HENRY HUGH PROCTOR, all prominent Atlanta pastors, were associate editors. The *Voice of the Negro* was a monthly periodical of high quality, carrying articles by such major figures as JOHN EDWARD BRUCE, W. E. B. DU BOIS, T. THOMAS FORTUNE, ARCHIBALD H. GRIMKÉ, PAULINE HOPKINS, KELLY MILLER, WILLIAM PICKENS, WILLIAM S. SCARBOROUGH, MARY CHURCH TERRELL, and FANNIE BARRIER WILLIAMS. Although the journal offered little fiction, it featured the poetry of WILLIAM STANLEY BEAUMONT BRAITHWAITE, BENJAMIN BRAWLEY, JAMES DAVID CORROTHERS, and GEORGIA DOUGLAS JOHNSON, as well as the art of John Henry Adams and William E. Scott.

Barber and the *Voice of the Negro* were engaged in the struggle between, on the one hand, BOOKER T. WASHINGTON's advocacy of industrial education for African Americans and Washington's accommodationist approach to racial politics and, on the other hand, Du Bois's insistence on the full exercise of civil rights by African Americans and a classical education for a black elite. The first issue of the *Voice of the Negro* included an article by Booker T. Washington, and Washington's secretary, EMMETT JAY SCOTT, served as the journal's fourth associate editor until August 1904, leaving after Barber objected to Washington's editorial interference. The Voice of the Negro's anti-Washington tone became more evident early in 1905 with the publication of Du Bois's attack on "hush money" used by Washington to control the black press, accompanied by an editorial attack on the "downright soulless materialism" of the Tuskegeean's policies.

Washington struck back with complaints to the journal's white owners, who had also published his autobiography, *Story of My Life and Work*. In September 1905 the *Voice of the Negro* endorsed the Niagara Movement organized by Du Bois, Barber, and others to protest African Americans' loss of civil rights. Four months later, the journal endorsed the Georgia Equal Rights League, which had similar objectives. *Voice of the Negro* was under attack by Washington-allied black journalists, such as BENJAMIN JEFFERSON DAVIS of the *Atlanta Independent* and Fortune of the *New York Age*. In June 1906 the journal's white owners offered the *Voice of the Negro* for sale just as it reached its maximum circulation of 15,000 in sales and subscriptions.

From 22 to 26 September 1906 white mobs swept across Atlanta, brutally attacking black people in the streets. Once white civilians were under control, the police entered the black community and disarmed its defenders. On 23 September John Temple Graves of the *Atlanta Georgian* telegraphed an account of the riot to the editor of the *New York World*, placing total blame on the African American community. Barber replied with a letter to the editor of the *World* blaming the racial sensationalism of venal politicians and the yellow journalism of men like Graves. Barber's letter was signed "A Colored Citizen," but white Atlantans discovered the name of its author and gave him a choice: leave town or face severe legal retribution. Barber fled the city, taking the *Voice of the Negro* with him to Chicago, where he continued its publication as *The Voice* for a year. In October 1907 the journal was sold to Fortune and ceased publication.

After the sale of *The Voice*, Washington's intervention cost Barber positions as editor of a newspaper, the *Chicago Conservator*, and as a teacher in Philadelphia. Barber discussed the possibility of launching a periodical for John E. Milholland's Constitutional League and addressed a session of the National Negro Political League, which was organized by WILLIAM MONROE TROTTER, JOHN MILTON WALDRON, and Bishop ALEXANDER WALTERS in 1908 to challenge Republican hegemony among African American voters. In 1909 Barber attended the National Negro Conference in New York, which led to the founding of the NAACP. When Du Bois began editing the organization's journal, *the Crisis*, Barber served as a contributing editor for three years.

Choosing a career in which Washington could not pursue him, Barber entered the Philadelphia

Dental School of Temple University in 1909. He graduated in 1912 and began practicing dentistry in the city. In 1912 Barber married Hattie B. Taylor, a Philadelphia public school teacher. After her death, he married another teacher, Elizabeth B. Miller.

Barber served as vice president and then president of the Philadelphia branch of the NAACP in its first decade. During the 1920s he was also a member of the NAACP's national board of directors. In 1922 Barber and T. Spotuas Burwell began a series of annual journeys to John Brown's grave in North Elba, New York, and organized the John Brown Memorial Association with the intention of garnering resources for a monument in honor of the famous abolitionist. As president of the association, Barber delivered the dedication address at a service at which its monument was unveiled in 1935. Barber continued to practice dentistry, and he engaged in little public activism after the dedication. Nine months after the death of his wife, Barber died in Philadelphia.

FURTHER READING

Aptheker, Herbert, ed. *The Correspondence of W. E. B. Du Bois* (1973–1978).

Bullock, Penelope L. *The Afro-American Periodical Press, 1838–1909* (1981).

Harlan, Louis, and Raymond Smock, eds. *The Booker T. Washington Papers* (1972–1989).

Johnson, Abby Arthur, and Ronald M. Johnson. *Propaganda and Aesthetics: The Literary Politics of Afro-American Magazines in the Twentieth Century* (1979).

Obituaries: *Philadelphia Independent*, 1 Oct. 1949; *Philadelphia Tribune*, 24 Sept. and 4 Oct. 1949.

This entry is taken from the *American National Biography* and is published here with the permission of the American Council of Learned Societies.

RALPH E. LUKER

Barboza, Anthony (10 May 1944–), photographer, writer, and historian, was born Anthony Barboza in New Bedford, Massachusetts, to Lillian Barboza, a homemaker, and Anthony Barboza Sr., a Fuller Brush salesman. Anthony Jr. was one of eight sons, one of whom was also an award-winning photographer and two of whom were well-known journalists. Barboza began his career in 1964, when he studied under Roy DeCarava in New York City at the Kamoinge Workshop, cofounded in 1963 as a response to the negative and biased representation of African Americans in mainstream media, with DeCarava serving as Kamoinge's first director. The group, which continued into the twenty-first century as Kamoinge, Inc., used photography to document and celebrate African American experiences.

Between 1965 and 1968 Barboza served as a photojournalist in the United States Navy. Upon opening his commercial photo studio in New York City a year after being discharged, he began shooting images in virtually all genres: commercial, documentary, editorial, and entertainment. He became one of the most widely published African American photographers, whose work has appeared in more than fifty publications worldwide, including *Ebony, Esquire, Essence, Life, National Geographic, Vanity Fair*, and *Vogue*. He has also photographed advertising campaigns for clients such as Adidas, Coca-Cola, HBO, Spike Lee Productions, and the United Negro College Fund. A survey of his work, however, demonstrates an interest in fine art portraiture, specifically of African American cultural and political icons.

Barboza paid homage to the tradition of Harlem Renaissance photographers, particularly JAMES AUGUSTUS JOSEPH VANDERZEE, one of the era's most popular studio photographers, whose work embodied and depicted the Great Migration's new, cosmopolitan African American culture, but in contrast to Barboza's subjects, primarily featured everyday, black New Yorkers. From 1975 to 1980 Barboza photographed a number of famous artists, musicians, and writers whose significant contributions to the African diaspora's cultural legacy went largely ignored by the dominant culture. AMIRI BARAKA, JAMES BALDWIN, ROMARE BEARDEN, and Miriam Makeba are only a small selection of the portraits included in the series that Barboza self-published as *Black Borders* (1980). His brother the journalist and author Steven Barboza and the poet NTOZAKE SHANGE—whose portrait is included in the book—contributed text to *Black Borders*, the publication of which was made possible by a grant from the National Endowment for the Arts. The New York State Council of the Arts awarded Barboza two additional grants while he was compiling the series.

In 1982 at the Studio Museum in Harlem, Barboza opened Introspect, a retrospective exhibit including a cross-range of his portraiture. The museum later compiled this work into the monograph also titled Introspect (1982). During the course of his long career, Barboza continued to artistically explore the personal yet contentious themes of his first book, the invisibility of African Americans and the pain of having their dreams denied and fears confirmed. Selections of this evolving body of work have been exhibited throughout the United States as well as in Taiwan and Germany; many pieces are also part of the permanent collections of more than ten museums, among them the Brooklyn Museum, the Museum of Modern Art in New York, the Schomburg Center for Research in Black Culture, and the Studio Museum in Harlem.

Barboza's dedication to photography extended beyond shooting and exhibiting his work; from the early 1970s he served the photographic community in a variety of capacities. He was a panelist-judge for the New York State Council of the Arts, the National Endowment for the Arts, and the Massachusetts Council of the Arts. He also lectured for several institutions, including the International Center of Photography, the School of the Museum of Fine Arts, the Rochester Institute of Technology, New York University's Tisch School of the Arts, and the Rhode Island School of Design. In 2001 Barboza served as assistant curator of the Brooklyn Museum's critically acclaimed show Committed to the Image: Contemporary Black Photographers. President of Kamoinge, Inc., as of 2005, he continued to operate into the twenty-first century his commercial studio in New York City, where he began *Black Dreams/White Sheets*, a project depicting blacks living in a dream state in America, with a planned publication date of 2009.

FURTHER READING

Barboza Studio, available online at http://www.barboza studio.com.

Kamoinge, available online at http://www.kamoinge. com.

CRYSTAL AM NELSON

Barès, Basile Jean (9 Jan. 1845–Sept. 1902), composer and pianist, was born in New Orleans, Louisiana, to Augustine Celestine, a slave, and Jean Barès, a white French-born carpenter. He was baptized at the age of one month in Saint Mary's Roman Catholic Church in the French Quarter. Basile Barès was born a slave of Adolphe Périer, the French-born owner of a music emporium, where Barès learned to tune pianos. Barès worked at this Royal Street business while receiving piano instruction under Eugène Prévost, former director of the Orleans Theater and the French Opera of New Orleans, and instruction in composition under C. A. Predigam. Barès played both piano and saxophone and composed for piano.

Barès's first-known published piece of sheet music, "Grande polka des Chasseurs à Pied de la Louisiane," was copyrighted to him in 1860, despite the illegality of this action because he was a sixteen-year-old slave. Very few slaves are known to have published works under their own names, and this could be the reason Barès was identified only by his first name as author on the sheet music. He is also known to have published and performed under the name Basile Périer while a slave, publicly using the surname Barès only after 1865. Despite previous suggestions that his use of the surname Périer may have meant that he was the son of his owner, recent evidence strongly suggests that this was not the case (Sullivan).

Barès took several business trips to Paris while working for the Périer business, where he remained employed once emancipated by the war. During a four-month visit in 1867, possibly his first, he performed frequently at the Paris International Exhibition. In the 1870s he began working in the New Orleans music shop of Louis Grunewald, whose music business became an empire in the burgeoning world of sheet-music publication. Grunewald published at least eight of Barès's compositions, including the 1875 "Les variétés du Carnaval," a collection of five dance pieces for piano. Between 1869 and the late 1880s Barès published at least nineteen dances for piano, many with carnival themes, such as the "Galop du Carnaval" in 1875. Because his published compositions do not include many that he had composed and performed publicly, the exact number of his compositions is unknown. At least twenty-eight published works are known to exist in a variety of Louisiana archives, including those of Tulane University and the Historic New Orleans Collection. Xavier University holds an unpublished composition as well as his autographed photograph taken while in Paris. More of Barès's published music is available today than for any other black composer of his era.

Barès's music could be heard in theaters, concert halls, ballrooms, and private homes; his compositional style has been given many labels, including popular, art, concert, salon, and classical. Because modern notions of separating popular music from high-culture music did not exist then, his pieces were used more flexibly within the musical climate of the city. His compositions were based on European models and published usually with French titles and, at times, lyrics. Barès reportedly loved France and things French. His existing published works are mostly dance numbers, including polkas, waltzes, quadrilles, and mazurkas. Some music scholars have suggested that forms used in these pieces contain elements later used in jazz.

In New Orleans, where he spent most of his life and career, Barès frequently performed with other Creole musicians of color, who were also local free blacks, including Victor-Eugène Macarty and Samuel Snaër. Some of these performances were benefits for groups favoring black male suffrage as well as for the Freedmen's Orphan Asylum. Creoles of color in New Orleans experienced tightening racial restrictions during Reconstruction and the late nineteenth century. The relative autonomy that free people of color had experienced in New Orleans before the Civil War, especially when compared with that of other American cities, began to disintegrate. It was in this changing climate that Barès lived and worked. New Orleans's Creole of color musicians could first use the Théâtre d'Orléans for their performances after the Civil War ended, but only during the off-season between May and October when the French and French-Creole population frequently fled the hot and sickly city. When the theater, which relied on the patronage of the large free black community of the city, tried to reinforce its strict segregation rules in 1875, Barès and other Creole of color musicians staged a boycott that helped cause serious financial problems for the theater. The repertoire at such performances varied greatly. Original compositions by Barès, such as "Magic Bells" and "Fusées musicales," were interspersed with pieces arranged from popular French and Italian operas. This would have been a common practice during all musical stage performances of the place and time, regardless of race, as original compositions were mixed with popular opera pieces.

Barès was recruited to play for both white and black audiences, including accompanying EDMOND DÉDÉ. On his return to New Orleans from his home in France, the famous New Orleans–born Creole of color violinist, composer, and orchestra leader performed a series of concerts in 1893 with Barès at the piano. Barès also helped many prominent white composers arrange vaudeville and opera orchestrations, and he led a string band for whites' carnival balls. Barès published no music after his 1884 "La Louisianaise: Valse brillante." This is likely because of a general decline in interest in locally composed French songs—fashions were moving toward more American musical styles—but could also be because of the increased segregation and

limitations on blacks in Jim Crow New Orleans. Barès died in New Orleans, leaving one son and three daughters.

FURTHER READING

Blassingame, John W. *Black New Orleans, 1860–1880* (1973).

Sullivan, Lester. "Composers of Color of Nineteenth-Century New Orleans: The History behind the Music," *Black Music Research Journal* 8 (1988).

Trotter, James M. *Music and Some Highly Musical People* (1878).

ANN OSTENDORF

Barker, Danny (13 Jan. 1909–13 Mar. 1994), jazz guitarist and banjoist, vocalist, and author, was born Daniel Moses Barker in New Orleans, Louisiana, to Moses Barker, a drayman, and Rose Barbarin Barker. Barker grew up in New Orleans with a largely absent Baptist father of rural origins and a mother whose familial connections to the Barbarin family, famed in New Orleans music, rooted him in the city's Creole of Color musical community. His childhood experiences immersed him in the cultures of both sides of his family: rural Protestant and urban Roman Catholic.

Barker's uncle, the drummer PAUL BARBARIN (composer of the jazz standard "Bourbon Street Parade"), started Danny on drums; after trying the clarinet, Danny decided to play multiple string instruments: guitar, banjo, and ukulele. A teenaged Barker played in "spasm bands," children's bands that featured rudimentary instruments often created from discarded objects. Playing ukulele, Barker led a spasm band named the Boozan (Creole patois for "Good Times") Kings, which played for tips from white and black barroom audiences. He later played banjo professionally in New Orleans before moving to New York in 1930 and finding work as a rhythm guitarist. In 1931 he married Louisa Dupont, and the couple had one child, Sylvia Barker. Barker played in numerous big bands, including that of LUCKY MILLINDER (1937–1938) and Benny Carter (1938) before joining CAB CALLOWAY's Orchestra (1939–1946). While with Calloway, Barker recorded his observations of working and traveling with the band. During this period Barker played in some of the most famous recordings and music film shorts featuring the Calloway orchestra, including "Blues in the Night" (1940) and "Minnie the Moocher" (1941). A few years earlier Barker had appeared as a musician in OSCAR MICHEAUX's 1933 film *The Girl from Chicago*.

The stress of long and regular absences from his wife and daughter induced Barker to leave Calloway's band and seek other ways to support his family. Sylvia Barker remembers her mother singing blues songs while doing the dishes at night whenever her father was on tour, and Danny and other musicians encouraged her to record. Louisa Barker first recorded with Danny and others in 1938, at which time the producer gave her the professional name of "Blu Lu." Two of their risqué songs, both written by Danny, gained special notice: "Don't You Feel My Leg (Don't You Make Me High)" (1938) and "I Got Ways Like the Devil" (1938). The former earned Barker a Grammy Award in the mid-1970s after Maria Muldaur covered the song.

The Barkers were signed to the Apollo Record label in 1946, and they toured into the late 1940s. Finding little commercial success, however, and wishing to resettle in New York City, Barker sought different ways of earning a living. He created King Zulu Records and released what are likely the earliest commercial recordings of New Orleans Mardi Gras Indian songs: "Chocko Mo Feendo Hey" and "My Indian Red" in the early 1950s. Barker found success as a songwriter when, among other triumphs, Johnny Mercer and NAT KING COLE both recorded versions of Barker's "Save the Bones for Henry Jones" (1947).

Barker played in bars both as a solo artist and in small groups. He was a regular in the Dixieland Revival movement in New York, playing at Ryan's and Condon's. Fluent in many styles, Barker also appeared with BILLIE HOLIDAY in the 1957 Sound of Jazz television program. Other artists Barker performed and recorded with included LEAD BELLY, JELLY ROLL MORTON, LOUIS ARMSTRONG, and WYNTON MARSALIS. He also initiated his own research project into the early history of New Orleans jazz. Barker started the "Jazzland Research Guild" in the early 1950s and asked his musician friends to fill out a survey and participate in his collecting efforts. According to his daughter Sylvia, few of Barker's black peers took him seriously, largely because of his race. Though stung by the lack of cooperation from his fellow musicians, Barker nevertheless cooperated with the many white authors who approached him regarding the same history. Barker is featured prominently in Nat Hentoff's Hear Me Talkin' to Ya (1955).

Playing in Greenwich Village and other New York City venues brought Barker into contact with many authors; a few were moved by his stories of New Orleans and jazz history and offered to provide

him with room and board in a New York City hotel while he wrote. This arrangement ended quickly, however, when Barker balked at the creative interference of his would-be patrons. Nevertheless, his writing continued until late in life and flourished following his return to New Orleans in 1965. Barker collaborated with the sociologist Jack Buerkle to produce Bourbon Street Black, a study of African American musicians. The music historian Alyn Shipton worked with Barker to compile his stories and transcriptions of interviews into A Life in Jazz, a blend of autobiography and fiction. The urban folk revival brought renewed interest in Barker's banjo work, and it was at least in part by playing at venues such as the popular Newport Folk Festival that Barker began to consider the importance of honoring jazz musicians with their own New Orleans festival.

Barker enjoyed playing traditional New Orleans jazz and studying its history. He worked as an assistant to the curator of the New Orleans Jazz Museum Club for the next several years, and he served as grand marshall of the Onward Brass Band from 1965 until 1972. These activities made Barker a central figure in plans for the first jazz festivals in the city, precursors to the New Orleans Jazz and Heritage Festival.

Barker was largely responsible for the revival of brass band music in New Orleans after he formed and mentored the Fairview Baptist Church Christian Marching Band in the early 1970s. He had formed the band in response to Reverend Andrew Darby's request that he help keep neighborhood children occupied. The Fairview Church Band served as an incubator for many of the musicians who would lead the brass band revival in the city during the last decades of the twentieth century. Barker had once observed that "no kids want to dance to their grandparents' music" (personal interview, 1993), so he supported these musicians in developing their own interpretations of the music.

Barker recorded with several traditional New Orleans jazz bands. He also fully developed his vocal performance style and recorded a 1988 solo record for Orleans Records that captured his impish sense of humor. Barker would mug for audiences and wear loud clothes when playing solo, when accompanying Blue Lu, or as leader of Danny Barker and his Jazz Hounds. He drew inspiration from the vaudeville and film star BERT WILLIAMS and developed a comic persona similar to that of the comedian whose films he had watched so eagerly as a child. In the last decade of his life Barker had become a cultural icon in his hometown, and he received national honors in 1991 when he was named a National Endowment for the Arts Jazz Master.

Barker's health deteriorated quickly after he was diagnosed with cancer. He did not want to have a jazz funeral because he felt that the tradition had been warped. Despite his wishes, musicians convinced the family to allow one, and Barker received one of the best attended jazz funerals in the city's history.

FURTHER READING

Much of the information in this essay stems from numerous personal interviews with the Barker family: Danny Barker (1991–1993); Louisa Barker (1993–1996); Sylvia Barker (1994 and 1996).

Barker, Danny. "A Memory of King Bolden," *Evergreen Review* 37 (1965).

Barker, Danny, and Alyn Shipton. *A Life in Jazz.* (1988).

Barker, Danny, and Alyn Shipton, eds. *Buddy Bolden and the Last Days of Storyville* (2001).

Buerkle, Jack V., and Danny Barker. *Bourbon Street Black: The New Orleans Jazzmen* (1974).

Hentoff, Nat. *Hear Me Talkin to Ya* (1955).

Obituaries: *New York Times*, 15 Mar. 1994, and (New Orleans) *Times-Picayune* 14 Mar. 1994.

MICHAEL MIZELL-NELSON

Barkley, Charles (20 Feb. 1963–), professional basketball player, was born Charles Wade Barkley in Leeds, Alabama, in 1963. Barkley was raised by his mother, Charcey Glenn, who supported the family by cleaning homes, and his grandmother, Johnnie Mae Edwards, who worked in a meat factory. In high school the five-foot-ten-inch Barkley harbored ambitions to play in the National Basketball Association (NBA) despite failing to make the varsity squad in the tenth grade. However, Barkley persevered by putting in long hours on the practice court and by honing his vertical leaping ability. During his senior year in high school, Auburn University offered Barkley (who then stood six feet four inches) a basketball scholarship.

At Auburn, Barkley earned the first of many nicknames he would garner throughout his career: the "round mound of rebound." He earned this nickname because he weighed three hundred pounds and was able to consistently out-rebound taller opponents. Barkley caught the eye of NBA scouts by starting at center and using his "God-given ability to rebound." However, he never averaged more than fourteen points per game in college.

Nonetheless, the Philadelphia 76ers decided to take a chance on the "round mound of rebound," making him the fifth pick in the 1984 NBA Draft. Widely considered the best NBA Draft ever, the 1984 Draft saw Barkley passed up for other outstanding players such as MICHAEL JORDAN and Hakeem Olajuwon before landing with the 76ers. When Barkley joined his new team, he was unsure of his scoring ability; he was also unsure of his ability to adjust to big city life. He was quickly schooled by NBA legends JULIUS "DR. J" ERVING and Moses Malone; they instructed him to invest his money wisely and get rid of most of his seven cars.

As an NBA player, Barkley more than met his goal of "scor[ing] ten points a game and get[ting] ten rebounds a game." During his first three years in the league, he was leading the NBA in rebounding and averaging over twenty points per game. From 1984 to 1992 Barkley played for the 76ers and became a household name, both for his scoring and rebounding as well as for his run-ins with bad-tempered fans and the media. Perhaps the most famous of these run-ins was in New Jersey, where he attempted to spit at a heckler who hurled a racial epithet at him; instead, he accidentally hit a young girl in the stands.

By 1992 Barkley had grown tired of the mediocrity of the 76ers players and hungered for a chance at the one prize that had eluded him: an NBA championship. Furthermore, Barkley's consistent outspoken opinions frustrated the 76ers' management. Throughout his eight years in Philadelphia, Barkley had publicly commented on everything from American racism to the idea that athletes should not have to be role models. Barkley's opinions were consistently in newspapers, on sports talk radio, and most famously on a 1993 Nike advertisement where he unapologetically proclaimed: "I am not a role model."

The 76ers rid themselves of the outspoken Barkley by trading him to the Phoenix Suns for Jeff Hornacek and Andrew Lang after the 1991–1992 season. Barkley seemed to be reenergized by the trade. Barkley was the highest scorer on the legendary 1992 Olympic "Dream Team" that dominated the Olympic field and won the gold medal. The 1992–1993 NBA season proved to be Barkley's most memorable, as he led the Suns to sixty-three victories and garnered his first and only appearance in the NBA finals, where the Suns lost to Jordan's Chicago Bulls in six games. Throughout the series Barkley turned in consistent play, posting respectable numbers in scoring, rebounds, and assists.

Although the Suns nearly made it to the NBA Finals again in 1993–1994, Barkley never again returned to the NBA Finals, even though he continued his torrid pace of rebounding and scoring. He would make one last run at the championship when he was traded to the Houston Rockets after the 1995–1996 season. He recommitted himself to conditioning and offered to come off the bench for a Houston Rockets team that included NBA superstars Olajuwon and Clyde Drexler. However, a career of battling bigger, stronger players had taken a toll on his body and he was not the same player he had once been. Barkley admitted he was a "good player, not a great player" at that stage in his career.

Despite the fact that Barkley never won a championship, he is still remembered as one of the best players in NBA history and his career statistics reflect that. As of 2007, he was one of only four players to have accumulated 23,000 points, 12,000 rebounds, and 4,000 assists. He was a fixture on the NBA All-Star team and was named one of the NBA's 50 greatest players in 1996. Barkley's career averages of twenty-three points per game and almost twelve rebounds a game are a tribute to his consistency and hard work on the court.

Off the court Barkley was an outspoken and persistent critic of racism and consistently fought for the rights of lower income families. He donated $3 million to Alabama schools, arguing that everyone should have a good education available. Barkley considered running for governor of his home state of Alabama as an independent and has written several books, including *Outrageous* (1994), *I May Be Wrong, but I Doubt It* (2002), and *Who's Afraid of a Large Black Man?* (2005), detailing his views on race, class, and the state of America. Barkley was also a basketball commentator for TNT and did not rule out a return to basketball on the administrative side, stating that he would "love to be a GM [general manager]" of an NBA team. Barkley lives in Arizona with his wife, Maureen, and daughter, Christiana.

FURTHER READING

Casstevens, David. *Somebody's Gotta Be Me: The Wide, Wide, World of the One and Only Charles Barkley* (1994).

Tulumello, Mike, and Dave Cruz. *Breaking the Rules: A Season with Sports' Most Colorful Team, Charles Barkley's Phoenix Suns* (1997).

DANIEL A. DALRYMPLE

Barksdale, Don (31 Mar. 1923–8 Mar. 1993), basketball player and track athlete, was born Donald Angelo Barksdale in Oakland, California, the son of Agee Barksdale, a Pullman porter, and Desiree Barksdale, a homemaker. Barksdale grew up in a predominantly black neighborhood and played sports as a youngster at San Pablo Park, just four blocks from his home. Dutch Redquist, the director of the playground, helped him develop his skills. JACKIE ROBINSON, the great UCLA athlete who broke the color barrier in Major League Baseball, visited the park and became another of Barksdale's mentors. Barksdale also accompanied his father to meetings of the Brotherhood of Sleeping Car Porters where he listened to black activists such as A. PHILIP RANDOLPH.

While Barksdale was a gifted athlete, he never played high school basketball. The Berkeley High School basketball coach refused to have more than one black player on the team, so Barksdale, who entered high school in 1937, was cut in three consecutive years by the school's coach. Barksdale continued to develop his skills playing recreational basketball. He lettered in track and field for three straight years and competed in the long jump, high jump, and triple jump. Upon graduation in 1940, his athletic skills earned him an invitation to compete in basketball and track and field at Marin Junior College (later the College of Marin) in Kentfield, California, where he led Marin to two California State Junior College championships. In the middle of the 1942–1943 season, Barksdale accepted a scholarship to the University of California, Los Angeles (UCLA). He played only five basketball games for the UCLA Bruins before he was drafted into the army, but in one of the games he played, Barksdale scored eighteen points and helped UCLA defeat the University of Southern California for the first time in forty-two consecutive games.

In the fall of 1942 Barksdale was stationed at Camp Ross in California and was a member of an army service team. In 1944–1945 he scored 780 points and the following season hit for 1,288, the highest point total in the history of armed forces basketball. In 1946–1947 Barksdale returned to UCLA and led the Bruins in scoring with 368 points, averaging 14.7 points per game. In 1947 he made several All-America teams, the first African American so honored.

At the end of the 1947 season Barksdale decided to extend his basketball career by playing with the Oakland Bittners, a team that played by rules governed by the Amateur Athletic Union (AAU).

Technically, AAU players were not paid to play but worked for a company that also sponsored a basketball team. Barksdale himself did not work for Lou Bittner but rather owned a Blue 'n Gold beer distributorship, becoming the first African American to own a distributorship for this company. He also worked as a disc jockey. Some of the most successful of the AAU teams were sponsored by the Phillips Petroleum Company, the Caterpillar Company, and the Goodyear Tire and Rubber Company. The Oakland Bittners, by comparison, were a much smaller operation. The owner, Lou Bittner, had a tax consulting and insurance business, as well as a passion for sports. Barksdale chose to play for the Bittners instead of a professional team because in the late 1940s all the professional teams were east of the Mississippi River and paid rather small salaries. Moreover, only a few African Americans played in these leagues, and then only briefly, reflecting the racism prevalent in the country as a whole. Given these realities, the Bittners were a good fit for Barksdale, and the team had some of the best basketball talent from California's Bay Area.

By 1947 Barksdale measured six feet six inches and weighed two hundred pounds. He jumped well and had a feathery jump shot, and in the 1947–1948 season, he led the American Basketball League in scoring with a 16.7 scoring average. On 7 January 1948 Barksdale made history when he became the first African American athlete to play in an integrated athletic contest in Oklahoma. In front of an overflow crowd in Bartlesville, the Bittners beat the Phillips 66ers 45–41, the first home-court loss for them since 1944. Barksdale scored seventeen points and held Bob Kurland, Phillips's great center, to five points.

In March 1948 all the outstanding AAU teams gathered in Denver for the annual AAU national basketball tournament. The stakes in this tournament were especially high because the top three teams would earn the right to play in a tournament to decide who would represent the United States in the 1948 Olympics. While Oakland lost in the semifinals to Phillips, the Bittners, with Barksdale scoring twenty-one points, won the game for third place. Barksdale was named to the AAU All-America team and earned a trip to Madison Square Garden to play in the tournament to select the U.S. Olympic basketball team. After the tournament, the U.S. Olympic Basketball Committee named Barksdale as one of the fourteen players to represent the United States in the 1948 London Olympics. This made him the first African American basketball player to compete in the Olympics.

Prior to sailing to London, Barksdale trained with the Phillips 66ers, who won the Olympic tournament and placed five players on the team. To raise money for the trip, the Olympic committee scheduled three exhibition games between the Phillips 66ers and the Kentucky Wildcats, the second-place team in the tournament, who also had five players on the Olympic team. On 9 July 1948 the two teams met in Lexington, Kentucky, and Barksdale became the first African American to play on an integrated team in the Bluegrass State. Barksdale did not allow an anonymous death threat or the refusal of Lexington hotels to allow him to stay with his team to affect his play, and he and Bob Kurland each scored thirteen points to give Phillips the victory. In 1948 the United States Olympic basketball team won the gold medal, and this brought an extremely eventful year in Barksdale's life to a close.

The 1949 AAU basketball tournament was held in Oklahoma City, Okalahoma. In the championship game, the Oakland Bittners edged the Phillips 66ers 55–51 as Barksdale led all scorers with seventeen points. Oakland's victory ended Phillips's streak of six consecutive AAU championships. Because of segregation, neither Barksdale nor Dave Minor, also an African American, was allowed to stay with their teammates while they stayed in Oklahoma. Nonetheless, when Barksdale was named to the all-tournament team, the crowd gave him a loud ovation.

The following year Lou Bittner dropped his team sponsorship and Barksdale played for the Oakland Blue 'n Gold. The team lost in the finals of the National AAU Tournament to Phillips although Barksdale won All-America honors for a third time. In March 1951 he led the United States to a victory in the Pan American Games, for which the AAU had the responsibility of organizing the U.S. basketball team. He played his last AAU game in the 1951 tournament when the Blue 'n Gold was upset in the second round. Despite his team's loss, Barksdale was named an AAU All-America for the fourth time. In 1951 Barksdale signed a professional contract with the Baltimore Bullets, along with Dave Minor becoming the team's first black players. He played with the Bullets from 1951 to 1953 and with the Boston Celtics from 1952 to 1955. In four years he averaged eleven points per game, and in 1953 he was the first African American to play in the NBA All-Star game.

Because of foot and ankle problems, Barksdale retired from basketball in 1955 and returned to Oakland, where until the 1960s he owned the

Sportsman and Showcase nightclubs and also worked as a popular disc jockey in the Bay Area until the 1970s. Later he worked as a scout for the Golden State Warriors. In 1962 he married Jewell Jackson. The Barksdales had two sons, Donald and Derek, before divorcing in 1975. In 1982 he created the Save High School Sports Foundation to help make high school sports affordable for children in the Bay Area. The organization raised more than a million dollars by holding Celebrity Waiter Luncheons, for which he recruited celebrities such as WILLIE MAYS, DANNY GLOVER, and Carol Channing. Barksdale died in 1993 of cancer of the esophagus. He was inducted into the UCLA Hall of Fame in 1987, the Bay Area Hall of Fame in 1996, and the Pacific Ten Hall of Fame in 2005.

FURTHER READING
Grundman, Adolph H. *The Golden Age of Amateur Basketball: The AAU Tournament, 1921–1968* (2004).
Thomas, Ron. *They Cleared the Lane: The NBA's Black Pioneers* (2002).
Obituary: *New York Times*, 11 Mar. 1993.

DOLPH GRUNDMAN

Barnes, Ernie (15 July 1938–27 Apr. 2009), football player and painter, was born Ernest Eugene Barnes Jr. in Durham, North Carolina, the son of Ernest Barnes Sr., a tobacco worker, and Fannie Mae Geer, who worked for a local legal official. On occasion Barnes talked with Mr. Fuller, his mother's employer, and from him learned about culture, art, and classical music.

Before the landmark Supreme Court case *Brown v. Board of Education* in 1954 it was uncommon for African Americans in North Carolina to have access to museums or other sources of information about ancient or world cultures. Segregation and racial inequalities in schools and other public institutions deprived most back children of avenues for artistic pursuits. Despite such constraints, Barnes's mother exposed her son to as much culture and art as she could: he studied dance and horn and percussion instruments as well as the visual arts. By the time Barnes completed high school he had already been exposed to the great masters of the classical arts. An awkward adolescent, Barnes was overweight, tall, and painfully introverted, characteristics for which he was frequently ridiculed. His only refuge, aside from the protection of his mother, was the vast openness of creativity. Barnes felt safest in the company of his sketchbook and drawing implements. Once the schoolchildren recognized that his skill for drawing overshadowed his shyness and his weight, he was no longer ridiculed; in fact, he became the center of attention.

As his talent grew, so did his body. Standing head and shoulders above most of his high school classmates, Barnes became involved in extracurricular sports. In 1952 he started playing football; he excelled on the field and off, becoming a team leader. He graduated from high school with offers of several college scholarships. Barnes accepted an athletic scholarship at North Carolina College (later North Carolina Central University), where he played football and studied to become an artist.

After college his large stature and presence on and off the field gained the attention of the American Football League (AFL). Barnes was drafted by the Baltimore Colts as a lineman in 1959. Although he had joined the ranks of well-paid and famous athletes, Barnes maintained his love for art. He returned to Durham to create his first notable painting, *The Bench*. This piece fused his experience of the world of sports with his emergence into the world of painting. The AFL was Barnes's introduction to the lucrative yet brutal world of professional sports in which this affable southerner was confronted with the truculent racist discourse of white America. During the civil rights movement in the 1960s Barnes was developing as a football player as well as an artist. Recognizing that neither painting nor any other form of art was commonly associated with a 263-pound lineman, Barnes was unsure if he would be accepted by his fellow teammates. Much to his surprise, however, he and his art were well received.

Barnes's professional football career ended in 1966, but his painting career continued. Reflectively, Barnes reconnected with his beginnings, his time as a professional athlete, and his heritage as an African American. From a wellspring of memories, Barnes created a lasting body of work, gaining widespread acclaim through word of mouth and showings at small social events. Barnes was sponsored, supported, and promoted by country clubs and sportswriters from the Midwest to New York. Blending its creator's memories of the football field, the civil rights struggles, and his love of music and black culture, Barnes's work was featured as set decoration on the television program *Good Times* and in other venues. In 1984 Barnes married Bernadine Gradney, a Los Angeles schoolteacher; the couple had five children. Ernie Barnes was able to sustain his career by staying true to his love of art and by contributing to the education of children through the promotion of learning and the arts. In 2003 he returned to Durham to Hillside High, his alma mater, to talk to the students about using the power of creativity to enrich their lives, an example of the importance Barnes placed on community outreach and on helping children appreciate the arts. Barnes, whose work could claim a diverse group of admirers—ALEX HALEY and Charleton Heston, to name a few—died in Los Angeles after complications from a blood disorder. He was seventy.

FURTHER READING

Barnes, Ernie. *Autobiography: From Pads to Palette* (1995).

Kirkpatrick, C. D. "Art Helps Build Hillside Dreams," *Herald Sun*, 15 Aug. 2003.

Nakao, Annie. "Barnes Draws from Life but It's No Still Life," *San Francisco Chronicle*, 12 Sept. 2002.

Robertson, Dale. "Football Helped Barnes Blend Colors, Career," *Houston Chronicle*, 30 Jan. 2004.

Obituary: *New York Times*, 30 Apr. 2009.

HASAAN A. KIRKLAND

Barnes, Samuel Edward (25 Jan. 1915–21 Jan. 1997), pioneer black naval officer, was born in Oberlin, Ohio, one of five children (two boys and three girls) of James and Margaret Barnes. James, from North Carolina, was a chef at Oberlin College, and Margaret, from Kentucky, ran a family laundry. Soon after they married, Barnes's parents settled in Oberlin to raise their family because of the community's liberal atmosphere. They were aware of the role the town had played as a way station on the Underground Railroad for fugitive slaves in the nineteenth century. Barnes received the bulk of his education in Oberlin. He graduated from high school there in 1932 and was elected to the National Honor Society. In 1936 he graduated from Oberlin College with a bachelor's degree in Physical Education. He was an outstanding athlete who played end on the college's football team and starred on the track team. He established a school record in the broad jump, ran the 100-yard dash, 220, 440, and was part of the mile relay team.

From 1936 to 1941 Barnes was on the staff of church-affiliated, all-black Livingstone College in Salisbury, North Carolina. He was director of athletics, head basketball and football coach, dormitory supervisor, and assistant to the dean of the college.

As he recounted in an oral history many years later, Barnes avoided contact with whites as much as possible. He went by his initials to avoid being addressed by his first name. Whites addressed him as "Professor" to avoid having to attach the word "Mister" before his last name.

From 1941 to 1942 Barnes was the boys' work secretary at a YMCA in Cincinnati, Ohio, before enlisting in the Navy in September 1942. He was honor man—deemed by his seniors to be the top-performing member—of his company in recruit training at the Great Lakes Naval Training Station, north of Chicago. His next assignment as an enlisted man was in the physical training section at Camp Robert Smalls, the segregated site of training for black naval personnel at Great Lakes. In December 1943 Barnes married Olga Lash of Salisbury, North Carolina. They had three children, Olga Michele Welch, Margaret Nadine "Alexa" Donaphin, and Michael David Lash Barnes.

In January 1944, shortly after his marriage, Barnes joined fifteen other enlisted petty officers at Camp Robert Smalls to form the first training course for black officers in the history of the U.S. Navy. The sixteen men were culled from a population of approximately one hundred thousand black sailors. Included in the selection process were detailed background checks by the FBI. Almost everyone in the group had college experience, and a few had advanced degrees. In two and a half months, they went through a cram course that included training in such areas as navigation, communications, gunnery, propulsion machinery, seamanship, naval history, and the navy disciplinary system. The members of the training class concluded that they were part of an experiment on the part of the navy and were determined to succeed or fail as a group, rather than compete with each other. Thus they pooled their knowledge in after-hours sessions. All sixteen passed, but only thirteen became officers—twelve ensigns and one warrant officer. The other three students remained as enlisted men. Years later the pioneering officers became known collectively as the Golden Thirteen. Barnes's sister Margaret was among the first black women officers of the Women's Army Corps (WAC) commissioned by the army during World War II.

After receiving his commission in March 1944, Ensign Barnes remained at Great Lakes until the spring of 1945. During that time he was in charge of physical training and recreation for the three camps that trained black sailors. In April 1945 he became officer in charge of Logistics Support Company #123, which was trained at Camp Peary, Williamsburg, Virginia. In May 1945 the company went overseas, first to Eniwetok Atoll in the Marshall Islands and later to Okinawa in the Ryukuyus chain. The men of his all-black company were stevedores, involved in loading and unloading ships in anticipation of the planned invasion of the Japanese home islands. One of the few white officers who welcomed Barnes on Okinawa was Lieutenant (junior grade) Stephen Belichick, whom Barnes had known from his college years in Ohio. Belichick's son Bill later coached the Cleveland Browns and New England Patriots of the National Football League.

Once World War II ended, Barnes, by now a lieutenant (junior grade), returned to the United States and left active service in 1946. He returned to Oberlin College to do graduate work toward his master's degree, which he received in 1949. In 1947 he had begun a long career at Howard University in Washington, D.C., one of the nation's foremost traditionally black schools. At various times he was assistant football coach, head boxing coach, head wrestling coach, and head track coach. In 1956 he completed a doctorate in Sports Administration from Ohio State University. From 1956 to 1970 Barnes was Howard's director of athletics and head of the men's physical education department. In 1957 and 1958 during a one-year sabbatical from Howard, he went to Iraq on behalf of the U.S. State Department. While there he worked as a "sports ambassador," teaching Iraqi students about American coaching techniques.

Barnes was a member of the National Collegiate Athletic Association (NCAA) Council from 1965 to 1970. From 1971 to 1973 he was secretary-treasurer of the NCAA, the first black person to be an officer of the organization. After leaving Howard University, Barnes moved on to the Federal City College in Washington, D.C., to work for two years as interim director of athletics. In 1974 he became chairman of the division of health and physical education for the District of Columbia Teachers College. He remained in that capacity when the University of the District of Columbia was formed by the merger of D.C. Teachers College and two other schools. He retired in 1984 but remained active in the community. Among other pursuits, he worked with the Navy's Recruiting District Advisory Committee in Washington. He helped get a junior Naval Reserve Officer Training Corps program established in a Washington high school and was instrumental in working with the Washington Redskins in establishing companies of Navy recruits named for that professional football team. Among his many honors, Barnes was selected in 1986 as a charter member of the Oberlin College Athletic Hall of Fame. He died in Washington, D.C., in 1997.

FURTHER READING

Reminiscences of Dr. Samuel E. Barnes, Member of the Golden Thirteen (1993). This volume is composed of interviews conducted in 1986 and 1988 and was published by the U.S. Naval Institute in Annapolis, Maryland.

Stillwell, Paul, ed. *The Golden Thirteen: Recollections of the First Black Naval Officers* (1993).

Obituary: *Washington Post*, 24 Jan. 1997.

PAUL STILLWELL

Barnes, William Harry (4 Apr. 1887–15 June 1945), physician, otolaryngologist (an ear, nose, and throat specialist), inventor, and administrator, was born in Philadelphia, Pennsylvania, the son of George W. Barnes, a laborer, and Eliza Webb. Barnes and his two sisters lived poverty-stricken lives on Lombard Street, in a very poor area of the city. Barnes decided at an early age to become a physician, a decision unheard of and regarded in his neighborhood as preposterous. His parents tried to discourage him from pursuing what to them seemed an impossible dream for a poor black youth, hoping rather that he would focus on finding realistic employment. Nevertheless determined, Barnes walked ten miles every day to and from school and from his after-school work as a porter and messenger for jewelry shops. During summers he worked as a porter in hotels. Seeing those who lived a far different and more elegant life than his own inspired him to work himself out of poverty. In 1908 Barnes graduated from Philadelphia's Central High School with a collegiate bachelor of arts degree and decided to compete for a four-year scholarship to medical school offered by the University of Pennsylvania. He spent the entire summer of 1908 in serious study, took the competitive examination, passed it, and became the first African American to win that scholarship. Four years later, in 1912, Barnes received an MD and began a year's internship at Douglass and Mercy hospitals in Philadelphia. Also that year he married Mattie E. Thomas; they had five children.

Barnes soon established several long-term relationships with hospitals and other medical facilities in and outside of Philadelphia. From 1913 to 1945 he was an ear, nose, and throat staff physician at Douglass Hospital. In 1921 he was chief of otolaryngology at Jefferson Medical School Hospital in Philadelphia. From 1913 to 1922 and again in 1931 he was lecturer in bronchoscopy at Howard University Medical School in Washington, D.C. At this time he was also a registrant of the American College of Surgeons. In 1918 Barnes served as acting assistant surgeon for the U.S. Public Health Service. In spite of a heavy schedule of professional responsibilities and a professionally stultifying racial environment, he managed to develop and maintain a growing private medical practice between 1922 and 1945. In 1922, against the advice of friends, associates, and relatives, he limited his medical practice to diseases of the ear, nose, and throat, making him the first black medical specialist in the United States. In the early 1930s he organized and headed the Department of Bronchoscopy at Mercy Hospital. He found time to do postgraduate work at Douglass and Mercy hospitals (1921), the University of Pennsylvania (1924, 1926), the University of Paris, and the University of Bordeaux (1924). In addition to formal coursework he also underwent advanced medical training in bronchoscopic technique with internationally known specialists, such as Sebileau and Baldenbeck in Paris, Moure in Bordeaux, Unger in New York, and Schatz and Lukens in Philadelphia. Barnes was the first black physician to master the technique of bronchoscopy. He was also the first black granted certification by an American medical certifying board, the American Board of Otolaryngology (1927), and therefore the first black physician officially recognized as a medical specialist in the United States.

Barnes was a medical and community activist who worked hard to increase the flow of medical information and its accessibility to the African American community. In addition he made great efforts to upgrade medical practice and standards among black physicians. One of his highest priorities was to improve general living conditions within black communities because he was acutely aware of the connection between decent housing and good public health. He was the thirty-seventh president of the National Medical Association (1935–1936), a parallel organization created by black physicians in 1895 because they were denied membership in the American Medical Association. Barnes was an active participant in NMA annual meetings, which he turned into teaching forums by presenting papers and demonstrating surgical procedures. In 1931 Barnes founded the Society for the Promotion

of Negro Specialists in Medicine, and from 1931 to 1933 he served as the organization's executive secretary. A member of Philadelphia's Zoar Methodist Church, where he regularly taught Sunday school and was president of the board of trustees for fifteen years, Barnes organized a well-baby clinic and taught first aid. At other churches in the community he also set up and taught first-aid classes. He founded the Zoar Community Building and Loan Association and served as its president from 1925 to 1945. A proponent of integration in public housing, he was one of the original members of the Philadelphia Housing Authority and served as its assistant secretary-treasurer from 1937 to 1945.

Barnes was a medical innovator. Between 1913 and 1938 he invented the hypophyscope, an instrument for seeing the pituitary gland by accessing it through the sphenoidal sinus; invented a lingual tonsillectome, a specialized scalpel used in performing tonsillectomies; developed a surgical modification of the Myles lingual tonsillectomy procedure; developed surgical procedures for more effectively treating tonsillar abscesses; and created improved medical record-keeping procedures for patient records. He was an early riser and a practitioner of strict punctuality. When chairing meetings he would begin at the appointed time regardless of who was, or was not, present. His surgical operations were often scheduled for seven o'clock in the morning, to the annoyance of his staff and nurses.

Barnes belonged to and was an officer in many civic and professional organizations, including the American Medical Association, once black membership became possible in the late 1920s and early 1930s; the American Board of Otolaryngology; the Negro Specialists Society, of which he was executive secretary from 1931 to 1938; the Philadelphia Academy of Medicine and Allied Sciences, of which he was president for three years in the early 1930s; the NAACP; and the Citizen's Republican Club, where he was president of the Forum Commission in the 1930s. He died in Philadelphia.

Barnes was an indefatigable worker who involved himself in every aspect of medical and community life. His personal motto, which he often expressed, was "failure comes from within." In his view, therefore, failure could be controlled and eliminated. He proved by his own example that despite growing up in poverty and despite the existence of racial barriers, one could achieve lofty goals. Having done that, Barnes actively tried to help as many other people as possible obtain better lives for themselves.

FURTHER READING

Barnes, William Harry. *National Medical Association Journal* 47 (1955).

"The President Elect." *National Medical Association Journal* 26 (1934).

Sammons, Vivian Ovelton. *Blacks in Science and Medicine* (1990).

This entry is taken from the *American National Biography* and is published here with the permission of the American Council of Learned Societies.

BILL SCOTT

Barnes, William Henry (c.1845–24 Dec. 1866), Civil War soldier and Medal of Honor recipient, was born in Saint Mary's County, Maryland. He was likely enslaved for most or perhaps all of his life prior to his military service. The 1860 Federal Census Slave Schedules for Saint Mary's County indicate that one J. A. Barnes owned eight slaves aged four to thirty, one of them a fourteen-year-old boy who was probably William Henry Barnes. How he came to join the Union Army is unknown; Barnes may have been freed prior to the war, or he may have run away from his master to seek military service. Whatever the circumstance, Barnes enlisted in the 38th U.S. Colored Troops (USCT) regiment at Norfolk, Virginia, on 11 February 1864, stating his age as twenty-three and his occupation as that of a farmer.

The 38th USCT spent its first months after its formation stationed in the area of Norfolk and Portsmouth, Virginia, where its men gained valuable training experience while performing garrison duty. In June 1864, Barnes and the men of the 38th were sent to the front during the siege of Petersburg and Richmond. There, in the months that followed, many black soldiers, among them Barnes, Edward Ratcliff, and James Harris, would earn their country's highest decoration for bravery.

By 1864, the style of battle in the Civil War had evolved into a different kind of fighting; gone were the pitched battles such as those that had occurred early in the war at Bull Run and Gettysburg. Now, it was a war of attrition, and the Confederacy was hanging on for dear life. Especially around the capital city of Richmond, Virginia, elaborate trenches and fortifications were built to keep the Union Army at bay. However, General Ulysses Grant was prepared to win at all costs; his army had enough manpower to sustain heavy losses, while the Confederate Army did not. Among the troops available to Grant late in the war were the soldiers of the U.S. Colored Troop regiments, consisting of free blacks and former slaves. Indeed, by the war's end, nearly 179,000 free blacks and former slaves had served in USCT regiments and eventually constituted 10 percent of the Union Army's manpower and suffered over 1,700 casualties.

Late September 1864 found William Barnes and the men of the 38th USCT stationed near New Market Heights, just south of Richmond on the James River. As the southern anchor in the Confederate chain of fortifications surrounding Richmond, New Market Heights was a keystone in the Confederate defense. The Battle of New Market Heights was to be a two-pronged assault against Confederate forts on both sides of the James River. The northern attack was carried out by General Edward Ord's XVIII Corps, including Barnes and the men of the 38th. The attack began on the morning of 29 September 1864 and would prove to be the Union's only success in a battle that lasted two days and cost five thousand casualties. Despite heavy fire and fierce hand-to-hand combat, black troops led the way when their officers were shot down and overwhelmed the Confederates at Fort Harrison, the only fort to be captured of the four that were the Union's objectives in the battle. Among the first men to enter the enemy works was a wounded William Barnes.

While the Battle of New Market Heights was but a minor victory that has been largely forgotten, the actions of the USCT men were both heroic and groundbreaking; as a result of their outstanding valor, thirteen African American soldiers, including Private William Barnes, were awarded the Medal of Honor for their actions.

Less than a year after the battle, on 1 July 1865, Barnes was promoted to sergeant and continued to serve in the army after the end of hostilities. Later stationed in Texas, William H. Barnes subsequently died of consumption at the army hospital in Indianola, Texas. He is buried at the San Antonio National Cemetery.

FURTHER READING

Hanna, Charles W. *African American Recipients of the Medal of Honor* (2002).

GLENN ALLEN KNOBLOCK

Barnett, Claude Albert (16 Sept. 1889–2 Aug. 1967), entrepreneur, journalist, and government adviser, was born in Sanford, Florida, the son of William Barnett, a hotel worker, and Celena Anderson. His father worked part of the year in Chicago and the rest of the time in Florida. Barnett's parents separated when he was young, and he lived with his mother's family in Oak Park, Illinois, where he attended school. His maternal ancestors were free blacks who migrated from Wake County, North Carolina, to the black settlement of Lost Creek, near Terre Haute, Indiana, during the 1830s. They then moved to Mattoon, Illinois, where Barnett's maternal grandfather was a teacher and later a barbershop owner, and finally to Oak Park. While attending high school in Oak Park, Barnett worked as a houseboy for Richard W. Sears, cofounder of Sears, Roebuck and Company. Sears offered him a job with the company after he graduated from high school, but Barnett's mother insisted that he receive a college education. He graduated from Tuskegee Institute with a degree in Engineering in 1906. His maternal grandfather and BOOKER T. WASHINGTON, founder and head of Tuskegee Institute, were the major influences on Barnett's life and values. He cherished the principles of hard work, self-help, thrift, economic development, and service to his race.

Following graduation from Tuskegee, Barnett worked as a postal clerk in Chicago. While still employed by the post office, in 1913 he started his own advertising agency, the Douglas Specialty Company, through which he sold mail-order portraits of famous black men and women. He left the post office in 1915 and in 1918, with several other entrepreneurs, founded the Kashmir Chemical Company, which manufactured Nile Queen haircare products and cosmetics. Barnett became Kashmir's advertising manager and he toured the country to market its products and his portraits. He helped to develop a national market for Kashmir and also pioneered the use of positive advertisements. Traditional advertisements featured an unattractive black woman with a message that others should use the company's products to avoid looking like her. In contrast, Barnett used good-looking black models and celebrities with positive messages about the beauty of black women. He visited local black newspapers to negotiate advertising space and discovered that they were desperate for national news but did not have the resources to subscribe to the established newswire services. Barnett recommended that the *Chicago Defender*, founded by ROBERT ABBOTT in 1905 and the most widely circulated black newspaper during the early twentieth century, establish a black news service. The newspaper rejected his proposal since it had enough sources for its own publication and feared harming its circulation by providing competitors with material.

In March 1919, with backing from Kashmir's board of directors, Barnett started the Associated Negro Press (ANP) in the company's office. In 1926 the Kashmir Chemical Company dissolved under legal pressure from Procter and Gamble, which made a similar line of products called Cashmere. Barnett was now free to devote his attention fully to ANP. During this era black newspapers published weekly, so ANP evolved as a mail service rather than as a wire service, thereby making it affordable to subscribers. Moreover, the major wire services did not offer much information about African Americans. Barnett began ANP with eighty subscribers, including almost all the black newspapers and several white papers. He charged $25 to join ANP and a monthly fee of $16 to $24, depending on whether newspapers received dispatches once or twice a week. Subscribers agreed to credit ANP for articles featured in their newspapers, to provide ANP with news about their communities, and to forfeit membership if they failed to pay for the service within sixty days.

The staff produced about seventy pages of copy a week, including news stories, opinion pieces, essays, poetry, books reviews, cartoons, and occasionally photographs; the copy was then mimeographed and sent to subscribers. It did not cost much to operate ANP. The service mined news stories from various sources, such as black newspapers, the white press, special correspondents, and news releases from government agencies, foundations, organizations, and businesses, creating one of the most comprehensive files of news stories about African Americans. Barnett wrote some of the stories himself under the pen name Albert Anderson, a combination of his middle name and his mother's maiden name. Because subscribers usually were late in paying their fees, Barnett struggled to keep ANP afloat. Sometimes he took advertising space in the newspapers in lieu of news service fees. His companies, first Associated Publishers Representatives and later the National Feature Service, then sold the space to advertisers, offering advertisers lower rates than they would get if they placed advertisements directly with the newspapers.

In 1932 Barnett became one of the first graduates to serve on Tuskegee Institute's board of trustees. He also served as president of the board of trustees of Provident Hospital in Chicago, director of the Supreme Liberty Life Insurance Company, member of the Red Cross's national board of governors, and trustee of the Phelps-Stokes Fund. During the late 1920s and early 1930s he headed the Republican Party's publicity campaign for the black vote. Some of his ANP subscribers became upset by his stories that favored the Republicans. After Franklin D. Roosevelt's election to the presidency in 1932 and First Lady Eleanor Roosevelt's growing popularity among African Americans, Barnett ended his relationship with the Republican Party.

Barnett married the popular concert singer and actress ETTA MOTEN BARNETT in 1934. She had three daughters from a previous marriage. Barnett managed her career until 1942, when she assumed the lead role in the Broadway show *Porgy and Bess* and began to require the attention of a full-time agent. Also in 1942, Barnett became special assistant to the secretary of agriculture, Claude R. Wickard, a position that he held with successive secretaries until 1952, when the Republicans regained the White House with the election of Dwight D. Eisenhower. During his tenure with the Department of Agriculture, Barnett was a strong advocate for black tenant farmers and sharecroppers and sought to make it possible for them to own land. He also tried to improve the condition of black farmers through federal aid for health, education, and insurance programs. He was particularly interested in strengthening black agricultural colleges.

During World War II, ANP employed eight people at its Chicago headquarters and had almost two hundred subscribers. The news service opened an office in Washington, D.C., and later one at the United Nations in New York City. Barnett penned many articles about segregation in the military and pressed the federal government to accredit black journalists as war correspondents. His advocacy of racial equality played an important role in President Harry S. Truman's decision in 1948 to desegregate the military.

With an expanding African independence movement after World War II, Barnett secured more than one hundred African newspapers as subscribers to ANP. In 1959 he organized the World News Service to provide copy to subscribers in Africa. Barnett traveled to Africa more than fifteen times to solicit subscribers and to collect material for articles on black progress. He and his wife became avid collectors of African art and were much sought after speakers on Africa to African American civic, fraternal, and religious organizations. Although he had no formal training as a newsman, Barnett helped to develop a generation of black journalists. Most of his featured columnists wrote for the benefit of a large black audience rather than for pay.

With the rise of the civil rights movement during the late 1950s, many white newspapers began to cover the black community in the United States. News organizations started hiring black correspondents, most of whom had broken into the industry with ANP. Barnett had established a means for the black press to secure national and later international news about black people. ANP, with its motto "Progress, Loyalty, Truth," set professional standards for the black press and nurtured black journalists who were well prepared to move into mainstream media with the success of the civil rights movement. Increased competition, persistent financial problems, and failing health forced Barnett to close ANP and to retire in 1963. He made several more trips to Africa and began writing an autobiography. He died of a cerebral hemorrhage at his Chicago home.

FURTHER READING

The Archives and Manuscript Department of the Chicago Historical Society house Barnett's papers and ANP files. Most of this material is available on microfilm.

Evans, Linda J. "Claude A. Barnett and the Associated Negro Press." *Chicago History* 12, no. 1 (Spring 1983): 44–56.

Hogan, Lawrence D. *A Black National News Service: The Associated Negro Press and Claude Barnett, 1919–1945* (1984).

Silverman, Robert Mark. "The Effects of Racism and Racial Discrimination on Minority Business Development: The Case of Black Manufacturers in Chicago's Ethnic Beauty Aids Industry." *Journal of Social History* 31, no. 3 (Spring 1998): 571–597.

Obituary: *New York Times*, 3 Aug. 1967.

ROBERT L. HARRIS JR.

Barnett, Etta Moten (5 Nov. 1901–2 Jan. 2004), actor, singer, and philanthropist, was born Etta Moten in Weimar, Texas, the only daughter of Reverend Freeman F. Moten and Ida Norman Moten. The ten-year-old Etta took an active part in church, singing in the choral group and instructing Sunday-school lessons. Standing on a makeshift step stool, in order to be at the same height level as the rest of the choir, she shared her voice with the congregation.

After high school Barnett wedded Lieutenant Curtis Brooks. During their seven-year marriage, she had four children, one of whom died at birth.

Following in the footsteps of her college-educated parents, she attended the University of Kansas in the 1920s; however, in order to receive her education, Barnett had to sacrifice her conventional family life. She divorced her husband and left her three daughters under her parents' supervision while she attended school. On weekends she cared for her children at her parents' house, but during the week Barnett was a full-time student, earning a degree in voice and drama in 1931. Once an unhappy wife but dedicated mother of three, Barnett changed her fate at a time when many people thought change for women, especially black women, was impossible.

Barnett sang with the EVA JESSYE Choir of New York after she finished her education. On the way to New York she met her future second husband, CLAUDE BARNETT, father of the Associated Negro Press. Claude, dazzled by Etta's ambition, wrote introductory letters to his New York acquaintances to smooth her entrance into the theater scene. Soon after she arrived in New York Etta joined the Broadway cast of *Fast and Furious* (1931). Her performance earned her a place in the touring cast of *Zombie* (1932), which coincidentally played in Chicago, where Etta became reacquainted with her future husband, Claude. Due to his affiliation with national newspapers, he also had connections in Hollywood; Etta headed to the West Coast.

Entering the ranks of the film industry, Barnett dubbed songs for actresses, including Barbara Stanwyck and Ginger Rogers, without getting recognition in the credits. However, she became famous for her on-screen portrayal of a widow in *Gold Diggers* (1933), singing "My Forgotten Man." Because her role was not that of the stereotypical housekeeper or nursemaid, Barnett's performance gave credence to the idea that black actors could portray realistic characters, something many Americans at the time considered impossible. Her role in the film sparked interest and pride among African Americans around the nation, and the black press anointed her "The New Negro Woman." In addition, *Gold Diggers* won Barnett national acclaim for her musical talent: she was the first black woman to perform at the White House, reprising her song from the film at Franklin D. Roosevelt's birthday party in 1934.

In her next film, *Flying down to Rio* (1933), with Fred Astaire and Ginger Rogers, Barnett appeared with large fruit placed strategically in her hair, a style that many people mistakenly believed originated with Carmen Miranda, as she sang "The Carioca." Her performance of the musical number increased her fame when the Academy Awards panel nominated the piece for best song. A dynamic duo, Etta and Claude Barnett married in 1934, and Etta's three daughters moved to their mother's new Chicago residence.

Barnett returned to New York to play the role of Bess in *Porgy and Bess* in 1942. According to Barnett, Gershwin sought her to fill the role in 1935, when he initially produced the show. However Barnett, a lush contralto, politely declined the role since Gershwin had composed the part for a soprano voice. Yet Barnett did play Bess in the production's longest stint, starting in New York in 1942 and traveling throughout the United States and Canada until 1945. Among Barnett's other Broadway credits are *Sugar Hill* (1931) and *Lysistrata* (1946). SIDNEY POITIER charmingly described her as "the most incredible, amazing, voluptuous, dignified, and sensual actress to grace the Broadway stage in my lifetime" (Kinnon, "Etta at 100," 62).

Though she enjoyed a successful career in film and theater, Barnett's influence reached beyond the artistic sphere and into the world of activism and philanthropy. Beginning in 1947 African governance and culture became a part of Etta and Claude life as they traveled to the continent several times on behalf of three United States presidents during the movement for African independence. In March of 1957 Etta interviewed MARTIN LUTHER KING JR. about Ghana's independence celebration. Though her husband died in 1967, she carried on their support of African progress for the next thirty-seven years. In the 1950s she broadcast her own radio show, *I Remember When*, to listeners in thirty-eight states. Various organizations, such as the African American Institute, the National Council for Negro Women, the DuSable Museum of African American History, and the Chicago Lyric Opera, received her support and membership. In 1979 her legendary work earned her a place in the Black Filmmakers Hall of Fame.

At the age of ninety-six, Barnett remarked, "I've always said that the only difference between a rut and a grave is the depth, and I'm not ready for either one" (Kinnon, "Etta Moten Barnett," 52–54). Having lived a long, fulfilling life Etta Moten Barnett died of pancreatic cancer in Chicago's Mercy Hospital at the age of 102. Barnett's diverse acting roles, her portrayal of Bess, and her philanthropy have left a lasting impression on American culture.

FURTHER READING

Kinnon, Joy Bennett. "A Diva for All Times," *Ebony* (2004).

Kinnon, Joy Bennett. "Etta at 100: Etta Moten Barnett, Pioneer Actress, Singer, and Activist, Celebrates Centennial," *Ebony* 57 (2001).

Kinnon, Joy Bennett. "Etta Moten Barnett: Still on the Case at 96," *Ebony* (1997).

Laskas, Jeanne Marie. "Her Heart Keeps on Singing," *Good Housekeeping* 226, issue 2 (1998).

"Pioneer Actress-Singer Etta Moten Barnett Celebrates 100th Birthday in Chicago," *Jet* 100 (Dec. 2001).

Obituaries: (London) *Independent*, 7 Jan. 2004; *Variety*, 12 Jan. 2004; *Jet*, 26 Jan. 2004.

ALLISON KELLAR

Barnett, Ida B. Wells. *See* Wells-Barnett, Ida Bell.

Barnett, Marguerite Ross. *See* Ross-Barnett, Marguerite.

Barney, Lem (8 Sept. 1945–), professional football player, was born Lemuel Jackson Barney in Gulfport, Mississippi. Information about his upbringing and personal life is difficult to come by. He played football as a young man, attending local schools in Gulfport and playing a multitude of positions—including punter and defensive back—on his high school team. In 1963 he matriculated at the historically black Jackson State, where he made the team and was again a standout. He played three seasons and had twenty-seven interceptions. He also served as the team's punter.

In 1967 Barney graduated with a bachelor's degree in Health and Science and only then entered the National Football League (NFL) draft. He was taken in the second round by the Detroit Lions, and it was with the Lions that Barney would spend his entire career. His life in the Lions' silver and blue got off to an auspicious start. Barney, playing defensive back, intercepted the very first pass that was thrown his way—in a game against the Green Bay Packers and the legendary quarterback Bart Starr—and returned it twenty-four yards for a touchdown. He went on to be named the league's Defensive Rookie of the Year. That same year, Barney married Martha [maiden name not known]. The couple went on to have two children.

Meanwhile, Barney became friendly with the Motown great MARVIN GAYE. At the time, Gaye was considering a career in professional football and considering trying out for the Lions. In the end, he chose not to, but he did invite Barney to

sing backup on his 1971 single "What's Going On?" Barney, who had no professional inclination toward performance, won a gold record.

On the football field, Barney continued to excel. His rookie performance earned him a Pro Bowl nod, and his ten interceptions represented that year's NFL best. More, Barney returned three of those ten for touchdowns, just one short of the all-time NFL record. Barney's time with the Lions was during a period of low ebb for the team, and the squad frequently ended their season with a losing record. Still, his individual performance ranks him not only as among the all-time Lion greats but also as one of the NFL's greatest. In his eleven-year career, Barney collected fifty-six interceptions. He scored eleven touchdowns on both interceptions and punt and kickoff returns. He was named to seven Pro Bowls and was seven times an All Pro. He was named to the NFL's 1960s All-Decade Team along with such greats as JIM BROWN, WILLIE DAVIS, and Johnny Unitas.

Barney retired from the NFL in 1977. He took work for a time with the Michigan Consolidated Gas Company, and did a turn as a football commentator on Black Entertainment Television (BET). In 1992 he was inducted into the NFL Hall of Fame, one of only a handful of players who played the defense back position to be so honored. Shortly thereafter Barney was arrested during a traffic stop on charges of drug possession. The charges were subsequently dropped, but the scandal served to diminish his reputation and led many to ask how a player who had led the way in NFL antidrug efforts among young people should have come to such an impasse. He went to work at an auto dealership owned by a former teammate and remained active in his community with various charities and serves as a lay minister at Hope United Methodist Church, keeping busy with area youth and antidrug campaigns as well as other charitable endeavors in the Detroit area.

FURTHER READING

Knight, Dawn Taliaferro. *Breaking Barriers from the NFL Draft to the Ivory Tower* (2007).

Murray, Mike. *Lions Pride: 60 Years of Detroit Lions Football* (1993).

JASON PHILIP MILLER

Barnhill, David (13 Oct. 1914–8 Jan. 1983), baseball player, was born in Greenville, North Carolina. As a teenager working in the tobacco fields he honed his skills as a pitcher. His first exposure to professional baseball came in 1936 when the manager of the visiting Wilson Stars from Wilson, North Carolina, spotted his burgeoning talent. After the team manager promised Barnhill's mother a dollar a day for her son's pitching duties, she consented to let her son join the team.

Barnhill barnstormed for two years with several independent teams. In 1938 he began his first of twelve Negro League seasons by joining the Jacksonville Red Caps. The following year, with the Ethiopian Clowns, Barnhill took part in the team's minstrel sideshows. Earning the nickname "Impo," Barnhill cut up with his teammates in clown makeup and wild wigs while performing comic displays to delighted fans.

In the winter of 1940–1941 Barnhill pitched in the Puerto Rican league. He boasted an 11–9 record and led the league with 193 strikeouts for the Humacao team.

Legitimizing his career back in the Negro Leagues, Barnhill left the Clowns for the more respected New York Cubans. In 1941 he racked up the first of three consecutive East-West All-Star game appearances. Pitching 124 innings that season, he had a career best of sixteen wins with three losses.

On 14 June 1942, before a capacity crowd at Detroit's Briggs Stadium, Barnhill pitched a twelve-inning game, giving up only four hits while striking out eleven. He retired the side in nine of the twelve innings in a 4–2 Cubans' victory over the Baltimore Elite Giants.

The 5-foot, six-inch, 160-pound hurler was often accused by batters of doctoring the ball, yet such claims were never proven. Dogged by speculation and allegations, Barnhill always maintained his innocence.

Opening day in 1943 featured Barnhill as starting pitcher in Yankee stadium. Fanning fourteen Black Yankee batters in the 12–2 Cubans' victory, he went on to boast a team-leading fifteen wins with three losses.

On 4 August, Barnhill, along with Baltimore Elite Giants catcher ROY CAMPANELLA and infielder Sammy Hughes, was scheduled to try out for the Pittsburgh Pirates—the first-ever opportunity for African Americans to try out for Major League consideration. But at the eleventh hour Pirates president William Benswanger reneged on the offer, fearing the public would believe he was tied to the American Communist Party, which was intensely pressuring owners to integrate. Incensed by the snub, Barnhill took out his frustration on the

diamond, finishing the season strongly and earning another All-Star appearance.

In 1947 Barnhill did not lose a single game and capped off a successful year by beating the Cleveland Buckeyes in the decisive game of the Negro League World Series. During the off-season in Cuba, he compiled a 2.26 ERA and struck out a league-leading best of 122 batters.

In 1950 thirty-five-year-old Barnhill received an offer from the New York Giants to report to their AAA Minneapolis farm club. His 11–3 record helped the squad win the American Association championship. However, citing Barnhill's age as a factor, the Giants did not advance him to the majors.

After playing the 1952 season with Miami in Florida's International League, where he was 13–8 with a 1.19 ERA, Barnhill spent the next year with Fort Lauderdale but in only pitched four games. After hanging up his spikes at the end of the 1953 season Barnhill settled in Miami, where he worked in the city's recreation department for thirty-five years.

FURTHER READING

Riley, James A. *The Biographical Encyclopedia of the Negro Baseball Leagues* (1994).

Lester, Larry. *Black Baseball's National Showcase* (2001).

BYRON MOTLEY

Barrett, Janie Porter (9 Aug. 1865–27 Aug. 1948), educator, school founder, and social welfare advocate, was born in Athens, Georgia, the daughter of Julia Porter.

Various biographical accounts indicate that Barrett's parents were former slaves, while others speculate that her father was white. Little is known about either parent. During her early childhood, Barrett resided in the home of the Skinners, a white family whom her mother served as housekeeper. After her mother's marriage to a railway worker, Barrett remained with the Skinners, who encouraged her to further her education.

Though the Skinners suggested that she move north, Barrett, at her mother's urging, attended Hampton Institute in Virginia, graduating in 1884. While at Hampton she became convinced that it was her duty as an educated black woman to work assiduously for the betterment of all African Americans. That belief led her to teach in Dawson, Georgia, and at LUCY CRAFT LANEY's Haines Normal and Industrial Institute in Augusta, Georgia, prior to securing a teaching position at Hampton in 1886. In 1889 she married Harris Barrett, a cashier at Hampton Institute. They had four children.

Janie Porter Barrett established an informal day-care school at her home in Hampton, Virginia. In 1890, it became the Locust Street Social Settlement, the first settlement house for African Americans. (Austin/Thompson Collection, by permission of Hampton University Museum and Archives.)

While rearing her own children, Barrett decided to share her skills with some neighborhood girls. Beginning with Tuesday afternoon sewing classes in her home for a few girls, she soon formed a club for "improving the homes and the moral and social life of that community." People of all ages and of both genders were actively involved in developing skills designed to improve the quality of their lives. In time, because of the overwhelming response to the club and its activities, Barrett sought larger quarters. In 1902 the Barretts constructed a building on their property to house the Locust Street Settlement, as the club was then called, the first of its kind in Virginia. An auxiliary group of prominent community members raised funds to pay the club's basic expenses and to expand its programs. Northern philanthropists also contributed to the expansion. In 1903 the Barretts added a kindergarten to the growing list of services, and by 1909 the Locust Street Settlement House included five girls' and women's clubs and four boys' clubs. Students and staff from Hampton Institute provided instruction in arts and crafts, domestic arts, and agricultural science.

Barrett enjoyed a continuing relationship with Hampton Institute that resulted in a commitment by staff, faculty, and students to her social service and self-help projects. In 1907 the institute supplied stationery and other support to the Virginia State Federation of Colored Women's Clubs, founded at that year's Hampton Negro Conference. Barrett served as the federation's first president.

After an encounter with an eight-year-old black girl who had been incarcerated, Barrett convinced the federation to adopt as its primary project the establishment of a rehabilitative home for "wayward colored" girls. In 1915 members founded the Industrial Home School for Delinquent Colored Girls at Peake in Hanover County, Virginia, set on a 147-acre farm. Initially Barrett served as secretary of the school's interracial board of trustees. Following her husband's death in 1915, however, Barrett accepted the position of superintendent.

Under her leadership the school gained national prominence and was able to secure a state subsidy and private donations. Largely owing to Barrett's innovative administrative efforts, including the introduction of social welfare principles that nurtured the girls and guided their lives in new directions, the Russell Sage Foundation ranked the school among the top five of its kind in the United States. The reformatory school's program stressed the personal and educational development of the residents rather than punishment for their past behavior. Many of the students flourished in the environment, where good conduct was rewarded and practical skills for living were taught. The girls received vocational training that included sewing, housekeeping, and laundering. The program was designed to provide an eighth-grade education. Those who earned good deportment records for two years were eligible for parole. After their release, contact was maintained with the girls through the school's publication and through personal communication from Barrett.

The school's many accomplishments and success stories brought Barrett numerous awards. Notable among her recognitions was the 1929 William E. Harmon Award for Distinguished Achievement among Negroes. The award was given by the Harmon Foundation, established in 1922 by the philanthropist William E. Harmon. Because of her national reputation as an expert in child rehabilitation, President Herbert Hoover invited Barrett in 1930 to participate in the White House Conference on Child Health and Protection.

Although kept busy by the school's management, Barrett remained active with the federation and with the National Association of Colored Women (NACW), serving as chairperson of the NACW executive board from 1924 to 1928. She also served on local boards such as that of the Richmond Urban League and, in keeping with her promotion of interracial cooperation in matters relating to racial uplift and equality, was a member of the Commission on Interracial Cooperation. The school's board, with its interracial membership, reflected Barrett's commitment to work with whites to achieve the school's goals.

Barrett remained superintendent of the Industrial Home School for Delinquent Colored Girls until her retirement in 1940. She left the school, now a model institution for those seeking to steer young black females away from delinquent behavior, to return to Hampton, Virginia, where she remained until her death. In honor of her achievements, the school that she had led for nearly twenty-five years was renamed the Janie Porter Barrett School for Girls.

FURTHER READING

Neverdon-Morton, Cynthia. *Afro-American Women of the South and the Advancement of the Race, 1895–1925* (1989).

Whitman, Alden. *American Reformers* (1985).

This entry is taken from the *American National Biography* and is published here with the permission of the American Council of Learned Societies.

CYNTHIA NEVERDON-MORTON

Barrier, Eric (Eric B.) (1965–), DJ, producer, and member of Eric B. and Rakim, was born in East Elmhurst, Queens, New York. In his youth Barrier showed a musical aptitude, playing trumpet and guitar before devoting his energy to DJing, a form which—by the mid-1970s—was a cornerstone of the burgeoning hip-hop movement arising in New York City's boroughs. Barrier's turntable talents eventually landed him a job as the mobile DJ for New York radio station WBLS while in high school. It was also during this period that Barrier met William Griffin Jr., a young MC who had adopted the name and stage persona of "Rakim Allah" in 1984 to signal his growing commitment to the Five-Percent sect of the Nation of Islam, a controversial but influential sect that promoted a broadly Afrocentric blend of political and spiritual advancement. A prodigiously talented lyricist, Rakim's complicated, sophisticated rhymes found their perfect complement in the busy, jazz-inflected soundscapes favored by his new partner.

In 1985 Eric B. and Rakim made their partnership official, releasing their debut single—"Eric B. Is President" backed by "My Melody"—for small, Harlem-based Zakia Records in 1986. Rakim soon became one of hip-hop's most respected lyricists, but the duo's first single was a celebration of its other member, spotlighting Barrier's pioneering work as DJ and producer. This DJ-centric focus was in keeping with much early hip-hop but remains ironic in light of Rakim's rising reputation. Barrier used multiple, overlapping samples, a style of "noize" whose juxtapositions created a multilayered, occasionally jarring collection of rhythms and melodic snippets; in short order this approach became preeminent within the genre. Eric B. was particularly fond of JAMES BROWN samples, using Brown's stabbing style and deeply polyrhythmic arrangements to construct his own post-industrial symphonies, whose dissonance was perfectly matched by Rakim's thoughtful, politicized rhymes. Mixing the sonic blasts of Barrier's turntables, with Rakim's "knowledge-dropping" rhymes, Eric B. and Rakim's music quickly distinguished itself.

Their 1987 debut full-length recording, *Paid in Full*, fulfilled the promise of their early singles with an album's worth of the explosive creative energy that marked their early work. Still praised as one of hip-hop's greatest works, *Paid in Full* includes "I Know You Got Soul," a hit built around a funk track by James Brown associate Bobby Byrd (which the writer Steve Huey suggests "kicked off hip-hop's fascination" with Brown-related samples), and "Paid in Full," whose rhythm track was later sampled on numerous occasions (Huey, 158–159). The album also included three tracks on which Eric B. is featured without Rakim, displaying his dizzying prowess on the "wheels of steel."

Their second album, *Follow the Leader*, followed in 1988, and its artistic and commercial success solidified Eric B. and Rakim's place at hip-hop's pinnacle. The title single is perhaps Rakim's greatest moment as an MC, a mind-altering journey through time and space, and more Rakim-less examples of Barrier's "turntablism" are featured on the record. As was evident on all their recordings, but particularly on the single "Follow the Leader," which is arguably their masterpiece, the duo displayed a deep jazz sensibility, a mindset reflected in their choice and manipulation of backing tracks, but more significantly by both members' innovative approach to their craft. Both Eric B. and Rakim envisioned a limitless creative palette for their art, within which they were able to re-imagine the possibilities and limitations previously inscribed within rap music, and even popular music more generally. While many of their records are highly danceable (thanks to Barrier's fondness for funk and soul), their artistic aim exceeds this benchmark. This boundary-busting style proved revolutionary: Rakim's lengthy, literate rhymes raised the stakes for all future MCs, and Eric B.'s turntable hurricanes provided perfect soundtrack for the genre's burst of desperate creativity. During this period, the group's devotees—including KRS-ONE and Public Enemy—made acclaimed, popular music that followed Eric B. and Rakim's groundbreaking example. After Follow the Leader the duo recorded the 1989 hit "Friends" with the R&B singer Jody Watley, and Barrier established production and management companies in 1992.

Though their first two albums proved an insurmountable legacy, even for such a talented partnership, both 1990's Let the Rhythm Hit 'Em and 1992's Don't Sweat the Technique have their highlights. The former features "In the Ghetto," an urgent call to arms built around a restless rhythm track, and the latter includes "Know the Ledge," on which Rakim sounds a note of caution about the perils of life in urban black America. Nonetheless as hip-hop entered a period dominated by the West Coast–based "gangsta" movement, the challenging collages of Eric B. and Rakim seemed increasingly out of place, even though the group's esteem within all sectors of the rap community remained high. The 1992 release of Don't Sweat the Technique completed the duo's contract with MCA Records, which had begun in 1988, and—in the ensuing confusion over the direction of their career, particularly over the possibility of each recording a solo album—they broke up.

For the next several years, legal disagreements prevented either member from capitalizing on their previous success. Although Rakim would stage a successful comeback in the late 1990s, Barrier's subsequent career was less storied. His legendary reputation and track record helped him score various unremarkable production jobs throughout the 1990s, including a brief partnership with the gangsta virtuoso DR. DRE, and he released a 1995 solo effort that met with little critical or commercial success. Despite Eric B.'s subsequent lack of chart presence, his legacy was felt throughout the hip-hop world, as his groundbreaking redefinition of sample-based hip-hop tracks (combined with the virtuosic lyrics of his collaborator Rakim) continued to inform and influence the genre and culture.

FURTHER READING

Chang, Jeff. *Can't Stop Won't Stop: A History of the Hip-Hop Generation* (2005).

George, Nelson. *Hip Hop America* (1998).

Huey, Steve. "Eric B. and Rakim," in *All Music Guide to Hip-Hop*, ed. Vladimir Bogdanov (2001).

Wang, Oliver. *Classic Material: The Hip-Hop Album Guide* (2003).

CHARLES L. HUGHES

Barrow, Peter (1841–1906), slave, Civil War soldier, politician, and Baptist minister, was born Peter Barnabas Barrow, a Virginia slave. The month and day of his birth are unknown. It is believed that he was born near Petersburg, Virginia, and may have been taken to Mississippi or Alabama with his owner. In 1864 Barrow joined Company A, 66th U.S. Colored Infantry and in 1865 became a sergeant. A year later Barrow was discharged because of an injury he received. He went on to teach school at Vicksburg, Mississippi.

Barrow, who was most likely self-educated, served as a member of the Mississippi House of Representatives for Warren County, Mississippi, from 1870 to 1871. From 1872 to 1875 he served in the Mississippi State Senate. He migrated to Spokane, Washington, in 1889 and settled there in the city's African American community. Barrow and other African Americans were determined to thrive by establishing businesses, seeking political rights, creating jobs, and developing churches. Barrow served as the president of a land development company established to help build a colony of black rural workers. Land was purchased at a location called Deer Lake in Stevens County, Washington, "[f]or the purpose of giving the Negroes of Spokane an opportunity to make good on the farm, and to prove their worth as farm laborers." Therefore, "a band of Spokane colored folks has organized a development company, bought 140 acres of land near Deer Lake and will start this spring to develop the land with Negro labor only. No similar company exists in the United States" (Franklin, 24–26).

Shortly after arriving in Spokane, Barrow engaged in the city's political and religious affairs, in which he earned respect from both blacks and whites of the community. One of the political organizations he was involved with was the John Logan Colored Republican Club, which he founded in 1889 or 1890. One of the purposes of the club was to decide on which candidates to endorse for political offices. This club was made up of some of Spokane's most prominent black citizens, including Fred E. Wilson, Charles Scrutchins, and Rudolph B. Scott. During a particular club meeting, the members debated which candidate to endorse as their congressional representative. They discussed the possibility of two representatives, John L. Wilson and Judge George Turner, who went to the U.S. Senate in 1897. The club finally adopted a resolution that read as follows:

> The present congressman, John L. Wilson has failed to give the Negro the proper consideration in our [judgment] as a Congressman from the State of Washington and failed to acknowledge the receipt of letters from our people in matters of gigantic importance, and has failed to comply with the resolution adopted in the last convention of the state (Franklin, 24–26).

The club's resolution stated that Wilson's conduct was inappropriate for a congressman due to his "entering into an altercation and again into a free fight." Therefore the club endorsed Judge Turner as its candidate. Wilson, however continued to serve in the House of Representatives until 1895, at which time he went to the U.S. Senate. In 1894, unhappy with the lack of response to African American issues from the Republicans, Barrow unsuccessfully ran for the state legislature on the Populist ticket. He remained with the radical party through the tempestuous election of 1896 and eventually became a presidential elector for Spokane and Whitman Counties.

After residing in Spokane for only a year, Barrow, his wife, and a few African American citizens helped found the first black church in the city. This group of citizens gathered "to consider the propriety of organizing a church." Barrow served as pastor of Calvary Baptist Church from 1895 until he traveled to attend a church convention in Tacoma, Washington, in 1906 and died there, most likely in a streetcar accident.

FURTHER READING

Franklin, Joseph. *All Through the Night: The History of Spokane Black Americans 1860–1940* (1989).

Taylor, Quintard. "The Emergence of Black Communities in the Pacific Northwest: 1865–1910," *Journal of Negro History* (Autumn 1979).

FLORENCE COLEMAN

Barrow, Willie Taplin (7 Dec. 1924–), social activist and spiritual adviser, was born Willie Taplin in the small rural town of Burton, Texas, the daughter of Nelson Taplin, a Baptist preacher, and Octavia, a Methodist congregant. A member of a large extended family, Barrow fondly recalled an upbringing steeped in strict traditional family values and old-time southern religion. She lived with her parents, six siblings, both sets of grandparents, and a great-grandmother in the family home, and they were sometimes joined by a cousin or two in need of temporary housing. The family lived together, worked together, and went to church together. Although they had limited economic resources, they grew the food that they needed on the family farm, and though she came to understand the family's poverty in later years, Barrow said that she never knew hunger as a child.

Barrow discovered her activist voice and spirit early in life. Under the state-sponsored segregation that plagued the South, she was required to travel miles from home to attend a black public school. When she spied a yellow school bus preparing to pick up white children in a nearby community in the late 1930s, however, Barrow organized her schoolmates and staged a protest. It was her first taste of confrontational politics. The sweetness of her victory placed her on a "warrior's" path that served her for decades to come.

Upon graduating from high school in 1941, Barrow decided to study the ministry and moved from the South to the West Coast to pursue her calling. With limited funds and no expectation of financial support from her family, she joined thousands of other African Americans and women who were joining the war industries, accepting full-time employment at the Kaiser Shipyards in Portland, Oregon, where she worked the night shift and learned how to be a welder. Barrow enrolled in the Warner School of Theology in Portland as a full-time day student. Despite these challenges, Barrow persevered. She continued to hone her organizing and leadership skills as she pursued her desire to do God's work. Before moving to Chicago to continue her studies at the Moody Bible School in 1958, Barrow organized the first Black Church of God in Portland. In the mid-1960s she went to Liberia to complete her divinity studies at the University of Monrovia, which later presented her with an honorary doctor of divinity degree.

In 1945 Barrow married Clyde Raymond Barrow. This too became part of her enduring legacy. The couple remained married for fifty-three years, until Clyde's death in 1998. Willie Barrow chronicled her successful marriage in her book *How to Get Married and Stay Married* (2004). She also decided that she wanted to be a mother. She first adopted a child, then she gave birth to a son, and she eventually accepted the role of "godmother" for more than two hundred children.

From 1953 through 1965 Barrow served as a field organizer for MARTIN LUTHER KING JR. and was part of the historic Selma to Montgomery march. She trained new recruits, organized boycotts and rallies, and encouraged participation in voter registration drives. In 1962 she joined forces with the Reverend JESSE JACKSON SR. to organize a new effort, Operation Breadbasket, an outgrowth of the economic arm of the Southern Christian Leadership Conference (SCLC) dedicated to social uplift and economic empowerment in the African American community. Operation Breadbasket was the model for People United to Serve Humanity (PUSH), founded by Jackson in 1971. Barrow maintained a lifelong affiliation with PUSH. Her leadership and organizing skills were easily transferred to the new civil rights organization. However, she faced gender restrictions, as she was asked to train a succession of young male leaders but was never given the opportunity to lead. She challenged the leadership of PUSH and was subsequently named national executive director, chairperson, CEO of operations, and co-chairperson of the Rainbow-PUSH Coalition.

Affectionately called the "Little Warrior," Barrow took the lead role in many social movements, including the student and civil rights movements, the labor movement, the peace movement, and—as a result of the loss of her son Keith Barrow to AIDS—the fight for gay and lesbian rights. An activist at home and abroad, Barrow fulfilled the role of associate pastor and minister of justice for the Vernon Park Church of God in Chicago, was the first executive director of the statewide Coalition against Hunger in Illinois, and traveled to Vietnam during the height of the war in search of peace. She served as campaign director and road manager for Jackson's presidential campaigns in 1984 and 1988. A lifelong member of the National Council of Negro Women, the National Political Congress of Black Women, and the National Urban League, Barrow left an indelible mark of activism on every community in which she served.

FURTHER READING

Barrow, Willie. *How to Get Married and Stay Married* (2004).

Reid-Merritt, Patricia. *Sister Power: How Phenomenal Black Women Are Rising to the Top* (1996).

PATRICIA REID-MERRITT

Barry, Marion Shepilov, Jr. (6 Mar. 1936–), four-time mayor of Washington, D.C., was born on a cotton plantation near the Delta hamlet of Itta Bena in northwestern Mississippi to sharecroppers Marion Barry Sr. and Mattie Barry. In 1940 Barry Sr. died, and in 1944 Barry, his mother, and his sister moved to Memphis, Tennessee, where Mattie worked as a maid and married Dave Cummings, a butcher. The combined family, which eventually included nine members, lived in a narrow, wooden "shotgun" house in South Memphis, one of four black enclaves in the city. Barry slept on the couch and rose early each morning to chop wood for the stove. He stuffed cardboard in his shoes to fill the holes and sold his sandwiches to other kids at school for pocket money. A bright, industrious child, he eventually became one of the first African American Eagle Scouts in Memphis. In the summer he traveled with his mother and sisters to pick cotton in Arkansas and Mississippi.

Barry graduated from Booker T. Washington High School, one of two black high schools in Memphis, in 1954. He then became the first in his family to attend college, choosing the predominantly black LeMoyne College in Memphis. After joining Alpha Phi Alpha fraternity, Barry headed the school chapter of the NAACP. At this time, he adopted the middle name of "Shepilov" by picking the name out of a newspaper story about Dmitri Shepilov, a high-ranking member of the Soviet Communist Party. He graduated in 1958 and then earned a master's degree in chemistry at Fisk University in Nashville. He organized the Fisk NAACP and participated in sit-ins at Nashville restaurants. Barry subsequently finished three years as the only black student in the chemistry doctoral program at the University of Tennessee but did not complete his degree. He then taught at the all-black Knoxville College. Increasingly involved with civil rights, Barry abandoned academe in 1964 to become immersed in the civil rights movement full time. Barry briefly worked as the first chair of the Student Nonviolent Coordinating Committee (SNCC) and was a member of the SNCC executive committee. In 1965 he moved to Washington, D.C., to work as an SNCC field secretary. He left SNCC in 1967.

Barry became a familiar figure in Washington as he agitated for civil rights. He gained particular fame for his efforts on behalf of poor blacks. In 1971 Barry was elected to serve on Washington, D.C.'s first school board, and he became board president in 1972. When Congress granted the District of Columbia limited home rule in 1973, Barry won a seat on the first D.C. city council in 1974 as the highest vote getter. He won reelection in 1976, and in 1978 he won election as mayor of Washington, D.C.

Barry inherited an unwieldy bureaucracy, a budget deficit that topped $100 million, and a government beholden to Congress for part of its revenues; Congress could veto any council decision and held approval power over the D.C. budget. To much acclaim, he balanced the budget in his first term and initially reduced the deficit.

Barry served two more terms before leaving office in 1990 as mayor; however, rumors of drug use dogged him. His 1986 reelection victory came despite allegations of drug use and womanizing, as well as such chronic and highly visible problems as soaring city budget deficits, a dramatic increase in drug-related homicides, and the conviction of top city officials on corruption charges. Many black Washington, D.C., residents saw Barry as the victim of a white conspiracy to destroy him and voted for him in response to racial politics. On 18 January 1990, when his former girlfriend Rasheeda Moore cooperated in an FBI sting investigation, Barry was filmed smoking crack cocaine and was arrested. Shortly afterward Barry entered the Hanley-Hazelden Clinic in West Palm Beach, Florida, for treatment for health concerns that included alcohol abuse. Barry and his press secretary were silent about any cocaine abuse. A planned absence of a month stretched to seven weeks when Barry transferred from Hanley-Hazelden to Fenwick Hall, a drug-treatment facility in South Carolina.

On 15 February 1990 Barry was indicted on three felony counts of lying to a grand jury about his drug use and on five misdemeanor counts of cocaine possession. Black newspapers and radio shows portrayed the mayor as the victim of a white federal conspiracy to dethrone him, and the FBI came under severe attack for using heavy-handed tactics to entrap him. Meanwhile, the media, notably the *Washington Post*, bashed Barry in editorials and daily exposés of the criminal investigation. Barry abandoned his reelection plans after conviction on a misdemeanor for cocaine possession. He served six months in prison.

Always a popular politician in racially polarized D.C., Barry won a seat on the city council in 1992.

He won a landslide victory to a fourth mayoral term in 1994. In May 1996 Barry abruptly took a leave from his mayoral duties to seek help at a retreat in rural Maryland and then at a more distant church facility near St. Louis, raising suspicions that his substance abuse problems had resurfaced. Barry's hiatus occurred not long after he underwent surgery for prostate cancer, and he described himself as suffering from physical and spiritual exhaustion. He retired from politics in 1998 and aborted a run for city council in 2002 after another drug incident. In April 2002 police working near an open-air drug market in the Buzzard Point section of Southwest Washington found a small rock of crack cocaine in Barry's car. Park police said that the officer who approached Barry's Jaguar saw the driver ingest something and noticed a powdery substance under Barry's nose. The incident attracted a lot of publicity but nothing more. Supporters worried publicly that Barry had relapsed into drug usage, but in 2004 Barry won the Ward 8 city council seat with 96 percent of the vote. Barry's legal troubles continued, however, when in March 2006, he received three years' probation after pleading guilty to two misdemeanor charges for failing to file tax returns for the year 2005.

Barry was married three times, first in 1972 to Mary M. Treadwell; this marriage ended in divorce in 1977. He then married Effi Slaughter in 1978; this marriage produced a son, Marion Christopher Barry, in 1983 but ended in divorce in 1991. In 1994 he married Cora Masters, but this marriage, too, ended in divorce in 2002.

FURTHER READING

Agronsky, Jonathan I. Z. *Marion Barry: The Politics of Race* (1991).

Barras, Jonetta Rose. *The Last of the Black Emperors: The Hollow Comeback of Marion Barry in a New Age of Black Leader* (1998).

CARYN E. NEUMANN

Barthé, Richmond (28 Jan. 1901–6 Mar. 1989), sculptor, was born in Bay St. Louis, Mississippi, the son of Richmond Barthé and Marie Clementine Roboteau, a seamstress. His father died when Barthé was one month old. Barthé began drawing as a child and first exhibited his work at the county fair in Mississippi at age twelve. He did not attend high school, but he learned about his African heritage from books borrowed from a local grocer and publications given to him by a wealthy white family that vacationed in Bay St. Louis. This family, which had connections to Africa through ambassadorships, hired Barthé as a butler when he was in his teens; he moved with them to New Orleans. At age eighteen Barthé won first prize for a drawing he sent to the Mississippi County Fair. Lyle Saxon, the literary critic for the *New Orleans Times Picayune*, then attempted to register Barthé in a New Orleans art school, but Barthé was denied admission because of his race.

In 1924 Barthé began classes at the School of the Art Institute of Chicago, his tuition paid by a Catholic priest, Harry Kane. Living with an aunt, Barthé paid for his board and art supplies by working as a porter and busboy. During his senior year Barthé began modeling in clay at the suggestion of his anatomy teacher, Charles Schroeder. His busts of two classmates were shown in the Negro History Week exhibition. These works, along with busts of the Haitian general Toussaint-Louverture and the painter HENRY OSSAWA TANNER (first exhibited at a children's home in Gary, Indiana), were included in the Chicago Art League annual exhibition in 1928, the year of Barthé's graduation.

Barthé achieved wide recognition for his bronze busts and figures in the 1930s and 1940s. Within a year after his move to New York City in February 1929, he completed thirty-five sculptures. He continued his education at the Art Students League with fellowships from the Rosenwald Foundation (1929–1930). Barthé's first solo exhibitions (favorably reviewed by the *New York Times*) were in 1934 at the Caz-Delbo Gallery in New York, the Grand Rapids Art Gallery in Michigan, and the Women's City Art Club in Chicago, followed by exhibitions in New York at Delphic Studios (1935), Arden Galleries (1939), DePorres Interracial Center (1945), International Print Society (1945), and Grand Central Art Galleries (1947). He also exhibited in numerous group shows at various institutions, including the Harmon Foundation (1929, 1931, and 1933), the New York World's Fair (1939), the Whitney Museum annual exhibitions (1933, 1940, 1944, and 1945), the Metropolitan Museum of Art's *Artists for Victory* (1942), and the Pennsylvania Academy of Fine Arts' annual exhibitions (1938, 1940, 1943, 1944, and 1948).

Many of Barthé's early works, such as *Masaai* (1933), *African Woman* (c. 1934), and *Wetta* (c. 1934), depict Africans. Barthé dreamed of visiting Africa, stating, "I'd really like to devote all my time to Negro subjects, and I plan shortly to spend a year and a half in Africa studying types, making sketches and models which I hope to finish off in Paris for a show there, and later in London

and New York" (Lewis, 11), but he never traveled to the continent. Other works by Barthé, such as *Feral Benga, Stevedore,* and *African Man Dancing* (all 1937), were among the first sculptures of black male nudes by an African American artist. In the mid-1930s Barthé moved from Harlem to midtown Manhattan for a larger studio and to be closer to major theaters, as many of his clients were theatrical celebrities. Among his portrait busts are *Cyrina* (from *Porgy and Bess*, c. 1934), *Sir John Gielgud as Hamlet* (commissioned for the Haymarket Theatre in London, 1937), *Maurice Evans as Richard II* (1938, in the Shakespeare Theatre in Stratford, Connecticut), and *Katherine Cornell as Juliet* (1942). Barthé later produced busts of other entertainers, such as *Josephine Baker* (1950) and *Paul Robeson as Othello* (1975).

Barthé's largest work was an eight-by-eighty-foot frieze, *Green Pastures: The Walls of Jericho* (1937–1938), which he completed under the U.S. Treasury Art Project at the Harlem River Housing Project. His other public works of art include portraits of Abraham Lincoln, in New York (1940) and India (1942); Arthur Brisbane, in Central Park; GEORGE WASHINGTON CARVER, in Nashville (1945), and BOOKER T. WASHINGTON, at New York University (1946).

Many of Barthé's busts, such as *Birth of the Spirituals* (1941) and *The Negro Looks Ahead* (1944), are imbued with a calm spirituality. Barthé described his representational work as an attempt to "capture the beauty that I've seen in people, and abstraction wouldn't satisfy me. ... My work is all wrapped up with my search for God. I am looking for God inside of people. I wouldn't find it in squares, triangles and circles" (Reynolds and Wright, 154). A strong believer in reincarnation, the artist often called himself an "Old Soul" who had been an artist in Egypt in an earlier life.

In the 1940s Barthé received numerous awards, beginning with Guggenheim fellowships in 1941 and 1942. In 1945 he was elected to the National Sculpture Society (sponsored by the sculptor Malvina Hoffman) and the American Academy of Arts and Letters. He also received the Audubon Artists Gold Medal of Honor and the James J. Hoey Award for interracial justice. The sculptor was also active in several artists' organizations: the Liturgical Arts Society, the International Print Society, the New York Clay Club, and the Sculptors Guild. He also had solo exhibitions at the South Side Art Center in Chicago (1942); the Sayville Playhouse on Long Island (1945); the Margaret Brown Gallery in

Boston (1947); and Montclair Art Museum in New Jersey (1949).

In 1950 Barthé received a commission from the Haitian government to sculpt a large monument to Toussaint-Louverture; it now stands in front of the Palace in the Haitian capital, Port-au-Prince. In 1947 Barthé had moved to Jamaica, where he remained through the late 1960s. His most notable works from this time are the General Dessalines monument in Port-au-Prince (1952) and a portrait of Norman Manley, the prime minister of Jamaica (1956). The Institute of Jamaica hosted Barthé's solo show in 1959. In 1964 the artist received the Key to the City from Bay St. Louis. He then sculpted contemplative black male nudes, such as *Meditation* (1964), *Inner Music* (1965), and *Seeker* (1965).

Barthé left the West Indies in 1969 because of increasing violence there and spent five years traveling in Switzerland, Spain, and Italy. He then settled in Pasadena, California, and worked on his memoirs. In 1978 he had a solo exhibition at the William Grant Still Center in Los Angeles and was subsequently honored by the League of Allied Arts there in 1981. He died in Pasadena. Following his death, a retrospective was held at the Museum of African American Art (1990). Barthé's work toured the United States with that of RICHARD HUNT in the Landau/Traveling Exhibition *Two Sculptors, Two Eras* in 1992. His work, which was eventually collected by the Metropolitan and Whitney museums in New York City, the Smithsonian Institution in Washington, D.C., and the Art Institute of Chicago, among many others, continues to be featured in exhibitions and survey texts on African American art.

FURTHER READING

Lewis, Samella. *Two Sculptors, Two Eras* (1992).

Reynolds, Gary A., and Beryl J. Wright. *Against the Odds: African American Artists and the Harmon Foundation* (1989).

This entry is taken from the *American National Biography* and is published here with the permission of the American Council of Learned Societies.

THERESA LEININGER-MILLER

Barthelemy, Sidney J. (17 Mar. 1942–), state legislator and fifty-eighth mayor of New Orleans, was born Sidney John Barthelemy, the third of six children of Lionel Barthelemy, an insurance businessman, and Ruth Barthelemy, a beautician, in New Orleans, Louisiana. Roman Catholic, he grew up in the largely creole and catholic Seventh Ward section of the city and attended parochial schools— Corpus Christi Elementary School and then, later, St. Augustine High School, where he won the Purple Knight Award recognizing him as the best all-around student in 1960. After high school, he attended the Epiphany Apostolic Junior College in Newburgh, New York, and then entered St. Joseph Seminary in Washington, D.C., where he received a Bachelor of Arts degree in Philosophy in 1967 and pursued graduate study in theology (though he did not finish). While in seminary, he worked summers as a laborer in a stevedoring company. In 1968 Barthelemy married Michaele "Mickey" Thibodeaux with whom he had a son, Sidney Jr., and two daughters, Bridget and Cherrie.

In 1967, having decided not to enter the priesthood, Barthelemy returned to New Orleans and worked as an administrative assistant in the office of Total Community Action. He interned in the former mayor Moon Landrieu's office while he completed a Masters of Social Work at Tulane University (1971) in New Orleans. Barthelemy also worked part-time for the Urban League of Greater New Orleans and assisted with various political campaigns, joining the board of the Community Organization of Urban Politics (COUP), an influential political organization. In 1972 Barthelemy was appointed the director of the Department of Welfare under the administration of Mayor Moon Landrieu.

In the early 1970s, court-ordered redistricting created more predominantly-black legislative districts in Louisiana, enabling Barthelemy, with the aid of COUP, to become the first African American elected to the Louisiana State Senate since Reconstruction (1974). While he served in the legislature, he also joined Xavier University as the assistant director of the Urbinvolve Program and as an instructor in the Department of Sociology and became an adjunct faculty member in the Applied Health Sciences Department, Maternal and Child Health Section, of Tulane University.

In 1978 Barthelemy was elected Councilmanat-Large. He became the first African American to hold an at-large seat on the New Orleans City Council, a position he held for two terms. While in the council, Barthelemy became known for his longstanding rivalry with Mayor ERNEST "DUTCH" MORIAL. In 1986 he garnered enough votes to succeed Morial, who was term-limited, and became the Mayor of the City of New Orleans, only the second African American to hold the position.

As mayor, Barthelemy inherited a city with budget deficits and 11 percent unemployment. He promised black economic development but was criticized for maintaining close contacts with the white civic and economic leadership, which failed to appreciably benefit the majority of New Orleans' black residents. However, under his tenure, a number of black business owners and professionals benefited from set-aside programs and city contract work. Additionally, under Barthelemy's leadership, blacks enjoyed greater access to municipal employment. Under Barthelemy's headship, the city passed a controversial "antidiscrimination" ordinance affecting the membership in Mardi Gras carnival krewes. Other achievements during his two terms in office include the realization of Harrah's Casino on a city-owned riverfront site, the construction of the Aquarium of the Americas, convention center expansions, the 1987 papal visit, the city's hosting of the 1988 Republican Convention, two NCAA Final Four's, and a Super Bowl. Under the Barthelemy administration, major industrial development occurred in Eastern New Orleans.

In 1986 Barthelemy received the Outstanding Alumnus award from Tulane University School of Social Welfare. In 1989 he received the President's Award, Louisiana Conference of Black Mayors. In 1990 the New Orleans Chapter of National Association for the Advancement of Colored People (NAACP) honored him with the Daniel E. Byrd Award. He was awarded the National League of Cities Leadership Award in 1994. After leaving public office, Mr. Barthelemy held executive positions in the private sector, most recently, as the vice president of government relations for the real estate development company, HRI Properties.

FURTHER READING

Information on Barthelemy's public and private career can be found in the Records of Mayor Sidney J. Barthelemy, 1986–1994, City Archives, New Orleans Public Library, Executive Office of the Mayor, and in the Sidney Barthelemy Papers, 1987–1994, Amistad Research Center, Tulane University, New Orleans.

Biles, Roger. "Black Mayors: A Historical Assessment." *Journal of Negro History* 77 (Summer 1992): 109–25.

"Mayor Sidney Barthelemy: New Orleans' Gentle Giant," *Ebony* 41 (July 1986): 120–124.

ALEXANDER J. CHENAULT

Bartholomew, Dave (24 Dec. 1920–), bandleader, songwriter, producer, and arranger, was born Dave Louis Bartholomew in Edgard, Louisiana, to Louis Bartholomew, a musician, and Marie Rousell, a housekeeper. Louis played Dixieland tuba in Kid Harrison's and Willie Humphrey's jazz bands. He moved the family to New Orleans while Dave was in high school. Young Dave became interested in performing music after watching his father play. He first took up the tuba but switched to the trumpet because it would allow him a place in the popular marching bands of New Orleans. As a high school student he enjoyed the tutelage of Peter Davis, LOUIS ARMSTRONG's teacher. Bartholomew honed his skills on the New Orleans scene in the late 1930s. He moved in and out of various jazz and brass bands in Louisiana, including Marshall Lawrence's Brass Band, Toots Johnson's Band, and Claiborne Williams's Band. The pianist Fats Pinchon asked Bartholomew to join his group in 1939. Shortly afterward Pinchon left to take another job, allowing Bartholomew to become bandleader. In 1941 he married Pearl King with whom he would have three children.

World War II soon intervened, and Bartholomew was drafted into the army in 1942. The military offered him an opportunity to continue his musical education. He served in the 196 AGF band, where he learned to write and arrange songs. After the war Bartholomew returned to New Orleans with a newfound confidence and a desire for success. He put together a new band and soon became known as the premier bandleader in the city. The Bartholomew group frequented such New Orleans clubs as the Greystone, Club Rocket, the Starlight, the Robin Hood, Al's Starlight, and the Dew Drop. It played a hard-driving rhythm and blues steeped in the Dixieland tradition and its changing lineup featured the cream of Crescent City musicians, including the saxophonists Alvin "Red" Taylor and Lee Allen, and the drummer Earl Ball. Bartholomew played and occasionally sang, although in early 1947, he hired Theard Johnson as a lead vocalist.

Bartholomew's early studio efforts included recordings of "High Society" and "Stardust." He scored a minor regional rhythm and blues hit in 1949 with "Country Boy." Over the next several years Bartholomew continued to issue solo recordings with a rollicking New Orleans R&B flavor, from the social commentary of "The Monkey" (1954) to the risqué romp of "My Ding-a-Ling" (1952). CHUCK BERRY scored a number-one hit twenty years later with a cover of the latter song.

Bartholomew's meeting with Lew Chudd, president of Los Angeles's Imperial Records, shifted his career in a different direction. Chudd hired the bandleader as a producer and a talent scout, empowering him to recruit new talent and using his band to back solo artists. Bartholomew experienced his biggest recruiting success with the pianist ANTOINE "FATS" DOMINO, whom he hired in 1949. He produced and arranged Domino's most famous performances, including "The Fat Man," "Ain't that a Shame," "Blue Monday," "I'm Walkin'," and "Blueberry Hill." The last three cracked *Billboard's* Top Ten in 1956 and 1957. His strong commercial sense failed him only occasionally. He believed, for instance, that the eventual multimillion seller "Blueberry Hill" would fail.

Bartholomew exercised a firm hand in the studio and crafted a clean, tight sound from his players. His self-proclaimed "Big Beat" sound helped Domino to become the most successful black rock 'n' roller of the 1950s. Noting current popular music trends, Bartholomew began sweetening Domino's records with strings and female voices while still preserving his original sound. The Bartholomew-Domino collaboration remained lucrative, turning out hits into the early 1960s when, like many other rhythm and blues artists, Domino suffered from shifts in the music industry as a result of the British Invasion.

Bartholomew and Domino shared songwriting credits on most of the pianist's 1950s and early 1960s output. The producer told interviewers that he and the performer worked out tunes in the studio, but it is likely that Bartholomew took the primary role in composing Domino's songs. Although this work earned him his greatest financial gains and some notoriety, Bartholomew also produced a variety of hit records for other artists. He sat behind the board for many high-charting singles, including Lloyd Price's "Lawdy Miss Clawdy" (1952), Shirley & Lee's "Let the Good Times Roll" (1957), and Smiley Lewis's "I Hear You Knocking" (1952) and "One Night" (1956).

During the 1960s Bartholomew moved away from production work and focused on live performances. He played with his orchestra and toured some with Domino. A shrewd businessman, Bartholomew carefully managed his money, buying commercial and residential real estate in the New Orleans area, and retaining a portion of his huge song catalog. Some music writers credited him with ownership of over 4,000 songs, although in 2007 Broadcast Music Incorporated (BMI) listed his song credits at 425. He established Broadmoor Records in the late 1960s. He also created three music publishing companies.

The last few decades of the twentieth century found Bartholomew in semiretirement, still performing and recording occasionally, but writing music constantly. In 1968 his wife, Pearl, died. Two years later he married Rhea Douse. They had two children and Douse brought three children from a previous marriage. Bartholomew was inducted into the Rock and Roll Hall of Fame in 1991 and the Songwriters Halls of Fame in 1998. The Rhythm and Blues Foundation, composed of musicians and industry executives, honored Bartholomew with its Pioneer Award in 1996. When Hurricane Katrina devastated New Orleans less than ten years later, he relocated to Balch Springs, Texas, a Dallas suburb.

Although he was the key figure behind 1950s New Orleans R&B, Bartholomew's emphasis on production and songwriting, as opposed to making records under his own name, as well as Fats Domino's formidable persona, contributed to his relative anonymity in the public consciousness. His influence on popular music, however, was immense. Hundreds of millions of records were sold bearing his songs and numerous artists covered his tunes. These acts included Elton John, the Rolling Stones, Paul McCartney, Hank Williams Jr., Bob Seger, the Fabulous Thunderbirds, Dave Edmunds, Cheap Trick, Elvis Costello, and Joe Cocker. Bartholomew was not only a critical figure in the history of twentieth-century New Orleans music but his songs and productions also helped to shape the transition from rhythm and blues into rock 'n' roll.

FURTHER READING

Berry, Jason, Jonathan Foose, and Tad Jones. *Up from the Cradle of Jazz: New Orleans Music since World War II* (1986).

Broven, John. *Rhythm and Blues in New Orleans* (1974).

Hannusch, Jeff. *I Hear You Knockin': The Sound of New Orleans Rhythm and Blues* (1985).

ZACHARY J. LECHNER

Bartz, Gary Lee (26 Sept. 1940–), musician and composer, was born in Baltimore, Maryland, to Floyd Bartz, a railroad employee and club owner, and Elizabeth E. Bartz, a club owner. Bartz grew up in West Baltimore during an era when the music scene in that city was thriving. The hub of African American entertainment in Baltimore was found on Pennsylvania Avenue, although there were numerous clubs throughout the city owned by African Americans. At the age of six Bartz heard his first CHARLIE PARKER recording at his grandmother's house. Bartz recalled this formative moment: "Not knowing what the music was, what the instrument was or who was playing, I thought it was the most beautiful thing I ever heard, I said right then, I want to do whatever that is" (Ouellette, 31). When Bartz was eleven, he began to play the alto saxophone, influenced to take up the instrument by his love of Parker and LOUIS JORDAN.

Bartz's parents were instrumental in nurturing his musical career. While Bartz was in his early teens, his father would take him around to different clubs in Baltimore. He would tell both local musicians and those who toured through town about his son's musical abilities. At the Comedy Club in Baltimore, Bartz's father touted his son's abilities to saxophonist SONNY STITT, and Stitt invited Bartz to play with him. Immediately after the session, the two developed a friendship.

Bartz graduated high school from Baltimore City College in 1958. After graduation, Bartz moved to New York, at the age of seventeen, to attend the Juilliard School of Music. Skillful at playing music by ear, he wanted to learn to read music. He continued his musical education outside the classroom by frequenting cabarets on the Lower East Side to hear musicians such as Chet Baker, RED GARLAND, Donald Byrd, LEE MORGAN, YUSEF LATEEF, and HANK MOBLEY.

Bartz continued his studies at Juilliard for two years. In 1959 he left school but continued his informal musical training by playing with many seasoned and up-and-coming musicians including CHARLES MINGUS, John Gilmore, Lee Morgan, Donald Byrd, Freddie Hubbard, and PHILLY JOE JONES in New York City. In 1960 Bartz's father bought the North End Lounge, which was located at 1869 N. Gay Street in Baltimore. His parents managed the club, and it became a venue in which Bartz could perfect his playing. Bartz began commuting to Baltimore from New York to work in his father's club on weekends.

In the meantime, Bartz organized a band. In 1961 the Gary Bartz Quartet began to perform regularly at the North End Lounge. In 1962, Bartz married Rosa Lindsay at the Douglass Memorial Church in Baltimore, in a ceremony officiated by the Reverend Marion C. Bascom. From 1962 to 1964 he played with the Charles Mingus Jazz Workshop, where he worked with ERIC DOLPHY and met MCCOY TYNER. While still in his early twenties, he took his first professional job with the MAX ROACH–ABBEY LINCOLN group in 1964.

Bartz's father hired ART BLAKEY to play at his club. He had heard that John Gilmore was leaving Blakey's group, and he called his son to come to Baltimore to sit in. Bartz made his recording debut on Blakey's *Soul Finger* album. He established himself as a solid musician and was considered by his peers as one of the best alto players since CANNONBALL ADDERLEY. Bartz became a leading sideman, playing with some of the top musicians in the field. His musical range allowed him to incorporate hard bop, acoustic hard bop, avant-garde, funk, fusion, soul, and R&B into his repertoire.

Bartz worked with Art Blakey's Jazz Messengers from 1965 to 1966. But by 1967 Bartz was recording regularly as a group leader for Prestige and Milestone records. In 1968 Bartz worked with McCoy Tyner and his Expansions band as the alto saxophonist. Working with Tyner was another high point in Bartz's life. Tyner's strong connection with JOHN COLTRANE was important to Bartz and his development as an up-and-coming saxophonist. In 1970 Bartz, along with Ron Carter, Andy Bey, and others created the group Harlem Bush Music. Bartz also formed his own band later that year, called Ntu Troop ("Ntu" is the Bantu word for "unity"). This ensemble fused African folk music, hard bop, vanguard jazz, soul, and funk, synthesizing these musical styles into a dynamic musical form. Keeping busy as a musician, Bartz also continued to tour with the Max Roach band.

In 1970, after hearing promising things about Bartz's musical talent, MILES DAVIS hired Bartz and featured him as a soloist on his *Live Evil* recording. He worked with Davis's fusion group from 1970 to 1971. Throughout his career, Bartz recorded with several music labels, including Milestone, Prestige, Capitol, Atlantic, and Steeple Chase. By the late 1970s Bartz was doing studio work in Los Angeles with the vocalist and producer Phyllis Hyman and the producer, bandleader, and drummer Norman Connors. In 1977 his album *Music Is My Sanctuary* was regarded as one of the best fusion recordings of that era.

In the 1980s Bartz collaborated with the writer, producer, and percussionist Mtume with the release of "Music," a single from his album *Bartz* (1980), which was a spirited blend of musical genres. He collaborated with jazz vocalist Leon Thomas on *Precious Energy* in the late 1980s. From the early 1980s until 1988 Bartz wandered around until he recorded *Reflections on Monk* in 1988. Bartz further developed his musical talents by combining various musical idioms as he became one of the favorite jazz innovators of the 1990s, continuing to make recordings throughout the decade.

Despite Bartz's numerous recordings, he was troubled by the music industry's control over musicians and their work. He noted in an interview that "a creative musician is counterproductive to the record industry. They don't want creative musicians; they want clones" (Nahigian and Enright, 4). Bartz understood that the music industry did not have musicians' best interests in mind, but instead was concerned with promotions and sales of music, and that the only means for musicians to control their livelihood in the industry was to create and own their own labels and retain rights to their music. To gain total control of his musical creativity, "to empower himself," and to "take this great black music back for the musicians," Bartz's created his own label in 1999, called OYO (Own Your Own) Recordings. In 2001 he joined the faculty of the Oberlin Conservatory of Music in Ohio as visiting professor of Jazz Saxophone. In 2005 Bartz released *Live at the Jazz Standard Vol. 1: Soulstice, Live at the Jazz Standard Vol. 2*, and *Soprano Stories*, all of which were released through the OYO label. That same year he won a Grammy for Best Jazz Instrumental Album, Individual or Group for his playing on McCoy Tyner's album *Illuminations*. Bartz continues to perform as special guest with the McCoy Tyner Trio nationally and internationally.

FURTHER READING

Cook, Richard, and Brian Morton. *The Penguin Guide to Jazz Recordings*, 8th ed. (2006).

Nahigian, Alan, and Ed Enright. "Gary Bartz: Take Back the Music," *Down Beat* (Sept. 1998).

Ouellette, Dan. "Saxophone Hand," *Down Beat* (March 2000).

Rogers, John. "Gary Bartz," *All about Jazz* (July 2005).

VIVIAN NJERI FISHER

Basie, Count (21 Aug. 1904–26 Apr. 1984), jazz pianist, composer, and bandleader, was born William James Basie in Red Bank, New Jersey, the son of African American parents Harvey Lee Basie, an estate groundskeeper, and Lillian Ann Chiles, a laundress. Basie was first exposed to music through his mother's piano playing. He took piano lessons, played the drums, and acted in school skits. An indifferent student, he left school after junior high and began performing. He organized bands with friends and played various jobs in Red Bank, among them working as a movie theater pianist. In his late teens he pursued work in nearby Asbury Park, but he met with little success. Then, in the early 1920s,

he moved to Harlem, where he learned from the leading pianists of the New York "stride" style, WILLIE "THE LION" SMITH, JAMES P. JOHNSON, LUCKEY ROBERTS, and especially FATS WALLER, his exact contemporary.

Basie remained undecided between a stage or musical career. Until 1929 he alternately combined playing in Harlem nightclubs and theaters (on piano and organ) and touring with bands for vaudeville and burlesque troupes, which took him as far from New York as New Orleans, Kansas City, and Oklahoma. In Kansas City, during a layover in 1927 or 1928, Basie was stricken with spinal meningitis. After recovering, he worked solo jobs and eventually joined WALTER PAGE's Blue Devils, a major regional dance band. The Blue Devils featured the southwestern boogie-woogie style of relatively spare blues-based melodies, effortless dance rhythms, and "swinging" syncopation (all hallmarks of the later Basie band style). Basie worked at devising arrangements for the band, assisted by the trombonist-guitarist EDDIE DURHAM. Basie's ability to read and write music improved over the years, but he continued to rely on staff and freelance arrangers. At this time Basie lost interest in the musical stage and dedicated himself to dance music.

Kansas City, a wide-open hub of speakeasies, gambling, and prostitution, offered an active job market for black musicians who specialized in the

Count Basie, at the Aquarium in New York City, c. 1947. (© William P. Gottlieb; www.jazzphotos.com.)

aggressively swinging southwestern (or Kansas City) blues style. While with the Blue Devils, Basie blended this style with his New York "stride" piano background, and in 1929 he was hired by BENNIE MOTEN, who led the most successful Kansas City band of the time. Basie later called this move both the greatest risk and the most important turning point of his career. The Moten band toured extensively and played to large crowds in Chicago and New York.

About 1930, while working as Moten's second pianist and arranger, Basie married Vivian Wynn, but they soon separated and later divorced. Also in 1929 or 1930, he met a young chorus dancer, Catherine Morgan. She and Basie married in 1942 and had one daughter.

During a touring break in 1934, Basie took some Moten band musicians to Little Rock, Arkansas, for a longer-term job at a single location, after which the Moten band broke up. Back in Kansas City, Basie worked as a church organist and was preparing to join Moten's newest group when the bandleader died unexpectedly in 1935. Since 1928 Basie had called himself "Count" in imitation of royal nicknames used by other Harlem musicians, but only on taking over the Moten band did he bill himself by that name. Basie soon had the best players from the Moten unit working for him at the Reno Club in Kansas City. This nucleus included the trombonists Dan Minor and Eddie Durham, who was the band's chief arranger during its early years; the tenor saxophonists Herschel Evans and LESTER YOUNG, a key innovator in jazz history; and the inimitable blues vocalist JIMMY RUSHING.

To many listeners, however, the heart of the band was its superb rhythm section: on drums, JO JONES, a keenly knowledgeable musician who revolutionized both big band and small group drumming; on guitar, CLAUDE WILLIAMS, who was replaced in 1937 by Freddie Green (the mainstay of the Basie group for five decades); and on bass, Walter Page, former leader of the Blue Devils. These three men, in concord with Basie's own idiomatic piano work, synchronized their playing with unmatched skill, lightening and shading the driving, four-to-a-bar Kansas City beat, and infusing the band's ensemble play with supple, flowing, danceable rhythms.

In 1935 the white writer, critic, and record producer John Hammond heard a Basie radio broadcast and made arrangements to give the band national exposure. Expanding the group to thirteen men, Basie took his musicians to Chicago, where six of them made their first, classic recordings under the pseudonym (for contractual reasons) Jones-Smith, Inc. In New York City the band played at the Roseland Ballroom and recorded for Decca Records, with which the inexperienced Basie signed a demanding, long-term contract that paid no royalties. Included in the larger band's initial recordings was Basie's signature tune, "One O'Clock Jump," which featured the leader's slyly spare opening piano solo and the repeated, haunting melody played by the band. By this time BUCK CLAYTON's often muted trumpet solos had become another of the band's features, while Ed Lewis on trumpet, Earle Warren on alto saxophone, and Jack Washington on baritone saxophone anchored those instrumental sections. The band later formed an association with Columbia Records, which continued into the 1940s.

The Basie orchestra had come to New York City at the height of the big band era, but the group's relaxed, unembellished, freely swinging style reportedly puzzled those mostly white East Coast listeners who were enthusiasts of the strictly disciplined, thoroughly professional Benny Goodman orchestra. Hammond worked with Basie to tighten the band's section work and solo presentations. Such New York musicians as the trombonists DICKY WELLS and BENNY MORTON and the trumpeter Harry Edison were hired. BILLIE HOLIDAY, who already had forged her own deeply personal jazz singing style, became the band's first woman vocalist, to be replaced a year later by HELEN HUMES. They each joined Jimmy Rushing, who solidified his position as the leading male blues singer of the big band era. The changes paid off in the late 1930s with successful stints at New York's Famous Door and Savoy Ballroom ("the home of happy feet"), followed by engagements in Chicago and San Francisco.

Basie later recalled that by 1940 "what that name [Count Basie] stood for now was me and the band as the same thing." The band undertook almost constant tours throughout the country and continued its prolific recording work. Among bandleaders Basie was matched only by DUKE ELLINGTON as a careful, tenacious master of a group of disparate individual artists. Both men were ambitious leaders who defined the basic sounds of their groups, and each of them was ready to step back and allow great freedom to their soloists. But although Ellington was a composer of major stature, Basie was the more successful in integrating his band into the lucrative, white-dominated entertainment industry of the 1940s through the 1970s.

With the start of World War II, Basie, like many other bandleaders, had to cope with myriad difficulties; some of these included restrictions on travel, the musicians' union's two-year recording ban, and above all the military draft's continual disruption of the band's roster. Basie again showed great skill in choosing talented replacements, at different times bringing in the trombonist J. J. JOHNSON, the trumpeter Joe Newman, the tenor saxophonists Lucky Thompson, Paul Gonsalves, and ILLINOIS JACQUET, and the drummer SHADOW WILSON, among others. All through the 1940s the orchestra worked at choice locations such as New York's Ritz-Carlton and Philadelphia's Academy of Music, while it also maintained nearly continuous nationwide touring. After the recording ban was lifted at the end of 1943, the band resumed making records until the close of the decade. In addition, the Basie group was featured in several Hollywood films—*Reveille with Beverly, Crazy House*, and *Top Man* (all 1943)—and made frequent appearances on Kate Smith's national radio show.

Following the war Basie continued to revise personnel and shuffle arrangers; he allowed younger players like WARDELL GRAY on tenor saxophone and CLARK TERRY on trumpet to introduce a few new bebop ideas. But by the late 1940s the band had become relatively unadventurous. That development coincided with waning public interest in swing-era orchestras, and in 1950 Basie was forced to disband.

Basie remained active for more than a year with a sextet that showcased Gray, Terry, and the clarinetist Buddy DeFranco. In 1952, at the urging of singer BILLY ECKSTINE, he assembled a new orchestra, which eventually would include Marshall Royal as first alto saxophonist and rehearsal director; the highly original trumpeter THAD JONES; the tenor saxophonists Frank Foster, Frank Wess, Paul Quinichette, and EDDIE "LOCKJAW" DAVIS; Basie's longtime rhythm colleague Freddie Green; the drummer Gus Johnson, soon replaced by Sonny Payne; and the blues and ballad singing of JOE WILLIAMS. Birdland, then the most thriving club for jazz in New York, served as an effective home base, though the band often played the Blue Note in Chicago and the Crescendo in Los Angeles as well.

This edition of the Basie orchestra placed new emphasis on arrangers and precisely played ensembles. The arrangers Neal Hefti, ERNIE WILKINS, QUINCY JONES, and "the two Franks" (Foster and Wess) played key roles in making the band sound more appealing to a wider audience. The Basie orchestra now served a varied range of popular tastes, recording with celebrity singers such as Frank Sinatra and Tony Bennett, and featuring everything from Wild Bill Davis's crowd-pleasing arrangement of "April in Paris," to popular television theme songs, to jazz versions of rhythm and blues hits. In 1963 the Basie orchestra was featured in four best-selling albums, including two instrumental records arranged by Quincy Jones. Such popularity had not been attained by any big band since World War II, and, with rock music coming to dominate the record industry, it was a feat not to be duplicated.

Basie and his musicians had made the first of thirty successful European tours in 1954, and in 1963 they made the first of eight trips across the Pacific Ocean. Frequent national tours continued, usually reaching the West Coast twice each year. By 1961, when it performed at one of President John F. Kennedy's inaugural celebrations, the band had become part of America's official culture. Further appearances at the White House culminated in a reception for Basie in 1981, which celebrated a Kennedy Center honor for his contributions to the performing arts. In 1982 he was given a tribute, sponsored by the Black Music Association, at New York's Radio City Music Hall.

Six years earlier, in 1976, Basie had suffered a heart attack that kept him away from the band for half a year. After returning, he continued the band's touring on a reduced schedule, while remaining active at work in the recording studios. But various illnesses further weakened him, and a year after his wife's death, he died in Hollywood, Florida.

Basie's unique ability to inspire a large jazz band with the rhythmic drive and ease of 1930s Kansas City small combos, to select and lead an ever-changing roster of talented and complementary musicians, to adapt to rapidly evolving and diverse musical tastes while maintaining artistic integrity, to integrate his band into the mainstream of American entertainment, and to give the band matchless worldwide exposure all show him to have been one of the major figures in twentieth-century American music.

FURTHER READING
Basie's memorabilia and papers are still in private hands, although they have been pledged to the Hampton University Library, Hampton, Virginia.

Basie, Count, with Albert L. Murray. *Good Morning Blues* (1985).

Dance, Stanley. *The World of Count Basie* (1980).

Schuller, Gunther. *The Swing Era* (1989).

Sheridan, Chris. *Count Basie: A Bio-Discography* (1986).

Obituary: *New York Times*, 27 Apr. 1984.

This entry is taken from the *American National Biography* and is published here with the permission of the American Council of Learned Societies.

BURTON W. PERETTI

Baskett, James F. (16 Feb. 1904–9 July 1948), actor, was born in Indianapolis, Indiana, the only son of Elizabeth Baskett, a homemaker, and John Baskett, a barber. He was among the first students to attend Arsenal Technical High School in Indianapolis, where he studied pharmacology. A lack of funds, though, forced him to forsake his plans to make that his career.

On a visit to Chicago as a teen, however, he was asked to fill in for a sick performer in a show and developed an interest in acting. On the stage, Baskett toured as singer, actor, and comic under the name Jimmie (sometimes Jimmy) Baskette for most of the top African American companies of the period. He performed with Henry Drake and Ethel Walker's touring variety troupe in *Go Get 'Em* (1926) and *Look Who's Here* (1927) and with the prolific Salem Tutt Whitney and J. Homer Tutt's Smart Set company in *Deep Harlem* (1929). He moved to New York where he performed with the Lafayette Players. He also appeared in *Hot Chocolates* (1929), with music by FATS WALLER, and in *Lew Leslie's Blackbirds of 1930*, for which EUBIE BLAKE composed the music. He performed in BILL "BOJANGLES" ROBINSON's revue, Hot from Harlem (1932), which opened at the prestigious Palace Theatre and toured the vaudeville circuit through 1934 after being renamed *Goin' to Town* in its second year. Baskett also appeared in several low-budget independent films, often called "race films," geared for African American audiences, including *Harlem Is Heaven* (1932), *Gone Harlem* (1939), and *Comes Midnight* (1940). He also served as a straight man for comedians at the Apollo Theater and traveled to Los Angeles in that capacity with DEWEY "PIGMEAT" MARKHAM, where they performed with great success in the early 1940s. Baskett relocated to Los Angles with his wife, Margaret, and there he met Freeman Gosden of the *Amos 'n' Andy* show and subsequently joined the cast of radio's

immensely popular, long-running comedy in 1943. He played the fast-talking lawyer Gabby Gibson, whose popularity came to rival that of the main characters', a role he continued until his death in 1948.

In 1945, in answer to an ad for voice actors, Baskett auditioned for the role of a talking butterfly in *Song of the South*, Walt Disney's planned adaptation of Joel Chandler Harris's *Uncle Remus* stories. Disney was so impressed with Baskett's talents that he cast him, ahead of many better-known black actors, in the lead role of Uncle Remus, the performance for which he is best known. In the 1946 film, set not long after the Civil War, the elderly Uncle Remus lives on a plantation and helps the owner's young son adjust to rural life and to the extended absence of his father by telling him exemplary tales of the adventures of Brer Rabbit, a trickster character, as he evades the attempts of Brer Fox and Brer Bear to catch and eat him. The film was Disney's first live-action feature, although Uncle Remus's stories were animated in Disney's usual style. In addition to playing Uncle Remus, Baskett also provided the voice for Brer Fox, who, like his radio character, was a fast talker. His delivery was so rapid, in fact, that even Disney's best animators had a difficult time matching the character's mouth movements to Baskett's dialogue. When Johnny Lee, who voiced Brer Rabbit, left on a USO tour, Baskett even provided some of that character's dialogue in one scene.

For his performance, the Board of Governors of the Academy of Motion Picture Arts and Sciences presented him with a Special Award statuette inscribed "For his able and heartwarming characterization of Uncle Remus, friend and storyteller to the children of the world." The board had serious reservations about giving him the award, however, because of the stereotypical nature of the role, until the actor-humanitarian Jean Hersholt threatened to make a scene at the award ceremony if Baskett did not receive the award. He thus became the first African American male to be honored by the academy. In the film he also sang "Zip-a-Dee-Doo-Dah," which won the Oscar for Best Song. The film was commercially successful in its original release and in several subsequent rereleases. At the time of its release, some black newspapers praised it for potentially furthering race relations, but over the years it drew the criticism of various African American groups over the stereotypical depiction of its black characters. As a result, Buena Vista, Disney's distribution company, announced in 1970 that it was withdrawing the film for good. In 1972, however, it was rereleased and grossed twice as much at the box office as it did in its initial release. It earned even more in a 1986 release, but this was its last public screening in the United States, and Disney has not issued it in video format.

After his success in *Song of the South*, Baskett continued to work on the *Amos 'n' Andy* show, despite serious health problems which sometimes interfered with the live broadcasts. In 1947 the producer Jean Dalrymple began planning a revival of Marc Connelly's Pulitzer Prize–winning play, *The Green Pastures*, with James Baskett to star as De Lawd. Baskett's declining health led to repeated postponements of the project, however, and his 1948 death in Hollywood from heart disease ultimately caused it to be canceled entirely.

FURTHER READING

Cohen, Karl F. *Forbidden Animation: Censored Cartoons and Blacklisted Animators in America* (1997).

Wiley, Mason, and Damien Bona. *Inside Oscar: The Unofficial History of the Academy Awards* (1996).

Obituary: *New York Times*, 14 July 1948.

RICHARD J. LESKOSKY

Basquiat, Jean-Michel (22 Dec. 1960–12 Aug. 1988), painter, was born in Brooklyn, New York, the son of Gerard Basquiat, an accountant originally from Haiti, and Matilde Andradas, of Puerto Rican descent. A precocious draftsman from childhood, Basquiat received little formal artistic training. The last school he attended was the experimental City-as-School program in Manhattan, where he befriended his fellow artist Al Diaz.

Before quitting school altogether in 1978, Basquiat created SAMO (meaning "same old shit"), which was variously a pseudo-religion, a fictional logo, a nom de plume, and a persona. Basquiat and Diaz spray-painted original aphorisms with a copyright symbol next to the word SAMO on walls and in alleys in lower Manhattan. Their mock epigrams and mottoes included "SAMO as an end to mind-wash religion, nowhere politics, and bogus philosophy," "SAMO saves idiots," and "plush safe he think, SAMO." Whereas other graffiti artists such as Fab 5 Freddy, Futura 2000, and Rammellzee painted multicolored and elaborately designed "tags" on subway cars and alleyways, Diaz and Basquiat focused on their concepts and text-based work rather than aesthetics. In the 11 December 1978 issue of the *Village Voice*, Basquiat and Diaz identified themselves as SAMO; soon thereafter, they parted ways.

Aside from his SAMO work, Basquiat drew and painted his own art on any available surface he could find, including refrigerator doors; he also made postcards and t-shirts, which he sold on the street. Using oil and acrylic paints, oil paint sticks, and collage materials, he blended roughly drawn visual elements and text. When asked about his subject matter, Basquiat responded that he painted "royalty, heroism, and the streets." Black male figures, skulls, crowns, and hobo symbols proliferated in his paintings. He sometimes included references to his personal heroes, such as the musician CHARLIE PARKER and the boxer JOE LOUIS, as well as art-historical references such as Leonardo da Vinci's sketchbooks. Basquiat used words not as expanded captions but as crucial components in the composition and meaning of the work, sometimes repeating words or crossing them out, as in *Horn Players* (1983, Eli and Edythe L. Broad Collection, Los Angeles). In this painting, the artist painted Charlie Parker's name and the word "ornithology" (referring to the musician's nickname "the Bird") several times on the canvas, overlaid with more paint and next to his painted images of the musician. Basquiat once said, "I cross out words so that you will see them more; the fact that they are obscured makes you want to read them." In 1980 Basquiat painted a large mural for his first group exhibition, the Times Square Show. Organized by Colab (Collaborative Projects Incorporated), the exhibition featured several artists early in their careers, including Jenny Holzer, Kenny Scharf, and Kiki Smith. The following year Basquiat took part in numerous exhibitions in New York, such as New York/New Wave at P.S.1, along with the artists Robert Mapplethorpe and Andy Warhol, and Beyond Words: Graffiti Based-Rooted-Inspired Works at the Mudd Club. The Galleria d'Arte Emilio Mazzoli in Modena, Italy, held Basquiat's first one-man exhibition in the spring of 1981.

In 1980 the New York art dealer Annina Nosei began selling Basquiat's work and offered him her gallery basement to use as his studio. Despite this unusual arrangement (Nosei was criticized for having Basquiat "on exhibit"), she exposed Basquiat's art to several important collectors and gave him his first U.S. one-man exhibition in 1982. Although Basquiat changed dealers often in his short career, he maintained steady relationships with the Los Angeles dealer Larry Gagosian and Bruno Bischofberger, who was based in Switzerland and was the artist's international representative.

Basquiat was the youngest artist in the prestigious Documenta 7 exhibition in Kassel, Germany (1982), and in the 1983 Biennial Exhibition at the Whitney Museum of American Art. The Museum of Modern Art included him in their International Survey of Recent Painting and Sculpture at MOMA (1983).

He continued to gain recognition when, in 1983, he became a close friend of Andy Warhol, who was also represented by Bischofberger. At the suggestion of the dealer, the two artists collaborated on several paintings in 1985. Warhol painted or silk-screened corporate logos such as those of GE and Arm & Hammer along with other images including Felix the Cat. Basquiat painted over and around Warhol's work with his repertoire of motifs and words. Their paintings, exhibited in New York at the Tony Shafrazi Gallery that same year, received mixed reviews. One *New York Times* critic wrote that Basquiat was an art world mascot and that Warhol used him to regain his own popularity. Warhol and Basquiat ended their friendship following the exhibition.

An article on Basquiat written by Cathleen McGuigan for the *New York Times Magazine* (10 Feb. 1985) exposed him to a popular audience but also posed questions about the consequences of an inflated art market on such a young career. Some critics claimed that Basquiat became more interested in making art that would satisfy his collectors than in creating innovative work. But many of his last works featured new developments, such as very dense accumulations of words and images, as in *Untitled (Stretch)* (1985, estate of the artist), or starkly powerful compositions, as exemplified by *Riding with Death* (1988, private collection), which shows a dark human skeleton riding a white skeleton of a horse.

Basquiat died of a drug overdose in New York at the age of twenty-seven. His death at such an early age commanded reflection in the art world, an environment where artistic ideals had been replaced by greed and the pursuit of fame due to a period of auspicious wealth and soaring art prices. Basquiat, who never hid his career aspirations, was hailed as the first African American art star. Bearing the burden of this title, he was sometimes viewed as an exotic novelty or as a traitor to his race in the predominantly white art world. But Basquiat refused to be labeled. He said, "I don't know if my being black has anything to do with my success. I don't think I should be compared to black artists but all artists."

Although not an organized movement, Basquiat and other painters grouped as "neo-expressionists"—including Julian Schnabel, Georg Baselitz, and Susan Rothenberg—returned a sense of bravura and improvisation to painting that harked back to the abstract expressionists. Influenced by pop art, Basquiat's wordplay and use of signs and symbols aligned him with other postmodern artists, particularly those like Robert Longo who combined specific and sometimes edited images inspired by the mass media to convey meaning. Basquiat also maintained a very personal vision in his work, painting his heroes (boxers and jazz musicians), his artistic influences (da Vinci and Warhol), and episodes from his own life (drug use and racism) in his idiosyncratic style. His poetic means of combining text with imagery and social issues with personal experiences resonates in the work of several contemporary artists such as GLEN LIGON and LORNA SIMPSON.

FURTHER READING

Basquiat, Jean-Michel, with Bruno Bischofberger. *Jean-Michel Basquiat* (1999).

Hoban, Phoebe. *Basquiat: A Quick Killing in Art* (1998).

Marshall, Richard, ed. *Jean-Michel Basquiat* (1992).

Tate, Greg. "Nobody Loves a Genius Child." *Village Voice*, 14 Nov. 1988: 31–35.

Wines, Michael. "Jean-Michel Basquiat: Hazards of Sudden Success and Fame." *New York Times*, 27 Aug. 1988.

This entry is taken from the *American National Biography* and is published here with the permission of the American Council of Learned Societies.

N. ELIZABETH SCHLATTER

Bass, Charlotta (Oct. 1880–Apr. 1969), journalist, activist, and vice presidential candidate, was born Charlotta Amanda Spears in Sumter, South Carolina, the sixth of eleven children of Hiram Spears and Kate (maiden name unknown). The details of her childhood are unknown, but sometime before her twentieth birthday she went to live with her brother in Providence, Rhode Island, and began work at the *Providence Watchman*, selling ads and helping in the office. After ten years, suffering from exhaustion, she went for a rest to California on the advice of her doctor.

At the beginning of what was to have been a two-year stay, Spears went against her doctor's orders and took a job at the *Eagle*, a newspaper with a largely black readership. Her job was to sell advertising and subscriptions. However, when the newspaper's editor, John Neimore, became ill, he began to turn the operations of the Eagle over to Spears. When he died, the paper's new owner put Spears in charge, in May 1912. Spears continued to publish news of black society but increasingly dealt with social and political issues in the paper she renamed the *California Eagle*. Her commitment to righting the wrongs of society quickly became apparent.

In 1912 Joseph Bass joined the paper as an editor. Bass had been one of the founders of the *Topeka Plain Dealer*, and he shared Spears's concerns about injustice and racial discrimination. The two were soon married and ran the paper together for the next two decades. Among the targets of their passionate attacks was D. W. Griffith's film *The Birth of a Nation*, which perpetuated the worst kind of racial stereotyping in order to glorify the Ku Klux Klan. (The Klan tried to sue the paper for libel in 1925, but the suit was unsuccessful.) The Basses powerfully championed the black soldiers of the Twenty-fourth Infantry who were unjustly sentenced in a 1917 race riot that took place in Houston, Texas. They also filled their newspaper with support for the SCOTTSBORO BOYS, nine young men who were framed and convicted of rape in Scottsboro, Alabama, in 1931. The Basses also strongly endorsed labor leader A. PHILIP RANDOLPH in his battle against racial discrimination in railroad employment. Away from the newspaper, Bass helped found the Industrial Business Council, which fought discrimination in employment practices and encouraged entrepreneurship among black people. In an effort to defeat housing covenants in all-white neighborhoods, she formed the Home Protective Association. In 1919 she attended the Pan-African Congress in Paris, organized by W. E. B. Du Bois, and during the 1920s was co-president of the Los Angeles chapter of MARCUS GARVEY's Universal Negro Improvement Association.

After Joseph Bass died in 1934, Charlotta Bass continued to run the *California Eagle* on her own. She also became more active in local and national politics. In 1940 the Republican Party chose her as western regional director for Wendell Willkie's presidential campaign. Three years later she became the first African American member of the Los Angeles County Superior Court grand jury. In 1945 Bass ran for the L.A. city council as a "people's candidate" in a landmark election for black Angelenos. Although she lost the race, her progressive platform and powerful campaigning united diverse black organizations throughout the city's Seventh District. Her campaign also laid the groundwork for later, more successful, African American candidates, notably the future L.A. city councilman and mayor TOM BRADLEY.

The immediate postwar years in the United States were marked by a growing demand for African American civil rights, which was met by an upsurge in Klan activity and other forms of racial violence. In her newspaper and in her political activities, Bass took an unyielding stand against these horrors. When blacklisting hit Hollywood, she spoke out in favor of the "Hollywood Ten," a group of screenwriters who had refused to testify before the House Un-American Activities Committee (HUAC) about alleged Communist infiltration of the film industry. She herself was called before the California equivalent of HUAC, the Tenney Committee, which she denounced as "fascist."

Believing that neither of the major parties was committed to civil rights, Bass left the Republican Party in the late 1940s to become one of the founders of the Progressive Party. Nearing the age of seventy, she campaigned heavily for the party's presidential candidate, Henry Wallace, in the 1948 election. Leaving the *California Eagle* in the early 1950s, she traveled to wherever she felt her voice might make a difference for the causes that she believed in. She went to Prague, Czechoslovakia, to support the Stockholm Appeal to ban the bomb at the peace committee of the World Congress. Like other members of the American left at the time, notably PAUL ROBESON, she traveled to the Soviet Union and commented on its apparent lack of racial discrimination.

In 1950, she ran for California's Fourteenth Congressional District, but lost again. Bass nonetheless believed that her campaign had been successful in raising the issues she felt were important. This realization led her to accept the Progressive Party's nomination for vice president of the United States in 1952, making her the first black woman to run for national office. Bass was a consistent thorn in the side of her Republican opponent, Senator Richard Nixon, attacking him fiercely throughout the campaign. Her platform called for civil rights, women's rights, an end to the Korean War, and peace with the Soviet Union.

By the early 1950s, however, the Progressive Party was perceived by many Americans to be too closely linked to the Communist Party. Some of those links were real; others the result of McCarthyite hysteria. Either way, Bass and her running mate fared poorly, even among African Americans in those states that allowed blacks to vote. Nationally, the Progressive Party won only 0.2 percent of the vote.

In 1960 Bass wrote an autobiography entitled "Forty Years: Memoirs from the Pages of a Newspaper." During her years of retirement, she maintained a library in her garage for the young people in her neighborhood. It was a continuation of her long fight to give all people opportunities and education. She died in Los Angeles.

With remarkable dedication, Bass used her role as editor of the oldest black-run newspaper on the West Coast to crusade against injustice and inequality. She may never have won an election, but, as she said in her 1952 campaign, "Win or lose, we win by raising the issues."

FURTHER READING

Bass's unpublished manuscript "Forty Years: Memoirs from the Pages of a Newspaper" is available at the Southern California Library for Social Studies and Research in Los Angeles and the Schomburg Center for Research in Black Culture of the New York Public Library.

Gill, Gerald R. "'Win or Lose—We Win': The 1952 Vice Presidential Campaign of Charlotta A. Bass," in *The Afro-American Woman: Struggles and Images* (1981).

Streitmatter, Rodger. *Raising Her Voice: African American Women Journalists Who Changed History* (1994).

Obituary: *Los Angeles Sentinel*, 17 Apr. 1969.

KATHLEEN THOMPSON

Bass, George Houston (23 Apr. 1938–19 Sept. 1990), playwright, academic, director, and producer, was born in Murfreesboro, Tennessee, near Nashville. One of nine children Bass grew up in a segregated area of the capital, the son of Clarence Bass, a Baptist minister, and Mabel Dixon Bass, a retired schoolteacher and health-care worker. The atmosphere of his childhood home was closely knit and disciplined; life revolved around education and religion. Bass earned his bachelor's degree in Mathematics with honors from Fisk University in 1959. While a senior, he met the Harlem Renaissance writer ARNA BONTEMPS, then a Fisk librarian, who

brokered the student's formative literary partnership with LANGSTON HUGHES. Bass then attended Columbia University's Graduate School of Business (1959–1960) to study finance, but quit because of what he felt was endemic racism in the academic and social milieu. He received an M.A. from New York University's Film School (1964) and attended Yale School of Drama (1966–1968) as a recipient of the John Golden Playwriting Fellowship.

The literary partnership between Hughes and Bass began in 1959 when Hughes visited Tennessee on a lecture tour. In exchange for financial support for studies at Columbia, Bass conducted research and performed various administrative tasks while living in the writer's Harlem brownstone. For five years Hughes's influence granted his protégé ample opportunity to mingle with the luminaries of the New York artistic and social scene, including his lifelong friend Carl Van Vechten, the musicians Noble Sissle and Eubie Blake, as well as the Nigerian dissident Wole Soyinka. Bass also traveled extensively with his mentor and attended theater rehearsals for Hughes's play *Black Nativity* (1961), a fusion of Christian scripture, poetry, and song. As a dramatist Hughes had already garnered praise for such pieces as *Mulatto* (1935), a successful Broadway production. Concerned about the prospective difficulties that a career playwright would face, Hughes urged Bass to consider film school instead. Although he was unable to secure steady employment as a film studies graduate, Bass found work as a freelance writer and director. In 1964 he received the Rosenthal Award from the American Society of Cinematologists for the most creative script written by a young American.

Aside from Hughes, Bass also worked with DAISY BATES, author of the memoir *The Long Shadow of Little Rock* (1962), and VINNETTE CARROLL, Broadway's first black woman director. When Hughes died in 1967 Bass nurtured the writer's legacy as literary executor of the estate. That same year *The Game*, a film adaptation of one of Bass's plays, won the Plaque of the Lion of St. Mark at the Venice Film Festival. From 1964 until 1970 Bass was artistic director of the Jacob Riis Amphitheatre in New York. From 1968 to 1969 he served as associate producer and story editor of *On Being Black*, a set of nationally broadcast teleplays for WGBH-TV in Boston. Bass also spent time as artistic director of the Black Arts Theater in New Haven, Connecticut.

In 1969 Bass was hired as a lecturer at Brown University to teach classes in English and theater. He eventually secured full tenure as a professor of theater arts and African American studies in 1985. There he met Ramona Wilkins, a theater student originally from New York, whom he married in 1974. They had three children: Kwame, Khari, and Ayana.

Bass is perhaps most renowned as the originator and artistic director of the Rites and Reason Theater (originally the Black Theater, 1970), a research organ of the Africana Studies Department at Brown. From 1973 onward he collaborated with his colleague, the historian Rhett S. Jones, to conceive of the research-to-performance method, an interdisciplinary approach to interpreting black culture through the dual prisms of dramatic theory and innovative artistic practice. Beginning in 1988 he teamed with Karen Allen Baxter, a respected producer and the theater's present managing director, to plan projects for both Rites and Reason and other black companies nationwide. As a scholar Bass was concerned with the revivification of folk history, mythology, and communal rituals through art. He produced and directed more than fifty of his and other playwrights' works while at Brown, the first of which was his historical play *Black Masque* (1971). Other notable works from his oeuvre include *Malacoff Blue* (1976), *De Dey of No Mo'* (1980), and *Brer Rabbit Whole* (1984). Brown's George Houston Bass Performing Arts Space, christened at Commencement in 1991, was named in honor of the founder of New England's oldest continually operating black theater.

The diversity of African American vernacular traditions and the centrality of religion in everyday life emerged as key themes in Bass's work. He demonstrated his appreciation for folklore by editing, along with the critic HENRY LOUIS GATES JR., *Mule Bone: A Comedy of Negro Life* (originally written in 1931). Hughes and his contemporary ZORA NEALE HURSTON had composed this controversial play together, but they became embroiled in a major feud before the work could reach fruition. This work was published in full and subsequently produced for the first time in only in 1991, with Bass and Gates serving as consultants. Apart from resurrecting *Mule Bone*, analyzing and anthologizing Hughes's poems and plays, and searching for a suitable literary biographer for Hughes (Bass ultimately chose Arnold Rampersad), Bass maintained his lifelong commitment to Hughes by co-founding the Langston Hughes Society in 1981 and editing its official publication, *The Langston Hughes Review*.

Bass's vision of a modern black theater focused upon the tension between community values and individual choices. It also integrated traditional forms with more contemporary, experimental approaches and themes. Formal recognition for his artistic achievements included a John Hay Whitney Fellowship (1963), a Harlem Cultural Council Grant (1969), a Howard Foundation Fellowship (1977), a Fulbright Research Scholarship (1977), and a Ford Foundation Travel and Study Grant (1978). In 1967 Yale School of Drama honored its respected alumnus by staging George Bass Day, a festival of his short works. Bass died of a heart attack at Miriam Hospital in Providence, Rhode Island.

FURTHER READING

Griffin, Sharon. "Artist in Residence—One Writer's Journey of Affirmation: Poet Langston Hughes Helped Brown's George Bass Uncover His Creative Contours," *Providence Journal*, 28 June 1987.

Peterson, Bernard L., Jr. *Contemporary Black American Playwrights and Their Plays: A Biographical Directory and Dramatic Index* (1988).

Obituary: *New York Times*, 21 Sept. 1990.

NANCY KANG

Bassett, Angela (16 Aug. 1958–), actress, was born Angela Evelyn Bassett in the Bronx, New York, to Betty Bassett, a social worker, and a father whose name and occupation are unknown. Soon after Angela's birth her parents divorced, and she moved with her mother and sister to St. Petersburg, Florida. Bassett first thought of a career in acting after a 1974 school trip to Washington, D.C., where she saw JAMES EARL JONES perform in *Of Mice and Men* at the Kennedy Center.

After graduating from Boca Ciega High School in St. Petersburg in 1976, Bassett won a scholarship to study at Yale University. She earned her B.A. in African American Studies in 1980 and a master of fine arts from the Yale School of Drama in 1983. After Yale, Bassett did a stint as a photo researcher for *U.S. News and World Report* while also pursuing theater roles in New York and performing at the Yale Repertory Theatre. Under the mentorship of the director Lloyd Richards, Bassett acted in the playwright AUGUST WILSON's *Ma Rainey's Black Bottom* and *Joe Turner's Come and Gone* in 1985 and 1988, respectively. She soon moved to television roles, first as a prostitute in *Doubletake* (1985) and next as a news reporter on FX (1986). In 1991 Bassett caught Hollywood's attention as Cuba Gooding Jr.'s mother in JOHN SINGLETON's

Angela Bassett, accepting her award for Outstanding Supporting Actress in a Motion Picture for *The Score*, at the 33rd Annual NAACP Image Awards Ceremony at the Universal Amphitheatre in Los Angeles, 23 February 2002. (AP Images.)

Boyz in the Hood. She also had a minor role in John Sayles's *Passion Fish* (1992). She followed by playing BETTY SHABAZZ opposite DENZEL WASHINGTON in *Malcolm X* (1992), but her career took off with her role as TINA TURNER in *What's Love Got to Do with It?* (1993). Bassett earned critical praise for her physical transformation to portray the famously sculpted singer. The performance earned Bassett a Golden Globe for Best Actress—the first African American to win the award—as well as an Oscar nomination for best actress.

After her pivotal role as Turner, Bassett reportedly never had to audition for a film. In 1994 the author TERRY MCMILLAN handpicked her to star in both *Waiting to Exhale* (1995) and *How Stella Got Her Groove Back* (1998). Critics singled out Bassett for her performances in both films, but it was in *Stella* that she attacked both race and gender stereotypes through her portrayal of a forty-year-old divorced executive and mother who falls in love with a twenty-year-old Jamaican. In 2001 the independent film producer Lee Daniels offered her

the opportunity to star in his *Monster's Ball*, which became critically acclaimed, but Bassett turned it down. A self-described private person, she publicly voiced her refusal to play Daniels's Leticia Musgrove, telling *Newsweek* magazine that she "wasn't going to be a prostitute on film"(Samuels, 54), and that she did not want to play to stereotypes about black women and sexuality. HALLE BERRY took the role, for which she won an Academy Award in 2001.

In 1997 Bassett married Courtney B. Vance, an actor she had met while studying at Yale. Having battled infertility for years, Bassett and Vance used a surrogate to have two children in January 2006.

Bassett mixed her traditional acting roles with more unique projects, such as *Vampire in Brooklyn* (1995) and *Strange Days* (1995), in the latter playing one of the few black female science fiction characters in film. In 2002 she reunited with Sayles (and returned to her native Florida) to star in his ensemble film *Sunshine State*. Staying true to her passions, Bassett continued her notable portrayals of powerful and courageous black women. She played ROSA PARKS in a television movie directed by JULIE DASH, *The Rosa Parks Story* (2002), for which Bassett earned the NAACP Image Award and was nominated for an Emmy for outstanding lead actress. In 2007 Bassett was cast to costar with Don Cheadle in *Toussaint*, a biographical film about the Haitian revolutionary Toussaint L'Ouverture. Devoted to children's assistance and charities, Bassett served as an active ambassador of UNICEF; she was appointed in 2003 along with her husband. She also supported the Royal Theater Boys and Girls Club in St. Petersburg.

FURTHER READING

Bassett, Angela, and Courtney B. Vance. *Friends: A Love Story* (2007).
Collier, Aldore. "Angela Bassett Talks about Love, Marriage, the Twins and the Joys of Motherhood," *Ebony* (May 2006).
Samuels, Allison. "Angela's Fire," *Newsweek* (July 2002).
LINDA CHAVERS

Bateman, Mildred Mitchell *See* Mitchell-Bateman, Mildred.

Bates, Daisy (11 Nov. 1914–4 Nov. 1999), journalist and civil rights activist, was born Daisy Lee Gatson in Huttig, Arkansas, to parents she would never know. She may also have had four brothers. Bates learned as a child that three white men had attempted to rape her mother, who died while

Daisy Bates, at her home in Little Rock, Arkansas, 11 September 1997. A portrait of her late husband L. C. Bates hangs on the wall behind her. (AP Images.)

of a white policeman's cold-blooded murder of a black soldier on the streets of Little Rock prompted white advertisers to withdraw their financial support of the paper in protest. The Bateses persisted in exposing police brutality, however, and by the end of the war the *State Press*'s campaigns had persuaded the Little Rock authorities to hire black policemen to patrol African American neighborhoods. The paper's crusading reputation greatly increased its circulation among blacks throughout Arkansas but also earned the Bateses the enmity of conservative whites. In 1946, for example, Daisy and L. C. were sentenced to ten days in prison for publishing an article criticizing the conviction of labor activists, but the couple was later released on bond, and the Arkansas Supreme Court quashed their sentences. In 1952 the Arkansas NAACP recognized Daisy Bates's tireless campaigning for civil rights by electing her its president, a post that placed her at the forefront of desegregation efforts two years later, when the U.S. Supreme Court delivered its *Brown v. Board of Education* decision. Commentators believed that Arkansas under Governor Orval Faubus, a racial moderate, might lead the region in compliance with the school desegregation ruling, and that progressive Little Rock would lead Arkansas. After 1955, however, the Court's implementation decree, *Brown II*, emboldened segregationist whites. *Brown II* required local authorities to desegregate with "all deliberate speed," a phrase that white-dominated school boards, including Little Rock's, interpreted as a signal to delay and obstruct integration. In 1956 Bates responded to white delaying tactics by urging readers of the *State Press* to support *Cooper v. Aaron*, an NAACP lawsuit recommending the speedy integration of the Little Rock schools.

resisting them. Realizing that a black man in Arkansas could not successfully prosecute whites for murder, and fearing reprisals if he attempted to do so, Daisy's father left town shortly afterward, leaving his infant daughter with his friends Orlie and Susie Smith, who adopted her. Daisy enjoyed the close love and attention that came from being an only child, but the Smiths could not protect her from the most pernicious manifestations of white supremacy in Jim Crow Arkansas: verbal and physical abuse from whites, substandard education, and minimal economic opportunities. Her childhood was also scarred by the presence in town of one of her mother's murderers, though Daisy, the image of her mother, exacted a kind of revenge by staring at and haunting the man referred to in her memoirs as the "drunken pig."

At the age of fifteen she met the twenty-eight-year-old Lucius Christopher "L. C." Bates, a journalist then working as an insurance agent. The couple courted for several years and married in 1942, moving to Little Rock, Arkansas, to establish the *Arkansas State Press*, a weekly newspaper for the black community. They had no children.

During World War II, the *State Press* exemplified the increasing determination of southern blacks to challenge their second-class citizenship. In 1942, for instance, its reporting

In September 1957 the Little Rock school board finally unveiled its plan to enroll nine black students in the previously all-white Central High School, but even that token effort enraged whites. Working-class whites were particularly aggrieved that their children would be integrated while the children of wealthier whites would not. Tensions were raised further on the first day of classes, when Governor Faubus enlisted the Arkansas National Guard to surround the school. Warning that "blood would run in the streets" if blacks entered the building, Faubus had essentially used military force to deny the "Little Rock Nine" their constitutional right to attend an integrated school. Such defiance encouraged other whites to resist violently. Someone threw a rock through Bates's window, threatening dynamite next. And when one of the students, Elizabeth Eckford, attempted to enter the school alone, white mobs jeered at, spat at, and physically threatened the fifteen-year-old.

Throughout the tension, Daisy Bates served as the main adviser and confidante of the children and their parents. She paid for private bodyguards, held strategy sessions in her home, tutored the children during the three weeks that the state of Arkansas refused to do so, and helped handle the demands of the world media. On 25 September 1957, after President Dwight Eisenhower had federalized the National Guard and sent one thousand Screaming Eagles paratroopers from the 101st Airborne Division to enforce the law, Bates escorted the students through the front door of Central High School. In the year that followed, she continued to act as a mentor for the students when they braved intimidation and assaults, and also when they fought back, as one student did when she emptied a bowl of hot chili on the head of a white youth who taunted her. Bates's defiance and the courage of the students earned them the NAACP's Spingarn Medal in 1958.

The successful, albeit minimal, integration of Central did not end conflicts between Bates and the Little Rock authorities. In October 1957 she resisted a local ordinance that required organizations to provide the city clerk with financial records and the names of staff and officers. Other municipalities used such information to harass and punish NAACP members, and Bates argued that compulsory disclosure of these records infringed citizens' rights to freedom of association. The local court duly convicted Bates of violating the ordinance in 1957, but that conviction was reversed in 1960 by a unanimous U.S. Supreme Court ruling, *Bates v. Little Rock*.

After the Little Rock crisis, Bates faded from the national spotlight but remained active in civil rights. She spoke at the 1963 March on Washington, worked in the Johnson administration's War on Poverty, and led a community revitalization project in rural Arkansas. In 1984 the University of Arkansas awarded her an honorary degree. Many other awards followed. The city of Little Rock named an elementary school in her honor in 1987, and she even carried the Olympic torch en route to Atlanta in 1996. She received her greatest honor posthumously, when President Bill Clinton, a fellow Arkansan and friend, awarded Bates and the Little Rock Nine the Congressional Gold Medal. As the Nine received their honors from the president in November 1999, Bates lay in state in the Arkansas Capitol, a few feet away from the spot where Governor Faubus had predicted blood in the streets in 1957.

Popular histories of the civil rights era often depict Daisy Bates as the epitome of virtuous, nonviolent resistance and grace under pressure, largely on the strength of her brave, motherly shepherding of the Little Rock Nine. Indeed she was nonviolent in her approach, but she was also a realist. Her journalism was confrontational. She challenged police brutality and, from the time she learned of her mother's murder, found it "hard to suppress certain feelings, when all around you see only hate" (Tyson, *Robert F. Williams and the Roots of Black Power*, 153). Such feelings were not unreasonable given that the Ku Klux Klan raised three fiery crosses on her lawn and that white supremacists bombed her home several times. In 1959 she was at first equivocal about the case of ROBERT WILLIAMS, a North Carolina NAACP leader who advocated that blacks arm themselves in self-defense. After the NAACP Executive Secretary WALTER WHITE promised Daisy an extra $600 a month to help the ailing *State Press*, however, she agreed to support White's campaign to censure Williams. That decision reflected Bates's pragmatism—white advertisers had withdrawn support from the *State Press*, and the paper would soon fold. Daisy Bates was certainly courageous, but like others in the civil rights movement—and like activists in all eras—she recognized that success often requires compromise.

FURTHER READING
There are three main manuscript sources for information on Bates. In 1966 she donated papers related to the Little Rock crisis to the State Historical Society in Madison, Wisconsin. Twenty years later, she donated papers to the Special Collections Library of the University of Arkansas in Fayetteville. For her tenure as president of the Arkansas NAACP, see the Papers of the NAACP in the Library of Congress, Washington, D.C.
Bates, Daisy Lee. *The Long Shadow of Little Rock* (1962).
Kirk, John A. *Redefining the Color Line: Black Activism in Little Rock, Arkansas, 1940–1970* (2002).
Jacoway, Elizabeth, and C. Fred Williams. *Understanding the Little Rock Crisis* (1999).
Obituary: *New York Times*, 5 Nov. 1999.

STEVEN J. NIVEN

Bates, Peg Leg (11 Oct. 1907–8 Dec. 1998), tap dancer and entrepreneur, was born Clayton Bates in Fountain Inn, South Carolina, the son of Rufus Bates, a laborer, and Emma Stewart, a sharecropper and housecleaner. He began dancing when he was five. At age twelve, while working in a cottonseed gin mill, he caught and mangled his left leg in a conveyor belt. The leg was amputated on the kitchen table at his home. Although he was left with only one leg and a wooden peg leg that his uncle carved for him, Bates resolved to continue dancing. "It somehow grew in my mind that I wanted to be as good a dancer as any two-legged dancer," he recalled. "It hurt me that the boys pitied me. I was pretty popular before, and I still wanted to be popular. I told them not to feel sorry for me." He meant it. He began imitating the latest rhythm steps of metal tap-shoe dancers, adding his own novelty and acrobatic steps. He worked his way from minstrel shows and carnivals to the vaudeville circuits. At fifteen, after becoming the undisputed king of one-legged dancers, able to execute acrobatic, graceful soft-shoe dancing and powerful rhythm-tapping all with one leg and a peg, Bates established a professional career as a tap dancer.

In 1930, after dancing in the Paris version of Lew Leslie's *Blackbirds of 1928*, Bates returned to New York to perform as a featured tap dancer at such famous Harlem nightclubs as the Cotton Club, Connie's Inn, and Club Zanzibar. On Broadway in the 1930s he reinvented such popular tap steps as the Shim Sham Shimmy, Susie-Q, and Truckin' by enhancing them with the rhythmic combination of his deep-toned left-leg peg and the high-pitched metallic right-foot tap. As one of the black tap dancers able to cross the color barrier, Bates joined performers on the white vaudeville circuit of Keith & Loew and performed on the same bill as BILL "BOJANGLES" ROBINSON, Fred Astaire, and Gene Kelly. In 1949 Bates sang and danced the role of the swashbuckling pirate Long John Silver in the musical review *Blackouts*. "Don't give up the ship, although you seem to lose the fight; life means do the best with all you got, give it all your might," he sang in the Ken Murray musical that played for three years at the Hollywood and Vine Theatre in Hollywood, California. Wearing a white suit and looking as debonair as Astaire, Bates made his first television appearance in 1948 on *This Is Show Business*, a show hosted by Clifton Fadiman and Arlene Francis, performing high-speed paddle-and-roll tapping and balancing on his rubber-tipped peg as though it were a ballet pointe shoe.

On the *Ed Sullivan Show* in 1955, Bates strutted his stuff as he competed in a tap challenge dance, countering Hal LeRoy's wiggly steps with airy wing steps. "You're not making it easy," Bates chided as he tossed off heel clicks and soared into a flash finish with trenches (in which the body leans forward on the diagonal and the legs kick high to the back). Bates made more than twenty appearances on the *Ed Sullivan Show*, last appearing in a tap challenge dance with "Little Buck" on 22 August 1965.

While television gave him greater fame than ever before, Bates continued to pursue a variety of performance venues. In 1951 he invested his earnings and, with his wife, Alice, purchased a large turkey farm in New York's Catskill Mountains and converted it into a resort. The date of his marriage to Alice is not known, but the marriage lasted until her death in 1987. They had one child. The Peg Leg Country Club, in Kerhonkson, New York, flourished as the largest resort in the country that was owned and operated by a black person, and it catered to a largely black clientele and featured hundreds of jazz musicians and tap dancers. "During the prejudice years, country clubs were not integrated," said Bates, "and I started thinking how blacks might like to have a country resort just like any other race of people." After selling the property in 1989, Bates continued to perform and teach. He appeared before youth groups, senior citizens, and handicapped groups, spreading his philosophy of being involved in spite of life's adversities and encouraging youngsters to be drug-free and pursue an education. "Life means, do the best you can with what you've got, with all your mind and heart. You can do anything in this world if you want to do it bad enough," he often said.

Bates's tap dancing was melodically and rhythmically enhanced by the combination of his deep-toned peg, made of leather and tipped with rubber, with the higher-pitched metallic tap shoe. He was also accomplished in acrobatics, flash dancing (that is, executing spectacularly difficult steps involving virtuosic aerial maneuvers), and novelty dancing. He consistently proved himself beyond his peg-legged specialty, surpassing many two-legged dancers to become one of the finest rhythm dancers in the history of tap dancing.

In 1992 Bates was master of ceremonies at the National Tap Dance Day celebration in Albany, New York, where he received a Distinguished Leadership in the Arts award. In 1991 Bates was honored with the Flo-Bert Award by the New

York Committee to Celebrate National Tap Dance Day. Bates died in Fountain Inn, South Carolina, just a mile and a half from the place where he lost his leg.

FURTHER READING
Hill, Constance Valis. "Tap Day to Receive a Peg Leg Flourish." *Albany Times Union*, 22 May 1992.
Frank, Rusty. *Tap! The Greatest Tap Dance Stars and Their Stories, 1900–1955* (1990, 1994).
Obituary: *New York Times*, 8 Dec. 1998.

This entry is taken from the *American National Biography* and is published here with the permission of the American Council of Learned Societies.

CONSTANCE VALIS HILL

Bath, Patricia (4 November 1942–), doctor of ophthalmology, inventor, medical researcher, and advocate for social equity in health care, was born in Harlem, New York, the daughter of Rupert and Gladys Bath. A one-time merchant marine and global traveler, her father emigrated from Trinidad, taking a position as the first black motorman for the New York City subways, and her mother, a descendant of African slaves and Cherokee Indians, Bath tells her biographers, "was a housewife who worked as a domestic after we entered middle school. … She scrubbed floors so I could go to medical school" (Davidson). A brilliant student, Bath attended New York's Charles Evans Hughes High School and in 1959 was selected for a National Science Foundation summer program at Yeshiva University. Working on a cancer research team, Bath demonstrated the future potential of her work in science and medicine and was recognized as one of *Mademoiselle* magazine's Merit Award winners in 1960.

Bath graduated, in 1964, with highest honors from Hunter College in New York City, receiving her bachelor's degree in Chemistry and Physics. A year later, when she entered Howard University's medical school, she was awarded fellowships by the National Institutes of Health and the National Institute of Mental Health. During the summer of 1967 Bath researched children's health in Yugoslavia, and in 1968 she served as medical coordinator for MARTIN LUTHER KING JR.'s Poor People's Campaign, which sponsored a mass march on Washington, D.C., to bring needed attention to poverty in America. Both experiences enhanced Bath's commitment to international medicine and equitable health care. After completing her

medical degree with honors, Bath returned to New York to pursue more specialized medical training. Between 1968 and 1973 she completed an internship at Harlem Hospital (1968–1969) and was the first African American resident training in ophthalmology and corneal transplant at Columbia University (1969–1970) and New York University (1970–1973). While completing postgraduate work at Columbia, she married, and in 1972 she had a daughter, Eraka.

While interning at Harlem Hospital, Bath observed that, while half the patients at the Harlem Hospital eye clinic were blind or visually impaired, she saw very few blind patients at Columbia. To test her observation, Bath conducted a study and found that the rate of blindness among blacks was indeed twice that among whites. Concluding that blacks lacked access to adequate eye care, Bath initiated what she called Community Ophthalmology, training volunteers to visit underserved people at day care and senior centers to provide eye exams and identify and treat eye problems. Community Ophthalmology and providing eye care for the underserved would remain one of Patricia Bath's lifelong concerns and ambitions.

Bath and her daughter moved to Los Angeles in 1974 so that she could join the faculties of UCLA and Charles R. Drew University as assistant professor of surgery and ophthalmology. After just one year, she became the first woman faculty member in the Department of Ophthalmology at UCLA's Jules Stein Eye Institute. In 1977 Bath traveled to Nigeria and became the chief of ophthalmology at Mercy Hospital. Between 1977 and 1978 she was on the White House Council for National and International Blindness Prevention Program, and by 1983 she cofounded and chaired the ophthalmology residency training program at Drew/UCLA—becoming the first woman in the country to hold such a position. Between 1976 and 1978 Bath and three colleagues founded the American Institute for the Prevention of Blindness (AIPB), which is funded through donations of time from surgeons and donations of equipment from manufacturers. An international organization, the AIPB aims to provide eye care to people who otherwise would not be able to afford it, including making preventive medicines and treatment available to children.

In the 1980s Bath began developing a new technology to be used in the surgical removal of cataracts. Almost everyone who lives long enough will eventually develop cataracts, one of the leading causes of blindness. For years surgeons removed cataracts and replaced them with artificial lenses, but the traditional surgery was highly invasive. Bath became convinced that a laser could be used to remove cataracts more accurately and less invasively. Despite discouragement and difficulties, Bath persisted, doing much of her research in Germany so that she could work with the most advanced medical laser equipment available and expedite the inventive process. Ultimately successful in designing a laser probe, she applied for a United States patent in 1986. Her first patent, number 4,744,360, was issued two years later for an instrument known as the laserphacoprobe, which uses a powerful beam of light to break up and destroy the cataract. Continuing to improve her invention—which began to be used throughout the country and the world—Bath eventually received three more patents in the United States, and she also holds patents in Japan, Canada, and five European countries. Bath was the first African American woman doctor to receive a patent for a medical invention.

When she retired in 1993, Bath became the first woman elected to the UCLA Medical Center's honorary medical staff, but her global advocacy for the extension of eye care to the poor and underserved was only beginning. She became a pioneer in the field of telemedicine, which uses electronic communications to provide medical services to remote areas where people have limited access to health care. While holding positions in telemedicine at Howard University Hospital and at St. George's University in Grenada, she served as a consultant to an Internet firm, eBioCare.com and continued to direct the AIPB.

Dr. Bath's medical innovations, including her patented laser equipment and new methodologies for removing cataracts, as well as the organizational changes she has brought to eye care through Community Ophthalmology and the American Institute for the Prevention of Blindness, have saved the vision of thousands around the globe. Her career has been marked by firsts both for women and for African Americans. Bath's contributions to science, medical technology, and socially conscious health care in the second half of the twentieth century cannot be overstated. She was elected to the Hunter College Hall of Fame in 1988 and was named a Howard University Pioneer of Academic Medicine in 1993.

FURTHER READING

Davidson, Martha. "The Right to Sight: Patricia Bath," Lemelson Center Invention Features, Smithsonian Institution (March 2005). Available online at http://invention.smithsonian.org/centerpieces/ilives/bath/bath.html

Sullivan, Otha Richard. *Black Stars: African American Women Scientists and Inventors* (2001).

PAMELA C. EDWARDS

Batson, Flora (16 Apr. 1864–1 Dec. 1906), singer, was born in Washington, D.C. Though her father's name is unknown, evidence suggests that he was a Union soldier. After her father died from injuries sustained during the Civil War, Batson moved with her mother, Mary Batson, to Providence, Rhode Island. She attended school and studied music in Providence; by the age of nine she was a featured soloist at Bethel Church as well as at other local churches in the Rhode Island and Boston, Massachusetts, region.

Batson's professional career began to blossom at a time when several black women were achieving renown as classically trained singers. Nellie Brown Mitchell, SISSIERETTA JONES, MARIE SELIKA—all classical singers and contemporaries of Batson—stood in stark contrast to the Jim Crow stereotypes that prevailed in a nation only recently rid of institutionalized slavery. In the early 1880s Batson was the featured soloist at People's Church in Boston. She also toured with Redpath's Lecture Lyceum Bureau, a popular booking agency in the Boston area, sang for Storer's College at Harpers Ferry, West Virginia, and beginning in 1883 became a featured singer with the temperance movement while under the management of Thomas Doutney.

In 1883 Batson came to the attention of James G. Bergen (named in some sources as Col. John Bergen), the owner of the Bergen Star Concert Company (sometimes called the Tennessee Star Concert Company). Bergen was known for promoting black talent in New England during the late 1800s, and his roster of artists included Sidney Woodward, Sissieretta Jones, Nellie Brown Mitchell, Carrie Melvin, and HARRY T. BURLEIGH. Bergen, who was white, also had a romantic interest in Batson, and although sources disagree on exactly when the nuptials occurred (the most oft-cited dates are the year 1885 and 13 December 1887), the two were married until 1896. Unusual for the time, their consensual, interracial union was covered by newspapers in the United States and abroad.

Batson's relationship with James Bergen and the Bergen Star Concert Company positioned her for international renown. Her major appearances during this period include her performance with Adelaide Smith and Sam Lucas at New York City's Steinway Hall in 1885 and her triumphant Philadelphia debut during that same year. The watershed moment of Batson's career came when she stepped in at the last minute to substitute for Nellie Brown Mitchell, who up until that point had been the leading soprano of the Bergen Company. A scheduling conflict prevented Mitchell from appearing at a concert in Providence, and Batson, singing in her stead, received rave reviews. From that point in 1885 Batson became the undisputed star of Bergen's Concert Company.

By 1887 Batson had become nationally known and the press had dubbed her the "Double-voiced Queen of Song" because of her vocal range, which extended from baritone to soprano. Her repertoire, equally broad in its range, included concert and operatic selections, dramatic pieces, ballads, and popular songs. She was most often requested to sing ballads such as "The Last Rose of Summer" and "The Cows Are in the Corn." The public frequently expressed its affection for her with necklaces, crowns, earrings, and other bejeweled gifts. Batson took pride in wearing these during her performances, and an extant portrait published in several sources shows her adorned in her trademark jewels and tiara.

While black prima donnas of the late nineteenth century enjoyed wide acclaim, they also endured a press that frequently compared them to their white counterparts. In newspapers, Batson was dubbed the "colored Jenny Lind" after the world-famous Swedish coloratura soprano who dominated the concert stage in the 1850s. The press also called Batson the "Patti of her race," a comparison to Adelina Patti, the Italian-born prima donna who came to fame in the late 1800s. Because these comparisons were so commonplace, it no doubt created confusion since another black singer and contemporary of Batson's, Sissieretta Jones, was also widely known as "the Black Patti."

Batson made no fewer than three world tours throughout the course of her career. She traveled to Europe, China, Japan, Africa, Great Britain, Australia, India, Fiji, and New Zealand. She sang for numerous dignitaries and crowned heads of state including Queen Victoria of Great Britain, Pope Leo XIII, the royal family of New Zealand, and Queen Lili'uokalani of Hawaii.

In 1896 Batson's relationship with James Bergen and the Bergen Star Concert Company came to an end. Sources differ, however, as to the exact reasons for this dissolution. Some sources claim that Batson herself severed their relationship, while others suggest that Bergen's death occurred at about this time. In either case, Batson signed with a new manager in 1896, Gerard Millar, who was an African American basso.

Batson and Millar toured and performed together and were the featured duo in the South Before the War Company. The two also sang with the Orpheus McAdoo Minstrels and Vaudeville Company, a career change indicative of the public's increasing appetite for popular and comedic forms of entertainment during the years surrounding the turn of the twentieth century. Batson and Millar were eventually married. Soon after her death, Millar published *Life, Travels, and Works of Miss Flora Batson, Deceased Queen of Song.*

Although she turned to vaudeville during the later years of her career, Batson favored performing for churches and charitable causes until the end of her life. A deeply religious woman, she gave her last concert at Bethel African Methodist Episcopal Church in Philadelphia. At the time of her sudden death in Philadelphia, Flora Batson was considered one of the leading singers of her time.

FURTHER READING

Live, Travels, and Works of Miss Flora Batson, Deceased Queen of Song (1906?) is part of the Music Collection of the Boston Public Library. Copies are also available at the Library of Congress and at Brown University.

Southern, Eileen. "Flora Batson Bergen," in *Biographical Dictionary of Afro-Americans and African Musicians* (1982).

Story, Rosalyn. *And So I Sing: African American Divas of Opera and Concert* (1990).

Wright, Josephine. "Black Women in Classical Music in Boston during the Late Nineteenth Century: Profiles of Leadership," in *New Perspectives on Music: Essays in Honor of Eileen Southern* (1992).

TERESA L. REED

Battey, Cornelius Marion (C. M.) (26 Aug. 1873–1927), photographer and educator, was born in Augusta, Georgia, to Florida and Robert Battey, both laborers. He was living in New York City by his late teens and had become one of the most famous African American photographers in the country by 1900, although nothing is known about his educational background. In 1900 Battey married Anna H. Stokes, who gave birth to two daughters, Edyphe F. (born 1901) and Antoinette (born 1908). Affiliated with studios in Cleveland and New York, his primary base, he enjoyed a lucrative career as a studio and commercial photographer with a respected reputation among Americans and Europeans. He was superintendent of the Bradley Studio in New York with such clientele as Sir Thomas Lipton and Prince Henry of Prussia, and was a partner in Battey and Warren Studio in the city.

Battey made classic photogravure portraits of the Tuskegee Normal and Industrial Institute founder and president BOOKER T. WASHINGTON, c. 1890 and 1908; the statesman and abolitionist leader and publisher FREDERICK DOUGLASS, c. 1895; the educator and Virginia congressman JOHN MERCER LANGSTON, c. 1890; the poet PAUL LAURENCE DUNBAR, c. 1905; and the scholar W. E. B. DU BOIS, 1908, along with numerous other statesmen, writers, performers, and national leaders. A selection from this body of portraiture of distinguished male figures was published in *Our Heroes of Destiny*, later titled *Our Master Minds*. He also photographed Margaret Murray, Washington's wife in 1914. The same year, he created a tender portrayal of his second wife, *"You"—Portrait of Mrs. C. M. Battey*, inscribed with the following: "Where the Birth of Love Was First Drawn / Into the Rosy, Reluctant Auroras of Life" and "This is a character / sketch of *my* Pal taken / by her husband."

In 1905 Booker T. Washington petitioned George Eastman, one of the institution's benefactors, to finance a chair in photography that would be a catalyst for student creative development toward professional art careers as well as provide technical training and a staff post for institutional documentation. Eastman agreed to provide funds, and Battey was offered the position. He appeared well educated and was reputed for his integrity, work ethic, and high standards. Battey stood out further as being a member of an elite group of photographers who succeeded at multitasking across the spectrum of photographic branches, techniques, and subjects.

Battey and first wife, Anna, had divorced by the fall of 1910, and soon after he married the photographer Elizabeth Rahn, with whom he had two children, a daughter Muriel (born in 1908) and a son Champlin (born 1911).

Battey arrived on Tuskegee's campus in January 1917, two years after Washington's death and during the presidential term of Washington's successor, ROBERT RUSSA MOTON, who offered only lukewarm support to the board-initiated program. As head of the photography division, Battey was the official photographer for the Institute as well as chair and instructor of the photography curriculum. Needing students to jump-start the department, he embarked upon a recruitment campaign. He seized the opportunity at a Tuskegee "Men's Meeting" (a male convocation), during which he announced his pilot course and encouraged those with an artistic temperament to visit his office the following day. PRENTICE HERMAN POLK, an evening student at the time, was the first to respond. Polk became his best-known student, having a distinguished career as a portrait photographer and assuming the leadership of the division at Tuskegee, where he also served as the official photographer for fifty years.

Battey produced sensitive portrayals of the campus community, placing particular artistic emphasis on the treatment of classroom scenes, student activities, and college rituals. In his first year he photographed the commencement ceremony by depicting it as a regal processional of young men in dark suits and hats and parasol-carrying young women wearing floor-length white gowns. He made equally sensitive photographs of well-dressed, poised, and attentive students engaged in various course instructions, posed in the gardens, and gathered outside buildings between sessions. One of his famous student subjects was WILLIAM LEVI DAWSON, who went on to organize the School of Music at Tuskegee in 1931. Battey's photographs of campus dignitaries, important visitors, various structures, the Tuskegee band, and other scenes in Macon County, Alabama, contributed to the comprehensive nature of his work as the official photographer. Battey headed up the program until his death in 1927.

Ellie Lee Weems and Elise Forrest Harleston were among the students who, like Polk, went on to have exemplary careers in the field. Weems, a fellow Georgian, operated a studio in Atlanta and later in Jacksonville, Florida. Harleston, from Charleston, South Carolina, was encouraged by the genre and portrait painter EDWIN AUGUSTUS HARLESTON, her future husband, to study further under Battey. She later opened a studio in Charleston.

The recipient of awards in American and European galleries, Battey was featured in the NAACP's *Crisis* magazine in 1917 and did cover photographs for *The Crisis*, the National Urban League publication *Opportunity Journal*, and *The Tuskegee Messenger*. At the time of his death, Battey was in the process of inventorying, packing, and shipping his negatives to South Carolina where he had planned to retire.

FURTHER READING

Battey photographs are in the collections of Tuskegee University in Tuskegee, Alabama; Library of Congress in Washington, D.C.; and Schomburg Center for Research in Black Culture in New York City.

Appiah, Kwame Anthony, and Henry Louis Gates Jr. *Africana: The Encyclopedia of the African and African American Experience* (1999).

Willis, Deborah. *Reflections in Black: A History of Black Photographers 1840 to the Present* (2000).

AMALIA K. AMAKI

Battey, Earl (5 Jan. 1935–15 Nov. 2003), baseball player, was born Earl Jesse Battey Jr. in Los Angeles, California, to Esther (maiden name unknown) and Earl Battey Sr. His parents—particularly Esther who, from 1938 to 1948, was a catcher on women's softball teams such as the Watts All-Stars, the Ebonettes, and the MacAfee All-Stars—encouraged him to play baseball as a youngster. As a freshman at Los Angeles's Jordan High School, Battey made the team, only to sit the bench for the first six games of the season as a backup outfielder. When the starting catcher split his finger during a game, however, coach Norm Forester looked to Battey, his only nonpitcher left on the twelve-man roster, to fill in. Battey turned out to be so good as catcher that he kept the position even after the previous catcher recovered. At six feet, one inch tall and 205 pounds, the thick, slow-footed Battey was a natural for his position, with a powerful arm that he attributed to practicing with a punching bag. While in high school Battey developed his skills by playing for an adult men's team, the Watts Giants, against such future major leaguers as Duke Snider, Bob Lemon, and Irv Noren. He was also aided by the coaching of his uncle, Clifford Prelow, a former Brooklyn Dodgers prospect, and BIZ MACKEY, a former Negro League catcher and manager who moved to Los Angeles when Major League Baseball's integration precipitated the dissolution of the Newark Eagles.

While in high school Battey was better known as a basketball player than as a baseball player. After graduating in 1953, however, he turned down offers from the Harlem Globetrotters and UCLA to sign with the Chicago White Sox. His early years in baseball presented several major challenges, both professional and personal. Arriving for spring training in Florida in 1954, Battey encountered overt segregation and racism for the first time when he was prevented from eating in white restaurants or attending jazz concerts with whites. Though he took these injustices in stride, at other times his temper was problematic. For instance, that season he punched the opposing team's catcher, incurring a fine of two hundred dollars. Professionally, Battey spent his time in the White Sox organization frustrated and undervalued. Elevated to the major leagues for five games at the end of the 1955 season, he returned for only four the next, spending most of 1956 in the minor leagues at Toronto and part of 1957 with Los Angeles of the Pacific Coast League.

Battey established himself as Chicago's backup catcher in 1957, though he batted only .174 in forty-eight games and improved only slightly over sixty-eight games the next season. Battey handled his backup role positively, using his time to study the game and work with Hall of Fame manager and catcher Al Lopez on improving defensively. "I never got discouraged," he said later. "It's different sitting on the bench for a contender than it would be for a second-division club" (Baseball Hall of Fame file). Indeed, in 1959 the White Sox reached the World Series, only to lose to the relocated Los Angeles Dodgers in six games. They did so with little help from Battey, who logged only twenty-six games while batting .219 and was the only Chicago player not to play in the World Series.

In 1960 Battey was traded to the Washington Senators. He was initially dismayed to leave the American League's championship team for its last-place team. Yet Washington's haplessness provided him with the opportunity to play every day. When he arrived in Washington it was clear that he had much work to do. According to Senators coach Clyde McCullough, a former major league catcher himself, "When we first got Battey he was raw as a pound of uncooked hamburger." But after 1960, a season in which Battey hit .270 with 15 home runs over 137 games as the starting catcher, McCullough could say that "from a mechanical standpoint he's the best [catcher] in baseball" (*Los Angeles Times*, 17 Feb. 1961). Manager Cookie Lavagetto even credited Battey with being the driving force behind Washington's climb from eighth to fifth place in the American League.

Battey soon established himself as the most dependable catcher in baseball, catching more games in the first half of the 1960s than anyone else and playing at least 131 games in every season. His record during this time is incredible considering the daunting string of injuries that he suffered, including dislocated fingers, chronic knee problems, two broken cheekbones, and a goiter that helped make him sixty pounds heavier than his officially listed playing weight. During the 1965 World Series he ran neck-first into an overhanging crossbar at Dodger Stadium while chasing a pop foul. Unable to speak above a whisper or turn his neck to the left, he nevertheless played effectively in the remaining four games of the series, throwing out five would-be base stealers, including the great MAURY WILLS twice.

The Washington Senators relocated prior to the 1961 season, becoming the Minnesota Twins. "I like it here," Battey commented on his new home. "People are friendly, business opportunities are good and I can't think of a better place to play ball" (Baseball Hall of Fame file). He thrived in Minnesota, hitting a career high. 302 in 1961. Despite trade rumors the following season, Battey continued to excel at and behind the plate, foiling twenty-four would-be base stealers and picking off thirteen runners. As a result he won his third consecutive Gold Glove and earned his first of four appearances at the All-Star game over the next five years. In 1965 Battey garnered the most votes of any American League All-Star, picked at the time by fellow ballplayers.

The acclamation of his colleagues represented the respect with which Battey was regarded, both as a player and as a person. With his sharp sense of humor and friendly demeanor Battey became one of the most popular players in the Minnesota clubhouse. Teammate Tony Oliva later recalled, "When I came into the league as a rookie, I spoke little English. But he spoke Spanish and he helped me out. … He took me under his wing" (*Star-Tribune*, 18 Nov. 2003).

After a 1964 season in which many speculated that he was washed up, Battey fought through thirteen separate injuries to bat .297 over 131 games, finish tenth in the Most Valuable Player voting, and help lead the Twins to the World Series. Despite his strong defensive performance in that series, Battey hit only .120 in the Twins' seven-game loss. Looking back at the end of his career, Battey stated, "What I remember most is the 1965 season, the World Series and all that—I guess that was the best thing that ever happened to me in baseball" (Baseball Hall of Fame file).

After the 1965 season Battey's fortunes were in clear descent. Off the field, in January 1966 he was sentenced to five days in jail for failing to file state income tax returns from 1961 to 1964. Nearly two years later he was fined one thousand dollars and was put on three years of probation for nonpayment of federal income taxes during that time. On the field his production dwindled to only .255 over 115 games in 1966. He retired in 1967 after playing only forty-eight games and batting a meager .165. Despondent over a bright career cut short by injuries, he sat at his locker after his final game repeating, "What a way to go." After clearing up his legal troubles in late 1967 he announced plans to return for the 1969 season, but they never materialized.

Battey's life after baseball was dedicated to helping children. After working during his baseball days as a sports and physical fitness promoter for General Mills, he became the baseball consultant for Consolidated Edison in 1968. The position entailed accompanying five thousand poor children to forty games at Yankee Stadium or Shea Stadium, at which he would answer questions over a loudspeaker concerning baseball strategy. Despite the significant cut in pay that this role required, Battey commented, "It's worth it. I always enjoyed working with children" (Baseball Hall of Fame file). He held his position for twenty-three years before coaching the Bethune Cookman College baseball team in Daytona Beach, Florida, from 1980 to 1982. While coaching there he earned a degree, and then he moved on to coach high school baseball and teach special education in Ocala, Florida. Battey also served as a scout for the Seattle Mariners during this time.

In 2000 Battey was named the all-time greatest catcher in Minnesota Twins history. Until his death from cancer on 15 November 2003 he continued to follow baseball avidly. According to A. J. Pierzynski, Minnesota's starting catcher at the time, "All he wanted to talk about was baseball. He was so ill, but all he wanted to do was talk about baseball" (*Pioneer Press*, 18 Nov. 2003). Battey left behind a wife, Sonia, and five children, as well as a legacy of greatness as a player and a man. As former teammate and Hall of Famer Harmon Killebrew said, "He was the best catcher I ever played with. Few realize how great a player he was. He was a leader on and off the field. He was a first-class guy" (*Star Tribune*, 18 Nov. 2003).

FURTHER READING

There is a file with information on and interviews with Earl Battey at the National Baseball Hall of Fame Library, Cooperstown, New York.

Shatzkin, Mike, ed. *The Ballplayers* (1990).

Thorn, John, and Pete Palmer, eds. *Total Baseball* (1989).

Obituaries: *Saint Paul Pioneer Press* and *Minneapolis Star-Tribune*, 18 Nov. 2003.

CHRISTOPHER DEVINE

Battle, Effie Dean Threat (12 Mar. 1881–3 July 1963), educator, poet, and community activist, was born in Okolona, Chickasaw County, Mississippi, the only child of former slaves Mary Johnson Threat and George W. Threat. Though illiterate, her mother understood the value of education. She took in laundry and sold eggs and vegetables to save for her daughter's education. After completing studies at the Okolona Public School in 1894, Battle continued her education at Rust College in Holly Springs, Mississippi, graduating with an AB degree in 1900. She was teaching away from home when she learned that WALLACE BATTLE had come to Okolona to establish an industrial school. Although she was in line to become principal of a Greenwood, Mississippi, school she chose to return home in 1902 to help with the development of the Okolona Industrial School. She married the school's founder the following year. They had five children.

Along with her role as the wife of the president of Okolona Industrial School, Battle taught math. She also devoted time to writing poetry, some of which was published in newspapers and magazines, and which was sometimes used to raise funds for the school when she traveled north to do readings. Battle's love of writing poetry led to the publication of a well-received, eighteen-page volume of ten of her poems under the title *Gleanings from Dixie Land in Ten Poems* (c. 1914).

When her husband took a leave in 1925 and subsequently resigned from the presidency of Okolona Industrial School in 1927, Battle assumed the position of acting president. She operated the school in that capacity until 1933, when a permanent replacement was named. Although she was offered the position of dean of the Teacher Training School, she decided that she could not continue at the school in a subordinate position.

After her departure from Okolona, Battle relocated to the Bedford-Stuyvesant and later Crown Heights sections of Brooklyn, New York. Her poetry continued to win her renown as she did readings and was published in newspapers. Her poem "June" was published in *Modern American Poetry* by Galleon Press in 1934. Battle's earlier work, *Gleanings From Dixie Land in Ten Poems*, received praise from JAMES WELDON JOHNSON, author of the *Autobiography of an Ex-Colored Man* (1912). After receiving a copy of her collection in 1934, he informed Battle that he was placing it in the Francis Collection, a collection for private use by his classes in creative literature at Fisk University. In August 1937 she received a monetary award when she won first prize in a poetry contest on radio station WHN in New York. "Going to See the President," an illustrated poem, was included in an exhibit at the 1939 World's Fair called *The Big Book of Poetry*, presented by the National Poetry Center, Radio City, New York. Battle also participated in church and other programs for which she held poetry readings and spoke about the experiences she and her husband had as educators and school administrators in the South. She kept abreast of conditions at Okolona Industrial School and regularly participated in its annual Founder's Day program.

Battle was an early member of the Women's Service League of Brooklyn, an organization founded in the 1930s by ADDIE HUNTON, a former YWCA official and club woman activist. The organization was dedicated to promoting an active interest in the civic and social problems of the black community and of black women in particular. During the years that she was a member, Battle served the organization as corresponding secretary, recording secretary, and historian.

Battle died in Brooklyn. In 1996 her book of poetry, *Gleanings from Dixie Land*, was republished as part of a collection titled *Six Poets of Racial Uplift*, with an introduction by Gayle Pemberton.

JOANNE H. EDEY-RHODES

Battle, Kathleen (13 Aug. 1948–), lyric coloratura soprano, was the youngest of seven children born in Portsmouth, Ohio, to Grady Battle, a steelworker from Alabama who belonged to a gospel quartet, and Ollie Layne Battle.

Together with her six older siblings, Kathleen Deanna Battle experienced the gospel music of her African Methodist Episcopal Church from a very early age. Battle studied at Portsmouth High School with Charles Varney and began piano lessons at the age of twelve.

She considered using her National Achievement Scholarship, which she was awarded in 1966, to study mathematics at the University of Cincinnati, but she graduated instead from the University of Cincinnati's College Conservatory of Music with

Kathleen Battle, performing at the opening gala for the Muhammad Ali Center in Louisville, Kentucky, 19 November 2005. (AP Images.)

a degree in music education in 1970. The following year, Battle received a master's degree from the same institution. After graduation, Battle worked as a music teacher for fifth- and sixth-graders in a Cincinnati inner-city school for two years. While teaching, she continued to audition as a performer, and in 1972 Thomas Schippers, conductor of the Cincinnati Symphony, selected Battle to sing at Italy's Spoleto Festival of Two Worlds, where she sang Brahms's *German Requiem*. The performance received unanimous commendation and served as a career watershed. Confident, she began to appear with the best American and European orchestras. In 1974 the conductor James Levine chose her to sing the "Mater Glorioso" in Mahler's eighth symphony at Cincinnati's May Festival, an event that began a long-lasting professional association. Battle then went to New York to work as an understudy for Carmen Balthrop, who had the leading role in Scott Joplin's *Treemonisha*. In 1975 she made her debut at the New York City Opera as Susanna in Mozart's *The Marriage of Figaro*, and two years later Battle first appeared at the Metropolitan Opera under Levine's direction as the Shepherd in Richard Wagner's *Tannhäuser*. Critics acclaimed her performances and praised her voice, which maintained its integrity at both ends of a two-and-one-half octave range, from low A to high E. Her successful New York debut established her as one of the Metropolitan's favorite artists. She also sang in the best opera houses around the world and worked with internationally renowned directors. Battle attained star status

with supporting roles that usually did not produce divas, such as Zerlina in Mozart's *Don Giovanni* and Sophie in Richard Strauss's *Der Rosenkavalier*. While she particularly specialized in Mozart roles, her repertoire was diverse, and included Baroque music and African American spirituals. In spite of being one of the few African Americans in a predominantly white milieu (she shared this lonely status with LEONTYNE PRICE and JESSYE NORMAN), Battle's presence in a cast became a guarantee of success.

The recipient of several honorary degrees from, among other institutions, her alma mater, the University of Cincinnati; Westminster Choir College in Princeton, New Jersey; Ohio University; Xavier University in Cincinnati; Amherst College; and Seton Hall University. She was also a five-time Grammy Award winner: 1986 Best Classical Soloist Performance for *Kathleen Battle Sings Mozart*, 1987 Best Opera Recording for Richard Strauss's *Ariadne Auf Naxos*, 1987 Best Classical Soloist Performance for *Kathleen Battle—Salzburg Recital*, 1992 Best Classical Vocal Performance for *Kathleen Battle at Carnegie Hall*, and 1993 Best Opera Recording for Handel's *Semele*. Battle often teamed up with the most distinguished artists of her time. She appeared in concert with conductors such as Herbert von Karajan, Riccardo Muti, Seiji Ozawa, Claudio Abbado, Sir Georg Solti, Lorin Maazel, and Sir Neville Marriner. She performed with tenors Luciano Pavarotti and Plácido Domingo, violinist Itzhak Perlman, trumpeter WYNTON MARSALIS, and saxophonist GROVER WASHINGTON JR. These partnerships were documented on numerous CD recordings, many of which were bestsellers. In 1984 Battle performed Mozart's "Coronation" Mass, conducted by Herbert von Karajan in the Vatican. In spite of her success, Battle always sought new challenges. In 1988 she accepted the role of Cleopatra in the first Met production of Handel's *Julius Caesar*, a difficult and almost unknown opera.

Yet with success Battle also acquired a reputation for being difficult and a perfectionist. She enraged managers across the globe and cancelled events at the last moment because she felt her requests had not been satisfied. In 1993, for example, she walked out of a Met production of *Der Rosenkavalier* over disagreements with the conductor Christian Thielemann. Battle was as loved by audiences as she was dreaded by the people who worked backstage and by some of her colleagues. This aspect of her personality received particular public attention in 1994 when she was fired from the Met production of Donizetti's *La Fille du Régiment* for acting unprofessionally. The termination ensued after Battle's insistent complaints against one of her co-stars. All future Met offers also were withdrawn, a decision that drew nearly unanimous consensus from opera house managers around the world. Scores of media articles portrayed Battle as fussy and unreliable, or, at best, as an apparent example of the insecurities that beset opera singers. Nevertheless, Battle emerged undamaged and her recording and recitals remained popular. Her fees for recitals exceeded forty thousand dollars per event. Her opera appearances in the United States became a rarity, however.

Battle's dismissal from the Metropolitan prompted the artist to expand her repertoire to more accessible material. Before then, Battle had made only one brief foray outside classical music for a 1993 duet with pop superstar Janet Jackson. Battle's newer focus on popular music, including gospel material, Gershwin songs, Vangelis's theme music for NASA's Mission to Mars program, folk songs, and lullabies, led her to record crossover albums such as *So Many Stars* (1995), *Grace* (1997), and *Classic Battle: A Portrait* (2002). Mixing classic arias, sacred music, and popular songs, these works have been instant successes. In 2000 Battle's voice was featured in the update of the Disney classic *Fantasia*, in the segment entitled "Pomp and Circumstance," and in 2004 she sang on the soundtrack of Zhang Yimou's *House of Flying Daggers*. Although Battle did not often talk about racial matters, in 1995 she recorded *Honey and Rue*, a song cycle about the African American experience, which she commissioned from composer André Previn and Nobel Prize winner TONI MORRISON. In 1999 she was inducted into the NAACP Image Hall of Fame.

FURTHER READING

Pniewski, Tom. "Bravo Battle," *World and I* (Aug. 1998).

Story, Rosalyn. *And So I Sing: African-American Divas of Opera and Concert* (1990).

DISCOGRAPHY

Classic Battle: A Portrait (Sony, 2002).

Grace (Sony, 1997).

So Many Stars (Sony, 1995).

Bel Canto: Italian Opera Arias (Deutsche Grammophon, 1993).

Baroque Duets (Sony, 1992).

LUCA PRONO

Battle, Wallace Aaron, Sr. (10 May 1872–6 Sept. 1946), educator, industrial school founder, and Episcopal Church school field secretary, was born in Hurtsboro, Russell County, Alabama, one of thirteen children of former slaves, Jeanetta (Redden) and Augustus Battle Sr.

Battle's parents sent him to the district school when he was eight years old. He had not progressed far in his education when, at the age of sixteen, he joined his older brother, Augustus Aaron Battle Jr., and two sisters at Talladega College in Talladega, Alabama. Only prepared to enter the third grade, he attended class with eight-year-olds. Wallace was so determined to move forward in his education that he completed three grades in one year. He remained in attendance at Talladega College from 1889 to 1898. In the later years of his college preparatory studies there, he taught during the summers at Duke Station, Calhoun County, Alabama. He also became involved with teaching in Mission Sunday Schools that were set up for the poor some distance from Talladega. It was during the course of this experience that he set his goal of establishing an industrial school. Soon after entering Talladega's freshman college class, Battle decided to leave Talladega for Berea College in Berea, Kentucky.

Founded in 1855 by John G. Fee, Berea was the first interracial and co-educational college in the South. It was based on the philosophy of promoting understanding and kinship among all people. The school had a profound effect on Battle, who sustained himself by working on campus in various capacities, including that of the school's bell ringer, and through small loans from one of his teachers at Talladega. His attention to punctuality gained him recognition on the campus, and when it came time to graduate, he was chosen as one of the speakers. The experience of losing his place in his speech and fumbling his lines taught him to never write a speech to be read but instead to study his subject matter so that the words would come to him as needed. He graduated from Berea in June 1901 with an AB degree and was subsequently awarded an AM degree in 1907. During the course of his life, Battle also attended summer sessions at the Universities of Illinois and Wisconsin and at New York University.

After graduating from Berea, he spent a year helping Augustus Jr. with his work as principal of the Anniston Industrial College in Anniston, Alabama. Battle was in charge of the normal and college preparatory department as well as the industry department. His experience at Anniston helped to prepare him for the founding of his own school in the fall of 1902.

Okolona, a town of 4,000 inhabitants in Chickasaw County, Mississippi, was chosen as the site for the establishment of the school that Battle had conceived of years before. He organized a local board of trustees consisting of six African Americans and two whites. The Okolona Industrial School, later Okolona College, was founded on 2 September 1902 and opened at a church with five teachers and thirty-nine students on 1 October 1902. They moved to the school's permanent site, which initially consisted of a sixty-acre farm, in November of the same year. Within the first nine months, $3,000 was raised and 205 students representing four states and thirty-five towns and cities had been enrolled. The curriculum was made up of a variety of industrial and academic courses.

In 1903, Battle married EFFIE DEAN THREAT BATTLE, a graduate of Rust College. They became the parents of five children, Thelma, Wallace Jr., Marie (Annie Marie), Madelon (Madeline), and another child who died in infancy. Battle's wife assisted him with the development of the school. Over time, Okolona's board expanded to include some prominent members and the school gained recognition and support from a number of private and institutional sources, including Andrew Carnegie and the General Education Board.

Battle authored *the Mississippi Letter*, a quarterly school publication that was distributed around the country. He served as president of the Mississippi State Teacher's Association for four years, and he was the founder and first president of the Welfare League of Okolona. During World War I, Battle acted as a spokesperson on behalf of liberty bonds and sought to boost morale in Mississippi. The school became a Student's Training Camp. His war effort coupled with the rigors of operating the school led to ill health, and Battle became a victim of the flu pandemic. He spent six months recuperating on the Gulf Coast of Mississippi and another three months out of state.

In order to secure the future of the Okolona Industrial School, it was put under the management and ownership of the Protestant Episcopal Church in October 1918 with Battle retaining the presidency. By the time he resigned in 1925, the school's property had increased to 380 acres, with 300 students, twelve buildings, and a value of $250,000. Battle settled on a farm in New Jersey for two years where he taught night school during the winters. In 1927, the Episcopal Church asked him to assume the newly created position of field secretary of the American Church Institute for Negroes. The appointment made him the first African American general staff officer of the National Council of the Episcopal Church. Among his duties was oversight of the church's nine schools and colleges in eight southern states.

In 1932, Battle was awarded a fellowship of $1,500 from the Julius Rosenwald Fund to investigate the possibilities for black immigrants in Brazil. In the same year, he was awarded an honorary LittD degree from his alma mater, Berea College. Battle remained in his position with the Episcopal Church until his retirement in 1940. Between that time and his death in 1946, he spent his retirement years in Chaplin, Connecticut.

Berea honored Battle posthumously on 12 October 2006 with the John G. Fee Award for his distinguished service to his community and his vision of education.

JOANNE H. EDEY-RHODES

Baugh, John (10 Dec. 1949–) linguistics professor, was born in Brooklyn, New York, to Barbara Ardis Goore, an elementary school teacher and principal, and John Gordon Baugh VI, a director of projects at Hughes Aircraft Company in El Segundo, California. Baugh, the eldest of their three children, had an early fascination with language that grew in part from observing the complexity of linguistic differences around him. In due course Baugh decided to focus on linguistics in part because of experiences derived from a familial move in 1958 to Los Angeles. The Baughs relocated to a working-class, multiethnic neighborhood where many residents were learning English as a second language. He was also influenced by later experiences when the family moved to the western San Fernando Valley in 1960, where they were one of the few African American families in a mainly upper-middle-class, white, affluent community.

While attending Chatsworth High School in suburban Los Angeles, California, between 1964 and 1967, Baugh once joined white students in ridiculing the strong southern accent of a math teacher from Alabama; the teacher was white and knew well that many of the affluent white students who populated the school belittled his intellect. That linguistic experience was later reinforced for Baugh across the country in Philadelphia at Temple University; in a public-speaking class, he noticed that most African American and Puerto Rican students got Ds and Fs on their speeches, while the majority of working-class white students received B's and C's. He came to believe that it was because of the linguistic dexterity afforded him by his background that he earned an A in the class. In high school Baugh combined a mathematics major with a minor in auto mechanics. In college he began by studying accounting, but he found the issue of linguistic differences so fascinating that he changed his major to speech and communication, focusing on rhetoric, persuasion, and argumentation.

During this time, Baugh read a now famous article titled "The Logic of Nonstandard English," written by William Labov, who would later be his dissertation supervisor. Labov compared the logical constructs of middle-class African American speech with the nonstandard grammar of teenage gang members and was able to show that from a logical point of view, the teenagers were more coherent semantically than the more educated African Americans. This article, which fascinated Baugh, was his formal introduction to the study of linguistics. Baugh earned his B.A. in Speech and Rhetoric at Temple University in 1972. He then studied at the University of Pennsylvania, earning an M.A. in Linguistics in 1976 and a Ph.D. in Linguistics in 1979. His doctoral dissertation was titled "Linguistic Style Shifting in Black English."

Throughout his academic career, Baugh sought to advance distinguished scholarship of and by people of African descent, beginning with linguistic science, and eventually extending to all academic disciplines in his administrative roles, including traditional studies and preprofessional training in medicine, law, and various professional endeavors. His academic appointments have been in linguistics, as well as the fields of psychology, anthropology, education, English, African American studies, sociology, and foreign language education. A thorough list of his research interests bridges theoretical and applied linguistics, with particular attention to matters of policy and social equity in the fields of education, medicine, and law—fields where fluency in the dominant language has clear social advantages. Some of his research explores the ways that linguistic variation reinforces social stratification in the United States, Austria, Brazil, Hungary, South Africa, and the United Kingdom. His work also examines the evolution and dissemination of English and other European languages in postcolonial contexts worldwide, particularly with respect to linguistic profiling—discrimination based on the sound of an individual's voice regarding various traits, such as race, sex, age, sexual orientation, region, and class in advanced industrialized societies.

While completing his graduate studies, Baugh worked as a lecturer and assistant professor at Swarthmore College in Pennsylvania from 1975 to 1979. In 1980 he began teaching at the University of Texas at Austin as an assistant professor and later as an associate professor with appointments in linguistics, anthropology, and foreign language education. He was a visiting scholar at the Center for Applied Linguistics in Washington, D.C., during the 1982–1983 academic year. In 1983 Baugh married Charla Larrimore; they had three children, Chenoa, John, and Ariel, and later two grandchildren—Braden and Brynja.

During the 1988–1989 academic year, Baugh was a research fellow at the Center for Advanced Study in the Behavioral Sciences in Stanford, California, and in 1990 he became a professor at Stanford University in Palo Alto, California, with appointments in education and linguistics. It was there that Baugh conducted research on what had become his most famous study, leading to the creation of the term "linguistic profiling." When Baugh had first arrived in Palo Alto to begin his time at the Center for Advanced Study in the Behavioral Sciences, he noticed a disturbing trend as he was trying to find a place to live. When he telephoned a landlord about an available rental property, he was often invited to look at it, but when the landlords saw him in person, they told him there must have been a mistake; no places were available. Baugh concluded that his identity as an African American had been concealed over the telephone. His resulting research eventually led him to detailed exploration of what he came to call linguistic profiling. In 2002 the Ford Foundation provided Baugh with a three-year, $500,000 grant.

Baugh received many honors and awards throughout his career. In addition to receiving various research and teaching awards, he was principal investigator, National Science Foundation: Linguistic Diversity, Literacy and Related Consequences for Human Health and Environmental Change (1991–1993). The U.S. Department of Housing and Urban Development named him Pioneer of Fair Housing, in support of advancing civil rights nationally (2004). Baugh is the author of numerous scholarly articles, including publications in *American Speech, Annual Review of Anthropology, Du Bois Review,* and *Journal of English Linguistics.* He also contributed to a number of books on Black English. His authored books include *Beyond Ebonics: Linguistic*

Pride and Racial Prejudice (2000), *Out of the Mouths of Slaves: African American Language and Educational Malpractice* (1999), and *Black Street Speech: Its History, Structure and Survival* (1983), for which he won the Choice Outstanding Academic Book Award in 1984.

Baugh's interest in promoting the education of people of African descent and low-income students led him to become a founding member of the highly successful Eastside College Preparatory School in East Palo Alto (after East Palo Alto's only high school closed in 1976). The school was founded in 1996 and became fully accredited in 2003. One hundred percent of its graduates have gone on to pursue higher education. In 2005 Baugh was the first appointed MARGARET BUSH WILSON Professor in Arts and Sciences, named in honor of the prominent civil rights attorney and emeritus trustee, and director of the African and African American studies program at Washington University in St. Louis. He also received appointments at Washington University in the departments of psychology, anthropology, education, English, and linguistics.

FURTHER READING

Baugh, John. *Beyond Ebonics: Linguistic Pride and Racial Prejudice* (2000).

Baugh, John. *It Ain't about Race: Some Lingering (Linguistic) Consequences of the African Slave Trade and Their Relevance to Your Personal Historical Hardship Index* (2006).

Baugh, John. *Out of the Mouths of Slaves: African American Language and Educational Malpractice* (1999).

BETHANY K. DUMAS

Baxter, Freddie (Aug. 1923–), author, was born Freddie Mae Baxter in Denmark, South Carolina, the seventh of eight children born to Julia Free, a domestic worker, and Henry Baxter, a farmer. In 1933 Baxter's father left home and moved to a nearby town. Undeterred, her mother continued to work as a domestic caring for the families of others to support her own five girls and three boys. The family lived in extreme poverty, residing in a tiny one-story shack with no bathroom, running water, or electricity. Throughout these early years Baxter picked cotton for a family that owned a hardware store. At age thirteen, the quick thinking and strong-minded young lady decided that she no longer wanted to work in the field. She convinced her boss to let her work inside the home, fixing breakfast for the owner's family before school. Baxter was extremely close to her mother and would often accompany her to clean the homes that she worked in. Unfortunately that bond came to an untimely end when on January 3, 1940, Julia Baxter died at age forty-nine of an undetermined cause. Freddie Mae was sixteen years old. Devastated by the unexpected loss of her mother she eventually quit school after completing the tenth grade.

At age seventeen, Baxter took the train and moved north to Elizabeth, New Jersey, to live with her aunt, uncle, and baby brother Julius. Upon arrival, she found a job cooking for a local family that owned a large clothing store. She received a rude awakening when her aunt forced her to give up half of her earnings, despite already doing household chores such as scrubbing floors and washing windows. Freddie was frustrated but realized she could not change the situation. After confiding in her boss, she was offered a live-in position in order to save money. However, out of respect for her aunt, she turned down the job and moved back home to South Carolina in July of that year.

Once there, she stayed with her sister Margaret and worked for a wealthy family but found she missed New Jersey. She wrote a letter to the woman she had previously worked for and this time asked to be her live in assistant. The woman not only allowed her to return but also sent a train ticket and raised her salary from twelve dollars a week to fifteen. Freddie worked for that woman for a year and a half. On her days off, she would meet and dance with boys at the famed Savoy Ballroom, an integrated hot spot known for its battle of the bands competitions and where CHICK WEBB, COUNT BASIE, and the Bennie Goodman Orchestra were frequent headliners. However, Freddie grew restless.

At age nineteen, Baxter moved to Harlem in New York. She arrived during the early 1940's at the end of the Harlem Renaissance, a period of great social, cultural and intellectual awakening amongst African Americans. She found herself consumed by the music and excitement of the city, often going to see performers such as BILLIE HOLIDAY.

When she first arrived in Harlem, she was mesmerized by a saxophone player in a group called the International Sweethearts of Rhythm, the first integrated all women's swing and jazz band. This interest eventually led Baxter to take saxophone classes with Walter "Foots" Thomas, the noted saxophone player and arranger in CAB CALLOWAY's orchestra. Thomas was known for training local girl groups, and invited the talented Baxter to join one of them. She soon found herself playing tenor saxophone with several bands.

Despite her musical exploration, Baxter never shirked her responsibilities, nor forgot her family. After the move to New York, she brought several of her family members to stay with her until they could get on their feet. She soon began working in a factory where she made decorations for hats. She quit that job because the boss would not let her rest her elbows on the table, suggesting that if you rested, you were not working. After that experience she decided that she would only work in private homes usually spending two or three years with each family. Baxter cooked and cleaned for the families as if they were her own, especially since she never married or personally bore children. She did this for almost fifty years until her retirement in 1988, proud of the fact that she never took a dime from unemployment. As fate would have it, she would soon find herself with an unexpected job title—author.

A prearranged encounter on a commuter train in 1996 would soon alter the course of Baxter's life. It was there that she would reconnect with semiretired writer and editor, Gloria Bley Miller, while visiting a mutual friend and former boss of Baxter's who lived in a nursing home. The two struck up a conversation about their lives. Miller was so impressed with Baxter's easygoing manner, humor, and candid storytelling style that she encouraged a reluctant Baxter to record the story. The two would meet every Friday in Miller's Greenwich apartment. In 1997 Miller began transcribing and arranging the material, completing the process in two years. She then began to shop the book to agents and publishers who were not impressed with the modest story. It received thirty rejection letters, including one from the publisher who would later take on the project. In May of 1998 another chance meeting with Mr. F Joseph Spieler (Baxter's future agent) concluded with him forwarding the book to Robin Desser, senior editor at Alfred A. Knopf, a major publisher, who quickly acquired the book

The Seventh Child: A Lucky Life was released on May 4, 1999, with a print run of 125,000 copies. The project netted Baxter a hefty advance of more than $100,000 that was split with Miller. The then seventy-five-year-old went from obscurity to an overnight sensation, drawing the attention of such major publications as the *New York Times* and *TIME* magazine.

FURTHER READING
Baxter, Freddie Mae, and Gloria Bley Miller, eds. *The Seventh Child: A Lucky Life*, (1999).
Carlin, Peter Ames. "Light on Her Feet: Maid-Turned-Author Freddie Mae Baxter, 75, Turns a Scrappy Life into a Joyous Memoir," *People*, 26 July 1999.
Stewart, Barbara. "The Unlikely Author of a Lucky Life; Ex Domestic Worker Finds Voice and a Book in the Ordinary," *New York Times*, 29 May 1999.

DALHIA PATRICE PERRYMAN

Bayley, Solomon (c. 1771–c. 1839), was born a slave near Camden, in Kent County, Delaware. Bayley wrote in his *Narrative* that his grandmother was a "Guinea woman" who had been transported from West Africa to Virginia when she was only eleven years old and sold to "one of the most barbarous families of that day." Despite this, she gave birth to fifteen children and "lived to a great age" (38). Bayley's mother had been born and raised with the same Virginia family. She had had several children with her husband, Abner, by the time her master and mistress died and one of their daughters and her husband moved to Delaware, taking the black family. A few years later Solomon Bayley was born, one of thirteen children.

Bayley grew to manhood in Kent County, Delaware. He took a slave named Thamar as his wife and they had two children. When the wife of the couple who owned them died, and her husband moved back to Virginia in 1799, Bayley and his family, along with his mother and father and siblings, were transported to Hunting Creek, which later became Alexandria, Virginia. Under Delaware law, slaveholders taking slaves out of the state were not permitted to put them up for immediate sale, but soon after they arrived the owner sold the entire family. Moreover, they were scattered in all directions, "some to the east, some west, north and south" (39). About one year after the sale, Bayley's father, brother, and sister were sold and taken to the Caribbean. His mother was more fortunate. She ran away with Bayley's infant brother, and made it to freedom in New Jersey.

In his reminiscence, Bayley explained that, shortly after arriving in Virginia, he began legal proceedings to secure his freedom. Not only did Delaware law prohibit his immediate sale, but a Virginia statute, passed in 1795, gave persons illegally detained as slaves the right to sue for their freedom. If they did not have enough money to launch a suit, they would be assigned counsel and allowed to sue in forma pauperis (as a poor person).

"I employed lawyers," Bayley wrote, "and went to court two days, to have a suit brought to obtain my freedom" (2). Two days before the trial date, he was "taken up and put on board a vessel out of Hunting Creek, bound to Richmond." Jailed and cast into irons, he was "brought very low." After some time, he was put into one of three wagons owned by his new master and began a journey toward the mountains. "Now consider, how great my distress must have been," he later confessed, "being carried from my wife and children" (2).

At this point, Bayley decided to run away. Waiting for the right moment, he slipped off the wagon and hid in some bushes until the other wagons had passed. He then set out across the countryside heading back toward Richmond. Thinking he would surely perish, he ran at night and with the aid of "a dreadful wind," thunder, lightning, and rain, he avoided capture. Twice slave catchers with their trained hunting dogs came close, but the rain covered up his scent. From Richmond, Bayley made it to Petersburg, remaining there three weeks before going down the James River in a small boat with another runaway. When they reached Chesapeake Bay, his companion was detected, captured, and after trying to escape by jumping over the side of a boat, was bludgeoned to death with an oar. Bayley, however, escaped detection. Having instructed his wife if they were ever parted to run away and meet him at a specific location on the Eastern Shore (perhaps the farm of an antislavery white or free black family), Bayley miraculously found his wife and his two children. Together, they set out to the North and freedom.

When Bayley and his family returned to Kent County in 1799, the white man who had illegally sold him and his family in Virginia confronted Bayley and threatened to enslave him again; Bayley, in turn, threatened to take him to court. In the end the two compromised; if Bayley paid the man eighty dollars, a fraction of his market value, he would be allowed to go free. Bayley agreed, purchased himself, and finally, as he put it, "the yoke was off my neck" (18). In freedom, the ambitious and energetic Bayley learned the trade of coopering. With the demand for barrels high, and his wages higher than those of many whites, he was able to save enough to purchase his wife and children. He made his final purchase in 1813, buying his son, described by the auctioneer as a "likely young negro," for $360 and one shilling. Several white men, including one whom Bayley described as a "great man," assisted him, paying him for his security bond and asking another bidder to allow Solomon to purchase his son.

During the Second Great Awakening in the early nineteenth century, Bayley experienced a religious conversion. He joined the Methodist Episcopal Church, became one of its most devout members, and, when one minister suggested it was a sin not to sanctify his marriage in the eyes of God, he married his wife (he was in the process of purchasing her freedom at the time) in a church ceremony. Bayley felt so strongly about his new faith that he gave up working as a cooper because the wooden barrels he made were used for whiskey. Following his conversion, he became a farm laborer and spent a good deal of time as a lay preacher.

In 1820 Robert Hurnard, a British abolitionist visiting Delaware, heard stories about Bayley's remarkable escape and invited him to talk about his life. Upon his return to England, Hurnard wrote to Bayley, asking him to write a memoir and some letters about his life. Hurnard learned that Bayley had placed his two daughters, Margaret and Leah, "out in the service of respectable families" (vi) but they, along with his son, Spence, had died prematurely. Although advanced in life, Bayley enjoyed good health, as did his wife, who was four years older.

In 1824 Bayley's recollections were published in England, with Hurnard promising to "transmit the whole of the profits of the publication to America, for the benefit of the aged couple" (viii). Although disjointed and containing lengthy Biblical quotations, A Narrative gives the reader a rare glimpse into the life of a runaway slave in the late eighteenth century. It emphasizes Bayley's fear, anxiety, and the remarkable obstacles confronting runaways. It also reveals the treachery of greedy whites, as well as the sympathy and support of those whites opposed to slavery. It also shows the primary importance of the black family, Christianity, and the triumph of human spirit over adversity.

In one of his letters, the self-taught Bayley observed that, for some time, he had followed the career of the Pan-Africanist PAUL CUFFE Sr. and was himself considering leaving the United States. In 1827 Solomon and Thamar Bayley decided to immigrate to Liberia, a fledgling colony in West Africa. Before departing, Bayley obtained a letter of commendation from Willard Hall, a U.S. District Court Judge and leader in the Delaware colonization movement, a group of whites who offered assistance to free blacks who wished to settle in West Africa; Hall wrote that despite his "unfavorable age" (Bayley was about fifty-six) "his character stands high not only among his people of colour, but among the most respectable of our citizens." The two former fugitive slaves then boarded the brig *Doris* out of Baltimore, and, along with eighty other passengers, mostly from New York and Maryland, they set sail via Norfolk, Virginia, for Liberia.

During the period when the Bayleys arrived in the Liberian capital of Monrovia, there were clashes between native inhabitants and the approximately twelve hundred settlers, and newcomers were dying from "the fever," or malaria. Nonetheless, the Bayleys cleared a seven-acre plot and began cultivating a small farm on the outskirts of Monrovia, near the St. Paul's River. Solomon built a platform overlooking the river under a large tree, where, time permitting, he read and wrote. Following the death of his wife in 1833, Bayley published *A Brief Account of the Colony of Liberia*, which discussed the agricultural and commercial progress of the colony and the relationship between settlers and native Africans. He returned to the United States that year and visited a number of cities, but returned to Liberia, where he remarried and continued to farm, preach, and participate in community life until his death.

FURTHER READING

Bayley, Solomon. *A Narrative of Some Remarkable Incidents in the Life of Solomon Bayley, Formerly a Slave in the State of Delaware, North America* (1825).

Dalleo, Peter. "The Growth of Delaware's Antebellum Free African American Community," in *A History of African Americans of Delaware and Maryland's Eastern Shore*, ed. Carole Marks (1997).

Williams, William H. *Slavery and Freedom in Delaware, 1639–1865* (1996).

LOREN SCHWENINGER

Baylor, Elgin Gay (16 Sept. 1934–), basketball player and executive, was born in Washington, D.C., the son of a railroad brakeman. Little else is known about his parents. Baylor grew up in a poor section of the District of Columbia and played basketball at the all-black Spingarn High School, where he scored sixty-eight points in a single game to establish a new record for a D.C. high schooler. Although he was the first African American to make the all-metropolitan team, his poor grades discouraged college recruiters. Thus Baylor started his college career with a football scholarship at the tiny College of Idaho, which had only 450 students. Sam Vokes coached both football and basketball

Elgin Gay Baylor, of the Los Angeles Lakers, making a fast break past Golden State Warriors' McCoy McLemore (32) during the season opening game at San Francisco Civic Auditorium, October 1965. (AP Images.)

and decided that it made good sense to keep the talented Baylor off the football field. Baylor proceeded to average thirty-one points a game and made the NAIA All-American team, which recognizes the achievements of small-school athletes. After that year Baylor transferred to the University of Seattle. After sitting out the 1955–1956 season, Baylor finished third in scoring in the 1956–1957 season.

Baylor caught the attention of the nation's basketball fans in the 1957–1958 season when he averaged 32.5 points per game in the regular season to lead the nation in scoring. In the 1958 NCAA tournament, Baylor led Seattle to the championship game, where they fell to the University of Kentucky. Baylor elected to skip his senior season to enter the NBA with the Minneapolis Lakers.

Although the Lakers had won four NBA championships in the first half of the 1950s, they had descended into mediocrity when Baylor joined them in 1958. At six feet five inches tall and 225 pounds, Baylor was easily the most creative player in the NBA. Blessed with a great vertical leap and unbelievable body control, Baylor combined fakes and power that made him virtually unstoppable. As the rookie of the year Baylor led the Lakers to the 1959 finals, where they lost to the Boston Celtics. The following season Baylor set a new NBA single-game scoring record when he poured in sixty-four points against the Boston Celtics on 8 November 1959. After struggling for several years, in 1960 the Lakers moved to Los Angeles. That same year the Lakers drafted Jerry West, another future NBA great who teamed up with Baylor to make the Lakers a frequent NBA finalist in the 1960s. In his first season in Los Angeles, Baylor averaged 34.8 points and scored 71 points on 15 November 1960 to break his own NBA record. After three years Baylor was one of the dominant players in the NBA and was the undisputed leader of the Lakers. Merv Harris of the *Los Angeles Herald Examiner* wrote, "Whenever Elgin wanted to play poker, they played poker. Wherever Elgin wanted to eat, they went to eat. Whatever Elgin wanted to talk about, they talked about."

As in the case of other black players, Baylor had to battle racism. When the Lakers played a game in Charleston, West Virginia, and a hotel refused to provide accommodations for Baylor and two teammates, the Lakers star boycotted the game. Active in the NBA Player's Association, he was one of the NBA stars prepared to boycott the 1964 All-Star game unless the league provided a pension program for the players.

In 1961–1962 Baylor had one of his finest seasons. Because he was required to fulfill U.S. Army reserve duty, Baylor played in only forty-eight regular season games, but he averaged an eye-popping 38.2 points per game. The Lakers took the Boston Celtics to the seventh game of the NBA finals only to lose in overtime. In the fifth game of the series Baylor set a new single-game play-off scoring record by sinking sixty-one points. He also snagged twenty-two rebounds. In 1962–1963 Baylor had another spectacular year, averaging thirty-four points and fourteen rebounds per game. The Lakers lost to the Celtics in the NBA finals but became the first NBA team to gross $1 million. By the 1963–1964 season Baylor's knees began to bother him, and during the following season, on 3 April 1965, his kneecap split and he severely damaged a knee ligament. Without Baylor the Lakers lost for the third time in four years in the NBA finals to the Boston Celtics.

Baylor fooled his doctors and managed to play in sixty-five games of the 1965–1966 season but averaged only 16.6 points per game. Once again the Lakers lost to the Celtics in the NBA finals. Baylor never fully recovered from his injury, which forced him to adjust his game and rely more on his jump shot than on the acrobatic moves that had been his trademark. Despite these limitations, Baylor was still an extraordinary player. In the 1966–1967 season Baylor averaged twenty-six points and made the all-NBA first team. The Lakers, however, were eliminated in the first round of the play-offs. The team bounced back in 1967–1968 when they won the Western Division but once again lost to their nemesis, the Boston Celtics, in the finals. Baylor

finished second in the NBA in scoring with twenty-six points per game.

For the 1968–1969 season the Lakers added WILT CHAMBERLAIN to the tandem of Baylor and West. Baylor averaged 24.8 points and made the all-NBA team for the eighth time. In the NBA finals the Lakers jumped out to a three games to one lead over the Celtics but could not close the series, and Boston won yet another NBA championship. In 1969–1970 knee injuries limited Baylor to fifty-four games, but he still averaged 24 points. The Lakers advanced to the NBA finals against the New York Knicks, setting up one of the most memorable championship series in NBA history. In the seventh game, inspired by an injured Willis Reed, the Knicks trounced the Lakers. Injuries limited Baylor to two games in 1970–1971, and nine games into the 1971–1972 season he retired.

In the 1970s Baylor served as an assistant for the expansion team the New Orleans Jazz (1974–1976) and then was the Jazz head coach for three years (1976–1979). Baylor's teams registered a record of 86 wins and 135 losses. In 1986 the Los Angeles Clippers named Baylor vice president of basketball operations.

In the 1950s Elgin Baylor, along with BILL RUSSELL, Wilt Chamberlain, and OSCAR ROBERTSON, changed the way that basketball was played and opened the door to the NBA for other African American players. When he was free of injuries, Baylor was virtually unstoppable and scored with a variety of unpredictable shots. As an outstanding rebounder and passer, Baylor was a complete player whose creativity helped make the NBA one of America's most popular professional sports. In 1976 Elgin Baylor was inducted into the Naismith Basketball Hall of Fame. In 1996 he was named to the Fiftieth Anniversary NBA All-Time team. A ten-time all-NBA player, Baylor scored 23,149 points for a 27.4 per-game average.

FURTHER READING

Lazenby, Roland. *The Lakers* (1993).

Pluto, Terry. *Tall Tales* (1992).

Thomas, Ron. *They Cleared the Lane: The NBA's Black Pioneers* (2002).

Whalen, Thomas J. *Dynasty's End: Bill Russell and the 1968–69 World Champion Boston Celtics* (2004).

DOLPH GRUNDMAN

Bayne, Thomas (1824–1889), dentist and politician, was born into slavery in North Carolina and was known as Samuel Nixon before his escape from bondage in 1855. Nothing is known about his parents. He was sold several times before being purchased by C. F. Martin, a dentist in Norfolk, Virginia. As Martin's slave, Nixon learned sufficient dentistry to serve as the doctor's assistant and to make dental house calls. He also developed bookkeeping skills and monitored the doctor's accounts.

In Norfolk, Nixon became involved with the Underground Railroad. Befriending the captains of many of the schooners sailing in and out of Norfolk, he often convinced them to hide fugitive slaves aboard ship and carry them north, usually to Philadelphia or to New Bedford, Massachusetts. After conducting many other slaves through the Underground Railroad, Nixon decided to become a passenger himself in March 1855. He and three other slaves disguised themselves and hid on board a schooner bound for Philadelphia. He left behind his wife, Edna (maiden name unknown), and one child, both of whom were owned by E. P. Tabb, a Norfolk hardware merchant. The ship landed in New Jersey, where Nixon was directed to Abigail Goodwin, a Quaker abolitionist. In a letter to a fellow abolitionist, Goodwin described Nixon as "a smart young man … well dressed in fine broadcloth coat and overcoat, and has a very active tongue in his head," but she worried that "they will be after him soon."

Nixon then traveled to New Bedford, where he changed his name to Thomas Bayne and began a dentistry practice while maintaining contact with Underground Railroad agents like WILLIAM STILL of Philadelphia. Letters between Bayne and Still reveal that Bayne sometimes sheltered fugitives in his New Bedford home and that Still aided Bayne's advancement by sending medical and dental textbooks. In January 1860 Bayne thanked Still for his "Vigilance as a colored man helping a colored man to get such knowledge as will give the lie to our enemies." Bayne also gained renown in New Bedford as a speaker at abolitionist and temperance meetings, and he served on the New Bedford City Council in 1865.

At the end of the Civil War, Bayne returned to Norfolk, Virginia, to rejoin his family. He immediately became involved in politics, and in May 1865 he chaired a public meeting at which the participants passed eight civil rights resolutions under the title of *Equal Suffrage: Address from the Colored Citizens of Norfolk, Virginia to the People of the United States.* These resolutions pledged Virginia's loyalty to the Union, decried race discrimination as abhorrent to "patriotism, humanity, and religion," and demanded equal suffrage for black and white Americans. As a member of a committee that testified on behalf of rights for freedmen, Bayne appeared before O. O. Howard of the Freedmen's Bureau in December 1865. The following year he was among a delegation of black men from Virginia who met with President Andrew Johnson to articulate demands for civil and political rights, especially the right to vote. Bayne also testified before the Joint Committee on Reconstruction, where he urged that the rights of former slaves be protected and that Reconstruction reforms be enforced.

An important black leader in the Virginia Republican Party, Bayne served as vice president of the April 1867 state Republican convention held in Richmond, where he earned a reputation for his elegant dress and commitment to public education. He was subsequently elected as a delegate from Norfolk to the Constitutional Convention of the State of Virginia, which was charged with the task of drawing up a new state constitution that would qualify Virginia for readmission to the Union. Bayne was one of twenty-four black delegates to the convention, which met during the winter of 1867–1868. In the convention, Bayne adamantly insisted that the residual injustices of slavery be redressed. He fervently supported the proposed state constitution's Declaration of Rights, which stated that "all men are, by nature, equally free and independent, and have certain inherent rights … namely, the enjoyment of life and liberty, with the means of … obtaining happiness and safety." In the debate that surrounded that preamble, Bayne claimed the promises of the Declaration of Independence and the Constitution for black as well as white Americans, and he pledged himself to a constitution "that should not have the word black or the word white anywhere in it." He repeatedly argued that the harmful aftereffects of slavery could best be combated with the protection of black voting rights and equal citizenship rights.

Bayne recognized education as a priority for Virginia's black community. At the Virginia state convention he spoke out against the prejudice faced by many uneducated blacks with the reminder that white Virginians had "robbed the black man of his education, … taken the money and labor of the black man to support themselves in grandeur, and now they curse the black man because he is not a grammarian. They are like the hunter who shot the bird through both wings, and when it fluttered and fell, damned it because it would not rise." In reparation Bayne proposed that Virginia's constitution should ensure that "the free public schools in this State shall be open free to all classes, and no child, pupil or scholar shall be ejected from said schools on account of race, color, or any invidious distinction," but the measure was defeated as too radical.

Following the state convention, Bayne retained interest in public affairs, attending an all-black political convention in May 1869. Reconstruction soon ended in Virginia, however, and Bayne turned increasingly to his dentistry practice. As political opportunities for black Virginians diminished, Bayne sought to maintain a public profile by engaging in periodic bouts of traveling ministry, but these efforts were cut short by the senility that plagued his later years. In 1888 he was admitted to the Central State Lunatic Asylum in Norfolk, where he died. For Bayne, as for many other freedmen and freedwomen, the promise of Reconstruction's early days, during which he played an important role in post–Civil War politics, proved brighter than the long-term reality.

FURTHER READING

Aptheker, Herbert, ed. *A Documentary History of the Negro People in the United States*, vol. 2 (1968).

Foner, Eric. *Freedom's Lawmakers: A Directory of Black Officeholders during Reconstruction* (1993).

Still, William. *The Underground Railroad: A Record of Facts, Authentic Narratives, Letters &c.* (1872).

Taylor, Alrutheus A. *The Negro in the Reconstruction of Virginia* (1926).

This entry is taken from the *American National Biography* and is published here with the permission of the American Council of Learned Societies.

CHANDRA M. MILLER

Beals, Melba Pattillo (7 Dec. 1941–), journalist, author, and public speaker, was born Melba Joy Pattillo in Little Rock, Arkansas, the daughter of Howell "Will" Pattillo, a hostler's helper for the Missouri Pacific Railroad, and Dr. Lois Marie Peyton Pattillo, a junior high school English teacher who was among the first African Americans to attend the University of Arkansas (graduating in 1954). In 1957, spurred by the 1954 Supreme Court ruling in *Brown v. Board of Education*, mandating public school desegregation, Beals, at the age of fifteen, became one of the first African American students—later known as the "Little Rock Nine"—to enroll in Central High School, then Arkansas' finest high school.

Prior to 1957 Beals's deepest anguish had been her parents' divorce when she was seven. She found solace in the hours she spent with her cherished grandmother, India Anette Peyton, while her mother worked and studied and her younger brother, Conrad, played. Convinced that the desegregation of Central High was key to the future of civil rights for her people, Beals tried to prepare herself. Yet despite her keen familiarity with the degradation and humiliation imposed by Jim Crow, nothing in her experience could inure her to the hostility and violence she faced. Aptly, her grandmother India had given her the work of Mohandas K. Gandhi, the Indian whose program of nonviolent resistance provided a practical means for fulfilling her destiny as a "warrior." The Bible, the primary source of her grandmother's teachings, gave the young Beals spiritual sustenance throughout her lengthy ordeal. Thus, she learned to conceal her terror, her disgust, and her physical pain, and to respond to monstrous assaults with a simple "thank you."

Ernest Green, a fellow member of the "Nine," became the first African American to graduate from Central High, but subsequent efforts by the National Association for the Advancement of Colored People (NAACP) to block Arkansas Governor Orville Faubus's plan to close all area high schools proved unsuccessful. At the same time, the Ku Klux Klan posted signs promising to pay for Beals's capture, dead or alive.

At age seventeen, Beals boarded a plane for San Francisco with little more than a promise from Daisy Lee Gatson Bates, president of the Arkansas State Conference of the NAACP, that Association members in Santa Rosa, California, would look after her. Having lost her grandmother, Beals was now forced to leave her mother and brother behind and begin the next phase of her life in the rural home of the McCabes, a white Quaker family that resembled her own solely in the wealth of love they shared. The transition to another predominantly white high school was made more difficult than necessary by her painful recollections of the brutality she had faced at Central High, and Beals found herself increasingly isolated and suffering a crisis in personal identity: the few black students had no interest in befriending her, and despite numerous offers she could not immerse herself in the white social set. A complete collapse of her physical and mental health led to one of her few trips home to Little Rock.

Although freedom in California was far from complete—Beals was denied admission to a Santa

Rosa swimming pool—it had been sufficient to make a return to oppressive southern customs intolerable. Beals found it impossible to avert her eyes in the presence of whites or accommodate herself to segregated public seating, which were widely practiced customs in the South. Upon her return to California, Beals registered at Santa Rosa Community College but transferred to San Francisco State College (SFSC), a move that required her to forgo the comfort and warmth of the McCabes' home.

Her encounters with members of the educated black community in San Francisco quickly dashed her hopes for acceptance, and she found racism thriving among some of the white students on campus. Beals's refusal to reveal the role she had played in the Crisis of 1957 left her in the odd position of listening for the first time to a discussion of those events as an "outsider." Clearly, there were segregationists in California, too, even if they were not in the majority. Unable to find community with fellow blacks, Beals moved into a previously all-white women's residence club where, finally, she managed to establish tentative friendships. In 1962, despite her mother's pointed objections, she married Matt Beals, a white man, and reveled in life with her new husband.

Her daughter Kellie Joy was born in August 1963. That same month and far removed from the mounting struggle for civil rights, Beals watched the television coverage of MARTIN LUTHER KING JR., whom she had previously had the privilege of meeting, as he delivered his legendary "I have a dream" speech at the historic March on Washington. No longer pursuing her education, Beals rationalized that after enduring the trauma of desegregating Central High, she had earned time off from sociopolitical concerns; however, with the stillbirth of her second child, a wedge emerged between her and her husband, who soon abandoned both mother and child. For the first time in her life, Beals had to face the harsh economic reality that she and her daughter would survive only if they received public assistance. In 1968 they moved to a housing project, subsisting on welfare and food stamps. Encouraged by her surrogate father George McCabe, Beals decided, against all odds, to complete her education.

Beals's talent as a writer had not escaped the attention of her journalism teacher at SFSC, who encouraged her to submit an application for a program funded by the Ford Foundation. In 1971 Beals graduated from San Francisco State College and, leaving Kellie with her mother in Little Rock,

enrolled in a master's degree program in broadcast journalism at Columbia University in New York City.

Her professional career began at KQED, the public television station in San Francisco. The following year, she accepted a position as an NBC newscaster with KRON-TV, also in San Francisco. Beals also published a number of articles for the *San Francisco Examiner, Essence*, and *People*. Her bestselling *Expose Yourself: Using the Power of Public Relations to Promote Your Business and Yourself* appeared in 1990 and soon became an industry standard work.

Beals offered gripping details of her experience as a student at Central High in *Warriors Don't Cry: A Searing Memoir of the Battle to Integrate Little Rock's Central High* (1994). Winner of the American Library Association's Notable Books Award (1995) and the Robert F. Kennedy Memorial Book Award (1995), this extraordinary volume remains a seminal account of early efforts to ensure quality public education for African Americans. A source of vital historical information and a testament to the raw courage of youthful conviction, *Warriors* revealed the buried truths behind events that brought a small city in a rural Southern state to the attention of the world. Although it took more than three decades for Beals to write and publish *Warriors*, she produced her second volume of memoirs, *White Is a State of Mind* (1999), in relatively short order, providing a helpful "update" of her experiences following her efforts to desegregate Central High.

Beals was a guest on many radio talk shows and appeared on C-Span's *Booknotes, Good Morning America, Nightline*, and *Oprah Winfrey*. In 1998 Beals—along with other members of the "Little Rock Nine"—was awarded the Congressional Gold Medal by President Bill Clinton. Founder of Melcon Communications, Beals developed a diversity seminar, "The Spirit of Diversity: Seeing Equal Being Equal," designed to aid in the resolution of conflicts arising from racial and religious differences. In 2002 Beals was inducted into the Marin Women's Hall of Fame for her contributions to social change.

FURTHER READING

Beals, Melba Pattillo. *Warriors Don't Cry: A Searing Memoir of the Battle to Integrate Little Rock's Central High* (1994).
Beals, Melba Pattillo. *White Is a State of Mind* (1999).
Bates, Daisy. *The Long Shadow of Little Rock* (1962).

MARINELLE RINGER

Beam, Joseph Fairchild (30 Dec. 1954–27 Dec. 1988), writer, poet, and activist, was born in Philadelphia, Pennsylvania, to Sun Fairchild Beam, a security guard, and Dorothy Saunders Beam, a teacher and school guidance counselor. Beam attended Philadelphia's public schools as well as the St. Joseph School for Boys (Clayton, Delaware), Malvern Preparatory (Paoli, Pennsylvania), and St. Thomas More (Philadelphia). In 1972, while still a teenager, Beam was honored with the Philadelphia School District's Volunteer Service Award. He later attended Franklin College in Franklin, Indiana, where he studied journalism and earned his B.A. in 1976. As an undergraduate Beam was active in the local Black Student Union and was a member of the Franklin Independent Men. He was also active in college journalism and radio programming and was awarded the Omega Psi Phi Fraternity Award for Broadcasting in 1974.

After graduation, Beam remained in the Midwest where he pursued a master's degree in communications. He returned to Philadelphia in 1979 and began working at Giovanni's Room, a local independent gay and lesbian bookstore. Beam continued the writing he had begun in college and was active in the struggle for social justice for the black gay community at the local and national level.

Beam's work appeared in many newspapers and publications, including *Au Courant, Black/Out, Blackheart, Changing Men, Gay Community News, The Painted Bride Quarterly, The Philadelphia Gay News, The Advocate, New York Native, Body Politic,* and *The Windy City Times.* Among his critically recognized short stories are "Brother to Brother" and "No Cheek to Turn." Beam also interviewed many of the influential community activists of his time, including AUDRE LORDE, BAYARD RUSTIN, and SONIA SANCHEZ. In these interviews, whose subjects often became lifelong friends, Beam won praise for the style and beauty of his writing. Prefacing his interview with Audre Lorde, he wrote:

Audre Lorde is like a diamond. Multi-faceted, she is a mother, poet, novelist, publisher, socialist, feminist and lesbian. Sharp, she cuts through the bramble of political correctness and does not bite her tongue. Reflective, she shows not only where we are, but where we wish to be (*Philadelphia Gay News,* 18–24 October 1996).

In 1984 Beam was recognized for outstanding achievement by a minority journalist by the Lesbian and Gay Press Association. In 1985, *the Philadelphia Gay News* awarded him its prestigious Lambda Award for Outstanding Achievement. Also in that year, Beam joined the Executive Committee of the National Coalition of Black Lesbians and Gays and became the editor of its journal, *Black/Out.* He also began to serve as a consultant for the Gay and Lesbian Task Force of the American Friends Service Committee.

1986 saw the publication of the work for which Beam is best known, *In the Life.* The first anthology of poetry and prose by and about black gay men, *In the Life* was groundbreaking and influential. Beam described the impetus for the volume, stating that "By mid-1983, I had grown weary of reading literature by white gay men. … None of them spoke to me as a black man. Their words offered the reflection of a sidewalk; their characters cast ominous shadows" (13). In this volume, to which he also contributed, Beam addresses many of the central themes that resonate throughout the pieces. With raw honesty, he confronts how the dominant culture renders black gay men invisible and describes the pain of being excluded by the African American community. *In the Life* features the work of nearly three dozen African American gay men who discuss issues of race, gender, and sexuality. In addition to describing the pain and costs of exclusion, prejudice, and invisibility, *In the Life* also highlights the beauty, character, and dignity of this community: "We are black men who are proudly gay. What we offer is our lives, our love, our visions. … We are coming home with our heads held up high" (18).

Soon after the publication of *In the Life,* Beam began a second anthology, *Brother to Brother,* named after his earlier, acclaimed short story. Beam died of an AIDS-related illness before he could finish *Brother to Brother,* so his mother, Dorothy, and friend, the poet ESSEX HEMPHILL, completed the book, which was published in 1991. *Brother to Brother* stands as yet another influential book that showcases essays, poetry, and other writing by black gay men. *In the Life* and *Brother to Brother* are lauded as critical, pioneering, and important books that document the lives and experiences of black gay men—who until *In the Life* were unrepresented in published work. These authors include Gilberto Gerald, A. Billy S. Jones, James Charles Roberts, and James S. Tinney.

Beam's life and legacy have been honored and continue to influence and inspire the work of others. The Joseph Beam Scholarship Prize, established by Beam's mother after his death, is awarded annually for any essay or literary work on gay, lesbian, or transgender issues written by an undergraduate or graduate student in the English department at Temple University in Philadelphia. The filmmaker MARLON RIGGS dedicated his critically acclaimed film *Tongues Untied* (1990) to Beam. The Joseph Beam Youth Collaborative in Philadelphia, a non-profit educational organization, was founded in 2003 and works with and for lesbian, gay, bisexual, transgender, and questioning (LGBTQ) youth of color.

FURTHER READING

Many of Joseph Beam's papers are available at the Schomburg Center for Research in Black Culture in New York. The collection includes letters, conference materials, Beam's stories and essays, files of the National Coalition of Black Lesbians and Gays and its journal, *Black/Out*, and other documents, photos, and films.

Beam, Joseph, ed. *In the Life: A Black Gay Anthology* (1986).

Hemphill, Essex, ed. *Brother to Brother: New Writings by Black Gay Men* (1991).

BILLIE GASTIC

Beamon, Bob (29 Aug. 1946–), track-and-field athlete, motivational speaker, and activist for youth, was born Robert Alfred Beamon in Jamaica, New York, to Naomi Brown Beamon and a father he never met. After his mother died from tuberculosis before Beamon's first birthday, his stepfather, James, assumed parental responsibility for Robert and his older, disabled brother Andrew. Robert's grandmother, Bessie Beamon, ultimately took over their care as a result of James's inadequate parenting skills. Rarely supervised, Beamon ran away from home when he was fourteen and joined a gang. When he struck a teacher who had attempted to break up one of Beamon's fights, he was expelled and charged with assault and battery.

Beamon's life might have become a tragedy if it weren't for a judge who was "thoughtful, compassionate, and obviously interested in helping kids" (*Second Chances*, 3). The judge took a chance and allowed Beamon to attend an alternative school in Manhattan for juvenile delinquents. Although teachers and the school were "tough," they taught Beamon a different kind of life. After leaving the alternative school, Beamon turned to athletics to escape his troubled past. In 1962, during junior high school, Beamon set a Junior Olympic record in the long jump of 24 feet 1 inch (Beamon, 62) and set his sights on going to the more academic Jamaica High School. The dean and head coach of the track

team, LARRY ELLIS (who would later become the first black head track coach at Princeton and for the U.S. Olympic team), recognized Beamon's talent and "took Beamon under his wing," motivating him to dream and work toward his goals (*Second Chances*, 21). At the age of 16 Beamon set citywide track records in New York City and also set the New York State record for the long jump in 1965. That year he ranked second among U.S. high school athletes with a best jump of 25 feet 3½ inches and ranked first among triple jumpers with a best of 53 feet 3¾ inches (Schaap, 59). "Now, he had a purpose, an opportunity, encouragement from others and an Olympic dream" (Second Chances, 21).

Following graduation from Jamaica High School in January 1966, Beamon enrolled in North Carolina Agricultural and Technical College for less than a year before transferring to University of Texas–El Paso (UTEP), where he and fellow athletes faced racism from peers and local residents as well as the school's athletic director (*Booklist*, May 1999). In 1967, while Beamon was at UTEP, the track coach told a friend, "One day soon, Bob Beamon is going to make a jump that you won't believe and I won't believe" (*New York Times*, Nov. 2006).

Beamon set out to qualify for the 1968 Olympic long jump, but faced a problem. He had a strong tendency to foul (go over the "take-off" board, the board from which the jump begins). At the time Beamon's unofficial coach was his fellow track-and-field star and record holder Ralph Boston, who worked with Beamon to overcome his fouling problem. Nevertheless, Beamon ran into trouble during the Olympics by fouling in his first two attempts at qualifying for the finals. Prior to the third attempt, "Boston reminded him he could take off from farther behind the board and still reach the finals" (New York *Daily News*, June 2006) and Beamon adjusted himself accordingly for a successful jump. In the finals Beamon came just about as close to fouling as humanly possible: "The shadow of his takeoff shoe's toe lay for an instant over the foul line, but he left no mark on the telltale Plasticine [marking material]" (*Sports Illustrated*, June 1987). In addition, during his jump the wind blew behind him at exactly 2.0 meters per second, the maximum allowed.

After Beamon landed, the judges attempted to measure his jump, but the optical sighting device could not extend past twenty-eight feet. One of the judges exclaimed, "Fantastic, fantastic. ... We will have to measure it with a tape" (*Sportstar Weekly*, Aug. 2006). As Beamon looked on, the officials measured the distance of the jump and announced it as 8.90 meters. Beamon did not understand what 8.90 meters measured to in feet, and so it took Boston telling Beamon that he had jumped 29 feet 21½ inches before Beamon realized the significance of what had just happened (*Sports Illustrated*, 66). Beamon immediately collapsed and broke into tears in the face of powerful emotions and was helped to his feet by teammates. It was later discovered that "he was suffering a cataplectic seizure as his muscles gave way under the emotion of it all" (*Sportstar Weekly*, Aug. 2006). The previous world record had been 27 feet 4¾ inches. In the thirty-three years prior to 1968, athletes had extended the world record by only 8½ inches past JESSE OWENS's 1935 record of 26 feet 8¼ inches, and Beamon was now first to jump over 28 feet and 29 feet. In January 1969 *Track and Field News* named him Track and Field Athlete of the Year for 1968 (Schaap, 115).

While Beamon's leap shattered the world record, his achievement was touched by controversy. Critics have pointed to Mexico City's high elevation and the maximum allowable wind as contributing factors in Beamon's achievement by allowing athletes to jump farther than normal. But Beamon's jump withstood the test of time, his record lasting for twenty-three years until 30 August 1991 when the American MIKE POWELL jumped 29 feet 4½ inches in the World Championships in Tokyo.

Beamon's life after the 1968 Olympics brought him mixed fortunes, and he never jumped as far as 27 feet again, though following a hamstring injury in early 1969, he did jump 26 feet 11 inches off his other leg in the Amateur Athletic Union championship in June 1969 (Schaap, 122). He was a fifteenth-round 1969 NBA draft pick by the Phoenix Suns, though a professional basketball career never materialized. In 1972 Beamon retired from track and graduated from Adelphi University, earning a degree in Cultural Anthropology. He received a master's degree in Counseling Psychology from San Diego State in 1975. He participated without distinction in professional track-and-field from 1973 to 1976. He worked for Home Federal Savings in San Diego and as a television commentator.

Beamon became an artist, developed and marketed a successful line of neckties, coached college track, and led the Youth Services division of the Parks and Recreation programs in the Miami-Dade County area in Florida. He was also involved in youth-centered civic work, worked as a philanthropist—organizing charity golf outings benefiting youth programs—and served as an advocate in the Florida Children's Court System for disadvantaged youth. Beamon warned that if children are being exposed to more and more violence, whether at school, on the streets, from television or in video games, and "parents are becoming less watchful over, and less involved with, their own kids. Families are far more fragmented and disconnected" (*Second Chances*, 4). He recognized the need to reach out to children in danger of becoming criminals and to show them there is a better way to live. He served as a national spokesperson for the Children's Courts and supported the fight against legislation that would prosecute juvenile offenders as adults.

Beamon is the owner of Bob Beamon Communications, Inc., and a professional speaker for Fortune 500 companies. In 1997 he married his fifth wife, Milana Walter Beamon, with whom he lived in Miami with his two daughters, Deanna, adopted with his previous wife in 1985, and Tameka. In 1999 he published his autobiography, *The Man Who Could Fly: The Bob Beamon Story*, with Milana. In 2000 he became the director of athletic development at Florida Atlantic University. A participant in the 1996 Atlanta Olympics opening ceremonies, he served on the board of the committee for the New York 2012 Olympic Bid. Elected to the U.S. Olympic Hall of Fame in 1983 (its first year of operation), he was also a member of the New York Track-and-Field Hall of Fame and was rated by ESPN as one of the top hundred athletes of the twentieth century.

FURTHER READING

Beamon, Bob, and Milana Walter Beamon. *The Man Who Could Fly: The Bob Beamon Story* (1999).

Beauregard, Sue-Ellen. "*The Man Who Could Fly: The Bob Beamon Story* (Young Adult Review)," *Booklist* (May 1999).

Justice Policy Institute and Children and Family Justice Center of Northwestern University School of Law. *Second Chances: 100 Years of the Children's Court, Giving Kids a Chance to Make a Better Choice* (May 2000).

"The Magic Leap," *Sportstar Weekly* (Aug. 2006).

Moore, Kenny. "Giants on the Earth (Bob Beamon's and Lee Evans's Records from 1968 Olympics Still Stand)," *Sports Illustrated* (June 1987).

Schaap, Dick. *The Perfect Jump* (1976).

RICHARD SOBEL

Beard, Andrew Jackson (1849–10 May 1921), inventor, was born in Jefferson County, Alabama, the son of Milton Beard and Creasey Tatum, both former slaves on the Beard family plantation. He adopted the name of his former master at age fifteen after he was liberated by Union forces. A year later, he married Edie Beard, about whom nothing else is known. The couple raised three children: John, Jack, and Andrew Jr.; the latter died following graduation from high school. Like most former slaves, however, Beard was illiterate and remained so throughout his life.

After the Civil War, Beard worked as a sharecropper on his former master's farm until he was about eighteen years old and then moved to St. Clair County, Alabama. In 1872, he made a three-week journey from Birmingham to Montgomery on an oxcart that carried fifty bushels of apples, which he sold for approximately two hundred dollars. He eventually advanced from sharecropping to owning an eighty-acre farm outside Center Point, Alabama, where he raised his family and had tenant farmers. He built a wooden church, which also served as a schoolhouse, for his African American tenants, one family of which adopted his surname.

Beard, like many nineteenth-century inventors, was known as a "tinker," yet the term did not convey the intricacies of his work. He built and operated a flour mill in Hardwicks, Alabama, while he developed the concept for his earliest invention, a double plow. He received a patent on the device on 26 April 1881, which three years later he sold for $4,000. Following the sale of his double plow he returned to his birthplace and farmed for four years. He then received a patent for a plow or cultivator on 10 August 1886, which he sold for $5,200. At that point, he entered the real estate business; by this time his net worth was reportedly in excess of $30,000.

Despite receiving little recognition, African American inventors made many contributions, ranging from small cost-saving or safety devices to mechanical instruments that proved to be of vital importance to the industrial development of the nation. In 1889 Beard invented the rotary steam engine, which was promoted as being more efficient than conventional models at one-tenth the cost and having the ability to conserve 20 percent of steam without risk of explosion. He received a patent for the rotary engine on 7 May 1892. A year earlier Beard had unsuccessfully labored on the concept of a fish plate for a railroad, though he did not receive a patent.

Nineteenth-century African Americans often found employment with the railroad as firemen and switchmen, where they made significant contributions. For example, ELIJAH MCCOY, who studied mechanical engineering in Scotland, earlier worked as a fireman for the Michigan Central Railroad, where he invented a drip cup lubricating system in 1872. This lubricating device was modified for use in numerous other industries. Beard's employment with the Alabama and Chattanooga Railroad increased his exposure to mechanized instruments and led to his most significant invention, the automatic car-coupling, called the Jenny Coupler, which reduced the loss of life and limb. The job of hooking railroad cars had been done by individual workers, who had to climb down between two cars to insert the heavy iron pin that would hold the cars together. As the speed at which two cars could be brought together to be coupled was not mechanically controlled, the cars could crash together hard and fast. Many railroad workers were seriously injured—Beard himself reportedly lost a leg trying to couple two railroad cars together—and some even lost their lives. Aware of the grave danger faced by switchmen, who lacked insurance, he worked tirelessly, sometimes going without meals, to invent a safety device that made it unnecessary for switchmen to risk bodily harm as they connected train cars. On 23 November 1897, he received a patent for the Jenny Coupler, which sold for $50,000 to a New York company. This was followed by subsequent patents issued for improvements on 28 May 1901 and 31 May 1904. Another patent for improvements was assigned to the Beard Automatic Coupler Company on 19 December 1905. He later received recognition as an honorary member of the Master Car Builders Association and exhibited his invention at the association's convention in Atlantic City, New Jersey.

The facts of his later life remain unclear, but it is known that Beard rode a shiny buggy and had the image of a successful businessman, dressed in a vest and suit jacket and wearing eyeglasses. He acquired considerable landholdings and owned the Beard's Jitney (Taxi) Line in Birmingham, yet illiteracy coupled by unwise business decisions likely contributed to economic hardship in his final years. How he disposed of his considerable wealth is not known. Some reported that he donated several lots in Montgomery to support a school for African American children, and others indicated that he provided money to the same school in his will. In his latter years he fell upon hard times and was admitted to the Jefferson County Alms House in Birmingham, Alabama, where he died.

FURTHER READING

"Andrew Jackson Beard." *The National Cyclopedia* (1893).

Sluby, Patricia Carter. *The Inventive Spirit of African Americans: Patented Ingenuity* (2004).

Sullivan, Otha Richard. *African American Inventors* (1998).

ROLAND BARKSDALE-HALL

Beard, Matthew (1 Jan. 1925–8 Jan. 1981), actor, was born Matthew Beard Jr. in Los Angeles, California, to Johnnie Mae Beard and Matthew Beard Sr. The oldest boy, he and his father were born on New Year's Day. Little is known about his parents, except that his father was a longtime minister in Los Angeles. Beard's father heard that there was an audition being held by Hal Roach, the creator and producer of the popular *Our Gang* film series, for a black child to replace Allen "Farina" Hoskins, who was growing too old for the role. Three hundred and fifty children auditioned, but director Bob McGowan was so impressed by little Matthew's confidence, nonchalance, expressive eyes, and contagious smile that he signed him up for five years without a screen test.

Matthew's younger sister, Betty Jane, preceded him in two earlier shorts. His other siblings and even his mother made later appearances in the series, but it was Matthew who became a regular in *Our Gang*, playing the role of Stymie from 1930 to 1935. Beard's first appearance in an *Our Gang* comedy was as Hercules in "Teacher's Pet" (1930). Beard was so curious and excited about being on a movie set that he constantly wandered around the studio examining the props and gimmicks. He interfered with the shoot so often that a frustrated Bob McGowan uttered, "This kid's beautiful, but he stymies me all the time" (Maltin and Bann, 259). Thereafter, his character was named Stymie.

Stymie may have gotten in the way, but he was also McGowan's favorite *Our Gang* kid. He wasn't alone. Beard was a crowd pleaser. His star power increased as he evolved from being a sidekick to a major player in *Our Gang*. Powered by an outsized personality and a charming, effervescent grin, he was a natural scene-stealer. Sporting his trademark oversized bowler hat that often sat askew on his shaved head, Beard's precociousness and comedic talent enabled him to transcend the stereotypes littering the *Our Gang* territory. DONALD BOGLE writes in his book *Toms, Coons, Mulattoes, Mammies, & Bucks* that race was not significant in the relationship between the black and white children despite the accepted notions and attitudes of the day. "Indeed, the charming sense of 'Our Gang' was that all the children were buffoons … forever plagued by setbacks and sidetracks as they set out to have fun, and everyone had his turn at being outwitted" (23). However, few could outsmart Stymie: "Stymie is one of the most self-reliant characters in the history of *Our Gang*. He can hold his own against any child or adult in the series just by using his wits, and never does he surrender his basic charm and appeal in the process" (Maltin and Bann, 106).

Beard delivered one-liners with a glint in his eye and the assurance of a seasoned pro. He mastered the art of deadpan expressions and hilarious double-takes. He was such an excellent performer that the studio nicknamed him "One-take Stymie." Beard later said, "A lot of my ability just came from the natural thing, that I guess was a gift from the Good Lord" (Maltin and Bann, 107). Beard proved he could be just as effective in dramatic scenes. It's hard not to feel Stymie's pain when he bursts into tears in "The Pooch" (1932) after being falsely accused of stealing the gang's beloved dog, Pete.

Beard remembered the Hal Roach lot as a special place filled with lots of fun and laughter. Between takes he observed many of the comedy stars of the era working on nearby sets. The one he watched the most, he remembered, was Stan Laurel, of Laurel and Hardy. "One day Laurel said, 'Well, give this kid a derby.' That's why it never fit me; it belonged to Stan Laurel!" (Maltin and Bann, 259). Later, Beard discovered that according to the English music hall tradition, the derby given to him by Laurel represented the crown of comedy. In later years Beard visited the ill comedian at his home in Santa Monica, California. Shortly before Laurel died Beard told him how much his friendship meant to him.

William Thomas, who played Buckwheat, eventually replaced Beard's Stymie. "They brought William out when I was beginning to get too large, and I just had that funny feeling. I heard the footsteps, but I didn't want to go" (Maltin and Bann, 156). The transition for Beard was difficult. As a movie star he received loving accolades from fans and attention from the director and such luminaries as Laurel and Hardy. But once he got home he had to survive the rough day-to-day existence that comes from living in poverty.

Beard went on to play minor parts (sometimes credited as Stymie Beard) in feature films including *Jezebel* (1938), *The Great Man Votes* (1939), *Stormy*

Weather (1943), Captain Blood (1935), Two Gun Man from Harlem (1938), Broken Strings (1940), and Way down South (1939). Two Gun Man from Harlem and Broken Strings were so-called race films. After a time, though, Beard stopped acting. He dropped out of high school and began a drug habit that would last for decades. Almost thirty years later, a heroin addict, Beard checked himself into Synanon, a drug rehabilitation facility. He cleaned himself up and made a comeback, winning minor roles in feature films such as Truck Turner (1974) and The Buddy Holly Story (1978), along with television shows like Sanford and Son, Good Times, Starsky and Hutch, Diff'rent Strokes, and The Jeffersons.

Acting was not Beard's only passion. After his recovery, he traveled around the country lecturing and inspiring others as he shared his personal stories about drug abuse. Beard was married once, but the marriage may have been short-lived and in any event produced no children. In 1981 Beard suffered a stroke, contracted pneumonia, and died at the University of Southern California Medical Center. He was buried with his trademark bowler beside him.

FURTHER READING

Bogle, Donald. Bright Boulevards, Bold Dreams: The Story of Black Hollywood (2005).

Bogle, Donald. Toms, Coons, Mulattoes, Mammies, & Bucks (2001).

Maltin, Leonard, and Richard W. Bann. The Little Rascals: The Life and Times of Our Gang (1977, 1992).

Richards, Larry. African American Films through 1959 (1998).

WAYNE L. WILSON

Bearden, Romare (2 Sept. 1911–11 Mar. 1988), artist, was born Romare Howard Bearden in Charlotte, North Carolina, the son of R. Howard Bearden, a grocer, and Bessye Johnson. When Bearden was about four years old, the family moved to New York, settling in Harlem, where he went to public school and his parents developed a wide network of acquaintances among the Harlem jazz musicians and intellectuals of the day. His father later became an inspector for the New York Board of Health; his mother, a civic leader. Bearden finished high school in Pittsburgh, however, having lived there for a time with his grandmother. In 1932, after two years at Boston University, he transferred to New York University, where he created illustrations for the undergraduate humor magazine and earned a B.S. degree in Education in 1935. For the next two years he contributed political cartoons to the Baltimore Afro-American. Unable to find steady work, he enrolled at the Art Students League and studied drawing with the German emigré artist George Grosz in 1936–1937.

At about this time, Bearden joined the 306 Group, an informal association of black artists and writers—among them JACOB LAWRENCE and RALPH ELLISON—who met in the studio of his cousin, the painter CHARLES ALSTON, at 306 West 141st Street. From 1938 to 1942, now beginning to paint, Bearden supported himself as a full-time caseworker with the New York City Department of Social Services, a job to which he returned after World War II. In 1940, at the Harlem studio of a friend, Ad Bates, Bearden exhibited some of the work he had completed over the past four years, including paintings in oil and gouache, watercolors, and drawings. Taking his own studio on 125th Street, located over the Apollo Theater, he began work on a series of paintings that evoked the rural South of his childhood. Typical of the series is Folk Musicians (1941–1942), painted in a bold and dramatic style with flat planes and simplified, colorful figures.

While serving with an all-black regiment in 1944, Bearden mounted a solo exhibition at the "G" Place Gallery in Washington, D.C., which brought him to the attention of the influential New York dealer Samuel Kootz. Bearden's first exhibition at the Kootz Gallery, in 1945, was devoted to the Passion of Christ series, a group of semiabstract, cubist-inspired watercolors on paper. The exhibition was highly successful in terms of reviews and sales; He Is Arisen, purchased by the Museum of Modern Art in New York, was the first of Bearden's works to enter a museum collection. The following year, Kootz exhibited Bearden's painting Lament for a Bullfighter, inspired by García Lorca's poem "Lament for the Death of a Bullfighter." Inclusion of Bearden's works in the 1945 and 1946 annuals at the Whitney Museum of American Art in New York and in the Abstract and Surrealist American Art show held at the Art Institute of Chicago in 1948 further boosted his growing reputation. In 1951 Bearden went to Paris on the GI Bill to study philosophy at the Sorbonne. In addition to meeting the Cubist masters Pablo Picasso and Georges Braque, Bearden joined the circle of black artists and writers inspired by the concept of negritude. As he later admitted, however, the most significant thing he learned during his year in France was how to relate the black experience to universal experience. Between 1952, when he returned to New York, and 1954, the year he married the West Indian dancer Nanette Rohan, Bearden devoted himself mainly to music; some twenty of the songs he wrote in this period were published and recorded. Bearden then returned to painting and set up a new studio in lower Manhattan, on Canal Street, where he and his wife lived for the rest of his life. (They had no children.) In 1961 he showed some of his now wholly abstract oil paintings in the first of several solo exhibitions at the Cordier & Ekstrom Gallery, his dealers from that year on.

Bearden, who had described art in the journal he began keeping in 1947 as "a kind of divine play" (Schwartzman, 217), was increasingly drawn to collage, a way of "playing" with assortments of materials to create a whole and a medium much employed by the Cubists. He created his first signed collage, *Circus*, in 1961; three years later collage became his chief method of expression. The beginning of the civil rights movement and his participation in the discussions of the Spiral Group (which he cofounded in 1963) on the role of black artists in a time of new challenges coincided with this profound change in Bearden's art. In 1964 he created a series of small montages composed of fragments of reproductions cut from newspapers, magazines, or postcards and pasted onto a paper backing; these assemblages were then photographed and enlarged. The resulting *Projections*, as Bearden titled them, were exhibited that year at Cordier & Ekstrom. Later, arranged in series by subject matter, they were developed into true collages. One such sequence, titled *The Prevalence of Ritual*, includes individual panels representing "The Funeral," "The Baptism," and "The Conjur Woman." Another collage series evokes Harlem street life, as in *The Dove*, a crowded assemblage of cutout figures set against a suggestion of city buildings. The bizarrely composite figures, the abrupt shifts in scale between heads and bodies, and the arbitrary spatial relationships convey the rich, kaleidoscopic variety of the scene. Other series recall the Harlem jazz world of the 1930s (*The Savoy*, for example) and southern life (the nostalgic *Train Whistle Blues*).

As Bearden developed his collage techniques into the 1970s, he began to incorporate more of his own painted touches, in acrylics or watercolors, as well as torn pieces of paper in various hand-painted colors and bits of fabric. Spaces were opened up and thus were easier to perceive. Coinciding with the start of annual visits to his wife's family home on Saint Martin, the artist's palette took on the lush colors of the Caribbean and the collage figures became overtly sensuous. One of these later collages, *The Block* (1971), a large six-panel composition, approached mixed-media work; with the accompaniment of taped gospel and blues music, children's voices, and actual street noises, it recreated the look, sounds, and "feel" of an urban street.

Besides working in collage, Bearden designed tapestries and posters; in 1968 he was represented in an international poster exhibition in Warsaw, Poland. He designed sets for the Alvin Ailey Dance Company in 1977 and continued to make prints, including the colored lithographs that illustrate a 1983 edition of the work of the Caribbean poet DEREK WALCOTT. He also created murals, such as *Quilting Time*, commissioned by the Detroit Institute of Arts and installed there in 1986. In it, the quilter and six onlookers form a frieze against a brilliantly hued tropical setting. The whole is a mosaic of glass tesserae, so combined and colored as to suggest the molding of bodies and the textures and folds of fabrics.

A large traveling retrospective of Bearden's work, organized by the Mint Museum in Charlotte, North Carolina, in 1980 and concluding its tour at the Brooklyn Museum in 1981, capped Bearden's career. Also in 1980 he taught at Yale University, one of several temporary teaching posts he held during the course of his career. Represented in every major museum in New York City and in others throughout the country, he is considered to have transformed collage, generally regarded as a minor art form, into a forceful means of expression with universal appeal. His biographer called him "An artist for all seasons and for all humankind" (Schwartzman, 305).

In addition to *The Painter's Mind: A Study of Structure and Space in Painting*, written with his longtime friend, the artist Carl Holty (1969), Bearden wrote (with Harry Henderson) *A History of Afro-American Artists from 1792 to the Present*, which was posthumously published in 1993. He and Henderson also wrote a book for young readers, *Six Black Masters of American Art* (1972).

Part of Bearden's legacy consists of his multiple roles as teacher; as art director of the Harlem Cultural Council, to which he was appointed in 1964; as organizer of the landmark exhibition, the Evolution of Afro-American Artists: 1800–1950, held at City College of New York in 1967; and as cofounder, in 1969, of the Cinque Gallery in New York, a showcase for younger artists from various minority groups. For these contributions, Bearden was inducted into the National Institute of Arts and Letters in 1966; he was honored by his home state in 1976 as recipient of the Governor's Medal of the State of North Carolina, and he also was awarded the National Medal of Arts in 1987. The Pratt Institute (1973) and Carnegie-Mellon University (1975) awarded him honorary doctorates. He died in New York City.

FURTHER READING

The Schomburg Center for Research in Black Culture of the New York Public Library is the primary source of archival material relating to Bearden: photographs, his sketchbook and notebooks, and correspondence. The center also maintains a collection of his posters as well as examples of his other work. The Archives of American Art in New York houses the Romare Bearden Papers.

Campbell, Mary Schmidt, and Sharon F. Patton. *Memory and Metaphor: The Art of Romare Bearden, 1940–1987* (1991).

Igoe, Lynn M., with James Igoe. *250 Years of Afro-American Art: An Annotated Bibliography* (1981).

Schwartzman, Marvin. *Romare Bearden: His Life and Art* (1990).

Obituary: *New York Times*, 13 Mar. 1988.

This entry is taken from the *American National Biography* and is published here with the permission of the American Council of Learned Societies.

ELEANOR F. WEDGE

Beasley, Delilah Leontium (9 Sept. 1871–18 Aug. 1934), journalist and historian of the early West, was born in Cincinnati, Ohio, the eldest of five children of Daniel Beasley, an engineer, and Margaret (Heines) Beasley, a homemaker. Although little is known about her childhood, at the age of twelve Beasley published her first writings in the black-owned newspaper, the *Cleveland Gazette*. By the time she was fifteen she was working as a columnist for the *Cincinnati Enquirer*, becoming the first African American woman to write for a mainstream newspaper on a regular basis.

Beasley lost both parents as a teenager and was forced to take a full-time job working as a domestic laborer for the family of a white judge named Hagan. Her career then took several unusual turns as Beasley, who was described by biographer Lorraine Crouchett as "short, well-proportioned, and speaking in a shrill, light voice" (perhaps because of a chronic hearing problem), did not hesitate to embark on unconventional professional pursuits. She was often viewed as "eccentric and ahead of her time." After traveling to Elmhurst, Illinois, with the Hagans to work in their summer home, Beasley decided to relocate to Chicago, where she was employed as a masseuse. During this period she also studied medical gymnastics, scalp treatment, and physical therapy. Again and again she relocated in pursuit of her studies and interests: back to Ohio, to New York to work with pregnant women at the Buffalo Sanitarium, and eventually to Michigan, where she became head masseuse at a family resort. While continuing her work and studies in the health sciences Beasley used her free time to research African American history, taking advantage of the private libraries of friends and clients who allowed her access to valuable books. This began what would become Beasley's lifelong passion: a study of the undocumented history of African Americans in the West.

When she was in her early forties, in 1910, Beasley was invited to move to Berkeley, California, to work as a nurse and physical therapist with a former patient. Over the next eight years Beasley, who never married, dedicated herself completely to her research projects. Initially planning for a mere lecture series on the topic she conducted numerous interviews with local figures and traveled throughout the state to gather oral histories; she compiled tax documents and real estate and hospital records; she attended classes at the University of California, Berkeley; and she poured over newspaper archives at Berkeley's Bancroft Library.

While in California Beasley returned to her journalistic beginnings, penning in 1915 a well-received series of articles for the *Oakland Tribune* in protest of D. W. Griffith's movie *The Birth of a Nation*. This work won the journalist praise and recognition from the NAACP and helped to inspire a nationwide boycott of the film. Although she could have made a comfortable living as a masseuse at any time Beasley instead devoted her energies to historical research, earning just $10 a week for her *Tribune* column. After hearing her first lecture on the topic of pioneering black figures in the West, titled "My City of Inspiration—San Francisco," Beasley's friend, the minister David R. Wallace, convinced her to publish the findings as a book. Unable to find a publisher she placed herself into debt by borrowing the necessary funds from a colleague at the *Oakland Tribune*. She eventually published *The Negro Trail Blazers of California* in 1919, offering biographies of notable black figures from the era of slavery through statehood, as well as reports of the ongoing accomplishments of the black middle class. Although the book was the first such history of its kind, it received poor reviews from some historians, among them CARTER GODWIN WOODSON, who considered the work amateurish and flawed. Others, however, praised the book's groundbreaking documentation of positive contributions by black Americans.

In 1923 Beasley began writing a regular column for the *Oakland Tribune*, "Activities among Negroes," in which she condemned vociferously the use of derogatory terms like "nigger," "darkie," and "coon." Her efforts were far-reaching, and she even traveled long distances to make personal visits with editors in her campaign against such disparaging treatment. During the 1920s Beasley also became increasingly active in women's organizations. Always an adamant integrationist she was the only black female member of the press at the 1925 National Convention of Women Voters in Richmond, Virginia. She also worked with the League of Nations Association, the National League of Women Voters, and the World Forum on issues of civil rights and world peace. Following her retirement from the *Oakland Tribune* in 1925, she became particularly active in the women's club movement, herself becoming a trailblazing member of the National Association of Colored Women, and spearheading efforts to bring the group's 1925 national convention to Oakland. In addition she was a founding member of the Oakland branch of the National Urban League.

Throughout her life Beasley suffered from poor health due to heart disease, illnesses that eventually led to her death. Beasley's crowning work, *The Negro Trail Blazers of California*, was neglected for a time after its initial publication and was not resurrected until 1968, when it was reprinted by the California Historical Society and the San Francisco Negro Historical and Cultural Society.

FURTHER READING

Crouchett, Lorraine J. *Delilah Leontium Beasley: Oakland's Crusading Journalist* (1989).

Dannett, Sylvia G. L. *Profiles of Negro Womanhood* (1964).

Dillon, Richard H. *Humbugs and Heroes: A Gallery of California Pioneers* (1970).

Streitmatter, Rodger. *Raising Her Voice: African-American Women Journalists Who Changed History* (1994).

KRISTAL BRENT ZOOK

Beasley, Mathilda Taylor (Nov. 1832?–20 Dec. 1903), Catholic nun, was born Mathilda Taylor in New Orleans, Louisiana, to Caroline Taylor, a slave owned by James C. Taylor, whose surname he gave to his slaves. Her father, whose name is not known, was Native American. Little is known about Mathilda's early years, except that she learned to read and write and that she somehow received her freedom and moved to Savannah. There she began operating a secret school for African American children in the late 1850s, an enterprise for which she risked imprisonment because state laws prohibited education for blacks.

Taylor supported herself by working a variety of jobs in Savannah. In the 1860s she was employed at the Railroad House, a restaurant owned by Abraham Beasley, a prosperous free black man. In 1869 she married Beasley. His ventures included a produce market, a saloon, a boardinghouse, and, at times, the slave trade. The two had no children, and Mathilda Beasley was widowed in 1877. She inherited her husband's property, an estate that included five acres of land worth more than three hundred dollars.

In the 1880s Beasley departed for England to train as a nun. Upon her return she donated her husband's estate to the Sacred Heart Catholic Church of Savannah in order to establish the Saint Francis Home for Colored Orphans. The all-female orphanage began operation in 1887. Two years later Beasley founded the Third Order of Saint Francis, a religious order for black nuns. The community struggled to gain financial backing and remained a small group; in 1896 the Catholic directory listed five African American sisters and nineteen black orphan girls in Savannah. The group founded by Beasley built on earlier efforts by black Catholic women to establish religious communities. In 1829 MARY ELIZABETH LANGE founded the first such order, the Oblate Sisters of Providence.

In 1893 Beasley traveled to Philadelphia, Pennsylvania, where she visited Katherine Drexel, the wealthy heiress who had established the Sisters of the Blessed Sacrament for Indians and Colored People in 1890 as a means of evangelizing to those minority groups. Beasley requested both spiritual and financial aid from Drexel for her own religious order. Drexel briefly considered merging the two orders and transferring the Pennsylvania community to South Carolina, but she ultimately decided against such action, primarily because of racial issues. Beasley also communicated with a Cardinal Gibbons, requesting aid for the society in the form of new members. Her efforts continued, with requests to Father John Slattery, unofficial overseer of African American Catholic works in the United States. Her letters to Slattery included requests for books, more sisters, and any other aid that could be allotted to the struggling community.

Despite her efforts Beasley was unable to obtain the resources necessary to maintain the religious order. In 1898 the Third Order of Saint Francis was suppressed and the Saint Francis orphanage fell under the auspices of the Missionary Franciscan Sisters of the Immaculate Conception. Upon the order's dissolution Beasley retired to a small cottage adjacent to the orphanage; there she died during her prayers at the age of seventy-one. Though the religious order she founded failed to survive, Beasley's efforts continued the work of black Catholic women and helped to establish a precedent for African American nuns.

FURTHER READING

Davis, Cyprian. *The History of Black Catholics in the United States* (1990).

Obituary: *Savannah Morning News*, 21 Dec. 1903.

TONIA M. COMPTON

Beasley, Phoebe (3 June 1943–), artist and businesswoman, was born in Cleveland, Ohio, to George A. Beasley and Annette P. Beasley, both of whom worked at a local country club. Like many artists, she revealed considerable talent in childhood, excelling in school art classes and enjoying parental support for her creativity. She graduated from John Adams High School in Cleveland in 1961, and began her formal training at Ohio University, where she earned a BFA in Visual Arts in 1965. After graduation, she started teaching art at Cleveland's Glenville High School; she held this position from 1965 to 1969. During that time, she had a brief marriage in 1968 to Louis Evans, about whom little is known. They divorced in 1969.

In 1969 she moved to Los Angeles. After a year as a layout artist for Sage Publications, a leading publisher of social science books and journals, she became an advertising executive for KFI/KOST radio stations in Los Angeles. Beasley achieved enormous success in the field, securing several

major accounts including McDonald's, Toyota, and Ford Motor Company. Beasley's enduring personal discipline enabled her to devote several hours a day to artwork on top of her corporate responsibilities, and she became accomplished in both advertising and art. She retired from the radio position in 1999 so she could focus primarily on art. Beasley found mainstream art institutions exclusionary and elitist: many white gallery owners bluntly expressed their unwillingness to feature African American art. Like most black artists in America, Beasley discovered early in her career the deeply ingrained racial biases of mainstream art institutions. White gallery owners repeatedly informed her of their unwillingness to carry works with African American subject matter.

In spite of the obstacles, Beasley developed a reputation as a leading African American artist of the late twentieth century. Resolved to use her art to communicate her observations about her own people, she created works with an African American focus while offering a deeper universal vision about the human condition.

Her first major breakthrough as an artist came through the efforts of basketball great BILL RUSSELL, who had seen her work in Los Angeles in 1970. In 1976 he arranged an individual show for her in Seattle's Polly Friedlander Gallery. Following that, Beasley exhibited her work in numerous individual and group shows in galleries and museums throughout the country. In addition to their representations in many public and corporate collections, her paintings have been acquired by several prominent private collectors, including African American luminaries OPRAH WINFREY, MAYA ANGELOU, BILL RUSSELL, and TAVIS SMILEY.

Her artwork demonstrated a unique personal style, combining figurative elements blended effectively with the abstract forms she learned as a student. Her early efforts in "hard edge" abstraction informed her mature paintings and collages, a fusion of European and American modernist styles marshaled to narrate episodes of African American history and culture. The artistic influences of her youth—Jackson Pollock, Oskar Kokoschka, and Willem de Kooning—were apparent in many of her figurally abstract paintings and energetic collages. Her skill in combining color and form with paint, tissue paper, found objects, and cloth provided her artworks with a compelling jazz-like rhythm reminiscent of the signature works of ROMARE BEARDEN. Her thematic focus revealed her sympathetic feeling for ordinary people engaged in the routine activities of life: sewing, reading, studying, cooking, waiting, and traveling. Her paintings simultaneously ennobled their subjects, encouraging audiences to view them with dignity and respect, in dramatic contrast to American popular culture's long history of racist caricature and stereotype. That vision reflected a profound humanism that built on the similar perspectives of several prominent figures of African American art, such as JACOB LAWRENCE, CHARLES WHITE, LOIS JONES, ELIZABETH CATLETT, and JOHN BIGGERS. Beasley's view of African American women was particularly striking; her engaging works with female subjects add an outstanding dimension to a theme pervading African American art since the nineteenth century.

Like many other African American artists of the twentieth and twenty-first century, Beasley's works often commented on institutionalized racism in the United States and the challenges of redressing it. *Executive Order 9981*, a mixed-media work on canvas, called dramatic attention to President Harry S. Truman's 1948 order that desegregated the United States military, fully three years after the Allied victory in World War II. Its bold composition and vibrant colors served to remind viewers to understand history and to appreciate both the progress and problems in implementing the ideals of a democratic society.

Beasley received the Presidential Seal of Official Artist from George H. W. Bush in 1989 and Bill Clinton in 1993; she was the only artist to be so honored twice. She also served as an official artist in President Clinton's administration. Her artistic excellence has brought her many public commissions, including service as an official artist of the 2000 Los Angeles Marathon and the 2000 Democratic National Convention. In 2005 she received an honorary Doctor of Fine Arts degree from her alma mater, Ohio University, where she delivered the commencement address to the graduating class.

Beyond her business and artistic successes, Beasley forged a durable commitment to civic activism in the Los Angeles area. From 1980 to 1984 she was president of the California Museum of African American Art, an institution founded by legendary art historian and artist SAMELLA LEWIS. She also served as a member of the Los Angeles County Arts Commission beginning in 1997, where her efforts advanced artistic creativity in the most populous county in the United States, through the commission's art grants program. In 1998 she

began working with the Story Project Foundation, an organization dedicated to building confidence and encouraging literacy among teenagers through after-school programs and mentoring. Finally, in collaboration with Maya Angelou, Beasley published *Sunrise Is Coming after While* (1998), a limited-edition book of text and serigraphs interpreting the poems of LANGSTON HUGHES.

FURTHER READING
Bain, Terry. "Phoebe Beasley," in *St. James Guide to Black Artists*, ed. Thomas Riggs (1997).
Hanks, Eric, ed. *Masterpieces of African American Art: An African American Perspective* (2007).
Hanks, Eric, ed. *Timeless Textured Threads: Artwork by Phoebe Beasley* (2005).
King-Hammond, Leslie, ed. *Gumbo Ya Ya: Anthology of Contemporary African-American Women Artists* (1995).
Lewis, Samella. *African American Art and Artists* (2003).

PAUL VON BLUM

Beatty, Talley (1919–29 Apr. 1995), choreographer, dancer, and teacher, was born in Cedar Grove, Louisiana, the son of a housepainter. His parents' names are unknown. In the small town of Cedar Grove, right outside Shreveport, Beatty's earliest dance influence was the legendary KATHERINE DUNHAM. According to the historian Joe Nash, a close friend and colleague of Beatty, Dunham invited him to "watch dances in progress" when he was eleven years old. Dunham was in rehearsal for Ruth Page's *La Guillablesse*, scheduled to open at the Chicago Civic Opera in 1933, and was trying to keep the young boy's playing from disrupting her work. Beatty danced onstage for the first time in the opera's 1934 season and emerged as a dancer of note after studying from 1937 to 1940 at Dunham's Studio de la Danse in Shreveport. He danced the role of a priest in Dunham's *Yanvalou*, a snakelike dance in honor of the voodoo deity Damballa, at the historic Negro Dance Evening, 7 March 1937, at the Ninety-Second Street Young Men's Hebrew Association in New York City.

Beatty toured with the Katherine Dunham Company for nineteen years. He was in the brief 1940–1941 run of *Cabin in the Sky* on Broadway and appeared in films with the Dunham company, including *Carnival of Rhythm* (1941), *Cuban Episode* (1942), *Flamingo* (1942), and *Stormy Weather* (1943). In the late 1940s he appeared in Maya Deren's innovative film *Choreography for Camera*. He danced in the 1946 revival of *Show Boat* with PEARL PRIMUS, Joe Nash, and Alma Sutton. He returned to New York around 1950. Beatty left Dunham's company to form a duo with the celebrated JANET COLLINS, who was the first black prima ballerina, from 1951 to 1954 at the Metropolitan Opera House.

Beatty's ballets have been classified as part of a jazz idiom; however, the movements are not vernacular, and they never fall into an unidentifiable heap of clichéd gesture. In fact his dances, which survive in the repertoire of the Philadelphia Dance Company, the Dayton Contemporary Dance Company, and the ALVIN AILEY American Dance Theater, are not only virtuoso tours de force but also transformative excursions into human need. Beatty's sagas of city living, depicted by fast-paced movement, convoluted interactions between text and subtext, and the tensions created by social challenges, are a testimony to his choreographic facility. Beatty's legacy is part of a long tradition of dance as social commentary and as a catalyst for social change.

The *New York Times* critic Anna Kisselgoff had this to say about his work in 1989: "What is a Beatty signature? It is primarily his genius for putting technical perfection at the service of emotional expression. Inventing a jazz idiom that has the continuum of classical dancing, he has composed dance poems of urban existence. Their structure is largely abstract, creating drama through pattern and composition." Despite the fact that Kisselgoff incorrectly labels the work as "a jazz idiom," probably because Beatty used classical jazz scores from the likes of MILES DAVIS, DUKE ELLINGTON, and BILLY STRAYHORN in his distillation of ideas and motifs, along with short, tight, isolated gestures to frame and accent large technical phrases, she is on target when she notes the structure of his dances. Beatty was a master craftsman of mood and innuendo. With just the right mix of gestural mapping, speed, rhythmic thrust, and abstraction, he created dances that challenged notions of dance patterning and stylistic classification.

Beatty's first major work, *Southern Landscapes* (1947), a response to Howard Fast's book *Freedom Road*, was reconstructed by the Philadelphia Dance Company in 1992. A ballet in four sections, *Southern Landscapes* comments on the rise of the Ku Klux Klan after the Civil War. Between 1947 and 1955 Beatty toured with his company, Tropicana, and created many memorable masterpieces, including *The Road of Phoebe Snow* (1959), which chronicles the journey of a luxury train that passes through the backyards of the United States witnessing people who are alienated from themselves and their communities, and *Come and Get the Beauty of It Hot* (1960), which takes audiences through a day in the lives of Harlemites. "Toccata," the opening segment of *Beauty*, is a collage of finger-popping, body-slapping moves atop technical ploys. Dancers take to their knees, twist in diverse directions, and end, hovering, in nearly upside-down balances; "Toccata" is often performed independently. The final section of *Beauty*, "Congo, Tango, Palace," which depicts the elegance and bravura of flamenco executed in a Spanish Harlem ballroom, is also performed as a solo work. The ballet, excerpted and in its entirety, is a staple of the Dayton Contemporary Dance Company. Other ballets that span Beatty's forty-eight years of dance making include *Tropicana* (1949); *Migration* (1964); *Bring My Servant Home* (1969), a tribute to MARTIN LUTHER KING JR.; *The Stack-Up* (1983); *A Rag, a Bone, and a Hank of Hair* (1985); and *Such Sweet Morning Songs* (1990).

In addition to his work on the concert stage as a dancer and a choreographer, Beatty created television specials, like Duke Ellington's "Black, Brown, and Beige" for CBS in 1974, and made movement for the Broadway show *Your Arms Too Short to Box with God*, which was nominated for a Tony Award in 1977. As a teacher Beatty also made his mark in the 1960s and 1970s. Students at the Alma Lewis School of Fine Arts in Boston and the Fred Benjamin Dance Company in New York as well as dance students in England, France, Sweden, and Israel had the opportunity to experience his rare gifts. Beatty had a wry sense of humor, an acute awareness of the human condition, and the courage to speak from his heart and soul. His death in New York City caused a silence in the dance world.

Declared a "living legend" in 1992 during the National Black Arts Festival in Atlanta, Georgia, and a recipient of the Samuel H. Scripps–American Dance Festival Award in 1993, Beatty was indeed a national treasure. He created more than fifty ballets that were performed by some fourteen companies in the United States, Europe, and western Asia. A member of Ballet Society (which became the New York City Ballet in 1933), Beatty not only defied the images ascribed to blacks during his time but also set a standard for performance that has become a model for contemporary dancers of all ethnic groups. Even when blacks were stereotyped as incapable of performing ballet, Beatty dared to dance and choreograph as he chose. A consummate ballet technician, he blended ballet with other ethnic styles. With the language of the body, he provided blueprints of everyday life for all humanity.

FURTHER READING

Barnes, Clive. "Dance: Beatty Winding Up City Center Season," *New York Times*, 21 May 1969.

Bartett, B. S. K. "Talley Beatty Company in Vivid Performance at John Hancock Hall," *Boston Globe*, 15 Jan. 1952.

Emery, Lynne Fauley. *Black Dance: From 1619 to Today*, 2d ed. (1988).

Long, Richard A. *The Black Tradition in American Dance* (1989).

This entry is taken from the *American National Biography* and is published here with the permission of the American Council of Learned Societies.

C. S'THEMBILE WEST

Beaty, Powhatan (1839?–6 Dec. 1916), Medal of Honor recipient, actor, and playwright, was born in Richmond, Virginia, of unknown parentage. Beaty (sometimes spelled Beatty) was born a slave, but little else is known of his early years or how he came to be free. Beaty left Richmond in 1849 for Cincinnati, where he would spend the majority of his life, and became a farmer. Later, Beaty's education consisted of an apprenticeship to a black cabinetmaker in Cincinnati, as well as a tutelage under James E. Murdock, a retired professional actor and dramatic coach.

On 5 September 1862 Powhatan Beaty, along with 706 other African American men, was forced to join Cincinnati's Black Brigade after Confederate troops repeatedly threatened the city. The Black Brigade was one of the earliest, but unofficial, African American military units organized during the Civil War, but it did not engage in any military action since the city was never attacked. Instead, the brigade was tasked with building fortifications for the city and digging tunnels beneath the Ohio River in northern Kentucky, work that the white brigades were not asked to perform. Moreover, police officers had violently forced the men from their homes and places of work with billy clubs and bayonet points, and they were paraded through the streets of the city like prisoners. Despite the insulting experience with the Black Brigade, and the nation's formal repudiation of black service in the army, as the war between the North and the South began to escalate, so did Beaty's thirst for real military action. After the Lincoln administration began allowing black recruitment, on 5 June 1863, at the

Powhatan Beaty, Civil War veteran, Congressional Medal of Honor recipient, actor, and playwright, c. 1900. (Library of Congress/Daniel Murray Collection.)

age of twenty-four, Beaty enlisted as a private in the Union Army at Camp Delaware, Ohio, an all-black recruiting camp for African American enlistees. Beaty enlisted for three years and became a part of Company G, Fifth United States Colored Troops (USCT). Only two days later, he was promoted to first sergeant, one of the highest ranks an African American soldier could attain. Beaty is best known for his role in the Battle of Chaffin's Farm (sometimes called Chapin's Farm), also known as the Battle of Fort Harrison or, more broadly, the Battle of New Market Heights, in Virginia on 29 September 1864. The Battle of New Market Heights was part of a larger effort by General Ulysses S. Grant to weaken Confederate Robert E. Lee's defenses in order to take back the city of Richmond and the surrounding area of Petersburg, Virginia. The clash primarily took place on New Market Road in Henrico County, later a suburb of Richmond, and the battle is most noteworthy because it resulted in the eventual and permanent possession of the fort by Union forces. Beaty's infantry was a part of the second wave of attacks in New Market Heights that took place at around 6 A.M. on 29 September

1864. The first wave was sent under the command of Union General Thomas Paine at around 5:30 A.M. and consisted of 685 men, of whom 365 died. After the white officers of his unit had all either been killed or wounded, Beaty, although wounded himself, took command of his company and led the soldiers into battle until he was ordered to retreat. During the retreat, he noticed that the color-bearer had been killed and that the flag was no longer in sight. Amidst increasing gunfire, Beaty returned to the scene of warfare and retrieved the flag. Beaty was awarded the Medal of Honor for his actions during this struggle, and his Medal of Honor citation states that he "took command of his company, all the officers having been killed or wounded, and gallantly led it" (Kelly, 284). Fourteen other African American soldiers received Medals of Honor for their valiant actions during this critical battle.

After the Civil War, Beaty briefly worked as a porter on the Mississippi River steamboat *City of Vicksburg*. Upon returning to Cincinnati, Beaty went back to cabinetmaking and again took up acting. In the 1870s he began to perform publicly, and near the end of the decade he attained some recognition for his theatrical performances. Earlier in his career, Beaty had played Spartacus in Robert Montgomery Bird's *The Gladiator* to favorable reviews in Cincinnati. Throughout the 1880s, he performed with the famed African American leading actress HENRIETTA VINTON DAVIS in Cincinnati, Washington, D.C., and Philadelphia. Beaty reportedly received high praise for his roles in *Macbeth*, *Richard III*, and *Ingomar, the Barbarian* in the *New York Globe*. In 1880 Beaty wrote a play about the transition from slavery to freedom titled *Delmar; or Scenes in Southland*. The play was performed publicly in 1881 with Beaty himself starring in the leading role as the plantation owner. While there are no official reviews of the play, according to Errol G. Hill, a newspaper commentator, the script "abounds in fine, dramatic situations" (Hill, 83). Finally, in 1888 Beaty became the drama director of the Literary and Dramatic Club of Cincinnati, a club that he had helped form.

Little is known about Beaty's life after 1890, but a historical marker that is a part of the Underground Railroad Heritage program states that he died on 6 December 1916, "leaving two sons, attorney and state representative A. Lee Beaty and John W. Beaty" (Grace, 50). As a testament to Beaty's important place in U.S. history, more specifically his involvement in the Civil War, House Bill 897, dated 10 February 2000, designates the Interstate Route 895 (Pocahontas Parkway) bridge over Virginia Route 5 the "Powhatan Beatty Memorial Bridge." Powhatan Beaty, along with many other prominent African American figures, is buried in the Union Baptist Cemetery in Cincinnati, the oldest African American religious burial ground still in use.

FURTHER READING
Claxton, Melvin, and Mark Puls. *Uncommon Valor: A Story of Race, Patriotism, and Glory in the Final Battles of the Civil War* (2006).
Claxton, Melvin, and Mark Puls. *Uncommon Valor: The Exploits of the New Market Heights Medal of Honor Winners* (2006).
Grace, Kevin, and Tom White. *Cincinnati's Cemeteries: The Queen City of Underground (OH)* (2004).
Hill, Errol G. *A History of African American Theatre* (2003).
Kelly, C. Brian, and Ingrid Smyer-Kelly. *Best Little Ironies, Oddities, and Mysteries of the Civil War* (2000).
Peterson, Bernard L. *Profiles of African American Stage Performers and Theatre People, 1816–1960* (2001).
MARLENE L. DAUT

Beavers, Louise (8 Mar. 1902–26 Oct. 1962), actress, was born in Cincinnati, Ohio, the daughter of William Beavers.

Her mother's identity is not known. As a child Louise moved with her musically inclined family to California, where in 1918 she graduated from Pasadena High School. She then joined the Ladies' Minstrel Troupe for a year before being recognized by talent scouts.

Beavers, who would appear in more than one hundred motion pictures, began her Hollywood career by playing a maid to leading lady Lilyan Tashman in *Gold Diggers* (1923). Early on, maid was a role that Beavers had to play offscreen as well as on. From 1920 to 1926 she worked first as a dressing room attendant and then as the personal maid of the actress Leatrice Joy. In 1927 Beavers landed a major role in *Uncle Tom's Cabin*, followed in 1929 by roles in *Coquette* and *Nix on Dames*. In the early 1930s she earned critical notices for her handling of subservient roles in *Ladies of the Big House* (1932), *What Price Hollywood?* (1932), *Bombshell* (1933), and *She Done Him Wrong* (1933). Big-boned, dark-skinned, and usually smiling on the screen, Beavers was best known for playing the good-natured maid or housekeeper for such stars as Mae West, Claudette Colbert, and Jean Harlow. Typecast as a maid for her entire

Louise Beavers, appearing as the star on the motion picture poster for "Prison Bait," c. 1939. (Library of Congress.)

career, Beavers was seen serving a cavalcade of other motion picture greats, including Clara Bow, Boris Karloff, Hedda Hopper, James Stewart, Joan Crawford, Spencer Tracy, Ralph Bellamy, Ginger Rogers, Joan Blondell, Jimmy Durante, Edward G. Robinson, Humphrey Bogart, Ronald Reagan, Jane Wyman, Rosalind Russell, Henry Fonda, Bing Crosby, John Wayne, Zero Mostel, Orson Welles, Marlene Dietrich, W. C. Fields, SIDNEY POITIER, June Allyson, Jack Lemmon, Debbie Reynolds, Lloyd Bridges, Natalie Wood, and PEARL BAILEY, among many others. As the film historian Donald Bogle has pointed out, Beavers came to epitomize the lovable, loyal, overweight "Mammy" figure seemingly capable of taking on all the troubles of the world. "She perfected the optimistic, sentimental black woman whose sweet, sunny disposition and kindheartedness almost always saved the day, the Depression era's embodiment of Christian stoicism and goodness, lending a friendly ear and hand to down-on-their-luck heroines, who knew

that when the rest of the world failed them, Louise would always be there" (Bogle, 73).

Beavers's professional breakthrough came in her powerful portrayal of the businesslike, pancake-flapping Aunt Delilah to Claudette Colbert's Bea in *Imitation of Life* (1934), a sensitive performance acclaimed by both the white and black press; many critics felt that Beavers deserved an Oscar nomination. Yet what Beavers mostly won from that performance was the "Aunt Jemima" label that would stick to her forever. Despite her screen persona as a domestic, Beavers never cooked, though she did maintain a high-calorie diet to keep her weight up, and she took elocution lessons to cultivate a southern drawl. She married LeRoy Moore in the late 1950s.

Beavers was proud to be featured in two pioneering black-cast films produced by Million Dollar Productions, *Life Goes On* (1938) and *Reform School* (1939), even though in *Reform School* her role as a probation officer was a Mammy-type character. Of note is that, whereas in these films her respective characters were named "Star" and "Mother Barton," in other movies her names were usually associated with black servitude, such as "Lulu" in *The Expert* (1932), "Ivory" in *Ladies of the Big House* (1932) and *Women without Names* (1940), "Pearl" in *She Done Him Wrong* (1933), "Loretta" in *Bombshell* (1933), "Magnolia" in *Pick Up* (1933), "Imogene" in *Hat, Coat, and Gloves* (1934), "Florabelle" in *Wives Never Know* (1936), "Ophelia" in *Virginia* (1941), "Ruby" in *The Big Street* (1942), "Maum Maria" in *Reap the Wild Wind* (1942), "Mammy Jenny" in *Jack London* (1943), "Bedelia" in *Barbary Coast Gent* (1944), "Petunia" in *Seven Sweethearts* (1942), "Gussie" in *Mr. Blandings Builds His Dream House* (1948), and "Mammy Lou" in *Belle Starr* (1941). More typically, however, Louise Beavers was listed in movie credits—if at all—simply as "maid" (*Night World, Street of Women*, and *Young America*, all 1932), "cook" (*Made for Each Other*, 1939), "Mammy" (*Too Busy to Work*, 1932), "Aunt [so-and-so]" (Tina in *The Lady's from Kentucky*, 1939), or "Mamie" (*Make Way for Tomorrow*, 1937).

Ending the 1940s with *Tell It to the Judge* (1949), Beavers then starred in *Girls' School*, THE JACKIE ROBINSON STORY, and *My Blue Heaven* in 1950; *Colorado Sundown, I Dream of Jeannie*, and *Never Wave at a WAC* in 1953; *Goodbye, My Lady, Teenage Rebel*, and *You Can't Run Away from It* in 1956; *Tammy and the Bachelor* in 1957; *The Goddess* in 1958; and *All the Fine Young Cannibals* in 1960.

Beavers also played roles on television. Following on the heels of two other prominent black actresses who had starred on the popular television series *Beulah* (ETHEL WATERS and HATTIE MCDANIEL), Beavers decided to play the Henderson household's good-natured domestic. Her brief tenure, begun in 1952, lasted until the next year, when the show went off the air because she decided to leave the role. Her other television credits include *Star Stage* (1956), "The Hostess with the Mostest" on *Playhouse 90* (1957), and "Swamp Fox" on *Walt Disney Presents* (1959). Perhaps it was appropriate that, after nearly three decades and more than 116 films, Beavers's final role was the "Gilbert maid," serving Bob Hope and Lucille Ball in the 1961 madcap comedy *The Facts of Life*. She died the following year in Los Angeles.

The career of Louise Beavers serves as a critical reminder of how, in the early days of Hollywood, the stock roles available to black actresses progressed from merely inhabiting the background to representing a servile and gratuitous stereotype. Just as Aunt Delilah in *Imitation of Life* selflessly shares her pancake recipe with Bea rather than cash in on it herself, Louise Beavers exemplifies the legions of other early black actresses whose talents were subordinated to the self-serving biases of the dominant society.

FURTHER READING

Bogle, Donald. *Brown Sugar: Eighty Years of America's Black Female Superstars* (1980).

Loukides, Paul, and Linda K. Fuller, eds. *Beyond the Stars: Stock Characters in American Popular Film* (1990).

Nesteby, James R. *Black Images in American Films, 1896–1954: The Interplay between Civil Rights and Film Culture* (1982).

This entry is taken from the *American National Biography* and is published here with the permission of the American Council of Learned Societies.

LINDA K. FULLER

Bechet, Sidney (14 May 1897–14 May 1959), clarinetist, soprano saxophonist, and composer, was born Sidney Joseph Bechet, the youngest of five sons and two daughters (three other children died in infancy) born to Omar Bechet, a shoemaker, and Josephine Michel in New Orleans, Louisiana. Bechet was raised as a middle-class Creole at the time when state law reclassified Creoles of color as Negro. The adoption of the black codes and de jure

Sidney Bechet, performing at an unknown location, possibly New York City, November 1946. (© William P. Gottlieb; www.jazzphotos.com.)

segregation had profound repercussions for the first generations of ragtime and jazz musicians in the Crescent City. Although Sidney spoke French in his childhood household and his grandfather, Jean Becher, was free and had owned property since 1817, Sidney Bechet identified himself as African American.

The Bechet family was decidedly musical. Sidney's father played the flute and trumpet for relaxation, and Sidney's brothers all played music as a hobby and developed skills in various trades for their vocations. Homer was a janitor and string bassist, Leonard a dentist and trombonist, Albert Eugene a butcher and violinist, Joseph a plasterer and guitarist. When he was only seven or eight years old, Sidney began playing a toy fife and soon began practicing on his brother's clarinet morning, noon, and night. He played in a band with his older brothers, but his family and other adult musicians quickly realized that Sidney was a prodigy whose technique outstripped that of some professionals.

Sidney's mother organized parties and hired professional bands to play in her home. When Sidney was just ten years old, she hired the great band of MANUEL PEREZ (who sent the equally legendary FREDDIE KEPPARD as a substitute) to play for her oldest son's twenty-first birthday. GEORGE

BAQUET, the band's clarinetist, was late for the engagement, and Sidney, sequestered in another room, began playing his brother's clarinet as Baquet arrived. Sidney played well enough to cause Keppard to believe that it was Baquet warming up. As a result, Baquet began giving Sidney clarinet lessons. Bechet learned from him certain rudiments of clarinet playing, but he had already developed an unorthodox set of fingerings and refused to learn to read music. Bechet also studied with Paul Chaligny and ALPHONSE PICOU. His most important influence, however, came from "Big Eye" Louis Nelson. Nelson did not play in the academic style and specialized in the rougher "uptown" styles of the black players. Another lasting influence was the opera, which his mother took him to listen to. He especially liked the tenors (his favorite was Enrico Caruso), and the heavy vibrato that characterized his playing was in part modeled after them. As Bechet began to play with professional organizations in parades, picnics, dance halls, and parties, he did not attend school regularly, despite his family's admonitions, and he reportedly ignored their advice about learning a trade other than music. At age fourteen he joined the Young Olympians, and soon he was playing with all the notable bands of New Orleans, including those led by Buddy Petit and BUNK JOHNSON. Bechet's family worried about the boy's exposure to the seamier aspects of musicians' nightlife. Yet, in this setting, Bechet developed into a soft-spoken and charming fellow who was very attractive to women. He also became a heavy drinker with a very short fuse and sometimes displayed a violent temper. As a teenager he was jailed for a violent incident. This odd mixture of musical virtuosity, charm, and violence would follow Bechet throughout his adult life.

Bechet went to Chicago in 1918, where he quickly found work within the various New Orleans cliques that dominated the scene. There he met and played for NOBLE SISSLE, JAMES REESE EUROPE, and WILL MARION COOK. Bechet's virtuosity and his ear for melodies and harmony were such that he amazed all three of these bandleaders, despite his not being able to read music, a skill normally required for these orchestras. In 1919 Bechet joined Cook's Southern Syncopated Orchestra, which brought him to New York, where his talents were much in demand. He then went to the British Isles with Cook's orchestra. British audiences received the orchestra warmly, and many critics singled out Bechet's playing as noteworthy. The most important review came from the Swiss conductor Ernst Ansermet, who wrote,

in what was the first truly insightful critical article on jazz, that Bechet was an "extraordinary clarinet virtuoso" and an "artist of genius."

While in England, Bechet bought a soprano saxophone. The soprano saxophone was used very little in jazz, in part because of the severe intonation problems it presents, especially in the early models. But Bechet had a strong embouchure and a highly developed vibrato that allowed him to express himself with the instrument, and his supremacy as the greatest soprano saxophonist in jazz was not challenged until JOHN COLTRANE took up the instrument years after Bechet's death. The saxophone was perfect for Bechet, as its brassier and louder projection facilitated his natural inclination to take the melodic lead, usually the prerogative of trumpeters in the jazz ensembles of the 1910s and 1920s.

Bechet's stay in London ended when he was charged with assaulting a woman. Bechet pleaded not guilty, as did his codefendant, George Clapham. The stories of the two defendants and the two women involved conflicted, and Bechet hinted that his troubles with the police in England had racial overtones. He was sentenced to fourteen days of hard labor and was then deported on 3 November 1922.

Upon his arrival in New York, Bechet began to work in the theater circuit. He joined Donald Heywood's show *How Come*, in which Bechet played the role of How Come, a Chinese laundryman who was also a jazz musician. He was later billed as the "Wizard of the Clarinet" in theater bookings under Will Marion Cook's leadership. Bechet also began his recording career in New York, through CLARENCE WILLIAMS, a shrewd talent scout who helped supply black talent to record companies eager to cash in on the blues craze that followed MAMIE SMITH's hit record "Crazy Blues." In 1923 Bechet recorded his soprano saxophone on "Wild Cat Blues" and "Kansas City Man Blues" on Okeh Records. These records were listened to by thousands and served as models of jazz phrasing and improvisation for young musicians, including the likes of JOHNNY HODGES, HARRY CARNEY, and LIONEL HAMPTON. Bechet's success led to other recordings, where he accompanied singers such as Sara Martin, Mamie Smith, Rosetta Crawford, Margaret Johnson, EVA TAYLOR, and SIPPIE WALLACE. Bechet also began composing and made a big impression with his "Ghost of the Blues." He also wrote significant portions of *Negro Nuances*, a musical cowritten with Will Marion Cook and his wife, ABBIE MITCHELL. While the musical was not successful, Cook praised Bechet's compositions lavishly in the *Chicago Defender*.

In 1925 Bechet joined the *Black Revue*, featuring JOSEPHINE BAKER. The show took them to France, where they both became expatriates. Bechet continued working under the leadership of Noble Sissle and others. He also worked extensively in Germany, where he met Elisabeth Ziegler in 1926. He would eventually marry her in 1951, after both of them had married and divorced others. His original plans to marry Ziegler, after bringing her back to Paris in 1928, were spoiled. An argument between Bechet and the banjoist Gilbert "Little Mike" McKendrick began over a dispute about the correct harmonies to a song they had just played. By the end of the night the two were shooting at each other. Neither Bechet nor McKendrick was hit, but the pianist Glover Compton was shot in the leg, the dancer Dolores Giblins was shot in the lung, and an innocent bystander was shot in the neck. Bechet was sentenced to fifteen months in jail and was then deported.

He moved to Berlin and later returned to the United States after rejoining Noble Sissle's orchestra. In New York he led the New Orleans Feetwarmers with the trumpeter Tommy Ladnier. The group was short-lived, and Bechet briefly went into retirement from music and opened the Southern Tailor Shop in Harlem. In addition to tailoring, Bechet held jam sessions in the back room and cooked and served Creole cuisine. In 1934 Bechet returned to music once again at the behest of Noble Sissle. By the end of the 1930s the market for Bechet's style of jazz had lessened, but his cachet increased by the 1940s during the crest of the jazz revival. He played as either a bandleader or a star soloist throughout the United States. In 1949 he returned to Europe, eventually settling in France again, where he was the acknowledged patron saint of the European jazz revival. In 1951 he married Ziegler, with whom he lived for the rest of his life. He also had another home with a woman named Jacqueline, with whom he had a son, Daniel, in 1954. Bechet penned his most famous composition, "Petite fleur," in 1952, and in 1953 the Paris Conservatory Orchestra debuted his *La Nuit est une Sorcière*, a ballet in seven movements. With the help of two amanuenses, Joan Reid and Desmond Flower, Bechet also wrote *Treat It Gentle*, one of the most literarily ambitious jazz autobiographies.

Bechet, along with LOUIS ARMSTRONG, was among the first great jazz improvisers to liberate their solos from the rhythms and contours of the melody. Bechet's fame might have been even more widespread had the clarinet not fallen out of favor and the soprano saxophone been less obscure. He was the first to fashion legato melodies on the instrument and influenced such saxophone giants as Johnny Hodges and COLEMAN HAWKINS. He died before two of his disciples on the instrument, Steve Lacy and John Coltrane, popularized the instrument in the 1960s.

FURTHER READING

Bechet, Sidney. *Treat It Gentle* (1960).
Chilton, John. *Sidney Bechet: The Wizard of Jazz* (1987).
Obituary: *New York Times*, 15 May 1959.

SALIM WASHINGTON

Beck, Robert "Iceberg Slim" (4 Aug. 1918– 30 April 1992), pimp-turned-novelist, autobiographer, essayist, and central figure of the black crime fiction movement that began in the 1960s, was born in Chicago, Illinois, as Robert Lee Maupin Jr., the only child of Mary Brown, a hairdresser, and Robert Maupin Sr., a hustler and one-time cook for Chicago mayor William "Big Bill" Thompson. In 1919, the year of the bloodiest race riots in Chicago's history, Robert Maupin Sr. tossed his infant son against a wall and abandoned the family. Beck survived, and Mary Brown supported her infant son by working as a door-to-door hairstylist. In 1924 she met Henry Upshaw, the owner of a cleaning and pressing shop, the only black business in Rockford, Illinois. Remembered by Beck as "the only father I had ever really known" (Iceberg Slim, 23), Upshaw provided Beck and his mother with a relatively stable middle-class life. However, in 1928, Brown left Upshaw to go to Chicago with a gambler named Steve, who abused the family for three years until Brown snuck out on him. After a short venture into the world of street hustling, Beck graduated at the age of fifteen in 1934 with a 98.4 average from Wendell Phillip High School, the first predominantly black high school in Chicago. Beck won an alumni scholarship to Tuskegee and attended BOOKER T. WASHINGTON's institution the same moment as fellow writer RALPH ELLISON. Beck and Ellison never knew one another, and emblematic of the distinct paths they would take as writers, Ellison left Tuskegee after two years for New York to become a novelist, and Robert Beck was expelled for bootlegging whiskey.

Returning to Chicago in 1936, Beck began his twenty-five-year career as a pimp and street hustler.

He was known early in his career as Youngblood, but he earned the moniker of Iceberg Slim when a stray bullet knocked his hat off at a bar. Mistaking his cocaine-induced high for coolness-under-pressure, Beck's friend Glass Top gave him his legendary name. Robert Beck's early years as a pimp came at a moment when working-class blacks in Chicago and other urban centers were being increasingly isolated in inner-city ghettos with poor or substandard housing, and few job opportunities. Pimping was his attempt to transcend these social, racial, and spatial conditions. As he tells it in his autobiography: "I was still black in the white man's world. My hope to be important and admired could be realized even behind this black stockade. It was simple, just pimp my ass off and get a ton of scratch. Everybody in both worlds kissed your ass black and blue if you had flash and front" (Iceberg Slim, 117). For the better part of two and a half decades, Beck used the skills of sweet-talk, hustle, and muscle to earn enough money, or "scratch," to try to make his way out of the "black stockade" of the American ghetto. His criminal exploits landed him in prison five times, where he served a total of almost seven years. Beck was first incarcerated in 1936 at Wisconsin Green Bay State Reformatory on the charge of "carnal knowledge and abuse," and beginning in 1937, he served twenty-one months at Waupun State Penitentiary for grand theft. Beck returned to jail in 1946, where he served an eighteen-month sentence at Leavenworth on the charge of "white slavery" for sending a minor across state lines. In 1947 Beck was detained at the Cook County House of Corrections for armed robbery. He made a spectacular escape from the institution only to be recaptured and forced to serve out the rest of his sentence in 1960. Ironically, Beck never served any time for pimping.

The turning point in Beck's life came in 1960, when, after serving ten months in solitary confinement at Cook County House of Corrections, he decided to give up what is commonly known by the criminal underclass as "the Life." He moved to Los Angeles to make amends with his ailing mother, and even took the last name Beck, the name of his mother's husband, William Beck. With his common-law wife, Betty, Beck would have three daughters, Camille, Melody, and Misty, born in 1965, 1967, and 1970, respectively. In 1967, after trying a variety of jobs, including selling insecticides door to door, he submitted his autobiography to a Los Angeles–based paperback publisher, Holloway House. The manuscript would eventually become *Pimp: The Story*

of My Life published in 1967. Because of the controversial title and content, Holloway House was unable to secure any advertising space for the book in mainstream venues like the *New York Times*, but the Holloway House founder and CEO, Bentley Morriss, a former Hollywood publicist, explored alternative ways of publicizing the book, and he secured guest appearances on television shows and at local universities for Beck.

Pimp became the best-selling book by a black American author ever, and its popularity inspired Beck to publish more. On the heels of *Pimp*, in 1967 he published *Trick Baby*, the story of a light-skinned African American named John Patrick O'Brian, nicknamed White Folks, whose ability to pass for white makes him one of the best con men in Chicago. Following in the literary tradition exemplified by JAMES WELDON JOHNSON's *The Autobiography of an Ex-Colored Man* (1912) and NELLA LARSEN's *Passing* (1929), among others, Trick Baby explores the possibilities and limits of racial passing as a viable form of overcoming racial oppression in America. In 1969 Beck published what is arguably his most powerful and sensitive work, *Mama Black Widow*, the story of a gay transvestite named Otis Tilson and his family. Based on taped interviews Beck conducted with Tilson months before his suicide and published the same year as the Stonewall Riot, *Mama Black Widow* is a haunting novel about the failed promises of the Great Migration and an extended meditation on the philosophies of nonviolence by the recently assassinated MARTIN LUTHER KING JR.

The subtle turn toward black politics in *Mama Black Widow* would come to full fruition in the only work published under the name Robert Beck, *The Naked Soul of Iceberg Slim* (1971). Dedicated to MALCOLM X, ANGELA DAVIS, and a number of members from the Black Panther Party, *Naked Soul* features a wide range of his political and personal thoughts, including a heartfelt letter to his biological father, a sketch of his visit to Black Panther headquarters in the Watts neighborhood of Los Angeles, and his theories on how hatred for the mother acts as the psychological motivation for pimping. Throughout the 1970s, Beck, continuing to use the pen name of Iceberg Slim, published three more best-selling books, including *Death Wish*, a crime drama about the mafia (1976); *Long White Con*, a sequel to *Trick Baby* about the further of exploits of White Folks (1977); and *Airtight Willie and Me*, a collection of short stories (1979). In 1982 Robert Beck married Los Angeles native

Diane Millman, a freelance typist/transcriber and a devoted fan of his work who had sent him a letter in 1980, and the woman with whom Beck remained until his death. Beck died in Culver City Hospital, later Brotman Memorial, on 30 April 1992 from complications stemming from diabetes, as Watts was aflame from the riots sparked by the acquittal of white police officers for the videotaped beating of motorist RODNEY KING. After his death, *Doom Fox*, the only book not published by Holloway House, was published by Grove Press in 1998.

Millions of copies of Beck's novels have sold in America's black communities, distributed through less traditional venues like barbershops, liquor stores, beauty salons, and other local black businesses. A hybrid of street slang, psychoanalysis, and crime narrative, Beck's stories about ghetto life from the inside made him a folk hero among many working-class African Americans. According to H. Bruce Franklin, in his important study of American prison fiction, Beck's autobiography about the plight of the criminal class in America places him in an African American literary tradition that extends from the slave narratives of FREDERICK DOUGLASS and HARRIET JACOBS to the prison and crime novels of CHESTER HIMES. The popular success of his work convinced Holloway House to proclaim itself the "world's largest publisher of the black experience novel," publishing hundreds of novels since the late 1960s that reflect the experiences of dispossessed urban minorities. Beck's literature paved the way for dozens of black writers, including DONALD GOINES, Odie Hawkins, Roosevelt Malloy, ROLAND JEFFERSON, Joe Nazel, and many others, and along with his protégé and fellow best-selling author Donald Goines, Beck is considered a literary godfather of hip-hop. His poetics and narratives have inspired the likes of ICE-T, ICE CUBE, DMX, TUPAC SHAKUR, SNOOP DOGGY DOGG, and JAY-Z.

FURTHER READING

Beck, Robert. *The Naked Soul of Iceberg Slim* (1971).

Franklin, H. Bruce. *The Victim as Criminal and Artist: Literature from the American Prison* (1978).

Graham, D. B. "Negative Glamor: The Pimp Hero in the Fiction of Iceberg Slim," *Obsidian* 1 (Summer 1975).

Iceberg Slim. *Pimp: The Story of My Life* (1967).

Muckley, Peter A. *Iceberg Slim: The Life as Art* (2003).

JUSTIN DAVID GIFFORD

Beckham, Albert Sidney (21 Sept. 1893–9 Feb. 1964), one of the first African American psychologists, who established at Howard University the first psychology laboratory at any historically black institute of higher education, was born in Camden, South Carolina, to Calvin and Elizabeth James Beckham. Evidence for his date of birth varies. While 21 September 1897 is commonly published, a World War I draft registration records his year of birth as 1893, a second World War I draft registration provides the date 21 August 1897 (it appears he registered again after moving to a new address), and his World War II draft registration card records 21 September 1894. The 1910 census lists his age as sixteen, supporting the 1893 date.

His father owned a retail grocery business in Camden, and his early education was in Presbyterian schools. By 1910 he was the middle of five children; Carrie and Willis were older, Ernest and Arline younger. Arthur Henry George was also raised in the household by Calvin Beckham, George's uncle. Census reports for Kershaw County, where Camden is located, and nearby Lancaster County, show a number of Beckham families, including several individuals named Albert, so there was likely a network of extended family relations.

Beckham earned a bachelor's degree at Lincoln University in 1915, another bachelor's degree from Ohio State University in 1916, then a master's degree in psychology from Ohio State in 1917. One of his early published papers was "Characteristics and Decline of Negro Dialects," in 1917. When the United States declared war on Germany, Beckham applied to the Army Air Corps, but was refused training, and instead was enrolled as a sergeant in the Army Training Corps, teaching psychology at Wilberforce University in Xenia, Ohio, where he remained as an assistant professor until 1920. While there, he had initial responsibility for establishing a department of journalism, on 2 January 1920 initiating the four-page weekly *Sun-Dial*.

Calvin and Elizabeth Beckham moved to New York in the postwar years, where their son joined them, editing the New York *Dispatch* from 1921 to 1922. He began work at Howard University in 1924, first as an instructor, then as assistant professor of psychology from 1925 to 1928.

In August 1924, *The Crisis* published his article "Applied Eugenics" (vol. 28, no. 4, pp. 177–178). "Improving the race" was a common preoccupation with leading African Americans at the time. Many white supremacists saw elimination of the entire African American population as a desirable eugenic goal. Eugenics being, at the time, a respectable field of research, Beckham viewed it as a tool for improvement of his race, rather than its elimination. "No one nowadays doubts unusual abilities in the individual Negro," he wrote. The urgent priority was not individuals of giant stature, but "more attention given to the group," or elevating the entire race. "The problem with most white scientists who study the problems of the Negro," he added, "is that they lack sympathetic understanding."

The sociologist E. Franklin Frazier's critique of Beckham's enthusiasm provides insight into the academic and cultural context of Beckham's proposals. "Eugenics and the Race Problem" appeared in *The Crisis* (vol. 31, no. 2, December 1925) while Frazier was teaching at Morehouse College. Arguing that "the Negro problem is essentially a problem of social adjustment," Frazier accepted that "the Negro in marrying should have due regard for his offspring by not mating with stocks that show signs of feeblemindedness and the grosser abnormal physical traits which follow the Mendelian principle." Frazier added an often overlooked factor: "The whole social system in the South favors the propagation of the least socially desirable among Negroes," because "the less energetic and resourceful fit easily into the role the white man has assigned the Negro, while the more energetic and resourceful leave or often fail to reproduce."

In 1928 Beckham returned to New York City, where he received a Ph.D. in Psychology in 1930 from New York University. While completing his degree, he moved to Chicago in 1929, initially as a fellow of the National Committee for Mental Hygiene at the Illinois Institute for Juvenile Research. He remained at the institute as a junior assistant psychologist, 1931–1935. During the early 1930s he published a number of papers, including "Juvenile Delinquency and the Negro" (*Opportunity*, October 1931), "Race and Intelligence"(*Opportunity*, August 1932), "A Study of the Intelligence of Colored Adolescents of Different Economic and Social Status in Typical Metropolitan Areas" (*Journal of Social Psychology*, vol. 5, no. 1, 1933), and "A Study of Race Attitudes in Negro Children of Adolescent Age" (*Journal of Abnormal and Social Psychology*, vol. 29, no. 1, April 1934).

In 1934 Beckham married the psychologist RUTH WINIFRED HOWARD, a specialist in child development. She had just completed a Ph.D. in Psychology from the University of Minnesota, and declined a staff appointment teaching in Washington, D.C., moving to Chicago to join her husband. Undertaking an internship at the Illinois Institute of Juvenile Research, she later worked for the National Youth Administration and as a psychologist at Provident Hospital School of Nursing. The Beckhams also shared a part-time private practice in psychology, the Center of Psychological Service, from 1940 to 1964.

Beckham worked at the Chicago Board of Education, Bureau of Child Study, from 1935 until the end of his life in 1964. Many of those years were devoted to the families of students at Du Sable High School, developing a school psychology clinic, parent counseling groups, and providing the results of his study of adolescence to assist anxious mothers and fathers. A number of students credited this work, and Beckham's cultivation of ties between churches, neighborhoods and schools, with enabling them to move on to productive careers. Beginning in 1959 he was staff psychologist for McKinley settlement house.

Dr. Beckham died in Passavant Hospital, Chicago, survived by his widow, and his youngest sister, Arline de Berry.

FURTHER READING

Graves, Scott L., Jr. "Albert Sidney Beckham: The First African American School Psychologist," *School Psychology International* (Feb. 2009).

Guthrie, Robert V. *Even the Rat Was White: A Historical View of Psychology* (1998).

Obituary: *Chicago Tribune*, 11 Feb. 1964.

CHARLES ROSENBERG

Beckham, Ruth Winifred Howard (25 Mar. 1900–12 Feb. 1997), psychologist, social worker, and educator, was born in Washington, D.C., the eighth and youngest child of Reverend and Mrs. William James Howard. Ruth Howard loved reading as a child and originally considered becoming a librarian but, after three years at Howard University, she transferred to Simmons College in Boston and changed her major to social work.

In the early decades of the twentieth century, social work was a new professional field for women, and especially for black women. Most African American women in the early decades of the twentieth century were confined to jobs as domestic workers, or, if they entered the professional class, as teachers. But at Simmons, Howard was introduced to new role models and new career possibilities. Through a summer internship with the National Urban League she became inspired by the need for community programs for disadvantaged youth, including education, recreation, and job training. She received her bachelor's degree in social work from Simmons College in 1921 and began her career in Ohio at the Cleveland Child Welfare Agency working with poor children and children in the foster care system. Howard was dismayed to find that most of the white social workers and medical professionals seemed prejudiced against the poor and non–white urban communities they served. Howard saw a need for greater attention to the group and family dynamics in these children's lives, including the role of racism, and to the institutional and cultural needs of the black community as a whole. Her professional interests began to shift from social work to social psychology.

After receiving a master's degree from Simmons in 1927, Howard received a fellowship to the Teachers College and School of Social Work at Columbia University for one year. She then transferred to the Institute of Child Development at the University of Minnesota, where nearly all of her professors and fellow students were white women. In 1934 she completed her Ph.D. in Psychology and child development with a thesis entitled, "A Study of the Development of Triplets." Although many sources honor Howard as the first African American woman to receive a Ph.D. in Psychology, she was more likely the second. Inez Beverly Prosser received a doctorate in educational psychology from the University of Cincinnati in 1933, but was tragically killed in a car accident the following year and thus her career was cut short. The same year Howard received her doctorate she married ALBERT BECKHAM, another prominent African American psychologist.

Ruth Howard's work on triplets was groundbreaking in both scope and depth. Although the psychological field had been interested in the social development of twins for some time, she was among the first to conduct a large-scale study of more than two hundred sets of triplets at varying ages and life stages over a long period of time. Her research combined several fields of inquiry, including sociology, education, genetics, the psychology of race and ethnicity, and developmental psychology. Most of these were still new areas of research in the 1920s and 1930s, and twins or triplets provided a unique opportunity for researchers to explore the nature–nurture dichotomy. Howard found that triplets did not perform as well in school as their single-birth counterparts, and she examined various factors, both biological and social, to explain this fact. Although she began this research in the 1920s, she continued her studies and published her results much later in the *Journal of Psychology* (1946) and the *Journal of Genetic Psychology* (1947).

Howard's long career as a developmental and clinical psychologist led to her affiliation with dozens of social work organizations, medical facilities, and universities. After their marriage, Albert Beckham and Ruth Howard (it appears she continued to use the name Howard professionally) moved to Chicago, where she secured an internship at the Institute of Juvenile Research at the University of Illinois, studying parent–child relations, and then secured a temporary position as director of a National Youth Administration job skills training program in Chicago. Between 1940 and 1964, when Albert Beckham died, the Beckhams operated their own private practice, the Center for Psychological Services. The couple never had children, and theirs was an unusual partnership in being able to work together for so many years while advancing their individual careers. Howard later recalled fondly that, "In professional activities, as in marriage relations, we were partners" (quoted in profile in O'Connell, et al.).

Throughout this time, and into the early 1970s, Howard also consulted for or was on the psychological or counseling staff of numerous institutions, schools, and hospitals in Chicago. These included the Abraham Lincoln Center, the McKinley Center for Retarded Children, and the Chicago Board of Health, Mental Health Division. She also taught at historically black nursing schools in Missouri and Florida, and her concern for the educational and employment opportunities of black women led to her role in organizing the National Association of College Women in the 1940s. Howard also continued her work with children as a school psychologist and as a researcher on literacy, play therapy, and children with developmental disabilities. She was active in numerous professional and social-political organizations, including the American Psychological Association, International Psychology Association, International Council of Women Psychologists, International Reading Association, Women's International League for Peace and Freedom, Friends of the Mentally Ill, and the American Association of University Women.

Howard died in Washington, D.C., in 1997. She had not only led the way into new educational and career paths for black women in psychology, but she insisted that race, ethnicity, and gender be accounted for in the research and methods used by educational and developmental psychologists.

FURTHER READING

Guthrie, Robert V. *Even the Rat Was White: A Historical View of Psychology* (1998).

O'Connell, Agnes N., and Nancy F. Russo, eds. *Models of Achievement: Reflections of Eminent Women in Psychology* (1983).

Saltzman, Ann L. "Ruth Winifred Howard," *Feminist Psychologist, Newsletter of the Society for the Psychology of Women* 28:2 (Spring 2001). Available at http://www.psych.yorku.ca/femhop/Ruth%20 Howard.htm.

Warren, Wini. *Black Women Scientists in the United States* (1999).

TIFFANY K. WAYNE

Beckwourth, Jim (26 April 1800?–1866?), mountain man, fur trapper and trader, scout, translator, and explorer, was born James Pierson Beckwith in Frederick County, Virginia, the son of Sir Jennings Beckwith, a white Revolutionary War veteran and the descendant of minor Irish aristocrats who became prominent Virginians. Little is known about Jim's mother, a mixed-race slave working in the Beckwith household. Although he was born into slavery, Jim was manumitted by his father in the 1820s. In the early 1800s, Beckwith moved his family, which reputedly included fourteen children, to Missouri, eventually settling in St. Louis. Some commentators suggest that Beckwith, an adventurous outdoorsman, was seeking an environment less hostile to his racially mixed family.

As a young teenager, after four years of schooling, Jim Beckwourth (as his name came to be spelled) was apprenticed to a blacksmith. Unhappy as a tradesman, he fled to the newly discovered lead mines in Illinois's Fever River region and then to New Orleans in search of greater adventure. Motivated by a lack of work and by the racism he encountered, Jim responded to a newspaper ad placed by the entrepreneurial fur traders Andrew Henry and William Henry Ashley. The ad called for "One Hundred MEN to ascend the Missouri to the Rocky Mountains"; Jim enlisted in 1824. The Ashley-Henry strategy, which Beckwourth emulated, combined direct beaver trapping with trading for furs at the Indian villages. He learned trapping and frontier skills alongside the legendary mountain men Jedediah Smith and Jim Bridger, becoming a crack shot and expert bowie knife and tomahawk handler. Beckwourth was present at the first Mountain Man rendezvous at Henry's Fork on the Green River in 1825. He claimed to have been married briefly to two Blackfoot Indian sisters during this period. While on a trapping expedition in the late 1820s, Beckwourth was captured by Crow Indians (Absaroke or Sparrowhawk people). How exactly Beckwourth came to live with the Crow remains unclear. During the years he lived with the tribe, Beckwourth became a valued Crow warrior and tribe member. He lived with a succession of Indian women and acknowledged one child, Black Panther or Little Jim. Beckwourth's tribal names—Morning Star, Antelope, Enemy of Horses, Bobtail Horse, Bloody Arm, Bull's Robe, and Medicine Calf—capture both the romance and the narrative value of his years living, hunting, and raiding with the Crow.

Leaving the tribe and the Ashley-Henry fur trading company behind in 1836, Beckwourth crisscrossed the Western frontier playing cards, prospecting, trapping, selling whiskey to Indians, stealing horses, brawling in saloons, and guiding settlers. Hired by the U.S. Army as a muleskinner, messenger, and scout during the Seminole War of 1837, he fought against the Seminole, a confederation of Native Americans and runaway slaves. Subsequently, Jim traveled the Southwest working as a fur trader and translator for Andrew Sublette and Louis Vasquez on the Santa Fe Trail and as a wagon loader at Bent's Fort in Taos. In 1842 Beckwourth opened a trading post with his current wife, Louise Sandoval, in what is presently Pueblo, Colorado. A few years later, abandoning yet another family, Beckwourth answered the siren call of California, where he survived as a horse thief (he claimed to have stolen over two thousand horses), a letter carrier, and from 1846 to 1847 as a guide for the American forces during the conquest of California.

The discovery of gold in 1848 brought Beckwourth to the Sierra mining camps. But while most forty-niners panned for gold, Jim invested in a more lucrative gamble: a passable travel route through the rugged mountain terrain. In 1850 he located the Beckwourth Pass near present-day Reno, Nevada. Capitalizing on his discovery, Jim built a wagon road servicing settlers and gold rushers and established a ranch and trading post in what came to be known as Beckwourth, California. A charming and personable host, Jim briefly reinvented himself as a hotel and saloonkeeper. The pass, which in its heyday accommodated ten thousand wagons annually, remained popular until the railroad supplanted wagon travel in 1855.

In 1858 Beckwourth traveled east to St. Louis, Denver, and Kansas City, until gold was discovered near Pikes Peak, Colorado. Beckwourth and his latest wife, Elizabeth Lettbetter, worked as shopkeepers in Denver, but Jim never quite adapted to city life; his marriage dissolved, and he subsequently married a Crow woman named Sue. The Colorado Volunteer Cavalry hired Beckwourth to locate Cheyenne and Arapaho Indian camps in 1864. Beckwourth's role in the subsequent Sand Creek Massacre permanently alienated him from the Indian tribes.

The facts of Beckwourth's life remain in contention. Even the year of his birth is debated among historians. Much of the historical perplexity is the result of obfuscations in the autobiography that Beckwourth dictated to Thomas D. Bonner in 1854. Most significantly, the autobiography omits any mention of Beckwourth's race. While it was Bonner who altered the spelling of the name "Beckwourth," Jim was responsible for confusing dates, omitting details, and lavishly embellishing the facts of his life, including his role in events, the number of rivals killed, money made, and battles waged. He may have taken as his own the heroic tales of other frontiersmen, including Edward Rose, who lived with the Crow a generation before Beckwourth. The book, published in 1856, put into print stories Beckwourth had been spinning for years. Storytelling was a valued skill and an important part of the period's oral tradition, and Beckwourth had spent a lifetime fashioning elaborate narratives with himself as the hero. The book found a ready audience among armchair travelers fascinated and titillated by the exoticism and liberation of frontier stories. Once the inaccuracies of his text were revealed, however, Beckwourth was quickly labeled a liar. As a result, many early historians wrote him off as an unreliable and purposeful braggart, while others, fueled by racism, attacked him on the basis of his "mixed blood." In the early twenty-first century, historians generally agree that much of the text's basic narrative can be believed and that it represents an invaluable documentary record.

An inveterate adventurer and explorer, Beckwourth looked and dressed the part. Dark-eyed, muscular, and taller than six feet, he often dressed in embroidered buckskin, Crow leggings, ribbons, earrings, and gold chains and wore his thick, dark hair loose to his waist or elaborately braided. Beckwourth was not, as has been claimed, completely illiterate. He spoke English with great skill, fluent French, some Spanish, and a number of Indian dialects. The elision of race in his autobiography has been compounded by numerous painted portraits that untruthfully depict him as very light-skinned and by the 1951 film *Tomahawk*, which cast Jack Oakie, a white actor, as Beckwourth.

Mystery still surrounds Beckwourth's death in Crow territory near the Bighorn River in 1866. While it is generally believed that he died of sickness or food poisoning, the rumor lingers that he was purposefully poisoned by the Crow after rejecting offers to rejoin the tribe.

FURTHER READING

Beckwourth, James P. *The Life and Times of James P. Beckwourth, Mountaineer, Scout, Pioneer, and Chief of the Crow Nation of Indians as told to Thomas D. Bonner* (1856).

Mumey, Nolie. *James Pierson Beckwourth: An Enigmatic Figure of the West, A History of the Latter Years of His Life* (1957).

Wilson, Elinor. *Jim Beckwourth: Black Mountain Man and War Chief of the Crows* (1972).

LISA E. RIVO

Bedford, Robert Edward (18 Apr. 1884–16 Sept. 1969), labor union activist in the Chicago stockyards, was born in Cleveland, Ohio, the son of John W. Bedford and Melcenah S. Bedford. His father was born in 1844 in Virginia and was employed in 1880 (shortly before Robert was born) in a stove foundry in Columbiana County, Ohio. His mother was born in 1852 in Ohio. Her mother was also born in Ohio. Her father, John Davis, born in Virginia, lived with the family in 1880, as did two brothers, Orville and John Davis (Census, 1880). By 1900 Melcenah Bedford was raising her children alone at 492 Central Avenue in Cleveland, Ohio, making a living washing clothes. No record has been found as to what happened in the intervening twenty years, during which Robert Edward Bedford was born and grew to the age of sixteen.

It is likely that he was at least eight years old when his father died. He had two older siblings, Lenora, born in 1875, and Carl, born in 1874, as well as two who died in early childhood, and three younger: Cornelia, born in 1888, Elizabeth in 1890, and John in 1892. Most people on the block of Central Avenue where they settled were classified by the census as "black," although two neighbor families were classified as "white," one German and one Irish. Carl, aged 21, worked as a porter (Census, 1900). In 1910, Robert, now age 26, and Cornelia, 22, remained at home with their mother and their older sister Lenora, whose surname had changed to Whittaker. Melcenah Bedford was a hairdresser, and Robert a porter at a hotel. They had moved to 3410 Central Avenue, where their native-born American neighbors were classified as "black," the rest being recent immigrants from Hungary, Italy, and Russia, with their American-born children (Census, 1910).

Melcenah Bedford died 23 February 1913; around this time, Bedford moved to Chicago and married a woman named Lucille; her maiden name is unknown (WWI Draft Registration). He obtained work at the Wilson meatpacking plant, one of the "big five" packers in Chicago. After some periods of layoff, he had steady work for over two years beginning in the early part of 1917 (Records of the Federal Mediation and Conciliation Service [FMCS], pp. 148, 153). He was inspired by the militant Stockyards Labor Council, initiated at the time by the Chicago Federation of Labor, to join a local of the Amalgamated Meatcutters union.

A good speaker, respected by both white and black coworkers, Bedford was elected shop steward around December 1918 by men on the beef killing floor (FMCS, p. 149). This was a period of fervent, intense union organizing, the first after a failed strike in 1904. Tensions were contained by federally administered mediation, intended to ensure meat production continued during World War I. Bedford's main duty was to take up grievances, although the process had little formal procedure, written reports, or documentation. He would "take it to the boss," verbally, and "if I can do nothing with it, to report it to the officials of the union" (FMCS, p. 160). A federal arbitrator noted that the union membership on the floor included 150 men considered "white" and another thirty to forty considered "black" (FMCS, p. 293).

A typical grievance concerned six union members laid off when work on the killing floor was reduced. Called back to work, they were told by a foreman he didn't need anybody, and five minutes later, six nonunion men came from an employment office and were put to work. Bedford remonstrated with the foreman, who said to talk to the plant superintendent, Mr. Rhodes, who in turn said to talk to the employment office. A man there, known as Mr. Cheeks, said the foreman hadn't asked for the union men back. Returning to the foreman, Bedford was told the matter was "out of my hands now, it's in Mr. Rhodes's hands." The superintendent insisted, "I ain't going to have them men, I have got the six men I want" (FMCS, p. 231).

The union members who had been laid off were entitled to be the first called back, under an arbitration agreement negotiated in 1917–1918 between the labor council, the packinghouse owners, and the Federal Mediation and Conciliation Service, overseen by federal judge Samuel Alschuler. By the time Bedford was able to secure compliance, five of the laid-off union members had gotten tired of waiting and gone home; ultimately only one was rehired. Bedford noted in testimony concerning this grievance that "all the men involved were colored" (FMCS, p. 237).

About 90 percent of Northern-born African Americans in the industry, like Bedford, had joined the union by 1918—about the same percentage as Polish and Lithuanian immigrants, and smaller numbers of second or third generation Irish, who made up the rest of the workforce. Recently arrived Southern-born African Americans were more skeptical. A group of a dozen or so from Texas, led by Austin "Heavy" Williams, was specifically used by company management to discourage union membership and pick fights with union men.

Bedford testified to an incident where an antiunion agitator named Wilson had exclaimed, "God damn that union," then hit one union member, telling him, Bedford, and another man wearing a union button, "You are nothing but a lot of white folks' niggers, or you wouldn't be wearing that button." (Upper management and owners of all the packinghouses in Chicago were, without exception, "white folks.") When a couple of nonunion men asked him to stop, Wilson responded, "God damn it, don't talk to me. I know what I do. I get my orders from the office what I do" (FMCS, p. 221).

Corroborating Wilson's claim that he got orders from the company, when he was tried for knocking down a union member and hitting him with a "pritch iron," Bedford was told by a foreman that "if you go off this floor and go to any trial, you won't have any job when you get back." Bedford had been subpoenaed to appear, but on arriving in the court room was confronted by a company representative demanding "what kind of men are you to appear against the company" and again threatening that he would not have a job anymore (FMCS, pp. 222–223).

Bedford and his fellow stewards on the Wilson killing floor are primarily known to history through one hearing conducted by Judge Alschuler, 20 June 1919, on a union demand to remove several antiunion agitators from the plant. Over the following two years, the Stockyards Labor Council was torn apart by a jurisdictional dispute between national Amalgamated Meatcutters leadership and the CFL, then decimated by an unsuccessful strike in late

1920 and early 1921. There is no record of Bedford's role in the final drama, but it is unlikely he would have been hired back after the strike.

Before 1940 Bedford returned to Cleveland, where he was employed at the outbreak of World War II as a bartender by Lawrence O. Payne, at 4901 Central Avenue, about a mile from where his family had once lived. He lived nearby at 4800 Carnegie Avenue (WW II draft registration card). He died at a long-term care facility in Youngstown, Ohio, widowed, at the age of eighty-five (Ohio death certificate and Social Security notice).

FURTHER READING
Barrett, James R. *Work and Community in the Jungle: Chicago's Packinghouse Workers 1894–1922* (1987).

Halpern, Rick, and Roger Horowitz. *Meatpackers: An Oral History of Black Packinghouse Workers and Their Struggle for Racial and Economic Equality* (1996).

Halpern, Rick. *Down on the Killing Floor: Black and White Workers in Chicago's Packinghouses, 1904–54* (1997).

Trotter, Joe William, Earl Lewis, and Tera W. Hunter. *African American Urban Experience: Perspectives from the Colonial Period to the Present* (2004).

Records of the Federal Mediation and Conciliation Service (FMCS). "Violation of Agreement by Employers," Honorable Samuel Alschuler, Arbitrator, 20 June 1919. National Archives, College Park, MD, RG 280, Case 33/864, Box 42.

CHARLES ROSENBERG

Bedou, Arthur (6 July 1880–June 1966), photographer and businessman. Paul Arthur Bedou was born in New Orleans, where he remained professionally based throughout his sixty-plus-year career.

The leading African American photographer in New Orleans in the first half of the twentieth century, Bedou saw his reputation grow to national proportions as a result of his images of the life and travel of Tuskegee Normal and Industrial Institute (later Tuskegee University) President BOOKER T. WASHINGTON from the early 1900s through 1915. He photographed Washington at public-speaking engagements addressing crowds in Arkansas, Florida, Louisiana, Mississippi, South Carolina, Tennessee, Texas, Virginia, California, and numerous other locations during his final tour, which ended in 1915. He recorded Washington in transit by coach, train, and automobile in addition to his famous portraits of the education leader posed upon his horse.

As official photographer for the Institute, Bedou covered any number of events for the school. He recorded the 24 October 1905 celebration and parade in honor of President Theodore Roosevelt's visit to the campus (Roosevelt would later serve as a trustee), Tuskegee's twenty-fifth anniversary ceremony in 1906, and the delegation of officials and students from Barbados who attended the International Conference on the Negro held at Tuskegee in 1912. In addition to making formal photographs of administrators, faculty, alumni, and students in classrooms, work being done on buildings, and various other activities, he documented Washington hosting business, civic, political, religious, humanities, and academic dignitaries; and visiting school groups from Hawaii and Japan. Bedou also captured him attending events in the company of the educator and activist MARY MCLEOD BETHUNE, c. 1910; R. C. Houston Jr., president of Provident Savings Bank in Fort Worth, Texas; I. B. Scott, bishop of the African Methodist Episcopal Church; Dr. ELIAS CAMP MORRIS, president of the National Baptist Convention; ROSCOE CONKLING SIMMONS, editor of the *National Review*; and Charles S. Tator of the *New York Evening Post*.

Bedou was one of the earliest African American photographers to enjoy considerable financial success and to have his imagery considered for its artistic merit as well as technical proficiency. His private-studio clients included many of the city's elite and crossed all walks of life and ancestral heritage. Despite his reputation as a portraitist, he was equally regarded for documentation of the New Orleans Creole community, jazz musicians, and the Louisiana and Mississippi countryside. Some of the images reflecting his creative ability in camera work were a sensitively crafted photograph of a praline candy box with a portrait of two women from 1908; an outdoor scene titled *Color Waterfall View*, c. 1910; and a number of recorded views taken in Alabama, Florida, Kansas, Maryland, Massachusetts, Tennessee, and Virginia. He also took photographs at the home of FREDERICK DOUGLASS in the Anacostia neighborhood of Washington, D.C.

After Washington's death in 1915, and the founding of Xavier University by Mother Katherine Drexel in the same year, Bedou left Tuskegee and became the official photographer of the New Orleans school. On the business front, he was a founder of Peoples Life Insurance Company of Louisiana in 1922.

At Xavier, the first Catholic institution of higher learning for African Americans in the country, Bedou made numerous portraits of the Sisters of the Holy Family; full-body, standing poses of newly ordained Roman Catholic priests, c. 1934; and countless images of students at pivotal moments in their matriculation. He also recorded many campus views of buildings and monuments like the Goodridge School of Nursing. As was the case at Tuskegee, he expanded his lens toward residences, community buildings, churches, and portraits of African American students at other schools in the South from the late 1920s to the 1940s. He took the last photographs of MARCUS GARVEY in the United States before Garvey was deported to Jamaica and continued his extensive documentation of musicians, street festivals, and the diverse cultural demographics of the city.

From 1942 until his death in 1966, Bedou operated out of a studio at South Rampart and Common Streets in New Orleans. Many of his images of people associated with Tuskegee and Washington were unique because they included personal inscriptions to the president. Bedou's photography was placed in the permanent collections and archives of Xavier University, Tuskegee University, Atlanta History Center, Schomburg Center for Research in Black Culture, and numerous public and private collections.

FURTHER READING

Bedou, Arthur. *The Tuskegee Institute* (1911).

Coar, Valencia Hollins. *A Century of Black Photographers: 1840–1960* (1983).

Willis, Deborah. *Reflections in Black: A History of Black Photographers 1840 to the Present* (2000).

AMALIA K. AMAKI

Belafonte, Harry (1 Mar. 1927–), singer, actor, activist, and producer, was born Harold George Belafonte Jr. in Harlem in New York City, the son of Harold George Belafonte Sr., a seaman, and Melvine Love, a domestic worker. Belafonte Sr. was an alcoholic who contributed little to family life, other than occasionally hitting his spouse, and the young Harry was brought up almost exclusively by his mother. Harold and Melvine, who were both from the Caribbean, had a difficult time adjusting to life in New York, and after the Harlem race riots of 1935, Melvine and her son moved to her native Jamaica, where Harry spent five years shielded from American racism. When World War II broke out, the Belafontes returned to Harlem. Hoping for better conditions, the family would often try to pass for white. With white relatives on both the mother's and father's sides, they were all fair-skinned enough to be taken for Greek, Italian, or even Irish. Duty bound, Belafonte joined local gangs, drafted to help defend his white enclaves from neighboring blacks.

Belafonte attended school in Harlem but struggled with dyslexia; by ninth grade he had had enough and dropped out. Soon thereafter he enlisted in the U.S. Navy and was assigned to an all-black unit. Because of his race—and his temper—Belafonte was assigned as a munitions loader, one of the most dangerous jobs on the home front. "The men who were stuck with munitions loading were very bitter, very angry," he recalls. "In our bitterness and anger we went out and got drunk. We wanted to beat up everybody we met, including each other" (Eldridge, 117–118). When feeling less pugilistic, Belafonte discovered a passion for politics. He enjoyed sitting in on discussions of race and racism in the United States and labored to understand pamphlets and essays by W. E. B. Du Bois.

Belafonte met his first wife, Margurite Byrd, while his unit was stationed in Norfolk, Virginia. Byrd was studying psychology at the nearby Hampton Institute; she remembers their early relationship as "one long argument over racial issues" (Gates, 160). Belafonte and Byrd married in 1948 and had their first child, Adrienne, a year later. By this time, Belafonte had finished his tour of duty and moved his family to New York. Here, at Harlem's American Negro Theatre (ANT), Belafonte saw a play that sparked his interest in acting. With support from the GI Bill, he was soon enrolled in a workshop at the New School for Social Research, together with Marlon Brando, Tony Curtis, and Bea Arthur. Working as a janitor's assistant to help pay the bills, Belafonte volunteered backstage at the ANT. This quickly led to a role in a production of Sean O'Casey's *Juno and the Paycock*.

It was also at the ANT that Belafonte met SIDNEY POITIER, another black actor of Caribbean extraction, who became a lifelong friend and who, some say, stole Belafonte's career. The two were almost exact contemporaries and competed for many of the same roles. In a 1948 show called *Days of Our Youth*, Poitier was working as Belafonte's understudy. When Belafonte could not perform one night owing to his janitorial duties, Poitier filled in. A producer happened to be in the audience that evening and approached Poitier after the show. It

Harry Belafonte, singer, civil rights advocate, and Goodwill Ambassador for the U.N. Children's Fund, at a school in the Guediyawe district Dakar, Senegal, 24 February 2004. (AP Images.)

was the actor's big break, the one that eventually landed him in Hollywood.

Belafonte soldiered on in the theater, but slowly began to turn his attention toward music. On a friend's suggestion he performed at amateur night at a midtown club called the Royal Roost and was immediately hired full time. His performance consisted of pop jazz standards, a repertoire Belafonte found less than edifying; after a year he called it quits. By this time he had saved up a tidy sum of money, and he used it to open a grill called the Sage in Greenwich Village. The restaurant folded after eight months, but during that time it had served Belafonte as a late-night rehearsal space. Belafonte began indulging his interest in folk music at the Sage, and, after it closed, he pursued his research at a more conventional venue, listening to field recordings in the Library of Congress. In 1951 Belafonte brought his new act to the stage. Folk hardly seemed a promising genre at the height of the McCarthy era, when many of its left-leaning practitioners such as PAUL ROBESON and Pete Seeger were blacklisted, but success came quickly, with sell-out crowds at big-name clubs and a recording contract from RCA. Harry Belafonte's voice alone cannot account for his success, but

combined with his stage persona—tight trousers, open shirt, and shiny, mocha skin—it wowed audiences. Belafonte sang the expected folk standards, but then veered off toward African, Caribbean, and even Hebrew songs like "Hava Nageela." (He claims most American Jews learned the tune from him.) In spite of his success, Belafonte suffered the same indignities as other black entertainers of the day and was routinely denied the right to eat or sleep at the same venues that paid dearly to book his act. But Belafonte was quick to have revenge; in 1954, after *Brown v. Board of Education* declared segregation unconstitutional, he cancelled his engagements in the South.

Belafonte released several folk albums, but it was not until 1956 that he fully embraced the Caribbean music that delighted his audiences. *Harry Belafonte—Calypso* proved an instant classic, and two songs in particular, "The Banana Boat Song (Day-O)" and "Jamaica Farewell," topped the charts. Some claimed Belafonte had bastardized true Trinidadian calypso, but Belafonte was unapologetic about tailoring the music to American audiences. It was clearly an astute commercial move; in a year's time the album had sold 1.5 million copies, more than any previous record by a single artist.

As audiences grew and shows sold out, Belafonte resumed acting, taking roles in films and plays, including John Murray Anderson's Broadway revue *Almanac*, which earned him a Tony Award. Perhaps his most personally significant performance was in *Carmen Jones* (1954), an all-black film version of Georges Bizet's opera *Carmen* that also starred DOROTHY DANDRIDGE and PEARL BAILEY. Belafonte and Marguerite Byrd's second daughter, Shari, was born in 1954, but Belafonte's marriage ended in divorce in 1957. That same year he married Julie Robinson, a dancer with the KATHERINE DUNHAM Company, with whom he would later have a son, David, and a daughter, Gina. Initially, Belafonte's divorce slipped under the media's radar screen, but word of his remarriage eventually did get out, not least because his new bride was white.

Belafonte continued to act, including a role in 1957's *Island in the Sun*, a controversial tale of interracial love, but he found himself increasingly put off by Hollywood's ham-fisted attempts to deal with race. The scripts that came his way ranged from the shallow to the offensive, and Belafonte seemed unable to get any of his own ideas produced. In the 1960s he abandoned the cinema and engrossed himself in politics.

Belafonte had met MARTIN LUTHER KING JR. in 1956 during the Montgomery bus boycott and was immediately taken with King's passion and candor. At that first meeting, King seemed uncertain about the fate of the civil rights movement. He asked Belafonte for support, and over the next decade Belafonte lent his name and energy to the cause. He proved instrumental in rallying celebrities at home and abroad, forging political connections, and organizing fund-raisers. Belafonte also devoted large sums of his own money, heavily insuring King's life and bailing out activists arrested during sit-ins and protest marches. When King was jailed in Birmingham, it was Belafonte who led the charge to raise the fifty-thousand-dollar bail. His efforts earned him a place on the board of directors of King's Southern Christian Leadership Conference. Over the years of their joint involvement, Belafonte and King developed a close personal friendship, which lasted until King's death in 1968.

After the civil rights movement began to wane, Belafonte shifted his focus to Africa. His appointment by President John F. Kennedy as a cultural adviser to the Peace Corps in 1961 had first sparked his interest, and through the coming decades he devoted boundless energy to campaigns for development aid and human rights. Chief among these was the anti-apartheid struggle in South Africa, which consumed Belafonte in the 1980s. In 1987 the United Nations Children's Fund recognized his efforts and made him a goodwill ambassador, a position he has used to draw attention to famine, war, and the plague of AIDS.

Belafonte's activism often drew on his connections in the entertainment world. For a week in 1968 he guest hosted Johnny Carson's *Tonight Show*, turning light entertainment into politics with guests like Robert F. Kennedy and Martin Luther King Jr. In his anti-apartheid efforts, he worked to introduce exiled South African musicians like Miriam Makeba and Hugh Masekela to listeners in the United States, and in 1988 he released *Paradise in Gazankulu*, his own album of South African–themed music. In 1985 Belafonte took a similar approach to relief efforts for famine in Ethiopia. Inspired by pop stars from the British Isles who launched Band Aid in 1984, Belafonte was the driving force behind "We Are the World," an American effort in 1985 which raised over $70 million in aid for Ethiopian famine victims.

Perhaps because his political and show-business interests have always been so entwined, Belafonte has never been forced to choose between the two. In the thick of the anti-apartheid movement, he resumed acting and found time to mount major concert tours. Earlier, at the height of the civil rights movement, Belafonte had begun what may be his most ambitious musical project, a series of records then called *Anthology of Negro Folk Music*. He wanted to showcase the richness and variety of the African American musical tradition with a collection that included work songs and spirituals, minstrel tunes and lullabies. But when recording was completed in 1971, the backers of the project, RCA and *Reader's Digest*, pulled out, citing lack of commercial prospects, and the tapes languished in RCA vaults. They were finally released in 2001 as *The Long Road to Freedom: An Anthology of Black Music* and were nominated for a Grammy Award for best historical album.

The release of *Long Road* topped off a flurry of show-business activity by Belafonte in the 1990s. In 1995 he starred in the independent film *White Man's Burden* and the following year played the gangster Seldom Seen in Robert Altman's *Kansas City*. Plans were afoot for Belafonte to produce yet another picture with an unusual take on race—a film version of *Amos 'n Andy*, the long-running radio and television show that was criticized by the NAACP, among others, for perpetuating racist stereotypes, but which nonetheless enjoyed a substantial audience among African Americans from the 1920s to the 1950s. After a short hiatus from film acting at the beginning of the twenty-first century, Belafonte returned to the big screen in 2006 with a role in Emilio Estevez's *Bobby*, a film about Senator Robert Kennedy.

Belafonte has also continued to play sold-out shows and has campaigned to raise awareness about prostate health among African American men and the need to curb gang violence. He provoked controversy, however, in a much-criticized 15 October 2002 appearance on CNN's *Larry King Live*, when he refused to apologize for his earlier denunciation of Secretary of State COLIN POWELL as President George W. Bush's "house slave." Powell called Belafonte's comments "an unfortunate throwback to another time and another place," but the entertainer insisted that the secretary of state was a "sell-out." Asked by King if the same term applied to CONDOLEEZZA RICE, Bush's national security adviser, Belafonte replied, "Yes. Absolutely. Absolutely. Even more so." Belafonte continued his polemics against the Bush administration in subsequent years. In January 2006, the Associated Press reported that during a meeting with Hugo Chavez, the president of Venezuela, Belafonte commented that Bush was "the greatest terrorist in the world."

In the final analysis, Harry Belafonte remains difficult to pigeonhole either as an activist or as an entertainer, but it hardly seems worth the effort. Whether his greatest achievements have taken place onstage or off remains open to debate; his success in both arenas does not.

FURTHER READING

Eldridge, Michael. "Remains of the Day-O." *Transition* 92: 110–137.

Gates, Henry Louis, Jr. *Thirteen Ways of Looking at a Black Man* (1997).

Ward, Brian. *Just My Soul Responding: Rhythm and Blues, Black Consciousness, and Race Relations* (1998).

CHRIS BEBENEK

Belinda (c.1713–?), a former slave who achieved renown in the era of the American Revolution by laying claim to a portion of the wealth of her former master's estate, was born in the region of West Africa known as the Gold Coast (later Ghana). Her early years were spent in a village on the Volta River. According to her later memories, it was an Edenic existence. However, when she was about age twelve, the Atlantic slave trade shattered this bucolic world. She was captured in a slaving raid, permanently separated from her parents, marched overland to the coast, and sold to European slave traders. For several weeks she endured the horrific Middle Passage with some three hundred other Africans in chains, who were "suffering the most excruciating torment" (Carretta, 143).

In about 1732, after six or seven years in North America, Belinda became the slave of Isaac Royall Jr., a member of a prominent family of sugar planters on the Caribbean island of Antigua. She would serve him in bondage for nearly five decades. Royall had recently moved his family and slaves to Medford, Massachusetts, where he became the largest slaveholder in the colony. Belinda lived in his sizeable slave quarters in Medford, a rare experience for a New England slave. As the American Revolution neared, Royall became an outspoken Loyalist, an unpopular stance in radical Massachusetts. Fearing for his safety, he fled the colonies for Britain in April 1775, a few days after the battles of Lexington and Concord. With her master gone Belinda became the property of the state of Massachusetts, which manumitted her in 1778; unfortunately it appears that a son, Joseph, was sold away from her at the time of her manumission. She left Medford for Boston, where she and an invalid daughter, Prine, were living in 1783, when the Massachusetts courts finally declared slavery unconstitutional in the case of *Commonwealth v. Jennison*.

In February 1783, as Massachusetts was ending slavery and the Revolution was coming to an end, Belinda petitioned the Massachusetts legislature, assembled as a general court, for a portion of the rents and profits of the Royall estate. PRINCE HALL, a local black abolitionist who had personally petitioned the legislature on several occasions, probably helped her author the petition. It is unclear what other individuals or ideas may have influenced her action, although Boston blacks and a local Patriot pamphleteer named James Swan had promoted biblical justifications for restitution to the slaves in the years before the Revolution. After recounting her suffering as a result of slavery and the slave trade, and noting her advanced age and extreme poverty, she used the bulk of the petition to explain her reasons for seeking a pension, noting that she had labored in slavery for Royall for nearly half a century. Drawing on emerging capitalist notions, she observed that, despite her years of unpaid labor, she was "denied the enjoyment of one morsel of that immense wealth, a part whereof hath been accumulated by her own industry, and the whole augmented by her servitude" (Carretta, 143). She pleaded with the legislature to grant her a pension out of the wealth of the Royall estate. Moved by her argument, the legislature granted her a £15 annual pension. In 1787, after the estate had failed to continue payment of the pension, she again petitioned the legislature to order that the payments be resumed. Her request was granted. Finally, in 1790, the executor of the Royall estate refused to continue payment "without a further interposition" by the legislature. Belinda petitioned a third time and a legislative committee determined the pension was still in "full force." Nothing further is known of Belinda's life after 1790.

Belinda's initial petition had a separate life in the public sphere, reaching readers on both sides of the Atlantic. It was reprinted verbatim in the 18 June 1783 issue of the *New Jersey Gazette*, a popular newspaper in the Middle Atlantic states. Two months later it circulated through a few British periodicals under the heading "The Complaint of Belinda, an African." Rewritten into a first-person slave narrative for use in the emerging British antislavery campaign, the latter version added a tale of rape to the list of sufferings in the original petition. There was another flurry of interest in Belinda's case when Matthew Carey published the petition in his widely-circulated *American Museum* magazine in 1787.

The petition has been remembered and reinterpreted by writers as diverse as the pioneering historian WILLIAM COOPER NELL in his *Colored Patriots of the American Revolution* (1855) and the former U.S. poet laureate RITA DOVE in her 1982 poem entitled "Belinda's Petition." Both of these writers and others have viewed the petition as a suit for freedom. By the early twenty-first century, however, scholars increasingly understood the petition as an early call for personal restitution for time spent in bondage. The anthropologist Stephanie Shaw labeled it "perhaps the earliest example of reparations for the slave trade and slavery" (Finkenbine, 96).

FURTHER READING

Carretta, Vincent, ed. *Unchained Voices: An Anthology of Black Authors in the English-Speaking World of the Eighteenth Century* (1996).

Finkenbine, Roy E. "Belinda's Petition: Reparations for Slavery in Revolutionary Massachusetts," *William and Mary Quarterly* 54 (Jan. 2007): 95–104.

ROY E. FINKENBINE

Bell, Al (1940/41–), record executive, producer, and activist, was born Alvertis Isbell in Brinkley, Arkansas, in 1940 or 1941. In 1945 his family moved to Little Rock, where Bell later graduated with a bachelor's degree in Political Science from the city's Philander Smith College, following this with uncompleted ministerial training; he worked as a disc jockey throughout high school and college. In 1959 Bell began working at workshops run by the Southern Christian Leadership Conference (SCLC) and Dr. MARTIN LUTHER KING JR. His SCLC involvement was short-lived, which Bell attributed to a difference in philosophy, explaining that King's strategy of nonviolent confrontation differed from his belief in the power of black capitalist entrepreneurship in effecting social change.

Bell then worked full time at several radio stations, first at WLOK in Memphis, where his laidback style helped boost ratings, and then at WUST in Washington, D.C., where he introduced releases by the fledgling Memphis label Stax Records. He soon became station manager and also produced releases by local R&B artists. In 1965, Stax—now requiring expanded advertising to support its nationally marketed hit recordings—hired the charismatic, ambitious Bell as its national promotions director. From his first days with the label Bell's charm and contacts helped push Stax toward new heights of exposure and profitability; 1966 and 1967 would be peak years for the company, and Bell would soon parlay his success into an increasingly prominent role. In 1967 the label's owner, Jim Stewart, promoted Bell to executive vice-president, and from then on Bell would become arguably the most important force within the company.

The year 1968 was a tumultuous one for Stax. In December 1967, OTIS REDDING—the label's biggest star—was killed in a plane crash. In April 1968 Dr. King was assassinated in Memphis. The same year also saw Atlantic Records break its distribution deal with Stax, with Atlantic seizing most of Stax's catalog and severing all business connections. This devastated the already weakened company, and it was during this crucial period that Bell's leadership proved vital.

Over the next several years, and not without controversy, Bell reinvented Stax Records. His goals were a tidy encapsulation of the cultural and economic goals of much of the era's Black Power rhetoric: he sought to help the company achieve financial autonomy, while simultaneously using its music and influence to advance causes of black equality and opportunity. He gained 10 percent ownership in the company in 1968, and soon held controlling interest, making Stax black owned for the first time in its history. From his first days at the label, Bell had pushed toward the diversification of Stax releases, attempting to carve out success in nearly every musical format, even those which the label and its first leaders had previously ignored. Some of these attempts, like comedy releases from RICHARD PRYOR, proved more successful than others (such as Bell's repeated attempts to find a successful white artist). Stax also helped promote MELVIN VAN PEEBLES's groundbreaking film *Sweet Sweetback's Baadasssss Song*, predicting the huge success of the Stax artist ISAAC HAYES's *Shaft* soundtrack. Musically, Bell hoped to employ a "crossover" strategy similar to that perfected by Detroit's Motown Records. Though Bell loved all the music made at Stax, and as promotions director helped codify the notion of "the Memphis sound," he encouraged Stax artists to constantly explore, rather than stick to what he sometimes derisively referred to as "that 'Bama music," the funky mixture of gospel and blues that characterized Stax's early creative approach (Bowman, 152). While apparently paradoxical, Bell's black-nationalist concept of uplift through economic independence did not render inconsistent his notions of pursuing a mainstream, white audience. Two key events of Bell's tenure exhibit this clearly. In May 1969, Bell oversaw the simultaneous release of twenty-seven LPs and thirty singles. Bell's goal was twofold: this decision—known most for the breakout success of Hayes's *Hot Buttered Soul*—sought to instantly create a new, Stax-controlled catalog and also to reorient the company toward the release of LPs. As the Stax historian Rob Bowman has argued, the suggestion that R&B audiences would purchase LPs was not a consensus view, and Bell's decision to do this was an example of both his genius and, perhaps, his madness (Bowman, 178–180). Bell's other triumph came in August 1972, at the "Wattstax" concert, where the Stax roster performed for 90,000 people in Los Angeles. Commemorating the 1965 Watts uprisings, and spotlighting both the top Stax artists of the day and several key figures in Black Power politics, most famously the Reverend JESSE JACKSON, *Wattstax* was released as a successful film in 1973. While many, including some company stalwarts, felt that Bell's personal vision ultimately overpowered the communal spirit of 1960s-era Stax, no one denies the magnitude of Bell's importance in the history of the label's success. After the disasters of 1968, Stax under Bell became more commercially successful than ever before. Throughout his time as head of Stax, black organizations like Jesse Jackson's PUSH, as well as industry groups such as the National Association of Radio and Television Announcers (NATRA), honored Bell's leadership.

Despite these achievements, Bell will also be remembered as the head of Stax at its final collapse in the mid-1970s. After a succession of bad business deals—among them one with Union Planters Bank—Stax's unstable finances finally brought about its downfall in 1975. Bell deserves some blame for this, though probably not all. After the closing, Bell was indicted for fraud, and activists including Jesse Jackson leaped to his defense. The historian Rob Bowman has argued that, while charges of racism leveled against Bell's accusers likely have some merit, Stax's incredibly tangled finances suggest that such accusations were not entirely based on race (Bowman, 358–360). Bell was ultimately cleared of all charges, though the combined effect of Stax's closing and the fraud case greatly depleted the financial resources of Bell and his wife, Lydia, Isbell.

Bell remained active in music throughout the 1980s and 1990s. He helped release Tag Team's "Whoomp! (There It Is)" and Duice's "Dazzey Duks," two hugely successful hip-hop singles of the early 1990s. He also continued to play a role in helping to preserve the legacy of Stax Records. Although there are many who blame Bell and his decisions for the company's collapse, Bell—through his belief in the dual Black Power pillars of economic strength and cultural nationalism—helped not only to save Stax Records at an hour of crisis but also to remake the company into a vibrant force that helped define the soul music of the 1970s.

FURTHER READING

Bowman, Rob. *Soulsville, U.S.A.: The Story of Stax Records* (1997).

Guralnick, Peter. *Sweet Soul Music: Rhythm and Blues and the Southern Dream of Freedom* (1986).

CHARLES L. HUGHES

Bell, Bobby Lee (17 June 1940–), professional football player, was one of six children born to Pink Bell, a textile millworker, and Janelee Cole, a domestic worker, in Shelby, North Carolina. As a boy, Bell worked alongside his father at the textile mill in Shelby, located in rural Cleveland County, moving bolts of fabric produced from the local commodity cotton. Cleveland County was known for producing more than eighty thousand bales of cotton per year during the 1940s. It was one of the largest cotton producing mill towns in North Carolina, as well as one of the richest. Bell enjoyed sports as a child, and he became a standout athlete at nearby Cleveland High School, where he received all-state honors as quarterback. Bell's excellent football skills and standout ability on the playing field made him one of the top athletes in the nation in 1958 and 1959, which made college football coaches like Jim Tatum nervous. As the head football coach at the University of North Carolina, a school in the segregated Atlantic Coast Conference, Tatum was not interested in having Bell play for the Tarheels; he actually campaigned to have the all-state quarterback recruited away from schools that would play against ACC teams. This push to relocate the best high school football player in the state of North Carolina netted Bell a football scholarship to the University of Minnesota in 1959.

As a freshman at the University of Minnesota, Bell played quarterback on the freshman team. After Bell's first year, his athletic ability and intelligence were quickly recognized by head coach Murray Warmath as valuable assets to the team. According to Bell, during his sophomore year Warmath called him into his office one day and said, "We want quick and strong guys so we're going to switch you to offensive tackle" (Hall of Fame interview with Bobby Bell). While playing on the offensive line, Bell was the long snapper for punts, extra points, and field goals, developing a skill he would later utilize as a member of the Kansas City Chiefs. But it was as a defensive tackle that the gifted athlete excelled. From 1961 to 1962, Bell blossomed as the premier defensive tackle in the country, garnering first-team honors in the Big Ten Conference and All-American honors. Having a nose for the ball and outstanding football instincts, Bell, along with teammate Carl Eller—a future National Football League (NFL) Hall of Famer—anchored the Minnesota defensive line for two seasons, helping the once last-place Gophers to achieve national success. Bell's play contributed to Minnesota's back-to-back Rose Bowl appearances and helped them win the coveted college bowl game in 1962. In that year, Bell's final season as a Gopher, he won the Outland Trophy as college football's most outstanding lineman and played on the College All-Star team that defeated the two-time NFL champion Green Bay Packers.

The college All-Star and highly sought-after All-American prospect was drafted in 1963 by the Los Angeles Rams in the second round of the NFL draft, and in the seventh round by the Dallas Texans in the upstart American Football League (AFL) draft. The six-foot-four, 230-pound Bell chose to play with the rebel league founded by Lamar Hunt, owner of the Dallas Texans. Becoming acclimated to the professional game alongside teammates such as defensive tackle JUNIOUS "BUCK" BUCHANAN, Bell became one of the AFL's top defensive players as a defensive end. Buchanan would state that Bell was the "best all-around football player" he had ever seen ("Gladiator," Pro Football Hall of Fame). In only his second year in the league, Bell won All-AFL honors for his ability to rush the passer and create havoc on the field. Hank Stram, the head coach of the Dallas Texans (which changed its name to the Kansas City Chiefs in 1963) recognized the depth of Bell's abilities and designed a defense that would allow the gifted athlete to thrive as an All-Pro linebacker. Stram's revolutionary "stack" defense permitted Bell to roam the line of scrimmage, as well as to drop into the secondary from his lineman position. Bell blossomed as the prototype linebacker by utilizing his exceptional quickness and agility to cover running backs out of the backfield and his speed to rush the passer. His productivity and resilience would come to define the featured position on future Kansas City Chiefs teams.

Bell's knowledge of the game of football became his biggest asset. It allowed him to flourish athletically and to create opportunities for the big plays for which he was known. By his third season, Bell had fully made the transition to outside linebacker, grabbing four interceptions, scoring one touchdown, and causing problems for offensive coordinators who were trying to figure out how to control the play maker. Over the span of his career Bell would intercept twenty-six passes and score six touchdowns, while netting nearly five hundred yards in offense. Bell also recovered fifteen fumbles, scoring twice, and he once returned a kickoff fifty-three yards for a touchdown.

From 1965 to 1971, Bell was voted to either the All-AFL or All-NFL teams, playing in the last six AFL All-Star games (1964, 1965, 1966, 1967, 1968, 1969) and the first three AFC-NFC Pro Bowls (1970, 1971, 1972). In the 1969 divisional play-off game against the New York Jets, Bell used his intelligence and football instincts to help his team advance to Super Bowl IV. Late in the third quarter Bell's performance solidified a Chiefs victory. As the game unfolded and anticipating a run fake, Bell played his instincts by dropping in between Jets quarterback Joe Namath and the running back Matt Snell. Bell disrupted the play and dashed the plans of Namath, the MVP of Super Bowl III, to return to the championship game. The Kansas City Chiefs would go on to play the Minnesota Vikings in Super Bowl IV, beating the Vikings 23–7. In 1974, Bell retired after playing in 168 consecutive outings over a period of twelve seasons with the Chiefs, never missing a game. As an athlete, Bell will be remembered as a fierce competitor who could change the game from wherever he lined up on the field. In that same year, Bell became a full-time employee of the General Motors Corporation, marketing automotive parts and services.

In 1983, Bell became the first Kansas City Chiefs player to be elected to the Pro Football Hall of Fame; only Lamar Hunt, the owner and founder of the Chiefs and the founder of the AFL, would precede him. Bell was enshrined in the College Football Hall of Fame in 1991 and in the Missouri Sports Hall of Fame in 1995.

Bell moved to Lee's Summit, Missouri, in 1982. He became a member of the Kansas City Chiefs Ambassadors in 1989, and became an active member of the NFL Alumni Association in 1987. Bell has three children—Bobby Jr., Tracy, and Joshua—from his two marriages.

FURTHER READING

Effrat, Louis. "Unbeaten Gophers Inflict First Loss on Hawkeyes," *New York Times* (6 Nov. 1960).

McKenzie, Michael. *Arrowhead: Home of the Chiefs* (1997).

Smith, Don R. *NFL Pro Football Hall Of Fame All-Time Greats* (1988).

"Warfield and Bell Gain Hall of Fame," *New York Times* (2 Feb. 1983).

PELLOM MCDANIELS III

Bell, Cool Papa (17 May 1903–7 Mar. 1991), baseball player and manager, was born James Thomas Bell in Starkville, Mississippi, the son of Jonas Bell, a farmer whose father was an American Indian, and Mary Nichols. James had six siblings, two sisters and four brothers, and said that his mother taught him to be an honest, clean-living man who cared about other people.

He was reared in the Oktoc community near Starkville and began playing pickup games on the local sandlots while attending the local school through the eighth grade. There was neither a high school nor gainful employment in his hometown,

so in 1920 Bell moved to St. Louis, Missouri, to live with his older brothers and attend high school, completing two years before ending his formal education. Soon after arriving in St. Louis, he met Clarabelle Thompson, and they were married in September 1920. The marriage lasted seventy years but was childless.

The young husband worked for the Independent Packing Company and played baseball with the semi-pro Compton Hill Cubs and the East St. Louis Cubs. At this stage of his career, Bell was a promising, left-handed pitcher with a varied repertoire of pitches that included a screwball, a curve, and a knuckleball. He was scouted and signed in 1922 by the St. Louis Stars of the Negro National League for ninety dollars a month. In his rookie season he acquired the colorful nickname by which he was known forever afterward. In a crucial game situation, Bell struck out the great OSCAR CHARLESTON, the best hitter in the Negro Leagues at the time and a future Hall-of-Famer. The manager Bill Gatewood, impressed by the youngster's poise under pressure, applied the appellation "Cool Papa" to his protégé, and the name stuck.

In 1924, after an arm injury ended his pitching career, Cool Papa became a full-time outfielder, where he could use his incredible speed to the greatest advantage. He played a shallow center field and routinely demonstrated extraordinary range in the field by making sensational catches. A natural right-handed batter, he learned to switch-hit to better utilize his speed from the left side of the batter's box. He was so fast going from the batter's box to first base that if he bunted and the ball bounced twice, the fielders would say "Put it in your pocket" because there was no chance to get him out. When JACKIE ROBINSON played in the Negro Leagues with the Kansas City Monarchs, he was a shortstop, but knowledgeable observers knew that it was not his best position and that if he wanted to break into the major leagues he would have to change position. To demonstrate this to him, Cool Papa would hit ground balls to Robinson's right and beat the throw to first base.

Once clocked at twelve seconds circling the bases, Cool Papa is recognized as the fastest player ever to play the game. He was so swift that some players said that it looked like his feet did not even touch the ground. His incredible speed also made him an omnipresent base-stealing threat, and in 1933 he was credited with 175 stolen bases in a 200-game season. He sometimes took two bases on a bunt or scored from second base on a sacrifice fly.

While his speed was real, it was often exaggerated. SATCHEL PAIGE, the legendary pitcher and a skilled raconteur known to embellish stories, said that Cool Papa was so fast that he could turn off the light switch and be in bed with the covers pulled up to his chin before the room got dark. Cool Papa confirmed that he had demonstrated this skill but added a detail that Paige had conveniently omitted: the light switch was faulty, which resulted in a delay before the light went out. In later years, the boxer MUHAMMAD ALI claimed for himself the ability to perform the same feat.

During his ten seasons in St. Louis, Bell consistently batted well over .300, with his best year coming in 1926, when he batted .362, with fifteen home runs and twenty-three stolen bases in the eighty-five-game season; moreover, the Stars won Negro National League pennants in 1928, 1930, and 1931. Following the 1931 season, both the franchise and the league fell victim to the economics of the Great Depression and disbanded. With the demise of the league, the 1932 season was one of chaos, as players scrambled to earn a spot on the roster of a surviving solvent franchise. Cool Papa was no exception and played with three teams, the Detroit Wolves, the Kansas City Monarchs, and the Homestead Grays. In 1933 he joined owner WILLIAM AUGUSTUS GREENLEE's Pittsburgh Crawfords, and for the next four years Bell continued to bat over .300 each season, as the Crawfords contended for the championship of the new Negro National League. In 1933 Greenlee, who was league president, claimed a disputed championship, and in 1934 the team again finished strong but missed the play-offs. In 1935 the Crawfords defeated the New York Cubans in a seven-game play-off for an undisputed title, and they repeated as champions in 1936. That season was interrupted when the league sent a select All-Star team to participate in the Denver Post Tournament, which they won with ease, as Bell batted .450 and topped the tournament in stolen bases. During each of his four seasons with the Crawfords, Bell was voted to start in the East-West All-Star game, where he always played centerfield and batted leadoff.

In 1937 Cool Papa left the Crawfords and spent the next five years in Latin America. In his first season he helped the dictator Rafael Trujillo's All-Stars win the 1937 championship in the Dominican Republic. Bell later said that the players were told that if they didn't win the championship they would be executed. In 1938 he went to Mexico, where he remained for the next four seasons. After two years with Tampico, where he batted .356 and .354, he split the 1940 season between Torreon and Veracruz and had his best year in Mexico, winning the Triple Crown with a batting average of .437, twelve home runs, and seventy-nine RBI. He also led in hits with 167 and in triples with fifteen in the eighty-nine-game season, as Veracruz won the pennant. Cool Papa played with Monterrey in 1941 and ended with a .367 career batting average in the Mexican League.

During his long baseball career, Cool Papa supplemented his summer income by playing in integrated winter baseball leagues in California and Cuba. In California he had a .368 career batting average for a dozen intermittent winters between 1922 and 1945, and in 1933–1934 he led the league with a .362 batting average. In 1928 he played the first of three consecutive winters in Cuba with Cienfuegos and batted .325, while leading the league in home runs, stolen bases, and runs scored. He returned to Cuba for the 1940–1941 season, playing with Almendares in his final season, to finish with a career .292 batting average in the Cuban winter league.

In 1942 Cool Papa returned to the United States, joined the Chicago American Giants of the Negro American League, and began a string of three additional appearances in the East-West All-Star game. In 1943 he joined the Homestead Grays, the dominant team in the Negro National League, and batted .356 as the Grays won the pennant and defeated the Negro American League's Birmingham Black Barons in the Negro World Series. In 1944 he batted .373, and the Grays defended their Negro League championship by defeating Birmingham in a Negro World Series rematch. The following year he batted .302, as the Grays won another pennant but were swept in the World Series by the Cleveland Buckeyes. Cool Papa's last year with the Grays was 1946, during which he batted .396. He later said that he had won the batting title that year but "gave" it to MONTE IRVIN to enhance his chances to play in the major leagues.

For the next four years Cool Papa was a playing manager with lesser teams, the Detroit Senators in 1947 and the Kansas City Stars, a farm team for the Monarchs, from 1948 through 1950. He finished his Negro Leagues career with a lifetime .341 batting average and also had a .391 average in exhibition games against major leaguers. In 1951 he became a part-time scout for the St. Louis Browns, until the franchise moved to Baltimore in 1954. After leaving baseball he worked as a custodian and night security officer at St. Louis City Hall until he retired around 1970.

In 1974 Cool Papa Bell was inducted into the National Baseball Hall of Fame in Cooperstown, New York. He died of a heart attack in St. Louis, Missouri in 1991, only a few weeks after his beloved wife, Clarabelle.

For a quarter-century, Bell showcased his exceptional speed and all-around excellence on baseball diamonds throughout the United States and Latin America, demonstrating that African Americans could compete successfully against white athletes. His career contributed significantly to the eventual elimination of baseball's color line.

FURTHER READING

Holway, John. *Voices from the Great Black Baseball Leagues* (1975).

Peterson, Robert. *Only the Ball Was White* (1970).

Riley, James A. *The Biographical Encyclopedia of the Negro Baseball Leagues* (1994).

JAMES A. RILEY

Bell, Dennis (28 December 1866–25 September 1953), U.S. Army soldier and Medal of Honor recipient, was born in Washington, D.C., the son of Judson and Adeline (Beans) Bell. Judson Bell worked as both a sailor and a household servant, while his wife worked as a domestic servant and laundress to support their large family, including daughters Emily and Julia, sons Rowsberry, Abraham, Dennis, Alton, and Frank, as well as Adeline's mother, Henrietta Beans. After completing his public education, Dennis Bell left Washington, D.C. at an unknown date and by 1892 was employed in Pittsburgh, Pennsylvania, as a coal miner. Dennis Bell enlisted in the U.S. Army for a term of five years on 3 December 1892 at Pittsburgh and was assigned for duty in the 10th Cavalry Regiment. This unit was one of four segregated army regiments—including the 9th Cavalry and the 24th and 25th Infantry regiments—in which African Americans could serve at this time, each of which was composed of black enlisted men and noncommissioned and junior officers, commanded by white senior officers. These regiments were first assigned for duty in the American west beginning in the late 1860s, and soon became collectively known as "Buffalo Soldiers." After joining the 10th Cavalry, Bell was assigned to Troop H and sent westward, serving in Montana at Fort Assinniboine during the final years of the ongoing military campaign, referred to as the Indian Wars, to subdue several Native American nations and force them onto reservations. At the end of his first enlistment period in December 1897, Private Bell was rated a good soldier, and subsequently re-enlisted for another term. Just months later, in April 1898, Bell and the rest of the 10th Cavalry were ordered to depart Montana for Lakeland, Florida to take part in the recently declared Spanish-American War. While in Florida, a detachment of about fifty cavalrymen from the 9th and 10th Cavalry regiments were chosen to take part in a special mission to link up with and provide supplies to rebel insurgents in Cuba. Among the men chosen by Lt. Carter Johnson for this duty was Dennis Bell. While Bell was among the least experienced of the men chosen, Johnson surely had a reason for choosing him, and Bell would soon prove his abilities to the highest degree. The force departed Florida on 25 June 1898 and four days later made their first attempt to land in Cuba, only to be repulsed near Cienfuegos. The next day another landing was attempted, this time at Tayabacao; while American forces made it ashore, heavy gunfire from an enemy blockhouse sank several landing boats and forced a withdrawal. However, fourteen men had to be left behind and were in danger of being captured. After four attempts to rescue them were beaten back, Lt. Johnson finally decided to send four black cavalrymen, DENNIS BELL, GEORGE WANTON, FITZ LEE, and WILLIAM THOMPKINS, led by one white officer. In the subsequent action, which Lt. Johnson termed "a brave and gallant deed, and deserving of a reward" (Schubert, p. 139), the black troopers quietly rowed ashore, rescued the wounded men while enduring a hail of enemy gunfire, and made it safely back. For this heroic mission, Dennis Bell and his fellow black cavalrymen were recommended for the Medal of Honor and by June 1899 the award was approved. Dennis Bell received his Medal of Honor while serving in Manzanillo, Cuba, after the war had ended.

The service of men like BELL, THOMPKINS, and EDWARD BAKER JR. is important not just for the deeds that earned them the nation's highest military decoration but also because it highlights the important contributions made by black soldiers in one of America's forgotten conflicts. Indeed, while posthumous Medal of Honor recipient Theodore Roosevelt, a cavalry officer and future president, is the most enduring historical figure to emerge from the Spanish American War, black cavalrymen and fellow Medal of Honor recipients such as Dennis Bell deserve to be better remembered for their valiant service.

After serving in the Spanish-American War, Bell continued as a soldier in the 10th Cavalry, serving at Fort Clark and Eagle Pass, Texas, where he was promoted to corporal, and later in the Philippines. By 1906, Bell had retired from the army and returned to Washington, D.C. where he lived the remainder of his life and worked a variety of jobs, including that of construction worker. He would later, after 1930, marry Rosa Williams, and at the time of his death lived with his stepdaughter, Leola Ewell. After a brief illness, Dennis Bell died at Mount Alto Hospital and was subsequently buried in Arlington National Cemetery with full military honors.

FURTHER READING

Schubert, Frank N. *Black Valor: Buffalo Soldiers and the Medal of Honor, 1870–1898* (1997).

Obituary: "Dennis Bell Dies at 87; Held Medal of Honor," *Washington Post.* (September 1953).

GLENN ALLEN KNOBLOCK

Bell, Derrick Albert, Jr. (6 Nov. 1930–5 Oct. 2011), lawyer and educator, was born in Pittsburgh, Pennsylvania, to Derrick A. Bell Sr. and Ada Elizabeth Bell. Bell was born during the Great Depression and grew up in the city's black neighborhood known as "the Hill." Bell's father was employed as a porter in a Pittsburgh department store and also earned extra money through the underground numbers racket. In 1939 Bell Sr. hit the number for $700 and at the urging of his wife purchased a three-bedroom home in a more prosperous neighborhood. Eventually, Bell's father opened his own business hauling refuse.

Throughout his early life, Bell had a newspaper route that provided him with spending money and made him aware of the rich diversity of Pittsburgh's middle-class black world. He met lawyers, doctors, laborers, ministers, and postal workers all living and working in the same segregated neighborhoods. It was at the urging of one of those black customers, Judge HOMER S. BROWN, that Bell first expressed an interest in becoming a lawyer.

Bell graduated in 1948 from Schenley High School in Pittsburgh, and like his three siblings, attended college. His parents' hard work paid off, too; they were able to actually pay for their children's education with their own money. Following high school, Bell attended Duquesne University in Pittsburgh and joined the ROTC. Following college, he served two years in the military, in Korea from 1952 to 1954. After his military service, Bell was accepted at the University of Pittsburgh School of Law. It was in law school that he began to excel intellectually. He also became interested in civil rights and was selected for law review after his first year, writing a number of articles for that publication. His interest in civil rights began to grow as he learned more about prominent black attorneys like CHARLES HAMILTON HOUSTON and THURGOOD MARSHALL.

Upon graduation, Bell realized that jobs were scarce in Pittsburgh for black law graduates, so he took a job as a lawyer at the Department of Justice. It did not last long. The Department of Justice asked Bell to resign his membership in the NAACP because it was a conflict of interest. Bell refused and was reassigned to meaningless work within the agency. He resigned from the Department of Justice in 1959 in protest. These actions foreshadowed his life's work as a dedicated civil rights advocate and educator in the area of racial justice.

He returned to his hometown of Pittsburgh and became head of the local NAACP, where he organized local efforts to try to integrate the city. In 1960 Thurgood Marshall, head of the NAACP Legal Defense Fund, offered him a job as an attorney. Bell soon was working with the legal giants of the civil rights era—Thurgood Marshall, Jack Greenberg, ROBERT LEE CARTER, CONSTANCE BAKER MOTLEY, and JAMES MADISON NABRIT JR.—to try to implement the mandate of the famous *Brown v. Board of Education* case through the courts. Bell litigated hundreds of school desegregation cases in the South.

Bell remained at the NAACP until 1965, when he took a position as an administrator with the Department of Health, Education, and Welfare. Here he was deputy director at the agency in charge of civil rights. In 1968 he was hired to teach at UCLA's Western Center on Law and Poverty. In 1969 he was hired to teach at Harvard Law School, and in 1971 he became the law school's first black tenured law professor. His biggest contribution to the field of civil rights law and racial issues in the law occurred at Harvard, where he developed a course on civil rights law and in 1973 published the standard textbook for the course, *Race, Racism, and American Law*, which was adopted by law schools throughout the country.

Bell spent eleven years teaching at Harvard, where he won the respect of his colleagues. After a visit in professorship at the University of Washington Law School in Seattle, he was named dean of the University of Oregon School of Law in 1980, but his years there proved to be contentious. He had hoped that more persons of color would be hired for teaching positions at the school, but he could not bring about the changes he was seeking. When the law school's faculty hiring committee refused to authorize him to hire an Asian American woman faculty member (after two white male candidates had turned down the position), Bell concluded that he could no longer tolerate the slow pace of change. He resigned and returned to Harvard Law School only to confront similar problems.

In 1987 Bell published a book of nonfiction parables, *And We Are Not Saved: The Elusive Quest for Racial Justice*, followed by *Faces at the Bottom of the Well: The Permanence of Racism* in 1993. As he began his writing career, Bell also began protesting Harvard Law School's refusal to hire a woman of color as a tenured law professor. His decision not to teach until Harvard offered tenure to a woman of color received intense press coverage. Ultimately, the protest, which lasted from 1990 to 1992 failed; the school did not offer tenure to a woman of color and Bell was fired. He documented his efforts in his 1994 memoir, *Confronting Authority: Reflections of an Ardent Protestor*. Bell had embarked on the protest around the time his wife, Jewel Bell, was diagnosed with cancer. Sadly, she died in 1990. The couple had three sons, Derrick III, Douglass Du Bois, and Carter Robeson.

Following his failed protest at Harvard, in 1991 Bell joined the faculty at New York University School of Law and subsequently produced several more books. In 1996 his book *Gospel Choirs* appeared; *Afrolantica Legacies* appeared in 1998, and *Ethical Ambition: Living a Life of Meaning and Worth* followed in 2002. Finally, Bell published *Silent Covenants: "Brown v. Board of Education" and the Unfulfilled Hopes for Racial Reform* in 2004. Bell received many honorary degrees for his tireless work on racial justice issues, and his textbook on civil rights law remained a key text in that field well into the twenty-first century. He died in New York City at the age of 80.

FURTHER READING

Essien, Victor. "Race in the Academy: Moving Beyond Diversity and toward the Incorporation of Faculty of Color in Predominantly White Colleges and Universities," *Journal of Black Studies*, vol. 34, no. 1 (Sep. 2003): 63–71.

Gilmore, Brian. "American Racial and Legal History According to Derrick Bell," *Crisis* 112 (Sept.–Oct. 2005): 40.

BRIAN GILMORE

Bell, James Madison (3 Apr. 1826–1902), abolitionist, poet, and lecturer, was born in Gallipolis, Ohio. His parents' identities are unknown. At age sixteen, in 1842, he moved to Cincinnati. While there, in 1848, he married Louisiana Sanderlin (or Sanderline), with whom he had several children. He also learned the plastering trade from his brother-in-law, George Knight. Bell worked as a plasterer during the day and attended Cincinnati High School for Colored People at night. Founded in 1844 by Reverend Hiram S. Gilmore, the school had a connection to Oberlin College and was said to have given impetus to the sentiment found in *Uncle Tom's Cabin* and the cause of human freedom. Through his studies Bell was thoroughly indoctrinated into the principles of radical abolitionism.

In 1854 Bell moved his family to Chatham, Ontario, Canada, feeling that he would be freer under the authority of the British government. While continuing his trade he became involved in political activities and met and befriended John Brown. As his ally, Bell raised money and enlisted men to support Brown's raid on Harpers Ferry. He probably was one of the last people to see Brown before the raid took place.

In 1860 Bell moved to San Francisco, California, where he became involved in the fight to ensure equal education for local black children. He also took a leading and active role at various state conventions protesting laws that discriminated against blacks. At one such convention, held by ministers of the African Methodist Episcopal (AME) Church, Bell addressed the role of the church and its relationship to the state. (He was an active member and steward of the AME Church in San Francisco.)

Although far removed from the battlefield, he worked as a crusader for abolition during the Civil War. He wrote some of his most rousing poems while living in California, including "Emancipation," "Lincoln," and "The Dawn of Freedom." His works were long, comprising as many as 950 lines, and were meant to be recited. However, while Bell is known as a poet today, poetry came second to his activism during his lifetime.

Bell left California and moved to Toledo, Ohio, in 1865. He arrived at the time of emancipation and began to work with the freedmen, focusing his energies on the struggle for civil rights. He later went to Canada to visit his family and eventually moved them to Toledo. He continued to be active in the AME Church, serving as superintendent of the Sunday school and as a lay worker. Active briefly in Republican politics, Bell was elected as a delegate from Lucas County to the state convention and as a delegate at large from the state of Ohio to the Republican National Convention in both 1868 and 1872. He was a vocal and enthusiastic supporter of the nomination of Ulysses S. Grant at both conventions.

Bell traveled frequently, preaching a doctrine of human liberty, enjoining blacks to use their freedom responsibly, and instructing freedmen in their political and civic duties, often reciting his long poems as the method of instruction. Bishop B. W. ARNETT, a friend who worked with Bell in the church, often traveled with him as he gave public readings of his poetry and lectured on educational and legal rights for black Americans. According to Arnett, no one instructed people better or had a more imposing manner than Bell. "Many a young man who was not an honor to his race and a blessing to his people received the first spark of inspiration for true greatness" while listening to his poems (Arnett, 10).

Bell addressed many issues in his poems, including slavery, war, emancipation, and Reconstruction, often referencing historical figures, such as John Brown, or events of historical significance. Although he tended to vary the lengths of stanzas, his poems have been described as "almost identical and dull" and "without any distinctive literary quality." Many of Bell's poems were published individually, though they were eventually compiled in Arnett's *The Poetical Works of James Madison Bell* (1901).

One of Bell's long poems, "The Progress of Liberty" (1866), was written for the third anniversary of the Emancipation Proclamation. Its 850 lines review the Civil War, the triumph of liberty, and the martyrdom of Abraham Lincoln:

The bondsman's gloomy night has passed;
The slavery of this land is dead;
No tyrant's power, however vast,
Can wake it from its gory bed.
...
Though slavery's dead, yet there remains
A work for those from whom the chains
Today are falling one by one;
Nor should they deem their labor done,
Nor shrink the task, however hard,
While it insures a great reward,
And bids them on its might depend
For perfect freedom in the end.

Bell also used poems to encourage blacks to be model citizens:

In this yourselves must take the lead;
You must yourselves first elevate;
Till then the world will ne'er concede
Your claims to manhood's high estate.

In addition, Bell used his works—and the reading of them—to denounce laws and policies that he deemed to be detrimental to blacks. He is said to have triumphed in his "daring, vigorous satire of President Andrew Johnson" in the poem "Modern Moses, or 'My Policy' Man" (1867). Called his "most inventive and readable work" because of its "shrewd humor and irony, concrete topicality and personal emotion" (Sherman, 192), the poem ridicules Johnson from a personal as well as political perspective. It portrays the president as a Judas who betrayed the people by vetoing the Freedmen's Bureau Bill:

Mark when that bill for the supply
Of starving millions met his eye;
A breadless, clotheless, houseless throng.
Thus rendered by his nation's wrong.
Does he the bill in haste receive
And sign, their suff'rings to relieve?
...
Then he in their deep hour of grief,
Did them relieve and kept his vow;
When with a dark and wrinkled brow,
He stamped his veto on their prayer,
And doomed the suppliants to despair.

In *From Slavery to Freedom*, the historian JOHN HOPE FRANKLIN argues that the overwhelming acclaim of the poet PAUL LAURENCE DUNBAR probably overshadowed the works of Bell and other black poets of his era. If not for Dunbar's fame, Bell might have been more highly regarded as a poet during an age that was critical to the political, social, and cultural development of black Americans.

FURTHER READING
Arnett, Bishop B. W. *The Poetical Works of James Madison Bell* (1901).
Sherman, Joan R. *African American Poetry of the Nineteenth Century: An Anthology* (1992).
This entry is taken from the *American National Biography* and is published here with the permission of the American Council of Learned Societies.

MAMIE E. LOCKE

Bell, Mary A. (1 May 1852–?), slave narrative author, was born Mary Rice to SPOTSWOOD RICE, an enslaved tobacco roller, and a slave woman perhaps named Caroline on a large plantation near Glasgow, Missouri. In addition to Mary, Caroline and Spotswood Rice had three sons and two daughters, who lived with their mother on a Missouri riverside plantation owned by Katherine Diggs. Spotswood Rice lived and worked on Benjamin Lewis's plantation nearby. Interviewed by the Federal Writers Project in St. Louis in 1937 Bell recalled that "slavery was a mighty hard life." Her narrative is significant in that it was one of the few of the over two thousand recorded for the Federal Writers Project in which one black woman interviewed another about her life in slavery. The historian Paul Escott's analysis of several hundred WPA narratives found that former slaves interviewed by black women reported significantly higher levels of dissatisfaction with life under slavery. Black female interviewers were more than twice as likely as white male interviewers to report rapes on a plantation and to elicit negative appraisals of their subjects' masters, and were three times more likely than were white female interviewers to record recollections of white masters fathering slave children. Bell's narrative is indeed strongly critical of slavery and of slaveowners, as well as one of the most eloquent in its depiction of slave resistance to bondage.

When Bell was only seven years old her mistress hired her out to a Presbyterian minister to look after his three children. In addition young Mary Bell was placed on a pony to ride out to the minister's large farm and call the field hands to dinner. The following year Diggs hired her out to a baker, again to look after his children and to perform various chores around the house. "Neither family was nice to me," Bell recalled. Difficult as her own life was, Bell noted that life for her parents under slavery was even worse since they were only allowed to visit each other twice a week, on Wednesdays and Saturdays. She recalled that on those rare visits her mother often had to remove Spotswood Rice's bloody clothes and bathe and grease the injuries he received from whippings by his master's black overseer. Bell's narrative reveals her considerable pride in her father's skills as a tobacco roller and leader of the slave community. She expresses an even greater admiration for her father's defiance of his master, first by learning to read and write, and then by leading eleven of Lewis's best slaves to freedom. Although Bell recalled that her father ran off to Kansas City, Missouri, to join the Union forces,

U.S. Army records show that he did not travel that far, enlisting close to his daughter's home in Glasgow in February 1864.

Bell was finally reunited with her father and mother at the end of the Civil War in 1865 at the Benton Barracks Hospital in St. Louis. While her father worked at the Barracks as a nurse, Mary helped her mother to take in laundry. A desire to reconnect the family ties broken by slavery was common to millions of emancipated slaves, as was the goal of gaining an education. Bell shared both. When she was thirteen she attended school for the first time, spending six months in classes at Benton Barracks, where, she recalled, "I was very apt and learned fast." So fast, in fact, that she found herself traveling throughout St. Louis in the late 1860s and early 1870s, attending different schools for six months to three years at a time, to further her education.

Bell converted to the African Methodist Episcopal (AME) Church in St. Louis in 1866, and later, in 1882, she married a man named Bell (his first name is unknown), with whom she had seven children, and who died in May 1896. Although she did not earn enough money to buy a home until 1916, when she was sixty-four years old, Bell was able to purchase her home outright within six and a half years, partly from her widow's pension.

Compared to many former slaves interviewed as part of the federal government's Slave Narrative Project, Bell enjoyed a relatively comfortable retirement, though her life in working-class St. Louis was not without its disappointments. At least five of her children preceded her in death. At the time of her interview in 1937 she had only a daughter, Virginia Miller, who lived next door to her in St. Louis, and a son, William A. Bell, at that time serving in the army in the Philippines. Immensely proud of her son's military service, Bell concluded her 1937 interview by also praising her father, brother, husband, and indeed any "man who will fight for his rights, and any person who wants to be something."

FURTHER READING

Interview of Mary A. Bell. St. Louis, Missouri, 19 August 1937, WPA Slave Narrative Project, volume 11, *Arkansas Narratives, Part 7 and Missouri Narratives*.

Berlin, Ira, et al. *Remembering Slavery: African Americans Talk about Their Personal Experiences of Slavery and Freedom* (1998).

Escott, Paul. *Slavery Remembered: A Record of Twentieth Century Slave Narratives* (1979).

STEVEN J. NIVEN

Bell, Mary A. (2 July 1873–20 Sept. 1941), artist, was born in Washington, D.C., the daughter of James F. Bell and Susanna County, probably laborers. Little is known about Bell's early life. She presumably attended segregated schools. It is unlikely that she ever received artistic training; she declared that she drew "without human teaching." She probably worked as a domestic servant, laundress, or seamstress, beginning in her teenage years, and she may have traveled extensively. Bell said she "lived all around" before World War I. Since she does not appear in early-twentieth-century city directories or census records in Washington, D.C., or Boston, Massachusetts, and because she apparently never married or had children, it is likely that she resided with her various employers.

By the mid-1920s Bell was working for Edward Peter Pierce, justice of the Supreme Judicial Court of Massachusetts from 1914 to 1937, and Adele Dutaud Pierce, his wife, as a live-in domestic servant in Boston and in their summer home in Georgetown, Maine. Bell may have also worked on occasion for the sculptor Gaston Lachaise and his wife, Isabel. Isabel Lachaise and Adele Pierce were sisters, and Lachaise family papers indicate they both had a fondness for their maid. Bell maintained a friendly written correspondence with both families, signing letters "your humble servant" after she left their employment sometime in the mid-1930s.

Around 1936 Bell moved into a lodging house in Boston. Her artistic career blossomed when she was in her sixties, and she produced at least 140 drawings between 1936 and 1939. Apparently self-taught, Bell usually drew at night after working odd jobs. Most of her wax crayon and colored pencil drawings on tissue paper are delicate, fanciful courtship scenes of well-dressed white couples in elegant parlors or luxurious gardens. Yet there are also depictions of Creole beauties, regal Ethiopians, burlesque performers, penitent sinners, and loving mothers. A small narrative label in flowing script glued to the top center of a fastidiously constructed double-tissue border announces the title of each stage-like scene.

Bell regularly featured women in her work, explaining that "a woman is the cream of the earth and everybody likes cream, so I put a woman in all my drawings." Typically, a large-scale woman and a small man float in between plants and multiple horizon lines or small household furnishings, the latter perhaps traced from magazines. One exemplary work is *Proposing*, which depicts a beautiful woman seated in a parlor amid tiny floating furniture, including a grand piano, a swag lamp, and a fringed hook rug. A Catholic who declared that God, rather than she, created her drawings—as do many self-taught artists—Bell occasionally included an oval portrait of the Virgin Mary in the background, as she does in *Proposing*. Bell explained that the Mother of God appeared in all of her drawings initially "just to introduce her to my friends; now they all know HER and I don't need to put her in pictures."

Another notable work is *American Mixtures of the Ethiopian Race*. Here three women prance in a floral landscape. Two wear fashionable clothing, elaborate coiffures, and sparkling jewelry. The largest and fanciest figure is also the lightest skinned. Bell reflects contemporary notions of hierarchical skin tones by inscribing: "The girl in the center is Octoroon. The girl on the left, the Creole type. The [girl on the] right is the so-called Chocolate type." The darkest-skinned woman wears a miserable sack and has unruly hair. Bell may have identified with her; the artist's monogram, a floral bell, appears just below the hem of her dress.

Such charming images depicted on fragile materials delighted a small group of patrons, mostly in the Boston area, who excitedly shared Bell's work, priced at just fifty cents each, with one another. After Gaston Lachaise died in 1935, Isabel introduced Bell's art to her grandniece Ruth Pierce, a journalist, and the artist Kate Buss. Buss in turn sent Bell's drawings to Gertrude Stein in Paris and to the New York writer and photographer Carl Van Vechten. Van Vechten's friend, the publicist Mark Lutz of Philadelphia, also became a patron, as did the art critic Henry McBride. McBride then convinced the artist Florine Stettheimer to purchase several pieces. Additionally some of Isabel Lachaise's other friends took Bell's drawings on vacation to share abroad. All admired Bell's flamboyant images of women and flowers, dreamlike spaces, vivid colors, and charming narratives.

For Stein and Van Vechten, Bell was all the more exotic and attractive because of her race and outsider status. Both befriended and supported African American writers and performers. Van Vechten, a bisexual, was known for his photographs of Harlemites, and Stein consented to an all-black cast for the performance of her operatic *Four Saints in Three Acts*. Further, African American writers commended her short story "Melanctha" for its nonpatronizing attitude toward black people. Stein also collected work by both modern masters and self-taught artists and even planned an exhibition of American folk art in Paris in 1939. World War II, however, prevented this event.

While Bell did not associate with other artists and never exhibited her art, she hoped that her drawings might lead to some renown and racial uplift. She wrote to Van Vechten, who purchased more than one hundred of her drawings, that she was reincarnated and that whispering spirits told her to send out her drawings and "make yourself known to the world." In 1936 Bell took six works to a movie producer, explaining that she wanted the glory of the Ethiopian race to be known to the world. The producer, apparently amused by the ambition of an elderly black domestic, informed her that her marvelous colors could not possibly be duplicated. Soon thereafter she realized she had been duped when she received a photographic postcard of one of her drawings made by Van Vechten.

Pleased with Van Vechten's patronage, Bell offered to sign her works any way he wished, and she adopted a monogram in the shape of a floral bell at his suggestion. Yet when he and Lutz paid Bell a surprise visit in 1938, she refused to see them for unknown reasons. She also denied Van Vechten's request to photograph her, stating that she would not be photographed until she was on "Ethiopian soil." While stereotypes about a racial hierarchy according to skin color are evident in the artist's work—she believed the most beautiful women were the lightest—Bell was proud of her racial heritage. She included flags and jewelry with the Pan-African colors (red, black, green, and gold or yellow) in her art and took interest in the career of Haile Selassie, emperor of Ethiopia.

Plagued with failing eyesight and asthma, Bell also suffered from smoke inhalation from a fire in her apartment, which forced her to move across the street in May 1938. She then hoped to secure a four-room apartment near the Charles River so she could have a gallery of her own. Soon, however, she lost her most loyal patrons. Two of Van Vechten's friends, Edward Pierce and JAMES WELDON JOHNSON, died in 1938. That year Van Vechten officially donated his entire collection of black memorabilia to the Beinecke Rare Book and Manuscript Library at Yale University in honor of Johnson.

By mid-December 1940 Bell was institutionalized at the Boston State Hospital, a public mental health facility. She had predicted her tragic demise two years earlier: "Fate has decreed a cruel ending for me." Bell died in the facility of heart disease and the hardening of the arteries, complicated by psychosis. It is not known how long she was mentally ill or whether the condition affected her art. Destitute, Bell was buried in a pauper's grave across the street from the hospital.

Recognized by such luminaries as Van Vechten, Lachaise, Stein, and Stettheimer in her own time, Bell's charming and provocative works and letters continue to offer a rare glimpse into the world of an intriguing, self-taught African American artist. While virtually unknown to the mainstream history of art, her works are significant for their fresh vision and their social commentary on escapist romance, black skin tones, religion, and Pan-African overtones. Exhibitions of Bell's drawings were held at the Beinecke Library (1945), the Galerie Brusberg in Berlin, Germany (1986), the Chicago International Art Exposition (1987), and the Yale University Art Gallery (1991).

FURTHER READING

Bell's papers are in the James Weldon Johnson
     Memorial Collection of American Negro Arts
     and Letters, Beinecke Rare Book and Manuscript
     Library, Yale University, New Haven, Connecticut.

THERESA LEININGER-MILLER

Bell, Philip Alexander (1808?–25 April 1889), newspaper editor and civil rights activist, was born in New York City, the third of three children, to Alexander Bell and Letty (maiden name unknown). A stutterer, the young Bell turned to writing to express himself, honing his natural talents under the teachers at New York City's African Free School, an institution respected for such alumni as the Shakespearean actor IRA ALDRIDGE and the Episcopal priest and Pan-Africanist ALEXANDER CRUMMELL. After finishing school, Bell set out to make journalism his life's work, hoping to use the press to advance black interests.

On 25 January 1831 Bell attended a meeting of the Colored Citizens of New York at the Boyer Lodge Room. The meeting's attendees rejected the idea of black colonization in Liberia, West Africa—a plan of the American Colonization Society—saying that blacks absolutely claimed "this country, the place of our birth, and not Africa, as our mother country." A few months later, Bell was one of New York's representatives at the First Annual Convention of the People of Colour, held in Philadelphia in 1831, to discuss colonization, the abolition of slavery, and ways of achieving equality for "every freeman born in this country." Bell attended a second Philadelphia convention in 1832, which revisited the previous year's proposal, the resettlement of former

Philip Alexander Bell, journalist and civil rights activist who campaigned actively for equal rights on both the East and West Coast. (Schomburg Center for Research in Black Culture, New York Public Library.)

migrate there, as did Bell's friend, the activist and future judge MIFFLIN WISTAR GIBBS. Sometime in 1859 or early 1860 Bell decided to move to San Francisco, California, arriving in 1860.

Almost immediately, Bell joined the black community's efforts to eliminate California state statutes that prevented blacks from testifying and acting as witnesses in court cases involving whites. To end such laws and to provide a voice for the community, Bell and PETER ANDERSON established the San Francisco *Pacific Appeal* in 1862. In one of his earliest editorials, Bell wrote, "Our paper is devoted to the interests of the Colored People of California and to their moral, intellectual and political advancement [and] … will advocate their rights, their claims to humanity and justice; it will oppose the wrongs inflicted on them." In another editorial, Bell assessed African American life:

Exiles in our native land, aliens in the country that gave us birth, outlaws for no crime, proscribed without offence, amenable to the laws without being protected by them, thus we stand, innocent victims of an unholy and unrighteous prejudice—truly our condition is most deplorable (*Pacific Appeal*, 12 April 1862).

Bell and Anderson soon disagreed over editorial policy, forcing Bell to quit the paper in July 1862. Bell remained in the newspaper business, however, as an agent for New York's *Anglo-African*, while continuing his effort to overturn the discriminatory testimony and witness laws. His struggle proved successful in March 1863, when Governor Leland Stanford signed a measure repealing these laws. For Bell, however, the struggle for rights did not stop there; African Americans needed equal education and the right to vote. To help achieve those ends, Bell established his own newspaper, the *Elevator*, in April 1865. Working in conjunction with the Colored State Convention of 1865, Bell and the delegates sent a petition to the California State Legislature requesting voting rights. When the California state senate tabled it, Bell responded, "We will continue to repeal slander and denounce injustice and oppression … and fearlessly contend for our inalienable rights." In other *Elevator* editorials, Bell explained community goals succinctly:

To "set us right before the law."
To "give us the common right of citizens—in *political franchise*, in the school system."
To "give us in common with the other races, civil liberties" and "equal advantages with

slaves in Canada, instead of Liberia. Throughout his journalistic career, Bell regularly attended similar conventions as a delegate from New York or, later, from San Francisco. As an activist and writer in 1837, Bell joined with CHARLES RAY to establish New York's *Weekly Advocate*, soon renamed the *Colored American*. Bell used the paper to underscore his basic themes: opposition to colonization, an end to slavery, and equal rights. After the paper's demise, he articulated the same themes in the Philadelphia *Elevator* and the New York *Anglo-African*. Not content with just writing his message, Bell also directed the New York Intelligence Office, where he helped escaped slaves to find work or to flee to Canada.

During the 1840s and 1850s, Bell had established himself as an important newspaperman and an advocate for East Coast blacks. Meanwhile, on the West Coast, California was undergoing transformation from a Mexican province to a state. Its new status encouraged free blacks and former slaves to them in the development of common resources of the country."

To end the United States as exclusively a "white man's country."

To provide "equal laws for our safeguard and protection."

Bell spent considerable time from 1865 to 1867 working to gain the right to vote for African Americans, but then a new challenge emerged. For many years, black children in San Francisco had attended a separate elementary school, staffed by black teachers, in a building located on Broadway Street. In 1868 the San Francisco school board decided to close the school's Broadway building, replace its black teachers, and move the students to an inferior facility at the old Greenwich Street School. Bell responded that black teachers "feel an interest in the education of their race," and parents showed their resolve by boycotting the school. Of 209 school-age children, only twenty attended the Greenwich School. This equal-education fight dragged on for several years, until Bell convinced superintendent of schools James Denman to open a new school on Taylor and Vallejo streets. This much-improved facility, however, still did not satisfy Bell or the black parents. They pushed to have children attend the regular grammar and high schools in an integrated environment. Finally in 1875 the school board acquiesced, and both white and black students began attending the same schools.

The decade of the 1870s brought further changes and challenges. Once the federal government passed the Fifteenth Amendment, blacks in California could vote, but Bell realized that they also needed to become politically involved. Although he supported the Republican Party of Lincoln, Bell urged his readers to vote not for a party's candidate, but for the most qualified individual. In the late 1870s he warned African Americans to be wary of Denis Kearney's Workingmen's Party and its anti-Chinese platform, not because he was sympathetic to the Chinese, but because he feared repercussions for African Americans. In 1878 Bell supported the National Labor Party, and at its state convention in San Francisco, he held the position of sergeant-at-arms. Bell realized that the problems of workers—white, black, and Asian—overshadowed group identity; he simply wanted all workers to benefit from the land, and from economic, social, and political reforms through effective political leadership.

Philip Bell had other talents besides political activism. With his stuttering under control, he appeared as an actor in the Colored Amateur Company productions of *Ion* and *Pizarro*. As a literary critic, he wrote reviews of both white and black community productions of Shakespeare's *Richard III, As You Like It*, and *The Merchant of Venice*. In a review of the latter, Bell commented, "I have always sympathized with Shylock, have considered him 'more sinned against than sinning.'"

The late 1870s and early 1880s saw a still vigorous Bell continuing his efforts toward achieving equal rights and "elevating the character of our race." In the mid-1880s, however, his health began to decline, forcing him to retire. During his newspaper career Bell had made very little money, and since he never married or had children, he had to depend for his support on the charity of local women. Bell never fully regained his health, and he died in San Francisco in 1889. Judge Mifflin W. Gibbs described Bell as "proud in his humanity and intellectually great as a journalist," but perhaps the best summation of Bell's life comes in his own words, "Action is necessary. Prompt and immediate. Agitate! Agitate! Agitate!"

FURTHER READING

The best sources of information on the life and activities of Bell are the files of the New York *Colored American* and *Anglo-African* and the San Francisco *Pacific Appeal* and the *Elevator* newspapers.

Montesano, Philip M. *Some Aspects of the Free Negro Question in San Francisco, 1849–1870* (1973).

Penn, I. Garland. *The Afro-American Press and Its Editors* (1891).

Obituaries: *San Francisco Bulletin*, 26 and 27 Apr. 1889.

PHILIP M. MONTESANO

Bell, Robert Mack (6 July 1943–), jurist and civil rights activist, was born in Rocky Mount, North Carolina, the son of Thomas Bell, a construction worker, and Rosa Lee (Jordan) Bell, a health-care practitioner and the daughter of sharecroppers. In the mid-1940s Robert M. Bell, his parents, and two older brothers moved to Baltimore, Maryland, where he entered public schools.

As a sixteen-year-old student at Baltimore's Dunbar High School, Bell was recruited by the Civic Interest Group, a student integrationist organization, along with classmates and students from the historically black Morgan State College, to enter whites-only restaurants and request service. Years later Bell recalled that at the time he did not tell his mother what he was doing because he considered it a "high risk" undertaking (Cox).

On 17 June 1960, some five months after the historic sit-in demonstrations at a segregated Woolworth's lunch counter in Greensboro, North Carolina, Bell and eleven other students walked into Hooper's Restaurant in downtown Baltimore, requested service, were turned down, but refused to leave. The students were subsequently arrested, convicted of violating the trespass law, and fined ten dollars each. The judgment was appealed by a legal team that included the National Association for the Advancement of Colored People (NAACP) legal counsel Juanita Jackson Mitchell and the future United States Supreme Court justice THURGOOD MARSHALL.

At the end of that summer Bell returned to Dunbar High School, where he was president of the class of 1961 and finished first among its 196 graduates. He has said that one of the people he has most admired throughout his life was the vice president of that high school class, REGINALD FRANCIS LEWIS, who years later became the chairman and chief executive officer of TLC Beatrice International, the largest black-owned business in the United States. Following high school graduation Bell entered Morgan State College, but after his first semester was diagnosed with tuberculosis. He withdrew from college and was hospitalized for nearly a year.

In 1962 the Maryland Court of Appeals upheld the lower court conviction of Bell and his fellow sit-in demonstrators. The case, which was to become known as *Bell v. Maryland*, was appealed to the United States Supreme Court. By the time it was argued there, on 14 and 15 October 1963, both the Baltimore city council and the Maryland general assembly had enacted laws prohibiting the denial of public accommodations based on race.

On 22 June 1964, however, the U.S. Supreme Court, by a 5–4 decision, declined to rule that city and state public accommodations laws nullified the trespass laws of those respective jurisdictions and remanded the case to the Maryland courts. One of the dissenters, Justice William O. Douglas, pronounced the refusal to grant public accommodations to African Americans "a relic of slavery." Justice Douglas wrote, "When the state police, the state prosecutor, and the state courts unite to convict Negroes for renouncing that relic of slavery, the 'state' violates the Fourteenth Amendment" (*Baltimore Sun*, 27 Oct. 1996).

On 22 October 1964 the Maryland Court of Appeals surprisingly upheld the convictions of the Hooper's Restaurant demonstrators on grounds that the Maryland and Baltimore public accommodations laws were not intended to repeal the state and city trespass laws. The decision was rendered three months after President Lyndon B. Johnson signed the Federal Civil Rights Act of 1964, which included a prohibition against the denial of a public service to a customer on the basis of race.

On 23 November 1964 Bell's legal team filed a petition with the Maryland Court of Appeals seeking reconsideration of its decision, contending that there was "a substantial likelihood that the (U.S.) Supreme Court may hold that the Civil Rights Act of 1964 abates such prosecutions (as the verdict in *Bell v. Maryland*)" (Reynolds). Indeed, on 14 December 1964 the Supreme Court, in deciding *Hamm v. City of Rock Hill*, held that the federal civil rights law did abate all pending prosecutions of those who had been arrested for activity that the law protected. The Maryland Court of Appeals accepted the Bell petition but did not set a hearing date. Without rendering a written opinion, the state's highest court, on 9 April 1965, almost five years after the arrest of the Hooper's demonstrators, overturned the convictions of Bell and his fellow students.

In 1966 Robert M. Bell graduated from Morgan State College, second in his class of 450, with a degree in History and Political Science. He was subsequently recruited by Harvard Law School, where he was an instant celebrity of sorts. One former Harvard Law School student recalled that Bell frequently would be pointed out in hallways as "Bob Bell of *Bell v. Maryland*" (*Baltimore Sun*, 24 Oct. 1996). Law students who have their names attached to cases argued before the Supreme Court are few and far between.

Following graduation from Harvard Law School in 1969, Bell became the first African American hired by Piper and Marbury, one of Maryland's leading law firms. In 1975 the Maryland governor Marvin Mandel appointed Bell to a judgeship on the District Court of Maryland, Baltimore City, where, at the age of thirty-one, he was the youngest ever to serve. In 1980 Governor Harry Hughes named Bell to the Circuit Court of Maryland for Baltimore. In 1984 he was appointed to the Maryland Court of Special Appeals, where he served until 1991, at which time he was named to fill a vacancy on the Maryland Court of Appeals, the court that twice upheld trespassing convictions against him before finally overturning the verdict and technically ending de facto segregation in the State of Maryland.

On 23 October 1996 Governor Parris N. Glendening appointed Bell to be the first African American chief judge of the Maryland Court of Appeals, replacing the retiring chief judge Robert C. Murphy, who, three and a half decades earlier, as a deputy state attorney general, represented Maryland in the Supreme Court case known as *Bell v. Maryland*.

FURTHER READING

Cox, Daniel. "Going the Second Mile," *Equal Justice* 3.3 (Fall, 2004).

Hylton, Wil S. "Burden of Proof," *Baltimore Magazine* (Mar. 1997).

Reynolds, William L. "The Legal History of the Great Sit-in Case of *Bell v. Maryland*," *Maryland Law Review* 61.4 (2002).

Smith, C. Fraser. "Bell's Sweet Victory: New Top Judge Overcomes Segregation," *Baltimore Sun*, 24 and 27 Oct. 1996.

HAROLD N. BURDETT

Bell, Travers, Jr. (31 Jan. 1941–25 Jan. 1988), investment banker and entrepreneur, was born in Chicago, Illinois, the third of four children of Travers Bell Sr., a clerk at a brokerage firm, and Iona St. Ange, a teaching aide. Growing up on the tough streets of Chicago's South Side could often be rough, and Bell would later credit his experiences for giving him the wherewithal to survive and succeed on Wall Street later in his life.

After graduating from high school, Bell planned to go to a teachers' college. At the time his father was working in the backroom of Dempsey-Tegeler, a Midwestern brokerage firm. One summer Bell needed money, so his father got him a job as a messenger at the firm. On Bell's first day on the job, a manager asked him to deliver a briefcase to a company across the street. While walking to the destination, Bell peeked into the briefcase and saw what appeared to be worn and crumpled papers. Upon arrival, he handed it over and in return received a check to the company for $175,000. Bell realized that this was a business where people actually paid for paper if it was stock certificates that represented ownership in companies. This fascinated him and soon he decided that he would make his career on Wall Street.

Bell threw himself into his work. He worked fifteen to seventeen hours a day, trying to learn about the securities industry by studying various materials and closely watching senior officials at the firm. Unlike most other blacks who had preceded him as messengers, he did not stay in the mailroom for long, thanks to Jerome Tegeler, the cofounder and driving force of the firm. One day Tegeler approached the young man and sat him down for a chat. "Travers, I wanted to help your father, but I couldn't because nobody was ready for that yet [having a black man move up because of his race]. However, I don't care anymore. You obviously learn real fast and want to learn even more, so I am going to do something many people are not going to like: I am going to teach you this business." With his mentor guiding him, Bell quickly rose through the ranks. In 1963 Dempsey-Tegeler bought the firm Strauss, Blosser, and McDowell, which had about fifteen offices around the United States. At age twenty-three, Bell was named the operations manager of the whole firm, and he moved to St. Louis, Missouri, the location of Dempsey's headquarters, and began studying economics and business at Washington University in his free time.

After graduating in 1967, Bell became vice president in charge of operations at a small firm called Fusz Schmelzle. As he acquired more experience in all aspects of the securities business, Bell began planning to open up his own firm; however, when he tried to raise capital he was denied at every turn because many were unwilling to invest in a black-owned firm. Then he heard that another African American stockbroker named Willie Daniels was trying to get a firm started on the East Coast. Bell joined Daniels in New York City in 1970, but their ambitions were tempered because of a lack of financing, difficulties in getting over regulatory hurdles, and a slow period in the securities market.

After nearly two years, they had their big breakthrough. On 24 June 1971, Daniels & Bell, Inc., became the first black-owned member firm in the 179-year history of the New York Stock Exchange. Despite this milestone, significant obstacles immediately confronted the firm. The American economy was disintegrating, and Wall Street's business was deteriorating. In just a few years, hundreds of brokerage firms had closed their doors. It was a tough time for all companies, but it was especially hard for a young, black-owned firm. Although there was very little prejudice on the floor of NYSE because it is a buy and sell institution and thus more numbers oriented than relationship oriented, Daniels & Bell had trouble getting into the lucrative business of corporate finance, in which corporations use Wall Street firms to raise money by issuing bonds or stocks. Because their histories and relationships were not rooted in the powerful networks on Wall Street, Daniels & Bell was shut out of the "old boys network" where these deals were made. They thus had little access to the corporate clubs where business titans socialized and formed relationships. Bell's solution was to enter the municipal finance business and raise money for cities and states as an increasing number of black elected officials across the country could give them a fair opportunity to pitch their ideas and proposals. In 1972 Daniels & Bell led a $1.2 million bond issue for Mound Bayou, Mississippi, the oldest black municipality in the United States. Around this time, Daniels left the firm for reasons that are unclear.

Moving forward, Bell began to travel all across the country to talk with elected officials and pitch his belief that minority-owned firms should be given a chance to participate in the business of municipalities. He established close relationships with many elected officials, such as Chicago Mayor HAROLD WASHINGTON and Los Angeles Mayor TOM BRADLEY, and slowly garnered more business. One of Bell's biggest deals came in 1984, when the state of Connecticut chose Daniels & Bell to comanage a $5.5 billion transportation infrastructure renewal financing program. After that the firm received a number of lucrative deals. In 1986 the firm participated in $9 billion worth of financings, ranking as one of the top twenty municipal houses on Wall Street. The firm had also attracted a number of noteworthy corporate clients such as Exxon, General Electric, and Chase Manhattan Bank. As a result, Bell is credited with opening up areas of finance for other minorities on Wall Street.

In addition to his work on Wall Street, Bell had bought a candy maker named Cocoline Chocolate Company in 1974. It ranked as one of *Black Enterprise* magazine's Top 100 businesses for more than a decade. He also was the principal stockholder in Freedom National Bank, financial adviser to the African Development Bank, and chair of the New York District of the Securities Industry Association.

In 1988 Bell, who had a history of heart problems, died of a massive heart attack in his New York City apartment. He was forty-six years old. Because Daniels & Bell was so dependent on his relationships and ability, its business began to decline almost immediately. Though it eventually closed its doors in 1994, Bell's legacy lives on. Both the

Securities Industry Association and the National Association of Securities Professionals created the Travers Bell Award to honor his lasting contributions to the world of finance.

FURTHER READING

Bell, Gregory S. *In the Black: A History of African Americans on Wall Street* (2001).

Dingle, Derek. "Travers Bell: Breaking Barriers on Wall Street," *Black Enterprise* (Apr. 2005).

Pershing, Amy C. "Travers Bell," *Institutional Investor* (June 1987).

Wayne, Leslie. "An Empire in Black Business," *New York Times*, 18 Apr. 1982.

GREGORY S. BELL

Bellamy, Sherry (12 Oct. 1952–), attorney, was born Sherry Franchesca Bellamy in Harlem, New York, the youngest of seven children of Athelston Alhama Bellamy and Mary Elizabeth Reeves. Sherry's father, born and raised in Harlem, was a career military officer who served with the Tuskegee Airmen and eventually rose to the rank of captain in the U.S. Air Force. After retiring from the military he became a court officer and court clerk in the Civil Court of the City of New York. Sherry's mother was born and raised on a race-horse breeding farm outside Charlottesville, Virginia. Sherry grew up in Harlem and graduated from Cardinal Spellman High School, a Roman Catholic high school whose graduates include many successful minority judges, attorneys, and other professionals.

In 1974 Bellamy graduated from Swarthmore College in Swarthmore, Pennsylvania, with a B.A. in Political Science. She later received her juris doctor in 1977 from Yale Law School. During that same year she married George Alexander Bumbray Jr., an architect who attended Howard University and completed his bachelor of arts degree at Yale School of Architecture. The two met in New Haven shortly after George completed two master's degrees in Architecture and Environmental Design at Yale. They had three children together.

During her time at Swarthmore and Yale, Bellamy worked with Dr. KENNETH CLARK, the psychologist who provided evidence in support of *Brown v. Board of Education*, the landmark 1954 U.S. Supreme Court decision. Bellamy also studied under Charles Black, who during his tenure as a professor at Columbia Law School had authored the briefs in *Brown v. Board of Education*. She was also fortunate to intern with Haywood Burns, founder of the National Conference of Black

Lawyers and the first African American dean of a law school in New York State, as well as MARIAN WRIGHT EDELMAN, founder of the Children's Defense Fund.

Bellamy began her own legal career in 1977 as a family and children's rights attorney with the New Haven Legal Assistance Association (NHLAA) in Connecticut, which provided legal services to the poor. At NHLAA Bellamy was instrumental in the creation of a unit for the civil representation of children, which represented children in cases involving neglect, abuse, rights to education for the handicapped, and other matters before state and federal courts in Connecticut.

After four years in nonprofit service Bellamy became an associate at law firms in New York and Washington, D.C. From 1985 to 1991, while at Jones, Day, Reavis & Pogue, an internationally recognized law firm that specialized in business, government regulation, litigation, and tax, she specialized in telecommunications law at a time when the entire telecommunications industry was undergoing dramatic changes. Her success continued as a corporate attorney for Bell Atlantic beginning in 1991, which coincided with the first major overhaul of telecommunications law in almost sixty-two years. In 1992 she became vice president and general counsel of Bell Atlantic-Washington, D.C., and in 1997 she became president and chief executive officer of Bell Atlantic-Maryland—the first African American woman to advance to senior management within the Bell Atlantic corporation.

Three years later, Bellamy became vice president and associate general counsel for the newly formed Verizon Communications (a merger of the telephone giants Bell Atlantic and GTE), overseeing state regulatory matters for the East Coast. In 2006 she was promoted to vice president and deputy general counsel of Verizon Business, a division of Verizon formed after the acquisition of MCI Communications. Verizon was at that time a leader in delivering broadband, voice, wireless, and video communications to mass market, business, government, and wholesale customers in the United States and in seventy-five countries across six continents. At Verizon Business, Bellamy oversaw the company's litigation and regulatory matters throughout the United States.

Bellamy maintained a connection with the African American community and recognized that she was given opportunities that her parents and other previous generations of blacks had never enjoyed. In 2003, commenting on affirmative action, she wrote, "I feel neither stigma nor concern about benefiting from the only privilege that American society has ever bestowed upon the descendants of African slaves. I recognize that without the affirmative action practiced at Swarthmore College in 1969, I would never have been in a position to achieve what I have been fortunate enough to achieve." Bellamy rejected the assumption that affirmative action explained her success and instead stated that she focused on the tasks at hand to deliver results. As a person committed to justice, Bellamy served on numerous boards and professional and business organizations, including John Hopkins Medicine, the Swarthmore College Board of Managers, and the Kennedy Krieger Institute, devoted to the treatment, education, and study of children with brain injuries. She was the recipient of various awards, and was named a Distinguished Woman in Business and one of Maryland's Top 100 Women. In 2005 she received an honorary degree of humane letters from Rosemont College in Pennsylvania.

FURTHER READING
Bentley, Kenneth W. *Woman of Courage II* (1998).
Neely, Esme. "Bellamy Takes on Greatest Challenge," *Baltimore Business Journal* (29 Sept. 1997).

GREER C. BOSWORTH

Bellinger, Charles (15 Apr. 1875–14 June 1937), entrepreneur and political organizer, was born to Louisa and Theodore Bellinger, a blacksmith in Lockhart, a small town in Caldwell County in south central Texas. As a teenager he began to work in Lockhart, Texas, for Jeff Howard, who owned a saloon. There he became a dealer for card games that involved betting.

Using his own savings along with loans he acquired from Howard and the Pearl Brewery, Bellinger moved to San Antonio, where by 1906 he had opened his own saloon. His success as a gambler grew into a regional and national reputation, with trips to Chicago and New York to gamble. As an entrepreneur he diversified his investments by adding a real estate office, a construction company, a café, a pool room, a barbershop, a theater, a baseball team, a lottery, and a taxi service. When Prohibition came in the 1920s rumors suggested he had a hand in bootlegging, although Bellinger always denied it. Perhaps most important in terms of his growing political aspirations Bellinger began to make loans available to the black community. When he extended this possibility to several churches he increased his influence with both preachers and their congregations. As Bellinger's economic status improved, his family also grew. Of the twelve children born to Bellinger and his wife, Celeste Pelliman, only three daughters and two sons reached adulthood. Following a divorce from his first wife, he married Addie Scott.

As early as 1910 Bellinger became involved in San Antonio and Bexar County politics. He helped organize African American voters to support a series of local officials, who in turn responded to the concerns of the black community and its leaders. In Texas the dominant Democrats, through the legislature, had created a state poll tax, effectively disenfranchising many working class voters, including most blacks and Hispanics. The Democratic Party also used a white primary to exclude African Americans from its candidate selection process. Local elections often followed a nonpartisan format, however, that allowed anyone who paid a poll tax to participate. To increase black political participation as well as his own influence, Bellinger paid poll taxes for African Americans and placed the receipts in a safe until election day. He also made clear to voters which candidates would respond favorably to the voters' interests. For the black community he had become the "political boss," who according to some estimates influenced up to five thousand voters by the 1930s.

The first candidate Bellinger supported was John W. Tobin, who served as county sheriff and later as mayor of San Antonio through most of the period from 1900 to 1927. When local government leaders allowed black voters into the Democratic Party primary in 1922 it stirred opposition and led the state legislature to require a white primary. In response African Americans initiated a series of court cases that resulted in the Supreme Court's 1944 determination in *Smith v. Allwright* at last outlawing the white primary. By 1918 Bellinger had increased his role in local politics and become the most influential figure in the black community, even before the death of John Grumbles, the local president of the NAACP, in 1926. Bellinger also threw his weight into mayoral politics, supporting C. M. Chambers from 1929 to 1933, and C. K. Quinn in the 1930s, which resulted in improvements to African American neighborhoods, including street paving and lighting, city sewer lines, an improved public library branch and auditorium, as well as better parks and schools. During the Depression of the 1930s Bellinger also sought public assistance for black citizens who had lost jobs.

Some white reformers, usually those with paternalistic views, became frustrated with what they saw as corruption, machine politics, boss rule, and a lack of influence for themselves. This view was shared by some middle-class blacks, who also suspected that Bellinger chose not to challenge segregation because it allowed him to more easily organize African American voters. When the editors of the black newspaper the *Inquirer* refused to print a Bellinger political ad in 1931, he launched a new paper, the *Register*, with his son Valmo as editor. The *Register* soon pushed its older competitor out of business. The white reformer Maury Maverick, a Democratic congressman who opposed lynching and favored equal pay for African Americans, nevertheless claimed corruption in local government and focused on Bellinger's role in it. Charges followed in 1936 that Bellinger had not paid enough income tax. His conviction brought a fine and an eighteen-month federal prison term. After Bellinger suffered a heart attack, however, Valmo and local Democratic leaders successfully lobbied President Franklin Roosevelt to pardon him. The physical and psychological strain had been too much, and after a second heart attack he died in San Antonio. Valmo Bellinger continued the *Register* and some business activities, but achieved only partial success in assuming his father's political role, which had made Charles Bellinger the most important African American leader in San Antonio during the first half of the twentieth century.

FURTHER READING

Barr, Alwyn. *Black Texans: A History of African Americans in Texas, 1528–1995* (1996).

Mason, Kenneth. *African Americans and Race Relations in San Antonio, Texas, 1867–1937* (1998).

Taylor, Quintard. *In Search of the Racial Frontier: African Americans in the American West, 1528–1990* (1998).

Obituary: *Houston Informer*, 16 June 1937.

ALWYN BARR

Belton, Ethel Lee (18 Apr. 1897–1984), teacher, civil rights activist, plaintiff in *Belton v. Gebhart* (1952), a companion case to *Brown v. Board of Education* (1954), was born in Hazelhurse, Georgia, the daughter of Glover and Ida Hall.

Around 1948, almost a decade after her husband Louis passed away, Ethel Belton moved with her

School integration. (from left to right) Linda Brown Smith, Harry Briggs, Jr., Ethel Louise Belton Brown, and Spottswood Bolling Jr. during press conference at Hotel Americana ten years after *Brown v. Board of Education*, 9 June 1964. (Library of Congress, New York World-Telegram, and the *Sun Newspaper* Photograph Collection, Al Ravenna, photographer.)

seven children to Claymont, Delaware, a suburban community northwest of Wilmington, Delaware, to join her extended family. There she taught general education in a one-room school. Her daughter, Ethel Louise Belton, was eleven years old at the time of the move and was later assigned to Howard High School—the only free public school for blacks in the entire state at the time. Located in Wilmington, it was a fifty-minute, nine-mile commute for Ethel Louise, who had a congenital heart condition. Although Claymont High School, the school for white children in the community, was but a short walk away, the state constitution mandated that black and white students attend racially segregated schools. Nonetheless, Belton pressed school officials to admit her daughter.

Belton's initial motivation for seeking her daughter's admission to Claymont was born not out of any deep-seated desire to overthrow Jim Crow segregation. She was interested, as she mentioned in a letter to the state board of education and as she later testified before the Delaware Court of Chancery, in enrolling her daughter in Claymont High School because of its proximity and the fact that she was a resident of the district. In her testimony before Judge Collins J. Seitz, she later asserted:

Well, first of all I live in the community of Claymont. I work in Claymont. I shop there, and I help to support the community in general, and I see no reasons of why my child should leave Claymont and travel all the way to Wilmington to attend high school when there is a public high school right in Claymont (Testimony of Witnesses, NAACP Papers, Group II, Box 139: 36–37).

Having exhausted all administrative remedies, she approached LOUIS REDDING, the local attorney for the NAACP, and with his assistance she filed suit along with four other groups of black parents from neighboring communities in Wilmington, Claymont, Newark, and New Castle against the state board of education. Redding, along with his co-counsel, Jack Greenberg, successfully argued her case, along with one other (*Bulah v. Gebhart*, 1952) in the Delaware Court of Chancery. The state appealed the decision to the Delaware Supreme Court, lost, and applied for a *writ of certiorari* from the U.S. Supreme Court. The high court then agreed to hear the case along with four others from South Carolina, Virginia, Kansas, and the District of Columbia in what came to be known as *Brown v. Board of Education*. In that landmark 1954 case Chief Justice Earl Warren ruled that racially segregated education was in violation of the equal protection clause of the Fourteenth Amendment.

On 4 September 1952 the Claymont School Board admitted, over the objections of the state attorney general, eleven of the twelve child plaintiffs to Claymont High School. But Ethel Louise Belton never made the transfer. She was a junior at Howard by the time the Delaware Supreme Court demanded the admission of the black students to the white school, and she chose to complete her coursework at Howard. That Ethel Louise was a plaintiff in such an important case but failed to take advantage of the opportunity to attend desegregated schools spoke to some of the problems inherent in this particular kind of civil rights activism. First, litigation was often a painfully slow process and students sometimes aged out of the schools in which they sought admission. Ethel Louise also had a fondness for the faculty at Howard and quite naturally wished to graduate with her friends. This desire highlighted a long-standing tension within African American communities between loyalties to historically black educational institutions that had nurtured generations of black students and commitments to desegregation and the promises afforded in often better-resourced schools that had been reserved for white students.

FURTHER READING

Copies of Ethel Belton's correspondence with the state board of education are located in the papers of the State Board of Education/Department of Public Instruction at the Delaware State Archives. Copies of court transcript are located in National Association for the Advancement of Colored People Collection in the Library of Congress, Washington, D.C.

Irons, Peter. *Jim Crow's Children: The Broken Promise of the Brown Decision* (2002).

Kluger, Richard. *Simple Justice: The History of Brown v. Board of Education and Black America's Struggle for Equality* (1975).

Peters, William. "The Schools That Broke the Color Line," *Redbook: The Magazine for Young Adults* (Oct. 1954, NAACP Papers, Library of Congress).

BRETT GADSDEN

Beman, Amos Gerry (1812–1874), clergyman and abolitionist, was born in Colchester, Connecticut, the son of Jehiel C. Beman, a clergyman. Nothing is known of his mother. He grew up and received a basic education in Middletown, Connecticut, where his father was pastor of the African church. A Wesleyan University student, L. P. Dole, volunteered to tutor Beman after the university refused his application for admission because he was an African American. Dole and Beman suffered ridicule and harassment from other students, and an anonymous threat of bodily harm from "Twelve of Us" caused Beman to give up the effort after six months. He went to Hartford, where he taught school for four years, and around 1836 he briefly attended the Oneida Institute in New York.

Beman was ordained as a Congregational minister in 1839. At about this time he married a woman whose name is not known. In 1841 he became the first named African American pastor of Temple Street African Church in New Haven, Connecticut, where he remained for seventeen years. Here he gained respect and support throughout the city from both blacks and whites. The church became a center for social, educational, and benevolent activities for the African American community. The Temple Street Church became the Dixwell Avenue Church and in the early twenty-first century was the oldest existing African American Congregational church in the nation.

Beman was an avid supporter of temperance throughout his life. His father had organized the Home Temperance Society of Middletown African Americans in 1833, and the younger Beman served as its secretary. He was also a participant in the founding of the Connecticut Temperance Society and served two years as its president. He was a leader in 1842 in effecting a merger of the African American temperance associations in Connecticut, Massachusetts, New York, and New Jersey into the States' Delavan Union Temperance Society of Colored People and was the principal speaker at its convention in 1845. For about a year, in 1842, Beman edited *Zion's Wesleyan*, a newspaper that provided a voice for temperance, abolition, and other reforms.

Beman was an ardent abolitionist and a member of the American Anti-Slavery Society from its founding in 1833. In 1840, with the great schism among antislavery supporters resulting from differences on women's rights, politics, and the role of the churches in the antislavery movement, Beman withdrew from the American Anti-Slavery Society. He then became one of the eight African Americans—his father was another—at the founding convention of the American and Foreign Anti-Slavery Society, for which he served as assistant secretary. In great demand as an antislavery speaker, Beman traveled more than five thousand miles between January and August 1856, crisscrossing the Northeast and making trips into Canada and Illinois. In his churches he held regular concerts for the enslaved, which combined protest, agitation, and prayer. Beman also was a frequent contributor to FREDERICK DOUGLASS's newspapers, the *North Star* and *Frederick Douglass' Paper*.

Civil and political rights for free African Americans also received Beman's attention and energy. He carried on a long campaign to get suffrage rights in Connecticut, and he was a leader in the Negro Convention Movement. He served as president of the national conventions that met in Buffalo in 1843 and in Philadelphia in 1854 and as vice president of the meeting that met in Rochester in 1853. It was at the Buffalo meeting that HENRY HIGHLAND GARNET gave his famous address in which he called on the slaves to rise in revolt. Beman stepped down from the chair and spoke for more than an hour against Garnet's address. Beman carried a majority of the convention with him in not endorsing force and violence. However, after John Brown's raid and capture, Beman assisted in a prayer meeting for him at the Siloan Presbyterian Church in Brooklyn, New York.

In 1841 Beman was one of the founders and served as the first secretary of the Union Missionary Society, established by African Americans to support antislavery missionary work at home and abroad. When that society joined with other organizations in 1846 to organize the American Missionary Association (AMA), Beman became a supporter and active worker for the new evangelical abolitionist organization.

In the winter of 1856–1857 Beman's wife and two of their four children died from typhoid fever. After about a year he remarried, this time to a white woman whose name is not known. As a result he lost favor with his New Haven congregation and submitted his resignation in 1858 to accept a call to the Abyssinian Congregational Church in Portland, Maine. This church was small and poor, although it was the only church serving a community of four hundred African Americans. To supplement the small salary pledged by the church, the AMA commissioned Beman as a city missionary. When the church failed to raise the pledged salary, and he again encountered resentment against his wife, he petitioned the AMA for a full-time commission and received an appointment in 1859 as the association's fundraising agent for New England. That year at a meeting in Brooklyn he was elected president of the Evangelical Association of Colored Ministers of Congregational and Presbyterian Churches.

Beman was a hard worker for the AMA, covering a territory from Maine to Sag Harbor, Long Island, and visiting both white and black churches of any denomination that would admit him as an agent of an abolitionist society. He usually prefaced his appeals with lectures on such topics as "The Origin and History of the African Race" and "What the Colored People Can under God Do for Themselves." Nevertheless his collections were small. Either he resigned or his commission was allowed to expire, and in 1863 he became pastor of a struggling Congregational church in Jamaica, Long Island. There his second wife died. In 1865 he went to be pastor of Mount Zion Congregational Church in Cleveland, Ohio. He married again in 1871.

Beman died in Pittsfield, Massachusetts, where he was pastor of the Second Congregational Church, which he had helped in establishing a quarter-century before.

FURTHER READING

The Beman Collection at the Beinecke Rare Book and Manuscript Library at Yale University contains clippings, pamphlets, and scrapbooks that Amos Beman organized and annotated. There are seventy-two letters and reports written by Beman from 1841 to 1869 in the American Missionary Association Archives at the Amistad Research Center at Tulane University.

Swift, David E. *Black Prophets of Justice: Activist Clergy before the Civil War* (1989).

Warner, Robert A. "Amos Gerry Beman—1812–1874: A Memoir of a Forgotten Leader," *Journal of Negro History* 22 (Apr. 1937): 200–221.

This entry is taken from the *American National Biography* and is published here with the permission of the American Council of Learned Societies.

CLIFTON H. JOHNSON

Beman, Jehiel C. (1789?–21 Dec. 1858), shoemaker, clergyman, and abolitionist, was born in Chatham, Connecticut, to Sarah Gerry and Cesar Beman, a manumitted slave and Revolutionary War veteran who may have chosen his surname to indicate his freedom to "be a man." By 1809 Jehiel had moved to Colchester, Connecticut, and married Fanny Condol, with whom he fathered seven children, including the noted abolitionist AMOS G. BEMAN. Jehiel worked in Colchester as a shoemaker and Methodist exhorter until 1830, when he moved to Middletown, Connecticut, to pastor the city's Cross Street African Methodist Episcopal Zion (AMEZ) Church. On 11 August of that same year Jehiel's first wife died, and he married Nancy Scott on 17 October. In 1832 he left Cross Street after being appointed an itinerant missionary by the annual AMEZ conference, but he remained in Middletown as a preacher, shoemaker, and reformer until 1838, at which time he moved to Boston to pastor the new First AMEZ Church.

In the 1830s Beman's activities revolved around abolitionism, temperance, and his church. Like other AMEZ leaders Beman favored separate black churches. Upon traveling to Providence in 1837 he reported "finding many who worship in white churches desirous to worship by themselves" and helped organize an independent congregation. Beman denounced white Christians who urged black congregants to "sit in the corners," receive communion last, and "wait for the crumbs after the white brethren have partaken" (*Colored American*, 23 Sept. 1837).

Beman's denunciation of prejudice in white churches dovetailed with his antislavery principles. He joined rising calls for immediate emancipation in the 1830s, and when William Lloyd Garrison founded the *Liberator* in Boston in 1831, Beman, who served as the paper's subscription agent in Middletown, was one of the many black abolitionists whose support kept the paper afloat in its early years. Beman signed the founding declaration of the American Anti-Slavery Society (AASS) in 1833 and helped organize AASS auxiliaries in Connecticut.

Beman was also deeply involved in the temperance movement. He believed, with many other abolitionists, that black Northerners could counteract prejudice and undermine racist defenses of slavery by pursuing "moral reform." Beman approved more than once of the "wisdom to live down oppression" (*Colored American*, 27 Jan. 1838). At one annual meeting of the AASS he sponsored a resolution encouraging education, entrepreneurship, and moral improvement in free black communities. Beman pursued those goals in Connecticut by founding a Middletown temperance society in 1833 and a state temperance society for African Americans in 1836.

Beman continued his activism as an AMEZ minister in Boston. He was involved in local protests mounted by Boston's activist community, signing a petition on behalf of the fugitive slave George Latimer in 1842, as well as a petition against school segregation in 1844. Under his leadership the First AMEZ Church grew rapidly, moving into a new building in 1841 and attracting into its pews many of the city's black abolitionists. The church also served as a center for community events, such as First of August ceremonies celebrating British emancipation.

But in Boston, Beman also became embroiled in controversy. His church experienced some dissension when JULIA FOOTE, a female preacher, claimed that Beman had refused to let her speak in his church. Beman's opposition to Foote was partly caused by her doctrinal heterodoxy but might also have been partly caused by conservative views about women. Many of Beman's African American contemporaries identified social uplift with masculine virtues, a broad cultural tendency implicitly suggested by Beman's own surname. To live down oppression also meant, as Beman put it, "to live the man" (*New York Emancipator*, 16 Nov. 1837).

A larger but not unrelated controversy arose in 1839 when Beman parted ways with Garrison and the AASS. Since 1837 tensions had increased between Boston's evangelical abolitionists and the Garrisonians, who defended female lecturers, opposed political abolitionism, and often espoused heretical religious beliefs. In 1839 Garrison's detractors founded the Massachusetts Abolition Society to oppose the local AASS auxiliary and offered Beman a job as agent for an African American employment service. Beman accepted, a move consistent with his belief in the need for separate black businesses and education. Garrisonians vilified Beman for desertion, but he responded that he had not found work with them—implying, as increasing numbers of black abolitionists did in the 1840s, that jobs in Garrisonian organizations were still closed to African Americans because of latent prejudices among their officers.

Yet the controversy was about more than a job. Beman probably agreed with those who thought that the Garrisonians' radical views on gender and religion were hampering the antislavery cause. In 1840 when a group led by Lewis Tappan seceded from the AASS to form the American and Foreign Anti-Slavery Society, Beman joined them. Thus when his name appeared with other Tappanites on an 1844 petition defending capital punishment—which leading Garrisonians opposed—the *Liberator* called Beman, one of its earliest supporters, "the colored cat's-paw of the clerical seceders from the anti-slavery platform" (*Liberator*, 23 Feb. 1844).

Beman left Boston not long afterward, returning to Middletown in 1844 or 1845. There he resumed his leadership role in the local community, presiding over temperance meetings and state conventions of black activists. In 1844 he traveled to Baltimore and Washington, D.C., to attend an AMEZ conference, and after touring the capital he wrote of "sighing to think that my father faced the cannon's mouth for this country's liberty" (*Boston Morning Chronicle*, 15 Aug. 1844). In the 1850s Beman supported antislavery politicians and suffrage for the state's black citizens. He lectured on behalf of the Free Soil Party in 1852 and attended the national conventions of black abolitionists held in 1853 and 1855. Evidence suggests that Beman also assisted fugitive slaves in Connecticut.

In 1856 Beman's second wife, Nancy, died, and his own death followed two years later in New Haven. But Beman's legacy—as a reformer committed to uplift, as a clergyman committed to independence, and as a committed abolitionist—lived on, primarily in the careers of his sons, Leverett Beman and Amos G. Beman.

FURTHER READING
Some of Beman's writings can be found in the
microfilmed edition of the *Black Abolitionist Papers*

(1981), edited by George E. Carter and C. Peter Ripley.

Horton, James O., and Lois E. Horton. *Black Bostonians: Family Life and Community Struggle in the Antebellum North* (1979).

Housley, Kathleen. "'Yours for the Oppressed': The Life of Jehiel C. Beman," *Journal of Negro History* 77.1 (Winter 1992).

Jacobs, Donald M., ed. *Courage and Conscience: Black and White Abolitionists in Boston* (1993).

James, Jennifer Lee. "Jehiel C. Beman: A Leader of the Northern Free Black Community," *Journal of Negro History* 82.1 (Winter 1997).

W. CALEB MCDANIEL

Ben Jochannan, Yosef Alfredo Antonio (31 Dec. 1918–), historian, Egyptologist, educator, and Pan-Africanist, known popularly as "Dr. Ben," was born in Gondar, Ethiopia, the son of Krstan ben Jochannan, a lawyer and diplomat, and Tulia Matta, a native of Puerto Rico, who was a homemaker and midwife. Both parents were Jewish: his father was a member of a Jewish Ethiopian people then called the "Falasha," or Beta Israel, and his mother was descended from Spanish Sephardic Jews. The couple met in Madrid, Spain, where Matta was attending college and the elder ben Jochannan was a diplomatic attaché. Soon after their marriage, they traveled from Spain to Ethiopia where their son, Yosef, was born.

Ben Jochannan spent his earliest years in Ethiopia, but after age five he was raised in the Americas. He said in later interviews that, in the 1920s, the Ethiopian government sent his father to Brazil to help develop the coffee trade of that country. They lived for about a year in Rio de Janeiro before a 1928 coup in Ethiopia saw the overthrow of Empress Zauditu and the consolidation of power under Emperor Haile Selassie. After the change in political leadership, the family decided not to return to Ethiopia but instead settled permanently in Puerto Rico. Yosef was raised primarily in the town of Fajardo, located on the eastern side of Puerto Rico, and the nearby islands of St. Croix and St. Thomas, where Matta had additional relatives. He was thus fluent in both Spanish and English from an early age.

After secondary school on the island, ben Jochannan attended the University of Puerto Rico at Rio Piedras. He first studied law, but later switched to civil engineering, graduating with a bachelor of science degree in 1939. In his senior year of college ben Jochannan wrote and self-published

a booklet titled *Nosotros los Hebreos Negros* (We the Black Hebrews) about his experience growing up black and Jewish on a predominately Catholic island where at the time people of African ancestry were commonly viewed as inferior (Gates and Appiah, *Africana*, 457). His father, a well-educated man fluent in several languages, spoke often with his son about the significance of Ethiopia's ancient past. However, at school and in the community, the young ben Jochannan frequently heard the view that Africa was a backward and wretched continent. Because of this, shortly after he graduated from the university, his father sent him to visit his grandparents in Ethiopia, where he stayed for several months. To get there, ben Jochannan traveled by ship to Egypt, then took a train through that country to Ethiopia, and thus, he said, began a life-long fascination with Africa's 4,000-mile-long Nile Valley.

Upon his return to Puerto Rico, ben Jochannan worked briefly as a lawyer. But his prosecution of a criminal case against a friend of his father's soon brought him into conflict with his father who, after the man was convicted, asked him to leave the island. In 1941, he traveled to New York City where he initially stayed with his maternal uncle, CASPER HOLSTEIN, a self-made millionaire and philanthropist who had become rich from the Harlem "numbers racket." Holstein was one of the largest contributors to MARCUS GARVEY's Universal Negro Improvement Association, and was also politically active in his native Virgin Islands. Through his uncle, ben Jochannan gained a unique insight into the rich cultural milieu of black New York, including its lively street life, informal "numbers" lotteries, street-corner preachers, and politics. At the time, Harlem was an epicenter of African American activism in support of Ethiopia, which had been invaded and occupied by Italy under Benito Mussolini during World War II. Although the occupation ended the year he arrived in New York, ben Jochannan joined such affinity groups as the Ethiopian World Federation and African Nationals in America.

Ben Jochannan initially found work as a draftsman, but he was drawn to the study of Africa, especially its ancient history. Though his students and supporters later referred to him as "Dr. Ben," the precise trajectory of his formal education remains unclear, partly because of conflicting claims he made over the years in interviews and in published works. He claimed to have obtained a doctorate in Cultural Anthropology at the University of Havana

(1940) and to have done doctoral research at the University of Barcelona in Spain (1941). Whatever his educational training may have been, ben Jochannan began to speak on Harlem street corners, mostly about African history, taking part in a tradition of public speechmaking that was one of the neighborhood's unique attributes, joining such noteworthy contemporaries as Arthur Reid, Carlos Cooks, and Wentworth Matthew. He came to know several of Harlem's leading intellectuals and historians such as JOHN HENRIK CLARKE, J. A. ROGERS, John G. Jackson, and RICHARD B. MOORE, all of whom were members of the Harlem History Club. In 1947, he returned to Ethiopia, again spending a portion of the voyage in Egypt.

During the late 1940s, ben Jochannan met and befriended a young man known as "Detroit Red," who used to hustle on the corner below his Harlem office. Their friendship deepened after "Red" was arrested, joined the Nation of Islam in prison, and returned to Harlem as MALCOLM X, and it continued until Malcolm's assassination in 1965.

Through this early period of his life in the United States, ben Jochannan maintained the Jewish faith of his upbringing, attending Harlem's Commandment Keeper's Ethiopian Hebrew Congregation led by rabbi WENTWORTH A. MATTHEW, as well as other synagogues. But in New York, he continued to struggle, as he had in Puerto Rico, with the prevailing societal presumption that tended to question his identity as an African Jew; while, at the same time, his study of ancient Egyptian history and spiritual practices was having an ever increasing impact on his thinking. As he later wrote in several of his books, his differences with other Jews and his intense identification with the African American struggle eventually caused his "complete break with Western man's Talmudic Judaism" (*Africa: Mother of Western Civilization* [1971], 585).

In the 1950s, ben Jochannan worked as a researcher for UNESCO and with the Zanzibar mission to the United Nations, work that he continued to do until that country merged with Tanganyika to become Tanzania in 1961. During this period, ben Jochannan also began teaching as an adjunct professor in New York, mostly as a lecturer on African history at such schools as Marymount College at Tarrytown and at Columbia Teacher's College.

In 1957, ben Jochannan led a group of nine African American educators to Egypt because he wanted to show them evidence of his contention that sites such as Abu Simbel, the temple of Isis at Philae Island, and the royal tombs of the Valley of the Kings were the remains of ancient black civilizations. This trip was the first of dozens of similar tours that he led, sometimes twice a year, of scholars and ordinary citizens alike. These trips not only facilitated his own study and writing, but they came to be a major part of his legacy as a teacher. He estimated that he led several thousand African Americans to Egypt, Sudan, and Ethiopia over the next four decades.

In 1960, ben Jochannan self-published his first work produced in the United States, an early version of Black *Man of the Nile*, which he sold for $5 a copy at LEWIS MICHAUX's National Memorial African Bookstore on Lenox Avenue.

In 1961, he married Gertrude England, of St. Croix. The couple would go on to have nine daughters and three sons. They also adopted six other children. Throughout his career as a writer and teacher, ben Jochannan remained a fixture of the Harlem community where he raised his family. When Harlem was engulfed by several days of social unrest during the summer of 1964, after the police slaying of a local teenager, ben Jochannan was one of several Harlem activists who met with the New York mayors Robert Wagner and, later, John Lindsay to address systemic problems facing the black community in New York (*New York Times*, 19 Feb. 1966).

As a historian and anthropologist, ben Jochannan would return to the Nile Valley more than fifty times and self-publish forty-two books—mostly on African pre-history, the civilizations of Egypt, Sudan, and Ethiopia, and on religion. His work argued that the creators of ancient Egyptian civilization—the builders of the pyramids, the Sphinx, and cities and lodges—were black Africans who first migrated north from the Central Rift Valley of present-day Tanzania and Uganda. He claimed that mainstream publishers refused to publish his work, saying that there was not sufficient public interest in them and that the publishers had no way to fact-check his claims.

His self-published books were known for their tendentious tone and, perhaps, crude presentation that included newspaper clippings, hand-drawn maps, and an informal, idiosyncratic writing style. However, these shortcomings did not reflect a disregard for academic standards such as citation, footnotes, and bibliography, which he supplied extensively. His work drew criticism for its assertions about the role of blacks in Egyptian history and was dismissed for its slipshod editing. Despite this, ben Jochannan frequently said that he did not seek the approval of other scholars but deliberately chose to write in a manner that could be readily absorbed by both lay readers and researchers with little more than a middle-school education (Alexander, 9). He also steadfastly criticized the overall presentation of African history in American universities and museums.

In the late 1960s, ben Jochannan worked briefly as a writer for a New York publishing company, W.H. Sadlier, where he wrote textbooks on African history such as *Southern Lands* (1969). Beginning in 1973, he served as an adjunct professor of History and Egyptology at Cornell University's Africana Research Center, where his longtime friend and colleague John Henrik Clarke was teaching. He taught there for fifteen years, a period during which he also served as a visiting lecturer at the Faculty of Languages at Al Azhar University in Cairo, Egypt. In 1979, after another of his tours to Egypt, he traveled to the South Pacific where he lectured in Papua New Guinea about the native population's origins on the African continent. In 1984, he became one of six founding members of the Association for the Study of Classical African Civilization (ASCAC), an organization of black scholars focusing on the ancient African world. The other founders were John Henrik Clarke, Asa G. Hilliard III, Jacob H. Carruthers, Leonard Jeffries, and MAULANA KARENGA.

Ben Jochannan was a popular and sought-after lecturer on college campuses nationally and internationally, celebrated for his direct, polemical style and wit. This popularity also drew criticism as when, in 1993, Mary Lefkowitz, a Wellesley classics professor, mentioned him prominently in a Wall Street Journal editorial that fueled an acerbic national debate about "Afrocentrism" in academia (*Wall Street Journal*, 7 Apr. 1993).

Outside of academia, however, ben Jochannan's reputation remained high, particularly among many black laypeople. He could be frequently spotted around Harlem where residents greeted him warmly as "Dr. Ben!," regaled him with personal stories, and posed for photographs with him. A lifelong bibliophile, ben Jochannan had amassed a personal library of over 15,000 books chronicling African and African American history.

His other most widely circulated books are *African Origins of the Major "Western Religions"* (1970), *Africa: Mother of Western Civilization* (1971), and *Our Black Seminarians & Black Clergy without a Black Theology* (1978). Ben Jochannan was a key influence on a generation of students, historians, and educators such as Hilliard, MOLEFI ASANTE, Carruthers, and Karenga.

FURTHER READING

The Schomburg Center for Research in Black Culture's Hatch-Billops Collection includes an audio interview with Yosef ben Jochannan from 1972.

Ben Jochannan, Yosef A. A. *Africa: Mother of Western Civilization* (1988).

Alexander, E. Curtis. *Doc Ben Speaks Out* (interview; 1982).

JODY BENJAMIN

Benberry, Cuesta Ray (8 Sept. 1923–23 Aug. 2007), quilt historian and researcher, was born in Cincinnati to Walter Ray Sr., a dining car steward for the Southern Railway Company, and Marie Jones, a seamstress and homemaker. After age six, following her mother's death, Benberry and her older brother, Walter Jr., lived in St. Louis with their maternal grandmother, Letha Jennings.

After earning a B.A. in 1945 from Stowe Teachers College (later Harris-Stowe State University) in Saint Louis, she married George L. Benberry in 1951. The couple had one son, George Jr., born in 1953. Benberry spent about forty years as a teacher, reading specialist, and librarian for the St. Louis public school system. She went on to get a certificate of Library Science, also from Stowe, in 1967, and a masters of Education in 1973 from the University of Missouri–St. Louis.

Benberry's interest in quilting began during a trip to her husband's family in rural Paducah, Kentucky. Her mother-in-law, Minnie Benberry, was a quilter. Minnie and other quilters in the area shared with Benberry their newest quilts, which they called by different names. Benberry began to study the history of the names of the patterns. Her investigations would have an impact on American quilt history for decades.

In the early 1950s Benberry began corresponding with quilters across America and Canada. She joined quilt pattern "round robins," an exchange wherein participants mailed quilt patterns to everyone else in the group, thus enlarging all the members' collections. Benberry collected patterns for their beauty and cataloged them to document their origins and various regional names. In time, her collection of quilt pattern blocks would number eight hundred. In 1965 Benberry designed an original quilt block, *Kennedy's Eternal Flame*, which later the same year received an honorable mention from *Aunt Kate's Quilting Bee Magazine*.

Quilting publications at the time were generally simple, photocopied newsletters. The first, more formal, magazine-style quilt publication started in 1969 with *Nimble Needle Treasures*, a quarterly that featured reprinted quilt patterns and articles on quilt history. From 1970 to 1975 Benberry regularly contributed to the quarterly.

Benberry outlined her seven-year effort to confirm a quilt legend about a black woman MARTHA ANN RICKS, who made Queen Victoria a quilt in 1892 ("A Quilt for Queen Victoria," *Quilter's Newsletter Magazine*, Feb. 1987, 24–25). Benberry was able to accurately determine, with the assistance of her extensive network of quilters, the name of the eight-pointed *Evening Star* pattern used in a cradle quilt sold at the 1836 Boston Female Anti-Slavery Society Ladies Fair ("A Quilt Research Surprise," *Quilters Newsletter Magazine*, July–Aug. 1981, 34–35). Over the years her articles on quilt history and quilt patterns appeared in many periodicals, including *American Quilter Magazine, Canada Quilts, Center for the History of American Needlework Magazine, Essence Magazine, International Review of African American Art, Lady's Circle Patchwork Quilts*, and *Quilter's Newsletter Magazine*. At her request, Benberry's articles often ran without bylines.

America's bicentennial in 1976 and an attendant emphasis on the study of Americans' various cultural heritages provided the impetus for Benberry's research into African American quilt history. Beginning her study through interviews with older quilters, she then moved to nonquilting sources such as antislavery journals, slave narratives, nineteenth-century autobiographies of black people, newspapers, farm journals, the Work Progress Administration's (WPA's) Federal Writers' Project narratives, and women's history books to gain insights into the quilts and motivations of early black quilters.

In 1980 Benberry wrote the landmark "Afro-American Women and Quilts: An Introductory Essay," one of the first articles to place black women's needlework in the context of American quilt history (*Uncovering 1980*, ed. Sally Garoutte, 64–67). She insisted in her essay that a complete picture should include quilts made by slaves, quilts made in traditional European styles, quilts made in African traditions, and those with black images made by white quilters. Also in 1980 Benberry stitched her only quilt, *Afro-American Women and Quilts*, a sampler quilt featuring twelve blocks, each block representing an African American–made quilt she had learned about during her years of research.

In 1983 Benberry was inducted into the Quilters Hall of Fame for her thirty-year investigative contributions to quilt history and pattern collecting. In her acceptance speech Benberry said, "What I see as the quilt investigator's obligation is the expansion and enrichment of quilt information, undergirded by accuracy and truth, set in a frame of serious scholarship" ("Hall of Fame '83," *Quilters' Journal*, no. 23, 1983, 18). Three years later she answered an advertisement from CAROLYN MAZLOOMI in the February 1986 issue of *Quilter's Newsletter Magazine* requesting correspondence with other African American quilters. Benberry became a founding member of the Women of Color Quilters Network (WOCQN), an outgrowth of the advertisement. She was also a frequent contributor to the Women of Color Quilters Network Newsletter, available in the Museum of Arts and Design library in New York City.

Benberry traveled to London in 1986 for the opening of an exhibit featuring the quilts of the Zamani Soweto Sisters Council of South Africa. She gave the opening lecture to the exhibit. In addition, the mayor of Brixton presented Benberry and the Zamani Soweto Sisters with the keys to this London neighborhood for bringing the quilt program to the community.

Over the years Benberry shared her expertise generously, lecturing on African American quilt history, pattern history, and the role of the quilt historian at more than one hundred venues since 1980. A charter member of the American Quilt Study Group, she presented papers at some of the group's conferences, and her appearance on the popular Home and Garden Television (HGTV) network program *Simply Quilts* (1998) reached a wide audience. Benberry served on the board of directors for the American Quilt Study Group (1983–1986) and Art Saint Louis (1995) as well as on the advisory board of the Elder Craftsmen of New York (1989–1994). Her publications include *Always There: The African American Presence in American Quilting* (1992); *A Patchwork of Pieces: An Anthology of Early Quilt Stories 1845–1940* (1993), edited with Carol Pinney Crabb; *Twentieth Century Quilts, 1900–1970: Women Make Their Mark* (1997), with Joyce Gross; *A Piece of My Soul: Quilts by Black Arkansans* (2000); and *Love of Quilts: A Treasury of Classic Quilting Stories* (2004), with Carol Pinney Crabb.

Esteemed for her accumulated knowledge, in 1993 Benberry curated the exhibit Hear My Quilt: 150 Years of African American Quilt Making, which opened at the St. Louis Art Museum. The following year the museum purchased the quilt *Jo Baker's Birthday*, created by FAITH RINGGOLD in Benberry's honor. In 2004 the Anyone Can Fly Foundation presented Benberry with its first Senior Scholar Lifetime Achievement Award for her life's work—researching the quilt art of the African diaspora. In the same year, she donated her extensive collection of rare quilt history books, patterns, exhibit catalogs, and ephemera materials amassed after fifty years of research to the American Folk Art Museum Library in New York. Benberry continued to encourage and inspire other established and budding researchers until she passed away.

FURTHER READING

Blair, Margot Carter. "An Interview with Cuesta Benberry," *The Flying Needle* (Feb. 1985).

Center for the Quilt Online. http://www.centerforthequilt.org. See 2002 video interview with Benberry.

Doering, Henry, ed. *Book of Buffs, Masters, Mavens, and Uncommon Experts* (1980).

Kogan, Lee, and James Mitchell. "Update: The Library," *Folk Art* (Winter 2004–2005).

"The Meeting Place: Cuesta Benberry," *Quilter's Newsletter Magazine* (Feb. 1980).

KYRA E. HICKS

Benga, Ota. *See* Otabenga.

Benjamin, Bennie (4 November 1907–2 May 1989), musician and songwriter, was born Claude Augustus Benjamin in Christiansted, St. Croix, Virgin Islands (then Danish West Indies), the son of Joseph Benjamin and Euphrasia Seteon (spelled Shöin on his Anglican baptismal certificate). Benjamin's early life was difficult. His father was a fisherman who died when Benjamin was an infant, and changes in the shipping industry, hurricanes, and World War I pushed the economy of the Virgin Islands into decline. After graduating from Virgin Islands High School in 1925, he abandoned his early hopes of becoming a physician for lack of tuition to enter medical school, and worked as a tailor and cabinetmaker instead. In 1927 he moved to New York City in search of better opportunity.

Inspired by a local island musician, Louis Stakemann, Benjamin had taught himself ukulele and banjo (by ear) as a youth. Upon arriving in New York, he added guitar to his skills at Hy Smith's School of Music, and after just six months of training he could read music and play well enough to begin performing in dance orchestras. He developed a distinctive guitar solo style that interspersed chords in his melodic lines and this earned him a job with Napoleon's Orchestra at the Savoy Ballroom where he played for five years (c. 1928–1933). He also toured with the vaudeville act Olson and Johnson and played at the Cotton Club. Yet despite these prominent gigs, he struggled to make a living and worked odd jobs to stay afloat financially.

Beginning about 1935, Benjamin tried songwriting in the mainstream Tin Pan Alley idiom, but was unable to publish a single song. In 1938 he joined with Sol Marcus, and along with Eddie Seiler and EDDIE DURHAM, revised a tune Benjamin had previously shopped around to publishers unsuccessfully to create the smash hit "I Don't Want to Set the World on Fire" in 1941. Introduced by the African American group HARLAN LEONARD's Kansas City Rockets, the song next hit number four on the pop charts as performed by the Ink Spots and rose to number one when Horace Heidt's version captured the mood of the country after the Pearl Harbor attack. It won a 1941 *Billboard Magazine* Top Songwriter's Award for its creators. Seiler, Marcus, and Benjamin hit number one again soon after in 1942 with "When the Lights Go on Again (All over the World)," as performed by Vaughn Monroe, which used the imagery of World War II blackouts to express the hope for peace.

Benjamin enlisted in the United States Army Air Corps as an entertainment specialist on 5 September 1942 and was stationed at Mitchel Field in New York. During three years of service he played guitar and produced camp shows (e.g., writing songs, casting talent, directing). He wed Martha Flores on 25 September 1944; they remained married until her death in 1983. He was honorably discharged at the rank of corporal on 21 September 1945.

Returning to civilian life, he joined with George David Weiss to form the most successful partnership of his career. This team produced twenty hit songs in ten years, including "Oh What It Seemed to Be" (1945; 1946, number 1 Pop with Frankie Carle and number 1 Pop with Frank Sinatra), "Rumors Are Flying" (1946, number 1 Pop, Frankie Carle and Les Paul), and "Wheel of Fortune" (1952, number 1 Pop, Kay Starr). "Wheel of Fortune" sold over 1 million copies of sheet music and gave its name to an early television game show (1952–1953) that rewarded good Samaritans with a spin of a prize wheel. Other hits by the pair included "Strictly Instrumental" (1942), "I Want to Thank Your Folks" (1946, number 21, Perry Como), "Surrender" (1946, number 2, Perry Como; later Elvis Presley, 1961), "I Don't See Me in Your Eyes Anymore" (1949, number 6), "Can Anyone Explain" (1950, number 5, Ames Brothers), "Can Anyone Explain? (No, No, No)" (1950, number 7, Ames Brothers), "Echoes" (1950, number 18, Jo Stafford and Gordon MacRae), "Jet" (1951, number 20, NAT KING COLE), "These Things I Offer You" (1951, SARAH VAUGHAN), and "Cross over the Bridge" (1954, number 2, Patti Page). The pair was named the top songwriting team of 1946 by *Billboard Magazine*, and Disney commissioned them to pen the title songs for the movies *Fun and Fancy Free* (1947) and *Melody Time* (1948).

Benjamin reportedly had a hand in more than a hundred songs that registered on the *Billboard* charts. He approached his work as a professional art, observing that "songwriting is a craft, an art, a gift—like a vocation to medicine or law or any other profession" (*Virgin Islands Daily News*, 29 April 1968). His songs have little direct reference to African American idioms but are rather in the popular mainstream styles of the day. His lyrics focus on the subject of love with an undercurrent of innocent sensuality. Like other Tin Pan Alley songs, dramatic emphasis has shifted to the chorus, with a brief introduction to set the stage. Unobtrusive rhyme and clever word choice enchant the listener. Although his tuneful melodies are easily sung by amateurs, their subtlety engages professional interpreters as well. Rhythmic variations keep the melody fresh as it spins out with gentle syncopations and triplet inflections. Wide intervallic leaps are used with deliberate expressive intent, especially at the song's climax. In sum, Benjamin's songs are masterful realizations of the popular idiom.

Around 1950 Benjamin founded his own publishing company; after his 1955 split with Weiss, he again teamed with Sol Marcus. This pair created such songs as "Fabulous Character" (1955, Sarah Vaughan), "I Am Blessed" (NINA SIMONE), "Our Love (Will See Us Through)" (Nina Simone), "Lonely Man (1960, Elvis Presley), and "Don't Let Me Be Misunderstood" (1965, number 15, The Animals).

Evoking classic themes of love and capturing the energy of their time, Benjamin's songs often appear in movie soundtracks. For example, "Anyone (Could Fall in Love with You)" was sung by Elvis Presley in the 1964 movie *Kissin' Cousins*. The fact that four

and five decades later, films continued to include his songs reveals their ability to connect with audiences. These long-lived songs and their respective films include "Wheel of Fortune" (*Household Saints*, 1993; *L.A. Confidential*, 1997), "Don't Let Me Be Misunderstood" (*Layer Cake*, 2004; *The Banger Sisters*, 2002), and "I Don't Want to Set the World on Fire" (*Iris*, 2001; *Ask the Dust*, 2006).

By 1965 his company was known as Benjamin Publishing, and by 1968 Benjamin was sole owner of Bennie Benjamin Music. He was a member of the American Society of Composers, Authors and Publishers (ASCAP), the National Academy of Popular Music, and the Songwriters Guild of America. He also served on the council of the American Guild of Authors and Composers. In 1979 he won an ASCAP Award for "I'll Never Be Free," and that same year he was honored at the dedication of St. Thomas's Reichhold Center for the Arts. Five years later, in 1984, he was inducted into the Songwriters Hall of Fame.

As he became more affluent, Benjamin invested to support the Virgin Islands, buying real estate and becoming the largest stockholder in the West Indies Bank and Trust. Benjamin sponsored benefits for the March of Dimes, the Red Cross, and various leagues and associations such as the Queensboro Tuberculosis and Health Association. In 1963 New York Congressman ADAM CLAYTON POWELL JR. persuaded President John F. Kennedy to appoint Benjamin a member of the board of directors of the Virgin Islands Corporation.

Benjamin died after a long illness in New York City at the age of eighty-one. Lacking children, his last will and testament created the Bennie and Martha Benjamin Foundation to support medical training and clinics in the Virgin Islands. Established in 1990 the foundation gave its first grant for medical equipment in 1992 and began awarding annual scholarships to students pursuing careers in healthcare who are committed to working in the islands. As of 2006 the foundation had donated almost $1.7 million to Virgin Island hospitals, students, and nonprofits.

FURTHER READING

Benjamin's personal papers are held in the Schomburg Center for Research in Black Culture (New York Public Library, New York City).

Hughes, Langston. *Famous Negro Music Makers* (1955).

Moolenaar, Ruth. *Profiles of Outstanding Virgin Islanders* (1992).

MARK CLAGUE

Benjamin, Fred (8 Sept. 1944–), dancer, choreographer, and educator, was born in Boston, Massachusetts, to a theatrical and musical family. One of New York's most superb and demanding jazz teachers, as well as an excellent choreographer, Benjamin began his career at the age of four, studying with Elma Lewis at her well-respected School of Fine Arts. Two years later, he started studying ballet, a requirement for all of Lewis's students, no matter which style they chose to focus on. When peer pressure led Benjamin to stop dancing briefly—a not uncommon situation for young male dancers—he shifted to acting, taking classes at Boston Children's Theatre. Two years later he returned to Lewis's school and found something new: George Howard, a teacher of Haitian dance. Still a child, Benjamin knew instantly that "that's the thing I wanted to do, with the drums and everything. It was so exciting to me" (Hall, 3).

Lewis provided Benjamin with a thorough grounding in a wide range of techniques—ballet, jazz, and what is commonly referred to as "ethnic dance"—that set the stage for his future work as a choreographer. And she offered yet more inspiration by taking Benjamin and a small group of pupils to New York City to expose them to other teachers and performances. While there Benjamin had the opportunity to study with such master jazz instructors as Luigi and Matt Mattox, as well as in the American Ballet Theatre's school, which he later attended on a partial scholarship after graduating from high school.

At nineteen Benjamin joined the company of TALLEY BEATTY, who was a former Dunham dancer and one of the major figures in African American dance. Benjamin remained with the company for three years, finding in Beatty a powerful influence and one who also fused various styles into a cohesive whole. Many years later, following Beatty's death in 1995, Benjamin created *Beattyville* for Philadanco as a tribute to his mentor. One of Benjamin's most successful works, it became a staple in the company's repertoire.

In 1968, shortly after Beatty's company dissolved, Benjamin formed his own dance troupe, the Fred Benjamin Dance Company. Initially he had not intended to become a company director, but Elma Lewis asked him to do a piece for her and he agreed, using some of the dancers who were then performing with him in a production of *Hello, Dolly!* on Broadway. At that point he began to realize that he needed a "larger canvas" to reach his artistic goals (Hall, 8); that small collection of friends formed the original core of his company, which eventually appeared on such TV shows as *Soul*.

Benjamin described his company's technique as modern jazz, and he, as well as others, referred to his works as soul ballets, many of which have been set to popular music by singers like PATTI LABELLE and GLADYS KNIGHT. His choreography created movement that was full of power, often with very long elegant lines: in Benjamin's words, dances that were "sensual, linear, and entertaining," but at the same time rhythmic, with jazz isolations that allowed the body to move polyrhythmically (*Attitude*, 11).

In November 1975, Benjamin scarcely eluded death when thieves attacked and stabbed him six times outside his New York apartment. His response was to create a dance, "Travels Just Outside the House" about the experience. He told the *New York Times* dance reviewer Anna Kisselgoff that in spite of the trauma, the dancers of his studio stayed together and kept the company running, and that their solidarity inspired Benjamin and kept him from becoming bitter.

Benjamin's influence extended in two different directions: first, as a teacher in such studios as the famed New York's Clark Center for the Performing Arts, the Steps studios, and June Lewis, he trained a generation of dancers who went on to modern dance companies (including ALVIN AILEY) and Broadway. Always demanding, Benjamin challenged his students with complex, professional-level combinations. Second, he strove to bring his work to the community and expose as many people as possible to dance; during the late 1970s and early 1980s, he participated in the Harlem Cultural Council's annual Dance Mobile series, which presented free performances outdoors in a non-theatrical setting.

The Fred Benjamin Dance Company dissolved in 1990, when it was restructured as the Tally/Benjamin Project. Benjamin served as chair of the jazz department and faculty adviser of the Alvin Ailey American Dance Center. He also worked internationally, and taught dance in the Netherlands, Japan, and Belgium, among other places.

FURTHER READING

The Dance Research Division of the New York Public Library at Lincoln Center maintains a clippings file on Fred Benjamin.

Emery, Lynne Fauley. *Black Dance from 1619 to Today* (1988).

Hall, Noel. "Interview with Fred Benjamin," for the Oral History Project, Dance Division, New York Public Library. Conducted 6 Oct. 1989.

Lewis, Julinda. "Fred Benjamin: A Tyrant Matures," *Attitude* (Sept.–Oct. 1983).

Perpener, John O., III. *African-American Concert Dance: The Harlem Renaissance and Beyond* (2001).

KAREN BACKSTEIN

Benjamin, Robert Charles O'Hara (31 Mar. 1855–2 Oct. 1900), journalist and lawyer, was born on the island of St. Kitts in the West Indies. Details about his early life, including the names of his parents and the nature of his education, are unknown. In the fall of 1869 he arrived in New York, where he worked as soliciting agent for the *New York Star* and then as city editor for the *Progressive American*. Benjamin apparently became a U.S. citizen in the early 1870s, and in 1876 he gave speeches in support of Rutherford B. Hayes, the Republican candidate for president. He was rewarded with a position as a letter carrier in New York City but quit after nine months and moved to Kentucky, where he taught school. While there Benjamin also took up the study of law. He continued his studies after being named principal of a school in Decatur, Alabama, and he was admitted to the bar at Nashville, Tennessee, in January 1880.

Before and after his admission to the bar, the peripatetic Benjamin continued his career in journalism. In total he edited or owned (or both edited and owned) at least eleven black newspapers, including the *Colored Citizen* of Pittsburgh, the *Chronicle* of Evansville, Illinois, the *Nashville Free Lance*—where, as contributing editor, he wrote under the name "Cicero"—the *Negro American* of Birmingham, Alabama, the *Los Angeles Observer*, and the *San Francisco Sentinel*. When Benjamin worked at each of these papers is unclear. He was apparently in Birmingham in 1887, in Los Angeles in 1888, and in San Francisco in 1891. He also worked for the *Daily Sun*, a white-owned newspaper in Los Angeles.

In addition to his journalism, Benjamin also published a number of books and pamphlets that reflected his wide range of interests. In 1883 he published *Poetic Gems*, a small collection of poetry, and in 1888 he published *Life of Toussaint L'Ouverture*. He was perhaps best known for *Southern Outrages: A Statistical Record of Lawless Doings* (1894). In 1886 Benjamin traveled to Canada on a speaking tour.

For twenty years Benjamin maintained a legal practice in the cities where he edited newspapers. One of his cases received widespread publicity: in 1884 in Richmond, Virginia, he won an acquittal of a black woman charged with murder. At a time when most white newspapers spoke of blacks in derogatory and racist terms, Benjamin's skills as a lawyer drew favorable comment from white newspapers in Richmond, Los Angeles, and Lexington, Kentucky.

Benjamin did not, however, court white favor, although he well understood the risk that African Americans ran in challenging whites in civil rights, politics, and race relations. Benjamin was a vocal critic of racial discrimination and went much further than most black leaders; instead of simply denouncing Jim Crow legislation, he urged blacks to defend themselves when attacked by whites. Such an outspoken attitude led to Benjamin's being forced to leave Brinkley, Arkansas, in 1879 and Birmingham in 1887. Irvine Garland Penn, author of *The Afro-American Press and Its Editors* (1891), said of Benjamin: "He is fearless in his editorial expression; and the fact that he is a negro does not lead him to withhold his opinions upon the live issues of the day, but to give them in a courageous manner."

In December 1892 Benjamin married Lula M. Robinson; they had a son and a daughter. The family settled in Lexington, Kentucky, in 1897. To the dismay of some whites, Benjamin quickly became involved in local politics. On 2 October 1900 he argued with Michael Moynahan, a Democratic precinct worker, over the white man's harassment of blacks who wished to register to vote. Late that evening Moynahan killed Benjamin. At the examining trial several days later Moynahan pleaded not guilty by reason of self-defense. The judge accepted Moynahan's claim and dismissed the case, even though Benjamin had been shot in the back.

FURTHER READING

A few letters written by Benjamin can be found in the Booker T. Washington Papers at the Library of Congress.

Simmons, William J. *Men of Mark: Eminent, Progressive, and Rising* (1887).

This entry is taken from the *American National Biography* and is published here with the permission of the American Council of Learned Societies.

GEORGE C. WRIGHT

Bennett, Estelle (22 July 1941–11 Feb. 2009), daughter of Beatrice and Louis Bennett, was born in New York City. With her sister Veronica (Ronnie) Bennett (later Spector) and first cousin Nedra Tally,

Bennett rose to prominence as a member of the 1960s music group, The Ronettes.

Bennett and her sister were raised in the Washington Heights section of Manhattan. According to a biography by Spector, the girls were taunted as children because of their mixed ethnicity. (Their mother was black and Cherokee, their father white). Although she had a shy demeanor, Bennett liked to dance and sing, and she often performed for family and friends with her sister and Tally. In these amateur home performances, the girls styled their three-part harmonies after the young male doo-wop groups of the era such as Little Anthony and the Imperials and FRANKIE LYMON and the Teenagers.

Going by the name the Darling Sisters, Bennett, Spector, and Tally won the amateur talent contest at the Apollo Theatre in Harlem in 1959. They then began to perform as regular twist dancers at the legendary Peppermint Lounge, at the club's New York and Miami locations. The trio then began to work as backup singers, recording with Joey Dee, Del Shannon, and Bobby Rydell. In 1961 the women landed a recording contract with Colpix records, and appeared as dancers in the film *Twist around the Clock*. First under the name Ronnie and the Relatives, and later as the Ronettes, the group released a string of singles on Colpix, "I Want A Boy," "Good Girls," "Silhouettes," and "I'm on the Wagon," none of which greatly impacted the current music scene. In 1963 however, the Ronettes began to collaborate with the famed music producer Phil Spector, going to some lengths to be released from their contract with Colpix in order to cement their new partnership. Their first recording under Spector's Phillies label was "Be My Baby," released in August of 1963, the song went on to sell two million copies and chart at number two on the Billboard Pop singles charts. *Rolling Stone* magazine would eventually list the song as number twenty-two on its list of the five hundred greatest songs of all time.

The group subsequently had four more top forty hits including the songs "Baby, I Love You," and "Walking in the Rain." In 1964 they performed in England with the Rolling Stones and opened for the Beatles on their first tour of America that same year. At the height of their success, Bennett was romantically linked to the singer Mick Jagger, the Beatles guitarist George Harrison, and the pop singer JOHNNY MATHIS.

As their fame swelled, the Ronettes increasingly became known for their style, and their signature look of high-piled beehive hairdos and heavily applied eye liner and mascara shaped popular culture as much as their sound. Bennett, who had studied briefly at the Fashion Institute of Technology in Manhattan, was often credited with influencing their distinct flair. Both their appearance and vocalization had social resonance, as the heavy makeup and forthright lyrical delivery (for example, "Baby, I love you" in place of "I love him,") connoted a tough, streetwise attitude, and marked a departure from the innocent, pristine image of previous all-female acts.

The singles "Is This What I Get for Loving You?" and "I Can Hear Music," released in 1965 and 1966, respectively, failed to garner the same degree of success as earlier songs, and the Ronettes disbanded in 1966. The breakup was particularly devastating for Bennett, as she desperately wanted the group to go on. After the group's demise, Bennett recorded the single "The Year 2000/The Naked Boy," in 1966, but was unable to kick start a solo career. In 1968 Bennett married the group's road manager, Jon Dong, and had her only child, daughter Toyin, shortly thereafter. Bennett's marriage eventually dissolved, and she struggled with mental illness and anorexia throughout the ensuing decades, and was at various points homeless.

For years Bennett was rarely ever seen in the public eye. She reemerged for court appearances in 1988, the year the group sued Phil Spector for unpaid royalties. The Ronettes initially received a favorable court ruling, but it was later overturned. On 11 February 2009 Bennett died of colon cancer in Englewood, New Jersey.

In 2007 the Ronettes were inducted into the Rock and Roll Hall of Fame by Keith Richards. Bennett opted out of performing at the induction concert along with her former group members, but she did offer a simple, straightforward acceptance speech: "I would just like to say, thank you very much for giving us this award. I'm Estelle of the Ronettes, thank you."

FURTHER READING

Spector, Ronnie, and Vince Waldron. *Be My Baby: How I Survived Mascara, Miniskirts, and Madness, or My Life as a Fabulous Ronette* (1990).

CAMILLE A. COLLINS

Bennett, Gwendolyn (8 July 1902–30 May 1981), writer and artist, was born in Giddings, Texas, the daughter of Joshua Robin Bennett and Mayme F. Abernathy, teachers on an Indian reservation. In 1906 the family moved to Washington, D.C., where

Gwendolyn's father studied law and her mother worked as a manicurist and hairdresser. When her parents divorced, her mother won custody, but her father kidnapped the seven-year-old Gwendolyn. The two, with Gwendolyn's stepmother, lived in hiding in various towns along the East Coast and in Pennsylvania before finally settling in New York.

At Brooklyn's Girls' High (1918–1921) Bennett participated in the drama and literary societies—the first African American to do so—and won first place in an art contest. She attended fine arts classes at Columbia University (1921) and the Pratt Institute, from which she graduated in 1924. While she was still an undergraduate, her poems "Nocturne" and "Heritage" were published in *Crisis* (Nov. 1923) and *Opportunity* (Dec. 1923), respectively.

Bennett's poetry generally dealt with racial uplift and pride in her African heritage. "To Usward," published in both *Opportunity* and *Crisis* in May 1924, was a tribute to the new generation and a call to those who have "a song to sing." She also produced symbolist-inspired and romantic lyrics, such as "Quatrains" (1927). It expressed the tension Bennett experienced, torn between art and literature:

> Brushes and paints are all I have
> To speak the music in my soul
> While silently there laughs at me
> A copper jar beside a pale green bowl.

Over the next nine years, twenty-two of Bennett's poems appeared in *Opportunity, Crisis, Palms*, and *Gypsy*. Additional poems were published in WILLIAM STANLEY BEAUMONT BRAITHWAITE's *Anthology of Magazine Verse for 1927 and Yearbook of American Poetry* (1927), COUNTÉE CULLEN's *Caroling Dusk* (1927), and JAMES WELDON JOHNSON's *The Book of American Negro Poetry* (1931).

Bennett also created cover illustrations for *Crisis* in December 1923 and March 1924; the latter, *Pipes of Pan*, was a line drawing of a young African American man listening to music produced by nymphs and satyrs. Her covers for *Opportunity* appeared in January and July 1926 and December 1930. She also produced oil landscapes, but she rarely exhibited her work publicly.

In 1924 Bennett began teaching design, watercolor, and crafts at Howard University in Washington, D.C., and was reunited with her mother. The following year, on a $1,000 Delta Sigma Theta sorority fellowship, she studied art in Paris at the Académies de la Grande Chaumière, Julian, and Colarossi and at the École du Panthéon. She published two short stories, "Wedding Day," published in *Fire!!* (1926), and "Tokens," published in CHARLES SPURGEON JOHNSON's *Ebony and Topaz: A Collectanea* (1927). Both express the isolation and loneliness she experienced in Paris and feature African American expatriates who remained in France after serving in World War I.

After Bennett returned to Washington, D.C., in 1926, her father died, and she lost most of the paintings and batiks she had produced abroad in a fire in her stepmother's home. She then spent two years (1927–1928) writing "The Ebony Flute," a "literary and social chit-chat" column for *Opportunity*, for which she had also written book reviews. During the summer of 1927 she taught art classes at Nashville's Tennessee Agricultural and Industrial State College. The same year she served as editor for the magazine *Black Opals*.

In 1928 Bennett received a scholarship to study art at the Barnes Foundation in Merion, Pennsylvania. That year she married Alfred Jackson and moved to Eustis, Florida, where her husband had a medical practice. Unhappy in the segregated South, Bennett gained sixty pounds in four years and wrote little. The couple moved to Hempstead, Long Island, in 1932, and Bennett took a job with the Department of Information and Education of the Welfare Council of New York writing feature articles that appeared in the *Amsterdam News*, the *New York Age*, the *Baltimore Afro-American*, and *Better Times*.

After Jackson died in 1936, Bennett lived alternately with her stepmother and with the sculptor AUGUSTA SAVAGE in New York. She worked as a teacher, then as a project supervisor in the Federal Art Teaching Project. When Savage resigned as director of the Harlem Community Art Center, a Federal Art Project endeavor, in 1939, Bennett took that position. She was also active in the Harlem Artists Guild, the National Negro Congress, the Artists Union, the Negro People's Theater, and the Negro Playwright's Company, serving on the board of directors of the last.

In 1941 Bennett gave a series of lectures on African American arts at the School for Democracy; she also married a white Harvard graduate and fellow teacher, Richard Crosscup. Three years later Bennett was suspended from the Harlem Community Art Center by the House Un-American Activities Committee (HUAC) for her leftist sympathies. She then cofounded and directed the George Carver Community School, an adult education center for African Americans in Harlem. HUAC investigated the school, and it closed in 1947. From the end of the 1940s until the late 1960s, Bennett worked for the Consumers Union as a correspondent.

Upon their retirement in 1968, Bennett and her husband moved to Kutztown, Pennsylvania, and opened an antique store. Bennett died of congestive heart failure in Reading, Pennsylvania. Although she was a minor writer and artist, Bennett contributed significantly to the New Negro movement with her editing, teaching, and leadership, aiding the careers of such better-known colleagues as AARON DOUGLAS, LANGSTON HUGHES, and Cullen.

FURTHER READING
Bennett's papers are in the Schomburg Center for Research in Black Culture and History at the New York Public Library.
Govan, Sandra. "After the Renaissance: Gwendolyn Bennett and the WPA Years," *MidAtlantic Writers Association* 3 (Dec. 1988).
Primeau, Ronald. "Frank Horne and the Second Echelon Poets of the Harlem Renaissance," in *The Harlem Renaissance Remembered*, ed. Arna Bontemps (1972).

This entry is taken from the *American National Biography* and is published here with the permission of the American Council of Learned Societies.

THERESA LEININGER-MILLER

Bennett, Hal (21 Apr. 1930–8 Sept. 2004), writer and journalist, was born George Harold Bennett in Buckingham, Virginia, the seventh of eight children born to Charles E. Bennett Sr. and Minnie P. (Bryant) Bennett, of whom little else is known. His family moved north to Orange, New Jersey, during the Great Migration, though he often spent his childhood summers in Buckingham. At age sixteen, Bennett worked part time as a features writer for the *Newark (N.J.) Herald News*. He attended Orange High School, graduating as class valedictorian, and had dreams of becoming a concert pianist.

After high school Bennett joined the air force and was stationed in Korea, where he was a writer for the Public Information Division and an editor for a military newspaper. When he was discharged in 1952, he continued his journalism career as the fiction editor for *African American News* in Baltimore, Maryland, and then became a partner in an unsuccessful newspaper in Westbury, Long Island.

Later, ill from ulcers and wanting to use his G.I. Bill, he left for Mexico to attend Mexico City College. He received two grants from the Centro Mexicano de Escritores (The Mexican Writer's Center) and was helped by the writer Margaret Shedd, who was director of the Writer's Center at Mexico City College. In 1961 he published a book of poetry, *The Mexico City Poems/House on Hay Street*.

In 1966, at age thirty-six, Bennett published his first novel, *A Wilderness of Vines*, written, according to him, with the constant strains of Beethoven's *Ninth Symphony* in his mind. This first novel won him a fellowship at the Bread Loaf Writer's Conference in Vermont during the summer of 1966. Over the next ten years he would publish a total of five novels and many short stories. The novels, besides *A Wilderness of Vines*, include *The Black Wine* (1968), *Lord of Dark Places* (1970), *Wait until the Evening* (1974), and *Seventh Heaven* (1976).

The major settings for these novels and stories were the fictional towns of Burnside, Virginia (Buckingham), and Cousinville, New Jersey (a combination of Newark and Orange). Bennett's fiction traced the migration of blacks from the rural South to the urban North and ranged in time from 1919 until Watergate in 1972, though his was not naturalistic or sociological literature. His characters were often macabre: preachers who glorify sexuality, a mad and vindictive teenager, a grandmother who kills her husband, a son who plots to kill his father, and a father who kills his baby. While it was a literature that dealt with and revealed the traumas of black life, it did so in subversive, irreverent ways. Most often Bennett's work was described as satire; he zeroed in on the disparity between what was and what should be without sparing anyone. For instance, in *Wilderness of Vines* he mocked the racism that existed among blacks based on their degrees of blackness.

Sometimes Bennett was compared to William Faulkner (he himself said that his influences included Southern Gothic writers like Eudora Welty, Carson McCullers, and Harper Lee as well as Faulkner) in that he created a mythological landscape and that many of his characters reappeared in numerous stories. In 1973 he won the Faulkner Award for fiction. But he could be more outrageous and more profane than Faulkner or any of the other Southern Gothic writers. Critics, including his former teacher Margaret Shedd, sometimes faulted Bennett for being too sexually explicit. In speaking of his own literary technique, he stated, "I think there are times when we need to distort in order to see reality" (Newman, 368).

In 1977 Bennett published *Insanity Runs in Our Family*, a collection of his short stories. One of these stories, "Dotson Gerber Resurrected," which had first appeared in a 1970 issue of *Playboy*, had won him the accolade as that year's most promising young writer in the same magazine. It was also republished in the 1971 edition of *Best American Short Stories*.

In 1979 Bennett's novel-writing took a radical turn. Responding to what he said was a remark he had heard, that black writers were only capable of writing about their own pain, he decided to write popular fiction under pseudonyms to prove that he could imagine anything and write like anybody he wanted to. His first attempt, under the name Harriet Janeway, was a woman's romance novel titled *This Passionate Land*.

During the 1980s Bennett spent a good deal of time in San Miguel de Allende, Mexico, and began writing a series of men's adventure novels, sometimes two a year. No doubt this made him some money, but it also made his point. The series (titled the Justin Perry Series) was written under the name John D. Revere and began in 1983 with *The Assassin*. It was followed by *Vatican Kill* (1983), *Born to Kill* (1984), *Death's Running Mate* (1985), and *Stud Service* (1985).

Bennett also continued to write literary short stories. He wrote "The Salamander Kind" in 1984 for *Callaloo* literary magazine and won the Callaloo Award for Fiction for the story. He also wrote "Miss Askew on Ice" in 1987 for Callaloo, "Chewing Gum" for *Black American Literature Forum* (1987), and "Wings of the Dove" (1989) also for *Black American Literature Forum*.

In a 1987 interview, Bennett said that he was working on a new literary novel, *The Bank Walkers*, as well as a new collection of short stories. Neither ever appeared. Bennett died in the Menlo Park Veterans Home in Edison, New Jersey.

FURTHER READING

Newman, Katherine. "An Evening with Hal Bennett: An Interview," *Black American Literature Forum* (Winter 1987).

Walcott, Ronald. "Hal Bennett," in *Dictionary of Literary Biography*, volume 33: *Afro-American Fiction Writers after 1955* (1984).

WILLIAM P. TOTH

Bennett, Lerone, Jr. (17 Oct. 1928–), journalist, editor, and social historian, was born in Clarksdale, Mississippi, to Lerone Bennett Sr., a chauffeur, and Alma Reed Bennett, a restaurant cook. Bennett's family later moved to Jackson, Mississippi, where Bennett went to public school. He was born into a family that emphasized the importance of education; his grandmother made college obtainable for each of her thirteen children, and it was expected that Bennett would have that option, too. Surprisingly, he failed his first year of formal schooling. With her son at her side, his mother confronted the principal and the teacher before deciding to enroll her son in a better school. This experience helped Bennett understand that education is an accessible and necessary tool needed to combat racism. An avid reader, he was inspired by his teachers, particularly Mrs. M. D. Manning, to develop an interest in history.

While in his early years he also became interested in journalism, reportedly writing his first article at age eleven. He observed how employees worked at both the *Jackson Advocate* and the *Mississippi Enterprise*, black newspapers in Jackson, where he eventually became a gofer and newsboy. Bennett once said,

> Before I was ten, I fell in love with the word. I believed the word was one of the few weapons available to save my life and my people's lives (Dawkins, 13).

During his teen years Bennett played clarinet and saxophone and edited his high school's yearbook and newspaper. After he graduated from Lenier High School in Jackson, he entered the historically black Morehouse College in Atlanta, Georgia. While there, he edited the school newspaper and found his professors, as well as the president of Morehouse, Dr. BENJAMIN MAYS, particularly inspiring and influential. In 1949 he graduated Phi Beta Kappa with a bachelor's degree in Journalism. He enrolled in graduate school at Atlanta University that same year. Once interested in pursuing a career in law, he worked as a reporter for the Atlanta Daily World newspaper, one of the oldest black-owned papers in Atlanta, from 1949 to 1952. In 1952 he became the paper's city editor.

The following year he met JOHN H. JOHNSON, who in 1945 had founded *Ebony* magazine. Johnson was interested in attracting the best professionals in the publishing industry to his publishing company. He chose Bennett in 1953 to work as an associate editor at *Jet* magazine. This was a major turning point for Bennett, beginning an alliance with Johnson's company that would span over fifty years. In 1954 Bennett became an associate editor at *Ebony*. Two years later he married Gloria Sylvester, and the couple had four children, including one set of twins. Bennett became *Ebony* magazine's first senior editor in 1958. He also was a visiting professor of history at Northwestern University from 1968 to 1969 and a senior fellow of the Institute of the Black World in 1969.

Bennett's first book, *Before the Mayflower: A History of Black America, 1619–1962*, based on articles written for *Ebony* in 1959, helped launch the book division of John H. Johnson's publishing house. Though the book did not garner immediate success, it eventually sold over one million copies and, from its 1962 publication, was revised and updated. *Before the Mayflower's* companion volume, *The Shaping of Black America: The Struggles and Triumphs of African-Americans, 1619 to the 1990s*, was published in 1975. It had two sections: "Foundations," which focused on the early stages of America's development, including the arrival of Africans in 1619, and "Directions," an exploration of black labor and capital. In 1964 *What Manner of Man: A Biography of Martin Luther King, Jr. 1929–1968* was published. That same year, Dr. MARTIN LUTHER KING JR., who had graduated from Morehouse a year before Bennett, won the Nobel Peace Prize, and in 1965 the Society of Midland Authors recognized Bennett's publication with the Patron Saints Award. The book focused on King's life from his birth in Atlanta, through his rise as a civil rights leader, until 1964, when he was named "Man of the Year" by *Time* magazine.

Bennett's other publications include *The Negro Mood, and Other Essays* (1964); *Confrontation: Black and White* (1965); *Black Power U.S.A.: The Human Side of Reconstruction, 1867–1877* (1967); *Pioneers in Protest* (1968); *The Challenge of Blackness* (1972); and *Wade in the Water: Great Moments in Black History* (1979). Bennett also co-wrote *Succeeding against the Odds* (1993), an autobiography of the publisher and entrepreneur John H. Johnson. His most controversial work, *Forced into Glory: Abraham Lincoln's White Dream* (2000), developed from an equally controversial essay in a 1968 issue of *Ebony*, "Was Abe Lincoln a White Supremacist?" Both works investigated the myths that surrounded Lincoln's participation in the demise of slavery. Bennett is often regarded as fair in his criticism of depictions of historical people and events. In 2003 he spoke out against offensive comments made about ROSA PARKS in the box-office hit *Barbershop* (2002). Using the pages of *Ebony* magazine, he told a more accurate story of the civil rights movement and Parks's participation in it.

Bennett also published fiction and poetry in a number of books, magazines, and journals. In 1987 he became executive editor of *Ebony*. He considered retiring from the position in 2003 after fifty years of working as a journalist, but decided against it when Johnson, chairman of *Ebony*, and LINDA JOHNSON RICE, the magazine's president and CEO, asked him not to retire.

Among Bennett's numerous awards and honors include the Literature Award of the American Academy of Arts and Letters in 1978, the Salute to Greatness Award for his contributions to civil rights efforts in 1996, the American Book Award's Lifetime Achievement Award in 2002, the CARTER G. WOODSON Lifetime Achievement Award in 2003, as well as numerous honorary doctorate degrees. After retiring in 2005, Bennett became executive editor emeritus, devoting most of his time to lecturing and working on several books.

FURTHER READING
Abbott, Dorothy. *Mississippi Writers: Reflections of Childhood and Youth* (1985).
Dawkins, Wayne. "Black America's Popular Historian," in *Black Issues Book Review*, (Jan.–Feb. 2004).

KAAVONIA HINTON

Bennett, Louise (7 Sept. 1919–26 July 2006), poet, short story writer, mythologist, and folklorist, was born in Kingston, Jamaica, to Cornelius A. Bennett, a baker, and Kerene Robinson Bennett, a seamstress. Bennett's father died when she was just seven years old, leaving her mother to support the family. Bennett received a typical colonial education at St. Simon's College (1933–1936) and Excelsior High School (1936–1938), which greatly influenced her later interest in elevating and legitimizing traditional Jamaican culture. Though in high school Bennett began writing poetry in English, she later switched to writing in West Indian English, which linguists would eventually come to recognize as a language rather than just a dialect.

Bennett also began performing versions of her poems to audiences in high school and her success caught the attention of Eric Coverley, who would later become Bennett's husband. Coverley, a draftsman and impresario, organized a popular Christmas concert in Jamaica at which Bennett made her professional debut in 1938. In 1940 Bennett published her first book of poetry, *Dialect Verses*. She also studied journalism in the late 1930s and began to do social work in 1943. Her volume *Jamaican Dialect Verses* was published in 1942, her work *Jamaican Humour in Dialect* in 1943, and her *Anancy Stories and Poems in Dialect* in 1944.

In recognition of her artistic abilities Bennett received a British Council scholarship to attend the Royal Academy of Dramatic Art in London and left for England in 1945. While there she worked for the BBC and had a weekly variety show called *Caribbean Carnival* (1945–1946) and a later show called *West Indian Guest Night* (1950–1953). Bennett moved to the United States in 1953, spending two years in New York, New Jersey, and Connecticut pursuing a career in radio and acting, performing at St. Martin's Little Theater in Harlem, singing folk songs at the Village Vanguard in Greenwich Village, and directing the folk musical *Day in Jamaica* with Coverley. Bennett and Coverley married on 30 May 1954, and the couple returned to Jamaica that same year.

Bennett worked for the Jamaica Social Welfare Commission as a drama officer from 1955 to 1959 and as director from 1959 to 1963, this latter position affording her the opportunity to travel around the island and further study Jamaican myth and folklore. During these years she produced several recordings, including *Jamaican Folk Songs* (1954), *Jamaican Singing Games* (1954), *Children's Jamaican Songs and Games* (1957), and *West Indies Festival of Arts* (1958). Bennett also served as a lecturer at the University of the West Indies in Kingston from 1955 to 1969, where she taught drama and Jamaican folklore.

After 1963 Bennett was a frequent performer on radio, television, and the stage, and from 1970 to 1982 she hosted a weekly children's television show called *Ring Ding*, through which she hoped to pass down Jamaican folklore to the young people of the island and to instill in them a sense of pride in their culture and history. The story of Brer Anancy, the African spider hero of many Jamaican folk tales, was a frequent feature of the show and Bennett also featured Anancy in many of her own publications, including *Anancy and Miss Lou* (1979).

Bennett's *Selected Poems* appeared in 1982 and went on to become one of her most popular works. Her poems often took the form of the ballad quatrain and while this form did give her poetry some structure on the page, the underlying orality of her work remained its most distinctive feature—her poems were meant to be heard. She made use of repetition and sharp images and often alluded to a variety of literary sources, from English literature to Jamaican folk songs. Constant throughout all her work, however, was the value she placed on traditional Jamaican culture and language.

Although Bennett was primarily thought of as a performer and an entertainer, as she stated in a 1968 interview, "I did start to write before I started to perform!" She lamented, "I have been set apart by other creative writers a long time ago because of the language I speak and work in. From the beginning nobody ever recognised me as a writer. … Up to now a lot of people don't even think I write. They say, 'Oh, you just stand up and say these things!'" She continued, "My work does lend itself so much to performance because it is oral in its tradition, legendary. People are not as accustomed to reading the dialect as they are to listening to it, and I found it a wonderful medium for the stage" (Scott, 98).

As one of the first West Indian poets to make extensive use of dialect and one of the leading Jamaican folklorists, Bennett had an undeniable influence on Caribbean poetry. As the critic Mervyn Morris noted, "In the final analysis, what most strongly recommends the work of Louise Bennett is not the sanity and generosity implicit in her creations, nor her steady and determined promotion of things Jamaican, but the fact that, for the last 40 years, her uncommon talent has been, for many people, a considerable source of pleasure" (Morris, xix). And, in Bennett's own words, "I think I speak to all Jamaica" (Scott, 100).

Bennett and Coverley lived their final years in Canada, where she nursed her husband through years of ill health until he died at age ninety-one. Bennett herself died in Toronto, survived by her stepson, Fabian Coverley, and three step-grandsons.

FURTHER READING
Hoenisch, Michael E. "Louise Bennett," *Dictionary of Literary Biography*, vol. 117 (1992).
"Louise (Simone) Bennett." *Contemporary Authors Online* (2003).
Morris, Mervyn. Introduction to *Selected Poems* by Louise Bennett (1987).
Rickards, Colin. "Bennett, (Simone) Louise," *Contemporary Poets*, 6th ed. (1996).
Scott, Dennis. "Bennett on Bennett," *Caribbean Quarterly* 14, no. 1–2 (1968).
Obituary: *New York Times*, 29 July 2006.

MALINDA WILLIAMS

Benson, Al (30 June 1908–6 Sept. 1978), disc jockey, impresario, and businessman, was born Arthur Bernard Leaner in Jackson, Mississippi. An ambitious young man, Benson sang with the family band, performed in black vaudeville, and produced shows at Jackson's black theater, the Alamo. He also attended Jackson Normal College. In the 1920s he moved to Chicago but returned to Jackson to weather the Great Depression. As the pains of the Depression eased, Benson moved back to Chicago, where he worked as a probation officer, a railroad cook, an interviewer for the Works Progress Administration (WPA), and a preacher before making his name as one of Chicago's leading radio personalities. He lived in Chicago with his wife, Norma, and their daughters, Arleta and Bertina, until he retired in 1967.

Benson began his radio career as Reverend Arthur Leaner, hosting a fifteen-minute Sunday morning broadcast from his storefront church on Chicago's South Side. When station owners objected to his selling of advertising on his religious broadcasts, Reverend Leaner adopted the name Al Benson and became a commercial disc jockey. By 1948 he was broadcasting ten hours a day on WGES, WAAF, and WJJD in Chicago. As Charles Walton relates in "Al Benson: The Godfather of Chicago Black Radio," it wasn't long before people across the city were tuning in to hear him say, "Good afternoon, ladies and gentlemen, this is your Old Swingmaster Al Benson bringing you sixty minutes of red hot, beat me down, swing tunes of the day, and that's for sure" (Walton, 1).

Benson became a disc jockey at a time when few blacks were heard on the radio. Since most owners and announcers were white and most radio content was directed at whites, the representations of African Americans heard on the radio often perpetuated the kinds of racist stereotypes popularized by blackface minstrelsy. One of the most popular shows of early radio was *The Amos 'n' Andy Show* in which the white entertainers Freeman Gosden and Charles Correll caricatured black dialect and culture with their contemporary reincarnation of Zip Coon, nineteenth- century minstrelsy's urban huckster, and Jim Crow, his country simpleton partner. Early African American radio announcers like Jack Cooper and Eddie Honesty challenged the stereotypes of Amos and Andy: they embraced middle class manners and propriety in their speech and musical choices and rejected black dialect and rural working class music like the blues. While this strategy countered prevailing stereotypes and opened doors for a few black announcers, it did not speak to the rapidly growing number of working-class African Americans migrating to Chicago from the rural South. Benson's mix of urban blues and down-home talk did. By 1948 a *Chicago Tribune* poll had voted him the most popular disc jockey in the city and in 1949 the *Chicago Defender* appointed him honorary mayor of Bronzeville, the thriving African American district of Chicago. At this time DJs were independent contractors who bought airtime from stations. As his popularity grew Benson was buying more airtime than he could cover by himself, and he employed numerous "satellite" disc jockeys, many of whom, like Big Bill Hill and Purvis Spann, also went on to successful careers in radio.

Benson did not appeal just to Chicago's new immigrants: he also appealed to advertisers. DJs made most of their money endorsing products, and Benson was a consummate pitchman. He was also one of the first to show that African Americans provided an important market. In his prime he counted many local businesses among his clients, along with Budweiser, Coca-Cola, Ace Beer, and California Swiss Colony Wine. His patronage and on-air commentary could make or break a nightclub, and his influence granted him—and consequently other blacks—entrée to previously segregated establishments.

Though best known as a radio personality, Benson also worked in Chicago's live music and recording industries. He hosted weekly rhythm and blues concerts at Chicago's Regal Theatre, often presiding in brightly colored custom suits. His recording career started in 1948 when he cut several tracks at the Pershing Hotel, followed shortly by recordings of the Benson All-Star Orchestra. He went on to start three record labels: Old Swing-Master, Parrot, and Blue Lake. The short-lived Old Swing-Master label that Benson started with Egmont Sonderling issued mostly jazz and rhythm and blues recordings acquired from defunct local labels like Rhumboogie and Planet. The Parrot and Blue Lake labels were started several years later and featured jazz, gospel, blues, and rhythm and blues. Many of Benson's musicians were unknowns, but he also worked with famous and soon-to-be famous artists like COLEMAN HAWKINS, AHMAD JAMAL, ALBERT KING, and JIMMY RUSHING. Benson's involvement in radio and recording led to claims that he was plugging his own recordings unfairly. Though Benson always maintained that he simply played records that he liked, he had the power to make a record a hit simply by playing it on his show. And it was not uncommon for recording companies to own radio stations that served as outlets for their products. Indeed, the relationships between independent record labels and small radio stations made it possible for many black musicians to find a place on the airwaves.

Benson's power, wealth, and prestige also afforded him many opportunities to advance the cause of civil rights. Besides making the sounds of African American speech and music acceptable on the radio, he frequently editorialized in favor of the civil rights movement. He also brought many African Americans into the broadcasting industry. In a particularly memorable gesture, he hired an airplane to drop copies of the U.S. Constitution on the Mississippi State Capitol on the eve of the 1956 presidential election "to wake up the citizens of Mississippi" (Spaulding, 81).

But by the late 1950s radio was experiencing major changes and Benson's influence began to fade. The sounds of the Old Swingmaster were being supplanted by new forms of African American music and popular culture—forms of expression that entered radio through the door Benson had opened. Benson's down-home patter began to sound old-fashioned in comparison to the more urban and sophisticated approaches of disc jockeys like Oscar Brown Jr. and Roy Wood, and younger audiences preferred the sounds of soul singers like Jerry Butler to the blues records that Benson played. Shakeups also rocked the industry, especially after revelations that record companies had been paying disc jockeys to play their records. While not illegal, the resulting payola scandal led to a loss of power for DJs. Stations switched to prescribed music formats, placing programming choices in the hands of executives and station managers. Advertising solicitation also shifted from DJs to station managers. Consequently the business opportunities that allowed Benson to become a millionaire all but disappeared. By the late 1960s the post–World War II immigrants Benson had spoken to and for were retiring and their children were creating new forms of music and radio. In 1967, facing declining health and diminishing popularity, he left broadcasting. After a brief return to preaching he and his wife retired to Michigan where he succumbed to pneumonia, leaving others like his daughter Arleta to continue the tradition of black radio, a tradition he helped to invent.

FURTHER READING

Barlow, William. *Voice Over: The Making Of Black Radio* (1999).

Spaulding, Norman. *History of Black Oriented Radio in Chicago, 1929–1963.* Ph.D. thesis, University of Illinois at Urbana (1981).

Walton, Charles. "Al Benson: The Godfather of Chicago Black Radio." Available online at http://www.jazzinchicago. org/Internal/ Articles/ tabid/43/ctl/ArticleView/mid/522/ articleId/ 81/ AlBensonTheGodfatherofChicago BlackRadio. Aspx.

Williams, Gilbert A. *Legendary Pioneers of Black Radio* (1998).

Obituaries: *Chicago Sun-Times*, 8 Sept. 1978; *Jet*, 28 Sept. 1978.

JOHN HARRIS-BEHLING

Benson, George (22 Mar. 1943–), jazz guitarist, musician, and singer, was born in the Hill District, the African American center of Pittsburgh, Pennsylvania. Little information about his early life is available, except that Benson enjoyed a musical upbringing and was considered something of a wunderkind. Indeed, he won his first singing contest at the age of four, and before he was ten years old he was performing publicly, winning more music contests, and appearing on local radio broadcasts. His favorite instrument was the guitar—he'd actually first picked up a ukulele—that had been handmade for him by his stepfather, but he sang as well, and at the age of ten he recorded his first single, "She Makes Me Mad," for an offshoot of the RCA label. At first, he was interested in rhythm and blues and rock and roll, but soon he fell under the influence of the jazz greats of the day, CHARLIE PARKER among them, and so his music soon turned in the direction of jazz. He attended schools in the Pittsburgh area, including Connelly High School, but he dropped out to pursue what he had determined would be a lifetime of music-making.

His first big move came with a gig with the great hard bop jazz organist Jack McDuff, for whom he played in the backup band. After four years with McDuff, he struck out on his own, relocating to New York and embarking on a solo career. The year 1964 saw the release of his first album, *The New Boss Guitar*, a soul-inflected offering backed by McDuff's band. Though *The New Boss Guitar* was largely unknown to the broader listening audience, it did bring Benson to the attention of Columbia Records' John Hammond, who in 1965 signed Benson to the label. In short order, Benson turned out a pair of albums, *It's Uptown* and *Benson Burner*, and played backup for many of the label's major stars, including MILES DAVIS. For a time, he jumped labels—first Verve, after leaving Columbia, then CTI. He tutored under the jazz guitarist WES

George Benson performs at the Universal Amphitheatre in Universal City, California, 6 July 1978. (AP Images.)

MONTGOMERY, who remained one of Benson's most important influences. Creed Taylor, the influential jazz producer, likewise took him under his wing.

In 1975 Benson found himself onboard the Warner Bros. label, and it was there that he achieved his first major success as a recording artist. His first album for Warner, *Breezin'* (1976), with its mix of jazz guitar and scat singing (Benson had fought with record executives for some time over the issue of his vocals; he wanted to use them, the executives were less enthusiastic), became a major cross-over success. Its single, "This Masquerade," reached number one on the Jazz charts and number ten on the Billboard Hot 100. The album's title track would itself become one of Benson's most immediately recognizable and enduringly popular hits. The album became so popular that it hit number one on the Pop charts as well and earned Benson three Grammy Awards. His follow-up albums, *In Flight* (1977), *Weekend in L.A.* (1978), and *Give Me the Night* (1980), were likewise commercial successes, though Benson occasionally suffered the slings and arrows of a critical opinion that faulted him for walking away from his pure jazz roots in favor of a more accessible and broadly popular style. Benson did indeed go on

to record more pure jazz albums, though he never strayed too far or too long from what appeared to be his conversant and easy-going style of light jazz. Among his most popular tracks was the original recording of Masser and Creed's "Greatest Love of All," a song rerecorded and made into a hit by Whitney Houston in 1986. The song was featured in the 1977 MUHAMMAD ALI biopic *The Greatest*. Also ranking high is his live version of "On Broadway," which won a Grammy in 1980.

Even as he enjoyed commercial success, however, Benson's personal life was often difficult. Three of his seven children died, two of natural causes and one of a gunshot wound suffered during an altercation in a bar. Through it all, Benson continued to perform, record, and tour. Among his numerous albums were *Twice the Love* (1988), *Tenderly* (1989), *Big Boss Band* (1990), *Love Remembers* (1993), *Standing Together* (1998), *After Hours* (2002), and *Songs and Stories* (2009). He frequently recorded with other artists—including MCCOY TYNER, the Count Basie Orchestra, and Chet Atkins—and made numerous television appearances. In 2009 the National Endowment of the Arts honored Benson as a Jazz Master, noting his contribution as a "distinguished artist whose excellence, impact, and significant contributions have helped to keep the important tradition of jazz alive" (NEA 2009).

FURTHER READING

Cohn, Lawrence. *Nothing but the Blues: The Music and the Musicians* (1993).

Floyd, Samuel A., Jr. *The Power of Black Music: Interpreting Its History from Africa to the United States* (1995).

JASON PHILIP MILLER

Bentley, Gladys (12 Aug. 1907–18 Jan. 1960), blues singer and pianist, was born Gladys Alberta Bentley in Philadelphia, Pennsylvania, the eldest of four children of George L. Bentley and Mary C. Mote, a native of Trinidad. The Bentley family was very poor. Later a lesbian, Bentley acknowledged that even as a child she felt more comfortable in boys' clothing than in girls' clothing; however, it was when Bentley developed a long-term crush on one of her female schoolteachers that her classmates began to ridicule her and her parents began to take Bentley from doctor to doctor in an effort to "fix" her. Finally at age sixteen Bentley left Philadelphia and traveled to Harlem, New York, where she quickly became immersed in the Harlem Renaissance and its "don't ask, don't tell" attitude about sexuality. Bentley became just one of many homosexual or bisexual celebrities, joining the likes of LANGSTON HUGHES, ETHEL WATERS, BESSIE SMITH, and MA RAINEY. Though Bessie Smith may have been the "Queen of the Blues," Bentley was known as the "Brown Bomber of Sophisticated Songs."

In Harlem, Bentley found acceptance among the participants in the "sporting life," which favored gambling, rent parties, female impersonators, sex shows, drugs, and alcohol. She began performing at the sporting life events, quickly becoming extremely popular. It was not uncommon to find Bentley, a talented pianist, playing and singing all night long at a piano. Writing to COUNTÉE CULLEN, a friend said of Bentley, "When Gladys sings 'St. James Infirmary,' it makes you weep your heart out" (Duberman, 324).

Bentley's first major job was at the Mad House, which later became Barbara's Exclusive Club. Starting at thirty-five dollars a week, Bentley soon received a hundred dollars a week when Carl Van Vechten and others began crowding into the clubs to see her perform. As Bentley's popularity increased, she moved on to clubs such as the Cotton Club, Connie's Inn, and the Clam House. Weighing anywhere from two hundred and fifty to three hundred

pounds she dressed in a tuxedo with tails and top hat, and her manly style of dress quickly became a feature of her shows. She was even more famous for her raunchy lyrics, full of sexual innuendos that she interpolated into the popular songs of the day. Bentley was so convincing as a man that the artist ROMARE BEARDEN thought that she was a female impersonator. In fact, she did sometimes perform under the name "Bobby Minton." Bentley was one of the few openly lesbian performers, flirting outrageously with the women in her audiences.

In 1928 Bentley began recording for Okeh Records, eventually making a total of eight records. Some of her more famous songs include "How Long, How Long Blues," "Worried Blues," "How Much Can I Stand?" and "Moanful Wailin' Blues." Bentley was at the height of her popularity during the 1920s and 1930s. In 1931 she was celebrated in Blair Nile's novel *Strange Brother*, being the basis of the character Sybil. Carl Van Vechten's book *Parties* and Clement Woods's book *Deep River* were reported to have characters based on the larger-than-life Gladys Bentley (Faderman, 1991). It was also in the early 1930s that Bentley married her white female lover in a much-publicized civil ceremony in New Jersey.

Advantages of the show business lifestyle for lesbians was the ability to earn a decent living, limit contact with men, and work within a predominantly female social world. During the early 1930s Bentley moved on to the New York jazz scene, performing primarily at the Ubangi Club on Fifty-second Street. By the late 1930s the Depression and Harlem's loss of fashionable status became contributing factors in her decision to move to California. There she lived with and cared for her elderly mother and sang at such gay clubs as Hollywood's Rose Room, Mona's in San Francisco, and Joaquin's El Rancho in Los Angeles. She began experiencing problems with the police while at Joaquin's El Rancho and at Mona's in early 1940. The clubs were required to obtain special permits that allowed Bentley to perform her act in men's clothing instead of women's clothing (*Gay and Lesbian Biography*, 1997). By the 1950s and the McCarthy era, Bentley was forced to perform in women's clothing and came under the scrutiny of the U.S. House Committee on Un-American Activities because of her same-sex marriage in New Jersey.

In 1945 Bentley made five recordings for the Excelsior label, including *Thrill Me till I Get My Fill*, *Find Out What He Likes*, and *Notoriety Papa*. She also worked with the Washboard Serenaders on the Victor label. In a 1952 interview with *Ebony* magazine, Bentley claimed to have overcome her lesbianism through the ingestion of female hormones and announced that she was happily married to a male newspaper columnist named J. T. Gibson. When interviewed, Gibson denied that a wedding had taken place. Bentley was married for a brief time to a cook named Charles Roberts. Bentley was forty-five and Roberts twenty-nine; on the marriage certificate she stated that she was thirty-five.

During the 1950s Bentley performed twice on Groucho Marx's live television show *You Bet Your Life*. Bentley also recorded a record for the Flame label. It was at this time that she became an active member in a Hollywood church called the Temple of Love in Christ. In the late 1950s Bentley began to study to become a minister, but she died during an influenza epidemic before she was able to become ordained. In 1992 Rosetta Records, a small feminist label, reissued five of Bentley's songs on a disc titled *Mean Mothers: Independent Women Blues, Volume 1*. In 2004 Sony Music released a DVD set titled *You Bet Your Life: The Best Episodes*, which includes a 1958 performance of Bentley singing "Them There Eyes."

FURTHER READING

Duberman, Martin Bauml. *Hidden from the History: Reclaiming the Gay and Lesbian Past* (1989).

Faderman, Lillian. *Odd Girls and Twilight Lovers: A History of Lesbian Life in Twentieth-Century America* (1991).

Rodger, Gillian. *GLBTQ: An Encyclopedia of Gay, Lesbian, Bisexual, Transgender & Queer Culture* (2002) Available at http://www.glbtq.com.

Tyrkus, Michael, ed. "Gladys Bentley (1907–1960): Classic Blues Singer," *St. James Press Gay and Lesbian Biography* (1997).

ANNE K. DRISCOLL

Berksteiner, Constance (5 July 1900–12 June 1999), singer, music educator, and choral director, was born in Sandfly, Georgia, a tiny hamlet of Savannah, one of thirteen children born to Daphne and Daniel Berksteiner. Her father worked as a carpenter, and her mother took in washing to make ends meet. In addition to the influence of her family, her early years were influenced by her church, the Speedwell Episcopal Church, and its school, Haven Home. It was at Speedwell and Haven Home that Constance received, first, religious instruction and, second, her introduction to academia.

Through her association with the church, she received her first scholarship, which enabled her to attend and graduate from the Boylan Home High School in Jacksonville, Florida. The specific point at which Constance realized she could sing is unrecorded. There was the singing in the church as a child and in the choir in her high school years. Perhaps the realization came when one of her teachers at Boylan took her to a program where she was one of the singers. The response to her song was so overwhelming that Constance asked her teacher, "What went wrong?" The teacher told her that the audience wanted an encore. "It means that they like your singing and want you to sing again." She received a second scholarship from the North West Indiana Conference of the Methodist Church, which led to her attending the Iowa National Training College in Des Moines, Iowa, earning a degree in Religious Education. Throughout her life, Constance emphasized the importance of education for advancement in life. Armed with her new degree, she taught at the Sager Brown School in Baldwin, Louisiana. Sager Brown was the only orphanage for black children at that time. The school offered little opportunities to advance, so Constance felt the call of the music world and moved to New York City, where she would spend the rest of her life.

In New York she began to make contacts with teachers and coaches who would push an aspiring young artist. Through her older sister, she met a Mrs. Howell, who helped arrange recitals at local churches, including Abyssinian Baptist Church in Harlem. Upon hearing her sing, Abyssinian's pastor, ADAM CLAYTON POWELL SR. was so impressed that he gave her a vase of flowers, water and all. She had learned the importance of training in her early years in order to be successful. She realized that to keep up with the pace in New York she had to study, and she studied with many teachers and coaches. She would attend 3:00 and 5:30 P.M. concerts at Town Hall and then go over to Carnegie Hall for the 8:30 P.M. concert. Opportunities began to open up for blacks, and the concert halls opened for them to perform. In 1948, Constance made her concert debut at Town Hall to great acclaim. She was described by one critic as an "exceptional artist of great talent." RAOUL ABDUL, music critic of the *New York Amsterdam News* described her as "The Grand Dame of the New York Music World." An appearance with the NBC Orchestra, in a coast-to-coast broadcast was a highlight in her stellar career. In 1952, she became a member of the National Association of Negro Musicians, Inc.

(NANM) as a state organizer, national board member, eastern regional director, and national second vice president, director of branches. A branch was named in her honor, the Collins-Berksteiner Branch. Constance served as president of the Opera Ebony Committee, founded in 1974 in New York, for many years and in 1990 was made president emeritus. She was also a member of the Queens Chapter, Delta Zeta Chapter of Zeta Phi Beta Sorority. When she no longer performed on stage, she turned her gifts and talents to teaching and established two vocal studios and formed the Berksteiner Chorale, which was in demand for many years. She was interested in community affairs and served as head of the Department of Music for Neighborhood Board #1 Schools in Harlem.

Constance Berksteiner was a member of Salem United Methodist Church in Harlem for seventy-one years. She joined the church shortly after she came to New York. She served the church in a number of positions including Sunday School Superintendent and teacher, director of the Chancel Choir, organizer of the Welcome Committee and chairperson of the Music Committee. The Methodist Church was a strong part of her life. Her favorite song, "Let All My Life Be Music," by Charles Gilbert Stross, was sung at her memorial at Salem United Methodist Church on 17 June 1999.

FURTHER READING
Archives E. Azalia Hackley Collection, Detroit Public Library, Detroit, Michigan.
Archives, the Schomburg Library. New York Public Library, New York, New York.
Obituary: *Daily Times,* Savannah, 18 June 1999.
This entry is taken from the *American National Biography* and is published here with the permission of the American Council of Learned Societies.

LOIS BELLAMY

Bernhardt, Clyde (11 July 1905–20 May 1986), jazz trombonist and singer, was born Clyde Edric Barnhardt in Gold Hill, North Carolina, the son of Washington Michael Barnhardt, a miner, and Elizabeth Mauney. When Clyde was a child, he added Barron to his name because his grandmother in slavery had been lent to a family named Barron who treated her kindly. He changed the spelling of his surname in 1930 on the advice of a psychic. Thus his full name became Clyde Edric Barron Bernhardt or Clyde E. B. Bernhardt.

In 1912, after his father suffered a heart attack and left mining, Bernhardt helped to peddle goods from a wagon. The family moved to New Hope (later absorbed into Badin), North Carolina, and in 1915 his father died. Bernhardt attended school for three months each year while holding various jobs, including work at Alcoa Aluminum in 1918. The following year his mother took the family to Harrisburg, Pennsylvania, and then to Steeltown, Pennsylvania. Bernhardt returned to Badin in November 1919 with the intent of resuming work at Alcoa, but instead he secured a better job, becoming a messenger boy for Western Union. After rejoining his mother and siblings in Steeltown in April 1921, he quit school, having reached eighth grade. He held various jobs over the next several years.

Although Bernhardt had been attracted to music in his preschool years, only in 1922 did he purchase a trombone and begin serious studies with teachers in Pennsylvania and Ohio, when his mother relocated the family and he moved out on his own. By 1925 he was working professionally, and in 1928, after affiliations with several little-known bandleaders, Bernhardt joined the Whitman Sisters—Alice Whitman and her sisters Essie, Mable, and Alberta—in their show in Harlem and toured with them until June 1929. In March 1931 he joined the cornetist KING OLIVER's band, touring for eight months. With Oliver's encouragement Bernhardt began doubling as a blues singer. In 1931 he thought that he had married a woman named Barbara, known as "Bobby" (maiden name unknown), only to discover a few months later that she was already married. He never attempted marriage again.

Bernhardt joined Marion Hardy's Alabamians in New York City in November 1931. He worked with Billy Fowler's band from September 1932 to April 1933, a gig that included jobs accompanying the pianist and singer FATS WALLER. Bernhardt was a member of Vernon Andrade's dance orchestra from 1934 to 1937, and in September 1934 he made his first recordings, "Ain't It Nice?" and "Functionizin," with Alex Hill's band. As a member of the pianist Edgar Hayes's big band from February 1937, Bernhardt performed in Europe in 1938 and made annual tours accompanying the dancer BILL ROBINSON; he also worked with the pianist HORACE HENDERSON's big band in 1941.

After leaving Hayes, Bernhardt toured briefly with Waller's big band, but he was bored by the lack of challenging parts or solos. In September 1942 he joined the pianist JAY MCSHANN's big band, touring until July 1943. He played in the tenor saxophonist Cecil Scott's band at the Ubangi Club in

New York City for five months. In 1944 he joined the orchestra of the pianist LUIS RUSSELL, who featured Bernhardt as a singer, most notably in well-received performances at the Apollo Theater in Harlem. Bernhardt suffered from bronchitis and was obliged to quit Russell's band in October. For the remainder of 1944 he worked in the pianist CLAUDE HOPKINS's band at the Club Zanzibar in New York. He joined the Bascomb Brothers' orchestra in 1945, and he spent the first four months of 1946 with Scott again.

From 1946 to 1948 Bernhardt for the first time led his own group, the Blue Blazers. He rejoined Russell from 1948 to 1951 while also working with other bands. In 1952 he began recording under the pseudonym Ed Barron, and he had a hit rhythm and blues song with his own "Cracklin' Bread," but he was cheated out of royalties by the record company. From 1952 to 1970 he played in Joe Garland's dance orchestra. During the course of this lengthy affiliation he resumed day work and general studies. He passed the high school equivalency examination in 1963 and then took a job as a custodian in Newark, New Jersey.

Interest in Bernhardt's musical activities was rekindled by a series of articles published by Derrick Stewart-Baxter in 1967 and 1968 and by a recording that Stewart-Baxter produced in the latter year and issued in 1971. Bernhardt retired as a custodian in February 1972 and vacationed for a few weeks in England, where he was treated as a musical celebrity. He worked with the bassist Hayes Alvis's band later that year, shortly before Alvis died. Bernhardt recorded his own albums *Blues and Jazz from Harlem* (1972) and *More Blues and Jazz from Harlem* (1973), the latter with the Harlem Blues and Jazz Band of which he eventually became the sole leader. A heart attack interrupted his new career in 1974, but he recovered and resumed playing and singing, touring Europe annually from 1976 to 1979 with his band. He spent his final years from 1979 onward as a member of drummer Barry Martyn's Legends of Jazz. Bernhardt died in Newark.

Though Bernhardt was not an important jazz or rhythm and blues performer, he is important for his detailed, levelheaded reminiscences of dozens of African American entertainers, including valuable essays on less well-known performers such as the Whitman Sisters, Hardy and his Alabamians, Andrade, Scott, and the Bascomb Brothers, among others, as well as important jazz musicians such as McShann and Russell. Bernhardt's several published recollections of a forceful, responsible, talented, shrewd King Oliver in late career provide an especially welcome antidote to the romantic but pathetic portrait of Oliver popularized in the famous early jazz book *Jazzmen* (1939).

FURTHER READING
Bernhardt, Clyde E. B. "Talking about King Oliver: An Oral History Excerpt," *Annual Review of Jazz Studies* 1 (1982).
Bernhardt, Clyde E. B., with Sheldon Harris. *I Remember: Eighty Years of Black Entertainment, Big Bands, and the Blues* (1986).
Gaster, Gilbert. "Clyde Bernhardt," *Storyville*, no. 44 (1 Dec. 1972).
Stewart-Baxter, Derricks, with Clyde E. B. Bernhardt. "The Clyde Bernhardt Story," *Jazz Journal* 20 (Sept.–Oct. 1967) and 21 (Jan.–Feb. 1968).
Obituary: *New York Times*, 31 May 1986.
This entry is taken from the *American National Biography* and is published here with the permission of the American Council of Learned Societies.

BARRY KERNFELD

Berry, Chu (13 Sept. 1908–30 Oct. 1941), tenor saxophonist, was born Leon Brown Berry in Wheeling, West Virginia. His parents' names and occupations are unknown. He played alto saxophone in high school and at West Virginia State College, which he attended for three years.

In 1929 Sammy Stewart hired Berry to play tenor in his Chicago band. In 1930 Berry moved to New York City and worked in several groups, including bands led by Benny Carter, Charlie Johnson, Spike Hughes, and Teddy Hill. An early highlight was a May 1933 recording for Hughes that included COLEMAN HAWKINS, with the two tenor giants striving to surpass each other in tunes like "Fanfare." Berry recorded with a variety of groups during the second half of the 1930s, including those led by Gene Krupa, Benny Goodman, RED ALLEN, HOT LIPS PAGE, and Wingy Manone. His superb work with various TEDDY WILSON groups is typified by his beautiful solo in BILLIE HOLIDAY's 1935 recording of "Twenty-Four Hours a Day," with Wilson's orchestra. Berry also played and recorded with the Count Basie Orchestra for a short while, soloing to particularly good effect in the 1939 Basie classic, "Lady Be Good."

Berry recorded much of his most important work with the FLETCHER HENDERSON orchestra in 1935 and 1936 and with CAB CALLOWAY from 1937 to 1941. He established his reputation with Henderson; Berry wrote "Christopher Columbus," one of the band's biggest hits, and played propulsive solos on pieces like "Sing, Sing, Sing." With Calloway he soloed in practically every recorded performance by the band and was featured more often than any other player; he swapped arrangements with other groups, such as the CHICK WEBB band, and was personally responsible for keeping the group steeped in good music. Examples of Berry's stellar work can be found in tunes like "Ghost of a Chance," "Lonesome Nights," and "Bye Bye Blues," and especially in his near-perfect solo in the 1939 recording of "Pluckin' the Bass."

While starring with the Calloway band, Berry also performed and recorded widely with his own groups. He recorded several sessions with his close friend ROY ELDRIDGE. Among the best of these sides are four outstanding tunes that the two musicians waxed for Commodore Records in 1938 (under the name Chu Berry and His Little Jazz Ensemble), in which Berry and Eldridge proved perfect foils for each other, particularly at the fast tempos at which both excelled. The Berry version of "Body and Soul" recorded at this time remains one of the few to rival the classic Coleman Hawkins rendition.

Berry's short life and compressed recording career provide a particularly accessible portrait of his playing style. From the beginning Hawkins loomed as Berry's major influence—hardly an unusual situation, since Hawkins did so for nearly every other tenor player until LESTER YOUNG appeared. But Berry was more successful in carving out a clear stylistic niche for himself than any of the others. He had a less rounded, less "voluptuous" sound than Hawkins had (though it was fuller than Young's) and was not as melodically imaginative as the older master, but Berry also had "a more emotive vibrato and a strange crying sound in his frequently-used upper register" (Carr, 40). He possessed a propulsive sense of swing and excelled at fast tempos that showed "an unerring sense of time" and a sophisticated "melodic-harmonic conception." On ballads Berry often played in double tempo with a wide, fast vibrato to compensate for his less warm tone. Toward the end of his life he grew less bombastic and more reflective in his ballad playing. Ballads such as "A Ghost of a Chance" and "Lonesome Nights," both recorded with the Calloway band in 1940, and "On the Sunny Side of the Street," from his own 1941 session with Chu Berry and His Jazz Ensemble,

illustrate this more subtle, sophisticated approach to balladry.

When Berry died in a car accident in Conneaut, Ohio, Calloway said that it was "like losing a brother, someone I had joked with and hollered at. There was a quiet around the band for weeks and we left his chair empty" (Carr, 40). Berry had what some described as a "tubby and chuckling" personality. His friendship with Eldridge is legendary. The two often played together at after-hours jam sessions, taking on all comers and cutting them mercilessly. Musically Berry just seemed to be coming into his own. A few months before Berry's death, Hawkins ranked him among his favorite tenor players, second only to BEN WEBSTER. Though long all but forgotten, Berry's music made something of a comeback in the 1970s and 1980s, influencing younger players like Frank Lowe.

FURTHER READING

Carr, Ian, Digby Fairweather, and Brian Priestley, eds. *Jazz: The Essential Companion* (1987).

Schuller, Gunther. *The Swing Era: The Development of Jazz, 1930–1945* (1989).

Obituary: *New York Times*, 31 Oct. 1941.

DISCOGRAPHY

Morgenstern, Dan. *The Complete Commodore Jazz Recordings, Vol. 1* (Mosaic, 1988).

Piazza, Tom. *The Guide to Classic Recorded Jazz* (1995).

This entry is taken from the *American National Biography* and is published here with the permission of the American Council of Learned Societies.

RONALD P. DUFOUR

Berry, Chuck (18 Oct. 1926–), singer, songwriter, and guitarist, was born Charles Edward Anderson Berry in St. Louis, Missouri, the fourth of six children of Henry William Berry, a carpenter and handyman, and Martha Bell Banks. The industrious Henry Berry instilled in his son a hunger for material success and a prodigious capacity for hard work, traits that were not entirely apparent in Berry as a youth. Martha Berry, a skilled pianist and accomplished singer, passed on to her son her love for music. By the time he was a teenager, however, Berry preferred jazz, blues, and the "beautiful harmony of country music" to his mother's Baptist hymns (Berry, 14).

In 1944 Berry and two friends hatched an ill-considered plan to drive across the country to

California. They soon ran out of money and committed a series of armed robberies in an attempt to return home. All three were arrested, convicted, and given ten-year sentences. In prison, Berry began to take music seriously, cofounding a gospel quartet and a rhythm and blues band popular with both black and white inmates. The quartet sang during services in the prison chapel and met with such success that prison officials allowed the group to sing for African American church congregations in Kansas City and St. Louis.

Berry was released on parole in 1947, and returned to St. Louis. In 1948 he married Themetta Suggs, with whom he had four children. While working menial day jobs, he studied guitar with Ira Harris, who laid the foundation of his guitar-playing style. The recordings of the guitarists CHARLIE CHRISTIAN, T-BONE WALKER, and Carl Hogan, who played in LOUIS JORDAN's band, further shaped his sound. NAT KING COLE, MUDDY WATERS, and BIG JOE TURNER were among the singers whose diverse styles he sometimes emulated. Berry's taste, although eclectic, was firmly rooted in both the urban blues and rhythm and blues of the era. By 1952 Berry was playing regularly in local St. Louis clubs and had developed a reputation as a capable sideman, whose flamboyant stage presence and willingness to indulge in "little gimmicks," such as singing country and western songs, delighted audiences. Among those who noticed the rising bluesman was the pianist JOHNNIE JOHNSON, leader of a popular trio whose repertoire included blues, rhythm and blues, and popular songs. When one of Johnson's sideman was indisposed, Johnson asked Berry to sit in with the band at the Cosmopolitan Club in East St. Louis.

Audiences at the Cosmopolitan Club responded enthusiastically to Berry and the club's owner immediately asked Johnson to hire him permanently. Johnson readily agreed, explaining that Berry's showmanship "brought something to the group that was missin'" (Pegg, 25). Berry's performance with Johnson's trio on New Year's Eve 1952 marked the beginning of a remarkable musical collaboration that produced "Roll Over Beethoven" (1956), "School Day" (1957), and "Rock and Roll Music" (1957), which, more than any other songs, defined the new musical genre of rock and roll. Although Johnson helped to shape the melodies, and his powerful left hand supplied much of the songs' rhythmic drive, the men were not equal partners. The lyrics were Berry's alone, and he was the

Chuck Berry, performing his "duck walk" on stage, 4 April 1980. (AP Images.)

sole author of songs such as "Maybellene" (1955), his first hit, and "Johnny B. Goode" (1958), one of the most honored songs in rock and roll history.

Within a few years, Berry's role in the trio overshadowed Johnson's, and he began to look beyond St. Louis's African American nightclubs toward a wider audience. In 1955 he visited Chicago, hoping to build on his local success by signing a recording contract. The blues musician Muddy Waters, whom Berry met after a concert, directed him to Leonard Chess, who ran a small independent record company. Like many of the era's independent labels, Chess Records produced the African American music that major labels tended to ignore. Chess agreed to record "Maybellene," a song similar to the country and western novelties that Berry often sang, and "Wee Wee Hours," a standard blues tune.

"Maybellene" fired Leonard Chess's imagination. He knew that young white consumers, bored with the music that major labels produced, were searching for something new. Many had gravitated toward rhythm and blues, which, beyond its musical excellence, possessed the lure of the forbidden.

Independent labels courted this emerging market, and disc jockeys, such as Alan Freed, who began calling the music "rock and roll," expanded it. Chess believed that "Maybellene," with its fusion of country and western and rhythm and blues, was the perfect song for the times. It proved to be a dazzling success.

Like most of Berry's songs, "Maybellene" sold well to both whites and blacks. Like all of his songs, it was an exercise in "signifyin'," drawing on African American vernacular forms to speak, simultaneously, in more than one voice. While whites heard something both familiar and unexpected—a frenetic homage to country and western—African Americans heard an affectionate parody. The song reached number two on *Billboard* magazine's pop chart (the "white" chart) and number one on the rhythm and blues chart (the "black" chart). "Maybellene" amalgamated black and white musical styles, exalted cars, girls, and—implicitly—sex, and moved the electric guitar to center stage, creating a musical template that generations of rock and roll musicians would follow.

Determined to repeat the success of "Maybellene," Berry began the process of transforming himself from a competent bluesman into a brilliant rock and roller. With one eye on the cash register and the other on his growing legions of young white fans, he wrote songs that were, above all, marketable. Although producing great art was the least of his concerns, many of the songs that Berry wrote between 1955 and the early 1960s were nothing less than miniature masterpieces. His lyrics blended irony, parody, and literal-minded observation into a coherent whole. His music, while grounded in rhythm and blues, continued to draw on country and western and other popular forms.

In late 1959 and early 1960, Berry's string of successes ended when he was arraigned on two counts of having violated the White Slave Traffic Act (Mann Act), a federal statute. The federal prosecutor in St. Louis alleged that Berry had, on two separate occasions during concert tours, transported Joan Mathis Bates, a white woman in her late teens, and Janice Norine Escalanti, a fourteen-year-old Native American girl, across state lines for immoral purposes. When the case involving Bates went to trial, both she and Berry admitted to having had a consensual sexual relationship, and Bates added that she was in love with him. The jury acquitted Berry, noting that the charges involved a voluntary relationship between two adults.

The Escalanti case, however, ended in a conviction. The jury accepted Escalanti's testimony that she and Berry had engaged in consensual sexual relations on several occasions. The fact that the relationship was consensual had no impact on the charges; prosecutors were only required to prove that, after transporting Escalanti across state lines, Berry's behavior had been "immoral." While Berry denied that he had had a sexual relationship with Escalanti, he proved a nervous and unconvincing witness. The behavior of trial judge George Moore, who repeatedly interjected remarks of a racial nature into the proceedings, compounded Berry's difficulties. Berry appealed his conviction, arguing that Moore's hostile and prejudicial conduct had deprived him of a fair trial. A federal appellate court agreed, and sent the case back to the district court. However, in 1961 Berry was convicted a second time, and entered federal prison in 1962.

By the time Berry was released in 1963, his music had begun to sound old-fashioned. Even though songs that he wrote in prison, such as "Promised Land" (1964), rank among his best, his career as a recording artist was waning. Berry enjoyed a brief revival in 1972, when he scored his first number one hit on the pop chart with the trifling, double-entendre–filled "My Ding-A-Ling." Although he rarely recorded after this point, Berry continued to tour, often with great success, well into his seventies.

In 2000 Johnny Johnson sued Berry, claiming that he had never received credit for cowriting many of the songs that Berry recorded in the 1950s and that he had thereby been defrauded of millions of dollars in royalties. Parts of the case were dismissed in 2001, with the court ruling that it would be impossible for Johnson to prove that he had cowritten the songs. The court also noted that because so much time had passed, many potential witnesses had died and that the memories of others had faded. In addition, Johnson had admitted in the *St. Louis Post-Dispatch* that he spent much of the 1950s in an alcoholic fog, rendering his testimony suspect. Although the precise nature of the relationship between the two men is likely to remain disputed, Johnson's role was almost certainly that of an arranger of Berry's musical ideas.

In his later years, Berry accrued honors that acknowledged his central role in reshaping popular music. He is a member of the Blues Foundation Hall of Fame, the National Academy of Popular Music Songwriter's Hall of Fame, and, in 1986 he was among the first artists inducted into the Rock and Roll Hall of Fame.

FURTHER READING

Berry, Chuck. *Chuck Berry: The Autobiography* (1987).

Collis, John. *Chuck Berry: The Biography* (2002).

Pegg, Bruce. *Brown Eyed Handsome Man: The Life and Hard Times of Chuck Berry, an Unauthorized Biography* (2002).

DISCOGRAPHY

Rothwell, Fred. *Long Distance Information: Chuck Berry's Recorded Legacy* (2001).

JOHN EDWIN MASON

Berry, Halle (14 Aug. 1966–), film actress and model, was born Halle Maria Berry in Cleveland, Ohio, the daughter of Jerome Berry, a hospital attendant, and Judith Hawkins, a psychiatric nurse. Her father, an alcoholic, abandoned the family when she was four, leaving her mother to raise Halle and her sister Heidi, first in predominantly black inner-city Cleveland and later in that city's white suburbs. Berry's childhood was troubled, in part because of the economic hardship of growing

Halle Berry, at the induction ceremony of her star on the Hollywood Walk of Fame in Los Angeles, 3 April 2007. (AP Images.)

up in a single-parent household. But as the light-skinned child of an interracial couple—her mother was white, her father African American—she also endured racial taunts from both blacks and whites. Fellow students called her "zebra" and on one occasion left an Oreo cookie in her school locker. Berry never had any doubts about her own identity, however, and states on her Web site that her "race" is African American and English.

An extremely shy teenager, Berry craved acceptance from her peers and worked energetically to be the most active and popular young woman at her high school. As a cheerleader, editor of the school newspaper, an honor student, and class president, she appeared to have succeeded, but when fellow students accused her of stuffing the ballot box in the voting for prom queen, she was forced to share the title with a white student. Although this reversal suggested to Berry that whites would not accept a standard of beauty that included people of color, her success in beauty pageants suggested otherwise. By the mid-1980s an African American woman as flawlessly beautiful as Halle Berry could win Miss Teen Ohio and Miss Ohio. As a runner-up in the 1986 Miss U.S.A. pageant, Berry, then a student at Cleveland's Cuyahoga Community College traveled to London to represent the United States in Miss World, the leading international beauty contest. Although Miss Trinidad & Tobago won the title, Berry placed sixth and created a sensation by appearing in the "national costume" segment of the pageant wearing a skimpy bikini with strands of beads and shooting stars. The outfit was purported to express "America's advancement in space," but it drew the ire of other contestants such as Miss Holland, who wore the traditionally bulky and much less revealing Dutch costume with clogs. Berry found participation in beauty pageants an ideal preparation for a career in Hollywood, since it taught her how to lose and not be devastated. Considered too short at five feet six inches to be a runway model, she won bit parts in the television sitcoms *Amen* and *A Different World*, but she was rejected at her first audition for a major television role in *Charlie's Angels '88*. She did win a regular spot as a teenage model in 1989's short-lived sitcom on ABC, *Living Dolls*, but increasingly found that her stunning looks and beauty pageant past kept her from landing the serious acting roles she desired. A minor but critically praised role as a crack addict in SPIKE LEE's *Jungle Fever* (1991) signaled a change in her fortunes. That performance marked Berry's first, but by no means last, effort to overcome critics, including Lee himself initially, who could not envision her as anything less than glamorous. In preparation for the role, she interviewed drug addicts and refused to bathe for ten days before shooting. Her next role, as a radio producer on the prime-time soap opera *Knots Landing*, was much less gritty, but it did ensure greater exposure and led to a series of prominent appearances in the film comedies *Strictly Business* and *Boomerang* (1992) and the television miniseries of ALEX HALEY's *Queen* (1993).

In the 1990s Berry became one of the most bankable actors in Hollywood, appearing in popular, though not critically acclaimed movies such as *Fatherhood* (1993), *The Flintstones* (1994), and *Executive Decision* (1996). She received favorable reviews for these parts, but the praise—the film critic Roger Ebert described her as "so warm and charming you want to cuddle her"—may have reinforced the view in Hollywood that she was best suited to light roles. At the same time, Berry's beauty and poise earned her an MTV award in 1993 for "most desirable female," an assessment shared by *People* magazine, which since 1992 has consistently listed her among the most beautiful and best dressed women in the world, and by the manufacturers of Revlon makeup, who named her their main spokesmodel in 1996. In an age of celebrity, when fashion has come to mean as much to the corporate world and consumers as films and television, such accolades have greatly enhanced Berry's fame, fortune, and clout. Indeed, in 2002 the *Wall Street Journal* reported that the financially ailing Revlon Company was relying on a line of Halle Berry Cosmetics as the primary means of halting its plummeting profits and share price.

Berry's growing fame and celebrity came at the price of endless media scrutiny. Her 1993 marriage to David Justice, a right fielder for the Atlanta Braves, delighted the tabloids, who printed scores of articles on the glamorous newlyweds, but the couple's troubled relationship and acrimonious divorce three years later was like manna from heaven for the *National Enquirer* and the *Star*. Though she continued to play an increasing variety of film roles, including a drug-addicted mother forced to give up her child to adoption by white parents in *Losing Isaiah* (1995), Berry's personal life provided greater publicity than her movies. In February 2000 a judge placed her on three years probation and ordered her to pay $13,500 in fines and perform 200 hours community service for leaving the scene of a traffic accident. Berry enjoyed better press in 2001, when she married the singer Eric Benet

and became stepmother to his daughter, India. However, Berry and Benet separated in 2003, and in January 2005, the couple divorced. In 2008 Berry had a daughter Nahla Ariela Aubry with Gabriel Aubry, a French Canadian model. Berry and Aubry separated in 2010.

Her first leading role, as DOROTHY DANDRIDGE in the television drama *Introducing Dorothy Dandridge* (1999), gave Berry the critical success she had long craved and won her an Emmy Award for outstanding lead actress. As a longtime admirer of Dandridge, Berry co-produced the biopic and lobbied hard to publicize this HBO film about an African American actress renowned for her poise and beauty who suffered from depression and several unhappy and tempestuous relationships. Although Berry never faced the full force of Jim Crow segregation, she strongly identified with Dandridge's determination to broaden the diversity of roles open to women of color.

The parallel with Dandridge continued with Berry's performance in *Monster's Ball* (2001), when she became the first black woman to win the Academy Award for best actress; in 1955, nearly half a century earlier, Dandridge had been the first African American nominated in that category. Some critics ridiculed the speech in which Berry accepted her award in the name of "every nameless, faceless woman of color that now has a chance because this door tonight has been opened." They noted that actresses like HATTIE McDANIEL and Dandridge, let alone thousands of unsung women in the civil rights movement, had already given that door an almighty push. Yet Berry was hardly the first Oscar-winning actress—or actor, for that matter—to be overcome by gushing hyperbole in receiving their profession's highest award. Others, including the members of the Academy, praised her portrayal of a poor southern black woman struggling to raise a son after the execution of her husband, and her complex relationship with one of his white executioners. In *the Nation* MICHAEL ERIC DYSON, a prominent black academic, lauded Berry's bravery in using her speech to speak up for "ordinary brothers and sisters."

Following her Oscar triumph, Berry became one of the highest paid actresses in Hollywood. She starred as Storm in the critically and commercially successful *X-Men* trilogy and had a voiceover role in the animated hit *Robots*. In the James Bond film *Die Another Day*, Berry revived memories of Ursula Andress with her role as Giacinta "Jinx" Johnson. Less successful was Berry's eponymous role in *Catwoman*

(2004). Widely panned, Berry's performance earned her the unfortunate worst actress award in the 2005 Golden Raspberry Foundation Awards, though she displayed self-deprecation and a great sense of humor in turning up to collect her "Razzie."

Berry's breakthrough in winning an Academy Award and the sharp criticisms of her acceptance speech captured the ambiguities facing prominent African Americans at the beginning of the twenty-first century. Black American talents and achievements were recognized and rewarded by America's dominant culture as never before, yet that same culture continued to debate those successes in highly racialized ways.

Although her motion picture appearances were limited as she focused on her family between 2006 and 2009, Berry appeared in *X-Men: The Last Stand* (2006), *Perfect Stranger* (2007), and *Things We Lost in the Fire* (2007). In 2010 she made a return to film in the psychological drama, *Frankie and Alice*, in which she portrayed a go-go dancer with dissociative identity disorder. For that role, she was nominated for a Best Actress Golden Globe, and won both the NAACP image award for Outstanding Actress in a Motion Picture and the Best Actress Award from the African American Film Critics Association.

FURTHER READING

Dyson, Michael Eric. "Oscar Opens the Door," *Nation*, 15 Apr. 2002.

Farley, Christopher J. *Introducing Halle Berry* (2002).

Norment, Lynn. "Halle's Big Year," *Ebony* (Nov. 2002).

STEVEN J. NIVEN

Berry, Lawrence S. (?–1871), political activist and journalist, was a slave who belonged to an influential antebellum lawyer from South Alabama. Little else is known about his life prior to the Civil War; however, it is known that during the early years of the Civil War, Berry was sent to toil in a hazardous saltworks that the Confederacy operated in Clarke County. Berry survived three years of intense labor there, and he emerged from the ordeal more experienced, as well as more militant, than many of the other African Americans he knew. After moving to the Gulf Coast city of Mobile, Berry became a member of the vanguard of black leaders who would help the state's black masses achieve legal and psychological freedom in the aftermath of the Civil War.

The Union victory and the federal effort to alter the legal status of black people deepened white Alabamians' resistance to change. State lawmakers were particularly devoted to preserving the status quo. In September 1865 delegates to a state constitutional convention adopted a body of laws that voided secession, repudiated the Confederate debt, and ratified section one of the Thirteenth Amendment, abolishing slavery. (Section two, which gave congressmen the power to enforce the amendment through appropriate legislation, was rejected.) Delegates also decided that representatives to Alabama's legislature would serve two-year terms and that only white men would be able to become legislators. A census for 1866 was approved, but representation would be based on the calculated population of white Alabamians only. Henceforth blacks would be allowed to serve as witnesses in open-court criminal cases that involved whites, which existing state law prevented, but marriage between whites and blacks would be forbidden. And because of a split between wealthy white planters (who thought that they could control black voters) and small merchants and farmers (who opposed black suffrage), a proposal for universal manhood suffrage was tabled.

On the heels of the constitutional convention, Berry and E. C. Branch, a white Republican from the North, organized a black convention to encourage political activism. The conference was held in Mobile from 20 to 22 November, with almost sixty black men in attendance. Most of them were ministers from the central and southern regions of the state, and E. S. Winn, an African Methodist Episcopal Zion (AMEZ) Church elder, presided. He and the other black delegates realized that that their newly acquired freedom presented tremendous opportunities and obligations. This, they agreed, was a task that they could achieve with God's help. The men therefore resolved to work hard to promote peace, goodwill, and friendship among all persons (especially the southern whites with whom their lot was cast), but they refused to relinquish any human or civil right. Over the next two years, Berry's influence grew. As a traveling (later general) agent and board member of the *Mobile Nationalist*, Alabama's first unofficial Republican newspaper, he encouraged black people to utilize the legal privileges that they had been afforded by the Thirteenth Amendment, the Civil Rights Act of 1866, and similar measures. A prominent AMEZ layman and one of Mobile's most respected union, or Loyal Leaguer, organizers, Berry led movements to integrate the port city's police force, municipal boards, and streetcars. When white carriers refused to treat black passengers fairly,

Berry utilized the federal civil rights act and filed charges against company executives.

Another statewide freemen's convention, led by Branch and Berry, was held on 4 March 1867, just two days after the First Reconstruction Act was passed. Among the matters addressed by convention leaders were white domination and black voters' supposed ignorance. In an extremely concise statement, Berry proclaimed that black Alabamians were smart enough to understand their newfound rights and privileges and were determined to enjoy them. Berry reiterated this point when he and Branch held a third statewide freedmen's conference from 1 to 4 May 1867.

Berry served on the resolutions committee, where he and his companions supported integrated public schools as well as relief programs for elderly and homeless people. The committee congratulated the Freedmen's Bureau for its work on behalf of black Alabamians, asked the central government to address the abuses that former slave owners and federal soldiers were carrying out against free persons, and drafted a resolution calling each delegate a member to the state and national Republican parties and thus eligible for any privilege that membership or federal law afforded. Specifically, the delegates wanted the same rights and privileges that white Republicans enjoyed, including holding public office, sitting on juries, riding on public conveyances, and sitting at public tables and places of amusement alongside other lawful citizens. In one of the strongest political pronouncements that any group of black Alabamians had ever made, Berry and other members of the resolutions committee called these inalienable rights that any respectful citizen should be able to enjoy freely.

In 1867 Mobile city officials opened a soup kitchen to aid the impoverished. The Freedmen's Bureau offered financial assistance, and Berry was hired to help coordinate activities. Blacks throughout the city praised him for his involvement, but they criticized Berry for opposing an all-black national labor convention that was in the works. According to Berry, segregated meetings would hamper black progress and was at odds with the intent of Reconstruction, but numerous black Mobilians disagreed. Consequently Berry changed his position, arguing that the racial history of the nation justified segregated meetings.

Ulysses S. Grant's presidential election in 1868 proved momentous for Berry and other black Republicans. At the state level William H. Smith, a white Republican, was elected governor, and a free public school system was established. In the wake of their victories, a cadre of influential black Mobilians was able to secure legislation allowing them to remove Mobile's mayor and municipal board members. Among the governor's appointments was Berry, who became an alderman. The same year Berry founded a school and opened a grocery store with two other prominent blacks.

The next two years were quite eventful for Berry. In 1869, he became embroiled in a sectarian and ethnic dispute about the composition of the county school board. The following year he supported a plan to allow the city physician to treat destitute citizens, especially blacks, led an official inquiry into police pay, and called on the state government to reform the chain-gang system for prisoners. Berry also backed free public schools and an economic subsidy scheme that might have benefited his black constituency if Governor Smith had been reelected in November 1870. However Smith was defeated by a Democrat named Robert Lindsay.

Lindsay's victory ushered in Alabama's first—and Mobile's only—restoration of Democratic (or home) rule. For the remainder of the nineteenth century, every major political office in Mobile was held by a Democrat. Among the politicians affected by the Democratic reemergence was Berry, who quickly fell on hard times. By January 1871 he was unemployed, having been removed from his sergeant-at-arms post in the Alabama House, and he was impoverished. Without property, money, a wife, or a job, Berry withdrew money from a joint banking account that he and two of his business partners had opened—without their knowledge—and squandered the money. He then began to wander the streets of Mobile, drinking heavily, until one Saturday morning his body was found in a small, run-down dwelling behind a tenement building on Conception Street. His throat was slit, and it was not determined whether he was murdered or if he had committed suicide.

FURTHER READING

Bailey, Richard. *Neither Carpetbaggers nor Scalawags: Black Officeholders during the Reconstruction of Alabama, 1867–1878* (1995).

Fitzgerald, Michael. *The Union League Movement in the Deep South: Politics and Agricultural Change during Reconstruction* (1989).

Fitzgerald, Michael. *Urban Emancipation: Popular Politics in Reconstruction Mobile, 1860–1890* (2002).

Foner, Eric. *Freedom's Lawmakers: A Directory of Black Officeholders during Reconstruction* (1996).

BERTIS ENGLISH

Berry, Leonidas (20 July 1902–4 Dec. 1995), physician and public service and church activist, was born Leonidas Harris Berry on a tobacco farm in Woodsdale, North Carolina, the son of the Reverend Llewellyn Longfellow Berry, general secretary of the Department of Home and Foreign Missions of the African Methodist Episcopal (AME) Church, and Beulah Harris. Leonidas acquired the desire to become a doctor at the age of five, when a distinguished-looking local doctor treated a small wound on his foot. The young boy was impressed by this "miraculous" event. His aspiration to go to medical school intensified while he was attending Booker T. Washington High School in Norfolk, Virginia. In 1924 Berry graduated from Wilberforce University and went on to obtain the SB in 1925 from the University of Chicago. In 1930 he also received his medical degree from the University of Chicago's Rush Medical College. Berry continued his medical training, earning an M.S. in Pathology at the University of Illinois Medical School in 1933. He completed his internship at Freedmen's Hospital (1929–1930), one of the nation's first black hospitals, and then his residency at Cook County Hospital in Chicago (1931–1935).

For most of his career, Berry resided in Chicago, becoming a nationally and internationally recognized clinician. His practice and research were centered at Chicago's Provident, Michael Reese, and Cook County Hospitals. From 1935 until 1970 Berry was a mainstay of the physician staff at Provident. This institution, which had been founded by DANIEL HALE WILLIAMS, was one of the nation's leading black hospitals. In 1946 Berry became the first black physician admitted to the staff at Michael Reese. At Cook County he was the first black internist, rising from assistant to senior attending physician during his long affiliation with this institution (1946–1976). He also served as clinical professor in medicine at the University of Illinois from 1960 until 1975.

Beginning in the 1930s Berry developed into a leader in the emerging specialty of gastroenterology. This branch of medicine focuses on the physiology and pathology of the stomach and intestines as well as their interconnected organs, such as the liver, esophagus, gallbladder, and pancreas. Berry's clinical accomplishments were at the forefront of his specialty. He became an international authority on digestive diseases and the technique of endoscopy. Berry helped revolutionize his field when he became the first American doctor to employ the fiberoptic gastro-camera to examine the inside of the digestive tract. The use of this instrument

became increasingly refined, enabling physicians to diagnose at much earlier stages various diseases, especially cancers, of the gastrointestinal organs. He invented the Eder-Berry gastrobiopsy scope, a device that made it possible to retrieve tissue samples from the stomach for microscopic study. This instrument has been exhibited at the Smithsonian Institution in Washington, D.C.

In addition to his extraordinary clinical achievements, Berry was a superb medical academician. During the course of his career, he authored or co-authored twelve books and eighty-four medical research articles and presented more than 180 medical lectures, exhibitions, and academic papers nationally and internationally. In 1941 Berry presented a research paper before the gastroenterology and proctology section at the American Medical Association's (AMA) annual convention in Cleveland, Ohio, the first time a black physician made a national presentation before this prestigious group.

The church activities and travels of Berry's father and mother deeply impressed him throughout his early life—so much so that Berry's autobiography, *I Wouldn't Take Nothin' for My Journey* (1981), was written primarily as a memoir dedicated to his parents and their lives. Even while achieving his clinical and academic successes, Berry, raised in the swirl of his parents' church work and community service, never lost touch with the traditional ideals of the black American community—ideals that emphasize charitable work and resistance to racial discrimination. He realized these ideals by expanding his duties and resources at the hospitals and medical schools where he worked, as well as by taking on leadership positions in AME Church and community organizations. From the early 1950s Berry served president of the mostly black Cook County Physicians Association. He led a citywide movement to set up medical services for young drug addicts and to prevent the spread of drug addiction. His plan involved organizing medical counseling clinics and follow-up services for drug addicts—a plan that became a program that he administered for eight years with finances provided by the Illinois state legislature and the Illinois Department of Public Health.

In 1965 Berry served as president of the National Medical Association (NMA), the nation's premier organization established for black physicians. The highlight of his tenure was spearheading the NMA's activities to integrate the AMA. At this time the AMA still maintained segregated local chapters throughout the nation. In addresses to his NMA constituents, Berry described his disdain for this discriminatory barrier faced by black doctors. He called this practice "a senseless social embargo … against licensed and practicing physicians based upon a criterion of race in some [AMA] societies and tokenism in others" (Morais, 220). In order to place the NMA on higher ground regarding the integration of physician associations, at the August 1965 annual convention, the association passed Berry's proposal that the NMA recruit white physicians. At the convention's press conference, Berry stated his rationale clearly: "We cannot remain a segregated [medical] society when we are pressing for integration ourselves" (Morais, 196).

Under Berry's leadership the NMA next held a series of formal meetings with AMA officials and trustees. These meetings, which took place between September 1965 and August 1966, resulted in the adoption of several cooperative measures. First, the two organizations agreed to increase recruitment efforts to attract more black Americans into medical careers. Second, the AMA resolved to appoint more black members of the two organizations to high-standing councils and committees of the AMA. Finally, the AMA appointed a special committee of the AMA board of trustees to serve as a watchdog body to work against segregation in local chapters and physician practices. The committee contacted segregated local chapters to persuade them to comply voluntarily with the AMA's national resolutions prohibiting racial discrimination in local societies, hospitals, and medical care.

Berry also was a deeply committed "churchman" for the AME Church. He strove to use his church ties to work with other denominations on projects for community betterment. For example, for many years Berry served as the medical director of the Health Commission of the AME Church. In this capacity, in the mid-1960s he developed means to support the integration drive in Cairo, Illinois. In response to Ku Klux Klan activities and entrenched neighborhood poverty, local community activists in Cairo launched an antiracism campaign known as the Black United Front. Berry organized a "flying health service to Cairo" called the Flying Black Doctors to assist the Cairo activists. Berry's group of thirty-two physicians, nurses, and technicians flew down to Cairo and gave medical exams to some three hundred persons. The Cairo activities of the Flying Black Doctors attracted the attention of the national news media, including NBC's famed television news show, *The Huntley-Brinkley Report*, with Chet Huntley and David Brinkley.

Berry liked to refer to himself as a "multidimensional doctor." In his autobiography he emphasizes that although he was a successful clinician, he was most pleased that he had never given in to the tendency to become too "circumscribed and perhaps obsessed with the pursuit of excellence in … matters purely medical" (405). Berry viewed his medical and public service achievements as much more than solo endeavors. Instead, he believed that they were the direct outgrowth of family and religious influences that stemmed from the slave communities of the pre–Civil War United States. In his autobiography Berry writes: "The success of my career [was] a high water mark in the destiny of the Berry family in its long odyssey through the generations. The strength of Afro-American culture to a great extent lies in the unique common bonds which tie together many [such] successful Black nuclear and multinuclear families in America" (Berry, 407). Berry and his extended family have left a permanent contribution at the highest levels of American and black American medical science and religious life.

FURTHER READING

The papers of Leonidas H. Berry, 1907–1982, are located in the Modern Manuscripts Collection, History of Medicine Division, National Library of Medicine, Bethesda, Maryland. There is also a body of Berry's personal papers at the Schomburg Manuscripts and Rare Books Collection, New York Public Library, New York City, under the title Leonidas H. Berry Papers, 1932–1988.

Berry, Leonidas H. *I Wouldn't Take Nothin' for My Journey: Two Centuries of an Afro-American Minister's Family* (1981).

Morais, H. M. *The History of the Negro in Medicine* (1968).

Obituary: *New York Times* (Late Edition), 12 December 1995.

DAVID MCBRIDE

Berry, Mary Frances (17 Feb. 1938–), scholar and civil rights advocate, was born in Nashville, Tennessee, to George Berry, a laborer, and Frances Southall, a beautician. She was the middle child between two brothers. After attending public schools in Nashville, she entered Howard University where she received her bachelor of arts degree in 1961 and her master of arts degree in 1962. During the 1962–1963 academic year she was a teaching fellow at Howard University, after which she

Mary Frances Berry, chairwoman of the U.S. Commission on Civil Rights, speaking in Washington, D.C., 7 December 2001. (AP Images.)

moved to Ann Arbor, Michigan, to pursue a doctorate in history at the University of Michigan. She served as a teaching assistant during the 1965–1966 academic year and, after completing work on her Ph.D. in 1966, was appointed assistant professor in the Department of History. In 1968 she was promoted to associate professor. Simultaneously she pursued the study of law and in 1970 received her J.D. degree from the University of Michigan Law School.

Berry rapidly rose through the ranks of academia, serving as acting director, then director of the Afroamerican Studies program at the University of Colorado from 1970 to 1974. She also acted as provost of the school's Division of Behavioral and Social Sciences and Education in 1974, and as chancellor in 1976 and 1977. From 1976 through 1980 she held the rank of professor in the Department of History, although with the election of President Jimmy Carter in 1976, she took a

leave of absence to enter government service. She became a member of his administration, serving as assistant secretary of education in the Department of Health, Education, and Welfare from April 1977 through January 1980. In this post Berry headed the Education Division, administering a substantial annual budget. She oversaw a number of programs, including those of the National Institute of Education, the Office of Education, the Fund for the Improvement of Postsecondary Education, the Institute of Museum and Library Services, and the National Center for Education Statistics. Her years in Washington prompted her departure from Colorado, where she had faced criticism from the faculty of the University of Colorado for her role in granting amnesty to student protestors. Berry returned to Howard University, where she was professor in the Department of History and Law from 1980 through 1987. In 1987 she was appointed Geraldine R. Segal Professor of American Social Thought at the University of Pennsylvania.

In 1980 the Carter administration appointed her to the United States Commission on Civil Rights. The 1957 Civil Rights Act, the first civil rights bill passed by Congress in more than eighty years, created the commission. The commission's objective was to investigate complaints regarding civil rights abuses, hold hearings, and generate briefings, reports, and papers on the state of civil rights in the country for the benefit of lawmakers and the education of the public.

From 1980 to 1982 Berry served as the commission's vice chairperson. During the 1980s the commission assumed a broad mantle; a number of reports and hearings addressed a spectrum of issues. Her persistence in advocating for civil rights during the Reagan administration—he twice tried to fire her—earned Berry a reputation in Washington as a fierce iconoclast, as did her strong condemnation of the Reverend Louis FARRAKHAN at the time of his Million Man March in 1995.

On 19 November 1993 President Clinton appointed Berry as chairperson of the commission and in January of 1999 reappointed her. Working with state advisory committees, the commission, under Berry's leadership, conducted a number of studies and generated reports and recommendations regarding civil rights issues across the nation, including police misconduct in West Virginia, civil rights issues facing Arab Americans after the terrorist attacks of 11 September 2001, and problems faced by women business owners.

Berry continued to serve as a lightning rod for controversy, disappointing some supporters on the political left for her silence in the wake of Clinton's 1996 welfare reform act. Meanwhile, congressional oversight of the commission raised questions of its financial management, leading to allegations of mismanagement, which Berry and some of her supporters attributed to racism. In 1999 Berry's actions in quelling protest at Pacifica Radio, a left-leaning network of radio stations whose board she had headed since 1997, caused many to accuse her of censorship. Following the 2000 presidential election, a major portion of the commission's attention came to focus on problems attending African American access to the ballot. In a report issued in June 2001, Berry stated that the consequences of Florida's voting problems during the 2000 election "fell most harshly on African Americans." The Civil Rights Commission held a series of meetings in Florida, listening to testimony from blacks who were blocked from voting and from various other parties involved in the debacle. African Americans made up 11 percent of the Florida electorate but cast 54 percent of the votes that were ultimately discarded. The commission found that the problem was nationwide: of the almost 2 million votes thrown out for one reason or another, more than half were cast by African Americans.

Following the Florida hearings Berry argued strongly before Congress on the need for electoral reform. As the 2004 presidential election neared, Berry renewed the call for oversight of the Florida electoral process. The Civil Rights Commission itself lacked enforcement powers of any sort, so Berry held hearings intended to create public awareness of obstacles to free and equal voting.

Even while guiding the Civil Rights Commission, Berry continued to be a productive scholar. Her books include *Black Resistance, White Law: A History of Constitutional Racism in America* (1971), *Why ERA Failed: Politics, Women's Rights and the Amending Process of the Constitution* (1986), *Long Memory: The Black Experience in America* (with John W. Blassingame, 1982), *The Pig Farmer's Daughter and Other Tales of American Justice: Episodes of Racism and Sexism in the Courts From 1865 to the Present* (1999), and *The Politics of Parenthood: Child Care, Women's Rights, and the Myth of the Good Mother* (1993).

The recipient of more than thirty honorary degrees, Berry also received a number of awards. Honorary degrees were conferred by, among others, the University of Akron (1977), Benedict College (1979), Grambling State University (1979), Bethune-Cookman (1980), Clark College (1980), Oberlin College (1983), and Colby College (1986). Her awards include the NAACP's Roy Wilkins Award, the Rosa Parks Award of the Southern Christian Leadership Conference, the *Ebony* Black Achievement Award, and a *Ms.* Woman of the Year Award. Berry was a member of the U.S. Commission on Civil Rights from 1980 to 2004, serving as chair from 1993 to 2004.

FURTHER READING

Neuman, Johanna. "Civil Rights Panel Changes May Cause Clash," *Los Angeles Times* (4 Dec. 2004).

Smith, Jessie Carney. *Notable Black American Women* (1992).

JOHN R. HOWARD

Berry, Nyas, James Berry, and Warren Berry

(18 Aug. 1913–5 Oct. 1951), (c. 1915–28 Jan. 1969), and (25 Dec. 1922–10 Aug. 1996), dancers, were the sons of Redna (maiden name unknown) and Ananias Berry, whose occupations are unknown. Nyas, whose given name was Ananias, and James were both born in New Orleans, Louisiana, and Warren was born in Denver, Colorado.

In 1919 Nyas and James began performing together, touring the church circuit in Chicago as elocutionists reciting poems by PAUL LAURENCE DUNBAR. After the family moved to Denver, the two elder brothers branched out and began playing carnivals. Their father, a religious man, had forbidden them to dance, but Nyas had memorized dances he had seen other performers do and had built upon them himself. He persuaded his father to let him enter an amateur dance contest, in which he floored the audience. The theater manager offered Nyas $75 a week; the elder Ananias insisted that Nyas and James continue as a team.

The brothers then put together an act based on the widely acclaimed BERT WILLIAMS and GEORGE WALKER, the most famous African American show business performance team of their time. Nyas and James named their act the Miniature Williams and Walker. In the mid-1920s the Berry family moved to Hollywood, California, where James danced at parties given by silent film stars, such as Mary Pickford and Clara Bow. The brothers also appeared in *Our Gang* comedies. Toward the end of the decade they opened as a duo, the Berry Brothers, with the already legendary DUKE ELLINGTON at Harlem's Cotton Club. Although the famous nightclub would remain their home base for the next four and a half years, they toured and performed in other groundbreaking shows. In 1929 they traveled to London and were featured performers in Lew Leslie's popular and highly acclaimed all–African American revue *Blackbirds of 1928*. They were the first African American act at the Copacabana in 1929. They appeared in *Rhythmania* at the Cotton Club and *Rhapsody in Black* in 1931. When Radio City Music Hall had its grand opening on 27 December 1932, the Berry Brothers were on the bill.

In 1934 Nyas left the act and married VALAIDA SNOW, a popular African American entertainer. During this time Warren, the youngest brother, was pulled out of school and formal dance classes and drafted into the act. James taught his younger brother every move of the Berry Brothers' act, and soon this new duo was performing steadily. When Nyas's marriage dissolved, he talked his brothers into forming a Berry Brothers act with three Berrys. Nyas also persuaded them to move back to Hollywood. The Berry Brothers enjoyed tremendous success in their newly formed trio and appeared extensively throughout the United States on stage, in clubs, and in film as well as throughout Europe. The brothers possessed three distinct personalities and styles: Nyas was the king of the strut, James was the comedian and singer, and Warren was the solid dancer and acrobat. Their act remained virtually unchanged for over twenty years. In addition to their work in the 1941 musical film *Lady Be Good*, the Berrys also appeared in *Panama Hattie* (1942), *Boarding House Blues* (1948), and *You're My Everything* (1949). Their club engagements over the years included the Apollo Theater, the Zanzibar Café, and the Savoy Ballroom in New York; the Moulin Rouge in Paris; and the Rio Cabana in Chicago.

In 1938, at the downtown Cotton Club, a legendary competition took place between the Berry Brothers and the Nicholas Brothers, another great dance act. The Berrys devised a memorable finish in which Nyas and James ran up side stairways onto an elevated balcony and took a flying leap twelve feet out and over the heads of the entire CAB CALLOWAY orchestra, while Warren, on the stage below, completed a flip-flop twist. On the last note of the music, all three landed simultaneously in splits. "People talked about that for a long time!" recalled Warren.

The secret of the Berry Brothers' success was timing, precision, and dynamics. They were masters of the "freeze and melt," the sparkling contrast between posed immobility and sudden flashing action. The act that the three brothers perfected stayed their act for over twenty years. This repetition was common throughout vaudeville, when acts toured the country year after year. During that time, audiences wanted to see exactly the same familiar act with no changes. When the Berry Brothers contemplated using a new song or creating a new dance routine, the bookers dissuaded them. Resigned, the Berrys kept their act intact until Nyas's death of heart failure at the age of thirty-nine in New York. Warren and James performed together and then as solo acts individually for a time, but a hip injury Warren had suffered as a teen finally disabled him. In 1969 James died in New York of complications of arteriosclerosis. Warren worked for over fifteen years as a film editor for Screen Gems in New York City. During his last years he worked in Los Angeles on several unpublished scripts; he died in Los Angeles.

The Berrys are remembered as one of the greatest dance acts in the history of the American stage and cinema in the twentieth century. At a time when tap dancers were "a dime a dozen," these brothers combined their talents to form a unique act that remains unsurpassed. Ironically, they never wore taps on their shoes because their work with canes and their acrobatics required leather-soled shoes for safety. Their mixture of the cakewalk strut, tap dancing, thrilling acrobatics, and amazing cane work was a winning and lasting formula.

FURTHER READING

Frank, Rusty E. *TAP! The Greatest Tap Dance Stars and Their Stories, 1900–1955* (1990; repr., 1994).

Stearns, Marshall, and Jean Stearns. *Jazz Dance: The Story of American Vernacular Dance* (1968; repr., 1994).

Obituaries: Nyas Berry, *New York Age*, 13 Oct. 1951; James Berry, *New York Amsterdam News*, 8 Feb. 1969; and Warren Berry, *Los Angeles Times*, 16 Aug. 1996.

This entry is taken from the *American National Biography* and is published here with the permission of the American Council of Learned Societies.

RUSTY E. FRANK

Berry, Theodore M. (8 Nov. 1905–15 Oct. 2000), first black mayor of Cincinnati, Ohio, was born in Maysville, Kentucky, to a white farmer whom he never knew and Cora Berry. When he was a toddler, Berry's mother brought him to Cincinnati, where they settled in the emerging African American community in the city's West End. Severely hearing impaired and with difficulty speaking, his mother earned little as a domestic, and Berry's sister Anna, fifteen years his senior, eventually assembled the family in her own household.

Berry attended the segregated Harriet Beecher Stowe Elementary School and graduated from the racially mixed Woodward High School in 1924 as valedictorian, the first black student in Cincinnati to achieve that honor in an integrated high school. Berry received his bachelor of arts degree from the University of Cincinnati in 1928 and his juris doctorate from the University of Cincinnati College of Law in 1931. He worked his way through school by selling newspapers and later working in the steel mills in nearby Newport, Kentucky.

Soon after graduation from law school, Berry became president of the Cincinnati branch of the National Association for the Advancement of Colored People (NAACP), a post he held from 1932 to 1938 and again from 1943 to 1946. Thereafter he served at various times as an officer or board member for the NAACP Cincinnati Branch, the Ohio NAACP state chapter, and the national organization. In June 1938 Berry married Johnnie Mae Newton, and the couple had three children, Faith Daryl, Gail Estelle, and Theodore Newton.

In 1939 Berry became Hamilton County's first black assistant prosecutor—a Republican Party political appointment. In 1942, when he went to work in Washington, D.C., in the federal Office of War Information, he became a Democrat. Upon returning to Cincinnati, Berry resumed his private law practice and his work with the NAACP and ran unsuccessfully as an independent for the Cincinnati City Council in 1947. During that campaign, however, Berry's outspoken support for the proportional representation system of voting then used to elect Cincinnati's city council played a crucial role in helping defeat a Republican-led repeal effort as he reminded black Cincinnatians that proportional representation had allowed them to elect an African American council member in every election since 1931.

Subsequently, Berry was elected to the city council in 1949 on the local Charter Party ticket. This put two blacks, including a Republican incumbent, on the nine-member council for the first time. Berry served on the council from 1949 to 1957, 1963 to 1965, and 1971 to 1975, during the last of which he also served as the city's first black mayor. As a city council member, Berry continued his civil rights activism. In 1953 he worked with civic housing reformers to legislate a ban on racial discrimination in housing to be constructed as part of the city's first postwar urban renewal project, and in 1953 and 1954 he attempted, unsuccessfully, to use Cincinnati's control of the waterworks that supplied the growing suburbs of Hamilton County as a tool to force developers to open a major housing development (later named the City of Forest Park) to African American residents.

Berry lost his 1957 bid for reelection after a successful Republican-led campaign to repeal proportional representation, a campaign widely believed to have prevailed because of white fears that Berry might become mayor. Indeed, Berry had been the top vote-getter of the majority party in the November 1955 election, which by local tradition would have made him mayor. Instead Berry had chosen to step aside in favor of a white council member from his party. With a larger black population and greater support from white voters, Berry was reelected to the council in 1963. He served until he was appointed Assistant Director for Community Action Programs in the federal Office of Economic Opportunity in 1965, which occurred, in part, because of his instrumental role in the early creation of Cincinnati's Community Action Program.

Berry resumed his private practice of law in Cincinnati in 1969. In 1971 he returned to the city council by appointment to fill a seat vacated by the death of a black incumbent. In council elections later that year, he was the top vote-getter in the Charter Party half of the majority Charter-Democratic coalition and as a result became mayor in December 1972, a position he held until he retired from political office in 1975. Berry remained active in Cincinnati municipal politics, including supporting younger black office seekers like Marian Spencer, whom he saw elected as the first woman president of the local NAACP branch, and then as the first black woman elected to the Cincinnati city council in 1983. Berry also continued to work for the reinstatement of proportional representation in the election of city council. While some local activists argued for a combined district/at-large method to assure a fair proportion of blacks on council, Berry worked to persuade the federal courts that the 1957 Republican attack on proportional representation had been racially motivated and had illegally denied Cincinnati blacks fair representation. Berry and his allies lost the suit in 1993, but Cincinnati finally saw the election of African Americans to its city council starting in the 1990s in numbers roughly proportionate to the city's black population.

In addition to Berry's political career and service to the NAACP, he played important roles in other civil rights organizations, including as president of the Ohio Committee for Civil Rights Legislation (1949–1965), which organized for state fair-employment (enacted 1959) and fair-housing legislation (enacted 1965). Between 1949 and 1958 he helped a group of black war veterans purchase, finance, and build a small subdivision in an otherwise white area of northern Hamilton County. In addition he worked with the North Avondale Neighborhood Association (founded in 1960), which helped that neighborhood make a successful transition from an upper-middle-class white neighborhood to an upper-middle-class integrated neighborhood. That same year he helped found Housing Opportunities Made Equal, which lobbied for local and state fair housing legislation and after 1965 worked to enforce Ohio's fair housing law and then federal fair housing law.

By the early 1990s Berry's age and health had begun to limit his participation in civic life. His death in 2000 was accompanied by accolades from a broad range of Cincinnatians, reflecting the decency, honesty, and effectiveness for which Berry had been known throughout his career.

FURTHER READING
This article was drawn primarily from materials in the Theodore M. Berry Collection, Department of Archives and Rare Books, University of Cincinnati Libraries. Additional material came from the Theodore M. Berry Collection, Cincinnati Historical Society Library. Berry appears prominently in the papers of a number of other Cincinnati organizations including the Better Housing League, Housing Opportunities Made Equal, and the Cincinnati Human Relations Commission, all at the University of Cincinnati, and in the Urban League of Greater Cincinnati Collection and the Cincinnati Development Committee Collection at the Cincinnati Historical Society Library. Numerous articles are available in Cincinnati newspapers indexed at http://newsdex.cincinnatilibrary.org. His obituary is available online at the *New York Times* (http://www.nytimes.com) and in the *Cincinnati Enquirer* and the *Cincinnati Post* at http://www.cincinnati.com. There is no complete biography of Berry available. The Cincinnati Historical Society Library's web site has a brief biography and a guide to other resources about him at http://library.cincymuseum.org/aag/bio/berry.html.

CHARLES F. CASEY-LEININGER

Berry Newman, Constance (8 Jul 1935–), political administrator and lawyer, was born Constance Ernestine Berry in Chicago, Illinois, the daughter of Ernestine Siggers and Joseph Alonzo Berry. Her mother was a social worker and a nurse, her father was a physician. Berry was young when the family relocated to Tuskegee, Alabama, where she was reared and attended Tuskegee Institute High School located on the campus of Tuskegee University a private historically black university established in 1881. She was a member of the Government Club and an honor roll student. Upon graduating from high school in 1952, Berry enrolled at Bates College in Lewiston, Maine, where she earned a Bachelor of Arts degree in Political Science in 1956. Three years later, in 1959, she graduated with a Juris Doctorate from the University of Minnesota Law School. The same year she was married to Theodore Newman, a member of the United States Air Force, and together they moved to France.

Berry Newman returned to the United States in 1962 and settled down in Washington, D.C., where she worked with the United States Interior Department first as a clerk typist, then personnel assistant, and finally a personnel manager. In 1967, she assumed a position in the Office of Economic Development assisting migrant farmers. Berry Newman went to work, in 1969, at the Department of Health, Education and Welfare—what is now called the Department of Health and Human Services—as special assistant to Secretary Elliot Richardson, head of the department. Two years later, in 1971, she was appointed by the Republican U.S. president Richard Nixon as the first African American national director of Volunteers in Service to America (VISTA), the domestic Peace Corps; the swearing-in ceremony was conducted by her husband, who was by then a Washington, DC, Superior Court judge. Berry Newman, herself a committed Republican, served in this capacity until 1973, when she became the commissioner of the Consumer Product Safety Commission; she became vice chair of the commission in 1975. For one year, from 1976 until 1977, she served as assistant director of the United States Department of Housing and Urban Development, presiding over the consumer unit focused on Indian and elderly affairs.

In 1977, Berry Newman cofounded Newman and Hermansome Company, a consulting firm and policy research company that worked in housing, transportation, international development, and urban development. She served as president of

Constance Berry Newman, Assistant Secretary for African Affairs, U.S. Department of State, speaking at a Washington Foreign Press Center briefing on economic cooperation in Senegal (2005). (United States Department of State.)

Newman and Hermansome until 1982, when the company was sold. In 1982, Berry Newman was employed by the Institute of American Business as president until 1984, when she went to work as a private consultant. She served as private consultant until 1987, advising the World Bank on issues related to Africa, a project that required that she live and work in Lesotho, near South Africa. Berry Newman continued her relationship with World Bank in Lesotho as consultant to the Cooperative Housing Foundation for a project to merge existing housing corporations into one unified body until 1988. From 1989 until 1992 she worked as the director of the United States Office of Personnel Management. Berry Newman served as the undersecretary of the Smithsonian Institution from 1992 until 2000. In 2001 she was employed by the United States Agency for International Development as the assistant administrator for Africa until June 2004.

Berry Newman was appointed by then U.S. president George W. Bush on 24 June 2004 to serve as the United States Assistant Secretary for African Affairs; she was central to the determination that genocide had been committed in the Darfur region of Sudan. One year later, in April 2005, she resigned from this position.

Berry Newman was honored with the Amherst College Award in 1980. In 1985, she was awarded the Secretary of Defense Medal for Outstanding Public Service. In 1991, Berry Newman was given an award by Central State University, a historically black university in Wilberforce, Ohio, established in 1887. The Smithsonian Institution granted Berry Newman their highest honor in 2000 with the Joseph Henry Medal for her achievements, extraordinary service, recognition, and development of the Smithsonian Institution during her tenure as undersecretary. Berry Newman served as a member of the board and vice chair of the District of Columbia Financial

Responsibility Management Assistance Authority from 1994 to 2000. She sat on the board as a member for the International Republican Institute from 1998 until 2001, an organization established in 1983 to perform international democratization initiatives. In 1998, Berry Newman received the Washingtonian of the Year award. In November 2010, Berry Newman was appointed by the newly elected mayor of Washington, D.C., Vincent C. Gray, to his transition team to serve as an advisor on government operations.

FURTHER READING

"Constance B. Newman of VISTA: Energetic Lawyer Heads Volunteers In Service To America." *Ebony*, Sept. 1972.

Lacey, Marc. "Riot Toll Mounts in Sudan after Rebel Leader's Death." *New York Times*, 4 Aug. 2005.

Prunier, Gerard. *Darfur: A 21st Century Genocide* (2008).

SAFIYA DALILAH HOSKINS

Bessent, Hattie (26 Dec. 1926–), nursing educator and administrator, was born in Jacksonville, Florida. Little information is available about her parents or other aspects of her personal background. When she was nine years old Bessent lost her mother. Her grandmother then raised her, instilling in her a strong belief that self-giving is the measure of personal worth. After graduating from high school in Jacksonville, Bessent worked as a laboratory and x-ray technician, an unusual job for a black woman of her time and place but one that led to her groundbreaking career in nursing.

During and after slavery, African Americans, especially women, often served as lay healers and tenders of the sick. Starting in the nineteenth century, as nursing became a more formally organized profession, the "color line" sliced through it. Even though black communities urgently needed more health care, black nurses were denied membership in the American Nurses Association (ANA), educational opportunities, and all but the lowest-paid, least prestigious jobs, usually in private duty work. In 1908 the National Association of Colored Graduate Nurses (NACGN) was founded to strive for professional equality, particularly for the desegregation of the ANA, the largest professional association. By the time of Hattie Bessent's birth, black nurses had created their own basic training programs but were still excluded from many good jobs, graduate education, and specialist training. This was still true in

1949, when the ANA finally accepted black members and the NACGN chose to disband, its chief mission having been attained.

Against this difficult yet newly promising historical backdrop, Bessent sought her B.S. in Nursing Education from Florida A&M University. After graduating in 1959 Bessent became the first black nursing head of any psychiatric unit in Jacksonville. She then earned an MSN in Psychiatric Nursing from Indiana University in 1962 and spent five years as assistant professor of this specialty at Florida A&M University. With her Ed.D. in Psychological Foundations of Education, obtained in 1970 at the University of Florida, Bessent became the first African American nurse in her home state to receive a doctorate. She was also a registered nurse (RN) and a fellow of the American Academy of Nursing (FAAN).

During the early to mid-1970s Bessent taught and researched on the nursing school faculties of the University of Florida and Vanderbilt University. In 1976 she became Vanderbilt's first African American nursing dean. From 1977 to 1992 Bessent directed the ANA's nationwide Ethnic Minority Fellowship Program (EMFP). Since 1974 the EMFP has offered doctoral fellowships in psychiatric nursing and related fields to African, Native, Asian, and Hispanic Americans. Psychiatric nursing addresses not only conditions like posttraumatic stress disorder and depression but also substance abuse and, since the 1980s, HIV and AIDS. Along with poverty and inadequate health care access, these problems have continued to disproportionately burden people of color. The EMFP increased minority representation, leadership, and wisdom in psychiatric nursing clinical practice, administration, teaching, research, and policy work. As EMFP director Bessent raised millions of dollars from private foundations and government agencies.

Through her congressional policy internships, many fellows witnessed the legislative process firsthand and better understood its day-to-day effects on health care workers and patients. Bessent regularly visited the fellows at each of the fifty-plus universities where they then were enrolled. She stressed the importance of assertiveness training, mentoring, and networking in their development as professionals. She also helped them with job placement, recruited new fellows, and raised awareness of the EMFP and diversity issues among nursing faculty and other health professionals. U.S. Senator Daniel Inouye of Hawaii praised her in the

Congressional Record as "an outstanding role model for both her professional colleagues and for future generations of minority students. She has ... demonstrated the positive long-term consequences of being actively involved in the political process.... Very few can match her accomplishments and dedication" (Inouye, S15443–S15444).

After her retirement as EMFP director, Bessent wrote *Strategies for Recruitment, Retention, and Graduation of Minority Nurses in Colleges of Nursing* (1997), *Minority Nurses in the New Century* (2002), and *Soul of Leadership* (2005). She continued to publish articles in professional journals and make presentations at scientific sessions of the World Federation of Mental Health. In 2002 the American Nurses Foundation of the ANA appointed her director of a new initiative to train minority nurse leaders at historically black colleges and universities. Bessent hoped that this training would empower minority nurses to skillfully challenge racial and ethnic disparities in health care and teach their patients how to do the same.

Along with the ANA, Bessent involved herself in such groups as the W.K. Kellogg Foundation's Project LEAD, the American Educational Research Association, the Association for Supervision and Curriculum Development, the National League for Nursing, the Delta Sigma Theta sorority, the Alachua County Mental Health Association, and the Gainesville Human Relations Board. She was awarded a lifetime membership by the National Black Nurses Association and the first honorary membership in the Association of Black Nursing Faculty. She was the first African American southerner inducted into the honorary nursing organizations Phi Delta Kappa, Sigma Theta Tau, and Pi Lambda Theta. Her other honors include a Career Teachers Grant; appointments by President Jimmy Carter to his Task Force for the Friendship Treaty to China and his Commission on Mental Health (1977); Distinguished Alumna Award, Florida A&M University (1980); Serwa Award, Virginia Chapter, National Coalition of 100 Black Women (1990); an honorary doctorate of science degree, Hunter College (2002); and the ANA's Mary Mahoney Award (2004).

The onetime ethnic minority fellow Beverly Malone aptly described Hattie Bessent as a "fighting spirit with a clear sense of mission" (Inouye, S15443–S15444). When she became one of the first black women to head the American Nurses Association, from 1996 to 2000, Malone expressed gratitude for Bessent's mentorship. In the opening years of the twenty-first century Bessent persisted as a leader in the long and still unfinished struggle for equality in the nursing profession and in health care access. Thanks to Bessent, Malone, and hundreds of other nursing leaders gained the opportunity to thrive and succeed in their profession, improve the life chances of the poor and minority Americans they serve, and cultivate still more nursing leaders of color.

FURTHER READING

Carnegie, M. Elizabeth. *The Path We Tread: Blacks in Nursing Worldwide, 1854–1994,* 3d ed. (1995).

Inouye, Daniel. "Tribute to Dr. Hattie Bessent for 16 Years of Placing Minority Nurse Interns on Capitol Hill," *Congressional Record*, 30 Oct. 1991, available online at http://thomas.loc.gov.

Taylor, Cheryl. "Bessent, Hattie," in *Black Women in America,* ed. Darlene Clark Hine (1993).

MARY KRANE DERR

Best, Denzil (27 Apr. 1917–25 May 1965), jazz drummer and composer, was born Denzil de Costa Best in New York City, the son of immigrant parents from Barbados; his mother was Josephine Best (his father's name is unknown). Denzil Best married Arline Riley (date unknown), with whom he had two daughters. Best began studying piano when he was six years old but later learned trumpet, which he played professionally in the mid-1930s with the drummer Chris Columbus (Joe Morris). By the end of the decade Best became associated with several seminal bop musicians playing at Minton's nightclub in New York, including THELONIOUS MONK, KENNY CLARKE, and house bandleader Joe Guy. Because of a lung disorder, Best stopped playing trumpet in 1941, returned to the piano, and later played string bass and drums.

After having worked as a drummer with locally led New York City bands (Saxie Payne, Eddie Williams, Leon Gross), Best made several recordings with the saxophonist BEN WEBSTER in September 1943. The next year he played drums on several recordings made by a number of well-known jazz musicians, including COLEMAN HAWKINS (replacing Jimmy Crawford), ILLINOIS JACQUET, CHARLIE SHAVERS, Clyde Hart, and MARY LOU WILLIAMS.

In 1947 Best was coleader on several quartet recordings with Webster before joining the bassist Chubby Jackson (with Conte Candoli, Frank Socolow, Terry Gibbs, and Lou Levy) on a Scandinavian tour. Throughout the late 1940s and into the 1950s Best played and recorded with swing-era musicians such as BUCK CLAYTON, TEDDY WILSON, Shavers, Jimmy Jones, STUFF SMITH, and Jack Teagarden. From 1949 to 1952 he played with the George Shearing quintet and helped originate the unique mellow sound that identified the group.

Best fractured his legs in an automobile accident in 1952 and was in temporary retirement until October of the next year, when he joined Artie Shaw's last Gramercy Five band, recording with the group in February and March 1954. Best then played with Erroll Garner in 1955–1956, recording on the pianist's milestone album *Concert by the Sea* (1955; Columbia CL883). During the late 1950s Best suffered from calcium deposits in his wrists, and although he continued to perform (with Lee Evans, Cecil Young, NINA SIMONE, Tyree Glenn, and Stuff Smith), his affliction seriously curtailed his professional career, and he worked sparingly during the 1960s. He died in New York City from head injuries that he received in a fall down a flight of subway stairs.

Best was one of several bop-era drummers who personified the subtle, understated style of accompaniment drumming first demonstrated by Jo JONES and Dave Tough and later by Connie Kay and Chuck Flores. His playing, characterized by his facile brushwork on the recordings that he made with Shearing and Garner, was in sharp contrast to the forceful style of most bop drummers of this period.

Although well known as a drummer, Best will most likely be remembered for his several compositions that have become bop standards. These include "Allen's Alley" ("Wee"), recorded first by Coleman Hawkins; "Dee Dee's Dance," recorded by Clyde Hart and Chubby Jackson; "Move," recorded by MILES DAVIS and later FATS NAVARRO; "Nothing but D Best," recorded by Shearing; and "Bemsha Swing," written with and recorded by Monk in 1952.

FURTHER READING

Gilter, Ira. *Jazz Masters of the Forties* (1966).

Harris, Pat. "None Better than Best with a Brush," *Down Beat* 18, no. 8 (Apr. 1951): 18.

Stewart, Doug. "The Forgotten Ones: Denzil Best," *Jazz Journal International* 39, no. 11 (1986): 18.

This entry is taken from the *American National Biography* and is published here with the permission of the American Council of Learned Societies.

T. DENNIS BROWN

Best, Willie (27 May 1916?–27 Feb. 1962), actor, was born in Sunflower, Mississippi. Little is known of his early life until Best was a teenager, when he took a job chauffeuring a white family from Mississippi to Southern California. Best remained in Los Angeles, where he found work in a touring stage show. He was discovered by a Hollywood agent who noticed both his comedic talent and his physical similarity to STEPIN FETCHIT (Lincoln Perry), the popular African American comic actor, and Best was signed to appear in feature films.

Best's film debut was the 1930 comedy *Feet First*. Because his roles were often small and his films were usually inexpensive and quickly made, Best has an extensive filmography of over 120 movies—in 1935 three films featuring Willie Best were released in the same month. Best's career received a major boost when Stepin Fetchit was fired from the Shirley Temple film *The Littlest Rebel* in 1935 and Best was brought in to replace him. Although he continued to work in small roles in numerous B-movies, after replacing Stepin Fetchit he began performing in films with bigger budgets and bigger stars. Best worked with Humphrey Bogart, the Marx Brothers, and Laurel and Hardy, as well as LOUIS ARMSTRONG, LENA HORNE, and the rest of the all-black cast of the classic *Cabin in the Sky* (1943).

Willy Best's onscreen characters were similar to Fetchit's; shuffling, dim-witted stereotypes with names like "Charcoal" or "Sambo." In some of his early films, Best performed under the Fetchit-like stage name "Sleep 'N' Eat," a name that director SPIKE LEE would later use for a lead character in his satire of Hollywood racism, *Bamboozled* (Best also appears in Lee's closing montage of ignominious moments in film history). In a 1934 interview Best said, "I often think about the roles I have to play. Most of them are pretty broad. Sometimes I tell the director and he cuts out the real bad parts.... But what's an actor going to do? Either you do it or you get out" (Watkins, p. 243).

Not all of his work was racially problematic. In *The Ghostbreakers* (1940), Best received the highest billing of his career, third lead behind the white stars Bob Hope and Paulette Goddard. Best's character is active rather than slothful (even fighting off a hulking zombie in one scene), and his comic fright is equaled by Hope's, turning a racist stereotype into an effective comedy double act between the black and white performers. Despite the film's financial success, it failed to elevate the sorts of roles that Best played, instead consigning him to a multitude of comedy-thrillers of greatly varying quality, where he continued quivering and cowering.

By the late 1940s, the public's tolerance of minstrel-show comedy began to deteriorate. Only a few years after praising Best as "very funny as a terrified blackamoor" (*New York Times*, 21 Sept. 1941), the same critic wrote in a 1947 review that Best's "old-fashioned Sambo performance … could very well have been left out of a modern-day juvenile film" (*New York Times*, 27 Nov. 1947). With this change of attitude, actors in the mold of Stepin Fetchit and Willie Best began to find film work hard to come by. Best's career was also hurt by a highly publicized arrest in May of 1951 on narcotics charges. *South of Caliente*, a Roy Rogers western released that year, would be Best's last feature film, although there was still work in television for him. From 1951 to 1955 he appeared as a regular or semiregular in the domestic comedies *My Little Margie* and *The Stu Erwin Show*, and in the drama *Waterfront*.

In 1962, terminally ill and with no immediate family, Best left his home in Los Angeles for the Motion Picture Country Hospital in Woodland Hills, California, where he passed away on 27 May. Although Best was buried in an unmarked grave, an Internet campaign lead by the website Celluloid Slammer raised money in early 2009 to purchase an elegant grave marker for the actor.

Whether or not he was, as AMIRI BARAKA wrote in "A Poem for Willie Best," "a renegade / behind the mask"(p. 53), Best's legacy is complicated. Although his film work is marked by the casual racism of a past era, he was a talented actor who was often genuinely very funny. His best work hints at the career that might have been available, under different circumstances, to the man Bob Hope called "the best actor I know."

FURTHER READING

Baraka, Amiri. *The LeRoi Jones/Amiri Baraka Reader* (1999).

Bogle, Donald. *Toms, Coons, Mulattoes, Mammies, and Bucks: An Interpretive History of Blacks in American Films* (1989).

Watkins, Mel. *On the Real Side: Laughing, Lying, and Signifying* (1994).

MALCOLM WOMACK

Bethea, Elvin (1 March 1946–), football player and labor activist, was born in Trenton, New Jersey, the first of nine children born to Jesse and Henrietta Bethea. Bethea grew up poor, with his father finding whatever jobs he could while his mother worked out of the home as a hairdresser. His father, who enforced a strict home environment, did not think much of football as he struggled in a low-paying factory job, but he did leave Elvin his blue-collar work ethic—a trait the son applied to his own life, especially in football. Bethea excelled in football at Trenton Central High School and was offered a football scholarship at North Carolina Agricultural & Technical University in Greensboro, where he made All-America as a two way lineman. At North Carolina A & T, Bethea played under the assistant coach Hornsby Howell, who pushed him to succeed not only in sports but also in life, and stressed the need to graduate. Bethea, also a world class shot putter in track and field, passed up an opportunity to make the 1968 U.S. Olympic squad to turn professional in football. He was drafted by the Houston Oilers in the third round in 1968—the second year the National Football League (NFL) and the American Football League (AFL) held a common draft—the fifth defensive end taken.

The Oilers had been AFL champions in 1967 but slowly declined over the next six seasons, winning only a single game in 1972 and 1973 and struggling after the two leagues merged in 1970. Bethea started his career in 1968 as an offensive lineman but in the eighth game of his rookie year moved to defense, soon becoming the bell cow (or leader) of the defensive line. Even though Houston lost on the field, Bethea was an impact player, recording fourteen and a half sacks in just his second season. Though sacks were not an official NFL statistic until 1982, teams kept their own records; Bethea ended his career with 105 sacks (still a franchise record), led his team six seasons, with a career high of sixteen in 1973. He played sixteen seasons and still holds the franchise record for sacks in a single season. In 1978 and 1979 Houston made it to the AFL championship game, one win shy of the Super Bowl. Led by running back Earl Campbell on offense and Bethea on defense, the Oilers fell to the Pittsburgh Steelers both years. For his achievements Bethea was named to eight NFL pro bowls, and was a first team All Pro in 1975 and second team three times. Until he was sidelined by a broken arm in 1977, Bethea had played in a total of 210 games, 135 consecutively, an enormous feat within professional football. He retired after the 1983 season, and his uniform number (65) was retired the same season. Although eligible in 1988 for the Pro Football Hall of Fame in Canton, Ohio, year after year passed without his induction. Twenty years after retirement, he received the call in what may

Elvin Bethea, Houston Oilers defensive end (1970). (AP Images.)

have been his last opportunity (after so many years of failing to earn enough Hall votes once eligible, players are eliminated from the ballot and can only be elected by the Veterans committee). Following his presenter, his old college coach Howell, Bethea credited parents, family, past coaches, and teammates in a seven-minute induction speech on 3 August 2003.

After his playing career Bethea spent years as a member of the NFL Players Association executive committee. Although Gene Upshaw (of the Oakland Raiders) was the more recognizable union representative, Bethea was a leading advocate for players to receive a fair share of the NFL's enormous television revenues and the right of free agency, which allowed players to sign more lucrative contracts. In 1982, breakdown in negotiations between owners and players led to a fifty-seven-day player strike that cut the sixteen-game schedule to nine and changed the future of professional football forever. Again, Bethea played a significant behind-the-scenes role.

For twenty years after his retirement Bethea worked as sales representative for Anheuser-Busch, a job he held since his early years in the NFL. He spent much of his time playing charity golf events

and making personal appearances. He attended a 2010 book signing for *The Unbroken Line*, an account of the business side of professional football, and is the author (with Mark Adams) of *Smash-Mouth: My Journey from Trenton to Canton* (2005), an autobiography. Married to Pat Bethea with three children (Lamont, Brittany, and Damon), Bethea has remained in Houston, working to protect former NFL players' rights.

FURTHER READING

Bethea, Elvin, with Mark Adams. *My Football Journey from Trenton to Canton* (2005).

DuPree, Billy Joe, and Spencer Kopf. *The Unbroken Line: The Untold Story of Gridiron Greats and Their Struggle to Save Professional Football* (2010).

Pirkle, John. *Oiler Blues: The Story of Pro Football's Most Frustrating Team* (1999).

BOYD CHILDRESS

Bethea, Rainey (16 Oct. 1913?–14 Aug. 1936), the last person publicly executed in the United States, was born Joseph Rainey Bethea in Roanoke, Virginia, to Rainey Bethea and Ella Louise Huggins. Most press reports of his execution state that Bethea Jr. was twenty-two at the time of his arrest, though he also claimed at times that he had been born in 1909. Since Bethea Jr.'s father would have been only fifteen years old in 1909, it appears more likely that the 1913 date is correct. The younger Bethea hardly knew his parents. He was still a child when his mother died in 1919 and barely a teenager when his father died seven years later in 1926, leaving Bethea, his sister Ora, and his brother as orphans. Around that time the siblings separated. While his brother remained in Virginia and his sister moved to Nichols, South Carolina, Bethea traveled west to Owensboro, Kentucky.

In 1933 Bethea began doing odd jobs for a white family, in whose basement he lived for a couple of years. Barely literate and with only three years of schooling, he took work where he could find it, but in rural Kentucky at the depth of the Great Depression there were few such opportunities for young black men like Bethea. He turned to a life of petty crime and began drinking heavily. He was fined twenty dollars for breach of the peace in Owensboro in early 1935, and he was indicted on May 31 of that year for stealing two purses at a beauty shop. Upon pleading guilty he was sentenced to one year at the Kentucky State Penitentiary in Eddyville, but he was released on parole on 1 December 1935 after serving the minimum sentence of six months.

Upon his return to Owensboro he found work as a laborer and odd-job man for his landlady, earning seven dollars a week and free room and board. Within a month of his release from prison, however, he was arrested again for housebreaking and public drunkenness. Unable to pay a one-hundred-dollar fine, Bethea remained in the Daviess County jail in Owensboro from January to 18 April 1936, when he was released. Since he had broken the terms of his parole, the county authorities ought to have returned him to the Kentucky State Penitentiary, but they failed to do so.

That administrative error proved costly both for Bethea and for Mrs. Lischia Edwards, a white, seventy-year-old widow whose Owensboro home a shoeless and drunken Bethea burgled on 7 June 1936. Having once worked for and boarded near Mrs. Edwards, he knew the basic layout of the home. Although the precise sequence of events is unclear, Bethea was arrested several days later and confessed in custody to having raped and assaulted Mrs. Edwards, who had subsequently died from the assault. Bethea, who frustrated his white, court-appointed lawyers by giving them conflicting accounts, later retracted that confession, but then entered a guilty plea at his trial. Despite that admission, the judge allowed the prosecution to make its case. An all-white jury found Bethea guilty after deliberating for only five minutes.

Condemned to hang on 31 July 1936, Bethea once again claimed his innocence and hired new counsel, five black lawyers from Louisville including CHARLES W. ANDERSON JR. Bethea's new attorneys made several procedural appeals concerning their client's lack of access to counsel, and compared his plight to that of the SCOTTSBORO BOYS, whose inadequate court-appointed counsel the U.S. Supreme Court had condemned in *Powell v. Alabama* (1932). Although Bethea's lawyers won him a temporary stay of execution, the courts swiftly rejected all of his appeals. Kentucky governor Albert B. "Happy" Chandler signed Bethea's death warrant on 6 August 1936, the same day he ordered the execution of John (Pete) Montjoy. Bethea's public hanging was set for the Daviess County courthouse on 14 August 1936.

Several factors resulted in the Bethea case becoming a national cause célèbre. Among these was the issue of interracial sex and the apparent rape of a popular and well-respected white woman by a black male drifter in a small southern town. Indeed, the mood in the wake of Bethea's arrest was such that many in the town expected him to be lynched. Another was that Owensboro had not seen a public hanging for more than eighty years and that Kentucky was now the last state in the Union to perform public executions. Such executions were reserved solely for crimes involving rape, because state lawmakers deemed the electric chair too humane for rapists. In a pattern common throughout the South at that time, Kentuckians condemned to death for rape were invariably African American and their victims white. The atmosphere at several contemporaneous public hangings had resembled the carnival of the SAM HOSE and other public lynchings, during which predominantly white crowds sought a combination of vengeance and souvenir items. To this already combustible mix was added the requirement that the local sheriff perform the execution; Owensboro's sheriff was a white woman, a factor that assured the case newspaper coverage throughout the nation. On the eve of the execution, however, the sheriff deputized a man to perform the task.

By then, accounts of the "hangman in skirts" in respectable newspapers like the *New York Times* and *the Louisville Courier-Journal*, as well as in the sensationalist "yellow press," had swelled the crowd at Bethea's hanging to between ten and twenty thousand people. Some of the spectators arrived at the gallows on horseback; most walked, came by car, truck, or train; a few arrived for pre-execution hanging parties and barbecues by airplane. They came from Kentucky, Indiana, and Illinois, but also as far away as Florida and the North. Newspaper accounts of the execution differ. The *New York Times* and other out-of-town newspapers reported that an angry white crowd jeered as a Roman Catholic priest read Bethea his last rites and that following the hanging the mob stormed the gallows, tearing Bethea's clothes and even the hangman's hood for souvenirs. Local newspapers disputed those accounts, claiming the crowd had observed the execution in respectful silence, and that the national press, denied the spectacle of a "hangman in skirts," decided to condemn a savage redneck mob instead. Whatever the precise sequence of events, the controversy surrounding the hanging of Rainey Bethea persuaded Kentucky to join the rest of the country in abolishing public executions.

FURTHER READING
Ryan, Perry T. *The Last Public Execution in America* (1992).

Wright, George C. *Racial Violence in Kentucky, 1865–1940: Lynchings, Mob Rule, and "Legal Lynchings"* (1990).

STEVEN J. NIVEN

Bethune, Mary McLeod (10 July 1875–18 May 1955), organizer of black women and advocate for social justice, was born Mary Jane McLeod in Mayesville, South Carolina, the child of the former slaves Samuel McLeod and Patsy McIntosh, farmers. After attending a school operated by the Presbyterian Board of Missions for Freedmen, she entered Scotia Seminary (later Barber-Scotia College) in Concord, North Carolina, in 1888 and graduated in May 1894. She spent the next year at Dwight Moody's evangelical Institute for Home and Foreign Missions in Chicago, Illinois. In 1898 she married Albertus Bethune. They both taught briefly at Kindell Institute in Sumter, South Carolina. The marriage was not happy. They had one child and separated late in 1907. After teaching in a number of schools, Bethune founded the Daytona Normal and Industrial Institute for Training Negro Girls in Daytona, Florida, in 1904. Twenty years later the school merged with a boys' school, the Cookman Institute, and was renamed Bethune-Cookman College in 1929. Explaining why she founded the training school, Bethune remarked, "Many homeless girls have been sheltered there and trained physically, mentally and spiritually. They have been helped and sent out to serve, to pass their blessings on to other needy children."

In addition to her career as an educator, Bethune helped found some of the most significant organizations in black America. In 1920 Bethune became vice president of the National Urban League and helped create the women's section of its Commission on Interracial Cooperation. From 1924 to 1928 she also served as the president of the National Association of Colored Women. In 1935, as founder and president of the National Council of Negro Women, Bethune forged a coalition of hundreds of black women's organizations across the country. She served from 1936 to 1950 as president of the Association for the Study of Negro Life and History, later known as the Association for the Study of Afro-American Life and History. In 1935 the National Association for the Advancement of Colored People awarded Bethune its highest honor, the Spingarn Medal. She received honorary degrees from ten universities, the Medal of Honor and Merit from Haiti (1949), and the Star of Africa Award from Liberia (1952). In 1938 she participated

along with liberal white southerners in the annual meetings of the Southern Conference for Human Welfare. Bethune's involvement in national government began in the 1920s during the Calvin Coolidge and Herbert Hoover presidential administrations, when she participated in child welfare conferences. In June 1936 Bethune became administrative assistant and, in January 1939, director in charge of Negro Affairs in the New Deal National Youth Administration (NYA). This made her the first black woman in U.S. history to occupy such a high-level federal position. Bethune was responsible for helping vast numbers of unemployed sixteen- to twenty-four-year-old black youths find jobs in private industry and in vocational training projects. The agency created work-relief programs that opened opportunities for thousands of black youths, which enabled countless black communities to survive the Depression. She served in this office until the NYA was closed in 1944.

During her service in the Franklin D. Roosevelt administration, Bethune organized a small but influential group of black officials who became known as the Black Cabinet. Prominent among them were

Mary McLeod Bethune, organizer of black women and advocate for social justice, 6 April 1949. (Library of Congress/Carl Van Vechten.)

WILLIAM HENRY HASTIE of the Department of the Interior and the War Department and ROBERT WEAVER, who served in the Department of the Interior and several manpower agencies. The Black Cabinet did more than advise the president; it articulated a black agenda for social change, beginning with demands for greater benefit from New Deal programs and equal employment opportunities.

In 1937 in Washington, D.C., Bethune orchestrated the National Conference on the Problems of the Negro and Negro Youth, which focused on concerns ranging from better housing and health care for African Americans to equal protection under the law. As an outspoken advocate for black civil rights, she fought for federal antipoll tax and antilynching legislation. Bethune's influence during the New Deal was further strengthened by her friendship with First Lady Eleanor Roosevelt.

During World War II, Bethune was special assistant to the secretary of war and assistant director of the Women's Army Corps. In this post she set up the first officer candidate schools for the corps. Throughout the war she pressed President Roosevelt and other governmental and military officials to make use of the many black women eager to serve in the national defense program; she also lobbied for increased appointments of black women to federal bureaus. After the war she continued to lecture and to write newspaper and magazine columns and articles until her death in Daytona Beach, Florida.

Urged by the National Council of Negro Women, the federal government dedicated the Mary McLeod Bethune Memorial Statue at Lincoln Park in southeastern Washington, D.C., on 10 July 1974. Bethune's life and work provide one of the major links between the social reform efforts of post-Reconstruction black women and the political protest activities of the generation emerging after World War II. The many strands of black women's struggle for education, political rights, racial pride, sexual autonomy, and liberation are united in the writings, speeches, and organization work of Bethune.

FURTHER READING

Holt, Rackman. *Mary McLeod Bethune: A Biography* (1964).

Ross, B. Joyce. "Mary McLeod Bethune and the National Youth Administration: A Case Study of Power Relationships in the Black Cabinet of Franklin D. Roosevelt," *Journal of Negro History* 60 (Jan. 1975): 1–28.

Smith, Elaine M. "Mary McLeod Bethune and the National Youth Administration," in *Clio Was a Woman: Studies in the History of American Women* (1980).

Obituary: *New York Times*, 19 May 1955.

This entry is taken from the *American National Biography* and is published here with the permission of the American Council of Learned Societies.

DARLENE CLARK HINE

Bethune, Thomas. *See* Blind Tom.

Betsch, MaVynee (13 Jan. 1935–5 Sept. 2005), activist and performer, was born in Jacksonville, Florida, one of three children born to John and Mary Betsch, both of whom worked for the Afro-American Life Insurance Company. The family was both well off and well known. Indeed, much of the Betsch family history can be traced through the important civil rights developments in the state of Florida. Her family was among the first black millionaires in the state. Of particular significance to MaVynee's life was the influence of her great-grandfather, Abraham Lincoln Lewis, who in the early 1930s founded American Beach, one of the only beach resorts and, eventually for African Americans, among the only available oceanfront properties in the state. It was in service of American Beach and its legacy that Betsch would spend most of her adult life and for which she became famous.

MaVynee's upbringing was steeped in both education and music. She began taking piano lessons as a young girl and soon settled on a career in musical performance. She attended local schools in Jacksonville and matriculated to Oberlin Conservatory of Music, where she studied performance and opera, graduating in 1955 with a bachelor's degree in Music. Shortly thereafter, Betsch traveled to Paris, France, where she continued her opera singing lessons and where she planned to launch a career on the musical stage. By 1959 she had relocated to Germany and made her operatic debut. In Braunschweig, she quickly became a celebrity and, as a black opera star, something of a novelty, too. Her fame spread, as did the difficulty and stress or maintaining a busy performance schedule. In 1965 she was informed that her mother had fallen into poor health, and she returned to Jacksonville. The homecoming was less than perfectly happy, however. Betsch's own health began to flag and she was soon diagnosed with ovarian cancer. She underwent a hysterectomy but soon grew frustrated by the quality of care she was receiving (and by what she perceived as her doctors' bumbling) and soon removed herself into her own care. Meanwhile, her family's ancestral home was seized through eminent domain and razed to make room for new construction at a local hospital. In 1975 both her mother and grandfather died, and Betsch inherited a great deal of money and property. She was a wealthy woman, though one without an immediate cause or occupation.

American Beach soon presented itself to her as both. She had moved there after the destruction of the family estate and became convinced that the beach house that had belonged to her grandfather was the cause of her apparent cure from cancer. Life on the beach turned her attention to environmental causes, and she began to give away her money to them in large donations. She gave away so much of her money, in fact, that she was eventually forced out of the beach house. An unscrupulous relative took over the Afro-American Life Insurance Company and mismanaged it into ruin. Betsch took up residence in the company's offices, but was forced to leave those, too. She was broke and homeless at the age of fifty.

Betsch returned to American Beach and lived there in any way she should could until her sister, Dr. JOHNNETTA COLE, bought her a small house. It was during that time that she became known as the "Beach Lady." The residents of American Beach knew her, or knew of her family and its long and proud history, and they helped her however they could, with food or a bit of money or a night's shelter. When, in 1994, a move to develop the beach with luxury condominiums and resorts was undertaken by various developers, Betsch became a singular voice for saving the beach and its homes from what she saw as a campaign by deep-pocketed whites to destroy the African American heritage of American Beach. Her crusade made her something of a local celebrity and her personality and idiosyncratic appearance—with her long, curled fingernails, uncut hair, and almost shamanistic style of dress—brought her to the national spotlight as well. She appeared on CNN and various network news programs, as well as in numerous publications like *Southern Living* and *Essence*. In 1997, and despite her tireless efforts, she lost her fight against the so-called Harrison Tract development, ironically initiated by the same relative who had run her family's insurance company into destitution. She

continued to educate visitors and residences alike about the history and legacy of American Beach, as well as the beauty and vitality of the natural world. When she died of cancer on the beach she'd spent much of her adult life defending, she was widely recognized as a hero of African American history and environmental causes alike. None other than the fourteenth Dalai Lama feted her as an Unsung Hero of Compassion. A movie in part about her life and experiences, as well as those of her family, *An American Beach*, was produced and directed by the filmmaker Kathleen Donaghy in 2000.

FURTHER READING

Rymer, Russ. *American Beach: A Saga of Race, Wealth, and Memory* (1998).

JASON PHILIP MILLER

Bettis, Jerome (16 Feb. 1972–), football player, was born Jerome Abram Bettis in Detroit, Michigan, the youngest of three children of Gladys and Johnnie Bettis. Throughout his childhood, Bettis was more interested in bowling than in football, because his mother, an accredited bowling instructor, encouraged bowling as a safe family hobby to deter her children from getting into trouble in their native Detroit. Bettis took up football in tenth grade, which disappointed his mother, who many years later remarked to a reporter from the Pittsburgh (PA) *Tribune-Review* (18 Jan. 2006) that she "hated the dreaded sport of football." However, Bettis was inspired to play partly because he hoped to earn a scholarship to ease the financial burden on his parents. During this early stage of his football career the Reggie McKenzie Football Camp, which was provided free of charge during the summer, aided Bettis significantly, and McKenzie, a former standout offensive linemen with the Buffalo Bills, helped to mold the young man into the 1990 Gatorade Circle of Champions Michigan Player of the Year by the time he was a senior at Detroit's Mackenzie High School. Bettis played on both sides of the ball as a linebacker on defense and as a running back on offense.

Bettis was heavily recruited coming out of high school, but he eventually settled on Notre Dame, where he went on to have a tremendous college career, rushing 337 times for 1,912 yards, a 5.7 yards per carry average. He gave credit to Lou Holtz, his college coach, for motivating him and preparing him for the NFL, claiming at a 2004 College Football Hall of Fame luncheon that "Coach Holtz always made sure he found a way to keep you going." The Notre Dame student newspaper gave him a nickname that defined him for the rest of his college and professional career: "The Bus."

Bettis's successful college career drew the attention of the National Football League, and in 1993, he entered the NFL Draft. He was drafted in the first round by the St. Louis Rams and wasted no time proving himself to be an NFL-caliber running back. He silenced early critics who wondered if his size made him better suited for the heavier fullback position and earned a plethora of honors after becoming the first Rams rookie running back since Eric Dickerson in 1983 to top 1,000 yards in a season, running for 1,429 yards on 294 carries. He was voted the 1993 Rookie of the Year by the Associated Press, *Pro Football Weekly*, the *Sporting News*, and the Pro Football Writers' Association, and he finished just 57 yards behind EMMITT SMITH for the NFL rushing title. Over the next couple years, however, Bettis fell out of favor with the Rams. In 1994, he again topped 1,000 yards, but by 1995 his carries were down to 183 from 319 in 1994. The Rams had lost faith in him and were looking to go in a different direction with the running back, and Bettis needed a change of scenery to jumpstart his career. Both Bettis and the Rams got their wish in 1996 when Bettis was traded to the Pittsburgh Steelers in a draft-day trade sometimes called the trade of the decade by football observers.

Bettis was revitalized in Pittsburgh, saying he felt like he was running downhill for his new team, and in 1996, his first year with the Steelers, he surpassed his rookie total rushing for 1,431 yards. He was also voted NFL Comeback Player of the Year for 1996. In 1997 Bettis followed up his amazing first year in Pittsburgh with his best statistical season as a pro when he rushed for 1,665 yards and removed all doubt about his viability as a starting NFL running back. He carried the majority of the load for the Steelers from 1996 to 2001, leading the Steelers to the AFC Championship game in 2001, where they lost to the eventual Super Bowl champions, the New England Patriots. Starting in 2001, Bettis accepted a reduced role in the offense but was nevertheless central to the Steelers play-off runs in 2002, 2004, and, perhaps most significantly, the Steelers' fifth Super Bowl title in 2005. The Steelers' desire for Bettis to retire as a champion became the rallying cry for the unlikely 2005 world champions. Often featuring Bettis in short yardage situations and in the fourth quarter, the 2005 Steelers reeled off nine straight wins to get Bettis home to Detroit for the Super Bowl. Bettis led the team onto the field before the 2005 Super Bowl and was greeted with a strong ovation from the heavily partisan Super Bowl crowd.

He earned a place as one of the Steelers' all-time greats, not just through his play, but by his unselfish mentoring of young running backs, his willingness to take significant pay cuts to stick with the Steelers, and his tireless community activism.

Bettis never forgot what the Reggie McKenzie football camp meant to him as a tenth grader and teamed up with McKenzie to help teach more than six hundred kids each summer about football and to help mentor them about life decisions. The McKenzie football camp became just one of many branches of Bettis' foundation, called The Bus Stops Here. The foundation provided scholarships to his old high school, donated football cleats to local high schools, and endowed a scholarship program at Notre Dame. In 2006, Bettis began the Cyber Bus Computer Literacy Program, which allowed underprivileged children to get valuable hands-on experience with computers. He partnered with the city of Pittsburgh in 2006 to renovate an inner-city park and made plans to help renovate the football field at Mackenzie High School.

Throughout his career, Bettis remained a positive role model both on and off the football field. He is almost assured a spot in the Hall of Fame with his 13,662 career rushing yards and has surpassed NFL greats such as Eric Dickerson, JIM BROWN, and Marcus Allen along the way. He made the Pro Bowl six times: in 1993, 1994, 1996, 1997, 2001, and 2005. However, what Bettis may be remembered most for is his community-first spirit and his good nature. Among his many honors for work off the gridiron was his selection as Pittsburgh Dapper Dan Man of the Year award in 1997 and the 2002 NFL Walter Payton Man of the Year award, both for his contributions to the community. Bettis married Trameka Boykin on 8 July 2006 and had one daughter, Jada, born in 2005.

FURTHER READING

Barger, James, ed. *Decade of Power: The Pittsburgh Steelers in the Cowher Era* (2002).

Schmalzbauer, Adam. *The History of the Pittsburgh Steelers* (2005).

"Fueling the Bus," Pittsburgh (PA) *Tribune-Review* (18 Jan. 2006). Available at http://www.pittsburghlive. com/ x/pittsburghtrib/living/fooddrink/ cookbookreviews/ s_414466.html.

"Jerome Bettis Tells College Football Luncheon Crowd How 'The Bus' Got Rolling" (23 Apr. 2004). Available at http://www.collegefootball.org/news. php?id=369.

DANIEL A. DALRYMPLE

Bevel, James (19 Oct. 1936–19 Dec. 2008), civil rights activist, was born in Itta Bena, Mississippi, to Dennis and Illie Bevel (originally Beverly, from James's white great-grandfather). His father, a farmer and lay minister nicknamed "Crazy Dennis Bevel" by local whites for his unwillingness to suffer the indignities of Jim Crow, served as an early model for James about how to live according to one's personal code. As a black landowner in Humphreys County, Dennis was a target for white repression, and the loss of his property scarred the family deeply. After his parents divorced James's childhood was divided between rural Mississippi and Cleveland, Ohio. He served in the U.S. Navy and then worked as a bricklayer's assistant in a Cleveland steel mill and moonlighted in a musical group. While making good money, and spending much of it in Cleveland's nightclubs, a neighbor prevailed upon him to join her at church. Here Bevel first heard the voice of God.

Stirred by this experience Bevel enrolled at American Baptist Theological Seminary in Nashville, Tennessee, in January 1957. He soon became well known around campus for his gorgeous singing voice, powerful preaching ability, deep-rooted evangelical beliefs, fondness for and skill at intellectual debate, and singular charisma. Although he pursued his studies and female students with equal ardor, Bevel was drawn into far different extracurricular activities. Late 1950s Nashville was a small but important incubator for civil rights activism, due chiefly to the presence of the Reverend JAMES LAWSON, a former Methodist missionary and representative of the Fellowship of Reconciliation (FOR). Steeped in the philosophy and techniques of nonviolent direct action, Lawson attracted local college students—mostly blacks, but also a handful of whites—to his workshops, which taught nonviolence as a radical form of Christianity that could liberate both blacks and whites from the sin of segregation. Participants in these workshops included the future civil rights activists DIANE NASH, JOHN LEWIS, MARION BARRY, and Bernard Lafayette, among others. Although initially skeptical Bevel became a fervent believer in Lawson's teachings, especially with Lawson's use of the Gandhian example. Bevel had read the Russian novelist and Christian pacifist Leo Tolstoy in the navy, and taken together these influences suggested to Bevel that nonviolent direct action was the logical manifestation of Christian witness, redemptive suffering, and social justice combined.

Lawson's workshops culminated in a sustained and successful sit-in campaign against Nashville's downtown lunch counters in early 1960. Although part of a wider campaign of lunch-counter protests across the South, the Nashvillians won particular attention for their nonviolent discipline and profession of Christian ideals. The group's influence continued after Bevel and his peers met with similar-minded activists from across the South to form the Student Nonviolent Coordinating Committee (SNCC). Bevel and the Nashvillians were regarded with both awe and derision. Some admired what they perceived as a confidence borne from experience, while others derided them as fanatic Christians devoted to nonviolence as a way of life. Such differences of opinion, particularly as the Nashvillians argued with a more pragmatic contingent from Atlanta that saw nonviolence as one tactic among many, would be a considerable source of creative tension within SNCC in subsequent years.

After helping found SNCC Bevel played a critical role in local and national movement activities. In 1961 he assisted the campaign to desegregate downtown Nashville with "stand-ins" outside movie theaters. That year he also joined other Nashvillians in reviving the Freedom Rides to integrate interstate travel accommodations, which the South kept segregated in violation of federal law. The rides resulted in Bevel's imprisonment in Mississippi; after his release he began grassroots organizing in Jackson, Laurel, and elsewhere in the state. He also married fellow activist Diane Nash in fall 1961; they would divorce four years later after having two children. Working both with SNCC and the Southern Christian Leadership Conference (SCLC), Bevel rose quickly in the latter organization, becoming by 1963 a member of the executive staff in addition to a field secretary. In 1964 he was named director of direct action and unofficially served as MARTIN LUTHER KING JR.'s conduit to the younger SNCC activists while continuing to fulfill his reputation as a daring strategist and skilled organizer, which he attributed to voices of divine inspiration. Perhaps most famously, Bevel orchestrated the 1963 Children's Crusade march in Birmingham, Alabama. By using children as protestors, Bevel revived the SCLC's flagging campaign and kept the city at the forefront of national headlines. Although many were aghast at the sight of children demonstrating, dramatic film of Police Commissioner Bull Connor's use of water hoses on black bystanders served the SCLC's cause.

Many also credited Bevel as being one of several who inspired the 1963 March on Washington. In September 1963 while organizing in Edenton, North Carolina, Bevel and Nash were shaken by the Klan bombing of Birmingham's Sixteenth Street Baptist Church that killed DENISE MCNAIR, CAROLE ROBERTSON, CYNTHIA WESLEY, and ADDIE MAE COLLINS. The couple returned to the Deep South and redoubled their efforts, particularly in devising the blueprint for SCLC's campaign in Selma, Alabama, for a voting rights bill. In Selma, Bevel directed the Selma-to-Montgomery March and endured a vicious beating and imprisonment that nearly killed him.

With the movement's focus widening as the 1960s continued, Bevel remained active on all fronts. He remained central to the SCLC's work for open housing in Chicago, lobbied Martin Luther King Jr. to oppose the Vietnam War, and worked on behalf of the antiwar and disarmament movements. After King's assassination in 1968 Bevel's eccentric qualities became increasingly erratic, and his opinionated outbursts, combined with his moralistic pronouncements, continued to rankle other members of the SCLC. He was especially fervent in insisting that the SCLC assist the defense of King's murderer, James Earl Ray. Worries about his mental health arose in 1970 after a lecture to Spelman College coeds degenerated into a weekend where he quarantined himself in a hotel room, ruined the walls with a marker in outlining a sermon, and challenged listeners to drink his urine to prove their commitment. Nonetheless Bevel continued his political and social activism in myriad ways. Through the 1970s he worked extensively on programs addressing mental health, poverty, and economic development, based mostly but not exclusively in Chicago. He ran a failed campaign to be the Republican congressman from his Chicago district in 1984. Eight years later he served as the vice presidential candidate on the perennial political gadfly Lyndon LaRouche's ticket. In the mid-1990s he was a catalyst for LOUIS FARRAKHAN's Million Man March.

Although his idiosyncrasies have perhaps overshadowed his role in history, Bevel was among the first rank of leaders in the modern African American freedom struggle. His talents combined a shrewd tactical cunning with the unyielding and passionate belief of a religious prophet. Outspoken and unconventionally brilliant, his activist career was emblematic of the civil rights movement's mix of strategy and belief. He died in Springfield, Virginia, at the age of 72.

FURTHER READING

Halberstam, David. *The Children* (1998).

Houston, Benjamin. "The Nashville Way: A Southern City Confronts Racial Change, 1945–1975," Ph.D. diss., University of Florida (2006).

Kryn, Randall L. "James L. Bevel: The Strategist of the 1960s Civil Rights Movement," in *We Shall Overcome: The Civil Rights Movement in the United States in the 1950's and 1960's*, ed. David J. Garrow (1989).

Lewis, John. *Walking with the Wind: A Memoir of the Movement* (1998).

BENJAMIN HOUSTON

Bey, Dawoud (25 Nov. 1953–), a portrait photographer, was born David Edward Smikle in Jamaica, Queens, New York, to Mary Smikle and Kenneth Smikle. He changed his name to Dawoud Bey in the early 1970s. Bey received his first camera, an Argus C3 rangefinder, in 1968 and began to learn how to take pictures. In 1973 he apprenticed to Levey J. Smith at MOT Photography Studio in Hollis, New York, and began spending time at the Studio Museum in Harlem. Bey then attended the School of Visual Arts in New York City for a year but left in 1978 to accept an artist's position with the Cultural Council Foundation CETA Artists Project in New York. He graduated with a B from Empire State College, State University of New York, in 1990. He also earned an M from the Yale University School of Art in 1993.

Bey emerged as a documentarian of African American life. African American images have been heavily influenced by a history of slavery, which defined black people as chattel and three-fifths human as well as inferior to whites. Bey's work reflects the African American fight for the imagery and the power to illustrate the self. His focus is on the face that blacks show to the world and the style in which they present themselves.

Bey's earliest professional photographs evolved into a five-year project chronicling the people and streets of Harlem. The collective portrait, *Harlem USA* (1975–1979), is in the documentary tradition of the New Deal federal photographic projects of the 1930s and 1940s as well as the practitioners of that period such as Walker Evans and Margaret Bourke-White. Bey has also been influenced by ROY DECARAVA and JAMES VAN DER ZEE. Like DeCarava, Bey has familial ties to Harlem. These photographs helped him identify where he was located, both geographically and socially.

Harlem served as Bey's focus because it had become his home. In 1976, he began teaching photography at the Studio Museum in Harlem while also teaching at the Jamaica Arts Center in Queens. He spent much of his free time at the Wesusi Nyumba Ya Sana Gallery in Harlem. He mounted his first exhibition, a three-person exhibit, with the photographers Frank Stewart and JEANNE MOUTOUSSAMY-ASHE at Benin Gallery in Harlem in 1976.

In the mid-1980s, Bey traded in his 35-mm camera for a 4 × 5-inch camera with a tripod and hood in order to slow down the way in which he worked and develop more sustained contact with subjects. Bey began to work almost exclusively with a view camera and Polaroid material beginning in 1988. Meanwhile, Bey married Candida Alvarez in 1982 (and they divorced in 2006). The couple had a son, Ramon Alvarez-Smikle, in 1991.

In the early 1990s Bey decided to change his practice once again by moving entirely into the studio. He found that, after making portraits in the streets, that the reading of the photograph is influenced by the environment. The environment becomes the key to identifying the subject but the reading is not always accurate. To remove the environment from the picture, Bey began to photograph his subjects using formal lighting, backdrop paper, and a 20 × 24-inch Polaroid camera, one of the Polaroid Corporation's largest cameras. This camera measures five feet high by three and a half feet wide. He used Polaroid Positive/Negative Type 55 film that enabled him to give a photograph to his model in slightly over a minute and still have a usable negative from which to print. Once in the studio, Bey also shifted his exploration into issues of reciprocity through the very construction of his prints. Accordingly, rather than photograph his subjects frontally and in the center of his compositions as he had done in so much of his large-format street work, Bey focused on different aspects of his subjects' bodies and photographed them from multiple angles or profiles.

Bey won a New York State Council on the Arts residency fellowship in 1984 and a National Endowment for the Arts fellowship in 1991. His solo exhibitions have been shown at the Walker Art Center in Minneapolis, the Museum of Contemporary Photography in Chicago, and the Fogg Art Museum at Harvard University. He has participated in group exhibitions at the Whitney Museum of American Art in New York State and the Museum of Modern Art in New York City. He has been a professor of photography at Columbia College in Chicago since 1998.

FURTHER READING
Halbreich, Kathy, et al. *Dawoud Bey: Portraits 1975–1995* (1995).
Reynolds, Jock, and Taro Nettleton. *Class Pictures: Photographs by Dawoud Bey* (2007).

CARYN E. NEUMANN

Bey, James Hawthorne (17 Apr. 1913–8 Apr. 2004), musician, composer, educator, priest, and artist, was born James Hawthorne in Yamassee, South Carolina, to Mary Hugee and Roland Hawthorne. When he was still a boy he and his family moved to New Jersey, then to New York City—first to Brooklyn and later to Harlem. In Brooklyn James and his parents lived with his grandparents, and his grandfather encouraged him to join the church choir.

His musical talents became more evident after his move to Harlem, when he began to study dance and percussion with Isame Andrews, a specialist in African music and dance and a student of ASADATA DAFORA. Attracting notice with his vocal skills, Hawthorne was admitted to both the EVA JESSYE and the FRANCIS HALL JOHNSON choirs. In the mid- to late 1930s he studied African drum making and performance, especially the ashiko drum, with Moses Miannes (Mianns), a Nigerian who had come to the United States to perform at the 1934 Chicago World's Fair.

Shortly before the beginning of World War II, Hawthorne married Louise Smith. He then enlisted in the military, serving in the United Stated Navy where he had the rank of Mate First Class. He saw action at Pearl Harbor when his ship was attacked and he earned an Asiatic Pacific One Star Victory Medal for his courage in battle. On his return to the United Sates he enrolled in a cosmetology school and began a family. He and his wife had three children—a son, David, and two daughters, Denise and Carolyn.

James Hawthorne's interest in African culture led him to the Moorish Science Temple and after joining he changed his name to Bey. By the 1950s he had developed a reputation for his knowledge and proficiency in African percussion, gospel, jazz, and other genres of African American music. His rich, deep bass voice continued to attract attention and in 1953 EVA JESSYE engaged him as a cast member for the international tour of *Porgy and Bess*, starring LEONTYNE PRICE, CAB CALLOWAY, and WILLIAM WARFIELD. The company traveled across Europe to great acclaim.

Returning to New York Bey began an extensive recording career, which included collaborations with HARRY BELAFONTE, ART BLAKEY, Herbie Mann, Babatunde Olatunji, MAX ROACH, PHAROAH SANDERS, Randy Weston, and many other renowned musicians. His career as a performer continued to blossom during the 1960s, taking him to premier jazz and concert venues throughout the United States performing with Belafonte, Clifford Jordan, Herbie Mann, Miriam Makeba, and the World Saxophone Quartet. Between 1958 and 1998 he performed on twenty-three recordings under five different names (Baba Hawthorne Bey, Chief Bey, Chief James Hawthorne Bey, Hawthorne Bey, and James Bey). However, Bey never let success interfere with his commitment to his people; he found time to return again and again to community centers, churches, schools, and local events to share his spirit and his talent. Always honing his skills, Bey developed a new way of tying and securing the skins on the heads of djembe drums, a technique that has been adopted by a number of African drum makers.

Bey had an affinity for dance as well as music and was engaged with a number of dance companies such as the ALVIN AILEY Dance Theatre, Charles Moore Dance Company, and the Syvilla Fort Dance Company. He performed extensively with PEARL PRIMUS, touring with her troupe in South America and Africa in addition to their appearances in the United States. While on tour in West Africa with Primus he was recognized by the Araba of Lagos, Fagbeni Ajaiku, who honored him with the title of Chief. Back in the United States, Bey organized a music group named Egbe Ife (Society of Love), which became a training ground for young percussionists; a number of his students went on to develop successful careers. From 1973–1975 he was in the cast of the Broadway musical *Raisin*, his role being *African Drummer*. On 17 April 1973 Bey married Barbara Ann Coleman, also known as Barbara Kenyatta, with whom he spent the rest of his life.

As Bey continued to seek connections to his African heritage that would fulfill his spiritual, intellectual, and creative destiny, he discovered Orisha Worship. In 1976 he became an initiated priest of Sango and his wife Barbara became a priest of Yemoja in the Yoruba Lucumi religious tradition. As a priest, Bey was generous with his time and energy—providing spiritual guidance to many people from all walks of life who recognized his sincere character and sought his counsel. He was fiercely honest, deeply aware of his own human weaknesses, extremely loving toward his family, and courageous in defense of his people. These qualities made him an exemplary leader in his community, where he was recognized as a revered elder and was often asked to give blessings, pour libations, lead prayer, and expound on Yoruba Lucumi religious teachings. Eventually he established Ile Omo Olofi, a religious house, with his wife Barbara and many godchildren.

Always interested in teaching and sharing information, Bey was a frequent guest speaker at such institutions as Duke University, City College, Drake University, Medgar Evers College, Princeton University, Temple University, the University of Hartford, and New York University. Interested also in reaching out to children, in the 1990s he accepted a position to teach shekere at Intermediate School 246, in Brooklyn.

Even at the age of ninety, after being diagnosed with stomach cancer, he continued his activities. Just months before his death, he performed in a drum symposium at New York University. By the time of his death, he had been the subject of many celebrations and tributes of all kinds in honor of his life. Hundreds attended his funeral at Friendship Missionary Baptist Church in Brooklyn, New York; he was buried on 14 April 2004 at Calverton National Cemetery, Long Island, New York. Just days later, on 17 April 2004, on the day that would have been his ninety-first birthday and the couple's thirty-first anniversary, his wife died. He was survived by his son, David, and daughters, Carol, Denise, and Ayodele, as well as four grandchildren and abundant godchildren, students, and friends.

FURTHER READING

James Hawthorne Bey's son, David Hawthorne, maintains Chief Bey's papers and archives, including recordings, photographs, and performance videos.

Frazier, E. "Rhythm (A Tribute to Chief Bey, P.J. and Drummers of the World)," *Essence*, vol. 5 (2002).

Olatunji, Babatunde, with Robert Atkinson, and Akinsola Akiwowo. *The Beat of My Drum, An Autobiography* (2005).

Obituaries: *Amsterdam News*, 14 April 2004; *Associated Press, New York Times*, 13 April 2004.

DISCOGRAPHY

Bey, Chief, and Ile Omo Olofi. *Explorations II* (Mapleshade, 1995).

Ilori, Solomon. *African Highlife* (Blue Note, 1963).

Mann, Herbie. *At the Village Gate* (Atlantic, 1961).

Olatunji, Babatunde. *Drums of Passion* (Columbia, 1959).

Olatunji, Babatunde. *More Drums of Passion* (Columbia, 1966).
Saunders, Pharaoh. *Izipho Zam* (Strata East, 1969).
World Saxophone Quartet. *Metamorphosis* (Elektra/ Nonesuch, 1990).

SUSAN RICHARDSON-SANABRIA

Bharucha-Reid, Albert Turner (13 Nov. 1927–26 Feb. 1985), mathematician, was born in Hampton, Virginia, the son of William Thaddeus Reid, who taught electricity at Hampton Institute's trade school, and Elaine Brown. Albert had a brother, William M., and a sister, Cora Mae. His strong interest in biology and mathematics led him to enroll at Iowa State University, where such joint disciplinary programs were encouraged. After obtaining his bachelor of science degree in 1949, Reid continued at Iowa State in the graduate program for mathematics and biology, but he left for the University of Chicago in 1950. There he studied mathematical biology, mathematics, probability and statistics, and physics, and he served as a research assistant in the mathematical biology program. In 1953 Reid accepted a position as a research associate in mathematical statistics at Columbia University. He did not complete the Ph.D. program at Chicago or Columbia because he did not believe that a doctorate was necessary to become a competent researcher in the mathematical sciences. This view was reinforced by the continuing publication of his work in significant research journals.

On 7 June 1954 Reid married Rodabe Phiroze Bharucha and from then on hyphenated his name to Bharucha-Reid. The couple had two children, Kurush in 1955, and Rustum in 1965.

In 1955 Bharucha-Reid took a yearlong appointment as assistant research statistician (equivalent to assistant professor) in the statistics department at the University of California at Berkeley. The following year he took a teaching position at the University of Oregon, where he remained until 1961. During the 1958–1959 academic year he continued his research efforts as a fellow at the Mathematical Institute of the Polish Academy of Sciences in Warsaw, Poland. In 1961 Bharucha Reid accepted a position as associate professor of mathematics at Wayne State University in Detroit. Two years later he took a yearlong leave from the university to travel to Madras, India, as a visiting professor on the faculty of applied mathematics in the Institute of Mathematical Sciences.

In 1965 he was promoted to full professor of mathematics at Wayne State, and he subsequently served there as director of the Center for Research in Probability from 1967 to 1981, as acting chair of the mathematics department from 1972 to 1973, and as dean and associate provost for graduate studies from 1976 to 1981. During this time he also held visiting professorships at the University of Wisconsin's Mathematics Research Center, from 1966 to 1967, and at the Georgia Institute of Technology, from 1973 to 1974. In 1981 Bharucha-Reid began working at the Georgia Institute of Technology in Atlanta as a professor in the School of Mathematics. In 1983 he left that position to assume duties at Atlanta University as distinguished professor of mathematics.

Bharucha-Reid's research covered a wide range of topics in mathematical biology, pure mathematics, physics, probability, and statistics. From 1953 to 1955 he engaged in research on two air force projects at Columbia University that involved him in basic research into stochastic processes and stochastic theories or epidemics. He continued this research during 1955 and 1956 at the University of California, Berkeley. From 1956 to 1962 he was director of an Army Research Office project concerned with stochastic processes and related statistical problems at the University of Oregon and Wayne State University. From 1962 to 1964 he was co-principal investigator for a National Science Foundation grant on stochastic processes and mathematical physics at Wayne, and he continued from 1966 to 1969 as director of a National Institutes of Health grant on stochastic processes in biology. Other Wayne projects included a National Science Foundation grant, from 1969 to 1971, on probability measures and random equations, and an Army Research office grant, from 1977 to 1981, on computational solution of random integral equations.

During his brief tenure at Atlanta University, from 1983 to 1985, Bharucha-Reid was active in the new graduate program for master of science in physics, and he made significant contributions to the research programs in computational and plasma physics. Two of his last papers were concerned with the numerical solutions of a random singular integral equation appearing in crack problems and the effect of random loading on the mechanics of fatigue and crack growth in solids.

Bharucha-Reid published his first book, *Elements of the Theory of Markov Processes and Their Applications*, in 1960. It provided one of the first concise introductions to the area of probabilistic analysis, and for many years it was successful as a textbook and guide for self-study. During his career he published more than seventy papers and wrote seven books on topics in the stochastic theory of epidemics, Markov processes, random integral and polynomial equations, and computational methods. His last book, with M. Sambandham, *Random Polynomials*, was published posthumously in 1986.

Bharucha-Reid traveled widely through North America, Europe, and India, and presented lectures at many universities, international conferences, and workshops. He served as editor of the *Journal of Integral Equations and Applications*, and associate editor for *Nonlinear Analysis* and the *Bulletin of Mathematical Biology*. He was on the editorial board of the *Journal of Mathematical and Physical Sciences* and was a member of the reviewing staff for *Mathematical Reviews* and *Zentralblatt für Mathematik*. He was also editor for the North-Holland series in Probability and Applied Mathematics.

Bharucha-Reid held active membership in numerous professional organizations, including the American Mathematical Society, the Polish Mathematical Society, the American Association for the Advancement of Science, the Institute of Mathematical Statistics, the Society for Mathematical Biology, and the Society for Industrial and Applied Mathematics. His other professional responsibilities included serving as vice president of the International Association for Mathematical Geology, from 1972 to 1976, member of the Russian Translation Committee of the American Mathematical Society and the Institute of Mathematical Statistics, from 1973 to 1981, and member of the American Mathematical Society's Committee on Academic Freedom, Tenure, and Employment Security, from 1977 to 1981.

Bharucha-Reid had fourteen students earn their doctoral degrees under his direction at Wayne State University, and many of them went on to enjoy successful careers as both academicians and researchers. Having benefited greatly from both his teaching and research abilities, most of his students published jointly with Bharucha-Reid, and several became major research collaborators, in particular, Dhandapani Kannan and Mark J. Christensen. A significant collaborator, who was not a student of Bharucha-Reid's, was M. Sambandham, who published several papers with him and coauthored a book on random polynomials.

Albert Turner Bharucha-Reid died at his home in Atlanta. His distinguished career as both a pure and applied research mathematician extended over three and a half decades, and his many contributions to research, student training and mentoring, and academic leadership were acknowledged by the large number of honors and awards he received throughout his life. In particular, he was granted an honorary doctorate of science from Syracuse University in 1984 and the National Association of Mathematicians established an annual lecture series in his name.

FURTHER READING

Bharucha-Reid's papers are housed at the Amistad Research Center, Tulane University, New Orleans, Louisiana.

Krapp, Kristine, ed. *Notable Black American Scientists* (1999).

Mickens, Ronald E. "Albert Turner Bharucha-Reid," *Physics Today* (Dec. 1985).

Newell, Virginia K., ed. *Black Mathematicians and Their Works* (1980).

Sammons, Vivian O. *Blacks in Science and Medicine* (1989).

RONALD E. MICKENS

Biassou, Jorge (Georges) (c. 1760–c. 1801), Haitian revolutionary, was born a slave in Cap Français (or Guarico, in Spanish), on the northern coast of Saint Domingue, in modern Haiti. Spanish documents give his parents' names as Carlos and Diana, and Biassou and his mother were the slaves of the Holy Fathers of Charity in Cap Français, where Biassou's mother worked in the Hospital of the Holy Fathers of Charity, probably as a laundress or cook. Biassou's father's owner and occupation are unknown.

In 1791 Biassou joined Boukman Dutty, a slave driver and coachman considered by the slaves to be a religious leader, and Jean-François, also a slave from the Northern Plains of Saint Domingue, in leading the largest slave revolt in the Western Hemisphere on–the richest sugar colony of its day, French Saint Domingue. Boukman was killed in November of 1791, only three months into the revolt, and Biassou and Jean-François assumed command of the rebel slave forces of the North. Jean-François decorated himself with the Cross of St. Louis, an aristocratic military order. Biassou titled himself the Viceroy of the Conquered Territories, and Toussaint-Louverture, a freeman who had once been a slave on the Bréda plantation, became aide and physician to Biassou's large army of forty thousand men, all former slaves.

Unable to feed and supply such a large force for very long, Jean-François and Biassou attempted to secure the general amnesty promised in late 1791 by the French Assembly. This decree promised to forgive "acts of revolution" for rebels who "returned to order" (Du Bois, 125). They sued for peace in exchange for their own freedom and political rights and those of their families and officers, but the reactionary planters of Saint Domingue unwisely rejected their offer. Biassou angrily ordered the execution of all his white prisoners, vowing that they would pay "for the insolence of the [Colonial] Assembly which has dared to write to me with so little respect" (Landers, 209). Toussaint stayed his superior's order, but the bloody fighting continued.

In the spring of 1793 England and Spain both declared war on France and began to court Biassou and Jean-François, whose troops by that time were almost in a starving state. Commissioner Léger Félicité Sonthonax, one of three civil commissioners sent to represent the new French Republic in Saint Domingue, also offered freedom and alliance in the name of the French Republic, but some rebels considered this a trick and believed only a king could make and keep such a promise. Jean-François and Biassou allegedly responded, "Since the beginning of the world we have obeyed the will of a king. We have lost the king of France but we are dear to him of Spain who constantly shows us reward and assistance. We therefore cannot recognize you until you have enthroned a king" (Landers, 210).

Spain designated its new armies of risen slaves the Black Auxiliaries of Charles IV. The Spanish captain general and governor of Santo Domingo (the Spanish name for Saint Domingue) ceremoniously decorated Jean-François, Biassou, and Toussaint with gold medals bearing the likeness of the king and presented them with documents expressing the gratitude and confidence of the Spanish government. Newly supplied and under a Spanish flag, the forces of Jean-François, Biassou, and Toussaint fought many bloody battles against the French, but when the French Assembly finally abolished slavery in May of 1794, Toussaint broke with the Spaniards and offered his services and loyalty to the French Republic. Jean-François and Biassou remained loyal to Spain.

In 1795 Spain and the directory of the French Republic, the ruling body of the new French Republic, finally concluded a peace treaty by which Spain ceded western Hispaniola to the French and agreed to disband the Black Auxiliaries of Carlos IV. On the last day of December 1795, the exiled black troops sailed away for Havana, Cuba, on a small flotilla of four ships, but Cuban officials refused to let them disembark. After much angry correspondence, Jean-François and twelve of his military subordinates, along with their extended families, totaling 136 persons, sailed away from Havana for Cádiz, Spain. The remainder of Jean-François's troops was dispersed to various parts of Central America. In January 1796 Biassou traveled with his immediate household of five, his slave, and seventeen other dependents to Spanish-held St. Augustine, Florida.

Biassou had enjoyed a position of command for five years before he settled in Florida, and his proud demeanor immediately alienated the Spanish governor, who had arranged lodging for Biassou and his immediate family and sent two nights' supper to the house, only to have Biassou complain that he had not been invited to dine at the governor's home. The black general walked the streets of St. Augustine in fine clothes trimmed in gold, a silver-trimmed saber, and a fancy ivory and silver dagger. The gold medal of Charles IV must also have impressed the townspeople, but the governor wrote, "The slave owners have viewed his arrival with great disgust, for they fear he will set a bad example for the rest of his class" (Landers, 212). Only three months after arriving, Biassou's brother-in-law and military heir, Sergeant Juan Jorge Jacobo, married Rafaela Witten, the daughter of PRINCE WITTEN. Like Biassou and Jorge Jacobo, Witten was a member of the free black militia and had served with distinction in 1795 against invaders sponsored by the French revolutionary Edmond Charles Genet, first minister of the French Republic to the United States.

The marriage of Biassou's heir, Jorge, and Witten's daughter, Rafaela, thus united the leading families of both groups of blacks who had allied with the cause of the Spanish king against the forces of French republicanism. Previously, no black militiaman in Florida who served in Spain had held a rank higher than sergeant, but by virtue of his service in Santo Domingo, Biassou still used the title of general. His elevated title thus raised the status of Florida's black militia. Biassou and his troops proved able defenders of Spanish interests in the next decades. In 1800 the Seminole Indians launched a series of violent attacks on outlying plantations; Biassou led the troops in expeditions against the raiders and in border patrols until his sudden illness and death in July 1801.

When Biassou died, his bereaved family and followers arranged a wake and buried him the following day with full honors in St. Augustine's Tolomato Cemetery. Despite rumors about his possible practice of vodun (the Afro-syncretic religion also known as vodou) in Santo Domingo, in his last years Biassou had apparently been baptized and so he received a full Catholic burial. After an elaborate mass that included songs, tolling bells, candles, and burning incense, Florida's governor and other persons of distinction accompanied Biassou's cortege to the graveyard. They were accompanied by drummers and an honor guard of twenty members of Biassou's troops, who discharged a volley of gunfire at the grave site. The obligations of military corporatism outweighed any racial distinctions in this ceremony, the public notary attesting that "every effort was made to accord him the decency due an officer Spain had recognized for military heroism" (Landers, 133). The parish priest entered Biassou in the death register as "the renowned *caudillo* (or military leader) of the black royalists of Santo Domingo" (Landers, *A Turbulent Time*, 169).

FURTHER READING

Du Bois, Laurent. *Avengers of the New World: The Story of the Haitian Revolution* (2004).

Gaspar, David Barry, and David Patrick Geggus, eds. *A Turbulent Time: The French Revolution and the Greater Caribbean* (1997).

Geggus, David. *Haitian Revolutionary Studies* (2002).

James, C. L. R. *Black Jacobins: Toussaint L'Ouverture and the San Domingo Revolution* (1963).

Landers, Jane. *Black Society in Spanish Florida* (1999).

Landers, Jane. "Rebellion and Royalism in Spanish Florida: The French Revolution on Spain's Northern Colonial Frontier," in *A Turbulent Time*, eds. David Barry Gaspar and David Patrick Geggus (1997).

JANE G. LANDERS

Bibb, Henry Walton (10 May 1815–1 Aug. 1854), author, editor, and antislavery lecturer, was born into slavery on the plantation of David White of Shelby County, Kentucky, the son of James Bibb, a slaveholding planter and state senator, and Mildred Jackson. White began hiring Bibb out as a laborer on several neighboring plantations before he had reached the age of ten. The constant change in living situations throughout his childhood, combined with the inhumane treatment he often received at the hands of strangers, set a pattern for life that he would later refer to in his autobiography as "my manner of living on the road." Bibb was sold more than six times between 1832 and 1840 and was forced to relocate to at least seven states throughout the South; later, as a free man, his campaign for abolition took him throughout eastern Canada and the northern United States. But such early instability also made the young Bibb both self-sufficient and resourceful, two characteristics that were useful against the day-to-day assault of slavery: "The only weapon of self defense that I could use successfully," he wrote, "was that of deception."

In 1833 Bibb met and married Malinda, a slave on William Gatewood's plantation in nearby Oldham County, Kentucky, and the following year she gave birth to Mary Frances, their only child to survive infancy. At about this time Gatewood purchased Bibb from the Whites in the vain hope that uniting the young family would pacify their desire for freedom. Living less than ten miles from the Ohio River, Bibb made his first escape from slavery by crossing the river into Madison, Indiana, in the winter of 1837. He boarded a steamboat bound for Cincinnati, escaping the notice of authorities because he was "so near the color of a slaveholder," a trait deemed undesirable by prospective slave buyers and for which he endured prolonged incarcerations at various slave markets. Bibb situated this first escape historically as "the commencement of what was called the underground railroad to Canada." Less than a year after achieving freedom, Bibb returned to Kentucky for his wife and daughter. He was captured and taken to the Louisville slave market, from which he again escaped, returning to Perrysburg, Ohio.

In July 1839 Bibb once more undertook to free his wife and child. Betrayed by another slave, Bibb was again taken to Louisville for sale; this time his wife and child accompanied him on the auction block. While awaiting sale, Bibb received the rudiments of an education from white felons in the prison, where he was forced to work at hard labor for a summer. Finally, a speculator purchased the Bibbs for resale at the lucrative markets of New Orleans. After being bought by Deacon Francis Whitfield of Claiborn Parish, Louisiana, Bibb and his family suffered unimaginable cruelty. They were physically beaten and literally overworked to the point of death, and they nearly perished for lack of food and adequate shelter. Bibb attempted two escapes from Whitfield, preferring that his family risk the perils of the surrounding Red River swamps than endure eighteen-hour days in the cotton fields.

The final escape attempt resulted in Bibb's permanent separation from his family in December 1840. First staked down and beaten nearly to death after his capture, Bibb was then sold to two professional gamblers. These men took him through Texas and Arkansas and into "Indian Territory," where they sold him to a Cherokee slave owner on the frontier of white settlement in what is probably present-day Oklahoma or southeastern Kansas. There Bibb received what he considered his only humane treatment in slavery. Because he was allotted a modicum of independence and respect, and because he was reluctant to desert his master, who was then terminally ill, Bibb delayed his final escape from slavery by a year, departing the night of his master's death. He traveled through wilderness, occasionally stumbling onto Indian encampments, before crossing into Missouri, where his route took him east along the Osage River into Jefferson City. From there he traveled by steamboat through St. Louis to Cincinnati and on to freedom in 1841.

In Detroit in the winter of 1842, Bibb briefly attended the school of the Reverend William C. Monroe, receiving his only formal education. Bibb's work as what he called an "advocate of liberty" began in earnest soon after his final escape from slavery; for the next decade he epitomized the black abolitionist, making his voice heard through lectures, a slave narrative, and the independent press. Like his contemporaries FREDERICK DOUGLASS, WILLIAM WELLS BROWN, and WILLIAM and ELLEN CRAFT, Bibb was among a first generation of African American fugitives from the South who used their firsthand experience in slavery as a compelling testimony against the atrocities of the southern institution.

Although his highly regarded *Narrative of the Life and Adventures of Henry Bibb, An American Slave* was not published until the spring of 1849, Bibb began telling the story of his life before antislavery crowds in Adrian, Michigan, in May 1844. His story proved so poignant in its depiction of human suffering and endurance, so heroic in its accounts of ingenious escapes, and so romantic in its adventures in the territories of the West that the Detroit Liberty Association undertook a full-scale investigation to allay public incredulity, an unprecedented response to a nineteenth-century slave narrative. Through correspondence with Bibb's former associates, "slave owners, slave dealers, fugitives from slavery, political friends and political foes," the committee found the facts of Bibb's account "corroborated beyond all question."

Lecturing for the Michigan Liberty Party, Bibb was sent to Ohio to speak along the north side of the Mason-Dixon Line, a region notorious for its proslavery sympathies. Bibb returned to the South one final time in the winter of 1845 in search of his wife and daughter. While visiting his mother in Kentucky, Bibb learned that his wife and daughter's escape from certain death on Whitfield's plantation came at the expense of their marriage; Malinda had been forced to become the mistress of a white southerner. In 1848, on a sabbatical from lecturing, Bibb met and married Mary E. Miles, an African American abolitionist from Boston. It is not known whether they had children. With the passage of the 1850 Fugitive Slave Law, the Bibbs fled to Sandwich, western Canada, where, in January 1851, Henry and Mary established the *Voice of the Fugitive*. This publication was a biweekly antislavery journal that reported on the condition of fugitives and advocated the abolition of slavery, black colonization to Canada, temperance, black education, and the development of black commercial enterprises.

With the aid of the black abolitionists JAMES T. HOLLY and J. T. Fisher, Bibb organized the North American League, an organization evolving out of the North American Convention of Colored People, held in Toronto and over which Bibb presided in September 1851. The league was meant to promote colonization to Canada and to serve as the central authority for blacks in the Americas. Although the league survived but a few short months, Bibb continued to work toward colonization, encouraging Michigan philanthropists a year later to help form the Refugee Home Society—a joint-stock company for the purpose of acquiring and selling Canadian farmland to black emigrants—to which Bibb attached his journal as its official organ. Tension among prominent black Canadians, however, brought about the society's demise. Bibb died in Windsor, Ontario, Canada, without realizing his vision for an African American colony.

FURTHER READING

Andrews, William L. *To Tell a Free Story: The First Century of Afro-American Autobiography, 1760–1865* (1988).

Hite, Roger W. "Voice of a Fugitive: Henry Bibb and Ante-bellum Black Separatism," *Journal of Black Studies* 4 (Mar. 1974): 269–284.

Quarles, Benjamin. *Black Abolitionists* (1969).

Ripley, C. Peter, ed. *The Black Abolitionist Papers*, vols. 3–4 (1985, 1991).

Silverman, Jason H. *Unwelcome Guests: Canada West's Response to American Fugitive Slaves, 1800–1865* (1985).

This entry is taken from the *American National Biography* and is published here with the permission of the American Council of Learned Societies.

GREGORY S. JACKSON

Bibb, Joseph Dandridge (21 Sept. 1895–Dec. 1966), editor, writer, publisher, lawyer, and government official, was born in Montgomery, Alabama, the son of Viola (Lovett) Bibb and Joseph D. Bibb, an African Methodist Episcopal (AME) minister and a prominent teacher and advocate for the employment of black teachers. Bibb used his earnings from working in the railroad industry and southern factories to pay for his college education; he attended Atlanta University, Livingstone College, and Howard University, and completed his legal training at Yale and Harvard Universities.

After the completion of his formal education, Bibb moved to Chicago, the destination of thousands of job-seeking African Americans from the South. This mass exodus from the South—the Great Migration—saw blacks pour into urban areas between 1915 and 1925. Chicago and other cities such as Detroit and New York saw their black populations double and triple; these cities offered relative freedom from the violence and lack of opportunity in the South, but it was still hard for blacks to find work. Consequently, African Americans created their own newspapers to address issues such as racial discrimination, violence, and poor living conditions. Black newspapers, however, continued to urge southern blacks to migrate to the North.

Realizing the growing need to empower black citizens and to address black issues, Bibb, along with William Linton, started the *Chicago Whip* in 1919 with a mere twenty-five cents. The *Whip* appeared on the scene when black newspapers were experiencing a renaissance in Chicago, one of the nation's most racially polarized cities. Such newspapers included the *Chicago Conservator* (1878–1914), the *Chicago Defender* (1905–present), and the *Chicago Bee* (1925–1947). Published weekly, the *Whip* reached a circulation of 65,000 within its first year, second only to the *Chicago Defender*. Throughout its twenty-year existence, the paper campaigned for black rights and often featured the civil rights leader MARCUS GARVEY. In his editorials Bibb urged complete integration and the hiring of black workers. Because of this, the paper was considered to be militant by politicians and members of the mainstream press; Bibb later recalled how he was labeled "Red, radical, revolutionary" (*Ebony*, Jan. 1956). While writing for the *Whip*, Bibb also practiced law, and in 1922 he married Goldie Thompson. In 1929 the *Whip* promoted the successful "Don't Buy Where You Can't Work" campaign to combat the practices of white-owned businesses that wouldn't hire blacks. Other black

newspapers throughout the country publicized similar boycotts. The *Whip* was liquidated during the Depression in 1939, and Bibb began working as managing editor of the Chicago edition of the *Pittsburgh Courier*, a popular black newspaper that published local and national editions. As an editor, he continued the spirit of the *Whip* in his columns on black civil rights.

Known for his biting editorials on behalf of civil rights, Bibb was also a staunch and loyal Republican, and this made him something of an anomaly at a time when most African Americans were gradually shifting their loyalty from the Republican to the Democratic party, seen as more committed to racial equality. For more than twenty-five years, Bibb served as a writer and speaker for the National Republican Committee. In 1952 Bibb was vocal about what he perceived as a smear campaign against then-vice presidential candidate Richard Nixon by Democratic campaigners to deter blacks from voting for Nixon and Dwight Eisenhower for president. Bibb urged the Republican Party to reach out to black voters.

During his campaign for governor of Illinois in 1952, the Republican candidate William G. Stratton had promised to appoint the first African American to state cabinet. Upon his 1953 inauguration Stratton named Bibb director of public safety. This made the fifty-seven-year-old Bibb the first African American to hold a cabinet post in Illinois and in any state since Reconstruction. Many saw this as a cynical move to court black voters. Nonetheless, Bibb described his new role as overseeing the "well-being and protection of the citizens of Illinois and visitors within its borders" (*Ebony*, Jan. 1956).

Bibb had to give up his law career and newspaper column for the state job, which paid $12,000 a year. From 1953 to 1961 Bibb served as director of public safety, overseeing four state penitentiaries, the state police, all state parole agents, and the Division of Criminal Investigation and Identification. Bibb reduced the prison population and pushed for prison reform and the efficiency of crime labs. He answered letters from inmates and investigated their complaints. When Bibb took office, Illinois had one of the largest populations in the United States, and traffic problems were becoming more of an issue. Bibb researched new techniques to control safety and noise on the Illinois expressways and pushed for a sixty-five-mile-per-hour speed limit in the state.

As the first black department director in the state of Illinois, Bibb restructured the Department of Public Safety to make it more efficient. But his major contributions are embodied in the written word—in his editorials and columns in the *Chicago Whip* and *Pittsburgh Courier*. Bibb remains an important figure in the history of the black newspapers that exhaustively fought for the rights and safety of black citizens.

FURTHER READING

"'Mr. Public Safety' Joseph Bibb is Guardian of Illinois Life and Property," *Ebony* (Jan. 1956)
Jet (Sept. 1967).

MARTHA PITTS

Bibb, Leon (7 Feb. 1922–), singer and actor, was born Charles Leon Arthello Bibb in Louisville, Kentucky. His father, also Leon Bibb, worked as a mail carrier and his mother, Elizabeth (McCloskey) Bibb, was a homemaker, although she sometimes assisted her mother, a domestic servant. Bibb's grandparents were born in slavery, and his forbears worked as slaves on vegetable plantations in western Kentucky. When he was a young child Bibb's aunt taught him spirituals, some of which he continued to sing throughout his career. His aunt recognized his vocal talent early, and she gave him a vision beyond the heavily segregated world of the South of the 1920s and 1930s by telling the young Bibb about ROLAND HAYES, a black concert singer who moved to Europe when he could not find career opportunities in the United States because of his race, and later returned to perform at Carnegie Hall. Bibb continued to sing in choruses in school and choirs at church, and in more informal groups with his friends during his teenage years.

After high school he attended Louisville Municipal College and was a soloist with the college glee club until he joined the army, where he was chosen for training as part of an all-black unit called the Tuskegee Airmen, the first African American pilots in the U.S. military who served with great distinction in World War II. Music was still on his mind, however, and immediately after his military service ended, Bibb headed to New York City to study voice.

Arriving in the city with just a few dollars in his pocket, he took a variety of jobs to support himself while searching for a way into music. He worked in restaurants, in the animation business, and in a factory making parts for radar equipment. At the invitation of an acquaintance, he attended a theater performance of *Othello* with PAUL ROBESON in the lead role. Bibb had the chance to meet Robeson,

and the encounter sparked a lifelong friendship and a mentorship for the younger man.

It did not, however, lead to immediate work opportunities in singing. That came when Bibb responded to a newspaper advertisement seeking "Colored Singers." Asked over the telephone if he was colored, Bibb replied that no, he was a Negro, and was invited to come down to audition. At that time Bibb's professional experience consisted of winning a talent contest at the Apollo Theater. As a result of that audition he was chosen to appear in the original cast of *Annie Get Your Gun*, which starred Ethel Merman and opened on Broadway in 1946.

The show was the first of a number of successful and increasingly prominent roles Bibb enjoyed in the New York theater. He sang in the chorus and joined the touring company of *Finian's Rainbow*, which saw art comment on life with a subplot concerning a racist southern senator who through a mistaken magic spell has to experience life as a black man. At this time, in the late 1940s and early 1950s, there were few roles for blacks on Broadway or off, and Bibb had uneven success in finding work. One of his highest-profile roles was in *Lost in the Stars*, a 1949 piece based on the work of South African writer Alan Paton and written by Kurt Weill and Maxwell Anderson.

Bibb also took roles in Off-Broadway projects, including the play *Sandhog*, and he worked in non-singing parts as well, including an appearance in the drama *Flight into Egypt*. Still, he could not earn a steady income with his acting roles. Considering ways to supplement his income, he created a singing repertoire comprising English and Irish folk ballads, the spirituals he remembered from his Kentucky childhood, and chain gang and prison songs. His timing was right; soon the folk music revival would capture the country's interest, with stars such as the Weavers, the Freedom Singers, and ODETTA, quickly followed on by the next generation of folk-based singers including Bob Dylan, Joan Baez, and Carolyn Hester. Bibb's folk repertoire, classically trained voice, and theater-honed professionalism engaged audiences and also caught the ears of organizers of the first Newport (Rhode Island) Folk Festival, who were drawing on their contacts in the New York city music scene to put together one of the first major festivals featuring contemporary folk singers, coffeehouse stars, and traditional artists all at the same venue. Bibb's eclectic mix of songs and his polished tenor also attracted interest from executives at Vanguard Recording Society, a company that had begun by focusing on classical music but, in part because of the owners' support for the social justice causes of the day, was moving into folk and protest music. Bibb was recorded live performing four songs at the Newport Folk Festival and subsequently released a number of albums with Vanguard and other labels.

The spirituals and prison songs Bibb recorded came into sharper focus as the singer lent his voice and presence to civil rights actions during the 1960s. On the personal side, Bibb had married during the 1950s and had three children, son Eric (who would go on to become a respected blues musician) and daughter Doria, who were twins, and daughter Amy. As the 1960s progressed, however, his first marriage dissolved. He continued to make his living through music and also took occasional roles in film, including an appearance in *For the Love of Ivy* with SIDNEY POITIER in 1968. Bibb often opened for comedians, and while on tour with BILL COSBY in 1971 Bibb visited Vancouver and decided to move there. In addition to recording and performing, Bibb founded Step Ahead, a program designed to start students and teachers talking about racism and bullying, and talking with each other about how to address these issues in their communities.

FURTHER READING

There are no archives or published biographies of Mr. Bibb. A personal interview with Mr. Bibb was conducted by telephone to obtain some of the material for this entry. Liner notes for his early recordings many be found in archival collections, and the program notes from *Live at the Newport Folk Festival, Volume One*, also provide a short biography.

DISCOGRAPHY

A Family Affair (Jericho Beach 2002).
Roots of Folk (Vanguard 2002).

KERRY DEXTER

Bigard, Barney (3 Mar. 1906–27 June 1980), jazz musician, was born Albany Leon Bigard in New Orleans, Louisiana, the son of Alexander Louis Bigard and Emanuella Marquez. Little is known of his family except that it produced musicians: his older brother Alex was a drummer, his uncle Emile was a violinist who played with musicians like KING OLIVER and KID ORY, and his cousin Anatie ("Natty") Dominique was a trumpet player and bandleader. Bigard studied clarinet under LORENZO TIO JR., whose students included JOHNNY

DODDS, ALBERT NICHOLAS, OMER SIMEON, and Jimmie Noone.

Raised mostly by his grandparents, Bigard worked in the cigar factory of his uncle Ulysses as a boy and also as a photoengraver, and he played music mostly with parade bands. At the age of sixteen, however, Bigard joined Albert Nicholas's band as a tenor saxophonist. He continued playing the tenor with other New Orleans bands, including LUIS RUSSELL's. In 1924, on the recommendations of Russell and Nicholas, King Oliver asked Bigard to join his band in Chicago, and so, like many other young New Orleans musicians of the day, he left town and headed north. Bigard's first wife, Arthemise or Artemise (maiden name unknown), whom he married in about 1924, accompanied him to Chicago. They had four children, but the couple drifted apart, and the marriage ended some years later.

Bigard joined King Oliver's Dixie Syncopators as a tenor saxophonist, later switching to clarinet. While in Chicago he recorded with Oliver, LOUIS ARMSTRONG, JELLY ROLL MORTON, and Johnny Dodds. A young DOC CHEATHAM, at the time a budding saxophonist before he took up the trumpet, heard Bigard play in Chicago; Cheatham said years later, "I thought he was the greatest tenor player I ever heard in my life!" (Dance, 307). It was with the clarinet, however, that Bigard's talent was fully realized. His sound is usually described as warm, clear, liquid, or woody, and his style as fluid or articulate. Bigard's playing employed the full range of the instrument but with a particular resonance in the lower register, which some critics have ascribed to the fact that unlike most clarinetists he used the older Albert fingering system instead of the newer Boehm system. Haywood Henry, as a young sax and clarinet player, first heard Bigard playing with DUKE ELLINGTON in 1930 and remembered that "Barney Bigard was my model from the first. I loved his sound and the way he flowed on the clarinet. What he played always made a lot of sense, and he always told a story" (Dance, 207).

Bigard played with the Oliver band, both in Chicago at the Plantation Café and on tour, until the summer of 1927, when, after a brief stint with Charlie Elgar's Creole Orchestra in Milwaukee, he went on to New York City to join a group led by Luis Russell. Bigard was spotted by WELLMAN BRAUD, the bassist for the Duke Ellington Orchestra, which was playing in Harlem at the Cotton Club. In January 1928 Ellington asked Bigard to join his band as the replacement for Rudy Jackson. Bigard remained with Ellington for fifteen years as a featured player on clarinet, working with such outstanding jazz musicians as COOTIE WILLIAMS, JOHNNY HODGES, SONNY GREER, HARRY CARNEY, and Sam Nanton. Bigard contributed his distinctive New Orleans voice to the Ellington sound, and in return Ellington, as he did with other key musicians, wrote Bigard's voice into many of his classic arrangements, such as "C-Jam Blues," "Azure," "Caravan," "Harlem Air Shaft," and "Clarinet Lament." Bigard claimed to have written one of the band's signature pieces, "Mood Indigo," based partly on a melody borrowed from Lorenzo Tio Jr., although the published score bears Ellington's name and seems to give him credit for its composition.

In a highly segregated era, Ellington's band was an all-black group playing for all-white audiences. Bigard's obituary in the *New York Times* noted that "because he was fair-skinned, Mr. Bigard often purchased food for members of the Ellington band when the musicians toured in the Deep South during the years of the Jim Crow racial practices." Also, when the Ellington orchestra played on screen in a 1930 Amos 'n' Andy film titled *Check and Double Check*, Bigard and the band's valve trombonist, Juan Tizol, both being very light-skinned, were required to appear in blackface.

From 1931 on, Ellington and his group were on the road much of the time. Finally, tired of constant touring, which he found grueling—especially after 1941, when the war disrupted transportation schedules—Bigard left the Ellington orchestra in 1942 and headed to the West Coast, where he played with local groups, briefly formed a small band with Kid Ory on trombone and CHARLIE MINGUS on bass, and did studio work. Also in 1942 he married Dorothy Edgecombe. He returned to New York in 1944 and for a few months led his own group at the Onyx Club on Fifty-second Street. Then in 1944 or 1945 he returned to California, where he played with Kid Ory. In 1947 Bigard appeared in the film *New Orleans* with Armstrong. After the filming, Armstrong asked him to join Jack Teagarden, COZY COLE, and Velma Middleton in a small Dixieland group to be called Louis Armstrong's All Stars. Bigard stayed with the All Stars for five years, making many tours and records, and later he rejoined the group twice for shorter stints. By 1962 he had retired from full-time playing but continued to appear for brief engagements, concerts, and festivals, leading his own bands or playing with groups headed by Cozy Cole, Ben Pollack, JOHNNY ST. CYR, Muggsy Spanier, REX STEWART,

EARL HINES, Art Hodes, Eddie Condon, and Wild Bill Davison.

Bigard died in Culver City, California. Over a period of sixty years he had been a quintessential sideman, playing in big bands and small, Dixieland and swing, associated with many of the great jazz figures of the first half of the twentieth century. Bigard was in that group of fine young New Orleans clarinetists—among them Albert Nicholas, BUSTER BAILEY, Omer Simeon, EDMOND HALL, SIDNEY BECHET, and GEORGE LEWIS—who brought their style of music north after World War I and helped spread the gospel of jazz. A French critic, Jacques Morgantini, assessed Bigard's accomplishments this way: "Apart from those multiple qualities as an instrumentalist, improviser, and swingman … Barney Bigard possessed the remarkable talent of being able to adapt the typically New Orleans clarinet style to the big band context" (album notes, *Barney Bigard Story*, Jazz Archives, no. 12).

FURTHER READING

Bigard, Barney, with Barry Martyn. *With Louis and the Duke* (1985).
Dance, Stanley. *The World of Swing* (1974).
Obituary: *New York Times*, 28 June 1980.
This entry is taken from the *American National Biography* and is published here with the permission of the American Council of Learned Societies.

BRUCE R. CARRICK

Biggers, John (13 Apr. 1924–25 Jan. 2001), artist and educator, later known as John "Anansa" Thomas Biggers, was born in Gastonia, North Carolina, to Cora Biggers, a homemaker who excelled in sewing and quiltmaking, and Paul Biggers, an educator, preacher, carpenter, and farmer. The youngest of seven children, John learned to appreciate the creativity, industry, and struggle of African American families in the example of his parents. When his father died in 1937, John was only thirteen. Cora Biggers took a job as a matron in an orphanage for black children and sent John and his brother Joe to Lincoln Academy, a boarding school that prepared black students to be teachers and ministers.

Biggers's artistic self-discovery began in 1941 when he enrolled at a black college in Virginia— Hampton Institute (later Hampton University). Although he intended to study the practical trade of plumbing, he ultimately majored in art because he was encouraged by his professor and mentor, Victor Lowenfeld, an Austrian Jewish psychologist and artist who had recently escaped Nazi persecution. Lowenfeld was the former director of an African art museum in Vienna, and he used Hampton's African art collection to teach African social, aesthetic, and spiritual values and their relevance to the lives of African Americans. Through his relationship with Lowenfeld, Biggers was inspired to learn about the art and culture of his ancestral heritage and to work from his life experiences. Describing his changing perspective about art, he reflected, "I began to see art not primarily as an individual expression of talent, but as a responsibility to reflect the spirit and style of the Negro people" (Biggers et al., *Black Art in Houston*, 7–8). His early paintings revealed this devotion to conveying the tenacity and dignity of African Americans. *Mother and Child* (1943) celebrated black women as pillars of communal and family life, and *Gleaners* (1943) showed the diligence and commitment of regular working people. Other works criticized the effects of racist laws and the impoverished conditions in which blacks lived. *Crossing the Bridge* (1942) showed African Americans striving for a better life, and *Crucifixion* (1942) attacked the racist oppression of blacks in the South.

At Hampton University Biggers was exposed to a variety of artists and art historical movements that defined his philosophy and early style. He was most impressed by the works of American regionalists such as Grant Wood, Thomas Hart Benton, and Harry Sternberg, and by the Mexican muralists Diego Rivera, David Alfaro Siqueiros, and Jose Clemente Orozco. He also studied the figures of the Harlem Renaissance, most notably, the writers W. E. B. Du Bois and Alain Locke, and the artists William Ellisworth Artis, Hale A. Woodruff, Elizabeth Catlett, and Charles White. White and Catlett visited Hampton, and they became mentors to and friends of Biggers; White painted Biggers into his campus mural *The Contribution of the Negro to American Democracy*.

In 1943 Biggers was drafted into the still-segregated U.S. Navy, where he served for two years as a visual arts specialist under the supervision of Joe Gilliard, his former ceramics teacher at Hampton. After his discharge in 1945 Biggers returned to Hampton for a semester and then followed Lowenfeld to Pennsylvania State University, where he received all three of his degrees: B.S. and M.S. degrees in 1948 and a Ph.D. in Education in 1954. Also at Pennsylvania he met Hazel Hales, an accounting major, and in 1948 they married. In 1949 the couple moved to Houston, where Biggers had accepted a position to establish an art department at Texas Southern University, then called Texas State University for Negroes. Initially he encountered many challenges. As a result of the segregated and substandard education for southern blacks, the majority of his students were barely literate, and he was frustrated in attempts to introduce art history to his curriculum, in addition to the foundations of creating art. Further, he lacked the supplies, equipment, and adequate studio space to set up his department, and the school administration was antagonistic to his ideas and requests. Describing the institutional reaction to his interest in digging for the African roots of African American culture, Biggers wrote, "The great majority of American blacks thought I was crazy.... These included members of my own department. Paris, London, and Rome were the foreign cities that our teachers, as well as most of those from other universities, wanted to visit" (Biggers et al., 16). Despite these obstacles, he persevered with the philosophic approach he developed at Hampton, and encouraged students to paint from their own insights and their identification with black cultural heritage.

Biggers soon adopted a workshop approach to teaching: the students were considered apprentices and the program fostered their personal growth, understanding of art materials, and exploration of black cultural heritage. The methodology of "learning by doing" is exemplified by Biggers's mural program for art majors in which every senior student was expected to complete a mural on campus; in the early 2000s there were 114 such murals on the Texas Southern campus (Biggers et al., 17). Having built the art department from the ground up, with allies in fellow faculty members and artists Joseph Mack and Carroll Simms, Biggers held his position at Texas Southern for thirty-four years.

In 1957 Biggers received a UNESCO grant to study art and culture in West Africa. With his wife, Hazel, he spent six months living in Ghana, Benin (then called Dahomey), Nigeria, and Togo, where he documented his experiences and observations in photographs, writing, and sketches. One of the first African American artists to travel extensively in Africa, he was particularly enthralled with the activity of marketplaces, the sanctity of shrines, and the daily life of fishermen, women, and children. Biggers's style of representation was transformed by the trip to Africa, and his subsequent work was less narrative and more symbolic, for it included

African emblems and complex layers of geometric patterning. Using his research and sketches, he created a visual diary, *Ananse: The Web of Life in Africa* (1962), which included eighty-nine drawings and accompanying text. Biggers said that he chose to focus on the spider Ananse, the heroic trickster of Ashanti proverbs, because "God gave Ananse the meaning of order.... This is symbolized by his web, which stands also for the sun and its rays, and the sun personifies God" (*Ananse*, title page). Inspired by the powerful symbol of the ananse, this series of drawings expresses the interconnectedness of African communal life. Perhaps this is why he later changed his own name to John "Anansa" Thomas Biggers (although the exact date of the name change is unknown).

Biggers created over twenty-three murals that make visible the contributions of African Americans and their heritage in a monumental form of public art. Before he retired from Texas Southern University in 1983, he made a fifty-foot mural as a legacy to the school and a source of inspiration for future generations of African American artists. Entitled *Family Unity*, the mural showed the human cycle of life and the persistence of cultural continuity. He later used a detail of the mural for his lithograph *The Upper Room*. By the early 1990s Biggers was including Native American, Asian, and African cultural symbols in works that suggested the unity of humankind and the interconnectedness of human beings, nature, and the universe.

From 1995 to 1997 Biggers's work was celebrated in a major traveling retrospective hosted by seven art museums across the United States: Museum of Fine Arts, Houston; Cincinnati Art Museum; Hampton University Museum; North Carolina Museum of Art; Wadsworth Atheneum, Hartford, Connecticut; Museum of Fine Arts, Boston; and California Afro-American Museum, Los Angeles. The exhibition included his prints, drawings, and paintings. He died in his Houston home at the age of seventy-six. He left behind a prolific legacy of murals and paintings that celebrated African American and African life. Remarkably, he spent a lifetime developing dual careers as both an outstanding artist and a groundbreaking educator. Like the songs of an African storyteller, Biggers's art keeps alive the histories of African American people and their vital connection with African heritage.

FURTHER READING

Biggers, John. *Ananse: The Web of Life in Africa* (1996).

Biggers, John, Carroll Simms, and John Edward Meems. *Black Art in Houston: The Texas Southern Experience* (1978).

Ritter, Rebecca E. *Five Decades: John Biggers and the Hampton Art Tradition* (1990).

Roberts, Kristin Schreiber. *Framing John Biggers' Shotguns (1987): African American Art and Identity* (1997).

Wardlaw, Alvia J., with essays by Edmund Barry Gaither, Alison de Lima Greene, and Robert Farris Thompson. *The Art of John Biggers: View from the Upper Room* (1995).

Obituary: *New York Times*, 30 Jan. 2001.

SOPHIE SANDERS

Biggie Smalls. *See* Notorious B. I. G.

Biggs, Bradley (29 Aug. 1920–16 Nov. 2004), soldier, author, and educator, was born in Newark, New Jersey, to Bradley Biggs, a bootlegger, and Julia DeFreece, a domestic. The couple divorced when Bradley was an infant, and he recalled his childhood as one of abject poverty. His mother struggled to earn enough to support him and his younger brother Burton, and the family lived in public housing.

In his high school years, consumed by a desire to escape his harsh surroundings, Biggs developed two interests that helped define his path: flying and athletics. As a member of the Falcon Aeronautical Club of East Orange, New Jersey—the first and perhaps only black flying club in the East—he was exposed to the basics of flight and the mechanics of airplanes. At a burly six feet three inches tall, he was also able to use his athleticism to win a place on the New York Brown Bombers professional football club. Sensing an opportunity to advance himself, however, he quit in 1939 to join the United States Army. Biggs would later speak of this decision as one motivated not only by a desire to escape the ghetto but also as a way to create more opportunities for people like himself.

Segregation was still rigidly enforced in the military at the time, and Biggs was assigned to a black infantry unit. Given his interest in aeronautics, he enthusiastically campaigned throughout the war for an assignment in an airborne division. Blacks were considered incapable of handling all but the most menial duties, a prejudice that provided stiff resistance to his ambition. However, an executive officer at the Army's Parachute School in Fort

Benning, Georgia, happened to be a former football star at West Point. He and Biggs shared a love of the game, and the officer was fond of him personally. As a result, Biggs, a commissioned second lieutenant, was a logical choice when the military brass planned to experiment with creating a black airborne infantry unit. In 1943 he received an order to report to Fort Benning, Georgia, and begin airborne training with twenty-two other black servicemen. He was the officer of the unit, the 555th Parachute Infantry Battalion, known as the "Triple Nickels." Under Biggs's command, Walter Morris became the first black soldier to receive airborne training.

The unit quickly dispelled the idea that blacks were incapable of succeeding in the same roles as white soldiers. Nevertheless, bigotry kept them from seeing combat duty. They served as "smoke jumpers" who parachuted into blazing forest fires on the West Coast set by Japanese bombs carried across the Pacific by balloons. The hazardous duty resulted in the highest casualty rate of any noncombat unit in World War II. Biggs and his men had successfully penetrated an elite segment of the military five years before the army would formally desegregate.

Where others saw segregation in the army, Biggs saw opportunities. He worked relentlessly for the betterment of black soldiers until the military desegregated in 1948. He continued his career with decorated combat duty in Korea from 1950 to 1951 and a post in Germany at the end of that conflict. While stationed in Germany he completed several programs at Tennessee A&I (later Tennessee State) and at the University of Nevada before receiving his degree from the University of Maryland. He retired in 1960 as a lieutenant colonel and became active in the University of Maryland overseas learning program for servicemen and the U.S. Army Education System, helping numerous soldiers under his command complete college programs.

When Biggs returned to the United States in 1960, a director from the Maryland program solicited his help in establishing a new college near Middletown, Connecticut. Biggs personally scouted a location with his private plane, and Middlesex Community College opened in 1968 with Biggs as its first dean of faculty and administration. While continuing to teach and serve in administrative roles at the college, he was also recruited to serve as deputy commissioner of public works for the State of Connecticut. In 1977 he moved to Boston to serve as both an administrator for the Boston Housing Authority,

drawing on his childhood experiences in public housing, and for the Department of Health and Hospitals. Seemingly tireless, he also founded Biggs International Development Corporation to perform municipal public works.

He could not shake his love of education, however. In 1978 he moved to Miami to teach at Florida International University, where he became vice president for administrative affairs in 1983. In the midst of these responsibilities he somehow found time to earn two additional degrees—a master's degree in 1969, and a master of arts for teachers in 1973, both from Wesleyan University—and build a family. He married Kunigunde "Gunde" Elsinger, a teacher, in July 1960, and they raised two children: Bradley III, a clinical psychologist, and Carina, an oncologist. To finish his career, he authored two books: *Gavin* (1980), a biography of Lieutenant General James M. Gavin, the white officer who worked with Biggs to integrate the 555th into the 82d Airborne, and *Triple Nickels: America's First All-Black Paratroop Unit* (1986). He returned to Connecticut in his later years, remaining active in the community and with educational institutions. Most of all, he cherished time with his wife of more than four decades. He died of heart failure in Middletown, near the college he almost singlehandedly founded.

FURTHER READING

Biggs, Bradley. *Gavin* (1980).

Biggs, Bradley. *Triple Nickels: America's First All-Black Paratroop Unit* (1986).

Obituary: *Hartford Courant*, 12 Dec. 2004.

EDWARD M. BURMILA

Bilali (c. 1760–1855), Muslim leader and plantation manager, was born in Africa, sold into slavery, and transported to the Bahamas and then to Sapelo Island, Georgia. His name is also given as Bilali Mahomet and Bul-Ali. Almost nothing is known about Bilali's life in Africa, but his fellow Fula or Peul (originally Malian) friend, SALIH BILALI, who was enslaved on the neighboring island of Saint Simons, said that Bilali came from the village of Timbo, in Futa Jallon (later Guinea). This was an important Muslim educational and political community and the homeland of another Fula, IBRAHIMA ABD AL-RAHMAN, who was enslaved in Mississippi. Bilali's strict adherence to Muslim ways and the book he wrote in Arabic show that he paid attention to his teachers in Africa. In the Bahamas

Bilali married at least one of his four known wives before being brought to Georgia around 1802. He had a proud bearing and insisted on the use of his African name. ("Bilali" was popular in West Africa as it was the name of the Prophet Muhammad's first *muezzin* or caller to prayer, a black African former slave and one of the first converts to Islam.) He reportedly persisted in dressing as he had in Africa in a robe and fez; he also prayed facing the east, followed Muslim dietary rules and prohibitions, and held himself aloof from non-Muslims.

Bilali is believed to have been buried with a Koran, prayer beads, and a prayer rug. He must have been an extraordinarily strong person to hold on to these items through the Middle Passage, during which most captives were stripped of their possessions. This seemingly unlikely possibility is not far-fetched since the single extant artifact from Bilali's possessions, his once mysterious book, known about for some time until bequeathed by Bilali to a friendly white writer in the late 1850s, written on eighteenth-century Venetian paper often traded on the coast of Africa, was found in America rather than Africa. Writing his book was Bilali's attempt, around 1830, after at least thirty-five years of slavery, to set down in Arabic some of the rituals required of the followers of Muhammad found on Sapelo Island.

The thirteen-page manuscript was not taken seriously until 1940, and linguists have as of this writing not translated the complete text. Despite apparent corrections and annotations by another hand, the main text admits numerous misspellings and other probable errors. It is possible, however, according to some readers, in light of other manuscripts from West Africa, that Bilali was using phonetic Arabic letters to write his own language, Fulfulde or Pular. Two unpolished pages offer rules about praying, four are still not translated, two describe ablution practices before prayer, while the next five pages include repetitive assertions on keeping the faith, hope in being accepted as a servant of God, and rules about when to pray.

Using skills he had probably learned or practiced in Futa Jallon, Bilali became the only manager needed to run the five-hundred-slave Sea Island plantation on which he lived. His politically prominent and agriculturally adventurous purchaser, Thomas Spalding, a sometime lawyer, wrote occasional newspaper articles—but none have been found about Bilali. Their plantation hosted several once-famous domestic and foreign travelers. Some of these travelers were Aaron Burr, shortly

after he had killed Alexander Hamilton in a duel; John D. Legare, editor of the important *Southern Agriculturist* journal; the British wanderers Basil and Margaret Hall; the actress Fanny Kemble; the scientist Charles Lyell; the courtier Amelia Murray; and Sweden's Fredrika Bremer. The travelers wrote positively about their visits and the good slave relations they saw, but though they marveled at how well the place was run, even though the master left for weeks at a time, no one mentioned Bilali or his role as the de facto manager in the absence of whites.

The first-known published notice of Bilali in 1829, written by the slaver Zephaniah Kingsley, does not include names but clearly refers to Bilali and Salih Bilali. He wrote that both had saved their slave charges in 1815 and 1824, and that both were Muslims. As a matter of fact, near the end of the War of 1812, Sapelo Island was in danger of being raided by the British, but the raid did not occur, so Bilali did not have to employ the eighty muskets his master left with him to fend off the invaders. However, the pending danger allowed Bilali, according to tradition, to declare: "I will answer for every negro of the true faith, but not for the Christian dogs you own" (Coulter, *Thomas Spalding of Sapelo*, 1940). (Salih Bilali had less luck in saving his slaves on his plantation on Saint Simons, as some two hundred fled to or were taken away by the British.) In the terrible hurricane of 1824, however, both Muslim leaders seemed to have been responsible for saving their fellow slaves while whites went inland and many coastal people were lost elsewhere.

Bilali was described in 1850—the year his master died—by a neighbor, Georgia B. Conrad, as being old, black, tall, well-formed, good-featured, and the father of many Muslim children. It was not only his children who were servants of Allah; Bilali seems also to have been the leader, *imam* or *amir*, of Sapelo's own Muslim community, which he strove to keep on the right path. Not long before he died, he gave his "book" to Francis Goulding, a local white writer—unable, apparently, to find literate Muslims or African Americans. It may be seen today in the University of Georgia library.

Few whites, including Goulding, paid serious attention to this remarkable man and his story. The famed storyteller Joel Chandler Harris borrowed tales of Bilali from several sources and tenderly recast them in the language of his black servants for the amusement of whites. Harris never allowed his narrator, Uncle Remus, to say anything positive about strong, independent African Americans though elsewhere Harris, stressing the *Arabic* as if Bilali and others were merely visitors in Africa, wrote positively about "Arabic-Africans." It would be a long time before Americans would accept black African agency and literacy. Consistent with contemporary notices that omitted anything about slave religious practices, Harris considered Arabs to be a light-skinned, improved mixed-race of people. He wrote two books, *The Story of Aaron, the Son of Ben Ali* and *Aaron in the Wildwoods*, with an "Arabic-African" hero who was called the son of "Bul Ali" and made to despise black Africans—misrepresenting the religious attitude as a racial attitude of black African Muslims like Bilali.

In the late 1930s, interviewers of former slaves on Sapelo Island were told stories about Bilali, his religious practices, artifacts, offspring, and others who maintained Muslim names and traditions for at least two generations. Later descendents of Sapelo Island slaves told the historian William McFeely about Bilali "the powerful 'old man,'" and in the late 1990s a descendant named Cornelia Walker Bailey told even more about Bilali and about the island's Baptist church whose members cover their heads, seat men and women separately, and all pray facing the east—as Muslims do around the world.

Bilali lived an extraordinary life. He was a renowned plantation manager, a practicing if not official *imam*, literate in Arabic, and a misused model for the hero of two books by Joel Chandler Harris. His life sheds light on the intelligence, strength, and dignity of enslaved people, many of whom have been all but forgotten in history.

FURTHER READING

Austin, Allan D. *African Muslims in Antebellum America: Transatlantic Stories and Spiritual Struggles* (1997).

Bailey, Cornelia, with Christena Bledsoe. *God, Dr. Buzzard, and the Bolito Man: A Saltwater Geechee Talks about Life on Sapelo Island* (2000).

Diouf, Sylviane A. *Servants of Allah: African Muslims Enslaved in the Americas* (1998).

Judy, Ronald A. T. *(Dis)Forming the American Canon: African-Arabic Slave Narratives and the Vernacular* (1993).

Martin, Bradford G. "Sapelo Island's Arabic Document … in Context," *Georgia Historical Quarterly* (Fall 1994).

McFeely, William S. *Sapelo's People: A Long Walk into Freedom* (1994).

Savannah Unit of the Georgia Writers Project of the Works Projects Administration. *Drums and Shadows: Survival Studies among the Georgia Coastal Negroes, 1940* (1986).

ALLAN D. AUSTIN

Bilali, Salih. *See* Salih Bilali.

Billingsley, Orzell, Jr. (24 Oct. 1924–13 Dec. 2001), civil rights attorney and political activist, was born in Birmingham, Alabama. One of three sons, he attended Birmingham public schools, including the city's first and oldest, and, at one time, the South's largest African American high school, Industrial (A. H. Parker) High.

After graduating from high school Billingsley attended two highly respected, historically black institutions of higher learning. The first was Talladega College, a private liberal arts college located in Alabama, fifty miles east of Birmingham. He graduated with high honors in 1946 and headed for Washington, D.C., where he attended Howard University School of Law. He earned his law degree there in 1950. Afterward, he returned to Alabama, where he was admitted to the Alabama state bar in 1951, one of the first ten African Americans to do so.

Instantly, Billingsley threw himself behind the post–World War II fight for full black citizenship in America. Always blunt, doggedly direct, and determined, he took no quarter with his opponents in the courtroom. Consequently, he served as either the chief or co-counsel in a number of major court cases. He served as one of the lead lawyers for MARTIN LUTHER KING JR. and the Montgomery Improvement Association during the historic 1955 Montgomery bus boycott. He also represented ROSA PARKS, whose refusal to surrender her seat to a white man triggered the boycott. Equally important, however, is that he represented the impoverished. As a result, he often did not receive any pay for his legal services.

Billingsley's perhaps most notable case began in 1957. His client, the Alabama native Caliph Washington, had been charged with capital murder by an all-white jury for the accidental death of a white police officer with whom he had scuffled. During the scuffle, the officer was killed when his own gun was accidentally discharged. Although it would take four trials and fifteen years, Billingsley eventually won an acquittal for his client in 1972. Washington, indeed, was only one of at least twenty men whose lives Billingsley saved by serving as their defense attorney. Billingsley's defense of Washington was also notable for helping to end the practice of selecting all-white juries in Jefferson County.

The Washington case also led to the historic *Reynolds v. Sims* (1964) U.S. Supreme Court case and its monumental "one man, one vote" decision. Some legal commentators rank that decision higher in importance than *Brown v. Board of Education* (1954).

Billingsley, who in 1963 demanded that Alabama's racist 1901 state constitution be replaced, gradually became a central figure in the legal life of his native state, serving as general counsel for the Alabama Cities, as a consultant for corporations, credit unions, and cooperatives, and as a Recorder's Court judge. He was also a municipal judge in Roosevelt City, an all-black town near Birmingham, that was one of the more than twenty small towns in Alabama that he organized and helped found in the 1960s and 1970s by soliciting financial assistance from the federal government and private corporations.

Billingsley was also active in electoral politics. In 1960, five years before the passage of the Voting Rights Act, he cofounded and became the president of the Alabama Democratic Conference (ADC), the first statewide black political organization in Alabama. Over time, the ADC became recognized as one of the most powerful African American political organizations in the nation. Birmingham served as its stronghold, but Billingsley traveled extensively and dangerously throughout Alabama's racially divided Black Belt region promoting the organization and its program.

As ADC president, Billingsley butted heads with the Alabama Democratic Party (ADP), then still dominated by segregationist whites. Primarily he did so by demanding that the ADP remove the "white supremacy" phrase from its official emblem and that African Americans have greater involvement in the ADP's activities. He also stressed the importance of political mass education and the need for more African American leaders to run for public and party office.

More a leader than a follower, Billingsley founded the Alabama Unit of the Southern Democratic Conference, and was general counsel for the National Democratic Party of Alabama (NDPA), serving as one of its delegates at the 1968 Democratic National Convention.

A staunch supporter of black economic development, Billingsley organized many corporations, including the Alabama Afro Contractors Association. He also served on the board of directors of both the Alabama State Conference of Counties and the Jefferson County Commission for Economic Opportunity. Moreover, he became a member of the Democratic Executive Commission of Jefferson County, the first black elected to that position.

Highly respected in both legal and political circles during the turbulent era of the civil rights movement, Billingsley would sometimes receive phone calls directly from either President Lyndon B. Johnson or his predecessor, John F. Kennedy. Both often called him to receive updates about the state of race relations in Alabama. So greatly impressed was Kennedy with Billingsley's legal expertise that, reportedly, he requested that Billingsley be appointed as attorney general. Various credible sources have also stated that Billingsley ranked high as a candidate for becoming America's first African American United States Supreme Court justice, prior to his fellow Howard law school alumnus and friend THURGOOD MARSHALL. Orzell Billingsley Jr. died in Birmingham, Alabama, after a long illness.

FURTHER READING

The Orzell Billingsley Jr. Papers are located in the Department of Archives and Manuscripts, Linn-Henley Research Library, Birmingham Public Library, Birmingham, Alabama.

Chestnut, J. L., Jr., and Julia Cass. *Black in Selma: The Uncommon Life of J. L. Chestnut, Jr.* (1990).

Johnson, John W. *Historic U.S. Court Cases, 1619–1990: An Encyclopedia* (1992).

Obituary: *Birmingham News*, 19 Dec. 2001.

J. D. JACKSON

Billops, Camille (12 Aug. 1933–), ceramist, sculptor, filmmaker, and cofounder (with her husband, James Hatch) of the Hatch-Billops Collection, an archive of African American cultural history, was born in Los Angeles, California, to Lucius Billops, a cook and merchant seaman, and Alma Gilmore, a dressmaker, maid, and aircraft assembly worker. Billops graduated from Catholic Girls High School in 1952, and in 1954 she began her studies at the University of Southern California. She majored in occupational therapy, which included drawing, sculpture, and ceramics. She transferred to Los Angeles State College in 1956 after she became pregnant, and then she changed her major to special education. Billops worked during the day as a bank bookkeeper and maintained a full academic workload in the evening. At the end of 1956 her daughter, Christa, was born, and Billops put her up for adoption. This was an experience she would explore in her 1992 autobiographical documentary, *Finding Christa*. After graduating from Los Angeles State College in 1960, Billops taught special-needs children at Huntington Park Grammar School in California.

In 1960 Camille Billops's stepsister, Josie Dotson, a student of UCLA theater professor James Hatch, introduced Billops to C. Bernard Jackson. Jackson led a multiracial chorus in Echo Park, which was under the auspices of the Los Angeles City Bureau of Music. In 1960 she was in the chorus of the Jackson and Hatch collaboration, *Fly Blackbird*. Billops had acted professionally once before, appearing in Otto Preminger's 1954 film *Carmen Jones* as an extra. Other participants in this production were Dotson, George Takei, and Francis Ford Coppola, who was a lighting and carpentry technician. In 1961 *Fly Blackbird* was produced in New York and won an Obie for Best Off-Broadway Play.

In 1961 Billops began studying sculpture at the Chouinard Art Institute in Los Angeles. At Chouinard she worked with the Dutch artist Heino. She also studied privately with Artpod Damjan, a Hungarian artist who had produced large-scale sculptures in Budapest.

In 1962, when Hatch (then in a relationship with Billops) received a three-year Fulbright grant to teach at the High Cinema Institute in Cairo, Egypt, she accompanied him. At this time Egypt was the center of the Pan Africanism that inspired the American civil rights movement. They met and became acquaintances of W. E. B. DU BOIS, his stepson David Du Bois, and Maya Make, who later took the name MAYA ANGELOU. Billops and Hatch completed their first collaboration during her second visit to Cairo in 1964: *Poems for Niggers and Crackers*, a satirical collection coauthored by Hatch and Ibrahim Ibn Ismail and illustrated by Billops.

Billops returned to Los Angeles in 1963. With recommendations from the artist CHARLES WHITE and the writer JOHN OLIVER KILLENS, she received a grant from the Huntington Hartford Foundation. The same year that Billops received the Huntington Hartford grant, four African American girls were killed in the bombing of the Sixteenth Street Baptist Church in Birmingham, Alabama. ROBERT F. WILLIAMS's book, *Negro with Guns*, was published in 1962 and launched the black self-defense movement; among the new organizations inspired by Williams's book was the Black Panther Party for Self Defense. In the tumultuous 1960s, Billops was among the artists producing politically relevant art—or "angry art," as she called it in an interview with the artist and art historian Samella Lewis. With the Huntington Hartford grant Billops produced two ceramic bas-reliefs, the *Birmingham Bombing* and *Marian Anderson*.

Billops returned to Egypt in 1964 and had her first solo exhibition at the Gallery Ahkenaton in 1965. Billops and Hatch returned to the United States in mid-1965, and Leo Hamalian, a writer and friend, helped Hatch get a teaching position at the City College in New York and Billops entered the MFA graduate art program at Hunter College. One of the first African American artists she met in New York was the painter Vivian E. Browne, who was also from California. Upon graduation Billops taught at the Goddard Riverside Community Center and was a substitute teacher in Spanish Harlem. The July 1965 riots in Newark, New Jersey, brought the problems that black Americans faced to the attention of mainstream America. The riots in the Watts section of Los Angeles the following month also focused national attention on inequity in employment and housing, and exposed recurring police brutality.

In 1967 Billops and Hatch traveled to India where Billops made drawings for masks and costumes and designed sets for the traveling production of *America Hurrah* by Jean-Claude van Itallie. The couple returned to New York in 1968 and acquired their first loft, where they presented plays, poetry readings, and exhibitions. Early plays produced in the loft on Eleventh Street include *Son of Zen* by Lee-Joo For from Kuala Lampur, Malaysia, and *If It Do Not Die, It Do Not Die*, a 1971 piece by Hatch and Larry Garvin about the Black Panthers. During this time, Billops met BENNY ANDREWS, who showed her how to hang and display an exhibition.

In 1970, while teaching in the City University of New York system, the lack of material on black playwrights, plays, and black theater history available for Hatch's theater classes precipitated the creation of the Hatch-Billops Collection—an assembly of art, artifacts, literature, oral histories, and interviews. Hatch also collaborated with the black-theater scholar and playwright Ted Shine to publish *Black Theatre USA, 45 Plays by Black Americans 1847–1974*. The Hatch-Billops Collection was incorporated in 1975 with a mission to accrue material to document the contributions of African American artists and activists. As part of their cultural mission Billops and Hatch inaugurated in 1981 the "Artist and Influence" series of interviews with artists, writers, cultural activists, filmmakers, and other cultural producers, publishing them in a yearly journal of the same name.

In the early 1980s Billops created and exhibited large-scale figural sculptures based on her family. *Smoke and Blue, 1986* referenced her parents by their nicknames, while *George and Phine, 1987* were inspired by her uncle and aunt who lived in Red Bank, New Jersey. *The Story of Mom, 1981* was inspired by her godmother's life, and its decorative characteristics resembled those in her color etching, *Firefighter.* The sale of Billops's sculpture, prints, and drawings helped fund her documentary films. Billops film, *Suzanne, Suzanne* (1982) was selected for the Museum of Modern Art's New Director New Film Series. *Older Women and Love* (1987) was followed by *Finding Christa,* which won the Grand Jury Prize at the Sundance Film Festival in 1992. *Finding Christa* is about finding the daughter Billops gave up for adoption in 1960. Two years later she completed the satirical play *KKK Boutique Ain't Just Rednecks.* In 1997 Camille Billops and James Hatch received an Obie for Distinguished Contributions to Off-Broadway theater. *A String of Pearls* (2000) was chosen as the Diaspora Film at the Toronto Film Festival. In 2003 Billops designed the sets for the New York experimental theater La Mama's production of the musical *Klub Ka: The Blues Legend,* based on Suzanne Noguere and James Hatch's book, *The Stone House: A Blues Legend.*

FURTHER READING

Estell, Kenneth. *African America: Portrait of a People* (1994).

Harris, Michael D. *Colored Pictures: Race and Visual Representation* (2003).

Henkes, Robert. *The Art of Black American Women: Works of Twenty-Four Artists of the Twentieth Century* (1993).

Moore, Sylvia, ed. *Gumbo Ya Ya: Anthology of Contemporary African American Women Artists* (1995).

Riggs, Thomas, ed. *St. James Guide to Black Artists* (1997).

CYNTHIA HAWKINS

Billy (fl. 1781), a mixed-race slave, also known as Will or William, was the subject of an alleged treason case during the American Revolution. Nothing is known about Billy's birth, family, or childhood.

The Billy, or Will, of the treason case was the slave of Colonel John Tayloe, a resident of Richmond County, Virginia. Billy and others were arrested and convicted of seizing an armed vessel on 2 April 1781

to wage war against Virginia. He was condemned to death by the court of Oyer and Terminer in Prince William County on 8 May. Henry Lee and William Carr, dissenting justices, noted that he was not a citizen and owed no allegiance to Virginia. Furthermore, Billy argued that others had forced him onto the vessel, and there was no evidence that he had gone aboard voluntarily.

Only Governor Thomas Jefferson could grant Billy a reprieve. Jefferson was profoundly ambivalent about the institution of slavery; his actions and writings reveal his often contradictory impulses. Like many planters, Jefferson had a financial interest in perpetuating slavery and believed in the innate inferiority of Africans. He owned many slaves and offered a reward for the return of his escaped slave Sandy in 1769. Yet as a member of Virginia's House of Burgesses, Jefferson also sought, albeit unsuccessfully, to permit slaveholders to free their slaves without approval of the legislature. When granting his own slaves freedom, he exiled them to the wilderness, providing them with the wherewithal for survival. In his draft of the Declaration of Independence, Jefferson condemned the king of England for his involvement in the African slave trade.

When deciding whether to grant Billy a reprieve, Jefferson had to consider his own ambivalence toward slavery as well as Lord Dunmore's 1775 proclamation urging slaves and indentured servants to escape behind British lines to freedom. Even though he considered Dunmore's proclamation an attempt by the king to incite racial massacres, Jefferson did not let his fears of a slave uprising or the loss of thirty of his own slaves to the British deter him from seeking justice for Billy. In May 1781, after accepting the opinion of Mann Page, one of Tayloe's executors, Jefferson signed a temporary reprieve for Billy. After a joint resolution of the Virginia house and senate on 14 June 1781, Billy was granted a permanent reprieve. He was free to return to the anonymity he had known before his brief encounter with American justice.

The case is more significant for what it says about the ambivalence toward slavery of Jefferson and other Virginians than for the light it sheds on the life of Billy, or Will. Ironically, in 1710 another slave named Will had a brief flirtation with history. This earlier Will was freed for "his fidelity ... in discovering a conspiracy of diverse negros ... for levying war" in Virginia.

FURTHER READING

Boyd, Julian P., ed. *The Papers of Thomas Jefferson,* vol. 5 (1952).

Catterall, Helen Tunnicliff, ed. *Judicial Cases concerning American Slavery and the Negro*, vol. 1 (1926).

Higginbotham, A. Leon, Jr. *In the Matter of Color: The Colonial Period*. Race and the American Legal Process series (1978).

Mellon, Matthew T. *Early American Views on Negro Slavery* (1969).

This entry is taken from the *American National Biography* and is published here with the permission of the American Council of Learned Societies.

WILLIAM SERAILE

Binga, Jesse (10 Apr. 1865–13 June 1950), businessman, banker, and real estate investor, was born in Detroit, Michigan, the son of Robert Binga Jr., a barber, and Adelphia Powers, a builder and real estate owner. Nearly all sources cite William W. Binga as Jesse Binga's father, but all are based on a December 1927 article by Inez V. Cantley in *Crisis*, which may not be reliable. A family member, Anthony J. Binga Sr., after conducting research in the census records from the Courts of Records of the Dominion of Canada, claimed that Jesse Binga's father was Robert Binga Jr. *Who's Who in Colored America* (1928–1929) also names Robert Binga as Jesse Binga's father.

The Binga family owned and managed real estate properties, and, according to a number of sources, it was Adelphia Binga who possessed most of the family's business acumen. As a youngster, Jesse helped his mother collect rents on the family's tenement properties along what was called "Binga Row." Tenants were mostly black migrants on their way to and from Canada.

Jesse dropped out of high school after only two years to learn the barber trade from his father. During this period he also worked for a young black attorney. In 1885 Binga left Detroit and set out on his own, working his way across the northwest with the goal of becoming an entrepreneur. After working as a barber in Kansas City, Missouri, St. Paul, Minnesota, and Missoula, Montana, Binga opened his own barbershops in Tacoma and Seattle, Washington. Each venture, however, was short-lived. In Oakland, California, Binga worked first as a barber and then as a porter for the Southern Pacific Railroad. Later, while in Ogden, Utah, he invested in a land deal on a former Indian reservation. The venture was profitable enough that, by the time he arrived in Chicago in 1893, Binga had sufficient capital to begin building his own empire.

Binga opened his first real estate office on State Street in 1898 and continued to prosper for the next three decades by acquiring rental properties throughout Chicago's South Side, regardless of racial restrictions. Binga would purchase the homes of more affluent whites who were fleeing the encroaching black population and then subdivide the houses into smaller units, which he would rent to single black men and families. In 1905 he leased a seven-story building on State Street and opened it to black tenants. Despite hostile reactions to his practice of "block busting" to bring black tenants into formerly white areas, Binga and others like him met housing needs that were not otherwise being addressed. Chicago's African American population, which had grown rapidly since 1900, could no longer be contained within the traditional black ghetto. Thus Binga's business activities served a crucial social need while at the same time turning a nice profit. By 1907 he was one of the most prosperous African American real estate agents in the city. A year later he opened the Binga Bank in a newly constructed office building on State Street. It was the first private bank in the North to be owned or controlled by blacks.

In 1912 Binga married Eudora Johnson, sister of John "Mushmouth" Johnson, the gambling kingpin of the South Side. Apparently Eudora Johnson was neither young nor attractive, and many Chicagoans were convinced that the handsome Binga married her for her money. Whatever the truth, at the time of their marriage she had inherited from her father after his death in 1906 an estate worth $200,000, which greatly enhanced Binga's economic prospects. According to Anthony J. Binga Sr., the couple had two children. Anthony Binga also claimed to have found a record of a second marriage in the U.S. Census records, but details are unknown.

Binga's bank and his personal fortune grew impressively in the wake of the massive black migration to northern cities in the years just before and after World War I, but white resentment in Chicago grew apace. His properties were vandalized on several occasions, and during the so-called Red Summer of 1919 both his real estate office and his home were bombed. Nonetheless at one point in the mid-1920s Binga owned 1,200 leaseholds on flats and residences, and by 1926 the *Chicago Broad Ax* was reporting that he owned more frontage on State Street south of Twelfth Street than anyone else.

All of this made possible the opening of Binga State Bank in January 1921. The bank's board of directors was composed of the leading African American businessmen in the community, and the *Broad Ax* viewed the bank's opening as a "history-making event among colored people residing in Chicago." By 1924 Binga had increased the capital and surplus of Binga State Bank to $235,000. He also opened the Binga Safe Deposit Company and organized a black insurance firm. However, although he had acquired a state charter for the bank, Binga continued to be its largest shareholder and ran the bank as if it were a private, solely owned corporation—practices for which he was later severely criticized.

The pinnacle of Binga's success came in 1929 when he constructed the Binga Arcade, a five-story building and ballroom at the corner of Thirty-fifth and State streets. Once the center of black business in Chicago, the area had badly deteriorated. Binga hoped that his development would help to revitalize the area, but instead his empire soon began to unravel. When the Binga State Bank failed in 1930, Binga lost his personal fortune of $400,000 as well as the savings of thousands of black Chicagoans. Although the Great Depression was partly to blame for the failure, the state banking examiner concluded that Binga had managed the financial institution in an illegal and unwise manner. Convicted of embezzlement in 1933, Binga was sentenced to ten years in prison; appeals delayed the start of his sentence until 1935.

Despite his mixed reputation in the community and even though many had lost their life savings when the bank failed, leading African Americans organized a petition to secure Binga's freedom. The effort was successful, and he was released from prison in 1938. Stripped of his former prominence, Binga spent the remainder of his life working as a custodian at St. Anselm's Catholic Church (having earlier converted to the faith). He died in Chicago after a fall at his nephew's home.

Binga's efforts to develop Chicago's black community brought him both praise and censure from the city's black and white communities. He was lauded for his business acumen and for his philanthropy, but he was also criticized for rent gouging and for having a hard-driving personality. Many years after Binga's death, the eminent African American leader EARL DICKERSON remembered Binga as "a mean son-of-a-bitch." In many ways Binga's career reflected the complex web of hope and despair that characterized the city's black business community during the early decades of the twentieth century.

FURTHER READING
Binga, Anthony J., Sr. "Jesse Binga: Founder and President, Binga State Bank, Chicago, Illinois," *Journal of the Afro-American History and Genealogy Society* 2, no. 4 (1981).
Harris, Abram L. *The Negro as Capitalist* (1936).
Major, Gerri. *Black Society* (1976).
Osthaus, Carl. "The Rise and Fall of Jesse Binga, Black Banker," *Journal of Negro History* 58 (Jan. 1973).
Obituaries: *Chicago Herald American*, 14 June 1950; *Chicago Defender*, 24 June 1950.

This entry is taken from the *American National Biography* and is published here with the permission of the American Council of Learned Societies.

JOHN N. INGHAM

Bingham, Howard (29 May 1939–), photographer and writer, was born in Jackson, Mississippi, the eldest son of eight children of Willie Everrett Bingham, a minister and baggage handler, and Emmaline Bingham, a homemaker whose maiden name is not now known. At the age of four, Bingham and his family moved from Mississippi to Los Angeles. Young Bingham was inspired by his photographer neighbors and developed a strong interest in photography. While attending Compton Junior College in the late 1950s, Bingham, a music major, enrolled in a photography course, for which he received a failing grade. Although he eventually left college, he continued to pursue photography and began an apprenticeship at the *Los Angeles Sentinel*, one of the largest black-owned newspapers in the United States. After one month at the *Sentinel*, he was hired as a staff photographer.

In 1962 the *Sentinel* sent Bingham to cover a press conference in Los Angeles for a new young boxer named Cassius Clay. Later that day, Bingham ran into Clay and his brother and offered them a tour of the city. This meeting would be the beginning of a friendship that spanned decades. In his book *Muhammad Ali: A Thirty Year Journey*, Bingham recounted his experiences photographing his close friend. Bingham not only captured images of the boxer but also accompanied Ali during travel and personal appearances. In 1963 Bingham met GORDON PARKS in Los Angeles while Parks was there to shoot pictures of MALCOLM X. Parks mentored Bingham and influenced the scope of his photography, even contributing an introduction to one of Bingham's books.

While working at the *Sentinel*, Bingham pursued a number of freelance jobs that eventually led to his firing after eighteen months at the newspaper. By the time of his termination from the *Sentinel*, however, Bingham had acquired the contacts necessary to move onto to the next phase of his career.

One of his assignments was to provide coverage of the Watts riots during the summer of 1966. *Life* magazine would later contract him to cover riots nationally, making him only the second black photographer to do contract work with the publication. He would also cover the 1968 National Democratic Convention in Chicago.

Traveling the country, Bingham captured American life, including representations that did not often garner front-page coverage. Bingham partnered with the writer Dick Hall in 1969 for a critically acclaimed photo essay of Mound Bayou, Mississippi. The essay told the story of an all-black town that was founded by former slaves in 1887 and remains one of the poorest communities in the country. Bingham gave a voice to Mound Bayou's citizens, who struggled to acquire basic amenities, such as clean, running water.

Although Bingham struggled with a severe stutter, he charmed and connected with people, including some significant historical figures of the twentieth century. In June 1968, he was one of the few photographers allowed access into the world of the Black Panthers: he photographed the group's leaders as well as its weapons cache. Although the photos were meant for a *Life* magazine feature that never ran, Bingham's work from that project was used in Gilbert Moore's book, *A Special Rage* (1971). Bingham also photographed MARTIN LUTHER KING JR., Elvis, the Beatles, and Nelson Mandela, his work appearing in issues of *Time, Sports Illustrated, Look, People, Newsweek,* and *Ebony*.

In 1969, while still traveling with Ali, Bingham met BILL COSBY on the set of his television show, *I Spy*. Blacks were not then allowed to join the Camera Guild (later the International Cinematographers' Guild), but Cosby later invited Bingham to shoot stills for his next television show, *The Bill Cosby Show*. As a nonunion photographer Bingham could not work on the set. As a result, a white union cameraman was present on the set as Bingham worked, photographing the show. Cosby wrote a letter urging the union to extend an offer of membership to Bingham; soon after he became the first black members admitted to the cameramen's union. He was a still photographer for many films,

including *The Candidate* (1972), *All the President's Men* (1976), and *Ghost Dad* (1990).

Bingham married Carolyn L. Turner in 1972; they would have two sons, Damon Howard and Dustin Lenoid, and divorced in 1986.

In 2001 Bingham served as an executive producer for the motion picture *Ali*. He was instrumental in the development of the film, which took eleven years to make. In *Ali*, Bingham was played by Jeffrey Wright. Bingham sought to ensure the depiction of Ali's life was accurate and remained as close to true events as possible.

Bingham's work and commitment to social change was recognized with a number of awards. In 1997 he received the International Award from the American Society of Photographers/Professional Photographers of America, and Photographer of the Year from the Photographic Marketing Distribution Association. Fusing his craft and commitment to the community, Bingham had an endowment established in his name to provide financial aid to minority photography students through the Eastman Kodak Company at the Rochester (N.Y.) Institute of Technology. In 2002 *Main Event: The Ali/Foreman Extravaganza through the Lens of Howard L. Bingham* was a featured exhibition at the Smithsonian Anacostia Community Museum in Washington, D.C.

FURTHER READING

Brada, Kristien. "Howard Bingham: Chronicles of a Celebrated Boxer," *Petersen's Photographic* (Mar. 1998).

Deford, Frank. "The Best of Friends," *Sports Illustrated* (13 July 1998).

Kelly, David. Review of *Muhammad Ali*. *New York Times Book Review*, 21 Nov. 1993.

LISA KAY DAVIS

Birtha, Becky (11 Oct. 1948–), poet and author, was born in Hampton, Virginia, the youngest daughter of Herbert Marshall Birtha, whose occupation is not known, and Jessie (Moore) Birtha, a librarian. She was named after her great-grandmother, Rebecca Burford, who had been a slave, and was possibly of Irish, Cherokee, and Catawba heritage. When she was three, Birtha's family moved to Salisbury, Maryland, but she mainly grew up in the Germantown section of Philadelphia, Pennsylvania, where the family moved in 1951. Birtha's mother introduced her daughters to the works of major African American writers, but she also grew up with such children's book classics as those written by Laura Ingalls Wilder, Edith Nesbitt, and Edward Eager; her favorite book was *A Little Princess* (1905) by Frances Hodgson Burnett. She took her first creative writing class at the public Philadelphia School for Girls, where she won a first prize for poetry in fifth grade. She began college at Case Western Reserve University, then moved in 1969 to Berkeley, California, but returned to school the following year to graduate from the State University of New York in Buffalo, with a degree in Children's Studies. In 1984 Birtha received an MFA in Creative Writing from Vermont College, and went on to teach at Goddard College and Bryn Mawr College.

Birtha described herself as a Quaker lesbian feminist writer, having declared her sexual identity in 1976. Many short stories in her published collections, *For Nights Like This One: Stories of Loving Women* (1983) and *Lovers' Choice* (1987), have a strong focus on African American women's lives and lesbian communities. But these collections also attest to her keen sensitivity to children, as someone who worked in her early years as a camp counselor, a day-care worker, and a preschool teacher, and this sustained interest in children's issues would continue to define the shape of her life. In "Ice Castle," her most widely known short story, published in *Lovers' Choice*, Birtha depicts a black lesbian poet, Maurie, whose fascination with European children's books complicates her adult identity as an African American writer. In this story Maurie must grapple with a similar but larger conflict in her private life, in having to find a way of reconciling what seems to her an irrational attraction she feels toward a young white woman.

Representative of the plot twists and open-endedness often seen in Birtha's work, and particularly of her masterful use of metaphor and imagery, the principal characters in "Ice Castle" wander forever in the whiteness of the snow. Emphasizing the value that lies in the process of confronting difficult questions, rather than in finding closure, the short story opens up a space for thinking about the complexity of one's racial and sexual identity that shifts depending on interpretation and context, resonating with the central concerns of major women writers like AUDRE LORDE, Paula Gunn Allen, and Gloria Anzaldúa.

Birtha lent her voice to many readings, conferences, and workshops throughout her career, and her interests ranged from serving on the editorial board of the Lesbian-Feminist Study Clearinghouse, established in 1978 by Carolyn Fontaine at the University of Pittsburgh, to working for the National Adoption Center and Freddie Mac Foundation's program, *Wednesday's Child*.

Birtha gained significant recognition for her writing over the years, winning an Individual Fellowship in Literature from the Pennsylvania Council for the Arts in 1985, a Creative Writing Fellowship in Literature from the National Endowment of the Arts in 1988, a Pushcart Prize that same year, and a Pew fellowship in the Arts in 1993. Her works appeared in nineteen anthologies and over fifty journals and periodicals such as the *Iowa Review, Sinister Wisdom, Conditions, off our backs*, and *Sojourner*. Most notably, her poem "Maria de Las Rosas" was included in *Home Girls: A Black Feminist Anthology* (1983) edited by the literary critic BARBARA SMITH, a landmark anthology influential in forging the aesthetics and politics of black feminist literature. Joining her voice with African American women writers such as ALICE WALKER, Cheryl Clarke, and Michelle Cliff, Birtha's poem thrives within a distinctive heritage of black feminism rooted in the home and the neighborhood. "Maria de las Rosas," about a young black lesbian woman bringing cream-colored brambly wild roses to a housewife across town and walking home with a single fragrant red rose given to her in friendly exchange, conveys a vital sense of acceptance that surrounds the awakening of the girl's lesbian sexuality. In a poem about a bond between two women that reaches across racial, ethnic, and sexual identity, Birtha's vision powerfully reflects black feminism's global purview and its urgent concern with the simultaneous oppression that affects the lives of women belonging to the Third World.

In 1991, as she published her first collection of poetry, *The Forbidden Poems*, Birtha adopted a daughter, Tasha Alfrieda Birtha. She was awarded the Golden Kite Award for her first book written for children, *Grandmama's Pride* (2005).

FURTHER READING

Brownworth, Victoria A. "The Mother's Tongue: Poet Becky Birtha Gives Voice to the Experience of Parenting," *Advocate* (23 Apr. 1991).

Ferrera, Miranda H., ed. "Becky Birtha," in *The Writers Directory*, 19th ed. (2003).

Mark, Rebecca. "Becky Birtha (1948–)," in *Contemporary Lesbian Writers of the United States* (1993).

Pullin, Faith. "Acts of Reclamation," *Times Literary Supplement*, 3–9 June 1988.

Roberts, J. R., comp. *Black Lesbians: An Annotated Bibliography* (1981).

REI MAGOSAKI

Bishop, Sanford Dixon, Jr. (4 Feb. 1947–), politician, was born in Mobile, Alabama, to Sanford Dixon Bishop, an educational administrator and first president of Bishop State Community College, and Minnie Bethany Slade Bishop, a librarian. When he was seven years old, the family moved to Toulminville, a transitional neighborhood in Mobile for poor and working-class whites, where a black subdivision had been built. The Deep South's segregation and hostility were not foreign to Bishop growing up: The Ku Klux Klan had been active with cross-burnings in the district, and the new black community began a neighborhood watch. As a youth, Bishop was heavily involved with the Boy Scouts, later becoming an Eagle Scout and member of the Order of the Arrow, the Scouts' honor society.

Bishop's schools—Booker T. Washington Junior High for blacks and Central High School for whites—were segregated, and the secondhand textbooks and supplements were not ideal for the son of two educators. Though his parents contemplated sending him to boarding school, Bishop stayed in the city and excelled academically. In his senior year, his essay on the importance of law in society won a contest sponsored by the local Bar Association; as a prize—along with a cash award—Bishop attended a naturalization ceremony at the federal courthouse, which stoked his interest in law. He graduated from high school in 1964 and decided to go to Morehouse to eventually pursue a J.D.

Bishop entered student politics in Morehouse, becoming Student Government Association president his senior year. Present when the Morehouse graduate Dr. MARTIN LUTHER KING JR. received his honorary degree at the campus, Bishop also walked in the late civil rights leader's processional at the university and sang at his funeral in 1968. Bishop graduated with a B in Political Science that year, and attended Emory Law School, hoping to use his education and legal training to improve conditions in the south.

His first year at Emory broadened his world view: he met civil rights leaders like JULIAN BOND and JOHN LEWIS at his part-time job as an archivist at the Institute of the Black World, and at the end of his first year, did Basic ROTC to begin his military requirement. Following his graduation from Emory in 1971, Bishop was granted a medical discharge from the army, and went to New York City for a fellowship in civil rights litigation with the NAACP's Legal Defense and Education Fund.

In 1972 Bishop returned south and opened a law practice in Columbus, Georgia. One of his major victories was a class-action suit on behalf of almost six thousand black inmates in Georgia State Prison; the judge agreed that the prison would have to alter its conditions to curb overcrowding, violence, and bias. Frustrated by the state legislature's tight purse strings in helping to enact prison reform, Bishop decided to run for state government. In 1976 Bishop won a State House seat and served in Georgia's House through 1990, and then in the State Senate for two years, while remaining a partner at his firm.

When reapportionment created a new black-majority district, Bishop entered the race for the U.S. House of Representatives in 1992. In the Democratic primary, he defeated the white incumbent, Charles Hatcher, who had been caught up in the House banking scandal, in which members routinely bounced checks and overdrew accounts from the House Bank. After easily beating his Republican opponent in the general election, Bishop was sworn in and attended a prison opening, where he noted, "I realized that I could win a case in court, and it would affect only my clients. But if I passed one good law in the legislature, it would affect everybody in the State of Georgia … if you pass one good law in Congress, you affect everybody in the United States" (Interview with *The History Makers*, http://www.idvl.org/thehistorymakers/iCoreClient.html).

Bishop made national news in the summer of 1994, after a flood from the tropical storm Alberto hit southern Georgia. His hands-on concern and requests for federal assistance eventually forced President Bill Clinton to come to the district himself and promise millions of dollars in relief.

In 1995, after the Supreme Court deemed that his district's reconfiguring was unconstitutional, Bishop's Congressional seat was once again redrawn, this time without a black majority: the state's newly mapped Second District saw its demographics shift from over half African American to 65 percent white, and from half urban to a largely rural population. His subsequent reelection victory in 1996 was attributed to two things: his popularity in the wake of the flood, and a rightward move in his politics. Though his 8 percent margin of victory was comfortable, it was a marked decrease from the 32 percent margin he won only two years earlier.

In what many regarded as an attempt to curry favor with his new constituency that summer, Bishop joined the National Rifle Association and the conservative Blue Dog Democrat coalition, and became a proponent of the issues popular among Republicans and conservative Democrats, such as the politically divisive welfare reform bill and the 1996 Defense of Marriage Act, in which the federal government explicitly defined marriage as between people of the opposite sex. Leading up to the 1996 election, he played down his skin color and its significance, saying in an interview, "Cotton, peanuts, and soybeans are all more important than my race." (*The New Republic*, 4 Nov. 1996, p. 20.) In 2002 Bishop was one of only four Congressional Black Caucus members to vote for the resolution authorizing the Iraq War. The others, WILLIAM JEFFERSON (D-LA), HAROLD FORD JR. (D-TN), and ALBERT WYNN (D-MD), were, like Bishop, representatives of southern and border states.

Through Bishop's career in Congress, he sat on the Appropriations Committee, taking an interest in agriculture and defense. He served the former by protecting the interests of peanut-growing constituents: the Farm Bill of 1996 kept subsidies intact for peanut farmers, and his district was the recipient of many funds for agricultural development and diversification.

In 2009 Bishop was criticized after an investigation into a youth program that had received earmarks from him was found to have hired his stepdaughter, Aayesha, and her husband. The next year, Bishop came under heavier charges of steering CBC Foundation Scholarships to two relatives and the fiancee of one of his aides. Those criticisms prompted many political observers to speculate that Bishop's ability to hold on to his Congressional seat would end in Georgia's 2010, 2nd Congressional district race. The electorate was evenly divided between blacks and whites, but Bishop faced a weak year for Democrats coupled with the deep unpopularity of BARACK OBAMA among southern whites.

Obama had won the 2nd Congressional district with 54% of the vote in 2008; that Bishop secured 68 percent indicated that he won a significant proportion of the electorate who had backed the Republican John McCain in the presidential race. In Obama's first-term agenda Bishop supported the administration's legislative reforms in health care reform, economic stimulus, and energy. In an era when incumbents usually held an edge in fund-raising and spending on elections, Bishop's Republican opponent nearly matched Bishop in terms of money raised. On the eve of the election, opinion polls—including that of the much-praised political blogger Nate Silver—suggested that Bishop

would be one of many Democratic Party losses. Yet on election day, and even though his majority declined by more than 40,000 votes, Bishop defied the odds and maintained his seat with 51% of the vote. His victory was testament to his ability to maintain solid support from the African American voters in his district, while winning a minority of white votes.

In 2001 Bishop married his longtime girlfriend Vivian Creighton, who served as elected Clerk of the Municipal Court of Columbus, the first African American female to be elected to a citywide post in Columbus. In the 2008 presidential primary, she supported U.S. Senator Hillary Clinton (D-NY), while her husband supported Obama.

FURTHER READING
Grann, David. "Whose Bishop? A Race for the House: Georgia," *New Republic*, 4 Nov. 1996.

ADAM W. GREEN

Bishop, Stephen (1821?–1857), slave and guide, achieved fame in the decades preceding the Civil War. Nothing is known of his parents or early life, but it is known that Bishop was a slave belonging to Kentucky lawyer Franklin Gorin, who in the 1830s purchased Mammoth Cave for $5,000. Previous cave guides had been local white men, but Gorin either saw something promising in the teenaged Bishop or reasoned that he could save money by training a slave to do the same work. Either way, beginning in the spring of 1838 Bishop received training from the previous guide and quickly took to the job, learning the several miles of trail and numerous pits, rock formations, and other attractions of his underground place of employment.

Bishop was allowed to spend many hours exploring the cave on his own. In the fall of 1838 he penetrated a confusing maze of trails known as the Labyrinth and discovered a formerly unseen vertical shaft that came to be known as Gorin's Dome. More important, he devised a way to cross Bottomless Pit, a chasm that had previously marked the end of the trail for visitors to the cave. That same year Bishop discovered the River Styx—the first time water had been found within Mammoth Cave. He also captured specimens of the bizarre eyeless fish that inhabited the river, bringing additional attention to the geological and biological treasures located at the site. As a result of Bishop's daring expeditions, many more miles of tunnel were opened to exploration and Mammoth Cave's fame began to spread beyond Kentucky and its neighboring states.

Stephen Bishop, renowned guide to Mammoth Cave, Kentucky. Illustrated in Hovey's *Mammoth Cave*, 1882. (Library of Congress.)

Franklin Gorin did not have the funds to develop Mammoth into a first-class tourist destination, and in 1839 John Croghan, a wealthy physician from Louisville, Kentucky, purchased the cave—and Bishop—from their previous owner. Croghan invested heavily in his new property, building a fashionable, large hotel and working with the state of Kentucky to improve the roads leading to the cave. He brought in two other young slaves to join Bishop on the guide staff, and Bishop taught them everything he had learned. Among the increasing number of visitors to the cave were geologists, biologists, and other scientists, who requested Bishop as their guide. Bishop appears to have learned from his visitors as much as he taught them, for he became an expert on the processes of stalactite and stalagmite formation, the action of water upon the limestone rock that made up the main structure of the cave, and the life cycles of the animals living within it. He learned to read and taught himself still more.

In winter 1842 Croghan took Bishop with him to Locust Grove, his farm outside of Louisville. There Bishop spent days drawing from memory a map of the many miles of trail that had been discovered since the previous map was drawn in 1835. Bishop's map became part of a book about Mammoth Cave that Croghan published as a souvenir and publicity device. Possibly during his stay at Locust Grove, Bishop met Charlotte, a young female slave also owned by Croghan. They were married in 1843; later that year their son, Thomas Bishop, was born.

Bishop continued to guide visitors through the cave for the next fourteen years. Travel writers reported on his extensive knowledge of the many attractions of the cave, but they also lauded his sense of humor and easy familiarity with visitors from many walks of life. "His great talent was a knowledge of man," Franklin Gorin once wrote about Bishop. Among the celebrities and royalty who visited Mammoth due to Bishop's discoveries and requested him as a guide were the Swedish singer Jenny Lind, the Norwegian violinist Ole Bull, Prince Alexis of Russia, and Dom Pedro, the emperor of Brazil. In 1849 John Croghan died. His will directed that after three years his slaves be allowed to hire themselves out for pay, and that four years following that they should all be manumitted. Bishop, who had been studying the law, reportedly considered moving to Liberia to become a lawyer, but ultimately stayed in Kentucky and invested money in a piece of land near Mammoth Cave. He died under unknown circumstances and is buried in the Old Guides' Cemetery, within what is now Mammoth Cave National Park. His monument, donated decades later by the Pittsburgh businessman James Mellon, was created from a discarded stone that had been engraved for a Union soldier but never paid for. It carries (incorrectly) 1859 as the year of death. Bishop's widow remarried another cave guide; it is not known what became of Thomas, their son.

As of 2007, with more than 350 miles of mapped trails, Mammoth Cave was the most extensive cave system in the world, and the national park was toured by nearly two million visitors a year.

FURTHER READING

Bullitt, Alexander Clark. *Rambles in the Mammoth Cave, During the Year 1844, By A Visitor* (1845, 1985).

Brucker, Roger W., and Richard A. Watson. *The Longest Cave* (1976).

ELIZABETH MITCHELL

Bivins, Horace Wayman (6 May 1866–?), decorated soldier and expert marksman, was born in Pungoteague, Accomack County, Virginia, the eighth of nine children born to Severn and Elizabeth Bivins. His father was a farmer who was also active in religious and educational endeavors. Four years before Horace Bivins was born, his father provided the money for the first church and schoolhouse for freed slaves built on the eastern shore of Virginia. The Accomack County census of 1870 said of Bivins's mother only that she "keeps house."

Bivins worked on his parents' farm until the age of fifteen, when he was put in charge of another farm near Keller Station, Virginia. Three years later he entered Hampton School as a work student and received his first military training. "Having a very great desire for adventure and to see the wild West," as Bivins later put it (Cashin, 58), he enlisted in the U.S. Army on 7 November 1887. After training in Missouri, Bivins was assigned to Troop E of the Tenth Cavalry, which he joined at Fort Grant, Arizona Territory, in June 1888. Over the next four years, Bivins later told a newspaper reporter, "My troop took a prominent part in the campaigns against Geronimo, Apache Kid, and other Indian chieftains of the southwest."

It was during his service in Arizona that Bivins took up shooting, placing second in a troop of sixty men the first time he ever shot a rifle during target practice. He was soon made a sharpshooter. His regiment was ordered to Montana in 1892, where he kept up his shooting record. He represented his troop in 1892, 1893, and 1894 at departmental competitions, and in 1894 he carried off the first army gold medal in carbine competition at Fort Sheridan, Illinois, where he also won two other gold medals.

In 1896 Buffalo Bill Cody, a buffalo hunter and flamboyant showman, offered Bivins a position in his Wild West show, shooting against Annie Oakley. Cody was said to have sought a furlough for Bivins and offered him one hundred dollars a month, but Bivins was in line to become an ordnance officer and said he preferred the army routine to circus life. Bivins's regiment was ordered south when war with Spain was declared in April 1898. The regiment left Montana in April, proceeded to Wisconsin, then south by train. Bivins said they were greeted by "great ovations all along the line" (Cashin, 61), but the welcome grew considerably more muted as they entered the South, where the Jim Crow laws astonished many of the black troopers. They arrived in Cuba in mid-June and were involved in much hard fighting and marching, often side by side with the First Volunteer Cavalry, perhaps more famously known as the Rough Riders. At the battle of Las Guasimas, elements of the Tenth Cavalry, including Bivins, saved the Rough Riders from a near disaster after they had been ambushed by Spanish troops. At the battle of San Juan Hill, Bivins, by then a sergeant, rendered notable service operating a Hotchkiss gun, a small artillery piece from which he was credited with single-handedly firing seventy-two shells, even after he had been wounded. He was awarded a Silver Star for his actions. After more service stateside and then a brief return to Cuba, Bivins's regiment was sent to the Philippines in April 1901 to "pacify" insurrectionist natives in the northeastern part of the main island.

He served there for a year before being transferred back to Montana, where he renewed a relationship with Claudia Browning of Billings, Montana, whom he had met during his earlier service in that state. In March 1904 he married Browning, a native of Deadwood, South Dakota. They lived at Fort Missoula, Montana, until 1906, when he was ordered back to the Philippines. His second tour of duty there was quiet enough that he was able to devote himself to collecting Philippine birds, shells, fossils, and other curios. He later donated artifacts to museums in Montana, California, and Minnesota. From 1908 to 1913, at which time he retired from active service as an ordnance sergeant, Bivins was transferred from fort to fort all over the country. With double-time for foreign service in Cuba and the Philippines, Bivins upon his retirement was given credit for thirty years in the regular army.

He settled down in Billings after his retirement, where he and his wife reared two sons and a daughter, and where Bivins was known for his flourishing vegetable gardens. His wife was an active member of the African Methodist Episcopal (AME) Church, vice president of the Montana Federation of Negro Women, a member of the Society of Eastern Montana Pioneers, and secretary of the Billings Federation of Women's Clubs. Bivins was recalled to active service in 1918, after the United States entered World War I, assigned by the War Department to the ordnance department in Newport News, Virginia. In June of that year the African republic of Liberia, founded in 1821 as a settlement for freed U.S. slaves, offered Bivins a commission to train 115,000 men who were going to fight against the Germans in West Africa, but Bivins declined. Bivins was soon made a captain of infantry, serving as a supply officer and then head of a labor battalion at a detention camp in Fort Dix, New Jersey. He retired from the army for good in

1919. He had thirty-two years of credit with the army and, coincidentally, had won thirty-two army medals.

He studied taxidermy after the war and followed that trade for many years. A newspaper article in 1935 described him as "industrious, sober and studious," and said he was six feet tall with broad, square-set shoulders (*Billings Gazette*, 3 Mar. 1935). Claudia Bivins died in 1943, and in 1949 it was reported in a newspaper article that Bivins had recently left Montana to live in Philadelphia, Pennsylvania. It is unknown whether Bivins ever returned to Montana or whether he died in Philadelphia.

FURTHER READING.

Cashin, Herschel V., et al. *Under Fire with the Tenth U.S. Cavalry* (1899).

EDWARD A. KEMMICK

Black Herman. *See* Rucker, Benjamin H. "Black Herman."

Black, John Lincoln (17 Aug. 1931–18 June 2004), stationary engineer, labor union president, was born John Lincoln Black in Burgin, Kentucky, the second child of Robert Lincoln Black, a laborer, and Bertha Ann Ball Boggs Black. After his birth the Black family moved to Keene, Kentucky, to live with John's paternal grandmother. Within a few years Bertha Black became ill with tuberculosis and sickle cell anemia, so young John was sent to live with his father's relatives while his older sister and younger brother remained with the family. After the death of his mother in 1934 Black continued to live with his great-aunt Martha while his two siblings, Anna Mae and Wallace, lived with their paternal grandmother. After the death of his great-aunt, John moved to Cincinnati and joined his father, stepmother, and siblings. John Black attended the Cincinnati public schools—the all-black Harriet Beecher Stowe Elementary School founded by Jennie Porter, Bloom Junior High, and William Woodward High School, from which he graduated in 1949.

After high school he enrolled at the University of Kentucky but transferred to the University of Cincinnati before enlisting in the U.S. Army on 1 February 1950. Training at Fort Benning, Georgia, and Fort Bragg, North Carolina, Black was a member of Battery B 376th Airborne Field Artillery Battalion. During his military service he was promoted to sergeant and awarded the Parachute/Glider Badge; he received an honorable discharge on 15 March 1953.

Black married Edna Earl McNeil of Holly Springs, North Carolina, a mother of two children, on 17 March 1953, and moved to Cincinnati. Together they had eleven children. In December 1955 Black gained employment as a janitor with the Cincinnati public schools eight days after ROSA PARKS was arrested for refusing to relinquish her seat on a bus in Montgomery, Alabama. After ten years as a janitor and working a second and sometimes a third job, Black began to study stationary engineering with the tutorial assistance of his cousin James Vinegar. He also took classes at the Ohio College of Applied Science in Cincinnati. In 1965 he received his state license for steam fireman boiler operator and was promoted to steam fireman and sent to Woodward High School. On 25 January 1971 he received his state license for stationary engineering, 3rd class. In 1973 he was promoted to Engineer/Custodian 4 and two years later was promoted to Plant Operator 6 at the School for the Creative and Performing Arts, where he remained for nineteen years. As plant operator he was in charge of the entire physical plant of the school facility. Overseeing the custodial, maintenance, and mechanical operations of the building, Black worked long hours and nearly every day of the week. Nine years later he was promoted to Plant Operator 7.

On 2 February 1967 he joined the International Union of Operating Engineers Local #20, of which he became a loyal member. Black embraced the union idea passed on to him by his father, a unionized forklift operator and clerk at the Cincinnati based Milling Machine Company (later Cincinnati Milacron). Black served as a chief steward of members working for the public schools and in 1975 became steward for Cincinnati public school engineers. He quickly moved up the ranks, becoming a member of Local #20 executive board, a trustee, and then an auditor. In 1978 Black was elected vice president of the local—he was just the second African American elected to that position in the local—and served for twelve years. During his term the local had a strike at the University of Cincinnati, which lasted for one week and involved grievances with contract issues. The strike was settled as the agreement with the University met Local #20 members' demands. The local had a long relationship with the university. Starting in 1966 the local established an apprenticeship program with the university as signatory and sanctioned by the Department of Labor. This program, similar to a co-op education program where students would get course credit for on-the-job work or apprenticeship, offered 144 hours per year on-the-job training in the physical plant, matriculation in the core courses of the university, and after four years the conferral of a bachelor's degree in Stationary Engineering. Black saw this as an opportunity for African American applicants. He actively recruited from the African American community in order to provide opportunities to an alternative engineering program at the university. He was also able to increase the number of African Americans in the stationary engineer field and in the ranks of Local #20.

In 1991 Black was elected president of Local #20, making him the first African American to hold such an office in the IUOE Local. In that position Black oversaw contract negotiations with the Cincinnati public schools and was able to increase the educational opportunities for prospective stationary engineers by instituting tutorial classes directly under his supervision.

Excluded from most labor unions for much of the early twentieth century, African American union activities increased in the postwar era. During the civil rights era African Americans in Local #20 moved quickly into officer positions. John Black worked for the Cincinnati public schools for thirty-eight years and was a member of the International Union of Operating Engineers Local #20 for twenty-six years. He served as an officer of the local for over fifteen years. His term as the first African American president of Local #20 ended July 1993. He retired from the Cincinnati public schools on 1 August 1993. After retirement Black volunteered with the Hamilton County Board of Elections, Democratic County Central Committee, and was steward of the Democratic Party 7th Ward. John L. Black died of cardiac arrest in Cincinnati.

FURTHER READING

The information for this article was gathered from the Personnel Records, Human Resources Department, Cincinnati Public Schools; and Archives, International Union of Operating Engineers, Local #20, Cincinnati, Ohio. The John L. Black papers are held in a private family collection in Cincinnati, Ohio.

Mason, Patrick L. *African Americans, Labor and Society: Organizing for a New Agenda* (2001).

SAMUEL W. BLACK

Black, Leonard (8 Mar. 1822–28 Apr. 1883), minister and author, was born a slave in Anne Arundel County, Maryland, about sixty miles from Baltimore. He is best known for his narrative, published in 1847, which describes his time in slavery, his escape, and his call to the ministry.

Though Black served several owners in his early life, he was eventually brought back to Maryland to live with his original owner, where he was reunited with his four brothers. Within six months of meeting them again, three of his brothers escaped, encouraging him to escape when he could. While enslaved in Baltimore, Black had the urge to read, and though he bought books on several occasions, his master found them and either burned them or gave them to his son. Black is quick in his narrative to make the observation that in this case the education of a white child was not simply gained at the expense of the slaves' education but was quite literally bought for them by slaves.

Ten terrible years passed after his brothers left before Black became inspired by the Bible to escape enslavement, though his escape plan was almost ruined by a fellow slave who reported his plan to the owner. In 1837 Black managed to make it all the way to Boston, where he began to inquire after his brothers, only to be led eventually to Portland, Maine, and the home of George Black, a man who was not his brother, but who welcomed him as one nonetheless. There Black began to learn to read, gained employment, became a Christian, and fell in love with George Black's daughter. He followed the Black family back to Boston, where he married. In time he moved with his wife to Providence, Rhode Island.

Black's narrative describes his more than twenty years in slavery, under several cruel masters, as brutal and demoralizing. He had a keen awareness of the slave owners' lack of economic logic, evident in the treatment of their slaves. Though he acknowledged that it may make sense to feed a slave as little as possible, he knew that hunger made them need to steal and that the punishments he received made it impossible for him to work.

One of the major points of his narrative concerned the distortion of Christianity in the South, such that white people could be considered Christians and own slaves at the same time. Black also outlined the contradictions and faulty logic of white southern pro-slavery advocates, but he was equally critical of white northerners who not only allowed slavery to exist but also profited from its continuance through industry that relied on the products of slave labor from the South. Typical of many slave narrative authors of the time, Black, in hindsight, judged the white men he met based on their adherence (or lack of adherence) to the Christian scriptures.

Filled with biblical references to Hagar, Judas, Joseph, and Ahab, Black's narrative also chronicles his conversion to Christianity and his work as a minister. In Providence he worked for the Reverend Doctor Francis Wayland, then president of Brown University and later founder of Wayland Seminary in Washington, D.C. After being tutored by Wayland, Black believed that he was ready to preach, but the minister and other church committee members declined his request on the supposed grounds that his education was deficient. Black subsequently despaired and temporarily abandoned his desire to preach until a horse accident left him immobile and unable to care for his family. He then had a vision that compelled him to make a commitment to preach the word of God upon his recovery.

Based on that promise he left Providence to search for a church. When he arrived in Nantucket, Massachusetts, he found a congregation with no preacher, a vacancy he succeeded in filling after delivering only one sermon before it. In Nantucket he raised the money to rebuild that church and also served as a missionary to the Native Americans.

Admittedly written as a means to earn money to invest in his education, Black's narrative is the source from which we know the most about the author's life. However, Black's life and achievements did not end with the publication of his life story. He later served as a member of the 25th New York Volunteer Infantry during the Civil War, and he voyaged to England, Scotland, and France in 1867. Ultimately, Black's greater significance relates less to his narrative (which is fairly typical of the genre and not widely read) but to his wide-reaching ministry.

During his time as a minister, Black served in Stonington and New Haven, Connecticut, as well as in Buffalo and Brooklyn, New York. In 1873 he moved to Virginia, first preaching in Norfolk before moving on to Petersburg to be the minister of a Baptist congregation there and to double the congregation during his tenure.

When Black died in 1883, he was mourned by more than five thousand people at one of the largest funerals held up to that time in Petersburg. His grave is in Petersburg's People's Memorial Cemetery, an African American burial ground, and it is marked with a monument in memory of his service to the community.

FURTHER READING

Black, Leonard. *The Life and Sufferings of Leonard Black, A Fugitive from Slavery, Written by Himself* (1847).

Bragg, George F. *Men of Maryland* (1925).

LAURA MURPHY

Blackburn, Alpha (16 Sept. 1939–), designer, businesswoman, and civic leader, was born Alpha Coles in Lynchburg, Virginia, the youngest of eight children of Alphonso Carroll Coles and Minnie Pugh Coles. Growing up, Blackburn attended a segregated school system, and went on to win a scholarship to Howard University, from which she graduated with honors, attaining a bachelor of arts in Design and a master of fine arts in painting and Art History. In 1964 she moved to Indianapolis, Indiana, with her husband, WALTER SCOTT BLACKBURN, who had completed his degree in architecture at Howard. She commenced work as a freelance designer of clothing and interiors.

Blackburn's petite figure and radiant good looks created opportunities for her to model, and she accepted a steady job at the prestigious L. S. Ayres & Company in downtown Indianapolis. Concurrently, she hosted a half-hour daily talk show from 1972 to 1978, *Indy Today*, on WISH-TV (a CBS affiliate), followed by a half-hour weekly talk show *Indiana Illustrated*, from 1978 to 1981 on WTHR-TV (an NBC affiliate). From 1980 to 1990 Blackburn was fashion editor for *Indianapolis Monthly* magazine. From 1980 to 2000 Blackburn was vice president of her husband's firm, Blackburn Architects, Inc., designing interiors and working with the company's architects to choose exterior colors and materials. In 1988 she incorporated a line of designer products as Alpha, Inc.

The Indianapolis Museum of Art commissioned Blackburn to design the "Dress of the Century" to present at its centennial celebration. Also in 1983 Blackburn was the recipient of Harvey's Bristol Cream nationwide Tribute to the Black Designer. Blackburn designed uniforms for the National Football League's Indianapolis Colts and the National Basketball Association's Indiana Pacers cheerleaders, and for Indianapolis's Methodist Hospital nurses. A featured designer and commentator for more than two hundred fashion shows and line showings, Blackburn received more than a dozen citations and awards as Designer of the Year. In 1985 the Indiana State Museum mounted Alpha, An Original, a twenty-year retrospective of her work as a fashion designer. Blackburn's "one-of-a-kind" gowns for clients are built on her philosophy that a design reflecting its owner is more important than one that mirrors the designer's artistry.

Blackburn's national clients included the singer Kenny Lattimore and the journalist and commentator TAVIS SMILEY. Her notable design projects include the National Underground Freedom Center in Cincinnati, Ohio; the Purdue University Black Culture Center in West Lafayette, Indiana; and, in Indianapolis, the renovation of the historic Madame Walker Theatre Center, the Lilly Endowment Building, offices of the Indiana State Housing Board and Indiana Arts Commission, and CONSECO Field House. Blackburn is respected because she is responsive to her clients' needs while introducing them to creative possibilities that reflect their personal styles. She believes that "Nothing falls into place. You have to put it into place."

Blackburn assumed the position of president and CEO of Blackburn Architects, Inc., in 2000, just prior to the death of her husband. With his designs firmly in place, she oversaw completion of the National Underground Railroad Freedom Center on the site between the Reds and Bengals stadiums along Cincinnati's Ohio River front. Alpha Blackburn had initially served as spokesperson for the firm, presenting a daring vision to win the 1998 competition. Turning from a traditional museum model of artifacts and labels, Blackburn Architects dramatized the site to create metaphors through structure and embellishment and present material culture and information in the context of past, present, and future. Even before the National Underground Railroad Freedom Center opened on 22 August 2004, Blackburn began plans for the creation of the Indiana Museum of African American History, scheduled to open in 2009, adjacent to the NCAA Hall of Champions in White River State Park in Indianapolis. As chair of the museum's founding board, she assumed the dual roles of spearheading the fund-raising and overseeing completion of the $52 million structure designed by Blackburn Architects. The limestone and metal building, which will feature a ninety-foot tower shingled with multicolored glass, bears little resemblance to the curvilinear, interconnected three-pavilion Freedom Center structure. While the Freedom Center's purpose is to explore universal issues surrounding the quest for freedom, the Indiana Museum is primarily focused on collecting, documenting, preserving, and educating the public about the history, life, and culture of African Americans in Indiana and beyond.

Blackburn has been a major fund-raiser for the United Negro College Fund. An American Society of Interior Design Allied member and American Institute of Architects (AIA) associate member, she serves on the AIA Diversity Task Force. She has been a juror of regional and university architectural competitions and has guest lectured on architecture at Miami University of Ohio and Ball State University. She is on the advisory committee of Ball State and Indiana University–Purdue University in Indianapolis. In 1983 Soroptimist International of Indianapolis, Inc., honored Blackburn for Outstanding Contributions to the Arts in Indiana. A commissioner of the Indiana Civil Rights Commission since 1987 and its chair since 1990, Blackburn has chaired the Indiana Business Hall of Fame, sat on the Indiana Cultural Tourism Commission, and served as technical adviser and co-coordinator of art in Indianapolis's airport. In 1993 she was named a distinguished alumna of Howard University. She is a recipient of the Hoosier Heritage Civic Leadership Award, Trailblazer Award, presented by Indiana Black Expo, and was chosen as one of five Indiana "Renaissance Women." She is a recipient of the Prodigy of Indianapolis Award for outstanding commitment to nonprofit organizations and charitable causes and has served on numerous corporate boards.

FURTHER READING

Hagen, Patricia. "Circle of Life," *Indianapolis Woman*, vol. 12, no. 2 (Feb. 2005): 36-41.

Slaughter, Ronnetta S. "Alpha," *Indianapolis Recorder*, 14 Apr. 2000, section C.

Way, Deborah. "Alpha's Bet," *Indianapolis Monthly*, vol. 25, no. 1 (Sept. 2001): 162-167, 250.

RITA KOHN

Blackburn, Robert Hamilton (12 Dec. 1920–21 Apr. 2003), master printer, artist, educator, and founder of the Printmaking Workshop, was born in Summit, New Jersey, the son of Jeannette Chambers Blackburn and Archibald Blackburn of Jamaica, West Indies. Robert, also known as Bob, had a younger sister, Gertrude, and a half brother. His father, although trained as a minister, found employment with the Lackawanna Railroad in Summit. When Blackburn was two, the family moved to rural Elmira, New York. Blackburn fondly recalled his early childhood in the rural town, where he listened to the train whistle from his bedroom window, attended church every Sunday, and won a toy car as a prize for a drawing he had done. During the Depression, when Blackburn was seven, his family moved to Harlem, where he attended public schools from 1932 to 1936.

At Frederick Douglass Junior High School, Blackburn was influenced by his teacher, the poet COUNTÉE CULLEN, who sparked his interest in literature and the history of art. Blackburn served as the art editor of the *Pilot*, the school paper, and was awarded the FREDERICK DOUGLASS Guidance and Art medals in 1936. Three years earlier he had met CHARLES HENRY ALSTON, a painter and sculptor, and enrolled in his Harlem Arts Workshop, a Public Works Art Project-sponsored program at the New York Public Library. Alston proved to be a major influence on Blackburn as a mentor and teacher, as were Ronald Joseph, another teacher at the Harlem Arts Workshop who introduced him to Chinese art, and Henry W. Bannarn, a sculptor. While Blackburn was initially too young to qualify for the $23.80 weekly project pay, he met and was influenced by a number of emerging artists and thinkers, including JACOB ARMSTEAD LAWRENCE, Sara Murrell, Norman Lewis, Ad Bates, ROMARE BEARDEN, and RICHARD WRIGHT. In the 1930s Blackburn was a member of the Harlem Artists Guild, founded by AUGUSTA SAVAGE, and he took classes at her Uptown Art Laboratory along with Lawrence and GWENDOLYN KNIGHT. Blackburn also attended after-school classes at the Harlem YMCA's Arts and Crafts Department (1934–1935), working with painters Richard W. Lindsey and Rex Gorleigh, as well as the sculptor WILLIAM ELLISWORTH ARTIS. He assisted Artis on a mural for the boys' recreation hall and received the YMCA's John Wanamaker Medal, the Spingarn Award, the Robert Pious Award, the Poussant Award, and the G.J. Pinckney Award.

In 1936 Blackburn entered DeWitt Clinton High School, where he was the art editor for the school's literary magazine, the *Magpie*, in which he published his poetry, stories, and prints. Among his fellow contributors to the *Magpie* were Richard Avedon, JAMES BALDWIN, and Sidney "Paddy" Chayefsky. While in high school Blackburn also attended the Harlem Community Art Center (HCAC). Directed by AUGUSTA SAVAGE, and later GWENDOLYN BENNETT, HCAC grew to be the largest WPA program in the country. At HCAC, Blackburn recalled hearing a lecture by the abstract painter Vaclav Vytlacil, one of several white artists who worked in this predominantly black circle (who would later become an important influence at the Art Students League). Another was Riva Helfond, a WPA artist, who first introduced Blackburn to lithography, etching, woodblock, and silk screening in 1938. Blackburn subsequently published twelve editions of lithographs, some in the *Magpie*, and entered into juried exhibits with the assistance of the Harmon Foundation. ALAIN LEROY LOCKE, his Howard University colleague, and JAMES AMOS PORTER were among the many critics who praised Blackburn's drawings and lithographs from this period.

Knowing that his family could not fund a college education during the Depression, Blackburn was determined to find ways to make his livelihood in art. He was a scholarship student at the Art Students League from 1940 to 1943, where he was instructed by Vytlacil and printmaker Will Barnet. In 1943 Blackburn graduated from the league, and for four years he worked as a freelance graphic artist for the Harmon Foundation, the China Institute of America, and Associated American Artists. In 1945 Blackburn moved from Harlem to downtown Manhattan, where he shared a loft with the painter ERNEST CRICHLOW. Two years later Blackburn purchased a lithographic press and began printing for other artists and taught three classes a week. In 1948 he officially opened the Creative Graphic Workshop. Although this workshop did not turn a profit, it provided Blackburn with studio space and enabled him to collaborate with a range of artists, including John Von Wicht, Ronald Joseph, Larry Potter, Tom Laidman, Stella Wright, Peter Bradley, and ELDZIER CORTOR.

In 1949 he also began printing for Cooper Union School of Art students. He did this job for twenty years before being offered a teaching position in the mid-1960s. Blackburn also taught printmaking at Brooklyn College, Maryland Institute College of Art, New York University, Pratt Institute, Rutgers University School of Visual Arts, and Columbia University (where he was a faculty member from 1970 to 1990). In the early 1950s, Blackburn studied drawing with Wallace Harrison and made plein air ink sketches with Ronald Joseph. In April 1952 *ARTnews* magazine highlighted his technical achievements and collaboration with Will Barnet on a suite of color lithographs created from 1951 to 1952.

The following year Blackburn left the workshop in charge of a group of artist friends and traveled to Europe on a John Hay Whitney Traveling Fellowship. He spent six months in Paris, working with André Lhote, an important Cubist painter, and spent a year touring Europe. From 1957 to 1963 Blackburn was employed as the first master printer at ULAE (Universal Limited Art Editions), Long Island, New York, founded by Tatyana and Maurice

Grosman. Blackburn printed the first seventy-nine editions of lithographs for major American artists, including Helen Frankenthaler, Grace Hartigan, Jasper Johns, Robert Rauschenberg, and Larry Rivers. After six years with ULAE, Blackburn returned as director to the Printmaking Workshop. In 1971 the PMW was incorporated as a nonprofit institution, eventually offering scholarships, international fellowships, and community programs to students of all ages in support of its mission to encourage and support creativity and training in the field of printmaking. Blackburn served as director, teacher, master printer, and friend to generations of artists working there.

Blackburn's most productive and mature period as a lithographer was the late 1950s through 1971, when his work was influenced by Cubism, as well as abstract expressionism and color field painting with the focus on abstraction, gesture, and color. Blackburn's experimentation and technical achievements in color lithography greatly affected the work of well-known ULAE artists and contributed to the popularity of the medium and print boom of the 1960s in the United States. Blackburn was unique among African American artists in terms of his artistic development from representation to abstraction and emphasis on the flat, two-dimensional surface of the printmaking stone. In 1971, the year PMW was incorporated as a nonprofit, Blackburn also created a board of trustees. While at ULAE he kept PMW running and eventually returned to full-time director. During the 1970s and 1980s, after ULAE, Blackburn, after twenty-five years of producing lithography, made the woodcut his primary medium. In both small- and large-scale woodcuts, Blackburn continued to maintain "his command of color, his sense of improvisation, and his control of compelling abstract balances" (Cullen, "A Life in Print").

The Printmaking Workshop has been described as "… the oldest continuously operating non-profit, artist-run printmaking studio in the country" (Cullen, "A Life in Print"). As an educational and artistic cooperative, it helped to produce the work of thousands of culturally diverse artists, promoting cultural exchange and advancement in the fields of art and education. Blackburn's passion for collaboration and cooperative learning was ignited by his experiences growing up in the artistic milieu of the late Harlem Renaissance and the WPA-sponsored art centers. He recreated the benefits of those experiences through his own workshop, which came to mentor artists in the same process. As director of the Printmaking Workshop, his interest in fostering the careers of young artists and creating a center for creative expression took precedence over his own artistic career. In spite of this, Blackburn created an outstanding body of work exhibited internationally and in the collections of the Library of Congress, the Brooklyn Museum, the Bronx Museum, the United Negro College Fund, the Baltimore Museum of Art, Asilah Museum (Morocco), and the Tel Aviv Museum. In 1997 more than 2,500 artworks from the Printmaking Workshop Print Collection, formed by donations from participating artists, were transferred to the Library of Congress, in Washington, D.C.

Blackburn received numerous awards, including the Skowhegan Governor's Award for Lifetime Service (1987), the New York Governor's Award (1988), the Mayor of New York City's Award of Honor for Arts and Culture (1992), the John T. and Catherine D. MacArthur Foundation Fellowship (1992), Lifetime Achievement Awards from the College Art Association and the National Fine Print Association (2002); and six honorary doctoral degrees.

FURTHER READING

Billops, Camille, and James V. Hatch. "Bob Blackburn (1920–2003)," *Artist and Influence,* vol. 5, no. 22 (2003).

Cullen, Deborah. "Appreciation: Robert Blackburn (1920–2003): A Printmaker's Printmaker," *American Art,* vol. 17, no. 3 (2003).

Cummings, Paul. "Interview with Bob Blackburn in the Printmaking Workshop," *Archives of American Art,* 4 December 1970.

Gaither, Edmund. "Millennium Portrait: Robert Blackburn," *American Visions* (Feb. 2000).

Parris, Nina. *Through a Master Printer: Robert Blackburn and the Printmaking Workshop,* Columbia Museum Exhibition Catalog (March–May 1985).

York, Hildreth. "Bob Blackburn and the Printmaking Workshop," *Black American Literature Forum,* vol. 20, no. 1–2 (Spring–Summer 1986).

Obituaries: *New York Times,* 25 Apr. 2003 and *Art in America* (June 2003).

LENA HYUN

Blackburn, Walter Scott (21 Feb. 1938–9 Aug. 2000), architect and civic leader, was born in Indianapolis, Indiana, the son of the Reverend Cleo W. Blackburn, executive director of Flanner

House, a social service center for Indianapolis's black community, president of Jarvis Christian College, and executive director and CEO of the Board of Fundamental Education (BFE), which received a national charter in 1954. Cleo Blackburn was born in Port Gibson, Mississippi, the son of a slave. At Butler University he earned a degree in social work and was ordained a minister of the Christian Church (Disciples of Christ). After earning a master's degree in Sociology at Fisk University in Nashville, Tennessee, Cleo Blackburn was director of research and records at Tuskegee Institute, Alabama. He returned to Indianapolis in 1936. In 2000 he was recognized posthumously as one of the fifty most influential people of the twentieth century in Indianapolis. Walter Blackburn's mother, Fannie Scott Blackburn, a civic leader, was born in Lynchburg, Virginia.

After attending Purdue University for two years, Walter Blackburn transferred to Howard University to obtain a degree in architecture. At Howard University he met and married Alpha Coles (ALPHA BLACKBURN), an artist, art historian, and designer. The couple would have two sons and a daughter. In 1964 they moved to Indianapolis, where Blackburn's first commission came from a Shortridge High School classmate for a funeral home, and commissions for house additions came from his mother's friends. His initial practice was established in partnership with David Snyder. In 1981 Blackburn Architects, Inc., was formed with five employees. The firm garnered praise for its award-winning, distinctive, and elegant rest stops along Indiana's interstates, police and fire stations, schools and churches. Blackburn's breakthrough came in 1984 with an award-winning, innovative design for inner-city housing and a high-profile commission, with Browning and Day, for the Hoosier Dome (later the RCA Dome), home of the National Football League's Indianapolis Colts.

During the next dozen years Blackburn Architects became one of Indianapolis's largest firms, with twenty-eight employees. It won eight major awards and amassed a roster of work stretching into the twenty-first century. Throughout, Blackburn maintained his focus on a high level of aesthetics to inject natural light, beauty, excitement, open space, and connections to community. Blackburn Architects' signature is its portals: brightly and diversely colored entrances that clearly announce the purpose of the structure as well as dramatic exits. Blackburn's Artsgarden, a 12,500-square-foot glass-clad public space, strikes a bold pose in downtown Indianapolis's skyline and spans the intersection of Illinois and Washington streets (known variously as the National Road and U.S. 40). Like his concept for a loggia to unify a new Indiana Government Center with the 1880 Statehouse, 500 Place Office Building seemingly floating along Indianapolis's downtown canal, and the College Avenue Branch Library in the shape of a boat, the Artsgarden is a destination drawing visitors and residents alike.

The commission of his lifetime came in 1998, when Blackburn was fighting the resurgence of the cancer that had been in remission. For the National Underground Railroad Freedom Center along Cincinnati's Ohio River front, Blackburn led a team of designers to encapsulate the significance of the African American migration within an inspiring setting. Multiple winding paths from the river lead to the building's carefully articulated entry, leading to a curvilinear structure. Inside, the perilous journey reverberates throughout interactive exhibits. Three pavilions, signifying Courage, Cooperation, and Perseverance, challenge visitors to consider ongoing universal issues about loss and maintenance of freedom. Also in 1998 he returned to Purdue University to design a Black Cultural Center, featuring elements of traditional African architecture, serving to invite and include everyone.

Blackburn's multifaceted civic life paralleled his professional philosophy of service. A fellow of the American Institute of Architects, he held multiple positions of leadership, including president of Indianapolis and Indiana chapters and vice president of the national AIA board of directors. He was twice awarded Indiana's highest civilian honor, named a distinguished alumnus of Howard University, and received an honorary doctorate from Purdue University's School of Engineering and Technology. He was visiting professor of architecture at Ball State University; a trustee of Rose Hulman Institute of Technology, Terre Haute, Indiana, and Bethany College, West Virginia; and a member of the Dean's Advisory Board for Indiana University–Purdue University, Indianapolis. He was appointed by President Ronald Reagan to the General Services Administration Review Board Region V. He was chairman of the Indiana State Housing Board, a commissioner of the Indiana Arts Commission, and on boards of the American Pianists Association, Indianapolis Opera Company, Second Century Society of the Indianapolis Museum of Art, Indianapolis Arts Council, and founded the Central Indiana Business Development Coalition. A National Kool Achiever awardee, he also was designated by the City of Indianapolis an Outstanding Role Model. He was a life member of the NAACP and the honoraries Sigma Pi Phi and Tau Beta Pi.

Blackburn died in Indianapolis.

FURTHER READING

Obituary: *Indianapolis Star*, 10 Aug. 2000.

RITA KOHN

Blackman, Pompey (c. 1756–20 May 1790), soldier, served in the militia and Continental army during the American Revolution. Blackman also went by the name of Pompey Fortune, and after the Revolution he used the name Pompey Freeman and often shortened his name to Pomp. Blackman enlisted at Concord, Massachusetts, in 1775 in a regiment commanded by Colonel Samuel Gerrish. His place of origin and civil status are unknown, but given the later change of his name to Freeman it seems probable that he had been a slave. His enlistment therefore may have been illegal, because the Massachusetts Committee of Safety had passed a resolution on 20 May 1775 that forbade slave enlistments. Later acts forbade service by any African American, but clearly Massachusetts continued to violate its own laws on this issue, because African American troops were found in numerous Massachusetts regiments in significant numbers. On 27 January 1777 Massachusetts legislators finally came to terms with the facts on the ground in a law that gave only Quakers exemption from enlistment. On 28 April 1778 the legislature at last passed a law that explicitly allowed for black enlistment.

Blackman fought in the first actions of the Revolution at Lexington and Concord on 19 April 1775. He served under a series of officers, first Captain John Woods and then Captain John Baker and Captain Joseph Pettengill. Blackman went on to serve under Captain John Bridge in Colonel Eleazar Brooks's militia regiment. In 1776 he served under Captain Charles Miles in a Massachusetts militia regiment under the overall command of Colonel Jonathan Reed that reinforced colonial forces at Fort Ticonderoga. New England often recruited African Americans to fill out regiments, but doing this was far less prevalent elsewhere in the colonies. The effect of the Revolution on slavery in Massachusetts was great; most slaves were freed during or after the Revolution, particularly those who served in the military, and Massachusetts was the only state not to number any slaves in its population in the first U.S. census, of 1790.

The Continental army raised by the Continental Congress was multiracial, but soon after George Washington took command in the spring of 1775 he ordered recruiting officers not to enlist African Americans. In a council of war on 8 October 1775 Washington and other prominent officers decided unanimously to bar all slaves and by a wide majority to bar all African Americans from enlisting in the Continental army. Washington quickly reversed this decision, though, given the manpower shortages of the Continental army. African Americans in the Continental army had on average longer enlistment periods than their white counterparts. As the war went on, states increasingly turned to African Americans to deal with manpower shortages in their regiments, and many Continental army officers began to realize the competence of African American soldiers.

In 1777 Blackman joined the Continental army when he took on a three-year enlistment in the Fifteenth Massachusetts, a regiment commanded by Colonel Timothy Bigelow. Blackman served under Captain Edmund Munroe. With this regiment Blackman fought at Saratoga in the autumn of 1777, a battle that led to the defeat and capture of the British general John Burgoyne and his army, an event that proved instrumental in gaining French support for the American war effort. With the rest of the army Blackman wintered at Valley Forge from 1777 to 1778, where the weather and incompetence on the part of American supply officers led to the suffering of the enlisted men. Blackman also fought at the Battle of Monmouth on 28 June 1778 when Captain Munroe was killed. At Monmouth, Washington attacked the rear of the British army of Sir Henry Clinton, though neither of the two held the field at the end of the day. Monmouth was the last major action of the war in the northern theater. After 1778 Blackman served in Rhode Island for a brief period. He was discharged from his regiment on 10 March 1780.

After his wartime service Blackman returned to Massachusetts. He filed an intent to marry Susanna Bay of Holliston, Massachusetts, in 1781, but the marriage never took place. Blackman moved back to Lexington and was admitted to the local congregational church in 1782. Some sources indicate that he died in Lexington on 1 January 1783, but it appears that he made his way to New Hampshire. In Jaffrey, New Hampshire, he worked as a tanner under a free black friend, AMOS FORTUNE, whom Blackman had designated as his legal representative during his wartime service. Loan documents for funds given by Fortune to a Pomp Freeman indicate his presence there. Another black veteran of the American Revolution, Christopher Mann, witnessed the loan document. Blackman continued to live in New Hampshire until his death on 20 May 1790.

The experience of individuals like Blackman as African American soldiers in the Revolution was used by black abolitionists like WILLIAM COOPER NELL in their works to justify claims for equality. In addition, advocates for African American participation in the armed forces of the United States used the experience and heroism of Blackman and others to argue that a multiracial fighting force was not a departure from American military tradition, because it was present at the very inception of the republic.

FURTHER READING

Greene, Robert Ewell. *Black Courage, 1775–1783: Documentation of Black Participation in the American Revolution* (1984).

Johnson, Edward Austin. *A School History of the Negro Race in America from 1619 to 1890* (1911).

Knoblock, Glenn A. *"Strong and Brave Fellows": New Hampshire's Black Soldiers and Sailors of the American Revolution, 1775–1784* (2003).

National Society Daughters of the American Revolution. *Minority Revolutionary War Service: Massachusetts, 1775–1783* (1999).

Nell, William Cooper. *Services of Colored American in the Wars of 1776 and 1812* (1851).

M. KELLY BEAUCHAMP

Blackwell, David (24 Apr. 1919–8 July 2010), mathematician and professor, was born David Harold Blackwell in Centralia, Illinois, the oldest of four children, to Grover Blackwell, a locomotive mechanic for the Illinois Central Railroad, and Mabel Johnson. Although much of Blackwell's hometown was segregated, he attended an integrated elementary school. He first became interested in mathematics in high school where, although not particularly interested in algebra or trigonometry, he immediately took an interest in geometry—the scientific study of the properties and relations of lines, surfaces, and solids in space. Later in his life Blackwell credited his high school geometry instructor for showing him the beauty and the usefulness of mathematics. He joined his high school's mathematics club where his instructor pushed students to submit solutions to the *School Science and Mathematics Journal*, which published one of Blackwell's solutions. It was with geometry that Blackwell first began to apply mathematical methods and formulas to games such as "crosses" in order to determine the probability of winning for the first player. When Blackwell entered college at the age of sixteen, he intended at first to become an elementary school teacher. In 1938 he earned an AB degree from the University of Illinois at Urbana-Champaign and went on to receive an AM in 1939 and a Ph.D. in 1941. Here, his interest in probability and statistics emerged and flourished. His dissertation, written under the direction of Joseph L. Doob, was entitled "Some Properties of Markoff Chains." When he completed the PhD, Blackwell was only twenty-two years old and was only the seventh African American to receive a Ph.D. in Mathematics.

After completing the Ph.D., Blackwell accepted a Rosenwald Postdoctoral Fellowship at the Institute for Advanced Study in Princeton, prompting outrage from some in the university community who vehemently opposed the appointment of an African American to this position at Princeton, which had not yet even enrolled African American students. The university's president, Harold D. Dodds, admonished the institute for making such an appointment against the wishes of the university community and sought unsuccessfully to block Blackwell's appointment.

Perhaps because of his experience in the Ivy League, Blackwell seemed to be aware of the limited opportunities for African American scholars in higher academia, and with the exception of an application and interview at the University of California at Berkeley, he applied for faculty positions at only historically black colleges and universities. After one year at Princeton he took short-term professorships at Southern University in Baton Rouge, Louisiana, and Clark Atlanta University.

In 1944 Blackwell joined the faculty of Howard University as an assistant professor at a time when the Washington, D.C., institution was a mecca for black scholars, including the historian RAYFORD W. LOGAN, the philosopher ALAIN LOCKE, and the sociologist E. FRANKLIN FRAZIER. Shortly after arriving at Howard, Blackwell married Ann Madison, and in just three years he had risen to the rank of full professor and chairman of the mathematics department.

David Blackwell, an innovator in statistical analysis, game theory, and mathematical decision-making. (Schomburg Center for Research in Black Culture, New York Public Library.)

At Howard, Blackwell also launched his career as a widely recognized and honored researcher in mathematics. Hearing a lecture and attending a subsequent meeting with the well-known statistician Abe Girshick stimulated Blackwell's interest in statistics and sequential analysis. Even while teaching and chairing the Department of Mathematics at Howard, Blackwell published over twenty research papers in mathematical statistics. Between 1948 and 1950 his interest in the theory of games—the method of applying logic to determine which of several available strategies is likely to maximize one's gain or minimize one's loss in a game or military solution—was revived by three summers of work at the Rand Corporation. Blackwell became particularly interested in the art of dueling with pistols and in determining the most statistically advantageous moment for a dueler to shoot. In the midst of the cold war, such statistical analyses of games became useful and pertinent for the federal government in thinking about U.S. military strategy, and Blackwell's work and Blackwell himself became a leader in the field of statistical analysis and game theory. In 1950–1951 Blackwell spent one year as a visiting professor of statistics at Stanford University.

All of Blackwell's work in game theory (including the art of dueling and the statistical analysis of bluffing as a strategy in poker) culminated in 1954 when he and Abe Girshick jointly wrote *Theory of Games and Statistical Decisions*. This book served as a mathematical textbook for students in statistical decision functions. Building upon the prior works of John von Neumann and A. Wald in the statistical and conceptual aspects of decision theory and theory of games, Blackwell and Girshick developed new and innovative concepts of mathematical decision making that were later used in military tactics, the business world, and engineering.

By the time of the book's publication in 1954, Blackwell's career was rising rapidly. Shortly after he gave an address on concepts of probability at the International Congress of Mathematicians in Amsterdam, he was offered and accepted a position as professor of statistics at the University of California at Berkeley. Serving as chair of the Berkeley statistics department from 1957 to 1961, Blackwell continued to be a prolific academic writer, publishing over fifty articles in the field of statistical analysis. Prominent appointments and accolades soon followed. In 1955 he was elected president of the Institute of Mathematical Statistics, and later served as president for the International Association for Statistics in Physical Sciences and the Bernoulli Society, and vice president of the International Statistical Institute, the American Statistical Association, and the American Mathematical Society.

In 1965 Blackwell became the first African American named to the National Academy of Sciences (NAS), a body used by the federal government and other agencies to investigate, experiment, and report on scientific matters. (Remarkably, nearly three decades later in 1996, *the Journal of Blacks in Higher Education* found that Blackwell had been joined by only two further black inductees at the NAS, the chemist PERCY LAVON JULIAN and the sociologist WILLIAM JULIUS WILSON.) In 1979 Blackwell received the prestigious von Neumann Theory Prize from the Operations Research Society of America for his work in dynamic programming, and in 1986 Blackwell received the R. A. Fisher Award from the Committee of Presidents of Statistical Societies. All of these awards and prizes acknowledged the continued relevance of his research in statistical analysis and game theory. In addition to being known as one of the world's best mathematicians, his scholarly work and professional activities have brought Blackwell honorary degrees from Howard, Harvard, Yale, the University of Illinois, Carnegie-Mellon, the University of Southern California, Michigan State, Syracuse, Southern Illinois University, the University of

Warwick in England, and the National University of Lesotho. Blackwell retired from Berkeley in 1989, although he remained on the faculty as professor emeritus and continued to publish in mathematical journals. Blackwell also advised over fifty graduate students. Blackwell's legacy in teaching and researching, and the pathbreaking trail he made for African Americans in the mathematics field, made him one of this century's most notable figures in this highly specialized area. He died in Berkeley, California, at the age of nintey-one.

FURTHER READING

Blackwell, David, et al. *Theory of Games and Statistical Decisions* (1954).

DeGroot, Morris H. "A Conversation with David Blackwell," *Statistical Science*, Feb. 1986: 40–53.

Guillen, Michael. "Normal, against the Odds," *New York Times*, 30 June 1985.

Martin, Donald A. "The Determinacy of Blackwell Games," *Journal of Symbolic Logic*, Dec. 1998: 1565–1581.

"The Mathematics of Poker Strategy," *New York Times*, 25 Dec. 1949.

"National Academy of Sciences: Nearly as White as a Posh Country Club in Alabama," *Journal of Blacks in Higher Education* (Summer 1996): 18–19.

KEITH WAILOO AND
RICHARD MIZELLE

Blackwell, Ed (10 Oct. 1929–8 Oct. 1992), jazz drummer, was born Edward Joseph in New Orleans, Louisiana, to unknown parents. He grew up steeped in his hometown's musical tradition, influenced by two tap-dancing siblings to take up the drums. New Orleans percussionists like PAUL BARBARIN were Blackwell's earliest models, making him one of several future avant-gardists whose roots were in jazz's oldest traditions.

In 1951 Blackwell relocated to Los Angeles, where he played in the rhythm and blues outfits of Plas and Raymond Johnson. More significantly he made the acquaintance the saxophonist ORNETTE COLEMAN, with whom he would be associated for his entire career. Coleman, also working with various degrees of success in the Los Angeles rhythm and blues scene, sought to introduce an unprecedented degree of melodic, harmonic, and rhythmic freedom into jazz. This new approach required an almost telepathic bond between band members, as interaction was governed by little more than improvisational ingenuity. In Blackwell, Coleman found not only a sympathetic collaborator but also a stylist whose loose-limbed, melodic sound provided the perfect complement for his plaintive, emotive alto.

It would be nearly a decade, however, before the rest of the world became aware of Coleman and Blackwell's unique rapport. In search of steady gigs, Blackwell moved first to Texas in 1953 before returning to his native New Orleans in 1956. Meanwhile, Coleman assembled a quartet with BILLY HIGGINS on drums, which arrived in New York in 1959 and was hailed as a revolution in jazz.

Blackwell rejoined Coleman in 1960, in time to appear on the canonical Atlantic recordings *This Is Our Music* and *Free Jazz* that year and *Ornette on Tenor* in 1961. Each of these albums was, in its own right, a major statement on the future of jazz. *Free Jazz* in particular gained such notoriety that its title became shorthand for an entire musical movement. This single, continuous piece, which sported a reproduction of a Jackson Pollock painting as its cover art, consisted of a double-quartet lineup in which Blackwell's exuberant playing was mirrored by Higgins's more fluid style. On all three albums, however, Blackwell's bare-bones drumming, which relied heavily on dance-like rhythms on the tom-toms and a deep-seated sense of swing, spurred Coleman's rootsy avant-garde to new expressive heights. *Ornette on Tenor* made the link between past and present almost tangible, as Coleman's evocation of the tenor's bluesy heritage brought out the New Orleans second-line heritage that was such an essential part of Blackwell's playing.

During this same period Blackwell performed at the Five Spot with a quintet co-led by the reedman ERIC DOLPHY (who appeared on *Free Jazz*) and the trumpeter BOOKER LITTLE, a forward-looking band arguably the equal of Coleman's ensembles. Work with the pianist Randy Weston and tenor ARCHIE SHEPP also demonstrated Blackwell's preeminent standing in the jazz world, as he showed his ability to excel in settings not directly indebted to Coleman's musical language.

Yet throughout the sixties and seventies Blackwell continued to be identified with Coleman's musical universe. He recorded several classic albums with DON CHERRY, best known as Coleman's trumpeter; their duo sessions, which yielded the two-part *Mu* (1969), are regarded as indispensable examples of interplay and spontaneous invention. In 1975 Blackwell entered academia, joining Connecticut's Wesleyan University as an artist in residence where he found some much-needed professional and financial stability in a particularly lean era for avant-garde jazz musicians.

In 1976 Blackwell joined up with fellow Coleman alumni Cherry, Dewey Redman (tenor), and Charlie Haden (bass) to form Old and New Dreams, an aptly named project devoted to performing Coleman's songbook and new compositions in the Coleman vein. While certainly a celebration of Coleman's legacy, this quintet's lively, engrossing performances proved that this idiom was anything but dated. And although Coleman cast a long, imposing shadow over Old and New Dreams, showcasing these musicians apart from the man himself underscored just how instrumental these sidemen had been in forging a sound that had been largely collective in nature. As both a tribute to their musical guru and an assertion of their own historical importance, Old and New Dreams struck the ideal balance between nostalgia and urgency, making it the ideal vehicle for former vanguardists at a crossroads.

Old and New Dreams served as a lodestar for these Coleman alumni throughout the eighties, and Blackwell was no exception. By the eighties the drummer and his onetime partners in the revolution had all become elder statesmen. For younger musicians, playing with Blackwell became an honor, and he became a regular on the festival circuit. Luckily, Blackwell himself was still every bit the creative force, making these late career efforts easily the equal of his earlier, seminal work in the Coleman orbit.

Blackwell was dogged by ill health throughout the eighties, as kidney problems (which required he undergo dialysis three times a day) limited his recordings and performances. His mounting health-care costs also posed a significant problem for a career jazz musician, but were alleviate somewhat by a series of high-profile benefits. Blackwell's skills remained undiminished; in 1992 he finally recorded as a leader, teaming with Redman for the joyous trio outing *Walls-Bridges*. Months later, his Ed Blackwell Project headlined the Bay Area's Eddie Moore Memorial Jazz Festival, leading to two albums' worth of spirited live blowing (released in 1992 and 1994 as *What It Is?* and *What It Be Like?*, respectively). But despite his continued excellence behind the drum kit, Blackwell's illness eventually caught up with him, and he passed away in Hartford, Connecticut, due to complications arising from his kidney ailments.

FURTHER READING
Palmer, Robert. "Ed Blackwell: Crescent City Thumper," *Downbeat* (19 May 1977).

Wilmer, Valerie. *As Serious As Your Life: The Story of the New Jazz* (1977).
Obituary: *New York Times*, 9 Oct. 1992.

DISCOGRAPHY
Coleman, Ornette. *This Is Our Music* (Atlantic, 1960).
Dolphy, Eric. *At the Five Spot Volume 1* (New Jazz, 1961).
Old and New Dreams. *Old and New Dreams* (Black Saint, 1979).

NATHANIEL FRIEDMAN

Blackwell, John Kenneth (Ken) (28 Feb. 1948–), politician, was born on Cincinnati's segregated west side, the older of two brothers born to George Blackwell, a meatpacker, and Dana Blackwell, a part-time nurse. Until he was six years old, the family lived in the Laurel Homes housing project. Blackwell would later attribute his character to his father's work ethic, his mother's reading and lessons from the Bible, and the parents' strong promotion of education. He graduated from Hughes High School in 1966, and attended Cincinnati's Xavier University on a football scholarship. A well-regarded and physically imposing athlete—he stood at 6 feet 4 inches, 220 pounds—Blackwell was also seen by his peers as a radical black campus leader, donning daishikis and wearing his hair in an Afro, serving as president of the black students association, and lobbying the administration in civil rights issues.

In his sophomore year, Blackwell married his childhood girlfriend, Rosa, whom he had known since the fourth grade. After he graduated Xavier in 1970 with a B in Psychology, he tried out with the National Football League's Dallas Cowboys. According to Blackwell, when the team attempted to shift him from linebacker to offensive lineman, he lost interest and left football. Returning to Xavier to get his master's degree in Education, he taught and worked for the university in recruiting black students and helping with university outreach to the surrounding communities.

In 1975, Blackwell made an unsuccessful run for the Cincinnati board of education, but won a seat on the City Council two years later as a member of the city's progressive political faction, the Charter Party. In 1979, the thirty-one-year-old Blackwell was named mayor of the city (through the City Council, who at the time appointed the then-mostly-nominal one-year-term position). Though he worked for the Democrat Jimmy Carter's 1980 presidential reelection campaign—which he would later ascribe to his wife's candidacy as an alternate delegate in the election—Blackwell underwent a political conversion by the early 1980s. Influenced by the former NFL star and political stalwart Jack Kemp's views on economic policy as well as a meeting with President Ronald Reagan at the White House, Blackwell became a conservative and shifted to the Republican Party.

A charismatic and outspoken politician, Blackwell served for twelve years on the City Council before becoming Kemp's undersecretary in the department of Housing and Urban Development in 1989 and 1990 under George H. W. Bush. Under Kemp's urging, Blackwell returned to Cincinnati to run for a vacant seat in the House of Representatives, but despite significant political power behind his run (Bush himself came and stumped), lost by two percentage points to Charlie Lueken, the son of the departing congressman.

By then a prominent African American Republican, Blackwell was named ambassador to the United Nations Human Rights Commission by Bush. After he was appointed state treasurer in 1994 by the Ohio governor George Voinovich, Blackwell was reelected to the position later that year, becoming the first black man to be elected to a state executive position in Ohio. Citing him as a Republican on the rise in August 1996, *Time* magazine captured Blackwell's distaste for big government and religious fervor with his quote, "Doomsday is the day we get all the government we pay for."

In 1998, Blackwell was elected Ohio's secretary of state. In 1999, he became the first African American to run a national campaign for a major white candidate, after the billionaire magazine heir Steve Forbes tapped him to chair his presidential bid. When Forbes was defeated in the primary, Blackwell moved on to help with the successful George W. Bush campaign.

After successfully defending his seat as secretary of state in 2002, Blackwell worked for the reelection of Bush in 2004 and was named a state election official. He became the subject of numerous lawsuits claiming voter irregularities and fraud, specifically his implementation of "provisional ballots," ones that would be counted only after verification of a voter's residency. In early 2006, he came under scrutiny for owning shares of stock in the voting-machine manufacturer Diebold, while his state office negotiated a controversial deal with the company.

Throughout his terms in statewide office, Blackwell pushed to move the Ohio Republican party further to the right. Along with supporting the fiscal conservatism of business deregulation and low taxes, he was also a social conservative, as a staunch antiabortion advocate and opponent of gay unions. His coauthored book Rebuilding America, an examination and criticism of Lyndon Johnson's War on Poverty, was meant to be a economic model for his own run for the governor's chair: Though he won a hotly contested gubernatorial primary in 2006, Blackwell lost to Ted Strickland in the general election.

Following his defeat in 2006, Blackwell became a columnist and senior fellow for the Family Research Council, a religious-political foundation. In 2009, Blackwell ran unsuccessfully for chair of the Republican National Committee; after withdrawing from the race, he supported the eventual winner, Michael Steele.

Blackwell and his wife, Rosa, a longtime educator who was named superintendent for the Cincinnati Public Schools in 2005, had two daughters, Kimberley and Kristin, and a son, Rahshann. Privately, Blackwell profited in 2001 when Blue Chip Broadcasting, a company he partly owned, sold fifteen radio stations to Radio One for $190 million.

FURTHER READING

Blackwell, John Kenneth, and Jerome Corsi. *Rebuilding America: A Prescription for Creating Strong Families, Building the Wealth of Working People, and Ending Welfare* (2006).

Fitzgerald, Frances. "Holy Toledo," *New Yorker*, 31 July 2008.

Merida, Kevin. "Campaign Commander," *Cincinnati Magazine*, Nov. 1999.

ADAM W. GREEN

Blackwell, Lucien Edward (1 Aug. 1931–24 Jan. 2003), politician, was born the son of Thomas Williams Blackwell, a grocery store owner, and Mary Ellen Blackwell in Whitsett, Pennsylvania. Blackwell was one of eleven children. After completing high school in 1949 he matriculated at St. Joseph's College in Philadelphia, Pennsylvania. He left college and worked as a dock worker. In 1953 he joined the U.S. Army and served in the Korean War. After a year he was discharged and returned to his previous job on the waterfront. He participated in labor activities and served as trustee, vice president, and business agent of Local 1332 of the International Longshoremen's Association (ILA). In 1973 he became president of the local chapter of the ILA, a position he retained until 1991.

Blackwell married Jannie L. Blackwell, a former schoolteacher, around 1973. At the time he was a single father with six children from a previous marriage. Blackwell's labor work led him to enter politics in 1973, and that year he was elected as a Democratic representative to the Pennsylvania legislature. There he was instrumental in establishing the Crisis Intervention Network to deal with gang crimes. He left state for local politics when he was elected to the Philadelphia city council in 1974.

Throughout his long tenure as councilman (1974–1991) Blackwell remained devoted to issues related to employment, housing, human rights, and public assistance. He sponsored ordinances that guaranteed quotas of work contracted by the city to minority-owned and women-led enterprises. He even undertook a six-week fast to protest the lack of maintenance and security in the public housing projects. He contributed to the organization of better public assistance for the homeless. Blackwell chaired the finance committee of the city council and the Philadelphia Gas Commission. His work on the finance committee led the city to divest its pension funds from financial institutions doing business in apartheid-era South Africa. By then LEON H. SULLIVAN, pastor of Mt. Zion Baptist Church (1950–1988), had made Philadelphia a center of activism against the apartheid system in South Africa.

Blackwell drafted ordinances authorizing the building of the Pennsylvania Convention Center and worked as a commissioner for the Delaware Port Authority. He ran unsuccessfully for mayor in 1979 and 1991. JESSE JACKSON chose him as the Pennsylvania coordinator of his 1988 presidential campaign. As councilman Blackwell served as mentor to John F. Street, who later became the second black mayor of Philadelphia in 2000. In 1991 Blackwell was elected to Congress and his wife, Jannie Blackwell, took his seat on the city council. His congressional district included west Philadelphia and sections of Delaware County.

Experienced in labor issues, Blackwell pursued the same interests in Congress. He introduced a bill for a thirty-hour workweek in order to allow more people to find employment during the 1990s recession. He sponsored bills meant to protect the credit ratings of the unemployed. As a member of the U.S. Committee on the Budget he strongly supported President Bill Clinton's economic policies. Blackwell was elected to one more Congressional term in 1992. He lost in the Democratic Primary election to CHAKA FATTAH in 1994 and then worked as a lobbyist for the city of Philadelphia. Blackwell later held the chairmanship of two African American organizations, Black Elected Officials and United Black Ward Leaders of Philadelphia. In late 2002 he was appointed to the transition team for Pennsylvania governor-elect Edward Rendell. Just before his death he worked as chairman of St. Hill and Associates, a debt-collection firm. He died in Philadelphia and is remembered as–an outstanding advocate for the poor and the homeless. In addition to his wife his political legacy was carried by his son, Thomas Blackwell, who was elected to the Pennsylvania House of Representatives in 2004.

FURTHER READING
Carey, Charles W. *African-American Political Leaders* (2004).
Obituary: *Philadelphia Inquirer*, 25 Jan. 2003.
DAVID MICHEL

Blackwell, Otis (16 Feb. 1932–6 May 2002), songwriter and musician, was born in Brooklyn, New York. Information on his family and early life is fragmented at best, but it is known that Blackwell was a musical child and learned to play the piano while he was young.

Upon leaving school at the end of the 1940s, Blackwell held jobs in a New York theater as a floor sweeper and as a laundry clothes presser. In 1952 his musical talents helped him win a talent contest at Harlem's Apollo Theater, arguably the capital of live black entertainment during the era of the chitlin circuit, the circuit of African American performance venues that supplied black performers with their steadiest and most stable source of employment. Blackwell subsequently signed a deal with RCA Victor Records, under the tutelage of the producer Joe Davis. Davis left RCA a year later to form Jay-Dee Records, and Blackwell followed his mentor to the new label. He recorded several sides for Jay-Dee, but none achieved much chart success. Perhaps most prominent among Blackwell's early recordings was his song "Daddy Rolling Stone," a pulsating R&B groove that would later become popular through versions by the Jamaican singer Derrick Martin and the British rock band the Who. Throughout the early 1950s Blackwell continued to record songs for Jay-Dee, RCA, and Groove Records, but his most outstanding accomplishments in the music business would not come in front of the microphone but as a songwriter.

Blackwell's breakthrough, and period of greatest success, came during the rock and roll explosion of the late 1950s, when he became a part of New York's prosperous community of tunesmiths that provided hits for a variety of black (and later white) artists. Blackwell not only distinguished himself through his talent, but also through the fact that he combined influences from both black and white musical spaces, linking music which—though popular across the color line—had rarely been combined by a professional songwriter to such a clear and effective extent. Blackwell was influenced by the blues and jazz singers of the era, but he also consistently acknowledged a debt to country and western culture, from recorded country music to the westerns of Gene Autry and Tex Ritter that Blackwell viewed regularly at his local cinema. Throughout his career, Blackwell maintained a connection with his cowboy heroes, from his affection for cowboy hats and boots to his ease at crafting country-influenced hits for both white and black artists. Though notably talented, Blackwell was not alone in his ability to bridge the gap between two genres that, symbolically at least, remained separated by a gulf of racial tension and cultural segregation. From country's interracial origins, through the genre-busting country work of R&B artists like RAY CHARLES or BOBBY WOMACK, to the involvement of southern soul musicians in the pioneering "Nashville sound" country of the 1960s, these two genres are closely intertwined, and Blackwell's work is a testament to this long-standing relationship.

On Christmas Eve 1955 Blackwell sold six of his songs, through a tape of homemade demo recordings, to the publisher Moe Gale for $150. Among the songs in this initial group was "Fever," which would become first an R&B hit for the blues singer Little Willie John and then a pop smash for the sultry white crooner Peggy Lee, and "Don't Be Cruel," which a young Elvis Presley recorded as his first national single release for RCA Victor in 1956, and which became one of Presley's first hits. This initial success led to Presley recording several of Blackwell's songs. The connection between Blackwell and Presley produced the number one record "All Shook Up" (1957) and the hits "Return to Sender" (1962) and "One Broken Heart for Sale" (1963).

Apart from the songs themselves—which perhaps more than any other early Presley recordings capture the singer's energetic blend of pop, country, and R&B elements—Presley was also influenced by Blackwell's vocal style and arrangements (which the pop star heard on Blackwell's demo versions of the material), and he incorporated many of Blackwell's characteristics into his own versions. Also, Presley's business arrangements often got him listed as a cowriter on Blackwell's compositions, a common (though semi-legal) form of compensation for pop singers who chose to record a particular song. (Presley never met Blackwell, never claimed to have actually written the songs, and has since been removed from the songwriter's credit. Blackwell never publicly expressed any resentment toward Presley or any other white artist he was associated with.)

Through the early 1960s Blackwell provided songs for many artists, both black and white; occasionally Blackwell would use the pseudonym John Davenport when copyrighting his songs, a move which some have theorized was an attempt to remove any racial stigma that his "black-sounding" real name may have caused. Blackwell's songs for wild rockabilly star Jerry Lee Lewis are second only to his work with Presley in terms of success; Blackwell wrote three hits for Lewis, most famously the number one hit "Great Balls of Fire." Like the Presley recordings, Lewis's versions of these Blackwell compositions demonstrate the way that early rock and roll blurred the lines between what constituted "white" and "black" music. An interracial coterie of the era's luminaries would record Blackwell's songs over the next several years.

Later in his career, Blackwell's famous catalog songs were recorded by white artists like Tanya Tucker and James Taylor (who revived Blackwell's hit for Jimmy Jones, "Handy Man"), and by black artists like Ray Charles and OTIS REDDING. Blackwell himself recorded an album in 1976, tellingly titled *These Are My Songs!*, for Inner City Records, and he recorded a tribute to Elvis Presley (titled *The #1 King of Rock and Roll*) in 1977. In 1986 Blackwell was inducted into the Nashville Songwriters Hall of Fame, and he joined the National Academy of Popular Music Songwriters' Hall of Fame in 1991. In 1992 he was the subject of a tribute album, called *Brace Yourself!*, featuring popular artists like Kris Kristofferson, Deborah Harry, and Ronnie Spector.

Otis Blackwell died in 2002, leaving his longtime wife, Mamie Wiggins Blackwell, and seven children, and he is buried in Nashville, Tennessee. Blackwell, who copyrighted more than one thousand songs and is one of the most successful songwriters of the late 1950s, left a body of work that speaks to the excitement and possibility of a time when music's racial lines were not entirely intransigent, and when a country-loving black man from New York could provide hits for rockers, pop crooners, country singers, and R&B performers. Although Blackwell's financial reward from his esteemed catalog never matched his creative success, his name is firmly, justifiably etched in the history of American popular music.

FURTHER READING

Dahl, Bill. "Otis Blackwell," *All Music Guide to Soul: The Definitive Guide to R&B and Soul*, ed. Vladimir Bogdanov (2003).

Guralnick, Peter. *Last Train to Memphis: The Rise of Elvis Presley* (1994).

Obituary: *New York Times*, 9 May 2002.

DISCOGRAPHY

All Shook Up (Shanachie Records 9204).

These Are My Songs! (Inner City Records 1032).

CHARLES L. HUGHES

Blackwell, Randolph Talmadge (10 Mar. 1927–21 May 1981), attorney, educator, and civil rights activist, was born in Greensboro, North Carolina, the son of Joe Blackwell and Blanche Mary Donnell. Randolph attended the city's public schools for African Americans and earned a B.S. in Sociology from North Carolina Agricultural and Technical University in Greensboro in 1949. Four years later he earned a J.D. degree from Howard University in Washington, D.C. In December 1954 Blackwell married Elizabeth Knox; the couple had one child. After teaching economics for a year at Alabama Agricultural and Mechanical College in Normal, Alabama, Blackwell became an associate professor of social sciences at Winston-Salem State Teachers College in North Carolina.

Because of Blackwell's legal background, WILEY BRANTON, the director of the Voter Education Project (VEP), hired Blackwell as its field director in 1962. Secretly encouraged by the Kennedy administration, the VEP was launched in April 1962 with funding from private foundations. Sheltered under the tax-exempt status of the Southern Regional Council, the VEP encouraged voter registration among African Americans throughout the South by regranting funds to civil rights organizations to underwrite their voter registration efforts. In Mississippi, where only 5 percent of eligible black adults were registered, the prospect of funding from the VEP encouraged the civil rights organizations to establish the Council of Federated Organizations (COFO) to coordinate voter registration efforts among African Americans. Faced with the threat of being jailed, beaten, bombed, or even killed at the hands of determined white opposition, voter registration workers produced only 3,228 newly registered black voters in 1962, despite $50,000 worth of funding from the VEP.

On 28 February 1963, eight days after an arsonist torched four black businesses in order to destroy COFO's voter registration office in Greenwood, Mississippi, Blackwell met with COFO organizers there. While Blackwell was at the office, Jimmy Travis, a COFO worker, reported that three white men in a Buick with no license plates had staked out the office. Travis then drove Blackwell and the civil rights activist ROBERT MOSES out of Greenwood toward Greenville. The Buick followed them. Seven miles out of Greenwood, white nightriders pulled up beside them and fired on their car. Hit in both the shoulder and the back of the neck, Travis slumped into Moses's lap as he pulled the car to a halt. Two days later, doctors at a Jackson hospital removed a bullet from Travis's spine. Branton quickly wired Attorney General Robert Kennedy with a demand for "immediate action by the federal government" in Greenwood. An appeal to MARTIN LUTHER KING JR.'s Southern Christian Leadership Conference (SCLC) brought trained voter education workers to Greenwood for citizenship education classes. Blackwell revisited Greenwood in March 1963 and found twenty to thirty people working in the COFO office, helping with canvassing and with voter registration, organizing clothing and food distribution, coordinating youth work, arranging both mass meetings and Sunday speaking engagements, and establishing citizenship schools.

When WYATT TEE WALKER left the staff of the SCLC in July 1964, ANDREW YOUNG became his successor, and Blackwell succeeded Young as program director. One of the few laymen to serve on the SCLC's executive staff, Blackwell attempted to restructure the organization by employing various administrative techniques meant to establish clear lines of authority, thus avoiding the confusion and antagonism that had previously permeated the SCLC. Blackwell suggested separating the organization into specific departments with designated department heads who reported to Blackwell, who in turn answered to Young. The proposal had little effect because charismatic preachers on the executive staff vied for control of the field staff and resented having to answer to anyone but King.

Blackwell was the SCLC's program director during the Alabama voting rights campaign that led to the march from Selma to Montgomery. After marchers were attacked on Selma's Edmund Pettus Bridge on "Bloody Sunday," 7 March 1965, Blackwell sent two hundred telegrams in King's name inviting religious leaders from across the nation to join him for the march from Selma. By 9 March, 450 white clergymen had gathered in Selma for the march to Montgomery. After the march, however, Blackwell found little enthusiasm in black Selma for the SCLC's continued presence there because of its staff's poor relationships with local community leaders.

In addition to fighting such external battles as the one in Selma, Blackwell was also plagued by internal battles within the SCLC. Blackwell doubted the ability of the SCLC executive staff member HOSEA WILLIAMS to manage its VEP-funded Southern Community Organization and Political Education (SCOPE) project in the summer of 1965. Later his worst fears were confirmed by SCOPE's incompetence, by Williams's misconduct and mismanagement, and by the incredible waste of the organization as a whole. Blackwell accused Williams of "empire building" and begged King to end the program immediately. "It has cost freedom contributors ten times what it should have," Blackwell wrote. "The operation has raised suspicion of financial dishonesty." Later Blackwell told King that "the conflict between myself and Mr. Williams … goes to the bottom of the philosophy of the organization. It raises in a very serious way the question of whether we can at this point develop the structural discipline needed" (Fairclough, 269). Although Blackwell agreed with Williams that the SCLC should maintain its focus on the South rather than open a campaign in a major northern city like Chicago, by October he was talking about leaving the SCLC. In February 1966 Blackwell's conflict with Williams was so intense that Blackwell appealed to King for the resolution of a whole series of issues within the organization, and by August of that year Blackwell had taken a leave of absence. SCLC staff turmoil worsened after Blackwell's departure, and King regretted not having dealt with his complaints and feared that Blackwell would not return to the SCLC staff. As late as June 1967 the SCLC's SEPTIMA CLARK urged King to bring Blackwell back to the organization to ease his personal burdens and to bring more discipline to the staff.

When Blackwell left the SCLC in 1966, he founded Southern Rural Action, Incorporated, an organization based in Atlanta that sought to develop black businesses and economic cooperatives. He was the director of this organization until 1977, when he became the director of the Department of Commerce's Office of Minority Business Enterprise in Washington, D.C. In 1979 Blackwell returned to Atlanta as director of the Office of Minority Enterprise Program and Development. He remained in that position until his death from cancer in Atlanta. A recipient of the Martin Luther King Jr. Peace Prize in 1976, Blackwell was also a member of the board of directors of the Martin Luther King Jr. Center for Nonviolent Social Change and of Southern Rural Action.

FURTHER READING

Blackwell's papers are at the Martin Luther King Jr. Center for Nonviolent Social Change in Atlanta, Georgia.

Fairclough, Adam. *To Redeem the Soul of America: The Southern Christian Leadership Conference and Martin Luther King, Jr.* (1987).

Garrow, David J. *Bearing the Cross: Martin Luther King, Jr., and the Southern Christian Leadership Conference* (1986).

Lawson, Steven F. *Black Ballots: Voting Rights in the South, 1944–1969* (1976).

Peake, Thomas R. *Keeping the Dream Alive: A History of the Southern Christian Leadership Conference from King to the Nineteen-Eighties* (1987).

Obituaries: *Atlanta Constitution*, 22 May 1981; *New York Times*, 23 May 1981.

This entry is taken from the *American National Biography* and is published here with the permission of the American Council of Learned Societies.

RALPH E. LUKER

Blackwell, Unita Z. (18 Mar. 1933–), civil rights activist and mayor, was born in Lula, Mississippi, the daughter of sharecroppers in Coahoma County, Mississippi. Her father had to leave Mississippi when he refused to obey his plantation owner's order to send his young daughter Unita to the fields to pick cotton. He found work in an icehouse in a neighboring state. Her mother was illiterate and determined that her children would learn to read and write. In the Mississippi Delta, everyone was required to pick and chop cotton, and the schools closed down to allow for this work except for two or three months a year. Consequently, Unita

Blackwell and her sister took the ferry across the Mississippi River to West Helena, Arkansas. She lived with her aunt for eight months of the year and attended Westside Junior High School, where she completed the eighth grade. Later, she received her high school equivalency diploma. Blackwell spent her younger years picking cotton—as much as three hundred bales a day. After she married, she and her husband went to Florida to pick tomatoes and work in a canning plant. She moved to Mayersville, Mississippi, in 1962 and picked cotton, while her husband worked for U.S. industries.

In 1964 she became a field worker for the Student Nonviolent Coordinating Committee under the supervision of STOKELY CARMICHAEL. She was in charge of voter registration in the Second Congressional District in Mississippi, and, along with seven other people, she registered to vote in Issaquena County. She became a close friend of FANNIE LOU HAMER, and they both became founding members of the Mississippi Freedom Democratic Party (MFDP), formed in 1964 to challenge the white supremacist Democratic Party in Mississippi. Along with Hamer, Blackwell was an MFDP delegate to the 1964 Democratic national convention in Atlantic City. Members of the MFDP challenged the seating of the all-white delegates from Mississippi, and Blackwell, Hamer, and others testified before the credentials committee. When Hamer presented her famous testimony before the committee, President Lyndon Johnson called a press conference to prevent television coverage of the powerful and inspirational speaker from Mississippi. After much political wrangling, the MFDP was awarded only two delegate seats, which the members refused.

In the summer of 1965 the MFDP marched on the state legislature in Jackson to support Governor Paul Johnson's request that the legislators repeal Mississippi's discriminatory voting laws. Over half of the five hundred demonstrators were in their teens. Police arrested more than two hundred of the marchers, including Blackwell, placing them in the stockyards of the state fairgrounds, where many of the women were tortured. Blackwell herself was imprisoned for eleven days (University of Southern Mississippi oral history interview, 35–36).

Blackwell continued to press for change in the Delta. In 1965 she demanded that the school board provide decent facilities, teachers, and books for her son's school. The board refused to hear the demands, and Blackwell sued for desegregation of the schools in *Sharkey and Issaquena County Consolidated Line v. Blackwell*. The black principal followed the orders of the school board and refused to cooperate and, in Blackwell's view, left them with no alternative but to sue. "Desegregation of school was not one [of] our favorites," she recalled. "Our thing was to have good schools, didn't care what color they were…. We was asking for books; we was asking for fixing of the schools, that they would be just as nice" (University of Southern Mississippi oral history interview, 44). She won her case.

Undaunted by intimidation, Blackwell continued her struggle for justice. In the winter of 1965 and 1966 poor people in the Delta were hungry and cold. Indeed, two people froze to death. Conditions were made worse when planters evicted sharecroppers for registering to vote and participating in civil rights activities; the planters then saw to it that officials denied the evicted sharecroppers access to the federal food commodity program. With no food to eat and no place to live, sharecroppers formed the Mississippi Freedom Labor Union in January of 1965. The union launched a strike, and domestic workers, tractor drivers, and field hands walked off their jobs all over the Delta.

As evictions and starvation continued, the union members Blackwell, Ida Mae Lawrence, and Isaac Foster, in the face of the federal government's refusal to answer their plea for help, decided to set up their own community and government. They led over seventy men, women, and children onto the empty Greenville Air Base, consisting of two thousand acres and three hundred buildings. There Blackwell eloquently expressed the goals of the group: "I feel that the federal government have proven that it don't care about poor people. Everything that we have asked for through these years has been handed down on paper. It's never been a reality. We the poor people of Mississippi is tired," she continued. "We're going to build for ourselves, because we don't have a government that represents us." A group of Air Police removed the squatters after thirty hours, but Blackwell and others had forced national attention on the dire poverty that many lived in and the limits of federal programs to address poor peoples' concerns.

Blackwell continued her efforts on behalf of poor people, becoming a national spokesperson on the issues of community economic development and low-income housing. In 1967, along with Hamer, ANNIE DEVINE, and AMZIE MOORE, she helped organize the Mississippi Action for Community Education Inc. (MACE) "to build and strengthen local human capacities and indigenous community development efforts" in the Mississippi Delta. MACE has trained local community organizers and leaders; conducts literacy, job training, career development, and arts education programs; and sponsors the Mississippi Delta Blues and Heritage Festival. In the late 1960s and early 1970s Blackwell worked with the National Council of Negro Women as a community-development specialist, establishing cooperative ventures in ownership of low-income housing. In 1983 she received a master's degree in Regional Planning from the University of Massachusetts at Amherst.

Blackwell has remained politically active on both a local and a national level. In 1976 she was elected mayor of Mayersville, becoming the first African American to hold mayoral office in Mississippi. In 1979 she attended President Jimmy Carter's Energy Summit at Camp David, and in 1984 she addressed the National Democratic Convention in San Francisco. In 1989 she chaired the National Mayor's Conference and, in 1991, the Black Women's Mayor's Conference. From 1976 to 1983 she was president of the U.S.–China Peoples' Friendship Association and traveled to China on numerous occasions. She has traveled extensively throughout Asia, Central America, and Europe.

In recognition of her achievements, in 1992 Blackwell was awarded the prized MacArthur Fellowship, also called the "genius" award, and the University of Massachusetts invited her to become the Eleanor Bateman Alumni Scholar. Her fighting spirit and faith in humanity persists. In 2000 she observed: "It seems like the whole century has been about overcoming. Fighting and then overcoming. You had women's suffrage, and apartheid and segregation. And we blacks lived in that lock-in, and somehow survived. How, I do not know. Nothing but a God I say. The whole era was full of hate, but we're trying to overcome it, and we're headed for something new, I just feel it. Maybe we are the group of people, the blacks in America, that brought everyone to their worst, and then to their best. Including ourselves" (*UMASS Online Magazine*).

FURTHER READING

The most extensive source of information on Blackwell is her interview, located in the Civil Rights in Mississippi Digital Archive, McCain Library and Archives, University of Southern Mississippi. Blackwell herself authored a memoir in 2006. See also the Mississippi Action for Community Education Inc. web site, and *UMASS Online Magazine* (Winter 2000).

"My Whole World Was My Kinfolks," *UMASS Online Magazine* (Winter 2000).

"Mississippi Freedom Labor Union, 1965 Origins," and "We Have No Government," in *Black Protest: History, Documents, and Analyses, 1619 to the Present*, ed. Jo Ann Grant, 498–505.

Blackwell, Unita, and Joanne Prichard Morris. *Barefootin': Life Lessons from the Road to Freedom* (2006).

Dittmer, John. *Local People: The Struggle for Civil Rights in Mississippi* (1994).

Mills, Kay. *This Little Light of Mine: The Life of Fannie Lou Hamer* (1993).

Payne, Charles. *I've Got the Light of Freedom: The Organizing Tradition and the Mississippi Freedom Struggle* (1995).

NAN ELIZABETH WOODRUFF

Blair, Norval (1829–1916), farmer, patriarch, and founder of the Sully County Colored Colony, Dakota Territory (South Dakota became a state in 1889), was born in slavery, probably in Tennessee, and was freed at Emancipation. He married Mary Elizabeth Bagby Blair, reported to be half Cherokee. With their six adult children they founded South Dakota's only successful black agricultural colony. Five years out of slavery the family was farming near Morris, Illinois, about fifty miles southwest of Chicago. With substantial personal property, they held their land "free and clear." An oral tradition among South Dakota African Americans suggests that Blair's successful bloodline of fast horses, his unseemly prosperity, and his interest in expanding his lands aroused jealousy among his white neighbors in Illinois, prompting him to consider relocating to Dakota Territory.

Sully County, just east of present-day Pierre, South Dakota, opened for settlement in April 1883. The following year Norval Blair sent two of his sons, Benjamin P. and Patrick Henry Blair, to reconnoiter and, if suitable, to purchase land where the clan could relocate. The Blair sons were personable, educated, and enthusiastic about Sully County, and they were well accepted by other speculators. They chose a home site with an excellent water supply not far from the village of Fairbank. Norval Blair brought the rest of the family to Sully County the following year, along with seeds, livestock, and a string of fine Morgan foundation stock intended for breeding purposes. Settlers to the Northern Great Plains, well into the twentieth century, often brought fine equine breed stock, since horses provided both transportation and power for the arduous work of breaking the prairie to agriculture. Morgan horses, developed in the early 1800s by Justin Morgan, were especially prized as carriage horses for their strength, speed, and beauty. Their bloodlines were foundation stock for American standardbreds, Tennessee Walkers, and other fine breeds.

The Blair family built a comfortable home and lived quietly in Sully County for more than twenty years, successfully farming the difficult and unforgiving land. They continued to breed their Morgan racing stock, which developed a considerable reputation throughout the Midwest. The Blairs' most famous horse was Johnny Bee, which held the state record for speed from 1907 to 1909.

In 1906 Norval Blair, with his sons and daughter Elizabeth (Betty), joined other black South Dakotans in the Northwestern Homestead Movement, a statewide effort to encourage black immigration to farming colonies in the state. Local black families throughout the state pledged to assist and sponsor the newcomers, and the Blair family offered 1,700 acres on their land for an agricultural college to train African American farmers in local farming techniques. Homesteaders from all backgrounds, tempted by the availability of free farmland on the Northern Great Plains, especially west of the Missouri River, found that pioneering unbroken land in a harsh country was difficult, challenging, and discouraging. Snowbound winters, sweltering summers, grasshopper plagues, tough and unyielding unbroken prairie, hailstorms, drought and unpredictable weather patterns, isolation, and falling grain prices proved too much for all but the most hearty and determined. Although the college never materialized, the colony did. Over the next twenty-five years, more than two hundred African Americans experienced Sully County farm life, some with considerable success, and all with the active encouragement of the Blairs.

Betty Blair became a real estate saleswoman for the King Real Estate Company, Iowa land speculators. Most of the black settlers purchased their land from "Miss Betty." The settlers ranged in age from very young couples with young children to elderly couples accompanied by their grown children. Although the population varied over the years, the community was close-knit and was centered on the country school that also served as a church. Like other Great Plains farms, the colony did not survive the Dust Bowl and Depression of the 1930s, although a few farms remained through the 1940s. A maintained cemetery on the original Blair farm is the last resting place of Norval and Mary Blair and others of the Sully County Colored Colony. The cemetery, now located on a private ranch, is maintained in perpetuity by the terms of the property's deed.

FURTHER READING
Linde, Martha. *Western Dakota Horse Stories* (1989).
Saxman, Michelle C. "To Better Oneself: Sully County's African American 'Colony,'" *South Dakota History* 34, no. 4 (Winter 2004): 319–328.
Sully County Centennial History Book Committee. *100 Years of a Proud People, 1883–1983: A History of Sully County* (1983).
Sully County Old Settlers Association. *The History of Sully County* (1939).
Thompson, Harry, Editor. *A New South Dakota History* (2005). See especially the chapters "Farming, Dependency and Depopulation" and "African Americans," the latter by Betti C. VanEpps-Taylor.
VanEpps-Taylor, Betti C. *Forgotten Americans: African Americans in South Dakota* (2007).

BETTI CAROL VANEPPS-TAYLOR

Blake, "Blind" Arthur (c. 1893–c. 1933), popular blues guitarist, composer, singer, and recording artist, was born in Jacksonville, Florida.

To date, researchers have not found much biographical information about Blind Blake, including the place and exact date of his birth and death. His birth and death certificates have never been found, and there is nothing available about his family background, including the name of his parents or if there were any siblings. His name is also a mystery. It is not certain if "Blake" was his surname or an epithet. On one of his recordings he does state that his name is Arthur Blake, and this is also the name his contemporaries said he mentioned. Some of his compositions have the imprint of Arthur Phelps, another name attributed to him. Other names he was known by included Billy James, Gorgeous Weed, and George Martin. It is also unknown when or how he lost his sight. The name Blind Blake was most likely given to him by Paramount, the company that recorded his performances. In early blues history, the word "Blind" was often a substitute for the artist's first name, used by the recording administrators and producers to sell the artist. It was also alleged that Blake had a son but this information is also not confirmed by any credible sources.

From the promotional material used by Paramount, the birthplace of Blake was given as Jacksonville, Florida. A small part of Blake's life and biography has been traced through his performances and recordings and from recollections by his contemporaries, some of whom performed with him. Similar to other blind blues musicians and according to the *Paramount Book of the Blues*, Blake learned to play the blues guitar and songs from blues sounds he heard: "He studied long and earnestly—listening to talented pianists and guitar players, and began to gradually draw out harmonious tunes to fit every mood."

Similar to other blues artists seeking a way out of a life of poverty and despair, Blake performed blues music on the streets, at parties, juke houses, barrelhouses, and saloons as a means of supporting himself. Quite early in his career, Blake became an itinerant blues musician; singing and performing on the guitar along the East Coast. He also had a gift for playing barrelhouse piano.

In his late teenage years, Blake made his way to Georgia, the Carolinas, and Tennessee, performing and living the life of a traveling musician. The lyrics to some of his songs even make reference to these places. He also performed with BLIND WILLIE MCTELL in Atlanta, Georgia. One of his contemporaries, JOSH WHITE, noted that he saw him in Charleston, West Virginia, and heard him perform during the early 1920s. Another guitarist who met and befriended Blake during the 1920s was Bill Williams. He stated in an interview with Woody Mann (*Six Black Blues Guitarists*), that Blake already knew how to play most of the classic blues works by the time he met him. They often played duets together in locations such as Bristol, Virginia. From Bill Williams's account, Blake was an upbeat person.

During the 1920s and early 1930s, Blake eventually took up residence in the Midwest; performing in Illinois, Indiana, Michigan, Ohio, and Wisconsin. His time in Chicago (1926–29); Richmond, Indiana (1929); and Grafton, Wisconsin (1929–32) can be traced through his recordings with Paramount and his contemporaries. Sometime in 1926 in Chicago, Blake was discovered by Mayo "Ink" Williams, the talent scout and head of Paramount. The first recording he made was the guitar solo "Early Mornin' Blues" followed by "West Coast Blues." Blake's first recording was such a huge success and sellout that Paramount released at least one or more recordings of Blake's each month.

Blake was a well-paid black blues artist earning around $50.00 per recording side. His works showcased his outstanding virtuoso finger-picking guitar style that included agile single-string passages, and thumb rolls, some of which had roots in ragtime piano. But the source of his guitar playing has been a mystery, and his naturally outstanding and unique finger-picking technique was unsurpassed. He was one of the earliest blind blues artists who popularized and greatly influenced this American style and form, recording over eighty songs for Paramount including: "Skeedle Loo Doo Blues" and "Tampa Bound" (1926); "Brownskin Mama Blues," "Southern Rag," and "That Will Never Happen No More" (1927); "Cold Hearted Mama Blues," "Detroit Bound Blues," "Ramblin' Boa Constrictor Blues," and "That Lovin' I Crave" (1928); and "Blind Arthur's Breakdown," "Chump Man Blues," and "Georgia Bound" (1929).

Blake made few recordings between 1930 and 1931, namely "Diddie Wa Diddie No. 2" (1930) and "Rope Stretchin' Blues" (1931). During this time, he performed with Bill Williams' s touring show, *Happy Go Lucky*. Blake's final recordings were in 1932 and included his original works, "Champagne Charlie Is My Name," "Depression's Gone from Me Blues," "Dissatisfied Blues," "Miss Emma Liza (Sweetness)," "Night and Day Blues," and "Sun to Sun." By 1932, Paramount was feeling the effects of the Great Depression era. With slumping sales, they eventually went out of business. Blake disappeared, and no one was able to trace his whereabouts or knew what happened to him. Some speculated that he died in a streetcar accident in 1933 in New York, but that was never confirmed. It was theorized that with the demise of Paramount, his main source of income, Blake may have returned to Jacksonville, Florida, and died around 1933.

Blake accompanied several noted blues artist on recordings. His blues songs and instrumental works were often upbeat, bouncy, and humorous, with difficult rhythmic passages. His overall skill, musicianship, and talent for improvisation were great. This prolific blues recording artist had a natural gift for composition. His stunning virtuosic and artistic guitar performance greatly influenced blues guitarists.

FURTHER READING

Balfour, Alan. "Notes, Blind Blake: The Complete Recorded Works in Chronological Order, vols. 1–4," Document DOCD-5024/5025/5026/5027 (1991).

"Blind Blake," in Gerard Herzhaft, ed., *Encyclopedia of the Blues* (1997).

Mann, Woody. "Blind Blake," in *Six Black Blues Guitarists* (1973).

Obrecht, Jas. "Blind Blake," *Blues Revue Quarterly*, no. 7 (Winter 1993): 18–21.

BARBARA BONOUS-SMIT